AF862005

Programming Language Pragmatics

FOURTH EDITION

Programming Language Pragmatics

FOURTH EDITION

Michael L. Scott

Department of Computer Science

University of Rochester

ELSEVIER

AMSTERDAM • BOSTON • HEIDELBERG • LONDON
NEW DELHI • NEW YORK • OXFORD • PARIS • SAN DIEGO
SAN FRANCISCO • SINGAPORE • SYDNEY • TOKYO
Butterworth-Heinemann is an imprint of Elsevier

MK
MORGAN KAUFMANN

ELSEVIER

RELX India Pvt. Ltd.
Registered Office: 818, Indraprakash Building, 8th Floor, 21, Barakhamba Road, New Delhi-110001
Corporate Office: 14th Floor, Building No. 10B, DLF Cyber City, Phase II, Gurgaon-122 002, Haryana, India

Programming Language Pragmatics, 4/e, Michael L. Scott

ISBN: 978-0-12-410409-9

This reprint of Programming Language Pragmatics, 4/e by Michael L. Scott was undertaken by RELX India Private Limited and is published by arrangement with Elsevier Inc.

Indian Reprint ISBN: 978-93-5107-366-6

First Printed in India 2018

Printed in India by Rajkamal Electric Press, Kundli, Haryana.

About the Author

Michael L. Scott is a professor and past chair of the Department of Computer Science at the University of Rochester. He received his Ph.D. in computer sciences in 1985 from the University of Wisconsin–Madison. From 2014–2015 he was a Visiting Scientist at Google. His research interests lie at the intersection of programming languages, operating systems, and high-level computer architecture, with an emphasis on parallel and distributed computing. His MCS mutual exclusion lock, co-designed with John Mellor-Crummey, is used in a variety of commercial and academic systems. Several other algorithms, co-designed with Maged Michael, Bill Scherer, and Doug Lea, appear in the `java.util.concurrent` standard library. In 2006 he and Dr. Mellor-Crummey shared the ACM SIGACT/SIGOPS Edsger W. Dijkstra Prize in Distributed Computing.

Dr. Scott is a Fellow of the Association for Computing Machinery, a Fellow of the Institute of Electrical and Electronics Engineers, and a member of Usenix, the Union of Concerned Scientists, and the American Association of University Professors. The author of more than 150 refereed publications, he served as General Chair of the 2003 ACM Symposium on Operating Systems Principles (SOSP) and as Program Chair of the 2007 ACM SIGPLAN Workshop on Transactional Computing (TRANSACT), the 2008 ACM SIGPLAN Symposium on Principles and Practice of Parallel Programming (PPoPP), and the 2012 International Conference on Architectural Support for Programming Languages and Operating Systems (ASPLOS). In 2001 he received the University of Rochester's Robert and Pamela Goergen Award for Distinguished Achievement and Artistry in Undergraduate Teaching.

To family and friends.

Contents

Foreword

Programming languages are universally accepted as one of the core subjects that every computer scientist must master. The reason is clear: these languages are the main notation we use for developing products and for communicating new ideas. They have influenced the field by enabling the development of those multimillion-line programs that shaped the information age. Their success is owed to the long-standing effort of the computer science community in the creation of new languages and in the development of strategies for their implementation. The large number of computer scientists mentioned in the footnotes and bibliographic notes in this book by Michael Scott is a clear manifestation of the magnitude of this effort as is the sheer number and diversity of topics it contains.

Over 75 programming languages are discussed. They represent the best and most influential contributions in language design across time, paradigms, and application domains. They are the outcome of decades of work that led initially to Fortran and Lisp in the 1950s, to numerous languages in the years that followed, and, in our times, to the popular dynamic languages used to program the Web. The 75 plus languages span numerous paradigms including imperative, functional, logic, static, dynamic, sequential, shared-memory parallel, distributed-memory parallel, dataflow, high-level, and intermediate languages. They include languages for scientific computing, for symbolic manipulations, and for accessing databases. This rich diversity of languages is crucial for programmer productivity and is one of the great assets of the discipline of computing.

Cutting across languages, this book presents a detailed discussion of control flow, types, and abstraction mechanisms. These are the representations needed to develop programs that are well organized, modular, easy to understand, and easy to maintain. Knowledge of these core features and of their incarnation in today's languages is a basic foundation to be an effective programmer and to better understand computer science today.

Strategies to implement programming languages must be studied together with the design paradigms. A reason is that success of a language depends on the quality of its implementation. Also, the capabilities of these strategies sometimes constraint the design of languages. The implementation of a language starts with parsing and lexical scanning needed to compute the syntactic structure of programs. Today's parsing techniques, described in Part I, are among the most beautiful algorithms ever developed and are a great example of the use of mathematical objects to create practical instruments. They are worthwhile studying just as an intellectual achievement. They are of course of great practical value, and a good way to appreciate the greatness of these strategies is to go back to the first Fortran compiler and study the ad hoc, albeit highly ingenious, strategy used to implement precedence of operators by the pioneers that built that compiler.

The other usual component of implementation are the compiler components that carry out the translation from the high-level language representation to a lower level form suitable for execution by real or virtual machines. The translation can be done ahead of time, during execution (just in time), or both. The book discusses these approaches and implementation strategies including the elegant mechanisms of translation driven by parsing. To produce highly efficient code, translation routines apply strategies to avoid redundant computations, make efficient use of the memory hierarchy, and take advantage of intra-processor parallelism. These, sometimes conflicting goals, are undertaken by the optimization components of compilers. Although this topic is typically outside the scope of a first course on compilers, the book gives the reader access to a good overview of program optimization in Part IV.

An important recent development in computing is the popularization of parallelism and the expectation that, in the foreseeable future, performance gains will mainly be the result of effectively exploiting this parallelism. The book responds to this development by presenting the reader with a range of topics in concurrent programming including mechanisms for synchronization, communication, and coordination across threads. This information will become increasingly important as parallelism consolidates as the norm in computing.

Programming languages are the bridge between programmers and machines. It is in them that algorithms must be represented for execution. The study of programming languages design and implementation offers great educational value by requiring an understanding of the strategies used to connect the different aspects of computing. By presenting such an extensive treatment of the subject, Michael Scott's *Programming Language Pragmatics*, is a great contribution to the literature and a valuable source of information for computer scientists.

David Padua
Siebel Center for Computer Science
University of Illinois at Urbana-Champaign

Preface

A course in computer programming provides the typical student's first exposure to the field of computer science. Most students in such a course will have used computers all their lives, for social networking, email, games, web browsing, word processing, and a host of other tasks, but it is not until they write their first programs that they begin to appreciate how applications *work*. After gaining a certain level of facility as programmers (presumably with the help of a good course in data structures and algorithms), the natural next step is to wonder how *programming languages* work. This book provides an explanation. It aims, quite simply, to be the most comprehensive and accurate languages text available, in a style that is engaging and accessible to the typical undergraduate. This aim reflects my conviction that students will understand more, and enjoy the material more, if we explain what is really going on.

In the conventional "systems" curriculum, the material beyond data structures (and possibly computer organization) tends to be compartmentalized into a host of separate subjects, including programming languages, compiler construction, computer architecture, operating systems, networks, parallel and distributed computing, database management systems, and possibly software engineering, object-oriented design, graphics, or user interface systems. One problem with this compartmentalization is that the list of subjects keeps growing, but the number of semesters in a Bachelor's program does not. More important, perhaps, many of the most interesting discoveries in computer science occur at the boundaries *between* subjects. Computer architecture and compiler construction, for example, have inspired each other for over 50 years, through generations of supercomputers, pipelined microprocessors, multicore chips, and modern GPUs. Over the past decade, advances in virtualization have blurred boundaries among the hardware, operating system, compiler, and language run-time system, and have spurred the explosion in cloud computing. Programming language technology is now routinely embedded in everything from dynamic web content, to gaming and entertainment, to security and finance.

Increasingly, both educators and practitioners have come to emphasize these sorts of interactions. Within higher education in particular, there is a growing trend toward integration in the core curriculum. Rather than give the typical student an in-depth look at two or three narrow subjects, leaving holes in all the others, many schools have revised the programming languages and computer organization courses to cover a wider range of topics, with follow-on electives in various specializations. This trend is very much in keeping with the ACM/IEEE-CS *Computer Science Curricula 2013* guidelines [SR13], which emphasize the need to manage the size of the curriculum and to cultivate both a "system-level perspective" and an appreciation of the interplay between theory and practice. In particular, the authors write,

> Graduates of a computer science program need to think at multiple levels of detail and abstraction. This understanding should transcend the implementation details of the various components to encompass an appreciation for the structure of computer systems and the processes involved in their construction and analysis [p. 24].

On the specific subject of this text, they write

> Programming languages are the medium through which programmers precisely describe concepts, formulate algorithms, and reason about solutions. In the course of a career, a computer scientist will work with many different languages, separately or together. Software developers must understand the programming models underlying different languages and make informed design choices in languages supporting multiple complementary approaches. Computer scientists will often need to learn new languages and programming constructs, and must understand the principles underlying how programming language features are defined, composed, and implemented. The effective use of programming languages, and appreciation of their limitations, also requires a basic knowledge of programming language translation and static program analysis, as well as run-time components such as memory management [p. 155].

The first three editions of *Programming Language Pragmatics* (PLP) had the good fortune of riding the trend toward integrated understanding. This fourth edition continues and strengthens the "systems perspective" while preserving the central focus on programming language design.

At its core, PLP is a book about *how programming languages work.* Rather than enumerate the details of many different languages, it focuses on concepts that underlie all the languages the student is likely to encounter, illustrating those concepts with a variety of concrete examples, and exploring the tradeoffs that explain *why* different languages were designed in different ways. Similarly, rather than explain how to build a compiler or interpreter (a task few programmers will undertake in its entirety), PLP focuses on what a compiler does to an input program, and why. Language design and implementation are thus explored together, with an emphasis on the ways in which they interact.

Changes in the Fourth Edition

In comparison to the third edition, PLP-4e includes

1. New chapters devoted to type systems and composite types, in place of the older single chapter on types

2. Updated treatment of functional programming, with extensive coverage of OCaml
3. Numerous other reflections of changes in the field
4. Improvements inspired by instructor feedback or a fresh consideration of familiar topics

Item 1 in this list is perhaps the most visible change. Chapter 7 was the longest in previous editions, and there is a natural split in the subject material. Reorganization of this material for PLP-4e afforded an opportunity to devote more explicit attention to the subject of type inference, and of its role in ML-family languages in particular. It also facilitated an update and reorganization of the material on parametric polymorphism, which was previously scattered across several different chapters and sections.

Item 2 reflects the increasing adoption of functional techniques into mainstream imperative languages, as well as the increasing prominence of SML, OCaml, and Haskell in both education and industry. Throughout the text, OCaml is now co-equal with Scheme as a source of functional programming examples. As noted in the previous paragraph, there is an expanded section (7.2.4) on the ML type system, and Section 11.4 includes an OCaml overview, with coverage of equality and ordering, bindings and lambda expressions, type constructors, pattern matching, and control flow and side effects. The choice of OCaml, rather than Haskell, as the ML-family exemplar reflects its prominence in industry, together with classroom experience suggesting that—at least for many students—the initial exposure to functional thinking is easier in the context of eager evaluation. To colleagues who wish I'd chosen Haskell, my apologies!

Other new material (Item 3) appears throughout the text. Wherever appropriate, reference has been made to features of the latest languages and standards, including C & C++11, Java 8, C# 5, Scala, Go, Swift, Python 3, and HTML 5. Section 3.6.4 pulls together previously scattered coverage of lambda expressions, and shows how these have been added to various imperative languages. Complementary coverage of object closures, including C++11's `std::function` and `std::bind`, appears in Section 10.4.4. Section c-5.4.5 introduces the x86-64 and ARM architectures in place of the x86-32 and MIPS used in previous editions. Examples using these same two architectures subsequently appear in the sections on calling sequences (9.2) and linking (15.6). Coverage of the x86 calling sequence continues to rely on `gcc`; the ARM case study uses LLVM. Section 8.5.3 introduces smart pointers. R-value references appear in Section 9.3.1. JavaFX replaces Swing in the graphics examples of Section 9.6.2. Appendix A has new entries for Go, Lua, Rust, Scala, and Swift.

Finally, Item 4 encompasses improvements to almost every section of the text. Among the more heavily updated topics are FOLLOW and PREDICT sets (Section 2.3.3); Wirth's error recovery algorithm for recursive descent (Section c-2.3.5); overloading (Section 3.5.2); modules (Section 3.3.4); duck typing (Section 7.3); records and variants (Section 8.1); intrusive lists (removed from the running example of Chapter 10); static fields and methods (Section 10.2.2);

mix-in inheritance (moved from the companion site back into the main text, and updated to cover Scala traits and Java 8 default methods); multicore processors (pervasive changes to Chapter 13); phasers (Section 13.3.1); memory models (Section 13.3.3); semaphores (Section 13.3.5); futures (Section 13.4.5); GIMPLE and RTL (Section c-15.2.1); QEMU (Section 16.2.2); DWARF (Section 16.3.2); and language genealogy (Figure A.1).

To accommodate new material, coverage of some topics has been condensed or even removed. Examples include modules (Chapters 3 and 10), variant records and `with` statements (Chapter 8), and metacircular interpretation (Chapter 11). Additional material—the Common Language Infrastructure (CLI) in particular—has moved to the companion site. Throughout the text, examples drawn from languages no longer in widespread use have been replaced with more recent equivalents wherever appropriate. Almost all remaining references to Pascal and Modula are merely historical. Most coverage of Occam and Tcl has also been dropped.

Overall, the printed text has grown by roughly 40 pages. There are 5 more "Design & Implementation" sidebars, 35 more numbered examples, and about 25 new end-of-chapter exercises and explorations. Considerable effort has been invested in creating a consistent and comprehensive index. As in earlier editions, Morgan Kaufmann has maintained its commitment to providing definitive texts at reasonable cost: PLP-4e is far less expensive than competing alternatives, but larger and more comprehensive.

The Companion Site

To minimize the physical size of the text, make way for new material, and allow students to focus on the fundamentals when browsing, over 350 pages of more advanced or peripheral material can be found on a companion web site: *booksite.elsevier.com/web/9780124104099*. Each companion-site (CS) section is represented in the main text by a brief introduction to the subject and an "In More Depth" paragraph that summarizes the elided material.

Note that placement of material on the companion site does *not* constitute a judgment about its technical importance. It simply reflects the fact that there is more material worth covering than will fit in a single volume or a single-semester course. Since preferences and syllabi vary, most instructors will probably want to assign reading from the CS, and most will refrain from assigning certain sections of the printed text. My intent has been to retain in print the material that is likely to be covered in the largest number of courses.

Also included on the CS are pointers to on-line resources and compilable copies of all significant code fragments found in the text (in more than two dozen languages).

Design & Implementation Sidebars

Like its predecessors, PLP-4e places heavy emphasis on the ways in which language design constrains implementation options, and the ways in which anticipated implementations have influenced language design. Many of these connections and interactions are highlighted in some 140 "Design & Implementation" sidebars. A more detailed introduction appears in Sidebar 1.1. A numbered list appears in Appendix B.

Numbered and Titled Examples

Examples in PLP-4e are intimately woven into the flow of the presentation. To make it easier to find specific examples, to remember their content, and to refer to them in other contexts, a number and a title for each is displayed in a marginal note. There are over 1000 such examples across the main text and the CS. A detailed list appears in Appendix C.

Exercise Plan

Review questions appear throughout the text at roughly 10-page intervals, at the ends of major sections. These are based directly on the preceding material, and have short, straightforward answers.

More detailed questions appear at the end of each chapter. These are divided into *Exercises* and *Explorations*. The former are generally more challenging than the per-section review questions, and should be suitable for homework or brief projects. The latter are more open-ended, requiring web or library research, substantial time commitment, or the development of subjective opinion. Solutions to many of the exercises (but not the explorations) are available to registered instructors from a password-protected web site: visit *textbooks.elsevier.com/web/9780124104099.*

How to Use the Book

Programming Language Pragmatics covers almost all of the material in the PL "knowledge units" of the *Computing Curricula 2013* report [SR13]. The languages course at the University of Rochester, for which this book was designed, is in fact one of the featured "course exemplars" in the report (pp. 369–371). Figure 1 illustrates several possible paths through the text.

For self-study, or for a full-year course (track F in Figure 1), I recommend working through the book from start to finish, turning to the companion site as each "In More Depth" section is encountered. The one-semester course at Rochester (track R) also covers most of the book, but leaves out most of the CS

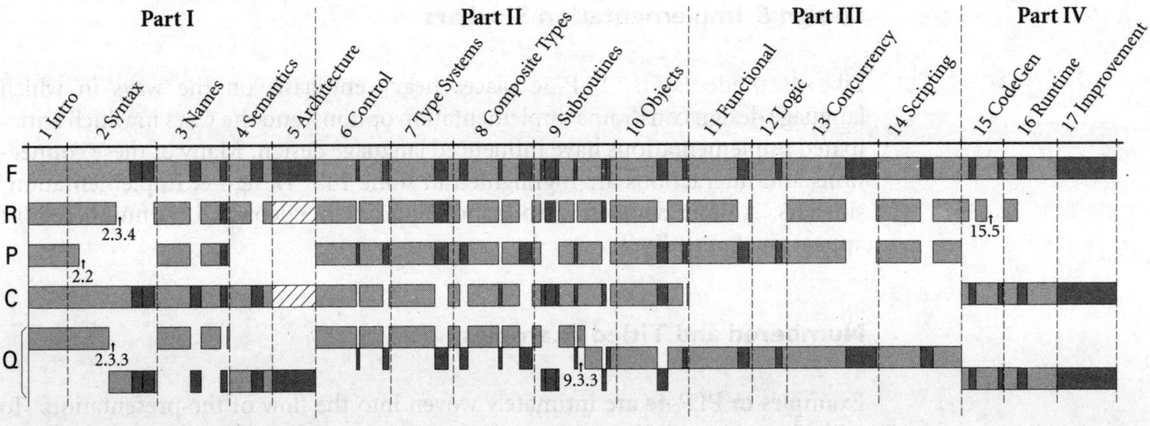

F: The full-year/self-study plan
R: The one-semester Rochester plan
P: The traditional Programming Languages plan; would also de-emphasize implementation material throughout the chapters shown
C: The compiler plan; would also de-emphasize design material throughout the chapters shown
Q: The 1+2 quarter plan: an overview quarter and two independent, optional follow-on quarters, one language-oriented, the other compiler-oriented

Figure 1 **Paths through the text.** Darker shaded regions indicate supplemental "In More Depth" sections on the companion site. Section numbers are shown for breaks that do not correspond to supplemental material.

sections, as well as bottom-up parsing (2.3.4), logic languages (Chapter 12), and the second halves of Chapters 15 (Building a Runnable Program) and 16 (Run-time Program Management). Note that the material on functional programming (Chapter 11 in particular) can be taught in either OCaml or Scheme.

Some chapters (2, 4, 5, 15, 16, 17) have a heavier emphasis than others on implementation issues. These can be reordered to a certain extent with respect to the more design-oriented chapters. Many students will already be familiar with much of the material in Chapter 5, most likely from a course on computer organization; hence the placement of the chapter on the companion site. Some students may also be familiar with some of the material in Chapter 2, perhaps from a course on automata theory. Much of this chapter can then be read quickly as well, pausing perhaps to dwell on such practical issues as recovery from syntax errors, or the ways in which a scanner differs from a classical finite automaton.

A traditional programming languages course (track P in Figure 1) might leave out all of scanning and parsing, plus all of Chapter 4. It would also de-emphasize the more implementation-oriented material throughout. In place of these, it could add such design-oriented CS sections as multiple inheritance (10.6), Smalltalk (10.7.1), lambda calculus (11.7), and predicate calculus (12.3).

PLP has also been used at some schools for an introductory compiler course (track C in Figure 1). The typical syllabus leaves out most of Part III (Chapters 11 through 14), and de-emphasizes the more design-oriented material throughout. In place of these, it includes all of scanning and parsing, Chapters 15 through 17, and a slightly different mix of other CS sections.

For a school on the quarter system, an appealing option is to offer an introductory one-quarter course and two optional follow-on courses (track Q in Figure 1). The introductory quarter might cover the main (non-CS) sections of Chapters 1, 3, 6, 7, and 8, plus the first halves of Chapters 2 and 9. A language-oriented follow-on quarter might cover the rest of Chapter 9, all of Part III, CS sections from Chapters 6 through 9, and possibly supplemental material on formal semantics, type theory, or other related topics. A compiler-oriented follow-on quarter might cover the rest of Chapter 2; Chapters 4–5 and 15–17, CS sections from Chapters 3 and 9–10, and possibly supplemental material on automatic code generation, aggressive code improvement, programming tools, and so on.

Whatever the path through the text, I assume that the typical reader has already acquired significant experience with at least one imperative language. Exactly which language it is shouldn't matter. Examples are drawn from a wide variety of languages, but always with enough comments and other discussion that readers without prior experience should be able to understand easily. Single-paragraph introductions to more than 60 different languages appear in Appendix A. Algorithms, when needed, are presented in an informal pseudocode that should be self-explanatory. Real programming language code is set in `"typewriter" font`. Pseudocode is set in a sans-serif font.

Supplemental Materials

In addition to supplemental sections, the companion site contains complete source code for all nontrivial examples, and a list of all known errors in the book. Additional resources are available on-line at *textbooks.elsevier.com/web/9780124104099*. For instructors who have adopted the text, a password-protected page provides access to

- Editable PDF source for all the figures in the book
- Editable PowerPoint slides
- Solutions to most of the exercises
- Suggestions for larger projects

Acknowledgments for the Fourth Edition

In preparing the fourth edition, I have been blessed with the generous assistance of a very large number of people. Many provided errata or other feedback on the third edition, among them Yacine Belkadi, Björn Brandenburg,

Bob Cochran, Daniel Crisman, Marcelino Debajo, Chen Ding, Peter Drake, Michael Edgar, Michael Glass, Sérgio Gomes, Allan Gottlieb, Hossein Hadavi, Chris Hart, Thomas Helmuth, Wayne Heym, Scott Hoge, Kelly Jones, Ahmed Khademzadeh, Eleazar Enrique Leal, Kyle Liddell, Annie Liu, Hao Luo, Dirk Müller, Holger Peine, Andreas Priesnitz, Mikhail Prokharau, Harsh Raju, and Jingguo Yao. I also remain indebted to the many individuals acknowledged in previous editions, and to the reviewers, adopters, and readers who made those editions a success.

Anonymous reviewers for the fourth edition provided a wealth of useful suggestions; my thanks to all of you! Special thanks to Adam Chlipala of MIT for his detailed and insightful suggestions on the coverage of functional programming. My thanks as well to Nelson Beebe (University of Utah) for pointing out that compilers cannot safely use integer comparisons for floating-point numbers that may be NaNs; to Dan Scarafoni for prompting me to distinguish between FIRST/EPS of symbols and FIRST/EPS of strings in the algorithm to generate PREDICT sets; to Dave Musicant for suggested improvements to the description of deep binding; to Allan Gottlieb (NYU) for several key clarifications regarding Ada semantics; and to Benjamin Kowarsch for similar clarifications regarding Objective-C. Problems that remain in all these areas are entirely my own.

In preparing the fourth edition, I have drawn on 25 years of experience teaching this material to upper-level undergraduates at the University of Rochester. I am grateful to all my students for their enthusiasm and feedback. My thanks as well to my colleagues and graduate students, and to the department's administrative, secretarial, and technical staff for providing such a supportive and productive work environment. Finally, my thanks to David Padua, whose work I have admired since I was in graduate school; I am deeply honored to have him as the author of the Foreword.

As they were on previous editions, the staff at Morgan Kaufmann has been a genuine pleasure to work with, on both a professional and a personal level. My thanks in particular to Nate McFadden, Senior Development Editor, who shepherded both this and the previous two editions with unfailing patience, good humor, and a fine eye for detail; to Mohana Natarajan, who managed the book's production; and to Todd Green, Publisher, who upholds the personal touch of the Morgan Kauffman imprint within the larger Elsevier universe.

Most important, I am indebted to my wife, Kelly, for her patience and support through endless months of writing and revising. Computing is a fine profession, but family is what really matters.

Michael L. Scott
Rochester, NY
August 2015

I Foundations

A central premise of *Programming Language Pragmatics* is that language design and implementation are intimately connected; it's hard to study one without the other.

The bulk of the text—Parts II and III—is organized around topics in language design, but with detailed coverage throughout of the many ways in which design decisions have been shaped by implementation concerns.

The first five chapters—Part I—set the stage by covering foundational material in both design and implementation. Chapter 1 motivates the study of programming languages, introduces the major language families, and provides an overview of the compilation process. Chapter 3 covers the high-level structure of programs, with an emphasis on *names*, the *binding* of names to objects, and the *scope rules* that govern which bindings are active at any given time. In the process it touches on storage management; subroutines, modules, and classes; polymorphism; and separate compilation.

Chapters 2, 4, and 5 are more implementation oriented. They provide the background needed to understand the implementation issues mentioned in Parts II and III. Chapter 2 discusses the *syntax*, or textual structure, of programs. It introduces *regular expressions* and *context-free grammars*, which designers use to describe program syntax, together with the *scanning* and *parsing* algorithms that a compiler or interpreter uses to recognize that syntax. Given an understanding of syntax, Chapter 4 explains how a compiler (or interpreter) determines the *semantics*, or meaning of a program. The discussion is organized around the notion of *attribute grammars*, which serve to map a program onto something else that has meaning, such as mathematics or some other existing language. Finally, Chapter 5 (entirely on the companion site) provides an overview of assembly-level computer architecture, focusing on the features of modern microprocessors most relevant to compilers. Programmers who understand these features have a better chance not only of understanding why the languages they use were designed the way they were, but also of using those languages as fully and effectively as possible.

1 Introduction

The first electronic computers were monstrous contraptions, filling several rooms, consuming as much electricity as a good-size factory, and costing millions of 1940s dollars (but with much less computing power than even the simplest modern cell phone). The programmers who used these machines believed that the computer's time was more valuable than theirs. They programmed in machine language. Machine language is the sequence of bits that directly controls a processor, causing it to add, compare, move data from one place to another, and so forth at appropriate times. Specifying programs at this level of detail is an enormously tedious task. The following program calculates the greatest common divisor (GCD) of two integers, using Euclid's algorithm. It is written in machine language, expressed here as hexadecimal (base 16) numbers, for the x86 instruction set.

EXAMPLE 1.1
GCD program in x86 machine language

```
55 89 e5 53  83 ec 04 83  e4 f0 e8 31  00 00 00 89  c3 e8 2a 00
00 00 39 c3  74 10 8d b6  00 00 00 00  39 c3 7e 13  29 c3 39 c3
75 f6 89 1c  24 e8 6e 00  00 00 8b 5d  fc c9 c3 29  d8 eb eb 90
```

As people began to write larger programs, it quickly became apparent that a less error-prone notation was required. Assembly languages were invented to allow operations to be expressed with mnemonic abbreviations. Our GCD program looks like this in x86 assembly language:

EXAMPLE 1.2
GCD program in x86 assembler

```
        pushl   %ebp                    jle     D
        movl    %esp, %ebp              subl    %eax, %ebx
        pushl   %ebx                B:  cmpl    %eax, %ebx
        subl    $4, %esp                jne     A
        andl    $-16, %esp          C:  movl    %ebx, (%esp)
        call    getint                  call    putint
        movl    %eax, %ebx              movl    -4(%ebp), %ebx
        call    getint                  leave
        cmpl    %eax, %ebx              ret
        je      C                   D:  subl    %ebx, %eax
    A:  cmpl    %eax, %ebx              jmp     B
```

Assembly languages were originally designed with a one-to-one correspondence between mnemonics and machine language instructions, as shown in this example.[1] Translating from mnemonics to machine language became the job of a systems program known as an *assembler*. Assemblers were eventually augmented with elaborate "macro expansion" facilities to permit programmers to define parameterized abbreviations for common sequences of instructions. The correspondence between assembly language and machine language remained obvious and explicit, however. Programming continued to be a machine-centered enterprise: each different kind of computer had to be programmed in its own assembly language, and programmers thought in terms of the instructions that the machine would actually execute.

As computers evolved, and as competing designs developed, it became increasingly frustrating to have to rewrite programs for every new machine. It also became increasingly difficult for human beings to keep track of the wealth of detail in large assembly language programs. People began to wish for a machine-independent language, particularly one in which numerical computations (the most common type of program in those days) could be expressed in something more closely resembling mathematical formulae. These wishes led in the mid-1950s to the development of the original dialect of Fortran, the first arguably high-level programming language. Other high-level languages soon followed, notably Lisp and Algol.

Translating from a high-level language to assembly or machine language is the job of a systems program known as a *compiler*.[2] Compilers are substantially more complicated than assemblers because the one-to-one correspondence between source and target operations no longer exists when the source is a high-level language. Fortran was slow to catch on at first, because human programmers, with some effort, could almost always write assembly language programs that would run faster than what a compiler could produce. Over time, however, the performance gap has narrowed, and eventually reversed. Increases in hardware complexity (due to pipelining, multiple functional units, etc.) and continuing improvements in compiler technology have led to a situation in which a state-of-the-art compiler will usually generate better code than a human being will. Even in cases in which human beings can do better, increases in computer speed and program size have made it increasingly important to economize on programmer effort, not only in the original construction of programs, but in subsequent

1 The 22 lines of assembly code in the example are encoded in varying numbers of bytes in machine language. The three `cmp` (compare) instructions, for example, all happen to have the same register operands, and are encoded in the two-byte sequence (`39 c3`). The four `mov` (move) instructions have different operands and lengths, and begin with `89` or `8b`. The chosen syntax is that of the GNU `gcc` compiler suite, in which results overwrite the last operand, not the first.

2 High-level languages may also be *interpreted* directly, without the translation step. We will return to this option in Section 1.4. It is the principal way in which scripting languages like Python and JavaScript are implemented.

program *maintenance*—enhancement and correction. Labor costs now heavily outweigh the cost of computing hardware.

1.1 The Art of Language Design

Today there are thousands of high-level programming languages, and new ones continue to emerge. Why are there so many? There are several possible answers:

Evolution. Computer science is a young discipline; we're constantly finding better ways to do things. The late 1960s and early 1970s saw a revolution in "structured programming," in which the `goto`-based control flow of languages like Fortran, Cobol, and Basic[3] gave way to `while` loops, `case` (`switch`) statements, and similar higher-level constructs. In the late 1980s the nested block structure of languages like Algol, Pascal, and Ada began to give way to the object-oriented structure of languages like Smalltalk, C++, Eiffel, and—a decade later—Java and C#. More recently, scripting languages like Python and Ruby have begun to displace more traditional compiled languages, at least for rapid development.

Special Purposes. Some languages were designed for a specific problem domain. The various Lisp dialects are good for manipulating symbolic data and complex data structures. Icon and Awk are good for manipulating character strings. C is good for low-level systems programming. Prolog is good for reasoning about logical relationships among data. Each of these languages can be used successfully for a wider range of tasks, but the emphasis is clearly on the specialty.

Personal Preference. Different people like different things. Much of the parochialism of programming is simply a matter of taste. Some people love the terseness of C; some hate it. Some people find it natural to think recursively; others prefer iteration. Some people like to work with pointers; others prefer the implicit dereferencing of Lisp, Java, and ML. The strength and variety of personal preference make it unlikely that anyone will ever develop a universally acceptable programming language.

Of course, some languages are more successful than others. Of the many that have been designed, only a few dozen are widely used. What makes a language successful? Again there are several answers:

Expressive Power. One commonly hears arguments that one language is more "powerful" than another, though in a formal mathematical sense they are all

3 The names of these languages are sometimes written entirely in uppercase letters and sometimes in mixed case. For consistency's sake, I adopt the convention in this book of using mixed case for languages whose names are pronounced as words (e.g., Fortran, Cobol, Basic), and uppercase for those pronounced as a series of letters (e.g., APL, PL/I, ML).

Turing complete—each can be used, if awkwardly, to implement arbitrary algorithms. Still, language features clearly have a huge impact on the programmer's ability to write clear, concise, and maintainable code, especially for very large systems. There is no comparison, for example, between early versions of Basic on the one hand, and C++ on the other. The factors that contribute to expressive power—abstraction facilities in particular—are a major focus of this book.

Ease of Use for the Novice. While it is easy to pick on Basic, one cannot deny its success. Part of that success was due to its very low "learning curve." Pascal was taught for many years in introductory programming language courses because, at least in comparison to other "serious" languages, it was compact and easy to learn. Shortly after the turn of the century, Java came to play a similar role; though substantially more complex than Pascal, it is simpler than, say, C++. In a renewed quest for simplicity, some introductory courses in recent years have turned to scripting languages like Python.

Ease of Implementation. In addition to its low learning curve, Basic was successful because it could be implemented easily on tiny machines, with limited resources. Forth had a small but dedicated following for similar reasons. Arguably the single most important factor in the success of Pascal was that its designer, Niklaus Wirth, developed a simple, portable implementation of the language, and shipped it free to universities all over the world (see Example 1.15).[4] The Java and Python designers took similar steps to make their language available for free to almost anyone who wants it.

Standardization. Almost every widely used language has an official international standard or (in the case of several scripting languages) a single canonical implementation; and in the latter case the canonical implementation is almost invariably written in a language that has a standard. Standardization—of both the language and a broad set of libraries—is the only truly effective way to ensure the portability of code across platforms. The relatively impoverished standard for Pascal, which was missing several features considered essential by many programmers (separate compilation, strings, static initialization, random-access I/O), was at least partially responsible for the language's drop from favor in the 1980s. Many of these features were implemented in different ways by different vendors.

Open Source. Most programming languages today have at least one open-source compiler or interpreter, but some languages—C in particular—are much more closely associated than others with freely distributed, peer-reviewed, community-supported computing. C was originally developed in the early

4 Niklaus Wirth (1934–), Professor Emeritus of Informatics at ETH in Zürich, Switzerland, is responsible for a long line of influential languages, including Euler, Algol W, Pascal, Modula, Modula-2, and Oberon. Among other things, his languages introduced the notions of enumeration, subrange, and set types, and unified the concepts of records (structs) and variants (unions). He received the annual ACM Turing Award, computing's highest honor, in 1984.

1970s by Dennis Ritchie and Ken Thompson at Bell Labs,[5] in conjunction with the design of the original Unix operating system. Over the years Unix evolved into the world's most portable operating system—the OS of choice for academic computer science—and C was closely associated with it. With the standardization of C, the language became available on an enormous variety of additional platforms. Linux, the leading open-source operating system, is written in C. As of June 2015, C and its descendants account for well over half of a variety of language-related on-line content, including web page references, book sales, employment listings, and open-source repository updates.

Excellent Compilers. Fortran owes much of its success to extremely good compilers. In part this is a matter of historical accident. Fortran has been around longer than anything else, and companies have invested huge amounts of time and money in making compilers that generate very fast code. It is also a matter of language design, however: Fortran dialects prior to Fortran 90 lacked recursion and pointers, features that greatly complicate the task of generating fast code (at least for programs that can be written in a reasonable fashion without them!). In a similar vein, some languages (e.g., Common Lisp) have been successful in part because they have compilers and supporting tools that do an unusually good job of helping the programmer manage very large projects.

Economics, Patronage, and Inertia. Finally, there are factors other than technical merit that greatly influence success. The backing of a powerful sponsor is one. PL/I, at least to first approximation, owed its life to IBM. Cobol and Ada owe their life to the U. S. Department of Defense. C# owes its life to Microsoft. In recent years, Objective-C has enjoyed an enormous surge in popularity as the official language for iPhone and iPad apps. At the other end of the life cycle, some languages remain widely used long after "better" alternatives are available, because of a huge base of installed software and programmer expertise, which would cost too much to replace. Much of the world's financial infrastructure, for example, still functions primarily in Cobol.

Clearly no single factor determines whether a language is "good." As we study programming languages, we shall need to consider issues from several points of view. In particular, we shall need to consider the viewpoints of both the programmer and the language implementor. Sometimes these points of view will be in harmony, as in the desire for execution speed. Often, however, there will be conflicts and tradeoffs, as the conceptual appeal of a feature is balanced against the cost of its implementation. The tradeoff becomes particularly thorny when the implementation imposes costs not only on programs that use the feature, but also on programs that do not.

---

5 Ken Thompson (1943–) led the team that developed Unix. He also designed the B programming language, a child of BCPL and the parent of C. Dennis Ritchie (1941–2011) was the principal force behind the development of C itself. Thompson and Ritchie together formed the core of an incredibly productive and influential group. They shared the ACM Turing Award in 1983.

In the early days of computing the implementor's viewpoint was predominant. Programming languages evolved as a means of telling a computer what to do. For programmers, however, a language is more aptly defined as a means of expressing algorithms. Just as natural languages constrain exposition and discourse, so programming languages constrain what can and cannot easily be expressed, and have both profound and subtle influence over what the programmer can *think*. Donald Knuth has suggested that programming be regarded as the art of telling another human being what one wants the computer to do [Knu84].[6] This definition perhaps strikes the best sort of compromise. It acknowledges that both conceptual clarity and implementation efficiency are fundamental concerns. This book attempts to capture this spirit of compromise, by simultaneously considering the conceptual and implementation aspects of each of the topics it covers.

DESIGN & IMPLEMENTATION

1.1 Introduction

Throughout the book, sidebars like this one will highlight the interplay of language design and language implementation. Among other things, we will consider

- Cases (such as those mentioned in this section) in which ease or difficulty of implementation significantly affected the success of a language
- Language features that many designers now believe were mistakes, at least in part because of implementation difficulties
- Potentially useful features omitted from some languages because of concern that they might be too difficult or slow to implement
- Language features introduced at least in part to facilitate efficient or elegant implementations
- Cases in which a machine architecture makes reasonable features unreasonably expensive
- Various other tradeoffs in which implementation plays a significant role

A complete list of sidebars appears in Appendix B.

---

6 Donald E. Knuth (1938–), Professor Emeritus at Stanford University and one of the foremost figures in the design and analysis of algorithms, is also widely known as the inventor of the TeX typesetting system (with which this book was produced) and of the *literate programming* methodology with which TeX was constructed. His multivolume *The Art of Computer Programming* has an honored place on the shelf of most professional computer scientists. He received the ACM Turing Award in 1974.

declarative	
functional	Lisp/Scheme, ML, Haskell
dataflow	Id, Val
logic, constraint-based	Prolog, spreadsheets, SQL
imperative	
von Neumann	C, Ada, Fortran, ...
object-oriented	Smalltalk, Eiffel, Java, ...
scripting	Perl, Python, PHP, ...

Figure 1.1 Classification of programming languages. Note that the categories are fuzzy, and open to debate. In particular, it is possible for a functional language to be object-oriented, and many authors do not consider functional programming to be declarative.

1.2 The Programming Language Spectrum

EXAMPLE 1.3
Classification of programming languages

The many existing languages can be classified into families based on their model of computation. Figure 1.1 shows a common set of families. The top-level division distinguishes between the *declarative* languages, in which the focus is on *what* the computer is to do, and the *imperative* languages, in which the focus is on *how* the computer should do it. ■

Declarative languages are in some sense "higher level"; they are more in tune with the programmer's point of view, and less with the implementor's point of view. Imperative languages predominate, however, mainly for performance reasons. There is a tension in the design of declarative languages between the desire to get away from "irrelevant" implementation details and the need to remain close enough to the details to at least control the outline of an algorithm. The design of efficient algorithms, after all, is what much of computer science is about. It is not yet clear to what extent, and in what problem domains, we can expect compilers to discover good algorithms for problems stated at a very high level of abstraction. In any domain in which the compiler cannot find a good algorithm, the programmer needs to be able to specify one explicitly.

Within the declarative and imperative families, there are several important subfamilies:

- *Functional* languages employ a computational model based on the recursive definition of functions. They take their inspiration from the *lambda calculus*, a formal computational model developed by Alonzo Church in the 1930s. In essence, a program is considered a function from inputs to outputs, defined in terms of simpler functions through a process of refinement. Languages in this category include Lisp, ML, and Haskell.
- *Dataflow* languages model computation as the flow of information (*tokens*) among primitive functional *nodes*. They provide an inherently parallel model: nodes are triggered by the arrival of input tokens, and can operate concurrently. Id and Val are examples of dataflow languages. Sisal, a descendant of Val, is more often described as a functional language.

- *Logic* or *constraint-based* languages take their inspiration from predicate logic. They model computation as an attempt to find values that satisfy certain specified relationships, using goal-directed search through a list of logical rules. Prolog is the best-known logic language. The term is also sometimes applied to the SQL database language, the XSLT scripting language, and programmable aspects of spreadsheets such as Excel and its predecessors.
- The *von Neumann* languages are probably the most familiar and widely used. They include Fortran, Ada, C, and all of the others in which the basic means of computation is the modification of variables.[7] Whereas functional languages are based on expressions that have values, von Neumann languages are based on statements (assignments in particular) that influence subsequent computation via the *side effect* of changing the value of memory.
- *Object-oriented* languages trace their roots to Simula 67. Most are closely related to the von Neumann languages, but have a much more structured and distributed model of both memory and computation. Rather than picture computation as the operation of a monolithic processor on a monolithic memory, object-oriented languages picture it as interactions among semi-independent *objects*, each of which has both its own internal state and subroutines to manage that state. Smalltalk is the purest of the object-oriented languages; C++ and Java are probably the most widely used. It is also possible to devise object-oriented functional languages (the best known of these are CLOS [Kee89] and OCaml), but they tend to have a strong imperative flavor.
- *Scripting* languages are distinguished by their emphasis on coordinating or "gluing together" components drawn from some surrounding context. Several scripting languages were originally developed for specific purposes: `csh` and `bash` are the input languages of job control (shell) programs; PHP and JavaScript are primarily intended for the generation of dynamic web content; Lua is widely used to control computer games. Other languages, including Perl, Python, and Ruby, are more deliberately general purpose. Most place an emphasis on rapid prototyping, with a bias toward ease of expression over speed of execution.

One might suspect that concurrent (parallel) languages would form a separate family (and indeed this book devotes a chapter to such languages), but the distinction between concurrent and sequential execution is mostly independent of the classifications above. Most concurrent programs are currently written using special library packages or compilers in conjunction with a sequential language such as Fortran or C. A few widely used languages, including Java, C#, and Ada, have explicitly concurrent features. Researchers are investigating concurrency in each of the language families mentioned here.

---

7 John von Neumann (1903–1957) was a mathematician and computer pioneer who helped to develop the concept of *stored program* computing, which underlies most computer hardware. In a stored program computer, both programs and data are represented as bits in memory, which the processor repeatedly fetches, interprets, and updates.

As a simple example of the contrast among language families, consider the greatest common divisor (GCD) problem introduced at the beginning of this chapter. The choice among, say, von Neumann, functional, or logic programming for this problem influences not only the appearance of the code, but how the programmer thinks. The von Neumann algorithm version of the algorithm is very imperative:

EXAMPLE 1.4
GCD function in C

> To compute the `gcd` of `a` and `b`, check to see if `a` and `b` are equal. If so, print one of them and stop. Otherwise, replace the larger one by their difference and repeat.

C code for this algorithm appears at the top of Figure 1.2.

EXAMPLE 1.5
GCD function in OCaml

In a functional language, the emphasis is on the mathematical relationship of outputs to inputs:

> The `gcd` of `a` and `b` is defined to be (1) `a` when `a` and `b` are equal, (2) the `gcd` of `b` and `a - b` when `a > b`, and (3) the `gcd` of `a` and `b - a` when `b > a`. To compute the `gcd` of a given pair of numbers, expand and simplify this definition until it terminates.

An OCaml version of this algorithm appears in the middle of Figure 1.2. The keyword `let` introduces a definition; `rec` indicates that it is permitted to be recursive (self-referential); arguments for a function come between the name (in this case, `gcd`) and the equals sign.

EXAMPLE 1.6
GCD rules in Prolog

In a logic language, the programmer specifies a set of axioms and proof rules that allows the system to find desired values:

> The proposition `gcd(a, b, g)` is true if (1) `a`, `b`, and `g` are all equal; (2) `a` is greater than `b` and there exists a number `c` such that `c` is `a - b` and `gcd(c, b, g)` is true; or (3) `a` is less than `b` and there exists a number `c` such that `c` is `b - a` and `gcd(c, a, g)` is true. To compute the `gcd` of a given pair of numbers, search for a number `g` (and various numbers `c`) for which these rules allow one to prove that `gcd(a, b, g)` is true.

A Prolog version of this algorithm appears at the bottom of Figure 1.2. It may be easier to understand if one reads "if" for `:-` and "and" for commas.

It should be emphasized that the distinctions among language families are not clear-cut. The division between the von Neumann and object-oriented languages, for example, is often very fuzzy, and many scripting languages are also object-oriented. Most of the functional and logic languages include some imperative features, and several recent imperative languages have added functional features. The descriptions above are meant to capture the general flavor of the families, without providing formal definitions.

Imperative languages—von Neumann and object-oriented—receive the bulk of the attention in this book. Many issues cut across family lines, however, and the interested reader will discover much that is applicable to alternative computational models in most chapters of the book. Chapters 11 through 14 contain additional material on functional, logic, concurrent, and scripting languages.

```
int gcd(int a, int b) {                                // C
    while (a != b) {
        if (a > b) a = a - b;
        else b = b - a;
    }
    return a;
}

let rec gcd a b =                                      (* OCaml *)
    if a = b then a
    else if a > b then gcd b (a - b)
        else gcd a (b - a)

gcd(A,B,G) :- A = B, G = A.                           % Prolog
gcd(A,B,G) :- A > B, C is A-B, gcd(C,B,G).
gcd(A,B,G) :- B > A, C is B-A, gcd(C,A,G).
```

Figure 1.2 The GCD algorithm in C (top), OCaml (middle), and Prolog (bottom). All three versions assume (without checking) that their inputs are positive integers.

1.3 Why Study Programming Languages?

Programming languages are central to computer science, and to the typical computer science curriculum. Like most car owners, students who have become familiar with one or more high-level languages are generally curious to learn about other languages, and to know what is going on "under the hood." Learning about languages is interesting. It's also practical.

For one thing, a good understanding of language design and implementation can help one choose the most appropriate language for any given task. Most languages are better for some things than for others. Few programmers are likely to choose Fortran for symbolic computing or string processing, but other choices are not nearly so clear-cut. Should one choose C, C++, or C# for systems programming? Fortran or C for scientific computations? PHP or Ruby for a web-based application? Ada or C for embedded systems? Visual Basic or Java for a graphical user interface? This book should help equip you to make such decisions.

Similarly, this book should make it easier to learn new languages. Many languages are closely related. Java and C# are easier to learn if you already know C++; Common Lisp if you already know Scheme; Haskell if you already know ML. More importantly, there are basic concepts that underlie all programming languages. Most of these concepts are the subject of chapters in this book: types, control (iteration, selection, recursion, nondeterminacy, concurrency), abstraction, and naming. Thinking in terms of these concepts makes it easier to assimilate the syntax (form) and semantics (meaning) of new languages, compared to picking them up in a vacuum. The situation is analogous to what happens in natural languages: a good knowledge of grammatical forms makes it easier to learn a foreign language.

Whatever language you learn, understanding the decisions that went into its design and implementation will help you use it better. This book should help you:

Understand obscure features. The typical C++ programmer rarely uses unions, multiple inheritance, variable numbers of arguments, or the `.*` operator. (If you don't know what these are, don't worry!) Just as it simplifies the assimilation of new languages, an understanding of basic concepts makes it easier to understand these features when you look up the details in the manual.

Choose among alternative ways to express things, based on a knowledge of implementation costs. In C++, for example, programmers may need to avoid unnecessary temporary variables, and use copy constructors whenever possible, to minimize the cost of initialization. In Java they may wish to use `Executor` objects rather than explicit thread creation. With certain (poor) compilers, they may need to adopt special programming idioms to get the fastest code: pointers for array traversal; `x*x` instead of `x**2`. In any language, they need to be able to evaluate the tradeoffs among alternative implementations of abstractions—for example between computation and table lookup for functions like bit set cardinality, which can be implemented either way.

Make good use of debuggers, assemblers, linkers, and related tools. In general, the high-level language programmer should not need to bother with implementation details. There are times, however, when an understanding of those details is virtually essential. The tenacious bug or unusual system-building problem may be dramatically easier to handle if one is willing to peek at the bits.

Simulate useful features in languages that lack them. Certain very useful features are missing in older languages, but can be emulated by following a deliberate (if unenforced) programming style. In older dialects of Fortran, for example, programmers familiar with modern control constructs can use comments and self-discipline to write well-structured code. Similarly, in languages with poor abstraction facilities, comments and naming conventions can help imitate modular structure, and the extremely useful *iterators* of Clu, C#, Python, and Ruby (which we will study in Section 6.5.3) can be imitated with subroutines and static variables.

Make better use of language technology wherever it appears. Most programmers will never design or implement a conventional programming language, but most will need language technology for other programming tasks. The typical personal computer contains files in dozens of structured formats, encompassing word processing, spreadsheets, presentations, raster and vector graphics, music, video, databases, and a wide variety of other application domains. Web content is increasingly represented in XML, a text-based format designed for easy manipulation in the XSLT scripting language (discussed in Section C-14.3.5). Code to parse, analyze, generate, optimize, and otherwise manipulate structured data can thus be found in almost any sophisticated program, and all of this code is based on language technology. Programmers with a strong grasp of this technology will be in a better position to write well-structured, maintainable tools.

In a similar vein, most tools themselves can be customized, via start-up configuration files, command-line arguments, input commands, or built-in *extension languages* (considered in more detail in Chapter 14). My home directory holds more than 250 separate configuration ("preference") files. My personal configuration files for the `emacs` text editor comprise more than 1200 lines of Lisp code. The user of almost any sophisticated program today will need to make good use of configuration or extension languages. The designers of such a program will need either to adopt (and adapt) some existing extension language, or to invent new notation of their own. Programmers with a strong grasp of language theory will be in a better position to design elegant, well-structured notation that meets the needs of current users and facilitates future development.

Finally, this book should help prepare you for further study in language design or implementation, should you be so inclined. It will also equip you to understand the interactions of languages with operating systems and architectures, should those areas draw your interest.

✓ CHECK YOUR UNDERSTANDING

1. What is the difference between machine language and assembly language?
2. In what way(s) are high-level languages an improvement on assembly language? Are there circumstances in which it still make sense to program in assembler?
3. Why are there so many programming languages?
4. What makes a programming language successful?
5. Name three languages in each of the following categories: von Neumann, functional, object-oriented. Name two logic languages. Name two widely used concurrent languages.
6. What distinguishes declarative languages from imperative languages?
7. What organization spearheaded the development of Ada?
8. What is generally considered the first high-level programming language?
9. What was the first functional language?
10. Why aren't concurrent languages listed as a separate family in Figure 1.1?

1.4 Compilation and Interpretation

EXAMPLE 1.7
Pure compilation

At the highest level of abstraction, the compilation and execution of a program in a high-level language look something like this:

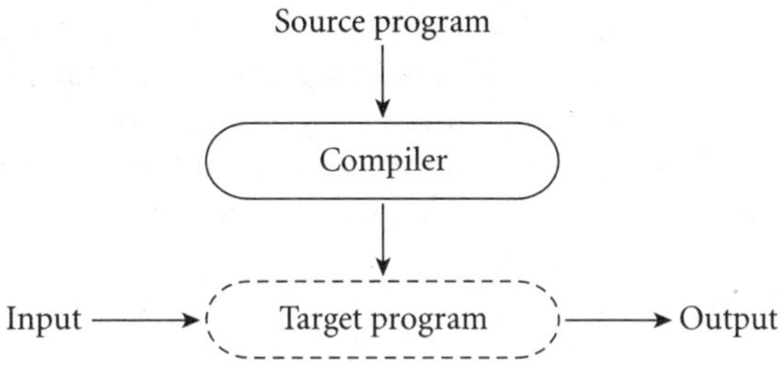

The compiler *translates* the high-level source program into an equivalent target program (typically in machine language), and then goes away. At some arbitrary later time, the user tells the operating system to run the target program. The compiler is the locus of control during compilation; the target program is the locus of control during its own execution. The compiler is itself a machine language program, presumably created by compiling some other high-level program. When written to a file in a format understood by the operating system, machine language is commonly known as *object code*.

EXAMPLE 1.8
Pure interpretation

An alternative style of implementation for high-level languages is known as *interpretation*:

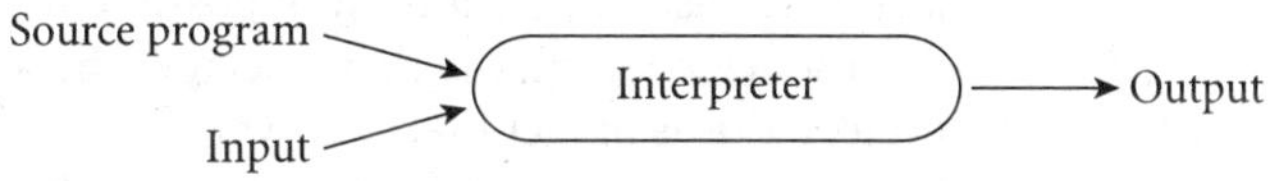

Unlike a compiler, an interpreter stays around for the execution of the application. In fact, the interpreter is the locus of control during that execution. In effect, the interpreter implements a virtual machine whose "machine language" is the high-level programming language. The interpreter reads statements in that language more or less one at a time, executing them as it goes along.

In general, interpretation leads to greater flexibility and better diagnostics (error messages) than does compilation. Because the source code is being executed directly, the interpreter can include an excellent source-level debugger. It can also cope with languages in which fundamental characteristics of the program, such as the sizes and types of variables, or even which names refer to which variables, can depend on the input data. Some language features are almost impossible to implement without interpretation: in Lisp and Prolog, for example, a program can write new pieces of itself and execute them on the fly. (Several scripting languages also provide this capability.) Delaying decisions about program implementation until run time is known as *late binding*; we will discuss it at greater length in Section 3.1.

Compilation, by contrast, generally leads to better performance. In general, a decision made at compile time is a decision that does not need to be made at run time. For example, if the compiler can guarantee that variable x will always lie at location 49378, it can generate machine language instructions that access this location whenever the source program refers to x. By contrast, an interpreter may need to look x up in a table every time it is accessed, in order to find its location. Since the (final version of a) program is compiled only once, but generally executed many times, the savings can be substantial, particularly if the interpreter is doing unnecessary work in every iteration of a loop.

EXAMPLE 1.9
Mixing compilation and interpretation

While the conceptual difference between compilation and interpretation is clear, most language implementations include a mixture of both. They typically look like this:

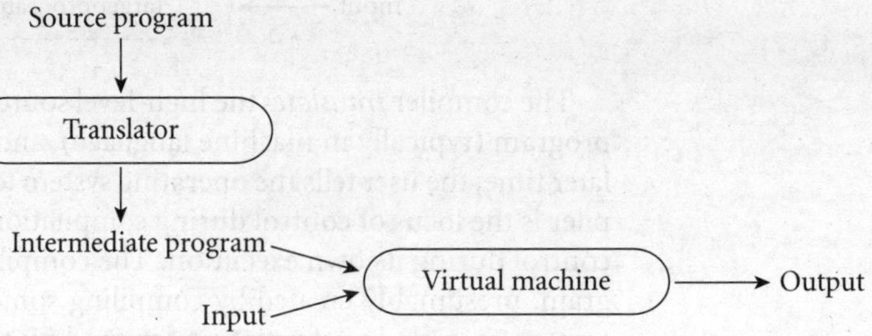

We generally say that a language is "interpreted" when the initial translator is simple. If the translator is complicated, we say that the language is "compiled." The distinction can be confusing because "simple" and "complicated" are subjective terms, and because it is possible for a compiler (complicated translator) to produce code that is then executed by a complicated virtual machine (interpreter); this is in fact precisely what happens by default in Java. We still say that a language is compiled if the translator analyzes it thoroughly (rather than effecting some "mechanical" transformation), and if the intermediate program does not bear a strong resemblance to the source. These two characteristics—thorough analysis and nontrivial transformation—are the hallmarks of compilation. ■

DESIGN & IMPLEMENTATION

1.2 Compiled and interpreted languages

Certain languages (e.g., Smalltalk and Python) are sometimes referred to as "interpreted languages" because most of their semantic error checking must be performed at run time. Certain other languages (e.g., Fortran and C) are sometimes referred to as "compiled languages" because almost all of their semantic error checking can be performed statically. This terminology isn't strictly correct: interpreters for C and Fortran can be built easily, and a compiler can generate code to perform even the most extensive dynamic semantic checks. That said, language design has a profound effect on "compilability."

In practice one sees a broad spectrum of implementation strategies:

EXAMPLE 1.10
Preprocessing

Most interpreted languages employ an initial translator (a *preprocessor*) that removes comments and white space, and groups characters together into *tokens* such as keywords, identifiers, numbers, and symbols. The translator may also expand abbreviations in the style of a macro assembler. Finally, it may identify higher-level syntactic structures, such as loops and subroutines. The goal is to produce an intermediate form that mirrors the structure of the source, but can be interpreted more efficiently.

In some very early implementations of Basic, the manual actually suggested removing comments from a program in order to improve its performance. These implementations were pure interpreters; they would re-read (and then ignore) the comments every time they executed a given part of the program. They had no initial translator.

EXAMPLE 1.11
Library routines and linking

The typical Fortran implementation comes close to pure compilation. The compiler translates Fortran source into machine language. Usually, however, it counts on the existence of a *library* of subroutines that are not part of the original program. Examples include mathematical functions (`sin`, `cos`, `log`, etc.) and I/O. The compiler relies on a separate program, known as a *linker*, to merge the appropriate library routines into the final program:

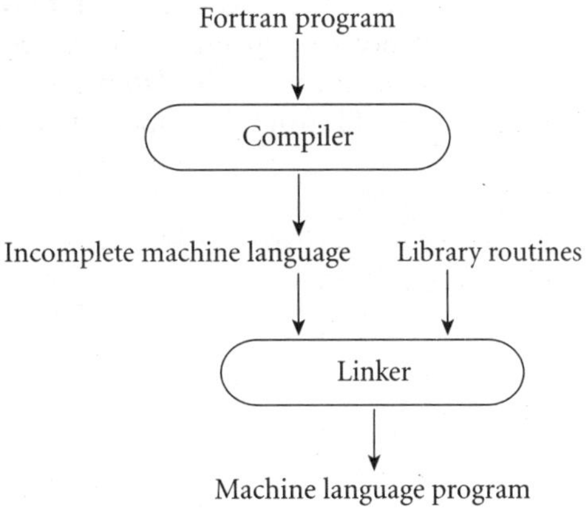

In some sense, one may think of the library routines as extensions to the hardware instruction set. The compiler can then be thought of as generating code for a virtual machine that includes the capabilities of both the hardware and the library.

In a more literal sense, one can find interpretation in the Fortran routines for formatted output. Fortran permits the use of `format` statements that control the alignment of output in columns, the number of significant digits and type of scientific notation for floating-point numbers, inclusion/suppression of leading zeros, and so on. Programs can compute their own formats on the fly. The output library routines include a format interpreter. A similar interpreter can be found in the `printf` routine of C and its descendants.

EXAMPLE 1.12
Post-compilation assembly

Many compilers generate assembly language instead of machine language. This convention facilitates debugging, since assembly language is easier for people to read, and isolates the compiler from changes in the format of machine language files that may be mandated by new releases of the operating system (only the assembler must be changed, and it is shared by many compilers):

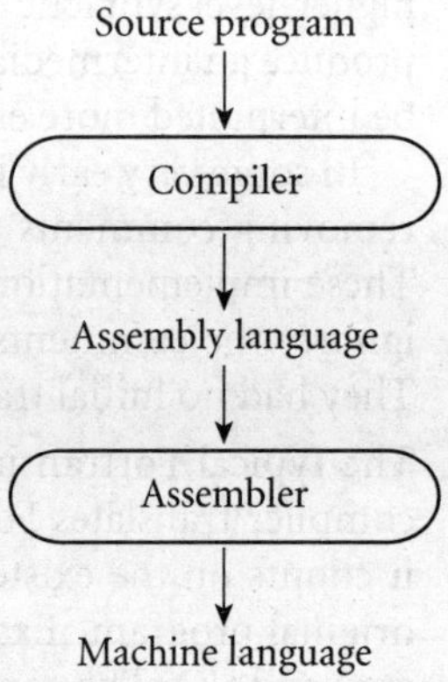

EXAMPLE 1.13
The C preprocessor

Compilers for C (and for many other languages running under Unix) begin with a preprocessor that removes comments and expands macros. The preprocessor can also be instructed to delete portions of the code itself, providing a *conditional compilation* facility that allows several versions of a program to be built from the same source:

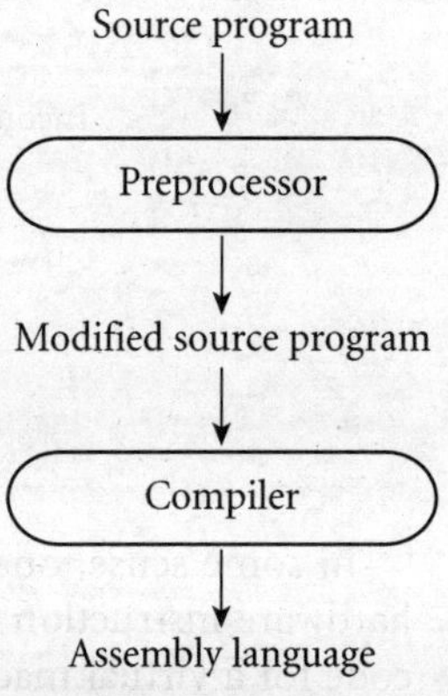

EXAMPLE 1.14
Source-to-source translation

A surprising number of compilers generate output in some high-level language—commonly C or some simplified version of the input language. Such *source-to-source* translation is particularly common in research languages and during the early stages of language development. One famous example was AT&T's original compiler for C++. This was indeed a true compiler, though it generated C instead of assembler: it performed a complete analysis of the syntax and semantics of the C++ source program, and with very few exceptions generated all of the error messages that a programmer would see prior to running the program. In fact, programmers were generally unaware that the C compiler was being used behind the scenes. The C++ compiler did not invoke the C compiler unless it had generated C code that would pass through the second round of compilation without producing any error messages:

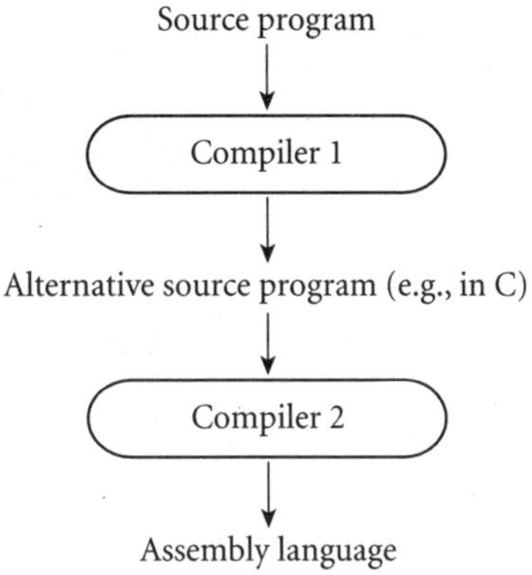

Occasionally one would hear the C++ compiler referred to as a preprocessor, presumably because it generated high-level output that was in turn compiled. I consider this a misuse of the term: compilers attempt to "understand" their source; preprocessors do not. Preprocessors perform transformations based on simple pattern matching, and may well produce output that will generate error messages when run through a subsequent stage of translation.

EXAMPLE 1.15
Bootstrapping

Many compilers are *self-hosting*: they are written in the language they compile—Ada compilers in Ada, C compilers in C. This raises an obvious question: how does one compile the compiler in the first place? The answer is to use a technique known as *bootstrapping*, a term derived from the intentionally ridiculous notion of lifting oneself off the ground by pulling on one's bootstraps. In a nutshell, one starts with a simple implementation—often an interpreter—and uses it to build progressively more sophisticated versions. We can illustrate the idea with an historical example.

Many early Pascal compilers were built around a set of tools distributed by Niklaus Wirth. These included the following:

- A Pascal compiler, written in Pascal, that would generate output in *P-code*, a stack-based language similar to the *bytecode* of modern Java compilers
- The same compiler, already translated into P-code
- A P-code interpreter, written in Pascal

To get Pascal up and running on a local machine, the user of the tool set needed only to translate the P-code interpreter (by hand) into some locally available language. This translation was not a difficult task; the interpreter was small. By running the P-code version of the compiler on top of the P-code interpreter, one could then compile arbitrary Pascal programs into P-code, which could in turn be run on the interpreter. To get a faster implementation, one could modify the Pascal version of the Pascal compiler to generate a locally available variety of assembly or machine language, instead of generating P-code (a somewhat more difficult task). This compiler could then be bootstrapped—run through itself—to yield a machine-code version of the compiler:

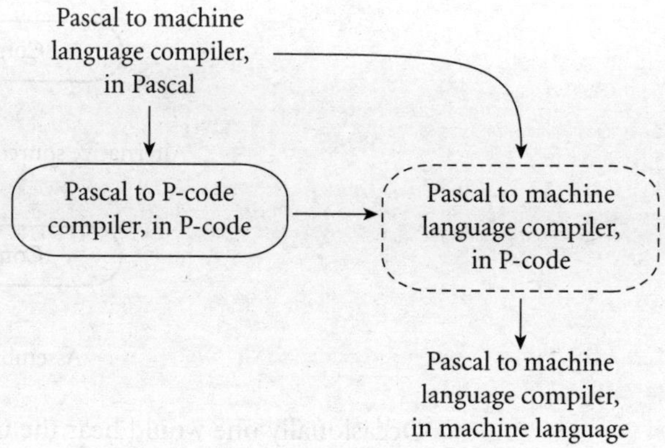

In a more general context, suppose we were building one of the first compilers for a new programming language. Assuming we have a C compiler on our target system, we might start by writing, in a simple subset of C, a compiler for an equally simple subset of our new programming language. Once this compiler was working, we could hand-translate the C code into (the subset of) our new language, and then run the new source through the compiler itself. After that, we could repeatedly extend the compiler to accept a larger subset

DESIGN & IMPLEMENTATION

1.3 The early success of Pascal

The P-code-based implementation of Pascal, and its use of bootstrapping, are largely responsible for the language's remarkable success in academic circles in the 1970s. No single hardware platform or operating system of that era dominated the computer landscape the way the x86, Linux, and Windows do today.[8] Wirth's toolkit made it possible to get an implementation of Pascal up and running on almost any platform in a week or so. It was one of the first great successes in system portability.

8 Throughout this book we will use the term "x86" to refer to the instruction set architecture of the Intel 8086 and its descendants, including the various Pentium, "Core," and Xeon processors. Intel calls this architecture the IA-32, but x86 is a more generic term that encompasses the offerings of competitors such as AMD as well.

of the new programming language, bootstrap it again, and use the extended language to implement an even larger subset. "Self-hosting" implementations of this sort are actually quite common.

EXAMPLE 1.16
Compiling interpreted languages

One will sometimes find compilers for languages (e.g., Lisp, Prolog, Smalltalk) that permit a lot of late binding, and are traditionally interpreted. These compilers must be prepared, in the general case, to generate code that performs much of the work of an interpreter, or that makes calls into a library that does that work instead. In important special cases, however, the compiler can generate code that makes reasonable assumptions about decisions that won't be finalized until run time. If these assumptions prove to be valid the code will run very fast. If the assumptions are not correct, a dynamic check will discover the inconsistency, and revert to the interpreter.

EXAMPLE 1.17
Dynamic and just-in-time compilation

In some cases a programming system may deliberately delay compilation until the last possible moment. One example occurs in language implementations (e.g., for Lisp or Prolog) that invoke the compiler on the fly, to translate newly created source into machine language, or to optimize the code for a particular input set. Another example occurs in implementations of Java. The Java language definition defines a machine-independent intermediate form known as Java *bytecode*. Bytecode is the standard format for distribution of Java programs; it allows programs to be transferred easily over the Internet, and then run on any platform. The first Java implementations were based on byte-code interpreters, but modern implementations obtain significantly better performance with a *just-in-time* compiler that translates bytecode into machine language immediately before each execution of the program:

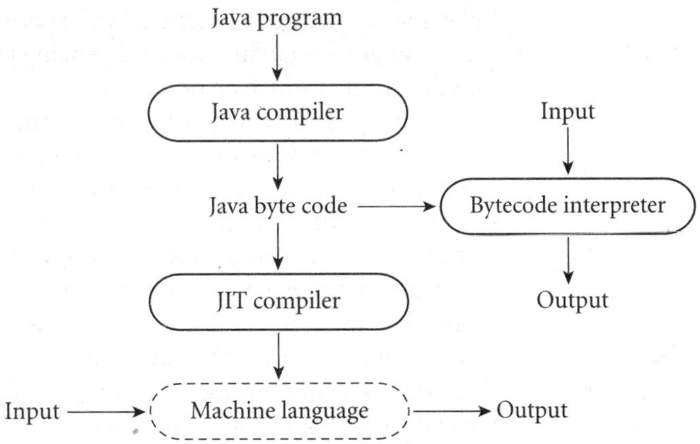

C#, similarly, is intended for just-in-time translation. The main C# compiler produces *Common Intermediate Language* (CIL), which is then translated into machine language immediately prior to execution. CIL is deliberately language independent, so it can be used for code produced by a variety of front-end compilers. We will explore the Java and C# implementations in detail in Section 16.1.

EXAMPLE 1.18
Microcode (firmware)

On some machines (particularly those designed before the mid-1980s), the assembly-level instruction set is not actually implemented in hardware, but in fact runs on an interpreter. The interpreter is written in low-level instructions called *microcode* (or *firmware*), which is stored in read-only memory and executed by the hardware. Microcode and microprogramming are considered further in Section C-5.4.1.

As some of these examples make clear, a compiler does not necessarily translate from a high-level programming language into machine language. Some compilers, in fact, accept inputs that we might not immediately think of as programs at all. Text formatters like TEX, for example, compile high-level document descriptions into commands for a laser printer or phototypesetter. (Many laser printers themselves contain pre-installed interpreters for the Postscript page-description language.) Query language processors for database systems translate languages like SQL into primitive operations on files. There are even compilers that translate logic-level circuit specifications into photographic masks for computer chips. Though the focus in this book is on imperative programming languages, the term "compilation" applies whenever we translate automatically from one nontrivial language to another, with full analysis of the meaning of the input.

1.5 Programming Environments

Compilers and interpreters do not exist in isolation. Programmers are assisted in their work by a host of other tools. Assemblers, debuggers, preprocessors, and linkers were mentioned earlier. Editors are familiar to every programmer. They may be augmented with cross-referencing facilities that allow the programmer to find the point at which an object is defined, given a point at which it is used. Pretty printers help enforce formatting conventions. Style checkers enforce syntactic or semantic conventions that may be tighter than those enforced by the compiler (see Exploration 1.14). Configuration management tools help keep track of dependences among the (many versions of) separately compiled modules in a large software system. Perusal tools exist not only for text but also for intermediate languages that may be stored in binary. Profilers and other performance analysis tools often work in conjunction with debuggers to help identify the pieces of a program that consume the bulk of its computation time.

In older programming environments, tools may be executed individually, at the explicit request of the user. If a running program terminates abnormally with a "bus error" (invalid address) message, for example, the user may choose to invoke a debugger to examine the "core" file dumped by the operating system. He or she may then attempt to identify the program bug by setting breakpoints, enabling tracing and so on, and running the program again under the control of the debugger. Once the bug is found, the user will invoke the editor to make an appropriate change. He or she will then recompile the modified program, possibly with the help of a configuration manager.

Modern environments provide more integrated tools. When an invalid address error occurs in an integrated development environment (IDE), a new window is likely to appear on the user's screen, with the line of source code at which the error occurred highlighted. Breakpoints and tracing can then be set in this window without explicitly invoking a debugger. Changes to the source can be made without explicitly invoking an editor. If the user asks to rerun the program after making changes, a new version may be built without explicitly invoking the compiler or configuration manager.

The editor for an IDE may incorporate knowledge of language syntax, providing templates for all the standard control structures, and checking syntax as it is typed in. Internally, the IDE is likely to maintain not only a program's source and object code, but also a partially compiled internal representation. When the source is edited, the internal representation will be updated automatically—often incrementally (without reparsing large portions of the source). In some cases, structural changes to the program may be implemented first in the internal representation, and then automatically reflected in the source.

IDEs are fundamental to Smalltalk—it is nearly impossible to separate the language from its graphical environment—and have been routinely used for Common Lisp since the 1980s. With the ubiquity of graphical interfaces, integrated environments have largely displaced command-line tools for many languages and systems. Popular open-source IDEs include Eclipse and NetBeans. Commercial systems include the Visual Studio environment from Microsoft and the XCode environment from Apple. Much of the appearance of integration can also be achieved within sophisticated editors such as `emacs`.

✓ CHECK YOUR UNDERSTANDING

11. Explain the distinction between interpretation and compilation. What are the comparative advantages and disadvantages of the two approaches?
12. Is Java compiled or interpreted (or both)? How do you know?
13. What is the difference between a compiler and a preprocessor?
14. What was the intermediate form employed by the original AT&T C++ compiler?

DESIGN & IMPLEMENTATION

1.4 Powerful development environments

Sophisticated development environments can be a two-edged sword. The quality of the Common Lisp environment has arguably contributed to its widespread acceptance. On the other hand, the particularity of the graphical environment for Smalltalk (with its insistence on specific fonts, window styles, etc.) made it difficult to port the language to systems accessed through a textual interface, or to graphical systems with a different "look and feel."

15. What is P-code?
16. What is bootstrapping?
17. What is a just-in-time compiler?
18. Name two languages in which a program can write new pieces of itself "on the fly."
19. Briefly describe three "unconventional" compilers—compilers whose purpose is not to prepare a high-level program for execution on a general-purpose processor.
20. List six kinds of tools that commonly support the work of a compiler within a larger programming environment.
21. Explain how an integrated development environment (IDE) differs from a collection of command-line tools.

1.6 An Overview of Compilation

Compilers are among the most well-studied computer programs. We will consider them repeatedly throughout the rest of the book, and in chapters 2, 4, 15, and 17 in particular. The remainder of this section provides an introductory overview.

EXAMPLE 1.19
Phases of compilation and interpretation

In a typical compiler, compilation proceeds through a series of well-defined *phases*, shown in Figure 1.3. Each phase discovers information of use to later phases, or transforms the program into a form that is more useful to the subsequent phase.

The first few phases (up through semantic analysis) serve to figure out the meaning of the source program. They are sometimes called the *front end* of the compiler. The last few phases serve to construct an equivalent target program. They are sometimes called the *back end* of the compiler.

An interpreter (Figure 1.4) shares the compiler's front-end structure, but "executes" (interprets) the intermediate form directly, rather than translating it into machine language. The execution typically takes the form of a set of mutually recursive subroutines that traverse ("walk") the syntax tree, "executing" its nodes in program order. Many compiler and interpreter phases can be created automatically from a formal description of the source and/or target languages. ■

One will sometimes hear compilation described as a series of *passes*. A pass is a phase or set of phases that is serialized with respect to the rest of compilation: it does not start until previous phases have completed, and it finishes before any subsequent phases start. If desired, a pass may be written as a separate program, reading its input from a file and writing its output to a file. Compilers are commonly divided into passes so that the front end may be shared by compilers

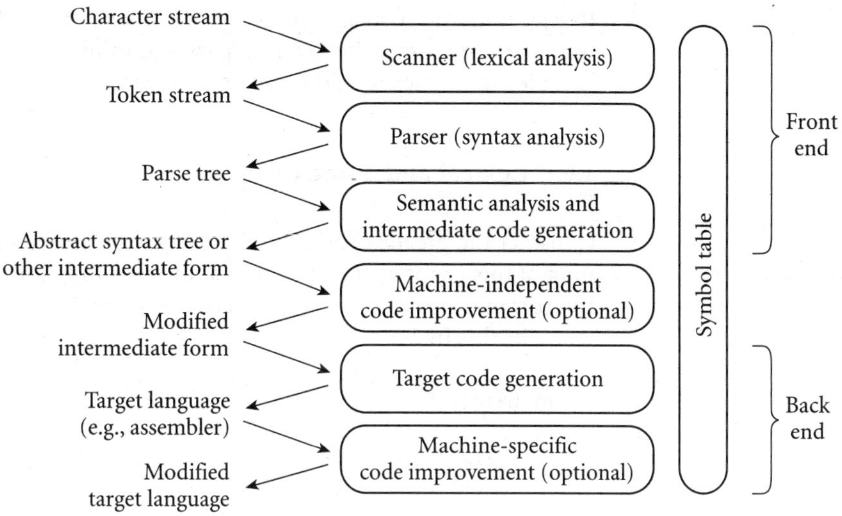

Figure 1.3 Phases of compilation. Phases are listed on the right and the forms in which information is passed between phases are listed on the left. The symbol table serves throughout compilation as a repository for information about identifiers.

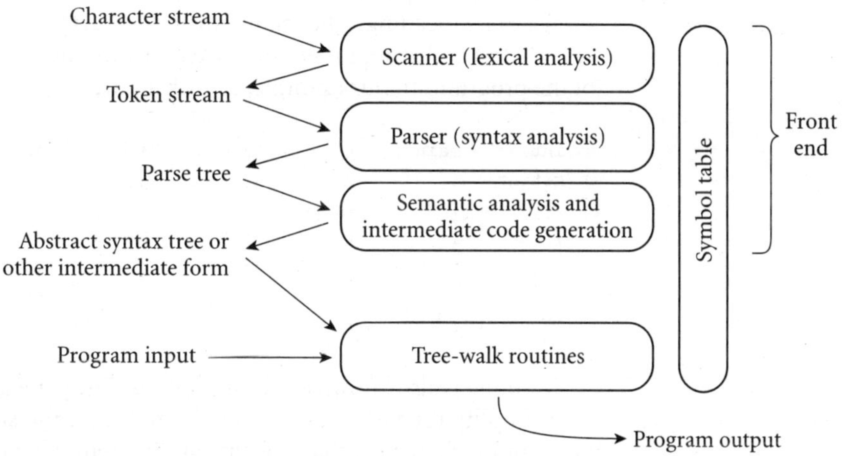

Figure 1.4 Phases of interpretation. The front end is essentially the same as that of a compiler. The final phase "executes" the intermediate form, typically using a set of mutually recursive subroutines that walk the syntax tree.

for more than one machine (target language), and so that the back end may be shared by compilers for more than one source language. In some implementations the front end and the back end may be separated by a "middle end" that is responsible for language- and machine-independent code improvement. Prior to the dramatic increases in memory sizes of the mid to late 1980s, compilers were also sometimes divided into passes to minimize memory usage: as each pass completed, the next could reuse its code space.

1.6.1 Lexical and Syntax Analysis

EXAMPLE 1.20
GCD program in C

Consider the greatest common divisor (GCD) problem introduced at the beginning of this chapter, and shown as a function in Figure 1.2. Hypothesizing trivial I/O routines and recasting the function as a stand-alone program, our code might look like this in C:

```
int main() {
    int i = getint(), j = getint();
    while (i != j) {
        if (i > j) i = i - j;
        else j = j - i;
    }
    putint(i);
}
```

EXAMPLE 1.21
GCD program tokens

Scanning and parsing serve to recognize the structure of the program, without regard to its meaning. The scanner reads characters (‘i’, ‘n’, ‘t’, ‘ ’, ‘m’, ‘a’, ‘i’, ‘n’, ‘(’, ‘)’, etc.) and groups them into *tokens*, which are the smallest meaningful units of the program. In our example, the tokens are

`int`	`main`	`(`	`)`	`{`	`int`	`i`	`=`
`getint`	`(`	`)`	`,`	`j`	`=`	`getint`	`(`
`)`	`;`	`while`	`(`	`i`	`!=`	`j`	`)`
`{`	`if`	`(`	`i`	`>`	`j`	`)`	`i`
`=`	`i`	`-`	`j`	`;`	`else`	`j`	`=`
`j`	`-`	`i`	`;`	`}`	`putint`	`(`	`i`
`)`	`;`	`}`					

Scanning is also known as *lexical analysis*. The principal purpose of the scanner is to simplify the task of the parser, by reducing the size of the input (there are many more characters than tokens) and by removing extraneous characters like white space. The scanner also typically removes comments and tags tokens with line and column numbers, to make it easier to generate good diagnostics in later phases. One could design a parser to take characters instead of tokens as input—dispensing with the scanner—but the result would be awkward and slow.

EXAMPLE 1.22
Context-free grammar and parsing

Parsing organizes tokens into a *parse tree* that represents higher-level constructs (statements, expressions, subroutines, and so on) in terms of their constituents. Each construct is a node in the tree; its constituents are its children. The root of the tree is simply "*program*"; the leaves, from left to right, are the tokens received from the scanner. Taken as a whole, the tree shows how the tokens fit together to make a valid program. The structure relies on a set of potentially recursive rules known as a *context-free grammar*. Each rule has an arrow sign (⟶) with the construct name on the left and a possible expansion on the right.[9] In C, for example, a `while` loop consists of the keyword `while` followed by a parenthesized Boolean expression and a statement:

iteration-statement ⟶ `while ( ` *expression* ` ) ` *statement*

The statement, in turn, is often a list enclosed in braces:

statement ⟶ *compound-statement*

compound-statement ⟶ `{` *block-item-list_opt* `}`

where

block-item-list_opt ⟶ *block-item-list*

or

block-item-list_opt ⟶ ϵ

and

block-item-list ⟶ *block-item*

block-item-list ⟶ *block-item-list block-item*

block-item ⟶ *declaration*

block-item ⟶ *statement*

Here ϵ represents the empty string; it indicates that *block-item-list_opt* can simply be deleted. Many more grammar rules are needed, of course, to explain the full structure of a program.

A context-free grammar is said to define the *syntax* of the language; parsing is therefore known as *syntax analysis*. There are many possible grammars for C (an infinite number, in fact); the fragment shown above is taken from the sample grammar contained in the official language definition [Int99]. A full parse tree for our GCD program (based on a full grammar not shown here) appears in Figure 1.5. While the size of the tree may seem daunting, its details aren't particularly important at this point in the text. What *is* important is that (1) each individual branching point represents the application of a single grammar rule, and (2) the resulting complexity is more a reflection of the grammar than it is of the input program. Much of the bulk stems from (a) the use of such artificial "constructs" as *block_item-list* and *block_item-list_opt* to generate lists of arbitrary

EXAMPLE 1.23
GCD program parse tree

9 Theorists also study *context-sensitive* grammars, in which the allowable expansions of a construct (the applicable rules) depend on the context in which the construct appears (i.e., on constructs to the left and right). Context sensitivity is important for natural languages like English, but it is almost never used in programming language design.

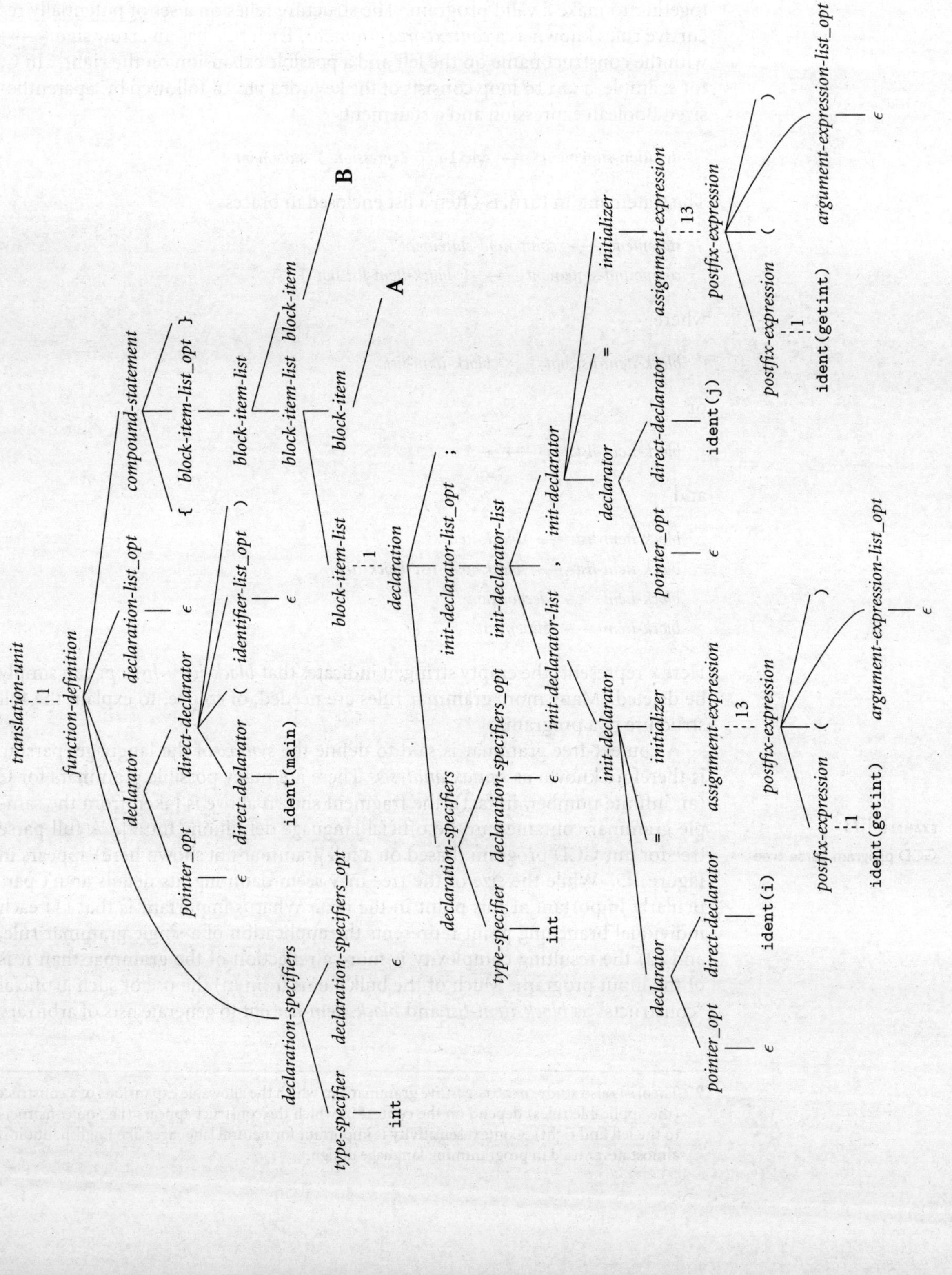
translation-unit
1
function-definition
declaration-specifiers
declarator
declaration-list_opt
compound-statement
type-specifier
declaration-specifiers_opt
pointer_opt
direct-declarator
ϵ
{
block-item-list_opt
}
int
ϵ
ϵ
direct-declarator
(
identifier-list_opt
)
block-item-list
ident(main)
ϵ
block-item-list
block-item
1
block-item-list
block-item
B
declaration
A
declaration-specifiers
init-declarator-list_opt
;
type-specifier
declaration-specifiers_opt
init-declarator-list
int
ϵ
init-declarator-list
,
init-declarator
init-declarator
declarator
=
initializer
declarator
=
initializer
pointer_opt
direct-declarator
assignment-expression
pointer_opt
direct-declarator
assignment-expression
ϵ
ident(i)
13
ϵ
ident(j)
13
postfix-expression
postfix-expression
postfix-expression
(
argument-expression-list_opt
)
postfix-expression
(
argument-expression-list_opt
)
1
1
ident(getint)
ϵ
ident(getint)
ϵ

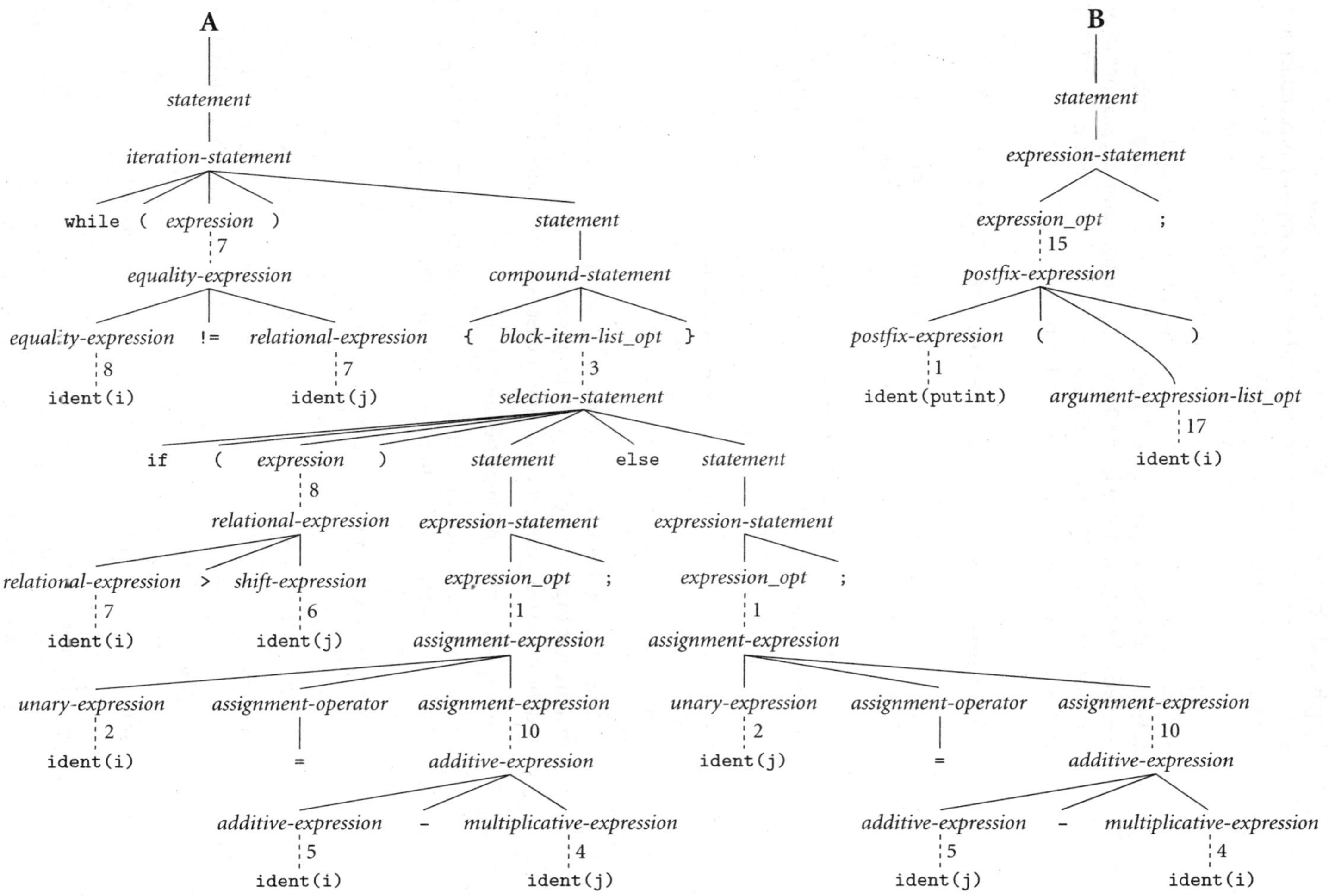

Figure 1.5 Parse tree for the GCD program. The symbol ϵ represents the empty string. Dotted lines indicate a chain of one-for-one replacements, elided to save space; the adjacent number indicates the number of omitted nodes. While the details of the tree aren't important to the current chapter, the sheer *amount* of detail is: it comes from having to fit the (much simpler) source code into the hierarchical structure of a context-free grammar.

length, and (b) the use of the equally artificial *assignment-expression*, *additive-expression*, *multiplicative-expression*, and so on, to capture precedence and associativity in arithmetic expressions. We shall see in the following subsection that much of this complexity can be discarded once parsing is complete. ■

In the process of scanning and parsing, the compiler or interpreter checks to see that all of the program's tokens are well formed, and that the sequence of tokens conforms to the syntax defined by the context-free grammar. Any malformed tokens (e.g., `123abc` or `$@foo` in C) should cause the scanner to produce an error message. Any syntactically invalid token sequence (e.g., `A = X Y Z` in C) should lead to an error message from the parser.

1.6.2 Semantic Analysis and Intermediate Code Generation

Semantic analysis is the discovery of *meaning* in a program. Among other things, the semantic analyzer recognizes when multiple occurrences of the same identifier are meant to refer to the same program entity, and ensures that the uses are consistent. In most languages it also tracks the *types* of both identifiers and expressions, both to verify consistent usage and to guide the generation of code in the back end of a compiler.

To assist in its work, the semantic analyzer typically builds and maintains a *symbol table* data structure that maps each identifier to the information known about it. Among other things, this information includes the identifier's type, internal structure (if any), and scope (the portion of the program in which it is valid).

Using the symbol table, the semantic analyzer enforces a large variety of rules that are not captured by the hierarchical structure of the context-free grammar and the parse tree. In C, for example, it checks to make sure that

- Every identifier is declared before it is used.
- No identifier is used in an inappropriate context (calling an integer as a subroutine, adding a string to an integer, referencing a field of the wrong type of `struct`, etc.).
- Subroutine calls provide the correct number and types of arguments.
- Labels on the arms of a `switch` statement are distinct constants.
- Any function with a non-`void` return type `returns` a value explicitly.

In many front ends, the work of the semantic analyzer takes the form of *semantic action routines*, invoked by the parser when it realizes that it has reached a particular point within a grammar rule.

Of course, not all semantic rules can be checked at compile time (or in the front end of an interpreter). Those that can are referred to as the *static semantics* of the language. Those that must be checked at run time (or in the later phases of an interpreter) are referred to as the *dynamic semantics* of the language. C has very little in the way of dynamic checks (its designers opted for performance over safety). Examples of rules that other languages enforce at run time include:

- Variables are never used in an expression unless they have been given a value.[10]
- Pointers are never dereferenced unless they refer to a valid object.
- Array subscript expressions lie within the bounds of the array.
- Arithmetic operations do not overflow.

When it cannot enforce rules statically, a compiler will often produce code to perform appropriate checks at run time, aborting the program or generating an *exception* if one of the checks then fails. (Exceptions will be discussed in Section 9.4.) Some rules, unfortunately, may be unacceptably expensive or impossible to enforce, and the language implementation may simply fail to check them. In Ada, a program that breaks such a rule is said to be *erroneous*; in C its behavior is said to be *undefined*.

EXAMPLE 1.24 GCD program abstract syntax tree

A parse tree is sometimes known as a *concrete syntax tree*, because it demonstrates, completely and concretely, how a particular sequence of tokens can be derived under the rules of the context-free grammar. Once we know that a token sequence is valid, however, much of the information in the parse tree is irrelevant to further phases of compilation. In the process of checking static semantic rules, the semantic analyzer typically transforms the parse tree into an *abstract syntax tree* (otherwise known as an *AST*, or simply a *syntax tree*) by removing most of the "artificial" nodes in the tree's interior. The semantic analyzer also *annotates* the remaining nodes with useful information, such as pointers from identifiers to their symbol table entries. The annotations attached to a particular node are known as its *attributes*. A syntax tree for our GCD program is shown in Figure 1.6.

EXAMPLE 1.25 Interpreting the syntax tree

Many interpreters use an annotated syntax tree to represent the running program: "execution" then amounts to tree traversal. In our GCD program, an interpreter would start at the root of Figure 1.6 and visit, in order, the statements on the main spine of the tree. At the first ":=" node, the interpreter would notice that the right child is a call: it would therefore call the `getint` routine (found in slot 3 of the symbol table) and assign the result into `i` (found in slot 5 of the symbol table). At the second ":=" node the interpreter would similarly assign the result of `getint` into `j`. At the while node it would repeatedly evaluate the left ("$\neq$") child and, if the result was true, recursively walk the tree under the right (if) child. Finally, once the while node's left child evaluated to false, the interpreter would move on to the final call node, and output its result.

In many compilers, the annotated syntax tree constitutes the intermediate form that is passed from the front end to the back end. In other compilers, semantic analysis ends with a traversal of the tree (typically single pass) that generates some other intermediate form. One common such form consists of a *control flow graph* whose nodes resemble fragments of assembly language for a simple

---

10 As we shall see in Section 6.1.3, Java and C# actually do enforce initialization at compile time, but only by adopting a conservative set of rules for "definite assignment," outlawing programs for which correctness is difficult or impossible to verify at compile time.

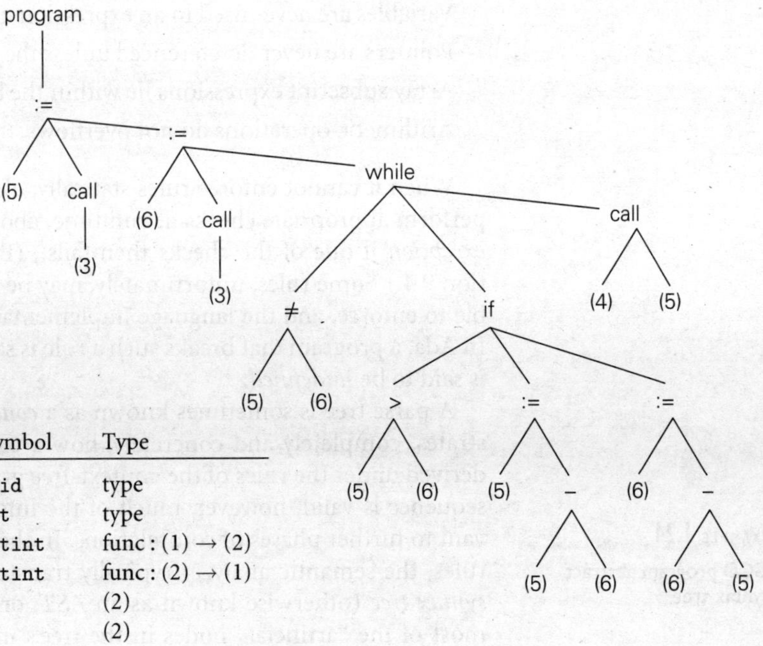

Index	Symbol	Type
1	`void`	type
2	`int`	type
3	`getint`	func : (1) → (2)
4	`putint`	func : (2) → (1)
5	`i`	(2)
6	`j`	(2)

Figure 1.6 Syntax tree and symbol table for the GCD program. Note the contrast to Figure 1.5: the syntax tree retains just the essential structure of the program, omitting details that were needed only to drive the parsing algorithm.

idealized machine. We will consider this option further in Chapter 15, where a control flow graph for our GCD program appears in Figure 15.3. In a suite of related compilers, the front ends for several languages and the back ends for several machines would share a common intermediate form.

1.6.3 Target Code Generation

EXAMPLE 1.26
GCD program assembly code

The code generation phase of a compiler translates the intermediate form into the target language. Given the information contained in the syntax tree, generating correct code is usually not a difficult task (generating *good* code is harder, as we shall see in Section 1.6.4). To generate assembly or machine language, the code generator traverses the symbol table to assign locations to variables, and then traverses the intermediate representation of the program, generating loads and stores for variable references, interspersed with appropriate arithmetic operations, tests, and branches. Naive code for our GCD example appears in Figure 1.7, in x86 assembly language. It was generated automatically by a simple pedagogical compiler.

The assembly language mnemonics may appear a bit cryptic, but the comments on each line (not generated by the compiler!) should make the correspon-

```
    pushl  %ebp               # \
    movl   %esp, %ebp         #  ) reserve space for local variables
    subl   $16, %esp          # /
    call   getint             # read
    movl   %eax, -8(%ebp)     # store i
    call   getint             # read
    movl   %eax, -12(%ebp)    # store j
A:  movl   -8(%ebp), %edi     # load i
    movl   -12(%ebp), %ebx    # load j
    cmpl   %ebx, %edi         # compare
    je     D                  # jump if i == j
    movl   -8(%ebp), %edi     # load i
    movl   -12(%ebp), %ebx    # load j
    cmpl   %ebx, %edi         # compare
    jle    B                  # jump if i < j
    movl   -8(%ebp), %edi     # load i
    movl   -12(%ebp), %ebx    # load j
    subl   %ebx, %edi         # i = i - j
    movl   %edi, -8(%ebp)     # store i
    jmp    C
B:  movl   -12(%ebp), %edi    # load j
    movl   -8(%ebp), %ebx     # load i
    subl   %ebx, %edi         # j = j - i
    movl   %edi, -12(%ebp)    # store j
C:  jmp    A
D:  movl   -8(%ebp), %ebx     # load i
    push   %ebx               # push i (pass to putint)
    call   putint             # write
    addl   $4, %esp           # pop i
    leave                     # deallocate space for local variables
    mov    $0, %eax           # exit status for program
    ret                       # return to operating system
```

Figure 1.7 Naive x86 assembly language for the GCD program.

dence between Figures 1.6 and 1.7 generally apparent. A few hints: esp, ebp, eax, ebx, and edi are registers (special storage locations, limited in number, that can be accessed very quickly). -8(%ebp) refers to the memory location 8 bytes before the location whose address is in register ebp; in this program, ebp serves as a *base* from which we can find variables i and j. The argument to a subroutine call instruction is passed by pushing it onto a stack, for which esp is the top-of-stack pointer. The return value comes back in register eax. Arithmetic operations overwrite their second argument with the result of the operation.[11] ■

11 As noted in footnote 1, these are GNU assembler conventions; Microsoft and Intel assemblers specify arguments in the opposite order.

Often a code generator will save the symbol table for later use by a symbolic debugger, by including it in a nonexecutable part of the target code.

1.6.4 Code Improvement

Code improvement is often referred to as *optimization*, though it seldom makes anything optimal in any absolute sense. It is an optional phase of compilation whose goal is to transform a program into a new version that computes the same result more efficiently—more quickly or using less memory, or both.

Some improvements are machine independent. These can be performed as transformations on the intermediate form. Other improvements require an understanding of the target machine (or of whatever will execute the program in the target language). These must be performed as transformations on the target program. Thus code improvement often appears twice in the list of compiler phases: once immediately after semantic analysis and intermediate code generation, and again immediately after target code generation.

EXAMPLE 1.27
GCD program optimization

Applying a good code improver to the code in Figure 1.7 produces the code shown in Example 1.2. Comparing the two programs, we can see that the improved version is quite a lot shorter. Conspicuously absent are most of the loads and stores. The machine-independent code improver is able to verify that `i` and `j` can be kept in registers throughout the execution of the main loop. (This would not have been the case if, for example, the loop contained a call to a subroutine that might reuse those registers, or that might try to modify `i` or `j`.) The machine-specific code improver is then able to assign `i` and `j` to actual registers of the target machine. For modern microprocessors, with complex internal behavior, compilers can usually generate better code than can human assembly language programmers. ■

✓ CHECK YOUR UNDERSTANDING

22. List the principal phases of compilation, and describe the work performed by each.
23. List the phases that are also executed as part of interpretation.
24. Describe the form in which a program is passed from the scanner to the parser; from the parser to the semantic analyzer; from the semantic analyzer to the intermediate code generator.
25. What distinguishes the front end of a compiler from the back end?
26. What is the difference between a phase and a pass of compilation? Under what circumstances does it make sense for a compiler to have multiple passes?
27. What is the purpose of the compiler's symbol table?
28. What is the difference between static and dynamic semantics?

29. On modern machines, do assembly language programmers still tend to write better code than a good compiler can? Why or why not?

1.7 Summary and Concluding Remarks

In this chapter we introduced the study of programming language design and implementation. We considered why there are so many languages, what makes them successful or unsuccessful, how they may be categorized for study, and what benefits the reader is likely to gain from that study. We noted that language design and language implementation are intimately tied to one another. Obviously an implementation must conform to the rules of the language. At the same time, a language designer must consider how easy or difficult it will be to implement various features, and what sort of performance is likely to result.

Language implementations are commonly differentiated into those based on interpretation and those based on compilation. We noted, however, that the difference between these approaches is fuzzy, and that most implementations include a bit of each. As a general rule, we say that a language is compiled if execution is preceded by a translation step that (1) fully analyzes both the structure (syntax) and meaning (semantics) of the program, and (2) produces an equivalent program in a significantly different form. The bulk of the implementation material in this book pertains to compilation.

Compilers are generally structured as a series of *phases*. The first few phases—scanning, parsing, and semantic analysis—serve to analyze the source program. Collectively these phases are known as the compiler's *front end*. The final few phases—target code generation and machine-specific code improvement—are known as the *back end*. They serve to build a target program—preferably a fast one—whose semantics match those of the source. Between the front end and the back end, a good compiler performs extensive machine-independent code improvement; the phases of this "middle end" typically comprise the bulk of the code of the compiler, and account for most of its execution time.

Chapters 3, 6, 7, 8, 9, and 10 form the core of the rest of this book. They cover fundamental issues of language design, both from the point of view of the programmer and from the point of view of the language implementor. To support the discussion of implementations, Chapters 2 and 4 describe compiler front ends in more detail than has been possible in this introduction. Chapter 5 provides an overview of assembly-level architecture. Chapters 15 through 17 discuss compiler back ends, including assemblers and linkers, run-time systems, and code improvement techniques. Additional language paradigms are covered in Chapters 11 through 14. Appendix A lists the principal programming languages mentioned in the text, together with a genealogical chart and bibliographic references. Appendix B contains a list of "Design & Implementation" sidebars; Appendix C contains a list of numbered examples.

1.8 Exercises

1.1 Errors in a computer program can be classified according to when they are detected and, if they are detected at compile time, what part of the compiler detects them. Using your favorite imperative language, give an example of each of the following.

(a) A lexical error, detected by the scanner
(b) A syntax error, detected by the parser
(c) A static semantic error, detected by semantic analysis
(d) A dynamic semantic error, detected by code generated by the compiler
(e) An error that the compiler can neither catch nor easily generate code to catch (this should be a violation of the language definition, not just a program bug)

1.2 Consider again the Pascal tool set distributed by Niklaus Wirth (Example 1.15). After successfully building a machine language version of the Pascal compiler, one could in principle discard the P-code interpreter and the P-code version of the compiler. Why might one choose *not* to do so?

1.3 Imperative languages like Fortran and C are typically compiled, while scripting languages, in which many issues cannot be settled until run time, are typically interpreted. Is interpretation simply what one "has to do" when compilation is infeasible, or are there actually some *advantages* to interpreting a language, even when a compiler is available?

1.4 The gcd program of Example 1.20 might also be written

```
int main() {
    int i = getint(), j = getint();
    while (i != j) {
        if (i > j) i = i % j;
        else j = j % i;
    }
    putint(i);
}
```

Does this program compute the same result? If not, can you fix it? Under what circumstances would you expect one or the other to be faster?

1.5 Expanding on Example 1.25, trace an interpretation of the gcd program on the inputs 12 and 8. Which syntax tree nodes are visited, in which order?

1.6 Both interpretation and code generation can be performed by traversal of a syntax tree. Compare these two kinds of traversals. In what ways are they similar/different?

1.7 In your local implementation of C, what is the limit on the size of integers? What happens in the event of arithmetic overflow? What are the implications of size limits on the portability of programs from one machine/compiler to another? How do the answers to these questions differ for Java? For Ada? For Pascal? For Scheme? (You may need to find a manual.)

1.8 The Unix `make` utility allows the programmer to specify *dependences* among the separately compiled pieces of a program. If file *A* depends on file *B* and file *B* is modified, `make` deduces that *A* must be recompiled, in case any of the changes to *B* would affect the code produced for *A*. How accurate is this sort of dependence management? Under what circumstances will it lead to unnecessary work? Under what circumstances will it fail to recompile something that needs to be recompiled?

1.9 Why is it difficult to tell whether a program is correct? How do you go about finding bugs in your code? What kinds of bugs are revealed by testing? What kinds of bugs are not? (For more formal notions of program correctness, see the bibliographic notes at the end of Chapter 4.)

1.9 Explorations

1.10 (a) What was the first programming language you learned? If you chose it, why did you do so? If it was chosen for you by others, why do you think they chose it? What parts of the language did you find the most difficult to learn?

(b) For the language with which you are most familiar (this may or may not be the first one you learned), list three things you wish had been differently designed. Why do you think they were designed the way they were? How would you fix them if you had the chance to do it over? Would there be any negative consequences, for example in terms of compiler complexity or program execution speed?

1.11 Get together with a classmate whose principal programming experience is with a language in a different category of Figure 1.1. (If your experience is mostly in C, for example, you might search out someone with experience in Lisp.) Compare notes. What are the easiest and most difficult aspects of programming, in each of your experiences? Pick a simple problem (e.g., sorting, or identification of connected components in a graph) and solve it using each of your favorite languages. Which solution is more elegant (do the two of you agree)? Which is faster? Why?

1.12 (a) If you have access to a Unix system, compile a simple program with the `-S` command-line flag. Add comments to the resulting assembly language file to explain the purpose of each instruction.

(b) Now use the `-o` command-line flag to generate a *relocatable object file*. Using appropriate local tools (look in particular for `nm`, `objdump`, or a symbolic debugger like `gdb` or `dbx`), identify the machine language corresponding to each line of assembler.

(c) Using `nm`, `objdump`, or a similar tool, identify the *undefined external symbols* in your object file. Now run the compiler to completion, to produce an *executable* file. Finally, run `nm` or `objdump` again to see what has happened to the symbols in part (b). Where did they come from—how did the linker resolve them?

(d) Run the compiler to completion one more time, using the `-v` command-line flag. You should see messages describing the various subprograms invoked during the compilation process (some compilers use a different letter for this option; check the `man` page). The subprograms may include a preprocessor, separate passes of the compiler itself (often two), probably an assembler, and the linker. If possible, run these subprograms yourself, individually. Which of them produce the files described in the previous subquestions? Explain the purpose of the various command-line flags with which the subprograms were invoked.

1.13 Write a program that commits a dynamic semantic error (e.g., division by zero, access off the end of an array, dereference of a null pointer). What happens when you run this program? Does the compiler give you options to control what happens? Devise an experiment to evaluate the cost of run-time semantic checks. If possible, try this exercise with more than one language or compiler.

1.14 C has a reputation for being a relatively "unsafe" high-level language. For example: it allows the programmer to mix operands of different sizes and types in many more ways than its "safer" cousins. The Unix `lint` utility can be used to search for potentially unsafe constructs in C programs. In effect, many of the rules that are enforced by the compiler in other languages are optional in C, and are enforced (if desired) by a separate program. What do you think of this approach? Is it a good idea? Why or why not?

1.15 Using an Internet search engine or magazine indexing service, read up on the history of Java and C#, including the conflict between Sun and Microsoft over Java standardization. Some have claimed that C# was, at least in part, an attempt by Microsoft to undermine the spread of Java. Others point to philosophical and practical differences between the languages, and argue that C# more than stands on its merits. In hindsight, how would you characterize Microsoft's decision to pursue an alternative to Java?

1.10 Bibliographic Notes

The compiler-oriented chapters of this book attempt to convey a sense of what the compiler does, rather than explaining how to build one. A much greater level of detail can be found in other texts. Leading options include the work of Aho et al. [ALSU07], Cooper and Torczon [CT04], and Fischer et al. [FCL10]. Other excellent, though less current texts include those of Appel [App97] and Grune et al. [GBJ+12]. Popular texts on programming language design include those of Louden [LL12], Sebesta [Seb15], and Sethi [Set96].

Some of the best information on the history of programming languages can be found in the proceedings of conferences sponsored by the Association for Computing Machinery in 1978, 1993, and 2007 [Wex78, Ass93, Ass07]. Another excellent reference is Horowitz's 1987 text [Hor87]. A broader range of historical material can be found in the quarterly *IEEE Annals of the History of Computing.* Given the importance of personal taste in programming language design, it is inevitable that some language comparisons should be marked by strongly worded opinions. Early examples include the writings of Dijkstra [Dij82], Hoare [Hoa81], Kernighan [Ker81], and Wirth [Wir85a].

Much modern software development takes place in integrated programming environments. Influential precursors to these environments include the Genera Common Lisp environment from Symbolics Corp. [WMWM87] and the Smalltalk [Gol84], Interlisp [TM81], and Cedar [SZBH86] environments at the Xerox Palo Alto Research Center.

2 Programming Language Syntax

Unlike natural languages such as English or Chinese, computer languages must be precise. Both their form (syntax) and meaning (semantics) must be specified without ambiguity, so that both programmers and computers can tell what a program is supposed to do. To provide the needed degree of precision, language designers and implementors use formal syntactic and semantic notation. To facilitate the discussion of language features in later chapters, we will cover this notation first: syntax in the current chapter and semantics in Chapter 4.

EXAMPLE 2.1
Syntax of Arabic numerals

As a motivating example, consider the Arabic numerals with which we represent numbers. These numerals are composed of digits, which we can enumerate as follows ('|' means "or"):

digit ⟶ 0 | 1 | 2 | 3 | 4 | 5 | 6 | 7 | 8 | 9

Digits are the syntactic building blocks for numbers. In the usual notation, we say that a natural number is represented by an arbitrary-length (nonempty) string of digits, beginning with a nonzero digit:

non_zero_digit ⟶ 1 | 2 | 3 | 4 | 5 | 6 | 7 | 8 | 9
natural_number ⟶ *non_zero_digit digit* *

Here the "Kleene[1] star" metasymbol (*) is used to indicate zero or more repetitions of the symbol to its left. ■

Of course, digits are only symbols: ink blobs on paper or pixels on a screen. They carry no meaning in and of themselves. We add semantics to digits when we say that they represent the natural numbers from zero to nine, as defined by mathematicians. Alternatively, we could say that they represent colors, or the days of the week in a decimal calendar. These would constitute alternative semantics for the same syntax. In a similar fashion, we define the semantics of natural numbers by associating a base-10, place-value interpretation with each

1 Stephen Kleene (1909–1994), a mathematician at the University of Wisconsin, was responsible for much of the early development of the theory of computation, including much of the material in Section C-2.4.

string of digits. Similar syntax rules and semantic interpretations can be devised for rational numbers, (limited-precision) real numbers, arithmetic, assignments, control flow, declarations, and indeed all of programming languages.

Distinguishing between syntax and semantics is useful for at least two reasons. First, different programming languages often provide features with very similar semantics but very different syntax. It is generally much easier to learn a new language if one is able to identify the common (and presumably familiar) semantic ideas beneath the unfamiliar syntax. Second, there are some very efficient and elegant algorithms that a compiler or interpreter can use to discover the syntactic structure (but not the semantics!) of a computer program, and these algorithms can be used to drive the rest of the compilation or interpretation process.

In the current chapter we focus on syntax: how we specify the structural rules of a programming language, and how a compiler identifies the structure of a given input program. These two tasks—specifying syntax rules and figuring out how (and whether) a given program was built according to those rules—are distinct. The first is of interest mainly to programmers, who want to write valid programs. The second is of interest mainly to compilers, which need to analyze those programs. The first task relies on *regular expressions* and *context-free grammars*, which specify how to generate valid programs. The second task relies on *scanners* and *parsers*, which recognize program structure. We address the first of these tasks in Section 2.1, the second in Sections 2.2 and 2.3.

In Section 2.4 (largely on the companion site) we take a deeper look at the formal theory underlying scanning and parsing. In theoretical parlance, a scanner is a *deterministic finite automaton* (DFA) that recognizes the tokens of a programming language. A parser is a deterministic *push-down automaton* (PDA) that recognizes the language's context-free syntax. It turns out that one can generate scanners and parsers automatically from regular expressions and context-free grammars. This task is performed by tools like Unix's `lex` and `yacc`,[2] among others. Possibly nowhere else in computer science is the connection between theory and practice so clear and so compelling.

2.1 Specifying Syntax: Regular Expressions and Context-Free Grammars

Formal specification of syntax requires a set of rules. How complicated (expressive) the syntax can be depends on the kinds of rules we are allowed to use. It turns out that what we intuitively think of as tokens can be constructed from individual characters using just three kinds of formal rules: concatenation, alternation (choice among a finite set of alternatives), and so-called "Kleene closure"

2 At many sites, `lex` and `yacc` have been superseded by the GNU `flex` and `bison` tools, which provide a superset of the original functionality.

(repetition an arbitrary number of times). Specifying most of the rest of what we intuitively think of as syntax requires one additional kind of rule: recursion (creation of a construct from simpler instances of the same construct). Any set of strings that can be defined in terms of the first three rules is called a *regular set*, or sometimes a *regular language*. Regular sets are generated by *regular expressions* and recognized by scanners. Any set of strings that can be defined if we add recursion is called a *context-free language* (CFL). Context-free languages are generated by *context-free grammars* (CFGs) and recognized by parsers. (Terminology can be confusing here. The meaning of the word "language" varies greatly, depending on whether we're talking about "formal" languages [e.g., regular or context-free], or programming languages. A formal language is just a set of strings, with no accompanying semantics.)

2.1.1 Tokens and Regular Expressions

Tokens are the basic building blocks of programs—the shortest strings of characters with individual meaning. Tokens come in many *kinds*, including keywords, identifiers, symbols, and constants of various types. Some kinds of token (e.g., the increment operator) correspond to only one string of characters. Others (e.g., *identifier*) correspond to a set of strings that share some common form. (In most languages, keywords are special strings of characters that have the right form to be identifiers, but are reserved for special purposes.) We will use the word "token" informally to refer to both the generic kind (an identifier, the increment operator) and the specific string (`foo`, `++`); the distinction between these should be clear from context.

EXAMPLE 2.2
Lexical structure of C11

Some languages have only a few kinds of token, of fairly simple form. Other languages are more complex. C, for example, has more than 100 kinds of tokens, including 44 keywords (`double`, `if`, `return`, `struct`, etc.); identifiers (`my_variable`, `your_type`, `sizeof`, `printf`, etc.); integer (0765, 0x1f5, 501), floating-point (6.022e23), and character (`'x'`, `'\''`, `'\0170'`) constants; string literals (`"snerk"`, `"say \"hi\"\n"`); 54 "punctuators" (`+`, `]`, `->`, `*=`, `:`, `||`, etc.), and two different forms of comments. There are provisions for international character sets, string literals that span multiple lines of source code, constants of varying precision (width), alternative "spellings" for symbols that are missing on certain input devices, and preprocessor macros that build tokens from smaller pieces. Other large, modern languages (Java, Ada) are similarly complex. ■

To specify tokens, we use the notation of *regular expressions*. A regular expression is one of the following:

1. A character
2. The empty string, denoted ϵ
3. Two regular expressions next to each other, meaning any string generated by the first one followed by (concatenated with) any string generated by the second one

4. Two regular expressions separated by a vertical bar (|), meaning any string generated by the first one *or* any string generated by the second one
5. A regular expression followed by a Kleene star, meaning the concatenation of zero or more strings generated by the expression in front of the star

Parentheses are used to avoid ambiguity about where the various subexpressions start and end.[3]

EXAMPLE 2.3
Syntax of numeric constants

Consider, for example, the syntax of numeric constants accepted by a simple hand-held calculator:

$$\begin{aligned}
\textit{number} &\longrightarrow \textit{integer} \mid \textit{real} \\
\textit{integer} &\longrightarrow \textit{digit digit} * \\
\textit{real} &\longrightarrow \textit{integer exponent} \mid \textit{decimal} \; (\, \textit{exponent} \mid \epsilon \,) \\
\textit{decimal} &\longrightarrow \textit{digit} * \; (\; \texttt{.} \;\; \textit{digit} \mid \textit{digit} \;\; \texttt{.} \;) \; \textit{digit} * \\
\textit{exponent} &\longrightarrow (\, \texttt{e} \mid \texttt{E} \,) \; (\, \texttt{+} \mid \texttt{-} \mid \epsilon \,) \; \textit{integer} \\
\textit{digit} &\longrightarrow \texttt{0} \mid \texttt{1} \mid \texttt{2} \mid \texttt{3} \mid \texttt{4} \mid \texttt{5} \mid \texttt{6} \mid \texttt{7} \mid \texttt{8} \mid \texttt{9}
\end{aligned}$$

The symbols to the left of the $\longrightarrow$ signs provide names for the regular expressions. One of these (*number*) will serve as a token name; the others are simply

DESIGN & IMPLEMENTATION

2.1 Contextual keywords

In addition to distinguishing between keywords and identifiers, some languages define so-called *contextual keywords*, which function as keywords in certain specific places in a program, but as identifiers elsewhere. In C#, for example, the word `yield` can appear immediately before `return` or `break`—a place where an identifier can never appear. In this context, it is interpreted as a keyword; anywhere else it is an identifier. It is therefore perfectly acceptable to have a local variable named `yield`: the compiler can distinguish it from the keyword by where it appears in the program.

C++11 has a small handful of contextual keywords. C# 4.0 has 26. Most were introduced in the course of revising the language to create a new standard version. Given a large user community, any short, intuitively appealing word is likely to have been used as an identifier by someone, in some existing program. Making that word a contextual keyword in the new version of the language, rather than a full keyword, reduces the risk that existing programs will suddenly fail to compile.

---

3 Some authors use λ to represent the empty string. Some use a period (.), rather than juxtaposition, to indicate concatenation. Some use a plus sign (+), rather than a vertical bar, to indicate alternation.

for convenience in building larger expressions.[4] Note that while we have allowed definitions to build on one another, nothing is ever defined in terms of itself, even indirectly. Such recursive definitions are the distinguishing characteristic of context-free grammars, described in Section 2.1.2. To generate a valid number, we expand out the sub-definitions and then scan the resulting expression from left to right, choosing among alternatives at each vertical bar, and choosing a number of repetitions at each Kleene star. Within each repetition we may make different choices at vertical bars, generating different substrings. ▒

Character Sets and Formatting Issues

Upper- and lowercase letters in identifiers and keywords are considered distinct in some languages (e.g., Perl, Python, and Ruby; C and its descendants), and identical in others (e.g., Ada, Common Lisp, and Fortran). Thus `foo`, `Foo`, and `FOO` all represent the same identifier in Ada, but different identifiers in C. Modula-2 and Modula-3 require keywords and predefined (built-in) identifiers to be written in uppercase; C and its descendants require them to be written in lowercase. A few languages allow only letters and digits in identifiers. Most allow underscores. A few (notably Lisp) allow a variety of additional characters. Some languages (e.g., Java and C#) have standard (but optional) conventions on the use of upper- and lowercase letters in names.[5]

With the globalization of computing, non-Latin character sets have become increasingly important. Many modern languages, including C, C++, Ada 95, Java, C#, and Fortran 2003 have introduced explicit support for multibyte character sets, generally based on the Unicode and ISO/IEC 10646 international standards. Most modern programming languages allow non-Latin characters to appear within comments and character strings; an increasing number allow them in identifiers as well. Conventions for portability across character sets and for *localization* to a given character set can be surprisingly complex, particularly when various forms of backward compatibility are required (the C99 Rationale devotes five full pages to this subject [Int03a, pp. 19–23]); for the most part we ignore such issues here.

Some language implementations impose limits on the maximum length of identifiers, but most avoid such unnecessary restrictions. Most modern languages are also more or less *free format*, meaning that a program is simply a sequence of tokens: what matters is their order with respect to one another, not their physical position within a printed line or page. "White space" (blanks, tabs, carriage returns, and line and page feed characters) between tokens is usually ignored, except to the extent that it is needed to separate one token from the next.

---

4 We have assumed here that all numeric constants are simply "numbers." In many programming languages, integer and real constants are separate kinds of token. Their syntax may also be more complex than indicated here, to support such features are multiple lengths or nondecimal bases.

5 For the sake of consistency we do not always obey such conventions in this book: most examples follow the common practice of C programmers, in which underscores, rather than capital letters, separate the "subwords" of names.

There are a few noteworthy exceptions to these rules. Some language implementations limit the maximum length of a line, to allow the compiler to store the current line in a fixed-length buffer. Dialects of Fortran prior to Fortran 90 use a *fixed format*, with 72 characters per line (the width of a paper punch card, on which programs were once stored), and with different columns within the line reserved for different purposes. Line breaks serve to separate statements in several other languages, including Go, Haskell, Python, and Swift. Haskell and Python also give special significance to indentation. The body of a loop, for example, consists of precisely those subsequent lines that are indented farther than the header of the loop.

Other Uses of Regular Expressions

Many readers will be familiar with regular expressions from the `grep` family of tools in Unix, the search facilities of various text editors, or such scripting languages and tools as Perl, Python, Ruby, `awk`, and `sed`. Most of these provide a rich set of extensions to the notation of regular expressions. Some extensions, such as shorthand for "zero or one occurrences" or "anything other than white space," do not change the power of the notation. Others, such as the ability to require a second occurrence, later in the input string, of the same character sequence that matched an earlier part of the expression, increase the power of the notation, so that it is no longer restricted to generating regular sets. Still other extensions are designed not to increase the expressiveness of the notation but rather to tie it to other language facilities. In many tools, for example, one can bracket portions of a regular expression in such a way that when a string is matched against it the contents of the corresponding substrings are assigned into named local variables. We will return to these issues in Section 14.4.2, in the context of scripting languages.

2.1.2 Context-Free Grammars

EXAMPLE 2.4
Syntactic nesting in expressions

Regular expressions work well for defining tokens. They are unable, however, to specify *nested* constructs, which are central to programming languages. Consider for example the structure of an arithmetic expression:

DESIGN & IMPLEMENTATION

2.2 Formatting restrictions

Formatting limitations inspired by implementation concerns—as in the punch-card-oriented rules of Fortran 77 and its predecessors—have a tendency to become unwanted anachronisms as implementation techniques improve. Given the tendency of certain word processors to "fill" or auto-format text, the line break and indentation rules of languages like Haskell, Occam, and Python are somewhat controversial.

expr ⟶ `id` | `number` | `-` *expr* | `(` *expr* `)`
  | *expr op expr*

op ⟶ `+` | `-` | `*` | `/`

Here the ability to define a construct in terms of itself is crucial. Among other things, it allows us to ensure that left and right parentheses are matched, something that cannot be accomplished with regular expressions (see Section C-2.4.3 for more details). The arrow symbol (⟶) means "can have the form"; for brevity it is sometimes pronounced "goes to."

Each of the rules in a context-free grammar is known as a *production*. The symbols on the left-hand sides of the productions are known as *variables*, or *nonterminals*. There may be any number of productions with the same left-hand side. Symbols that are to make up the strings derived from the grammar are known as *terminals* (shown here in `typewriter` font). They cannot appear on the left-hand side of any production. In a programming language, the terminals of the context-free grammar are the language's tokens. One of the nonterminals, usually the one on the left-hand side of the first production, is called the *start symbol*. It names the construct defined by the overall grammar.

The notation for context-free grammars is sometimes called Backus-Naur Form (BNF), in honor of John Backus and Peter Naur, who devised it for the definition of the Algol-60 programming language [NBB$^+$63].[6] Strictly speaking, the Kleene star and meta-level parentheses of regular expressions are not allowed in BNF, but they do not change the expressive power of the notation, and are commonly included for convenience. Sometimes one sees a "Kleene plus" ($^+$) as well; it indicates one or more instances of the symbol or group of symbols in front of it.[7] When augmented with these extra operators, the notation is often called extended BNF (EBNF). The construct

EXAMPLE 2.5
Extended BNF (EBNF)

id_list ⟶ `id ( , id )*`

is shorthand for

id_list ⟶ `id`
id_list ⟶ *id_list* `, id`

"Kleene plus" is analogous. Note that the parentheses here are metasymbols. In Example 2.4 they were part of the language being defined, and were written in fixed-width font.[8]

---

6 John Backus (1924–2007) was also the inventor of Fortran. He spent most of his professional career at IBM Corporation, and was named an IBM Fellow in 1987. He received the ACM Turing Award in 1977.

7 Some authors use curly braces ({ }) to indicate zero or more instances of the symbols inside. Some use square brackets ([ ]) to indicate zero or one instances of the symbols inside—that is, to indicate that those symbols are optional.

8 To avoid confusion, some authors place quote marks around any single character that is part of the language being defined: *id_list* ⟶ `id (`','` id)*`; *expr* ⟶ '(' *expr* ')'. In both regular and extended BNF, many authors use ::= instead of ⟶.

Like the Kleene star and parentheses, the vertical bar is in some sense superfluous, though it was provided in the original BNF. The construct

op ⟶ `+ | - | * | /`

can be considered shorthand for

op ⟶ `+`
op ⟶ `-`
op ⟶ `*`
op ⟶ `/`

which is also sometimes written

op ⟶ `+`
⟶ `-`
⟶ `*`
⟶ `/`

Many tokens, such as `id` and `number` above, have many possible spellings (i.e., may be represented by many possible strings of characters). The parser is oblivious to these; it does not distinguish one identifier from another. The semantic analyzer does distinguish them, however; the scanner must save the spelling of each such "interesting" token for later use.

2.1.3 Derivations and Parse Trees

A context-free grammar shows us how to generate a syntactically valid string of terminals: Begin with the start symbol. Choose a production with the start symbol on the left-hand side; replace the start symbol with the right-hand side of that production. Now choose a nonterminal *A* in the resulting string, choose a production *P* with *A* on its left-hand side, and replace *A* with the right-hand side of *P*. Repeat this process until no nonterminals remain.

EXAMPLE 2.6
Derivation of `slope * x + intercept`

As an example, we can use our grammar for expressions to generate the string "`slope * x + intercept`":

expr ⟹ *expr op* <u>*expr*</u>
⟹ *expr* <u>*op*</u> `id`
⟹ <u>*expr*</u> `+ id`
⟹ *expr op* <u>*expr*</u> `+ id`
⟹ *expr* <u>*op*</u> `id + id`
⟹ <u>*expr*</u> `* id + id`
⟹ `id * id + id`
`(slope) (x) (intercept)`

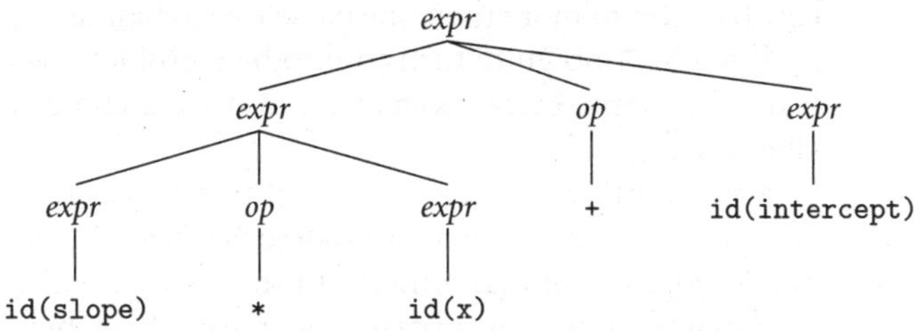

Figure 2.1 Parse tree for `slope * x + intercept` (grammar in Example 2.4).

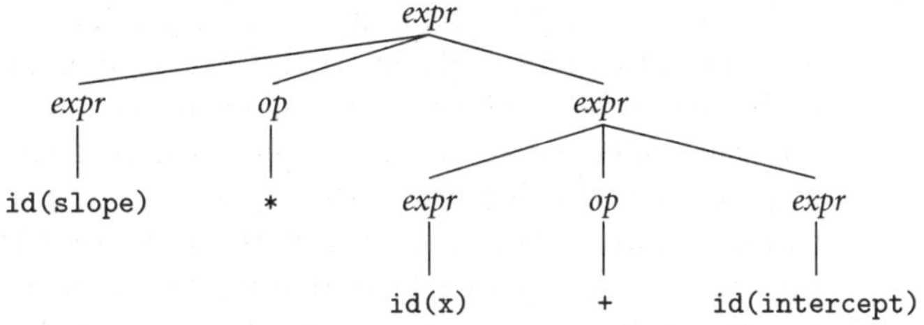

Figure 2.2 Alternative (less desirable) parse tree for `slope * x + intercept` (grammar in Example 2.4). The fact that more than one tree exists implies that our grammar is ambiguous.

The $\Longrightarrow$ metasymbol is often pronounced "derives." It indicates that the right-hand side was obtained by using a production to replace some nonterminal in the left-hand side. At each line we have underlined the symbol A that is replaced in the following line.

A series of replacement operations that shows how to derive a string of terminals from the start symbol is called a *derivation*. Each string of symbols along the way is called a *sentential form*. The final sentential form, consisting of only terminals, is called the *yield* of the derivation. We sometimes elide the intermediate steps and write *expr* $\Longrightarrow^*$ `slope * x + intercept`, where the metasymbol $\Longrightarrow^*$ means "derives after zero or more replacements." In this particular derivation, we have chosen at each step to replace the right-most nonterminal with the right-hand side of some production. This replacement strategy leads to a *right-most* derivation. There are many other possible derivations, including *left-most* and options in-between.

We saw in Chapter 1 that we can represent a derivation graphically as a *parse tree*. The root of the parse tree is the start symbol of the grammar. The leaves of the tree are its yield. Each internal node, together with its children, represents the use of a production.

EXAMPLE 2.7
Parse trees for `slope * x + intercept`

A parse tree for our example expression appears in Figure 2.1. This tree is not unique. At the second level of the tree, we could have chosen to turn the operator into a `*` instead of a `+`, and to further expand the expression on the right, rather than the one on the left (see Figure 2.2). A grammar that allows the construction of more than one parse tree for some string of terminals is said to be *ambiguous*. Ambiguity turns out to be a problem when trying to build a parser: it requires some extra mechanism to drive a choice between equally acceptable alternatives. ■

A moment's reflection will reveal that there are infinitely many context-free grammars for any given context-free language.[9] Some grammars, however, are much more useful than others. In this text we will avoid the use of ambiguous grammars (though most parser generators allow them, by means of *disambiguating* rules). We will also avoid the use of so-called *useless* symbols: nonterminals that cannot generate any string of terminals, or terminals that cannot appear in the yield of any derivation.

When designing the grammar for a programming language, we generally try to find one that reflects the internal structure of programs in a way that is useful to the rest of the compiler. (We shall see in Section 2.3.2 that we also try to find one that can be parsed efficiently, which can be a bit of a challenge.) One place in which structure is particularly important is in arithmetic expressions, where we can use productions to capture the *associativity* and *precedence* of the various operators. Associativity tells us that the operators in most languages group left to right, so that `10 - 4 - 3` means `(10 - 4) - 3` rather than `10 - (4 - 3)`. Precedence tells us that multiplication and division in most languages group more tightly than addition and subtraction, so that `3 + 4 * 5` means `3 + (4 * 5)` rather than `(3 + 4) * 5`. (These rules are not universal; we will consider them again in Section 6.1.1.)

EXAMPLE 2.8
Expression grammar with precedence and associativity

Here is a better version of our expression grammar:

1. *expr* ⟶ *term* | *expr add_op term*
2. *term* ⟶ *factor* | *term mult_op factor*
3. *factor* ⟶ `id` | `number` | `-` *factor* | `(` *expr* `)`
4. *add_op* ⟶ `+` | `-`
5. *mult_op* ⟶ `*` | `/`

This grammar is unambiguous. It captures precedence in the way *factor*, *term*, and *expr* build on one another, with different operators appearing at each level. It captures associativity in the second halves of lines 1 and 2, which build sub*exprs* and sub*terms* to the left of the operator, rather than to the right. In Figure 2.3, we can see how building the notion of precedence into the grammar makes it clear that multiplication groups more tightly than addition in `3 + 4 * 5`, even without parentheses. In Figure 2.4, we can see that subtraction groups more tightly to the left, so that `10 - 4 - 3` would evaluate to `3`, rather than to `9`. ■

9 Given a specific grammar, there are many ways to create other equivalent grammars. We could, for example, replace A with some new symbol B everywhere it appears in the right-hand side of a production, and then create a new production $B \longrightarrow A$.

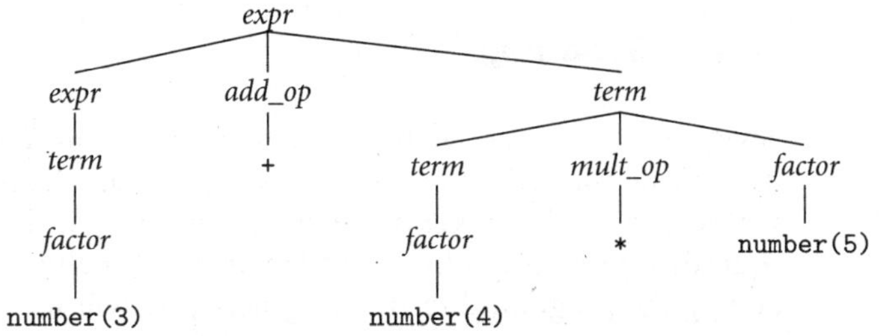

Figure 2.3 Parse tree for 3 + 4 * 5, with precedence (grammar in Example 2.8).

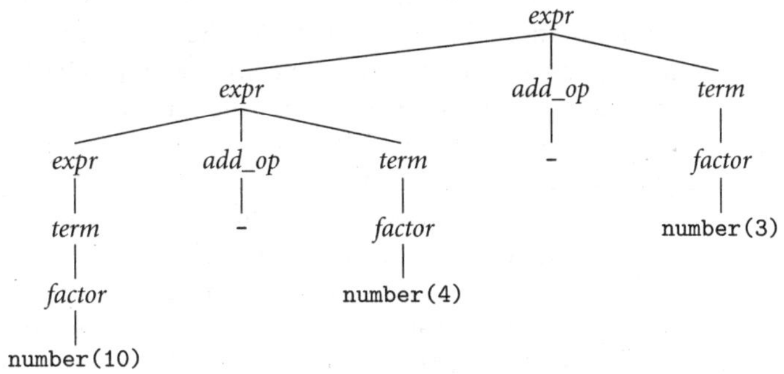

Figure 2.4 Parse tree for 10 – 4 – 3, with left associativity (grammar in Example 2.8).

✓ CHECK YOUR UNDERSTANDING

1. What is the difference between syntax and semantics?
2. What are the three basic operations that can be used to build complex regular expressions from simpler regular expressions?
3. What additional operation (beyond the three of regular expressions) is provided in context-free grammars?
4. What is *Backus-Naur form*? When and why was it devised?
5. Name a language in which indentation affects program syntax.
6. When discussing context-free languages, what is a *derivation*? What is a *sentential form*?
7. What is the difference between a *right-most* derivation and a *left-most* derivation?
8. What does it mean for a context-free grammar to be *ambiguous*?
9. What are *associativity* and *precedence*? Why are they significant in parse trees?

2.2 Scanning

Together, the scanner and parser for a programming language are responsible for discovering the syntactic structure of a program. This process of discovery, or *syntax analysis*, is a necessary first step toward translating the program into an equivalent program in the target language. (It's also the first step toward interpreting the program directly. In general, we will focus on compilation, rather than interpretation, for the remainder of the book. Most of what we shall discuss either has an obvious application to interpretation, or is obviously irrelevant to it.)

By grouping input characters into tokens, the scanner dramatically reduces the number of individual items that must be inspected by the more computationally intensive parser. In addition, the scanner typically removes comments (so the parser doesn't have to worry about them appearing throughout the context-free grammar—see Exercise 2.20); saves the text of "interesting" tokens like identifiers, strings, and numeric literals; and tags tokens with line and column numbers, to make it easier to generate high-quality error messages in subsequent phases.

EXAMPLE 2.9
Tokens for a calculator language

In Examples 2.4 and 2.8 we considered a simple language for arithmetic expressions. In Section 2.3.1 we will extend this to create a simple "calculator language" with input, output, variables, and assignment. For this language we will use the following set of tokens:

assign ⟶ `:=`
plus ⟶ `+`
minus ⟶ `-`
times ⟶ `*`
div ⟶ `/`
lparen ⟶ `(`
rparen ⟶ `)`
id ⟶ *letter* (*letter* | *digit*)*
  except for `read` and `write`
number ⟶ *digit digit* * | *digit* * (. *digit* | *digit* .) *digit* *

In keeping with Algol and its descendants (and in contrast to the C-family languages), we have used := rather than = for assignment. For simplicity, we have omitted the exponential notation found in Example 2.3. We have also listed the tokens `read` and `write` as exceptions to the rule for `id` (more on this in Section 2.2.2). To make the task of the scanner a little more realistic, we borrow the two styles of comment from C:

comment ⟶ `/*` (*non-*∗ | ∗ *non-/*)* ∗⁺ `/`
  | `//` (*non-newline*)* *newline*

Here we have used *non-*∗, *non-/*, and *non-newline* as shorthand for the alternation of all characters other than ∗, /, and *newline*, respectively. ■

EXAMPLE 2.10
An ad hoc scanner for calculator tokens

How might we go about recognizing the tokens of our calculator language? The simplest approach is entirely ad hoc. Pseudocode appears in Figure 2.5. We can structure the code however we like, but it seems reasonable to check the simpler and more common cases first, to peek ahead when we need to, and to embed loops for comments and for long tokens such as identifiers and numbers.

After finding a token the scanner returns to the parser. When invoked again it repeats the algorithm from the beginning, using the next available characters of input (including any that were peeked at but not consumed the last time). ■

As a rule, we accept the longest possible token in each invocation of the scanner. Thus `foobar` is always `foobar` and never `f` or `foo` or `foob`. More to the point, in a language like C, `3.14159` is a real number and never `3`, `.`, and `14159`. White space (blanks, tabs, newlines, comments) is generally ignored, except to the extent that it separates tokens (e.g., `foo bar` is different from `foobar`).

Figure 2.5 could be extended fairly easily to outline a scanner for some larger programming language. The result could then be fleshed out, by hand, to create code in some implementation language. Production compilers often use such ad hoc scanners; the code is fast and compact. During language development, however, it is usually preferable to build a scanner in a more structured way, as an explicit representation of a *finite automaton*. Finite automata can be generated automatically from a set of regular expressions, making it easy to regenerate a scanner when token definitions change.

EXAMPLE 2.11
Finite automaton for a calculator scanner

An automaton for the tokens of our calculator language appears in pictorial form in Figure 2.6. The automaton starts in a distinguished initial state. It then moves from state to state based on the next available character of input. When it reaches one of a designated set of final states it recognizes the token associated with that state. The "longest possible token" rule means that the scanner returns to the parser only when the next character cannot be used to continue the current token. ■

DESIGN & IMPLEMENTATION

2.3 Nested comments

Nested comments can be handy for the programmer (e.g., for temporarily "commenting out" large blocks of code). Scanners normally deal only with nonrecursive constructs, however, so nested comments require special treatment. Some languages disallow them. Others require the language implementor to augment the scanner with special-purpose comment-handling code. C and C++ strike a compromise: `/* ... */` style comments are not allowed to nest, but `/* ... */` and `//...` style comments can appear inside each other. The programmer can thus use one style for "normal" comments and the other for "commenting out." (The C99 designers note, however, that conditional compilation (`#if`) is preferable [Int03a, p. 58].)

```
skip any initial white space (spaces, tabs, and newlines)
if cur_char ∈ {'(', ')', '+', '-', '*'}
    return the corresponding single-character token
if cur_char = ':'
    read the next character
    if it is '=' then return assign else announce an error
if cur_char = '/'
    peek at the next character
    if it is '*' or '/'
        read additional characters until "*/" or newline is seen, respectively
        jump back to top of code
    else return div
if cur_char = .
    read the next character
    if it is a digit
        read any additional digits
        return number
    else announce an error
if cur_char is a digit
    read any additional digits and at most one decimal point
    return number
if cur_char is a letter
    read any additional letters and digits
    check to see whether the resulting string is read or write
    if so then return the corresponding token
    else return id
else announce an error
```

Figure 2.5 Outline of an ad hoc scanner for tokens in our calculator language.

2.2.1 Generating a Finite Automaton

While a finite automaton can in principle be written by hand, it is more common to build one automatically from a set of regular expressions, using a *scanner generator* tool. For our calculator language, we should like to covert the regular expressions of Example 2.9 into the automaton of Figure 2.6. That automaton has the desirable property that its actions are *deterministic*: in any given state with a given input character there is never more than one possible outgoing transition (arrow) labeled by that character. As it turns out, however, there is no obvious one-step algorithm to convert a set of regular expressions into an equivalent deterministic finite automaton (DFA). The typical scanner generator implements the conversion as a series of three separate steps.

The first step converts the regular expressions into a *nondeterministic* finite automaton (NFA). An NFA is like a DFA except that (1) there may be more than one transition out of a given state labeled by a given character, and (2) there may be so-called *epsilon transitions*: arrows labeled by the empty string symbol, ϵ. The NFA is said to accept an input string (token) if there exists a path from the start

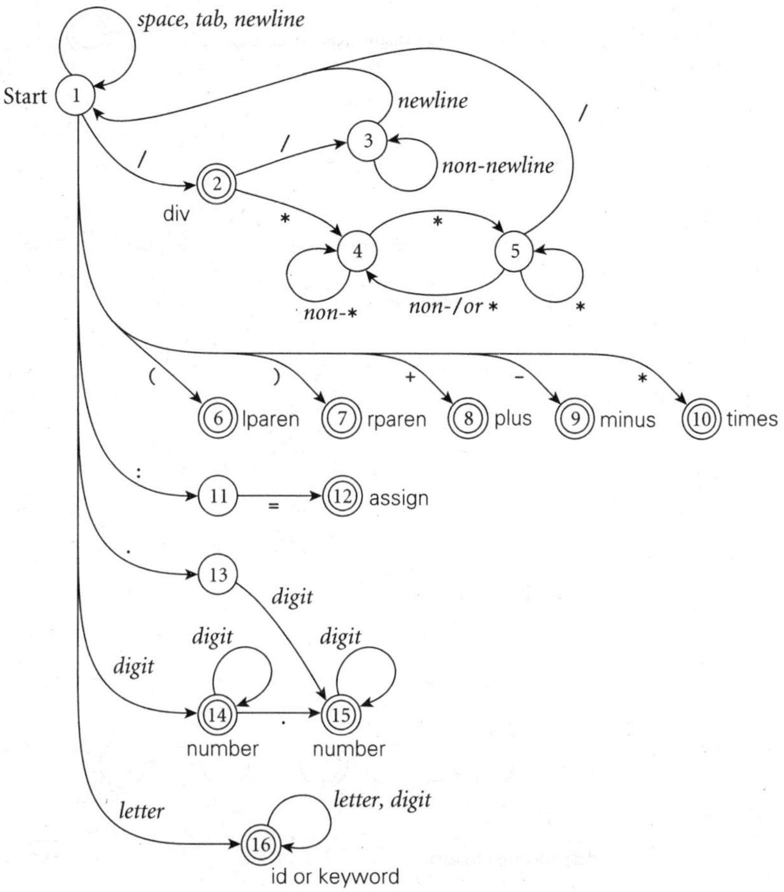

Figure 2.6 Pictorial representation of a scanner for calculator tokens, in the form of a finite automaton. This figure roughly parallels the code in Figure 2.5. States are numbered for reference in Figure 2.12. Scanning for each token begins in the state marked "Start." The *final* states, in which a token is recognized, are indicated by double circles. Comments, when recognized, send the scanner back to its start state, rather than a final state.

state to a final state whose non-epsilon transitions are labeled, in order, by the characters of the token.

To avoid the need to search all possible paths for one that "works," the second step of a scanner generator translates the NFA into an equivalent DFA: an automaton that accepts the same language, but in which there are no epsilon transitions, and no states with more than one outgoing transition labeled by the same character. The third step is a space optimization that generates a final DFA with the minimum possible number of states.

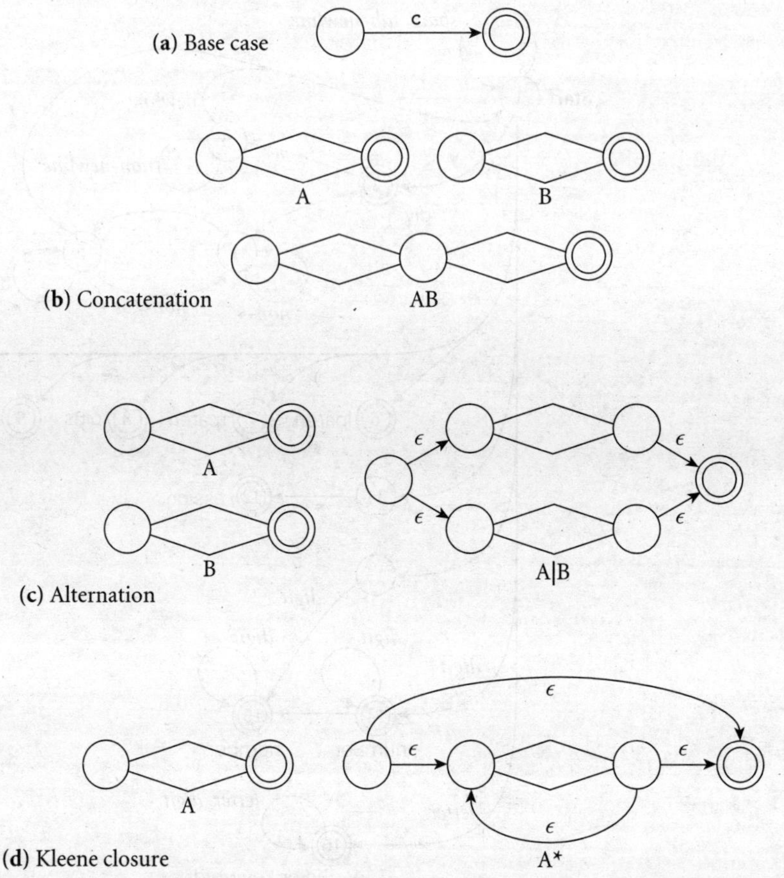

Figure 2.7 **Construction of an NFA equivalent to a given regular expression.** Part (a) shows the base case: the automaton for the single letter c. Parts (b), (c), and (d), respectively, show the constructions for concatenation, alternation, and Kleene closure. Each construction retains a unique start state and a single final state. Internal detail is hidden in the diamond-shaped center regions.

From a Regular Expression to an NFA

EXAMPLE 2.12

Constructing an NFA for a given regular expression

A trivial regular expression consisting of a single character c is equivalent to a simple two-state NFA (in fact, a DFA), illustrated in part (a) of Figure 2.7. Similarly, the regular expression ϵ is equivalent to a two-state NFA whose arc is labeled by ϵ. Starting with this base we can use three subconstructions, illustrated in parts (b) through (d) of the same figure, to build larger NFAs to represent the concatenation, alternation, or Kleene closure of the regular expressions represented by smaller NFAs. Each step preserves three invariants: there are no transitions into the initial state, there is a single final state, and there are no transitions out of the final state. These invariants allow smaller automata to be joined into larger

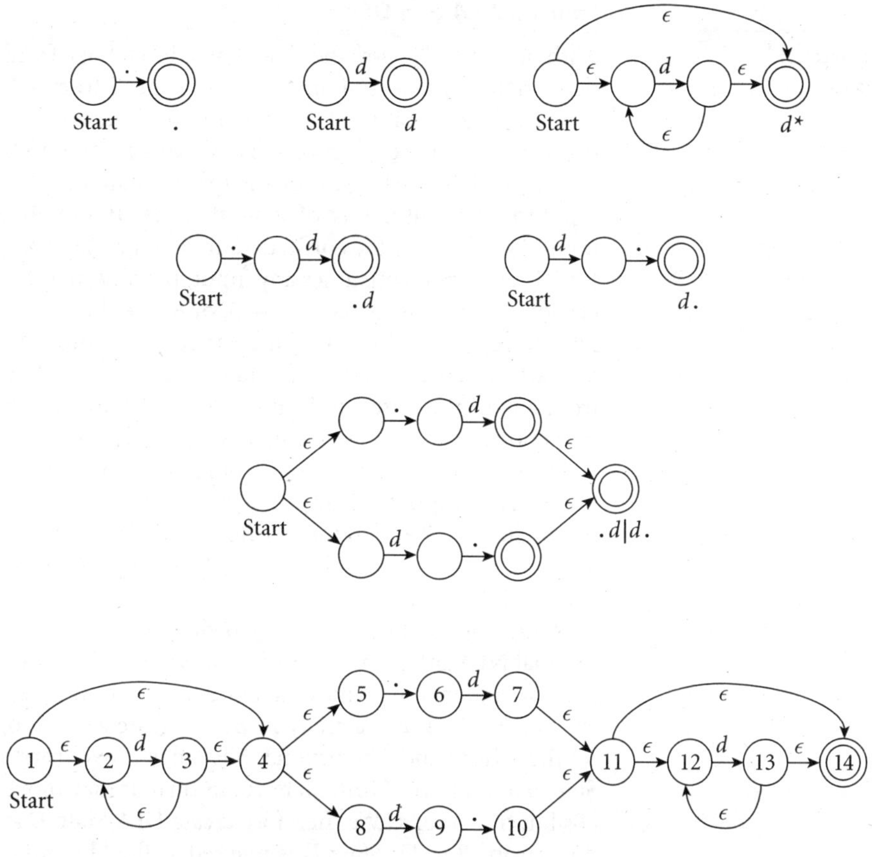

Figure 2.8 Construction of an NFA equivalent to the regular expression d*(. d | d .) d*. In the top row are the primitive automata for . and d, and the Kleene closure construction for d*. In the second and third rows we have used the concatenation and alternation constructions to build . d, d ., and (. d | d .) . The fourth row uses concatenation again to complete the NFA. We have labeled the states in the final automaton for reference in subsequent figures.

ones without any ambiguity about where to create the connections, and without creating any unexpected paths.

EXAMPLE 2.13

NFA for d*(. d | d .) d*

To make these constructions concrete, we consider a small but nontrivial example—the *decimal* strings of Example 2.3. These consist of a string of decimal digits containing a single decimal point. With only one digit, the point can come at the beginning or the end: (. d | d .), where for brevity we use d to represent any decimal digit. Arbitrary numbers of digits can then be added at the beginning or the end: d*(. d | d .) d*. Starting with this regular expression and using the constructions of Figure 2.7, we illustrate the construction of an equivalent NFA in Figure 2.8.

From an NFA to a DFA

EXAMPLE 2.14
DFA for $d*(.d \mid d.) d*$

With no way to "guess" the right transition to take from any given state, any practical implementation of an NFA would need to explore all possible transitions, concurrently or via backtracking. To avoid such a complex and time-consuming strategy, we can use a "set of subsets" construction to transform the NFA into an equivalent DFA. The key idea is for the state of the DFA after reading a given input to represent the *set* of states that the NFA might have reached on the same input. We illustrate the construction in Figure 2.9 using the NFA from Figure 2.8. Initially, before it consumes any input, the NFA may be in State 1, or it may make epsilon transitions to States 2, 4, 5, or 8. We thus create an initial State *A* for our DFA to represent this set. On an input of *d*, our NFA may move from State 2 to State 3, or from State 8 to State 9. It has no other transitions on this input from any of the states in *A*. From State 3, however, the NFA may make epsilon transitions to any of States 2, 4, 5, or 8. We therefore create DFA State *B* as shown.

On a ., our NFA may move from State 5 to State 6. There are no other transitions on this input from any of the states in *A*, and there are no epsilon transitions out of State 6. We therefore create the singleton DFA State *C* as shown. None of States *A*, *B*, or *C* is marked as final, because none contains a final state of the original NFA.

Returning to State *B* of the growing DFA, we note that on an input of *d* the original NFA may move from State 2 to State 3, or from State 8 to State 9. From State 3, in turn, it may move to States 2, 4, 5, or 8 via epsilon transitions. As these are exactly the states already in *B*, we create a self-loop in the DFA. Given a ., on the other hand, the original NFA may move from State 5 to State 6, or from State 9 to State 10. From State 10, in turn, it may move to States 11, 12, or 14 via epsilon transitions. We therefore create DFA State *D* as shown, with a transition on . from *B* to *D*. State *D* is marked as final because it contains state 14 of the original NFA. That is, given input *d*., there exists a path from the start state to the end state of the original NFA. Continuing our enumeration of state sets, we end up creating three more, labeled *E*, *F*, and *G* in Figure 2.9. Like State *D*, these all contain State 14 of the original NFA, and thus are marked as final. ■

In our example, the DFA ends up being smaller than the NFA, but this is only because our regular language is so simple. In theory, the number of states in the DFA may be exponential in the number of states in the NFA, but this extreme is also uncommon in practice. For a programming language scanner, the DFA tends to be larger than the NFA, but not outlandishly so. We consider space complexity in more detail in Section C-2.4.1.

Minimizing the DFA

EXAMPLE 2.15
Minimal DFA for $d*(.d \mid d.) d*$

Starting from a regular expression, we have now constructed an equivalent DFA. Though this DFA has seven states, a bit of thought suggests that a smaller one should exist. In particular, once we have seen both a *d* and a ., the only valid transitions are on *d*, and we ought to be able to make do with a single final state.

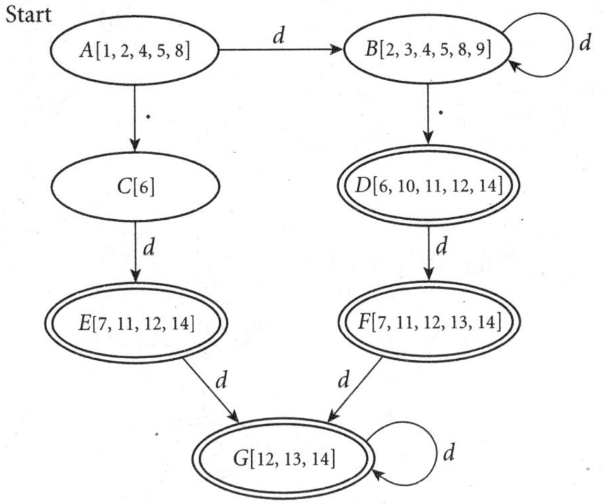

Figure 2.9 **A DFA equivalent to the NFA at the bottom of Figure 2.8.** Each state of the DFA represents the *set* of states that the NFA could be in after seeing the same input.

We can formalize this intuition, allowing us to apply it to any DFA, via the following inductive construction.

Initially we place the states of the (not necessarily minimal) DFA into two equivalence classes: final states and nonfinal states. We then repeatedly search for an equivalence class $\mathcal{X}$ and an input symbol c such that when given c as input, the states in $\mathcal{X}$ make transitions to states in $k > 1$ different equivalence classes. We then partition $\mathcal{X}$ into k classes in such a way that all states in a given new class would move to a member of the same old class on c. When we are unable to find a class to partition in this fashion we are done.

In our example, the original placement puts States *D*, *E*, *F*, and *G* in one class (final states) and States *A*, *B*, and *C* in another, as shown in the upper left of Figure 2.10. Unfortunately, the start state has ambiguous transitions on both *d* and .. To address the *d* ambiguity, we split *ABC* into *AB* and *C*, as shown in the upper right. New State *AB* has a self-loop on *d*; new State *C* moves to State *DEFG*. State *AB* still has an ambiguity on ., however, which we resolve by splitting it into States *A* and *B*, as shown at the bottom of the figure. At this point there are no further ambiguities, and we are left with a four-state minimal DFA.

2.2.2 Scanner Code

We can implement a scanner that explicitly captures the "circles-and-arrows" structure of a DFA in either of two main ways. One embeds the automaton in the control flow of the program using gotos or nested case (switch) statements; the other, described in the following subsection, uses a table and a driver. As a general rule, handwritten automata tend to use nested case statements, while

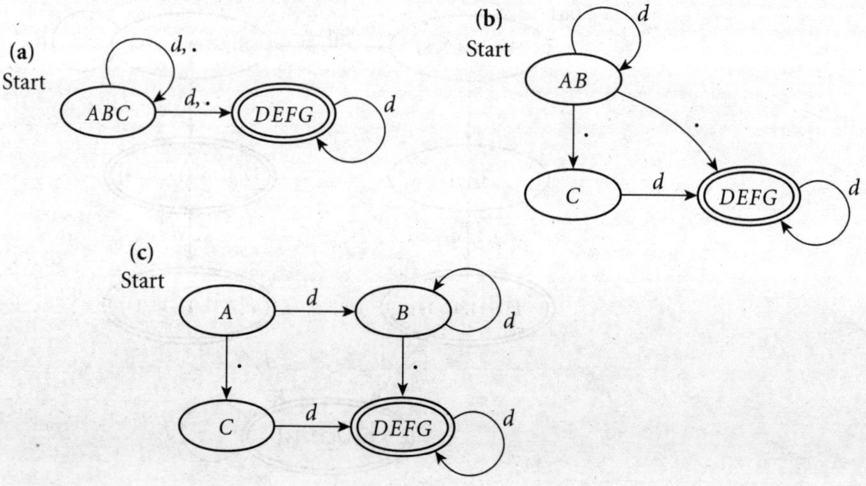

Figure 2.10 Minimization of the DFA of Figure 2.9. In each step we split a set of states to eliminate a transition ambiguity.

most automatically generated automata use tables. Tables are hard to create by hand, but easier than code to create from within a program. Likewise, nested case statements are easier to write and to debug than the ad hoc approach of Figure 2.5, if not quite as efficient. Unix's `lex/flex` tool produces C language output containing tables and a customized driver.

EXAMPLE 2.16
Nested case statement automaton

The nested case statement style of automaton has the following general structure:

```
state := 1          -- start state
loop
    read cur_char
    case state of
        1 : case cur_char of
                ' ', '\t', '\n' : ...
                'a'... 'z' :      ...
                '0'... '9' :      ...
                '>' :             ...
                ...
        2 : case cur_char of
                ...
        ...
        n: case cur_char of
```

The outer case statement covers the states of the finite automaton. The inner case statements cover the transitions out of each state. Most of the inner clauses simply set a new state. Some return from the scanner with the current token. (If the current character should not be part of that token, it is pushed back onto the input stream before returning.) ▪

Two aspects of the code typically deviate from the strict form of a formal finite automaton. One is the handling of keywords. The other is the need to peek ahead when a token can validly be extended by two or more additional characters, but not by only one.

As noted at the beginning of Section 2.1.1, keywords in most languages look just like identifiers, but are reserved for a special purpose (some authors use the term *reserved word* instead of keyword). It is possible to write a finite automaton that distinguishes between keywords and identifiers, but it requires a *lot* of states (see Exercise 2.3). Most scanners, both handwritten and automatically generated, therefore treat keywords as "exceptions" to the rule for identifiers. Before return-

DESIGN & IMPLEMENTATION

2.4 Recognizing multiple kinds of token

One of the chief ways in which a scanner differs from a formal DFA is that it *identifies* tokens in addition to recognizing them. That is, it not only determines whether characters constitute a valid token; it also indicates *which one*. In practice, this means that it must have separate final states for every kind of token. We glossed over this issue in our RE-to-DFA constructions.

To build a scanner for a language with n different kinds of tokens, we begin with an NFA of the sort suggested in the figure here. Given NFAs M_i, $1 \le i \le n$ (one automaton for each kind of token), we create a new start state with epsilon transitions to the start states of the M_is. In contrast to the alternation construction of Figure 2.7(c), however, we do *not* create a single final state; we keep the existing ones, each labeled by the token for which it is final. We then apply the NFA-to-DFA construction as before. (If final states for different tokens in the NFA ever end up in the same state of the DFA, then we have ambiguous token definitions. These may be resolved by changing the regular expressions from which the NFAs were derived, or by wrapping additional logic around the DFA.)

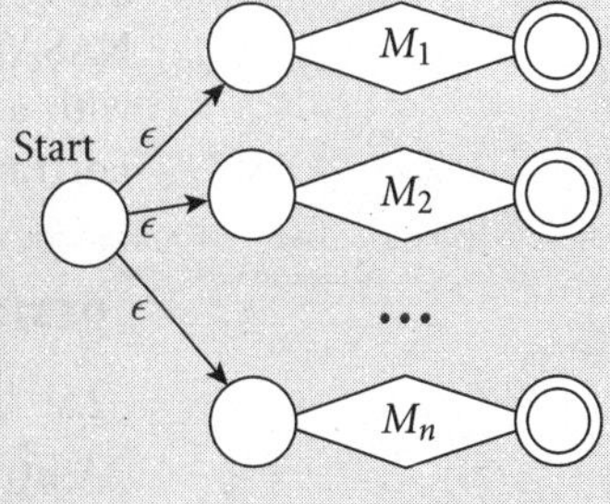

In the DFA minimization construction, instead of starting with two equivalence classes (final and nonfinal states), we begin with $n + 1$, including a separate class for final states for each of the kinds of token. Exercise 2.5 explores this construction for a scanner that recognizes both the *integer* and *decimal* types of Example 2.3.

ing an identifier to the parser, the scanner looks it up in a hash table or trie (a tree of branching paths) to make sure it isn't really a keyword.[10]

Whenever one legitimate token is a prefix of another, the "longest possible token" rule says that we should continue scanning. If some of the intermediate strings are not valid tokens, however, we can't tell whether a longer token is possible without looking more than one character ahead. This problem arises with dot characters (periods) in C. Suppose the scanner has just seen a `3` and has a dot coming up in the input. It needs to peek at characters beyond the dot in order to distinguish between `3.14` (a single token designating a real number), `3 . foo` (three tokens that the scanner should accept, even though the parser will object to seeing them in that order), and `3 ... foo` (again not syntactically valid, but three separate tokens nonetheless). In general, upcoming characters that a scanner must examine in order to make a decision are known as its *look-ahead*. In Section 2.3 we will see a similar notion of look-ahead *tokens* in parsing. ■

EXAMPLE 2.17
The nontrivial prefix problem

In messier languages, a scanner may need to look an arbitrary distance ahead. In Fortran IV, for example, `DO 5 I = 1,25` is the header of a loop (it executes the statements up to the one labeled `5` for values of `I` from 1 to 25), while `DO 5 I = 1.25` is an assignment statement that places the value `1.25` into the variable `DO5I`. Spaces are ignored in (pre-Fortran 90) Fortran input, even in the middle of variable names. Moreover, variables need not be declared, and the terminator for a `DO` loop is simply a label, which the parser can ignore. After seeing `DO`, the scanner cannot tell whether the `5` is part of the current token until it reaches the comma or dot. It has been widely (but apparently incorrectly) claimed that NASA's Mariner 1 space probe was lost due to accidental replacement of a comma with a dot in a case similar to this one in flight control software.[11] Dialects of Fortran starting with Fortran 77 allow (in fact encourage) the use of alternative

EXAMPLE 2.18
Look-ahead in Fortran scanning

DESIGN & IMPLEMENTATION

2.5 Longest possible tokens

A little care in syntax design—avoiding tokens that are nontrivial prefixes of other tokens—can dramatically simplify scanning. In straightforward cases of prefix ambiguity, the scanner can enforce the "longest possible token" rule automatically. In Fortran, however, the rules are sufficiently complex that no purely lexical solution suffices. Some of the problems, and a possible solution, are discussed in an article by Dyadkin [Dya95].

10 Many languages include *predefined* identifiers (e.g., for standard library functions), but these are not keywords. The programmer can redefine them, so the scanner must treat them the same as other identifiers. Contextual keywords, similarly, must be treated by the scanner as identifiers.

11 In actuality, the faulty software for Mariner 1 appears to have stemmed from a missing "bar" punctuation mark (indicating an average) in handwritten notes from which the software was derived [Cer89, pp. 202–203]. The Fortran `DO` loop error does appear to have occurred in at least one piece of NASA software, but no serious harm resulted [Web89].

syntax for loop headers, in which an extra comma makes misinterpretation less likely: `DO 5,I = 1,25`. ▪

In C, the dot character problem can easily be handled as a special case. In languages requiring larger amounts of look-ahead, the scanner can take a more general approach. In any case of ambiguity, it assumes that a longer token will be possible, but remembers that a shorter token could have been recognized at some point in the past. It also buffers all characters read beyond the end of the shorter token. If the optimistic assumption leads the scanner into an error state, it "unreads" the buffered characters so that they will be seen again later, and returns the shorter token.

2.2.3 Table-Driven Scanning

EXAMPLE 2.19
Table-driven scanning

In the preceding subsection we sketched how control flow—a loop and nested `case` statements—can be used to represent a finite automaton. An alternative approach represents the automaton as a data structure: a two-dimensional *transition table*. A driver program (Figure 2.11) uses the current state and input character to index into the table. Each entry in the table specifies whether to move to a new state (and if so, which one), return a token, or announce an error. A second table indicates, for each state, whether we might be at the end of a token (and if so, which one). Separating this second table from the first allows us to notice when we pass a state that might have been the end of a token, so we can back up if we hit an error state. Example tables for our calculator tokens appear in Figure 2.12.

Like a handwritten scanner, the table-driven code of Figure 2.11 looks tokens up in a table of keywords immediately before returning. An outer loop serves to filter out comments and "white space"—spaces, tabs, and newlines. ▪

2.2.4 Lexical Errors

The code in Figure 2.11 explicitly recognizes the possibility of *lexical errors*. In some cases the next character of input may be neither an acceptable continuation of the current token nor the start of another token. In such cases the scanner must print an error message and perform some sort of recovery so that compilation can continue, if only to look for additional errors. Fortunately, lexical errors are relatively rare—most character sequences do correspond to token sequences—and relatively easy to handle. The most common approach is simply to (1) throw away the current, invalid token; (2) skip forward until a character is found that can legitimately begin a new token; (3) restart the scanning algorithm; and (4) count on the error-recovery mechanism of the parser to cope with any cases in which the resulting sequence of tokens is not syntactically valid. Of course the need for error recovery is not unique to table-driven scanners; any scanner must cope with errors. We did not show the code in Figure 2.5, but it would have to be there in practice.

```
state = 0 .. number_of_states
token = 0 .. number_of_tokens
scan_tab : array [char, state] of record
    action : (move, recognize, error)
    new_state : state
token_tab : array [state] of token          -- what to recognize
keyword_tab : set of record
    k_image : string
    k_token : token
-- these three tables are created by a scanner generator tool

tok : token
cur_char : char
remembered_chars : list of char
repeat
    cur_state : state := start_state
    image : string := null
    remembered_state : state := 0        -- none
    loop
        read cur_char
        case scan_tab[cur_char, cur_state].action
            move:
                if token_tab[cur_state] ≠ 0
                    -- this could be a final state
                    remembered_state := cur_state
                    remembered_chars := ε
                add cur_char to remembered_chars
                cur_state := scan_tab[cur_char, cur_state].new_state
            recognize:
                tok := token_tab[cur_state]
                unread cur_char        -- push back into input stream
                exit inner loop
            error:
                if remembered_state ≠ 0
                    tok := token_tab[remembered_state]
                    unread remembered_chars
                    remove remembered_chars from image
                    exit inner loop
                -- else print error message and recover; probably start over
        append cur_char to image
    -- end inner loop
until tok ∉ {white_space, comment}
look image up in keyword_tab and replace tok with appropriate keyword if found
return ⟨tok, image⟩
```

Figure 2.11 Driver for a table-driven scanner, with code to handle the ambiguous case in which one valid token is a prefix of another, but some intermediate string is not.

State	*space, tab*	*newline*	/	*	(	)	+	-	:	=	.	*digit*	*letter*	*other*	
	Current input character														
1	17	17	2	10	6	7	8	9	11	–	13	14	16	–	
2	–	–	3	4	–	–	–	–	–	–	–	–	–	–	div
3	3	18	3	3	3	3	3	3	3	3	3	3	3	3	
4	4	4	4	5	4	4	4	4	4	4	4	4	4	4	
5	4	4	18	5	4	4	4	4	4	4	4	4	4	4	
6	–	–	–	–	–	–	–	–	–	–	–	–	–	–	lparen
7	–	–	–	–	–	–	–	–	–	–	–	–	–	–	rparen
8	–	–	–	–	–	–	–	–	–	–	–	–	–	–	plus
9	–	–	–	–	–	–	–	–	–	–	–	–	–	–	minus
10	–	–	–	–	–	–	–	–	–	–	–	–	–	–	times
11	–	–	–	–	–	–	–	–	–	12	–	–	–	–	
12	–	–	–	–	–	–	–	–	–	–	–	–	–	–	assign
13	–	–	–	–	–	–	–	–	–	–	–	15	–	–	
14	–	–	–	–	–	–	–	–	–	–	15	14	–	–	number
15	–	–	–	–	–	–	–	–	–	–	–	15	–	–	number
16	–	–	–	–	–	–	–	–	–	–	–	16	16	–	identifier
17	17	17	–	–	–	–	–	–	–	–	–	–	–	–	white_space
18	–	–	–	–	–	–	–	–	–	–	–	–	–	–	comment

Figure 2.12 Scanner tables for the calculator language. These could be used by the code of Figure 2.11. States are numbered as in Figure 2.6, except for the addition of two states—17 and 18—to "recognize" white space and comments. The right-hand column represents table token_tab; the rest of the figure is scan_tab. Numbers in the table indicate an entry for which the corresponding action is move. Dashes appear where there is no way to extend the current token: if the corresponding entry in token_tab is nonempty, then action is recognize; otherwise, action is error. Table keyword_tab (not shown) contains the strings `read` and `write`.

The code in Figure 2.11 also shows that the scanner must return both the kind of token found and its character-string image (spelling); again this requirement applies to all types of scanners. For some tokens the character-string image is redundant: all semicolons look the same, after all, as do all `while` keywords. For other tokens, however (e.g., identifiers, character strings, and numeric constants), the image is needed for semantic analysis. It is also useful for error messages: "undeclared identifier" is not as nice as "`foo` has not been declared."

2.2.5 Pragmas

Some languages and language implementations allow a program to contain constructs called *pragmas* that provide directives or hints to the compiler. Pragmas that do not change program semantics—only the compilation process—are sometimes called *significant comments.* In some languages the name is also appropriate because, like comments, pragmas can appear anywhere in the source program. In this case they are usually processed by the scanner: allowing them anywhere in the grammar would greatly complicate the parser. In most languages, however, pragmas are permitted only at certain well-defined places in the grammar. In this case they are best processed by the parser or semantic analyzer.

Pragmas that serve as directives may

- Turn various kinds of run-time checks (e.g., pointer or subscript checking) on or off
- Turn certain code improvements on or off (e.g., on in inner loops to improve performance; off otherwise to improve compilation speed)
- Enable or disable performance profiling (statistics gathering to identify program bottlenecks)

Some directives "cross the line" and change program semantics. In Ada, for example, the `unchecked` pragma can be used to disable type checking. In OpenMP, which we will consider in Chapter 13, pragmas specify significant parallel extensions to Fortran, C and C++: creating, scheduling, and synchronizing threads. In this case the principal rationale for expressing the extensions as pragmas rather than more deeply integrated changes is to sharply delineate the boundary between the core language and the extensions, and to share a common set of extensions across languages.

Pragmas that serve (merely) as hints provide the compiler with information about the source program that may allow it to do a better job:

- Variable `x` is very heavily used (it may be a good idea to keep it in a register).
- Subroutine `F` is a pure function: its only effect on the rest of the program is the value it returns.
- Subroutine `S` is not (indirectly) recursive (its storage may be statically allocated).
- 32 bits of precision (instead of 64) suffice for floating-point variable `x`.

The compiler may ignore these in the interest of simplicity, or in the face of contradictory information.

Standard syntax for pragmas was introduced in C++11 (where they are known as "attributes"). A function that prints an error message and terminates execution, for example, can be labeled `[[noreturn]]`, to allow the compiler to optimize code around calls, or to issue more helpful error or warning messages. As of this writing, the set of supported attributes can be extended by vendors (by modifying the compiler), but not by ordinary programmers. The extent to which these attributes should be limited to hints (rather than directives) has been somewhat controversial. New pragmas in Java (which calls them "annotations") and C# (which calls them "attributes") *can* be defined by the programmer; we will return to these in Section 16.3.1.

CHECK YOUR UNDERSTANDING

10. List the tasks performed by the typical scanner.
11. What are the advantages of an automatically generated scanner, in comparison to a handwritten one? Why do many commercial compilers use a handwritten scanner anyway?
12. Explain the difference between deterministic and nondeterministic finite automata. Why do we prefer the deterministic variety for scanning?
13. Outline the constructions used to turn a set of regular expressions into a minimal DFA.
14. What is the "longest possible token" rule?
15. Why must a scanner sometimes "peek" at upcoming characters?
16. What is the difference between a *keyword* and an *identifier*?
17. Why must a scanner save the text of tokens?
18. How does a scanner identify lexical errors? How does it respond?
19. What is a *pragma*?

2.3 Parsing

The parser is the heart of a typical compiler. It calls the scanner to obtain the tokens of the input program, assembles the tokens together into a syntax tree, and passes the tree (perhaps one subroutine at a time) to the later phases of the compiler, which perform semantic analysis and code generation and improvement. In effect, the parser is "in charge" of the entire compilation process; this style of compilation is sometimes referred to as *syntax-directed translation*.

As noted in the introduction to this chapter, a context-free grammar (CFG) is a *generator* for a CF language. A parser is a language *recognizer*. It can be shown that for any CFG we can create a parser that runs in $O(n^3)$ time, where n is the length of the input program.[12] There are two well-known parsing algorithms that achieve this bound: Earley's algorithm [Ear70] and the Cocke-Younger-Kasami (CYK) algorithm [Kas65, You67]. Cubic time is much too slow for parsing sizable programs, but fortunately not all grammars require such a general and slow parsing algorithm. There are large classes of grammars for which we can build parsers that run in linear time. The two most important of these classes are called LL and LR (Figure 2.13).

---

12 In general, an algorithm is said to run in time $O(f(n))$, where n is the length of the input, if its running time $t(n)$ is proportional to $f(n)$ in the worst case. More precisely, we say $t(n) = O(f(n)) \iff \exists c, m\, [n > m \longrightarrow t(n) < cf(n)]$.

Class	Direction of scanning	Derivation discovered	Parse tree construction	Algorithm used
LL	left-to-right	left-most	top-down	predictive
LR	left-to-right	right-most	bottom-up	shift-reduce

Figure 2.13 Principal classes of linear-time parsing algorithms.

LL stands for "Left-to-right, Left-most derivation." LR stands for "Left-to-right, Right-most derivation." In both classes the input is read left-to-right, and the parser attempts to discover (construct) a derivation of that input. For LL parsers, the derivation will be left-most; for LR parsers, right-most. We will cover LL parsers first. They are generally considered to be simpler and easier to understand. They can be written by hand or generated automatically from an appropriate grammar by a parser-generating tool. The class of LR grammars is larger (i.e., more grammars are LR than LL), and some people find the structure of the LR grammars more intuitive, especially in the handling of arithmetic expressions. LR parsers are almost always constructed by a parser-generating tool. Both classes of parsers are used in production compilers, though LR parsers are more common.

LL parsers are also called "top-down," or "predictive" parsers. They construct a parse tree from the root down, predicting at each step which production will be used to expand the current node, based on the next available token of input. LR parsers are also called "bottom-up" parsers. They construct a parse tree from the leaves up, recognizing when a collection of leaves or other nodes can be joined together as the children of a single parent.

EXAMPLE 2.20
Top-down and bottom-up parsing

We can illustrate the difference between top-down and bottom-up parsing by means of a simple example. Consider the following grammar for a comma-separated list of identifiers, terminated by a semicolon:

id_list ⟶ `id` *id_list_tail*
id_list_tail ⟶ `, id` *id_list_tail*
id_list_tail ⟶ `;`

These are the productions that would normally be used for an identifier list in a top-down parser. They can also be parsed bottom-up (most top-down grammars can be). In practice they would not be used in a bottom-up parser, for reasons that will become clear in a moment, but the ability to handle them either way makes them good for this example.

Progressive stages in the top-down and bottom-up construction of a parse tree for the string `A, B, C;` appear in Figure 2.14. The top-down parser begins by predicting that the root of the tree (*id_list*) will expand to `id` *id_list_tail*. It then matches the `id` against a token obtained from the scanner. (If the scanner produced something different, the parser would announce a syntax error.) The parser then moves down into the first (in this case only) nonterminal child and predicts that *id_list_tail* will expand to `, id` *id_list_tail*. To make this prediction it needs

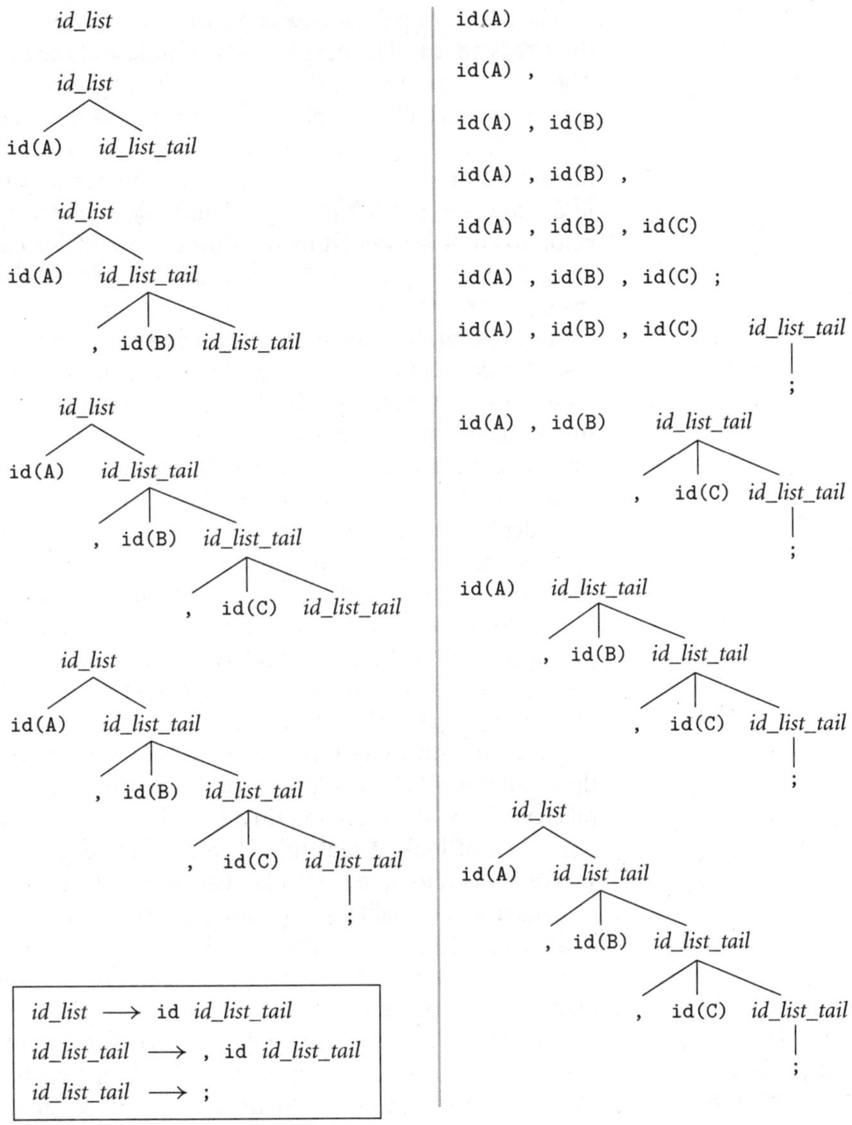

id_list	⟶	`id` *id_list_tail*
id_list_tail	⟶	`,` `id` *id_list_tail*
id_list_tail	⟶	`;`

Figure 2.14 Top-down (*left*) and bottom-up parsing (*right*) of the input string `A, B, C;`. Grammar appears at lower left.

to peek at the upcoming token (a comma), which allows it to choose between the two possible expansions for *id_list_tail*. It then matches the comma and the `id` and moves down into the next *id_list_tail*. In a similar, recursive fashion, the top-down parser works down the tree, left-to-right, predicting and expanding nodes and tracing out a left-most derivation of the fringe of the tree.

The bottom-up parser, by contrast, begins by noting that the left-most leaf of the tree is an `id`. The next leaf is a comma and the one after that is another `id`. The parser continues in this fashion, shifting new leaves from the scanner into a forest of partially completed parse tree fragments, until it realizes that some of those fragments constitute a complete right-hand side. In this grammar, that doesn't occur until the parser has seen the semicolon—the right-hand side of *id_list_tail* ⟶ ; . With this right-hand side in hand, the parser reduces the semicolon to an *id_list_tail*. It then reduces , `id` *id_list_tail* into another *id_list_tail*. After doing this one more time it is able to reduce `id` *id_list_tail* into the root of the parse tree, *id_list*.

At no point does the bottom-up parser predict what it will see next. Rather, it shifts tokens into its forest until it recognizes a right-hand side, which it then reduces to a left-hand side. Because of this behavior, bottom-up parsers are sometimes called *shift-reduce* parsers. Moving up the figure, from bottom to top, we can see that the shift-reduce parser traces out a right-most derivation, in reverse. Because bottom-up parsers were the first to receive careful formal study, right-most derivations are sometimes called *canonical*. ■

There are several important subclasses of LR parsers, including SLR, LALR, and "full LR." SLR and LALR are important for their ease of implementation, full LR for its generality. LL parsers can also be grouped into SLL and "full LL" subclasses. We will cover the differences among them only briefly here; for further information see any of the standard compiler-construction or parsing theory textbooks [App97, ALSU07, AU72, CT04, FCL10, GBJ+12].

One commonly sees LL or LR (or whatever) written with a number in parentheses after it: LL(2) or LALR(1), for example. This number indicates how many tokens of look-ahead are required in order to parse. Most real compilers use just one token of look-ahead, though more can sometimes be helpful. The open-source ANTLR tool, in particular, uses multitoken look-ahead to enlarge the class of languages amenable to top-down parsing [PQ95]. In Section 2.3.1 we will look at LL(1) grammars and handwritten parsers in more detail. In Sections 2.3.3 and 2.3.4 we will consider automatically generated LL(1) and LR(1) (actually SLR(1)) parsers.

EXAMPLE 2.21
Bounding space with a bottom-up grammar

The problem with our example grammar, for the purposes of bottom-up parsing, is that it forces the compiler to shift all the tokens of an *id_list* into its forest before it can reduce any of them. In a very large program we might run out of space. Sometimes there is nothing that can be done to avoid a lot of shifting. In this case, however, we can use an alternative grammar that allows the parser to reduce prefixes of the *id_list* into nonterminals as it goes along:

id_list ⟶ *id_list_prefix* ;
id_list_prefix ⟶ *id_list_prefix* , `id`
⟶ `id`

This grammar cannot be parsed top-down, because when we see an `id` on the input and we're expecting an *id_list_prefix*, we have no way to tell which of the two

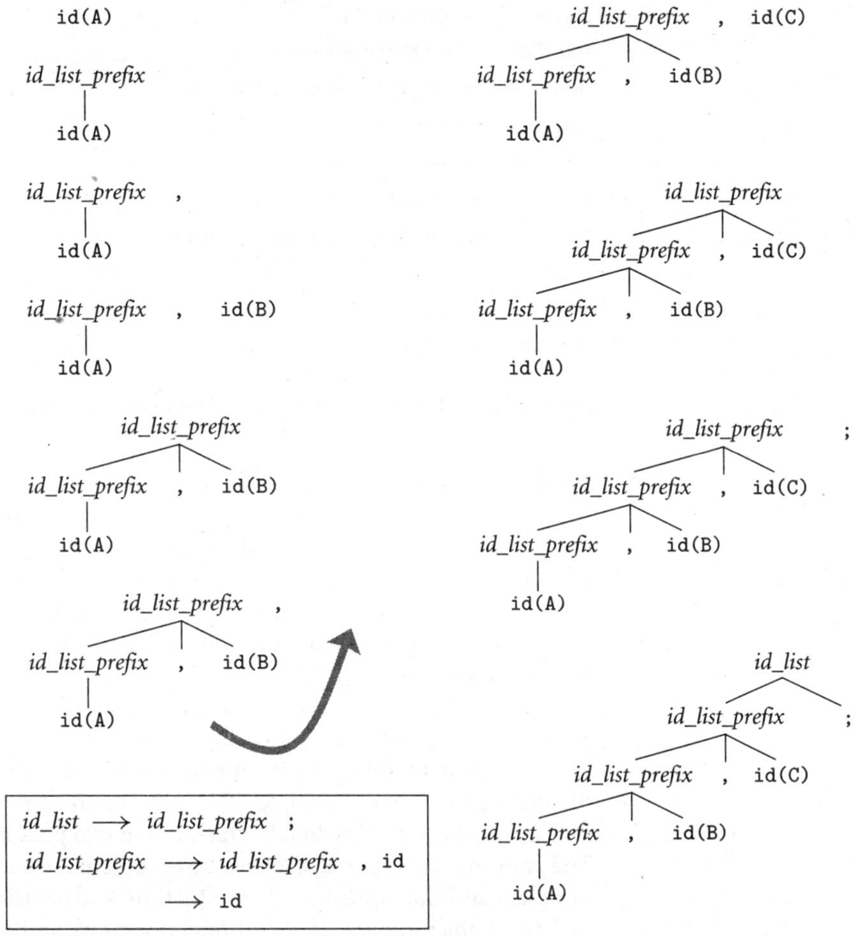

Figure 2.15 Bottom-up parse of `A, B, C;` using a grammar (lower left) that allows lists to be collapsed incrementally.

possible productions we should predict (more on this dilemma in Section 2.3.2). As shown in Figure 2.15, however, the grammar works well bottom-up.

2.3.1 Recursive Descent

EXAMPLE 2.22
Top-down grammar for a calculator language

To illustrate top-down (predictive) parsing, let us consider the grammar for a simple "calculator" language, shown in Figure 2.16. The calculator allows values to be read into named variables, which may then be used in expressions. Expressions in turn may be written to the output. Control flow is strictly linear (no loops, `if` statements, or other jumps). In a pattern that will repeat in many of our examples, we have included an initial *augmenting* production, *program* ⟶ *stmt_list* `$$`, *program* ⟶ *stmt_list* `$$`

stmt_list ⟶ *stmt stmt_list* | ϵ

stmt ⟶ `id :=` *expr* | `read id` | `write` *expr*

expr ⟶ *term term_tail*

term_tail ⟶ *add_op term term_tail* | ϵ

term ⟶ *factor factor_tail*

factor_tail ⟶ *mult_op factor factor_tail* | ϵ

factor ⟶ `(` *expr* `)` | `id` | `number`

add_op ⟶ `+` | `-`

mult_op ⟶ `*` | `/`

Figure 2.16 LL(1) grammar for a simple calculator language.

which arranges for the "real" body of the program (*stmt_list*) to be followed by a special *end marker* token, `$$`. The end marker is produced by the scanner at the end of the input. Its presence allows the parser to terminate cleanly once it has seen the entire program, and to decline to accept programs with extra garbage tokens at the end. As in regular expressions, we use the symbol ϵ to denote the empty string. A production with ϵ on the right-hand side is sometimes called an *epsilon production.*

It may be helpful to compare the *expr* portion of Figure 2.16 to the expression grammar of Example 2.8. Most people find that previous, LR grammar to be significantly more intuitive. It suffers, however, from a problem similar to that of the *id_list* grammar of Example 2.21: if we see an `id` on the input when expecting an *expr*, we have no way to tell which of the two possible productions to predict. The grammar of Figure 2.16 avoids this problem by merging the common prefixes of right-hand sides into a single production, and by using new symbols (*term_tail* and *factor_tail*) to generate additional operators and operands as required. The transformation has the unfortunate side effect of placing the operands of a given operator in separate right-hand sides. In effect, we have sacrificed grammatical elegance in order to be able to parse predictively. ■

So how do we parse a string with our calculator grammar? We saw the basic idea in Figure 2.14. We start at the top of the tree and predict needed productions on the basis of the current left-most nonterminal in the tree and the current input token. We can formalize this process in one of two ways. The first, described in the remainder of this subsection, is to build a *recursive descent parser* whose subroutines correspond, one-one, to the nonterminals of the grammar. Recursive descent parsers are typically constructed by hand, though the ANTLR parser generator constructs them automatically from an input grammar. The second approach, described in Section 2.3.3, is to build an *LL parse table* which is then read by a driver program. Table-driven parsers are almost always constructed automatically by a parser generator. These two options—recursive descent and table-driven—are reminiscent of the nested case statements and table-driven approaches to building a scanner that we saw in Sections 2.2.2 and 2.2.3. It should be emphasized that they implement the same basic parsing algorithm.

Handwritten recursive descent parsers are most often used when the language to be parsed is relatively simple, or when a parser-generator tool is not available. There are exceptions, however. In particular, recursive descent appears in recent versions of the GNU compiler collection (`gcc`). Earlier versions used `bison` to create a bottom-up parser automatically. The change was made in part for performance reasons and in part to enable the generation of higher-quality syntax error messages. (The `bison` code was easier to write, and arguably easier to maintain.)

EXAMPLE 2.23
Recursive descent parser for the calculator language

Pseudocode for a recursive descent parser for our calculator language appears in Figure 2.17. It has a subroutine for every nonterminal in the grammar. It also has a mechanism input_token to inspect the next token available from the scanner and a subroutine (match) to consume and update this token, and in the process verify that it is the one that was expected (as specified by an argument). If match or any of the other subroutines sees an unexpected token, then a syntax error has occurred. For the time being let us assume that the parse_error subroutine simply prints a message and terminates the parse. In Section 2.3.5 we will consider how to recover from such errors and continue to parse the remainder of the input. ■

EXAMPLE 2.24
Recursive descent parse of a "sum and average" program

Suppose now that we are to parse a simple program to read two numbers and print their sum and average:

```
read A
read B
sum := A + B
write sum
write sum / 2
```

The parse tree for this program appears in Figure 2.18. The parser begins by calling the subroutine program. After noting that the initial token is a `read`, program calls stmt_list and then attempts to match the end-of-file pseudotoken. (In the parse tree, the root, *program*, has two children, *stmt_list* and `$$`.) Procedure stmt_list again notes that the upcoming token is a `read`. This observation allows it to determine that the current node (*stmt_list*) generates *stmt stmt_list* (rather than ϵ). It therefore calls stmt and stmt_list before returning. Continuing in this fashion, the execution path of the parser traces out a left-to-right depth-first traversal of the parse tree. This correspondence between the dynamic execution trace and the structure of the parse tree is the distinguishing characteristic of recursive descent parsing. Note that because the *stmt_list* nonterminal appears in the right-hand side of a *stmt_list* production, the stmt_list subroutine must call itself. This recursion accounts for the name of the parsing technique. ■

Without additional code (not shown in Figure 2.17), the parser merely verifies that the program is syntactically correct (i.e., that none of the otherwise parse_error clauses in the case statements are executed and that match always sees what it expects to see). To be of use to the rest of the compiler—which must produce an equivalent target program in some other language—the parser must

```
procedure match(expected)
    if input_token = expected then consume_input_token()
    else parse_error

-- this is the start routine:
procedure program()
    case input_token of
        id, read, write, $$ :
            stmt_list()
            match($$)
        otherwise parse_error

procedure stmt_list()
    case input_token of
        id, read, write : stmt(); stmt_list()
        $$ : skip    -- epsilon production
        otherwise parse_error

procedure stmt()
    case input_token of
        id : match(id); match(:=); expr()
        read : match(read); match(id)
        write : match(write); expr()
        otherwise parse_error

procedure expr()
    case input_token of
        id, number, ( : term(); term_tail()
        otherwise parse_error

procedure term_tail()
    case input_token of
        +, - : add_op(); term(); term_tail()
        ), id, read, write, $$ :
            skip    -- epsilon production
        otherwise parse_error

procedure term()
    case input_token of
        id, number, ( : factor(); factor_tail()
        otherwise parse_error
```

Figure 2.17 **Recursive descent parser for the calculator language.** Execution begins in procedure program. The recursive calls trace out a traversal of the parse tree. Not shown is code to save this tree (or some similar structure) for use by later phases of the compiler. *(continued)*

```
procedure factor_tail()
    case input_token of
        *, / : mult_op(); factor(); factor_tail()
        +, -, ), id, read, write, $$ :
            skip        -- epsilon production
        otherwise parse_error

procedure factor()
    case input_token of
        id : match(id)
        number : match(number)
        ( : match( (); expr(); match( ))
        otherwise parse_error

procedure add_op()
    case input_token of
        + : match(+)
        - : match(-)
        otherwise parse_error

procedure mult_op()
    case input_token of
        * : match(*)
        / : match(/)
        otherwise parse_error
```

Figure 2.17 *(continued)*

save the parse tree or some other representation of program fragments as an explicit data structure. To save the parse tree itself, we can allocate and link together records to represent the children of a node immediately before executing the recursive subroutines and match invocations that represent those children. We shall need to pass each recursive routine an argument that points to the record that is to be expanded (i.e., whose children are to be discovered). Procedure match will also need to save information about certain tokens (e.g., character-string representations of identifiers and literals) in the leaves of the tree.

As we saw in Chapter 1, the parse tree contains a great deal of irrelevant detail that need not be saved for the rest of the compiler. It is therefore rare for a parser to construct a full parse tree explicitly. More often it produces an abstract syntax tree or some other more terse representation. In a recursive descent compiler, a syntax tree can be created by allocating and linking together records in only a subset of the recursive calls.

The trickiest part of writing a recursive descent parser is figuring out which tokens should label the arms of the case statements. Each arm represents one production: one possible expansion of the symbol for which the subroutine was named. The tokens that label a given arm are those that *predict* the production. A token X may predict a production for either of two reasons: (1) the right-hand

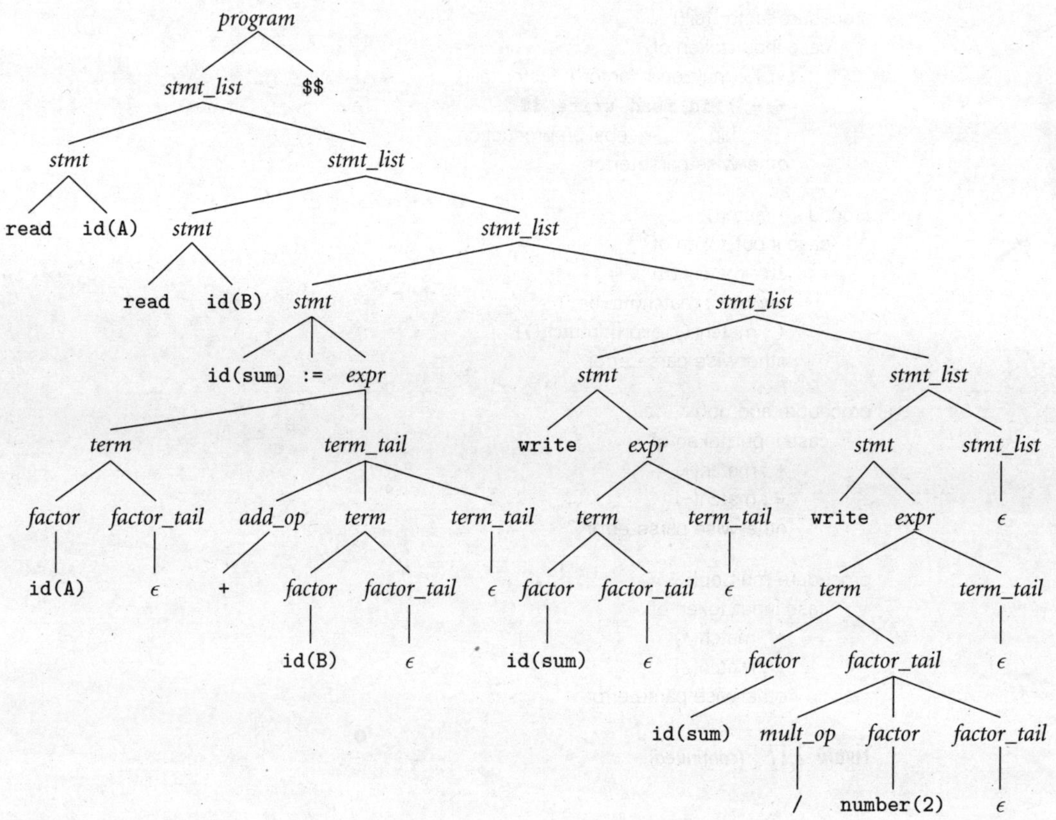

Figure 2.18 Parse tree for the sum-and-average program of Example 2.24, using the grammar of Figure 2.16.

side of the production, when recursively expanded, may yield a string beginning with `X`, or (2) the right-hand side may yield nothing (i.e., it is ϵ, or a string of nonterminals that may recursively yield ϵ), and `X` may begin the yield of what comes *next*. We will formalize this notion of prediction in Section 2.3.3, using sets called FIRST and FOLLOW, and show how to derive them automatically from an LL(1) CFG.

✓ CHECK YOUR UNDERSTANDING

20. What is the inherent "big-O" complexity of parsing? What is the complexity of parsers used in real compilers?
21. Summarize the difference between LL and LR parsing. Which one of them is also called "bottom-up"? "Top-down"? Which one is also called "predictive"? "Shift-reduce"? What do "LL" and "LR" stand for?

22. What kind of parser (top-down or bottom-up) is most common in production compilers?
23. Why are right-most derivations sometimes called *canonical*?
24. What is the significance of the "1" in LR(1)?
25. Why might we want (or need) different grammars for different parsing algorithms?
26. What is an *epsilon production*?
27. What are *recursive descent* parsers? Why are they used mostly for small languages?
28. How might a parser construct an explicit parse tree or syntax tree?

2.3.2 Writing an LL(1) Grammar

When designing a recursive-descent parser, one has to acquire a certain facility in writing and modifying LL(1) grammars. The two most common obstacles to "LL(1)-ness" are *left recursion* and *common prefixes.*

EXAMPLE 2.25
Left recursion

A grammar is said to be left recursive if there is a nonterminal A such that $A \Longrightarrow^{+} A\ \alpha$ for some α.[13] The trivial case occurs when the first symbol on the right-hand side of a production is the same as the symbol on the left-hand side. Here again is the grammar from Example 2.21, which cannot be parsed top-down:

id_list ⟶ *id_list_prefix* ;
id_list_prefix ⟶ *id_list_prefix* , `id`
⟶ `id`

The problem is in the second and third productions; in the *id_list_prefix* parsing routine, with `id` on the input, a predictive parser cannot tell which of the productions it should use. (Recall that left recursion is *desirable* in bottom-up grammars, because it allows recursive constructs to be discovered incrementally, as in Figure 2.15.)

EXAMPLE 2.26
Common prefixes

Common prefixes occur when two different productions with the same left-hand side begin with the same symbol or symbols. Here is an example that commonly appears in languages descended from Algol:

13 Following conventional notation, we use uppercase Roman letters near the beginning of the alphabet to represent nonterminals, uppercase Roman letters near the end of the alphabet to represent arbitrary grammar symbols (terminals or nonterminals), lowercase Roman letters near the beginning of the alphabet to represent terminals (tokens), lowercase Roman letters near the end of the alphabet to represent token strings, and lowercase Greek letters to represent strings of arbitrary symbols.

$stmt \longrightarrow$ `id := ` $expr$

$\longrightarrow$ `id (` $argument\_list$ `)` -- procedure call

With `id` at the beginning of both right-hand sides, we cannot choose between them on the basis of the upcoming token. ■

Both left recursion and common prefixes can be removed from a grammar mechanically. The general case is a little tricky (Exercise 2.25), because the prediction problem may be an indirect one (e.g., $S \longrightarrow A\ \alpha$ and $A \longrightarrow S\ \beta$, or $S \longrightarrow A\ \alpha$, $S \longrightarrow B\ \beta$, $A \Longrightarrow^* \texttt{c}\ \gamma$, and $B \Longrightarrow^* \texttt{c}\ \delta$). We can see the general idea in the examples above, however.

EXAMPLE 2.27
Eliminating left recursion

Our left-recursive definition of *id_list* can be replaced by the right-recursive variant we saw in Example 2.20:

$id\_list \longrightarrow$ `id` id_list_tail

$id\_list\_tail \longrightarrow$ `,` `id` id_list_tail

$id\_list\_tail \longrightarrow$ `;` ■

EXAMPLE 2.28
Left factoring

Our common-prefix definition of *stmt* can be made LL(1) by a technique called *left factoring*:

$stmt \longrightarrow$ `id` $stmt\_list\_tail$

$stmt\_list\_tail \longrightarrow$ `:=` $expr$ | `(` $argument\_list$ `)` ■

Of course, simply eliminating left recursion and common prefixes is *not* guaranteed to make a grammar LL(1). There are infinitely many non-LL *languages*—languages for which no LL grammar exists—and the mechanical transformations to eliminate left recursion and common prefixes work on their grammars just fine. Fortunately, the few non-LL languages that arise in practice can generally be handled by augmenting the parsing algorithm with one or two simple heuristics.

EXAMPLE 2.29
Parsing a "dangling `else`"

The best known example of a "not quite LL" construct arises in languages like Pascal, in which the `else` part of an `if` statement is optional. The natural grammar fragment

$stmt \longrightarrow$ `if` $condition\ then\_clause\ else\_clause$ | $other\_stmt$

$then\_clause \longrightarrow$ `then` $stmt$

$else\_clause \longrightarrow$ `else` $stmt$ | ϵ

is ambiguous (and thus neither LL nor LR); it allows the `else` in `if` $\texttt{C}_1$ `then if` $\texttt{C}_2$ `then` $\texttt{S}_1$ `else` $\texttt{S}_2$ to be paired with either `then`. The less natural grammar fragment

$stmt \longrightarrow balanced\_stmt$ | $unbalanced\_stmt$

$balanced\_stmt \longrightarrow$ `if` $condition$ `then` $balanced\_stmt$ `else` $balanced\_stmt$
| $other\_stmt$

$unbalanced\_stmt \longrightarrow$ `if` $condition$ `then` $stmt$
| `if` $condition$ `then` $balanced\_stmt$ `else` $unbalanced\_stmt$

can be parsed bottom-up but not top-down (there is *no* pure top-down grammar for Pascal `else` statements). A *balanced_stmt* is one with the same number of `then`s and `else`s. An *unbalanced_stmt* has more `then`s.

The usual approach, whether parsing top-down or bottom-up, is to use the ambiguous grammar together with a "disambiguating rule," which says that in the case of a conflict between two possible productions, the one to use is the one that occurs first, textually, in the grammar. In the ambiguous fragment above, the fact that *else_clause* $\longrightarrow$ `else` *stmt* comes before *else_clause* $\longrightarrow \epsilon$ ends up pairing the `else` with the nearest `then`.

Better yet, a language designer can avoid this sort of problem by choosing different syntax. The ambiguity of the *dangling else* problem in Pascal leads to problems not only in parsing, but in writing and maintaining correct programs. Most Pascal programmers at one time or another ended up writing a program like this one:

EXAMPLE 2.30
"Dangling `else`" program bug

```
if P <> nil then
    if P^.val = goal then
        foundIt := true
else
    endOfList := true
```

Indentation notwithstanding, the Pascal manual states that an `else` clause matches the closest unmatched `then`—in this case the inner one—which is clearly not what the programmer intended. To get the desired effect, the Pascal programmer needed to write

```
if P <> nil then begin
    if P^.val = goal then
        foundIt := true
end
else
    endOfList := true
```

EXAMPLE 2.31
End markers for structured statements

Many other Algol-family languages (including Modula, Modula-2, and Oberon, all more recent inventions of Pascal's designer, Niklaus Wirth) require explicit *end markers* on all structured statements. The grammar fragment for `if` statements in Modula-2 looks something like this:

DESIGN & IMPLEMENTATION

2.6 The dangling `else`

A simple change in language syntax—eliminating the dangling `else`—not only reduces the chance of programming errors, but also significantly simplifies parsing. For more on the dangling `else` problem, see Exercise 2.24 and Section 6.4.

stmt ⟶ IF *condition then_clause else_clause* END | *other_stmt*

then_clause ⟶ THEN *stmt_list*

else_clause ⟶ ELSE *stmt_list* | ϵ

The addition of the END eliminates the ambiguity.

Modula-2 uses END to terminate all its structured statements. Ada and Fortran 77 end an if with end if (and a while with end while, etc.). Algol 68 creates its terminators by spelling the initial keyword backward (if...fi, case...esac, do...od, etc.).

EXAMPLE 2.32
The need for elsif

One problem with end markers is that they tend to bunch up. In Pascal one could write

```
if A = B then ...
else if A = C then ...
else if A = D then ...
else if A = E then ...
else ...
```

With end markers this becomes

```
if A = B then ...
else if A = C then ...
else if A = D then ...
else if A = E then ...
else ...
end end end end
```

To avoid this awkwardness, languages with end markers generally provide an elsif keyword (sometimes spelled elif):

```
if A = B then ...
elsif A = C then ...
elsif A = D then ...
elsif A = E then ...
else ...
end
```

2.3.3 Table-Driven Top-Down Parsing

EXAMPLE 2.33
Driver and table for top-down parsing

In a recursive descent parser, each arm of a case statement corresponds to a production, and contains parsing routine and match calls corresponding to the symbols on the right-hand side of that production. At any given point in the parse, if we consider the calls beyond the program counter (the ones that have yet to occur) in the parsing routine invocations currently in the call stack, we obtain a list of the symbols that the parser expects to see between here and the end of the program. A table-driven top-down parser maintains an explicit stack containing this same list of symbols.

```
terminal = 1 .. number_of_terminals
non_terminal = number_of_terminals + 1 .. number_of_symbols
symbol = 1 .. number_of_symbols
production = 1 .. number_of_productions

parse_tab : array [non_terminal, terminal] of record
    action : (predict, error)
    prod : production
prod_tab : array [production] of list of symbol
-- these two tables are created by a parser generator tool

parse_stack : stack of symbol

parse_stack.push(start_symbol)
loop
    expected_sym : symbol := parse_stack.pop()
    if expected_sym ∈ terminal
        match(expected_sym)                    -- as in Figure 2.17
        if expected_sym = $$ then return       -- success!
    else
        if parse_tab[expected_sym, input_token].action = error
            parse_error
        else
            prediction : production := parse_tab[expected_sym, input_token].prod
            foreach sym : symbol in reverse prod_tab[prediction]
                parse_stack.push(sym)
```

Figure 2.19 Driver for a table-driven LL(1) parser.

Pseudocode for such a parser appears in Figure 2.19. The code is language independent. It requires a language-*dependent* parsing table, generally produced by an automatic tool. For the calculator grammar of Figure 2.16, the table appears in Figure 2.20.

EXAMPLE 2.34
Table-driven parse of the "sum and average" program

To illustrate the algorithm, Figure 2.21 shows a trace of the stack and the input over time, for the sum-and-average program of Example 2.24. The parser iterates around a loop in which it pops the top symbol off the stack and performs the following actions: If the popped symbol is a terminal, the parser attempts to match it against an incoming token from the scanner. If the match fails, the parser announces a syntax error and initiates some sort of error recovery (see Section 2.3.5). If the popped symbol is a nonterminal, the parser uses that nonterminal together with the next available input token to index into a two-dimensional table that tells it which production to predict (or whether to announce a syntax error and initiate recovery).

Initially, the parse stack contains the start symbol of the grammar (in our case, *program*). When it predicts a production, the parser pushes the right-hand-side symbols onto the parse stack in reverse order, so the first of those symbols ends up at top-of-stack. The parse completes successfully when we match the end marker

Top-of-stack nonterminal	**Current input token**											
	`id`	`number`	`read`	`write`	`:=`	`(`	`)`	`+`	`-`	`*`	`/`	`$$`
program	1	–	1	1	–	–	–	–	–	–	–	1
stmt_list	2	–	2	2	–	–	–	–	–	–	–	3
stmt	4	–	5	6	–	–	–	–	–	–	–	–
expr	7	7	–	–	–	7	–	–	–	–	–	–
term_tail	9	–	9	9	–	–	9	8	8	–	–	9
term	10	10	–	–	–	10	–	–	–	–	–	–
factor_tail	12	–	12	12	–	–	12	12	12	11	11	12
factor	14	15	–	–	–	13	–	–	–	–	–	–
add_op	–	–	–	–	–	–	–	16	17	–	–	–
mult_op	–	–	–	–	–	–	–	–	–	18	19	–

Figure 2.20 **LL(1) parse table for the calculator language.** Table entries indicate the production to predict (as numbered in Figure 2.23). A dash indicates an error. When the top-of-stack symbol is a terminal, the appropriate action is always to match it against an incoming token from the scanner. An auxiliary table, not shown here, gives the right-hand-side symbols for each production.

token, `$$`. Assuming that `$$` appears only once in the grammar, at the end of the first production, and that the scanner returns this token only at end-of-file, any syntax error is guaranteed to manifest itself either as a failed match or as an error entry in the table. ■

As we hinted at the end of Section 2.3.1, predict sets are defined in terms of simpler sets called FIRST and FOLLOW, where FIRST(A) is the set of all tokens that could be the start of an A and FOLLOW(A) is the set of all tokens that could come after an A in some valid program. If we extend the domain of FIRST in the obvious way to include *strings* of symbols, we then say that the predict set of a production $A \longrightarrow \beta$ is FIRST(β), plus FOLLOW(A) if $\beta \Longrightarrow^* \epsilon$. For notational convenience, we define the predicate EPS such that EPS(β) $\equiv \beta \Longrightarrow^* \epsilon$.

EXAMPLE 2.35

Predict sets for the calculator language

We can illustrate the algorithm to construct these sets using our calculator grammar (Figure 2.16). We begin with "obvious" facts about the grammar and build on them inductively. If we recast the grammar in plain BNF (no EBNF '|' constructs), then it has 19 productions. The "obvious" facts arise from adjacent pairs of symbols in right-hand sides. In the first production, we can see that `$$` $\in$ FOLLOW(*stmt_list*). In the third (*stmt_list* $\longrightarrow \epsilon$), EPS(*stmt_list*) = true. In the fourth production (*stmt* $\longrightarrow$ `id` `:=` *expr*), `id` $\in$ FIRST(*stmt*) (also `:=` $\in$ FOLLOW(`id`), but it turns out we don't need FOLLOW sets for nonterminals). In the fifth and sixth productions (*stmt* $\longrightarrow$ `read` `id` | `write` *expr*), {`read`, `write`} $\subset$ FIRST(*stmt*). The complete set of "obvious" facts appears in Figure 2.22.

From the "obvious" facts we can deduce a larger set of facts during a second pass over the grammar. For example, in the second production (*stmt_list* $\longrightarrow$ *stmt stmt_list*) we can deduce that {`id`, `read`, `write`} $\subset$ FIRST(*stmt_list*), because we already know that {`id`, `read`, `write`} $\subset$ FIRST(*stmt*), and a *stmt_list* can

Parse stack	Input stream	Comment
program	read A read B ...	initial stack contents
stmt_list $$	read A read B ...	predict *program* ⟶ *stmt_list* $$
stmt stmt_list $$	read A read B ...	predict *stmt_list* ⟶ *stmt stmt_list*
read id *stmt_list* $$	read A read B ...	predict *stmt* ⟶ read id
id *stmt_list* $$	A read B ...	match read
stmt_list $$	read B sum := ...	match id
stmt stmt_list $$	read B sum := ...	predict *stmt_list* ⟶ *stmt stmt_list*
read id *stmt_list* $$	read B sum := ...	predict *stmt* ⟶ read id
id *stmt_list* $$	B sum := ...	match read
stmt_list $$	sum := A + B ...	match id
stmt stmt_list $$	sum := A + B ...	predict *stmt_list* ⟶ *stmt stmt_list*
id := *expr stmt_list* $$	sum := A + B ...	predict *stmt* ⟶ id := *expr*
:= *expr stmt_list* $$	:= A + B ...	match id
expr stmt_list $$	A + B ...	match :=
term term_tail stmt_list $$	A + B ...	predict *expr* ⟶ *term term_tail*
factor factor_tail term_tail stmt_list $$	A + B ...	predict *term* ⟶ *factor factor_tail*
id *factor_tail term_tail stmt_list* $$	A + B ...	predict *factor* ⟶ id
factor_tail term_tail stmt_list $$	+ B write sum ...	match id
term_tail stmt_list $$	+ B write sum ...	predict *factor_tail* ⟶ ϵ
add_op term term_tail stmt_list $$	+ B write sum ...	predict *term_tail* ⟶ *add_op term term_tail*
+ *term term_tail stmt_list* $$	+ B write sum ...	predict *add_op* ⟶ +
term term_tail stmt_list $$	B write sum ...	match +
factor factor_tail term_tail stmt_list $$	B write sum ...	predict *term* ⟶ *factor factor_tail*
id *factor_tail term_tail stmt_list* $$	B write sum ...	predict *factor* ⟶ id
factor_tail term_tail stmt_list $$	write sum ...	match id
term_tail stmt_list $$	write sum write ...	predict *factor_tail* ⟶ ϵ
stmt_list $$	write sum write ...	predict *term_tail* ⟶ ϵ
stmt stmt_list $$	write sum write ...	predict *stmt_list* ⟶ *stmt stmt_list*
write *expr stmt_list* $$	write sum write ...	predict *stmt* ⟶ write *expr*
expr stmt_list $$	sum write sum / 2	match write
term term_tail stmt_list $$	sum write sum / 2	predict *expr* ⟶ *term term_tail*
factor factor_tail term_tail stmt_list $$	sum write sum / 2	predict *term* ⟶ *factor factor_tail*
id *factor_tail term_tail stmt_list* $$	sum write sum / 2	predict *factor* ⟶ id
factor_tail term_tail stmt_list $$	write sum / 2	match id
term_tail stmt_list $$	write sum / 2	predict *factor_tail* ⟶ ϵ
stmt_list $$	write sum / 2	predict *term_tail* ⟶ ϵ
stmt stmt_list $$	write sum / 2	predict *stmt_list* ⟶ *stmt stmt_list*
write *expr stmt_list* $$	write sum / 2	predict *stmt* ⟶ write *expr*
expr stmt_list $$	sum / 2	match write
term term_tail stmt_list $$	sum / 2	predict *expr* ⟶ *term term_tail*
factor factor_tail term_tail stmt_list $$	sum / 2	predict *term* ⟶ *factor factor_tail*
id *factor_tail term_tail stmt_list* $$	sum / 2	predict *factor* ⟶ id
factor_tail term_tail stmt_list $$	/ 2	match id
mult_op factor factor_tail term_tail stmt_list $$	/ 2	predict *factor_tail* ⟶ *mult_op factor factor_tail*
/ *factor factor_tail term_tail stmt_list* $$	/ 2	predict *mult_op* ⟶ /
factor factor_tail term_tail stmt_list $$	2	match /
number *factor_tail term_tail stmt_list* $$	2	predict *factor* ⟶ number
factor_tail term_tail stmt_list $$		match number
term_tail stmt_list $$		predict *factor_tail* ⟶ ϵ
stmt_list $$		predict *term_tail* ⟶ ϵ
$$		predict *stmt_list* ⟶ ϵ

Figure 2.21 Trace of a table-driven LL(1) parse of the sum-and-average program of Example 2.24.

program ⟶ *stmt_list* $$	$$ ∈ FOLLOW(*stmt_list*)
stmt_list ⟶ *stmt* *stmt_list*	
stmt_list ⟶ ϵ	EPS(*stmt_list*) = true
stmt ⟶ id := *expr*	id ∈ FIRST(*stmt*)
stmt ⟶ read id	read ∈ FIRST(*stmt*)
stmt ⟶ write *expr*	write ∈ FIRST(*stmt*)
expr ⟶ *term* *term_tail*	
term_tail ⟶ *add_op* *term* *term_tail*	
term_tail ⟶ ϵ	EPS(*term_tail*) = true
term ⟶ *factor* *factor_tail*	
factor_tail ⟶ *mult_op* *factor* *factor_tail*	
factor_tail ⟶ ϵ	EPS(*factor_tail*) = true
factor ⟶ (*expr*)	(∈ FIRST(*factor*) and) ∈ FOLLOW(*expr*)
factor ⟶ id	id ∈ FIRST(*factor*)
factor ⟶ number	number ∈ FIRST(*factor*)
add_op ⟶ +	+ ∈ FIRST(*add_op*)
add_op ⟶ -	- ∈ FIRST(*add_op*)
mult_op ⟶ *	* ∈ FIRST(*mult_op*)
mult_op ⟶ /	/ ∈ FIRST(*mult_op*)

Figure 2.22 "Obvious" facts (right) about the LL(1) calculator grammar (left).

DESIGN & IMPLEMENTATION

2.7 Recursive descent and table-driven LL parsing

When trying to understand the connection between recursive descent and table-driven LL parsing, it is tempting to imagine that the explicit stack of the table-driven parser mirrors the implicit call stack of the recursive descent parser, but this is not the case.

A better way to visualize the two implementations of top-down parsing is to remember that both are discovering a parse tree via depth-first left-to-right traversal. When we are at a given point in the parse—say the circled node in the tree shown here—the implicit call stack of a recursive descent parser holds a frame for each of the nodes on the path back to the root, created when the routine corresponding to that node was called. (This path is shown in grey.)

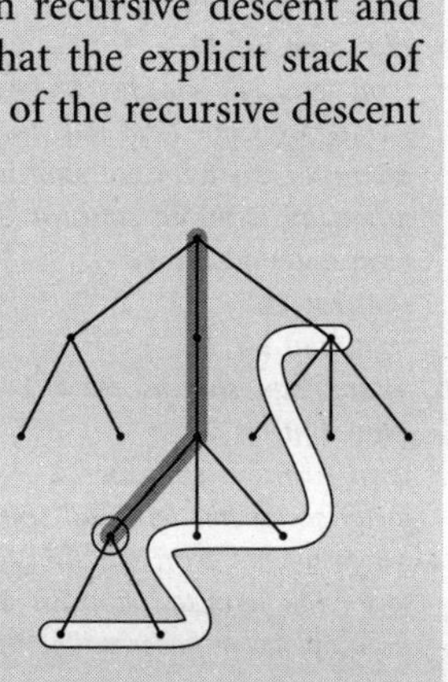

But these nodes are immaterial. What matters for the rest of the parse—as shown on the white path here—are the *upcoming calls* on the case statement arms of the recursive descent routines. Those calls—those parse tree nodes—are precisely the contents of the explicit stack of a table-driven LL parser.

FIRST

program {`id`, `read`, `write`, `$$`}
stmt_list {`id`, `read`, `write`}
stmt {`id`, `read`, `write`}
expr {`(`, `id`, `number`}
term_tail {`+`, `-`}
term {`(`, `id`, `number`}
factor_tail {`*`, `/`}
factor {`(`, `id`, `number`}
add_op {`+`, `-`}
mult_op {`*`, `/`}

FOLLOW

program ∅
stmt_list {`$$`}
stmt {`id`, `read`, `write`, `$$`}
expr {`)`, `id`, `read`, `write`, `$$`}
term_tail {`)`, `id`, `read`, `write`, `$$`}
term {`+`, `-`, `)`, `id`, `read`, `write`, `$$`}
factor_tail {`+`, `-`, `)`, `id`, `read`, `write`, `$$`}
factor {`+`, `-`, `*`, `/`, `)`, `id`, `read`, `write`, `$$`}
add_op {`(`, `id`, `number`}
mult_op {`(`, `id`, `number`}

PREDICT

1. *program* ⟶ *stmt_list* `$$` {`id`, `read`, `write`, `$$`}
2. *stmt_list* ⟶ *stmt stmt_list* {`id`, `read`, `write`}
3. *stmt_list* ⟶ ϵ {`$$`}
4. *stmt* ⟶ `id :=` *expr* {`id`}
5. *stmt* ⟶ `read id` {`read`}
6. *stmt* ⟶ `write` *expr* {`write`}
7. *expr* ⟶ *term term_tail* {`(`, `id`, `number`}
8. *term_tail* ⟶ *add_op term term_tail* {`+`, `-`}
9. *term_tail* ⟶ ϵ {`)`, `id`, `read`, `write`, `$$`}
10. *term* ⟶ *factor factor_tail* {`(`, `id`, `number`}
11. *factor_tail* ⟶ *mult_op factor factor_tail* {`*`, `/`}
12. *factor_tail* ⟶ ϵ {`+`, `-`, `)`, `id`, `read`, `write`, `$$`}
13. *factor* ⟶ `(` *expr* `)` {`(`}
14. *factor* ⟶ `id` {`id`}
15. *factor* ⟶ `number` {`number`}
16. *add_op* ⟶ `+` {`+`}
17. *add_op* ⟶ `-` {`-`}
18. *mult_op* ⟶ `*` {`*`}
19. *mult_op* ⟶ `/` {`/`}

Figure 2.23 FIRST, FOLLOW, and PREDICT sets for the calculator language. FIRST(c) = {c} ∀ tokens c. EPS(*A*) is true iff *A* ∈ {*stmt_list*, *term_tail*, *factor_tail*}.

begin with a *stmt*. Similarly, in the first production, we can deduce that `$$` ∈ FIRST(*program*), because we already know that EPS(*stmt_list*) = true.

In the eleventh production (*factor_tail* ⟶ *mult_op factor factor_tail*), we can deduce that {`(`, `id`, `number`} ⊂ FOLLOW(*mult_op*), because we already know that {`(`, `id`, `number`} ⊂ FIRST(*factor*), and *factor* follows *mult_op* in the right-hand side. In the production *expr* ⟶ *term term_tail*, we can deduce that `)` ∈ FOLLOW(*term_tail*), because we already know that `)` ∈ FOLLOW(*expr*), and a *term_tail* can be the last part of an *expr*. In this same production, we can also deduce that `)` ∈ FOLLOW(*term*), because the *term_tail* can generate ϵ (EPS(*term_tail*) = true), allowing a *term* to be the last part of an *expr*.

There is more that we can learn from our second pass through the grammar, but the examples above cover all the different kinds of cases. To complete our calculation, we continue with additional passes over the grammar until we don't learn any more (i.e., we don't add anything to any of the FIRST and FOLLOW sets). We then construct the PREDICT sets. Final versions of all three sets appear in Figure 2.23. The parse table of Figure 2.20 follows directly from PREDICT.

The algorithm to compute EPS, FIRST, FOLLOW, and PREDICT sets appears, a bit more formally, in Figure 2.24. It relies on the following definitions:

```
-- EPS values and FIRST sets for all symbols:
    for all terminals c, EPS(c) := false; FIRST(c) := {c}
    for all nonterminals X, EPS(X) := if X ⟶ ε then true else false; FIRST(X) := ∅
    repeat
        ⟨outer⟩ for all productions X ⟶ Y1 Y2 ... Yk,
            ⟨inner⟩ for i in 1..k
                add FIRST(Yi) to FIRST(X)
                if not EPS(Yi) (yet) then continue outer loop
            EPS(X) := true
    until no further progress

-- Subroutines for strings, similar to inner loop above:

    function string_EPS(X1 X2 ... Xn)
        for i in 1..n
            if not EPS(Xi) then return false
        return true

    function string_FIRST(X1 X2 ... Xn)
        return_value := ∅
        for i in 1..n
            add FIRST(Xi) to return_value
            if not EPS(Xi) then return

-- FOLLOW sets for all symbols:
    for all symbols X, FOLLOW(X) := ∅
    repeat
        for all productions A ⟶ α B β,
            add string_FIRST(β) to FOLLOW(B)
        for all productions A ⟶ α B
                or A ⟶ α B β, where string_EPS(β) = true,
            add FOLLOW(A) to FOLLOW(B)
    until no further progress

-- PREDICT sets for all productions:
    for all productions A ⟶ α
        PREDICT(A ⟶ α) := string_FIRST(α) ∪ (if string_EPS(α) then FOLLOW(A) else ∅)
```

Figure 2.24 **Algorithm to calculate FIRST, FOLLOW, and PREDICT sets.** The grammar is LL(1) if and only if all PREDICT sets for productions with the same left-hand side are disjoint.

$$\text{EPS}(\alpha) \equiv \textbf{if } \alpha \Longrightarrow^{*} \epsilon \textbf{ then } \text{true} \textbf{ else } \text{false}$$
$$\text{FIRST}(\alpha) \equiv \{\texttt{c} : \alpha \Longrightarrow^{*} \texttt{c}\ \beta\}$$
$$\text{FOLLOW}(A) \equiv \{\texttt{c} : S \Longrightarrow^{+} \alpha\ A\ \texttt{c}\ \beta\}$$
$$\text{PREDICT}(A \longrightarrow \alpha) \equiv \text{FIRST}(\alpha) \cup (\textbf{ if } \text{EPS}(\alpha) \textbf{ then } \text{FOLLOW}(A) \textbf{ else } \varnothing\ )$$

The definition of PREDICT assumes that the language has been augmented with an end marker—that is, that FOLLOW(S) = {\$\$}. Note that FIRST sets and EPS values for strings of length greater than one are calculated on demand; they are not stored explicitly. The algorithm is guaranteed to terminate (i.e., converge on a solution), because the sizes of the FIRST and FOLLOW sets are bounded by the number of terminals in the grammar.

If in the process of calculating PREDICT sets we find that some token belongs to the PREDICT set of more than one production with the same left-hand side, then the grammar is not LL(1), because we will not be able to choose which of the productions to employ when the left-hand side is at the top of the parse stack (or we are in the left-hand side's subroutine in a recursive descent parser) and we see the token coming up in the input. This sort of ambiguity is known as a *predict-predict conflict*; it can arise either because the same token can begin more than one right-hand side, or because it can begin one right-hand side and can also appear after the left-hand side in some valid program, and one possible right-hand side can generate ϵ.

✓ CHECK YOUR UNDERSTANDING

29. Describe two common idioms in context-free grammars that cannot be parsed top-down.
30. What is the "dangling `else`" problem? How is it avoided in modern languages?
31. Discuss the similarities and differences between recursive descent and table-driven top-down parsing.
32. What are FIRST and FOLLOW sets? What are they used for?
33. Under what circumstances does a top-down parser predict the production $A \longrightarrow \alpha$?
34. What sorts of "obvious" facts form the basis of FIRST set and FOLLOW set construction?
35. Outline the algorithm used to complete the construction of FIRST and FOLLOW sets. How do we know when we are done?
36. How do we know when a grammar is not LL(1)?

2.3.4 Bottom-Up Parsing

Conceptually, as we saw at the beginning of Section 2.3, a bottom-up parser works by maintaining a forest of partially completed subtrees of the parse tree, which it joins together whenever it recognizes the symbols on the right-hand side of some production used in the right-most derivation of the input string. It creates a new internal node and makes the roots of the joined-together trees the children of that node.

In practice, a bottom-up parser is almost always table-driven. It keeps the roots of its partially completed subtrees on a stack. When it accepts a new token from the scanner, it *shifts* the token into the stack. When it recognizes that the top few symbols on the stack constitute a right-hand side, it *reduces* those symbols to their left-hand side by popping them off the stack and pushing the left-hand side in their place. The role of the stack is the first important difference between top-down and bottom-up parsing: a top-down parser's stack contains a list of what the parser expects to see in the future; a bottom-up parser's stack contains a record of what the parser has already seen in the past.

Canonical Derivations

We also noted earlier that the actions of a bottom-up parser trace out a right-most (canonical) derivation in reverse. The roots of the partial subtrees, left-to-right, together with the remaining input, constitute a sentential form of the right-most derivation. On the right-hand side of Figure 2.14, for example, we have the following series of steps:

EXAMPLE 2.36
Derivation of an id list

```
Stack contents (roots of partial trees)   Remaining input

ϵ                                          A, B, C;
id (A)                                      , B, C;
id (A) ,                                      B, C;
id (A) , id (B)                                , C;
id (A) , id (B) ,                                C;
id (A) , id (B) , id (C)                          ;
id (A) , id (B) , id (C) ;
id (A) , id (B) , id (C) id_list_tail
id (A) , id (B) id_list_tail
id (A) id_list_tail
id_list
```

The last four lines (the ones that don't just shift tokens into the forest) correspond to the right-most derivation:

```
id_list ⟹ id id_list_tail
        ⟹ id , id id_list_tail
        ⟹ id , id , id id_list_tail
        ⟹ id , id , id ;
```

The symbols that need to be joined together at each step of the parse to represent the next step of the backward derivation are called the *handle* of the sentential form. In the parse trace above, the handles are underlined. ■

EXAMPLE 2.37
Bottom-up grammar for the calculator language

In our *id_list* example, no handles were found until the entire input had been shifted onto the stack. In general this will not be the case. We can obtain a more realistic example by examining an LR version of our calculator language, shown in Figure 2.25. While the LL grammar of Figure 2.16 can be parsed bottom-up, the version in Figure 2.25 is preferable for two reasons. First, it uses a left-recursive production for *stmt_list*. Left recursion allows the parser to collapse long statement lists as it goes along, rather than waiting until the entire list is

1. *program* ⟶ *stmt_list* $$
2. *stmt_list* ⟶ *stmt_list stmt*
3. *stmt_list* ⟶ *stmt*
4. *stmt* ⟶ id := *expr*
5. *stmt* ⟶ read id
6. *stmt* ⟶ write *expr*
7. *expr* ⟶ *term*
8. *expr* ⟶ *expr add_op term*
9. *term* ⟶ *factor*
10. *term* ⟶ *term mult_op factor*
11. *factor* ⟶ (*expr*)
12. *factor* ⟶ id
13. *factor* ⟶ number
14. *add_op* ⟶ +
15. *add_op* ⟶ -
16. *mult_op* ⟶ *
17. *mult_op* ⟶ /

Figure 2.25 **LR(1) grammar for the calculator language.** Productions have been numbered for reference in future figures.

on the stack and then collapsing it from the end. Second, it uses left-recursive productions for *expr* and *term*. These productions capture left associativity while still keeping an operator and its operands together in the same right-hand side, something we were unable to do in a top-down grammar.

Modeling a Parse with LR Items

EXAMPLE 2.38
Bottom-up parse of the "sum and average" program

Suppose we are to parse the sum-and-average program from Example 2.24:

```
read A
read B
sum := A + B
write sum
write sum / 2
```

The key to success will be to figure out when we have reached the end of a right-hand side—that is, when we have a handle at the top of the parse stack. The trick is to keep track of the set of productions we might be "in the middle of" at any particular time, together with an indication of where in those productions we might be.

When we begin execution, the parse stack is empty and we are at the beginning of the production for *program*. (In general, we can assume that there is only one production with the start symbol on the left-hand side; it is easy to modify any grammar to make this the case.) We can represent our location—more specifically, the location represented by the top of the parse stack—with a • in the right-hand side of the production:

program ⟶ • *stmt_list* `$$`

When augmented with a •, a production is called an LR *item*. Since the • in this item is immediately in front of a nonterminal—namely *stmt_list*—we may be about to see the yield of that nonterminal coming up on the input. This possibility implies that we may be at the beginning of some production with *stmt_list* on the left-hand side:

program ⟶ • *stmt_list* `$$`
stmt_list ⟶ • *stmt_list stmt*
stmt_list ⟶ • *stmt*

And, since *stmt* is a nonterminal, we may also be at the beginning of any production whose left-hand side is *stmt*:

program ⟶ • *stmt_list* `$$` (State 0)
stmt_list ⟶ • *stmt_list stmt*
stmt_list ⟶ • *stmt*
stmt ⟶ • `id := ` *expr*
stmt ⟶ • `read id`
stmt ⟶ • `write` *expr*

Since all of these last productions begin with a terminal, no additional items need to be added to our list. The original item (*program* ⟶ • *stmt_list* `$$`) is called the *basis* of the list. The additional items are its *closure*. The list represents the initial state of the parser. As we shift and reduce, the set of items will change, always indicating which productions *may* be the right one to use next in the derivation of the input string. If we reach a state in which some item has the • at the end of the right-hand side, we can reduce by that production. Otherwise, as in the current situation, we must shift. Note that if we need to shift, but the incoming token cannot follow the • in any item of the current state, then a syntax error has occurred. We will consider error recovery in more detail in Section C-2.3.5.

Our upcoming token is a `read`. Once we shift it onto the stack, we know we are in the following state:

stmt ⟶ `read` • `id` (State 1)

This state has a single basis item and an empty closure—the • precedes a terminal. After shifting the `A`, we have

stmt ⟶ `read id` • (State 1′)

We now know that `read id` is the handle, and we must reduce. The reduction pops two symbols off the parse stack and pushes a *stmt* in their place, but what should the new state be? We can see the answer if we imagine moving back in time to the point at which we shifted the `read`—the first symbol of the right-hand side. At that time we were in the state labeled "State 0" above, and the upcoming tokens on the input (though we didn't look at them at the time) were `read id`. We have now consumed these tokens, and we know that they constituted a *stmt*. By pushing a *stmt* onto the stack, we have in essence replaced `read id` with *stmt* on the input stream, and have then "shifted" the nonterminal, rather than its yield, into the stack. Since one of the items in State 0 was

stmt_list ⟶ • *stmt*

we now have

stmt_list ⟶ *stmt* • (State 0′)

Again we must reduce. We remove the *stmt* from the stack and push a *stmt_list* in its place. Again we can see this as "shifting" a *stmt_list* when in State 0. Since two of the items in State 0 have a *stmt_list* after the •, we don't know (without looking ahead) which of the productions will be the next to be used in the derivation, but we don't have to know. The key advantage of bottom-up parsing over top-down parsing is that we don't need to predict ahead of time which production we shall be expanding.

Our new state is as follows:

program ⟶ *stmt_list* • `$$` (State 2)
stmt_list ⟶ *stmt_list* • *stmt*
stmt ⟶ • `id :=` *expr*
stmt ⟶ • `read id`
stmt ⟶ • `write` *expr*

The first two productions are the basis; the others are the closure. Since no item has a • at the end, we shift the next token, which happens again to be a `read`, taking us back to State 1. Shifting the `B` takes us to State 1′ again, at which point we reduce. This time however, we go back to State 2 rather than State 0 before shifting the left-hand-side *stmt*. Why? Because we were in State 2 when we began to read the right-hand side. ▪

The Characteristic Finite-State Machine and LR Parsing Variants

An LR-family parser keeps track of the states it has traversed by pushing them into the parse stack, along with the grammar symbols. It is in fact the states (rather than the symbols) that drive the parsing algorithm: they tell us what state we were in at the beginning of a right-hand side. Specifically, when the combination of state and input tells us we need to reduce using production $A \longrightarrow \alpha$, we pop $length(\alpha)$ symbols off the stack, together with the record of states we moved through while shifting those symbols. These pops expose the state we were in immediately prior to the shifts, allowing us to return to that state and proceed as if we had seen A in the first place.

We can think of the shift rules of an LR-family parser as the transition function of a finite automaton, much like the automata we used to model scanners. Each state of the automaton corresponds to a list of items that indicate where the parser might be at some specific point in the parse. The transition for input symbol X (which may be either a terminal or a nonterminal) moves to a state whose basis consists of items in which the $\bullet$ has been moved across an X in the right-hand side, plus whatever items need to be added as closure. The lists are constructed by a bottom-up parser generator in order to build the automaton, but are not needed during parsing.

It turns out that the simpler members of the LR family of parsers—LR(0), SLR(1), and LALR(1)—all use the same automaton, called the *characteristic finite-state machine*, or CFSM. Full LR parsers use a machine with (for most grammars) a much larger number of states. The differences between the algorithms lie in how they deal with states that contain a *shift-reduce conflict*—one item with the $\bullet$ in front of a terminal (suggesting the need for a shift) and another with the $\bullet$ at the end of the right-hand side (suggesting the need for a reduction). An LR(0) parser works only when there are no such states. It can be proven that with the addition of an end-marker (i.e., `$$`), any language that can be deterministically parsed bottom-up has an LR(0) grammar. Unfortunately, the LR(0) grammars for real programming languages tend to be prohibitively large and unintuitive.

SLR (simple LR) parsers peek at upcoming input and use FOLLOW sets to resolve conflicts. An SLR parser will call for a reduction via $A \longrightarrow \alpha$ only if the upcoming token(s) are in FOLLOW(α). It will still see a conflict, however, if the tokens are also in the FIRST set of any of the symbols that follow a $\bullet$ in other items of the state. As it turns out, there are important cases in which a token may follow a given nonterminal somewhere in a valid program, but never in a context described by the current state. For these cases global FOLLOW sets are too crude. LALR (look-ahead LR) parsers improve on SLR by using *local* (state-specific) look-ahead instead.

Conflicts can still arise in an LALR parser when the same set of items can occur on two different paths through the CFSM. Both paths will end up in the same state, at which point state-specific look-ahead can no longer distinguish between them. A full LR parser duplicates states in order to keep paths disjoint when their local look-aheads are different.

LALR parsers are the most common bottom-up parsers in practice. They are the same size and speed as SLR parsers, but are able to resolve more conflicts. Full LR parsers for real programming languages tend to be very large. Several researchers have developed techniques to reduce the size of full-LR tables, but LALR works sufficiently well in practice that the extra complexity of full LR is usually not required. `Yacc/bison` produces C code for an LALR parser.

Bottom-Up Parsing Tables

Like a table-driven LL(1) parser, an SLR(1), LALR(1), or LR(1) parser executes a loop in which it repeatedly inspects a two-dimensional table to find out what action to take. However, instead of using the current input token and top-of-stack nonterminal to index into the table, an LR-family parser uses the current input token and the current parser state (which can be found at the top of the stack). "Shift" table entries indicate the state that should be pushed. "Reduce" table entries indicate the number of states that should be popped and the nonterminal that should be pushed back onto the input stream, to be shifted by the state uncovered by the pops. There is always one popped state for every symbol on the right-hand side of the reducing production. The state to be pushed next can be found by indexing into the table using the uncovered state and the newly recognized nonterminal.

EXAMPLE 2.39
CFSM for the bottom-up calculator grammar

The CFSM for our bottom-up version of the calculator grammar appears in Figure 2.26. States 6, 7, 9, and 13 contain potential shift-reduce conflicts, but all of these can be resolved with global FOLLOW sets. SLR parsing therefore suffices. In State 6, for example, FIRST(*add_op*) $\cap$ FOLLOW(*stmt*) $= \varnothing$. In addition to shift and reduce rules, we allow the parse table as an optimization to contain rules of the form "shift and then reduce." This optimization serves to eliminate trivial states such as $1'$ and $0'$ in Example 2.38, which had only a single item, with the • at the end.

A pictorial representation of the CFSM appears in Figure 2.27. A tabular representation, suitable for use in a table-driven parser, appears in Figure 2.28. Pseudocode for the (language-independent) parser driver appears in Figure 2.29. A trace of the parser's actions on the sum-and-average program appears in Figure 2.30.

Handling Epsilon Productions

EXAMPLE 2.40
Epsilon productions in the bottom-up calculator grammar

The careful reader may have noticed that the grammar of Figure 2.25, in addition to using left-recursive rules for *stmt_list*, *expr*, and *term*, differs from the grammar of Figure 2.16 in one other way: it defines a *stmt_list* to be a sequence of one or more *stmts*, rather than zero or more. (This means, of course, that it defines a different language.) To capture the same language as Figure 2.16, production 3 in Figure 2.25,

stmt_list ⟶ *stmt*

would need to be replaced with

stmt_list ⟶ ϵ

Note that it does in general make sense to have an empty statement list. In the calculator language it simply permits an empty program, which is admittedly silly. In real languages, however, it allows the body of a structured statement to be empty, which can be very useful. One frequently wants one arm of a `case` or multiway `if... then ... else` statement to be empty, and an empty `while` loop allows

	State	Transitions
0.	*program* → • *stmt_list* `$$`	on *stmt_list* shift and goto 2
	stmt_list → • *stmt_list stmt*	
	stmt_list → • *stmt*	on *stmt* shift and reduce (pop 1 state, push *stmt_list* on input)
	stmt → • `id` `:=` *expr*	on `id` shift and goto 3
	stmt → • `read` `id`	on `read` shift and goto 1
	stmt → • `write` *expr*	on `write` shift and goto 4
1.	*stmt* → `read` • `id`	on `id` shift and reduce (pop 2 states, push *stmt* on input)
2.	*program* → *stmt_list* • `$$`	on `$$` shift and reduce (pop 2 states, push *program* on input)
	stmt_list → *stmt_list* • *stmt*	on *stmt* shift and reduce (pop 2 states, push *stmt_list* on input)
	stmt → • `id` `:=` *expr*	on `id` shift and goto 3
	stmt → • `read` `id`	on `read` shift and goto 1
	stmt → • `write` *expr*	on `write` shift and goto 4
3.	*stmt* → `id` • `:=` *expr*	on `:=` shift and goto 5
4.	*stmt* → `write` • *expr*	on *expr* shift and goto 6
	expr → • *term*	on *term* shift and goto 7
	expr → • *expr add_op term*	
	term → • *factor*	on *factor* shift and reduce (pop 1 state, push *term* on input)
	term → • *term mult_op factor*	
	factor → • `(` *expr* `)`	on `(` shift and goto 8
	factor → • `id`	on `id` shift and reduce (pop 1 state, push *factor* on input)
	factor → • `number`	on `number` shift and reduce (pop 1 state, push *factor* on input)
5.	*stmt* → `id` `:=` • *expr*	on *expr* shift and goto 9
	expr → • *term*	on *term* shift and goto 7
	expr → • *expr add_op term*	
	term → • *factor*	on *factor* shift and reduce (pop 1 state, push *term* on input)
	term → • *term mult_op factor*	
	factor → • `(` *expr* `)`	on `(` shift and goto 8
	factor → • `id`	on `id` shift and reduce (pop 1 state, push *factor* on input)
	factor → • `number`	on `number` shift and reduce (pop 1 state, push *factor* on input)
6.	*stmt* → `write` *expr* •	on FOLLOW(*stmt*) = {`id`, `read`, `write`, `$$`} reduce (pop 2 states, push *stmt* on input)
	expr → *expr* • *add_op term*	on *add_op* shift and goto 10
	add_op → • `+`	on `+` shift and reduce (pop 1 state, push *add_op* on input)
	add_op → • `-`	on `-` shift and reduce (pop 1 state, push *add_op* on input)

Figure 2.26 CFSM for the calculator grammar (Figure 2.25). Basis and closure items in each state are separated by a horizontal rule. Trivial reduce-only states have been eliminated by use of "shift and reduce" transitions. *(continued)*

	State	Transitions
7.	*expr* ⟶ *term* •	on FOLLOW(*expr*) = {`id`, `read`, `write`, `$$`, `)`, `+`, `-`} reduce
	term ⟶ *term* • *mult_op* *factor*	(pop 1 state, push *expr* on input)
		on *mult_op* shift and goto 11
	mult_op ⟶ • `*`	on `*` shift and reduce (pop 1 state, push *mult_op* on input)
	mult_op ⟶ • `/`	on `/` shift and reduce (pop 1 state, push *mult_op* on input)
8.	*factor* ⟶ `(` • *expr* `)`	on *expr* shift and goto 12
	expr ⟶ • *term*	on *term* shift and goto 7
	expr ⟶ • *expr* *add_op* *term*	
	term ⟶ • *factor*	on *factor* shift and reduce (pop 1 state, push *term* on input)
	term ⟶ • *term* *mult_op* *factor*	
	factor ⟶ • `(` *expr* `)`	on `(` shift and goto 8
	factor ⟶ • `id`	on `id` shift and reduce (pop 1 state, push *factor* on input)
	factor ⟶ • `number`	on `number` shift and reduce (pop 1 state, push *factor* on input)
9.	*stmt* ⟶ `id` `:=` *expr* •	on FOLLOW(*stmt*) = {`id`, `read`, `write`, `$$`} reduce
	expr ⟶ *expr* • *add_op* *term*	(pop 3 states, push *stmt* on input)
		on *add_op* shift and goto 10
	add_op ⟶ • `+`	on `+` shift and reduce (pop 1 state, push *add_op* on input)
	add_op ⟶ • `-`	on `-` shift and reduce (pop 1 state, push *add_op* on input)
10.	*expr* ⟶ *expr* *add_op* • *term*	on *term* shift and goto 13
	term ⟶ • *factor*	on *factor* shift and reduce (pop 1 state, push *term* on input)
	term ⟶ • *term* *mult_op* *factor*	
	factor ⟶ • `(` *expr* `)`	on `(` shift and goto 8
	factor ⟶ • `id`	on `id` shift and reduce (pop 1 state, push *factor* on input)
	factor ⟶ • `number`	on `number` shift and reduce (pop 1 state, push *factor* on input)
11.	*term* ⟶ *term* *mult_op* • *factor*	on *factor* shift and reduce (pop 3 states, push *term* on input)
	factor ⟶ • `(` *expr* `)`	on `(` shift and goto 8
	factor ⟶ • `id`	on `id` shift and reduce (pop 1 state, push *factor* on input)
	factor ⟶ • `number`	on `number` shift and reduce (pop 1 state, push *factor* on input)
12.	*factor* ⟶ `(` *expr* • `)`	on `)` shift and reduce (pop 3 states, push *factor* on input)
	expr ⟶ *expr* • *add_op* *term*	on *add_op* shift and goto 10
	add_op ⟶ • `+`	on `+` shift and reduce (pop 1 state, push *add_op* on input)
	add_op ⟶ • `-`	on `-` shift and reduce (pop 1 state, push *add_op* on input)
13.	*expr* ⟶ *expr* *add_op* *term* •	on FOLLOW(*expr*) = {`id`, `read`, `write`, `$$`, `)`, `+`, `-`} reduce
	term ⟶ *term* • *mult_op* *factor*	(pop 3 states, push *expr* on input)
		on *mult_op* shift and goto 11
	mult_op ⟶ • `*`	on `*` shift and reduce (pop 1 state, push *mult_op* on input)
	mult_op ⟶ • `/`	on `/` shift and reduce (pop 1 state, push *mult_op* on input)

Figure 2.26 *(continued)*

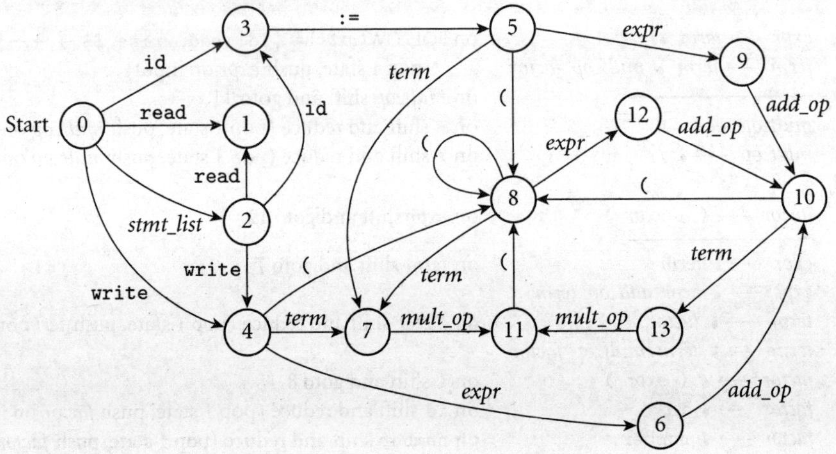

Figure 2.27 Pictorial representation of the CFSM of Figure 2.26. Reduce actions are not shown.

Top-of-stack state	Current input symbol																	
	sl	*s*	*e*	*t*	*f*	*ao*	*mo*	`id`	`lit`	`r`	`w`	:=	(	)	+	-	*	/	$$
0	s2	b3	–	–	–	–	–	s3	–	s1	s4	–	–	–	–	–	–	–	–
1	–	–	–	–	–	–	–	b5	–	–	–	–	–	–	–	–	–	–	–
2	–	b2	–	–	–	–	–	s3	–	s1	s4	–	–	–	–	–	–	–	b1
3	–	–	–	–	–	–	–	–	–	–	–	s5	–	–	–	–	–	–	–
4	–	–	s6	s7	b9	–	–	b12	b13	–	–	–	s8	–	–	–	–	–	–
5	–	–	s9	s7	b9	–	–	b12	b13	–	–	–	s8	–	–	–	–	–	–
6	–	–	–	–	–	s10	–	r6	–	r6	r6	–	–	–	b14	b15	–	–	r6
7	–	–	–	–	–	–	s11	r7	–	r7	r7	–	–	r7	r7	r7	b16	b17	r7
8	–	–	s12	s7	b9	–	–	b12	b13	–	–	–	s8	–	–	–	–	–	–
9	–	–	–	–	–	s10	–	r4	–	r4	r4	–	–	–	b14	b15	–	–	r4
10	–	–	–	s13	b9	–	–	b12	b13	–	–	–	s8	–	–	–	–	–	–
11	–	–	–	–	b10	–	–	b12	b13	–	–	–	s8	–	–	–	–	–	–
12	–	–	–	–	–	s10	–	–	–	–	–	–	–	b11	b14	b15	–	–	–
13	–	–	–	–	–	–	s11	r8	–	r8	r8	–	–	r8	r8	r8	b16	b17	r8

Figure 2.28 SLR(1) parse table for the calculator language. Table entries indicate whether to shift (s), reduce (r), or shift and then reduce (b). The accompanying number is the new state when shifting, or the production that has been recognized when (shifting and) reducing. Production numbers are given in Figure 2.25. Symbol names have been abbreviated for the sake of formatting. A dash indicates an error. An auxiliary table, not shown here, gives the left-hand-side symbol and right-hand-side length for each production.

```
state = 1 .. number_of_states
symbol = 1 .. number_of_symbols
production = 1 .. number_of_productions
action_rec = record
    action : (shift, reduce, shift_reduce, error)
    new_state : state
    prod : production

parse_tab : array [symbol, state] of action_rec
prod_tab : array [production] of record
    lhs : symbol
    rhs_len : integer
-- these two tables are created by a parser generator tool

parse_stack : stack of record
    sym : symbol
    st : state

parse_stack.push(⟨null, start_state⟩)
cur_sym : symbol := scan()                  -- get new token from scanner
loop
    cur_state : state := parse_stack.top().st  -- peek at state at top of stack
    if cur_state = start_state and cur_sym = start_symbol
        return                              -- success!
    ar : action_rec := parse_tab[cur_state, cur_sym]
    case ar.action
        shift:
            parse_stack.push(⟨cur_sym, ar.new_state⟩)
            cur_sym := scan()               -- get new token from scanner
        reduce:
            cur_sym := prod_tab[ar.prod].lhs
            parse_stack.pop(prod_tab[ar.prod].rhs_len)
        shift_reduce:
            cur_sym := prod_tab[ar.prod].lhs
            parse_stack.pop(prod_tab[ar.prod].rhs_len−1)
        error:
            parse_error
```

Figure 2.29 Driver for a table-driven SLR(1) parser. We call the scanner directly, rather than using the global input_token of Figures 2.17 and 2.19, so that we can set cur_sym to be an arbitrary symbol. We pass to the pop() routine a parameter that indicates the number of symbols to remove from the stack.

Parse stack	Input stream	Comment
0	read A read B ...	
0 read **1**	A read B ...	shift read
0	*stmt* read B ...	shift id(A) & reduce by *stmt* ⟶ read id
0	*stmt_list* read B ...	shift *stmt* & reduce by *stmt_list* ⟶ *stmt*
0 *stmt_list* **2**	read B sum ...	shift *stmt_list*
0 *stmt_list* **2** read **1**	B sum := ...	shift read
0 *stmt_list* **2**	*stmt* sum := ...	shift id(B) & reduce by *stmt* ⟶ read id
0	*stmt_list* sum := ...	shift *stmt* & reduce by *stmt_list* ⟶ *stmt_list stmt*
0 *stmt_list* **2**	sum := A ...	shift *stmt_list*
0 *stmt_list* **2** id **3**	:= A + ...	shift id(sum)
0 *stmt_list* **2** id **3** := **5**	A + B ...	shift :=
0 *stmt_list* **2** id **3** := **5**	*factor* + B ...	shift id(A) & reduce by *factor* ⟶ id
0 *stmt_list* **2** id **3** := **5**	*term* + B ...	shift *factor* & reduce by *term* ⟶ *factor*
0 *stmt_list* **2** id **3** := **5** *term* **7**	+ B write ...	shift *term*
0 *stmt_list* **2** id **3** := **5**	*expr* + B write ...	reduce by *expr* ⟶ *term*
0 *stmt_list* **2** id **3** := **5** *expr* **9**	+ B write ...	shift *expr*
0 *stmt_list* **2** id **3** := **5** *expr* **9**	*add_op* B write ...	shift + & reduce by *add_op* ⟶ +
0 *stmt_list* **2** id **3** := **5** *expr* **9** *add_op* **10**	B write sum ...	shift *add_op*
0 *stmt_list* **2** id **3** := **5** *expr* **9** *add_op* **10**	*factor* write sum ...	shift id(B) & reduce by *factor* ⟶ id
0 *stmt_list* **2** id **3** := **5** *expr* **9** *add_op* **10**	*term* write sum ...	shift *factor* & reduce by *term* ⟶ *factor*
0 *stmt_list* **2** id **3** := **5** *expr* **9** *add_op* **10** *term* **13**	write sum ...	shift *term*
0 *stmt_list* **2** id **3** := **5**	*expr* write sum ...	reduce by *expr* ⟶ *expr add_op term*
0 *stmt_list* **2** id **3** := **5** *expr* **9**	write sum ...	shift *expr*
0 *stmt_list* **2**	*stmt* write sum ...	reduce by *stmt* ⟶ id := *expr*
0	*stmt_list* write sum ...	shift *stmt* & reduce by *stmt_list* ⟶ *stmt*
0 *stmt_list* **2**	write sum ...	shift *stmt_list*
0 *stmt_list* **2** write **4**	sum write sum ...	shift write
0 *stmt_list* **2** write **4**	*factor* write sum ...	shift id(sum) & reduce by *factor* ⟶ id
0 *stmt_list* **2** write **4**	*term* write sum ...	shift *factor* & reduce by *term* ⟶ *factor*
0 *stmt_list* **2** write **4** *term* **7**	write sum ...	shift *term*
0 *stmt_list* **2** write **4**	*expr* write sum ...	reduce by *expr* ⟶ *term*
0 *stmt_list* **2** write **4** *expr* **6**	write sum ...	shift *expr*
0 *stmt_list* **2**	*stmt* write sum ...	reduce by *stmt* ⟶ write *expr*
0	*stmt_list* write sum ...	shift *stmt* & reduce by *stmt_list* ⟶ *stmt_list stmt*
0 *stmt_list* **2**	write sum / ...	shift *stmt_list*
0 *stmt_list* **2** write **4**	sum / 2 ...	shift write
0 *stmt_list* **2** write **4**	*factor* / 2 ...	shift id(sum) & reduce by *factor* ⟶ id
0 *stmt_list* **2** write **4**	*term* / 2 ...	shift *factor* & reduce by *term* ⟶ *factor*
0 *stmt_list* **2** write **4** *term* **7**	/ 2 $$	shift *term*
0 *stmt_list* **2** write **4** *term* **7**	*mult_op* 2 $$	shift / & reduce by *mult_op* ⟶ /
0 *stmt_list* **2** write **4** *term* **7** *mult_op* **11**	2 $$	shift *mult_op*
0 *stmt_list* **2** write **4** *term* **7** *mult_op* **11**	*factor* $$	shift number(2) & reduce by *factor* ⟶ number
0 *stmt_list* **2** write **4**	*term* $$	shift *factor* & reduce by *term* ⟶ *term mult_op factor*
0 *stmt_list* **2** write **4** *term* **7**	$$	shift *term*
0 *stmt_list* **2** write **4**	*expr* $$	reduce by *expr* ⟶ *term*
0 *stmt_list* **2** write **4** *expr* **6**	$$	shift *expr*
0 *stmt_list* **2**	*stmt* $$	reduce by *stmt* ⟶ write *expr*
0	*stmt_list* $$	shift *stmt* & reduce by *stmt_list* ⟶ *stmt_list stmt*
0 *stmt_list* **2**	$$	shift *stmt_list*
0	*program*	shift $$ & reduce by *program* ⟶ *stmt_list* $$
[done]		

Figure 2.30 Trace of a table-driven SLR(1) parse of the sum-and-average program. States in the parse stack are shown in boldface type. Symbols in the parse stack are for clarity only; they are not needed by the parsing algorithm. Parsing begins with the initial state of the CFSM (State 0) in the stack. It ends when we reduce by *program* ⟶ *stmt_list* $$, uncovering State 0 again and pushing *program* onto the input stream.

a parallel program (or the operating system) to wait for a signal from another process or an I/O device.

EXAMPLE 2.41
CFSM with epsilon productions

If we look at the CFSM for the calculator language, we discover that State 0 is the only state that needs to be changed in order to allow empty statement lists. The item

stmt_list ⟶ • *stmt*

becomes

stmt_list ⟶ • ϵ

which is equivalent to

stmt_list ⟶ ϵ •

or simply

stmt_list ⟶ •

The entire state is then

program ⟶ • *stmt_list* $$	on *stmt_list* shift and goto 2
stmt_list ⟶ • *stmt_list stmt*	
stmt_list ⟶ •	on $$ reduce (pop 0 states, push *stmt_list* on input)
stmt ⟶ • `id` `:=` *expr*	on `id` shift and goto 3
stmt ⟶ • `read` `id`	on `read` shift and goto 1
stmt ⟶ • `write` *expr*	on `write` shift and goto 4

The look-ahead for item

stmt_list ⟶ •

is FOLLOW(*stmt_list*), which is the end-marker, $$. Since $$ does not appear in the look-aheads for any other item in this state, our grammar is still SLR(1). It is worth noting that epsilon productions commonly prevent a grammar from being LR(0): if such a production shares a state with an item in which the dot precedes a terminal, we won't be able to tell whether to "recognize" ϵ without peeking ahead.

✓ CHECK YOUR UNDERSTANDING

37. What is the *handle* of a right sentential form?
38. Explain the significance of the characteristic finite-state machine in LR parsing.
39. What is the significance of the dot (•) in an LR item?
40. What distinguishes the *basis* from the *closure* of an LR state?
41. What is a *shift-reduce conflict*? How is it resolved in the various kinds of LR-family parsers?

42. Outline the steps performed by the driver of a bottom-up parser.
43. What kind of parser is produced by `yacc/bison`? By ANTLR?
44. Why are there never any epsilon productions in an LR(0) grammar?

2.3.5 Syntax Errors

EXAMPLE 2.42
A syntax error in C

Suppose we are parsing a C program and see the following code fragment in a context where a statement is expected:

```
A = B : C + D;
```

We will detect a syntax error immediately after the `B`, when the colon appears from the scanner. At this point the simplest thing to do is just to print an error message and halt. This naive approach is generally not acceptable, however: it would mean that every run of the compiler reveals no more than one syntax error. Since most programs, at least at first, contain numerous such errors, we really need to find as many as possible now (we'd also like to continue looking for semantic errors). To do so, we must modify the state of the parser and/or the input stream so that the upcoming token(s) are acceptable. We shall probably want to turn off code generation, disabling the back end of the compiler: since the input is not a valid program, the code will not be of use, and there's no point in spending time creating it. ■

In general, the term *syntax error recovery* is applied to any technique that allows the compiler, in the face of a syntax error, to continue looking for other errors later in the program. High-quality syntax error recovery is essential in any production-quality compiler. The better the recovery technique, the more likely the compiler will be to recognize additional errors (especially nearby errors) correctly, and the less likely it will be to become confused and announce spurious *cascading errors* later in the program.

IN MORE DEPTH

On the companion site we explore several possible approaches to syntax error recovery. In *panic mode*, the compiler writer defines a small set of "safe symbols" that delimit clean points in the input. Semicolons, which typically end a statement, are a good choice in many languages. When an error occurs, the compiler deletes input tokens until it finds a safe symbol, and then "backs the parser out" (e.g., returns from recursive descent subroutines) until it finds a context in which that symbol might appear. *Phrase-level recovery* improves on this technique by employing different sets of "safe" symbols in different productions of the grammar (right parentheses when in an expression; semicolons when in a declaration). *Context-specific look-ahead* obtains additional improvements by differentiating among the various contexts in which a given production might appear in a syntax tree. To respond gracefully to certain common programming errors, the compiler writer may augment the grammar with *error productions* that capture language-specific idioms that are incorrect but are often written by mistake.

Niklaus Wirth published an elegant implementation of phrase-level and context-specific recovery for recursive descent parsers in 1976 [Wir76, Sec. 5.9]. *Exceptions* (to be discussed further in Section 9.4) provide a simpler alternative if supported by the language in which the compiler is written. For table-driven top-down parsers, Fischer, Milton, and Quiring published an algorithm in 1980 that automatically implements a well-defined notion of *locally least-cost syntax repair*. Locally least-cost repair is also possible in bottom-up parsers, but it is significantly more difficult. Most bottom-up parsers rely on more straightforward phrase-level recovery; a typical example can be found in `yacc/bison`.

2.4 Theoretical Foundations

Our understanding of the relative roles and computational power of scanners, parsers, regular expressions, and context-free grammars is based on the formalisms of *automata theory*. In automata theory, a *formal language* is a set of strings of symbols drawn from a finite *alphabet*. A formal language can be specified either by a set of rules (such as regular expressions or a context-free grammar) that generates the language, or by a *formal machine* that *accepts* (*recognizes*) the language. A formal machine takes strings of symbols as input and outputs either "yes" or "no." A machine is said to accept a language if it says "yes" to all and only those strings that are in the language. Alternatively, a language can be defined as the set of strings for which a particular machine says "yes."

Formal languages can be grouped into a series of successively larger classes known as the *Chomsky hierarchy*.[14] Most of the classes can be characterized in two ways: by the types of rules that can be used to generate the set of strings, or by the type of formal machine that is capable of recognizing the language. As we have seen, *regular languages* are defined by using concatenation, alternation, and Kleene closure, and are recognized by a scanner. *Context-free languages* are a proper superset of the regular languages. They are defined by using concatenation, alternation, and recursion (which subsumes Kleene closure), and are recognized by a parser. A scanner is a concrete realization of a *finite automaton*, a type of formal machine. A parser is a concrete realization of a *push-down automaton*. Just as context-free grammars add recursion to regular expressions, push-down automata add a stack to the memory of a finite automaton. There are additional levels in the Chomsky hierarchy, but they are less directly applicable to compiler construction, and are not covered here.

---

14 Noam Chomsky (1928–), a linguist and social philosopher at the Massachusetts Institute of Technology, developed much of the early theory of formal languages.

It can be proven, constructively, that regular expressions and finite automata are equivalent: one can construct a finite automaton that accepts the language defined by a given regular expression, and vice versa. Similarly, it is possible to construct a push-down automaton that accepts the language defined by a given context-free grammar, and vice versa. The grammar-to-automaton constructions are in fact performed by scanner and parser generators such as `lex` and `yacc`. Of course, a real scanner does not accept just one token; it is called in a loop so that it keeps accepting tokens repeatedly. As noted in Sidebar 2.4, this detail is accommodated by having the scanner accept the alternation of all the tokens in the language (with distinguished final states), and by having it continue to consume characters until no longer token can be constructed.

IN MORE DEPTH

On the companion site we consider finite and pushdown automata in more detail. We give an algorithm to convert a DFA into an equivalent regular expression. Combined with the constructions in Section 2.2.1, this algorithm demonstrates the equivalence of regular expressions and finite automata. We also consider the sets of grammars and languages that can and cannot be parsed by the various linear-time parsing algorithms.

2.5 Summary and Concluding Remarks

In this chapter we have introduced the formalisms of regular expressions and context-free grammars, and the algorithms that underlie scanning and parsing in practical compilers. We also mentioned syntax error recovery, and presented a quick overview of relevant parts of automata theory. Regular expressions and context-free grammars are language *generators*: they specify how to construct valid strings of characters or tokens. Scanners and parsers are language *recognizers*: they indicate whether a given string is valid. The principal job of the scanner is to reduce the quantity of information that must be processed by the parser, by grouping characters together into tokens, and by removing comments and white space. Scanner and parser generators automatically translate regular expressions and context-free grammars into scanners and parsers.

Practical parsers for programming languages (parsers that run in linear time) fall into two principal groups: top-down (also called LL or predictive) and bottom-up (also called LR or shift-reduce). A top-down parser constructs a parse tree starting from the root and proceeding in a left-to-right depth-first traversal. A bottom-up parser constructs a parse tree starting from the leaves, again working left-to-right, and combining partial trees together when it recognizes the children of an internal node. The stack of a top-down parser contains a prediction of what will be seen in the future; the stack of a bottom-up parser contains a record of what has been seen in the past.

Top-down parsers tend to be simple, both in the parsing of valid strings and in the recovery from errors in invalid strings. Bottom-up parsers are more powerful, and in some cases lend themselves to more intuitively structured grammars, though they suffer from the inability to embed action routines at arbitrary points in a right-hand side (we discuss this point in more detail in Section C-4.5.1). Both varieties of parser are used in real compilers, though bottom-up parsers are more common. Top-down parsers tend to be smaller in terms of code and data size, but modern machines provide ample memory for either.

Both scanners and parsers can be built by hand if an automatic tool is not available. Handbuilt scanners are simple enough to be relatively common. Handbuilt parsers are generally limited to top-down recursive descent, and are most commonly used for comparatively simple languages. Automatic generation of the scanner and parser has the advantage of increased reliability, reduced development time, and easy modification and enhancement.

Various features of language design can have a major impact on the complexity of syntax analysis. In many cases, features that make it difficult for a compiler to scan or parse also make it difficult for a human being to write correct, maintainable code. Examples include the lexical structure of Fortran and the `if`... `then`... `else` statement of languages like Pascal. This interplay among language design, implementation, and use will be a recurring theme throughout the remainder of the book.

2.6 Exercises

2.1 Write regular expressions to capture the following.

(a) Strings in C. These are delimited by double quotes (`"`), and may not contain newline characters. They may contain double-quote or backslash characters if and only if those characters are "escaped" by a preceding backslash. You may find it helpful to introduce shorthand notation to represent any character that is *not* a member of a small specified set.

(b) Comments in Pascal. These are delimited by `(*` and `*)` or by `{` and `}`. They are not permitted to nest.

(c) Numeric constants in C. These are octal, decimal, or hexadecimal integers, or decimal or hexadecimal floating-point values. An octal integer begins with `0`, and may contain only the digits `0`–`7`. A hexadecimal integer begins with `0x` or `0X`, and may contain the digits `0`–`9` and `a`/`A`–`f`/`F`. A decimal floating-point value has a fractional portion (beginning with a dot) or an exponent (beginning with `E` or `e`). Unlike a decimal integer, it is allowed to start with `0`. A hexadecimal floating-point value has an optional fractional portion and a mandatory exponent (beginning with `P` or `p`). In either decimal or hexadecimal, there may be digits to the left of the dot, the right of the dot, or both, and the exponent itself is given in decimal, with an optional leading `+` or `-` sign. An integer may end with an optional `U` or `u` (indicating "unsigned"), and/or `L` or `l` (indicating "long") or `LL` or `ll` (indicating "long long"). A floating-point value may end with an optional `F` or `f` (indicating "float"—single precision) or `L` or `l` (indicating "long"—double precision).

(d) Floating-point constants in Ada. These match the definition of *real* in Example 2.3, except that (1) a digit is required on both sides of the decimal point, (2) an underscore is permitted between digits, and (3) an alternative numeric base may be specified by surrounding the nonexponent part of the number with pound signs, preceded by a base in decimal (e.g., `16#6.a7#e+2`). In this latter case, the letters `a..f` (both upper- and lowercase) are permitted as digits. Use of these letters in an inappropriate (e.g., decimal) number is an error, but need not be caught by the scanner.

(e) Inexact constants in Scheme. Scheme allows real numbers to be explicitly *inexact* (imprecise). A programmer who wants to express all constants using the same number of characters can use sharp signs (`#`) in place of any lower-significance digits whose values are not known. A base-10 constant without exponent consists of one or more digits followed by zero of more sharp signs. An optional decimal point can be placed at the beginning, the end, or anywhere in-between. (For the record, numbers in Scheme are actually a good bit more complicated than this. For the purposes of this exercise, please ignore anything you may know about sign, exponent, radix, exactness and length specifiers, and complex or rational values.)

(f) Financial quantities in American notation. These have a leading dollar sign (`$`), an optional string of asterisks (`*`—used on checks to discourage fraud), a string of decimal digits, and an optional fractional part consisting of a decimal point (`.`) and two decimal digits. The string of digits to the left of the decimal point may consist of a single zero (`0`). Otherwise it must not start with a zero. If there are more than three digits to the left of the decimal point, groups of three (counting from the right) must be separated by commas (`,`). Example: `$**2,345.67`. (Feel free to use "productions" to define abbreviations, so long as the language remains regular.)

2.2 Show (as "circles-and-arrows" diagrams) the finite automata for Exercise 2.1.

2.3 Build a regular expression that captures all nonempty sequences of letters other than `file`, `for`, and `from`. For notational convenience, you may assume the existence of a **not** operator that takes a set of letters as argument and matches any *other* letter. Comment on the practicality of constructing a regular expression for all sequences of letters other than the keywords of a large programming language.

2.4 (a) Show the NFA that results from applying the construction of Figure 2.7 to the regular expression *letter* (*letter* | *digit*)*.

(b) Apply the transformation illustrated by Example 2.14 to create an equivalent DFA.

(c) Apply the transformation illustrated by Example 2.15 to minimize the DFA.

2.5 Starting with the regular expressions for *integer* and *decimal* in Example 2.3, construct an equivalent NFA, the set-of-subsets DFA, and the minimal equivalent DFA. Be sure to keep separate the final states for the two different kinds of token (see Sidebar 2.4). You may find the exercise easier if you undertake it by modifying the machines in Examples 2.13 through 2.15.

2.6 Build an ad hoc scanner for the calculator language. As output, have it print a list, in order, of the input tokens. For simplicity, feel free to simply halt in the event of a lexical error.

2.7 Write a program in your favorite scripting language to remove comments from programs in the calculator language (Example 2.9).

2.8 Build a nested-`case`-statements finite automaton that converts all letters in its input to lower case, except within Pascal-style comments and strings. A Pascal comment is delimited by `{` and `}`, or by `(*` and `*)`. Comments do not nest. A Pascal string is delimited by single quotes (`' ... '`). A quote character can be placed in a string by doubling it (`'Madam, I''m Adam.'`). This upper-to-lower mapping can be useful if feeding a program written in standard Pascal (which ignores case) to a compiler that considers upper- and lowercase letters to be distinct.

2.9 (a) Describe in English the language defined by the regular expression `a* ( b a* b a* )*`. Your description should be a high-level characterization—one that would still make sense if we were using a different regular expression for the same language.

(b) Write an unambiguous context-free grammar that generates the same language.

(c) Using your grammar from part (b), give a canonical (right-most) derivation of the string `b a a b a a a b b`.

2.10 Give an example of a grammar that captures right associativity for an exponentiation operator (e.g., `**` in Fortran).

2.11 Prove that the following grammar is LL(1):

decl ⟶ `ID` *decl_tail*
decl_tail ⟶ `,` *decl*
⟶ `: ID ;`

(The final `ID` is meant to be a type name.)

2.12 Consider the following grammar:

$G \longrightarrow S$ $$
$S \longrightarrow A\ M$
$M \longrightarrow S \mid \epsilon$
$A \longrightarrow$ a $E \mid$ b $A\ A$
$E \longrightarrow$ a $B \mid$ b $A \mid \epsilon$
$B \longrightarrow$ b $E \mid$ a $B\ B$

(a) Describe in English the language that the grammar generates.

(b) Show a parse tree for the string `a b a a`.

(c) Is the grammar LL(1)? If so, show the parse table; if not, identify a prediction conflict.

2.13 Consider the following grammar:

stmt ⟶ *assignment*
⟶ *subr_call*
assignment ⟶ `id := ` *expr*
subr_call ⟶ `id (` *arg_list* `)`
expr ⟶ *primary expr_tail*
expr_tail ⟶ *op expr*
⟶ ϵ
primary ⟶ `id`
⟶ *subr_call*
⟶ `(` *expr* `)`
op ⟶ `+ | - | * | /`
arg_list ⟶ *expr args_tail*
args_tail ⟶ `,` *arg_list*
⟶ ϵ

(a) Construct a parse tree for the input string `foo(a, b)`.

(b) Give a canonical (right-most) derivation of this same string.

(c) Prove that the grammar is not LL(1).

(d) Modify the grammar so that it *is* LL(1).

2.14 Consider the language consisting of all strings of properly balanced parentheses and brackets.

(a) Give LL(1) and SLR(1) grammars for this language.

(b) Give the corresponding LL(1) and SLR(1) parsing tables.

(c) For each grammar, show the parse tree for `([]([]))[](())`.

(d) Give a trace of the actions of the parsers in constructing these trees.

2.15 Consider the following context-free grammar.

$$
\begin{aligned}
G &\longrightarrow G\ B \\
&\longrightarrow G\ N \\
&\longrightarrow \epsilon \\
B &\longrightarrow (\ E\ ) \\
E &\longrightarrow E\ (\ E\ ) \\
&\longrightarrow \epsilon \\
N &\longrightarrow (\ L\ ] \\
L &\longrightarrow L\ E \\
&\longrightarrow L\ (\\
&\longrightarrow \epsilon
\end{aligned}
$$

(a) Describe, in English, the language generated by this grammar. (Hint: B stands for "balanced"; N stands for "nonbalanced".) (Your description should be a high-level characterization of the language—one that is independent of the particular grammar chosen.)

(b) Give a parse tree for the string `(( ] ( )`.

(c) Give a canonical (right-most) derivation of this same string.

(d) What is FIRST(E) in our grammar? What is FOLLOW(E)? (Recall that FIRST and FOLLOW sets are defined for symbols in an arbitrary CFG, regardless of parsing algorithm.)

(e) Given its use of left recursion, our grammar is clearly not LL(1). Does this language have an LL(1) grammar? Explain.

2.16 Give a grammar that captures all levels of precedence for arithmetic expressions in C, as shown in Figure 6.1. (Hint: This exercise is somewhat tedious. You'll probably want to attack it with a text editor rather than a pencil.)

2.17 Extend the grammar of Figure 2.25 to include `if` statements and `while` loops, along the lines suggested by the following examples:

```
abs := n
if n < 0 then abs := 0 - abs fi

sum := 0
read count
while count > 0 do
    read n
    sum := sum + n
    count := count - 1
od
write sum
```

Your grammar should support the six standard comparison operations in conditions, with arbitrary expressions as operands. It should also allow an arbitrary number of statements in the body of an `if` or `while` statement.

2.18 Consider the following LL(1) grammar for a simplified subset of Lisp:

$P \longrightarrow E$ `$$`
$E \longrightarrow$ `atom`
$\longrightarrow$ `'` E
$\longrightarrow$ `(` $E\ Es$ `)`
$Es \longrightarrow E\ Es$
$\longrightarrow$

(a) What is FIRST(Es)? FOLLOW(E)? PREDICT($Es \longrightarrow \epsilon$)?

(b) Give a parse tree for the string `(cdr '(a b c)) $$`.

(c) Show the left-most derivation of `(cdr '(a b c)) $$`.

(d) Show a trace, in the style of Figure 2.21, of a table-driven top-down parse of this same input.

(e) Now consider a recursive descent parser running on the same input. At the point where the quote token (`'`) is matched, which recursive descent routines will be active (i.e., what routines will have a frame on the parser's run-time stack)?

2.19 Write top-down and bottom-up grammars for the language consisting of all well-formed regular expressions. Arrange for all operators to be left-associative. Give Kleene closure the highest precedence and alternation the lowest precedence.

2.20 Suppose that the expression grammar in Example 2.8 were to be used in conjunction with a scanner that did *not* remove comments from the input, but rather returned them as tokens. How would the grammar need to be modified to allow comments to appear at arbitrary places in the input?

2.21 Build a complete recursive descent parser for the calculator language. As output, have it print a trace of its matches and predictions.

2.22 Extend your solution to Exercise 2.21 to build an explicit parse tree.

2.23 Extend your solution to Exercise 2.21 to build an abstract syntax tree directly, without constructing a parse tree first.

2.24 The dangling `else` problem of Pascal was not shared by its predecessor Algol 60. To avoid ambiguity regarding which `then` is matched by an `else`, Algol 60 prohibited `if` statements immediately inside a `then` clause. The Pascal fragment

```
if C1 then if C2 then S1 else S2
```

had to be written as either

```
if C1 then begin if C2 then S1 end else S2
```

or

```
if C1 then begin if C2 then S1 else S2 end
```

in Algol 60. Show how to write a grammar for conditional statements that enforces this rule. (Hint: You will want to distinguish in your grammar between conditional statements and nonconditional statements; some contexts will accept either, some only the latter.)

2.25 Flesh out the details of an algorithm to eliminate left recursion and common prefixes in an arbitrary context-free grammar.

2.26 In some languages an assignment can appear in any context in which an expression is expected: the value of the expression is the right-hand side of the assignment, which is placed into the left-hand side as a side effect. Consider the following grammar fragment for such a language. Explain why it is not LL(1), and discuss what might be done to make it so.

expr ⟶ `id :=` *expr*
  ⟶ *term term_tail*
term_tail ⟶ `+` *term term_tail* | ε
term ⟶ *factor factor_tail*
factor_tail ⟶ `*` *factor factor_tail* | ε
factor ⟶ `(` *expr* `)` | `id`

2.27 Construct the CFSM for the *id_list* grammar in Example 2.20 and verify that it can be parsed bottom-up with *zero* tokens of look-ahead.

2.28 Modify the grammar in Exercise 2.27 to allow an *id_list* to be empty. Is the grammar still LR(0)?

2.29 Repeat Example 2.36 using the grammar of Figure 2.15.

2.30 Consider the following grammar for a declaration list:

decl_list ⟶ *decl_list decl* `;` | *decl* `;`
decl ⟶ `id :` *type*
type ⟶ `int` | `real` | `char`
  ⟶ `array const .. const of` *type*
  ⟶ `record` *decl_list* `end`

Construct the CFSM for this grammar. Use it to trace out a parse (as in Figure 2.30) for the following input program:

```
foo : record
        a : char;
        b : array 1 .. 2 of real;
    end;
```

2.31–2.37 In More Depth.

2.7 Explorations

2.38 Some languages (e.g., C) distinguish between upper- and lowercase letters in identifiers. Others (e.g., Ada) do not. Which convention do you prefer? Why?

2.39 The syntax for type casts in C and its descendants introduces potential ambiguity: is `(x)-y` a subtraction, or the unary negation of `y`, cast to type `x`? Find out how C, C++, Java, and C# answer this question. Discuss how you would implement the answer(s).

2.40 What do you think of Haskell, Occam, and Python's use of indentation to delimit control constructs (Section 2.1.1)? Would you expect this convention to make program construction and maintenance easier or harder? Why?

2.41 Skip ahead to Section 14.4.2 and learn about the "regular expressions" used in scripting languages, editors, search tools, and so on. Are these really regular? What can they express that cannot be expressed in the notation introduced in Section 2.1.1?

2.42 Rebuild the automaton of Exercise 2.8 using `lex/flex`.

2.43 Find a manual for `yacc/bison`, or consult a compiler textbook [ALSU07, Secs. 4.8.1 and 4.9.2] to learn about *operator precedence parsing*. Explain how it could be used to simplify the grammar of Exercise 2.16.

2.44 Use `lex/flex` and `yacc/bison` to construct a parser for the calculator language. Have it output a trace of its shifts and reductions.

2.45 Repeat the previous exercise using ANTLR.

2.46–2.47 In More Depth.

2.8 Bibliographic Notes

Our coverage of scanning and parsing in this chapter has of necessity been brief. Considerably more detail can be found in texts on parsing theory [AU72] and compiler construction [ALSU07, FCL10, App97, GBJ+12, CT04]. Many compilers of the early 1960s employed recursive descent parsers. Lewis and Stearns [LS68] and Rosenkrantz and Stearns [RS70] published early formal studies of LL grammars and parsing. The original formulation of LR parsing is due to Knuth [Knu65]. Bottom-up parsing became practical with DeRemer's discovery of the SLR and LALR algorithms [DeR71]. W. L. Johnson et al. [JPAR68] describe an early scanner generator. The Unix `lex` tool is due to Lesk [Les75]. `Yacc` is due to S. C. Johnson [Joh75].

Further details on formal language theory can be found in a variety of textbooks, including those of Hopcroft, Motwani, and Ullman [HMU07] and

Sipser [Sip13]. Kleene [Kle56] and Rabin and Scott [RS59] proved the equivalence of regular expressions and finite automata.[15] The proof that finite automata are unable to recognize nested constructs is based on a theorem known as the *pumping lemma*, due to Bar-Hillel, Perles, and Shamir [BHPS61]. Context-free grammars were first explored by Chomsky [Cho56] in the context of natural language. Independently, Backus and Naur developed BNF for the syntactic description of Algol 60 [NBB$^+$63]. Ginsburg and Rice [GR62] recognized the equivalence of the two notations. Chomsky [Cho62] and Evey [Eve63] demonstrated the equivalence of context-free grammars and push-down automata.

Fischer et al.'s text [FCL10] contains an excellent survey of error recovery and repair techniques, with references to other work. The phrase-level recovery mechanism for recursive descent parsers described in Section C-2.3.5 is due to Wirth [Wir76, Sec. 5.9]. The locally least-cost recovery mechanism for table-driven LL parsers described in Section C-2.3.5 is due to Fischer, Milton, and Quiring [FMQ80]. Dion published a locally least-cost bottom-up repair algorithm in 1978 [Dio78]. It is quite complex, and requires very large precomputed tables. McKenzie, Yeatman, and De Vere subsequently showed how to effect the same repairs without the precomputed tables, at a higher but still acceptable cost in time [MYD95].

15 Dana Scott (1932–), Professor Emeritus at Carnegie Mellon University, is known principally for inventing domain theory and launching the field of denotational semantics, which provides a mathematically rigorous way to formalize the meaning of programming languages. Michael Rabin (1931–), of Harvard University, has made seminal contributions to the concepts of nondeterminism and randomization in computer science. Scott and Rabin shared the ACM Turing Award in 1976.

3 Names, Scopes, and Bindings

Early languages such as Fortran, Algol, and Lisp were termed "high level" because their syntax and semantics were significantly more *abstract*—farther from the hardware—than those of the assembly languages they were intended to supplant. Abstraction made it possible to write programs that would run well on a wide variety of machines. It also made programs significantly easier for human beings to understand. While machine independence remains important, it is primarily ease of programming that continues to drive the design of modern languages. This chapter is the first of six to address core issues in language design. (The others are Chapters 6 through 10.) Much of the current discussion will revolve around the notion of *names*.

A name is a mnemonic character string used to represent something else. Names in most languages are identifiers (alphanumeric tokens), though certain other symbols, such as + or :=, can also be names. Names allow us to refer to variables, constants, operations, types, and so on using symbolic identifiers rather than low-level concepts like addresses. Names are also essential in the context of a second meaning of the word *abstraction*. In this second meaning, abstraction is a process by which the programmer associates a name with a potentially complicated program fragment, which can then be thought of in terms of its purpose or function, rather than in terms of how that function is achieved. By hiding irrelevant details, abstraction reduces conceptual complexity, making it possible for the programmer to focus on a manageable subset of the program text at any particular time. Subroutines are *control abstractions*: they allow the programmer to hide arbitrarily complicated code behind a simple interface. Classes are *data abstractions*: they allow the programmer to hide data representation details behind a (comparatively) simple set of operations.

We will look at several major issues related to names. Section 3.1 introduces the notion of *binding time*, which refers not only to the binding of a name to the thing it represents, but also in general to the notion of resolving any design decision in a language implementation. Section 3.2 outlines the various mechanisms used to allocate and deallocate storage space for objects, and distinguishes between the lifetime of an object and the lifetime of a binding of a name to that object.[1] Most name-to-object bindings are usable only within a limited region of a given high-level program. Section 3.3 explores the *scope* rules that define this region; Section 3.4 (mostly on the companion site) considers their implementation.

The complete set of bindings in effect at a given point in a program is known as the current *referencing environment*. Section 3.5 discusses aliasing, in which more than one name may refer to a given object in a given scope, and overloading, in which a name may refer to more than one object in a given scope, depending on the context of the reference. Section 3.6 expands on the notion of scope rules by considering the ways in which a referencing environment may be bound to a subroutine that is passed as a parameter, returned from a function, or stored in a variable. Section 3.7 discusses macro expansion, which can introduce new names via textual substitution, sometimes in ways that are at odds with the rest of the language. Finally, Section 3.8 (mostly on the companion site) discusses separate compilation.

3.1 The Notion of Binding Time

A *binding* is an association between two things, such as a name and the thing it names. *Binding time* is the time at which a binding is created or, more generally, the time at which any implementation decision is made (we can think of this as binding an answer to a question). There are many different times at which decisions may be bound:

Language design time: In most languages, the control-flow constructs, the set of fundamental (primitive) types, the available *constructors* for creating complex types, and many other aspects of language semantics are chosen when the language is designed.

Language implementation time: Most language manuals leave a variety of issues to the discretion of the language implementor. Typical (though by no means universal) examples include the precision (number of bits) of the fundamental types, the coupling of I/O to the operating system's notion of files, and the organization and maximum sizes of the stack and heap.

Program writing time: Programmers, of course, choose algorithms, data structures, and names.

Compile time: Compilers choose the mapping of high-level constructs to machine code, including the layout of statically defined data in memory.

1 For want of a better term, we will use the term "object" throughout Chapters 3–9 to refer to anything that might have a name: variables, constants, types, subroutines, modules, and others. In many modern languages "object" has a more formal meaning, which we will consider in Chapter 10.

Link time: Since most compilers support *separate compilation*—compiling different modules of a program at different times—and depend on the availability of a library of standard subroutines, a program is usually not complete until the various modules are joined together by a linker. The linker chooses the overall layout of the modules with respect to one another, and resolves inter-module references. When a name in one module refers to an object in another module, the binding between the two is not finalized until link time.

Load time: Load time refers to the point at which the operating system loads the program into memory so that it can run. In primitive operating systems, the choice of machine addresses for objects within the program was not finalized until load time. Most modern operating systems distinguish between virtual and physical addresses. Virtual addresses are chosen at link time; physical addresses can actually change at run time. The processor's memory management hardware translates virtual addresses into physical addresses during each individual instruction at run time.

Run time: Run time is actually a very broad term that covers the entire span from the beginning to the end of execution. Bindings of values to variables occur at run time, as do a host of other decisions that vary from language to language. Run time subsumes program start-up time, module entry time, elaboration time (the point at which a declaration is first "seen"), subroutine call time, block entry time, and expression evaluation time/statement execution.

The terms *static* and *dynamic* are generally used to refer to things bound before run time and at run time, respectively. Clearly "static" is a coarse term. So is "dynamic."

Compiler-based language implementations tend to be more efficient than interpreter-based implementations because they make earlier decisions. For example, a compiler analyzes the syntax and semantics of global variable declarations once, before the program ever runs. It decides on a layout for those variables in memory and generates efficient code to access them wherever they appear in the program. A pure interpreter, by contrast, must analyze the declarations every time the program begins execution. In the worst case, an interpreter may reanalyze the local declarations within a subroutine each time that subroutine is called. If a call appears in a deeply nested loop, the savings achieved by a compiler that is able to analyze the declarations only once may be very large. As we shall see in

DESIGN & IMPLEMENTATION

3.1 Binding time

It is difficult to overemphasize the importance of binding times in the design and implementation of programming languages. In general, early binding times are associated with greater efficiency, while later binding times are associated with greater flexibility. The tension between these goals provides a recurring theme for later chapters of this book.

the following section, a compiler will not usually be able to predict the address of a local variable at compile time, since space for the variable will be allocated dynamically on a stack, but it can arrange for the variable to appear at a fixed offset from the location pointed to by a certain register at run time.

Some languages are difficult to compile because their semantics require fundamental decisions to be postponed until run time, generally in order to increase the flexibility or expressiveness of the language. Most scripting languages, for example, delay all type checking until run time. References to objects of arbitrary types (classes) can be assigned into arbitrary named variables, as long as the program never ends up applying an operator to (invoking a method of) an object that is not prepared to handle it. This form of *polymorphism*—applicability to objects or expressions of multiple types—allows the programmer to write unusually flexible and general-purpose code. We will mention polymorphism again in several future sections, including 7.1.2, 7.3, 10.1.1, and 14.4.4.

3.2 Object Lifetime and Storage Management

In any discussion of names and bindings, it is important to distinguish between names and the objects to which they refer, and to identify several key events:

- Creation and destruction of objects
- Creation and destruction of bindings
- Deactivation and reactivation of bindings that may be temporarily unusable
- References to variables, subroutines, types, and so on, all of which use bindings

The period of time between the creation and the destruction of a name-to-object binding is called the binding's *lifetime*. Similarly, the time between the creation and destruction of an object is the object's lifetime. These lifetimes need not necessarily coincide. In particular, an object may retain its value and the potential to be accessed even when a given name can no longer be used to access it. When a variable is passed to a subroutine by *reference*, for example (as it typically is in Fortran or with '`&`' parameters in C++), the binding between the parameter name and the variable that was passed has a lifetime shorter than that of the variable itself. It is also possible, though generally a sign of a program bug, for a name-to-object binding to have a lifetime *longer* than that of the object. This can happen, for example, if an object created via the C++ `new` operator is passed as a `&` parameter and then deallocated (`delete`-ed) before the subroutine returns. A binding to an object that is no longer live is called a *dangling reference*. Dangling references will be discussed further in Sections 3.6 and 8.5.2.

Object lifetimes generally correspond to one of three principal *storage allocation* mechanisms, used to manage the object's space:

1. *Static* objects are given an absolute address that is retained throughout the program's execution.

2. *Stack* objects are allocated and deallocated in last-in, first-out order, usually in conjunction with subroutine calls and returns.
3. *Heap* objects may be allocated and deallocated at arbitrary times. They require a more general (and expensive) storage management algorithm.

3.2.1 Static Allocation

Global variables are the obvious example of static objects, but not the only one. The instructions that constitute a program's machine code can also be thought of as statically allocated objects. We shall see examples in Section 3.3.1 of variables that are local to a single subroutine, but retain their values from one invocation to the next; their space is statically allocated. Numeric and string-valued constant literals are also statically allocated, for statements such as `A = B/14.7` or `printf("hello, world\n")`. (Small constants are often stored within the instruction itself; larger ones are assigned a separate location.) Finally, most compilers produce a variety of tables that are used by run-time support routines for debugging, dynamic type checking, garbage collection, exception handling, and other purposes; these are also statically allocated. Statically allocated objects whose value should not change during program execution (e.g., instructions, constants, and certain run-time tables) are often allocated in protected, read-only memory, so that any inadvertent attempt to write to them will cause a processor interrupt, allowing the operating system to announce a run-time error.

EXAMPLE 3.1
Static allocation of local variables

Logically speaking, local variables are created when their subroutine is called, and destroyed when it returns. If the subroutine is called repeatedly, each invocation is said to create and destroy a separate *instance* of each local variable. It is not always the case, however, that a language implementation must perform work at run time corresponding to these create and destroy operations. Recursion was not originally supported in Fortran (it was added in Fortran 90). As a result, there can never be more than one invocation of a subroutine active in an older Fortran program at any given time, and a compiler may choose to use static allocation for local variables, effectively arranging for the variables of different invocations to share the same locations, and thereby avoiding any run-time overhead for creation and destruction. ■

DESIGN & IMPLEMENTATION

3.2 Recursion in Fortran

The lack of recursion in (pre-Fortran 90) Fortran is generally attributed to the expense of stack manipulation on the IBM 704, on which the language was first implemented. Many (perhaps most) Fortran implementations choose to use a stack for local variables, but because the language definition permits the use of static allocation instead, Fortran programmers were denied the benefits of language-supported recursion for over 30 years.

In many languages a named constant is required to have a value that can be determined at compile time. Usually the expression that specifies the constant's value is permitted to include only other known constants and built-in functions and arithmetic operators. Named constants of this sort, together with constant literals, are sometimes called *manifest constants* or *compile-time constants.* Manifest constants can always be allocated statically, even if they are local to a recursive subroutine: multiple instances can share the same location.

In other languages (e.g., C and Ada), constants are simply variables that cannot be changed after elaboration (initialization) time. Their values, though unchanging, can sometimes depend on other values that are not known until run time. Such *elaboration-time constants,* when local to a recursive subroutine, must be allocated on the stack. C# distinguishes between compile-time and elaboration-time constants using the `const` and `readonly` keywords, respectively.

3.2.2 Stack-Based Allocation

If a language permits recursion, static allocation of local variables is no longer an option, since the number of instances of a variable that may need to exist at the same time is conceptually unbounded. Fortunately, the natural nesting of subroutine calls makes it easy to allocate space for locals on a stack. A simplified picture of a typical stack appears in Figure 3.1. Each instance of a subroutine at run time has its own *frame* (also called an *activation record*) on the stack, containing arguments and return values, local variables, temporaries, and bookkeeping information. Temporaries are typically intermediate values produced in complex calculations. Bookkeeping information typically includes the subroutine's return address, a reference to the stack frame of the caller (also called the *dynamic link*), saved values of registers needed by both the caller and the callee, and various other values that we will study later. Arguments to be passed to subsequent routines lie at the top of the frame, where the callee can easily find them. The organization of the remaining information is implementation-dependent: it varies from one language, machine, and compiler to another.

EXAMPLE 3.2
Layout of the run-time stack

Maintenance of the stack is the responsibility of the subroutine *calling sequence*—the code executed by the caller immediately before and after the call—and of the *prologue* (code executed at the beginning) and *epilogue* (code executed at the end) of the subroutine itself. Sometimes the term "calling sequence" is used to refer to the combined operations of the caller, the prologue, and the epilogue. We will study calling sequences in more detail in Section 9.2.

While the location of a stack frame cannot be predicted at compile time (the compiler cannot in general tell what other frames may already be on the stack), the offsets of objects *within* a frame usually *can* be statically determined. Moreover, the compiler can arrange (in the calling sequence or prologue) for a particular register, known as the *frame pointer* to always point to a known location within the frame of the current subroutine. Code that needs to access a local variable within the current frame, or an argument near the top of the calling frame,

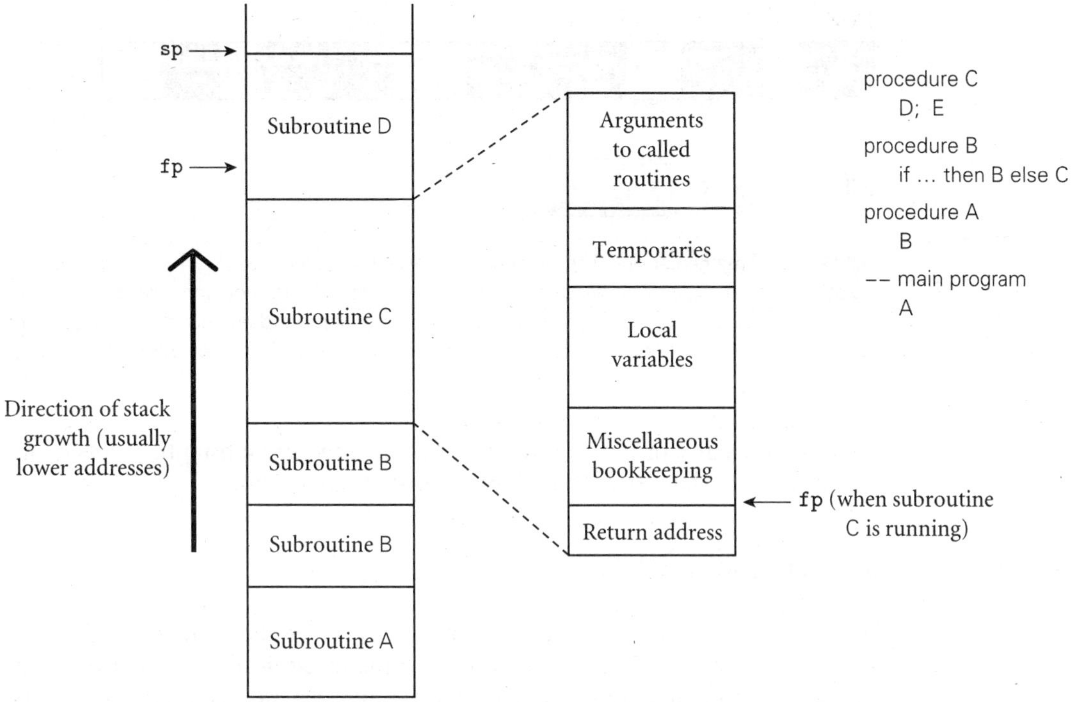

Figure 3.1 Stack-based allocation of space for subroutines. We assume here that subroutines have been called as shown in the upper right. In particular, B has called itself once, recursively, before calling C. If D returns and C calls E, E's frame (activation record) will occupy the same space previously used for D's frame. At any given time, the stack pointer (`sp`) register points to the first unused location on the stack (or the last used location on some machines), and the frame pointer (`fp`) register points to a known location within the frame of the current subroutine. The relative order of fields within a frame may vary from machine to machine and compiler to compiler.

can do so by adding a predetermined offset to the value in the frame pointer. As we discuss in Section C-5.3.1, almost every processor provides a *displacement addressing* mechanism that allows this addition to be specified implicitly as part of an ordinary `load` or `store` instruction. The stack grows "downward" toward lower addresses in most language implementations. Some machines provide special `push` and `pop` instructions that assume this direction of growth. Local variables, temporaries, and bookkeeping information typically have negative offsets from the frame pointer. Arguments and returns typically have positive offsets; they reside in the caller's frame.

Even in a language without recursion, it can be advantageous to use a stack for local variables, rather than allocating them statically. In most programs the pattern of potential calls among subroutines does not permit all of those subroutines to be active at the same time. As a result, the total space needed for local variables of currently active subroutines is seldom as large as the total space across *all*

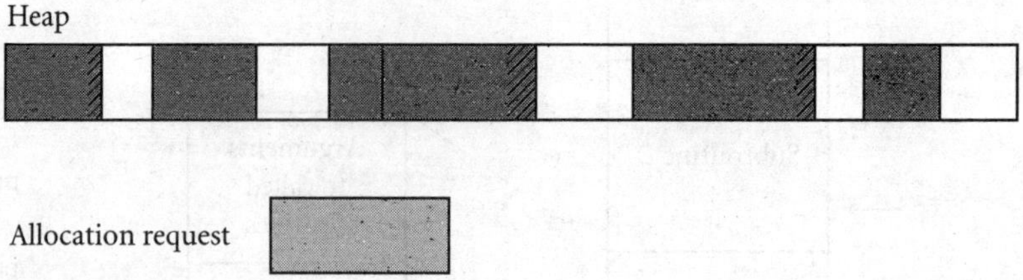

Figure 3.2 **Fragmentation.** The shaded blocks are in use; the clear blocks are free. Cross-hatched space at the ends of in-use blocks represents internal fragmentation. The discontiguous free blocks indicate external fragmentation. While there is more than enough total free space remaining to satisfy an allocation request of the illustrated size, no single remaining block is large enough.

subroutines, active or not. A stack may therefore require substantially less memory at run time than would be required for static allocation.

3.2.3 Heap-Based Allocation

A *heap* is a region of storage in which subblocks can be allocated and deallocated at arbitrary times.[2] Heaps are required for the dynamically allocated pieces of linked data structures, and for objects such as fully general character strings, lists, and sets, whose size may change as a result of an assignment statement or other update operation.

There are many possible strategies to manage space in a heap. We review the major alternatives here; details can be found in any data-structures textbook. The principal concerns are speed and space, and as usual there are tradeoffs between them. Space concerns can be further subdivided into issues of internal and external *fragmentation*. Internal fragmentation occurs when a storage-management algorithm allocates a block that is larger than required to hold a given object; the extra space is then unused. External fragmentation occurs when the blocks that have been assigned to active objects are scattered through the heap in such a way that the remaining, unused space is composed of multiple blocks: there may be quite a lot of free space, but no one piece of it may be large enough to satisfy some future request (see Figure 3.2).

EXAMPLE 3.3
External fragmentation in the heap

Many storage-management algorithms maintain a single linked list—the *free list*—of heap blocks not currently in use. Initially the list consists of a single block comprising the entire heap. At each allocation request the algorithm searches the list for a block of appropriate size. With a *first fit* algorithm we select the first block on the list that is large enough to satisfy the request. With a *best fit* algorithm we search the entire list to find the smallest block that is large enough to satisfy the

2 Unfortunately, the term "heap" is also used for the common tree-based implementation of a priority queue. These two uses of the term have nothing to do with one another.

request. In either case, if the chosen block is significantly larger than required, then we divide it into two and return the unneeded portion to the free list as a smaller block. (If the unneeded portion is below some minimum threshold in size, we may leave it in the allocated block as internal fragmentation.) When a block is deallocated and returned to the free list, we check to see whether either or both of the physically adjacent blocks are free; if so, we coalesce them.

Intuitively, one would expect a best fit algorithm to do a better job of reserving large blocks for large requests. At the same time, it has higher allocation cost than a first fit algorithm, because it must always search the entire list, and it tends to result in a larger number of very small "left-over" blocks. Which approach—first fit or best fit—results in lower external fragmentation depends on the distribution of size requests.

In any algorithm that maintains a single free list, the cost of allocation is linear in the number of free blocks. To reduce this cost to a constant, some storage management algorithms maintain separate free lists for blocks of different sizes. Each request is rounded up to the next standard size (at the cost of internal fragmentation) and allocated from the appropriate list. In effect, the heap is divided into "pools," one for each standard size. The division may be static or dynamic. Two common mechanisms for dynamic pool adjustment are known as the *buddy system* and the *Fibonacci heap*. In the buddy system, the standard block sizes are powers of two. If a block of size 2^k is needed, but none is available, a block of size 2^{k+1} is split in two. One of the halves is used to satisfy the request; the other is placed on the kth free list. When a block is deallocated, it is coalesced with its "buddy"—the other half of the split that created it—if that buddy is free. Fibonacci heaps are similar, but use Fibonacci numbers for the standard sizes, instead of powers of two. The algorithm is slightly more complex, but leads to slightly lower internal fragmentation, because the Fibonacci sequence grows more slowly than 2^k.

The problem with external fragmentation is that the ability of the heap to satisfy requests may degrade over time. Multiple free lists may help, by clustering small blocks in relatively close physical proximity, but they do not eliminate the problem. It is always possible to devise a sequence of requests that cannot be satisfied, even though the total space required is less than the size of the heap. If memory is partitioned among size pools statically, one need only exceed the maximum number of requests of a given size. If pools are dynamically readjusted, one can "checkerboard" the heap by allocating a large number of small blocks and then deallocating every other one, in order of physical address, leaving an alternating pattern of small free and allocated blocks. To eliminate external fragmentation, we must be prepared to *compact* the heap, by moving already-allocated blocks. This task is complicated by the need to find and update all outstanding references to a block that is being moved. We will discuss compaction further in Section 8.5.3.

3.2.4 Garbage Collection

Allocation of heap-based objects is always triggered by some specific operation in a program: instantiating an object, appending to the end of a list, assigning a long value into a previously short string, and so on. Deallocation is also explicit in some languages (e.g., C, C++, and Rust). As we shall see in Section 8.5, however, many languages specify that objects are to be deallocated implicitly when it is no longer possible to reach them from any program variable. The run-time library for such a language must then provide a *garbage collection* mechanism to identify and reclaim unreachable objects. Most functional and scripting languages require garbage collection, as do many more recent imperative languages, including Java and C#.

The traditional arguments in favor of explicit deallocation are implementation simplicity and execution speed. Even naive implementations of automatic garbage collection add significant complexity to the implementation of a language with a rich type system, and even the most sophisticated garbage collector can consume nontrivial amounts of time in certain programs. If the programmer can correctly identify the end of an object's lifetime, without too much run-time bookkeeping, the result is likely to be faster execution.

The argument in favor of automatic garbage collection, however, is compelling: manual deallocation errors are among the most common and costly bugs in real-world programs. If an object is deallocated too soon, the program may follow a *dangling reference*, accessing memory now used by another object. If an object is *not* deallocated at the end of its lifetime, then the program may "leak memory," eventually running out of heap space. Deallocation errors are notoriously difficult to identify and fix. Over time, many language designers and programmers have come to consider automatic garbage collection an essential language feature. Garbage-collection algorithms have improved, reducing their run-time overhead; language implementations have become more complex in general, reducing the marginal complexity of automatic collection; and leading-edge applications have become larger and more complex, making the benefits of automatic collection ever more compelling.

✓ CHECK YOUR UNDERSTANDING

1. What is *binding time*?

2. Explain the distinction between decisions that are bound statically and those that are bound dynamically.

3. What is the advantage of binding things as early as possible? What is the advantage of delaying bindings?

4. Explain the distinction between the *lifetime* of a name-to-object binding and its *visibility*.

5. What determines whether an object is allocated statically, on the stack, or in the heap?
6. List the objects and information commonly found in a stack frame.
7. What is a *frame pointer*? What is it used for?
8. What is a *calling sequence*?
9. What are internal and external *fragmentation*?
10. What is *garbage collection*?
11. What is a *dangling reference*?

3.3 Scope Rules

The textual region of the program in which a binding is active is its *scope*. In most modern languages, the scope of a binding is determined statically, that is, at compile time. In C, for example, we introduce a new scope upon entry to a subroutine. We create bindings for local objects and deactivate bindings for global objects that are hidden (made invisible) by local objects of the same name. On subroutine exit, we destroy bindings for local variables and reactivate bindings for any global objects that were hidden. These manipulations of bindings may at first glance appear to be run-time operations, but they do not require the execution of any code: the portions of the program in which a binding is active are completely determined at compile time. We can look at a C program and know which names refer to which objects at which points in the program based on purely textual rules. For this reason, C is said to be *statically scoped* (some authors say *lexically scoped*[3]). Other languages, including APL, Snobol, Tcl, and early dialects of Lisp, are *dynamically scoped*: their bindings depend on the flow of execution at run time. We will examine static and dynamic scoping in more detail in Sections 3.3.1 and 3.3.6.

In addition to talking about the "scope of a binding," we sometimes use the word "scope" as a noun all by itself, without a specific binding in mind. Informally, a scope is a program region of maximal size in which no bindings change (or at least none are destroyed—more on this in Section 3.3.3). Typically, a scope is the body of a module, class, subroutine, or structured control-flow statement, sometimes called a *block*. In C family languages it would be delimited with `{...}` braces.

3 *Lexical scope* is actually a better term than *static scope*, because scope rules based on nesting can be enforced at run time instead of compile time if desired. In fact, in Common Lisp and Scheme it is possible to pass the unevaluated text of a subroutine declaration into some other subroutine as a parameter, and then use the text to create a lexically nested declaration at run time.

Algol 68 and Ada use the term *elaboration* to refer to the process by which declarations become active when control first enters a scope. Elaboration entails the creation of bindings. In many languages, it also entails the allocation of stack space for local objects, and possibly the assignment of initial values. In Ada it can entail a host of other things, including the execution of error-checking or heap-space-allocating code, the propagation of exceptions, and the creation of concurrently executing *tasks* (to be discussed in Chapter 13).

At any given point in a program's execution, the set of active bindings is called the current *referencing environment*. The set is principally determined by static or dynamic *scope rules*. We shall see that a referencing environment generally corresponds to a sequence of scopes that can be examined (in order) to find the current binding for a given name.

In some cases, referencing environments also depend on what are (in a confusing use of terminology) called *binding rules*. Specifically, when a reference to a subroutine *S* is stored in a variable, passed as a parameter to another subroutine, or returned as a function value, one needs to determine when the referencing environment for *S* is chosen—that is, when the binding between the reference to *S* and the referencing environment of *S* is made. The two principal options are *deep binding*, in which the choice is made when the reference is first created, and *shallow binding*, in which the choice is made when the reference is finally used. We will examine these options in more detail in Section 3.6.

3.3.1 Static Scoping

In a language with static (lexical) scoping, the bindings between names and objects can be determined at compile time by examining the text of the program, without consideration of the flow of control at run time. Typically, the "current" binding for a given name is found in the matching declaration whose block most closely surrounds a given point in the program, though as we shall see there are many variants on this basic theme.

The simplest static scope rule is probably that of early versions of Basic, in which there was only a single, global scope. In fact, there were only a few hundred possible names, each of which consisted of a letter optionally followed by a digit. There were no explicit declarations; variables were declared implicitly by virtue of being used.

Scope rules are somewhat more complex in (pre-Fortran 90) Fortran, though not much more. Fortran distinguishes between global and local variables. The scope of a local variable is limited to the subroutine in which it appears; it is not visible elsewhere. Variable declarations are optional. If a variable is not declared, it is assumed to be local to the current subroutine and to be of type `integer` if its name begins with the letters I–N, or `real` otherwise. (Different conventions for implicit declarations can be specified by the programmer. In Fortran 90 and its successors, the programmer can also turn off implicit declarations, so that use of an undeclared variable becomes a compile-time error.)

```
/*
    Place into *s a new name beginning with the letter 'L' and
    continuing with the ASCII representation of a unique integer.
    Parameter s is assumed to point to space large enough to hold any
    such name; for the short ints used here, 7 characters suffice.
*/
void label_name (char *s) {
    static short int n;          /* C guarantees that static locals
                                    are initialized to zero */
    sprintf (s, "L%d\0", ++n);   /* "print" formatted output to s */
}
```

Figure 3.3 C code to illustrate the use of static variables.

Semantically, the lifetime of a local Fortran variable (both the object itself and the name-to-object binding) encompasses a single execution of the variable's subroutine. Programmers can override this rule by using an explicit `save` statement. (Similar mechanisms appear in many other languages: in C one declares the variable `static`; in Algol one declares it `own`.) A `save`-ed (`static`, `own`) variable has a lifetime that encompasses the entire execution of the program. Instead of a logically separate object for every invocation of the subroutine, the compiler creates a single object that retains its value from one invocation of the subroutine to the next. (The name-to-variable binding, of course, is inactive when the subroutine is not executing, because the name is out of scope.)

EXAMPLE 3.4
Static variables in C

As an example of the use of static variables, consider the code in Figure 3.3. The subroutine `label_name` can be used to generate a series of distinct character-string names: `L1`, `L2`, ... A compiler might use these names in its assembly language output.

3.3.2 Nested Subroutines

The ability to nest subroutines inside each other, introduced in Algol 60, is a feature of many subsequent languages, including Ada, ML, Common Lisp, Python, Scheme, Swift, and (to a limited extent) Fortran 90. Other languages, including C and its descendants, allow classes or other scopes to nest. Just as the local variables of a Fortran subroutine are not visible to other subroutines, any constants, types, variables, or subroutines declared within a scope are not visible outside that scope in Algol-family languages. More formally, Algol-style nesting gives rise to the *closest nested scope rule* for bindings from names to objects: a name that is introduced in a declaration is known in the scope in which it is declared, and in each internally nested scope, unless it is *hidden* by another declaration of the same name in one or more nested scopes. To find the object corresponding to a given use of a name, we look for a declaration with that name in the current, innermost scope. If there is one, it defines the active binding for the name. Otherwise, we look for a declaration in the immediately surrounding scope. We continue outward, examining successively surrounding scopes, until we reach the outer nesting level of the program, where global objects are declared. If no declaration is found at any level, then the program is in error.

Many languages provide a collection of *built-in*, or *predefined objects*, such as I/O routines, mathematical functions, and in some cases types such as `integer` and `char`. It is common to consider these to be declared in an extra, invisible, outermost scope, which surrounds the scope in which global objects are declared. The search for bindings described in the previous paragraph terminates at this extra, outermost scope, if it exists, rather than at the scope in which global objects are declared. This outermost scope convention makes it possible for a programmer to define a global object whose name is the same as that of some predefined object (whose "declaration" is thereby hidden, making it invisible).

EXAMPLE 3.5
Nested scopes

An example of nested scopes appears in Figure 3.4.[4] In this example, procedure `P2` is called only by `P1`, and need not be visible outside. It is therefore declared inside `P1`, limiting its scope (its region of visibility) to the portion of the program shown here. In a similar fashion, `P4` is visible only within `P1`, `P3` is visible only within `P2`, and `F1` is visible only within `P4`. Under the standard rules for nested scopes, `F1` could call `P2` and `P4` could call `F1`, but `P2` could not call `F1`.

Though they are hidden from the rest of the program, nested subroutines are able to access the parameters and local variables (and other local objects) of the surrounding scope(s). In our example, `P3` can name (and modify) `A1`, `X`, and `A2`, in addition to `A3`. Because `P1` and `F1` both declare local variables named `X`, the inner declaration hides the outer one within a portion of its scope. Uses of `X` in `F1` refer to the inner `X`; uses of `X` in other regions of the code refer to the outer `X`. ■

A name-to-object binding that is hidden by a nested declaration of the same name is said to have a *hole* in its scope. In some languages, the object whose name is hidden is simply inaccessible in the nested scope (unless it has more than one name). In others, the programmer can access the outer meaning of a name by applying a *qualifier* or *scope resolution operator*. In Ada, for example, a name may be prefixed by the name of the scope in which it is declared, using syntax that resembles the specification of fields in a record. `My_proc.X`, for example, refers to the declaration of `X` in subroutine `My_proc`, regardless of whether some other `X` has been declared in a lexically closer scope. In C++, which does not allow subroutines to nest, `::X` refers to a global declaration of `X`, regardless of whether the current subroutine also has an `X`.[5]

Access to Nonlocal Objects

We have already seen (Section 3.2.2) that the compiler can arrange for a frame pointer register to point to the frame of the currently executing subroutine at run

4 This code is not contrived; it was extracted from an implementation (originally in Pascal) of the FMQ error repair algorithm described in Section C-2.3.5.

5 The C++ `::` operator is also used to name members (fields or methods) of a base class that are hidden by members of a derived class; we will consider this use in Section 10.2.2.

```
procedure P1(A1)
    var X           -- local to P1
    ...
    procedure P2(A2)
        ...
        procedure P3(A3)
            ...
        begin
            ...         -- body of P3
        end
        ...
    begin
        ...             -- body of P2
    end
    ...
    procedure P4(A4)
        ...
        function F1(A5)
            var X   -- local to F1
            ...
        begin
            ...         -- body of F1
        end
        ...
    begin
        ...             -- body of P4
    end
    ...
begin
    ...                 -- body of P1
end
```

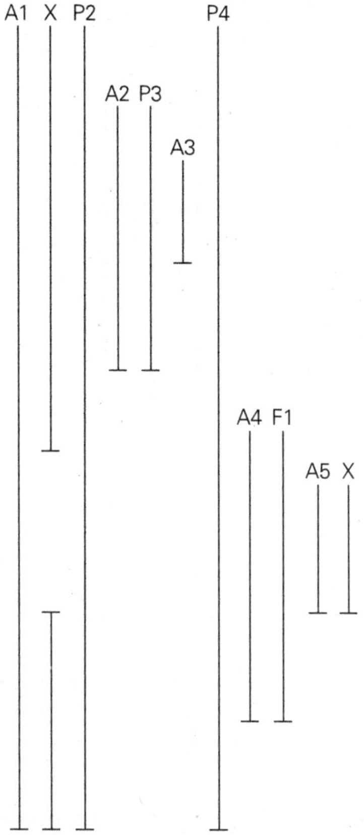

Figure 3.4 **Example of nested subroutines, shown in pseudocode.** Vertical bars indicate the scope of each name, for a language in which declarations are visible throughout their subroutine. Note the hole in the scope of the outer X.

time. Using this register as a base for *displacement* (register plus offset) addressing, target code can access objects within the current subroutine. But what about objects in lexically surrounding subroutines? To find these we need a way to find the frames corresponding to those scopes at run time. Since a nested subroutine may call a routine in an outer scope, the order of stack frames at run time may not necessarily correspond to the order of lexical nesting. Nonetheless, we can be sure that there *is* some frame for the surrounding scope already in the stack, since the current subroutine could not have been called unless it was visible, and it could not have been visible unless the surrounding scope was active. (It is actually possible in some languages to save a reference to a nested subroutine, and then call it when the surrounding scope is no longer active. We defer this possibility to Section 3.6.2.)

The simplest way in which to find the frames of surrounding scopes is to maintain a *static link* in each frame that points to the "parent" frame: the frame of the

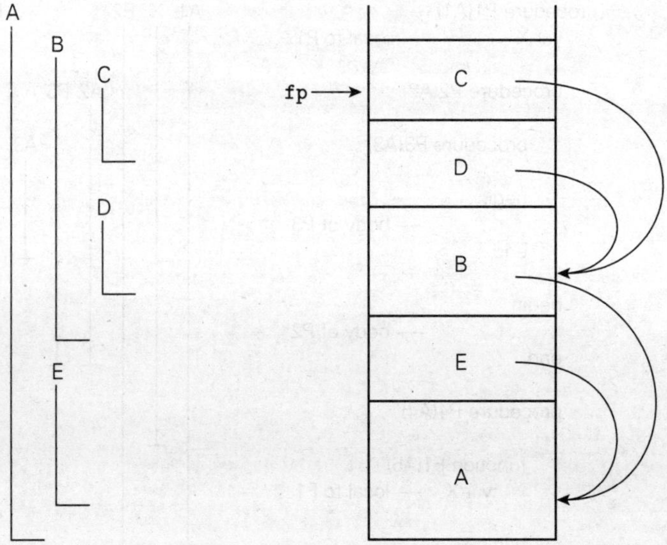

Figure 3.5 **Static chains.** Subroutines A, B, C, D, and E are nested as shown on the left. If the sequence of nested calls at run time is A, E, B, D, and C, then the static links in the stack will look as shown on the right. The code for subroutine C can find local objects at known offsets from the frame pointer. It can find local objects of the surrounding scope, B, by dereferencing its static chain once and then applying an offset. It can find local objects in B's surrounding scope, A, by dereferencing its static chain twice and then applying an offset.

most recent invocation of the lexically surrounding subroutine. If a subroutine is declared at the outermost nesting level of the program, then its frame will have a null static link at run time. If a subroutine is nested k levels deep, then its frame's static link, and those of its parent, grandparent, and so on, will form a *static chain* of length k at run time. To find a variable or parameter declared j subroutine scopes outward, target code at run time can dereference the static chain j times, and then add the appropriate offset. Static chains are illustrated in Figure 3.5. We will discuss the code required to maintain them in Section 9.2. ■

EXAMPLE 3.6
Static chains

3.3.3 Declaration Order

In our discussion so far we have glossed over an important subtlety: suppose an object `x` is declared somewhere within block `B`. Does the scope of `x` include the portion of `B` before the declaration, and if so can `x` actually be used in that portion of the code? Put another way, can an expression E refer to any name declared in the current scope, or only to names that are declared *before* E in the scope?

Several early languages, including Algol 60 and Lisp, required that all declarations appear at the beginning of their scope. One might at first think that this rule would avoid the questions in the preceding paragraph, but it does not, because declarations may refer to one another.[6]

EXAMPLE 3.7
A "gotcha" in declare-before-use

In an apparent attempt to simplify the implementation of the compiler, Pascal modified the requirement to say that names must be declared before they are used. There are special mechanisms to accommodate recursive types and subroutines, but in general, a *forward reference* (an attempt to use a name before its declaration) is a static semantic error. At the same time, however, Pascal retained the notion that the scope of a declaration is the entire surrounding block. Taken together, whole-block scope and declare-before-use rules can interact in surprising ways:

```
1.  const N = 10;
2.  ...
3.  procedure foo;
4.  const
5.      M = N;        (* static semantic error! *)
6.      ...
7.      N = 20;       (* local constant declaration; hides the outer N *)
```

Pascal says that the second declaration of `N` covers all of `foo`, so the semantic analyzer should complain on line 5 that `N` is being used before its declaration. The error has the potential to be highly confusing, particularly if the programmer meant to use the outer `N`:

```
const N = 10;
...
procedure foo;
const
    M = N;              (* static semantic error! *)
var
    A : array [1..M] of integer;
    N : real;           (* hiding declaration *)
```

Here the pair of messages "`N` used before declaration" and "`N` is not a constant" are almost certainly not helpful.

DESIGN & IMPLEMENTATION

3.3 Mutual recursion

Some Algol 60 compilers were known to process the declarations of a scope in program order. This strategy had the unfortunate effect of implicitly outlawing mutually recursive subroutines and types, something the language designers clearly did not intend [Atk73].

6 We saw an example of mutually recursive subroutines in the recursive descent parsing of Section 2.3.1. Mutually recursive types frequently arise in linked data structures, where nodes of two types may need to point to each other.

In order to determine the validity of any declaration that appears to use a name from a surrounding scope, a Pascal compiler must scan the remainder of the scope's declarations to see if the name is hidden. To avoid this complication, most Pascal successors (and some dialects of Pascal itself) specify that the scope of an identifier is not the entire block in which it is declared (excluding holes), but rather the portion of that block from the declaration to the end (again excluding holes). If our program fragment had been written in Ada, for example, or in C, C++, or Java, no semantic errors would be reported. The declaration of `M` would refer to the first (outer) declaration of `N`. ■

C++ and Java further relax the rules by dispensing with the define-before-use requirement in many cases. In both languages, members of a class (including those that are not defined until later in the program text) are visible inside all of the class's methods. In Java, classes themselves can be declared in any order.

EXAMPLE 3.8
Whole-block scope in C#

Interestingly, while C# echos Java in requiring declaration before use for local variables (but not for classes and members), it returns to the Pascal notion of whole-block scope. Thus the following is invalid in C#:

```
class A {
    const int N = 10;
    void foo() {
        const int M = N;      // uses inner N before it is declared
        const int N = 20;
```

■

Perhaps the simplest approach to declaration order, from a conceptual point of view, is that of Modula-3, which says that the scope of a declaration is the entire block in which it appears (minus any holes created by nested declarations), and that the order of declarations doesn't matter. The principal objection to this approach is that programmers may find it counterintuitive to use a local variable before it is declared.

EXAMPLE 3.9
"Local if written" in Python

Python takes the "whole block" scope rule one step further by dispensing with variable declarations altogether. In their place it adopts the unusual convention that the local variables of subroutine `S` are precisely those variables that are written by some statement in the (static) body of `S`. If `S` is nested inside of `T`, and the name `x` appears on the left-hand side of assignment statements in both `S` and `T`, then the `x`'s are distinct: there is one in `S` and one in `T`. Non-local variables are read-only unless explicitly imported (using Python's `global` statement). We will consider these conventions in more detail in Section 14.4.1, as part of a general discussion of scoping in scripting languages. ■

EXAMPLE 3.10
Declaration order in Scheme

In the interest of flexibility, modern Lisp dialects tend to provide several options for declaration order. In Scheme, for example, the `letrec` and `let*` constructs define scopes with, respectively, whole-block and declaration-to-end-of-block semantics. The most frequently used construct, `let`, provides yet another option:

```
(let ((A 1))            ; outer scope, with A defined to be 1
  (let ((A 2)           ; inner scope, with A defined to be 2
        (B A))          ;            and B defined to be A
    B))                 ; return the value of B
```

Here the nested declarations of `A` and `B` don't take effect until after the end of the declaration list. Thus when `B` is defined, the redefinition of `A` has not yet taken effect. `B` is defined to be the *outer* `A`, and the code as a whole returns 1.

Declarations and Definitions

Recursive types and subroutines introduce a problem for languages that require names to be declared before they can be used: how can two declarations each appear before the other? C and C++ handle the problem by distinguishing between the *declaration* of an object and its *definition*. A declaration introduces a name and indicates its scope, but may omit certain implementation details. A definition describes the object in sufficient detail for the compiler to determine its implementation. If a declaration is not complete enough to be a definition, then a separate definition must appear somewhere else in the scope. In C we can write

EXAMPLE 3.11
Declarations vs definitions in C

```
struct manager;                      /* declaration only */
struct employee {
    struct manager *boss;
    struct employee *next_employee;
    ...
};
struct manager {                     /* definition */
    struct employee *first_employee;
    ...
};
```

and

```
void list_tail(follow_set fs);       /* declaration only */
void list(follow_set fs)
{
    switch (input_token) {
        case id : match(id); list_tail(fs);
    ...
}
void list_tail(follow_set fs)        /* definition */
{
    switch (input_token) {
        case comma : match(comma); list(fs);
    ...
}
```

The initial declaration of `manager` needed only to introduce a name: since pointers are generally all the same size, the compiler can determine the implementation of `employee` without knowing any `manager` details. The initial declaration of `list_tail`, however, must include the return type and parameter list, so the compiler can tell that the call in `list` is correct.

Nested Blocks

In many languages, including Algol 60, C89, and Ada, local variables can be declared not only at the beginning of any subroutine, but also at the top of any `begin... end` (`{...}`) block. Other languages, including Algol 68, C, and all of C's descendants, are even more flexible, allowing declarations wherever a statement may appear. In most languages a nested declaration hides any outer declaration with the same name (Java and C# make it a static semantic error if the outer declaration is local to the current subroutine).

DESIGN & IMPLEMENTATION

3.4 Redeclarations

Some languages, particularly those that are intended for interactive use, permit the programmer to redeclare an object: to create a new binding for a given name in a given scope. Interactive programmers commonly use redeclarations to experiment with alternative implementations or to fix bugs during early development. In most interactive languages, the new meaning of the name replaces the old in all contexts. In ML dialects, however, the old meaning of the name may remain accessible to functions that were elaborated before the name was redeclared. This design choice can sometimes be counterintuitive. Here's an example in OCaml (the lines beginning with # are user input; the others are printed by the interpreter):

```
# let x = 1;;
val x : int = 1
# let f y = x + y;;
val f : int -> int = <fun>
# let x = 2;;
val x : int = 2
# f 3;;
- : int = 4
```

The second line of user input defines `f` to be a function of one argument (`y`) that returns the sum of that argument and the previously defined value `x`. When we redefine `x` to be 2, however, the function does not notice: it still returns `y` plus 1. This behavior reflects the fact that OCaml is usually compiled, bit by bit on the fly, rather than interpreted. When `x` is redefined, `f` has already been compiled into a form (bytecode or machine code) that accesses the old meaning of `x` directly. By comparison, a language like Scheme, which is lexically scoped but usually interpreted, stores the bindings for names in known locations. Programs always access the meanings of names indirectly through those locations: if the meaning of a name changes, all accesses to the name will use the new meaning.

EXAMPLE 3.12
Inner declarations in C

Variables declared in nested blocks can be very useful, as for example in the following C code:

```
{
    int temp = a;
    a = b;
    b = temp;
}
```

Keeping the declaration of `temp` lexically adjacent to the code that uses it makes the program easier to read, and eliminates any possibility that this code will interfere with another variable named `temp`. ■

No run-time work is needed to allocate or deallocate space for variables declared in nested blocks; their space can be included in the total space for local variables allocated in the subroutine prologue and deallocated in the epilogue. Exercise 3.9 considers how to minimize the total space required.

✓ CHECK YOUR UNDERSTANDING

12. What do we mean by the *scope* of a name-to-object binding?
13. Describe the difference between static and dynamic scoping.
14. What is *elaboration*?
15. What is a *referencing environment*?
16. Explain the *closest nested scope rule.*
17. What is the purpose of a *scope resolution operator*?
18. What is a *static chain*? What is it used for?
19. What are *forward references*? Why are they prohibited or restricted in many programming languages?
20. Explain the difference between a *declaration* and a *definition*. Why is the distinction important?

3.3.4 Modules

An important challenge in the construction of any large body of software is to divide the effort among programmers in such a way that work can proceed on multiple fronts simultaneously. This modularization of effort depends critically on the notion of *information hiding*, which makes objects and algorithms invisible, whenever possible, to portions of the system that do not need them. Properly modularized code reduces the "cognitive load" on the programmer by minimizing the amount of information required to understand any given portion of the system. In a well-designed program the interfaces among modules are as "narrow" (i.e., simple) as possible, and any design decision that is likely to change is hidden inside a single module.

Information hiding is crucial for software maintenance (bug fixes and enhancement), which tends to significantly outweigh the cost of initial development for most commercial software. In addition to reducing cognitive load, hiding reduces the risk of name conflicts: with fewer visible names, there is less chance that a newly introduced name will be the same as one already in use. It also safeguards the integrity of data abstractions: any attempt to access an object outside of the module to which it belongs will cause the compiler to issue an "undefined symbol" error message. Finally, it helps to compartmentalize run-time errors: if a variable takes on an unexpected value, we can generally be sure that the code that modified it is in the variable's scope.

Encapsulating Data and Subroutines

Unfortunately, the information hiding provided by nested subroutines is limited to objects whose lifetime is the same as that of the subroutine in which they are hidden. When control returns from a subroutine, its local variables will no longer be live: their values will be discarded. We have seen a partial solution to this problem in the form of the `save` statement in Fortran and the `static` and `own` variables of C and Algol.

Static variables allow a subroutine to have "memory"—to retain information from one invocation to the next—while protecting that memory from accidental access or modification by other parts of the program. Put another way, static variables allow programmers to build single-subroutine abstractions. Unfortunately, they do not allow the construction of abstractions whose interface needs to consist of more than one subroutine. Consider, for example, a simple pseudorandom number generator. In addition to the main `rand_int` routine, we might want a `set_seed` routine that primes the generator for a specific pseudorandom sequence (e.g., for deterministic testing). We should like to make the state of the generator, which determines the next pseudorandom number, visible to both `rand_int` and `set_seed`, but hide it from the rest of the program. We can achieve this goal in many languages through use of a *module* construct. ■

EXAMPLE 3.13
Pseudorandom numbers as a motivation for modules

Modules as Abstractions

A module allows a collection of objects—subroutines, variables, types, and so on—to be encapsulated in such a way that (1) objects inside are visible to each other, but (2) objects on the inside may not be visible on the outside unless they are *exported*, and (3) objects on the outside may not be visible on the inside unless they are *imported*. Import and export conventions vary significantly from one language to another, but in all cases, only the *visibility* of objects is affected; modules do not affect the lifetime of the objects they contain.

```
#include <time.h>
namespace rand_mod {
    unsigned int seed = time(0);       // initialize from current time of day
    const unsigned int a = 48271;
    const unsigned int m = 0x7fffffff;

    void set_seed(unsigned int s) {
        seed = s;
    }
    unsigned int rand_int() {
        return seed = (a * seed) % m;
    }
}
```

Figure 3.6 Pseudorandom number generator module in C++. Uses the linear congruential method, with a default seed taken from the current time of day. While there exist much better (more random) generators, this one is simple, and acceptable for many purposes.

Modules were one of the principal language innovations of the late 1970s and early 1980s; they appeared in Clu[7] (which called them *clusters*), Modula (1, 2, and 3), Turing, and Ada 83, among others. In more modern form, they also appear in Haskell, C++, Java, C#, and all the major scripting languages. Several languages, including Ada, Java, and Perl, use the term *package* instead of module. Others, including C++, C#, and PHP, use *namespace*. Modules can be emulated to some degree through use of the separate compilation facilities of C; we discuss this possibility in Section C-3.8.

EXAMPLE 3.14
Pseudorandom number generator in C++

As an example of the use of modules, consider the pseudorandom number generator shown in Figure 3.6. As discussed in Sidebar 3.5, this module (namespace) would typically be placed in its own file, and then imported wherever it is needed in a C++ program.

Bindings of names made inside the namespace may be partially or totally hidden (inactive) on the outside—but not destroyed. In C++, where namespaces can appear only at the outermost level of lexical nesting, integer `seed` would retain its value throughout the execution of the program, even though it is visible only to `set_seed` and `rand_int`.

Outside the `rand_mod` namespace, C++ allows `set_seed` and `rand_int` to be accessed as `rand_mod::set_seed` and `rand_mod::rand_int`. The `seed` variable could also be accessed as `rand_mod::seed`, but this is probably not a good idea, and the need for the `rand_mod` prefix means it's unlikely to happen by accident.

---

7 Barbara Liskov (1939–), the principal designer of Clu, is one of the leading figures in the history of abstraction mechanisms. A faculty member at MIT since 1971, she was also the principal designer of the Argus programming language, which combined language and database technology to improve the reliability and programmability of distributed systems. She received the ACM Turing Award in 2008.

The need for the prefix can be eliminated, on a name-by-name basis, with a `using` directive:

```
using rand_mod::rand_int;
...
int r = rand_int();
```

Alternatively, the full set of names declared in a namespace can be made available at once:

```
using namespace rand_mod;
...
set_seed(12345);
int r = rand_int();
```

Unfortunately, such wholesale exposure of a module's names increases both the likelihood of conflict with names in the importing context and the likelihood that objects like `seed`, which are logically private to the module, will be accessed accidentally. ■

Imports and Exports

Some languages allow the programmer to specify that names exported from modules be usable only in restricted ways. Variables may be exported read-only, for example, or types may be exported *opaquely*, meaning that variables of that type may be declared, passed as arguments to the module's subroutines, and possibly compared or assigned to one another, but not manipulated in any other way.

Modules into which names must be explicitly imported are said to be *closed scopes*. By extension, modules that do not require imports are said to be *open scopes*. Imports serve to document the program: they increase modularity by requiring a module to specify the ways in which it depends on the rest of the program. They also reduce name conflicts by refraining from importing anything that isn't needed. Modules are closed in Modula (1, 2, and 3) and Haskell. C++ is representative of an increasingly common option, in which names are automatically exported, but are available on the outside only when *qualified* with the module name—unless they are explicitly "imported" by another scope (e.g., with the C++ `using` directive), at which point they are available unqualified. This option, which we might call *selectively open* modules, also appears in Ada, Java, C#, and Python, among others.

Modules as Managers

EXAMPLE 3.15
Module as "manager" for a type

Modules facilitate the construction of abstractions by allowing data to be made private to the subroutines that use them. When used as in Figure 3.6, however, each module defines a single abstraction. Continuing our previous example, there are times when it may be desirable to have more than one pseudorandom number generator. When debugging a game, for example, we might want to obtain deterministic (repeatable) behavior in one particular game module (a particular

```
#include <time.h>
namespace rand_mgr {
    const unsigned int a = 48271;
    const unsigned int m = 0x7fffffff;

    typedef struct {
        unsigned int seed;
    } generator;

    generator* create() {
        generator* g = new generator;
        g->seed = time(0);
        return g;
    }
    void set_seed(generator* g, unsigned int s) {
        g->seed = s;
    }
    unsigned int rand_int(generator* g) {
        return g->seed = (a * g->seed) % m;
    }
}
```

Figure 3.7 Manager module for pseudorandom numbers in C++.

character, perhaps), regardless of uses of pseudorandom numbers elsewhere in the program. If we want to have several generators, we can make our namespace a "manager" for instances of a generator *type*, which is then exported from the module, as shown in Figure 3.7. The manager idiom requires additional subroutines to create/initialize and possibly destroy generator instances, and it requires that every subroutine (`set_seed`, `rand_int`, `create`) take an extra parameter, to specify the generator in question.

Given the declarations in Figure 3.7, we could create and use an arbitrary number of generators:

```
using rand_mgr::generator;
generator *g1 = rand_mgr::create();
generator *g2 = rand_mgr::create();
...
using rand_mgr::rand_int;
int r1 = rand_int(g1);
int r2 = rand_int(g2);
```

In more complex programs, it may make sense for a module to export several related types, instances of which can then be passed to its subroutines.

3.3.5 Module Types and Classes

An alternative solution to the multiple instance problem appeared in Euclid, which treated each module as a *type*, rather than a simple encapsulation construct. Given a module type, the programmer could declare an arbitrary number of similar module objects. As it turns out, the classes of modern object-oriented languages are an extension of module types. Access to a module instance typically looks like access to an object, and we can illustrate the ideas in any object-oriented language. For our C++ pseudorandom number example, the syntax

EXAMPLE 3.16
A pseudorandom number generator type

```
generator *g = rand_mgr::create();
...
int r = rand_int(g);
```

might be replaced by

```
rand_gen *g = new rand_gen();
...
int r = g->rand_int();
```

where the `rand_gen` class is declared as in Figure 3.8. Module types or classes allow the programmer to think of the `rand_int` routine as "belonging to" the generator, rather than as a separate entity to which the generator must be passed

DESIGN & IMPLEMENTATION

3.5 Modules and separate compilation

One of the hallmarks of a good abstraction is that it tends to be useful in multiple contexts. To facilitate code reuse, many languages make modules the basis of separate compilation. Modula-2 actually provided two different kinds of modules: one (external modules) for separate compilation, the other (internal modules) for textual nesting within a larger scope. Experience with these options eventually led Niklaus Wirth, the designer of Modula-2, to conclude that external modules were by far the more useful variety; he omitted the internal version from his subsequent language, Oberon. Many would argue, however, that internal modules find their real utility only when extended with instantiation and inheritance. Indeed, as noted near the end of this section, many object-oriented languages provide both modules *and* classes. The former support separate compilation and serve to minimize name conflicts; the latter are for data abstraction.

To facilitate separate compilation, modules in many languages (Modula-2 and Oberon among them) can be divided into a declaration part (*header*) and an implementation part (*body*), each of which occupies a separate file. Code that uses the exports of a given module can be compiled as soon as the header exists; it is not dependent on the body. In particular, work on the bodies of cooperating modules can proceed concurrently once the headers exist. We will return to the subjects of separate compilation and code reuse in Sections C-3.8 and 10.1, respectively.

```
class rand_gen {
    unsigned int seed = time(0);
    const unsigned int a = 48271;
    const unsigned int m = 0x7fffffff;

public:
    void set_seed(unsigned int s) {
        seed = s;
    }
    unsigned int rand_int() {
        return seed = (a * seed) % m;
    }
};
```

Figure 3.8 Pseudorandom number generator class in C++.

as an argument. Conceptually, there is a dedicated `rand_int` routine for every generator (`rand_gen` object). In practice, of course, it would be highly wasteful to create multiple copies of the code. As we shall see in Chapter 10, `rand_gen` instances really share a single pair of `set_seed` and `rand_int` routines, and the compiler arranges for a pointer to the relevant instance to be passed to the routine as an extra, hidden parameter. The implementation turns out to be very similar to that of Figure 3.7, but the programmer need not think of it that way.

Object Orientation

The difference between module types and classes is a powerful pair of features found together in the latter but not the former—namely, *inheritance* and *dynamic method dispatch*.[8] Inheritance allows new classes to be defined as extensions or refinements of existing classes. Dynamic method dispatch allows a refined class to *override* the definition of an operation in its parent class, and for the choice among definitions to be made at run time, on the basis of whether a particular object belongs to the child class or merely to the parent.

Inheritance facilitates a programming style in which all or most operations are thought of as belonging to objects, and in which new objects can inherit many of their operations from existing objects, without the need to rewrite code. Classes have their roots in Simula-67, and were further developed in Smalltalk. They appear in many modern languages, including Eiffel, OCaml, C++, Java, C#, and several scripting languages, notably Python and Ruby. Inheritance mechanisms can also be found in certain languages that are not usually considered object-oriented, including Modula-3, Ada 95, and Oberon. We will examine inheritance, dynamic dispatch, and their impact on scope rules in Chapter 10 and in Section 14.4.4.

8 A few languages—notably members of the ML family—have module types with inheritance—but still without dynamic method dispatch. Modules in most languages are missing both features.

Module types and classes (ignoring issues related to inheritance) require only simple changes to the scope rules defined for modules in Section 3.3.4. Every instance `A` of a module type or class (e.g., every `rand_gen`) has a separate copy of the module or class's variables. These variables are then visible when executing one of `A`'s operations. They may also be indirectly visible to the operations of some other instance `B` if `A` is passed as a parameter to one of those operations. This rule makes it possible in most object-oriented languages to construct binary (or more-ary) operations that can manipulate the variables (fields) of more than one instance of a class.

Modules Containing Classes

EXAMPLE 3.17 Modules and classes in a large application

While there is a clear progression from modules to module types to classes, it is not necessarily the case that classes are an adequate replacement for modules in all cases. Suppose we are developing an interactive "first person" game. Class hierarchies may be just what we need to represent characters, possessions, buildings, goals, and a host of other data abstractions. At the same time, especially on a project with a large team of programmers, we will probably want to divide the functionality of the game into large-scale subsystems such as graphics and rendering, physics, and strategy. These subsystems are really not data abstractions, and we probably don't *want* the option to create multiple instances of them. They are naturally captured with traditional modules, particularly if those modules are designed for separate compilation (Section 3.8). Recognizing the need for both multi-instance abstractions and functional subdivision, many languages, including C++, Java, C#, Python, and Ruby, provide separate class and module mechanisms. ■

3.3.6 Dynamic Scoping

In a language with dynamic scoping, the bindings between names and objects depend on the flow of control at run time, and in particular on the order in which subroutines are called. In comparison to the static scope rules discussed in the previous section, dynamic scope rules are generally quite simple: the "current" binding for a given name is the one encountered most recently *during execution*, and not yet destroyed by returning from its scope.

Languages with dynamic scoping include APL, Snobol, Tcl, TEX (the typesetting language with which this book was created), and early dialects of Lisp [MAE+65, Moo78, TM81] and Perl.[9] Because the flow of control cannot in general be predicted in advance, the bindings between names and objects in a language with dynamic scoping cannot in general be determined by a compiler. As a

---

9 Scheme and Common Lisp are statically scoped, though the latter allows the programmer to specify dynamic scoping for individual variables. Static scoping was added to Perl in version 5; the programmer now chooses static or dynamic scoping explicitly in each variable declaration. (We consider this choice in more detail in Section 14.4.1.)

```
1.  n : integer                 -- global declaration

2.  procedure first()
3.      n := 1

4.  procedure second()
5.      n : integer             -- local declaration
6.      first()

7.  n := 2
8.  if read_integer() > 0
9.      second()
10. else
11.     first()
12. write_integer(n)
```

Figure 3.9 **Static versus dynamic scoping.** Program output depends on both scope rules and, in the case of dynamic scoping, a value read at run time.

result, many semantic rules in a language with dynamic scoping become a matter of dynamic semantics rather than static semantics. Type checking in expressions and argument checking in subroutine calls, for example, must in general be deferred until run time. To accommodate all these checks, languages with dynamic scoping tend to be interpreted, rather than compiled.

EXAMPLE 3.18
Static vs dynamic scoping

Consider the program in Figure 3.9. If static scoping is in effect, this program prints a 1. If dynamic scoping is in effect, the output depends on the value read at line 8 at run time: if the input is positive, the program prints a 2; otherwise it prints a 1. Why the difference? At issue is whether the assignment to the variable n at line 3 refers to the global variable declared at line 1 or to the local variable declared at line 5. Static scope rules require that the reference resolve to the closest lexically enclosing declaration, namely the global n. Procedure first changes n to 1, and line 12 prints this value. Dynamic scope rules, on the other hand, require that we choose the most recent, active binding for n at run time.

DESIGN & IMPLEMENTATION

3.6 Dynamic scoping

It is not entirely clear whether the use of dynamic scoping in Lisp and other early interpreted languages was deliberate or accidental. One reason to think that it may have been deliberate is that it makes it very easy for an interpreter to look up the meaning of a name: all that is required is a stack of declarations (we examine this stack more closely in Section C-3.4.2). Unfortunately, this simple implementation has a very high run-time cost, and experience indicates that dynamic scoping makes programs harder to understand. The modern consensus seems to be that dynamic scoping is usually a bad idea (see Exercise 3.17 and Exploration 3.36 for two exceptions).

We create a binding for `n` when we enter the main program. We create another when and if we enter procedure `second`. When we execute the assignment statement at line 3, the `n` to which we are referring will depend on whether we entered `first` through `second` or directly from the main program. If we entered through `second`, we will assign the value 1 to `second`'s local `n`. If we entered from the main program, we will assign the value 1 to the global `n`. In either case, the write at line 12 will refer to the global `n`, since `second`'s local `n` will be destroyed, along with its binding, when control returns to the main program. ■

EXAMPLE 3.19
Run-time errors with dynamic scoping

With dynamic scoping, errors associated with the referencing environment may not be detected until run time. In Figure 3.10, for example, the declaration of local variable `max_score` in procedure `foo` accidentally redefines a global variable used by function `scaled_score`, which is then called from `foo`. Since the global `max_score` is an integer, while the local `max_score` is a floating-point number, dynamic semantic checks in at least some languages will result in a type clash message at run time. If the local `max_score` had been an integer, no error would have been detected, but the program would almost certainly have produced incorrect results. This sort of error can be very hard to find. ■

3.4 Implementing Scope

To keep track of the names in a statically scoped program, a compiler relies on a data abstraction called a *symbol table*. In essence, the symbol table is a dictionary: it maps names to the information the compiler knows about them. The most basic operations are to insert a new mapping (a name-to-object binding) or to look up the information that is already present for a given name. Static scope rules add complexity by allowing a given name to correspond to different objects—and thus to different information—in different parts of the program. Most variations on static scoping can be handled by augmenting a basic dictionary-style symbol table with `enter_scope` and `leave_scope` operations to keep track of visibility. Nothing is ever deleted from the table; the entire structure is retained throughout compilation, and then saved for use by debuggers or run-time reflection (type lookup) mechanisms.

In a language with dynamic scoping, an interpreter (or the output of a compiler) must perform operations analogous to symbol table insert and lookup at run time. In principle, any organization used for a symbol table in a compiler could be used to track name-to-object bindings in an interpreter, and vice versa. In practice, implementations of dynamic scoping tend to adopt one of two specific organizations: an *association list* or a *central reference table*.

IN MORE DEPTH

A symbol table with visibility support can be implemented in several different ways. One appealing approach, due to LeBlanc and Cook [CL83], is described on the companion site, along with both association lists and central reference tables.

```
max_score : integer        -- maximum possible score

function scaled_score(raw_score : integer) : real
    return raw_score / max_score * 100
...
procedure foo()
    max_score : real := 0        -- highest percentage seen so far
    ...
    foreach student in class
        student.percent := scaled_score(student.points)
        if student.percent > max_score
            max_score := student.percent
```

Figure 3.10 **The problem with dynamic scoping.** Procedure scaled_score probably does not do what the programmer intended when dynamic scope rules allow procedure foo to change the meaning of max_score.

An association list (or *A-list* for short) is simply a list of name/value pairs. When used to implement dynamic scoping it functions as a stack: new declarations are pushed as they are encountered, and popped at the end of the scope in which they appeared. Bindings are found by searching down the list from the top. A central reference table avoids the need for linear-time search by maintaining an explicit mapping from names to their current meanings. Lookup is faster, but scope entry and exit are somewhat more complex, and it becomes substantially more difficult to save a referencing environment for future use (we discuss this issue further in Section 3.6.1).

3.5 The Meaning of Names within a Scope

So far in our discussion of naming and scopes we have assumed that there is a one-to-one mapping between names and visible objects at any given point in a program. This need not be the case. Two or more names that refer to the same object at the same point in the program are said to be *aliases.* A name that can refer to more than one object at a given point in the program is said to be *overloaded.* Overloading is in turn related to the more general subject of *polymorphism,* which allows a subroutine or other program fragment to behave in different ways depending on the types of its arguments.

3.5.1 Aliases

Simple examples of aliases occur in the variant records and unions of many programming languages (we will discuss these features detail in Section C-8.1.3).

They also arise naturally in programs that make use of pointer-based data structures. A more subtle way to create aliases in many languages is to pass a variable by reference to a subroutine that also accesses that variable directly. Consider the following code in C++:

EXAMPLE 3.20
Aliasing with parameters

```
double sum, sum_of_squares;
...
void accumulate(double& x) {        // x is passed by reference
    sum += x;
    sum_of_squares += x * x;
}
```

If we pass sum as an argument to accumulate, then sum and x will be aliases for one another inside the called routine, and the program will probably not do what the programmer intended. ■

As a general rule, aliases tend to make programs more confusing than they otherwise would be. They also make it much more difficult for a compiler to perform certain important code improvements. Consider the following C code:

EXAMPLE 3.21
Aliases and code improvement

```
int a, b, *p, *q;
...
a = *p;      /* read from the variable referred to by p */
*q = 3;      /* assign to the variable referred to by q */
b = *p;      /* read from the variable referred to by p */
```

DESIGN & IMPLEMENTATION

3.7 Pointers in C and Fortran

The tendency of pointers to introduce aliases is one of the reasons why Fortran compilers tended, historically, to produce faster code than C compilers: pointers are heavily used in C, but missing from Fortran 77 and its predecessors. It is only in recent years that sophisticated alias analysis algorithms have allowed C compilers to rival their Fortran counterparts in speed of generated code. Pointer analysis is sufficiently important that the designers of the C99 standard decided to add a new keyword to the language. The `restrict` qualifier, when attached to a pointer declaration, is an assertion on the part of the programmer that the object to which the pointer refers has no alias in the current scope. It is the programmer's responsibility to ensure that the assertion is correct; the compiler need not attempt to check it. C99 also introduced *strict aliasing*. This allows the compiler to assume that pointers of different types will never refer to the same location in memory. Most compilers provide a command-line option to disable optimizations that exploit this rule; otherwise (poorly written) legacy programs may behave incorrectly when compiled at higher optimization levels.

```
declare
    type month is (jan, feb, mar, apr, may, jun,
                   jul, aug, sep, oct, nov, dec);
    type print_base is (dec, bin, oct, hex);
    mo : month;
    pb : print_base;
begin
    mo := dec;        -- the month dec (since mo has type month)
    pb := oct;        -- the print_base oct (since pb has type print_base)
    print(oct);       -- error!  insufficient context
                      --         to decide which oct is intended
```

Figure 3.11 Overloading of enumeration constants in Ada.

The initial assignment to a will, on most machines, require that *p be loaded into a register. Since accessing memory is expensive, the compiler will want to hang on to the loaded value and reuse it in the assignment to b. It will be unable to do so, however, unless it can verify that p and q cannot refer to the same object—that is, that *p and *q are not aliases. While compile-time verification of this sort is possible in many common cases, in general it's undecidable.

3.5.2 Overloading

Most programming languages provide at least a limited form of overloading. In C, for example, the plus sign (+) is used to name several different functions, including signed and unsigned integer and floating-point addition. Most programmers don't worry about the distinction between these two functions—both are based on the same mathematical concept, after all—but they take arguments of different types and perform very different operations on the underlying bits. A slightly more sophisticated form of overloading appears in the enumeration constants of Ada. In Figure 3.11, the constants oct and dec refer either to months or to numeric bases, depending on the context in which they appear.

EXAMPLE 3.22
Overloaded enumeration constants in Ada

Within the symbol table of a compiler, overloading must be handled (*resolved*) by arranging for the lookup routine to return a *list* of possible meanings for the requested name. The semantic analyzer must then choose from among the elements of the list based on context. When the context is not sufficient to decide, as in the call to print in Figure 3.11, then the semantic analyzer must announce an error. Most languages that allow overloaded enumeration constants allow the programmer to provide appropriate context explicitly. In Ada, for example, one can say

EXAMPLE 3.23
Resolving ambiguous overloads

```
print(month'(oct));
```

In Modula 3 and C#, *every* use of an enumeration constant must be prefixed with a type name, even when there is no chance of ambiguity:

```
struct complex {
    double real, imaginary;
};
enum base {dec, bin, oct, hex};

int i;
complex x;

void print_num(int n) { ...
void print_num(int n, base b) { ...
void print_num(complex c) { ...

print_num(i);         // uses the first function above
print_num(i, hex);    // uses the second function above
print_num(x);         // uses the third function above
```

Figure 3.12 **Simple example of overloading in C++.** In each case the compiler can tell which function is intended by the number and types of arguments.

```
mo := month.dec;                  (* Modula-3 *)

pb = print_base.oct;              // C#
```

In C, one cannot overload enumeration constants at all; every constant visible in a given scope must be distinct. C++11 introduced new syntax to give the programmer control over this behavior: `enum` constants must be distinct; `enum class` constants must be qualified with the class name (e.g., month::oct). ■

EXAMPLE 3.24
Overloading in C++

Both Ada and C++ have elaborate facilities for overloading subroutine names. Many of the C++ facilities carry over to Java and C#. A given name may refer to an arbitrary number of subroutines in the same scope, so long as the subroutines differ in the number or types of their arguments. C++ examples appear in Figure 3.12. ■

Redefining Built-in Operators

EXAMPLE 3.25
Operator overloading in Ada

Many languages also allow the built-in arithmetic operators (`+`, `-`, `*`, etc.) to be overloaded with user-defined functions. Ada, C++, and C# do this by defining alternative *prefix* forms of each operator, and defining the usual infix forms to be abbreviations (or "syntactic sugar") for the prefix forms. In Ada, `A + B` is short for `"+"(A, B)`. If `"+"` (the prefix form) is overloaded, then `+` (the infix form) will work for the new types as well. It must be possible to resolve the overloading (determine which `+` is intended) from the types of `A` and `B`. ■

EXAMPLE 3.26
Operator overloading in C++

Fortran 90 provides a special `interface` construct that can be used to associate an operator with some named binary function. In C++ and C#, which are object-oriented, `A + B` may be short for either `operator+(A, B)` or `A.operator+(B)`. In the latter case, `A` is an instance of a class (module type) that defines an `operator+` function. In C++ one might say

```
class complex {
    double real, imaginary;
    ...
public:
    complex operator+(complex other) {
        return complex(real + other.real, imaginary + other.imaginary);
    }
    ...
};
...
complex A, B, C;
...
C = A + B;              // uses user-defined operator+
```

C# syntax is similar. ■

EXAMPLE 3.27
Infix operators in Haskell

In Haskell, user-defined infix operators are simply functions whose names consist of non-alphanumeric characters:

```
let a @@ b = a * 2 + b
```

Here we have defined a 2-argument operator named `@@`. We could also have declared it with the usual prefix notation, in which case we would have needed to enclose the name in parentheses:

```
let (@@) a b = a * 2 + b
```

Either way, both `3 @@ 4` and `(@@) 3 4` will evaluate to `10`. (An arbitrary function can also be used as infix operator in Haskell by enclosing its name in backquotes. With an appropriate definition, `gcd 8 12` and ``8 `gcd` 12`` will both evaluate to `4`.)

Unlike most languages, Haskell allows the programmer to specify both the associativity and the precedence of user-defined operators. We will return to this subject in Section 6.1.1. ■

EXAMPLE 3.28
Overloading with type classes

Both operators and ordinary functions can be overloaded in Haskell, using a mechanism known as *type classes*. Among the simplest of these is the class `Eq`, declared in the standard library as

DESIGN & IMPLEMENTATION

3.8 User-defined operators in OCaml

OCaml does not support overloading, but it does allow the user to create new operators, whose names—as in Haskell—consist of non-alphanumeric characters. Each such name must begin with the name of one of the built-in operators, from which the new operator inherits its syntactic role (prefix, infix, or postfix) and precedence. So, for example, `+.` is used for floating-point addition; `+/` is used for "bignum" (arbitrary precision) integer addition.

```
class Eq a, where
  (==) :: a -> a -> Bool
```

This declaration establishes Eq as the set of types that provide an == operator. Any instance of ==, for some particular type a, must take two arguments (each of type a) and return a Boolean result. In other words, == is an overloaded operator, supported by all types of class Eq; each such type must provide its own equality definition. The definition for integers, again from the standard library, looks like this:

```
instance Eq Integer where
  x == y = x `integerEq` y
```

Here integerEq is the built-in, non-overloaded integer equality operator. ■

Type classes can build upon themselves. The Haskell Ord class, for example, encompasses all Eq types that also support the operators <, >, <=, and >=. The Num class (simplifying a bit) encompasses all Eq types that also support addition, subtraction, and multiplication. In addition to making overloading a bit more explicit than it is in most languages, type classes make it possible to specify that certain polymorphic functions can be used only when their arguments are of a type that supports some particular overloaded function (for more on this subject, see Sidebar 7.7).

Related Concepts

When considering function and subroutine calls, it is important to distinguish overloading from the related concepts of *coercion* and *polymorphism*. All three can be used, in certain circumstances, to pass arguments of multiple types to (or return values of multiple types from) what appears to be a single named routine. The syntactic similarity, however, hides significant differences in semantics and pragmatics.

Coercion, which we will cover in more detail in Section 7.2.2, is the process by which a compiler automatically converts a value of one type into a value of another type when that second type is required by the surrounding context. Polymorphism, which we will consider in Sections 7.1.2, 7.3, 10.1.1, and 14.4.4, allows a single subroutine to accept arguments of multiple types.

EXAMPLE 3.29
Printing objects of multiple types

Consider a print routine designed to display its argument on the standard output stream, and suppose that we wish to be able to display objects of multiple types. With overloading, we might write a separate print routine for each type of interest. Then when it sees a call to print(my_object), the compiler would choose the appropriate routine based on the type of my_object.

Now suppose we already have a print routine that accepts a floating-point argument. With coercion, we might be able to print integers by passing them to this existing routine, rather than writing a new one. When it sees a call to print(my_integer), the compiler would coerce (convert) the argument automatically to floating-point type prior to the call.

Finally, suppose we have a language in which many types support a to_string operation that will generate a character-string representation of an object of that type. We might then be able to write a polymorphic print routine that accepts an argument of any type for which to_string is defined. The to_string operation might itself be polymorphic, built in, or simply overloaded; in any of these cases, print could call it and output the result.

In short, overloading allows the programmer to give the same name to multiple objects, and to disambiguate (*resolve*) them based on context—for subroutines, on the number or types of arguments. Coercion allows the compiler to perform an automatic type conversion to make an argument conform to the expected type of some existing routine. Polymorphism allows a single routine to accept arguments of multiple types, provided that it attempts to use them only in ways that their types support.

✓ CHECK YOUR UNDERSTANDING

21. Explain the importance of information hiding.
22. What is an *opaque* export?
23. Why might it be useful to distinguish between the *header* and the *body* of a module?
24. What does it mean for a scope to be *closed*?
25. Explain the distinction between "modules as managers" and "modules as types."
26. How do classes differ from modules?
27. Why might it be useful to have modules and classes in the same language?
28. Why does the use of dynamic scoping imply the need for run-time type checking?
29. Explain the purpose of a compiler's symbol table.
30. What are *aliases*? Why are they considered a problem in language design and implementation?
31. Explain the value of the `restrict` qualifier in C.
32. What is *overloading*? How does it differ from *coercion* and *polymorphism*?
33. What are *type classes* in Haskell? What purpose do they serve?

3.6 The Binding of Referencing Environments

We have seen in Section 3.3 how scope rules determine the referencing environment of a given statement in a program. Static scope rules specify that the referencing environment depends on the lexical nesting of program blocks in which names are declared. Dynamic scope rules specify that the referencing environment depends on the order in which declarations are encountered at run time. An additional issue that we have not yet considered arises in languages that allow one to create a *reference* to a subroutine—for example, by passing it as a parameter. When should scope rules be applied to such a subroutine: when the reference is first created, or when the routine is finally called? The answer is particularly important for languages with dynamic scoping, though we shall see that it matters even in languages with static scoping.

EXAMPLE 3.30
Deep and shallow binding

A dynamic scoping example appears as pseudocode in Figure 3.13. Procedure print_selected_records is assumed to be a general-purpose routine that knows how to traverse the records in a database, regardless of whether they represent people, sprockets, or salads. It takes as parameters a database, a predicate to make print/don't print decisions, and a subroutine that knows how to format the data in the records of this particular database. We have hypothesized that procedure print_person uses the value of nonlocal variable line_length to calculate the number and width of columns in its output. In a language with dynamic scoping, it is natural for procedure print_selected_records to declare and initialize this variable locally, knowing that code inside print_routine will pick it up if needed. For this coding technique to work, the referencing environment of print_routine must not be created until the routine is actually called by print_selected_records. This late binding of the referencing environment of a subroutine that has been passed as a parameter is known as *shallow binding*. It is usually the default in languages with dynamic scoping.

For function older_than_threshold, by contrast, shallow binding may not work well. If, for example, procedure print_selected_records happens to have a local variable named threshold, then the variable set by the main program to influence the behavior of older_than_threshold will not be visible when the function is finally called, and the predicate will be unlikely to work correctly. In such a situation, the code that originally passes the function as a parameter has a particular referencing environment (the current one) in mind; it does not want the routine to be called in any other environment. It therefore makes sense to bind the environment at the time the routine is first passed as a parameter, and then restore that environment when the routine is finally called. That is, we arrange for older_than_threshold to see, when it is eventually called, the same referencing environment it would have seen if it had been called at the point where the reference was created. This early binding of the referencing environment is known as *deep binding*. It is almost always the default in languages with static scoping, and is sometimes available as an option with dynamic scoping as well. ■

```
type person = record
    ...
    age : integer
    ...
threshold : integer
people : database

function older_than_threshold(p : person) : boolean
    return p.age ≥ threshold

procedure print_person(p : person)
    -- Call appropriate I/O routines to print record on standard output.
    -- Make use of nonlocal variable line_length to format data in columns.
    ...

procedure print_selected_records(db : database;
        predicate, print_routine : procedure)
    line_length : integer

    if device_type(stdout) = terminal
        line_length := 80
    else      -- Standard output is a file or printer.
        line_length := 132
    foreach record r in db
        -- Iterating over these may actually be
        -- a lot more complicated than a 'for' loop.
        if predicate(r)
            print_routine(r)

-- main program
...
threshold := 35
print_selected_records(people, older_than_threshold, print_person)
```

Figure 3.13 Program (in pseudocode) to illustrate the importance of binding rules. One might argue that deep binding is appropriate for the environment of function older_than_threshold (for access to threshold), while shallow binding is appropriate for the environment of procedure print_person (for access to line_length).

3.6.1 Subroutine Closures

Deep binding is implemented by creating an explicit representation of a referencing environment (generally the one in which the subroutine would execute if called at the present time) and bundling it together with a reference to the subroutine. The bundle as a whole is referred to as a *closure*. Usually the subroutine itself can be represented in the closure by a pointer to its code. In a language with dynamic scoping, the representation of the referencing environment depends on whether the language implementation uses an association list or a

```
def A(I, P):

    def B():
        print(I)

    # body of A:
    if I > 1:
        P()
    else:
        A(2, B)

def C():
    pass        # do nothing

A(1, C)         # main program
```

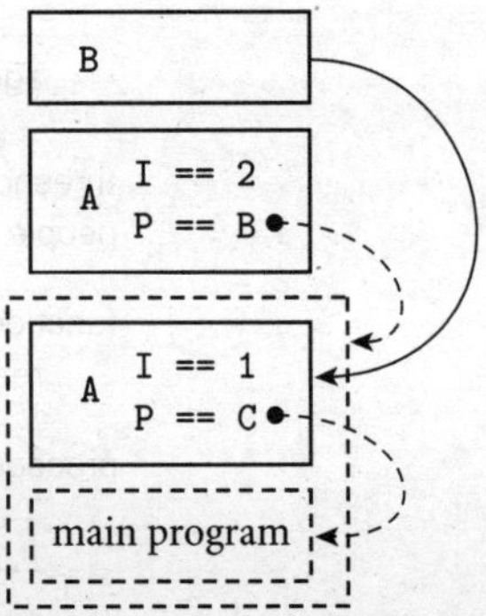

Figure 3.14 Deep binding in Python. At right is a conceptual view of the run-time stack. Referencing environments captured in closures are shown as dashed boxes and arrows. When `B` is called via formal parameter `P`, two instances of `I` exist. Because the closure for `P` was created in the initial invocation of `A`, `B`'s static link (solid arrow) points to the frame of that earlier invocation. `B` uses that invocation's instance of `I` in its `print` statement, and the output is a `1`.

central reference table for run-time lookup of names; we consider these alternatives at the end of Section C-3.4.2.

In early dialects of Lisp, which used dynamic scoping, deep binding was available via the built-in primitive `function`, which took a function as its argument and returned a closure whose referencing environment was the one in which the function would have executed if called at that moment in time. The closure could then be passed as a parameter to another function. If and when it was eventually called, it would execute in the saved environment. (Closures work slightly differently from "bare" functions in most Lisp dialects: they must be called by passing them to the built-in primitives `funcall` or `apply`.)

At first glance, one might be tempted to think that the binding time of referencing environments would not matter in a language with static scoping. After all, the meaning of a statically scoped name depends on its lexical nesting, not on the flow of execution, and this nesting is the same whether it is captured at the time a subroutine is passed as a parameter or at the time the subroutine is called. The catch is that a running program may have more than one *instance* of an object that is declared within a recursive subroutine. A closure in a language with static scoping captures the current instance of every object, at the time the closure is created. When the closure's subroutine is called, it will find these captured instances, even if newer instances have subsequently been created by recursive calls.

EXAMPLE 3.31 Binding rules with static scoping

One could imagine combining static scoping with shallow binding [VF82], but the combination does not seem to make much sense, and does not appear to have been adopted in any language. Figure 3.14 contains a Python program that illustrates the impact of binding rules in the presence of static scoping. This program prints a 1. With shallow binding it would print a 2. ■

It should be noted that binding rules matter with static scoping only when accessing objects that are neither local nor global, but are defined at some intermediate level of nesting. If an object is local to the currently executing subroutine, then it does not matter whether the subroutine was called directly or through a closure; in either case local objects will have been created when the subroutine started running. If an object is global, there will never be more than one instance, since the main body of the program is not recursive. Binding rules are therefore irrelevant in languages like C, which has no nested subroutines, or Modula-2, which allows only outermost subroutines to be passed as parameters, thus ensuring that any variable defined outside the subroutine is global. (Binding rules are also irrelevant in languages like PL/I and Ada 83, which do not permit subroutines to be passed as parameters at all.)

Suppose then that we have a language with static scoping in which nested subroutines can be passed as parameters, with deep binding. To represent a closure for subroutine *S*, we can simply save a pointer to *S*'s code together with the static link that *S* would use if it were called right now, in the current environment. When *S* is finally called, we temporarily restore the saved static link, rather than creating a new one. When *S* follows its static chain to access a nonlocal object, it will find the object instance that was current at the time the closure was created. This instance may not have the *value* it had at the time the closure was created, but its identity, at least, will reflect the intent of the closure's creator.

3.6.2 First-Class Values and Unlimited Extent

In general, a value in a programming language is said to have *first-class* status if it can be passed as a parameter, returned from a subroutine, or assigned into a variable. Simple types such as integers and characters are first-class values in most programming languages. By contrast, a "second-class" value can be passed as a parameter, but not returned from a subroutine or assigned into a variable, and a "third-class" value cannot even be passed as a parameter. As we shall see in Section 9.3.2, labels (in languages that have them) are usually third-class values, but they are second-class values in Algol. Subroutines display the most variation. They are first-class values in all functional programming languages and most scripting languages. They are also first-class values in C# and, with some restrictions, in several other imperative languages, including Fortran, Modula-2 and -3, Ada 95, C, and C++.[10] They are second-class values in most other imperative languages, and third-class values in Ada 83.

Our discussion of binding so far has considered only second-class subroutines. First-class subroutines in a language with nested scopes introduce an additional level of complexity: they raise the possibility that a reference to a subroutine may

---

10 Some authors would say that first-class status requires anonymous function definitions—lambda expressions—that can be embedded in other expressions. C#, several scripting languages, and all functional languages meet this requirement, but many imperative languages do not.

EXAMPLE 3.32 Returning a first-class subroutine in Scheme

outlive the execution of the scope in which that routine was declared. Consider the following example in Scheme:

```
1. (define plus-x
2.   (lambda (x)
3.     (lambda (y) (+ x y))))
4. ...
5. (let ((f (plus-x 2)))
6.   (f 3))                   ; returns 5
```

Here the `let` construct on line 5 declares a new function, `f`, which is the result of calling `plus-x` with argument 2. Function `plus-x` is defined at line 1. It returns the (unnamed) function declared at line 3. But that function refers to parameter `x` of `plus-x`. When `f` is called at line 6, its referencing environment will include the `x` in `plus-x`, despite the fact that `plus-x` has already returned (see Figure 3.15). Somehow we must ensure that `x` remains available. ■

If local objects were destroyed (and their space reclaimed) at the end of each scope's execution, then the referencing environment captured in a long-lived closure might become full of dangling references. To avoid this problem, most functional languages specify that local objects have *unlimited extent*: their lifetimes continue indefinitely. Their space can be reclaimed only when the garbage collection system is able to prove that they will never be used again. Local objects (other than `own`/`static` variables) in most imperative languages have *limited extent*: they are destroyed at the end of their scope's execution. (C# and Smalltalk are exceptions to the rule, as are most scripting languages.) Space for local objects with limited extent can be allocated on a stack. Space for local objects with unlimited extent must generally be allocated on a heap.

Given the desire to maintain stack-based allocation for the local variables of subroutines, imperative languages with first-class subroutines must generally adopt alternative mechanisms to avoid the dangling reference problem for closures. C and (pre-Fortran 90) Fortran, of course, do not have nested subroutines. Modula-2 allows references to be created only to outermost subroutines (outermost routines are first-class values; nested routines are third-class values). Modula-3 allows nested subroutines to be passed as parameters, but only outer-

DESIGN & IMPLEMENTATION

3.9 Binding rules and extent

Binding mechanisms and the notion of extent are closely tied to implementation issues. A-lists make it easy to build closures (Section C-3.4.2), but so do the non-nested subroutines of C and the rule against passing nonglobal subroutines as parameters in Modula-2. In a similar vein, the lack of first-class subroutines in many imperative languages reflects in large part the desire to avoid heap allocation, which would be needed for local variables with unlimited extent.

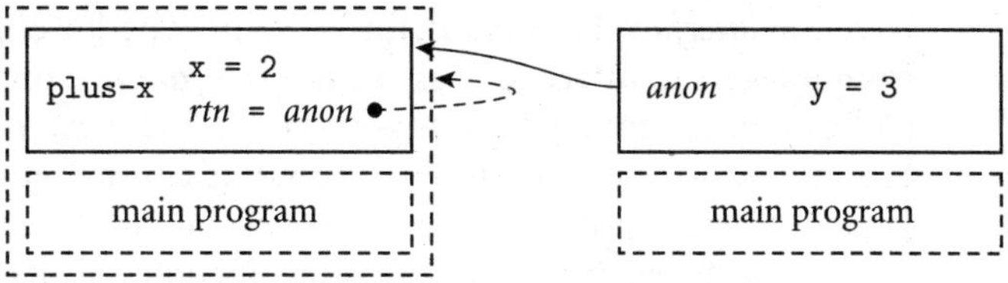

Figure 3.15 **The need for unlimited extent.** When function `plus-x` is called in Example 3.32, it returns (left side of the figure) a closure containing an anonymous function. The referencing environment of that function encompasses both `plus-x` and `main`—including the local variables of `plus-x` itself. When the anonymous function is subsequently called (right side of the figure), it must be able to access variables in the closure's environment—in particular, the `x` inside `plus-x`—despite the fact that `plus-x` is no longer active.

most routines to be returned or stored in variables (outermost routines are first-class values; nested routines are second-class values). Ada 95 allows a nested routine to be returned, but only if the scope in which it was declared is the same as, or larger than, the scope of the declared return type. This containment rule, while more conservative than strictly necessary (it forbids the Ada equivalent of Figure 3.14), makes it impossible to propagate a subroutine reference to a portion of the program in which the routine's referencing environment is not active.

3.6.3 Object Closures

As noted in Section 3.6.1, the referencing environment in a closure will be non-trivial only when passing a nested subroutine. This means that the implementation of first-class subroutines is trivial in a language without nested subroutines. At the same time, it means that a programmer working in such a language is missing a useful feature: the ability to pass a subroutine *with context*. In object-oriented languages, there is an alternative way to achieve a similar effect: we can encapsulate our subroutine as a method of a simple object, and let the object's fields hold context for the method. In Java we might write the equivalent of Example 3.32 as follows:

EXAMPLE 3.33
An object closure in Java

```
interface IntFunc {
    public int call(int i);
}
class PlusX implements IntFunc {
    final int x;
    PlusX(int n) { x = n; }
    public int call(int i) { return i + x; }
}
...
IntFunc f = new PlusX(2);
System.out.println(f.call(3));      // prints 5
```

Here the *interface* IntFunc defines a static type for objects enclosing a function from integers to integers. Class PlusX is a concrete implementation of this type, and can be instantiated for any integer constant x. Where the Scheme code in Example 3.32 captured x in the subroutine closure returned by (plus-x 2), the Java code here captures x in the object closure returned by new PlusX(2). ■

An object that plays the role of a function and its referencing environment may variously be called an *object closure*, a *function object*, or a *functor*. (This is unrelated to use of the term *functor* in Prolog, ML, or Haskell.) In C#, a first-class subroutine is an instance of a *delegate* type:

EXAMPLE 3.34
Delegates in C#

```
delegate int IntFunc(int i);
```

This type can be instantiated for any subroutine that matches the specified argument and return types. That subroutine may be static, or it may be a method of some object:

```
static int Plus2(int i)  return i + 2;
...
IntFunc f = new IntFunc(Plus2);
Console.WriteLine(f(3));          // prints 5

class PlusX
    int x;
    public PlusX(int n)  x = n;
    public int call(int i)  return i + x;

...
IntFunc g = new IntFunc(new PlusX(2).call);
Console.WriteLine(g(3));          // prints 5
```

■

EXAMPLE 3.35
Delegates and unlimited extent

Remarkably, though C# does not permit subroutines to nest in the general case, it does allow delegates to be instantiated in-line from *anonymous* (unnamed) methods. These allow us to mimic the code of Example 3.32:

```
static IntFunc PlusY(int y) {
    return delegate(int i) { return i + y; };
}
...
IntFunc h = PlusY(2);
```

Here y has unlimited extent! The compiler arranges to allocate it in the heap, and to refer to it indirectly through a hidden pointer, included in the closure. This implementation incurs the cost of dynamic storage allocation (and eventual garbage collection) only when it is needed; local variables remain in the stack in the common case. ■

EXAMPLE 3.36
Function objects in C++

Object closures are sufficiently important that some languages support them with special syntax. In C++, an object of a class that overrides operator() can be called as if it were a function:

```
class int_func {
public:
    virtual int operator()(int i) = 0;
};
class plus_x : public int_func {
    const int x;
public:
    plus_x(int n) : x(n) { }
    virtual int operator()(int i) { return i + x; }
};
...
plus_x f(2);
cout << f(3) << "\n";                    // prints 5
```

Object `f` could also be passed to any function that expected a parameter of class `int_func`.

3.6.4 Lambda Expressions

In most of our examples so far, closures have corresponded to subroutines that were declared—and named—in the usual way. In the Scheme code of Example 3.32, however, we saw an anonymous function—a *lambda expression*. Similarly, in Example 3.35, we saw an anonymous delegate in C#. That example can be made even simpler using C#'s lambda syntax:

EXAMPLE 3.37
A lambda expression in C#

```
static IntFunc PlusY(int y) {
    return i => i + y;
}
```

Here the keyword `delegate` of Example 3.35 has been replaced by an `=>` sign that separates the anonymous function's parameter list (in this case, just `i`) from its body (the expression `i + y`). In a function with more than one parameter, the parameter list would be parenthesized; in a longer, more complicated function, the body could be a code block, with one or more explicit `return` statements.

The term "lambda expression" comes from the *lambda calculus*, a formal notation for functional programming that we will consider in more detail in Chapter 11. As one might expect, lambda syntax varies quite a bit from one language to another:

EXAMPLE 3.38
Variety of lambda syntax

```
(lambda (i j) (> i j) i j)              ; Scheme

(int i, int j) => i > j ? i : j         // C#

fun i j -> if i > j then i else j       (* OCaml *)

->(i, j){ i > j ? i : j }               # Ruby
```

Each of these expressions evaluates to the larger of two parameters.

In Scheme and OCaml, which are predominately functional languages, a lambda expression simply *is* a function, and can be called in the same way as any other function:

```
; Scheme:
((lambda (i j) (> i j) i j) 5 8)              ; evaluates to 8

(* OCaml: *)
(fun i j -> if i > j then i else j) 5 8      (* likewise *)
```

In Ruby, which is predominately imperative, a lambda expression must be called explicitly:

```
print ->(i, j){ i > j ? i : j }.call(5, 8)
```

In C#, the expression must be assigned into a variable (or passed into a parameter) before it can be invoked:

```
Func<int, int, int> m = (i, j) => i > j ? i : j;
Console.WriteLine(m.Invoke(5, 8));
```

Here `Func<int, int, int>` is how one names the type of a function taking two integer parameters and returning an integer result. ■

In functional programming languages, lambda expressions make it easy to manipulate functions as values—to combine them in various ways to create new functions on the fly. This sort of manipulation is less common in imperative languages, but even there, lambda expressions can help encourage code reuse and generality. One particularly common idiom is the *callback*—a subroutine, passed into a library, that allows the library to "call back" into the main program when appropriate. Examples of callbacks include a comparison operator passed into a sorting routine, a predicate used to filter elements of a collection, or a handler to be called in response to some future event (see Section 9.6.2).

With the increasing popularity of first-class subroutines, lambda expressions have even made their way into C++, where the lack of garbage collection and the emphasis on stack-based allocation make it particularly difficult to solve the problem of variable capture. The adopted solution, in keeping with the nature of the language, stresses efficiency and expressiveness more than run-time safety.

EXAMPLE 3.39
A simple lambda expression in C++11

In the simple case, no capture of nonlocal variables is required. If `V` is a vector of integers, the following will print all elements less than 50:

```
for_each(V.begin(), V.end(),
    [](int e){ if (e < 50) cout << e << " "; }
);
```

Here `for_each` is a standard library routine that applies its third parameter—a function—to every element of a collection in the range specified by its first two parameters. In our example, the function is denoted by a lambda expression, introduced by the empty square brackets. The compiler turns the lambda expression into an anonymous function, which is then passed to `for_each` via C++'s usual mechanism—a simple pointer to the code. ■

EXAMPLE 3.40
Variable capture in C++ lambda expressions

Suppose, however, that we wanted to print all elements less than `k`, where `k` is a variable outside the scope of the lambda expression. We now have two options in C++:

```
[=](int e){ if (e < k) cout << e << " "; }

[&](int e){ if (e < k) cout << e << " "; }
```

Both of these cause the compiler to create an object closure (a *function object* in C++), which could be passed to (and called from) `for_each` in the same way as an ordinary function. The difference between the two options is that `[=]` arranges for a copy of each captured variable to be placed in the object closure; `[&]` arranges for a reference to be placed there instead. The programmer must choose between these options. Copying can be expensive for large objects, and any changes to the object made after the closure is created will not be seen by the code of the lambda expression when it finally executes. References allow changes to be seen, but will lead to undefined (and presumably incorrect) behavior if the closure's lifetime exceeds that of the captured object: C++ does *not* have unlimited extent. In particularly complex situations, the programmer can specify capture on an object-by-object basis:

```
[j, &k](int e){ ...    // capture j's value and a reference to k,
                       // so they can be used in here
```
■

DESIGN & IMPLEMENTATION

3.10 Functions and function objects

The astute reader may be wondering: In Example 3.40, how does `for_each` manage to "do the right thing" with two different implementations of its third parameter? After all, sometimes that parameter is implemented as a simple pointer; other times it is a pointer to an object with an `operator()`, which requires a different kind of call. The answer is that `for_each` is a *generic* routine (a *template* in C++). The compiler generates customized implementations of `for_each` on demand. We will discuss generics in more detail in Section 7.3.1.

In some situations, it may be difficult to use generics to distinguish among "function-like" parameters. As an alternative, C++ provides a standard `function` *class*, with constructors that allow it to be instantiated from a function, a function pointer, a function object, or a manually created object closure. Something like `for_each` could then be written as an ordinary (nongeneric) subroutine whose third parameter was a object of class `function`. In any given call, the compiler would coerce the provided argument to be a function object.

EXAMPLE 3.41
Lambda expressions in Java 8

Lambda expressions appear in Java 8 as well, but in a restricted form. In situations where they might be useful, Java has traditionally relied on an idiom known as a *functional interface*. The `Arrays.sort` routine, for example, expects a parameter of type `Comparator`. To sort an array of personnel records by age, we would (traditionally) have written

```
class AgeComparator implements Comparator<Person> {
    public int compare(Person p1, Person p2) {
        return Integer.compare(p1.age, p2.age);
    }
}
Person[] People = ...
...
Arrays.sort(People, new AgeComparator());
```

Significantly, `Comparator` has only a single abstract method: the `compare` routine provided by our `AgeComparator` class. With lambda expressions in Java 8, we can omit the declaration of `AgeComparator` and simply write

```
Arrays.sort(People, (p1, p2) -> Integer.compare(p1.age, p2.age));
```

The key to the simpler syntax is that `Comparator` is a functional interface, and thus has only a single abstract method. When a variable or formal parameter is declared to be of some functional interface type, Java 8 allows a lambda expression whose parameter and return types match those of the interface's single method to be assigned into the variable or passed as the parameter. In effect, the compiler uses the lambda expression to create an instance of an anonymous class that implements the interface. ■

As it turns out, coercion to functional interface types is the *only* use of lambda expressions in Java. In particular, lambda expressions have no types of their own: they are not really objects, and cannot be directly manipulated. Their behavior with respect to variable capture is entirely determined by the usual rules for nested classes. We will consider these rules in more detail in Section 10.2.3; for now, suffice it to note that Java, like C++, does not support unlimited extent.

3.7 Macro Expansion

EXAMPLE 3.42
A simple assembly macro

Prior to the development of high-level programming languages, assembly language programmers could find themselves writing highly repetitive code. To ease the burden, many assemblers provided sophisticated *macro expansion* facilities. Consider the task of loading an element of a two-dimensional array from memory into a register. As we shall see in Section 8.2.3, this operation can easily require half a dozen instructions, with details depending on the hardware instruction set; the size of the array elements; and whether the indices are constants, values in memory, or values in registers. In many early assemblers, one could define a macro that would replace an expression like ld2d(target_reg, array_name, row, column, row_size, element_size) with the appropriate multi-instruction sequence. In a numeric program containing hundreds or thousands of array access operations, this macro could prove extremely useful.

EXAMPLE 3.43
Preprocessor macros in C

When C was created in the early 1970s, it was natural to include a macro preprocessing facility:

```
#define LINE_LEN 80
#define DIVIDES(a,n) (!((n) % (a)))
    /* true iff n has zero remainder modulo a */
#define SWAP(a,b) {int t = (a); (a) = (b); (b) = t;}
#define MAX(a,b) ((a) > (b) ? (a) : (b))
```

Macros like `LINE_LEN` avoided the need (in early versions of C) to support named constants in the language itself. Perhaps more important, parameterized macros like `DIVIDES`, `MAX`, and `SWAP` were much more efficient than equivalent C functions. They avoided the overhead of the subroutine call mechanism (including register saves and restores), and the code they generated could be integrated into any code improvements that the compiler was able to effect in the code surrounding the call.

EXAMPLE 3.44
"Gotchas" in C macros

Unfortunately, C macros suffer from several limitations, all of which stem from the fact that they are implemented by textual substitution, and are not understood by the rest of the compiler. Put another way, they provide a naming and binding mechanism that is separate from—and often at odds with—the rest of the programming language.

In the definition of `DIVIDES`, the parentheses around the occurrences of `a` and `n` are essential. Without them, `DIVIDES(y + z, x)` would be replaced by `(!(x % y + z))`, which is the same as `(!((x % y) + z))`, according to the rules of precedence. In a similar vein, `SWAP` may behave unexpectedly if the programmer writes `SWAP(x, t)`: textual substitution of arguments allows the macro's declaration of `t` to *capture* the `t` that was passed. `MAX(x++, y++)` may also behave unexpectedly, since the increment side effects will happen more than once. Unfortunately,

DESIGN & IMPLEMENTATION

3.11 Generics as macros

In some sense, the ability to import names into an ordinary module provides a primitive sort of generic facility. A stack module that imports its element type, for example, can be inserted (with a text editor) into any context in which the appropriate type name has been declared, and will produce a "customized" stack for that context when compiled. Early versions of C++ formalized this mechanism by using macros to implement templates. Later versions of C++ have made templates (generics) a fully supported language feature, giving them much of the flavor of hygienic macros. (More on templates and on *template metaprogramming* can be found in Section C-7.3.2.)

in standard C we cannot avoid the extra side effects by assigning the parameters into temporary variables: a C macro that "returns" a value must be an expression, and declarations are one of many language constructs that cannot appear inside (see also Exercise 3.23). ■

Modern languages and compilers have, for the most part, abandoned macros as an anachronism. Named constants are type-safe and easy to implement, and *in-line* subroutines (to be discussed in Section 9.2.4) provide almost all the performance of parameterized macros without their limitations. A few languages (notably Scheme and Common Lisp) take an alternative approach, and integrate macros into the language in a safe and consistent way. So-called *hygienic* macros implicitly encapsulate their arguments, avoiding unexpected interactions with associativity and precedence. They rename variables when necessary to avoid the capture problem, and they can be used in any expression context. Unlike subroutines, however, they are expanded during semantic analysis, making them generally unsuitable for unbounded recursion. Their appeal is that, like all macros, they take *unevaluated* arguments, which they evaluate lazily on demand. Among other things, this means that they preserve the multiple side effect "gotcha" of our `MAX` example. Delayed evaluation was a bug in this context, but can sometimes be a feature. We will return to it in Sections 6.1.5 (short-circuit Boolean evaluation), 9.3.2 (call-by-name parameters), and 11.5 (normal-order evaluation in functional programming languages).

✓ CHECK YOUR UNDERSTANDING

34. Describe the difference between deep and shallow *binding* of referencing environments.

35. Why are binding rules particularly important for languages with dynamic scoping?

36. What are *first-class* subroutines? What languages support them?

37. What is a *subroutine closure*? What is it used for? How is it implemented?

38. What is an *object closure*? How is it related to a subroutine closure?

39. Describe how the *delegates* of C# extend and unify both subroutine and object closures.

40. Explain the distinction between limited and unlimited *extent* of objects in a local scope.

41. What is a *lambda expression*? How does the support for lambda expressions in functional languages compare to that of C# or Ruby? To that of C++ or Java?

42. What are *macros*? What was the motivation for including them in C? What problems may they cause?

3.8 Separate Compilation

Since most large programs are constructed and tested incrementally, and since the compilation of a very large program can be a multihour operation, any language designed to support large programs must provide for separate compilation.

IN MORE DEPTH

On the companion site we consider the relationship between modules and separate compilation. Because they are designed for encapsulation and provide a narrow interface, modules are the natural choice for the "compilation units" of many programming languages. The separate module headers and bodies of Modula-3 and Ada, for example, are explicitly intended for separate compilation, and reflect experience gained with more primitive facilities in other languages. C and C++, by contrast, must maintain backward compatibility with mechanisms designed in the early 1970s. Modern versions of C and C++ include a *namespace* mechanism that provides module-like data hiding, but names must still be declared before they are used in every compilation unit, and the mechanisms used to accommodate this rule are purely a matter of convention. Java and C# break with the C tradition by requiring the compiler to infer header information automatically from separately compiled class definitions; no header files are required.

3.9 Summary and Concluding Remarks

This chapter has addressed the subject of names, and the *binding* of names to objects (in a broad sense of the word). We began with a general discussion of the notion of *binding time*—the time at which a name is associated with a particular object or, more generally, the time at which an answer is associated with any open question in language or program design or implementation. We defined the notion of *lifetime* for both objects and name-to-object bindings, and noted that they need not be the same. We then introduced the three principal storage allocation mechanisms—static, stack, and heap—used to manage space for objects.

In Section 3.3 we described how the binding of names to objects is governed by *scope rules*. In some languages, scope rules are dynamic: the meaning of a name is found in the most recently entered scope that contains a declaration and that has not yet been exited. In most modern languages, however, scope rules are static, or *lexical*: the meaning of a name is found in the closest lexically surrounding scope that contains a declaration. We found that lexical scope rules vary in important but sometimes subtle ways from one language to another. We considered what sorts of scopes are allowed to nest, whether scopes are *open* or *closed*, whether the scope of a name encompasses the entire block in which it is declared, and whether a name must be declared before it is used. We explored the implementation of scope rules in Section 3.4.

In Section 3.5 we examined several ways in which bindings relate to one another. Aliases arise when two or more names in a given scope are bound to the same object. Overloading arises when one name is bound to multiple objects. We noted that while behavior reminiscent of overloading can sometimes be achieved through coercion or polymorphism, the underlying mechanisms are really very different. In Section 3.6 we considered the question of when to bind a referencing environment to a subroutine that is passed as a parameter, returned from a function, or stored in a variable. Our discussion touched on the notions of *closures* and *lambda expressions*, both of which will appear repeatedly in later chapters. In Sections 3.7 and 3.8 we considered macros and separate compilation.

Some of the more complicated aspects of lexical scoping illustrate the evolution of language support for data abstraction, a subject to which we will return in Chapter 10. We began by describing the `own` or `static` variables of languages like Fortran, Algol 60, and C, which allow a variable that is local to a subroutine to retain its value from one invocation to the next. We then noted that simple modules can be seen as a way to make long-lived objects local to a group of subroutines, in such a way that they are not visible to other parts of the program. By selectively exporting names, a module may serve as the "manager" for one or more abstract data types. At the next level of complexity, we noted that some languages treat modules *as* types, allowing the programmer to create an arbitrary number of instances of the abstraction defined by a module. Finally, we noted that object-oriented languages extend the module-as-type approach (as well as the notion of lexical scope) by providing an inheritance mechanism that allows new abstractions (classes) to be defined as extensions or refinements of existing classes.

Among the topics considered in this chapter, we saw several examples of useful features (recursion, static scoping, forward references, first-class subroutines, unlimited extent) that have been omitted from certain languages because of concern for their implementation complexity or run-time cost. We also saw an example of a feature (the private part of a module specification) introduced expressly to facilitate a language's implementation, and another (separate compilation in C) whose design was clearly intended to mirror a particular implementation. In several additional aspects of language design (late vs early binding, static vs dynamic scoping, support for coercions and conversions, toleration of pointers and other aliases), we saw that implementation issues play a major role.

In a similar vein, apparently simple language rules can have surprising implications. In Section 3.3.3, for example, we considered the interaction of whole-block scope with the requirement that names be declared before they can be used. Like the `do` loop syntax and white space rules of Fortran (Section 2.2.2) or the `if... then... else` syntax of Pascal (Section 2.3.2), poorly chosen scoping rules can make program analysis difficult not only for the compiler, but for human beings as well. In future chapters we shall see several additional examples of features that are both confusing and hard to compile. Of course, semantic utility and ease of implementation do not always go together. Many easy-to-compile features (e.g., `goto` statements) are of questionable value at best. We will also see several examples of highly useful and (conceptually) simple features, such as garbage collection (Section 8.5.3) and unification (Sections 7.2.4, C-7.3.2, and 12.2.1), whose implementations are quite complex.

3.10 Exercises

3.1 Indicate the binding time (when the language is designed, when the program is linked, when the program begins execution, etc.) for each of the following decisions in your favorite programming language and implementation. Explain any answers you think are open to interpretation.

- The number of built-in functions (math, type queries, etc.)
- The variable declaration that corresponds to a particular variable reference (use)
- The maximum length allowed for a constant (literal) character string
- The referencing environment for a subroutine that is passed as a parameter
- The address of a particular library routine
- The total amount of space occupied by program code and data

3.2 In Fortran 77, local variables were typically allocated statically. In Algol and its descendants (e.g., Ada and C), they are typically allocated in the stack. In Lisp they are typically allocated at least partially in the heap. What accounts for these differences? Give an example of a program in Ada or C that would not work correctly if local variables were allocated statically. Give an example of a program in Scheme or Common Lisp that would not work correctly if local variables were allocated on the stack.

3.3 Give two examples in which it might make sense to delay the binding of an implementation decision, even though sufficient information exists to bind it early.

3.4 Give three concrete examples drawn from programming languages with which you are familiar in which a variable is live but not in scope.

3.5 Consider the following pseudocode:

```
procedure main()
    a : integer := 1
    b : integer := 2

    procedure middle()
        b : integer := a

        procedure inner()
            print a, b
```

```
        a : integer := 3

        -- body of middle
        inner()
        print a, b

    -- body of main
    middle()
    print a, b
```

Suppose this was code for a language with the declaration-order rules of C (but with nested subroutines)—that is, names must be declared before use, and the scope of a name extends from its declaration through the end of the block. At each print statement, indicate which declarations of a and b are in the referencing environment. What does the program print (or will the compiler identify static semantic errors)? Repeat the exercise for the declaration-order rules of C# (names must be declared before use, but the scope of a name is the entire block in which it is declared) and of Modula-3 (names can be declared in any order, and their scope is the entire block in which they are declared).

3.6 Consider the following pseudocode, assuming nested subroutines and static scope:

```
procedure main()
    g : integer

    procedure B(a : integer)
        x : integer

        procedure A(n : integer)
            g := n

        procedure R(m : integer)
            write_integer(x)
            x /:= 2 -- integer division
            if x > 1
                R(m + 1)
            else
                A(m)

        -- body of B
        x := a × a
        R(1)

    -- body of main
    B(3)
    write_integer(g)
```

(a) What does this program print?

```
typedef struct list_node {
    void* data;
    struct list_node* next;
} list_node;

list_node* insert(void* d, list_node* L) {
    list_node* t = (list_node*) malloc(sizeof(list_node));
    t->data = d;
    t->next = L;
    return t;
}

list_node* reverse(list_node* L) {
    list_node* rtn = 0;
    while (L) {
        rtn = insert(L->data, rtn);
        L = L->next;
    }
    return rtn;
}

void delete_list(list_node* L) {
    while (L) {
        list_node* t = L;
        L = L->next;
        free(t->data);
        free(t);
    }
}
```

Figure 3.16 List management routines for Exercise 3.7.

(b) Show the frames on the stack when A has just been called. For each frame, show the static and dynamic links.

(c) Explain how A finds g.

3.7 As part of the development team at MumbleTech.com, Janet has written a list manipulation library for C that contains, among other things, the code in Figure 3.16.

(a) Accustomed to Java, new team member Brad includes the following code in the main loop of his program:

```
list_node* L = 0;
while (more_widgets()) {
    L = insert(next_widget(), L);
}
L = reverse(L);
```

Sadly, after running for a while, Brad's program always runs out of memory and crashes. Explain what's going wrong.

(b) After Janet patiently explains the problem to him, Brad gives it another try:

```
list_node* L = 0;
while (more_widgets()) {
        L = insert(next_widget(), L);
}
list_node* T = reverse(L);
delete_list(L);
L = T;
```

This seems to solve the insufficient memory problem, but where the program used to produce correct results (before running out of memory), now its output is strangely corrupted, and Brad goes back to Janet for advice. What will she tell him this time?

3.8 Rewrite Figures 3.6 and 3.7 in C. You will need to use separate compilation for name hiding.

3.9 Consider the following fragment of code in C:

```
{   int a, b, c;
    ...
    {   int d, e;
        ...
        {   int f;
            ...
        }
        ...
    }
    ...
    {   int g, h, i;
        ...
    }
    ...
}
```

(a) Assume that each integer variable occupies four bytes. How much total space is required for the variables in this code?

(b) Describe an algorithm that a compiler could use to assign stack frame offsets to the variables of arbitrary nested blocks, in a way that minimizes the total space required.

3.10 Consider the design of a Fortran 77 compiler that uses static allocation for the local variables of subroutines. Expanding on the solution to the previous question, describe an algorithm to minimize the total space required for these variables. You may find it helpful to construct a *call graph* data structure in which each node represents a subroutine, and each directed arc indicates that the subroutine at the tail may sometimes call the subroutine at the head.

3.11 Consider the following pseudocode:

```
procedure P(A, B : real)
    X : real

    procedure Q(B, C : real)
        Y : real
        ...

    procedure R(A, C : real)
        Z : real
        ...                         -- (*)
    ...
```

Assuming static scope, what is the referencing environment at the location marked by (*)?

3.12 Write a simple program in Scheme that displays three different behaviors, depending on whether we use `let`, `let*`, or `letrec` to declare a given set of names. (Hint: To make good use of `letrec`, you will probably want your names to be functions [`lambda` expressions].)

3.13 Consider the following program in Scheme:

```
(define A
  (lambda()
    (let* ((x 2)
           (C (lambda (P)
                (let ((x 4))
                  (P))))
           (D (lambda ()
                x))
           (B (lambda ()
                (let ((x 3))
                  (C D)))))
      (B))))
```

What does this program print? What would it print if Scheme used dynamic scoping and shallow binding? Dynamic scoping and deep binding? Explain your answers.

3.14 Consider the following pseudocode:

```
x : integer        -- global

procedure set_x(n : integer)
    x := n
```

```
procedure print_x()
    write_integer(x)

procedure first()
    set_x(1)
    print_x()

procedure second()
    x : integer
    set_x(2)
    print_x()

set_x(0)
first()
print_x()
second()
print_x()
```

What does this program print if the language uses static scoping? What does it print with dynamic scoping? Why?

3.15 The principal argument in *favor* of dynamic scoping is that it facilitates the customization of subroutines. Suppose, for example, that we have a library routine print_integer that is capable of printing its argument in any of several bases (decimal, binary, hexadecimal, etc.). Suppose further that we want the routine to use decimal notation most of the time, and to use other bases only in a few special cases: we do not want to have to specify a base explicitly on each individual call. We can achieve this result with dynamic scoping by having print_integer obtain its base from a nonlocal variable print_base. We can establish the default behavior by declaring a variable print_base and setting its value to 10 in a scope encountered early in execution. Then, any time we want to change the base temporarily, we can write

```
begin       -- nested block
    print_base : integer := 16      -- use hexadecimal
    print_integer(n)
```

The problem with this argument is that there are usually other ways to achieve the same effect, without dynamic scoping. Describe at least two for the print_integer example.

3.16 As noted in Section 3.6.3, C# has unusually sophisticated support for first-class subroutines. Among other things, it allows *delegates* to be instantiated from anonymous nested methods, and gives local variables and parameters unlimited extent when they may be needed by such a delegate. Consider the implications of these features in the following C# program:

```
using System;
public delegate int UnaryOp(int n);
   // type declaration: UnaryOp is a function from ints to ints

public class Foo {
    static int a = 2;
    static UnaryOp b(int c) {
        int d = a + c;
        Console.WriteLine(d);
        return delegate(int n) { return c + n; };
    }
    public static void Main(string[] args) {
        Console.WriteLine(b(3)(4));
    }
}
```

What does this program print? Which of `a`, `b`, `c`, and `d`, if any, is likely to be statically allocated? Which could be allocated on the stack? Which would need to be allocated in the heap? Explain.

3.17 If you are familiar with structured exception handling, as provided in Ada, C++, Java, C#, ML, Python, or Ruby, consider how this mechanism relates to the issue of scoping. Conventionally, a `raise` or `throw` statement is thought of as referring to an exception, which it passes as a parameter to a handler-finding library routine. In each of the languages mentioned, the exception itself must be declared in some surrounding scope, and is subject to the usual static scope rules. Describe an alternative point of view, in which the `raise` or `throw` is actually a reference to a *handler*, to which it transfers control directly. Assuming this point of view, what are the scope rules for handlers? Are these rules consistent with the rest of the language? Explain. (For further information on exceptions, see Section 9.4.)

3.18 Consider the following pseudocode:

```
x : integer      -- global

procedure set_x(n : integer)
    x := n

procedure print_x()
    write_integer(x)

procedure foo(S, P : function; n : integer)
    x : integer := 5
    if n in {1, 3}
        set_x(n)
    else
        S(n)
```

```
    if n in {1, 2}
        print_x()
    else
        P

set_x(0); foo(set_x, print_x, 1); print_x()
set_x(0); foo(set_x, print_x, 2); print_x()
set_x(0); foo(set_x, print_x, 3); print_x()
set_x(0); foo(set_x, print_x, 4); print_x()
```

Assume that the language uses dynamic scoping. What does the program print if the language uses shallow binding? What does it print with deep binding? Why?

3.19 Consider the following pseudocode:

```
x : integer := 1
y : integer := 2

procedure add()
    x := x + y

procedure second(P : procedure)
    x : integer := 2
    P()

procedure first
    y : integer := 3
    second(add)

first()
write_integer(x)
```

(a) What does this program print if the language uses static scoping?

(b) What does it print if the language uses dynamic scoping with deep binding?

(c) What does it print if the language uses dynamic scoping with shallow binding?

3.20 Consider mathematical operations in a language like C++, which supports both overloading and coercion. In many cases, it may make sense to provide multiple, overloaded versions of a function, one for each numeric type or combination of types. In other cases, we might use a single version—probably defined for double-precision floating point arguments—and rely on coercion to allow that function to be used for other numeric types (e.g., integers). Give an example in which overloading is clearly the preferable approach. Give another in which coercion is almost certainly better.

3.21 In a language that supports operator overloading, build support for rational numbers. Each number should be represented internally as a (numerator, denominator) pair in simplest form, with a positive denominator. Your code should support unary negation and the four standard arithmetic operators. For extra credit, create a conversion routine that accepts two floating-point parameters—a value and a error bound—and returns the simplest (smallest denominator) rational number within the given error bound of the given value.

3.22 In an imperative language with lambda expressions (e.g., C#, Ruby, C++, or Java), write the following higher-level functions. (A higher-level function, as we shall see in Chapter 11, takes other functions as argument and/or returns a function as a result.)

- `compose(g, f)`—returns a function `h` such that `h(x) == g(f(x))`.
- `map(f, L)`—given a function `f` and a list `L` returns a list `M` such that the *i*th element of `M` is `f(`*e*`)`, where *e* is the *i*th element of `L`.
- `filter(L, P)`—given a list `L` and a predicate (Boolean-returning function) `P`, returns a list containing all and only those elements of `L` for which `P` is true.

Ideally, your code should work for any argument or list element type.

3.23 Can you write a macro in standard C that "returns" the greatest common divisor of a pair of arguments, without calling a subroutine? Why or why not?

3.24–3.31 In More Depth.

3.11 Explorations

3.32 Experiment with naming rules in your favorite programming language. Read the manual, and write and compile some test programs. Does the language use lexical or dynamic scoping? Can scopes nest? Are they open or closed? Does the scope of a name encompass the entire block in which it is declared, or only the portion after the declaration? How does one declare mutually recursive types or subroutines? Can subroutines be passed as parameters, returned from functions, or stored in variables? If so, when are referencing environments bound?

3.33 List the keywords (reserved words) of one or more programming languages. List the predefined identifiers. (Recall that every keyword is a separate token. An identifier cannot have the same spelling as a keyword.) What criteria do you think were used to decide which names should be keywords and which should be predefined identifiers? Do you agree with the choices? Why or why not?

3.34 If you have experience with a language like C, C++, or Rust, in which dynamically allocated space must be manually reclaimed, describe your experience with dangling references or memory leaks. How often do these bugs arise? How do you find them? How much effort does it take? Learn about open-source or commercial tools for finding storage bugs (*Valgrind* is a popular open-source example). Do such tools weaken the argument for automatic garbage collection?

3.35 A few languages—notably Euclid and Turing, make every subroutine a closed scope, and require it to explicitly import any nonlocal names it uses. The import lists can be thought of as explicit, mandatory documentation of a part of the subroutine interface that is usually implicit. The use of import lists also makes it easy for Euclid and Turing to prohibit passing a variable, by reference, to a subroutine that also accesses that variable directly, thereby avoiding the errors alluded to in Example 3.20.

In programs you have written, how hard would it have been to document every use of a nonlocal variable? Would the effort be worth the improvement in the quality of documentation and error rates?

3.36 We learned in Section 3.3.6 that modern languages have generally abandoned dynamic scoping. One place it can still be found is in the so-called *environment variables* of the Unix programming environment. If you are not familiar with these, read the manual page for your favorite shell (command interpreter—`ksh`/`bash`, `csh`/`tcsh`, etc.) to learn how these behave. Explain why the usual alternatives to dynamic scoping (default parameters and static variables) are not appropriate in this case.

3.37 Compare the mechanisms for overloading of enumeration names in Ada and in Modula-3 or C# (Section 3.5.2). One might argue that the (historically more recent) Modula-3/C# approach moves responsibility from the compiler to the programmer: it requires even an unambiguous use of an enumeration constant to be annotated with its type. Why do you think this approach was chosen by the language designers? Do you agree with the choice? Why or why not?

3.38 Learn about *tied variables* in Perl. These allow the programmer to associate an ordinary variable with an (object-oriented) object in such a way that operations on the variable are automatically interpreted as method invocations on the object. As an example, suppose we write `tie $my_var, "my_class";`. The interpreter will create a new object of class `my_class`, which it will associate with scalar variable `$my_var`. For purposes of discussion, call that object *O*. Now, any attempt to read the value of `$my_var` will be interpreted as a call to method *O*`->FETCH()`. Similarly, the assignment `$my_var = `*value* will be interpreted as a call to *O*`->STORE(`*value*`)`. Array, hash, and filehandle variables, which support a larger set of built-in operations, provide access to a larger set of methods when tied.

Compare Perl's tying mechanism to the operator overloading of C++. Which features of each language can be conveniently emulated by the other?

3.39 Do you think coercion is a good idea? Why or why not?

3.40 The syntax for lambda expressions in Ruby evolved over time, with the result that there are now four ways to pass a *block* into a method as a closure:

by placing it after the end of the argument list (in which case it become an extra, final parameter); by passing it to `Proc.new`; or, within the argument list, by prefixing it with the keyword `lambda` or by writing it in `->` lambda notation. Investigate these options. Which came first? Which came later? What are their comparative advantages? Are their any minor differences in their behavior?

3.41 Lambda expressions were a late addition to the Java programming language: they were strongly resisted for many years. Research the controversy surrounding them. Where do your sympathies lie? What alternative proposals were rejected? Do you find any of them appealing?

3.42 Give three examples of features that are *not* provided in some language with which you are familiar, but that are common in other languages. Why do you think these features are missing? Would they complicate the implementation of the language? If so, would the complication (in your judgment) be justified?

3.43–3.47 In More Depth.

3.12 Bibliographic Notes

This chapter has traced the evolution of naming and scoping mechanisms through a very large number of languages, including Fortran (several versions), Basic, Algol 60 and 68, Pascal, Simula, C and C++, Euclid, Turing, Modula (1, 2, and 3), Ada (83 and 95), Oberon, Eiffel, Perl, Tcl, Python, Ruby, Rust, Java, and C#. Bibliographic references for all of these can be found in Appendix A.

Both modules and objects trace their roots to Simula, which was developed by Dahl, Nygaard, Myhrhaug, and others at the Norwegian Computing Center in the mid-1960s. (Simula I was implemented in 1964; descriptions in this book pertain to Simula 67.) The encapsulation mechanisms of Simula were refined in the 1970s by the developers of Clu, Modula, Euclid, and related languages. Other Simula innovations—inheritance and dynamic method binding in particular—provided the inspiration for Smalltalk, the original and arguably purest of the object-oriented languages. Modern object-oriented languages, including Eiffel, C++, Java, C#, Python, and Ruby, represent to a large extent a reintegration of the evolutionary lines of encapsulation on the one hand and inheritance and dynamic method binding on the other.

The notion of information hiding originates in Parnas's classic paper, "On the Criteria to be Used in Decomposing Systems into Modules" [Par72]. Comparative discussions of naming, scoping, and abstraction mechanisms can be found, among other places, in Liskov et al.'s discussion of Clu [LSAS77], Liskov and Guttag's text [LG86, Chap. 4], the Ada Rationale [IBFW91, Chaps. 9–12], Harbison's text on Modula-3 [Har92, Chaps. 8–9], Wirth's early work on modules [Wir80], and his later discussion of Modula and Oberon [Wir88a, Wir07]. Further information on object-oriented languages can be found in Chapter 10.

For a detailed discussion of overloading and polymorphism, see the survey by Cardelli and Wegner [CW85]. Cailliau [Cai82] provides a lighthearted discussion of many of the scoping pitfalls noted in Section 3.3.3. Abelson and Sussman [AS96, p. 11n] attribute the term "syntactic sugar" to Peter Landin.

Lambda expressions for C++ are described in the paper of Järvi and Freeman [JF10]. Lambda expressions for Java were developed under JSR 335 of the Java Community Process (documentation at *jcp.org*).

4 Semantic Analysis

In Chapter 2 we considered the topic of programming language syntax. In the current chapter we turn to the topic of semantics. Informally, syntax concerns the *form* of a valid program, while semantics concerns its *meaning*. Meaning is important for at least two reasons: it allows us to enforce rules (e.g., type consistency) that go beyond mere form, and it provides the information we need in order to generate an equivalent output program.

It is conventional to say that the syntax of a language is precisely that portion of the language definition that can be described conveniently by a context-free grammar, while the semantics is that portion of the definition that cannot. This convention is useful in practice, though it does not always agree with intuition. When we require, for example, that the number of arguments contained in a call to a subroutine match the number of formal parameters in the subroutine definition, it is tempting to say that this requirement is a matter of syntax. After all, we can count arguments without knowing what they mean. Unfortunately, we cannot count them with context-free rules. Similarly, while it is possible to write a context-free grammar in which every function must contain at least one `return` statement, the required complexity makes this strategy very unattractive. In general, any rule that requires the compiler to compare things that are separated by long distances, or to count things that are not properly nested, ends up being a matter of semantics.

Semantic rules are further divided into *static* and *dynamic* semantics, though again the line between the two is somewhat fuzzy. The compiler enforces static semantic rules at compile time. It generates code to enforce dynamic semantic rules at run time (or to call library routines that do so). Certain errors, such as division by zero, or attempting to index into an array with an out-of-bounds subscript, cannot in general be caught at compile time, since they may occur only for certain input values, or certain behaviors of arbitrarily complex code. In special cases, a compiler may be able to tell that a certain error will always or never occur, regardless of run-time input. In these cases, the compiler can generate an error message at compile time, or refrain from generating code to perform the check at run time, as appropriate. Basic results from computability theory, however, tell us that no algorithm can make these predictions correctly for arbitrary programs:

there will inevitably be cases in which an error will always occur, but the compiler cannot tell, and must delay the error message until run time; there will also be cases in which an error can never occur, but the compiler cannot tell, and must incur the cost of unnecessary run-time checks.

Both semantic analysis and intermediate code generation can be described in terms of annotation, or *decoration* of a parse tree or syntax tree. The annotations themselves are known as *attributes*. Numerous examples of static and dynamic semantic rules will appear in subsequent chapters. In this current chapter we focus primarily on the mechanisms a compiler uses to enforce the static rules. We will consider intermediate code generation (including the generation of code for dynamic semantic checks) in Chapter 15.

In Section 4.1 we consider the role of the semantic analyzer in more detail, considering both the rules it needs to enforce and its relationship to other phases of compilation. Most of the rest of the chapter is then devoted to the subject of *attribute grammars*. Attribute grammars provide a formal framework for the decoration of a tree. This framework is a useful conceptual tool even in compilers that do not build a parse tree or syntax tree as an explicit data structure. We introduce the notion of an attribute grammar in Section 4.2. We then consider various ways in which such grammars can be applied in practice. Section 4.3 discusses the issue of *attribute flow*, which constrains the order(s) in which nodes of a tree can be decorated. In practice, most compilers require decoration of the parse tree (or the evaluation of attributes that would reside in a parse tree if there were one) to occur in the process of an LL or LR parse. Section 4.4 presents *action routines* as an ad hoc mechanism for such "on-the-fly" evaluation. In Section 4.5 (mostly on the companion site) we consider the management of space for parse tree attributes.

Because they have to reflect the structure of the CFG, parse trees tend to be very complicated (recall the example in Figure 1.5). Once parsing is complete, we typically want to replace the parse tree with a syntax tree that reflects the input program in a more straightforward way (Figure 1.6). One particularly common compiler organization uses action routines during parsing solely for the purpose of constructing the syntax tree. The syntax tree is then decorated during a separate traversal, which can be formalized, if desired, with a separate attribute grammar. We consider the decoration of syntax trees in Section 4.6.

4.1 The Role of the Semantic Analyzer

Programming languages vary dramatically in their choice of semantic rules. Lisp dialects, for example, allow "mixed-mode" arithmetic on arbitrary numeric types, which they will automatically promote from integer to rational to floating-point or "bignum" (extended) precision, as required to maintain precision. Ada, by contract, assigns a specific type to every numeric variable, and requires the programmer to convert among these explicitly when combining them in expressions.

Languages also vary in the extent to which they require their implementations to perform dynamic checks. At one extreme, C requires no checks at all, beyond those that come "free" with the hardware (e.g., division by zero, or attempted access to memory outside the bounds of the program). At the other extreme, Java takes great pains to check as many rules as possible, in part to ensure that an untrusted program cannot do anything to damage the memory or files of the machine on which it runs. The role of the semantic analyzer is to enforce all static semantic rules and to annotate the program with information needed by the intermediate code generator. This information includes both clarifications (this is floating-point addition, not integer; this is a reference to the global variable `x`) and requirements for dynamic semantic checks.

In the typical compiler, analysis and intermediate code generation mark the end of *front end* computation. The exact division of labor between the front end and the back end, however, may vary from compiler to compiler: it can be hard to say exactly where analysis (figuring out what the program means) ends and synthesis (expressing that meaning in some new form) begins (and as noted in Section 1.6 there may be a "middle end" in between). Many compilers also carry a program through more than one intermediate form. In one common organization, described in more detail in Chapter 15, the semantic analyzer creates an annotated syntax tree, which the intermediate code generator then translates into a linear form reminiscent of the assembly language for some idealized machine. After machine-independent code improvement, this linear form is then translated into yet another form, patterned more closely on the assembly language of the target machine. That form may undergo machine-specific code improvement.

Compilers also vary in the extent to which semantic analysis and intermediate code generation are interleaved with parsing. With fully separated phases, the parser passes a full parse tree on to the semantic analyzer, which converts it to a syntax tree, fills in the symbol table, performs semantic checks, and passes it on to the code generator. With fully interleaved phases, there may be no need to build either the parse tree or the syntax tree in its entirety: the parser can call semantic check and code generation routines on the fly as it parses each expression, statement, or subroutine of the source. We will focus on an organization in which construction of the syntax tree is interleaved with parsing (and the parse tree is not built), but semantic analysis occurs during a separate traversal of the syntax tree.

Dynamic Checks

Many compilers that generate code for dynamic checks provide the option of disabling them if desired. It is customary in some organizations to enable dynamic checks during program development and testing, and then disable them for production use, to increase execution speed. The wisdom of this practice is questionable: Tony Hoare, one of the key figures in programming language design,[1] has likened the programmer who disables semantic checks to a sailing enthusiast who wears a life jacket when training on dry land, but removes it when going to sea [Hoa89, p. 198]. Errors may be less likely in production use than they are in testing, but the consequences of an undetected error are significantly worse. Moreover, on modern processors it is often possible for dynamic checks to execute in pipeline slots that would otherwise go unused, making them virtually free. On the other hand, some dynamic checks (e.g., ensuring that pointer arithmetic in C remains within the bounds of an array) are sufficiently expensive that they are rarely implemented.

Assertions

When reasoning about the correctness of their algorithms (or when formally proving properties of programs via axiomatic semantics) programmers frequently write logical *assertions* regarding the values of program data. Some programming languages make these assertions a part of the language syntax. The compiler then generates code to check the assertions at run time. An assertion is a statement that a specified condition is expected to be true when execution reaches a certain point in the code. In Java one can write

EXAMPLE 4.1
Assertions in Java

DESIGN & IMPLEMENTATION

4.1 Dynamic semantic checks

In the past, language theorists and researchers in programming methodology and software engineering tended to argue for more extensive semantic checks, while "real-world" programmers "voted with their feet" for languages like C and Fortran, which omitted those checks in the interest of execution speed. As computers have become more powerful, and as companies have come to appreciate the enormous costs of software maintenance, the "real-world" camp has become much more sympathetic to checking. Languages like Ada and Java have been designed from the outset with safety in mind, and languages like C and C++ have evolved (to the extent possible) toward increasingly strict definitions. In scripting languages, where many semantic checks are deferred until run time in order to avoid the need for explicit types and variable declarations, there has been a similar trend toward stricter rules. Perl, for example (one of the older scripting languages), will typically attempt to infer a possible meaning for expressions (e.g., `3 + "four"`) that newer languages (e.g., Python or Ruby) will flag as run-time errors.

---

1 Among other things, C. A. R. Hoare (1934–) invented the quicksort algorithm and the `case` statement, contributed to the design of Algol W, and was one of the leaders in the development of axiomatic semantics. In the area of concurrent programming, he refined and formalized the *monitor* construct (to be described in Section 13.4.1), and designed the CSP programming model and notation. He received the ACM Turing Award in 1980.

```
assert denominator != 0;
```

An `AssertionError` exception will be thrown if the semantic check fails at run time.

Some languages (e.g., Euclid, Eiffel, and Ada 2012) also provide explicit support for *invariants*, *preconditions*, and *postconditions*. These are essentially structured assertions. An invariant is expected to be true at all "clean points" of a given body of code. In Eiffel, the programmer can specify an invariant on the data inside a class: the invariant will be checked, automatically, at the beginning and end of each of the class's methods (subroutines). Similar invariants for loops are expected to be true before and after every iteration. Pre- and postconditions are expected to be true at the beginning and end of subroutines, respectively. In Euclid, a postcondition, specified once in the header of a subroutine, will be checked not only at the end of the subroutine's text, but at every `return` statement as well.

EXAMPLE 4.2
Assertions in C

Many languages support assertions via standard library routines or macros. In C, for example, one can write

```
assert(denominator != 0);
```

If the assertion fails, the program will terminate abruptly with the message

```
myprog.c:42: failed assertion `denominator != 0'
```

The C manual requires `assert` to be implemented as a macro (or built into the compiler) so that it has access to the textual representation of its argument, and to the file name and line number on which the call appears.

Assertions, of course, could be used to cover the other three sorts of checks, but not as clearly or succinctly. Invariants, preconditions, and postconditions are a prominent part of the header of the code to which they apply, and can cover a potentially large number of places where an assertion would otherwise be required. Euclid and Eiffel implementations allow the programmer to disable assertions and related constructs when desired, to eliminate their run-time cost.

Static Analysis

In general, compile-time algorithms that predict run-time behavior are known as *static analysis*. Such analysis is said to be *precise* if it allows the compiler to determine whether a given program will always follow the rules. Type checking, for example, is static and precise in languages like Ada and ML: the compiler ensures that no variable will ever be used at run time in a way that is inappropriate for its type. By contrast, languages like Lisp, Smalltalk, Python, and Ruby obtain greater flexibility, while remaining completely type-safe, by accepting the run-time overhead of dynamic type checks. (We will cover type checking in more detail in Chapter 7.)

Static analysis can also be useful when it isn't precise. Compilers will often check what they can at compile time and then generate code to check the rest dynamically. In Java, for example, type checking is mostly static, but dynamically loaded classes and type casts may require run-time checks. In a similar vein, many compilers perform extensive static analysis in an attempt to eliminate the need for dynamic checks on array subscripts, variant record tags, or potentially dangling pointers (to be discussed in Chapter 8).

If we think of the omission of unnecessary dynamic checks as a performance optimization, it is natural to look for other ways in which static analysis may enable code improvement. We will consider this topic in more detail in Chapter 17. Examples include *alias analysis*, which determines when values can be safely cached in registers, computed "out of order," or accessed by concurrent threads; *escape analysis*, which determines when all references to a value will be confined to a given context, allowing the value to be allocated on the stack instead of the heap, or to be accessed without locks; and *subtype analysis*, which determines when a variable in an object-oriented language is guaranteed to have a certain subtype, so that its methods can be called without dynamic dispatch.

An optimization is said to be *unsafe* if it may lead to incorrect code in certain programs. It is said to be *speculative* if it usually improves performance, but may degrade it in certain cases. A compiler is said to be *conservative* if it applies optimizations only when it can guarantee that they will be both safe and effective. By contrast, an *optimistic* compiler may make liberal use of speculative optimizations. It may also pursue unsafe optimizations by generating two versions of the code, with a dynamic check that chooses between them based on information not available at compile time. Examples of speculative optimization include *nonbinding prefetches*, which try to bring data into the cache before they are needed, and *trace scheduling*, which rearranges code in hopes of improving the performance of the processor pipeline and the instruction cache.

To eliminate dynamic checks, language designers may choose to tighten semantic rules, banning programs for which conservative analysis fails. The ML type system, for example (Section 7.2.4), avoids the dynamic type checks of Lisp, but disallows certain useful programming idioms that Lisp supports. Similarly, the *definite assignment* rules of Java and C# (Section 6.1.3) allow the compiler to ensure that a variable is always given a value before it is used in an expression, but disallow certain programs that are legal (and correct) in C.

4.2 Attribute Grammars

EXAMPLE 4.3

Bottom-up CFG for constant expressions

In Chapter 2 we learned how to use a context-free grammar to specify the syntax of a programming language. Here, for example, is an LR (bottom-up) grammar for arithmetic expressions composed of constants, with precedence and associativity:[2]

2 The addition of semantic rules tends to make attribute grammars quite a bit more verbose than context-free grammars. For the sake of brevity, many of the examples in this chapter use very short symbol names: *E* instead of *expr*, *TT* instead of *term_tail*.

$E \longrightarrow E$ + T
$E \longrightarrow E$ - T
$E \longrightarrow T$
$T \longrightarrow T$ * F
$T \longrightarrow T$ / F
$T \longrightarrow F$
$F \longrightarrow$ - F
$F \longrightarrow$ (E)
$F \longrightarrow$ const

EXAMPLE 4.4
Bottom-up AG for constant expressions

This grammar will generate all properly formed constant expressions over the basic arithmetic operators, but it says nothing about their meaning. To tie these expressions to mathematical concepts (as opposed to, say, floor tile patterns or dance steps), we need additional notation. The most common is based on *attributes*. In our expression grammar, we can associate a val attribute with each E, T, F, and const in the grammar. The intent is that for any symbol S, S.val will be the meaning, as an arithmetic value, of the token string derived from S. We assume that the val of a const is provided to us by the scanner. We must then invent a set of rules for each production, to specify how the vals of different symbols are related. The resulting *attribute grammar* (AG) is shown in Figure 4.1.

In this simple grammar, every production has a single rule. We shall see more complicated grammars later, in which productions can have several rules. The rules come in two forms. Those in productions 3, 6, 8, and 9 are known as *copy rules*; they specify that one attribute should be a copy of another. The other rules invoke *semantic functions* (sum, quotient, additive_inverse, etc.). In this example, the semantic functions are all familiar arithmetic operations. In general, they can be arbitrarily complex functions specified by the language designer. Each semantic function takes an arbitrary number of arguments (each of which must be an attribute of a symbol in the current production—no global variables are allowed), and each computes a single result, which must likewise be assigned into an attribute of a symbol in the current production. When more than one symbol of a production has the same name, subscripts are used to distinguish them. These subscripts are solely for the benefit of the semantic functions; they are not part of the context-free grammar itself.

In a strict definition of attribute grammars, copy rules and semantic function calls are the only two kinds of permissible rules. In our examples we use a ▷ symbol to introduce each code fragment corresponding to a single rule. In practice, it is common to allow rules to consist of small fragments of code in some well-defined notation (e.g., the language in which a compiler is being written), so that simple semantic functions can be written out "in-line." In this relaxed notation, the rule for the first production in Figure 4.1 might be simply E_1.val := E_2.val + T.val. As another example, suppose we wanted to count the elements of a comma-separated list:

EXAMPLE 4.5
Top-down AG to count the elements of a list

1. $E_1 \longrightarrow E_2$ + T ▷ E_1.val := sum(E_2.val, T.val)
2. $E_1 \longrightarrow E_2$ - T ▷ E_1.val := difference(E_2.val, T.val)
3. $E \longrightarrow T$ ▷ E.val := T.val
4. $T_1 \longrightarrow T_2$ * F ▷ T_1.val := product(T_2.val, F.val)
5. $T_1 \longrightarrow T_2$ / F ▷ T_1.val := quotient(T_2.val, F.val)
6. $T \longrightarrow F$ ▷ T.val := F.val
7. $F_1 \longrightarrow$ - F_2 ▷ F_1.val := additive_inverse(F_2.val)
8. $F \longrightarrow$ (E) ▷ F.val := E.val
9. $F \longrightarrow$ const ▷ F.val := const.val

Figure 4.1 **A simple attribute grammar for constant expressions, using the standard arithmetic operations.** Each semantic rule is introduced by a ▷ sign.

$L \longrightarrow$ id LT ▷ L.c := 1 + LT.c
$LT \longrightarrow$, L ▷ LT.c := L.c
$LT \longrightarrow \epsilon$ ▷ LT.c := 0

Here the rule on the first production sets the c (count) attribute of the left-hand side to one more than the count of the tail of the right-hand side. Like explicit semantic functions, in-line rules are not allowed to refer to any variables or attributes outside the current production. We will relax this restriction when we introduce action routines in Section 4.4. ■

Neither the notation for semantic functions (whether in-line or explicit) nor the types of the attributes themselves is intrinsic to the notion of an attribute grammar. The purpose of the grammar is simply to associate meaning with the nodes of a parse tree or syntax tree. Toward that end, we can use any notation and types whose meanings are already well defined. In Examples 4.4 and 4.5, we associated numeric values with the symbols in a CFG—and thus with parse tree nodes—using semantic functions drawn from ordinary arithmetic. In a compiler or interpreter for a full programming language, the attributes of tree nodes might include

- for an identifier, a reference to information about it in the symbol table
- for an expression, its type
- for a statement or expression, a reference to corresponding code in the compiler's intermediate form
- for almost any construct, an indication of the file name, line, and column where the corresponding source code begins
- for any internal node, a list of semantic errors found in the subtree below

For purposes other than translation—e.g., in a theorem prover or machine-independent language definition—attributes might be drawn from the disciplines of *denotational*, *operational*, or *axiomatic* semantics. Interested readers can find references in the Bibliographic Notes at the end of the chapter.

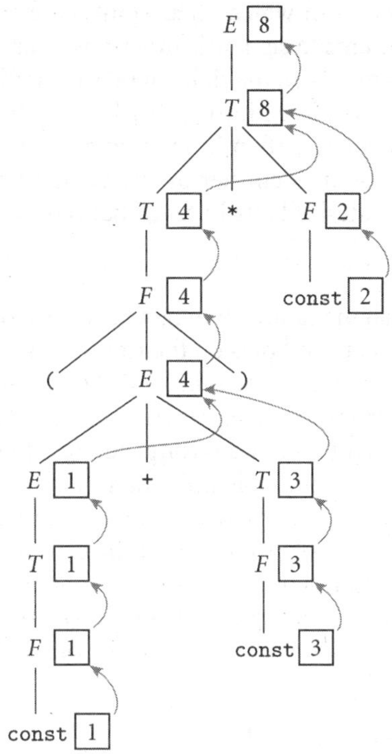

Figure 4.2 Decoration of a parse tree for `(1 + 3) * 2`, using the attribute grammar of Figure 4.1. The val attributes of symbols are shown in boxes. Curving arrows show the attribute flow, which is strictly upward in this case. Each box holds the output of a single semantic rule; the arrow(s) entering the box indicate the input(s) to the rule. At the second level of the tree, for example, the two arrows pointing into the box with the 8 represent application of the rule T_1.val := product(T_2.val, F.val).

4.3 Evaluating Attributes

EXAMPLE 4.6
Decoration of a parse tree

The process of evaluating attributes is called *annotation* or *decoration* of the parse tree. Figure 4.2 shows how to decorate the parse tree for the expression `(1 + 3) * 2`, using the AG of Figure 4.1. Once decoration is complete, the value of the overall expression can be found in the val attribute of the root of the tree.

Synthesized Attributes

The attribute grammar of Figure 4.1 is very simple. Each symbol has at most one attribute (the punctuation marks have none). Moreover, they are all so-called *synthesized attributes*: their values are calculated (synthesized) only in productions in which their symbol appears on the left-hand side. For annotated parse trees like the one in Figure 4.2, this means that the *attribute flow*—the pattern in which information moves from node to node—is entirely bottom-up.

An attribute grammar in which all attributes are synthesized is said to be *S-attributed.* The arguments to semantic functions in an S-attributed grammar are always attributes of symbols on the right-hand side of the current production, and the return value is always placed into an attribute of the left-hand side of the production. Tokens (terminals) often have intrinsic properties (e.g., the character-string representation of an identifier or the value of a numeric constant); in a compiler these are synthesized attributes initialized by the scanner.

Inherited Attributes

In general, we can imagine (and will in fact have need of) attributes whose values are calculated when their symbol is on the right-hand side of the current production. Such attributes are said to be *inherited.* They allow contextual information to flow into a symbol from above or from the side, so that the rules of that production can be enforced in different ways (or generate different values) depending on surrounding context. Symbol table information is commonly passed from symbol to symbol by means of inherited attributes. Inherited attributes of the root of the parse tree can also be used to represent the external environment (characteristics of the target machine, command-line arguments to the compiler, etc.).

EXAMPLE 4.7
Top-down CFG and parse tree for subtraction

As a simple example of inherited attributes, consider the following fragment of an LL(1) expression grammar (here covering only subtraction):

expr ⟶ `const` *expr_tail*
expr_tail ⟶ `-` `const` *expr_tail* | ϵ

For the expression `9 - 4 - 3`, we obtain the following parse tree:

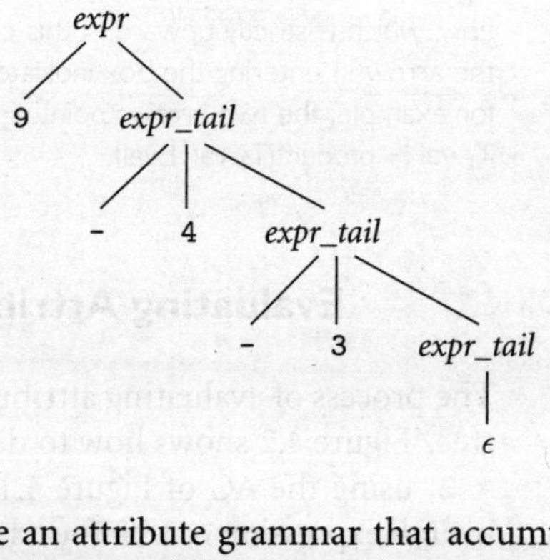

If we want to create an attribute grammar that accumulates the value of the overall expression into the root of the tree, we have a problem: because subtraction is left associative, we cannot summarize the right subtree of the root with a single numeric value. If we want to decorate the tree bottom-up, with an S-attributed grammar, we must be prepared to describe an arbitrary number of right operands in the attributes of the top-most *expr_tail* node (see Exercise 4.4). This is indeed possible, but it defeats the purpose of the formalism: in effect, it requires us to embed the entire tree into the attributes of a single node, and do all the real work inside a single semantic function.

EXAMPLE 4.8
Decoration with left-to-right attribute flow

If, however, we are allowed to pass attribute values not only bottom-up but also left-to-right in the tree, then we can pass the 9 into the top-most *expr_tail* node, where it can be combined (in proper left-associative fashion) with the 4. The resulting 5 can then be passed into the middle *expr_tail* node, combined with the 3 to make 2, and then passed upward to the root:

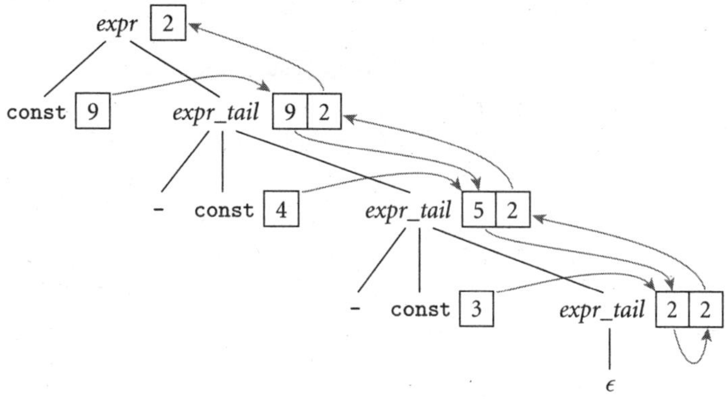

EXAMPLE 4.9
Top-down AG for subtraction

To effect this style of decoration, we need the following attribute rules:

expr ⟶ `const` *expr_tail*
▷ expr_tail.st := const.val
▷ expr.val := expr_tail.val

$expr\_tail_1$ ⟶ `-` `const` $expr\_tail_2$
▷ expr_tail_2.st := expr_tail_1.st − const.val
▷ expr_tail_1.val := expr_tail_2.val

expr_tail ⟶ ϵ
▷ expr_tail.val := expr_tail.st

In each of the first two productions, the first rule serves to copy the left context (value of the expression so far) into a "subtotal" (st) attribute; the second rule copies the final value from the right-most leaf back up to the root. In the *expr_tail* nodes of the picture in Example 4.8, the left box holds the st attribute; the right holds val.

EXAMPLE 4.10
Top-down AG for constant expressions

We can flesh out the grammar fragment of Example 4.7 to produce a more complete expression grammar, as shown (with shorter symbol names) in Figure 4.3. The underlying CFG for this grammar accepts the same language as the one in Figure 4.1, but where that one was SLR(1), this one is LL(1). Attribute flow for a parse of `(1 + 3) * 2`, using the LL(1) grammar, appears in Figure 4.4. As in the grammar fragment of Example 4.9, the value of the left operand of each operator is carried into the *TT* and *FT* productions by the st (subtotal) attribute. The relative complexity of the attribute flow arises from the fact that operators are left associative, but the grammar cannot be left recursive: the left and right operands of a given operator are thus found in separate productions. Grammars to perform

1. $E \longrightarrow T\ TT$
   ▷ TT.st := T.val ▷ E.val := TT.val
2. $TT_1 \longrightarrow +\ T\ TT_2$
   ▷ TT_2.st := TT_1.st + T.val ▷ TT_1.val := TT_2.val
3. $TT_1 \longrightarrow -\ T\ TT_2$
   ▷ TT_2.st := TT_1.st − T.val ▷ TT_1.val := TT_2.val
4. $TT \longrightarrow \epsilon$
   ▷ TT.val := TT.st
5. $T \longrightarrow F\ FT$
   ▷ FT.st := F.val ▷ T.val := FT.val
6. $FT_1 \longrightarrow *\ F\ FT_2$
   ▷ FT_2.st := FT_1.st × F.val ▷ FT_1.val := FT_2.val
7. $FT_1 \longrightarrow /\ F\ FT_2$
   ▷ FT_2.st := FT_1.st ÷ F.val ▷ FT_1.val := FT_2.val
8. $FT \longrightarrow \epsilon$
   ▷ FT.val := FT.st
9. $F_1 \longrightarrow -\ F_2$
   ▷ F_1.val := − F_2.val
10. $F \longrightarrow (\ E\ )$
   ▷ F.val := E.val
11. $F \longrightarrow$ const
   ▷ F.val := const.val

Figure 4.3 **An attribute grammar for constant expressions based on an LL(1) CFG.** In this grammar several productions have two semantic rules.

semantic analysis for practical languages generally require some non-S-attributed flow.

Attribute Flow

Just as a context-free grammar does not specify how it should be parsed, an attribute grammar does not specify the order in which attribute rules should be invoked. Put another way, both notations are *declarative*: they define a set of valid trees, but they don't say how to build or decorate them. Among other things, this means that the order in which attribute rules are listed for a given production is immaterial; attribute flow may require them to execute in any order. If, in Figure 4.3, we were to reverse the order in which the rules appear in productions 1, 2, 3, 5, 6, and/or 7 (listing the rule for symbol.val first), it would be a purely cosmetic change; the grammar would not be altered.

We say an attribute grammar is *well defined* if its rules determine a unique set of values for the attributes of every possible parse tree. An attribute grammar is *noncircular* if it never leads to a parse tree in which there are cycles in the attribute flow graph—that is, if no attribute, in any parse tree, ever depends (transitively)

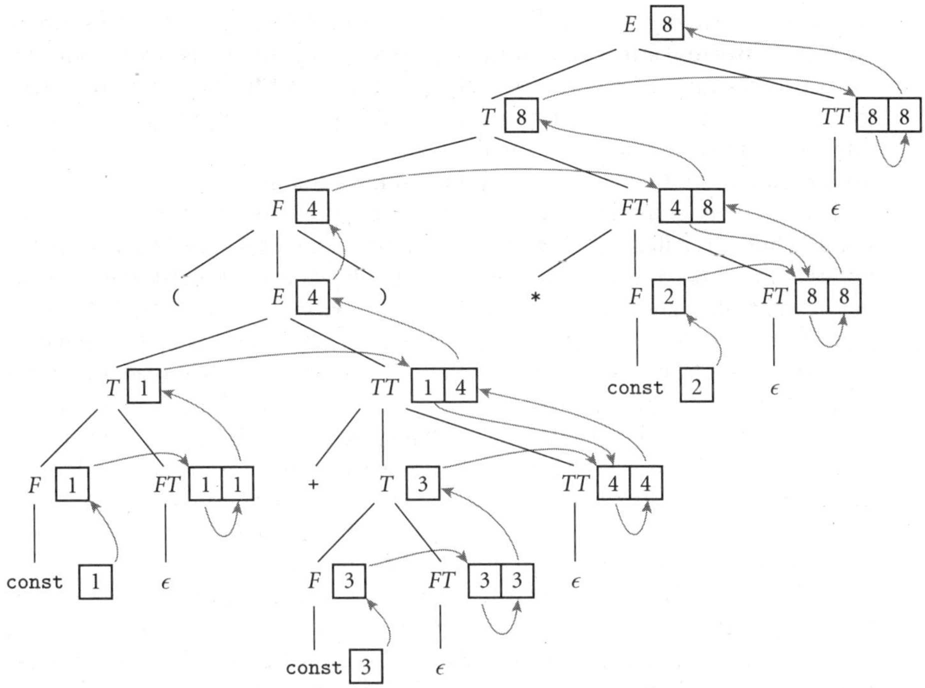

Figure 4.4 Decoration of a top-down parse tree for `(1 + 3) * 2`, using the AG of Figure 4.3. Curving arrows again indicate attribute flow; the arrow(s) entering a given box represent the application of a single semantic rule. Flow in this case is no longer strictly bottom-up, but it is still left-to-right. At *FT* and *TT* nodes, the left box holds the `st` attribute; the right holds `val`.

on itself. (A grammar can be circular and still be well defined if attributes are guaranteed to converge to a unique value.) As a general rule, practical attribute grammars tend to be noncircular.

An algorithm that decorates parse trees by invoking the rules of an attribute grammar in an order consistent with the tree's attribute flow is called a *translation scheme*. Perhaps the simplest scheme is one that makes repeated passes over a tree, invoking any semantic function whose arguments have all been defined, and stopping when it completes a pass in which no values change. Such a scheme is said to be *oblivious*, in the sense that it exploits no special knowledge of either the parse tree or the grammar. It will halt only if the grammar is well defined. Better performance, at least for noncircular grammars, may be achieved by a *dynamic* scheme that tailors the evaluation order to the structure of a given parse tree—for example, by constructing a topological sort of the attribute flow graph and then invoking rules in an order consistent with the sort.

The fastest translation schemes, however, tend to be *static*—based on an analysis of the structure of the attribute grammar itself, and then applied mechanically to any tree arising from the grammar. Like LL and LR parsers, linear-time static translation schemes can be devised only for certain restricted classes of grammars. S-attributed grammars, such as the one in Figure 4.1, form the simplest such class. Because attribute flow in an S-attributed grammar is strictly bottom-up, attributes can be evaluated by visiting the nodes of the parse tree in exactly the same order that those nodes are generated by an LR-family parser. In fact, the attributes can be evaluated on the fly during a bottom-up parse, thereby interleaving parsing and semantic analysis (attribute evaluation).

The attribute grammar of Figure 4.3 is a good bit messier than that of Figure 4.1, but it is still *L-attributed*: its attributes can be evaluated by visiting the nodes of the parse tree in a single left-to-right, depth-first traversal (the same order in which they are visited during a top-down parse—see Figure 4.4). If we say that an attribute A.s *depends on* an attribute B.t if B.t is ever passed to a semantic function that returns a value for A.s, then we can define L-attributed grammars more formally with the following two rules: (1) each synthesized attribute of a left-hand-side symbol depends only on that symbol's own inherited attributes or on attributes (synthesized or inherited) of the production's right-hand-side symbols, and (2) each inherited attribute of a right-hand-side symbol depends only on inherited attributes of the left-hand-side symbol or on attributes (synthesized or inherited) of symbols to its left in the right-hand side.

Because L-attributed grammars permit rules that initialize attributes of the left-hand side of a production using attributes of symbols on the right-hand side, every S-attributed grammar is also an L-attributed grammar. The reverse is not the case: S-attributed grammars do not permit the initialization of attributes on the right-hand side, so there are L-attributed grammars that are not S-attributed.

S-attributed attribute grammars are the most general class of attribute grammars for which evaluation can be implemented on the fly during an LR parse. L-attributed grammars are the most general class for which evaluation can be implemented on the fly during an LL parse. If we interleave semantic analysis (and possibly intermediate code generation) with parsing, then a bottom-up parser must in general be paired with an S-attributed translation scheme; a top-down parser must be paired with an L-attributed translation scheme. (Depending on the structure of the grammar, it is often possible for a bottom-up parser to accommodate some non-S-attributed attribute flow; we consider this possibility in Section C-4.5.1.) If we choose to separate parsing and semantic analysis into separate passes, then the code that builds the parse tree or syntax tree must still use an S-attributed or L-attributed translation scheme (as appropriate), but the semantic analyzer can use a more powerful scheme if desired. There are certain tasks, such as the generation of code for "short-circuit" Boolean expressions (to be discussed in Sections 6.1.5 and 6.4.1), that are easiest to accomplish with a non-L-attributed scheme.

One-Pass Compilers

A compiler that interleaves semantic analysis and code generation with parsing is said to be a *one-pass compiler*.[3] It is unclear whether interleaving semantic analysis with parsing makes a compiler simpler or more complex; it's mainly a matter of taste. If intermediate code generation is interleaved with parsing, one need not build a syntax tree at all (unless of course the syntax tree *is* the intermediate code). Moreover, it is often possible to write the intermediate code to an output file on the fly, rather than accumulating it in the attributes of the root of the parse tree. The resulting space savings were important for previous generations of computers, which had very small main memories. On the other hand, semantic analysis is easier to perform during a separate traversal of a syntax tree, because that tree reflects the program's semantic structure better than the parse tree does, especially with a top-down parser, and because one has the option of traversing the tree in an order other than that chosen by the parser.

Building a Syntax Tree

EXAMPLE 4.11
Bottom-up and top-down AGs to build a syntax tree

If we choose not to interleave parsing and semantic analysis, we still need to add attribute rules to the context-free grammar, but they serve only to create the syntax tree—not to enforce semantic rules or generate code. Figures 4.5 and 4.6 contain bottom-up and top-down attribute grammars, respectively, to build a syntax tree for constant expressions. The attributes in these grammars hold neither numeric values nor target code fragments; instead they point to nodes of the syntax tree. Function make_leaf returns a pointer to a newly allocated syntax tree node containing the value of a constant. Functions make_un_op and make_bin_op return pointers to newly allocated syntax tree nodes containing a unary or

DESIGN & IMPLEMENTATION

4.2 Forward references

In Sections 3.3.3 and C-3.4.1 we noted that the scope rules of many languages require names to be declared before they are used, and provide special mechanisms to introduce the forward references needed for recursive definitions. While these rules may help promote the creation of clear, maintainable code, an equally important motivation, at least historically, was to facilitate the construction of one-pass compilers. With increases in memory size, processing speed, and programmer expectations regarding the quality of code improvement, multipass compilers have become ubiquitous, and language designers have felt free (as, for example, in the class declarations of C++, Java, and C#) to abandon the requirement that declarations precede uses.

3 Most authors use the term *one-pass* only for compilers that translate all the way from source to target code in a single pass. Some authors insist only that intermediate code be generated in a single pass, and permit additional pass(es) to translate intermediate code to target code.

$E_1 \longrightarrow E_2 + T$
▷ E_1.ptr := make_bin_op("+", E_2.ptr, T.ptr)

$E_1 \longrightarrow E_2 - T$
▷ E_1.ptr := make_bin_op("−", E_2.ptr, T.ptr)

$E \longrightarrow T$
▷ E.ptr := T.ptr

$T_1 \longrightarrow T_2 * F$
▷ T_1.ptr := make_bin_op("×", T_2.ptr, F.ptr)

$T_1 \longrightarrow T_2 / F$
▷ T_1.ptr := make_bin_op("÷", T_2.ptr, F.ptr)

$T \longrightarrow F$
▷ T.ptr := F.ptr

$F_1 \longrightarrow - F_2$
▷ F_1.ptr := make_un_op("+/_", F_2.ptr)

$F \longrightarrow (E)$
▷ F.ptr := E.ptr

$F \longrightarrow$ `const`
▷ F.ptr := make_leaf(const.val)

Figure 4.5 **Bottom-up (S-attributed) attribute grammar to construct a syntax tree.** The symbol +/_ is used (as it is on calculators) to indicate change of sign.

binary operator, respectively, and pointers to the supplied operand(s). Figures 4.7 and 4.8 show stages in the decoration of parse trees for `(1 + 3) * 2`, using the grammars of Figures 4.5 and 4.6, respectively. Note that the final syntax tree is the same in each case. ■

✓ CHECK YOUR UNDERSTANDING

1. What determines whether a language rule is a matter of syntax or of static semantics?
2. Why is it impossible to detect certain program errors at compile time, even though they can be detected at run time?
3. What is an *attribute grammar*?
4. What are programming *assertions*? What is their purpose?
5. What is the difference between *synthesized* and *inherited* attributes?
6. Give two examples of information that is typically passed through inherited attributes.
7. What is *attribute flow*?
8. What is a *one-pass* compiler?

$E \longrightarrow T\ TT$
▷ TT.st := T.ptr
▷ E.ptr := TT.ptr

$TT_1 \longrightarrow$ + $T\ TT_2$
▷ TT_2.st := make_bin_op("+", TT_1.st, T.ptr)
▷ TT_1.ptr := TT_2.ptr

$TT_1 \longrightarrow$ - $T\ TT_2$
▷ TT_2.st := make_bin_op("−", TT_1.st, T.ptr)
▷ TT_1.ptr := TT_2.ptr

$TT \longrightarrow \epsilon$
▷ TT.ptr := TT.st

$T \longrightarrow F\ FT$
▷ FT.st := F.ptr
▷ T.ptr := FT.ptr

$FT_1 \longrightarrow$ * $F\ FT_2$
▷ FT_2.st := make_bin_op("×", FT_1.st, F.ptr)
▷ FT_1.ptr := FT_2.ptr

$FT_1 \longrightarrow$ / $F\ FT_2$
▷ FT_2.st := make_bin_op("÷", FT_1.st, F.ptr)
▷ FT_1.ptr := FT_2.ptr

$FT \longrightarrow \epsilon$
▷ FT.ptr := FT.st

$F_1 \longrightarrow$ - F_2
▷ F_1.ptr := make_un_op("+/_", F_2.ptr)

$F \longrightarrow$ (E)
▷ F.ptr := E.ptr

$F \longrightarrow$ **const**
▷ F.ptr := make_leaf(const.val)

Figure 4.6 Top-down (L-attributed) attribute grammar to construct a syntax tree. Here the st attribute, like the ptr attribute (and unlike the st attribute of Figure 4.3), is a pointer to a syntax tree node.

9. What does it mean for an attribute grammar to be *S-attributed*? *L-attributed*? *Noncircular*? What is the significance of these grammar classes?

4.4 Action Routines

Just as there are automatic tools that will construct a parser for a given context-free grammar, there are automatic tools that will construct a semantic analyzer (attribute evaluator) for a given attribute grammar. Attribute evaluator gen-

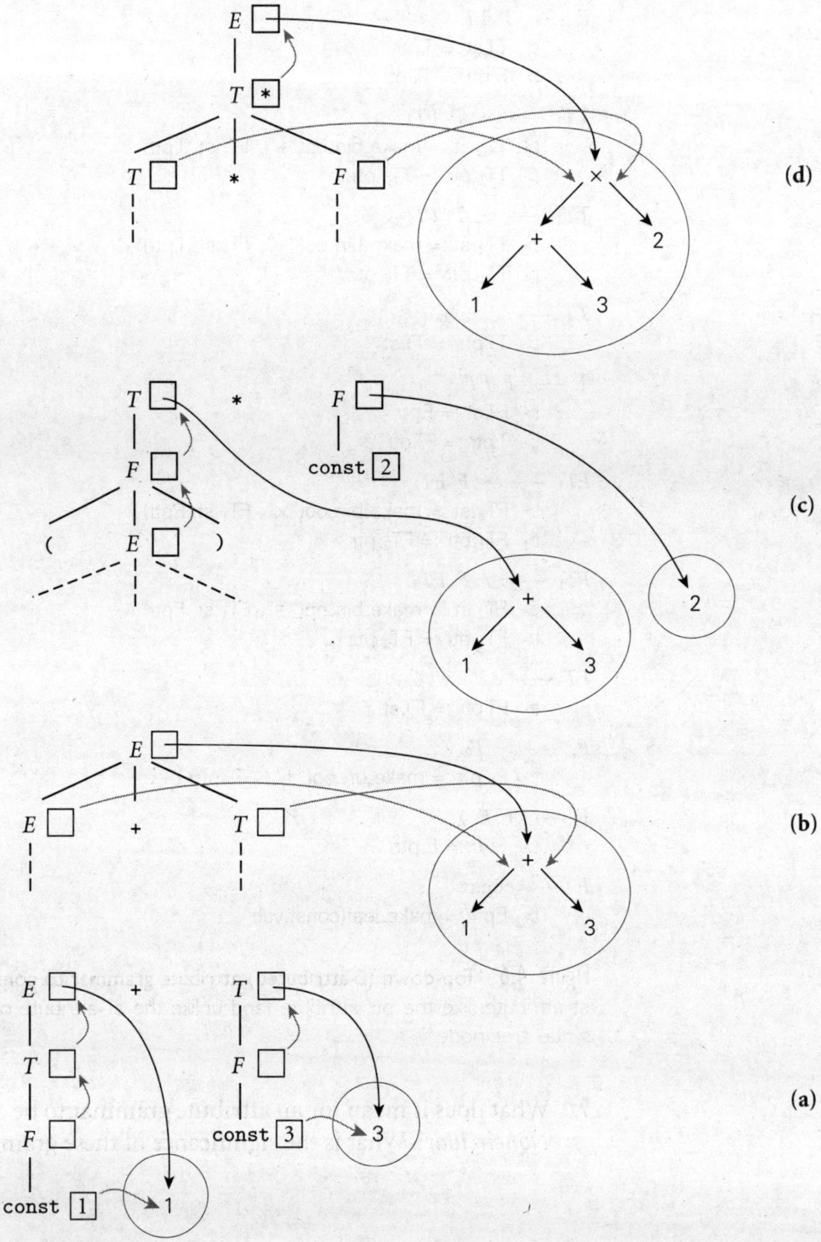

Figure 4.7 **Construction of a syntax tree for `(1 + 3) * 2` via decoration of a bottom-up parse tree, using the grammar of Figure 4.5.** This figure reads from bottom to top. In diagram (a), the values of the constants 1 and 3 have been placed in new syntax tree leaves. Pointers to these leaves propagate up into the attributes of E and T. In (b), the pointers to these leaves become child pointers of a new internal + node. In (c) the pointer to this node propagates up into the attributes of T, and a new leaf is created for 2. Finally, in (d), the pointers from T and F become child pointers of a new internal × node, and a pointer to this node propagates up into the attributes of E.

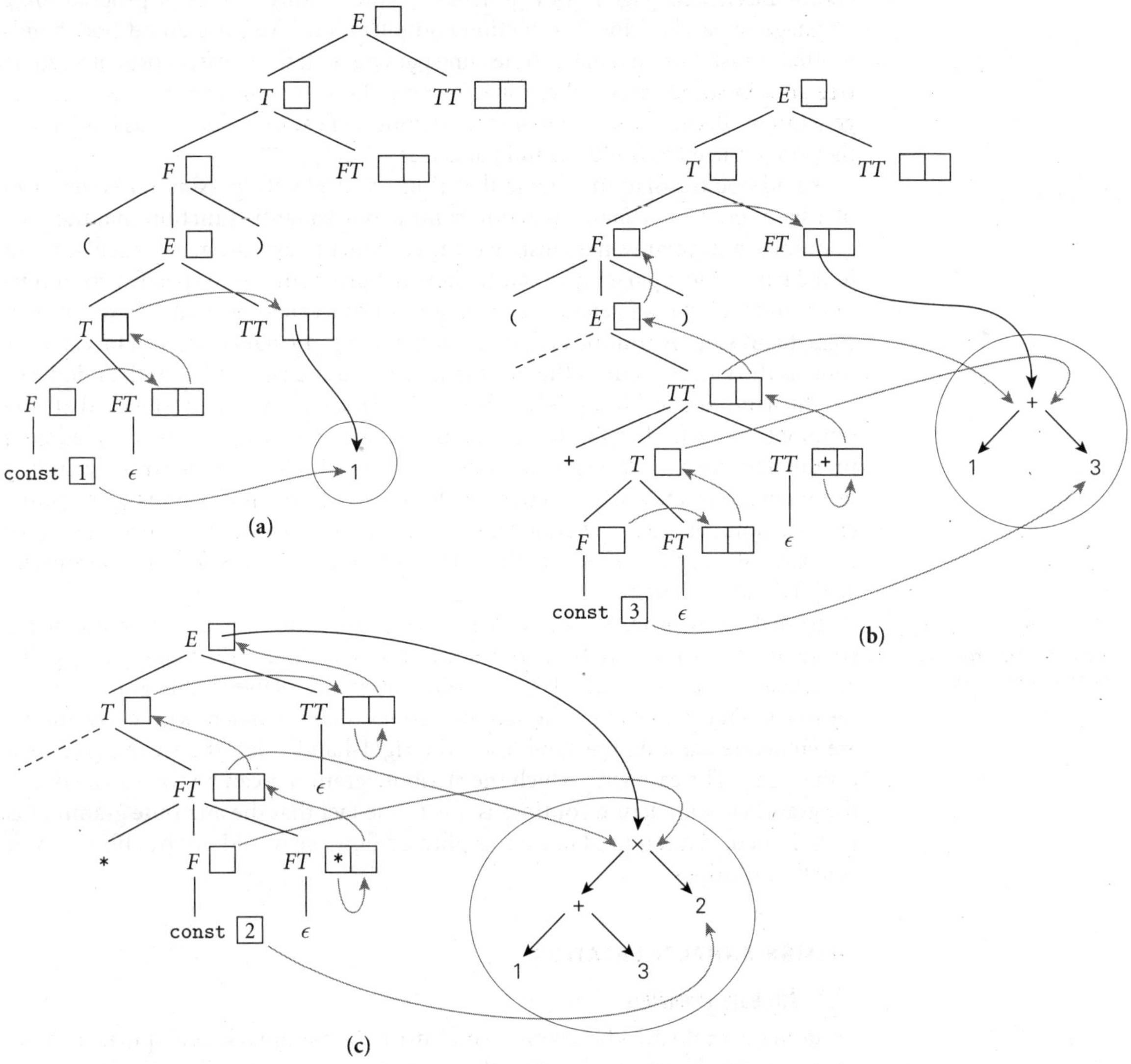

Figure 4.8 Construction of a syntax tree via decoration of a top-down parse tree, using the grammar of Figure 4.6. In the top diagram, (a), the value of the constant 1 has been placed in a new syntax tree leaf. A pointer to this leaf then propagates to the st attribute of *TT*. In (b), a second leaf has been created to hold the constant 3. Pointers to the two leaves then become child pointers of a new internal + node, a pointer to which propagates from the st attribute of the bottom-most *TT*, where it was created, all the way up and over to the st attribute of the top-most *FT*. In (c), a third leaf has been created for the constant 2. Pointers to this leaf and to the + node then become the children of a new × node, a pointer to which propagates from the st of the lower *FT*, where it was created, all the way to the root of the tree.

erators have been used in syntax-based editors [RT88], incremental compilers [SDB84], web-page layout [MTAB13], and various aspects of programming language research. Most production compilers, however, use an ad hoc, handwritten translation scheme, interleaving parsing with the construction of a syntax tree and, in some cases, other aspects of semantic analysis or intermediate code generation. Because they evaluate the attributes of each production as it is parsed, they do not need to build the full parse tree.

An ad hoc translation scheme that is interleaved with parsing takes the form of a set of *action routines*. An action routine is a semantic function that the programmer (grammar writer) instructs the compiler to execute at a particular point in the parse. Most parser generators allow the programmer to specify action routines. In an LL parser generator, an action routine can appear anywhere within a right-hand side. A routine at the beginning of a right-hand side will be called as soon as the parser predicts the production. A routine embedded in the middle of a right-hand side will be called as soon as the parser has matched (the yield of) the symbol to the left. The implementation mechanism is simple: when it predicts a production, the parser pushes *all* of the right-hand side onto the stack, including terminals (to be matched), nonterminals (to drive future predictions), and pointers to action routines. When it finds a pointer to an action routine at the top of the parse stack, the parser simply calls it, passing (pointers to) the appropriate attributes as arguments.

EXAMPLE 4.12
Top-down action routines to build a syntax tree

To make this process more concrete, consider again our LL(1) grammar for constant expressions. Action routines to build a syntax tree while parsing this grammar appear in Figure 4.9. The only difference between this grammar and the one in Figure 4.6 is that the action routines (delimited here with curly braces) are embedded among the symbols of the right-hand sides; the work performed is the same. The ease with which the attribute grammar can be transformed into the grammar with action routines is due to the fact that the attribute grammar is L-attributed. If it required more complicated flow, we would not be able to cast it as action routines. ■

DESIGN & IMPLEMENTATION

4.3 Attribute evaluators

Automatic evaluators based on formal attribute grammars are popular in language research projects because they save developer time when the language definition changes. They are popular in syntax-based editors and incremental compilers because they save execution time: when a small change is made to a program, the evaluator may be able to "patch up" tree decorations significantly faster than it could rebuild them from scratch. For the typical compiler, however, semantic analysis based on a formal attribute grammar is overkill: it has higher overhead than action routines, and doesn't really save the compiler writer that much work.

$E \longrightarrow T$ { TT.st := T.ptr } TT { E.ptr := TT.ptr }
$TT_1 \longrightarrow$ + T { TT_2.st := make_bin_op("+", TT_1.st, T.ptr) } TT_2 { TT_1.ptr := TT_2.ptr }
$TT_1 \longrightarrow$ - T { TT_2.st := make_bin_op("−", TT_1.st, T.ptr) } TT_2 { TT_1.ptr := TT_2.ptr }
$TT \longrightarrow \epsilon$ { TT.ptr := TT.st }
$T \longrightarrow F$ { FT.st := F.ptr } FT { T.ptr := FT.ptr }
$FT_1 \longrightarrow$ * F { FT_2.st := make_bin_op("×", FT_1.st, F.ptr) } FT_2 { FT_1.ptr := FT_2.ptr }
$FT_1 \longrightarrow$ / F { FT_2.st := make_bin_op("÷", FT_1.st, F.ptr) } FT_2 { FT_1.ptr := FT_2.ptr }
$FT \longrightarrow \epsilon$ { FT.ptr := FT.st }
$F_1 \longrightarrow$ - F_2 { F_1.ptr := make_un_op("+/_", F_2.ptr) }
$F \longrightarrow$ (E) { F.ptr := E.ptr }
$F \longrightarrow$ const { F.ptr := make_leaf(const.ptr) }

Figure 4.9 LL(1) grammar with action routines to build a syntax tree.

```
procedure term_tail(lhs : tree_node_ptr)
    case input_token of
        +, - :
            op : string := add_op()
            return term_tail(make_bin_op(op, lhs, term()))
                -- term() is a recursive call with no arguments
        ), id, read, write, $$ :        -- epsilon production
            return lhs
        otherwise parse_error
```

Figure 4.10 **Recursive descent parsing with embedded "action routines."** Compare with the routine of the same name in Figure 2.17, and with productions 2 through 4 in Figure 4.9.

EXAMPLE 4.13
Recursive descent and action routines

As in ordinary parsing, there is a strong analogy between recursive descent and table-driven parsing with action routines. Figure 4.10 shows the term_tail routine from Figure 2.17, modified to do its part in constructing a syntax tree. The behavior of this routine mirrors that of productions 2 through 4 in Figure 4.9. The routine accepts as a parameter a pointer to the syntax tree fragment contained in the attribute grammar's TT_1. Then, given an upcoming + or - symbol on the input, it (1) calls add_op to parse that symbol (returning a character string representation); (2) calls term to parse the attribute grammar's T; (3) calls make_bin_op to create a new tree node; (4) passes that node to term_tail, which parses the attribute grammar's TT_2; and (5) returns the result. ■

Bottom-Up Evaluation

In an LR parser generator, one cannot in general embed action routines at arbitrary places in a right-hand side, since the parser does not in general know what production it is in until it has seen all or most of the yield. LR parser generators therefore permit action routines only in the portion (suffix) of the right-hand side in which the production being parsed can be identified unambiguously (this is known as the *trailing part*; the ambiguous prefix is the *left corner*). If the attribute flow of the action routines is strictly bottom-up (as it is in an S-attributed attribute grammar), then execution at the end of right-hand sides is all that is needed. The attribute grammars of Figures 4.1 and 4.5, in fact, are essentially identical to the action routine versions. If the action routines are responsible for a significant part of semantic analysis, however (as opposed to simply building a syntax tree), then they will often need contextual information in order to do their job. To obtain and use this information in an LR parse, they will need some (necessarily limited) access to inherited attributes or to information outside the current production. We consider this issue further in Section C-4.5.1.

4.5 Space Management for Attributes

Any attribute evaluation method requires space to hold the attributes of the grammar symbols. If we are building an explicit parse tree, then the obvious approach is to store attributes in the nodes of the tree themselves. If we are not building a parse tree, then we need to find a way to keep track of the attributes for the symbols we have seen (or predicted) but not yet finished parsing. The details differ in bottom-up and top-down parsers.

For a bottom-up parser with an S-attributed grammar, the obvious approach is to maintain an *attribute stack* that directly mirrors the parse stack: next to every state number on the parse stack is an attribute record for the symbol we shifted when we entered that state. Entries in the attribute stack are pushed and popped automatically by the parser driver; space management is not an issue for the writer of action routines. Complications arise if we try to achieve the effect of inherited attributes, but these can be accommodated within the basic attribute-stack framework.

For a top-down parser with an L-attributed grammar, we have two principal options. The first option is automatic, but more complex than for bottom-up grammars. It still uses an attribute stack, but one that does not mirror the parse stack. The second option has lower space overhead, and saves time by "short-cutting" copy rules, but requires action routines to allocate and deallocate space for attributes explicitly.

In both families of parsers, it is common for some of the contextual information for action routines to be kept in global variables. The symbol table in particular is usually global. Rather than pass its full contents through attributes from one production to the next, we pass an indication of the currently active scope. Lookups in the global table then use this scope information to obtain the right referencing environment.

program ⟶ *stmt_list* `$$`

stmt_list ⟶ *stmt_list decl* | *stmt_list stmt* | ϵ

decl ⟶ `int id` | `real id`

stmt ⟶ `id :=` *expr* | `read id` | `write` *expr*

expr ⟶ *term* | *expr add_op term*

term ⟶ *factor* | *term mult_op factor*

factor ⟶ `(` *expr* `)` | `id` | `int_const` | `real_const` |
`float (` *expr* `)` | `trunc (` *expr* `)`

add_op ⟶ `+` | `-`

mult_op ⟶ `*` | `/`

Figure 4.11 Context-free grammar for a calculator language with types and declarations. The intent is that every identifier be declared before use, and that types not be mixed in computations.

IN MORE DEPTH

We consider attribute space management in more detail on the companion site. Using bottom-up and top-down grammars for arithmetic expressions, we illustrate automatic management for both bottom-up and top-down parsers, as well as the ad hoc option for top-down parsers.

4.6 Tree Grammars and Syntax Tree Decoration

In our discussion so far we have used attribute grammars solely to decorate parse trees. As we mentioned in the chapter introduction, attribute grammars can also be used to decorate syntax trees. If our compiler uses action routines simply to build a syntax tree, then the bulk of semantic analysis and intermediate code generation will use the syntax tree as base.

EXAMPLE 4.14 Bottom-up CFG for calculator language with types

Figure 4.11 contains a bottom-up CFG for a calculator language with types and declarations. The grammar differs from that of Example 2.37 in three ways: (1) we allow declarations to be intermixed with statements, (2) we differentiate between integer and real constants (presumably the latter contain a decimal point), and (3) we require explicit conversions between integer and real operands. The intended semantics of our language requires that every identifier be declared before it is used, and that types not be mixed in computations. ■

EXAMPLE 4.15 Syntax tree to average an integer and a real

Extrapolating from the example in Figure 4.5, it is easy to add semantic functions or action routines to the grammar of Figure 4.11 to construct a syntax tree for the calculator language (Exercise 4.21). The obvious structure for such a tree would represent expressions as we did in Figure 4.7, and would represent a program as a linked list of declarations and statements. As a concrete example, Figure 4.12 contains the syntax tree for a simple program to print the average of an integer and a real. ■

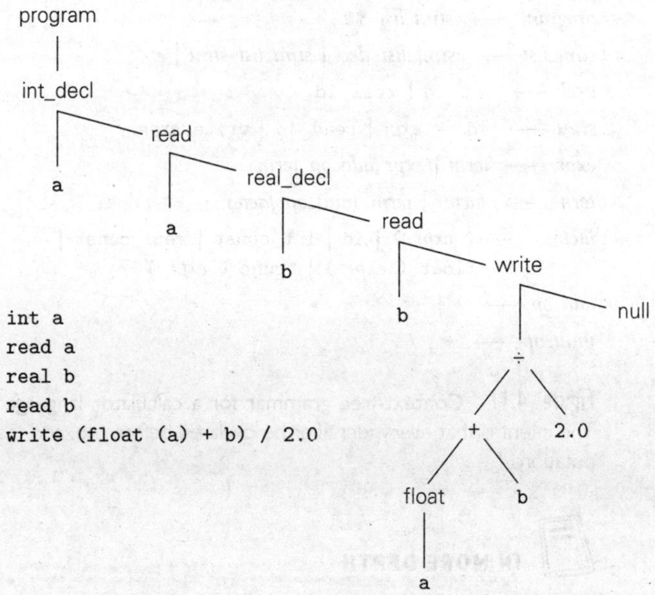

Figure 4.12 Syntax tree for a simple calculator program.

EXAMPLE 4.16
Tree grammar for the calculator language with types

Much as a context-free grammar describes the possible structure of parse trees for a given programming language, we can use a *tree grammar* to represent the possible structure of syntax trees. As in a CFG, each production of a tree grammar represents a possible relationship between a parent and its children in the tree. The parent is the symbol on the left-hand side of the production; the children are the symbols on the right-hand side. The productions used in Figure 4.12 might look something like the following:

program ⟶ *item*
int_decl : *item* ⟶ *id item*
read : *item* ⟶ *id item*
real_decl : *item* ⟶ *id item*
write : *item* ⟶ *expr item*
null : *item* ⟶ ϵ
'÷' : *expr* ⟶ *expr expr*
'+' : *expr* ⟶ *expr expr*
float : *expr* ⟶ *expr*
id : *expr* ⟶ ϵ
real_const : *expr* ⟶ ϵ

Here the notation $A : B$ on the left-hand side of a production means that A is one variant of B, and may appear anywhere a B is expected on a right-hand side. ■

Class of node	Variants	Attributes Inherited	Synthesized
program	—	—	location, errors
item	*int_decl, real_decl, read, write, :=, null*	symtab, errors_in	location, errors_out
expr	*int_const, real_const, id,* +, −, ×, ÷, *float, trunc*	symtab	location, type, errors, name (*id* only)

Figure 4.13 Classes of nodes for the syntax tree attribute grammar of Figure 4.14. With the exception of name, all variants of a given class have all the class's attributes.

Tree grammars and context-free grammars differ in important ways. A context-free grammar is meant to define (generate) a language composed of strings of tokens, where each string is the fringe (yield) of a parse tree. Parsing is the process of finding a tree that has a given yield. A tree grammar, as we use it here, is meant to define (or generate) the trees themselves. We have no need for a notion of parsing: we can easily inspect a tree and determine whether (and how) it can be generated by the grammar. Our purpose in introducing tree grammars is to provide a framework for the decoration of syntax trees. Semantic rules attached to the productions of a tree grammar can be used to define the attribute flow of a syntax tree in exactly the same way that semantic rules attached to the productions of a context-free grammar are used to define the attribute flow of a parse tree. We will use a tree grammar in the remainder of this section to perform static semantic checking. In Chapter 15 we will show how additional semantic rules can be used to generate intermediate code.

EXAMPLE 4.17
Tree AG for the calculator language with types

A complete tree attribute grammar for our calculator language with types can be constructed using the node classes, variants, and attributes shown in Figure 4.13. The grammar itself appears in Figure 4.14. Once decorated, the *program* node at the root of the syntax tree will contain a list, in a synthesized attribute, of all static semantic errors in the program. (The list will be empty if the program is free of such errors.) Each *item* or *expr* node has an inherited attribute symtab that contains a list, with types, of all identifiers declared to the left in the tree. Each *item* node also has an inherited attribute errors_in that lists all static semantic errors found to its left in the tree, and a synthesized attribute errors_out to propagate the final error list back to the root. Each *expr* node has one synthesized attribute that indicates its type and another that contains a list of any static semantic errors found inside.

Our handling of semantic errors illustrates a common technique. In order to continue looking for other errors, we must provide values for any attributes that would have been set in the absence of an error. To avoid cascading error messages, we choose values for those attributes that will pass quietly through subsequent checks. In this specific case we employ a pseudotype called error, which

program ⟶ *item*
▷ item.symtab := null
▷ program.errors := item.errors_out
▷ item.errors_in := null

int_decl : $item_1$ ⟶ *id* $item_2$
▷ declare_name(id, $item_1$, $item_2$, int)
▷ $item_1$.errors_out := $item_2$.errors_out

real_decl : $item_1$ ⟶ *id* $item_2$
▷ declare_name(id, $item_1$, $item_2$, real)
▷ $item_1$.errors_out := $item_2$.errors_out

read : $item_1$ ⟶ *id* $item_2$
▷ $item_2$.symtab := $item_1$.symtab
▷ if ⟨id.name, ?⟩ ∈ $item_1$.symtab
  $item_2$.errors_in := $item_1$.errors_in
else
  $item_2$.errors_in := $item_1$.errors_in + [id.name "undefined at" id.location]
▷ $item_1$.errors_out := $item_2$.errors_out

write : $item_1$ ⟶ *expr* $item_2$
▷ expr.symtab := $item_1$.symtab
▷ $item_2$.symtab := $item_1$.symtab
▷ $item_2$.errors_in := $item_1$.errors_in + expr.errors
▷ $item_1$.errors_out := $item_2$.errors_out

':=' : $item_1$ ⟶ *id expr* $item_2$
▷ expr.symtab := $item_1$.symtab
▷ $item_2$.symtab := $item_1$.symtab
▷ if ⟨id.name, A⟩ ∈ $item_1$.symtab -- for some type A
  if A ≠ error and expr.type ≠ error and A ≠ expr.type
    $item_2$.errors_in := $item_1$.errors_in + ["type clash at" $item_1$.location]
  else
    $item_2$.errors_in := $item_1$.errors_in + expr.errors
else
  $item_2$.errors_in := $item_1$.errors_in + [id.name "undefined at" id.location]
    + expr.errors
▷ $item_1$.errors_out := $item_2$.errors_out

null : *item* ⟶ ϵ
▷ item.errors_out := item.errors_in

Figure 4.14 **Attribute grammar to decorate an abstract syntax tree for the calculator language with types.** We use square brackets to delimit error messages and pointed brackets to delimit symbol table entries. Juxtaposition indicates concatenation within error messages; the '+' and '−' operators indicate insertion and removal in lists. We assume that every node has been initialized by the scanner or by action routines in the parser to contain an indication of the location (line and column) at which the corresponding construct appears in the source (see Exercise 4.22). The '?' symbol is used as a "wild card"; it matches any type. *(continued)*

```
id : expr ⟶ ε
    ▷ if ⟨id.name, A⟩ ∈ expr.symtab                -- for some type A
            expr.errors := null
            expr.type := A
        else
            expr.errors := [id.name "undefined at" id.location]
            expr.type := error

int_const : expr ⟶ ε
    ▷ expr.type := int

real_const : expr ⟶ ε
    ▷ expr.type := real

'+' : expr1 ⟶ expr2 expr3
    ▷ expr2.symtab := expr1.symtab
    ▷ expr3.symtab := expr1.symtab
    ▷ check_types(expr1, expr2, expr3)

'−' : expr1 ⟶ expr2 expr3
    ▷ expr2.symtab := expr1.symtab
    ▷ expr3.symtab := expr1.symtab
    ▷ check_types(expr1, expr2, expr3)

'×' : expr1 ⟶ expr2 expr3
    ▷ expr2.symtab := expr1.symtab
    ▷ expr3.symtab := expr1.symtab
    ▷ check_types(expr1, expr2, expr3)

'÷' : expr1 ⟶ expr2 expr3
    ▷ expr2.symtab := expr1.symtab
    ▷ expr3.symtab := expr1.symtab
    ▷ check_types(expr1, expr2, expr3)

float : expr1 ⟶ expr2
    ▷ expr2.symtab := expr1.symtab
    ▷ convert_type(expr2, expr1, int, real, "float of non-int")

trunc : expr1 ⟶ expr2
    ▷ expr2.symtab := expr1.symtab
    ▷ convert_type(expr2, expr1, real, int, "trunc of non-real")
```

Figure 4.14 *(continued on next page)*

we associate with any symbol table entry or expression for which we have already generated a message.

Though it takes a bit of checking to verify the fact, our attribute grammar is noncircular and well defined. No attribute is ever assigned a value more than once. (The helper routines at the end of Figure 4.14 should be thought of as macros, rather than semantic functions. For the sake of brevity we have passed them entire tree nodes as arguments. Each macro calculates the values of two different attributes. Under a strict formulation of attribute grammars each macro

```
macro declare_name(id, cur_item, next_item : syntax_tree_node; t : type)
    if ⟨id.name, ?⟩ ∈ cur_item.symtab
        next_item.errors_in := cur_item.errors_in + ["redefinition of" id.name "at" cur_item.location]
        next_item.symtab := cur_item.symtab – ⟨id.name, ?⟩ + ⟨id.name, error⟩
    else
        next_item.errors_in := cur_item.errors_in
        next_item.symtab := cur_item.symtab + ⟨id.name, t⟩
macro check_types(result, operand1, operand2)
    if operand1.type = error or operand2.type = error
        result.type := error
        result.errors := operand1.errors + operand2.errors
    else if operand1.type ≠ operand2.type
        result.type := error
        result.errors := operand1.errors + operand2.errors + ["type clash at" result.location]
    else
        result.type := operand1.type
        result.errors := operand1.errors + operand2.errors
macro convert_type(old_expr, new_expr : syntax_tree_node; from_t, to_t : type; msg : string)
    if old_expr.type = from_t or old_expr.type = error
        new_expr.errors := old_expr.errors
        new_expr.type := to_t
    else
        new_expr.errors := old_expr.errors + [msg "at" old_expr.location]
        new_expr.type := error
```

Figure 4.14 *(continued)*

would be replaced by two separate semantic functions, one per calculated attribute.) ■

EXAMPLE 4.18
Decorating a tree with the AG of Example 4.17

Figure 4.15 uses the grammar of Figure 4.14 to decorate the syntax tree of Figure 4.12. The pattern of attribute flow appears considerably messier than in previous examples in this chapter, but this is simply because type checking is more complicated than calculating constants or building a syntax tree. Symbol table information flows along the chain of *items* and down into *expr* trees. The *int_decl* and *real_decl* nodes add new information; other nodes simply pass the table along. Type information is synthesized at *id : expr* leaves by looking up an identifier's name in the symbol table. The information then propagates upward within an expression tree, and is used to type-check operators and assignments (the latter don't appear in this example). Error messages flow along the chain of *items* via the errors_in attributes, and then back to the root via the errors_out attributes. Messages also flow up out of *expr* trees. Wherever a type check is performed, the type attribute may be used to help create a new message to be appended to the growing message list. ■

In our example grammar we accumulate error messages into a synthesized attribute of the root of the syntax tree. In an ad hoc attribute evaluator we might be tempted to print these messages on the fly as the errors are discovered. In prac-

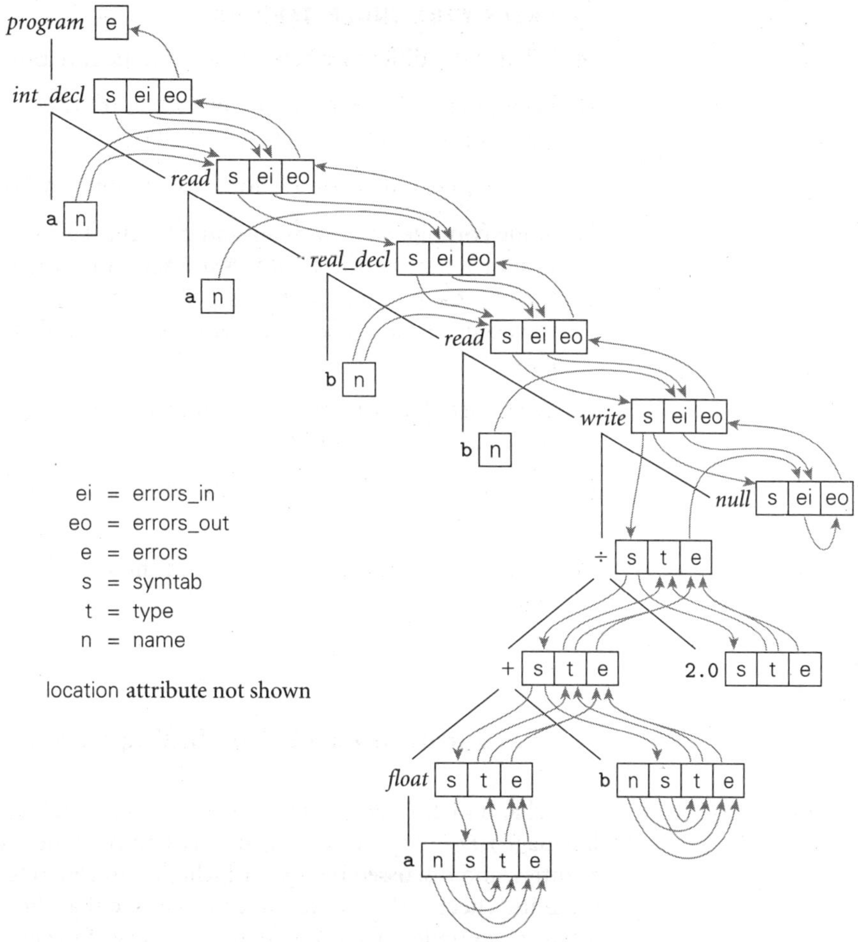

Figure 4.15 Decoration of the syntax tree of Figure 4.12, using the grammar of Figure 4.14. Location information, which we assume has been initialized in every node by the parser, contributes to error messages, but does not otherwise propagate through the tree.

tice, however, particularly in a multipass compiler, it makes sense to buffer the messages, so they can be interleaved with messages produced by other phases of the compiler, and printed in program order at the end of compilation.

One could convert our attribute grammar into executable code using an automatic attribute evaluator generator. Alternatively, one could create an ad hoc evaluator in the form of mutually recursive subroutines (Exercise 4.20). In the latter case attribute flow would be explicit in the calling sequence of the routines. We could then choose if desired to keep the symbol table in global variables, rather than passing it from node to node through attributes. Most compilers employ the ad hoc approach.

✓ CHECK YOUR UNDERSTANDING

10. What is the difference between a semantic function and an action routine?
11. Why can't action routines be placed at arbitrary locations within the right-hand side of productions in an LR CFG?
12. What patterns of attribute flow can be captured easily with action routines?
13. Some compilers perform all semantic checks and intermediate code generation in action routines. Others use action routines to build a syntax tree and then perform semantic checks and intermediate code generation in separate traversals of the syntax tree. Discuss the tradeoffs between these two strategies.
14. What sort of information do action routines typically keep in global variables, rather than in attributes?
15. Describe the similarities and differences between context-free grammars and tree grammars.
16. How can a semantic analyzer avoid the generation of cascading error messages?

4.7 Summary and Concluding Remarks

This chapter has discussed the task of semantic analysis. We reviewed the sorts of language rules that can be classified as syntax, static semantics, and dynamic semantics, and discussed the issue of whether to generate code to perform dynamic semantic checks. We also considered the role that the semantic analyzer plays in a typical compiler. We noted that both the enforcement of static semantic rules and the generation of intermediate code can be cast in terms of annotation, or *decoration*, of a parse tree or syntax tree. We then presented attribute grammars as a formal framework for this decoration process.

An attribute grammar associates *attributes* with each symbol in a context-free grammar or tree grammar, and *attribute rules* with each production. In a CFG, *synthesized* attributes are calculated only in productions in which their symbol appears on the left-hand side. The synthesized attributes of tokens are initialized by the scanner. *Inherited* attributes are calculated in productions in which their symbol appears within the right-hand side; they allow calculations in the subtree below a symbol to depend on the context in which the symbol appears. Inherited attributes of the start symbol (goal) can represent the external environment of the compiler. Strictly speaking, attribute grammars allow only *copy rules* (assignments of one attribute to another) and simple calls to *semantic functions*, but we usually relax this restriction to allow more or less arbitrary code fragments in some existing programming language.

Just as context-free grammars can be categorized according to the parsing algorithm(s) that can use them, attribute grammars can be categorized according to the complexity of their pattern of *attribute flow*. S-attributed grammars, in which all attributes are synthesized, can naturally be evaluated in a single bottom-up pass over a parse tree, in precisely the order the tree is discovered by an LR-family parser. L-attributed grammars, in which all attribute flow is depth-first left-to-right, can be evaluated in precisely the order that the parse tree is predicted and matched by an LL-family parser. Attribute grammars with more complex patterns of attribute flow are not commonly used for the parse trees of production compilers, but are valuable for syntax-based editors, incremental compilers, and various other tools.

While it is possible to construct automatic tools to analyze attribute flow and decorate parse trees, most compilers rely on *action routines*, which the compiler writer embeds in the right-hand sides of productions to evaluate attribute rules at specific points in a parse. In an LL-family parser, action routines can be embedded at arbitrary points in a production's right-hand side. In an LR-family parser, action routines must follow the production's *left corner*. Space for attributes in a bottom-up compiler is naturally allocated in parallel with the parse stack, but this complicates the management of inherited attributes. Space for attributes in a top-down compiler can be allocated automatically, or managed explicitly by the writer of action routines. The automatic approach has the advantage of regularity, and is easier to maintain; the ad hoc approach is slightly faster and more flexible.

In a *one-pass* compiler, which interleaves scanning, parsing, semantic analysis, and code generation in a single traversal of its input, semantic functions or action routines are responsible for all of semantic analysis and code generation. More commonly, action routines simply build a syntax tree, which is then decorated during separate traversal(s) in subsequent pass(es). The code for these traversals is usually written by hand, in the form of mutually recursive subroutines, allowing the compiler to accommodate essentially arbitrary attribute flow on the syntax tree.

In subsequent chapters (6–10 in particular) we will consider a wide variety of programming language constructs. Rather than present the actual attribute grammars required to implement these constructs, we will describe their semantics informally, and give examples of the target code. We will return to attribute grammars in Chapter 15, when we consider the generation of intermediate code in more detail.

4.8 Exercises

4.1 Basic results from automata theory tell us that the language $L = \mathtt{a}^n\mathtt{b}^n\mathtt{c}^n = \epsilon$, `abc`, `aabbcc`, `aaabbbccc`, ... is not context free. It can be captured, however, using an attribute grammar. Give an underlying CFG and a set of attribute rules that associates a Boolean attribute `ok` with the root `R` of each

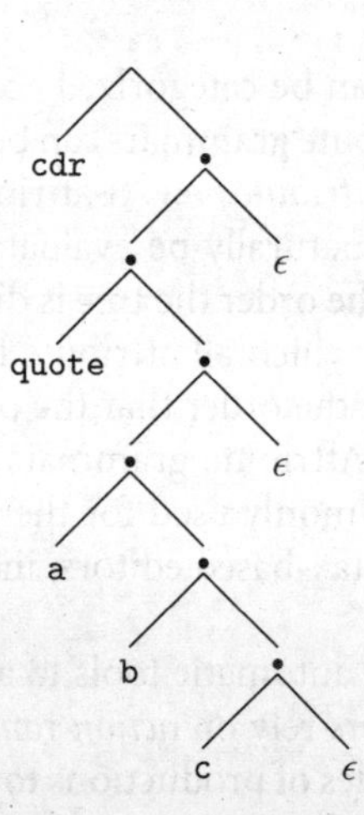

Figure 4.16 Natural syntax tree for the Lisp expression `(cdr '(a b c))`.

parse tree, such that R.ok = true if and only if the string corresponding to the fringe of the tree is in *L*.

4.2 Modify the grammar of Figure 2.25 so that it accepts only programs that contain at least one `write` statement. Make the same change in the solution to Exercise 2.17. Based on your experience, what do you think of the idea of using the CFG to enforce the rule that every function in C must contain at least one `return` statement?

4.3 Give two examples of reasonable semantic rules that *cannot* be checked at reasonable cost, either statically or by compiler-generated code at run time.

4.4 Write an S-attributed attribute grammar, based on the CFG of Example 4.7, that accumulates the value of the overall expression into the root of the tree. You will need to use dynamic memory allocation so that individual attributes can hold an arbitrary amount of information.

4.5 Lisp has the unusual property that its programs take the form of parenthesized lists. The natural syntax tree for a Lisp program is thus a tree of binary cells (known in Lisp as `cons` cells), where the first child represents the first element of the list and the second child represents the rest of the list. The syntax tree for `(cdr '(a b c))` appears in Figure 4.16. (The notation `'L` is syntactic sugar for `(quote L)`.)

Extend the CFG of Exercise 2.18 to create an attribute grammar that will build such trees. When a parse tree has been fully decorated, the root should have an attribute v that refers to the syntax tree. You may assume that each atom has a synthesized attribute v that refers to a syntax tree node that holds information from the scanner. In your semantic functions, you may assume the availability of a `cons` function that takes two references as arguments and returns a reference to a new `cons` cell containing those references.

4.6 Refer back to the context-free grammar of Exercise 2.13. Add attribute rules to the grammar to accumulate into the root of the tree a count of the maximum depth to which parentheses are nested in the program string. For example, given the string `f1(a, f2(b * (c + (d - (e - f)))))`, the *stmt* at the root of the tree should have an attribute with a count of 3 (the parentheses surrounding argument lists don't count).

4.7 Suppose that we want to translate constant expressions into the postfix, or "reverse Polish" notation of logician Jan Łukasiewicz. Postfix notation does not require parentheses. It appears in stack-based languages such as Postscript, Forth, and the P-code and Java bytecode intermediate forms mentioned in Section 1.4. It also served, historically, as the input language of certain hand-held calculators made by Hewlett-Packard. When given a number, a postfix calculator would push the number onto an internal stack. When given an operator, it would pop the top two numbers from the stack, apply the operator, and push the result. The display would show the value at the top of the stack. To compute $2 \times (15 - 3)/4$, for example, one would push `2` [E] `1 5` [E] `3` [E] `- * 4` [E] `/` (here [E] is the "enter" key, used to end the string of digits that constitute a number).

Using the underlying CFG of Figure 4.1, write an attribute grammar that will associate with the root of the parse tree a sequence of postfix calculator button pushes, seq, that will compute the arithmetic value of the tokens derived from that symbol. You may assume the existence of a function buttons(c) that returns a sequence of button pushes (ending with [E] on a postfix calculator) for the constant `c`. You may also assume the existence of a concatenation function for sequences of button pushes.

4.8 Repeat the previous exercise using the underlying CFG of Figure 4.3.

4.9 Consider the following grammar for reverse Polish arithmetic expressions:

$$E \longrightarrow E\ E\ op \mid \texttt{id}$$

$$op \longrightarrow \texttt{+} \mid \texttt{-} \mid \texttt{*} \mid \texttt{/}$$

Assuming that each `id` has a synthesized attribute name of type string, and that each E and op has an attribute val of type string, write an attribute grammar that arranges for the val attribute of the root of the parse tree to contain a translation of the expression into conventional infix notation. For example, if the leaves of the tree, left to right, were "`A A B - * C /`," then the val field of the root would be "`( ( A * ( A - B ) ) / C )`." As an extra challenge, write a version of your attribute grammar that exploits the usual arithmetic precedence and associativity rules to use as few parentheses as possible.

4.10 To reduce the likelihood of typographic errors, the digits comprising most credit card numbers are designed to satisfy the so-called *Luhn formula*, standardized by ANSI in the 1960s, and named for IBM mathematician Hans Peter Luhn. Starting at the right, we double every other digit (the second-to-last, fourth-to-last, etc.). If the doubled value is 10 or more, we add the resulting digits. We then sum together all the digits. In any valid number the result will be a multiple of 10. For example, 1234 5678 9012 3456 becomes 2264 1658 9022 6416, which sums to 64, so this is not a valid number. If the last digit had been 2, however, the sum would have been 60, so the number would potentially be valid.

Give an attribute grammar for strings of digits that accumulates into the root of the parse tree a Boolean value indicating whether the string is valid according to Luhn's formula. Your grammar should accommodate strings of arbitrary length.

4.11 Consider the following CFG for floating-point constants, without exponential notation. (Note that this exercise is somewhat artificial: the language in question is regular, and would be handled by the scanner of a typical compiler.)

C ⟶ *digits* . *digits*

digits ⟶ *digit more_digits*

more_digits ⟶ *digits* | ϵ

digit ⟶ `0` | `1` | `2` | `3` | `4` | `5` | `6` | `7` | `8` | `9`

Augment this grammar with attribute rules that will accumulate the value of the constant into a val attribute of the root of the parse tree. Your answer should be S-attributed.

4.12 One potential criticism of the obvious solution to the previous problem is that the values in internal nodes of the parse tree do not reflect the value, in context, of the fringe below them. Create an alternative solution that addresses this criticism. More specifically, create your grammar in such a way that the val of an internal node is the sum of the `val`s of its children. Illustrate your solution by drawing the parse tree and attribute flow for `12.34`. (Hint: You will probably want a different underlying CFG, and non-L-attributed flow.)

4.13 Consider the following attribute grammar for variable declarations, based on the CFG of Exercise 2.11:

decl ⟶ `ID` *decl_tail*
- ▷ decl.t := decl_tail.t
- ▷ decl_tail.in_tab := insert (decl.in_tab, ID.n, decl_tail.t)
- ▷ decl.out_tab := decl_tail.out_tab

decl_tail ⟶ , *decl*
- ▷ decl_tail.t := decl.t
- ▷ decl.in_tab := decl_tail.in_tab
- ▷ decl_tail.out_tab := decl.out_tab

decl_tail ⟶ `: ID ;`
- ▷ decl_tail.t := ID.n
- ▷ decl_tail.out_tab := decl_tail.in_tab

Show a parse tree for the string `A, B : C;`. Then, using arrows and textual description, specify the attribute flow required to fully decorate the tree. (Hint: Note that the grammar is *not* L-attributed.)

4.14 A CFG-based attribute evaluator capable of handling non-L-attributed attribute flow needs to take a parse tree as input. Explain how to build a parse tree automatically during a top-down or bottom-up parse (i.e., without explicit action routines).

4.15 Building on Example 4.13, modify the remainder of the recursive descent parser of Figure 2.17 to build syntax trees for programs in the calculator language.

4.16 Write an LL(1) grammar with action routines and automatic attribute space management that generates the reverse Polish translation described in Exercise 4.7.

4.17 **(a)** Write a context-free grammar for polynomials in x. Add semantic functions to produce an attribute grammar that will accumulate the polynomial's derivative (as a string) in a synthesized attribute of the root of the parse tree.

(b) Replace your semantic functions with action routines that can be evaluated during parsing.

4.18 **(a)** Write a context-free grammar for `case` or `switch` statements in the style of Pascal or C. Add semantic functions to ensure that the same label does not appear on two different arms of the construct.

(b) Replace your semantic functions with action routines that can be evaluated during parsing.

4.19 Write an algorithm to determine whether the rules of an arbitrary attribute grammar are noncircular. (Your algorithm will require exponential time in the worst case [JOR75].)

4.20 Rewrite the attribute grammar of Figure 4.14 in the form of an ad hoc tree traversal consisting of mutually recursive subroutines in your favorite programming language. Keep the symbol table in a global variable, rather than passing it through arguments.

4.21 Write an attribute grammar based on the CFG of Figure 4.11 that will build a syntax tree with the structure described in Figure 4.14.

4.22 Augment the attribute grammar of Figure 4.5, Figure 4.6, or Exercise 4.21 to initialize a synthesized attribute in every syntax tree node that indicates the location (line and column) at which the corresponding construct appears in the source program. You may assume that the scanner initializes the location of every token.

4.23 Modify the CFG and attribute grammar of Figures 4.11 and 4.14 to permit mixed integer and real expressions, without the need for `float` and `trunc`. You will want to add an annotation to any node that must be coerced to the opposite type, so that the code generator will know to generate code to do so. Be sure to think carefully about your coercion rules. In the expression `my_int + my_real`, for example, how will you know whether to coerce the integer to be a real, or to coerce the real to be an integer?

4.24 Explain the need for the $A : B$ notation on the left-hand sides of productions in a tree grammar. Why isn't similar notation required for context-free grammars?

4.25 A potential objection to the tree attribute grammar of Example 4.17 is that it repeatedly copies the entire symbol table from one node to another. In this particular tiny language, it is easy to see that the referencing environment never shrinks: the symbol table changes only with the addition of new identifiers. Exploiting this observation, show how to modify the pseudocode of Figure 4.14 so that it copies only pointers, rather than the entire symbol table.

4.26 Your solution to the previous exercise probably doesn't generalize to languages with nontrivial scoping rules. Explain how an AG such as that in Figure 4.14 might be modified to use a global symbol table similar to the one described in Section C-3.4.1. Among other things, you should consider nested scopes, the hiding of names in outer scopes, and the requirement (not enforced by the table of Section C-3.4.1) that variables be declared before they are used.

4.27–4.31 In More Depth.

4.9 Explorations

4.32 One of the most influential applications of attribute grammars was the Cornell Synthesizer Generator [Rep84, RT88]. Learn how the Generator used attribute grammars not only for incremental update of semantic information in a program under edit, but also for automatic creation of language based editors from formal language specifications. How general is this technique? What applications might it have beyond syntax-directed editing of computer programs?

4.33 The attribute grammars used in this chapter are all quite simple. Most are S- or L-attributed. All are noncircular. Are there any practical uses for more complex attribute grammars? How about automatic attribute evaluators? Using the Bibliographic Notes as a starting point, conduct a survey of attribute evaluation techniques. Where is the line between practical techniques and intellectual curiosities?

4.34 The first validated Ada implementation was the Ada/Ed interpreter from New York University [DGAFS+80]. The interpreter was written in the set-based language SETL [SDDS86] using a denotational semantics definition of Ada. Learn about the Ada/Ed project, SETL, and denotational semantics. Discuss how the use of a formal definition aided the development process.

Also discuss the limitations of Ada/Ed, and expand on the potential role of formal semantics in language design, development, and prototype implementation.

4.35 Version 5 of the Scheme language manual [KCR+98] included a formal definition of Scheme in denotational semantics. How long is this definition, compared to the more conventional definition in English? How readable is it? What do the length and the level of readability say about Scheme? About denotational semantics? (For more on denotational semantics, see the texts of Stoy [Sto77] or Gordon [Gor79].)

Version 6 of the manual [SDF+07] switched to operational semantics. How does this compare to the denotational version? Why do you suppose the standards committee made the change? (For more information, see the paper by Matthews and Findler [MF08].)

4.36–4.37 In More Depth.

4.10 Bibliographic Notes

Much of the early theory of attribute grammars was developed by Knuth [Knu68]. Lewis, Rosenkrantz, and Stearns [LRS74] introduced the notion of an L-attributed grammar. Watt [Wat77] showed how to use marker symbols to emulate inherited attributes in a bottom-up parser. Jazayeri, Ogden, and Rounds [JOR75] showed that exponential time may be required in the worst case to decorate a parse tree with arbitrary attribute flow. Articles by Courcelle [Cou84] and Engelfriet [Eng84] survey the theory and practice of attribute evaluation.

Language-based program editing based on attribute grammars was pioneered by the Synthesizer Generator [RT88] (a follow-on to the language-specific Cornell Program Synthesizer [TR81]) of Reps and Teitelbaum. Magpie [SDB84] was an early incremental compiler, again based on attribute grammars. Meyerovich et al. [MTAB13] have recently used attribute grammars to parallelize a variety of tree-traversal tasks—notably for web page rendering and GPU-accelerated animation.

Action routines to implement many language features can be found in the texts of Fischer et al. or Appel [App97]. Further notes on attribute grammars can be found in the texts of Cooper and Torczon [CT04, pp. 171–188] or Aho et al. [ALSU07, Chap. 5].

Marcotty, Ledgard, and Bochmann [MLB76] provide an early survey of formal notations for programming language semantics. More detailed but still somewhat dated treatment can be found in the texts of Winskel [Win93] and Slonneger and Kurtz [SK95]. Nipkow and Klein cover the topic from a modern and mathematically rigorous perspective, integrating their text with an executable theorem-proving system [NK15].

The seminal paper on axiomatic semantics is by Hoare [Hoa69]. An excellent book on the subject is Gries's *The Science of Programming* [Gri81]. The seminal paper on denotational semantics is by Scott and Strachey [SS71]. Early texts on the subject include those of Stoy [Sto77] and Gordon [Gor79].

5 Target Machine Architecture

As described in Chapter 1, a compiler is simply a translator. It translates programs written in one language into programs written in another language. This second language can be almost anything—some other high-level language, phototypesetting commands, VLSI (chip) layouts—but most of the time it's the machine language for some available computer.

Just as there are many different programming languages, there are many different machine languages, though the latter tend to display considerably less diversity than the former. Each machine language corresponds to a different *processor architecture.* Formally, an architecture is the interface between the hardware and the software—that is, the language generated by a compiler, or by a programmer writing for the bare machine. The *implementation* of the processor is a concrete realization of the architecture, generally in hardware. To generate correct code, it suffices for a compiler writer to understand the target architecture. To generate *fast* code, it is generally necessary to understand the implementation as well, because it is the implementation that determines the relative speeds of alternative translations of a given language construct.

IN MORE DEPTH

Chapter 5 can be found in its entirety on the companion site. It provides a brief overview of those aspects of processor architecture and implementation of particular importance to compiler writers, and may be worth reviewing even by readers who have seen the material before. Principal topics include data representation, instruction set architecture, the evolution of implementation techniques, and the challenges of compiling for modern processors. Examples are drawn largely from the x86, a legacy CISC (complex instruction set) architecture that dominates the desktop/laptop market, and the ARM, a more modern RISC (reduced instruction set) design that dominates the embedded, smart phone, and tablet markets.

DESIGN & IMPLEMENTATION

5.1 Pseudo-assembly notation

At various times throughout the remainder of this book, we shall need to consider sequences of machine instructions corresponding to some high-level language construct. Rather than present these sequences in the assembly language of some particular processor architecture, we will (in most cases) rely on a simple notation designed to represent a generic RISC machine. The following is a brief example that sums the elements of an n-element floating-point vector, V, and places the results in s:

```
    r1 = &V
    r2 := n
    f1 := 0
    goto L2
L1: f2 := *r1           -- load
    f1 +:= f2
    r1 +:= 8            -- floating-point numbers are 8 bytes long
    r2 −:= 1
L2: if r2 > 0 goto L1
    s := f1
```

The notation should in most cases be self-explanatory. It uses "assignment statements" and operators reminiscent of high-level languages, but each line of code corresponds to a single machine instruction, and registers are named explicitly (the names of integer registers begin with 'r'; those of floating-point registers begin with 'f'). Control flow is based entirely on gotos and subroutine calls (not shown). Conditional tests assume that the hardware can perform a comparison and branch in a single instruction, where the comparison tests the contents of a register against a small constant or the contents of another register.

Main memory in our notation can be accessed only by load and store instructions, which look like assignments to or from a register, with no arithmetic. We do, however, assume the availability of *displacement addressing*, which allows us to access memory at some constant offset from the address held in a register. For example, to store register r1 to a local variable at an offset of 12 bytes from the frame pointer (fp) register, we could say *(fp−12) := r1.

II

Core Issues in Language Design

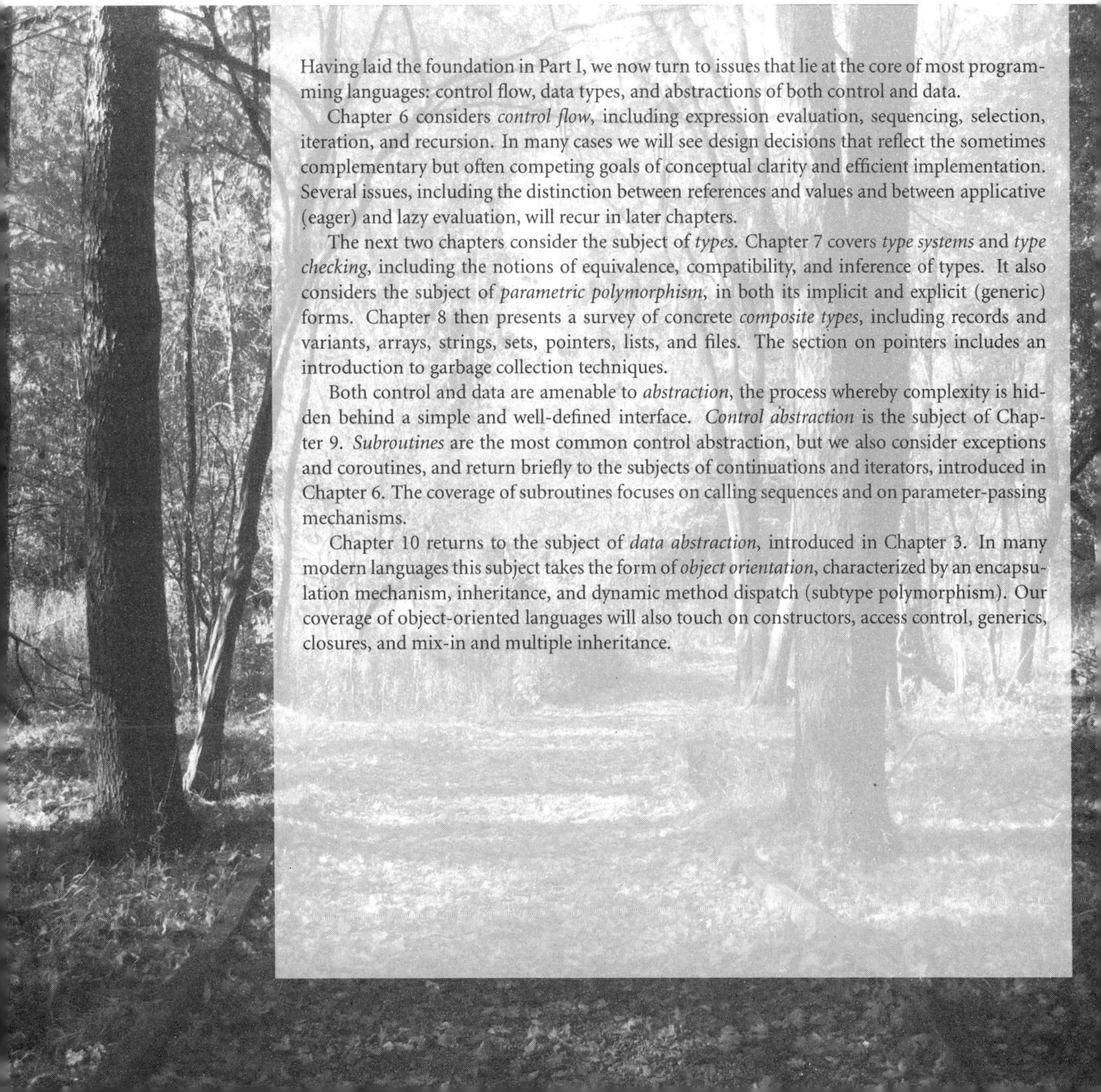

Having laid the foundation in Part I, we now turn to issues that lie at the core of most programming languages: control flow, data types, and abstractions of both control and data.

Chapter 6 considers *control flow*, including expression evaluation, sequencing, selection, iteration, and recursion. In many cases we will see design decisions that reflect the sometimes complementary but often competing goals of conceptual clarity and efficient implementation. Several issues, including the distinction between references and values and between applicative (eager) and lazy evaluation, will recur in later chapters.

The next two chapters consider the subject of *types*. Chapter 7 covers *type systems* and *type checking*, including the notions of equivalence, compatibility, and inference of types. It also considers the subject of *parametric polymorphism*, in both its implicit and explicit (generic) forms. Chapter 8 then presents a survey of concrete *composite types*, including records and variants, arrays, strings, sets, pointers, lists, and files. The section on pointers includes an introduction to garbage collection techniques.

Both control and data are amenable to *abstraction*, the process whereby complexity is hidden behind a simple and well-defined interface. *Control abstraction* is the subject of Chapter 9. *Subroutines* are the most common control abstraction, but we also consider exceptions and coroutines, and return briefly to the subjects of continuations and iterators, introduced in Chapter 6. The coverage of subroutines focuses on calling sequences and on parameter-passing mechanisms.

Chapter 10 returns to the subject of *data abstraction*, introduced in Chapter 3. In many modern languages this subject takes the form of *object orientation*, characterized by an encapsulation mechanism, inheritance, and dynamic method dispatch (subtype polymorphism). Our coverage of object-oriented languages will also touch on constructors, access control, generics, closures, and mix-in and multiple inheritance.

6 Control Flow

Having considered the mechanisms that a compiler uses to enforce semantic rules (Chapter 4) and the characteristics of the target machines for which compilers must generate code (Chapter 5), we now return to core issues in language design. Specifically, we turn in this chapter to the issue of *control flow* or *ordering* in program execution. Ordering is fundamental to most models of computing. It determines what should be done first, what second, and so forth, to accomplish some desired task. We can organize the language mechanisms used to specify ordering into several categories:

1. *Sequencing:* Statements are to be executed (or expressions evaluated) in a certain specified order—usually the order in which they appear in the program text.
2. *Selection:* Depending on some run-time condition, a *choice* is to be made among two or more statements or expressions. The most common selection constructs are `if` and `case` (`switch`) statements. Selection is also sometimes referred to as *alternation*.
3. *Iteration:* A given fragment of code is to be executed repeatedly, either a certain number of times, or until a certain run-time condition is true. Iteration constructs include `for`/`do`, `while`, and `repeat` loops.
4. *Procedural abstraction:* A potentially complex collection of control constructs (a *subroutine*) is encapsulated in a way that allows it to be treated as a single unit, usually subject to parameterization.
5. *Recursion:* An expression is defined in terms of (simpler versions of) itself, either directly or indirectly; the computational model requires a stack on which to save information about partially evaluated instances of the expression. Recursion is usually defined by means of self-referential subroutines.
6. *Concurrency:* Two or more program fragments are to be executed/evaluated "at the same time," either in parallel on separate processors, or interleaved on a single processor in a way that achieves the same effect.
7. *Exception handling* and *speculation:* A program fragment is executed optimistically, on the assumption that some expected condition will be true. If that con-

dition turns out to be false, execution branches to a handler that executes in place of the remainder of the protected fragment (in the case of exception handling), or in place of the *entire* protected fragment (in the case of speculation). For speculation, the language implementation must be able to undo, or "roll back," any visible effects of the protected code.

8. *Nondeterminacy:* The ordering or choice among statements or expressions is deliberately left unspecified, implying that any alternative will lead to correct results. Some languages require the choice to be random, or fair, in some formal sense of the word.

Though the syntactic and semantic details vary from language to language, these categories cover all of the control-flow constructs and mechanisms found in most programming languages. A programmer who thinks in terms of these categories, rather than the syntax of some particular language, will find it easy to learn new languages, evaluate the tradeoffs among languages, and design and reason about algorithms in a language-independent way.

Subroutines are the subject of Chapter 9. Concurrency is the subject of Chapter 13. Exception handling and speculation are discussed in those chapters as well, in Sections 9.4 and 13.4.4. The bulk of the current chapter (Sections 6.3 through 6.7) is devoted to the five remaining categories. We begin in Section 6.1 by considering the evaluation of *expressions*—the building blocks on which all higher-level ordering is based. We consider the syntactic form of expressions, the precedence and associativity of operators, the order of evaluation of operands, and the semantics of the assignment statement. We focus in particular on the distinction between variables that hold a *value* and variables that hold a *reference to* a value; this distinction will play an important role many times in future chapters. In Section 6.2 we consider the difference between *structured* and *unstructured* (`goto`-based) control flow.

The relative importance of different categories of control flow varies significantly among the different classes of programming languages. Sequencing is central to imperative (von Neumann and object-oriented) languages, but plays a relatively minor role in functional languages, which emphasize the evaluation of expressions, de-emphasizing or eliminating statements (e.g., assignments) that affect program output in any way other than through the return of a value. Similarly, functional languages make heavy use of recursion, while imperative languages tend to emphasize iteration. Logic languages tend to de-emphasize or hide the issue of control flow entirely: The programmer simply specifies a set of inference rules; the language implementation must find an order in which to apply those rules that will allow it to deduce values that satisfy some desired property.

6.1 Expression Evaluation

An expression generally consists of either a simple object (e.g., a literal constant, or a named variable or constant) or an *operator* or function applied to a collection of operands or arguments, each of which in turn is an expression. It is conventional to use the term *operator* for built-in functions that use special, simple syntax, and to use the term *operand* for an argument of an operator. In most imperative languages, function calls consist of a function name followed by a parenthesized, comma-separated list of arguments, as in

EXAMPLE 6.1 A typical function call

```
my_func(A, B, C)
```

EXAMPLE 6.2 Typical operators

Operators are typically simpler, taking only one or two arguments, and dispensing with the parentheses and commas:

```
a + b
- c
```

As we saw in Section 3.5.2, some languages define their operators as *syntactic sugar* for more "normal"-looking functions. In Ada, for example, `a + b` is short for `"+"(a, b)`; in C++, `a + b` is short for `a.operator+(b)` or `operator+(a, b)` (whichever is defined).

In general, a language may specify that function calls (operator invocations) employ prefix, infix, or postfix notation. These terms indicate, respectively, whether the function name appears before, among, or after its several arguments:

prefix:	*op* a b	or	*op* (a, b)	or	(*op* a b)
infix:	a *op* b				
postfix:	a b *op*				

Most imperative languages use infix notation for binary operators and prefix notation for unary operators and (with parentheses around the arguments) other functions. Lisp uses prefix notation for all functions, but with the third of the variants above: in what is known as *Cambridge Polish*[1] notation, it places the function name *inside* the parentheses:

EXAMPLE 6.3 Cambridge Polish (prefix) notation

```
(* (+ 1 3) 2)              ; that would be (1 + 3) * 2 in infix
(append a b c my_list)
```

EXAMPLE 6.4 Juxtaposition in ML

ML-family languages dispense with the parentheses altogether, except when they are required for disambiguation:

```
max (2 + 3) 4;;            ⟹ 5
```

1 Prefix notation was popularized by Polish logicians of the early 20th century; Lisp-like parenthesized syntax was first employed (for noncomputational purposes) by philosopher W. V. Quine of Harvard University (Cambridge, MA).

A few languages, notably ML and the R scripting language, allow the user to create new infix operators. Smalltalk uses infix notation for *all* functions (which it calls messages), both built-in and user-defined. The following Smalltalk statement sends a "`displayOn: at:`" message to graphical object `myBox`, with arguments `myScreen` and `100@50` (a pixel location). It corresponds to what other languages would call the invocation of the "`displayOn: at:`" function with arguments `myBox`, `myScreen`, and `100@50`.

EXAMPLE 6.5
Mixfix notation in Smalltalk

```
myBox displayOn: myScreen at: 100@50
```

EXAMPLE 6.6
Conditional expressions

This sort of multiword infix notation occurs occasionally in other languages as well.[2] In Algol one can say

```
a := if b <> 0 then a/b else 0;
```

Here "`if`... `then` ... `else`" is a three-operand infix operator. The equivalent operator in C is written "... `?` ... `:` ...":

```
a = b != 0 ? a/b : 0;
```

Postfix notation is used for most functions in Postscript, Forth, the input language of certain hand-held calculators, and the intermediate code of some compilers. Postfix appears in a few places in other languages as well. Examples include the pointer dereferencing operator (`^`) of Pascal and the post-increment and decrement operators (`++` and `--`) of C and its descendants.

6.1.1 Precedence and Associativity

Most languages provide a rich set of built-in arithmetic and logical operators. When written in infix notation, without parentheses, these operators lead to ambiguity as to what is an operand of what. In Fortran, for example, which uses `**` for exponentiation, how should we parse `a + b * c**d**e/f`? Should this be grouped as

EXAMPLE 6.7
A complicated Fortran expression

```
((((a + b) * c)**d)**e)/f
```

or

```
a + (((b * c)**d)**(e/f))
```

or

2 Most authors use the term "infix" only for binary operators. Multiword operators may be called "mixfix," or left unnamed.

```
a + ((b * (c**(d**e)))/f)
```

or yet some other option? (In Fortran, the answer is the last of the options shown.)

In any given language, the choice among alternative evaluation orders depends on the *precedence* and *associativity* of operators, concepts we introduced in Section 2.1.3. Issues of precedence and associativity do not arise in prefix or postfix notation.

EXAMPLE 6.8 Precedence in four influential languages

Precedence rules specify that certain operators, in the absence of parentheses, group "more tightly" than other operators. In most languages multiplication and division group more tightly than addition and subtraction, so $2 + 3 \times 4$ is 14 and not 20. Details vary widely from one language to another, however. Figure 6.1 shows the levels of precedence for several well-known languages.

The precedence structure of C (and, with minor variations, of its descendants, C++, Java, and C#) is substantially richer than that of most other languages. It is, in fact, richer than shown in Figure 6.1, because several additional constructs, including type casts, function calls, array subscripting, and record field selection, are classified as operators in C. It is probably fair to say that most C programmers do not remember all of their language's precedence levels. The intent of the language designers was presumably to ensure that "the right thing" will usually happen when parentheses are not used to force a particular evaluation order. Rather than count on this, however, the wise programmer will consult the manual or add parentheses.

EXAMPLE 6.9 A "gotcha" in Pascal precedence

It is also probably fair to say that the relatively flat precedence hierarchy of Pascal was a mistake. Novice Pascal programmers would frequently write conditions like

```
if A < B and C < D then (* ouch *)
```

Unless `A`, `B`, `C`, and `D` were all of type Boolean, which is unlikely, this code would result in a static semantic error, since the rules of precedence cause it to group as `A < (B and C) < D`. (And even if all four operands were of type Boolean, the result was almost certain to be something other than what the programmer intended.) Most languages avoid this problem by giving arithmetic operators higher precedence than relational (comparison) operators, which in turn have higher precedence than the logical operators. Notable exceptions include APL and Smalltalk, in which all operators are of equal precedence; parentheses *must* be used to specify grouping.

EXAMPLE 6.10 Common rules for associativity

Associativity rules specify whether sequences of operators of equal precedence group to the right or to the left. Conventions here are somewhat more uniform across languages, but still display some variety. The basic arithmetic operators almost always associate left-to-right, so `9 - 3 - 2` is `4` and not `8`. In Fortran, as noted above, the exponentiation operator (`**`) follows standard mathematical convention, and associates right-to-left, so `4**3**2` is `262144` and not `4096`. In Ada, exponentiation does not associate: one must write either `(4**3)**2` or

Fortran	Pascal	C	Ada
		++, -- (post-inc., dec.)	
**	not	++, -- (pre-inc., dec.), +, - (unary), &, * (address, contents of), !, ~ (logical, bit-wise not)	abs (absolute value), not, **
*, /	*, /, div, mod, and	* (binary), /, % (modulo division)	*, /, mod, rem
+, - (unary and binary)	+, - (unary and binary), or	+, - (binary)	+, - (unary)
		<<, >> (left and right bit shift)	+, - (binary), & (concatenation)
.eq., .ne., .lt., .le., .gt., .ge. (comparisons)	<, <=, >, >=, =, <>, IN	<, <=, >, >= (inequality tests)	=, /= , <, <=, >, >=
.not.		==, != (equality tests)	
		& (bit-wise and)	
		^ (bit-wise exclusive or)	
		| (bit-wise inclusive or)	
.and.		&& (logical and)	and, or, xor (logical operators)
.or.		|| (logical or)	
.eqv., .neqv. (logical comparisons)		?: (if...then...else)	
		=, +=, -=, *=, /=, %=, >>=, <<=, &=, ^=, |= (assignment)	
		, (sequencing)	

Figure 6.1 Operator precedence levels in Fortran, Pascal, C, and Ada. The operators at the top of the figure group most tightly.

`4**(3**2)`; the language syntax does not allow the unparenthesized form. In languages that allow assignments inside expressions (an option we will consider more in Section 6.1.2), assignment associates right-to-left. Thus in C, `a = b = a + c` assigns `a + c` into `b` and then assigns the same value into `a`. ■

EXAMPLE 6.11
User-defined precedence and associativity in Haskell

Haskell is unusual in allowing the programmer to specify both the associativity and the precedence of user-defined operators. The predefined `^` operator, for example, which indicates integer exponentiation, is declared in the standard library (and could be redefined by the programmer) as

```
infixr 8 ^
```

Here `infixr` means "right associative infix operator," so `4 ^ 3 ^ 2` groups as `4 ^ (3 ^ 2)` rather than as `(4 ^ 3) ^ 2`. The similar `infixl` and `infix` declarations specify left associativity and nonassociativity, respectively. Precedence levels run from 0 (loosest) to 9 (tightest). If no "fixity" declaration is provided, newly defined operators are left associative by default, and group at level 9. Function application (specified simply via juxtaposition in Haskell) groups tightest of all—effectively at level 10.

Because the rules for precedence and associativity vary so much from one language to another, a programmer who works in several languages is wise to make liberal use of parentheses.

6.1.2 Assignments

In a purely functional language, expressions are the building blocks of programs, and computation consists entirely of expression evaluation. The effect of any individual expression on the overall computation is limited to the value that expression provides to its surrounding context. Complex computations employ recursion to generate a potentially unbounded number of values, expressions, and contexts.

In an imperative language, by contrast, computation typically consists of an ordered series of changes to the values of variables in memory. Assignments provide the principal means by which to make the changes. Each assignment takes a pair of arguments: a value and a reference to a variable into which the value should be placed.

In general, a programming language construct is said to have a *side effect* if it influences subsequent computation (and ultimately program output) in any way other than by returning a value for use in the surrounding context. Assignment is perhaps the most fundamental side effect: while the evaluation of an assignment may sometimes yield a value, what we really care about is the fact that it changes the value of a variable, thereby influencing the result of any later computation in which the variable appears.

Many imperative languages distinguish between *expressions*, which always produce a value, and may or may not have side effects, and *statements*, which are executed *solely* for their side effects, and return no useful value. Given the centrality of assignment, imperative programming is sometimes described as "computing by means of side effects."

At the opposite extreme, purely functional languages have no side effects. As a result, the value of an expression in such a language depends only on the referencing environment in which the expression is evaluated, *not* on the time at which the evaluation occurs. If an expression yields a certain value at one point in time, it is guaranteed to yield the same value at any point in time. In fancier terms, expressions in a purely functional language are said to be *referentially transparent*.

Haskell and Miranda are purely functional. Many other languages are mixed: ML and Lisp are mostly functional, but make assignment available to programmers who want it. C#, Python, and Ruby are mostly imperative, but provide a variety of features (first-class functions, polymorphism, functional values and aggregates, garbage collection, unlimited extent) that allow them to be used in a largely functional style. We will return to functional programming, and the features it requires, in several future sections, including 6.2.2, 6.6, 7.3, 8.5.3, 8.6, and all of Chapter 11.

References and Values

On the surface, assignment appears to be a very straightforward operation. Below the surface, however, there are some subtle but important differences in the semantics of assignment in different imperative languages. These differences are often invisible, because they do not affect the behavior of simple programs. They have a major impact, however, on programs that use pointers, and will be explored in further detail in Section 8.5. We provide an introduction to the issues here.

EXAMPLE 6.12
L-values and r-values

Consider the following assignments in C:

```
d = a;
a = b + c;
```

In the first statement, the right-hand side of the assignment refers to the *value* of a, which we wish to place into d. In the second statement, the left-hand side refers to the *location* of a, where we want to put the sum of b and c. Both interpretations—value and location—are possible because a variable in C (as in many other languages) is a named container for a value. We sometimes say that languages like C use a *value model* of variables. Because of their use on the left-hand side of assignment statements, expressions that denote locations are referred to as *l-values*. Expressions that denote values (possibly the value stored in a location) are referred to as *r-values*. Under a value model of variables, a given expression can be either an l-value or an r-value, depending on the context in which it appears. ■

EXAMPLE 6.13
L-values in C

Of course, not all expressions can be l-values, because not all values have a location, and not all names are variables. In most languages it makes no sense to say `2 + 3 = a`, or even `a = 2 + 3`, if a is the name of a constant. By the same token, not all l-values are simple names; both l-values and r-values can be complicated expressions. In C one may write

```
(f(a)+3)->b[c] = 2;
```

In this expression `f(a)` returns a pointer to some element of an array of pointers to structures (records). The assignment places the value 2 into the c-th element

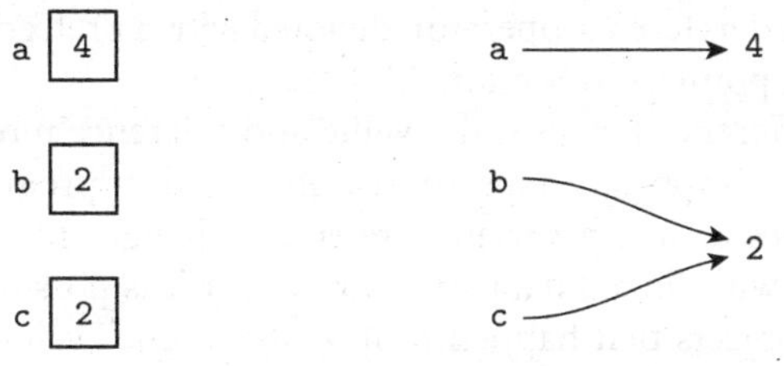

Figure 6.2 **The value (left) and reference (right) models of variables.** Under the reference model, it becomes important to distinguish between variables that refer to the same object and variables that refer to different objects whose values happen (at the moment) to be equal.

of field `b` of the structure pointed at by the third array element after the one to which `f`'s return value points.

EXAMPLE 6.14
L-values in C++

In C++ it is even possible for a function to return a reference to a structure, rather than a pointer to it, allowing one to write

```
g(a).b[c] = 2;
```

We will consider references further in Section 9.3.1.

A language can make the distinction between l-values and r-values more explicit by employing a *reference model* of variables. Languages that do this include Algol 68, Clu, Lisp/Scheme, ML, and Smalltalk. In these languages, a variable is not a named container for a value; rather, it is a named *reference to* a value. The following fragment of code is syntactically valid in both Pascal and Clu:

EXAMPLE 6.15
Variables as values and references

```
b := 2;
c := b;
a := b + c;
```

A Pascal programmer might describe this code by saying: "We put the value 2 in `b` and then copy it into `c`. We then read these values, add them together, and place the resulting 4 in `a`." The Clu programmer would say: "We let `b` refer to 2 and then let `c` refer to it also. We then pass these references to the `+` operator, and let `a` refer to the result, namely 4."

These two ways of thinking are illustrated in Figure 6.2. With a value model of variables, any integer variable can contain the value 2. With a reference model of variables, there is (at least conceptually) only *one* 2—a sort of Platonic Ideal—to which any variable can refer. The practical effect is the same in this example, because integers are *immutable*: the value of 2 never changes, so we can't tell the difference between two copies of the number 2 and two references to "the" number 2.

In a language that uses the reference model, every variable is an l-value. When it appears in a context that expects an r-value, it must be *dereferenced* to obtain the value to which it refers. In most languages with a reference model (including Clu), the dereference is implicit and automatic. In ML, the programmer must use an explicit dereference operator, denoted with a prefix exclamation point. We will revisit ML pointers in Section 8.5.1.

The difference between the value and reference models of variables becomes particularly important (specifically, it can affect program output and behavior) if the values to which variables refer can change "in place," as they do in many programs with linked data structures, or if it is possible for variables to refer to different objects that happen to have the "same" value. In this latter case it becomes important to distinguish between variables that refer to the same object and variables that refer to different objects whose values happen (at the moment) to be equal. (Lisp, as we shall see in Sections 7.4 and 11.3.3, provides more than one notion of equality, to accommodate this distinction.) We will discuss the value and reference models of variables further in Section 8.5.

Java uses a value model for built-in types and a reference model for user-defined types (classes). C# and Eiffel allow the programmer to choose between the value and reference models for each individual user-defined type. A C# `class` is a reference type; a `struct` is a value type.

Boxing

EXAMPLE 6.16
Wrapper classes

A drawback of using a value model for built-in types is that they can't be passed uniformly to methods that expect class-typed parameters. Early versions of Java required the programmer to "wrap" objects of built-in types inside corresponding predefined class types in order to insert them in standard container (collection) classes:

```
import java.util.Hashtable;
...
Hashtable ht = new Hashtable();
...
Integer N = new Integer(13);        // Integer is a "wrapper" class
ht.put(N, new Integer(31));
Integer M = (Integer) ht.get(N);
int m = M.intValue();
```

The wrapper class was needed here because `Hashtable` expects a parameter of object type, and an `int` is not an object. ■

DESIGN & IMPLEMENTATION

6.1 Implementing the reference model

It is tempting to assume that the reference model of variables is inherently more expensive than the value model, since a naive implementation would require a level of indirection on every access. As we shall see in Section 8.5.1, however, most compilers for languages with a reference model use multiple copies of immutable objects for the sake of efficiency, achieving exactly the same performance for simple types that they would with a value model.

EXAMPLE 6.17
Boxing in Java 5 and C#

C# and more recent versions of Java perform automatic *boxing* and *unboxing* operations that avoid the wrapper syntax in many cases:

```
ht.put(13, 31);
int m = (Integer) ht.get(13);
```

Here the Java compiler creates hidden `Integer` objects to hold the values `13` and `31`, so they may be passed to `put` as references. The `Integer` cast on the return value is still needed, to make sure that the hash table entry for `13` is really an integer and not, say, a floating-point number or string. Generics, which we will consider in Section 7.3.1, allow the programmer to declare a table containing only integers. In Java, this would eliminate the need to cast the return value. In C#, it would eliminate the need for boxing.

Orthogonality

A common design goal is to make the various features of a language as *orthogonal* as possible. Orthogonality means that features can be used in any combination, the combinations all make sense, and the meaning of a given feature is *consistent*, regardless of the other features with which it is combined.

Algol 68 was one of the first languages to make orthogonality a principal design goal, and in fact few languages since have given the goal such weight. Among other things, Algol 68 is said to be *expression-oriented*: it has no separate notion of statement. Arbitrary expressions can appear in contexts that would call for a statement in many other languages, and constructs that are considered to be statements in other languages can appear within expressions. The following, for example, is valid in Algol 68:

EXAMPLE 6.18
Expression orientation in Algol 68

```
begin
    a := if b < c then d else e;
    a := begin f(b); g(c) end;
    g(d);
    2 + 3
end
```

Here the value of the `if... then ... else` construct is either the value of its `then` part or the value of its `else` part, depending on the value of the condition. The value of the "statement list" on the right-hand side of the second assignment is the value of its final "statement," namely the return value of `g(c)`. There is no need to distinguish between procedures and functions, because every subroutine call returns a value. The value returned by `g(d)` is discarded in this example. Finally, the value of the code fragment as a whole is 5, the sum of 2 and 3.

C takes an intermediate approach. It distinguishes between statements and expressions, but one of the classes of statement is an "expression statement," which computes the value of an expression and then throws it away; in effect, this allows an expression to appear in any context that would require a statement in most other languages. Unfortunately, as we noted in Section 3.7, the reverse is not the case: statements cannot in general be used in an expression context. C provides special expression forms for selection and sequencing. Algol 60 defines `if... then ... else` as both a statement and an expression.

Both Algol 68 and C allow assignments within expressions. The value of an assignment is simply the value of its right-hand side. Where most of the descendants of Algol 60 use the := token to represent assignment, C follows Fortran in simply using =. It uses == to represent a test for equality (Fortran uses `.eq.`). Moreover, in any context that expects a Boolean value, C accepts anything that can be coerced to be an integer. It interprets zero as false; any other value is true.[3] As a result, both of the following constructs are valid—common—in C:

EXAMPLE 6.19
A "gotcha" in C conditions

```
if (a == b) {
    /* do the following if a equals b */
    ...

if (a = b) {
    /* assign b into a and then do
       the following if the result is nonzero */
    ...
```

Programmers who are accustomed to Ada or some other language in which = is the equality test frequently write the second form above when the first is what is intended. This sort of bug can be very hard to find. ■

Though it provides a true Boolean type (`bool`), C++ shares the problem of C, because it provides automatic coercions from numeric, pointer, and enumeration types. Java and C# eliminate the problem by disallowing integers in Boolean contexts. The assignment operator is still =, and the equality test is still ==, but the statement `if (a = b) ...` will generate a compile-time type clash error unless `a` and `b` are both of Boolean type.

Combination Assignment Operators

EXAMPLE 6.20
Updating assignments

Because they rely so heavily on side effects, imperative programs must frequently *update* a variable. It is thus common in many languages to see statements like

```
a = a + 1;
```

or, worse,

```
b.c[3].d = b.c[3].d * e;
```

Such statements are not only cumbersome to write and to read (we must examine both sides of the assignment carefully to see if they really are the same), they also

3 Historically, C lacked a separate Boolean type. C99 added `_Bool`, but it's really just a 1-bit integer.

result in redundant address calculations (or at least extra work to eliminate the redundancy in the code improvement phase of compilation).

EXAMPLE 6.21
Side effects and updates

If the address calculation has a side effect, then we may need to write a pair of statements instead. Consider the following code in C:

```
void update(int A[], int index_fn(int n)) {
    int i, j;
    /* calculate i */
    ...
    j = index_fn(i);
    A[j] = A[j] + 1;
}
```

Here we cannot safely write

```
A[index_fn(i)] = A[index_fn(i)] + 1;
```

We have to introduce the temporary variable `j` because we don't know whether `index_fn` has a side effect or not. If it is being used, for example, to keep a log of elements that have been updated, then we shall want to make sure that `update` calls it only once.

EXAMPLE 6.22
Assignment operators

To eliminate the clutter and compile- or run-time cost of redundant address calculations, and to avoid the issue of repeated side effects, many languages, beginning with Algol 68, and including C and its descendants, provide so-called *assignment operators* to update a variable. Using assignment operators, the statements in Example 6.20 can be written as follows:

```
a += 1;
b.c[3].d *= e;
```

and the two assignments in the `update` function can be replaced with

```
A[index_fn(i)] += 1;
```

In addition to being aesthetically cleaner, the assignment operator form guarantees that the address calculation and any side effects happen only once.

EXAMPLE 6.23
Prefix and postfix inc/dec

As shown in Figure 6.1, C provides 10 different assignment operators, one for each of its binary arithmetic and bit-wise operators. C also provides prefix and postfix increment and decrement operations. These allow even simpler code in `update`:

```
A[index_fn(i)]++;
```

or

```
++A[index_fn(i)];
```

More significantly, increment and decrement operators provide elegant syntax for code that uses an index or a pointer to traverse an array:

```
A[--i] = b;
*p++ = *q++;
```

When prefixed to an expression, the ++ or -- operator increments or decrements its operand *before* providing a value to the surrounding context. In the postfix form, ++ or -- updates its operand *after* providing a value. If `i` is 3 and `p` and `q` point to the initial elements of a pair of arrays, then `b` will be assigned into `A[2]` (not `A[3]`), and the second assignment will copy the initial elements of the arrays (not the second elements).

EXAMPLE 6.24
Advantages of postfix inc/dec

The prefix forms of ++ and -- are syntactic sugar for += and -=. We could have written

```
A[i -= 1] = b;
```

above. The postfix forms are not syntactic sugar. To obtain an effect similar to the second statement above we would need an auxiliary variable and a lot of extra notation:

```
*(t = p, p += 1, t) = *(t = q, q += 1, t);
```

Both the assignment operators (+=, -=) and the increment and decrement operators (++, --) do "the right thing" when applied to pointers in C (assuming those pointers point into an array). If `p` points to element i of an array, where each element occupies n bytes (including any bytes required for alignment, as discussed in Section C-5.1), then `p += 3` points to element $i+3$, $3n$ bytes later in memory. We will discuss pointers and arrays in C in more detail in Section 8.5.1.

Multiway Assignment

EXAMPLE 6.25
Simple multiway assignment

We have already seen that the right associativity of assignment (in languages that allow assignment in expressions) allows one to write things like `a = b = c`. In several languages, including Clu, ML, Perl, Python, and Ruby, it is also possible to write

```
a, b = c, d;
```

Here the comma in the right-hand side is *not* the sequencing operator of C. Rather, it serves to define an expression, or *tuple*, consisting of multiple r-values. The comma operator on the left-hand side produces a tuple of l-values. The effect of the assignment is to copy `c` into `a` and `d` into `b`.[4]

EXAMPLE 6.26
Advantages of multiway assignment

While we could just as easily have written

4 The syntax shown here is for Perl, Python, and Ruby. Clu uses := for assignment. ML requires parentheses around each tuple.

```
a = c; b = d;
```

the multiway (tuple) assignment allows us to write things like

```
a, b = b, a;            (* swap a and b *)
```

which would otherwise require auxiliary variables. Moreover, multiway assignment allows functions to return tuples, as well as single values:

```
a, b, c = foo(d, e, f);
```

This notation eliminates the asymmetry (nonorthogonality) of functions in most programming languages, which allow an arbitrary number of arguments, but only a single return.

✓ CHECK YOUR UNDERSTANDING

1. Name eight major categories of control-flow mechanisms.
2. What distinguishes *operators* from other sorts of functions?
3. Explain the difference between *prefix*, *infix*, and *postfix* notation. What is *Cambridge Polish* notation? Name two programming languages that use postfix notation.
4. Why don't issues of associativity and precedence arise in Postscript or Forth?
5. What does it mean for an expression to be *referentially transparent*?
6. What is the difference between a *value* model of variables and a *reference* model of variables? Why is the distinction important?
7. What is an *l-value*? An *r-value*?
8. Why is the distinction between *mutable* and *immutable* values important in the implementation of a language with a reference model of variables?
9. Define *orthogonality* in the context of programming language design.
10. What is the difference between a *statement* and an *expression*? What does it mean for a language to be *expression-oriented*?
11. What are the advantages of updating a variable with an *assignment operator*, rather than with a regular assignment in which the variable appears on both the left- and right-hand sides?

6.1.3 Initialization

Because they already provide a construct (the assignment statement) to set the value of a variable, imperative languages do not always provide a means of specifying an initial value for a variable in its declaration. There are several reasons, however, why such initial values may be useful:

1. As suggested in Figure 3.3, a `static` variable that is local to a subroutine needs an initial value in order to be useful.
2. For any statically allocated variable, an initial value that is specified in the declaration can be preallocated in global memory by the compiler, avoiding the cost of assigning an initial value at run time.
3. Accidental use of an uninitialized variable is one of the most common programming errors. One of the easiest ways to prevent such errors (or at least ensure that erroneous behavior is repeatable) is to give every variable a value when it is first declared.

Most languages allow variables of built-in types to be initialized in their declarations. A more complete and orthogonal approach to initialization requires a notation for *aggregates*: built-up structured values of user-defined composite types. Aggregates can be found in several languages, including C, C++, Ada, Fortran 90, and ML; we will discuss them further in Section 7.1.3.

It should be emphasized that initialization saves time only for variables that are statically allocated. Variables allocated in the stack or heap at run time must be initialized at run time.[5] It is also worth noting that the problem of using an uninitialized variable occurs not only after elaboration, but also as a result of any operation that destroys a variable's value without providing a new one. Two of the most common such operations are explicit deallocation of an object referenced through a pointer and modification of the *tag* of a variant record. We will consider these operations further in Sections 8.5 and C-8.1.3, respectively.

If a variable is not given an initial value explicitly in its declaration, the language may specify a default value. In C, for example, statically allocated variables for which the programmer does not provide an initial value are guaranteed to be represented in memory as if they had been initialized to zero. For most types on most machines, this is a string of zero bits, allowing the language implementation to exploit the fact that most operating systems (for security reasons) fill newly allocated memory with zeros. Zero-initialization applies recursively to the subcomponents of variables of user-defined composite types. Java and C# provide a similar guarantee for the fields of all class-typed objects, not just those that are statically allocated. Most scripting languages provide a default initial value for *all* variables, of all types, regardless of scope or lifetime.

---

5 For variables that are accessed indirectly (e.g., in languages that employ a reference model of variables), a compiler can often reduce the cost of initializing a stack or heap variable by placing the initial value in static memory, and only creating the pointer to it at elaboration time.

Dynamic Checks

Instead of giving every uninitialized variable a default value, a language or implementation can choose to define the use of an uninitialized variable as a dynamic semantic error, and can catch these errors at run time. The advantage of the semantic checks is that they will often identify a program bug that is masked or made more subtle by the presence of a default value. With appropriate hardware support, uninitialized variable checks can even be as cheap as default values, at least for certain types. In particular, a compiler that relies on the IEEE standard for floating-point arithmetic can fill uninitialized floating-point numbers with a *signaling NaN* value, as discussed in Section C-5.2.2. Any attempt to use such a value in a computation will result in a hardware interrupt, which the language implementation may catch (with a little help from the operating system), and use to trigger a semantic error message.

For most types on most machines, unfortunately, the costs of catching all uses of an uninitialized variable at run time are considerably higher. If every possible bit pattern of the variable's representation in memory designates some legitimate value (and this is often the case), then extra space must be allocated somewhere to hold an initialized/uninitialized flag. This flag must be set to "uninitialized" at elaboration time and to "initialized" at assignment time. It must also be checked (by extra code) at every use, or at least at every use that the code improver is unable to prove is redundant.

Definite Assignment

EXAMPLE 6.27
Programs outlawed by definite assignment

For local variables of methods, Java and C# define a notion of *definite assignment* that precludes the use of uninitialized variables. This notion is based on the control flow of the program, and can be statically checked by the compiler. Roughly speaking, every possible control path to an expression must assign a value to every variable in that expression. This is a conservative rule; it can sometimes prohibit programs that would never actually use an uninitialized variable. In Java:

```
int i;
int j = 3;
...
if (j > 0) {
    i = 2;
}
...                         // no assignments to j in here
if (j > 0) {
    System.out.println(i);  // error: "i might not have been initialized"
}
```

While a human being might reason that `i` will be used only when it has previously been given a value, such determinations are undecidable in the general case, and the compiler does not attempt them.

Constructors

Many object-oriented languages (Java and C# among them) allow the programmer to define types for which initialization of dynamically allocated variables occurs automatically, even when no initial value is specified in the declaration. Some—notably C++—also distinguish carefully between initialization and assignment. Initialization is interpreted as a call to a *constructor* function for the variable's type, with the initial value as an argument. In the absence of coercion, assignment is interpreted as a call to the type's assignment operator or, if none has been defined, as a simple bit-wise copy of the value on the assignment's right-hand side. The distinction between initialization and assignment is particularly important for user-defined abstract data types that perform their own storage management. A typical example occurs in variable-length character strings. An assignment to such a string must generally deallocate the space consumed by the old value of the string before allocating space for the new value. An initialization of the string must simply allocate space. Initialization with a nontrivial value is generally cheaper than default initialization followed by assignment, because it avoids deallocation of the space allocated for the default value. We will return to this issue in Section 10.3.2.

Neither Java nor C# distinguishes between initialization and assignment: an initial value can be given in a declaration, but this is the same as an immediate subsequent assignment. Java uses a reference model for all variables of user-defined object types, and provides for automatic storage reclamation, so assignment never copies values. C# allows the programmer to specify a value model when desired (in which case assignment does copy values), but otherwise mirrors Java.

6.1.4 Ordering within Expressions

While precedence and associativity rules define the order in which binary infix operators are applied within an expression, they do not specify the order in which the operands of a given operator are evaluated. For example, in the expression

EXAMPLE 6.28
Indeterminate ordering

```
a - f(b) - c * d
```

we know from associativity that `f(b)` will be subtracted from `a` before performing the second subtraction, and we know from precedence that the right operand of that second subtraction will be the result of `c * d`, rather than merely `c`, but without additional information we do not know whether `a - f(b)` will be evaluated before or after `c * d`. Similarly, in a subroutine call with multiple arguments

```
f(a, g(b), h(c))
```

we do not know the order in which the arguments will be evaluated. ■

There are two main reasons why the order can be important:

EXAMPLE 6.29
A value that depends on ordering

1. *Side effects:* If `f(b)` may modify `d`, then the value of `a - f(b) - c * d` will depend on whether the first subtraction or the multiplication is performed first. Similarly, if `g(b)` may modify `a` and/or `c`, then the values passed to `f(a, g(b), h(c))` will depend on the order in which the arguments are evaluated. ■

EXAMPLE 6.30
An optimization that depends on ordering

2. *Code improvement:* The order of evaluation of subexpressions has an impact on both register allocation and instruction scheduling. In the expression `a * b + f(c)`, it is probably desirable to call `f` before evaluating `a * b`, because the product, if calculated first, would need to be saved during the call to `f`, and `f` might want to use all the registers in which it might easily be saved. In a similar vein, consider the sequence

```
a := B[i];
c := a * 2 + d * 3;
```

On an in-order processor, it is probably desirable to evaluate `d * 3` before evaluating `a * 2`, because the previous statement, `a := B[i]`, will need to load a value from memory. Because loads are slow, if the processor attempts to use the value of `a` in the next instruction (or even the next few instructions on many machines), it will have to wait. If it does something unrelated instead (i.e., evaluate `d * 3`), then the load can proceed in parallel with other computation. ■

Because of the importance of code improvement, most language manuals say that the order of evaluation of operands and arguments is undefined. (Java and C# are unusual in this regard: they require left-to-right evaluation.) In the absence of an enforced order, the compiler can choose whatever order is likely to result in faster code.

DESIGN & IMPLEMENTATION

6.2 Safety versus performance

A recurring theme in any comparison between C++ and Java is the latter's willingness to accept additional run-time cost in order to obtain cleaner semantics or increased reliability. Definite assignment is one example: it may force the programmer to perform "unnecessary" initializations on certain code paths, but in so doing it avoids the many subtle errors that can arise from missing initialization in other languages. Similarly, the Java specification mandates automatic garbage collection, and its reference model of user-defined types forces most objects to be allocated in the heap. As we shall see in future chapters, Java also requires both dynamic binding of all method invocations and run-time checks for out-of-bounds array references, type clashes, and other dynamic semantic errors. Clever compilers can reduce or eliminate the cost of these requirements in certain common cases, but for the most part the Java design reflects an evolutionary shift away from performance as *the* overriding design goal.

Applying Mathematical Identities

Some language implementations (e.g., for dialects of Fortran) allow the compiler to *rearrange* expressions involving operators whose mathematical abstractions are commutative, associative, and/or distributive, in order to generate faster code. Consider the following Fortran fragment:

EXAMPLE 6.31

Optimization and mathematical "laws"

```
a = b + c
d = c + e + b
```

Some compilers will rearrange this as

```
a = b + c
d = b + c + e
```

They can then recognize the *common subexpression* in the first and second statements, and generate code equivalent to

```
a = b + c
d = a + e
```

Similarly,

```
a = b/c/d
e = f/d/c
```

may be rearranged as

```
t = c * d
a = b/t
e = f/t
```

Unfortunately, while mathematical arithmetic obeys a variety of commutative, associative, and distributive laws, computer arithmetic is not as orderly. The

DESIGN & IMPLEMENTATION

6.3 Evaluation order

Expression evaluation presents a difficult tradeoff between semantics and implementation. To limit surprises, most language definitions require the compiler, if it ever reorders expressions, to respect any ordering imposed by parentheses. The programmer can therefore use parentheses to prevent the application of arithmetic "identities" when desired. No similar guarantee exists with respect to the order of evaluation of operands and arguments. It is therefore unwise to write expressions in which a side effect of evaluating one operand or argument can affect the value of another. As we shall see in Section 6.3, some languages, notably Euclid and Turing, outlaw such side effects.

EXAMPLE 6.32
Overflow and arithmetic "identities"

problem is that numbers in a computer are of limited precision. Suppose `a`, `b`, and `c` are all integers between two billion and three billion. With 32-bit arithmetic, the expression `b - c + d` can be evaluated safely left-to-right (2^{32} is a little less than 4.3 billion). If the compiler attempts to reorganize this expression as `b + d - c`, however (e.g., in order to delay its use of `c`), then arithmetic overflow will occur. Despite our intuition from math, this reorganization is unsafe.

Many languages, including Pascal and most of its descendants, provide dynamic semantic checks to detect arithmetic overflow. In some implementations these checks can be disabled to eliminate their run-time overhead. In C and C++, the effect of arithmetic overflow is implementation-dependent. In Java, it is well defined: the language definition specifies the size of all numeric types, and requires two's complement integer and IEEE floating-point arithmetic. In C#, the programmer can explicitly request the presence or absence of checks by tagging an expression or statement with the `checked` or `unchecked` keyword. In a completely different vein, Scheme, Common Lisp, and several scripting languages place no a priori limit on the size of integers; space is allocated to hold extra-large values on demand.

EXAMPLE 6.33
Reordering and numerical stability

Even in the absence of overflow, the limited precision of floating-point arithmetic can cause different arrangements of the "same" expression to produce significantly different results, invisibly. Single-precision IEEE floating-point numbers devote one bit to the sign, eight bits to the exponent (power of two), and 23 bits to the mantissa. Under this representation, `a + b` is guaranteed to result in a loss of information if $|\log_2(a/b)| > 23$. Thus if `b = -c`, then `a + b + c` may appear to be zero, instead of `a`, if the magnitude of `a` is small, while the magnitudes of `b` and `c` are large. In a similar vein, a number like 0.1 cannot be represented precisely, because its binary representation is a "repeating decimal": 0.0001001001.... For certain values of `x`, `(0.1 + x) * 10.0` and `1.0 + (x * 10.0)` can differ by as much as 25%, even when `0.1` and `x` are of the same magnitude.

6.1.5 Short-Circuit Evaluation

EXAMPLE 6.34
Short-circuited expressions

Boolean expressions provide a special and important opportunity for code improvement and increased readability. Consider the expression `(a < b) and (b < c)`. If `a` is greater than `b`, there is really no point in checking to see whether `b` is less than `c`; we know the overall expression must be false. Similarly, in the expression `(a > b) or (b > c)`, if `a` is indeed greater than `b` there is no point in checking to see whether `b` is greater than `c`; we know the overall expression must be true. A compiler that performs *short-circuit evaluation* of Boolean expressions will generate code that skips the second half of both of these computations when the overall value can be determined from the first half.

EXAMPLE 6.35
Saving time with short-circuiting

Short-circuit evaluation can save significant amounts of time in certain situations:

```
if (very_unlikely_condition && very_expensive_function()) ...
```

EXAMPLE 6.36
Short-circuit pointer chasing

But time is not the only consideration, or even the most important. Short-circuiting changes the *semantics* of Boolean expressions. In C, for example, one can use the following code to search for an element in a list:

```
p = my_list;
while (p && p->key != val)
    p = p->next;
```

C short-circuits its `&&` and `||` operators, and uses zero for both null and false, so `p->key` will be accessed if and only if `p` is non-null. The syntactically similar code in Pascal does not work, because Pascal does not short-circuit `and` and `or`:

```
p := my_list;
while (p <> nil) and (p^.key <> val) do      (* ouch! *)
    p := p^.next;
```

Here both of the `<>` relations will be evaluated before `and`-ing their results together. At the end of an unsuccessful search, `p` will be `nil`, and the attempt to access `p^.key` will be a run-time (dynamic semantic) error, which the compiler may or may not have generated code to catch. To avoid this situation, the Pascal programmer must introduce an auxiliary Boolean variable and an extra level of nesting:

```
p := my_list;
still_searching := true;
while still_searching do
    if p = nil then
        still_searching := false
    else if p^.key = val then
        still_searching := false
    else
        p := p^.next;
```

EXAMPLE 6.37
Short-circuiting and other errors

Short-circuit evaluation can also be used to avoid out-of-bound subscripts:

```
const int MAX = 10;
int A[MAX];                /* indices from 0 to 9 */
...
if (i >= 0 && i < MAX && A[i] > foo) ...
```

division by zero:

```
if (d == 0 || n/d < threshold) ...
```

and various other errors.

There are situations, however, in which short circuiting may not be appropriate. In particular, if expressions *E1* and *E2* both have side effects, we may want the conjunction *E1* and *E2* (and likewise *E1* or *E2*) to evaluate both halves (Exercise 6.12). To accommodate such situations while still allowing short-circuit evaluation in scenarios like those of Examples 6.35 through 6.37, a few languages include both regular *and* short-circuit Boolean operators. In Ada, for example, the regular Boolean operators are `and` and `or`; the short-circuit versions are the two-word combinations `and then` and `or else`:

EXAMPLE 6.38
Optional short-circuiting

```
found_it := p /= null and then p.key = val;
...
if d = 0.0 or else n/d < threshold then ...
```

(Ada uses `/=` for "not equal.") In C, the bit-wise `&` and `|` operators can be used as non-short-circuiting alternatives to `&&` and `||` when their arguments are logical (zero or one) values.

If we think of `and` and `or` as binary operators, short circuiting can be considered an example of delayed or *lazy* evaluation: the operands are "passed" unevaluated. Internally, the operator evaluates the first operand in any case, the second only when needed. In a language like Algol 68, which allows arbitrary control flow constructs to be used inside expressions, conditional evaluation can be specified explicitly with `if... then ... else`; see Exercise 6.13.

When used to determine the flow of control in a selection or iteration construct, short-circuit Boolean expressions do not really have to calculate a Boolean value; they simply have to ensure that control takes the proper path in any given situation. We will look more closely at the generation of code for short-circuit expressions in Section 6.4.1.

✓ CHECK YOUR UNDERSTANDING

12. Given the ability to assign a value into a variable, why is it useful to be able to specify an *initial* value?
13. What are *aggregates*? Why are they useful?
14. Explain the notion of *definite assignment* in Java and C#.
15. Why is it generally expensive to catch all uses of uninitialized variables at run time?
16. Why is it impossible to catch all uses of uninitialized variables at compile time?
17. Why do most languages leave unspecified the order in which the arguments of an operator or function are evaluated?
18. What is *short-circuit* Boolean evaluation? Why is it useful?

6.2 Structured and Unstructured Flow

EXAMPLE 6.39
Control flow with `goto`s in Fortran

Control flow in assembly languages is achieved by means of conditional and unconditional jumps (branches). Early versions of Fortran mimicked the low-level approach by relying heavily on `goto` statements for most nonprocedural control flow:

```
if (A .lt. B) goto 10        ! ".lt." means "<"
...
10
```

The `10` on the bottom line is a *statement label.* `Goto` statements also featured prominently in other early imperative languages. ■

Beginning in the late 1960s, largely in response to an article by Edsger Dijkstra [Dij68b],[6] language designers hotly debated the merits and evils of `goto`s. It seems fair to say the detractors won. Ada and C# allow `goto`s only in limited contexts. Modula (1, 2, and 3), Clu, Eiffel, Java, and most of the scripting languages do not allow them at all. Fortran 90 and C++ allow them primarily for compatibility with their predecessor languages. (Java reserves the token `goto` as a keyword, to make it easier for a Java compiler to produce good error messages when a programmer uses a C++ `goto` by mistake.)

The abandonment of `goto`s was part of a larger "revolution" in software engineering known as *structured programming.* Structured programming was the "hot trend" of the 1970s, in much the same way that object-oriented programming was the trend of the 1990s. Structured programming emphasizes top-down design (i.e., progressive refinement), modularization of code, structured types (records, sets, pointers, multidimensional arrays), descriptive variable and constant names, and extensive commenting conventions. The developers of structured programming were able to demonstrate that within a subroutine, almost any well-designed imperative algorithm can be elegantly expressed with only sequencing, selection, and iteration. Instead of labels, structured languages rely on the boundaries of lexically nested constructs as the targets of branching control.

Many of the structured control-flow constructs familiar to modern programmers were pioneered by Algol 60. These include the `if... then... else` construct and both enumeration (`for`) and logically (`while`) controlled loops. The modern `case` (`switch`) statement was introduced by Wirth and Hoare in Algol W [WH66] as an alternative to the more unstructured computed `goto` and `switch` constructs of Fortran and Algol 60, respectively. (The `switch` statement of C bears a closer resemblance to the Algol W `case` statement than to the Algol 60 `switch`.)

---

6 Edsger W. Dijkstra (1930–2002) developed much of the logical foundation of our modern understanding of concurrency. He was also responsible, among many other contributions, for the semaphores of Section 13.3.5 and for much of the practical development of structured programming. He received the ACM Turing Award in 1972.

6.2.1 Structured Alternatives to goto

Once the principal structured constructs had been defined, most of the controversy surrounding `goto`s revolved around a small number of special cases, each of which was eventually addressed in structured ways. Where once a `goto` might have been used to jump to the end of the current subroutine, most modern languages provide an explicit `return` statement. Where once a `goto` might have been used to escape from the middle of a loop, most modern languages providc a `break` or `exit` statement for this purpose. (Some languages also provide a statement that will skip the remainder of the current iteration only: `continue` in C; `cycle` in Fortran 90; `next` in Perl.) More significantly, several languages allow a program to return from a nested chain of subroutine calls in a single operation, and many provide a way to raise an *exception* that propagates out to some surrounding context. Both of these capabilities might once have been attempted with (nonlocal) `goto`s.

Multilevel Returns

EXAMPLE 6.40
Escaping a nested subroutine

Returns and (local) `goto`s allow control to return from the current subroutine. On occasion it may make sense to return from a *surrounding* routine. Imagine, for example, that we are searching for an item matching some desired pattern within a collection of files. The `search` routine might invoke several nested routines, or a single routine multiple times, once for each place in which to search. In such a situation certain historic languages, including Algol 60, PL/I, and Pascal, permitted a `goto` to branch to a lexically visible label *outside* the current subroutine:

```
function search(key : string) : string;
var rtn : string;
...
    procedure search_file(fname : string);
    ...
    begin
        ...
        for ... (* iterate over lines *)
            ...
            if found(key, line) then begin
                rtn := line;
                goto 100;
            end;
            ...
    end;
...
begin (* search *)
    ...
```

```
            for ... (* iterate over files *)
                ...
                search_file(fname);
                ...
    100:    return rtn;
        end;
```

In the event of a nonlocal goto, the language implementation must guarantee to repair the run-time stack of subroutine call information. This repair operation is known as *unwinding*. It requires not only that the implementation deallocate the stack frames of any subroutines from which we have escaped, but also that it perform any bookkeeping operations, such as restoration of register contents, that would have been performed when returning from those routines.

As a more structured alternative to the nonlocal goto, Common Lisp provides a return-from statement that names the lexically surrounding function or block from which to return, and also supplies a return value (eliminating the need for the artificial rtn variable in Example 6.40).

But what if search_file were not nested inside of search? We might, for example, wish to call it from routines that search files in different orders. Algol 60, Algol 68, and PL/I allowed labels to be passed as parameters, so a dynamically nested subroutine could perform a goto to a caller-defined location. Common Lisp again provides a more structured alternative, also available in Ruby. In either language an expression can be surrounded with a catch block, whose value can be provided by any dynamically nested routine that executes a matching throw. In Ruby we might write

EXAMPLE 6.41
Structured nonlocal transfers

```
def searchFile(fname, pattern)
    file = File.open(fname)
    file.each {|line|
        throw :found, line if line =~ /#{pattern}/
    }
end

match = catch :found do
    searchFile("f1", key)
    searchFile("f2", key)
    searchFile("f3", key)
    "not found\n"                # default value for catch,
end                              # if control gets this far
print match
```

Here the throw expression specifies a *tag*, which must appear in a matching catch, together with a value (line) to be returned as the value of the catch. (The if clause attached to the throw performs a regular-expression pattern match, looking for pattern within line. We will consider pattern matching in more detail in Section 14.4.2.)

Errors and Other Exceptions

The notion of a multilevel return assumes that the callee knows what the caller expects, and can return an appropriate value. In a related and arguably more common situation, a deeply nested block or subroutine may discover that it is unable to proceed with its usual function, and moreover lacks the contextual information it would need to recover in any graceful way. Eiffel formalizes this notion by saying that every software component has a *contract*—a specification of the function it performs. A component that is unable to fulfill its contract is said to *fail*. Rather than return in the normal way, it must arrange for control to "back out" to some context in which the program is able to recover. Conditions that require a program to "back out" are usually called *exceptions*. We mentioned an example in Section C-2.3.5, where we considered phrase-level recovery from syntax errors in a recursive descent parser.

EXAMPLE 6.42
Error checking with status codes

The most straightforward but generally least satisfactory way to cope with exceptions is to use auxiliary Boolean variables within a subroutine (`if still_ok then ...`) and to return status codes from calls:

```
status := my_proc(args);
if status = ok then ...
```

The auxiliary Booleans can be eliminated by using a nonlocal `goto` or multilevel return, but the caller to which we return must still inspect status codes explicitly. As a structured alternative, many modern languages provide an *exception-handling* mechanism for convenient, nonlocal recovery from exceptions. We will discuss exception handling in more detail in Section 9.4. Typically the programmer appends a block of code called a *handler* to any computation in which an exception may arise. The job of the handler is to take whatever remedial action is required to recover from the exception. If the protected computation completes in the normal fashion, execution of the handler is skipped.

Multilevel returns and structured exceptions have strong similarities. Both involve a control transfer from some inner, nested context back to an outer context, unwinding the stack on the way. The distinction lies in where the computing occurs. In a multilevel return the inner context has all the information it needs. It completes its computation, generating a return value if appropriate, and transfers to the outer context in a way that requires no post-processing. At an exception, by contrast, the inner context cannot complete its work—it cannot fulfill its contract. It performs an "abnormal" return, triggering execution of the handler.

Common Lisp and Ruby provide mechanisms for both multilevel returns and exceptions, but this dual support is relatively rare. Most languages support only exceptions; programmers implement multilevel returns by writing a trivial handler. In an unfortunate overloading of terminology, the names `catch` and `throw`, which Common Lisp and Ruby use for multilevel returns, are used for exceptions in several other languages.

6.2.2 Continuations

The notion of nonlocal `goto`s that unwind the stack can be generalized by defining what are known as *continuations*. In low-level terms, a continuation consists of a code address, a referencing environment that should be established (or restored) when jumping to that address, and a reference to another continuation that represents what to do in the event of a subsequent subroutine return. (The chain of return continuations constitutes a *backtrace* of the run-time stack.) In higher-level terms, a continuation is an abstraction that captures a *context* in which execution might continue. Continuations are fundamental to denotational semantics. They also appear as first-class values in several programming languages (notably Scheme and Ruby), allowing the programmer to define new control-flow constructs.

Continuation support in Scheme takes the form of a function named `call-with-current-continuation`, often abbreviated `call/cc`. This function takes a single argument *f*, which is itself a function of one argument. `Call/cc` calls *f*, passing as argument a continuation *c* that captures the current program counter, referencing environment, and stack backtrace. The continuation is implemented as a closure, indistinguishable from the closures used to represent subroutines passed as parameters. At any point in the future, *f* can call *c*, passing it a value, *v*. The call will "return" *v* into *c*'s captured context, as if it had been returned by the original call to `call/cc`.

EXAMPLE 6.43
A simple Ruby continuation

Ruby support is similar:

```
def foo(i, c)
    printf "start %d; ", i
    if i < 3 then foo(i+1, c) else c.call(i) end
    printf "end %d; ", i
end

v = callcc { |d| foo(1, d) }
printf "got %d\n", v
```

Here the parameter to `callcc` is a *block*—roughly, a lambda expression. The block's parameter is the continuation `c`, which its body passes, together with the

DESIGN & IMPLEMENTATION

6.4 Cleaning up continuations

The implementation of continuations in Scheme and Ruby is surprisingly straightforward. Because local variables have unlimited extent in both languages, activation records must in general be allocated on the heap. As a result, explicit deallocation of frames in the current context is neither required nor appropriate when jumping through a continuation: if those frames are no longer accessible, they will eventually be reclaimed by the standard garbage collector (more on this in Section 8.5.3).

number 1, to subroutine foo. The subroutine then calls itself twice recursively before executing `c.call(i)`. Finally, the `call` method jumps into the context captured by `c`, making `i` (that is, 3) appear to have been returned by `callcc`. The final program output is `start 1; start 2; start 3; got 3.` ■

In this simple example, the jump into the continuation behaved much as an exception would, popping out of a series of nested calls. But continuations can do much more. Like other closures, they can be saved in variables, returned from subroutines, or called repeatedly, even after control has returned out of the context in which they were created (this means that they require *unlimited extent*; see Section 3.6). Consider the following more subtle example:

EXAMPLE 6.44
Continuation reuse and unlimited extent

```
def here
    return callcc { |a| return a }
end

def bar(i)
    printf "start %d; ", i
    b = if i < 3 then bar(i+1) else here end
    printf "end %d; ", i
    return b
end

n = 3
c = bar(1)
n -= 1
puts     # print newline
if n > 0 then c.call(c) end
puts "done"
```

This code performs three nested calls to `bar`, returning a continuation created by function `here` in the middle of the innermost call. Using that continuation, we can jump back into the nested calls of `bar`—in fact, we can do so repeatedly. Note that while `c`'s captured referencing environment remains the same each time, the value of `n` can change. The final program output is

```
start 1; start 2; start 3; end 3; end 2; end 1;
end 3; end 2; end 1;
end 3; end 2; end 1;
done
```

■

`Call/cc` suffices to build a wide variety of control abstractions, including `goto`s, midloop `exit`s, multilevel returns, exceptions, iterators (Section 6.5.3), call-by-name parameters (Section 9.3.1), and coroutines (Section 9.5). It even subsumes the notion of returning from a subroutine, though it seldom replaces it in practice. Used in a disciplined way, continuations make a language surprisingly extensible. At the same time, they allow the undisciplined programmer to construct completely inscrutable programs.

6.3 Sequencing

Like assignment, sequencing is central to imperative programming. It is the principal means of controlling the order in which side effects (e.g., assignments) occur: when one statement follows another in the program text, the first statement executes before the second. In most imperative languages, lists of statements can be enclosed with `begin... end` or `{...}` delimiters and then used in any context in which a single statement is expected. Such a delimited list is usually called a *compound statement*. A compound statement optionally preceded by a set of declarations is sometimes called a *block*.

In languages like Algol 68, which blur or eliminate the distinction between statements and expressions, the value of a statement (expression) list is the value of its final element. In Common Lisp, the programmer can choose to return the value of the first element, the second, or the last. Of course, sequencing is a useless operation unless the subexpressions that do not play a part in the return value have side effects. The various sequencing constructs in Lisp are used only in program fragments that do not conform to a purely functional programming model.

Even in imperative languages, there is debate as to the value of certain kinds of side effects. In Euclid and Turing, for example, functions (i.e., subroutines that return values, and that therefore can appear within expressions) are not permitted to have side effects. Among other things, side-effect freedom ensures that a Euclid or Turing function, like its counterpart in mathematics, is always *idempotent*: if called repeatedly with the same set of arguments, it will always return the same value, and the number of consecutive calls (after the first) will not affect the results of subsequent execution. In addition, side-effect freedom for functions means that the value of a subexpression will never depend on whether that subexpression is evaluated before or after calling a function in some other subexpression. These properties make it easier for a programmer or theorem-proving system to reason about program behavior. They also simplify code improvement, for example by permitting the safe rearrangement of expressions.

EXAMPLE 6.45
Side effects in a random number generator

Unfortunately, there are some situations in which side effects in functions are highly desirable. We saw one example in the label_name function of Figure 3.3. Another arises in the typical interface to a pseudorandom number generator:

```
procedure srand(seed : integer)
    -- Initialize internal tables.
    -- The pseudorandom generator will return a different
    -- sequence of values for each different value of seed.

function rand() : integer
    -- No arguments; returns a new "random" number.
```

Obviously rand needs to have a side effect, so that it will return a different value each time it is called. One could always recast it as a procedure with a reference parameter:

```
procedure rand(ref n : integer)
```

but most programmers would find this less appealing. Ada strikes a compromise: it allows side effects in functions in the form of changes to static or global variables, but does not allow a function to modify its parameters.

6.4 Selection

EXAMPLE 6.46
Selection in Algol 60

Selection statements in most imperative languages employ some variant of the `if... then ... else` notation introduced in Algol 60:

```
if condition then statement
else if condition then statement
else if condition then statement
...
else statement
```

As we saw in Section 2.3.2, languages differ in the details of the syntax. In Algol 60 and Pascal both the `then` clause and the `else` clause were defined to contain a single statement (this could of course be a `begin... end` compound statement). To avoid grammatical ambiguity, Algol 60 required that the statement after the `then` begin with something other than `if` (`begin` is fine). Pascal eliminated this restriction in favor of a "disambiguating rule" that associated an `else` with the closest unmatched `then`. Algol 68, Fortran 77, and more modern languages avoid the ambiguity by allowing a statement *list* to follow either `then` or `else`, with a terminating keyword at the end of the construct.

EXAMPLE 6.47
`elsif/elif`

To keep terminators from piling up at the end of nested `if` statements, most languages with terminators provide a special `elsif` or `elif` keyword. In Ruby, one writes

```
if a == b then
    ...
elsif a == c then
    ...
elsif a == d then
    ...
else
    ...
end
```

EXAMPLE 6.48
cond in Lisp

In Lisp, the equivalent construct is

```
(cond
    ((= A B)
        (...))
```

```
((= A C)
      (...))
((= A D)
      (...))
(T
      (...)))
```

Here cond takes as arguments a sequence of pairs. In each pair the first element is a condition; the second is an expression to be returned as the value of the overall construct if the condition evaluates to T (T means "true" in most Lisp dialects).

6.4.1 Short-Circuited Conditions

While the condition in an `if... then ... else` statement is a Boolean expression, there is usually no need for evaluation of that expression to result in a Boolean value in a register. Most machines provide conditional branch instructions that capture simple comparisons. Put another way, the purpose of the Boolean expression in a selection statement is not to compute a value to be stored, but to cause control to branch to various locations. This observation allows us to generate particularly efficient code (called *jump code*) for expressions that are amenable to the short-circuit evaluation of Section 6.1.5. Jump code is applicable not only to selection statements such as `if... then... else`, but to logically controlled loops as well; we will consider the latter in Section 6.5.5.

In the usual process of code generation, a synthesized attribute of the root of an expression subtree acquires the name of a register into which the value of the expression will be computed at run time. The surrounding context then uses this register name when generating code that uses the expression. In jump code, *inherited* attributes of the root inform it of the addresses to which control should branch if the expression is true or false, respectively.

EXAMPLE 6.49

Code generation for a Boolean condition

Suppose, for example, that we are generating code for the following source:

```
if ((A > B) and (C > D)) or (E ≠ F) then
      then_clause
else
      else_clause
```

In a language without short-circuit evaluation, the output code would look something like this:

```
r1 := A          -- load
r2 := B
r1 := r1 > r2
r2 := C
r3 := D
```

```
        r2 := r2 > r3
        r1 := r1 & r2
        r2 := E
        r3 := F
        r2 := r2 ≠ r3
        r1 := r1 | r2
        if r1 = 0 goto L2
    L1: then_clause          -- (label not actually used)
        goto L3
    L2: else_clause
    L3:
```

The root of the subtree for ((A > B) and (C > D)) or (E ≠ F) would name r1 as the register containing the expression value.

EXAMPLE 6.50
Code generation for short-circuiting

In jump code, by contrast, the inherited attributes of the condition's root would indicate that control should "fall through" to L1 if the condition is true, or branch to L2 if the condition is false. Output code would then look something like this:

```
        r1 := A
        r2 := B
        if r1 <= r2 goto L4
        r1 := C
        r2 := D
        if r1 > r2 goto L1
    L4: r1 := E
        r2 := F
        if r1 = r2 goto L2
    L1: then_clause
        goto L3
    L2: else_clause
    L3:
```

Here the value of the Boolean condition is never explicitly placed into a register. Rather it is implicit in the flow of control. Moreover for most values of A, B, C, D, and E, the execution path through the jump code is shorter and therefore faster (assuming good branch prediction) than the straight-line code that calculates the value of every subexpression.

DESIGN & IMPLEMENTATION

6.5 Short-circuit evaluation

Short-circuit evaluation is one of those happy cases in programming language design where a clever language feature yields both more useful semantics *and* a faster implementation than existing alternatives. Other at least arguable examples include `case` statements, local scopes for `for` loop indices (Section 6.5.1), and Ada-style parameter modes (Section 9.3.1).

EXAMPLE 6.51
Short-circuit creation of a Boolean value

If the value of a short-circuited expression is needed explicitly, it can of course be generated, while still using jump code for efficiency. The Ada fragment

```
found_it := p /= null and then p.key = val;
```

is equivalent to

```
if p /= null and then p.key = val then
    found_it := true;
else
    found_it := false;
end if;
```

and can be translated as

```
        r1 := p
        if r1 = 0 goto L1
        r2 := r1→key
        if r2 ≠ val goto L1
        r1 := 1
        goto L2
L1:     r1 := 0
L2:     found_it := r1
```

The astute reader will notice that the first goto L1 can be replaced by goto L2, since r1 already contains a zero in this case. The code improvement phase of the compiler will notice this also, and make the change. It is easier to fix this sort of thing in the code improver than it is to generate the better version of the code in the first place. The code improver has to be able to recognize jumps to redundant instructions for other reasons anyway; there is no point in building special cases into the short-circuit evaluation routines. ■

6.4.2 `Case/Switch` Statements

EXAMPLE 6.52
`case` statements and nested `if`s

The `case` statements of Algol W and its descendants provide alternative syntax for a special case of nested `if... then ... else`. When each condition compares the same expression to a different compile-time constant, then the following code (written here in Ada)

```
i := ... -- potentially complicated expression
if i = 1 then
    clause_A
elsif i = 2 or i = 7 then
    clause_B
elsif i in 3..5 then
    clause_C
elsif i = 10 then
    clause_D
else
    clause_E
end if;
```

can be rewritten as

```
case ... -- potentially complicated expression
is
    when 1        => clause_A
    when 2 | 7    => clause_B
    when 3..5     => clause_C
    when 10       => clause_D
    when others   => clause_E
end case;
```

The elided code fragments (*clause_A*, *clause_B*, etc.) after the arrows are called the *arms* of the `case` statement. The lists of constants in front of the arrows are `case` statement *labels*. The constants in the label lists must be disjoint, and must be of a type compatible with the tested ("controlling") expression. Most languages allow this type to be anything whose values are discrete: integers, characters, enumerations, and subranges of the same. C# and (recent versions of) Java allow strings as well.

The `case` statement version of the code above is certainly less verbose than the `if... then ... else` version, but syntactic elegance is not the principal motivation for providing a `case` statement in a programming language. The principal motivation is to facilitate the generation of efficient target code. The `if... then ... else` statement is most naturally translated as follows:

EXAMPLE 6.53
Translation of nested `if`s

```
    r1 := ...              -- calculate controlling expression
    if r1 ≠ 1 goto L1
    clause_A
    goto L6
L1: if r1 = 2 goto L2
    if r1 ≠ 7 goto L3
L2: clause_B
    goto L6
L3: if r1 < 3 goto L4
    if r1 > 5 goto L4
    clause_C
    goto L6
L4: if r1 ≠ 10 goto L5
    clause_D
    goto L6
L5: clause_E
L6:
```

Rather than test its controlling expression sequentially against a series of possible values, the `case` statement is meant to *compute* an address to which it jumps in a single instruction. The general form of the anticipated target code appears in Figure 6.3. The elided calculation at label L6 can take any of several forms. The most common of these simply indexes into an array, as shown in Figure 6.4.

EXAMPLE 6.54
Jump tables

```
      goto L6            -- jump to code to compute address
L1:  clause_A
      goto L7
L2:  clause_B
      goto L7
L3:  clause_C
      goto L7
      ...
L4:  clause_D
      goto L7
L5:  clause_E
      goto L7
L6:  r1 := ...           -- computed target of branch
      goto *r1
L7:
```

Figure 6.3 General form of target code generated for a five-arm case statement.

```
T:   &L1                 -- controlling expression = 1
     &L2
     &L3
     &L3
     &L3
     &L5
     &L2
     &L5
     &L5
     &L4                 -- controlling expression = 10
L6:  r1 := ...           -- calculate controlling expression
     if r1 < 1 goto L5
     if r1 > 10 goto L5     -- L5 is the "else" arm
     r1 -:= 1               -- subtract off lower bound
     r1 := T[r1]
     goto *r1
L7:
```

Figure 6.4 **Jump table to control branching in a case statement.** This code replaces the last three lines of Figure 6.3.

The "code" at label T in that figure is in fact an array of addresses, known as a *jump table*. It contains one entry for each integer between the lowest and highest values, inclusive, found among the case statement labels. The code at L6 checks to make sure that the controlling expression is within the bounds of the array (if not, we should execute the others arm of the case statement). It then fetches the corresponding entry from the table and branches to it. ■

Alternative Implementations

A jump table is fast: it begins executing the correct arm of the `case` statement in constant time, regardless of the value of the controlling expression. It is also space efficient when the overall set of `case` statement labels is dense and does not contain large ranges. It can consume an extraordinarily large amount of space, however, if the set of labels is nondense, or includes large value ranges. Alternative methods to compute the address to which to branch include sequential testing, hashing, and binary search. Sequential testing (as in an `if... then ... else` statement) is the method of choice if the total number of `case` statement labels is small. It chooses an arm in $O(n)$ time, where n is the number of labels. A hash table is attractive if the set of label values is large, but has many missing values and no large ranges. With an appropriate hash function it will choose the right arm in $O(1)$ time. Unfortunately, a hash table, like a jump table, requires a separate entry for each possible value of the controlling tested expression, making it unsuitable for statements with large value ranges. Binary search can accommodate ranges easily. It chooses an arm in $O(\log n)$ time.

To generate good code for all possible `case` statements, a compiler needs to be prepared to use a variety of strategies. During compilation it can generate code for the various arms of the case statement as it finds them, while simultaneously building up an internal data structure to describe the label set. Once it has seen all the arms, it can decide which form of target code to generate. For the sake of simplicity, most compilers employ only some of the possible implementations. Some use binary search in lieu of hashing. Some generate only jump tables; others only that plus sequential testing. Users of less sophisticated compilers may need to restructure their `case` statements if the generated code turns out to be unexpectedly large or slow.

Syntax and Label Semantics

As with `if... then ... else` statements, the syntactic details of `case` statements vary from language to language. Different languages use different punctuation to delimit labels and arms. More significantly, languages differ in whether they permit label ranges, whether they permit (or require) a default (`others`) clause, and in how they handle a value that fails to match any label at run time.

In some languages (e.g., Modula), it is a dynamic semantic error for the controlling expression to have a value that does not appear in the label lists. Ada

DESIGN & IMPLEMENTATION

6.6 `Case` statements

`Case` statements are one of the clearest examples of language design driven by implementation. Their primary reason for existence is to facilitate the generation of jump tables. Ranges in label lists (not permitted in Pascal or C) may reduce efficiency slightly, but binary search is still dramatically faster than the equivalent series of `if`s.

requires the labels to cover *all possible* values in the domain of the controlling expression's type; if the type has a very large number of values, then this coverage must be accomplished using ranges or an `others` clause. In some languages, notably C and Fortran 90, it is *not* an error for the tested expression to evaluate to a missing value. Rather, the entire construct has no effect when the value is missing.

The C `switch` Statement

C's syntax for case (`switch`) statements (retained by C++ and Java) is unusual in several respects:

```
switch (... /* controlling expression */) {
    case 1:  clause_A
             break;
    case 2:
    case 7:  clause_B
             break;
    case 3:
    case 4:
    case 5:  clause_C
             break;
    case 10: clause_D
             break;
    default: clause_E
             break;
}
```

Here each possible value for the tested expression must have its own label within the `switch`; ranges are not allowed. In fact, lists of labels are not allowed, but the effect of lists can be achieved by allowing a label (such as 2, 3, and 4 above) to have an *empty* arm that simply "falls through" into the code for the subsequent label. Because of the provision for fall-through, an explicit `break` statement must be used to get out of the `switch` at the end of an arm, rather than falling through into the next. There are rare circumstances in which the ability to fall through is convenient:

EXAMPLE 6.55
Fall-through in C `switch` statements

```
letter_case = lower;
switch (c) {
    ...
    case 'A' :
        letter_case = upper;
        /* FALL THROUGH! */
    case 'a' :
        ...
        break;
    ...
}
```

■

Most of the time, however, the need to insert a `break` at the end of each arm—and the compiler's willingness to accept arms without breaks, silently—is a recipe for unexpected and difficult-to-diagnose bugs. C# retains the familiar C syntax, including multiple consecutive labels, but requires every nonempty arm to end with a `break`, `goto`, `continue`, or `return`.

✓ CHECK YOUR UNDERSTANDING

19. List the principal uses of `goto`, and the structured alternatives to each.
20. Explain the distinction between exceptions and multilevel returns.
21. What are *continuations*? What other language features do they subsume?
22. Why is sequencing a comparatively unimportant form of control flow in Lisp?
23. Explain why it may sometimes be useful for a function to have side effects.
24. Describe the *jump code* implementation of short-circuit Boolean evaluation.
25. Why do imperative languages commonly provide a `case` or `switch` statement in addition to `if... then ... else`?
26. Describe three different search strategies that might be employed in the implementation of a `case` statement, and the circumstances in which each would be desirable.
27. Explain the use of `break` to terminate the arms of a C `switch` statement, and the behavior that arises if a `break` is accidentally omitted.

6.5 Iteration

Iteration and recursion are the two mechanisms that allow a computer to perform similar operations repeatedly. Without at least one of these mechanisms, the running time of a program (and hence the amount of work it can do and the amount of space it can use) would be a linear function of the size of the program text. In a very real sense, it is iteration and recursion that make computers useful for more than fixed-size tasks. In this section we focus on iteration. Recursion is the subject of Section 6.6.

Programmers in imperative languages tend to use iteration more than they use recursion (recursion is more common in functional languages). In most languages, iteration takes the form of *loops*. Like the statements in a sequence, the iterations of a loop are generally executed for their side effects: their modifications of variables. Loops come in two principal varieties, which differ in the mechanisms used to determine how many times to iterate. An *enumeration-controlled* loop is executed once for every value in a given finite set; the number of iterations is known before the first iteration begins. A *logically controlled* loop is executed until some Boolean condition (which must generally depend on values altered in the loop) changes value. Most (though not all) languages provide separate constructs for these two varieties of loop.

6.5.1 Enumeration-Controlled Loops

Enumeration-controlled iteration originated with the do loop of Fortran I. Similar mechanisms have been adopted in some form by almost every subsequent language, but syntax and semantics vary widely. Even Fortran's own loop has evolved considerably over time. The modern Fortran version looks something like this:

EXAMPLE 6.56
Fortran 90 do loop

```
do i = 1, 10, 2
    ...
enddo
```

Variable `i` is called the *index* of the loop. The expressions that follow the equals sign are `i`'s *initial value*, its *bound*, and the *step size*. With the values shown here, the *body* of the loop (the statements between the loop header and the `enddo` delimiter) will execute five times, with `i` set to 1, 3, ..., 9 in successive iterations. ■

EXAMPLE 6.57
Modula-2 `for` loop

Many other languages provide similar functionality. In Modula-2 one would say

```
FOR i := first TO last BY step DO
    ...
END
```

By choosing different values of `first`, `last`, and `step`, we could arrange to iterate over an arbitrary arithmetic sequence of integers, namely `i` = `first`, `first` + `step`, ..., `first` + ⌊(`last` − `first`)/`step`⌋ × `step`. ■

Following the lead of Clu, many modern languages allow enumeration-controlled loops to iterate over much more general finite sets—the nodes of a tree, for example, or the elements of a collection. We consider these more general *iterators* in Section 6.5.3. For the moment we focus on arithmetic sequences. For the sake of simplicity, we use the name "`for` loop" as a general term, even for languages that use a different keyword.

Code Generation for `for` *Loops*

EXAMPLE 6.58
Obvious translation of a `for` loop

Naively, the loop of Example 6.57 can be translated as

```
    r1 := first
    r2 := step
    r3 := last
L1: if r1 > r3 goto L2
    ...                         -- loop body; use r1 for i
    r1 := r1 + r2
    goto L1
L2:
```

■

EXAMPLE 6.59

`for` loop translation with test at the bottom

A slightly better if less straightforward translation is

```
    r1 := first
    r2 := step
    r3 := last
    goto L2
L1: ...                     -- loop body; use r1 for i
    r1 := r1 + r2
L2: if r1 ≤ r3 goto L1
```

This version is likely to be faster, because each iteration contains a single conditional branch, rather than a conditional branch at the top and an unconditional branch at the bottom. (We will consider yet another version in Exercise C-17.4.)

Note that both of these translations employ a loop-ending test that is fundamentally *directional*: as shown, they assume that all the realized values of `i` will be smaller than `last`. If the loop goes "the other direction"—that is, if `first` > `last`, and `step` < 0—then we will need to use the inverse test to end the loop. To allow the compiler to make the right choice, many languages restrict the generality of their arithmetic sequences. Commonly, `step` is required to be a compile-time constant. Ada actually limits the choices to ±1. Several languages, including both Ada and Pascal, require special syntax for loops that iterate "backward" (`for i in reverse 10..1` in Ada; `for i := 10 downto 1` in Pascal).

EXAMPLE 6.60

`for` loop translation with an iteration count

Obviously, one can generate code that checks the sign of `step` at run time, and chooses a test accordingly. The obvious translations, however, are either time or space inefficient. An arguably more attractive approach, adopted by many Fortran compilers, is to precompute the number of iterations, place this *iteration count* in a register, decrement the register at the end of each iteration, and branch back to the top of the loop if the count is not yet zero:

```
    r1 := first
    r2 := step
    r3 := max(⌊(last − first + step)/step⌋, 0)     -- iteration count
            -- NB: this calculation may require several instructions.
            -- It is guaranteed to result in a value within the precision of the machine,
            -- but we may have to be careful to avoid overflow during its calculation.
    if r3 ≤ 0 goto L2
L1: ...                     -- loop body; use r1 for i
    r1 := r1 + r2
    r3 := r3 − 1
    if r3 > 0 goto L1
    i := r1
L2:
```

EXAMPLE 6.61

A "gotcha" in the naive loop translation

The use of the iteration count avoids the need to test the sign of `step` within the loop. Assuming we have been suitably careful in precomputing the count, it also avoids a problem we glossed over in the naive translations of Examples 6.58

and 6.59: If `last` is near the maximum value representable by integers on our machine, naively adding `step` to the final legitimate value of `i` may result in arithmetic overflow. The "wrapped" number may then appear to be smaller (much smaller!) than `last`, and we may have translated perfectly good source code into an infinite loop. ■

Some processors, including the Power family, PA-RISC, and most CISC machines, can decrement the iteration count, test it against zero, and conditionally branch, all in a single instruction. For many loops this results in very efficient code.

Semantic Complications

The astute reader may have noticed that use of an iteration count is fundamentally dependent on being able to predict the number of iterations before the loop begins to execute. While this prediction is possible in many languages, including Fortran and Ada, it is *not* possible in others, notably C and its descendants. The difference stems largely from the following question: is the `for` loop construct *only* for iteration, or is it simply meant to make enumeration easy? If the language insists on enumeration, then an iteration count works fine. If enumeration is only *one possible* purpose for the loop—more specifically, if the number of iterations or the sequence of index values may change as a result of executing the first few iterations—then we may need to use a more general implementation, along the lines of Example 6.59, modified if necessary to handle dynamic discovery of the direction of the terminating test.

DESIGN & IMPLEMENTATION

6.7 Numerical imprecision

Among its many changes to the `do` loop of Fortran IV, Fortran 77 allowed the index, bounds, and step size of the loop to be floating-point numbers, not just integers. Interestingly, this feature was taken back out of the language in Fortran 90.

The problem with real-number sequences is that limited precision can cause comparisons (e.g., between the index and the bound) to produce unexpected or even implementation-dependent results when the values are close to one another. Should

```
for x := 1.0 to 2.0 by 1.0 / 3.0
```

execute three iterations or four? It depends on whether 1.0 / 3.0 is rounded up or down. The Fortran 90 designers appear to have decided that such ambiguity is philosophically inconsistent with the idea of finite enumeration. The programmer who wants to iterate over floating-point values must use an explicit comparison in a pretest or post-test loop (Section 6.5.5).

The choice between requiring and (merely) enabling enumeration manifests itself in several specific questions:

1. Can control enter or leave the loop in any way other than through the enumeration mechanism?
2. What happens if the loop body modifies variables that were used to compute the end-of-loop bound?
3. What happens if the loop body modifies the index variable itself?
4. Can the program read the index variable after the loop has completed, and if so, what will its value be?

Questions (1) and (2) are relatively easy to resolve. Most languages allow a `break/exit` statement to leave a `for` loop early. Fortran IV allowed a `goto` to jump *into* a loop, but this was generally regarded as a language flaw; Fortran 77 and most other languages prohibit such jumps. Similarly, most languages (but not C; see Section 6.5.2) specify that the bound is computed only once, before the first iteration, and kept in a temporary location. Subsequent changes to variables used to compute the bound have no effect on how many times the loop iterates.

EXAMPLE 6.62
Changing the index in a `for` loop

Questions (3) and (4) are more difficult. Suppose we write (in no particular language)

```
for i := 1 to 10 by 2
    ...
    if i = 3
        i := 6
```

What should happen at the end of the `i=3` iteration? Should the next iteration have `i` = 5 (the next element of the arithmetic sequence specified in the loop header), `i` = 8 (2 more than 6), or even conceivably `i` = 7 (the next value of the sequence after 6)? One can imagine reasonable arguments for each of these options. To avoid the need to choose, many languages prohibit changes to the loop index within the body of the loop. Fortran makes the prohibition a matter of programmer discipline: the implementation is not required to catch an erroneous update. Pascal provided an elaborate set of conservative rules [Int90, Sec. 6.8.3.9] that allowed the compiler to catch all possible updates. These rules were complicated by the fact that the index variable was declared outside the loop; it might be visible to subroutines called from the loop even if it was not passed as a parameter. ■

EXAMPLE 6.63
Inspecting the index after a `for` loop

If control escapes the loop with a `break/exit`, the natural value for the index would seem to be the one that was current at the time of the escape. For "normal" termination, on the other hand, the natural value would seem to be the first one that exceeds the loop bound. Certainly that is the value that will be produced by the implementation of Example 6.59. Unfortunately, as we noted in Example 6.60, the "next" value for some loops may be outside the range of integer precision. For other loops, it may be semantically invalid:

```
c : 'a'..'z'            -- character subrange
...
for c := 'a' to 'z' do
    ...
-- what comes after 'z'?
```

Requiring the post-loop value to always be the index of the final iteration is unattractive from an implementation perspective: it would force us to replace Example 6.59 with a translation that has an extra branch instruction in every iteration:

```
    r1 := 'a'
    r2 := 'z'
    if r1 > r2 goto L3       -- Code improver may remove this test,
                             -- since 'a' and 'z' are constants.
L1: ...                      -- loop body; use r1 for i
    if r1 = r2 goto L2
    r1 := r1 + 1
    goto L1
L2: i := r1
L3:
```

Of course, the compiler must generate this sort of code in any event (or use an iteration count) if arithmetic overflow may interfere with testing the terminating condition. To permit the compiler to use the fastest correct implementation in all cases, several languages, including Fortran 90 and Pascal, say that the value of the index is undefined after the end of the loop. ■

An attractive solution to both the index modification problem and the post-loop value problem was pioneered by Algol W and Algol 68, and subsequently adopted by Ada, Modula 3, and many other languages. In these, the header of the loop is considered to contain a *declaration* of the index. Its type is inferred from the bounds of the loop, and its scope is the loop's body. Because the index is not visible outside the loop, its value is not an issue. Of course, the programmer must not give the index the same name as any variable that must be accessed within the loop, but this is a strictly local issue: it has no ramifications outside the loop.

6.5.2 Combination Loops

Algol 60 provided a single loop construct that subsumed the properties of more modern enumeration and logically controlled loops. It allowed the programmer to specify an arbitrary number of "enumerators," each of which could be a single value, a range of values similar to those of modern enumeration-controlled loops, or an expression with a terminating condition. Common Lisp provides an even more powerful facility, with four separate sets of clauses, to initialize index variables (of which there may be an arbitrary number), test for loop termination (in any of several ways), evaluate body expressions, and clean up at loop termination.

A much simpler form of combination loop appears in C and its successors. Semantically, the C `for` loop is logically controlled. It was designed, however, to make enumeration easy. Our Modula-2 example

EXAMPLE 6.64

Combination (`for`) loop in C

```
FOR i := first TO last BY step DO
    ...
END
```

would usually be written in C as

```
for (i = first; i <= last; i += step) {
    ...
}
```

With caveats for a few special cases, C defines this to be equivalent to

```
{
    i = first;
    while (i <= last) {
        ...
        i += step;
    }
}
```

This definition means that it is the programmer's responsibility to worry about the effect of overflow on testing of the terminating condition. It also means that both the index and any variables contained in the terminating condition can be modified by the body of the loop, or by subroutines it calls, and these changes *will* affect the loop control. This, too, is the programmer's responsibility.

Any of the three clauses in the `for` loop header can be null (the condition is considered true if missing). Alternatively, a clause can consist of a sequence of comma-separated expressions. The advantage of the C `for` loop over its `while` loop equivalent is compactness and clarity. In particular, all of the code affecting

DESIGN & IMPLEMENTATION

6.8 `for` loops

Modern `for` loops reflect the impact of both semantic and implementation challenges. Semantic challenges include changes to loop indices or bounds from within the loop, the scope of the index variable (and its value, if any, outside the loop), and `goto`s that enter or leave the loop. Implementation challenges include the imprecision of floating-point values, the direction of the bottom-of-loop test, and overflow at the end of the iteration range. The "combination loops" of C (Section 6.5.2) move responsibility for these challenges out of the compiler and into the application program.

the flow of control is localized within the header. In the `while` loop, one must read both the top and the bottom of the loop to know what is going on.

While the logical iteration semantics of the C `for` loop eliminate any ambiguity about the value of the index variable after the end of the loop, it may still be convenient to make the index local to the body of the loop, by declaring it in the header's initialization clause. In Example 6.64, variable `i` must be declared in the surrounding scope. If we instead write

EXAMPLE 6.65
C `for` loop with a local index

```
for (int i = first; i <= last; i += step) {
    ...
}
```

then `i` will not be visible outside. It will still, however, be vulnerable to (deliberate or accidental) modification within the loop. ■

6.5.3 Iterators

In all of the examples we have seen so far (with the possible exception of the combination loops of Algol 60, Common Lisp, or C), a `for` loop iterates over the elements of an arithmetic sequence. In general, however, we may wish to iterate over the elements of any well-defined set (what are often called *collections*, or instances of a *container* class, in object-oriented code). Clu introduced an elegant *iterator* mechanism (also found in Python, Ruby, and C#) to do precisely that. Euclid and several more recent languages, notably C++, Java, and Ada 2012, define a standard interface for *iterator objects* (sometimes called *enumerators*) that are equally easy to use, but not as easy to write. Icon, conversely, provides a generalization of iterators, known as *generators*, that combines enumeration with backtracking search.[7]

True Iterators

Clu, Python, Ruby, and C# allow any container abstraction to provide an *iterator* that enumerates its items. The iterator resembles a subroutine that is permitted to contain `yield` statements, each of which produces a loop index value. `For` loops are then designed to incorporate a call to an iterator. The Modula-2 fragment

EXAMPLE 6.66
Simple iterator in Python

```
FOR i := first TO last BY step DO
    ...
END
```

would be written as follows in Python:

7 Unfortunately, terminology is not consistent across languages. Euclid uses the term "generator" for what are called "iterator objects" here. Python uses it for what are called "true iterators" here.

```
class BinTree:
    def __init__(self):      # constructor
        self.data = self.lchild = self.rchild = None
    ...
    # other methods: insert, delete, lookup, ...

    def preorder(self):
        if self.data != None:
            yield self.data
        if self.lchild != None:
            for d in self.lchild.preorder():
                yield d
        if self.rchild != None:
            for d in self.rchild.preorder():
                yield d
```

Figure 6.5 Python iterator for preorder enumeration of the nodes of a binary tree. Because Python is dynamically typed, this code will work for any data that support the operations needed by `insert`, `lookup`, and so on (probably just <). In a statically typed language, the `BinTree` class would need to be generic.

```
for i in range(first, last, step):
    ...
```

Here `range` is a built-in iterator that yields the integers from `first` to `first` + $\lfloor$(`last` − `first`)/`step`$\rfloor$ × `step` in increments of `step`. ■

When called, the iterator calculates the first index value of the loop, which it returns to the main program by executing a `yield` statement. The `yield` behaves like `return`, except that when control transfers back to the iterator after completion of the first iteration of the loop, the iterator continues where it last left off—*not* at the beginning of its code. When the iterator has no more elements to yield it simply returns (without a value), thereby terminating the loop.

In effect, an iterator is a separate thread of control, with its own program counter, whose execution is interleaved with that of the `for` loop to which it supplies index values.[8] The iteration mechanism serves to "decouple" the algorithm required to enumerate elements from the code that uses those elements.

EXAMPLE 6.67
Python iterator for tree enumeration

The `range` iterator is predefined in Python. As a more illustrative example, consider the preorder enumeration of values stored in a binary tree. A Python iterator for this task appears in Figure 6.5. Invoked from the header of a `for` loop, it yields the value in the root node (if any) for the first iteration and then calls itself recursively, twice, to enumerate values in the left and right subtrees. ■

8 Because iterators are interleaved with loops in a very regular way, they can be implemented more easily (and cheaply) than fully general threads. We will consider implementation options further in Section C-9.5.3.

Iterator Objects

As realized in most imperative languages, iteration involves both a special form of `for` loop and a mechanism to enumerate values for the loop. These concepts can be separated. Euclid, C++, Java, and Ada 2012 all provide enumeration-controlled loops reminiscent of those of Python. They have no `yield` statement, however, and no separate thread-like context to enumerate values; rather, an iterator is an ordinary object (in the object-oriented sense of the word) that provides methods for initialization, generation of the next index value, and testing for completion. Between calls, the state of the iterator must be kept in the object's data members.

EXAMPLE 6.68 Java iterator for tree enumeration

Figure 6.6 contains the Java equivalent of the `BinTree` class of Figure 6.5. Given this code, we can write

```
BinTree<Integer> myTree = ...
...
for (Integer i : myTree) {
    System.out.println(i);
}
```

The loop here is syntactic sugar for

```
for (Iterator<Integer> it = myTree.iterator(); it.hasNext();) {
    Integer i = it.next();
    System.out.println(i);
}
```

The expression following the colon in the more concise version of the loop must be an object that supports the standard `Iterable` interface. This interface includes an `iterator()` method that returns an `Iterator` object. ■

EXAMPLE 6.69 Iteration in C++11

C++ takes a related but somewhat different approach. With appropriate definitions, the Java `for` loop of the previous example could be written as follows in C++11:

```
tree_node* my_tree = ...
...
for (int n : *my_tree) {
    cout << n << "\n";
}
```

DESIGN & IMPLEMENTATION

6.9 "True" iterators and iterator objects

While the `iterator` library mechanisms of C++ and Java are highly useful, it is worth emphasizing that they are *not* the functional equivalents of "true" iterators, as found in Clu, Python, Ruby, and C#. Their key limitation is the need to maintain all intermediate state in the form of explicit data structures, rather than in the program counter and local variables of a resumable execution context.

```
class BinTree<T> implements Iterable<T> {
    BinTree<T> left;
    BinTree<T> right;
    T val;
    ...
    // other methods: insert, delete, lookup, ...

    public Iterator<T> iterator() {
        return new TreeIterator(this);
    }
    private class TreeIterator implements Iterator<T> {
        private Stack<BinTree<T>> s = new Stack<BinTree<T>>();
        TreeIterator(BinTree<T> n) {
            if (n.val != null) s.push(n);
        }
        public boolean hasNext() {
            return !s.empty();
        }
        public T next() {
            if (!hasNext()) throw new NoSuchElementException();
            BinTree<T> n = s.pop();
            if (n.right != null) s.push(n.right);
            if (n.left != null) s.push(n.left);
            return n.val;
        }
        public void remove() {
            throw new UnsupportedOperationException();
        }
    }
}
```

Figure 6.6 Java code for preorder enumeration of the nodes of a binary tree. The nested `TreeIterator` class uses an explicit `Stack` object (borrowed from the standard library) to keep track of subtrees whose nodes have yet to be enumerated. Java generics, specified as <T> type arguments for `BinTree`, `Stack`, `Iterator`, and `Iterable`, allow `next` to return an object of the appropriate type, rather than the undifferentiated `Object`. The `remove` method is part of the `Iterator` interface, and must therefore be provided, if only as a placeholder.

This loop is syntactic sugar for

```
for (tree_node::iterator it = my_tree->begin();
                            it != my_tree->end(); ++it) {
    int n = *it;
    cout << n << "\n";
}
```

Where a Java iterator has methods to produce successive elements of a collection on demand (and to indicate when there are no more), a C++ iterator is designed to act as a special kind of pointer. Support routines in the standard library leverage the language's unusually flexible operator overloading and reference mechanisms to redefine comparison (`!=`), increment (`++`), dereference (`*`), and so on in a way that makes iterating over the elements of a collection look very much like using pointer arithmetic to traverse a conventional array ("Pointers and Arrays in C," Section 8.5.1).

As in the Java example, iterator `it` encapsulates all the state needed to find successive elements of the collection, and to determine when there are no more. To obtain the current element, we "dereference" the iterator, using the `*` or `->` operators. The initial value of the iterator is produced by a collection's `begin` method. To advance to the following element, we use the increment (`++`) operator. The end method returns a special iterator that "points beyond the end" of the collection. The increment (`++`) operator must return a reference that tests equal to this special iterator when the collection has been exhausted. ■

Code to implement our C++ tree iterator is somewhat messier than the Java version of Figure 6.6, due to operator overloading, the value model of variables (which requires explicit references and pointers), and the lack of garbage collection. We leave the details to Exercise 6.19.

Iterating with First-Class Functions

EXAMPLE 6.70
Passing the "loop body" to an iterator in Scheme

In functional languages, the ability to specify a function "in line" facilitates a programming idiom in which the body of a loop is written as a function, with the loop index as an argument. This function is then passed as the final argument to an iterator, which is itself a function. In Scheme we might write

```
(define uptoby
  (lambda (low high step f)
    (if (<= low high)
        (begin
          (f low)
          (uptoby (+ low step) high step f))
        '())))
```

We could then sum the first 50 odd numbers as follows:

```
(let ((sum 0))
  (uptoby 1 100 2
          (lambda (i)
            (set! sum (+ sum i))))
  sum)                                  ⟹ 2500
```

Here the body of the loop, `(set! sum (+ sum i))`, is an assignment. The ⟹ symbol (not a part of Scheme) is used here to mean "evaluates to." ■

EXAMPLE 6.71
Iteration with blocks in Smalltalk

Smalltalk, which we consider in Section C-10.7.1, supports a similar idiom:

```
sum <- 0.
1 to: 100 by: 2 do:
    [:i | sum <- sum + i]
```

Like a `lambda` expression in Scheme, a square-bracketed *block* in Smalltalk creates a first-class function, which we then pass as argument to the `to: by: do:` iterator. The iterator calls the function repeatedly, passing successive values of the index variable `i` as argument. ■

Iterators in Ruby are also similar, with functional semantics but syntax reminiscent of Python or C#. Our `uptoby` iterator in Ruby could be written as follows:

EXAMPLE 6.72 Iterating with procs in Ruby

```
def uptoby(first, last, inc)
    while first <= last do
        yield first
        first += inc
    end
end
...
sum = 0
uptoby(1, 100, 2) { |i| sum += i }
puts sum                                    ⟹ 2500
```

This code is defined as syntactic sugar for

```
def uptoby(first, last, inc, block)
    while first <= last do
        block.call(first)
        first += inc
    end
end
...
sum = 0
uptoby(1, 100, 2, Proc.new { |i| sum += i })
puts sum
```

When a block, delimited by braces or `do`... `end`, follows the parameter list of a function invocation, Ruby passes a closure representing the block (a "proc") as an implicit extra argument to the function. Within the body of the function, `yield` is defined as a call to the function's last parameter, which must be a proc, and need not be explicitly declared.

For added convenience, all of Ruby's collection objects (arrays, ranges, mappings, and sets) support a method named `each` that will invoke a block for every element of the collection. To sum the first 100 integers (without the step size of 2), we could say

```
sum = 0
(1..100).each { |i| sum += i }
puts sum                                    ⟹ 5050
```

This code serves as the definition of conventional `for`-loop syntax, which is further syntactic sugar:

```
sum = 0
for i in (1..100) do
    sum += i
end
puts sum
```

In Lisp and Scheme, one can define similar syntactic sugar using continuations (Section 6.2.2) and lazy evaluation (Section 6.6.2); we consider this possibility in Exercises 6.34 and 6.35. ■

Iterating without Iterators

EXAMPLE 6.73
Imitating iterators in C

In a language with neither true iterators nor iterator objects, we can still decouple the enumeration of a collection from actual use of the elements by adopting appropriate programming conventions. In C, for example, we might define a `tree_iter` type and associated functions that could be used in a loop as follows:

```
bin_tree *my_tree;
tree_iter ti;
...
for (ti_create(my_tree, &ti); !ti_done(ti); ti_next(&ti)) {
    bin_tree *n = ti_val(ti);
    ...
}
ti_delete(&ti);
```

There are two principal differences between this code and the more structured alternatives: (1) the syntax of the loop is a good bit less elegant (and arguably more prone to accidental errors), and (2) the code for the iterator is simply a type and some associated functions—C provides no abstraction mechanism to group them together as a module or a class. By providing a standard interface for iterator abstractions, object-oriented languages facilitate the design of higher-order mechanisms that manipulate whole collections: sorting them, merging them, finding their intersection or difference, and so on. We leave the C code for `tree_iter` and the various `ti_` functions to Exercise 6.20. ■

6.5.4 Generators in Icon

Icon generalizes the concept of iterators, providing a *generator* mechanism that causes any expression in which it is embedded to enumerate multiple values on demand.

IN MORE DEPTH

We consider Icon generators in more detail on the companion site. The language's enumeration-controlled loop, the `every` loop, can contain not only a generator, but any expression that *contains* a generator. Generators can also be used in constructs like `if` statements, which will execute their nested code if *any* generated value makes the condition true, automatically searching through all the possibilities. When generators are nested, Icon explores all possible combinations of generated values, and will even *backtrack* where necessary to undo unsuccessful control-flow branches or assignments.

6.5.5 Logically Controlled Loops

EXAMPLE 6.74
`while` loop in Algol-W

In comparison to enumeration-controlled loops, logically controlled loops have many fewer semantic subtleties. The only real question to be answered is where within the body of the loop the terminating condition is tested. By far the most common approach is to test the condition before each iteration. The familiar `while` loop syntax for this was introduced in Algol-W:

```
while condition do statement
```

To allow the body of the loop to be a statement list, most modern languages use an explicit concluding keyword (e.g., `end`), or bracket the body with delimiters (e.g., `{...}`). A few languages (notably Python) indicate the body with an extra level of indentation.

Post-test Loops

EXAMPLE 6.75
Post-test loop in Pascal and Modula

Occasionally it is handy to be able to test the terminating condition at the bottom of a loop. Pascal introduced special syntax for this case, which was retained in Modula but dropped in Ada. A *post-test loop* allows us, for example, to write

```
repeat
    readln(line)
until line[1] = '$';
```

instead of

```
readln(line);
while line[1] <> '$' do
    readln(line);
```

The difference between these constructs is particularly important when the body of the loop is longer. Note that the body of a post-test loop is always executed at least once.

EXAMPLE 6.76
Post-test loop in C

C provides a post-test loop whose condition works "the other direction" (i.e., "while" instead of "until"):

```
do {
    line = read_line(stdin);
} while (line[0] != '$');
```

Mid-test Loops

Finally, as we noted in Section 6.2.1, it is sometimes appropriate to test the terminating condition in the middle of a loop. In many languages this "mid-test" can be accomplished with a special statement nested inside a conditional: exit in Ada, break in C, last in Perl. In Section 6.4.2 we saw a somewhat unusual use of break to leave a C switch statement. More conventionally, C also uses break to exit the closest for, while, or do loop:

EXAMPLE 6.77
break statement in C

```
for (;;) {
    line = read_line(stdin);
    if (all_blanks(line)) break;
    consume_line(line);
}
```

Here the missing condition in the for loop header is assumed to always be true. (C programmers have traditionally preferred this syntax to the equivalent while (1), presumably because it was faster in certain early C compilers.)

EXAMPLE 6.78
Exiting a nested loop in Ada

In some languages, an exit statement takes an optional loop-name argument that allows control to escape a nested loop. In Ada we might write

```
outer: loop
    get_line(line, length);
    for i in 1..length loop
        exit outer when line(i) = '$';
        consume_char(line(i));
    end loop;
end loop outer;
```

EXAMPLE 6.79
Exiting a nested loop in Perl

In Perl this would be

```
outer: while (<>) {                 # iterate over lines of input
    foreach $c (split //) {         # iterate over remaining chars
        last outer if ($c =~ '\$'); # exit main loop if we see a $ sign
        consume_char($c);
    }
}
```

Java extends the C/C++ break statement in a similar fashion, with optional labels on loops.

✓ CHECK YOUR UNDERSTANDING

28. Describe three subtleties in the implementation of enumeration-controlled loops.

29. Why do most languages not allow the bounds or increment of an enumeration-controlled loop to be floating-point numbers?

30. Why do many languages require the step size of an enumeration-controlled loop to be a compile-time constant?
31. Describe the "iteration count" loop implementation. What problem(s) does it solve?
32. What are the advantages of making an index variable local to the loop it controls?
33. Does C have enumeration-controlled loops? Explain.
34. What is a *collection* (a *container* instance)?
35. Explain the difference between true iterators and iterator objects.
36. Cite two advantages of iterator objects over the use of programming conventions in a language like C.
37. Describe the approach to iteration typically employed in languages with first-class functions.
38. Give an example in which a *mid-test* loop results in more elegant code than does a pretest or post-test loop.

6.6 Recursion

Unlike the control-flow mechanisms discussed so far, recursion requires no special syntax. In any language that provides subroutines (particularly functions), all that is required is to permit functions to call themselves, or to call other functions that then call them back in turn. Most programmers learn in a data structures class that recursion and (logically controlled) iteration provide equally powerful means of computing functions: any iterative algorithm can be rewritten, automatically, as a recursive algorithm, and vice versa. We will compare iteration and recursion in more detail in the first subsection below. In the following subsection we will consider the possibility of passing *unevaluated* expressions into a function. While usually inadvisable, due to implementation cost, this technique will sometimes allow us to write elegant code for functions that are only defined on a subset of the possible inputs, or that explore logically infinite data structures.

6.6.1 Iteration and Recursion

As we noted in Section 3.2, Fortran 77 and certain other languages do not permit recursion. A few functional languages do not permit iteration. Most modern languages, however, provide both mechanisms. Iteration is in some sense the more "natural" of the two in imperative languages, because it is based on the repeated modification of variables. Recursion is the more natural of the two in functional languages, because it does *not* change variables. In the final analysis, which to use in which circumstance is mainly a matter of taste. To compute a sum,

EXAMPLE 6.80
A "naturally iterative" problem

$$\sum_{1 \le i \le 10} f(i)$$

it seems natural to use iteration. In C one would say

```
typedef int (*int_func) (int);
int summation(int_func f, int low, int high) {
    /* assume low <= high */
    int total = 0;
    int i;
    for (i = low; i <= high; i++) {
        total += f(i);   // (C will automatically dereference
                         // a function pointer when we attempt to call it.)
    }
    return total;
}
```

EXAMPLE 6.81
A "naturally recursive" problem

To compute a value defined by a recurrence,

$$\gcd(a, b) \equiv \begin{cases} a & \text{if } a = b \\ \gcd(a-b, b) & \text{if } a > b \\ \gcd(a, b-a) & \text{if } b > a \end{cases} \quad \text{(positive integers, } a, b\text{)}$$

recursion may seem more natural:

```
int gcd(int a, int b) {
    /* assume a, b > 0 */
    if (a == b) return a;
    else if (a > b) return gcd(a-b, b);
    else return gcd(a, b-a);
}
```

EXAMPLE 6.82
Implementing problems "the other way"

In both these cases, the choice could go the other way:

```
typedef int (*int_func) (int);
int summation(int_func f, int low, int high) {
    /* assume low <= high */
    if (low == high) return f(low);
    else return f(low) + summation(f, low+1, high);
}
```

```
int gcd(int a, int b) {
    /* assume a, b > 0 */
    while (a != b) {
        if (a > b) a = a-b;
        else b = b-a;
    }
    return a;
}
```

Tail Recursion

It is sometimes argued that iteration is more efficient than recursion. It is more accurate to say that *naive implementation* of iteration is usually more efficient than naive implementation of recursion. In the examples above, the iterative implementations of summation and greatest divisors will be more efficient than the recursive implementations if the latter make real subroutine calls that allocate space on a run-time stack for local variables and bookkeeping information. An "optimizing" compiler, however, particularly one designed for a functional language, will often be able to generate excellent code for recursive functions. It is particularly likely to do so for *tail-recursive* functions such as gcd above. A tail-recursive function is one in which additional computation never follows a recursive call: the return value is simply whatever the recursive call returns. For such functions, dynamically allocated stack space is unnecessary: the compiler can *reuse* the space belonging to the current iteration when it makes the recursive call. In effect, a good compiler will recast the recursive gcd function above as follows:

EXAMPLE 6.83
Iterative implementation of tail recursion

```
int gcd(int a, int b) {
    /* assume a, b > 0 */
start:
    if (a == b) return a;
    else if (a > b) {
        a = a-b; goto start;
    } else {
        b = b-a; goto start;
    }
}
```

Even for functions that are not tail-recursive, automatic, often simple transformations can produce tail-recursive code. The general case of the transformation employs conversion to what is known as *continuation-passing style* [FWH01, Chaps. 7–8]. In effect, a recursive function can always avoid doing any work after returning from a recursive call by passing that work into the recursive call, in the form of a continuation.

Some specific transformations (not based on continuation passing) are often employed by skilled users of functional languages. Consider, for example, the recursive summation function above, written here in Scheme:

EXAMPLE 6.84
By-hand creation of tail-recursive code

```
(define summation
  (lambda (f low high)
    (if (= low high)
      (f low)                                          ; then part
      (+ (f low) (summation f (+ low 1) high)))))      ; else part
```

Recall that Scheme, like all Lisp dialects, uses Cambridge Polish notation for expressions. The `lambda` keyword is used to introduce a function. As recursive calls return, our code calculates the sum from "right to left": from `high` down to `low`. If the programmer (or compiler) recognizes that addition is associative, we can rewrite the code in a tail-recursive form:

```
(define summation
  (lambda (f low high subtotal)
    (if (= low high)
      (+ subtotal (f low))
      (summation f (+ low 1) high (+ subtotal (f low))))))
```

Here the `subtotal` parameter accumulates the sum from left to right, passing it into the recursive calls. Because it is tail recursive, this function can be translated into machine code that does not allocate stack space for recursive calls. Of course, the programmer won't want to pass an explicit `subtotal` parameter to the initial call, so we hide it (the parameter) in an auxiliary, "helper" function:

```
(define summation
  (lambda (f low high)
    (letrec ((sum-helper
               (lambda (low subtotal)
                 (let ((new_subtotal (+ subtotal (f low))))
                   (if (= low high)
                       new_subtotal
                       (sum-helper (+ low 1) new_subtotal))))))
      (sum-helper low 0))))
```

The `let` construct in Scheme serves to introduce a nested scope in which local names (e.g., `new_subtotal`) can be defined. The `letrec` construct permits the definition of recursive functions (e.g., `sum-helper`). ■

Thinking Recursively

EXAMPLE 6.85

Naive recursive Fibonacci function

Detractors of functional programming sometimes argue, incorrectly, that recursion leads to *algorithmically inferior* programs. Fibonacci numbers, for example, are defined by the mathematical recurrence

$$\underset{\text{(non-negative integer } n)}{F_n} \equiv \begin{cases} 1 & \text{if } n = 0 \text{ or } n = 1 \\ F_{n-1} + F_{n-2} & \text{otherwise} \end{cases}$$

The naive way to implement this recurrence in Scheme is

```
(define fib
  (lambda (n)
    (cond ((= n 0) 1)
          ((= n 1) 1)
          (#t (+ (fib (- n 1)) (fib (- n 2)))))))
          ; #t means 'true' in Scheme
```

EXAMPLE 6.86
Linear iterative Fibonacci function

Unfortunately, this algorithm takes exponential time, when linear time is possible.[9] In C, one might write

```
int fib(int n) {
    int f1 = 1; int f2 = 1;
    int i;
    for (i = 2; i <= n; i++) {
        int temp = f1 + f2;
        f1 = f2; f2 = temp;
    }
    return f2;
}
```

EXAMPLE 6.87
Efficient tail-recursive Fibonacci function

One can write this iterative algorithm in Scheme: the language includes (non-functional) iterative features. It is probably better, however, to draw inspiration from the tail-recursive version of the summation example above, and write the following $O(n)$ recursive function:

```
(define fib
  (lambda (n)
    (letrec ((fib-helper
              (lambda (f1 f2 i)
                (if (= i n)
                    f2
                    (fib-helper f2 (+ f1 f2) (+ i 1))))))
      (fib-helper 0 1 0))))
```

For a programmer accustomed to writing in a functional style, this code is perfectly natural. One might argue that it isn't "really" recursive; it simply casts an iterative algorithm in a tail-recursive form, and this argument has some merit. Despite the algorithmic similarity, however, there is an important difference between the iterative algorithm in C and the tail-recursive algorithm in Scheme: the latter has no side effects. Each recursive call of the `fib-helper` function creates a new scope, containing new variables. The language implementation may be able to reuse the space occupied by previous instances of the same scope, but it guarantees that this optimization will never introduce bugs.

9 Actually, one can do substantially better than linear time using algorithms based on binary matrix multiplication or closest-integer rounding of continuous functions, but these approaches suffer from high constant-factor costs or problems with numeric precision. For most purposes the linear-time algorithm is a reasonable choice.

6.6.2 Applicative- and Normal-Order Evaluation

Throughout the discussion so far we have assumed implicitly that arguments are evaluated before passing them to a subroutine. This need not be the case. It is possible to pass a representation of the *unevaluated* arguments to the subroutine instead, and to evaluate them only when (if) the value is actually needed. The former option (evaluating before the call) is known as *applicative-order evaluation*; the latter (evaluating only when the value is actually needed) is known as *normal-order evaluation*. Normal-order evaluation is what naturally occurs in macros (Section 3.7). It also occurs in short-circuit Boolean evaluation (Section 6.1.5), *call-by-name* parameters (to be discussed in Section 9.3.1), and certain functional languages (to be discussed in Section 11.5).

Algol 60 uses normal-order evaluation by default for user-defined functions (applicative order is also available). This choice was presumably made to mimic the behavior of macros (Section 3.7). Most programmers in 1960 wrote mainly in assembler, and were accustomed to macro facilities. Because the parameter-passing mechanisms of Algol 60 are part of the language, rather than textual abbreviations, problems like misinterpreted precedence or naming conflicts do not arise. Side effects, however, are still very much an issue. We will discuss Algol 60 parameters in more detail in Section 9.3.1.

Lazy Evaluation

From the points of view of clarity and efficiency, applicative-order evaluation is generally preferable to normal-order evaluation. It is therefore natural for it to be employed in most languages. In some circumstances, however, normal-order evaluation can actually lead to faster code, or to code that works when applicative-order evaluation would lead to a run-time error. In both cases, what matters is that normal-order evaluation will sometimes not evaluate an argument at all, if its value is never actually needed. Scheme provides for optional normal-order

DESIGN & IMPLEMENTATION

6.10 Normal-order evaluation

Normal-order evaluation is one of many examples we have seen where arguably desirable semantics have been dismissed by language designers because of fear of implementation cost. Other examples in this chapter include side-effect freedom (which allows normal order to be implemented via lazy evaluation), iterators (Section 6.5.3), and nondeterminacy (Section 6.7). As noted in Sidebar 6.2, however, there has been a tendency over time to trade a bit of speed for cleaner semantics and increased reliability. Within the functional programming community, Haskell and its predecessor Miranda are entirely side-effect free, and use normal-order (lazy) evaluation for all parameters.

evaluation in the form of built-in functions called `delay` and `force`.[10] These functions provide an implementation of *lazy evaluation*. In the absence of side effects, lazy evaluation has the same semantics as normal-order evaluation, but the implementation keeps track of which expressions have already been evaluated, so it can reuse their values if they are needed more than once in a given referencing environment.

A `delay`ed expression is sometimes called a *promise*. The mechanism used to keep track of which promises have already been evaluated is sometimes called *memoization*.[11] Because applicative-order evaluation is the default in Scheme, the programmer must use special syntax not only to pass an unevaluated argument, but also to use it. In Algol 60, subroutine headers indicate which arguments are to be passed which way; the point of call and the uses of parameters within subroutines look the same in either case.

EXAMPLE 6.88
Lazy evaluation of an infinite data structure

One important use of lazy evaluation is to create so-called *infinite* or *lazy data structures*, which are "fleshed out" on demand. The following example, adapted from version 5 of the Scheme manual [KCR+98, p. 28], creates a "list" of all the natural numbers:

```
(define naturals
  (letrec ((next (lambda (n) (cons n (delay (next (+ n 1)))))))
    (next 1)))
(define head car)
(define tail (lambda (stream) (force (cdr stream))))
```

Here `cons` can be thought of, roughly, as a concatenation operator. `Car` returns the head of a list; `cdr` returns everything but the head. Given these definitions, we can access as many natural numbers as we want:

```
(head naturals)                  ⟹ 1
(head (tail naturals))           ⟹ 2
(head (tail (tail naturals)))    ⟹ 3
```

The list will occupy only as much space as we have actually explored. More elaborate lazy data structures (e.g., trees) can be valuable in combinatorial search problems, in which a clever algorithm may explore only the "interesting" parts of a potentially enormous search space. ▒

6.7 Nondeterminacy

Our final category of control flow is nondeterminacy. A nondeterministic construct is one in which the choice between alternatives (i.e., between control paths)

10 More precisely, `delay` is a *special form*, rather than a function. Its argument is passed to it unevaluated.

11 Within the functional programming community, the term "lazy evaluation" is often used for any implementation that declines to evaluate unneeded function parameters; this includes both naive implementations of normal-order evaluation and the memoizing mechanism described here.

is deliberately unspecified. We have already seen examples of nondeterminacy in the evaluation of expressions (Section 6.1.4): in most languages, operator or subroutine arguments may be evaluated in any order. Some languages, notably Algol 68 and various concurrent languages, provide more extensive nondeterministic mechanisms, which cover statements as well.

IN MORE DEPTH

Further discussion of nondeterminism can be found on the companion site. Absent a nondeterministic construct, the author of a code fragment in which order does not matter must choose some arbitrary (artificial) order. Such a choice can make it more difficult to construct a formal correctness proof. Some language designers have also argued that it is inelegant. The most compelling uses for nondeterminacy arise in concurrent programs, where imposing an arbitrary choice on the order in which a thread interacts with its peers may cause the system as a whole to deadlock. For such programs one may need to ensure that the choice among nondeterministic alternatives is *fair* in some formal sense.

✓ CHECK YOUR UNDERSTANDING

39. What is a *tail-recursive* function? Why is tail recursion important?
40. Explain the difference between *applicative-* and *normal-order* evaluation of expressions. Under what circumstances is each desirable?
41. What is *lazy evaluation*? What are *promises*? What is *memoization*?
42. Give two reasons why lazy evaluation may be desirable.
43. Name a language in which parameters are always evaluated lazily.
44. Give two reasons why a programmer might sometimes want control flow to be *nondeterministic*.

6.8 Summary and Concluding Remarks

In this chapter we introduced the principal forms of control flow found in programming languages: sequencing, selection, iteration, procedural abstraction, recursion, concurrency, exception handling and speculation, and nondeterminacy. Sequencing specifies that certain operations are to occur in order, one after the other. Selection expresses a choice among two or more control-flow alternatives. Iteration and recursion are the two ways to execute operations repeatedly. Recursion defines an operation in terms of simpler instances of itself; it depends on procedural abstraction. Iteration repeats an operation for its side effect(s). Sequencing and iteration are fundamental to imperative programming. Recursion is fundamental to functional programming. Nondeterminacy allows the programmer to leave certain aspects of control flow deliberately unspecified. We touched on concurrency only briefly; it will be the subject of Chapter 13. Procedural abstractions (subroutines) are the subject of Chapter 9. Exception handling and speculation will be covered in Sections 9.4 and 13.4.4.

Our survey of control-flow mechanisms was preceded by a discussion of expression evaluation. We considered the distinction between l-values and r-values, and between the value model of variables, in which a variable is a named container for data, and the reference model of variables, in which a variable is a reference to a data object. We considered issues of precedence, associativity, and ordering within expressions. We examined short-circuit Boolean evaluation and its implementation via jump code, both as a semantic issue that affects the correctness of expressions whose subparts are not always well defined, and as an implementation issue that affects the time required to evaluate complex Boolean expressions.

In our survey we encountered many examples of control-flow constructs whose syntax and semantics have evolved considerably over time. An important early example was the phasing out of `goto`-based control flow and the emergence of a consensus on structured alternatives. While convenience and readability are difficult to quantify, most programmers would agree that the control-flow constructs of a language like Ada are a dramatic improvement over those of, say, Fortran IV. Examples of features in Ada that are specifically designed to rectify control-flow problems in earlier languages include explicit terminators (`end if`, `end loop`, etc.) for structured constructs; `elsif` clauses; label ranges and default (`others`) clauses in `case` statements; implicit declaration of `for` loop indices as read-only local variables; explicit `return` statements; multilevel loop `exit` statements; and exceptions.

The evolution of constructs has been driven by many goals, including ease of programming, semantic elegance, ease of implementation, and run-time efficiency. In some cases these goals have proved complementary. We have seen for example that short-circuit evaluation leads both to faster code and (in many cases) to cleaner semantics. In a similar vein, the introduction of a new local scope for the index variable of an enumeration-controlled loop avoids both the semantic problem of the value of the index after the loop and (to some extent) the implementation problem of potential overflow.

In other cases improvements in language semantics have been considered worth a small cost in run-time efficiency. We saw this in the development of iterators: like many forms of abstraction, they add a modest amount of run-time cost in many cases (e.g., in comparison to explicitly embedding the implementation of the enumerated collection in the control flow of the loop), but with a large pay-back in modularity, clarity, and opportunities for code reuse. In a similar vein, the developers of Java would argue that for many applications the portability and safety provided by extensive semantic checking, standard-format numeric types, and so on are far more important than speed.

In several cases, advances in compiler technology or in the simple willingness of designers to build more complex compilers have made it possible to incorporate features once considered too expensive. Label ranges in Ada `case` statements require that the compiler be prepared to generate code employing binary search. In-line functions in C++ eliminate the need to choose between the inefficiency of tiny functions and the messy semantics of macros. Exceptions (as we shall see in Section 9.4.3) can be implemented in such a way that they incur no cost in the common case (when they do not occur), but the implementation is quite tricky. Iterators, boxing, generics (Section 7.3.1), and first-class functions are likewise rather tricky, but are increasingly found in mainstream imperative languages.

Some implementation techniques (e.g., rearranging expressions to uncover common subexpressions, or avoiding the evaluation of guards in a nondeterministic construct once an acceptable choice has been found) are sufficiently important to justify a modest burden on the programmer (e.g., adding parentheses where necessary to avoid overflow or ensure numeric stability, or ensuring that expressions in guards are side-effect-free). Other semantically useful mechanisms (e.g., lazy evaluation, continuations, or truly random nondeterminacy) are usually considered complex or expensive enough to be worthwhile only in special circumstances (if at all).

In comparatively primitive languages, we can often obtain some of the benefits of missing features through programming conventions. In early dialects of Fortran, for example, we can limit the use of `goto`s to patterns that mimic the control flow of more modern languages. In languages without short-circuit evaluation, we can write nested selection statements. In languages without iterators, we can write sets of subroutines that provide equivalent functionality.

6.9 Exercises

6.1 We noted in Section 6.1.1 that most binary arithmetic operators are left-associative in most programming languages. In Section 6.1.4, however, we also noted that most compilers are free to evaluate the operands of a binary operator in either order. Are these statements contradictory? Why or why not?

6.2 As noted in Figure 6.1, Fortran and Pascal give unary and binary minus the same level of precedence. Is this likely to lead to nonintuitive evaluations of certain expressions? Why or why not?

6.3 In Example 6.9 we described a common error in Pascal programs caused by the fact that `and` and `or` have precedence comparable to that of the arithmetic operators. Show how a similar problem can arise in the stream-based I/O of C++ (described in Section C-8.7.3). (Hint: Consider the precedence of << and >>, and the operators that appear below them in the C column of Figure 6.1.)

6.4 Translate the following expression into postfix and prefix notation:

$$[-b + \text{sqrt}(b \times b - 4 \times a \times c)]/(2 \times a)$$

Do you need a special symbol for unary negation?

6.5 In Lisp, most of the arithmetic operators are defined to take two or more arguments, rather than strictly two. Thus `(* 2 3 4 5)` evaluates to 120, and `(- 16 9 4)` evaluates to 3. Show that parentheses are necessary to disambiguate arithmetic expressions in Lisp (in other words, give an example of an expression whose meaning is unclear when parentheses are removed).

In Section 6.1.1 we claimed that issues of precedence and associativity do not arise with prefix or postfix notation. Reword this claim to make explicit the hidden assumption.

6.6 Example 6.33 claims that "For certain values of `x`, `(0.1 + x) * 10.0` and `1.0 + (x * 10.0)` can differ by as much as 25%, even when `0.1` and `x` are of the same magnitude." Verify this claim. (*Warning:* If you're using an x86 processor, be aware that floating-point calculations [even on single-precision variables] are performed internally with 80 bits of precision. Roundoff errors will appear only when intermediate results are stored out to memory [with limited precision] and read back in again.)

6.7 Is `&(&i)` ever valid in C? Explain.

6.8 Languages that employ a reference model of variables also tend to employ automatic garbage collection. Is this more than a coincidence? Explain.

6.9 In Section 6.1.2 ("Orthogonality"), we noted that C uses = for assignment and == for equality testing. The language designers state: "Since assignment is about twice as frequent as equality testing in typical C programs, it's appropriate that the operator be half as long" [KR88, p. 17]. What do you think of this rationale?

6.10 Consider a language implementation in which we wish to catch every use of an uninitialized variable. In Section 6.1.3 we noted that for types in which every possible bit pattern represents a valid value, extra space must be used to hold an initialized/uninitialized flag. Dynamic checks in such a system can be expensive, largely because of the address calculations needed to access the flags. We can reduce the cost in the common case by having the compiler generate code to automatically initialize every variable with a distinguished *sentinel* value. If at some point we find that a variable's value is different from the sentinel, then that variable must have been initialized. If its value *is* the sentinel, we must double-check the flag. Describe a plausible allocation strategy for initialization flags, and show the assembly language sequences that would be required for dynamic checks, with and without the use of sentinels.

6.11 Write an attribute grammar, based on the following context-free grammar, that accumulates jump code for Boolean expressions (with short-circuiting) into a synthesized attribute code of *condition*, and then uses this attribute to generate code for `if` statements.

stmt ⟶ `if` *condition* `then` *stmt* `else` *stmt*
⟶ *other_stmt*
condition ⟶ *c_term* | *condition* `or` *c_term*
c_term ⟶ *c_factor* | *c_term* `and` *c_factor*
c_factor ⟶ `ident` *relation* `ident` | `(` *condition* `)` | `not` `(` *condition* `)`
relation ⟶ `<` | `<=` | `=` | `<>` | `>` | `>=`

You may assume that the code attribute has already been initialized for *other_stmt* and `ident` nodes. (For hints, see Fischer et al.'s compiler book [FCL10, Sec. 14.1.4].)

6.12 Describe a plausible scenario in which a programmer might wish to avoid short-circuit evaluation of a Boolean expression.

6.13 Neither Algol 60 nor Algol 68 employs short-circuit evaluation for Boolean expressions. In both languages, however, an `if... then ... else` construct can be used as an expression. Show how to use `if... then ... else` to achieve the effect of short-circuit evaluation.

6.14 Consider the following expression in C: `a/b > 0 && b/a > 0`. What will be the result of evaluating this expression when `a` is zero? What will be the result when `b` is zero? Would it make sense to try to design a language in which this expression is guaranteed to evaluate to `false` when either `a` or `b` (but not both) is zero? Explain your answer.

6.15 As noted in Section 6.4.2, languages vary in how they handle the situation in which the controlling expression in a `case` statement does not appear among the labels on the arms. C and Fortran 90 say the statement has no effect. Pascal and Modula say it results in a dynamic semantic error. Ada says that the labels must *cover* all possible values for the type of the expression, so the question of a missing value can never arise at run time. What are the tradeoffs among these alternatives? Which do you prefer? Why?

6.16 The equivalence of `for` and `while` loops, mentioned in Example 6.64, is not precise. Give an example in which it breaks down. Hint: think about the `continue` statement.

6.17 Write the equivalent of Figure 6.5 in C# or Ruby. Write a second version that performs an in-order enumeration, rather than preorder.

6.18 Revise the algorithm of Figure 6.6 so that it performs an in-order enumeration, rather than preorder.

6.19 Write a C++ preorder iterator to supply tree nodes to the loop in Example 6.69. You will need to know (or learn) how to use pointers, references, inner classes, and operator overloading in C++. For the sake of (relative) simplicity, you may assume that the data in a tree node is always an `int`; this will save you the need to use generics. You may want to use the `stack` abstraction from the C++ standard library.

6.20 Write code for the `tree_iter` type (`struct`) and the `ti_create`, `ti_done`, `ti_next`, `ti_val`, and `ti_delete` functions employed in Example 6.73.

6.21 Write, in C#, Python, or Ruby, an iterator that yields

(a) all permutations of the integers $1\,..\,n$

(b) all combinations of k integers from the range $1\,..\,n$ $(0 \le k \le n)$.

You may represent your permutations and combinations using either a list or an array.

6.22 Use iterators to construct a program that outputs (in some order) all *structurally distinct* binary trees of n nodes. Two trees are considered structurally distinct if they have different numbers of nodes or if their left or right subtrees are structurally distinct. There are, for example, five structurally distinct trees of three nodes:

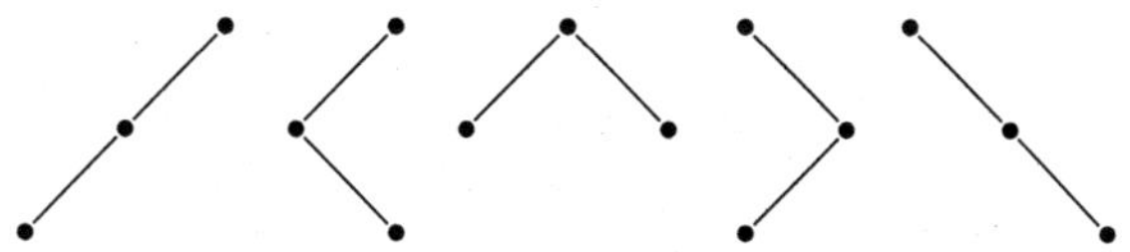

These are most easily output in "dotted parenthesized form":

```
(((.).).)
((.(.)).)
((.).(.))
(.((.).))
(.(.(.)))
```

(Hint: Think recursively! If you need help, see Section 2.2 of the text by Finkel [Fin96].)

6.23 Build true iterators in Java using threads. (This requires knowledge of material in Chapter 13.) Make your solution as clean and as general as possible. In particular, you should provide the standard `Iterator` or `IEnumerable` interface, for use with extended `for` loops, but the programmer should not have to write these. Instead, he or she should write a class with an `Iterate` method, which should in turn be able to call a `Yield` method, which you should also provide. Evaluate the cost of your solution. How much more expensive is it than standard Java iterator objects?

6.24 In an expression-oriented language such as Algol 68 or Lisp, a `while` loop (a `do` loop in Lisp) has a value as an expression. How do you think this value should be determined? (How is it determined in Algol 68 and Lisp?) Is the value a useless artifact of expression orientation, or are there reasonable programs in which it might actually be used? What do you think should happen if the condition on the loop is such that the body is never executed?

6.25 Consider a mid-test loop, here written in C, that looks for blank lines in its input:

```
for (;;) {
    line = read_line();
    if (all_blanks(line)) break;
    consume_line(line);
}
```

Show how you might accomplish the same task using a `while` or `do` (`repeat`) loop, if mid-test loops were not available. (Hint: One alternative duplicates part of the code; another introduces a Boolean flag variable.) How do these alternatives compare to the mid-test version?

6.26 Rubin [Rub87] used the following example (rewritten here in C) to argue in favor of a `goto` statement:

```
int first_zero_row = -1;            /* none */
int i, j;
for (i = 0; i < n; i++) {
    for (j = 0; j < n; j++) {
        if (A[i][j]) goto next;
    }
    first_zero_row = i;
    break;
next: ;
}
```

The intent of the code is to find the first all-zero row, if any, of an $n \times n$ matrix. Do you find the example convincing? Is there a good structured alternative in C? In any language?

6.27 Bentley [Ben00, Chap. 4] provides the following informal description of binary search:

> We are to determine whether the sorted array `X[1..N]` contains the element `T`.... Binary search solves the problem by keeping track of a range within the array in which `T` must be if it is anywhere in the array. Initially, the range is the entire array. The range is shrunk by comparing its middle element to `T` and discarding half the range. The process continues until `T` is discovered in the array or until the range in which it must lie is known to be empty.

Write code for binary search in your favorite imperative programming language. What loop construct(s) did you find to be most useful? NB: when he asked more than a hundred professional programmers to solve this problem, Bentley found that only about 10% got it right the first time, without testing.

6.28 A *loop invariant* is a condition that is guaranteed to be true at a given point within the body of a loop on every iteration. Loop invariants play a major role in *axiomatic semantics*, a formal reasoning system used to prove properties of programs. In a less formal way, programmers who identify (and write down!) the invariants for their loops are more likely to write correct code. Show the loop invariant(s) for your solution to the preceding exercise.

(Hint: You will find the distinction between $<$ and $\leq$ [or between $>$ and $\geq$] to be crucial.)

6.29 If you have taken a course in automata theory or recursive function theory, explain why `while` loops are strictly more powerful than `for` loops. (If you haven't had such a course, skip this question!) Note that we're referring here to Ada-style `for` loops, not C-style.

6.30 Show how to calculate the number of iterations of a general Fortran 90-style `do` loop. Your code should be written in an assembler-like notation, and should be guaranteed to work for all valid bounds and step sizes. Be careful of overflow! (Hint: While the bounds and step size of the loop can be either positive or negative, you can safely use an unsigned integer for the iteration count.)

6.31 Write a tail-recursive function in Scheme or ML to compute n factorial ($n! = \prod_{1 \leq i \leq n} i = 1 \times 2 \times \cdots \times n$). (Hint: You will probably want to define a "helper" function, as discussed in Section 6.6.1.)

6.32 Is it possible to write a tail-recursive version of the classic quicksort algorithm? Why or why not?

6.33 Give an example in C in which an in-line subroutine may be significantly faster than a functionally equivalent macro. Give another example in which the macro is likely to be faster. (Hint: Think about applicative vs normal-order evaluation of arguments.)

6.34 Use lazy evaluation (`delay` and `force`) to implement iterator objects in Scheme. More specifically, let an iterator be either the null list or a pair consisting of an element and a promise which when `force`d will return an iterator. Give code for an `uptoby` function that returns an iterator, and a `for-iter` function that accepts as arguments a one-argument function and an iterator. These should allow you to evaluate such expressions as

```
(for-iter (lambda (e) (display e) (newline)) (uptoby 10 50 3))
```

Note that unlike the standard Scheme `for-each`, `for-iter` should not require the existence of a list containing the elements over which to iterate; the intrinsic space required for `(for-iter f (uptoby 1 n 1))` should be only $O(1)$, rather than $O(n)$.

6.35 (Difficult) Use `call-with-current-continuation` (`call/cc`) to implement the following structured nonlocal control transfers in Scheme. (This requires knowledge of material in Chapter 11.) You will probably want to consult a Scheme manual for documentation not only on `call/cc`, but on `define-syntax` and `dynamic-wind` as well.

(a) Multilevel returns. Model your syntax after the `catch` and `throw` of Common Lisp.

(b) True iterators. In a style reminiscent of Exercise 6.34, let an iterator be a function which when `call/cc`-ed will return either a null list or a pair consisting of an element and an iterator. As in that previous exercise, your implementation should support expressions like

```
(for-iter (lambda (e) (display e) (newline)) (uptoby 10 50 3))
```

Where the implementation of uptoby in Exercise 6.34 required the use of delay and force, however, you should provide an iterator macro (a Scheme *special form*) and a yield function that allows uptoby to look like an ordinary tail-recursive function with an embedded yield:

```
(define uptoby
  (iterator (low high step)
    (letrec ((helper (lambda (next)
                       (if (> next high) '()
                         (begin                ; else clause
                           (yield next)
                           (helper (+ next step)))))))
      (helper low))))
```

6.36–6.40 In More Depth.

6.10 Explorations

6.41 *Loop unrolling* (described in Exercise C-5.21 and Section C-17.7.1) is a code transformation that replicates the body of a loop and reduces the number of iterations, thereby decreasing loop overhead and increasing opportunities to improve the performance of the processor pipeline by reordering instructions. Unrolling is traditionally implemented by the code improvement phase of a compiler. It can be implemented at source level, however, if we are faced with the prospect of "hand optimizing" time-critical code on a system whose compiler is not up to the task. Unfortunately, if we replicate the body of a loop k times, we must deal with the possibility that the original number of loop iterations, n, may not be a multiple of k. Writing in C, and letting $k = 4$, we might transform the main loop of Exercise C-5.21 from

```
i = 0;
do {
    sum += A[i]; squares += A[i] * A[i]; i++;
} while (i < N);
```

to

```
i = 0;   j = N/4;
do {
    sum += A[i]; squares += A[i] * A[i]; i++;
    sum += A[i]; squares += A[i] * A[i]; i++;
    sum += A[i]; squares += A[i] * A[i]; i++;
    sum += A[i]; squares += A[i] * A[i]; i++;
} while (--j > 0);
do {
    sum += A[i]; squares += A[i] * A[i]; i++;
} while (i < N);
```

In 1983, Tom Duff of Lucasfilm realized that code of this sort can be "simplified" in C by interleaving a `switch` statement and a loop. The result is rather startling, but perfectly valid C. It's known in programming folklore as "Duff's device":

```
i = 0; j = (N+3)/4;
switch (N%4) {
    case 0: do{ sum += A[i]; squares += A[i] * A[i]; i++;
    case 3:     sum += A[i]; squares += A[i] * A[i]; i++;
    case 2:     sum += A[i]; squares += A[i] * A[i]; i++;
    case 1:     sum += A[i]; squares += A[i] * A[i]; i++;
            } while (--j > 0);
}
```

Duff announced his discovery with "a combination of pride and revulsion." He noted that "Many people... have said that the worst feature of C is that `switch`es don't `break` automatically before each `case` label. This code forms some sort of argument in that debate, but I'm not sure whether it's for or against." What do you think? Is it reasonable to interleave a loop and a `switch` in this way? Should a programming language permit it? Is automatic fall-through ever a good idea?

6.42 Using your favorite language and compiler, investigate the order of evaluation of subroutine parameters. Are they usually evaluated left-to-right or right-to-left? Are they ever evaluated in the other order? (Can you be sure?) Write a program in which the order makes a difference in the results of the computation.

6.43 Consider the different approaches to arithmetic overflow adopted by Pascal, C, Java, C#, and Common Lisp, as described in Section 6.1.4. Speculate as to the differences in language design goals that might have caused the designers to adopt the approaches they did.

6.44 Learn more about container classes and the *design patterns* (structured programming idioms) they support. Explore the similarities and differences among the standard container libraries of C++, Java, and C#. Which of these libraries do you find the most appealing? Why?

6.45 In Examples 6.43 and 6.72 we suggested that a Ruby *proc* (a block, passed to a function as an implicit extra argument) was "roughly" equivalent to a lambda expression. As it turns out, Ruby has both procs *and* lambda expressions, and they're almost—but not quite—the same. Learn about the details, and the history of their development. In what situations will a proc and a lambda behave differently, and why?

6.46 One of the most popular idioms for large-scale systems is the so-called *visitor pattern*. It has several uses, one of which resembles the "iterating with first-class functions" idiom of Examples 6.70 and 6.71. Briefly, elements of a container class provide an `accept` method that expects as argument an object that implements the `visitor` interface. This interface in turn has a method named `visit` that expects an argument of element type. To iterate over a collection, we implement the "loop body" in the `visit` method of a visitor object. This object constitutes a closure of the sort described in Section 3.6.3. Any information that `visit` needs (beyond the identify of the "loop index" element) can be encapsulated in the object's fields. An iterator method for the collection passes the visitor object to the `accept` method of each element. Each element in turn calls the `visit` method of the visitor object, passing itself as argument.

Learn more about the visitor pattern. Use it to implement iterators for a collection—preorder, inorder, and postorder traversals of a binary tree, for example. How do visitors compare with equivalent iterator-based code? Do they add new functionality? What else are visitors good for, in addition to iteration?

6.47–6.50 In More Depth.

6.11 Bibliographic Notes

Many of the issues discussed in this chapter feature prominently in papers on the history of programming languages. Pointers to several such papers can be found in the Bibliographic Notes for Chapter 1. Fifteen papers comparing Ada, C, and Pascal can be found in the collection edited by Feuer and Gehani [FG84]. References for individual languages can be found in Appendix A.

Niklaus Wirth has been responsible for a series of influential languages over a 30-year period, including Pascal [Wir71], its predecessor Algol W [WH66], and the successors Modula [Wir77b], Modula-2 [Wir85b], and Oberon [Wir88b]. The `case` statement of Algol W is due to Hoare [Hoa81]. Bernstein [Ber85] considers a variety of alternative implementations for `case`, including multilevel versions appropriate for label sets consisting of several dense "clusters" of values. Guarded commands (Section C-6.7) are due to Dijkstra [Dij75]. Duff's device (Exploration 6.41) was originally posted to netnews, an early on-line discussion group system, in May of 1984. The original posting appears to have been lost, but Duff's commentary on it can be found at many Internet sites, including *www.lysator.liu.se/c/duffs-device.html.*

Debate over the supposed merits or evils of the `goto` statement dates from at least the early 1960s, but became a good bit more heated in the wake of a 1968 article by Dijkstra ("Go To Statement Considered Harmful" [Dij68b]). The structured programming movement of the 1970s took its name from the text of Dahl, Dijkstra, and Hoare [DDH72]. A dissenting letter by Rubin in 1987 ("'GOTO Considered Harmful' Considered Harmful" [Rub87]; Exercise 6.26) elicited a flurry of responses.

What has been called the "reference model of variables" in this chapter is called the "object model" in Clu; Liskov and Guttag describe it in Sections 2.3 and 2.4.2 of their text on abstraction and specification [LG86]. Clu iterators are described in an article by Liskov et al. [LSAS77], and in Chapter 6 of the Liskov and Guttag text. Icon generators are discussed in Chapters 11 and 14 of the text by Griswold and Griswold [GG96]. Ruby blocks, procs, and iterators are discussed in Chapter 4 of the text by Thomas et al. [TFH13]. The tree-enumeration algorithm of Exercise 6.22 was originally presented (without iterators) by Solomon and Finkel [SF80].

Several texts discuss the use of invariants (Exercise 6.28) as a tool for writing correct programs. Particularly noteworthy are the works of Dijkstra [Dij76] and Gries [Gri81]. Kernighan and Plauger provide a more informal discussion of the art of writing good programs [KP78].

The Blizzard [SFL$^+$94] and Shasta [SG96] systems for software distributed shared memory (S-DSM) make use of sentinels (Exercise 6.10). We will discuss S-DSM in Section 13.2.1.

Michaelson [Mic89, Chap. 8] provides an accessible formal treatment of applicative-order, normal-order, and lazy evaluation. The concept of memoization is originally due to Michie [Mic68]. Friedman, Wand, and Haynes provide an excellent discussion of continuation-passing style [FWH01, Chaps. 7–8].

7 Type Systems

Most programming languages include a notion of *type* for expressions and/or objects.[1] Types serve several important purposes:

EXAMPLE 7.1
Operations that leverage type information

1. Types provide implicit context for many operations, so that the programmer does not have to specify that context explicitly. In C, for instance, the expression `a + b` will use integer addition if `a` and `b` are of integer (`int`) type; it will use floating-point addition if `a` and `b` are of floating-point (`double` or `float`) type. Similarly, the operation `new p` in Pascal, where `p` is a pointer, will allocate a block of storage from the heap that is the right size to hold an object of the type pointed to by `p`; the programmer does not have to specify (or even know) this size. In C++, Java, and C#, the operation `new my_type()` not only allocates (and returns a pointer to) a block of storage sized for an object of type `my_type`; it also automatically calls any user-defined initialization (*constructor*) function that has been associated with that type. ■

EXAMPLE 7.2
Errors captured by type information

2. Types limit the set of operations that may be performed in a semantically valid program. They prevent the programmer from adding a character and a record, for example, or from taking the arctangent of a set, or passing a file as a parameter to a subroutine that expects an integer. While no type system can promise to catch every nonsensical operation that a programmer might put into a program by mistake, good type systems catch enough mistakes to be highly valuable in practice. ■
3. If types are specified explicitly in the source program (as they are in many but not all languages), they can often make the program easier to read and understand. In effect, they serve as stylized documentation, whose correctness is checked by the compiler. (On the flip side, the need for this documentation can sometimes make the program harder to write.)
4. If types are known at compile time (either because the programmer specifies them explicitly or because the compiler is able to infer them), they can be used

1 Recall that unless otherwise noted we are using the term "object" informally to refer to anything that might have a name. Object-oriented languages, which we will study in Chapter 10, assign a narrower, more formal, meaning to the term.

EXAMPLE 7.3

Types as a source of "may alias" information

to drive important performance optimizations. As a simple example, recall the concept of *aliases*, introduced in Section 3.5.1, and discussed in Sidebar 3.7. If a program performs an assignment through a pointer, the compiler may be able to infer that objects of unrelated types cannot possibly be affected; their values can safely remain in registers, even if loaded prior to the assignment. ■

Section 7.1 looks more closely at the meaning and purpose of types. It presents some basic definitions, and introduces the notions of polymorphism and orthogonality. Section 7.2 takes a closer look at type checking; in particular, it considers *type equivalence* (when can we say that two types are the same?), *type compatibility* (when can we use a value of a given type in a given context?), and *type inference* (how do we deduce the type of an expression from the types of its components and that of the surrounding context?).

As an example of both polymorphism and sophisticated inference, Section 7.2.4 surveys the type system of ML, which combines, to a large extent, the efficiency and early error reporting of compilation with the convenience and flexibility of interpretation. We continue the study of polymorphism in Section 7.3, with a particular emphasis on *generics*, which allow a body of code to be parameterized explicitly for multiple types. Finally, in Section 7.4, we consider what it means to compare two complex objects for equality, or to assign one into the other. In Chapter 8 we will consider syntactic, semantic, and pragmatic issues for some of the most important *composite* types: records, arrays, strings, sets, pointers, lists, and files.

7.1 Overview

Computer hardware can interpret bits in memory in several different ways: as instructions, addresses, characters, and integer and floating-point numbers of various lengths. The bits themselves, however, are untyped: the hardware on most machines makes no attempt to keep track of which interpretations correspond to which locations in memory. Assembly languages reflect this lack of typing: operations of any kind can be applied to values in arbitrary locations. High-level languages, by contrast, almost always associate types with values, to provide the contextual information and error checking alluded to above.

Informally, a *type system* consists of (1) a mechanism to define types and associate them with certain language constructs, and (2) a set of rules for *type equivalence*, *type compatibility*, and *type inference*. The constructs that must have types are precisely those that have values, or that can refer to objects that have values. These constructs include named constants, variables, record fields, parameters, and sometimes subroutines; literal constants (e.g., `17`, `3.14`, `"foo"`); and more complicated expressions containing these. Type equivalence rules determine when the types of two values are the same. Type compatibility rules determine when a value of a given type can be used in a given context. Type inference rules define the type of an expression based on the types of its constituent parts or (sometimes) the surrounding context. In a language with polymorphic variables or parameters, it may be important to distinguish between the type of a reference or pointer and the type of the object to which it refers: a given name may refer to objects of different types at different times.

Subroutines are considered to have types in some languages, but not in others. Subroutines need to have types if they are first- or second-class values (i.e., if they can be passed as parameters, returned by functions, or stored in variables). In each of these cases there is a construct in the language whose value is a dynamically determined subroutine; type information allows the language to limit the set of acceptable values to those that provide a particular subroutine interface (i.e., particular numbers and types of parameters). In a statically scoped language that never creates references to subroutines dynamically (one in which subroutines are always third-class values), the compiler can always identify the subroutine to which a name refers, and can ensure that the routine is called correctly without necessarily employing a formal notion of subroutine types.

Type checking is the process of ensuring that a program obeys the language's type compatibility rules. A violation of the rules is known as a *type clash*. A language is said to be *strongly typed* if it prohibits, in a way that the language implementation can enforce, the application of any operation to any object that is not intended to support that operation. A language is said to be *statically typed* if it is strongly typed and type checking can be performed at compile time. In the strictest sense of the term, few languages are statically typed. In practice, the term is often applied to languages in which most type checking can be performed at compile time, and the rest can be performed at run time.

Since the mid 1970s, most newly developed languages have tended to be strongly (though not necessarily statically) typed. Interestingly, C has become more strongly typed with each successive version of the language, though various loopholes remain; these include unions, nonconverting type casts, subroutines with variable numbers of parameters, and the interoperability of pointers and arrays (to be discussed in Section 8.5.1). Implementations of C rarely check anything at run time.

DESIGN & IMPLEMENTATION

7.1 Systems programming

The standard argument against complete type safety in C is that systems programs need to be able to "break" types on occasion. Consider, for example, the code that implements dynamic memory management (e.g., `malloc` and `free`). This code must interpret the same bytes, at different times, as unallocated space, metadata, or (parts of) user-defined data structures. "By fiat" conversions between types are inescapable. Such conversions need not, however, be subtle. Largely in reaction to experience with C, the designers of C# chose to permit operations that break the type system only within blocks of code that have been explicitly labeled `unsafe`.

Dynamic (run-time) type checking can be seen as a form of late binding, and tends to be found in languages that delay other issues until run time as well. Static typing is thus the norm in languages intended for performance; dynamic typing is more common in languages intended for ease of programming. Lisp and Smalltalk are dynamically (though strongly) typed. Most scripting languages are also dynamically typed; some (e.g., Python and Ruby) are strongly typed. Languages with dynamic scoping are generally dynamically typed (or not typed at all): if the compiler can't identify the object to which a name refers, it usually can't determine the type of the object either.

7.1.1 The Meaning of "Type"

While every programmer has at least an informal notion of what is meant by "type," that notion can be formalized in several different ways. Three of the most popular are what we might call the *denotational*, *structural*, and *abstraction-based* points of view. From the denotational point of view, a type is simply a set of values. A value has a given type if it belongs to the set; an object has a given type if its value is guaranteed to be in the set. From the structural point of view, a type is either one of a small collection of *built-in* types (integer, character, Boolean, real, etc.; also called *primitive* or *predefined* types), or a *composite* type created by

DESIGN & IMPLEMENTATION

7.2 Dynamic typing

The growing popularity of scripting languages has led a number of prominent software developers to publicly question the value of static typing. They ask: given that we can't check everything at compile time, how much pain is it worth to check the things we can? As a general rule, it is easier to write type-correct code than to prove that we have done so, and static typing requires such proofs. As type systems become more complex (due to object orientation, generics, etc.), the complexity of static typing increases correspondingly.

Anyone who has written extensively in Ada or C++ on the one hand, and in Python or Scheme on the other, cannot help but be struck at how much easier it is to write code, at least for modest-sized programs, without complex type declarations. Dynamic checking incurs some run-time overhead, of course, and may delay the discovery of bugs, but this is increasingly seen as insignificant in comparison to the potential increase in human productivity. An intermediate position, epitomized by the ML family of languages but increasingly adopted (in limited form) by others, retains the requirement that types be statically known, but relies on the compiler to infer them automatically, without the need for some (or—in the case of ML—most) explicit declarations. We will discuss this topic more in Section 7.2.3. Static and dynamic typing and the role of inference promise to provide some of the most interesting language debates of the coming decade.

applying a type *constructor* (`record`, `array`, `set`, etc.) to one or more simpler types. (This use of the term "constructor" is unrelated to the initialization functions of object-oriented languages. It also differs in a more subtle way from the use of the term in ML.) From the abstraction-based point of view, a type is an *interface* consisting of a set of operations with well-defined and mutually consistent semantics. For both programmers and language designers, types may also reflect a mixture of these viewpoints.

In denotational semantics (one of several ways to formalize the meaning of programs), a set of values is known as a *domain*. Types are domains, and the meaning of an expression is a value from the domain that represents the expression's type. Some domains—the integers, for example—are simple and familiar. Others are more complex. An array can be thought of as a value from a domain whose elements are functions; each of these functions maps values from some finite *index* type (typically a subset of the integers) to values of some other *element* type. As it turns out, denotational semantics can associate a type with *everything* in a program—even statements with side effects. The meaning of an assignment statement is a value from a domain of higher-level functions, each of whose elements maps a *store*—a mapping from names to values that represents the current contents of memory—to another store, which represents the contents of memory after the assignment.

One of the nice things about the denotational view of types is that it allows us in many cases to describe user-defined composite types (records, arrays, etc.) in terms of mathematical operations on sets. We will allude to these operations again under "Composite Types" in Section 7.1.4. Because it is based on mathematical objects, the denotational view of types usually ignores such implementation issues as limited precision and word length. This limitation is less serious than it might at first appear: Checks for such errors as arithmetic overflow are usually implemented outside of the type system of a language anyway. They result in a run-time error, but this error is not called a type clash.

When a programmer defines an enumerated type (e.g., `enum hue {red, green, blue}` in C), he or she certainly thinks of this type as a set of values. For other varieties of user-defined type, this denotational view may not be as natural. Instead, the programmer may think in terms of the way the type is built from simpler types, or in terms of its meaning or purpose. These ways of thinking reflect the structural and abstraction-based points of view, respectively. The structural point of view was pioneered by Algol W and Algol 68, and is characteristic of many languages designed in the 1970s and 1980s. The abstraction-based point of view was pioneered by Simula-67 and Smalltalk, and is characteristic of modern object-oriented languages; it can also be found in the module constructs of various other languages, and it can be adopted as a matter of programming discipline in almost any language. We will consider the structural point of view in more detail in Chapter 8, and the abstraction-based in Chapter 10.

7.1.2 Polymorphism

Polymorphism, which we mentioned briefly in Section 3.5.2, takes its name from the Greek, and means "having multiple forms." It applies to code—both data structures and subroutines—that is designed to work with values of multiple types. To maintain correctness, the types must generally have certain characteristics in common, and the code must not depend on any other characteristics. The commonality is usually captured in one of two main ways. In *parametric polymorphism* the code takes a type (or set of types) as a parameter, either explicitly or implicitly. In *subtype polymorphism*, the code is designed to work with values of some specific type *T*, but the programmer can define additional types to be extensions or refinements of *T*, and the code will work with these *subtypes* as well.

Explicit parametric polymorphism, also known as *generics* (or *templates* in C++), typically appears in statically typed languages, and is usually implemented at compile time. The implicit version can also be implemented at compile time—specifically, in ML-family languages; more commonly, it is paired with dynamic typing, and the checking occurs at run time.

Subtype polymorphism appears primarily in object-oriented languages. With static typing, most of the work required to deal with multiple types can be performed at compile time: the principal run-time cost is an extra level of indirection on method invocations. Most languages that envision such an implementation, including C++, Eiffel, OCaml, Java, and C#, provide a separate mechanism for generics, also checked mainly at compile time. The combination of subtype and parametric polymorphism is particularly useful for *container* (*collection*) classes such as "list of `T`" (`List<T>`) or "stack of `T`" (`Stack<T>`), where `T` is initially unspecified, and can be instantiated later as almost any type.

By contrast, dynamically typed object-oriented languages, including Smalltalk, Python, and Ruby, generally use a single mechanism for both parametric and subtype polymorphism, with checking delayed until run time. A unified mechanism also appears in Objective-C, which provides dynamically typed objects on top of otherwise static typing.

We will consider parametric polymorphism in more detail in Section 7.3, after our coverage of typing in ML. Subtype polymorphism will largely be deferred to Chapter 10, which covers object orientation, and to Section 14.4.4, which focuses on objects in scripting languages.

7.1.3 Orthogonality

In Section 6.1.2 we discussed the importance of orthogonality in the design of expressions, statements, and control-flow constructs. In a highly orthogonal language, these features can be used, with consistent behavior, in almost any combination. Orthogonality is equally important in type system design. A highly orthogonal language tends to be easier to understand, to use, and to reason about in a formal way. We have noted that languages like Algol 68 and C enhance orthogonality by eliminating (or at least blurring) the distinction between statements and expressions. To characterize a statement that is executed for its side effect(s), and that has no useful values, some languages provide a trivial type with a single value. In C and Algol 68, for example, a subroutine that is meant to be used as a procedure is generally declared with a return type of `void`. In ML, the trivial type is called `unit`. If the programmer wishes to call a subroutine that does return a value, but the value is not needed in this particular case (all that matters is the side effect[s]), then the return value in C can be discarded by "casting" it to `void`:

EXAMPLE 7.4
`void` (trivial) type

```
foo_index = insert_in_symbol_table(foo);
...
(void) insert_in_symbol_table(bar);      /* don't care where it went */
    /* cast is optional; implied if omitted */
```

EXAMPLE 7.5
Making do without `void`

In a language (e.g., Pascal) without a trivial type, the latter of these two calls would need to use a dummy variable:

```
var dummy : symbol_table_index;
...
dummy := insert_in_symbol_table(bar);
```

As another example of orthogonality, consider the common need to "erase" the value of a variable—to indicate that it does not hold a valid value of its type. For pointer types, we can often use the value `null`. For enumerations, we can add an extra "none of the above" alternative to the set of possible values. But these two techniques are very different, and they don't generalize to types that already make use of all available bit patterns in the underlying implementation.

EXAMPLE 7.6
Option types in OCaml

To address the need for "none of the above" in a more orthogonal way, many functional languages—and some imperative languages as well—provide a special type constructor, often called `Option` or `Maybe`. In OCaml, we can write

```
let divide n d : float option =   (* n and d are parameters *)
  match d with                    (* "float option" is the return type *)
  | 0. -> None
  | _  -> Some (n /. d);;         (* underscore means "anything else" *)

let show v : string =
  match v with
  | None   -> "??"
  | Some x -> string_of_float x;;
```

Here function `divide` returns `None` if asked to divide by zero; otherwise it returns `Some` x, where x is the desired quotient. Function `show` returns either `"??"` or the string representation of x, depending on whether parameter `v` is `None` or `Some` x.

Option types appear in a variety of other languages, including Haskell (which calls them `Maybe`), Scala, C#, Swift, and (as generic library classes) Java and C++. In the interest of brevity, C# and Swift use a trailing question mark instead of the `option` constructor. Here is the previous example, rewritten in Swift:

EXAMPLE 7.7 Option types in Swift

```
func divide(n : Double, d : Double) -> Double? {
    if d == 0 { return nil }
    return n / d
}

func show(v : Double?) -> String {
    if v == nil { return "??" }
    return "\(v!)"                      // interpolate v into string
}
```

With these definitions, `show(divide(3.0, 4.0))` will evaluate to `"0.75"`, while `show(divide(3.0, 0.0))` will evaluate to `"??"`. ■

Yet another example of orthogonality arises when specifying literal values for objects of composite type. Such literals are sometimes known as *aggregates.* They are particularly valuable for the initialization of static data structures; without them, a program may need to waste time performing initialization at run time.

EXAMPLE 7.8 Aggregates in Ada

Ada provides aggregates for all its structured types. Given the following declarations

```
type person is record
        name : string (1..10);
        age : integer;
    end record;
p, q : person;
A, B : array (1..10) of integer;
```

we can write the following assignments:

```
p := ("Jane Doe  ", 37);
q := (age => 36, name => "John Doe  ");
A := (1, 0, 3, 0, 3, 0, 3, 0, 0, 0);
B := (1 => 1, 3 | 5 | 7 => 3, others => 0);
```

Here the aggregates assigned into `p` and `A` are *positional*; the aggregates assigned into `q` and `B` name their elements explicitly. The aggregate for `B` uses a shorthand notation to assign the same value (`3`) into array elements `3`, `5`, and `7`, and to assign a `0` into all unnamed fields. Several languages, including C, C++, Fortran 90, and Lisp, provide similar capabilities. ■

ML provides a very general facility for composite expressions, based on the use of *constructors* (discussed in Section 11.4.3). Lambda expressions, which we saw in Section 3.6.4 and will discuss again in Chapter 11, amount to aggregates for values that are functions.

7.1.4 Classification of Types

The terminology for types varies some from one language to another. This subsection presents definitions for the most common terms. Most languages provide built-in types similar to those supported in hardware by most processors: integers, characters, Booleans, and real (floating-point) numbers.

Booleans (sometimes called *logicals*) are typically implemented as single-byte quantities, with `1` representing `true` and `0` representing `false`. In a few languages and implementations, Booleans may be packed into arrays using only one bit per value. As noted in Section 6.1.2 ("Orthogonality"), C was historically unusual in omitting a Boolean type: where most languages would expect a Boolean value, C expected an integer, using zero for `false` and anything else for `true`. C99 introduced a new `_Bool` type, but it is effectively an integer that the compiler is permitted to store in a single bit. As noted in Section C-6.5.4, Icon replaces Booleans with a more general notion of *success* and *failure*.

Characters have traditionally been implemented as one-byte quantities as well, typically (but not always) using the ASCII encoding. More recent languages (e.g., Java and C#) use a two-byte representation designed to accommodate (the commonly used portion of) the *Unicode* character set. Unicode is an international standard designed to capture the characters of a wide variety of languages (see Sidebar 7.3). The first 128 characters of Unicode (`\u0000` through `\u007f`) are identical to ASCII. C and C++ provide both regular and "wide" characters, though for wide characters both the encoding and the actual width are implementation dependent. Fortran 2003 supports four-byte Unicode characters.

Numeric Types

A few languages (e.g., C and Fortran) distinguish between different lengths of integers and real numbers; most do not, and leave the choice of precision to the implementation. Unfortunately, differences in precision across language implementations lead to a lack of portability: programs that run correctly on one system may produce run-time errors or erroneous results on another. Java and C# are unusual in providing several lengths of numeric types, with a specified precision for each.

A few languages, including C, C++, C#, and Modula-2, provide both signed and unsigned integers (Modula-2 calls unsigned integers *cardinals*). A few languages (e.g., Fortran, C, Common Lisp, and Scheme) provide a built-in complex type, usually implemented as a pair of floating-point numbers that represent the real and imaginary Cartesian coordinates; other languages support these as a standard library class. A few languages (e.g., Scheme and Common Lisp) provide a built-in rational type, usually implemented as a pair of integers that represent the numerator and denominator. Most varieties of Lisp also support integers of arbitrary precision, as do most scripting languages; the implementation uses multiple words of memory where appropriate. Ada supports *fixed-point* types, which are represented internally by integers, but have an implied decimal point at a programmer-specified position among the digits. Several languages support *decimal* types that use a base-10 encoding to avoid round-off anomalies in financial and human-centered arithmetic (see Sidebar 7.4).

Integers, Booleans, and characters are all examples of *discrete* types (also called *ordinal* types): the domains to which they correspond are countable (they have a one-to-one correspondence with some subset of the integers), and have a well-defined notion of predecessor and successor for each element other than the first and the last. (In most implementations the number of possible integers is finite, but this is usually not reflected in the type system.) Two varieties of user-defined types, enumerations and subranges, are also discrete. Discrete, rational, real, and

DESIGN & IMPLEMENTATION

7.3 Multilingual character sets

The *ISO 10646* international standard defines a *Universal Character Set (UCS)* intended to include all characters of all known human languages. (It also sets aside a "private use area" for such artificial [constructed] languages as Klingon, Tengwar, and Cirth [Tolkien Elvish]. Allocation of this private space is coordinated by a volunteer organization known as the ConScript Unicode Registry.) All natural languages currently employ codes in the 16-bit *Basic Multilingual Plane (BMP)*: `0x0000` through `0xfffd`.

Unicode is an expanded version of ISO 10646, maintained by an international consortium of software manufacturers. In addition to mapping tables, it covers such topics as rendering algorithms, directionality of text, and sorting and comparison conventions.

While recent languages have moved toward 16- or 32-bit internal character representations, these cannot be used for external storage—text files—without causing severe problems with backward compatibility. To accommodate Unicode without breaking existing tools, Ken Thompson in 1992 proposed a multibyte "expanding" code known as *UTF-8* (UCS/Unicode Transformation Format, 8-bit), and codified as a formal annex (appendix) to ISO 10646. UTF-8 characters occupy a maximum of 6 bytes—3 if they lie in the BMP, and only 1 if they are ordinary ASCII. The trick is to observe that ASCII is a 7-bit code; in any legacy text file the most significant bit of every byte is 0. In UTF-8 a most significant bit of 1 indicates a multibyte character. Two-byte codes begin with the bits `110`. Three-byte codes begin with `1110`. Second and subsequent bytes of multibyte characters always begin with `10`.

On some systems one also finds files encoded in one of ten variants of the older 8-bit ISO 8859 standard, but these are inconsistently rendered across platforms. On the web, non-ASCII characters are typically encoded with *numeric character references*, which bracket a Unicode value, written in decimal or hex, with an ampersand and a semicolon. The copyright symbol (©), for example, is `©`. Many characters also have symbolic *entity names* (e.g., `©`), but not all browsers support these.

complex types together constitute the *scalar* types. Scalar types are also sometimes called *simple* types.

Enumeration Types

Enumerations were introduced by Wirth in the design of Pascal. They facilitate the creation of readable programs, and allow the compiler to catch certain kinds of programming errors. An enumeration type consists of a set of named elements.

EXAMPLE 7.9
Enumerations in Pascal

In Pascal, one could write

```
type weekday = (sun, mon, tue, wed, thu, fri, sat);
```

The values of an enumeration type are ordered, so comparisons are generally valid (`mon < tue`), and there is usually a mechanism to determine the predecessor or successor of an enumeration value (in Pascal, `tomorrow := succ(today)`). The

DESIGN & IMPLEMENTATION

7.4 Decimal types

A few languages, notably Cobol and PL/I, provide a *decimal* type for fixed-point representation of integer quantities. These types were designed primarily to exploit the *binary-coded decimal (BCD)* integer format supported by many traditional CISC machines. BCD devotes one *nibble* (four bits—half a byte) to each decimal digit. Machines that support BCD in hardware can perform arithmetic directly on the BCD representation of a number, without converting it to and from binary form. This capability is particularly useful in business and financial applications, which treat their data as both numbers and character strings.

With the growth in on-line commerce, the past few years have seen renewed interest in decimal arithmetic. The 2008 revision of the IEEE 754 floating-point standard includes decimal floating-point types in 32-, 64-, and 128-bit lengths. These represent both the mantissa (significant bits) and exponent in binary, but interpret the exponent as a power of ten, not a power of two. At a given length, values of decimal type have greater precision but smaller range than binary floating-point values. They are ideal for financial calculations, because they capture decimal fractions precisely. Designers hope the new standard will displace existing incompatible decimal formats, not only in hardware but also in software libraries, thereby providing the same portability and predictability that the original 754 standard provided for binary floating-point.

C# includes a 128-bit `decimal` type that is compatible with the new standard. Specifically, a C# decimal variable includes 96 bits of precision, a sign, and a decimal *scaling factor* that can vary between 10^{-28} and 10^{28}. IBM, for which business and financial applications have always been an important market, has included a hardware implementation of the standard (64- and 128-bit widths) in its pSeries RISC machines, beginning with the POWER6.

ordered nature of enumerations facilitates the writing of enumeration-controlled loops:

```
for today := mon to fri do begin ...
```

It also allows enumerations to be used to index arrays:

```
var daily_attendance : array [weekday] of integer;
```

■

EXAMPLE 7.10
Enumerations as constants

An alternative to enumerations, of course, is simply to declare a collection of constants:

```
const sun = 0; mon = 1; tue = 2; wed = 3; thu = 4; fri = 5; sat = 6;
```

In C, the difference between the two approaches is purely syntactic:

```
enum weekday {sun, mon, tue, wed, thu, fri, sat};
```

is essentially equivalent to

```
typedef int weekday;
const weekday sun = 0, mon = 1, tue = 2,
              wed = 3, thu = 4, fri = 5, sat = 6;
```

■

In Pascal and most of its descendants, however, the difference between an enumeration and a set of integer constants is much more significant: the enumeration is a full-fledged type, incompatible with integers. Using an integer or an enumeration value in a context expecting the other will result in a type clash error at compile time.

EXAMPLE 7.11
Converting to and from enumeration type

Values of an enumeration type are typically represented by small integers, usually a consecutive range of small integers starting at zero. In many languages these *ordinal values* are semantically significant, because built-in functions can be used to convert an enumeration value to its ordinal value, and sometimes vice versa. In Ada, these conversions employ the *attributes* `pos` and `val`: `weekday'pos(mon) = 1` and `weekday'val(1) = mon`. ■

EXAMPLE 7.12
Distinguished values for enums

Several languages allow the programmer to specify the ordinal values of enumeration types, if the default assignment is undesirable. In C, C++, and C#, one could write

```
enum arm_special_regs {fp = 7, sp = 13, lr = 14, pc = 15};
```

(The intuition behind these values is explained in Sections C-5.4.5 and C-9.2.2.)

In Ada this declaration would be written

```
type arm_special_regs is (fp, sp, lr, pc);          -- must be sorted
for arm_special_regs use (fp => 7, sp => 13, lr => 14, pc => 15);
```

■

EXAMPLE 7.13
Emulating distinguished enum values in Java

In recent versions of Java one can obtain a similar effect by giving values an extra field (here named `register`):

```
enum arm_special_regs { fp(7), sp(13), lr(14), pc(15);
    private final int register;
    arm_special_regs(int r) { register = r; }
    public int reg() { return register; }
}
...
int n = arm_special_regs.fp.reg();
```

As noted in Section 3.5.2, Pascal and C do not allow the same element name to be used in more than one enumeration type in the same scope. Java and C# do, but the programmer must identify elements using fully qualified names: `arm_special_regs.fp`. Ada relaxes this requirement by saying that element names are overloaded; the type prefix can be omitted whenever the compiler can infer it from context (Example 3.22). C++ historically mirrored C in prohibiting duplicate `enum` names. C++11 introduced a new variety of `enum` that mirrors Java and C# (Example 3.23).

Subrange Types

Like enumerations, subranges were first introduced in Pascal, and are found in many subsequent languages. A subrange is a type whose values compose a contiguous subset of the values of some discrete *base* type (also called the *parent* type). In Pascal and most of its descendants, one can declare subranges of integers, characters, enumerations, and even other subranges. In Pascal, subranges looked like this:

EXAMPLE 7.14
Subranges in Pascal

```
type test_score = 0..100;
     workday = mon..fri;
```

DESIGN & IMPLEMENTATION

7.5 Multiple sizes of integers

The space savings possible with (small-valued) subrange types in Pascal and Ada is achieved in several other languages by providing more than one size of built-in integer type. C and C++, for example, support integer arithmetic on signed and unsigned variants of `char`, `short`, `int`, `long`, and `long long` types, with monotonically nondecreasing sizes.[2]

---

2 More specifically, C requires ranges for these types corresponding to lengths of at least 1, 2, 2, 4, and 8 bytes, respectively. In practice, one finds implementations in which plain `int`s are 2, 4, or 8 bytes long, including some in which they are the same size as `short`s but shorter than `long`s, and some in which they are the same size as `long`s, and longer than `short`s.

EXAMPLE 7.15
Subranges in Ada

In Ada one would write

```
type test_score is new integer range 0..100;
subtype workday is weekday range mon..fri;
```

The `range...` portion of the definition in Ada is called a type *constraint*. In this example `test_score` is a *derived* type, incompatible with integers. The `workday` type, on the other hand, is a *constrained subtype*; `workday`s and `weekday`s can be more or less freely intermixed. The distinction between derived types and subtypes is a valuable feature of Ada; we will discuss it further in Section 7.2.1. ■

One could of course use integers to represent test scores, or a `weekday` to represent a `workday`. Using an explicit subrange has several advantages. For one thing, it helps to document the program. A comment could also serve as documentation, but comments have a bad habit of growing out of date as programs change, or of being omitted in the first place. Because the compiler analyzes a subrange declaration, it knows the expected range of subrange values, and can generate code to perform dynamic semantic checks to ensure that no subrange variable is ever assigned an invalid value. These checks can be valuable debugging tools. In addition, since the compiler knows the number of values in the subrange, it can sometimes use fewer bits to represent subrange values than it would need to use to represent arbitrary integers. In the example above, `test_score` values can be stored in a single byte.

EXAMPLE 7.16
Space requirements of subrange type

Most implementations employ the same bit patterns for integers and subranges, so subranges whose values are large require large storage locations, even if the number of distinct values is small. The following type, for example,

```
type water_temperature = 273..373;   (* degrees Kelvin *)
```

would be stored in at least two bytes. While there are only 101 distinct values in the type, the largest (373) is too large to fit in a single byte in its natural encoding. (An unsigned byte can hold values in the range `0..255`; a signed byte can hold values in the range $-128..127$.) ■

Composite Types

Nonscalar types are usually called *composite* types. They are generally created by applying a *type constructor* to one or more simpler types. *Options*, which we introduced in Example 7.6, are arguably the simplest composite types, serving only to add an extra "none of the above" to the values of some arbitrary base type. Other common composite types include records (structures), variant records (unions), arrays, sets, pointers, lists, and files. All but pointers and lists are easily described in terms of mathematical set operations (pointers and lists can be described mathematically as well, but the description is less intuitive).

Records (structs) were introduced by Cobol, and have been supported by most languages since the 1960s. A record consists of collection of *fields*, each of which belongs to a (potentially different) simpler type. Records are akin to mathematical *tuples*; a record type corresponds to the Cartesian product of the types of the fields.

Variant records (unions) differ from "normal" records in that only one of a variant record's fields (or collections of fields) is valid at any given time. A variant record type is the *disjoint union* of its field types, rather than their Cartesian product.

Arrays are the most commonly used composite types. An array can be thought of as a function that maps members of an *index* type to members of a *component* type. Arrays of characters are often referred to as *strings*, and are often supported by special-purpose operations not available for other arrays.

Sets, like enumerations and subranges, were introduced by Pascal. A set type is the mathematical powerset of its base type, which must often be discrete. A variable of a set type contains a collection of distinct elements of the base type.

Pointers are l-values. A pointer value is a *reference* to an object of the pointer's base type. Pointers are often but not always implemented as addresses. They are most often used to implement *recursive* data types. A type T is recursive if an object of type T may contain one or more references to other objects of type T.

Lists, like arrays, contain a sequence of elements, but there is no notion of mapping or indexing. Rather, a list is defined recursively as either an empty list or a pair consisting of a head element and a reference to a sublist. While the length of an array must be specified at elaboration time in most (though not all) languages, lists are always of variable length. To find a given element of a list, a program must examine all previous elements, recursively or iteratively, starting at the head. Because of their recursive definition, lists are fundamental to programming in most functional languages.

Files are intended to represent data on mass-storage devices, outside the memory in which other program objects reside. Like arrays, most files can be conceptualized as a function that maps members of an index type (generally integer) to members of a component type. Unlike arrays, files usually have a notion of *current position*, which allows the index to be implied implicitly in consecutive operations. Files often display idiosyncrasies inherited from physical input/output devices. In particular, the elements of some files must be accessed in sequential order.

We will examine composite types in more detail in Chapter 8.

✓ **CHECK YOUR UNDERSTANDING**

1. What purpose(s) do types serve in a programming language?
2. What does it mean for a language to be *strongly typed*? *Statically typed*? What prevents, say, C from being strongly typed?

3. Name two programming languages that are strongly but dynamically typed.
4. What is a *type clash*?
5. Discuss the differences among the *denotational*, *structural*, and *abstraction-based* views of types.
6. What does it mean for a set of language features (e.g., a type system) to be *orthogonal*?
7. What are *aggregates*?
8. What are *option* types? What purpose do they serve?
9. What is *polymorphism*? What distinguishes its *parametric* and *subtype* varieties? What are *generics*?
10. What is the difference between *discrete* and *scalar* types?
11. Give two examples of languages that lack a Boolean type. What do they use instead?
12. In what ways may an enumeration type be preferable to a collection of named constants? In what ways may a subrange type be preferable to its base type? In what ways may a string be preferable to an array of characters?

7.2 Type Checking

In most statically typed languages, every definition of an object (constant, variable, subroutine, etc.) must specify the object's type. Moreover, many of the contexts in which an object might appear are also typed, in the sense that the rules of the language constrain the types that an object in that context may validly possess. In the subsections below we will consider the topics of *type equivalence*, *type compatibility*, and *type inference*. Of the three, type compatibility is the one of most concern to programmers. It determines when an object of a certain type can be used in a certain context. At a minimum, the object can be used if its type and the type expected by the context are equivalent (i.e., the same). In many languages, however, compatibility is a looser relationship than equivalence: objects and contexts are often compatible even when their types are different. Our discussion of type compatibility will touch on the subjects of type *conversion* (also called *casting*), which changes a value of one type into a value of another; type *coercion*, which performs a conversion automatically in certain contexts; and *nonconverting* type casts, which are sometimes used in systems programming to interpret the bits of a value of one type as if they represented a value of some other type.

Whenever an expression is constructed from simpler subexpressions, the question arises: given the types of the subexpressions (and possibly the type expected by the surrounding context), what is the type of the expression as a whole? This question is answered by type inference. Type inference is often trivial: the sum of two integers is still an integer, for example. In other cases (e.g., when dealing with sets) it is a good bit trickier. Type inference plays a particularly important role in ML, Miranda, and Haskell, in which almost all type annotations are optional, and will be inferred by the compiler when omitted.

7.2.1 Type Equivalence

In a language in which the user can define new types, there are two principal ways of defining type equivalence. *Structural equivalence* is based on the *content* of type definitions: roughly speaking, two types are the same if they consist of the same components, put together in the same way. *Name equivalence* is based on the *lexical occurrence* of type definitions: roughly speaking, each definition introduces a new type. Structural equivalence is used in Algol-68, Modula-3, and (with various wrinkles) C and ML. Name equivalence appears in Java, C#, standard Pascal, and most Pascal descendants, including Ada.

The exact definition of structural equivalence varies from one language to another. It requires that one decide which potential differences between types are important, and which may be considered unimportant. Most people would probably agree that the format of a declaration should not matter—identical declarations that differ only in spacing or line breaks should still be considered equivalent. Likewise, in a Pascal-like language with structural equivalence,

EXAMPLE 7.17
Trivial differences in type

```
type R1 = record
    a, b : integer
end;
```

should probably be considered the same as

```
type R2 = record
    a : integer;
    b : integer
end;
```

But what about

```
type R3 = record
    b : integer;
    a : integer
end;
```

Should the reversal of the order of the fields change the type? ML says no; most languages say yes. ■

EXAMPLE 7.18
Other minor differences in type

In a similar vein, consider the following arrays, again in a Pascal-like notation:

```
type str = array [1..10] of char;

type str = array [0..9] of char;
```

Here the length of the array is the same in both cases, but the index values are different. Should these be considered equivalent? Most languages say no, but some (including Fortran and Ada) consider them compatible. ■

To determine if two types are structurally equivalent, a compiler can expand their definitions by replacing any embedded type names with their respective definitions, recursively, until nothing is left but a long string of type constructors, field names, and built-in types. If these expanded strings are the same, then the types are equivalent, and conversely. Recursive and pointer-based types complicate matters, since their expansion does not terminate, but the problem is not insurmountable; we consider a solution in Exercise 8.15.

EXAMPLE 7.19
The problem with structural equivalence

Structural equivalence is a straightforward but somewhat low-level, implementation-oriented way to think about types. Its principal problem is an inability to distinguish between types that the programmer may think of as distinct, but which happen by coincidence to have the same internal structure:

```
1.  type student = record
2.      name, address : string
3.      age : integer

4.  type school = record
5.      name, address : string
6.      age : integer

7.  x : student;
8.  y : school;
9.  ...
10. x := y;                -- is this an error?
```

Most programmers would probably want to be informed if they accidentally assigned a value of type school into a variable of type student, but a compiler whose type checking is based on structural equivalence will blithely accept such an assignment.

Name equivalence is based on the assumption that if the programmer goes to the effort of writing two type definitions, then those definitions are probably meant to represent different types. In the example above, variables x and y will be considered to have different types under name equivalence: x uses the type declared at line 1; y uses the type declared at line 4. ■

Variants of Name Equivalence

EXAMPLE 7.20
Alias types

One subtlety in the use of name equivalence arises in the simplest of type declarations:

```
type new_type = old_type;          (* Algol family syntax *)

typedef old_type new_type;         /* C family syntax */
```

Here new_type is said to be an *alias* for old_type. Should we treat them as two names for the same type, or as names for two different types that happen to have the same internal structure? The "right" approach may vary from one program to another.

EXAMPLE 7.21
Semantically equivalent alias types

Users of any Unix-like system will be familiar with the notion of *permission* bits on files. These specify whether the file is readable, writable, and/or executable by its owner, group members, or others. Within the system libraries, the set of permissions for a file is represented as a value of type mode_t. In C, this type is commonly defined as an alias for the predefined 16-bit unsigned integer type:

```
typedef uint16_t mode_t;
```

While C uses structural equivalence for scalar types,[3] we can imagine the issue that would arise if it used name equivalence uniformly. By convention, permission sets are manipulated using bitwise integer operators:

```
mode_t my_permissions = S_IRUSR | S_IWUSR | S_IRGRP;
/* I can read and write; members of my group can read. */
...
if (my_permissions & S_IWUSR) ...
```

This convention depends on the equivalence of mode_t and uint16_t. One could ask programmers to convert mode_t objects explicitly to uint_16 before applying an integer operator—or even suggest that mode_t be an abstract type, with insert, remove, and lookup operations that hide the internal representation—but C programmers would probably regard either of these options as unnecessarily cumbersome: in "systems" code, it seems reasonable to treat mode_t and uint16_t the same.

EXAMPLE 7.22
Semantically distinct alias types

Unfortunately, there are other times when aliased types should probably not be the same:

```
type celsius_temp = real;
     fahrenheit_temp = real;
var  c : celsius_temp;
     f : fahrenheit_temp;
...
f := c;              (* this should probably be an error *)
```

A language in which aliased types are considered distinct is said to have *strict name equivalence*. A language in which aliased types are considered equivalent is said to have *loose name equivalence*. Most Pascal-family languages use loose name equivalence. Ada achieves the best of both worlds by allowing the programmer to indicate whether an alias represents a *derived* type or a *subtype*. A subtype is

EXAMPLE 7.23
Derived types and subtypes in Ada

3 Ironically, it uses name equivalence for structs.

compatible with its base (parent) type; a derived type is incompatible. (Subtypes of the same base type are also compatible with each other.) Our examples above would be written

```
subtype mode_t is integer range 0..2**16-1;    -- unsigned 16-bit integer
...
type celsius_temp is new integer;
type fahrenheit_temp is new integer;
```

One way to think about the difference between strict and loose name equivalence is to remember the distinction between declarations and definitions (Section 3.3.3). Under strict name equivalence, a declaration `type A = B` is considered a definition. Under loose name equivalence it is merely a declaration; `A` shares the definition of `B`.

EXAMPLE 7.24 Name vs structural equivalence

Consider the following example:

```
1. type cell    = ...          -- whatever
2. type alink   = pointer to cell
3. type blink   = alink
4. p, q : pointer to cell
5. r    : alink
6. s    : blink
7. t    : pointer to cell
8. u    : alink
```

Here the declaration at line 3 is an alias; it defines blink to be "the same as" alink. Under strict name equivalence, line 3 is both a declaration and a definition, and blink is a new type, distinct from alink. Under loose name equivalence, line 3 is just a declaration; it uses the definition at line 2.

Under strict name equivalence, p and q have the same type, because they both use the *anonymous* (unnamed) type definition on the right-hand side of line 4, and r and u have the same type, because they both use the definition at line 2. Under loose name equivalence, r, s, and u all have the same type, as do p and q. Under structural equivalence, all six of the variables shown have the same type, namely pointer to whatever cell is.

Both structural and name equivalence can be tricky to implement in the presence of separate compilation. We will return to this issue in Section 15.6.

Type Conversion and Casts

In a language with static typing, there are many contexts in which values of a specific type are expected. In the statement

EXAMPLE 7.25 Contexts that expect a given type

a := *expression*

we expect the right-hand side to have the same type as a. In the expression

a + b

the overloaded + symbol designates either integer or floating-point addition; we therefore expect either that a and b will both be integers, or that they will both be reals. In a call to a subroutine,

```
foo(arg1, arg2, . . . , argN)
```

we expect the types of the arguments to match those of the formal parameters, as declared in the subroutine's header.

Suppose for the moment that we require in each of these cases that the types (expected and provided) be exactly the same. Then if the programmer wishes to use a value of one type in a context that expects another, he or she will need to specify an explicit *type conversion* (also sometimes called a type *cast*). Depending on the types involved, the conversion may or may not require code to be executed at run time. There are three principal cases:

1. The types would be considered structurally equivalent, but the language uses name equivalence. In this case the types employ the same low-level representation, and have the same set of values. The conversion is therefore a purely conceptual operation; no code will need to be executed at run time.
2. The types have different sets of values, but the intersecting values are represented in the same way. One type may be a subrange of the other, for example, or one may consist of two's complement signed integers, while the other is unsigned. If the provided type has some values that the expected type does not, then code must be executed at run time to ensure that the current value is among those that are valid in the expected type. If the check fails, then a dynamic semantic error results. If the check succeeds, then the underlying representation of the value can be used, unchanged. Some language implementations may allow the check to be disabled, resulting in faster but potentially unsafe code.
3. The types have different low-level representations, but we can nonetheless define some sort of correspondence among their values. A 32-bit integer, for example, can be converted to a double-precision IEEE floating-point number with no loss of precision. Most processors provide a machine instruction to effect this conversion. A floating-point number can be converted to an integer by rounding or truncating, but fractional digits will be lost, and the conversion will overflow for many exponent values. Again, most processors provide a machine instruction to effect this conversion. Conversions between different lengths of integers can be effected by discarding or sign-extending high-order bytes.

EXAMPLE 7.26
Type conversions in Ada

We can illustrate these options with the following examples of type conversions in Ada:

```
n : integer;          -- assume 32 bits
r : long_float;       -- assume IEEE double-precision
t : test_score;       -- as in Example 7.15
c : celsius_temp;     -- as in Example 7.23
```

```
t := test_score(n);    -- run-time semantic check required
n := integer(t);       -- no check req.; every test_score is an int
r := long_float(n);    -- requires run-time conversion
n := integer(r);       -- requires run-time conversion and check
n := integer(c);       -- no run-time code required
c := celsius_temp(n);  -- no run-time code required
```

In each of the six assignments, the name of a type is used as a pseudofunction that performs a type conversion. The first conversion requires a run-time check to ensure that the value of `n` is within the bounds of a `test_score`. The second conversion requires no code, since every possible value of `t` is acceptable for `n`. The third and fourth conversions require code to change the low-level representation of values. The fourth conversion also requires a semantic check. It is generally understood that converting from a floating-point value to an integer results in the loss of fractional digits; this loss is not an error. If the conversion results in integer overflow, however, an error needs to result. The final two conversions require no run-time code; the `integer` and `celsius_temp` types (at least as we have defined them) have the same sets of values and the same underlying representation. A purist might say that `celsius_temp` should be defined as `new integer range -273..integer'last`, in which case a run-time semantic check would be required on the final conversion. ■

EXAMPLE 7.27
Type conversions in C

A type conversion in C (what C calls a type cast) is specified by using the name of the desired type, in parentheses, as a prefix operator:

```
r = (float) n;   /* generates code for run-time conversion */
n = (int) r;     /* also run-time conversion, with no overflow check */
```

C and its descendants do not by default perform run-time checks for arithmetic overflow on any operation, though such checks can be enabled if desired in C#. ■

Nonconverting Type Casts Occasionally, particularly in systems programs, one needs to change the type of a value *without* changing the underlying implementation; in other words, to interpret the bits of a value of one type as if they were another type. One common example occurs in memory allocation algorithms, which use a large array of bytes to represent a heap, and then reinterpret portions of that array as pointers and integers (for bookkeeping purposes), or as various user-allocated data structures. Another common example occurs in high-performance numeric software, which may need to reinterpret a floating-point number as an integer or a record, in order to extract the exponent, significand, and sign fields. These fields can be used to implement special-purpose algorithms for square root, trigonometric functions, and so on.

A change of type that does not alter the underlying bits is called a *nonconverting type cast*, or sometimes a *type pun*. It should not be confused with

EXAMPLE 7.28
Unchecked conversions in Ada

use of the term *cast* for conversions in languages like C. In Ada, nonconverting casts can be effected using instances of a built-in generic subroutine called `unchecked_conversion`:

```
-- assume 'float' has been declared to match IEEE single-precision
function cast_float_to_int is
    new unchecked_conversion(float, integer);
function cast_int_to_float is
    new unchecked_conversion(integer, float);
...
f := cast_int_to_float(n);
n := cast_float_to_int(f);
```

EXAMPLE 7.29
Conversions and nonconverting casts in C++

C++ inherits the casting mechanism of C, but also provides a family of semantically cleaner alternatives. Specifically, `static_cast` performs a type conversion, `reinterpret_cast` performs a nonconverting type cast, and `dynamic_cast` allows programs that manipulate pointers of polymorphic types to perform assignments whose validity cannot be guaranteed statically, but can be checked at run time (more on this in Chapter 10). Syntax for each of these is that of a generic function:

DESIGN & IMPLEMENTATION

7.6 Nonconverting casts

C programmers sometimes attempt a nonconverting type cast (type pun) by taking the address of an object, converting the type of the resulting pointer, and then dereferencing:

```
r = *((float *) &n);
```

This arcane bit of hackery usually incurs no run-time cost, because most (but not all!) implementations use the same representation for pointers to integers and pointers to floating-point values—namely, an address. The ampersand operator (`&`) means "address of," or "pointer to." The parenthesized `(float *)` is the type name for "pointer to float" (float is a built-in floating-point type). The prefix `*` operator is a pointer dereference. The overall construct causes the compiler to interpret the bits of `n` as if it were a `float`. The reinterpretation will succeed only if `n` is an l-value (has an address), and `int`s and `float`s have the same size (again, this second condition is often but not always true in C). If `n` does not have an address then the compiler will announce a static semantic error. If `int` and `float` do not occupy the same number of bytes, then the effect of the cast may depend on a variety of factors, including the relative size of the objects, the alignment and "endian-ness" of memory (Section C-5.2), and the choices the compiler has made regarding what to place in adjacent locations in memory. Safer and more portable nonconverting casts can be achieved in C by means of `unions` (variant records); we consider this option in Exercise C-8.24.

```
double d = ...
int n = static_cast<int>(d);
```

There is also a `const_cast` that can be used to remove read-only qualification. C-style type casts in C++ are defined in terms of `const_cast`, `static_cast`, and `reinterpret_cast`; the precise behavior depends on the source and target types.

Any nonconverting type cast constitutes a dangerous subversion of the language's type system. In a language with a weak type system such subversions can be difficult to find. In a language with a strong type system, the use of explicit nonconverting type casts at least labels the dangerous points in the code, facilitating debugging if problems arise.

7.2.2 Type Compatibility

Most languages do not require equivalence of types in every context. Instead, they merely say that a value's type must be *compatible* with that of the context in which it appears. In an assignment statement, the type of the right-hand side must be compatible with that of the left-hand side. The types of the operands of + must both be compatible with some common type that supports addition (integers, real numbers, or perhaps strings or sets). In a subroutine call, the types of any arguments passed into the subroutine must be compatible with the types of the corresponding formal parameters, and the types of any formal parameters passed back to the caller must be compatible with the types of the corresponding arguments.

The definition of type compatibility varies greatly from language to language. Ada takes a relatively restrictive approach: an Ada type S is compatible with an expected type T if and only if (1) S and T are equivalent, (2) one is a subtype of the other (or both are subtypes of the same base type), or (3) both are arrays, with the same numbers and types of elements in each dimension. Pascal was only slightly more lenient: in addition to allowing the intermixing of base and subrange types, it allowed an integer to be used in a context where a real was expected.

Coercion

Whenever a language allows a value of one type to be used in a context that expects another, the language implementation must perform an automatic, implicit conversion to the expected type. This conversion is called a *type coercion*. Like the explicit conversions of Section 7.2.1, coercion may require run-time code to perform a dynamic semantic check or to convert between low-level representations.

EXAMPLE 7.30
Coercion in C

C, which has a relatively weak type system, performs quite a bit of coercion. It allows values of most numeric types to be intermixed in expressions, and will coerce types back and forth "as necessary." Consider the following declarations:

```
short int s;
unsigned long int l;
char c;       /* may be signed or unsigned -- implementation-dependent */
float f;      /* usually IEEE single-precision */
double d;     /* usually IEEE double-precision */
```

Suppose that these variables are 16, 32, 8, 32, and 64 bits in length, respectively—as is common on 32-bit machines. Coercion may have a variety of effects when a variable of one type is assigned into another:

```
s = l;  /* l's low-order bits are interpreted as a signed number. */
l = s;  /* s is sign-extended to the longer length, then
            its bits are interpreted as an unsigned number. */
s = c;  /* c is either sign-extended or zero-extended to s's length;
            the result is then interpreted as a signed number. */
f = l;  /* l is converted to floating-point.  Since f has fewer
            significant bits, some precision may be lost. */
d = f;  /* f is converted to the longer format; no precision is lost. */
f = d;  /* d is converted to the shorter format; precision may be lost.
            If d's value cannot be represented in single-precision, the
            result is undefined, but NOT a dynamic semantic error. */
```

Coercion is a somewhat controversial subject in language design. Because it allows types to be mixed without an explicit indication of intent on the part of the programmer, it represents a significant weakening of type security. At the same time, some designers have argued that coercions are a natural way in which to support abstraction and program extensibility, by making it easier to use new types in conjunction with existing ones. This extensibility argument is particularly compelling in scripting languages (Chapter 14), which are dynamically typed and emphasize ease of programming. Most scripting languages support a wide variety of coercions, though there is some variation: Perl will coerce almost anything; Ruby is much more conservative.

Among statically typed languages, there is even more variety. Ada coerces nothing but explicit constants, subranges, and in certain cases arrays with the same type of elements. Pascal would coerce integers to floating-point in expressions and assignments. Fortran will also coerce floating-point values to integers in assignments, at a potential loss of precision. C will perform these same coercions on arguments to functions.

Some compiled languages even support coercion on arrays and records. Fortran 90 permits this whenever the expected and actual types have the same *shape*. Two arrays have the same shape if they have the same number of dimensions, each dimension has the same size (i.e., the same number of elements), and the individual elements have the same shape. Two records have the same shape if they have the same number of fields, and corresponding fields, in order, have the same shape. Field *names* do not matter, nor do the actual high and low bounds of array dimensions. Ada's coercion rules for arrays are roughly equivalent to those of Fortran 90. C provides no operations that take an entire array as an operand.

C does, however, allow arrays and *pointers* to be intermixed in many cases; we will discuss this unusual form of type compatibility further in Section 8.5.1. Neither Ada nor C allows records (structures) to be intermixed unless their types are name equivalent.

C++ provides what may be the most extreme example of coercion in a statically typed language. In addition to a rich set of built-in rules, C++ allows the programmer to define coercion operations to and from existing types when defining a new type (a *class*). The rules for applying these operations interact in complicated ways with the rules for resolving overloading (Section 3.5.2); they add significant flexibility to the language, but are one of the most difficult C++ features to understand and use correctly.

Overloading and Coercion

We have noted (in Section 3.5) that overloading and coercion (as well as various forms of polymorphism) can sometimes be used to similar effect. It is worth elaborating on the distinctions here. An overloaded name can refer to more than one object; the ambiguity must be resolved by context. Consider the addition of numeric quantities. In the expression `a + b`, `+` may refer to either the integer or the floating-point addition operation. In a language without coercion, `a` and `b` must either both be integer or both be real; the compiler chooses the appropriate interpretation of `+` depending on their type. In a language with coercion, `+` refers to the floating-point addition operation if either `a` or `b` is real; otherwise it refers to the integer addition operation. If only one of `a` and `b` is real, the other is coerced to match. One could imagine a language in which `+` was not overloaded, but rather referred to floating-point addition in all cases. Coercion could still allow `+` to take integer arguments, but they would always be converted to real. The problem with this approach is that conversions from integer to floating-point format take a non-negligible amount of time, especially on machines without hardware conversion instructions, and floating-point addition is significantly more expensive than integer addition. ■

EXAMPLE 7.31
Coercion vs overloading of addends

In most languages, literal constants (e.g., numbers, character strings, the empty set `[ ]` or the null pointer `[nil]`) can be intermixed in expressions with values of many types. One might say that constants are overloaded: `nil` for example might be thought of as referring to the null pointer value for whatever type is needed in the surrounding context. More commonly, however, constants are simply treated as a special case in the language's type-checking rules. Internally, the compiler considers a constant to have one of a small number of built-in "constant types" (int const, real const, string, null), which it then coerces to some more appropriate type as necessary, even if coercions are not supported elsewhere in the language. Ada formalizes this notion of "constant type" for numeric quantities: an integer constant (one without a decimal point) is said to have type `universal_integer`; a real-number constant (one with an embedded decimal point and/or an exponent) is said to have type `universal_real`. The `universal_integer` type is compatible with any integer type; `universal_real` is compatible with any fixed-point or floating-point type.

Universal Reference Types

For systems programming, or to facilitate the writing of general-purpose *container* (*collection*) objects (lists, stacks, queues, sets, etc.) that hold references to other objects, several languages provide a *universal* reference type. In C and C++, this type is called `void*`. In Clu it is called `any`; in Modula-2, `address`; in Modula-3, `refany`; in Java, `Object`; in C#, `object`. Arbitrary l-values can be assigned into an object of universal reference type, with no concern about type safety: because the type of the object referred to by a universal reference is unknown, the compiler will not allow any operations to be performed on that object. Assignments back into objects of a particular reference type (e.g., a pointer to a programmer-specified record type) are a bit trickier, if type safety is to be maintained. We would not want a universal reference to a floating-point number, for example, to be assigned into a variable that is supposed to hold a reference to an integer, because subsequent operations on the "integer" would interpret the bits of the object incorrectly. In object-oriented languages, the question of how to ensure the validity of a universal-to-specific assignment generalizes to the question of how to ensure the validity of any assignment in which the type of the object on left-hand side supports operations that the object on the right-hand side may not.

One way to ensure the safety of universal to specific assignments (or, in general, less specific to more specific assignments) is to make objects self-descriptive—that is, to include in the representation of each object a *tag* that indicates its type. This approach is common in object-oriented languages, which generally need it for dynamic method binding. Type tags in objects can consume a nontrivial amount of space, but allow the implementation to prevent the assignment of an object of one type into a variable of another. In Java and C#, a universal to specific assignment requires a type cast, and will generate an exception if the universal reference does not refer to an object of the casted type. In Eiffel, the equivalent operation uses a special assignment operator (?= instead of `:=`); in C++ it uses a `dynamic_cast` operation.

EXAMPLE 7.32
Java container of `Object`

In early versions of Java and C#, programmers would often create container classes that held objects of the universal reference class (`Object` or `object`, respectively). This idiom has become less common with the introduction of generics (to be discussed in Section 7.3.1), but it is still occasionally used for containers that hold objects of more than one class. When an object is removed from such a container, it must be assigned (with a type cast) into a variable of an appropriate class before anything interesting can be done with it:

```
import java.util.*;      // library containing Stack container class
...
Stack myStack = new Stack();
String s = "Hi, Mom";
Foo f = new Foo();       // f is of user-defined class type Foo
...
```

```
myStack.push(s);
myStack.push(f);           // we can push any kind of object on a stack
...
s = (String) myStack.pop();
    // type cast is required, and will generate an exception at run
    // time if element at top-of-stack is not a string
```

In a language without type tags, the assignment of a universal reference into an object of a specific reference type cannot be checked, because objects are not self-descriptive: there is no way to identify their type at run time. The programmer must therefore resort to an (unchecked) type conversion.

7.2.3 Type Inference

We have seen how type checking ensures that the components of an expression (e.g., the arguments of a binary operator) have appropriate types. But what determines the type of the overall expression? In many cases, the answer is easy. The result of an arithmetic operator usually has the same type as the operands (possibly after coercing one of them, if their types were not the same). The result of a comparison is usually Boolean. The result of a function call has the type declared in the function's header. The result of an assignment (in languages in which assignments are expressions) has the same type as the left-hand side. In a few cases, however, the answer is not obvious. Operations on subranges and composite objects, for example, do not necessarily preserve the types of the operands. We examine these cases in the remainder of this subsection. In the following section, we consider a more elaborate form of type inference found in ML, Miranda, and Haskell.

Subranges and Sets

EXAMPLE 7.33
Inference of subrange types

For arithmetic operators, a simple example of inference arises when one or more operands have subrange types. Given the following Pascal definitions, for example,

```
type Atype = 0..20;
     Btype = 10..20;
var  a : Atype;
     b : Btype;
```

what is the type of `a + b`? Certainly it is neither `Atype` nor `Btype`, since the possible values range from 10 to 40. One could imagine it being a new anonymous subrange type with 10 and 40 as bounds. The usual answer is to say that the result of any arithmetic operation on a subrange has the subrange's base type—in this case, integer.

If the result of an arithmetic operation is assigned into a variable of a subrange type, then a dynamic semantic check may be required. To avoid the expense of some unnecessary checks, a compiler may keep track at compile time of the largest and smallest possible values of each expression, in essence computing the anonymous `10...40` type. More sophisticated techniques can be used to eliminate many checks in loops; we will consider these in Section C-17.5.2. ■

EXAMPLE 7.34
Type inference for sets

Operations with type implications also occur when manipulating sets. Pascal and Modula, for example, supported union (+), intersection (∗), and difference (-) on sets of discrete values. Set operands were said to have compatible types if their elements had the same base type `T`. The result of a set operation was then of type `set of T`. As with subranges, a compiler could avoid the need for run-time bounds checks in certain cases by keeping track of the minimum and maximum possible members of the set expression. ■

Declarations

Ada was among the first languages to make the index of a `for` loop a new, local variable, accessible only in the loop. Rather than require the programmer to specify the type of this variable, the language implicitly assigned it the base type of the expressions provided as bounds for the loop.

Extensions of this idea appear in several more recent languages, including Scala, C# 3.0, C++11, Go, and Swift, all of which allow the programmer to omit type information from a variable declaration when the intent of the declaration can be inferred from context. In C#, for example, one can write

EXAMPLE 7.35
`var` declarations in C#

```
var i = 123;                              // equiv. to int i = 123;
var map = new Dictionary<string, int>();  // equiv. to
    // Dictionary<string, int> map = new Dictionary<string, int>();
```

Here the (easily determined) type of the right-hand side of the assignment can be used to infer the variable's type, freeing us from the need to declare it explicitly. We can achieve a similar effect in C++ with the `auto` keyword; in Scala we simply omit the type name when declaring an initialized variable or constant. ■

EXAMPLE 7.36
Avoiding messy declarations

The convenience of inference increases with complex declarations. Suppose, for example, that we want to perform what mathematicians call a *reduction* on the elements of a list—a "folding together" of values using some binary function. Using C++ lambda syntax (Section 3.6.4), we might write

```
auto reduce = [](list<int> L, int f(int, int), int s) {
        // the initial value of s should be the identity element for f
        for (auto e : L) {
            s = f(e, s);
        }
        return s;
    };
}
...
int sum = reduce(my_list, [](int a, int b){return a+b;}, 0);
int product = reduce(my_list, [](int a, int b){return a*b;}, 1);
```

Here the `auto` keyword allows us to omit what would have been a rather daunting indication of type:

```
int (*reduce) (list<int>, int (*)(int, int), int) = ...
    = [](list<int> L, int f(int, int), int s){...
```

EXAMPLE 7.37
decltype in C++11

C++ in fact goes one step further, with a `decltype` keyword that can be used to match the type of any existing expression. The `decltype` keyword is particularly handy in templates, where it is sometimes impossible to provide an appropriate static type name. Consider, for example, a generic arithmetic package, parameterized by operand types `A` and `B`:

```
template <typename A, typename B>
...
    A a;  B b;
    decltype(a + b) sum;
```

Here the type of `sum` depends on the types of `A` and `B` under the C++ coercion rules. If `A` and `B` are both `int`, for example, then `sum` will be an `int`. If one of `A` and `B` is `double` and the other is `int`, then `sum` will be a `double`. With appropriate (user-provided) coercion rules, `sum` might be inferred to have a complex (real + imaginary) or arbitrary-precision ("bignum") type.

7.2.4 Type Checking in ML

The most sophisticated form of type inference occurs in the ML family of functional languages, including Haskell, F#, and the OCaml and SML dialects of ML itself. Programmers have the option of declaring the types of objects in these languages, in which case the compiler behaves much like that of a more traditional statically typed language. As we noted near the beginning of Section 7.1, however, programmers may also choose not to declare certain types, in which case the compiler will infer them, based on the known types of literal constants, the explicitly declared types of any objects that have them, and the syntactic structure of the program. ML-style type inference is the invention of the language's creator, Robin Milner.[4]

The key to the inference mechanism is to *unify* the (partial) type information available for two expressions whenever the rules of the type system say that their types must be the same. Information known about each is then known about the other as well. Any discovered inconsistencies are identified as static semantic errors. Any expression whose type remains incompletely specified after inference is automatically polymorphic; this is the *implicit parametric polymorphism* referred to in Section 7.1.2. ML family languages also incorporate a powerful run-time pattern-matching facility and several unconventional structured types, including ordered tuples, (unordered) records, lists, a `datatype` mechanism that subsumes unions and recursive types, and a rich module system with inheritance (type extension) and explicit parametric polymorphism (generics). We will consider ML types in more detail in Section 11.4.

EXAMPLE 7.38
Fibonacci function in OCaml

The following is an OCaml version of the tail-recursive Fibonacci function introduced in Example 6.87:

```
1.  let fib n =
2.    let rec fib_helper n1 n2 i =
3.      if i = n then n2
4.      else fib_helper n2 (n1 + n2) (i + 1) in
5.    fib_helper 0 1 0;;
```

The inner `let` construct introduces a nested scope: function `fib_helper` is nested inside `fib`. The body of the outer function, `fib`, is the expression `fib_helper 0 1 0`. The body of `fib_helper` is an `if`... `then`... `else` expression; it evaluates to either `n2` or to `fib_helper n2 (n1 + n2) (i + 1)`, depending on whether the third argument to `fib_helper` is `n` or not. The keyword `rec` indicates that `fib_helper` is recursive, so its name should be made available within its own body—not just in the body of the `let`.

Given this function definition, an OCaml compiler will reason roughly as follows: Parameter `i` of `fib_helper` must have type `int`, because it is added to 1 at line 4. Similarly, parameter `n` of `fib` must have type `int`, because it is compared to `i` at line 3. In the call to `fib_helper` at line 5, the types of all three arguments are `int`, and since this is the only call, the types of `n1` and `n2` are `int`. Moreover the type of `i` is consistent with the earlier inference, namely `int`, and the types of the arguments to the recursive call at line 4 are similarly consistent. Since `fib_helper` returns `n2` at line 3, the result of the call at line 5 will be an `int`. Since `fib` immediately returns this result as its own result, the return type of `fib` is `int`. ■

4 Robin Milner (1934–2010), of Cambridge University's Computer Laboratory, was responsible not only for the development of ML and its type system, but for the Logic of Computable Functions, which provides a formal basis for machine-assisted proof construction, and the Calculus of Communicating Systems, which provides a general theory of concurrency. He received the ACM Turing Award in 1991.

EXAMPLE 7.39
Checking with explicit types

Of course, if any of our functions or parameters had been declared with explicit types, these would have been checked for consistency with all the other evidence. We might, for example, have begun with

```
let fib (n : int) : int = ...
```

to indicate that the function's parameter and return value were both expected to be integers. In a sense, explicit type declarations in OCaml serve as compiler-checked documentation.

EXAMPLE 7.40
Expression types

Because OCaml is a functional language, every construct is an expression. The compiler infers a type for every object and every expression. Because functions are first-class values, they too have types. The type of `fib` above is `int -> int`; that is, a function from integers to integers. The type of `fib_helper` is `int -> int -> int -> int`; that is, a function that takes three integer arguments and produces an integer result. Note that parentheses are generally omitted in both declarations of and calls to multiargument functions. If we had said

```
let rec fib_helper (n1, n2, i) =
  if i = n then n2
  else fib_helper (n2, n1+n2, i+1) in ...
```

then `fib_helper` would have accepted a *single* expression—a three-element *tuple*—as argument.[5]

Type correctness in the ML family amounts to what we might call type *consistency*: a program is type correct if the type checking algorithm can reason out a unique type for every expression, with no contradictions and no ambiguous occurrences of overloaded names. If the programmer uses an object inconsistently, the compiler will complain. In a program containing the following definition,

EXAMPLE 7.41
Type inconsistency

```
let circum r = r *. 2.0 *. 3.14159;;
```

the compiler will infer that `circum`'s parameter is of type `float`, because it is combined with the floating-point constants `2.0` and `3.14159`, using `*.`, the floating-point multiplication operator (here the dot is part of the operator name; there is a separate integer multiplication operator, `*`). If we attempt to apply `circum` to an integer argument, the compiler will produce a type clash error message.

Though the language is usually compiled in production environments, the standard OCaml distribution also includes an interactive interpreter. The programmer can interact with the interpreter "on line," giving it input a line at a

5 Multiple arguments are actually somewhat more complicated than suggested here, due to the fact that functions in OCaml are automatically *curried*; see Section 11.6 for more details.

time. The interpreter processes this input incrementally, generating an intermediate representation for each source code function, and producing any appropriate static error messages. This style of interaction blurs the traditional distinction between interpretation and compilation. While the language implementation remains active during program execution, it performs all possible semantic checks—everything that the production compiler would check—before evaluating a given program fragment.

In comparison to languages in which programmers must declare all types explicitly, the type inference of ML-family languages has the advantage of brevity and convenience for interactive use. More important, it provides a powerful form of implicit parametric polymorphism more or less for free. While all uses of objects in an OCaml program must be consistent, they do not have to be completely specified. Consider the OCaml function shown in Figure 7.1. Here the equality test (=) is a built-in polymorphic function of type `'a -> 'a -> bool`; that is, a function that takes two arguments of the same type and produces a Boolean result. The token `'a` is called a *type variable*; it stands for any type,

EXAMPLE 7.42
Polymorphic functions

DESIGN & IMPLEMENTATION

7.7 Type classes for overloaded functions in Haskell

In the OCaml code of Figure 7.1, parameters `x`, `p`, and `q` must support the equality operator (=). OCaml makes this easy by allowing anything to be compared for equality, and then checking at run time to make sure that the comparison actually makes sense. An attempt to compare two functions, for example, will result in a run-time error. This is unfortunate, given that most other type checking in OCaml (and in other ML-family languages) can happen at compile time. In a similar vein, OCaml provides a built-in definition of ordering (<, >, <=, and >=) on almost all types, even when it doesn't make sense, so that the programmer can create polymorphic functions like `min`, `max`, and `sort`, which require it. A function like `average`, which might plausibly work in a polymorphic fashion for all numeric types (presumably with roundoff for integers) cannot be defined in OCaml: each numeric type has its own addition and division operations; there is no operator overloading.

Haskell overcomes these limitations using the machinery of *type classes*. As mentioned in Example 3.28, these explicitly identify the types that support a particular overloaded function or set of functions. Elements of any type in the `Ord` class, for example, support the <, >, <=, and >= operations. Elements of any type in the `Enum` class are countable; `Num` types support addition, subtraction, and multiplication; `Fractional` and `Real` types additionally support division. In the Haskell equivalent of the code in Figure 7.1, parameters `x`, `p`, and `q` would be inferred to belong to some type in the class `Eq`. Elements of an array passed to `sort` would be inferred to belong to some type in the class `Ord`. Type consistency in Haskell can thus be verified entirely at compile time: there is no need for run-time checks.

```
let compare x p q =
  if x = p then
    if x = q then "both"
    else "first"
  else
    if x = q then "second"
    else "neither";;
```

Figure 7.1 An OCaml program to illustrate checking for type consistency.

and takes, implicitly, the role of an explicit type parameter in a generic construct (Sections 7.3.1 and 10.1.1). Every instance of `'a` in a given call to `=` must represent the same type, but instances of `'a` in different calls can be different. Starting with the type of `=`, an OCaml compiler can reason that the type of `compare` is `'a -> 'a -> 'a -> string`. Thus `compare` is polymorphic; it does not depend on the types of `x`, `p`, and `q`, so long as they are all the same. The key point to observe is that the programmer did not have to do anything special to make `compare` polymorphic: polymorphism is a natural consequence of ML-style type inference. ■

Type Checking

An OCaml compiler verifies type consistency with respect to a well-defined set of constraints. For example,

- All occurrences of the same identifier (subject to scope rules) have the same type.
- In an `if...then...else` expression, the condition is of type `bool`, and the `then` and `else` clauses have the same type.
- A programmer-defined function has type `'a -> 'b -> ... -> 'r`, where `'a`, `'b`, and so forth are the types of the function's parameters, and `'r` is the type of its result (the expression that forms its body).
- When a function is applied (called), the types of the arguments that are passed are the same as the types of the parameters in the function's definition. The type of the application (i.e., the expression constituted by the call) is the same as the type of the result in the function's definition.

EXAMPLE 7.43
A simple instance of unification

In any case where two types *A* and *B* are required to be "the same," the OCaml compiler must *unify* what it knows about *A* and *B* to produce a (potentially more detailed) description of their common type. The inference can work in either direction, or both directions at once. For example, if the compiler has determined that `E1` is an expression of type `'a * int` (that is, a two-element tuple whose second element is known to be an integer), and that `E2` is an expression of type `string * 'b`, then in the expression `if x then E1 else E2`, it can infer that `'a` is `string` and `'b` is `int`. Thus `x` is of type `bool`, and `E1` and `E2` are of type `string * int`. ■

DESIGN & IMPLEMENTATION

7.8 Unification

Unification is a powerful technique. In addition to its role in type inference (which also arises in the templates [generics] of C++), unification plays a central role in the computational model of Prolog and other logic languages. We will consider this latter role in Section 12.1. In the general case the cost of unifying the types of two expressions can be exponential [Mai90], but the pathological cases tend not to arise in practice.

✓ CHECK YOUR UNDERSTANDING

13. What is the difference between *type equivalence* and *type compatibility*?
14. Discuss the comparative advantages of *structural* and *name* equivalence for types. Name three languages that use each approach.
15. Explain the difference between *strict* and *loose* name equivalence.
16. Explain the distinction between *derived* types and *subtypes* in Ada.
17. Explain the differences among *type conversion*, *type coercion*, and *nonconverting type casts*.
18. Summarize the arguments for and against coercion.
19. Under what circumstances does a type conversion require a run-time check?
20. What purpose is served by *universal* reference types?
21. What is *type inference*? Describe three contexts in which it occurs.
22. Under what circumstances does an ML compiler announce a type clash?
23. Explain how the type inference of ML leads naturally to polymorphism.
24. Why do ML programmers often declare the types of variables, even when they don't have to?
25. What is *unification*? What is its role in ML?

7.3 Parametric Polymorphism

As we have seen in the previous section, functions in ML-family languages are naturally polymorphic. Consider the simple task of finding the minimum of two values. In OCaml, the function

EXAMPLE 7.44
Finding the minimum in OCaml or Haskell

```
let min x y = if x < y then x else y;;
```

can be applied to arguments of any type, though sometimes the built-in definition of < may not be what the programmer would like. In Haskell the same function (minus the trailing semicolons) could be applied to arguments of any type in the class `Ord`; the programmer could add new types to this class by providing a definition of <. Sophisticated type inference allows the compiler to perform most checking at compile time in OCaml, and all of it in Haskell (see Sidebar 7.7 for details).

In OCaml, our `min` function would be said to have type `'a -> 'a -> 'a`; in Haskell, it would be `Ord a => a -> a -> a`. While the explicit parameters of `min` are `x` and `y`, we can think of `a` as an extra, implicit parameter—a *type parameter*. For this reason, ML-family languages are said to provide *implicit parametric polymorphism*. ■

Languages without compile-time type inference can provide similar convenience and expressiveness, if we are willing to delay type checking until run time.

EXAMPLE 7.45
Implicit polymorphism in Scheme

In Scheme, our `min` function would be written like this:

```
(define min (lambda (a b) (if (< a b) a b)))
```

As in OCaml or Haskell, it makes no mention of types. The typical Scheme implementation employs an interpreter that examines the arguments to `min` and determines, at run time, whether they are mutually compatible and support a < operator. Given the definition above, the expression `(min 123 456)` evaluates to `123`; `(min 3.14159 2.71828)` evaluates to `2.71828`. The expression `(min "abc" "def")` produces a run-time error when evaluated, because the string comparison operator is named `string<?`, not <. ■

Similar run-time checks for object-oriented languages were pioneered by Smalltalk, and appear in Objective C, Swift, Python, and Ruby, among others. In these languages, an object is assumed to have an acceptable type if it supports whatever method is currently being invoked.

EXAMPLE 7.46
Duck typing in Ruby

In Ruby, for example, `min` is a predefined method supported by collection classes. Assuming that the elements of collection `C` support a comparison (`<=>` operator), `C.min` will return the minimum element:

```
[5, 9, 3, 6].min                 # 3  (array)
(2..10).min                      # 2  (range)
["apple", "pear", "orange"].min  # "apple" (lexicographic order)
["apple", "pear", "orange"].min {
    |a,b| a.length <=> b.length
}                                # "pear"
```

For the final call to `min`, we have provided, as a trailing block, an alternative definition of the comparison operator. ■

This operational style of checking (an object has an acceptable type if it supports the requested method) is sometimes known as *duck typing*. It takes its name from the notion that "if it walks like a duck and quacks like a duck, then it must be a duck."[6]

6 The origins of this "duck test" colloquialism are uncertain, but they go back at least as far as the early 20th century. Among other things, the test was widely cited in the 1940s and 50s as a means of identifying supposed Communist sympathizers.

7.3.1 Generic Subroutines and Classes

The disadvantage of polymorphism in Scheme, Smalltalk, Ruby, and the like is the need for run-time checking, which incurs nontrivial costs, and delays the reporting of errors. The implicit polymorphism of ML-family languages avoids these disadvantages, but requires advanced type inference. For other compiled languages, *explicit* parametric polymorphism (otherwise known as *generics*) allows the programmer to specify type parameters when declaring a subroutine or class. The compiler then uses these parameters in the course of static type checking.

EXAMPLE 7.47 Generic `min` function in Ada

Languages that provide generics include Ada, C++ (which calls them *templates*), Eiffel, Java, C#, and Scala. As a concrete example, consider the overloaded `min` functions on the left side of Figure 7.2. Here the integer and floating-point versions differ only in the types of the parameters and return value. We can exploit this similarity to define a single version that works not only for integers and reals, but for any type whose values are totally ordered. This code appears on the right side of Figure 7.2. The initial (bodyless) declaration of `min` is preceded by a `generic` clause specifying that two things are required in order to create a concrete instance of a minimum function: a type, `T`, and a corresponding comparison routine. This declaration is followed by the actual code for `min`, and instantiations of this code for integer and floating-point types. Given appropriate comparison routines (not shown), we can also instantiate versions for types like `string` and `date`, as shown on the last two lines. (The `"<"` operation mentioned in the definition of `string_min` is presumably overloaded; the compiler resolves the overloading by finding the version of `"<"` that takes arguments of type `T`, where `T` is already known to be `string`.) ■

EXAMPLE 7.48 Generic queues in C++

In an object-oriented language, generics are most often used to parameterize entire classes. Among other things, such classes may serve as *containers*—data abstractions whose instances hold a collection of other objects, but whose operations are generally oblivious to the type of the objects they contain. Examples of containers include stack, queue, heap, set, and dictionary (mapping) abstractions, implemented as lists, arrays, trees, or hash tables. In the absence of generics, it is possible in some languages (C is an obvious example, as were early versions of Java and C#) to define a queue of references to arbitrary objects, but use of such a queue requires type casts that abandon compile-time checking (Exercise 7.8). A simple generic queue in C++ appears in Figure 7.3. ■

EXAMPLE 7.49 Generic parameters

We can think of generic parameters as supporting compile-time customization, allowing the compiler to create an appropriate version of the parameterized subroutine or class. In some languages—Java and C#, for example—generic parameters must always be types. Other languages are more general. In Ada and C++, for example, a generic can be parameterized by values as well. We can see an example in Figure 7.3, where an integer parameter has been used to specify the

```
function min(x, y : integer)
    return integer is
begin
    if x < y then return x;
    else return y;
    end if;
end min;

function min(x, y : long_float)
    return long_float is
begin
    if x < y then return x;
    else return y;
    end if;
end min;
```

```
generic
    type T is private;
    with function "<"(x, y : T) return Boolean;
function min(x, y : T) return T;

function min(x, y : T) return T is
begin
    if x < y then return x;
    else return y;
    end if;
end min;

function int_min is new min(integer, "<");
function real_min is new min(long_float, "<");
function string_min is new min(string, "<");
function date_min is new min(date, date_precedes);
```

Figure 7.2 Overloading (*left*) versus generics (*right*) in Ada.

maximum length of the queue. In C++, this value must be a compile-time constant; in Ada, which supports dynamic-size arrays (Section 8.2.2), its evaluation can be delayed until elaboration time. ■

Implementation Options

Generics can be implemented several ways. In most implementations of Ada and C++ they are a purely static mechanism: all the work required to create and use multiple instances of the generic code takes place at compile time. In the usual case, the compiler creates a *separate copy* of the code for every instance. (C++

DESIGN & IMPLEMENTATION

7.9 Generics in ML

Perhaps surprisingly, given the implicit polymorphism that comes "for free" with type inference, both OCaml and SML provide explicit polymorphism—generics—as well, in the form of parameterized modules called *functors*. Unlike the implicit polymorphism, functors allow the OCaml or SML programmer to indicate that a collection of functions and other values (i.e., the contents of a module) share a common set of generic parameters. This sharing is then enforced by the compiler. Moreover, any types exported by a functor invocation (generic instantiation) are guaranteed to be distinct, even though their signatures (interfaces) are the same. As in Ada and C++, generic parameters in ML can be values as well as types.

NB: While Haskell also provides something called a `Functor` (specifically, a type class that supports a mapping function), its use of the term has little in common with that of OCaml and SML.

```
template<class item, int max_items = 100>
class queue {
    item items[max_items];
    int next_free, next_full, num_items;
public:
    queue() : next_free(0), next_full(0), num_items(0) { }
    bool enqueue(const item& it) {
        if (num_items == max_items) return false;
        ++num_items;  items[next_free] = it;
        next_free = (next_free + 1) % max_items;
        return true;
    }
    bool dequeue(item* it) {
        if (num_items == 0) return false;
        --num_items;  *it = items[next_full];
        next_full = (next_full + 1) % max_items;
        return true;
    }
};
...
queue<process> ready_list;
queue<int, 50> int_queue;
```

Figure 7.3 Generic array-based queue in C++.

goes farther, and arranges to type-check each of these instances independently.) If several queues are instantiated with the same set of arguments, then the compiler may share the code of the `enqueue` and `dequeue` routines among them. A clever compiler may arrange to share the code for a queue of integers with the code for a queue of floating-point numbers, if the two types happen to have the same size, but this sort of optimization is not required, and the programmer should not be surprised if it doesn't occur.

Java, by contrast, guarantees that *all* instances of a given generic will share the same code at run time. In effect, if `T` is a generic type parameter in Java, then objects of class `T` are treated as instances of the standard base class `Object`, except that the programmer does not have to insert explicit casts to use them as objects of class `T`, and the compiler guarantees, statically, that the elided casts will never fail. C# plots an intermediate course. Like C++, it will create specialized implementations of a generic for different primitive or value types. Like Java, however, it requires that the generic code itself be demonstrably type safe, independent of the arguments provided in any particular instantiation. We will examine the tradeoffs among C++, Java, and C# generics in more detail in Section C-7.3.2.

Generic Parameter Constraints

Because a generic is an abstraction, it is important that its interface (the header of its declaration) provide all the information that must be known by a user of the abstraction. Several languages, including Ada, Java, C#, Scala, OCaml, and SML, attempt to enforce this rule by *constraining* generic parameters. Specifically, they require that the operations permitted on a generic parameter type be explicitly declared.

EXAMPLE 7.50
with constraints in Ada

In Ada, the programmer can specify the operations of a generic type parameter by means of a trailing `with` clause. We saw a simple example in the "minimum" function of Figure 7.2 (right side). The declaration of a generic sorting routine in Ada might be similar:

```
generic
    type T is private;
    type T_array is array (integer range <>) of T;
    with function "<"(a1, a2 : T) return boolean;
procedure sort(A : in out T_array);
```

Without the `with` clause, procedure `sort` would be unable to compare elements of `A` for ordering, because type `T` is `private`—it supports only assignment, testing for equality and inequality, and a few other standard attributes (e.g., `size`).

Java and C# employ a particularly clean approach to constraints that exploits the ability of object-oriented types to *inherit* methods from a parent type or interface. We defer a full discussion of inheritance to Chapter 10. For now, we note that it allows the Java or C# programmer to require that a generic parameter support a particular set of methods, much as the type classes of Haskell constrain the types of acceptable parameters to an implicitly polymorphic function. In Java, we might declare and use a sorting routine as follows:

EXAMPLE 7.51
Generic sorting routine in Java

DESIGN & IMPLEMENTATION

7.10 Overloading and polymorphism

Given that a compiler will often create multiple instances of the code for a generic subroutine, specialized to a given set of generic parameters, one might be forgiven for wondering: what exactly is the difference between the left and right sides of Figure 7.2? The answer lies in the generality of the polymorphic code. With overloading the programmer must write a separate `min` routine for every type, and while the compiler will choose among these automatically, the fact that they do something similar with their arguments is purely a matter of convention. Generics, on the other hand, allow the *compiler* to create an appropriate version for every needed type. The similarity of the calling syntax (and of the generated code, when conventions are followed) has led some authors to refer to overloading as *ad hoc* (special case) *polymorphism*. There is no particular reason, however, for the programmer to think of polymorphism in terms of multiple copies: from a semantic (conceptual) point of view, overloaded subroutines use a single name for more than one thing; a polymorphic subroutine *is* a single thing.

```
public static <T extends Comparable<T>> void sort(T A[]) {
    ...
    if (A[i].compareTo(A[j]) >= 0) ...
    ...
}
...
Integer[] myArray = new Integer[50];
...
sort(myArray);
```

Where C++ requires a `template<`*type_args*`>` prefix before a generic method, Java puts the type parameters immediately in front of the method's return type. The `extends` clause constitutes a generic constraint: `Comparable` is an interface (a set of required methods) from the Java standard library; it includes the method `compareTo`. This method returns −1, 0, or 1, respectively, depending on whether the current object is less than, equal to, or greater than the object passed as a parameter. The compiler checks to make sure that the objects in any array passed to `sort` are of a type that implements `Comparable`, and are therefore guaranteed to provide `compareTo`. If `T` had needed additional interfaces (that is, if we had wanted more constraints), they could have been specified with a comma-separated list: `<T extends I1, I2, I3>`. ■

EXAMPLE 7.52
Generic sorting routine in C#

C# syntax is similar:

```
static void sort<T>(T[] A) where T : IComparable {
    ...
    if (A[i].CompareTo(A[j]) >= 0) ...
    ...
}
...
int[] myArray = new int[50];
sort(myArray);
```

C# puts the type parameters after the name of the subroutine, and the constraints (the `where` clause) after the regular parameter list. The compiler is smart enough to recognize that `int` is a primitive type, and generates a customized implementation of `sort`, eliminating the need for Java's `Integer` wrapper class, and producing faster code. ■

EXAMPLE 7.53
Generic sorting routine in C++

A few languages forgo explicit constraints, but still check how parameters are used. In C++, for example, the header of a generic sorting routine can be extremely simple:

```
template<typename T>
void sort(T A[], int A_size) { ...
```

No mention is made of the need for a comparison operator. The body of a generic can (attempt to) perform arbitrary operations on objects of a generic parameter type, but if the generic is instantiated with a type that does not support that operation, the compiler will announce a static semantic error. Unfortunately, because the header of the generic does not necessarily specify which operations will be required, it can be difficult for the programmer to predict whether a particular instantiation will cause an error message. Worse, in some cases the type provided in a particular instantiation may support an operation required by the generic's code, but that operation may not do "the right thing." Suppose in our C++ sorting example that the code for `sort` makes use of the < operator. For `int`s and `double`s, this operator will do what one would expect. For character strings, however, it will compare pointers, to see which referenced character has a lower address in memory. If the programmer is expecting comparison for lexicographic ordering, the results may be surprising!

To avoid surprises, it is best to avoid implicit use of the operations of a generic parameter type. The next version of the C++ standard is likely to incorporate syntax for explicit template constraints [SSD13]. For now, the comparison routine can be provided as a method of class `T`, an extra argument to the `sort` routine, or an extra generic parameter. To facilitate the first of these options, the programmer may choose to emulate Java or C#, encapsulating the required methods in an abstract base class from which the type `T` may inherit.

Implicit Instantiation

EXAMPLE 7.54
Generic class instance in C++

Because a class is a type, one must generally create an instance of a generic class (i.e., an object) before the generic can be used. The declaration provides a natural place to provide generic arguments:

```
queue<int, 50> *my_queue = new queue<int, 50>();        // C++
```

EXAMPLE 7.55
Generic subroutine instance in Ada

Some languages (Ada among them) also require generic subroutines to be instantiated explicitly before they can be used:

```
procedure int_sort is new sort(integer, int_array, "<");
...
int_sort(my_array);
```

EXAMPLE 7.56
Implicit instantiation in C++

Other languages (C++, Java, and C# among them) do not require this. Instead they treat generic subroutines as a form of overloading. Given the C++ sorting routine of Example 7.53 and the following objects:

```
int ints[10];
double reals[50];
string strings[30];  // library class string has lexicographic operator<
```

we can perform the following calls without instantiating anything explicitly:

```
sort(ints, 10);
sort(reals, 50);
sort(strings, 30);
```

	Explicit (generics)				Implicit	
	Ada	C++	Java	C#	Lisp	ML
Applicable to	subroutines, modules	subroutines, classes	subroutines, classes	subroutines, classes	functions	functions
Abstract over	types; subroutines; values of arbitrary types	types; enum, int, and pointer constants	types only	types only	types only	types only
Constraints	explicit (varied)	implicit	explicit (inheritance)	explicit (inheritance)	implicit	implicit
Checked at	compile time (definition)	compile time (instantiation)	compile time (definition)	compile time (definition)	run time	compile time (inferred)
Natural implementation	multiple copies	multiple copies	single copy (erasure)	multiple copies (reification)	single copy	single copy
Subroutine instantiation	explicit	implicit	implicit	implicit	—	—

Figure 7.4 Mechanisms for parametric polymorphism in Ada, C++, Java, C#, Lisp, and ML. Erasure and reification are discussed in Section C-7.3.2.

In each case, the compiler will implicitly instantiate an appropriate version of the `sort` routine. Java and C# have similar conventions. To keep the language manageable, the rules for implicit instantiation in C++ are more restrictive than the rules for resolving overloaded subroutines in general. In particular, the compiler will not coerce a subroutine argument to match a type expression containing a generic parameter (Exercise C-7.26). ■

Figure 7.4 summarizes the features of Ada, C++, Java, and C# generics, and of the implicit parametric polymorphism of Lisp and ML. Further explanation of some of the details appears in Section C-7.3.2.

7.3.2 Generics in C++, Java, and C#

Several of the key tradeoffs in the design of generics can be illustrated by comparing the features of C++, Java, and C#. C++ is by far the most ambitious of the three. Its templates are intended for almost any programming task that requires substantially similar but not identical copies of an abstraction. Java and C# provide generics purely for the sake of polymorphism. Java's design was heavily influenced by the desire for backward compatibility, not only with existing versions of the language, but with existing virtual machines and libraries. The C# designers, though building on an existing language, did not feel as constrained. They had been planning for generics from the outset, and were able to engineer substantial new support into the .NET virtual machine.

IN MORE DEPTH

On the companion site we discuss C++, Java, and C# generics in more detail, and consider the impact of their differing designs on the quality of error messages, the speed and size of generated code, and the expressive power of the notation. We note in particular the very different mechanisms used to make generic classes and methods support as broad a class of generic arguments as possible.

7.4 Equality Testing and Assignment

For simple, primitive data types such as integers, floating-point numbers, or characters, equality testing and assignment are relatively straightforward operations, with obvious semantics and obvious implementations (bit-wise comparison or copy). For more complicated or abstract data types, both semantic and implementation subtleties arise.

Consider for example the problem of comparing two character strings. Should the expression `s = t` determine whether `s` and `t`

- are aliases for one another?
- occupy storage that is bit-wise identical over its full length?
- contain the same sequence of characters?
- would appear the same if printed?

The second of these tests is probably too low level to be of interest in most programs; it suggests the possibility that a comparison might fail because of garbage in currently unused portions of the space reserved for a string. The other three alternatives may all be of interest in certain circumstances, and may generate different results.

In many cases the definition of equality boils down to the distinction between l-values and r-values: in the presence of references, should expressions be considered equal only if they refer to the same object, or also if the objects to which they refer are in some sense equal? The first option (refer to the same object) is known as a *shallow* comparison. The second (refer to equal objects) is called a *deep* comparison. For complicated data structures (e.g., lists or graphs) a deep comparison may require recursive traversal.

In imperative programming languages, assignment operations may also be deep or shallow. Under a reference model of variables, a shallow assignment `a := b` will make `a` refer to the object to which `b` refers. A deep assignment will create a copy of the object to which `b` refers, and make `a` refer to the copy. Under a value model of variables, a shallow assignment will copy the value of `b` into `a`, but if that value is a pointer (or a record containing pointers), then the objects to which the pointer(s) refer will not be copied.

EXAMPLE 7.57 Equality testing in Scheme

Most programming languages employ both shallow comparisons and shallow assignment. A few (notably Python and the various dialects of Lisp and ML) provide more than one option for comparison. Scheme, for example, has three general-purpose equality-testing functions:

```
(eq? a b)       ; do a and b refer to the same object?
(eqv? a b)      ; are a and b known to be semantically equivalent?
(equal? a b)    ; do a and b have the same recursive structure?
```

Both `eq?` and `eqv?` perform a shallow comparison. The former may be faster for certain types in certain implementations; in particular, `eqv?` is required to detect the equality of values of the same discrete type, stored in different locations; `eq?` is not. The simpler `eq?` behaves as one would expect for Booleans, symbols (names), and pairs (things built by `cons`), but can have implementation-defined behavior on numbers, characters, and strings:

```
(eq? #t #t)            ⟹  #t (true)
(eq? 'foo 'foo)        ⟹  #t
(eq? '(a b) '(a b))    ⟹  #f (false); created by separate cons-es
(let ((p '(a b)))
  (eq? p p))           ⟹  #t; created by the same cons
(eq? 2 2)              ⟹  implementation dependent
(eq? "foo" "foo")      ⟹  implementation dependent
```

In any particular implementation, numeric, character, and string tests will always work the same way; if `(eq? 2 2)` returns `true`, then `(eq? 37 37)` will return `true` also. Implementations are free to choose whichever behavior results in the fastest code.

The exact rules that govern the situations in which `eqv?` is guaranteed to return `true` or `false` are quite involved. Among other things, they specify that `eqv?` should behave as one might expect for numbers, characters, and nonempty strings, and that two objects will never test `true` for `eqv?` if there are any circumstances under which they would behave differently. (Conversely, however, `eqv?` is allowed to return `false` for certain objects—functions, for example—that would behave identically in all circumstances.)[7] The `eqv?` predicate is "less discriminating" than `eq?`, in the sense that `eqv?` will never return `false` when `eq?` returns `true`.

For structures (lists), `eqv?` returns `false` if its arguments refer to different root `cons` cells. In many programs this is not the desired behavior. The `equal?` predicate recursively traverses two lists to see if their internal structure is the same and their leaves are `eqv?`. The `equal?` predicate may lead to an infinite loop if the programmer has used the imperative features of Scheme to create a circular list. ■

---

7 Significantly, `eqv?` is also allowed to return false when comparing numeric values of different types: `(eqv? 1 1.0)` may evaluate to `#f`. For numeric code, one generally wants the separate `=` function: `(= val1 val2)` will perform the necessary coercion and test for numeric equality (subject to rounding errors).

Deep assignments are relatively rare. They are used primarily in distributed computing, and in particular for parameter passing in remote procedure call (RPC) systems. These will be discussed in Section C-13.5.4.

For user-defined abstractions, no single language-specified mechanism for equality testing or assignment is likely to produce the desired results in all cases. Languages with sophisticated data abstraction mechanisms usually allow the programmer to define the comparison and assignment operators for each new data type—or to specify that equality testing and/or assignment is not allowed.

✓ CHECK YOUR UNDERSTANDING

26. Explain the distinction between implicit and explicit parametric polymorphism. What are their comparative advantages?
27. What is *duck typing*? What is its connection to polymorphism? In what languages does it appear?
28. Explain the distinction between overloading and generics. Why is the former sometimes called *ad hoc* polymorphism?
29. What is the principal purpose of generics? In what sense do generics serve a broader purpose in C++ and Ada than they do in Java and C#?
30. Under what circumstances can a language implementation share code among separate instances of a generic?
31. What are *container* classes? What do they have to do with generics?
32. What does it mean for a generic parameter to be *constrained*? Explain the difference between explicit and implicit constraints. Describe how interface classes can be used to specify constraints in Java and C#.
33. Why will C# accept `int` as a generic argument, but Java won't?
34. Under what circumstances will C++ instantiate a generic function implicitly?
35. Why is equality testing more subtle than it first appears?

7.5 Summary and Concluding Remarks

This chapter has surveyed the fundamental concept of *types*. In the typical programming language, types serve two principal purposes: they provide implicit context for many operations, freeing the programmer from the need to specify that context explicitly, and they allow the compiler to catch a wide variety of common programming errors. When discussing types, we noted that it is sometimes helpful to distinguish among denotational, structural, and abstraction-based points of view, which regard types, respectively, in terms of their values, their substructure, and the operations they support.

In a typical programming language, the *type system* consists of a set of built-in types, a mechanism to define new types, and rules for *type equivalence*, *type compatibility*, and *type inference*. Type equivalence determines when two values or named objects have the same type. Type compatibility determines when a value of one type may be used in a context that "expects" another type. Type inference determines the type of an expression based on the types of its components or (sometimes) the surrounding context. A language is said to be *strongly typed* if it never allows an operation to be applied to an object that does not support it; a language is said to be *statically typed* if it enforces strong typing at compile time.

We introduced terminology for the common built-in types and for enumerations, subranges, and the common type *constructors* (more on the latter will appear in Chapter 8). We discussed several different approaches to type equivalence, compatibility, and inference. We also examined type *conversion*, *coercion*, and *nonconverting casts*. In the area of type equivalence, we contrasted the *structural* and *name*-based approaches, noting that while name equivalence appears to have gained in popularity, structural equivalence retains its advocates.

Expanding on material introduced in Section 3.5.2, we explored several styles of *polymorphism*, all of which allow a subroutine—or the methods of a class—to operate on values of multiple types, so long as they only use those values in ways their types support. We focused in particular on *parametric* polymorphism, in which the types of the values on which the code will operate are passed to it as extra parameters, implicitly or explicitly. The implicit alternative appears in the static typing of ML and its descendants, and in the dynamic typing of Lisp, Smalltalk, and many other languages. The explicit alternative appears in the *generics* of many modern languages. In Chapter 10 we will consider the related topic of *subtype polymorphism.*

In our discussion of implicit parametric polymorphism, we devoted considerable attention to type checking in ML, where the compiler uses a sophisticated system of inference to determine, at compile time, whether a type error (an attempt to perform an operation on a type that doesn't support it) could ever occur at run time—all without access to type declarations in the source code. In our discussion of generics we explored alternative ways to express *constraints* on generic parameters. We also considered implementation strategies. As examples, we contrasted (on the companion site) the generic facilities of C++, Java, and C#.

More so, perhaps, than in previous chapters, our study of types has highlighted fundamental differences in philosophy among language designers. As we have seen, some languages use variables to name values; others, references. Some languages do all or most of their type checking at compile time; others wait until run time. Among those that check at compile time, some use name equivalence; others, structural equivalence. Some languages avoid type coercions; others embrace them. Some avoid overloading; others again embrace them. In each case, the choice among design alternatives reflects nontrivial tradeoffs among competing language goals, including expressiveness, ease of programming, quality and timing of error discovery, ease of debugging and maintenance, compilation cost, and run-time performance.

7.6 Exercises

7.1 Most statically typed languages developed since the 1970s (including Java, C#, and the descendants of Pascal) use some form of name equivalence for types. Is structural equivalence a bad idea? Why or why not?

7.2 In the following code, which of the variables will a compiler consider to have compatible types under structural equivalence? Under strict name equivalence? Under loose name equivalence?

```
type T = array [1..10] of integer
     S = T
A : T
B : T
C : S
D : array [1..10] of integer
```

7.3 Consider the following declarations:

```
1. type cell              -- a forward declaration
2. type cell_ptr = pointer to cell
3. x : cell
4. type cell = record
5.       val : integer
6.       next : cell_ptr
7. y : cell
```

Should the declaration at line 4 be said to introduce an alias type? Under strict name equivalence, should x and y have the same type? Explain.

7.4 Suppose you are implementing an Ada compiler, and must support arithmetic on 32-bit fixed-point binary numbers with a programmer-specified number of fractional bits. Describe the code you would need to generate to add, subtract, multiply, or divide two fixed-point numbers. You should assume that the hardware provides arithmetic instructions only for integers and IEEE floating-point. You may assume that the integer instructions preserve full precision; in particular, integer multiplication produces a 64-bit result. Your description should be general enough to deal with operands and results that have different numbers of fractional bits.

7.5 When Sun Microsystems ported Berkeley Unix from the Digital VAX to the Motorola 680x0 in the early 1980s, many C programs stopped working, and had to be repaired. In effect, the 680x0 revealed certain classes of program bugs that one could "get away with" on the VAX. One of these classes of bugs occurred in programs that use more than one size of integer (e.g., `short` and `long`), and arose from the fact that the VAX is a little-endian machine, while the 680x0 is big-endian (Section C-5.2). Another class of bugs occurred in programs that manipulate both null and empty strings. It arose from the fact that location zero in a Unix process's address space on the VAX always contained a zero, while the same location on the 680x0 is not in the address space, and will generate a protection error if used. For both of these classes of bugs, give examples of program fragments that would work on a VAX but not on a 680x0.

7.6 Ada provides two "remainder" operators, `rem` and `mod` for integer types, defined as follows [Ame83, Sec. 4.5.5]:

> Integer division and remainder are defined by the relation `A = (A/B)*B + (A rem B)`, where `(A rem B)` has the sign of `A` and an absolute value less than the absolute value of `B`. Integer division satisfies the identity `(-A)/B = -(A/B) = A/(-B)`.
>
> The result of the modulus operation is such that `(A mod B)` has the sign of `B` and an absolute value less than the absolute value of `B`; in addition, for some integer value `N`, this result must satisfy the relation `A = B*N + (A mod B)`.

Give values of `A` and `B` for which `A rem B` and `A mod B` differ. For what purposes would one operation be more useful than the other? Does it make sense to provide both, or is it overkill?

Consider also the `%` operator of C and the `mod` operator of Pascal. The designers of these languages could have picked semantics resembling those of either Ada's `rem` or its `mod`. Which did they pick? Do you think they made the right choice?

7.7 Consider the problem of performing range checks on set expressions in Pascal. Given that a set may contain many elements, some of which may be known at compile time, describe the information that a compiler might maintain in order to track both the elements known to belong to the set and the possible range of unknown elements. Then explain how to update this information for the following set operations: union, intersection, and difference. The goal is to determine (1) when subrange checks can be eliminated at run time and (2) when subrange errors can be reported at compile time. Bear in mind that the compiler *cannot* do a perfect job: some unnecessary run-time checks will inevitably be performed, and some operations that must always result in errors will not be caught at compile time. The goal is to do as good a job as possible at reasonable cost.

7.8 In Section 7.2.2 we introduced the notion of a *universal reference type* (`void *` in C) that refers to an object of unknown type. Using such references, implement a "poor man's generic queue" in C, as suggested in Section 7.3.1. Where do you need type casts? Why? Give an example of a use of the queue that will fail catastrophically at run time, due to the lack of type checking.

7.9 Rewrite the code of Figure 7.3 in Ada, Java, or C#.

7.10 **(a)** Give a generic solution to Exercise 6.19.

(b) Translate this solution into Ada, Java, or C#.

7.11 In your favorite language with generics, write code for simple versions of the following abstractions:

(a) a stack, implemented as a linked list

(b) a priority queue, implemented as a skip list or a partially ordered tree embedded in an array

(c) a dictionary (mapping), implemented as a hash table

7.12 Figure 7.3 passes integer `max_items` to the `queue` abstraction as a generic parameter. Write an alternative version of the code that makes `max_items` a parameter to the `queue` constructor instead. What is the advantage of the generic parameter version?

7.13 Rewrite the generic sorting routine of Examples 7.50–7.52 (with constraints) using OCaml or SML functors.

7.14 Flesh out the C++ sorting routine of Example 7.53. Demonstrate that this routine does "the wrong thing" when asked to sort an array of `char*` strings.

7.15 In Example 7.53 we mentioned three ways to make the need for comparisons more explicit when defining a generic sort routine in C++: make the comparison routine a method of the generic parameter class `T`, an extra argument to the sort routine, or an extra generic parameter. Implement these options and discuss their comparative strengths and weaknesses.

7.16 Yet another solution to the problem of the previous exercise is to make the sorting routine a method of a `sorter` class. The comparison routine can then be passed into the class as a constructor argument. Implement this option and compare it to those of the previous exercise.

7.17 Consider the following code skeleton in C++:

```
#include <list>
using std::list;

class foo { ...
class bar : public foo { ...

static void print_all(list<foo*> &L) { ...


list<foo*> LF;
list<bar*> LB;
...
print_all(LF);        // works fine
print_all(LB);        // static semantic error
```

Explain why the compiler won't allow the second call. Give an example of bad things that could happen if it did.

7.18 Bjarne Stroustrup, the original designer of C++, once described templates as "a clever kind of macro that obeys the scope, naming, and type rules of C++" [Str13, 2nd ed., p. 257]. How close is the similarity? What can templates do that macros can't? What do macros do that templates don't?

7.19 In Section 9.3.1 we noted that Ada 83 does not permit subroutines to be passed as parameters, but that some of the same effect can be achieved with generics. Suppose we want to apply a function to every member of an array. We might write the following in Ada 83:

```
generic
    type item is private;
    type item_array is array (integer range <>) of item;
    with function F(it : in item) return item;
procedure apply_to_array(A : in out item_array);

procedure apply_to_array(A : in out item_array) is
begin
    for i in A'first..A'last loop
        A(i) := F(A(i));
    end loop;
end apply_to_array;
```

Given an array of integers, `scores`, and a function on integers, `foo`, we can write:

```
procedure apply_to_ints is
    new apply_to_array(integer, int_array, foo);
...
apply_to_ints(scores);
```

How general is this mechanism? What are its limitations? Is it a reasonable substitute for formal (i.e., second-class, as opposed to third-class) subroutines?

7.20 Modify the code of Figure 7.3 or your solution to Exercise 7.12 to throw an exception if an attempt is made to enqueue an item in a full queue, or to dequeue an item from an empty queue.

7.21–7.27 In More Depth.

7.7 Explorations

7.28 Some language definitions specify a particular representation for data types in memory, while others specify only the semantic behavior of those types. For languages in the latter class, some implementations guarantee a particular representation, while others reserve the right to choose different representations in different circumstances. Which approach do you prefer? Why?

7.29 Investigate the *typestate* mechanism employed by Strom et al. in the Hermes programming language [SBG+91]. Discuss its relationship to the notion of definite assignment in Java and C# (Section 6.1.3).

7.30 Several recent projects attempt to blur the line between static and dynamic typing by adding optional type declarations to scripting languages. These declarations support a strategy of *gradual typing*, in which programmers initially write in a traditional scripting style and then add declarations incrementally to increase reliability or decrease run-time cost. Learn about the Dart, Hack, and TypeScript languages, promoted by Google, Facebook, and Microsoft, respectively. What are your impressions? How easy do you think it will be in practice to retrofit declarations into programs originally developed without them?

7.31 Research the type systems of Standard ML, OCaml, Haskell, and F#. What are the principal differences? What might explain the different choices made by the language designers?

7.32 Write a program in C++ or Ada that creates at least two concrete types or subroutines from the same template/generic. Compile your code to assembly language and look at the result. Describe the mapping from source to target code.

7.33 While Haskell does not include generics (its parametric polymorphism is implicit), its type classes can be considered a generalization of type constraints. Learn more about type classes. Discuss their relevance to polymorphic functions, as well as more general uses. You might want to look ahead to the discussion of *monads* in Section 11.5.2.

7.34 Investigate the notion of *type conformance*, employed by Black et al. in the Emerald programming language [BHJL07]. Discuss how conformance relates to the type inference of ML and to the class-based typing of object-oriented languages.

7.35 C++11 introduces so-called *variadic templates*, which take a variable number of generic parameters. Read up on how these work. Show how they might be used to replace the usual `cout` << $expr_1$ << … << $expr_n$ syntax of formatted output with `print(`$expr_1$`, ... ,` $expr_n$`)`, while retaining full static type checking.

7.36–7.38 In More Depth.

7.8 Bibliographic Notes

References to general information on the various programming languages mentioned in this chapter can be found in Appendix A, and in the Bibliographic Notes for Chapters 1 and 6. Welsh, Sneeringer, and Hoare [WSH77] provide a critique of the original Pascal definition, with a particular emphasis on its type system. Tanenbaum's comparison of Pascal and Algol 68 also focuses largely on types [Tan78]. Cleaveland [Cle86] provides a book-length study of many of the issues in this chapter. Pierce [Pie02] provides a formal and detailed modern coverage of the subject. The ACM Special Interest Group on Programming Languages launched a biennial workshop on *Types in Language Design and Implementation* in 2003.

What we have referred to as the denotational model of types originates with Hoare [DDH72]. Denotational formulations of the overall semantics of programming languages are discussed in the Bibliographic Notes for Chapter 4. A related but distinct body of work uses algebraic techniques to formalize data abstraction; key references include Guttag [Gut77] and Goguen et al. [GTW78]. Milner's original paper [Mil78] is the seminal reference on type inference in ML. Mairson [Mai90] proves that the cost of unifying ML types is $O(2^n)$, where n is the length of the program. Fortunately, the cost is linear in the size of the program's type expressions, so the worst case arises only in programs whose semantics are too complex for a human being to understand anyway.

Hoare [Hoa75] discusses the definition of recursive types under a reference model of variables. Cardelli and Wegner survey issues related to polymorphism, overloading, and abstraction [CW85]. The Character Model standard for the World Wide Web provides a remarkably readable introduction to the subtleties and complexities of multilingual character sets [Wor05].

Garcia et al. provide a detailed comparison of generic facilities in ML, C++, Haskell, Eiffel, Java, and C# [GJL$^+$03]. The C# generic facility is described by Kennedy and Syme [KS01]. Java generics are based on the work of Bracha et al. [BOSW98]. Erwin Unruh is credited with discovering that C++ templates could trick the compiler into performing nontrivial computation. His specific example (*www.erwin-unruh.de/primorig.html*) did not compile, but caused the compiler to generate a sequence of n error messages, embedding the first n primes. Abrahams and Gurtovoy provide a book-length treatment of *template metaprogramming* [AG05], the field that grew out of this discovery.

8 Composite Types

Chapter 7 introduced the notion of types as a way to organize the many values and objects manipulated by computer programs. It also introduced terminology for both built-in and *composite* types. As we noted in Section 7.1.4, composite types are formed by joining together one or more simpler types using a *type constructor*. From a denotational perspective, the constructors can be modeled as operations on sets, with each set representing one of the simpler types.

In the current chapter we will survey the most important type constructors: records, arrays, strings, sets, pointers, lists, and files. In the section on records we will also consider both variants (unions) and tuples. In the section on pointers, we will take a more detailed look at the value and reference models of variables introduced in Section 6.1.2, and the heap management issues introduced in Section 3.2. The section on files (mostly on the companion site) will include a discussion of input and output mechanisms.

8.1 Records (Structures)

Record types allow related data of heterogeneous types to be stored and manipulated together. Originally introduced by Cobol, records also appeared in Algol 68, which called them *structures*, and introduced the keyword `struct`. Many modern languages, including C and its descendants, employ the Algol terminology. Fortran 90 simply calls its records "types": they are the only form of programmer-defined type other than arrays, which have their own special syntax. Structures in C++ are defined as a special form of *class* (one in which members are globally visible by default). Java has no distinguished notion of `struct`; its programmers use classes in all cases. C# and Swift use a reference model for variables of `class` types, and a value model for variables of `struct` types. In these languages, `struct`s do not support inheritance. For the sake of simplicity, we will use the term "record" in most of our discussion to refer to the relevant construct in all these languages.

8.1.1 Syntax and Operations

EXAMPLE 8.1
A C struct

In C, a simple record might be defined as follows:

```
struct element {
    char name[2];
    int atomic_number;
    double atomic_weight;
    _Bool metallic;
};
```

Each of the record components is known as a *field*. To refer to a given field of a record, most languages use "dot" notation:

EXAMPLE 8.2
Accessing record fields

```
element copper;
const double AN = 6.022e23;        /* Avogadro's number */
...
copper.name[0] = 'C'; copper.name[1] = 'u';
double atoms = mass / copper.atomic_weight * AN;
```

In Fortran 90 one would say `copper%name` and `copper%atomic_weight`. Cobol reverses the order of the field and record names: `name of copper` and `atomic_weight of copper`. In Common Lisp, one would say `(element-name copper)` and `(element-atomic_weight copper)`.

EXAMPLE 8.3
Nested records

Most languages allow record definitions to be nested. Again in C:

```
struct ore {
    char name[30];
    struct {
        char name[2];
        int atomic_number;
        double atomic_weight;
        _Bool metallic;
    } element_yielded;
};
```

Alternatively, one could say

```
struct ore {
    char name[30];
    struct element element_yielded;
};
```

In Fortran 90 and Common Lisp, only the second alternative is permitted: record fields can have record types, but the declarations cannot be lexically nested. Naming for nested records is straightforward: `malachite.element_` `yielded.atomic_number` in C; `atomic_number of element_yielded of malachite` in Cobol; `(element-atomic_number (ore-element_yielded malachite))` in Common Lisp. ■

EXAMPLE 8.4
OCaml records and tuples

As noted in Example 7.17, ML and its relatives differ from most languages in specifying that the order of record fields is insignificant. The OCaml record value `{name = "Cu"; atomic_number = 29; atomic_weight = 63.546; metallic = true}` is the same as the value `{atomic_number = 29; name = "Cu"; atomic_weight = 63.546; metallic = true}`—they will test `true` for equality.

OCaml's *tuples*, which we mentioned briefly in Section 7.2.4, and will visit again in Section 11.4.3, resemble records whose fields *are* ordered, but unnamed. In SML, the other leading ML dialect, the resemblance is actually equivalence: tuples are defined as syntactic sugar for records whose field names are small integers. The values `("Cu", 29)`, `{1 = "Cu", 2 = 29}`, and `{2 = 29, 1 = "Cu"}` will all test `true` for equality in SML. ■

8.1.2 Memory Layout and Its Impact

The fields of a record are usually stored in adjacent locations in memory. In its symbol table, the compiler keeps track of the offset of each field within each record type. When it needs to access a field, the compiler will often generate a load or store instruction with displacement addressing. For a local object, the base register is typically the frame pointer; the displacement is then the sum of the record's offset from the register and the field's offset within the record.

EXAMPLE 8.5
Memory layout for a record type

A likely layout for our `element` type on a 32-bit machine appears in Figure 8.1. Because the `name` field is only two characters long, it occupies two bytes in memory. Since `atomic_number` is an integer, and must (on most machines) be word-aligned, there is a two-byte "hole" between the end of `name` and the beginning of `atomic_number`. Similarly, since Boolean variables (in most language implementations) occupy a single byte, there are three bytes of empty space between the end of the `metallic` field and the next aligned location. In an array of `element`s, most compilers would devote 20 bytes to every member of the array. ■

DESIGN & IMPLEMENTATION

8.1 Struct tags and `typedef` in C and C++

One of the peculiarities of the C type system is that `struct` tags are not exactly type names. In Example 8.1, the name of the type is the two-word phrase `struct element`. We used this name to declare the `element_yielded` field of the second struct in Example 8.3. To obtain a one-word name, one can say `typedef struct element element_t`, or even `typedef struct element element`: struct tags and `typedef` names have separate name spaces, so the same name can be used in each. C++ eliminates this idiosyncrasy by allowing the struct tag to be used as a type name without the `struct` prefix; in effect, it performs the `typedef` implicitly.

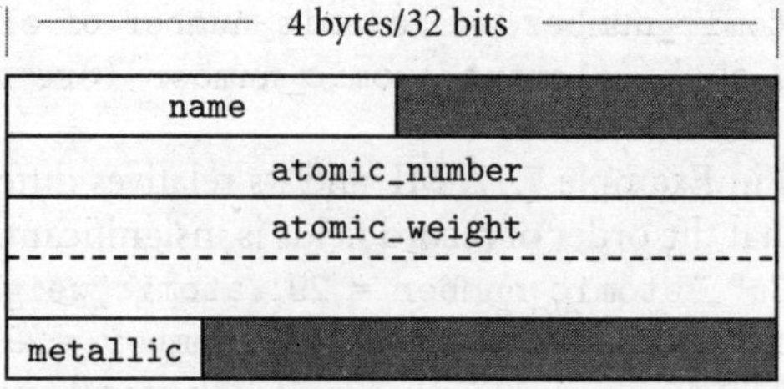

Figure 8.1 Likely layout in memory for objects of type `element` on a 32-bit machine. Alignment restrictions lead to the shaded "holes."

In a language with a value model of variables, nested records are naturally embedded in the parent record, where they function as large fields with word or double-word alignment. In a language with a reference model of variables, fields of record type are typically references to data in another location. The difference is a matter not only of memory layout, but also of semantics. We can see the difference in Figure 8.2. In C, with a value model of variables, data is laid out as shown at the top of the figure. In the following code, using the declarations at the top of the figure, the assignment of `s1` into `s2` copies the embedded `T`:

EXAMPLE 8.6
Nested records as values

```
struct S s1;
struct S s2;
s1.n.j = 0;
s2 = s1;
s2.n.j = 7;
printf("%d\n", s1.n.j);          /* prints 0 */
```

EXAMPLE 8.7
Nested records as references

In Java, by contrast, with a reference model of variables, data is laid out as shown at the bottom of the figure. In the following code, using the declarations at the bottom of the figure, assignment of `s1` into `s2` copies only the reference, so `s2.n.j` is an alias for `s1.n.j`:

```
S s1 = new S();
s1.n = new T();                  // fields initialized to 0
S s2 = s1;
s2.n.j = 7;
System.out.println(s1.n.j);      // prints 7
```

EXAMPLE 8.8
Layout of packed types

A few languages and implementations allow the programmer to specify that a record type (or an array, set, or file type) should be *packed*. In Ada, one uses a pragma:

```
type element = record
    ...
end;
pragma Pack(element);
```

```
struct T {
    int j;
    int k;
};
struct S {
    int i;
    struct T n;
};
```

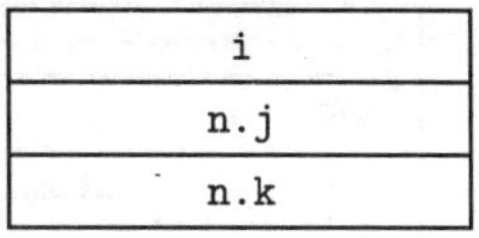


```
class T {
    public int j;
    public int k;
}
class S {
    public int i;
    public T n;
}
```

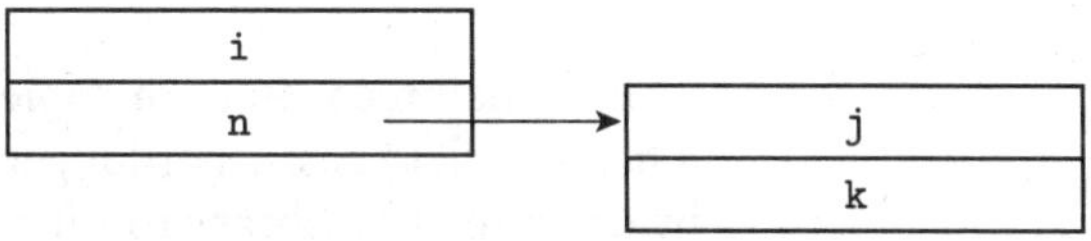

Figure 8.2 Layout of memory for a nested `struct` (`class`) in C (top) and Java (bottom). This layout reflects the fact that `n` is an embedded value in C, but a reference in Java. We have assumed here that integers and pointers have equal size.

When compiling with `gcc`, one uses an *attribute*:

```
struct __attribute__ ((__packed__)) element {
    ...
}
```

The Ada syntax is built into the language; the `gcc` syntax is a GNU extension. In either case, the directive asks the compiler to optimize for space instead of speed. Typically, a compiler will implement a packed record without holes, by simply "pushing the fields together." To access a nonaligned field, however, it will have to issue a multi-instruction sequence that retrieves the pieces of the field from memory and then reassembles them in a register. A likely packed layout for our `element` type (again for a 32-bit machine) appears in Figure 8.3. It is 15 bytes in length. An array of packed `element` records would probably devote 16 bytes to each member of the array; that is, it would align each element. A packed array of packed records might devote only 15 bytes to each; only every fourth element would be aligned. ■

EXAMPLE 8.9
Assignment and comparison of records

Most languages allow a value to be assigned to an entire record in a single operation:

```
my_element := copper;
```

Ada also allows records to be compared for equality (`if my_element = copper then ...`). Many other languages (including C and its successors) support assignment but not equality testing, though C++ allows the programmer to define the latter for individual record types. ■

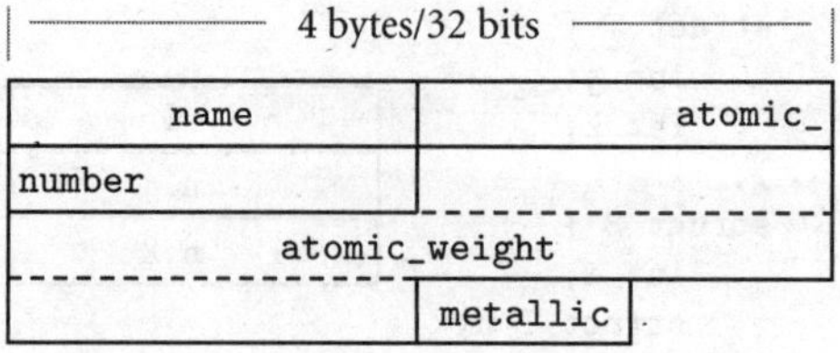

Figure 8.3 **Likely memory layout for packed `element` records.** The `atomic_number` and `atomic_weight` fields are nonaligned, and can only be read or written (on most machines) via multi-instruction sequences.

For small records, both copies and comparisons can be performed in-line on a field-by-field basis. For longer records, we can save significantly on code space by deferring to a library routine. A `block_copy` routine can take source address, destination address, and length as arguments, but the analogous `block_compare` routine would fail on records with different (garbage) data in the holes. One solution is to arrange for all holes to contain some predictable value (e.g., zero), but this requires code at every elaboration point. Another is to have the compiler generate a customized field-by-field comparison routine for every record type. Different routines would be called to compare records of different types.

EXAMPLE 8.10
Minimizing holes by sorting fields

In addition to complicating comparisons, holes in records waste space. Packing eliminates holes, but at potentially heavy cost in access time. A compromise, adopted by some compilers, is to sort a record's fields according to the size of their alignment constraints. All byte-aligned fields might come first, followed by any half-word aligned fields, word-aligned fields, and (if the hardware requires) double-word-aligned fields. For our `element` type, the resulting rearrangement is shown in Figure 8.4. ■

In most cases, reordering of fields is purely an implementation issue: the programmer need not be aware of it, so long as all instances of a record type are reordered in the same way. The exception occurs in systems programs, which sometimes "look inside" the implementation of a data type with the expectation that it will be mapped to memory in a particular way. A kernel programmer, for example, may count on a particular layout strategy in order to define a record

DESIGN & IMPLEMENTATION

8.2 The order of record fields

Issues of record field order are intimately tied to implementation tradeoffs: Holes in records waste space, but alignment makes for faster access. If holes contain garbage we can't compare records by looping over words or bytes, but zeroing out the holes would incur costs in time and code space. Predictable layout is important for mirroring hardware structures in "systems" languages, but reorganization may be advantageous in large records if we can group frequently accessed fields together, so they lie in the same cache line.

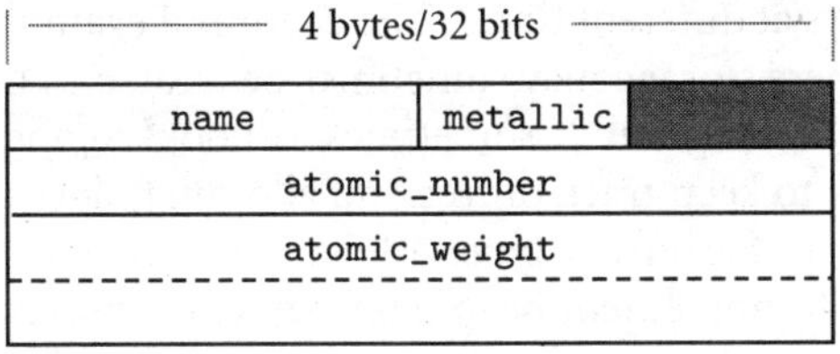

Figure 8.4 **Rearranging record fields to minimize holes.** By sorting fields according to the size of their alignment constraint, a compiler can minimize the space devoted to holes, while keeping the fields aligned.

that mimics the organization of memory-mapped control registers for a particular Ethernet device. C and C++, which are designed in large part for systems programs, guarantee that the fields of a `struct` will be allocated in the order declared. The first field is guaranteed to have the coarsest alignment required by the hardware for any type (generally a four- or eight-byte boundary). Subsequent fields have the natural alignment for their type. Fortran 90 allows the programmer to specify that fields must not be reordered; in the absence of such a specification the compiler can choose its own order. To accommodate systems programs, Ada, C, and C++ all allow the programmer to specify exactly how many bits to devote to each field of a record. Where a "packed" directive is essentially a nonbinding indication of the programmer's priorities, bit lengths on field declarations are a binding specification of assembly-level layout.

8.1.3 Variant Records (Unions)

Programming languages of the 1960s and 1970s were designed in an era of severe memory constraints. Many allowed the programmer to specify that certain variables (presumably ones that would never be used at the same time) should be allocated "on top of" one another, sharing the same bytes in memory. C's syntax, heavily influenced by Algol 68, looks very much like a struct:

EXAMPLE 8.11
A union in C

```
union {
    int i;
    double d;
    _Bool b;
};
```

The overall size of this *union* would be that of its largest member (presumably `d`). Exactly which bytes of `d` would be overlapped by `i` and `b` is implementation dependent, and presumably influenced by the relative sizes of types, their alignment constraints, and the endian-ness of the hardware.

In practice, unions have been used for two main purposes. The first arises in systems programs, where unions allow the same set of bytes to be interpreted in different ways at different times. The canonical example occurs in memory management, where storage may sometimes be treated as unallocated space (perhaps in need of "zeroing out"), sometimes as bookkeeping information (length and header fields to keep track of free and allocated blocks), and sometimes as user-allocated data of arbitrary type. While nonconverting type casts (Section 7.2.1) can be used to implement heap management routines, unions are a better indication of the programmer's intent: the bits are not being reinterpreted, they are being used for independent purposes.[1]

EXAMPLE 8.12
Motivation for variant records

The second, historical purpose for unions was to represent alternative sets of fields within a record. A record representing an employee, for example, might have several common fields (name, address, phone, department, ID number) and various other fields depending on whether the person in question works on a salaried, hourly, or consulting basis. Traditional C unions were awkward when used for this purpose. A much cleaner syntax appeared in the *variant records* of Pascal and its successors, which allow the programmer to specify that certain fields within a record should overlap in memory. Similar functionality was added to C11 and C++11 in the form of *anonymous* unions. ■

IN MORE DEPTH

We discuss unions and variant records in more detail on the companion site. Topics we consider include syntax, safety, and memory layout issues. Safety is a particular concern: where nonconverting type casts allow a programmer to circumvent the language's type system explicitly, a naive realization of unions makes it easy to do so by accident. Ada imposes limits on the use of unions and variant records that allow the compiler to verify, statically, that all programs are type-safe. We also note that inheritance in object-oriented languages provides an attractive alternative to type-safe variant records in most cases. This observation largely accounts for the omission of unions and variant records from most more recent languages.

✓ CHECK YOUR UNDERSTANDING

1. What are *struct tags* in C? How are they related to type names? How did they change in C++?

2. How do the records of ML differ from those of most other languages?

3. Discuss the significance of "holes" in records. Why do they arise? What problems do they cause?

1 By contrast, the other example mentioned under Nonconverting Type Casts in Section 7.2.1—examination of the internal structure of a floating-point number—does indeed reinterpret bits. Unions can also be used in this case (Exercise C-8.24), but here a nonconverting cast is a better indication of intent.

4. Why is it easier to implement assignment than comparison for records?
5. What is *packing*? What are its advantages and disadvantages?
6. Why might a compiler reorder the fields of a record? What problems might this cause?
7. Briefly describe two purposes for unions/variant records.

8.2 Arrays

Arrays are the most common and important composite data types. They have been a fundamental part of almost every high-level language, beginning with Fortran I. Unlike records, which group related fields of disparate types, arrays are usually homogeneous. Semantically, they can be thought of as a mapping from an *index type* to a *component* or *element type*. Some languages (e.g., Fortran) require that the index type be `integer`; many languages allow it to be any discrete type. Some languages (e.g., Fortran 77) require that the element type of an array be scalar. Most (including Fortran 90) allow any element type.

Some languages (notably scripting languages, but also some newer imperative languages, including Go and Swift) allow nondiscrete index types. The resulting *associative* arrays must generally be implemented with hash tables or search trees; we consider them in Section 14.4.3. Associative arrays also resemble the *dictionary* or *map* types supported by the standard libraries of many object-oriented languages. In C++, operator overloading allows these types to use conventional array-like syntax. For the purposes of this chapter, we will assume that array indices are discrete. This admits a (much more efficient) contiguous allocation scheme, to be described in Section 8.2.3. We will also assume that arrays are *dense*—that a large fraction of their elements are not equal to zero or some other default value. The alternative—*sparse* arrays—arises in many important scientific problems. For these, libraries (or, in rare cases, the language itself) may support an alternative implementation that explicitly enumerates only the non-default values.

8.2.1 Syntax and Operations

Most languages refer to an element of an array by appending a subscript—usually delimited by square brackets—to the name of the array: `A[3]`. A few languages—notably Fortran and Ada—use parentheses instead: `A(3)`.

EXAMPLE 8.13
Array declarations

In some languages one declares an array by appending subscript notation to the syntax that would be used to declare a scalar. In C:

```
char upper[26];
```

In Fortran:

```
character, dimension (1:26) :: upper
character (26) upper        ! shorthand notation
```

In C, the lower bound of an index range is always zero: the indices of an n-element array are $0 \ldots n-1$. In Fortran, the lower bound of the index range is one by default. Fortran 90 allows a different lower bound to be specified if desired, using the notation shown in the first of the two declarations above.

Many Algol descendants use an `array` constructor instead. In Ada, for example, one might say

```
upper : array (character range 'a'..'z') of character;
```

EXAMPLE 8.14
Multidimensional arrays

Most languages make it easy to declare multidimensional arrays:

```
mat : array (1..10, 1..10) of long_float;      -- Ada

real, dimension (10,10) :: mat                 ! Fortran
```

In some languages, one can also declare a multidimensional array by using the array constructor more than once in the same declaration. In Modula-3, for example,

```
VAR mat : ARRAY [1..10], [1..10] OF REAL;
```

is syntactic sugar for

```
VAR mat : ARRAY [1..10] OF ARRAY [1..10] OF REAL;
```

and `mat[3, 4]` is syntactic sugar for `mat[3][4]`.

EXAMPLE 8.15
Multidimensional vs built-up arrays

In Ada, by contrast,

```
mat1 : array (1..10, 1..10) of long_float;
```

is not the same as

```
type vector is array (integer range <>) of long_float;
type matrix is array (integer range <>) of vector (1..10);
mat2 : matrix (1..10);
```

Variable `mat1` is a two-dimensional array; `mat2` is an array of one-dimensional arrays. With the former declaration, we can access individual real numbers as `mat1(3, 4)`; with the latter we must say `mat2(3)(4)`. The two-dimensional array is arguably more elegant, but the array of arrays supports additional operations: it allows us to name the rows of `mat2` individually (`mat2(3)` is a 10-element, single-dimensional array), and it allows us to take *slices*, as discussed below (`mat2(3)(2..6)` is a five-element array of real numbers; `mat2(3..7)` is a five-element array of ten-element arrays).

EXAMPLE 8.16
Arrays of arrays in C

In C, one must also declare an array of arrays, and use two-subscript notation, but C's integration of pointers and arrays (to be discussed in Section 8.5.1) means that slices are not supported:

```
double mat[10][10];
```

Given this definition, `mat[3][4]` denotes an individual element of the array, but `mat[3]` denotes a *reference*, either to the third row of the array or to the first element of that row, depending on context.

DESIGN & IMPLEMENTATION

8.3 Is [ ] an operator?

Associative arrays in C++ are typically defined by overloading `operator[]`. C#, like C++, provides extensive facilities for operator overloading, but it does not use these facilities to support associative arrays. Instead, the language provides a special *indexer* mechanism, with its own unique syntax:

```
class directory {
    Hashtable table;                        // from standard library
    ...
    public directory() {                    // constructor
        table = new Hashtable();
    }
    ...
    public string this[string name] {       // indexer method
        get {
            return (string) table[name];
        }
        set {
            table[name] = value;            // value is implicitly
} } }                                       // a parameter of set
...
directory d = new directory();
...
d["Jane Doe"] = "234-5678";
Console.WriteLine(d["Jane Doe"]);
```

Why the difference? In C++, `operator[]` can return a *reference* (an explicit l-value), which can be used on either side of an assignment (further information can be found under "References in C++" in Section 9.3.1). C# has no comparable l-value mechanism, so it needs separate methods to get and set the value of `d["Jane Doe"]`.

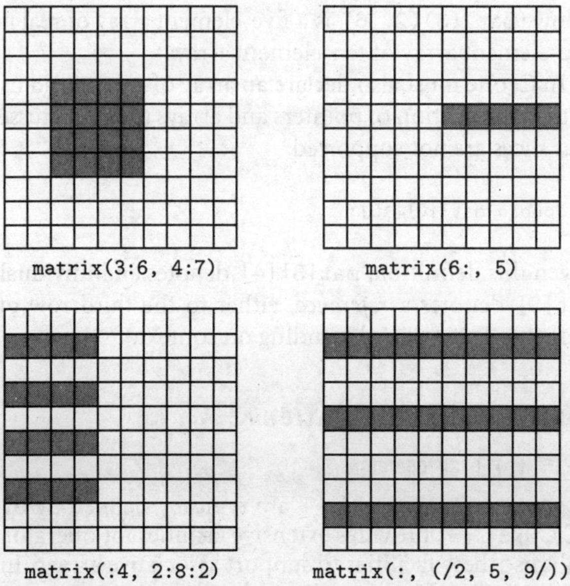

Figure 8.5 Array slices (sections) in Fortran 90. Much like the values in the header of an enumeration-controlled loop (Section 6.5.1), $a : b : c$ in a subscript indicates positions a, $a + c$, $a + 2c$, ... through b. If a or b is omitted, the corresponding bound of the array is assumed. If c is omitted, 1 is assumed. It is even possible to use negative values of c in order to select positions in reverse order. The slashes in the second subscript of the lower right example delimit an explicit list of positions.

Slices and Array Operations

EXAMPLE 8.17
Array slice operations

A *slice* or *section* is a rectangular portion of an array. Fortran 90 provides extensive facilities for slicing, as do Go and many scripting languages. Figure 8.5 illustrates some of the possibilities in Fortran 90, using the declaration of `mat` from Example 8.14. Ada provides more limited support: a slice is simply a contiguous range of elements in a one-dimensional array. As we saw in Example 8.15, the elements can themselves be arrays, but there is no way to extract a slice along both dimensions as a single operation. ■

In most languages, the only operations permitted on an array are selection of an element (which can then be used for whatever operations are valid on its type), and assignment. A few languages (e.g., Ada and Fortran 90) allow arrays to be compared for equality. Ada allows one-dimensional arrays whose elements are discrete to be compared for *lexicographic ordering*: `A < B` if the first element of `A` that is not equal to the corresponding element of `B` is less than that corresponding element. Ada also allows the built-in logical operators (`or`, `and`, `xor`) to be applied to Boolean arrays.

Fortran 90 has a very rich set of *array operations*: built-in operations that take entire arrays as arguments. Because Fortran uses structural type equivalence, the operands of an array operator need only have the same element type and shape. In particular, slices of the same shape can be intermixed in array operations, even if the arrays from which they were sliced have very different shapes. Any of the built-in arithmetic operators will take arrays as operands; the result is an array, of the same shape as the operands, whose elements are the result of applying the operator to corresponding elements. As a simple example, `A + B` is an array each of whose elements is the sum of the corresponding elements of `A` and `B`. Fortran 90 also provides a huge collection of *intrinsic*, or built-in functions. More than 60 of these (including logic and bit manipulation, trigonometry, logs and exponents, type conversion, and string manipulation) are defined on scalars, but will also perform their operation element-wise if passed arrays as arguments. The function `tan(A)`, for example, returns an array consisting of the tangents of the elements of `A`. Many additional intrinsic functions are defined solely on arrays. These include searching and summarization, transposition, and reshaping and subscript permutation.

Fortran 90 draws significant inspiration from APL, an array manipulation language developed by Iverson and others in the early to mid-1960s.[2] APL was designed primarily as a terse mathematical notation for array manipulations. It employs an enormous character set that made it difficult to use with traditional keyboards and textual displays. Its variables are all arrays, and many of the special characters denote array operations. APL implementations are designed for interpreted, interactive use. They are best suited to "quick and dirty" solution of mathematical problems. The combination of very powerful operators with very terse notation makes APL programs notoriously difficult to read and understand. J, a successor to APL, uses a conventional character set.

8.2.2 Dimensions, Bounds, and Allocation

In all of the examples in the previous subsection, the shape of the array (including bounds) was specified in the declaration. For such static shape arrays, storage can be managed in the usual way: static allocation for arrays whose lifetime is the entire program; stack allocation for arrays whose lifetime is an invocation of a subroutine; heap allocation for dynamically allocated arrays with more general lifetime.

Storage management is more complex for arrays whose shape is not known until elaboration time, or whose shape may change during execution. For these the compiler must arrange not only to allocate space, but also to make shape information available at run time (without such information, indexing would not be possible). Some dynamically typed languages allow run-time binding of

2 Kenneth Iverson (1920–2004), a Canadian mathematician, joined the faculty at Harvard University in 1954, where he conceived APL as a notation for describing mathematical algorithms. He moved to IBM in 1960, where he helped develop the notation into a practical programming language. He was named an IBM Fellow in 1970, and received the ACM Turing Award in 1979.

both the number and bounds of dimensions. Compiled languages may allow the bounds to be dynamic, but typically require the number of dimensions to be static. A local array whose shape is known at elaboration time may still be allocated in the stack. An array whose size may change during execution must generally be allocated in the heap.

In the first subsection below we consider the *descriptors*, or *dope vectors*,[3] used to hold shape information at run time. We then consider stack- and heap-based allocation, respectively, for dynamic shape arrays.

Dope Vectors

During compilation, the symbol table maintains dimension and bounds information for every array in the program. For every record, it maintains the offset of every field. When the number and bounds of array dimensions are statically known, the compiler can look them up in the symbol table in order to compute the address of elements of the array. When these values are not statically known, the compiler must generate code to look them up in a dope vector at run time.

In the general case a dope vector must specify the lower bound of each dimension and the size of each dimension other than the last (which is always the size of the element type, and will thus be statically known). If the language implementation performs dynamic semantic checks for out-of-bounds subscripts in array references, then the dope vector may contain upper bounds as well. Given lower bounds and sizes, the upper bound information is redundant, but including it avoids the need to recompute repeatedly at run time.

The contents of the dope vector are initialized at elaboration time, or whenever the number or bounds of dimensions change. In a language like Fortran 90, whose notion of shape includes dimension sizes but not lower bounds, an assignment statement may need to copy not only the data of an array, but dope vector contents as well.

In a language that provides both a value model of variables and arrays of dynamic shape, we must consider the possibility that a record will contain a field whose size is not statically known. In this case the compiler may use dope vectors not only for dynamic shape arrays, but also for dynamic shape records. The dope vector for a record typically indicates the offset of each field from the beginning of the record.

Stack Allocation

Subroutine parameters and local variables provide the simplest examples of dynamic shape arrays. Early versions of Pascal required the shape of all arrays to be specified statically. Standard Pascal allowed dynamic arrays as subroutine parameters, with shape fixed at subroutine call time. Such parameters are sometimes

3 The name "dope vector" presumably derives from the notion of "having the dope on (something)," a colloquial expression that originated in horse racing: advance knowledge that a horse has been drugged ("doped") is of significant, if unethical, use in placing bets.

```
void square(int n, double M[n][n]) {
    double T[n][n];
    for (int i = 0; i < n; i++) {        // compute product into T
        for (int j = 0; j < n; j++) {
            double s = 0;
            for (int k = 0; k < n; k++) {
                s += M[i][k] * M[k][j];
            }
            T[i][j] = s;
        }
    }
    for (int i = 0; i < n; i++) {        // copy T back into M
        for (int j = 0; j < n; j++) {
            M[i][j] = T[i][j];
        }
    }
}
```

Figure 8.6 **A dynamic local array in C.** Function `square` multiplies a matrix by itself and replaces the original with the product. To do so it needs a scratch array of the same shape as the parameter. Note that the declarations of `M` and `T` both rely on parameter `n`.

known as *conformant arrays.* Among other things, they facilitate the construction of linear algebra libraries, whose routines must typically work on arrays of arbitrary size. To implement such an array, the compiler arranges for the caller to pass both the data of the array and an appropriate dope vector. If the array is of dynamic shape in the caller's context, the dope vector may already be available. If the array is of static shape in the caller's context, an appropriate dope vector will need to be created prior to the call.

EXAMPLE 8.18
Local arrays of dynamic shape in C

Ada and C (though not C++) support dynamic shape for both parameters and local variables. Among other things, local arrays can be declared to match the shape of conformant array parameters, facilitating the implementation of algorithms that require temporary space for calculations. Figure 8.6 contains a simple example in C. Function `square` accepts an array parameter `M` of dynamic shape and allocates a local variable `T` of the same dynamic shape. ■

EXAMPLE 8.19
Stack allocation of elaborated arrays

In many languages, including Ada and C, the shape of a local array becomes fixed at elaboration time. For such arrays it is still possible to place the space for the array in the stack frame of its subroutine, but an extra level of indirection is required (see Figure 8.7). In order to ensure that every local object can be found using a known offset from the frame pointer, we divide the stack frame into a *fixed-size part* and a *variable-size part.* An object whose size is statically known goes in the fixed-size part. An object whose size is not known until elaboration time goes in the variable-size part, and a pointer to it, together with a dope vector, goes in the fixed-size part. If the elaboration of the array is buried in a nested block, the compiler delays allocating space (i.e., changing the stack pointer) until the block is entered. It still allocates space for the pointer and the dope vector

```
-- Ada:
procedure foo(size : integer) is
M : array (1..size, 1..size)
      of long_float;
...
begin
    ...
end foo;
```

```
// C99:
void foo(int size) {
    double M[size][size];
    ...
}
```

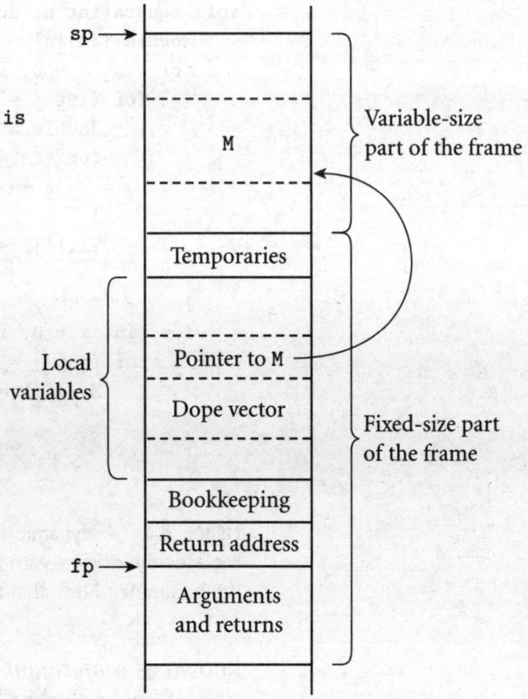

Figure 8.7 **Elaboration-time allocation of arrays.** Here `M` is a square two-dimensional array whose bounds are determined by a parameter passed to `foo` at run time. The compiler arranges for a pointer to `M` and a dope vector to reside at static offsets from the frame pointer. `M` cannot be placed among the other local variables because it would prevent those higher in the frame from having static offsets. Additional variable-size arrays or records are easily accommodated.

among the local variables when the subroutine itself is entered. Records of dynamic shape are handled in a similar way. ■

EXAMPLE 8.20 Elaborated arrays in Fortran 90

Fortran 90 allows specification of the bounds of an array to be delayed until after elaboration, but it does not allow those bounds to change once they have been defined:

```
real, dimension (:,:), allocatable :: mat
    ! mat is two-dimensional, but with unspecified bounds
...
allocate (mat (a:b, 0:m-1))
    ! first dimension has bounds a..b; second has bounds 0..m-1
...
deallocate (mat)
    ! implementation is now free to reclaim mat's space
```

Execution of an `allocate` statement can be treated like the elaboration of a dynamic shape array in a nested block. Execution of a `deallocate` statement can be treated like the end of the nested block (restoring the previous stack pointer) if there are no other arrays beyond the specified one in the stack. Alternatively, dynamic shape arrays can be allocated in the heap, as described in the following subsection.

Heap Allocation

Arrays that can change shape at arbitrary times are sometimes said to be *fully dynamic.* Because changes in size do not in general occur in FIFO order, stack allocation will not suffice; fully dynamic arrays must be allocated in the heap.

EXAMPLE 8.21
Dynamic strings in Java and C#

Several languages, including all the major scripting languages, allow strings—arrays of characters—to change size after elaboration time. Java and C# provide a similar capability (with a similar implementation), but describe the semantics differently: string variables in these languages are references to immutable string objects:

```
String s = "short";       // This is Java; use lower-case 'string' in C#
...
s = s + " but sweet";     // + is the concatenation operator
```

Here the declaration `String s` introduces a string variable, which we initialize with a reference to the constant string `"short"`. In the subsequent assignment, `+` creates a new string containing the concatenation of the old `s` and the constant `" but sweet"`; `s` is then set to refer to this new string, rather than the old. Note that arrays of characters are not the same as strings in Java and C#: the length of an array is fixed at elaboration time, and its elements can be modified in place.

Dynamically resizable arrays (other than strings) appear in APL, Common Lisp, and the various scripting languages. They are also supported by the `vector`, `Vector`, and `ArrayList` classes of the C++, Java, and C# libraries, respectively. In contrast to the `allocate`-able arrays of Fortran 90, these arrays can change their shape—in particular, can grow—while retaining their current content. In many cases, increasing the size will require that the run-time system allocate a larger block, copy any data that are to be retained from the old block to the new, and then deallocate the old.

If the number of dimensions of a fully dynamic array is statically known, the dope vector can be kept, together with a pointer to the data, in the stack frame of the subroutine in which the array was declared. If the number of dimensions can change, the dope vector must generally be placed at the beginning of the heap block instead.

In the absence of garbage collection, the compiler must arrange to reclaim the space occupied by fully dynamic arrays when control returns from the subroutine in which they were declared. Space for stack-allocated arrays is of course reclaimed automatically by popping the stack.

8.2.3 Memory Layout

Arrays in most language implementations are stored in contiguous locations in memory. In a one-dimensional array, the second element of the array is stored immediately after the first; the third is stored immediately after the second, and so forth. For arrays of records, alignment constraints may result in small holes between consecutive elements.

For multidimensional arrays, it still makes sense to put the first element of the array in the array's first memory location. But which element comes next? There are two reasonable answers, called *row-major* and *column-major* order. In row-major order, consecutive locations in memory hold elements that differ by one in the final subscript (except at the ends of rows). `A[2, 4]`, for example, is followed by `A[2, 5]`. In column-major order, consecutive locations hold elements that differ by one in the *initial* subscript: `A[2, 4]` is followed by `A[3, 4]`. These options are illustrated for two-dimensional arrays in Figure 8.8. The layouts for three or more dimensions are analogous. Fortran uses column-major order; most other languages use row-major order. (Correspondence with Fran Allen[4] suggests that column-major order was originally adopted in order to accommodate idiosyncrasies of the console debugger and instruction set of the IBM model 704 computer, on which the language was first implemented.) The advantage of row-major order is that it makes it easy to define a multidimensional array as an array of subarrays, as described in Section 8.2.1. With column-major order, the elements of the subarray would not be contiguous in memory. ■

EXAMPLE 8.22 Row-major vs column-major array layout

The difference between row- and column-major layout can be important for programs that use nested loops to access all the elements of a large, multidimensional array. On modern machines the speed of such loops is often limited by memory system performance, which depends heavily on the effectiveness of caching (Section C-5.1). Figure 8.8 shows the orientation of cache lines for row- and column-major layout of arrays. When code traverses a small array, all or most of its elements are likely to remain in the cache through the end of the nested loops, and the orientation of cache lines will not matter. For a large array, however, lines that are accessed early in the traversal are likely to be evicted to make room for lines accessed later in the traversal. If array elements are accessed in order of consecutive addresses, then each miss will bring into the cache not only the desired element, but the next several elements as well. If elements are accessed *across* cache lines instead (i.e., along the rows of a Fortran array, or the columns of an array in most other languages), then there is a good chance that almost every

EXAMPLE 8.23 Array layout and cache performance

4 Fran Allen (1932–) joined IBM's T. J. Watson Research Center in 1957, and stayed for her entire professional career. Her seminal paper, *Program Optimization* [All69] helped launch the field of code improvement. Her PTRAN (Parallel TRANslation) group, founded in the early 1980s, developed much of the theory of automatic parallelization. In 1989 Dr. Allen became the first woman to be named an IBM Fellow. In 2006 she became the first to receive the ACM Turing Award.

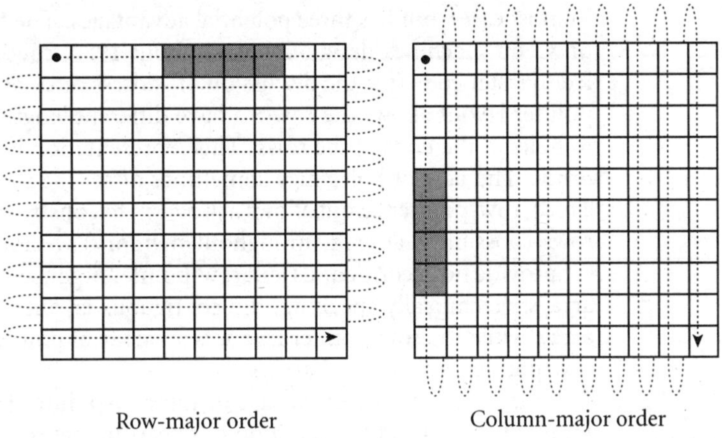

Figure 8.8 **Row- and column-major memory layout for two-dimensional arrays.** In row-major order, the elements of a row are contiguous in memory; in column-major order, the elements of a column are contiguous. The second cache line of each array is shaded, on the assumption that each element is an eight-byte floating-point number, that cache lines are 32 bytes long (a common size), and that the array begins at a cache line boundary. If the array is indexed from A[0,0] to A[9,9], then in the row-major case elements A[0,4] through A[0,7] share a cache line; in the column-major case elements A[4,0] through A[7,0] share a cache line.

access will result in a cache miss, dramatically reducing the performance of the code. In C, one should write

```
for (i = 0; i < N; i++) {          /* rows */
    for (j = 0; j < N; j++) {      /* columns */
        ... A[i][j] ...
    }
}
```

In Fortran:

```
do j = 1, N                        ! columns
    do i = 1, N                    ! rows
        ... A(i, j) ...
    end do
end do
```

Row-Pointer Layout

Some languages employ an alternative to contiguous allocation for some arrays. Rather than require the rows of an array to be adjacent, they allow them to lie anywhere in memory, and create an auxiliary array of pointers to the rows. If the array has more than two dimensions, it may be allocated as an array of pointers to arrays of pointers to .... This *row-pointer* memory layout requires more space in most cases, but has three potential advantages. The first is of historical interest only: on machines designed before about 1980, row-pointer layout sometimes led to faster code (see the discussion of address calculations below). Second, row-pointer layout allows the rows to have different lengths, without devoting space to holes at the ends of the rows. This representation is sometimes called a *ragged array*. The lack of holes may sometimes offset the increased space for pointers. Third, row-pointer layout allows a program to construct an array from preexisting rows (possibly scattered throughout memory) without copying. C, C++, and C# provide both contiguous and row-pointer organizations for multidimensional arrays. Technically speaking, the contiguous layout is a true multidimensional array, while the row-pointer layout is an array of pointers to arrays. Java uses the row-pointer layout for all arrays.

EXAMPLE 8.24
Contiguous vs row-pointer array layout

By far the most common use of the row-pointer layout in C is to represent arrays of strings. A typical example appears in Figure 8.9. In this example (representing the days of the week), the row-pointer memory layout consumes 57 bytes for the characters themselves (including a `NUL` byte at the end of each string), plus 28 bytes for pointers (assuming a 32-bit architecture), for a total of 85 bytes. The contiguous layout alternative devotes 10 bytes to each day (room enough for `Wednesday` and its `NUL` byte), for a total of 70 bytes. The additional space required for the row-pointer organization comes to 21 percent. In some cases, row pointers may actually save space. A Java compiler written in C, for example, would probably use row pointers to store the character-string representations of the 51 Java keywords and word-like literals. This data structure would use $55 \times 4 = 220$ bytes for the pointers (on a 32-bit machine), plus 366 bytes for the keywords, for a total of 586 bytes. Since the longest keyword (`synchronized`) requires 13 bytes (including space for the terminating `NUL`), a contiguous two-dimensional array would consume $55 \times 13 = 715$ bytes (716 when aligned). In this case, row pointers *save* a little over 18%. ■

DESIGN & IMPLEMENTATION

8.4 Array layout

The layout of arrays in memory, like the ordering of record fields, is intimately tied to tradeoffs in design and implementation. While column-major layout appears to offer no advantages on modern machines, its continued use in Fortran means that programmers must be aware of the underlying implementation in order to achieve good locality in nested loops. Row-pointer layout, likewise, has no performance advantage on modern machines (and a likely performance *penalty*, at least for numeric code), but it is a more natural fit for the "reference to object" data organization of languages like Java. Its impacts on space consumption and locality may be positive or negative, depending on the details of individual applications.

```
char days[][10] = {
    "Sunday", "Monday", "Tuesday",
    "Wednesday", "Thursday",
    "Friday", "Saturday"
};
...
days[2][3] == 's';  /* in Tuesday */
```

```
char *days[] = {
    "Sunday", "Monday", "Tuesday",
    "Wednesday", "Thursday",
    "Friday", "Saturday"
};
...
days[2][3] == 's';  /* in Tuesday */
```

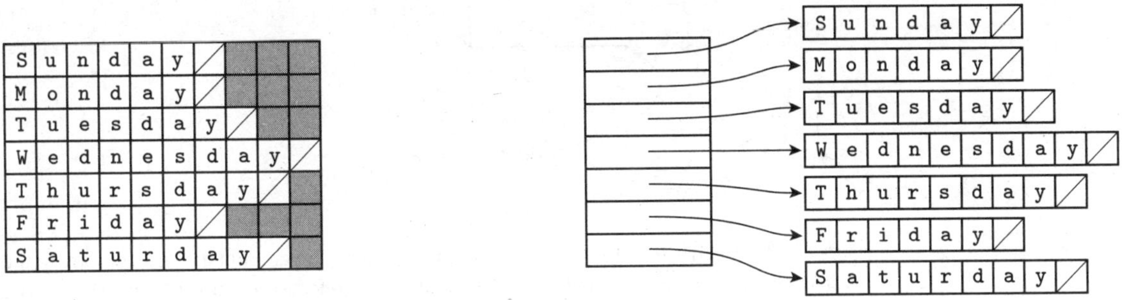

Figure 8.9 **Contiguous array allocation vs row pointers in C.** The declaration on the left is a true two-dimensional array. The slashed boxes are `NUL` bytes; the shaded areas are holes. The declaration on the right is a ragged array of pointers to arrays of characters. The arrays of characters may be located anywhere in memory—next to each other or separated, and in any order. In both cases, we have omitted bounds in the declaration that can be deduced from the size of the initializer (aggregate). Both data structures permit individual characters to be accessed using double subscripts, but the memory layout (and corresponding address arithmetic) is quite different.

Address Calculations

EXAMPLE 8.25
Indexing a contiguous array

For the usual contiguous layout of arrays, calculating the address of a particular element is somewhat complicated, but straightforward. Suppose a compiler is given the following declaration for a three-dimensional array:

A : array $[L_1 \,..\, U_1]$ of array $[L_2 \,..\, U_2]$ of array $[L_3 \,..\, U_3]$ of elem_type;

Let us define constants for the sizes of the three dimensions:

$$S_3 = \text{size of elem\_type}$$
$$S_2 = (U_3 - L_3 + 1) \times S_3$$
$$S_1 = (U_2 - L_2 + 1) \times S_2$$

Here the size of a row (S_2) is the size of an individual element (S_3) times the number of elements in a row (assuming row-major layout). The size of a plane (S_1) is the size of a row (S_2) times the number of rows in a plane. The address of A[i, j, k] is then

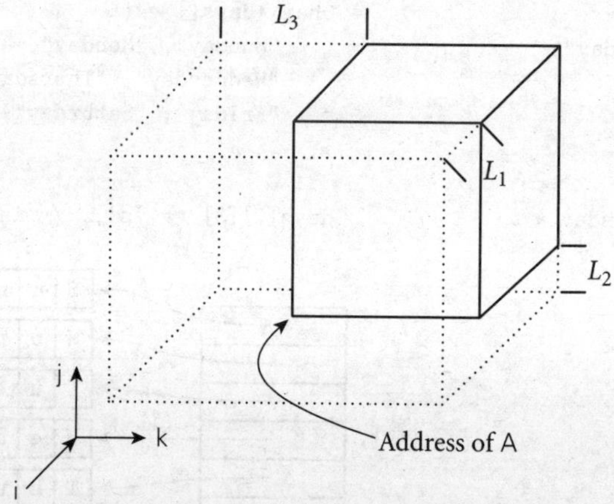

Figure 8.10 Virtual location of an array with nonzero lower bounds. By computing the constant portions of an array index at compile time, we effectively index into an array whose starting address is offset in memory, but whose lower bounds are all zero.

$$\begin{aligned} &\text{address of A} \\ &+\ (i - L_1) \times S_1 \\ &+\ (j - L_2) \times S_2 \\ &+\ (k - L_3) \times S_3 \end{aligned}$$

As written, this computation involves three multiplications and six additions/subtractions. We could compute the entire expression at run time, but in most cases a little rearrangement reveals that much of the computation can be performed at compile time. In particular, if the bounds of the array are known at compile time, then S_1, S_2, and S_3 are compile-time constants, and the subtractions of lower bounds can be distributed out of the parentheses:

$$\begin{aligned} &(i \times S_1) + (j \times S_2) + (k \times S_3) + \text{address of A} \\ &\quad -[(L_1 \times S_1) + (L_2 \times S_2) + (L_3 \times S_3)] \end{aligned}$$

The bracketed expression in this formula is a compile-time constant (assuming the bounds of A are statically known). If A is a global variable, then the address of A is statically known as well, and can be incorporated in the bracketed expression. If A is a local variable of a subroutine (with static shape), then the address of A can be decomposed into a static offset (included in the bracketed expression) plus the contents of the frame pointer at run time. We can think of the address of A plus the bracketed expression as calculating the location of an imaginary array whose [i, j, k]th element coincides with that of A, but whose lower bound in each dimension is zero. This imaginary array is illustrated in Figure 8.10. ■

EXAMPLE 8.26
Static and dynamic portions of an array index

If i, j, and/or k is known at compile time, then additional portions of the calculation of the address of A[i, j, k] will move from the dynamic to the static part of the formula shown above. If all of the subscripts are known, then the entire address can be calculated statically. Conversely, if any of the bounds of the array are not known at compile time, then portions of the calculation will move from the static to the dynamic part of the formula. For example, if L_1 is not known until run time, but k is known to be 3 at compile time, then the calculation becomes

$$(i \times S_1) + (j \times S_2) - (L_1 \times S_1) + \text{address of A} - [(L_2 \times S_2) + (L_3 \times S_3) - (3 \times S_3)]$$

Again, the bracketed part can be computed at compile time. If lower bounds are always restricted to zero, as they are in C, then they never contribute to run-time cost.

In all our examples, we have ignored the issue of dynamic semantic checks for out-of-bound subscripts. We explore the code for these in Exercise 8.10. In Section C-17.5.2 we will consider code improvement techniques that can be used to eliminate many checks statically, particularly in enumeration-controlled loops.

EXAMPLE 8.27
Indexing complex structures

The notion of "static part" and "dynamic part" of an address computation generalizes to more than just arrays. Suppose, for example, that V is a messy local array of records containing a nested, two-dimensional array in field M. The address of V[i].M[3, j] could be calculated as

DESIGN & IMPLEMENTATION

8.5 Lower bounds on array indices

In C, the lower bound of every array dimension is always zero. It is often assumed that the language designers adopted this convention in order to avoid subtracting lower bounds from indices at run time, thereby avoiding a potential source of inefficiency. As our discussion has shown, however, the compiler can avoid any run-time cost by translating to a virtual starting location. (The one exception to this statement occurs when the lower bound has a very large absolute value: if any index (scaled by element size) exceeds the maximum offset available with displacement mode addressing [typically 2^{15} bytes on RISC machines], then subtraction may still be required at run time.)

A more likely explanation lies in the interoperability of arrays and pointers in C (Section 8.5.1): C's conventions allow the compiler to generate code for an index operation on a pointer without worrying about the lower bound of the array into which the pointer points. Interestingly, Fortran array dimensions have a default lower bound of 1; unless the programmer explicitly specifies a lower bound of 0, the compiler must always translate to a virtual starting location.

$$
\begin{array}{ll}
i \times S_1^{\mathsf{V}} & \\
 & -L_1^{\mathsf{V}} \times S_1^{\mathsf{V}} \\
 & +\mathsf{M}\text{'s offset as a field} \\
 & +(3 - L_1^{\mathsf{M}}) \times S_1^{\mathsf{M}} \\
+j \times S_2^{\mathsf{M}} & \\
 & -L_2^{\mathsf{M}} \times S_2^{\mathsf{M}} \\
+\mathsf{fp} & \\
 & +\text{offset of V in frame}
\end{array}
$$

Here the calculations on the left must be performed at run time; the calculations on the right can be performed at compile time. (The notation for bounds and size places the name of the variable in a superscript and the dimension in a subscript: L_2^{M} is the lower bound of the second dimension of M.) ■

EXAMPLE 8.28
Indexing a row-pointer array

Address calculation for arrays that use row pointers is comparatively straightforward. Using our three-dimensional array A as an example, the expression `A[i, j, k]` is equivalent, in C notation, to `(*(*A[i])[j])[k]`. If the intermediate pointer loads both hit in the cache, the code to evaluate this expression is likely to be comparable in cost to that of the contiguous allocation case (Example 8.26). If the intermediate loads miss in the cache, it will be substantially slower. On a 1970s CISC machine, the balance would probably have tipped the other way: multiplies would have been slower, and memory accesses faster. In any event (contiguous or row-pointer allocation, old or new machine), important code improvements will often be possible when several array references use the same subscript expression, or when array references are embedded in loops. ■

✓ CHECK YOUR UNDERSTANDING

8. What is an array *slice*? For what purposes are slices useful?

9. Is there any significant difference between a two-dimensional array and an array of one-dimensional arrays?

10. What is the *shape* of an array?

11. What is a *dope vector*? What purpose does it serve?

12. Under what circumstances can an array declared within a subroutine be allocated in the stack? Under what circumstances must it be allocated in the heap?

13. What is a *conformant* array?

14. Discuss the comparative advantages of *contiguous* and *row-pointer* layout for arrays.

15. Explain the difference between *row-major* and *column-major* layout for contiguously allocated arrays. Why does a programmer need to know which lay-

out the compiler uses? Why do most language designers consider row-major layout to be better?

16. How much of the work of computing the address of an element of an array can be performed at compile time? How much must be performed at run time?

8.3 Strings

In some languages, a string is simply an array of characters. In other languages, strings have special status, with operations that are not available for arrays of other sorts. Scripting languages like Perl, Python, and Ruby have extensive suites of built-in string operators and functions, including sophisticated pattern matching facilities based on regular expressions. Some special-purpose languages—Icon, in particular—provide even more sophisticated mechanisms, including general-purpose *generators* and backtracking search. We will consider the string and pattern-matching facilities of scripting languages in more detail in Section 14.4.2. Icon was discussed in Section C-6.5.4. In the remainder of the current section we focus on the role of strings in more traditional languages.

Almost all programming languages allow literal strings to be specified as a sequence of characters, usually enclosed in single or double quote marks. Most languages distinguish between literal characters (often delimited with single quotes) and literal strings (often delimited with double quotes). A few languages make no such distinction, defining a character as simply a string of length one. Most languages also provide *escape sequences* that allow nonprinting characters and quote marks to appear inside literal strings.

EXAMPLE 8.29
Character escapes in C and C++

C and C++ provide a very rich set of escape sequences. An arbitrary character can be represented by a backslash followed by (a) 1 to 3 octal (base 8) digits, (b) an `x` and one or more hexadecimal (base-16) digits, (c) a `u` and exactly four hexadecimal digits, or (d) a `U` and exactly eight hexadecimal digits. The `\U` notation is meant to capture the four-byte (32-bit) Unicode character set described in Sidebar 7.3. The `\u` notation is for characters in the Basic Multilingual Plane. Many of the most common control characters also have single-character escape sequences, many of which have been adopted by other languages as well. For example, `\n` is a line feed; `\t` is a tab; `\r` is a carriage return; `\\` is a backslash. C# omits the octal sequences of C and C++; Java also omits the 32-bit extended sequences. ■

The set of operations provided for strings is strongly tied to the implementation envisioned by the language designer(s). Several languages that do not in general allow arrays to change size dynamically do provide this flexibility for strings. The rationale is twofold. First, manipulation of variable-length strings is fundamental to a huge number of computer applications, and in some sense "deserves" special treatment. Second, the fact that strings are one-dimensional, have one-byte elements, and never contain references to anything else makes dynamic-size strings easier to implement than general dynamic arrays.

Some languages require that the length of a string-valued variable be bound no later than elaboration time, allowing the variable to be implemented as a contiguous array of characters in the current stack frame. Ada supports a few string operations, including assignment and comparison for lexicographic ordering. C, on the other hand, provides only the ability to create a pointer to a string literal. Because of C's unification of arrays and pointers, even assignment is not supported. Given the declaration `char *s`, the statement `s = "abc"` makes `s` point to the constant `"abc"` in static storage. If `s` is declared as an array, rather than a pointer (`char s[4]`), then the statement will trigger an error message from the compiler. To assign one array into another in C, the program must copy the characters individually. ■

EXAMPLE 8.30
`char*` assignment in C

Other languages allow the length of a string-valued variable to change over its lifetime, requiring that the variable be implemented as a block or chain of blocks in the heap. ML and Lisp provide strings as a built-in type. C++, Java, and C# provide them as predefined classes of object, in the formal, object-oriented sense. In all these languages a string variable is a *reference* to a string. Assigning a new value to such a variable makes it refer to a different object—each such object is immutable. Concatenation and other string operators implicitly create new objects. The space used by objects that are no longer reachable from any variable is reclaimed automatically.

8.4 Sets

A programming language set is an unordered collection of an arbitrary number of distinct values of a common type. Sets were introduced by Pascal, and have been supported by many subsequent languages. The type from which elements of a set are drawn is known as the *base* or *universe* type. Pascal sets were restricted to discrete base types, and overloaded `+`, `*`, and `-` to provide set union, intersection, and difference operations, respectively. The intended implementation was a *characteristic array*—a bit vector whose length (in bits) is the number of distinct values of the base type. A one in the *k*th position in the bit vector indicates that the *k*th element of the base type is a member of the set; a zero indicates that it is not. In a language that uses ASCII, a set of characters would occupy 128 bits—16 bytes. Operations on bit-vector sets can make use of fast logical instructions on most machines. Union is bit-wise `or`; intersection is bit-wise `and`; difference is bit-wise `not`, followed by bit-wise `and`. ■

EXAMPLE 8.31
Set types in Pascal

Unfortunately, bit vectors do not work well for large base types: a set of integers, represented as a bit vector, would consume some 500 megabytes on a 32-bit machine. With 64-bit integers, a bit-vector set would consume more memory than is currently contained on all the computers in the world. Because of this problem, some languages (including early versions of Pascal, though not the ISO standard) limited sets to base types of fewer than some fixed number of values.

For sets of elements drawn from a large universe, most modern languages use alternative implementations, whose size is proportional to the number of elements present, rather than to the number of values in the base type. Most languages also provide a built-in iterator (Section 6.5.3) to yield the elements of the set. A distinction is often made between *sorted* lists, whose base type must support some notion of ordering, and whose iterators yield the elements smallest-to-largest, and *unordered* lists, whose iterators yield the elements in arbitrary order. Ordered sets are commonly implemented with skip lists or various sorts of trees. Unordered sets are commonly implemented with hash tables.

Some languages (Python and Swift, for example) provide sets as a built-in type constructor. The Python version can be seen in Example 14.67. In many object-oriented languages, sets are supported by the standard library instead. A few languages and libraries have no built-in set constructor, but do provide associative arrays (also known as "hashes," "dictionaries," or "maps"). These can be used to emulate unordered sets, by mapping all (and only) the desired elements to some dummy value. In Go, for example, we can write

EXAMPLE 8.32
Emulating a set with a map in Go

```
my_set := make(map[int]bool)    // mapping from int to bool
my_set[3] = true                // inserts <3, true> in mapping
...
delete(my_set, i)               // removes <i, true>, if present
...
if my_set[j] { ...              // true if present
```

If `M` is a mapping from type D to type R in Go, and if `k` $\in D$ is not mapped to anything in R, the expression `M[k]` will return the "zero value" of type R. For Booleans, the zero value happens to be `false`, so the test in the last line of our example will return `false` if `j` is not in `my_set`. Deleting a no-longer-present element is preferable to mapping it explicitly to `false`, because deletion reclaims the space in the underlying hash table; mapping to `false` does not.

8.5 Pointers and Recursive Types

A recursive type is one whose objects may contain one or more references to other objects of the type. Most recursive types are records, since they need to contain something in addition to the reference, implying the existence of heterogeneous fields. Recursive types are used to build a wide variety of "linked" data structures, including lists and trees.

In languages that use a reference model of variables, it is easy for a record of type `foo` to include a reference to another record of type `foo`: every variable (and hence every record field) *is* a reference anyway. In languages that use a value model of variables, recursive types require the notion of a *pointer*: a variable (or field) whose value is a reference to some object. Pointers were first introduced in PL/I.

In some languages (e.g., Pascal, Modula-3, and Ada 83), pointers were restricted to point only to objects in the heap. The only way to create a new pointer value (without using variant records or casts to bypass the type system) was to call a built-in function that allocated a new object in the heap and returned a pointer to it. In other languages, both old and new, one can create a pointer to a nonheap object by using an "address of" operator. We will examine pointer operations and the ramifications of the reference and value models in more detail in the first subsection below.

In any language that permits new objects to be allocated from the heap, the question arises: how and when is storage reclaimed for objects that are no longer needed? In short-lived programs it may be acceptable simply to leave the storage unused, but in most cases unused space must be reclaimed, to make room for other things. A program that fails to reclaim the space for objects that are no longer needed is said to "leak memory." If such a program runs for an extended period of time, it may run out of space and crash.

Some languages, including C, C++, and Rust, require the programmer to reclaim space explicitly. Other languages, including Java, C#, Scala, Go, and all the functional and scripting languages, require the language implementation to reclaim unused objects automatically. Explicit storage reclamation simplifies the language implementation, but raises the possibility that the programmer will forget to reclaim objects that are no longer live (thereby leaking memory), or will accidentally reclaim objects that are still in use (thereby creating *dangling references*). Automatic storage reclamation (otherwise known as *garbage collection*) dramatically simplifies the programmer's task, but imposes certain run-time costs, and raises the question of how the language implementation is to distinguish garbage from active objects. We will discuss dangling references and garbage collection further in Sections 8.5.2 and 8.5.3, respectively.

8.5.1 Syntax and Operations

Operations on pointers include allocation and deallocation of objects in the heap, dereferencing of pointers to access the objects to which they point, and assign-

DESIGN & IMPLEMENTATION

8.6 Implementation of pointers

It is common for programmers (and even textbook writers) to equate pointers with addresses, but this is a mistake. A pointer is a high-level concept: a reference to an object. An address is a low-level concept: the location of a word in memory. Pointers are often implemented as addresses, but not always. On a machine with a *segmented* memory architecture, a pointer may consist of a segment id and an offset within the segment. In a language that attempts to catch uses of dangling references, a pointer may contain both an address and an access key.

ment of one pointer into another. The behavior of these operations depends heavily on whether the language is functional or imperative, and on whether it employs a reference or value model for variables/names.

Functional languages generally employ a reference model for names (a purely functional language has no variables or assignments). Objects in a functional language tend to be allocated automatically as needed, with a structure determined by the language implementation. Variables in an imperative language may use either a value or a reference model, or some combination of the two. In C or Ada, which employ a value model, the assignment `A = B` puts the value of `B` into `A`. If we want `B` to refer to an object, and we want `A = B` to make `A` refer to the object to which `B` refers, then `A` and `B` must be pointers. In Smalltalk or Ruby, which employ a reference model, the assignment `A = B` always makes `A` refer to the same object to which `B` refers.

Java charts an intermediate course, in which the usual implementation of the reference model is made explicit in the language semantics. Variables of built-in Java types (integers, floating-point numbers, characters, and Booleans) employ a value model; variables of user-defined types (strings, arrays, and other objects in the object-oriented sense of the word) employ a reference model. The assignment `A = B` in Java places the value of `B` into `A` if `A` and `B` are of built-in type; it makes `A` refer to the object to which `B` refers if `A` and `B` are of user-defined type. C# mirrors Java by default, but additional language features, explicitly labeled "`unsafe`," allow systems programmers to use pointers when desired.

Reference Model

EXAMPLE 8.33
Tree type in OCaml

In ML-family languages, the *variant* mechanism can be used to declare recursive types (shown here in OCaml syntax):

```
type chr_tree = Empty | Node of char * chr_tree * chr_tree;;
```

Here a `chr_tree` is either an `Empty` leaf or a `Node` consisting of a character and two child trees. (Further details can be found in Section 11.4.3.)

It is natural in OCaml to include a `chr_tree` within a `chr_tree` because every variable is a reference. The tree `Node ('R', Node ('X', Empty, Empty), Node ('Y', Node ('Z', Empty, Empty), Node ('W', Empty, Empty)))` would most likely be represented in memory as shown in Figure 8.11. Each individual rectangle in the right-hand portion of this figure represents a block of storage allocated from the heap. In effect, the tree is a tuple (record) tagged to indicate that it is a `Node`. This tuple in turn refers to two other tuples that are also tagged as `Node`s. At the fringe of the tree are tuples that are tagged as `Empty`; these contain no further references. Because all `Empty` tuples are the same, the implementation is free to use just one, and to have every reference point to it. ■

EXAMPLE 8.34
Tree type in Lisp

In Lisp, which uses a reference model of variables but is not statically typed, our tree could be specified textually as `'(#\R (#\X ()()) (#\Y (#\Z ()()) (#\W ()())))`. Each level of parentheses brackets the elements of a *list*. In this case, the outermost such list contains three elements: the character `R` and nested

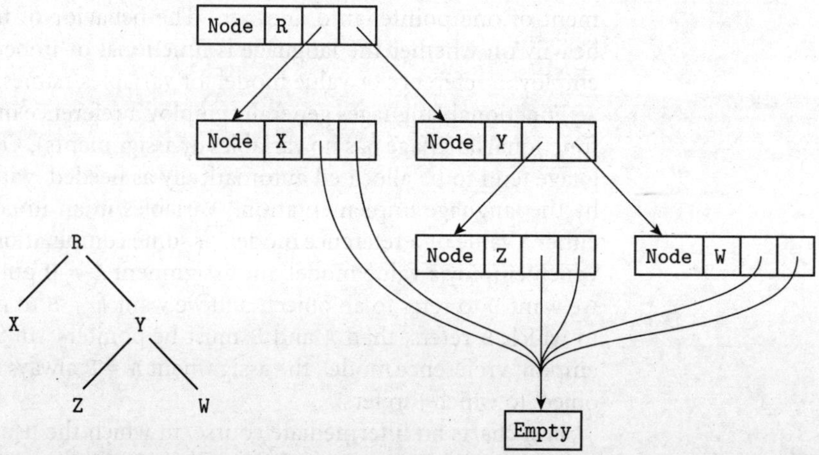

Figure 8.11 Implementation of a tree in ML. The abstract (conceptual) tree is shown at the lower left.

lists to represent the left and right subtrees. (The prefix #\ notation serves the same purpose as surrounding quotes in other languages.) Semantically, each list is a pair of references: one to the head and one to the remainder of the list. As we noted in Section 8.5.1, these semantics are almost always reflected in the implementation by a `cons` cell containing two pointers. A binary tree can thus be represented as a three-element (three `cons` cell) list, as shown in Figure 8.12. At the top level of the figure, the first `cons` cell points to `R`; the second and third point to nested lists representing the left and right subtrees. Each block of memory is tagged to indicate whether it is a `cons` cell or an *atom*. An atom is anything other than a `cons` cell; that is, an object of a built-in type (integer, real, character, string, etc.), or a user-defined structure (record) or array. The uniformity of Lisp lists (everything is a `cons` cell or an atom) makes it easy to write polymorphic functions, though without the static type checking of ML. ■

If one programs in a purely functional style in ML or in Lisp, the data structures created with recursive types turn out to be acyclic. New objects refer to old ones, but old ones never change, and thus never point to new ones. Circular structures are typically defined by using the imperative features of the languages. (For an exception to this rule, see Exercise 8.21.) In ML, the imperative features include an explicit notion of pointer, discussed briefly under "Value Model" below.

EXAMPLE 8.35
Mutually recursive types in OCaml

Even when writing in a functional style, one often finds a need for *types* that are *mutually recursive*. In a compiler, for example, it is likely that symbol table records and syntax tree nodes will need to refer to each other. A syntax tree node that represents a subroutine call will need to refer to the symbol table record that represents the subroutine. The symbol table record, for its part, will need to refer to the syntax tree node at the root of the subtree that represents the subroutine's code. If types are declared one at a time, and if names must be declared before they can be used, then whichever mutually recursive type is declared first will be

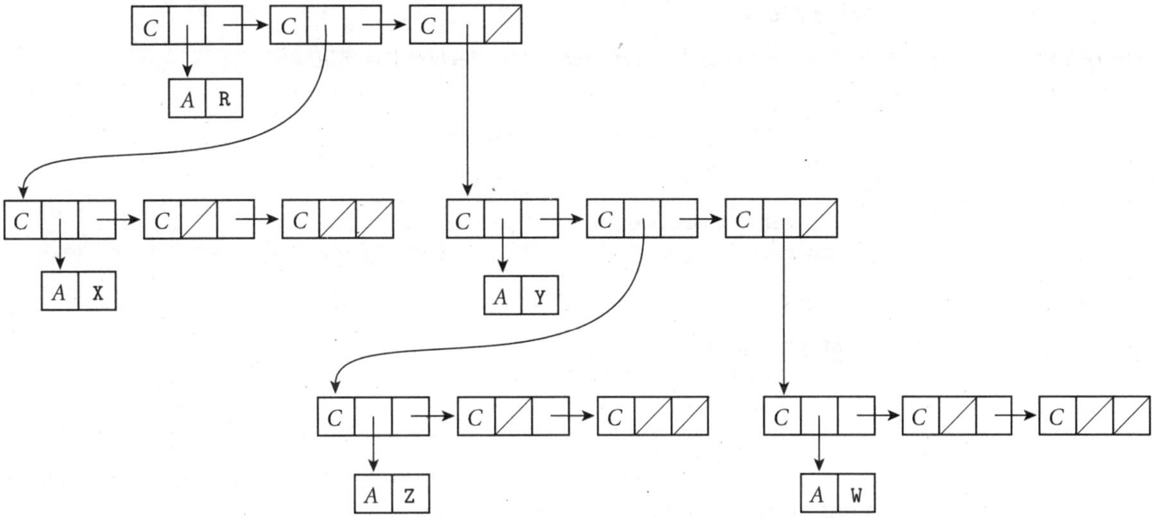

Figure 8.12 **Implementation of a tree in Lisp.** A diagonal slash through a box indicates a null pointer. The *C* and *A* tags serve to distinguish the two kinds of memory blocks: cons cells and blocks containing atoms.

unable to refer to the other. ML family languages address this problem by allowing types to be declared together as a group. Using OCaml syntax,

```
type subroutine_info = {code: syn_tree_node; ...}   (* record *)
 and subr_call_info  = {subr: sym_tab_rec; ...}     (* record *)
 and sym_tab_rec =                                  (* variant *)
    Variable of ...
  | Type of ...
  | ...
  | Subroutine of subroutine_info
 and syn_tree_node =                                (* variant *)
    Expression of ...
  | Loop of ...
  | ...
  | Subr_call of subr_call_info;;
```

Mutually recursive types of this sort are trivial in Lisp, since it is dynamically typed. (Common Lisp includes a notion of structures, but field types are not declared. In simpler Lisp dialects programmers use nested lists in which fields are merely positional conventions.) ■

Value Model

EXAMPLE 8.36
Tree types in Ada and C

In Ada, our tree data type would be declared as follows:

```
type chr_tree;
type chr_tree_ptr is access chr_tree;
type chr_tree is record
    left, right : chr_tree_ptr;
    val : character;
end record;
```

In C, the equivalent declaration is

```
struct chr_tree {
    struct chr_tree *left, *right;
    char val;
};
```

As mentioned in Section 3.3.3, Ada and C both rely on incomplete type declarations to accommodate recursive definition. ■

EXAMPLE 8.37
Allocating heap nodes

No aggregate syntax is available for linked data structures in Ada or C; a tree must be constructed node by node. To allocate a new node from the heap, the programmer calls a built-in function. In Ada:

```
my_ptr := new chr_tree;
```

In C:

```
my_ptr = malloc(sizeof(struct chr_tree));
```

C's `malloc` is defined as a library function, not a built-in part of the language (though many compilers recognize and optimize it as a special case). The programmer must specify the size of the allocated object explicitly, and while the return value (of type `void*`) can be assigned into any pointer, the assignment is not type safe. ■

EXAMPLE 8.38
Object-oriented allocation of heap nodes

C++, Java, and C# replace `malloc` with a built-in, type-safe `new`:

```
my_ptr = new chr_tree( arg_list );
```

In addition to "knowing" the size of the requested type, the C++/Java/C# `new` will automatically call any user-specified *constructor* (initialization) function, passing the specified argument list. In a similar but less flexible vein, Ada's `new` may specify an initial value for the allocated object:

```
my_ptr := new chr_tree'(null, null, 'X');
```

■

EXAMPLE 8.39
Pointer-based tree

After we have allocated and linked together appropriate nodes in C or Ada, our tree example is likely to be implemented as shown in Figure 8.13. A leaf is distinguished from an internal node simply by the fact that its two pointer fields are null. ■

EXAMPLE 8.40
Pointer dereferencing

To access the object referred to by a pointer, most languages use an explicit dereferencing operator. In Pascal and Modula this operator took the form of a postfix "up-arrow":

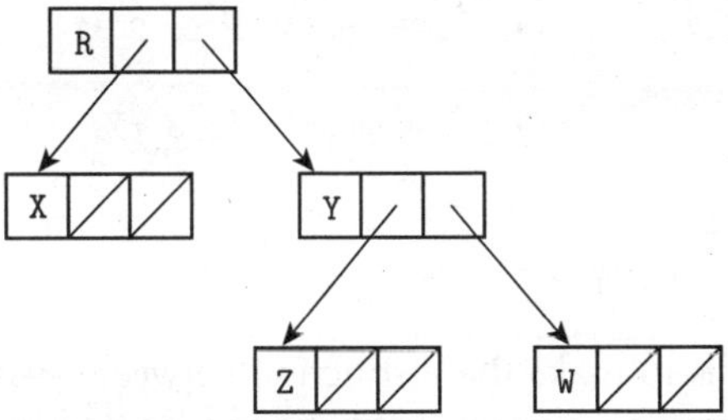

Figure 8.13 Typical implementation of a tree in a language with explicit pointers. As in Figure 8.12, a diagonal slash through a box indicates a null pointer.

```
my_ptr^.val := 'X';
```

In C it is a prefix star:

```
(*my_ptr).val = 'X';
```

Because pointers so often refer to records (`structs`), for which the prefix notation is awkward, C also provides a postfix "right-arrow" operator that plays the role of the "up-arrow dot" combination in Pascal:

```
my_ptr->val = 'X';
```

EXAMPLE 8.41
Implicit dereferencing in Ada

On the assumption that pointers almost always refer to records, Ada dispenses with dereferencing altogether. The same dot-based syntax can be used to access either a field of the record `foo` or a field of the record *pointed to* by `foo`, depending on the type of `foo`:

```
T : chr_tree;
P : chr_tree_ptr;
...
T.val := 'X';
P.val := 'Y';
```

In those cases in which one actually wants to name the *entire* object referred to by a pointer, Ada provides a special "pseudofield" called `all`:

```
T := P.all;
```

In essence, pointers in Ada are automatically dereferenced when needed.

EXAMPLE 8.42
Pointer dereferencing in OCaml

The imperative features of OCaml and other ML dialects include an assignment statement, but this statement requires that the left-hand side be a pointer: its effect is to make the pointer refer to the object on the right-hand side. To access the object referred to by a pointer, one uses an exclamation point as a prefix dereferencing operator:

```
let p = ref 2;;        (* p is a pointer to 2 *)
...
p := 3;;               (* p now points to 3 *)
...
let n = !p in ...
    (* n is simply 3 *)
```

The net result is to make the distinction between l-values and r-values very explicit. Most languages blur the distinction by implicitly dereferencing variables on the right-hand side of every assignment statement. Ada and Go blur the distinction further by dereferencing pointers automatically in certain circumstances. ■

The imperative features of Lisp do not include a dereferencing operator. Since every object has a self-evident type, and assignment is performed using a small set of built-in operators, there is never any ambiguity as to what is intended.

EXAMPLE 8.43
Assignment in Lisp

Assignment in Common Lisp employs the `setf` operator (Scheme uses `set!`, `set-car!`, and `set-cdr!`), rather than the more common = or `:=`. For example, if `foo` refers to a list, then `(cdr foo)` is the right-hand ("rest of list") pointer of the first node in the list, and the assignment `(set-cdr! foo foo)` makes this pointer refer back to `foo`, creating a one-node circular list:

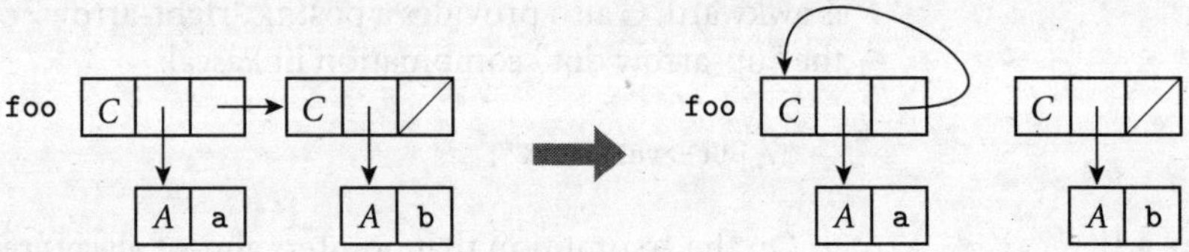

■

Pointers and Arrays in C

EXAMPLE 8.44
Array names and pointers in C

Pointers and arrays are closely linked in C. Consider the following declarations:

```
int n;
int *a;                 /* pointer to integer */
int b[10];              /* array of 10 integers */
```

Now all of the following are valid:

```
1.  a = b;              /* make a point to the initial element of b */
2.  n = a[3];
3.  n = *(a+3);         /* equivalent to previous line */
4.  n = b[3];
5.  n = *(b+3);         /* equivalent to previous line */
```

In most contexts, an unsubscripted array name in C is automatically converted to a pointer to the array's first element (the one with index zero), as shown here in line 1. (Line 5 embodies the same conversion.) Lines 3 and 5 illustrate *pointer arithmetic*: Given a pointer to an element of an array, the addition of an integer *k* produces a pointer to the element *k* positions later in the array (earlier if *k* is negative). The prefix * is a pointer dereference operator. Pointer arithmetic is valid only within the bounds of a single array, but C compilers are not required to check this.

Remarkably, the subscript operator `[]` in C is actually defined in terms of pointer arithmetic: lines 2 and 4 are syntactic sugar for lines 3 and 5, respectively. More precisely, `E1[E2]`, for any expressions `E1` and `E2`, is defined to be `(*((E1)+(E2)))`, which is of course the same as `(*((E2)+(E1)))`. (Extra parentheses have been used in this definition to avoid any questions of precedence if `E1` and `E2` are complicated expressions.) Correctness requires only that one operand of `[]` have an array or pointer type and the other have an integral type. Thus `A[3]` is equivalent to `3[A]`, something that comes as a surprise to most programmers. ■

DESIGN & IMPLEMENTATION

8.7 Stack smashing

The lack of bounds checking on array subscripts and pointer arithmetic is a major source of bugs and security problems in C. Many of the most infamous Internet viruses have propagated by means of *stack smashing*, a particularly nasty form of *buffer overflow attack*. Consider a (very naive) routine designed to read a number from an input stream:

```
int get_acct_num(FILE *s) {
    char buf[100];
    char *p = buf;
    do {
        /* read from stream s: */
        *p = getc(s);
    } while (*p++ != '\n');
    *p = '\0';
    /* convert ascii to int: */
    return atoi(buf);
}
```

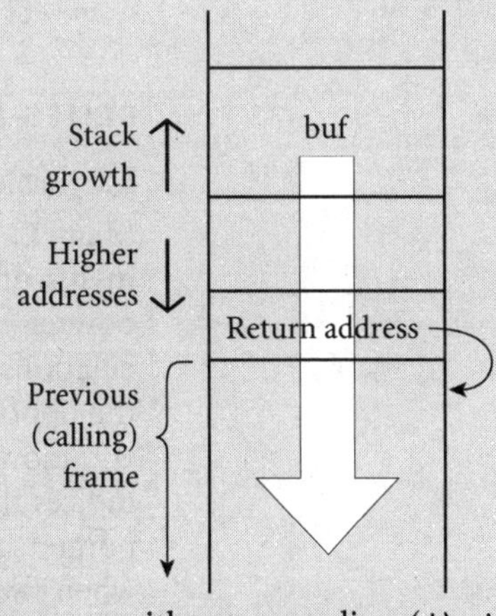

If the stream provides more than 100 characters without a newline (`'\n'`), those characters will overwrite memory beyond the confines of `buf`, as shown by the large white arrow in the figure. A careful attacker may be able to invent a string whose bits include both a sequence of valid machine instructions and a replacement value for the subroutine's return address. When the routine attempts to return, it will jump into the attacker's instructions instead.

Stack smashing can be prevented by manually checking array bounds in C, or by configuring the hardware to prevent the execution of instructions in the stack (see Sidebar C-9.10). It would never have been a problem in the first place, however, if C had been designed for automatic bounds checks.

EXAMPLE 8.45

Pointer comparison and subtraction in C

In addition to allowing an integer to be added to a pointer, C allows pointers to be subtracted from one another or compared for ordering, provided that they refer to elements of the same array. The comparison `p < q`, for example, tests to see if `p` refers to an element closer to the beginning of the array than the one referred to by `q`. The expression `p - q` returns the number of array positions that separate the elements to which `p` and `q` refer. All arithmetic operations on pointers "scale" their results as appropriate, based on the size of the referenced objects. For multidimensional arrays with row-pointer layout, `a[i][j]` is equivalent to `(*(a+i))[j]` or `*(a[i]+j)` or `*(*(a+i)+j)`. ■

EXAMPLE 8.46

Pointer and array declarations in C

Despite the interoperability of pointers and arrays in C, programmers need to be aware that the two are not the same, particularly in the context of variable declarations, which need to allocate space when elaborated. The declaration of a pointer variable allocates space to hold a pointer, while the declaration of an array variable allocates space to hold the whole array. In the case of an array the declaration must specify a size for each dimension. Thus `int *a[n]`, when elaborated, will allocate space for *n* row pointers; `int a[n][m]` will allocate space for a two-dimensional array with contiguous layout.[5] As a convenience, a variable declaration that includes initialization to an aggregate can omit the size of the outermost dimension if that information can be inferred from the contents of the aggregate:

```
int a[][2] = {{1, 2}, {3, 4}, {5, 6}};    // three rows
```
■

DESIGN & IMPLEMENTATION

8.8 Pointers and arrays

Many C programs use pointers instead of subscripts to iterate over the elements of arrays. Before the development of modern optimizing compilers, pointer-based array traversal often served to eliminate redundant address calculations, thereby leading to faster code. With modern compilers, however, the opposite may be true: redundant address calculations can be identified as common subexpressions, and certain other code improvements are easier for indices than they are for pointers. In particular, as we shall see in Chapter 17, pointers make it significantly more difficult for the code improver to determine when two l-values may be *aliases* for one other.

Today the use of pointer arithmetic is mainly a matter of personal taste: some C programmers consider pointer-based algorithms to be more elegant than their array-based counterparts, while others find them harder to read. Certainly the fact that arrays are passed as pointers makes it natural to write subroutines in the pointer style.

---

5 To read declarations in C, it is helpful to follow the following rule: start at the name of the variable and work right as far as possible, subject to parentheses; then work left as far as possible; then jump out a level of parentheses and repeat. Thus `int *a[n]` means that `a` is an *n*-element array of pointers to integers, while `int (*a)[n]` means that `a` is a pointer to an *n*-element array of integers.

EXAMPLE 8.47
Arrays as parameters in C

When an array is included in the argument list of a function call, C passes a pointer to the first element of the array, not the array itself. For a one-dimensional array of integers, the corresponding formal parameter may be declared as `int a[]` or `int *a`. For a two-dimensional array of integers with row-pointer layout, the formal parameter may be declared as `int *a[]` or `int **a`. For a two-dimensional array with contiguous layout, the formal parameter may be declared as `int a[][m]` or `int (*a)[m]`. The size of the first dimension is irrelevant; all that is passed is a pointer, and C performs no dynamic checks to ensure that references are within the bounds of the array. ■

In all cases, a declaration must allow the compiler (or human reader) to determine the size of the *elements* of an array or, equivalently, the size of the objects referred to by a pointer. Thus neither `int a[][]` nor `int (*a)[]` is a valid variable or parameter declaration: neither provides the compiler with the size information it needs to generate code for `a + i` or `a[i]`.

EXAMPLE 8.48
`sizeof` in C

The built-in `sizeof` operator returns the size in bytes of an object or type. When given an array as argument it returns the size of the entire array. When given a pointer as argument it returns the size of the pointer itself. If `a` is an array, `sizeof(a) / sizeof(a[0])` returns the number of elements in the array. Similarly, if pointers occupy 4 bytes and double-precision floating-point numbers occupy 8 bytes, then given

```
double *a;          /* pointer to double */
double (*b)[10];    /* pointer to array of 10 doubles */
```

we have `sizeof(a)` = `sizeof(b)` = 4, `sizeof(*a)` = `sizeof(*b[0])` = 8, and `sizeof(*b)` = 80. In most cases, `sizeof` can be evaluated at compile time. The principal exception occurs for variable-length arrays, whose size may not be known until elaboration time:

```
void f(int len) {
    int A[len];         /* sizeof(A) == len * sizeof(int) */
```
■

✓ CHECK YOUR UNDERSTANDING

17. Name three languages that provide particularly extensive support for character strings.

18. Why might a language permit operations on strings that it does not provide for arrays?

19. What are the strengths and weaknesses of the bit-vector representation for sets? How else might sets be implemented?

20. Discuss the tradeoffs between pointers and the recursive types that arise naturally in a language with a reference model of variables.

21. Summarize the ways in which one dereferences a pointer in various programming languages.

22. What is the difference between a *pointer* and an *address*? Between a pointer and a *reference*?

23. Discuss the advantages and disadvantages of the interoperability of pointers and arrays in C.

24. Under what circumstances must the bounds of a C array be specified in its declaration?

8.5.2 Dangling References

When a heap-allocated object is no longer live, a long-running program needs to reclaim the object's space. Stack objects are reclaimed automatically as part of the subroutine calling sequence. How are heap objects reclaimed? There are two alternatives. Languages like C, C++, and Rust require the programmer to reclaim an object explicitly. In C, for example, one says `free(my_ptr);` in C++, `delete my_ptr`. C++ provides additional functionality: prior to reclaiming the space, it automatically calls any user-provided *destructor* function for the object. A destructor can reclaim space for subsidiary objects, remove the object from indices or tables, print messages, or perform any other operation appropriate at the end of the object's lifetime.

EXAMPLE 8.49 Explicit storage reclamation

A *dangling reference* is a live pointer that no longer points to a valid object. In languages like C and C++, which allow the programmer to create pointers to stack objects, a dangling reference may be created when a subroutine returns while some pointer in a wider scope still refers to a local object of that subroutine:

EXAMPLE 8.50 Dangling reference to a stack variable in C++

```
int i = 3;
int *p = &i;
...
void foo() { int n = 5;  p = &n; }
...
cout << *p;                    // prints 3
foo();
...
cout << *p;                    // undefined behavior: n is no longer live
```

EXAMPLE 8.51 Dangling reference to a heap variable in C++

In a language with explicit reclamation of heap objects, a dangling reference is created whenever the programmer reclaims an object to which pointers still refer:

```
int *p = new int;
*p = 3;
...
cout << *p;          // prints 3
delete p;
...
cout << *p;          // undefined behavior: *p has been reclaimed
```

Note that even if the reclamation operation were to change its argument to a null pointer, this would not solve the problem, because *other* pointers might still refer to the same object.

Because a language implementation may reuse the space of reclaimed stack and heap objects, a program that uses a dangling reference may read or write bits in memory that are now part of some other object. It may even modify bits that are now part of the implementation's bookkeeping information, corrupting the structure of the stack or heap.

Algol 68 addressed the problem of dangling references to stack objects by forbidding a pointer from pointing to any object whose lifetime was briefer than that of the pointer itself. Unfortunately, this rule is difficult to enforce. Among other things, since both pointers and objects to which pointers might refer can be passed as arguments to subroutines, dynamic semantic checks are possible only if reference parameters are accompanied by a hidden indication of lifetime. Ada has a more restrictive rule that is easier to enforce: it forbids a pointer from pointing to any object whose lifetime is briefer than that of the pointer's *type*.

IN MORE DEPTH

On the companion site we consider two mechanisms that are sometimes used to catch dangling references at run time. *Tombstones* introduce an extra level of indirection on every pointer access. When an object is reclaimed, the indirection word (tombstone) is marked in a way that invalidates future references to the object. *Locks* and *keys* add a word to every pointer and to every object in the heap; these words must match for the pointer to be valid. Tombstones can be used in languages that permit pointers to nonheap objects, but they introduce the secondary problem of reclaiming the tombstones themselves. Locks and keys are somewhat simpler, but they work only for objects in the heap.

8.5.3 Garbage Collection

Explicit reclamation of heap objects is a serious burden on the programmer and a major source of bugs (memory leaks and dangling references). The code required to keep track of object lifetimes makes programs more difficult to design, implement, and maintain. An attractive alternative is to have the language implementation notice when objects are no longer useful and reclaim them automatically.

Automatic reclamation (otherwise known as *garbage collection*) is more or less essential for functional languages: `delete` is a very imperative sort of operation, and the ability to construct and return arbitrary objects from functions means that many objects that would be allocated on the stack in an imperative language must be allocated from the heap in a functional language, to give them unlimited extent.

Over time, automatic garbage collection has become popular for imperative languages as well. It can be found in, among others, Java, C#, Scala, Go, and all the major scripting languages. Automatic collection is difficult to implement, but the difficulty pales in comparison to the convenience enjoyed by programmers once the implementation exists. Automatic collection also tends to be slower than manual reclamation, though it eliminates any need to check for dangling references.

Reference Counts

When is an object no longer useful? One possible answer is: when no pointers to it exist.[6] The simplest garbage collection technique simply places a counter in each object that keeps track of the number of pointers that refer to the object. When the object is created, this *reference count* is set to one, to represent the pointer

DESIGN & IMPLEMENTATION

8.9 Garbage collection

Garbage collection presents a classic tradeoff between convenience and safety on the one hand and performance on the other. Manual storage reclamation, implemented correctly by the application program, is almost invariably faster than any automatic garbage collector. It is also more predictable: automatic collection is notorious for its tendency to introduce intermittent "hiccups" in the execution of real-time or interactive programs.

Ada takes the unusual position of refusing to take a stand: the language design makes automatic garbage collection possible, but implementations are not required to provide it, and programmers can request manual reclamation with a built-in routine called `Unchecked_Deallocation`. Newer versions of the language provide extensive facilities whereby programmers can implement their own storage managers (garbage collected or not), with different types of pointers corresponding to different storage "pools."

In a similar vein, the Real Time Specification for Java allows the programmer to create so-called *scoped memory* areas that are accessible to only a subset of the currently running threads. When all threads with access to a given area terminate, the area is reclaimed in its entirety. Objects allocated in a scoped memory area are never examined by the garbage collector; performance anomalies due to garbage collection can therefore be avoided by providing scoped memory to every real-time thread.

6 Throughout the following discussion we will use the pointer-based terminology of languages with a value model of variables. The techniques apply equally well, however, to languages with a reference model of variables.

returned by the `new` operation. When one pointer is assigned into another, the run-time system decrements the reference count of the object (if any) formerly referred to by the assignment's left-hand side, and increments the count of the object referred to by the right-hand side. On subroutine return, the calling sequence epilogue must decrement the reference count of any object referred to by a local pointer that is about to be destroyed. When a reference count reaches zero, its object can be reclaimed. Recursively, the run-time system must decrement counts for any objects referred to by pointers within the object being reclaimed, and reclaim those objects if their counts reach zero. To prevent the collector from following garbage addresses, each pointer must be initialized to null at elaboration time.

In order for reference counts to work, the language implementation must be able to identify the location of every pointer. When a subroutine returns, it must be able to tell which words in the stack frame represent pointers; when an object in the heap is reclaimed, it must be able to tell which words within the object represent pointers. The standard technique to track this information relies on *type descriptors* generated by the compiler. There is one descriptor for every distinct type in the program, plus one for the stack frame of each subroutine, and one for the set of global variables. Most descriptors are simply a table that lists the offsets within the type at which pointers can be found, together with the addresses of descriptors for the types of the objects referred to by those pointers. For a tagged variant record (discriminated union) type, the descriptor is a bit more complicated: it must contain a list of values (or ranges) for the tag, together with a table for the corresponding variant. For *untagged* variant records, there is no acceptable solution: reference counts work only if the language is strongly typed (but see the discussion of "Conservative Collection" at the end of Section 8.5.3).

EXAMPLE 8.52
Reference counts and circular structures

The most important problem with reference counts stems from their definition of a "useful object." While it is definitely true that an object is useless if no references to it exist, it may also be useless when references *do* exist. As shown in Figure 8.14, reference counts may fail to collect circular structures. They work well only for structures that are guaranteed to be noncircular. Many language implementations use reference counts for variable-length strings; strings never contain references to anything else. Perl uses reference counts for all dynamically allocated data; the manual warns the programmer to break cycles manually when data aren't needed anymore. Some purely functional languages may also be able to use reference counts safely in all cases, if the lack of an assignment statement prevents them from introducing circularity. Finally, reference counts can be used to reclaim tombstones. While it is certainly possible to create a circular structure with tombstones, the fact that the programmer is responsible for explicit deallocation of heap objects implies that reference counts will fail to reclaim tombstones only when the programmer has failed to reclaim the objects to which they refer. ■

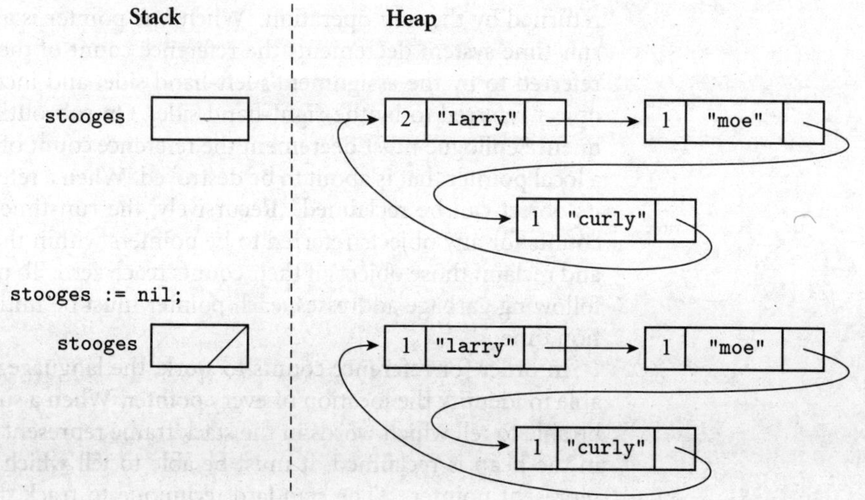

Figure 8.14 **Reference counts and circular lists.** The list shown here cannot be found via any program variable, but because it is circular, every cell contains a nonzero count.

Smart Pointers The general term *smart pointer* refers to a program-level object (implemented on top of the language proper) that mimics the behavior of a pointer, but with additional semantics. The most common use of smart pointers is to implement reference counting in a language that normally supports only manual storage reclamation. Other uses include bounds checking on pointer arithmetic, instrumentation for debugging or performance analysis, and tracking of references to external objects—e.g., open files.

Particularly rich support for smart pointers can be found in the C++ standard library, whose `unique_ptr`, `shared_ptr`, and `weak_ptr` classes leverage operator overloading, constructors, destructors, and *move semantics* to simplify the otherwise difficult task of manual reclamation. A `unique_ptr` is what its name implies—the only reference to an object. If the `unique_ptr` is destroyed (typically because the function in which it was declared returns), then the object to which it points is reclaimed by the pointer's destructor, as suggested in Section 8.5.2. If one `unique_ptr` is assigned into another (or passed as a parameter), the overloaded assignment operator or constructor *transfers* ownership of the pointed-to object by changing the old pointer to `null`. (Move semantics, which we will describe in more detail in under "References in C++" in Section 9.3.1, often allow the compiler to optimize away the cost of the ownership transfer.)

The `shared_ptr` type implements a reference count for the pointed-to object, typically storing it in a hidden, tombstone-like intermediate object. Counts are incremented in `shared_ptr` constructors, decremented in destructors, and adjusted (in both directions) by assignment operations. When circular structures are required, or when the programmer wants to maintain bookkeeping information without artificially extending object lifetimes, a `weak_ptr` can be used to point to an object *without* contributing to reference counting. The C++ library will reclaim an object when no `shared_ptr` to it remains; any remaining `weak_ptr`s will subsequently behave as if they were `null`.

Tracing Collection

As we have seen, reference counting defines an object to be useful if there exists a pointer to it. A better definition might say that an object is useful if it can be reached by following a chain of valid pointers starting from something that has a name (i.e., something outside the heap). According to this definition, the blocks in the bottom half of Figure 8.14 are useless, even though their reference counts are nonzero. Tracing collectors work by recursively exploring the heap, starting from external pointers, to determine what is useful.

Mark-and-Sweep The classic mechanism to identify useless blocks, under this more accurate definition, is known as *mark-and-sweep*. It proceeds in three main steps, executed by the garbage collector when the amount of free space remaining in the heap falls below some minimum threshold:

1. The collector walks through the heap, tentatively marking every block as "useless."

DESIGN & IMPLEMENTATION

8.10 What exactly is garbage?

Reference counting implicitly defines a garbage object as one to which no pointers exist. Tracing implicitly defines it as an object that is no longer reachable from outside the heap. Ideally, we'd like an even stronger definition: a garbage object is one that the program will never use again. We settle for nonreachability because this ideal definition is undecidable. The difference can matter in practice: if a program maintains a pointer to an object it will never use again, then the garbage collector will be unable to reclaim it. If the number of such objects grows with time, then the program has a memory leak, despite the presence of a garbage collector. (Trivially we could imagine a program that added every newly allocated object to a global list, but never actually perused the list. Such a program would defeat the collector entirely.)

For the sake of space efficiency, programmers are advised to "zero out" any pointers they no longer need. Doing this can be difficult, but not as difficult as fully manually reclamation—in particular, we do not need to realize when we are zeroing the *last* pointer to a given object. For the same reason, dangling references can never arise: the garbage collector will refrain from reclaiming any object that is reachable along some other path.

2. Beginning with all pointers outside the heap, the collector recursively explores all linked data in the program, marking each newly discovered block as "useful." (When it encounters a block that is already marked as "useful," the collector knows it has reached the block over some previous path, and returns without recursing.)
3. The collector again walks through the heap, moving every block that is still marked "useless" to the free list.

Several potential problems with this algorithm are immediately apparent. First, both the initial and final walks through the heap require that the collector be able to tell where every "in-use" block begins and ends. In a language with variable-size heap blocks, every block must begin with an indication of its size, and of whether it is currently free. Second, the collector must be able in Step 2 to find the pointers contained within each block. The standard solution is to place a pointer to a type descriptor near the beginning of each block.

Pointer Reversal The exploration step (Step 2) of mark-and-sweep collection is naturally recursive. The obvious implementation needs a stack whose maximum depth is proportional to the longest chain through the heap. In practice, the space for this stack may not be available: after all, we run garbage collection when we're about to run out of space![7] An alternative implementation of the exploration step uses a technique first suggested by Schorr and Waite [SW67] to embed the equivalent of the stack in already-existing fields in heap blocks. More specifically, as the collector explores the path to a given block, it *reverses* the pointers it follows, so that each points *back* to the previous block instead of forward to the next. This pointer-reversal technique is illustrated in Figure 8.15. As it explores, the collector keeps track of the current block and the block from whence it came.

EXAMPLE 8.53
Heap tracing with pointer reversal

To return from block X to block U (after part (d) of the figure), the collector will use the reversed pointer in U to restore its notion of previous block (T). It will then flip the reversed pointer back to X and update its notion of current block to U. If the block to which it has returned contains additional pointers, the collector will proceed forward again; otherwise it will return across the previous reversed pointer and try again. At most one pointer in every block will be reversed at any given time. This pointer must be marked, probably by means of another bookkeeping field at the beginning of each block. (We could mark the pointer by setting one of its low-order bits, but the cost in time would probably be prohibitive: we'd have to search the block on every visit.) ■

Stop-and-Copy In a language with variable-size heap blocks, the garbage collector can reduce external fragmentation by performing storage compaction.

7 In many language implementations, the stack and heap grow toward each other from opposite ends of memory (Section 15.4); if the heap is full, the stack can't grow. In a system with virtual memory the distance between the two may theoretically be enormous, but the space that backs them up on disk is still limited, and shared between them.

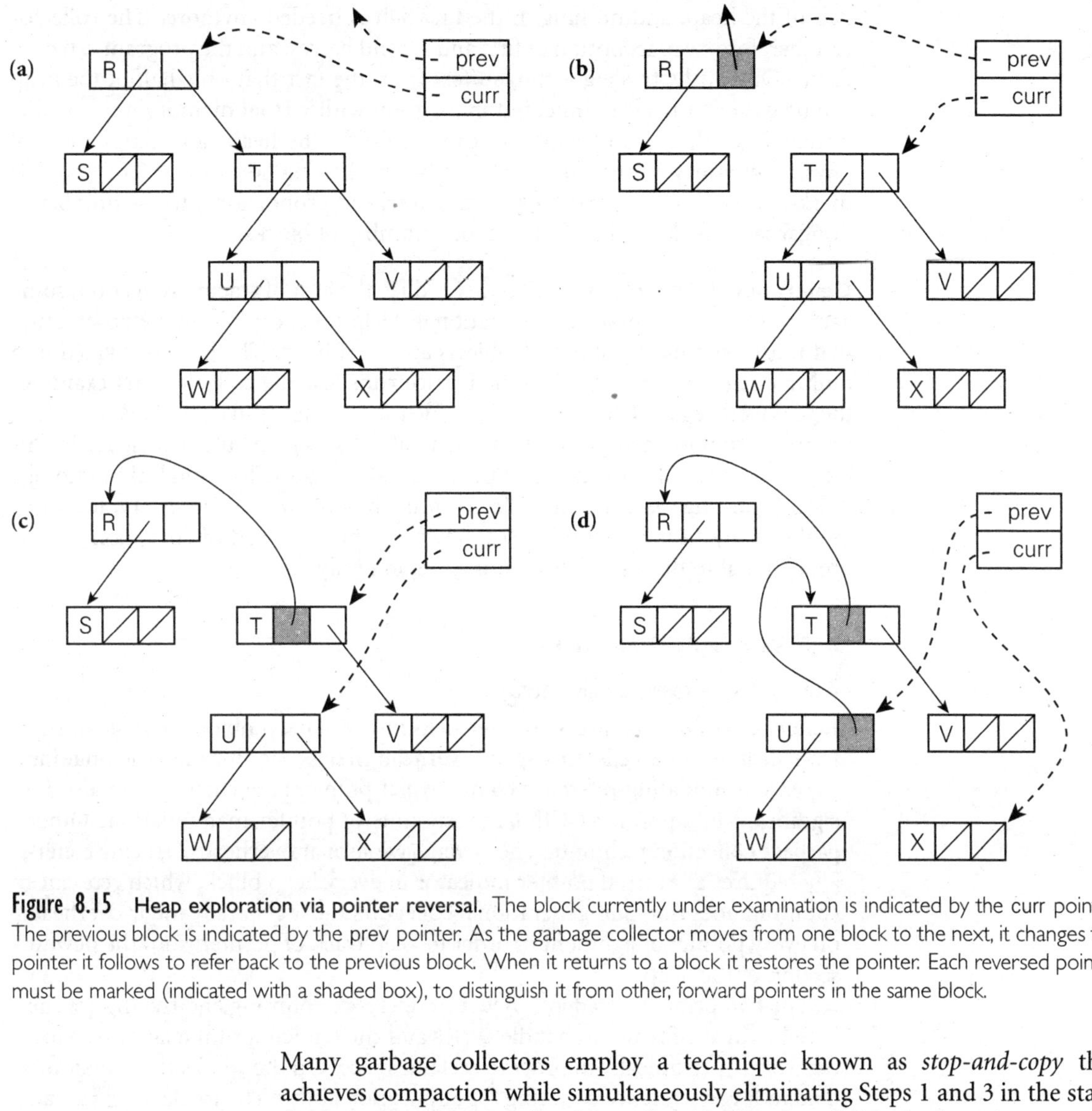

Figure 8.15 **Heap exploration via pointer reversal.** The block currently under examination is indicated by the curr pointer. The previous block is indicated by the prev pointer. As the garbage collector moves from one block to the next, it changes the pointer it follows to refer back to the previous block. When it returns to a block it restores the pointer. Each reversed pointer must be marked (indicated with a shaded box), to distinguish it from other, forward pointers in the same block.

Many garbage collectors employ a technique known as *stop-and-copy* that achieves compaction while simultaneously eliminating Steps 1 and 3 in the standard mark-and-sweep algorithm. Specifically, they divide the heap into two regions of equal size. All allocation happens in the first half. When this half is (nearly) full, the collector begins its exploration of reachable data structures. Each reachable block is copied into contiguous locations in the second half of the heap, with no external fragmentation. The old version of the block, in the first half of the heap, is overwritten with a "useful" flag and a pointer to the new location. Any other pointer that refers to the same block (and is found later in the exploration) is set to point to the new location. When the collector finishes its exploration, all useful objects have been moved (and compacted) into the second half of the heap, and nothing in the first half is needed anymore. The collector can therefore swap its notion of first and second halves, and the program can continue. Obviously, this algorithm suffers from the fact that only half of the heap can be used at any given time, but in a system with virtual memory it is only the virtual space that is underutilized; each "half" of the heap can occupy most of physical memory as needed. Moreover, by eliminating Steps 1 and 3 of standard mark-and-sweep, stop-and-copy incurs overhead proportional to the number of nongarbage blocks, rather than the total number of blocks.

Generational Collection To further reduce the cost of tracing collection, some garbage collectors employ a "generational" technique, exploiting the observation that most dynamically allocated objects are short lived. The heap is divided into multiple regions (often two). When space runs low the collector first examines the youngest region (the "nursery"), which it assumes is likely to have the highest proportion of garbage. Only if it is unable to reclaim sufficient space in this region does the collector examine the next-older region. To avoid leaking storage in long-running systems, the collector must be prepared, if necessary, to examine the entire heap. In most cases, however, the overhead of collection will be proportional to the size of the youngest region only.

DESIGN & IMPLEMENTATION

8.11 Reference counts versus tracing

Reference counts require a counter field in every heap object. For small objects such as `cons` cells, this space overhead may be significant. The ongoing expense of updating reference counts when pointers are changed can also be significant in a program with large amounts of pointer manipulation. Other garbage collection techniques, however, have similar overheads. Tracing generally requires a reversed pointer indicator in every heap block, which reference counting does not, and generational collectors must generally incur overhead on every pointer assignment in order to keep track of pointers into the newest section of the heap.

The two principal tradeoffs between reference counting and tracing are the inability of the former to handle cycles and the tendency of the latter to "stop the world" periodically in order to reclaim space. On the whole, implementors tend to favor reference counting for applications in which circularity is not an issue, and tracing collectors in the general case. Some real-world systems mix the two approaches, using reference counts on an ongoing basis, with an occasional tracing collection to catch any circular structures. The "stop the world" problem can also be addressed with *incremental* or *concurrent* collectors, which interleave their execution with the rest of the program, but these tend to have higher total overhead. Efficient, effective garbage collection techniques remain an active area of research.

Any object that survives some small number of collections (often one) in its current region is promoted (moved) to the next older region, in a manner reminiscent of stop-and-copy. Tracing of the nursery requires, of course, that pointers from old objects to new objects we treated as external "roots" of exploration. Promotion likewise requires that pointers from old objects to new objects be updated to reflect the new locations. While old-space-to-new-space pointers tend to be rare, a generational collector must be able to find them all quickly. At each pointer assignment, the compiler generates code to check whether the new value is an old-to-new pointer; if so, it adds the pointer to a hidden list accessible to the collector. This instrumentation on assignments is known as a *write barrier*.[8]

Conservative Collection Language implementors have traditionally assumed that automatic storage reclamation is possible only in languages that are strongly typed: both reference counts and tracing collection require that we be able to find the pointers within an object. If we are willing to admit the possibility that some garbage will go unreclaimed, it turns out that we can implement mark-and-sweep collection without being able to find pointers [BW88]. The key is to observe that any given block in the heap spans a relatively small number of addresses. There is only a very small probability that some word in memory that is not a pointer will happen to contain a bit pattern that looks like one of those addresses.

If we assume, conservatively, that everything that seems to point into a heap block is in fact a valid pointer, then we can proceed with mark-and-sweep collection. When space runs low, the collector (as usual) tentatively marks all blocks in the heap as useless. It then scans all word-aligned quantities in the stack and in global storage. If any of these words appears to contain the address of something in the heap, the collector marks the block that contains that address as useful. Recursively, the collector then scans all word-aligned quantities in the block, and marks as useful any other blocks whose addresses are found therein. Finally (as usual), the collector reclaims any blocks that are still marked useless.

The algorithm is completely safe (in the sense that it never reclaims useful blocks) so long as the programmer never "hides" a pointer. In C, for example, the collector is unlikely to function correctly if the programmer casts a pointer to `int` and then `xor`s it with a constant, with the expectation of restoring and using the pointer at a later time. In addition to sometimes leaving garbage unclaimed, conservative collection suffers from the inability to perform compaction: the collector can never be sure which "pointers" should be changed.

---

8 Unfortunately, the word "barrier" is heavily overloaded. Garbage collection barriers are unrelated to the synchronization barriers of Section 13.3.1, the memory barriers of Section 13.3.3, or the RTL barriers of Section C-15.2.1.

✓ **CHECK YOUR UNDERSTANDING**

25. What are *dangling references*? How are they created, and why are they a problem?
26. What is *garbage*? How is it created, and why is it a problem? Discuss the comparative advantages of *reference counts* and *tracing collection* as a means of solving the problem.
27. What are *smart pointers*? What purpose do they serve?
28. Summarize the differences among mark-and-sweep, stop-and-copy, and generational garbage collection.
29. What is *pointer reversal*? What problem does it address?
30. What is "conservative" garbage collection? How does it work?
31. Do dangling references and garbage ever arise in the same programming language? Why or why not?
32. Why was automatic garbage collection so slow to be adopted by imperative programming languages?
33. What are the advantages and disadvantages of allowing pointers to refer to objects that do not lie in the heap?

8.6 Lists

A list is defined recursively as either the empty list or a pair consisting of an initial object (which may be either a list or an atom) and another (shorter) list. Lists are ideally suited to programming in functional and logic languages, which do most of their work via recursion and higher-order functions (to be described in Section 11.6).

Lists can also be used in imperative programs. They are supported by built-in type constructors in a few traditional compiled languages (e.g., Clu) and in most modern scripting languages. They are also commonly supported by library classes in object-oriented languages, and programmers can build their own in any language with records and pointers. Since many of the standard list operations tend to generate garbage, lists tend to work best in a language with automatic garbage collection.

EXAMPLE 8.54
Lists in ML and Lisp

One key aspect of lists is very different in the two main functional language families. Lists in ML are *homogeneous*: every element of the list must have the same type. Lisp lists, by contrast, are *heterogeneous*: any object may be placed in a list, so long as it is never used in an inconsistent fashion.[9] These different

9 Recall that objects are self-descriptive in Lisp. The only type checking occurs when a function "deliberately" inspects an argument to see whether it is a list or an atom of some particular type.

approaches lead to different implementations. An ML list is usually a chain of blocks, each of which contains an element and a pointer to the next block. A Lisp list is a chain of `cons` cells, each of which contains *two* pointers, one to the element and one to the next `cons` cell (see Figures 8.11 and 8.12). For historical reasons, the two pointers in a `cons` cell are known as the `car` and the `cdr`; they represent the head of the list and the remaining elements, respectively. In both semantics (homogeneity vs heterogeneity) and implementation (chained blocks vs `cons` cells), Clu resembles ML, while Python and Prolog (to be discussed in Section 12.2) resemble Lisp.

EXAMPLE 8.55
List notation

Both ML and Lisp provide convenient notation for lists. In the OCaml dialect of ML, a list is enclosed in square brackets, with elements separated by semicolons: `[a; b; c; d]`. A Lisp list is enclosed in parentheses, with elements separated by white space: `(a b c d)`. In both cases, the notation represents a *proper* list—one whose innermost pair consists of the final element and the empty list. In Lisp, it is also possible to construct an *improper* list, whose final pair contains two elements. (Strictly speaking, such a list does not conform to the standard recursive definition.) Lisp systems provide a more general, but cumbersome *dotted* list notation that captures both proper and improper lists. A dotted list is either an atom (possibly null) or a pair consisting of two dotted lists separated by a period and enclosed in parentheses. The dotted list `(a . (b . (c . (d . null))))` is the same as `(a b c d)`. The list `(a . (b . (c . d)))` is improper; its final `cons` cell contains a pointer to `d` in the second position, where a pointer to a list is normally required.

Both ML and Lisp provide a wealth of built-in polymorphic functions to manipulate arbitrary lists. Because programs are lists in Lisp, Lisp must distinguish between lists that are to be evaluated and lists that are to be left "as is,"

DESIGN & IMPLEMENTATION

8.12 `car` and `cdr`

The names of the functions `car` and `cdr` are historical accidents: they derive from the original (1959) implementation of Lisp on the IBM 704 at MIT. The machine architecture included 15-bit "address" and "decrement" fields in some of the (36-bit) loop-control instructions, together with additional instructions to load an index register from, or store it to, one of these fields within a 36-bit memory word. The designers of the Lisp interpreter decided to make `cons` cells mimic the internal format of instructions, so they could exploit these special instructions. In now archaic usage, memory words were also known as "registers." What might appropriately have been called "first" and "rest" pointers thus came to be known as the `CAR` (contents of address field of register) and `CDR` (contents of decrement field of register). The 704, incidentally, was also the machine on which Fortran was first developed, and the first commercial machine to include hardware floating-point and magnetic core memory.

as structures. To prevent a literal list from being evaluated, the Lisp programmer may quote it: `(quote (a b c d))`, abbreviated `'(a b c d)`. To evaluate an internal list (e.g., one returned by a function), the programmer may pass it to the built-in function `eval`. In ML, programs are not lists, so a literal list is always a structural aggregate.

EXAMPLE 8.56
Basic list operations in Lisp

The most fundamental operations on lists are those that construct them from their components or extract their components from them. In Lisp:

```
(cons 'a '(b))              ⟹ (a b)
(car '(a b))                ⟹ a
(car nil)                   ⟹ ??
(cdr '(a b c))              ⟹ (b c)
(cdr '(a))                  ⟹ nil
(cdr nil)                   ⟹ ??
(append '(a b) '(c d))      ⟹ (a b c d)
```

Here we have used ⟹ to mean "evaluates to." The `car` and `cdr` of the empty list (`nil`) are defined to be `nil` in Common Lisp; in Scheme they result in a dynamic semantic error. ■

EXAMPLE 8.57
Basic list operations in OCaml

In OCaml the equivalent operations are written as follows:

```
a :: [b]            ⟹ [a; b]
hd [a, b]           ⟹ a
hd []               ⟹ run-time exception
tl [a, b, c]        ⟹ [b, c]
tl [a]              ⟹ []
tl []               ⟹ run-time exception
[a, b] @ [c, d]     ⟹ [a; b; c; d]
```

Run-time exceptions may be *caught* by the program if desired; further details will appear in Section 9.4. ■

Both ML and Lisp provide many additional list functions, including ones that test a list to see if it is empty; return the length of a list; return the *n*th element of a list, or a list consisting of all but the first *n* elements; reverse the order of the elements of a list; search a list for elements matching some predicate; or apply a function to every element of a list, returning the results as a list.

Several languages, including Miranda, Haskell, Python, and F#, provide lists that resemble those of ML, but with an important additional mechanism, known as *list comprehensions*. These are adapted from traditional mathematical set notation. A common form comprises an expression, an enumerator, and one or more filters. In Haskell, the following denotes a list of the squares of all odd numbers less than 100:

EXAMPLE 8.58
List comprehensions

```
[i*i | i <- [1..100], i `mod` 2 == 1]
```

In Python we would write

```
[i*i for i in range(1, 100) if i % 2 == 1]
```

In F# the equivalent is

```
[for i in 1..100 do if i % 2 = 1 then yield i*i]
```

All of these are meant to capture the mathematical

$$\{i \times i \mid i \in \{1, \ldots, 100\} \wedge i \bmod 2 = 1\}$$

We could of course create an equivalent list with a series of appropriate function calls. The brevity of the list comprehension syntax, however, can sometimes lead to remarkably elegant programs (see, e.g., Exercise 8.22).

8.7 Files and Input/Output

Input/output (I/O) facilities allow a program to communicate with the outside world. In discussing this communication, it is customary to distinguish between *interactive* I/O and I/O with files. Interactive I/O generally implies communication with human users or physical devices, which work in parallel with the running program, and whose input to the program may depend on earlier output from the program (e.g., prompts). Files generally refer to off-line storage implemented by the operating system. Files may be further categorized into those that are *temporary* and those that are *persistent*. Temporary files exist for the duration of a single program run; their purpose is to store information that is too large to fit in the memory available to the program. Persistent files allow a program to read data that existed before the program began running, and to write data that will continue to exist after the program has ended.

I/O is one of the most difficult aspects of a language to design, and one that displays the least commonality from one language to the next. Some languages provide built-in `file` data types and special syntactic constructs for I/O. Others relegate I/O entirely to library packages, which export a (usually opaque) `file` type and a variety of input and output subroutines. The principal advantage of language integration is the ability to employ non-subroutine-call syntax, and to perform operations (e.g., type checking on subroutine calls with varying numbers of parameters) that may not otherwise be available to library routines. A purely library-based approach to I/O, on the other hand, may keep a substantial amount of "clutter" out of the language definition.

IN MORE DEPTH

An overview of language-level I/O mechanisms can be found on the companion site. After a brief introduction to interactive and file-based I/O, we focus mainly on the common case of *text files*. The data in a text file are stored in character form, but may be converted to and from internal types during `read` and `write` operations. As examples, we consider the text I/O facilities of Fortran, Ada, C, and C++.

✓ **CHECK YOUR UNDERSTANDING**

34. Why are lists so heavily used in functional programming languages?
35. What are *list comprehensions*? What languages support them?
36. Compare and contrast the support for lists in ML- and Lisp-family languages.
37. Explain the distinction between *interactive* and *file-based* I/O; between *temporary* and *persistent* files.
38. What are some of the tradeoffs between supporting I/O in the language proper versus supporting it in libraries?

8.8 Summary and Concluding Remarks

This section concludes the fourth of our six core chapters on language design (names [from Part I], control flow, type systems, composite types, subroutines, and classes). In our survey of composite types, we spent the most time on records, arrays, and recursive types. Key issues for records include the syntax and semantics of variant records, whole-record operations, type safety, and the interaction of each of these with memory layout. Memory layout is also important for arrays, in which it interacts with binding time for shape; static, stack, and heap-based allocation strategies; efficient array traversal in numeric applications; the interoperability of pointers and arrays in C; and the available set of whole-array and *slice*-based operations.

For recursive data types, much depends on the choice between the *value* and *reference models* of variables/names. Recursive types are a natural fallout of the reference model; with the value model they require the notion of a *pointer*: a variable whose value is a reference. The distinction between values and references is important from an implementation point of view: it would be wasteful to implement built-in types as references, so languages with a reference model generally implement built-in and user-defined types differently. Java reflects this distinction in the language semantics, calling for a value model of built-in types and a reference model for objects of user-defined class types.

Recursive types are generally used to create linked data structures. In most cases these structures must be allocated from a heap. In some languages, the programmer is responsible for deallocating heap objects that are no longer needed. In other languages, the language run-time system identifies and reclaims such *garbage* automatically. Explicit deallocation is a burden on the programmer, and leads to the problems of *memory leaks* and *dangling references*. While language implementations almost never attempt to catch memory leaks (see Exploration 3.34 and Exercise C-8.28, however, for some ideas on this subject) *tombstones* or *locks* and *keys* are sometimes used to catch dangling references. Automatic garbage collection can be expensive, but has proved increasingly popular. Most garbage-collection techniques rely either on *reference counts* or on some form of recursive exploration (*tracing*) of currently accessible structures. Techniques in this latter category include *mark-and-sweep*, *stop-and-copy*, and *generational* collection.

Few areas of language design display as much variation as I/O. Our discussion (largely on the companion site) distinguished between *interactive I/O*, which tends to be very platform specific, and *file-based I/O*, which subdivides into *temporary files*, used for voluminous data within a single program run, and *persistent files*, used for off-line storage. Files also subdivide into those that represent their information in a binary form that mimics layout in memory and those that convert to and from character-based *text*. In comparison to binary files, text files generally incur both time and space overhead, but they have the important advantages of portability and human readability.

In our examination of types, we saw many examples of language innovations that have served to improve the clarity and maintainability of programs, often with little or no performance overhead. Examples include the original idea of user-defined types (Algol 68), enumeration and subrange types (Pascal), the integration of records and variants (Pascal), and the distinction between subtypes and derived types in Ada. In Chapter 10 we will examine what many consider the most important language innovation of the past 30 years, namely object orientation.

As in previous chapters, we saw several cases in which a language's convenience, orthogonality, or type safety appears to have been compromised in order to simplify the compiler, or to make compiled programs smaller or faster. Examples include the lack of an equality test for records in many languages, the requirement in Pascal and Ada that the variant portion of a record lie at the end, the limitations in many languages on the maximum size of sets, the lack of type checking for I/O in C, and the general lack of dynamic semantic checks in many language implementations. We also saw several examples of language features introduced at least in part for the sake of efficient implementation. These include `packed` types, multilength numeric types, decimal arithmetic, and C-style pointer arithmetic.

At the same time, one can identify a growing willingness on the part of language designers and users to tolerate complexity and cost in language implementation in order to improve semantics. Examples here include the type-safe variant records of Ada; the standard-length numeric types of Java and C#; the variable-length strings and string operators of modern scripting languages; the late binding of array bounds in Ada, C, and the various scripting languages; and the wealth of whole-array and slice-based array operations in Fortran 90. One might also include the polymorphic type inference of ML and its descendants. Certainly one should include the widespread adoption of automatic garbage collection. Once considered too expensive for production-quality imperative languages, garbage collection is now standard not only in functional and scripting languages, but in Ada, Java, C#, Scala, and Go, among others.

8.9 Exercises

8.1 Suppose we are compiling for a machine with 1-byte characters, 2-byte shorts, 4-byte integers, and 8-byte reals, and with alignment rules that require the address of every primitive data element to be an even multiple of the element's size. Suppose further that the compiler is not permitted to reorder fields. How much space will be consumed by the following array? Explain.

```
A : array [0..9] of record
    s : short
    c : char
    t : short
    d : char
    r : real
    i : integer
```

8.2 In Example 8.10 we suggested the possibility of sorting record fields by their alignment requirement, to minimize holes. In the example, we sorted smallest-alignment-first. What would happen if we sorted longest-alignment-first? Do you see any advantages to this scheme? Any disadvantages? If the record as a whole must be an even multiple of the longest alignment, do the two approaches ever differ in total space required?

8.3 Give Ada code to map from lowercase to uppercase letters, using

(a) an array
(b) a function

Note the similarity of syntax: in both cases `upper('a')` is `'A'`.

8.4 In Section 8.2.2 we noted that in a language with dynamic arrays and a value model of variables, records could have fields whose size is not known at compile time. To accommodate these, we suggested using a dope vector for the record, to track the offsets of the fields.

Suppose instead that we want to maintain a static offset for each field. Can we devise an alternative strategy inspired by the stack frame layout of Figure 8.7, and divide each record into a fixed-size part and a variable-size part? What problems would we need to address? (Hint: Consider nested records.)

8.5 Explain how to extend Figure 8.7 to accommodate subroutine arguments that are passed by value, but whose shape is not known until the subroutine is called at run time.

8.6 Explain how to obtain the effect of Fortran 90's `allocate` statement for one-dimensional arrays using pointers in C. You will probably find that your solution does not generalize to multidimensional arrays. Why not? If you are familiar with C++, show how to use its `class` facilities to solve the problem.

8.7 Example 8.24, which considered the layout of a two-dimensional array of characters, counted only the space devoted to characters and pointers. This is appropriate if the space is allocated statically, as a global array of days or keywords known at compile time. Supposed instead that space is allocated in the heap, with 4 or 8 bytes of overhead for each contiguous block of storage. How does this change the tradeoffs in space efficiency?

8.8 Consider the array indexing calculation of Example 8.25. Suppose that `i`, `j`, and `k` are already loaded into registers, and that A's elements are integers, allocated contiguously in memory on a 32-bit machine. Show, in the pseudo-assembly notation of Sidebar 5.1, the instruction sequence to load `A[i, j, k]` into a register. You may assume the existence of an indexed addressing mode capable of scaling by small powers of two. Assuming the final memory load is a cache hit, how many cycles is your code likely to require on a modern processor?

8.9 Continuing the previous exercise, suppose that `A` has row-pointer layout, and that `i`, `j`, and `k` are again available in registers. Show pseudo-assembler code to load `A[i, j, k]` into a register. Assuming that all memory loads are cache hits, how many cycles is your code likely to require on a modern processor?

8.10 Repeat the preceding two exercises, modifying your code to include run-time checking of array subscript bounds.

8.11 In Section 8.2.3 we discussed how to differentiate between the constant and variable portions of an array reference, in order to efficiently access the subparts of array and record objects. An alternative approach is to generate naive code and count on the compiler's code improver to find the constant portions, group them together, and calculate them at compile time. Discuss the advantages and disadvantages of each approach.

8.12 Consider the following C declaration, compiled on a 64-bit x86 machine:

```
struct {
    int n;
    char c;
} A[10][10];
```

If the address of `A[0][0]` is 1000 (decimal), what is the address of `A[3][7]`?

8.13 Suppose we are generating code for an imperative language on a machine with 8-byte floating-point numbers, 4-byte integers, 1-byte characters, and 4-byte alignment for both integers and floating-point numbers. Suppose further that we plan to use contiguous row-major layout for multidimensional arrays, that we do not wish to reorder fields of records or pack either records or arrays, and that we will assume without checking that all array subscripts are in bounds.

(a) Consider the following variable declarations:

```
A : array [1..10, 10..100] of real
i : integer
x : real
```

Show the code that our compiler should generate for the following assignment: x := A[3,i]. Explain how you arrived at your answer.

(b) Consider the following more complex declarations:

```
r : record
    x : integer
    y : char
    A : array [1..10, 10..20] of record
        z : real
        B : array [0..71] of char
j, k : integer
```

Assume that these declarations are local to the current subroutine. Note the lower bounds on indices in A; the first element is A[1,10].

Describe how r would be laid out in memory. Then show code to load r.A[2,j].B[k] into a register. Be sure to indicate which portions of the address calculation could be performed at compile time.

8.14 Suppose A is a 10×10 array of (4-byte) integers, indexed from [0][0] through [9][9]. Suppose further that the address of A is currently in register r1, the value of integer i is currently in register r2, and the value of integer j is currently in register r3.

Give pseudo-assembly language for a code sequence that will load the value of A[i][j] into register r1 (a) assuming that A is implemented using (row-major) contiguous allocation; (b) assuming that A is implemented using row pointers. Each line of your pseudocode should correspond to a single instruction on a typical modern machine. You may use as many registers as you need. You need not preserve the values in r1, r2, and r3. You may assume that i and j are in bounds, and that addresses are 4 bytes long.

Which code sequence is likely to be faster? Why?

8.15 Pointers and recursive type definitions complicate the algorithm for determining structural equivalence of types. Consider, for example, the following definitions:

```
type A = record
    x : pointer to B
    y : real
```

```
type B = record
    x : pointer to A
    y : real
```

The simple definition of structural equivalence given in Section 7.2.1 (expand the subparts recursively until all you have is a string of built-in types and type constructors; then compare them) does not work: we get an infinite expansion (type A = record x : pointer to record x : pointer to record x : pointer to record . . .). The obvious reinterpretation is to say two types A and B are equivalent if any sequence of field selections, array subscripts, pointer dereferences, and other operations that takes one down into the structure of A, and that ends at a built-in type, always encounters the same field names, and ends at the same built-in type when used to dive into the structure of B—and vice versa. Under this reinterpretation, A and B above have the same type. Give an algorithm based on this reinterpretation that could be used in a compiler to determine structural equivalence. (Hint: The fastest approach is due to J. Král [Krá73]. It is based on the algorithm used to find the smallest deterministic finite automaton that accepts a given regular language. This algorithm was outlined in Example 2.15; details can be found in any automata theory textbook [e.g., [HMU07]].)

8.16 Explain the meaning of the following C declarations:

```
double *a[n];
double (*b)[n];
double (*c[n])();
double (*d())[n];
```

8.17 In Ada 83, pointers (`access` variables) can point only to objects in the heap. Ada 95 allows a new kind of pointer, the `access all` type, to point to other objects as well, provided that those objects have been declared to be `aliased`:

```
type int_ptr is access all Integer;
foo : aliased Integer;
ip : int_ptr;
...
ip := foo'Access;
```

The `'Access` attribute is roughly equivalent to C's "address of" (`&`) operator. How would you implement `access all` types and `aliased` objects? How would your implementation interact with automatic garbage collection (assuming it exists) for objects in the heap?

8.18 As noted in Section 8.5.2, Ada 95 forbids an `access all` pointer from referring to any object whose lifetime is briefer than that of the pointer's type. Can this rule be enforced completely at compile time? Why or why not?

8.19 In much of the discussion of pointers in Section 8.5, we assumed implicitly that every pointer into the heap points to the *beginning* of a dynamically allocated block of storage. In some languages, including Algol 68 and C, pointers may also point to data *inside* a block in the heap. If you were trying to implement dynamic semantic checks for dangling references or, alternatively, automatic garbage collection (precise or conservative), how would your task be complicated by the existence of such "internal pointers"?

8.20 **(a)** Occasionally one encounters the suggestion that a garbage-collected language should provide a `delete` operation as an optimization: by explicitly `delete`-ing objects that will never be used again, the programmer might save the garbage collector the trouble of finding and reclaiming those objects automatically, thereby improving performance. What do you think of this suggestion? Explain.

(b) Alternatively, one might allow the programmer to "tenure" an object, so that it will never be a candidate for reclamation. Is this a good idea?

8.21 In Example 8.52 we noted that functional languages can safely use reference counts since the lack of an assignment statement prevents them from introducing circularity. This isn't strictly true; constructs like the Lisp `letrec` can also be used to make cycles, so long as uses of circularly defined names are hidden inside `lambda` expressions in each definition:

```
(define foo
  (lambda ()
    (letrec ((a (lambda(f) (if f #\A b)))
             (b (lambda(f) (if f #\B c)))
             (c (lambda(f) (if f #\C a))))
      a)))
```

Each of the functions `a`, `b`, and `c` contains a reference to the next:

```
((foo) #t)                        ⇒ #\A
(((foo) #f) #t)                   ⇒ #\B
((((foo) #f) #f) #t)              ⇒ #\C
(((((foo) #f) #f) #f) #t)         ⇒ #\A
```

How might you address this circularity without giving up on reference counts?

8.22 Here is a skeleton for the standard quicksort algorithm in Haskell:

```
quicksort [] = []
quicksort (a : l) = quicksort [...] ++ [a] ++ quicksort [...]
```

The `++` operator denotes list concatenation (similar to `@` in ML). The `:` operator is equivalent to ML's `::` or Lisp's `cons`. Show how to express the two elided expressions as list comprehensions.

8.23–8.31 In More Depth.

8.10 Explorations

8.32 If you have access to a compiler that provides optional dynamic semantic checks for out-of-bounds array subscripts, use of an inappropriate record variant, and/or dangling or uninitialized pointers, experiment with the cost of these checks. How much do they add to the execution time of programs that make a significant number of checked accesses? Experiment with different levels of optimization (code improvement) to see what effect each has on the overhead of checks.

8.33 Write a library package that might be used by a language implementation to manage sets of elements drawn from a very large base type (e.g., `integer`). You should support membership tests, union, intersection, and difference. Does your package allocate memory from the heap? If so, what would a compiler that assumed the use of your package need to do to make sure that space was reclaimed when no longer needed?

8.34 Learn about SETL [SDDS86], a programming language based on sets, designed by Jack Schwartz of New York University. List the mechanisms provided as built-in set operations. Compare this list with the set facilities of other programming languages. What data structure(s) might a SETL implementation use to represent sets in a program?

8.35 The HotSpot Java compiler and virtual machine implements an entire suite of garbage collectors: a traditional generational collector, a compacting collector for the old generation, a low pause-time parallel collector for the nursery, a high-throughput parallel collector for the old generation, and a "mostly concurrent" collector for the old generation that runs in parallel with the main program. Learn more about these algorithms. When is each used, and why?

8.36 Implement your favorite garbage collection algorithm in Ada. Alternatively, implement a simplified version of the `shared_ptr` class in C++, for which storage is garbage collected. You'll want to use templates (generics) so that your class can be instantiated for arbitrary pointed-to types.

8.37 Experiment with the cost of garbage collection in your favorite language implementation. What kind of collector does it use? Can you create artificial programs for which it performs particularly well or poorly?

8.38 Learn about *weak references* in Java. How do they interact with garbage collection? How do they compare to `weak_ptr` objects in C++? Describe several scenarios in which they may be useful.

8.39–8.41 In More Depth.

8.11 Bibliographic Notes

While arrays are the oldest composite data type, they remain an active subject of language design. Representative contemporary work can be found in the proceedings of the 2014 SIGPLAN International Workshop on Libraries, Languages, and Compilers for Array Programming [Hen14]. Implementation issues for arrays and records are discussed in all the standard compiler texts. Chamberlain and Snyder describe support for sparse arrays in the ZPL programming language [CS01].

Tombstones are due to Lomet [Lom75, Lom85]. Locks and keys are due to Fischer and LeBlanc [FL80]. The latter also discuss how to check for various other dynamic semantic errors in Pascal, including those that arise with variant records.

Garbage collection remains a very active topic of research. Much of the ongoing work is reported at ISMM, the annual International Symposium on Memory Management (*www.sigplan.org/Conferences/ISMM*). Constant-space (pointer-reversing) mark-and-sweep garbage collection is due to Schorr and Waite [SW67]. Stop-and-copy collection was developed by Fenichel and Yochelson [FY69], based on ideas due to Minsky. Deutsch and Bobrow [DB76] describe an *incremental* garbage collector that avoids the "stop-the-world" phenomenon. Wilson and Johnstone [WJ93] describe a later incremental collector. The conservative collector described at the end of Section 8.5.3 is due to Boehm and Weiser [BW88]. Cohen [Coh81] surveys garbage-collection techniques as of 1981; Wilson [Wil92b] and Jones and Lins [JL96] provide somewhat more recent views. Bacon et al. [BCR04] argue that reference counting and tracing are really dual views of the same underlying storage problem.

9 Subroutines and Control Abstraction

In the introduction to Chapter 3, we defined *abstraction* as a process by which the programmer can associate a name with a potentially complicated program fragment, which can then be thought of in terms of its purpose or function, rather than in terms of its implementation. We sometimes distinguish between *control abstraction*, in which the principal purpose of the abstraction is to perform a well-defined operation, and *data abstraction*, in which the principal purpose of the abstraction is to represent information.[1] We will consider data abstraction in more detail in Chapter 10.

Subroutines are the principal mechanism for control abstraction in most programming languages. A subroutine performs its operation on behalf of a *caller*, who waits for the subroutine to finish before continuing execution. Most subroutines are parameterized: the caller passes arguments that influence the subroutine's behavior, or provide it with data on which to operate. Arguments are also called *actual parameters*. They are mapped to the subroutine's *formal parameters* at the time a call occurs. A subroutine that returns a value is usually called a *function*. A subroutine that does not return a value is usually called a *procedure*. Statically typed languages typically require a declaration for every called subroutine, so the compiler can verify, for example, that every call passes the right number and types of arguments.

As noted in Section 3.2.2, the storage consumed by parameters and local variables can in most languages be allocated on a stack. We therefore begin this chapter, in Section 9.1, by reviewing the layout of the stack. We then turn in Section 9.2 to the *calling sequences* that serve to maintain this layout. In the process, we revisit the use of static chains to access nonlocal variables in nested subroutines, and consider (on the companion site) an alternative mechanism, known as a *display*, that serves a similar purpose. We also consider subroutine inlining and the representation of closures. To illustrate some of the possible implementation alternatives, we present (again on the companion site) case studies of the LLVM compiler for

1 The distinction between control and data abstraction is somewhat fuzzy, because the latter usually encapsulates not only information but also the operations that access and modify that information. Put another way, most data abstractions include control abstraction.

the ARM instruction set and the `gcc` compiler for 32- and 64-bit x86. We also discuss the *register window* mechanism of the SPARC instruction set.

In Section 9.3 we look more closely at subroutine parameters. We consider parameter-passing *modes*, which determine the operations that a subroutine can apply to its formal parameters and the effects of those operations on the corresponding actual parameters. We also consider named and default parameters, variable numbers of arguments, and function return mechanisms.

In Section 9.4, we consider the handling of exceptional conditions. While exceptions can sometimes be confined to the current subroutine, in the general case they require a mechanism to "pop out of" a nested context without returning, so that recovery can occur in the calling context. In Section 9.5, we consider *coroutines*, which allow a program to maintain two or more execution contexts, and to switch back and forth among them. Coroutines can be used to implement iterators (Section 6.5.3), but they have other uses as well, particularly in simulation and in server programs. In Chapter 13 we will use them as the basis for concurrent ("quasiparallel") threads. Finally, in Section 9.6 we consider asynchronous *events*—things that happen outside a program, but to which it needs to respond.

9.1 Review of Stack Layout

EXAMPLE 9.1
Layout of run-time stack (reprise)

In Section 3.2.2 we discussed the allocation of space on a subroutine call stack (Figure 3.1). Each routine, as it is called, is given a new *stack frame*, or *activation record*, at the top of the stack. This frame may contain arguments and/or return values, bookkeeping information (including the return address and saved registers), local variables, and/or temporaries. When a subroutine returns, its frame is popped from the stack. ■

EXAMPLE 9.2
Offsets from frame pointer

At any given time, the *stack pointer* register contains the address of either the last used location at the top of the stack or the first unused location, depending on convention. The *frame pointer* register contains an address within the frame. Objects in the frame are accessed via displacement addressing with respect to the frame pointer. If the size of an object (e.g., a local array) is not known at compile time, then the object is placed in a variable-size area at the top of the frame; its address and dope vector (descriptor) are stored in the fixed-size portion of the frame, at a statically known offset from the frame pointer (Figure 8.7). If there are no variable-size objects, then every object within the frame has a statically known offset from the stack pointer, and the implementation may dispense with the frame pointer, freeing up a register for other use. If the size of an argument is not known at compile time, then the argument may be placed in a variable-size portion of the frame *below* the other arguments, with its address and dope vector at known offsets from the frame pointer. Alternatively, the caller may simply pass a temporary address and dope vector, counting on the called routine to copy the argument into the variable-size area at the top of the frame. ■

EXAMPLE 9.3
Static and dynamic links

In a language with nested subroutines and static scoping (e.g., Ada, Common Lisp, ML, Scheme, or Swift), objects that lie in surrounding subroutines, and

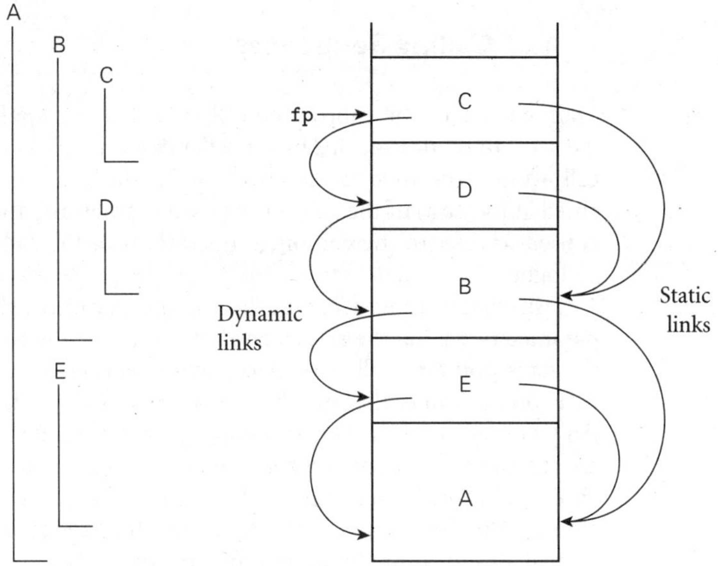

Figure 9.1 **Example of subroutine nesting, taken from Figure 3.5.** Within B, C, and D, all five routines are visible. Within A and E, routines A, B, and E are visible, but C and D are not. Given the calling sequence A, E, B, D, C, in that order, frames will be allocated on the stack as shown at right, with the indicated static and dynamic links.

that are thus neither local nor global, can be found by maintaining a *static chain* (Figure 9.1). Each stack frame contains a reference to the frame of the lexically surrounding subroutine. This reference is called the *static link.* By analogy, the saved value of the frame pointer, which will be restored on subroutine return, is called the *dynamic link.* The static and dynamic links may or may not be the same, depending on whether the current routine was called by its lexically surrounding routine, or by some other routine nested in that surrounding routine.

EXAMPLE 9.4
Visibility of nested routines

Whether or not a subroutine is called directly by the lexically surrounding routine, we can be sure that the surrounding routine is active; there is no other way that the current routine could have been visible, allowing it to be called. Consider, for example, the subroutine nesting shown in Figure 9.1. If subroutine D is called directly from B, then clearly B's frame will already be on the stack. How else could D be called? It is not visible in A or E, because it is nested inside of B. A moment's thought makes clear that it is only when control enters B (placing B's frame on the stack) that D comes into view. It can therefore be called by C, or by any other routine (not shown) that is nested inside C or D, but only because these are also within B.

9.2 Calling Sequences

Maintenance of the subroutine call stack is the responsibility of the *calling sequence*—the code executed by the caller immediately before and after a subroutine call—and of the *prologue* (code executed at the beginning) and *epilogue* (code executed at the end) of the subroutine itself. Sometimes the term "calling sequence" is used to refer to the combined operations of the caller, the prologue, and the epilogue.

Tasks that must be accomplished on the way into a subroutine include passing parameters, saving the return address, changing the program counter, changing the stack pointer to allocate space, saving registers (including the frame pointer) that contain values that may be overwritten by the callee but are still *live* (potentially needed) in the caller, changing the frame pointer to refer to the new frame, and executing initialization code for any objects in the new frame that require it. Tasks that must be accomplished on the way out include passing return parameters or function values, executing finalization code for any local objects that require it, deallocating the stack frame (restoring the stack pointer), restoring other saved registers (including the frame pointer), and restoring the program counter. Some of these tasks (e.g., passing parameters) must be performed by the caller, because they differ from call to call. Most of the tasks, however, can be performed either by the caller or the callee. In general, we will save space if the callee does as much work as possible: tasks performed in the callee appear only once in the target program, but tasks performed in the caller appear at every call site, and the typical subroutine is called in more than one place.

Saving and Restoring Registers

Perhaps the trickiest division-of-labor issue pertains to saving registers. The ideal approach (see Section C-5.5.2) is to save precisely those registers that are both live in the caller and needed for other purposes in the callee. Because of separate compilation, however, it is difficult (though not impossible) to determine this intersecting set. A simpler solution is for the caller to save all registers that are in use, or for the callee to save all registers that it will overwrite.

Calling sequence conventions for many processors, including the ARM and x86 described in the case studies of Section C-9.2.2, strike something of a compromise: registers not reserved for special purposes are divided into two sets of approximately equal size. One set is the caller's responsibility, the other is the callee's responsibility. A callee can assume that there is nothing of value in any of the registers in the caller-saves set; a caller can assume that no callee will destroy the contents of any registers in the callee-saves set. In the interests of code size, the compiler uses the callee-saves registers for local variables and other long-lived values whenever possible. It uses the caller-saves set for transient values, which are less likely to be needed across calls. The result of these conventions is that the caller-saves registers are seldom saved by either party: the callee knows that they are the caller's responsibility, and the caller knows that they don't contain anything important.

Maintaining the Static Chain

In languages with nested subroutines, at least part of the work required to maintain the static chain must be performed by the caller, rather than the callee, because this work depends on the lexical nesting depth of the caller. The standard approach is for the caller to compute the callee's static link and to pass it as an extra, hidden parameter. Two subcases arise:

1. The callee is nested (directly) inside the caller. In this case, the callee's static link should refer to the caller's frame. The caller therefore passes its own frame pointer as the callee's static link.
2. The callee is $k \geq 0$ scopes "outward"—closer to the outer level of lexical nesting. In this case, all scopes that surround the callee also surround the caller (otherwise the callee would not be visible). The caller dereferences its own static link k times and passes the result as the callee's static link.

A Typical Calling Sequence

EXAMPLE 9.5
A typical calling sequence

Figure 9.2 shows one plausible layout for a stack frame, consistent with Figure 3.1. The stack pointer (sp) points to the first unused location on the stack (or the last used location, depending on the compiler and machine). The frame pointer (fp) points to a location near the bottom of the frame. Space for all arguments is reserved in the stack, even if the compiler passes some of them in registers (the callee will need a standard place to save them if it ever calls a nested routine that may try to reach a lexically surrounding parameter via the static chain).

To maintain this stack layout, the calling sequence might operate as follows. The caller

1. saves any caller-saves registers whose values may be needed after the call
2. computes the values of arguments and moves them into the stack or registers
3. computes the static link (if this is a language with nested subroutines), and passes it as an extra, hidden argument
4. uses a special subroutine call instruction to jump to the subroutine, simultaneously passing the return address on the stack or in a register

In its prologue, the callee

1. allocates a frame by subtracting an appropriate constant from the sp
2. saves the old frame pointer into the stack, and updates it to point to the newly allocated frame
3. saves any callee-saves registers that may be overwritten by the current routine (including the static link and return address, if they were passed in registers)

After the subroutine has completed, the epilogue

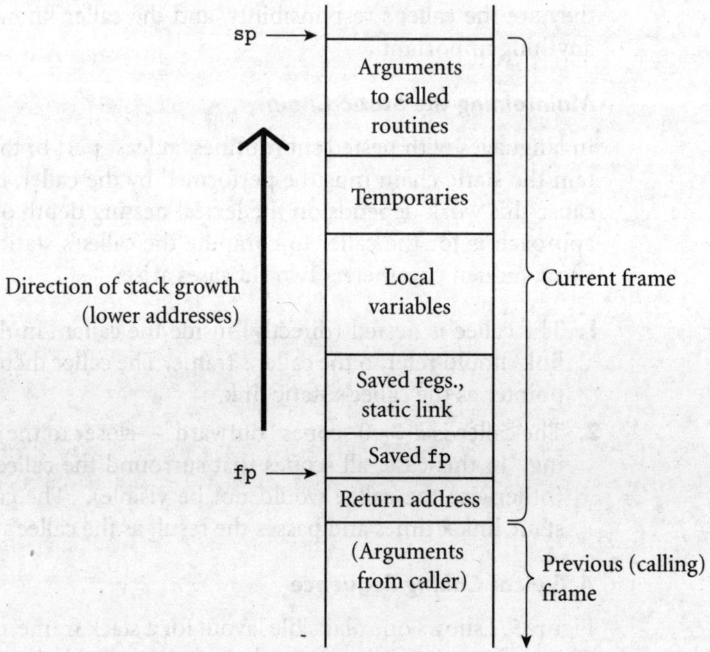

Figure 9.2 **A typical stack frame.** Though we draw it growing upward on the page, the stack actually grows downward toward lower addresses on most machines. Arguments are accessed at positive offsets from the fp. Local variables and temporaries are accessed at negative offsets from the fp. Arguments to be passed to called routines are assembled at the top of the frame, using positive offsets from the sp.

1. moves the return value (if any) into a register or a reserved location in the stack
2. restores callee-saves registers if needed
3. restores the fp and the sp
4. jumps back to the return address

Finally, the caller

1. moves the return value to wherever it is needed
2. restores caller-saves registers if needed

Special-Case Optimizations

Many parts of the calling sequence, prologue, and epilogue can be omitted in common cases. If the hardware passes the return address in a register, then a *leaf routine* (a subroutine that makes no additional calls before returning)[2] can simply

2 A leaf routine is so named because it is a leaf of the *subroutine call graph*, a data structure mentioned in Exercise 3.10.

leave it there; it does not need to save it in the stack. Likewise it need not save the static link or any caller-saves registers.

A subroutine with no local variables and nothing to save or restore may not even need a stack frame on a RISC machine. The simplest subroutines (e.g., library routines to compute the standard mathematical functions) may not touch memory at all, except to fetch instructions: they may take their arguments in registers, compute entirely in (caller-saves) registers, call no other routines, and return their results in registers. As a result they may be extremely fast.

9.2.1 Displays

One disadvantage of static chains is that access to an object in a scope k levels out requires that the static chain be dereferenced k times. If a local object can be loaded into a register with a single (displacement mode) memory access, an object k levels out will require $k + 1$ memory accesses. This number can be reduced to a constant by use of a *display*.

IN MORE DEPTH

As described on the companion site, a display is a small array that replaces the static chain. The jth element of the display contains a reference to the frame of the most recently active subroutine at lexical nesting level j. If the currently active routine is nested $i > 3$ levels deep, then elements $i - 1$, $i - 2$, and $i - 3$ of the display contain the values that would have been the first three links of the static chain. An object k levels out can be found at a statically known offset from the address stored in element $j = i - k$ of the display.

For most programs the cost of maintaining a display in the subroutine calling sequence tends to be slightly higher than that of maintaining a static chain. At the same time, the cost of dereferencing the static chain has been reduced by modern compilers, which tend to do a good job of caching the links in registers when appropriate. These observations, combined with the trend toward languages (those descended from C in particular) in which subroutines do not nest, have made displays less common today than they were in the 1970s.

9.2.2 Stack Case Studies: LLVM on ARM; gcc on x86

Calling sequences differ significantly from machine to machine and even compiler to compiler, though hardware vendors typically publish suggested conventions for their respective architectures, to promote interoperability among program components produced by different compilers. Many of the most significant differences reflect an evolution over time toward heavier use of registers and lighter use of memory. This evolution reflects at least three important technological trends: the increasing size of register sets, the increasing gap in speed between registers and memory (even L1 cache), and the increasing ability of both compilers and processors to improve performance by reordering instructions—at least when operands are all in registers.

Older compilers, particularly for machines with a small number of registers, tend to pass arguments on the stack; newer compilers, particularly for machines with larger register sets, tend to pass arguments in registers. Older architectures tend to provide a subroutine call instruction that pushes the return address onto the stack; newer architectures tend to put the return address in a register.

Many machines provide special instructions of use in the subroutine-call sequence. On the x86, for example, `enter` and `leave` instructions allocate and deallocate stack frames, via simultaneous update of the frame pointer and stack pointer. On the ARM, `stm` (store multiple) and `ldm` (load multiple) instructions save and restore arbitrary groups of registers; in one common idiom, the saved set includes the return address ("link register"); when the restored set includes the program counter (in the same position), `ldm` can pop a set of registers and return from the subroutine in a single instruction.

There has also been a trend—though a less consistent one—away from the use of a dedicated frame pointer register. In older compilers, for older machines, it was common to use `push` and `pop` instructions to pass stack-based arguments. The resulting instability in the value of the `sp` made it difficult (though not impossible) to use that register as the base for access to local variables. A separate frame pointer simplified both code generation and symbolic debugging. At the same time, it introduced additional instructions into the subroutine calling sequence, and reduced by one the number of registers available for other purposes. Modern compiler writers are increasingly willing to trade complexity for performance, and often dispense with the frame pointer, at least in simple routines.

IN MORE DEPTH

On the companion site we look in some detail at the stack layout conventions and calling sequences of a representative pair of compilers: the LLVM compiler for the 32-bit ARMv7 architecture, and the `gcc` compiler for the 32- and 64-bit x86. LLVM is a middle/back end combination originally developed at the University of Illinois and now used extensively in both academia and industry. Among other things, it forms the backbone of the standard tool chains for both iPhone (iOS) and Android devices. The GNU compiler collection, `gcc`, is a cornerstone of the open source movement, used across a huge variety of laptops, desktops, and servers. Both LLVM and `gcc` have back ends for many target architectures, and front ends for many programming languages. We focus on their support for C, whose conventions are in some sense a "lowest common denominator" for other languages.

9.2.3 Register Windows

As an alternative to saving and restoring registers on subroutine calls and returns, the original Berkeley RISC machines [PD80, Pat85] introduced a hardware mechanism known as *register windows*. The basic idea is to map the ISA's limited set of register names onto some subset (window) of a much larger collection of physical registers, and to change the mapping when making subroutine calls. Old and new mappings overlap a bit, allowing arguments to be passed (and function results returned) in the intersection.

IN MORE DEPTH

We consider register windows in more detail on the companion site. They have appeared in several commercial processors, most notably the Sun SPARC and the Intel IA-64 (Itanium).

9.2.4 In-Line Expansion

As an alternative to stack-based calling conventions, many language implementations allow certain subroutines to be expanded in-line at the point of call. A copy of the "called" routine becomes a part of the "caller"; no actual subroutine call occurs. In-line expansion avoids a variety of overheads, including space allocation, branch delays from the call and return, maintaining the static chain or display, and (often) saving and restoring registers. It also allows the compiler to perform code improvements such as global register allocation, instruction scheduling, and common subexpression elimination across the boundaries between subroutines—something that most compilers can't do otherwise.

In many implementations, the compiler chooses which subroutines to expand in-line and which to compile conventionally. In some languages, the programmer can suggest that particular routines be in-lined. In C and C++, the keyword `inline` can be prefixed to a function declaration:

EXAMPLE 9.6 Requesting an `inline` subroutine

```
inline int max(int a, int b) {return a > b ? a : b;}
```

In Ada, the programmer can request in-line expansion with a *significant comment*, or *pragma*:

```
function max(a, b : integer) return integer is
begin
    if a > b then return a; else return b; end if;
end max;
pragma inline(max);
```

Like the `inline` of C and C++, this pragma is a hint; the compiler is permitted to ignore it. ■

In Section 3.7 we noted the similarity between in-line expansion and macros, but argued that the former is semantically preferable. In fact, in-line expansion is semantically neutral: it is purely an implementation technique, with no effect on the meaning of the program. In comparison to real subroutine calls, in-line expansion has the obvious disadvantage of increasing code size, since the entire body of the subroutine appears at every call site. In-line expansion is also not an option in the general case for recursive subroutines.

EXAMPLE 9.7

In-lining and recursion

For the occasional case in which a recursive call is possible but unlikely, it may be desirable to generate a true recursive subroutine, but to expand one level of that routine in-line at each call site. As a simple example, consider a binary tree whose leaves contain character strings. A routine to return the fringe of this tree (the left-to-right concatenation of the values in its leaves) might look like this in C++:

```
string fringe(bin_tree *t) {
    // assume both children are nil or neither is
    if (t->left == 0) return t->val;
    return fringe(t->left) + fringe(t->right);
}
```

A compiler can expand this code in-line if it makes each nested invocation a true subroutine call. Since half the nodes in a binary tree are leaves, this expansion will eliminate half the dynamic calls at run time. If we expand not only the root

DESIGN & IMPLEMENTATION

9.1 Hints and directives

The `inline` keyword in C and C++ suggests but does not require that the compiler expand the subroutine in-line. A conventional implementation may be used when `inline` has been specified—or an in-line implementation when `inline` has *not* been specified—if the compiler has reason to believe that this will result in better code. (In both languages, the `inline` keyword also has an impact on the rules regarding separate compilation. In particular, to facilitate their inclusion in header files, `inline` functions are allowed to have multiple definitions. C++ says all the definitions must be the same; in C, the choice among them is explicitly unspecified.)

In effect, the inclusion of hints like `inline` in a programming language represents an acknowledgment that advice from the expert programmer may sometimes be useful with current compiler technology, but that this may change in the future. By contrast, the use of pointer arithmetic in place of array subscripts, as discussed in Sidebar 8.8, is more of a *directive* than a hint, and may complicate the generation of high-quality code from legacy programs.

calls but also (one level of) the two calls within the true subroutine version, only a quarter of the original dynamic calls will remain.

✓ CHECK YOUR UNDERSTANDING

1. What is a subroutine *calling sequence*? What does it do? What is meant by the subroutine *prologue* and *epilogue*?
2. How do calling sequences typically differ in older (CISC) and newer (RISC) instruction sets?
3. Describe how to maintain the *static chain* during a subroutine call.
4. What is a *display*? How does it differ from a static chain?
5. What are the purposes of the *stack pointer* and *frame pointer* registers? Why does a subroutine often need both?
6. Why do modern machines typically pass subroutine parameters in registers rather than on the stack?
7. Why do subroutine calling conventions often give the caller responsibility for saving half the registers and the callee responsibility for saving the other half?
8. If work can be done in either the caller or the callee, why do we typically prefer to do it in the callee?
9. Why do compilers typically allocate space for arguments in the stack, even when they pass them in registers?
10. List the optimizations that can be made to the subroutine calling sequence in important special cases (e.g., *leaf routines*).
11. How does an *in-line subroutine* differ from a *macro*?
12. Under what circumstances is it desirable to expand a subroutine in-line?

DESIGN & IMPLEMENTATION

9.2 In-lining and modularity

Probably the most important argument for in-line expansion is that it allows programmers to adopt a very modular programming style, with lots of tiny subroutines, without sacrificing performance. This modular programming style is essential for object-oriented languages, as we shall see in Chapter 10. The benefit of in-lining is undermined to some degree by the fact that changing the definition of an in-lined function forces the recompilation of every user of the function; changing the definition of an ordinary function (without changing its interface) forces relinking only. The best of both worlds may be achieved in systems with just-in-time compilation (Section 16.2.1).

9.3 Parameter Passing

Most subroutines are parameterized: they take arguments that control certain aspects of their behavior, or specify the data on which they are to operate. Parameter names that appear in the declaration of a subroutine are known as *formal parameters*. Variables and expressions that are passed to a subroutine in a particular call are known as *actual parameters*. We have been referring to actual parameters as *arguments*. In the following two subsections, we discuss the most common parameter-passing *modes*, most of which are implemented by passing values, references, or closures. In Section 9.3.3 we will look at additional mechanisms, including default (optional) parameters, named parameters, and variable-length argument lists. Finally, in Section 9.3.4 we will consider mechanisms for returning values from functions.

EXAMPLE 9.8
Infix operators

As we noted in Section 6.1, most languages use a prefix notation for calls to user-defined subroutines, with the subroutine name followed by a parenthesized argument list. Lisp places the function name inside the parentheses, as in `(max a b)`. ML dispenses with the parentheses entirely, except when needed for disambiguation: `max a b`. ML also allows the programmer to specify that certain names represent infix operators, which appear between a pair of arguments. In Standard ML one can even specify their precedence:

```
infixr 8 tothe;      (* exponentiation *)
fun x tothe 0 = 1.0
  | x tothe n = x * (x tothe(n-1));     (* assume n >= 0 *)
```

The `infixr` declaration indicates that `tothe` will be a right-associative binary infix operator, at precedence level 8 (multiplication and division are at level 7, addition and subtraction at level 6). Fortran 90 also allows the programmer to define new infix operators, but it requires their names to be bracketed with periods (e.g., `A .cross. B`), and it gives them all the same precedence. Smalltalk uses infix (or "mixfix") notation (without precedence) for all its operations. ■

EXAMPLE 9.9
Control abstraction in Lisp and Smalltalk

The uniformity of Lisp and Smalltalk syntax makes control abstraction particularly effective: user-defined subroutines (functions in Lisp, "messages" in Smalltalk) use the same style of syntax as built-in operations. As an example, consider `if... then ... else`:

```
if a > b then max := a; else max := b; end if;          -- Ada

(if (> a b) (setf max a) (setf max b))                  ; Lisp

(a > b) ifTrue: [max <- a] ifFalse: [max <- b].         "Smalltalk"
```

In Ada (as in most imperative languages) it is clear that `if... then ... else` is a built-in language construct: it does not look like a subroutine call. In Lisp and

Smalltalk, on the other hand, the analogous conditional constructs are syntactically indistinguishable from user-defined operations. They are in fact defined in terms of simpler concepts, rather than being built in, though they require a special mechanism to evaluate their arguments in normal, rather than applicative, order (Section 6.6.2).

9.3.1 Parameter Modes

In our discussion of subroutines so far, we have glossed over the semantic rules that govern parameter passing, and that determine the relationship between actual and formal parameters. Some languages, including C, Fortran, ML, and Lisp, define a single set of rules, which apply to all parameters. Other languages, including Ada, C++, and Swift, provide two or more sets of rules, corresponding to different parameter-passing *modes*. As in many aspects of language design, the semantic details are heavily influenced by implementation issues.

EXAMPLE 9.10 Passing an argument to a subroutine

Suppose for the moment that x is a global variable in a language with a value model of variables, and that we wish to pass x as a parameter to subroutine p:

```
p(x);
```

From an implementation point of view, we have two principal alternatives: we may provide p with a copy of x's value, or we may provide it with x's address. The two most common parameter-passing modes, called *call by value* and *call by reference*, are designed to reflect these implementations.

With value parameters, each actual parameter is assigned into the corresponding formal parameter when a subroutine is called; from then on, the two are independent. With reference parameters, each formal parameter introduces, within the body of the subroutine, a new name for the corresponding actual parameter. If the actual parameter is also visible within the subroutine under its original name (as will generally be the case if it is declared in a surrounding scope), then the two names are *aliases* for the same object, and changes made through one will be visible through the other. In most languages (Fortran is an exception; see below) an actual parameter that is to be passed by reference must be an l-value; it cannot be the result of an arithmetic operation, or any other value without an address.

EXAMPLE 9.11 Value and reference parameters

As a simple example, consider the following pseudocode:

```
x : integer                    -- global
procedure foo(y : integer)
    y := 3
    print x
...
x := 2
foo(x)
print x
```

If y is passed to foo by value, then the assignment inside foo has no visible effect—y is private to the subroutine—and the program prints 2 twice. If y is passed to foo by reference, then the assignment inside foo changes x—y is just a local name for x—and the program prints 3 twice. ■

Variations on Value and Reference Parameters

If the purpose of call by reference is to allow the called routine to modify the actual parameter, we can achieve a similar effect using *call by value/result*, a mode first introduced in Algol W. Like call by value, call by value/result copies the actual parameter into the formal parameter at the beginning of subroutine execution. Unlike call by value, it *also* copies the formal parameter back into the actual parameter when the subroutine returns. In Example 9.11, value/result would copy x into y at the beginning of foo, and y into x at the end of foo. Because foo accesses x directly in between, the program's visible behavior would be different than it was with call by reference: the assignment of 3 into y would not affect x until after the inner print statement, so the program would print 2 and then 3. ■

EXAMPLE 9.12
Call by value/result

In Pascal, parameters were passed by value by default; they were passed by reference if preceded by the keyword var in their subroutine header's formal parameter list. Parameters in C are always passed by value, though the effect for arrays is unusual: because of the interoperability of arrays and pointers in C (Section 8.5.1), what is passed by value is a pointer; changes to array elements accessed through this pointer are visible to the caller. To allow a called routine to modify a variable other than an array in the caller's scope, the C programmer must pass a pointer to the variable explicitly:

EXAMPLE 9.13
Emulating call-by-reference in C

```
void swap(int *a, int *b) { int t = *a; *a = *b; *b = t; }
...
swap(&v1, &v2);
```
■

Fortran passes all parameters by reference, but does not require that every actual parameter be an l-value. If a built-up expression appears in an argument list, the compiler creates a temporary variable to hold the value, and passes this variable by reference. A Fortran subroutine that needs to modify the values of its formal parameters without modifying its actual parameters must copy the values into local variables, and modify those instead.

DESIGN & IMPLEMENTATION

9.3 Parameter modes

While it may seem odd to introduce parameter modes (a semantic issue) in terms of implementation, the distinction between value and reference parameters is fundamentally an implementation issue. Most languages with more than one mode (Ada and Swift are notable exceptions) might fairly be characterized as an attempt to paste acceptable semantics onto the desired implementation, rather than to find an acceptable implementation of the desired semantics.

Call by Sharing Call by value and call by reference make the most sense in a language with a value model of variables: they determine whether we copy the variable or pass an alias for it. Neither option really makes sense in a language like Smalltalk, Lisp, ML, or Ruby, in which a variable is already a reference. Here it is most natural simply to pass the reference itself, and let the actual and formal parameters refer to the same object. Clu called this mode *call by sharing*. It is different from call by value because, although we do copy the actual parameter into the formal parameter, both of them are references; if we modify the object to which the formal parameter refers, the program will be able to see those changes through the actual parameter after the subroutine returns. Call by sharing is also different from call by reference, because although the called routine can change the value of the object to which the actual parameter refers, it cannot make the argument refer to a different object.

As we noted in Sections 6.1.2 and 8.5.1, a reference model of variables does not necessarily require that every object be accessed indirectly by address: the implementation can create multiple copies of immutable objects (numbers, characters, etc.) and access them directly. Call by sharing is thus commonly implemented the same as call by value for small objects of immutable type.

In keeping with its hybrid model of variables, Java uses call by value for variables of primitive, built-in types (all of which are values), and call by sharing for variables of user-defined class types (all of which are references). An interesting consequence is that a Java subroutine cannot change the value of an actual parameter of primitive type. A similar approach is the default in C#, but because the language allows users to create both value (`struct`) and reference (`class`) types, both cases are considered call by value. That is, whether a variable is a value or a reference, we always pass it by copying. (Some authors describe Java the same way.)

When desired, parameters in C# can be passed by reference instead, by labeling both a formal parameter *and each corresponding argument* with the `ref` or `out` keyword. Both of these modes are implemented by passing an address; they differ in that a `ref` argument must be *definitely assigned* prior to the call, as described in Section 6.1.3; an `out` argument need not. In contrast to Java, therefore, a C# subroutine *can* change the value of an actual parameter of primitive type, if the parameter is passed `ref` or `out`. Similarly, if a variable of `class` (reference) type is passed as a `ref` or `out` parameter, it may end up referring to a different object as a result of subroutine execution—something that is not possible with call by sharing.

The Purpose of Call by Reference Historically, there were two principal issues that a programmer might consider when choosing between value and reference parameters in a language (e.g., Pascal or Modula) that provided both. First, if the called routine was supposed to change the value of an actual parameter (argument), then the programmer had to pass the parameter by reference. Conversely, to ensure that the called routine could not modify the argument, the programmer could pass the parameter by value. Second, the implementation of value parameters would copy actuals to formals, a potentially time-consuming operation when arguments were large. Reference parameters can be implemented simply by passing an address. (Of course, accessing a parameter that is passed by reference requires an extra level of indirection. If the parameter were used often enough, the cost of this indirection might outweigh the cost of copying the argument.)

The potential inefficiency of large value parameters may prompt programmers to pass an argument by reference when passing by value would be semantically more appropriate. Pascal programmers, for example, were commonly taught to use `var` (reference) parameters both for arguments that need to be modified and for arguments that are very large. In a similar vein, C programmers today are commonly taught to pass pointers (created with `&`) for both to-be-modified and very large arguments. Unfortunately, the latter justification tends to lead to buggy code, in which a subroutine modifies an argument that the caller meant to leave unchanged.

Read-Only Parameters To combine the efficiency of reference parameters and the safety of value parameters, Modula-3 provided a `READONLY` parameter mode. Any formal parameter whose declaration was preceded by `READONLY` could not be changed by the called routine: the compiler prevented the programmer from using that formal parameter on the left-hand side of any assignment statement, reading it from a file, or passing it by reference to any other subroutine. Small `READONLY` parameters were generally implemented by passing a value; larger `READONLY` parameters were implemented by passing an address. As in Fortran, a Modula-3 compiler would create a temporary variable to hold the value of any built-up expression passed as a large `READONLY` parameter.

EXAMPLE 9.14
`const` parameters in C

The equivalent of `READONLY` parameters is also available in C, which allows any variable or parameter declaration to be preceded by the keyword `const`. `Const` variables are "elaboration-time constants," as described in Section 3.2. `Const` parameters are particularly useful when passing pointers to large structures:

```
void append_to_log(const huge_record* r) { ...
...
append_to_log(&my_record);
```

Here the keyword `const` applies to the record to which `r` points;[3] the callee will be unable to change the record's contents. Note, however, that in C the caller must create a pointer to the record explicitly, and the compiler does not have the option of passing by value. ■

One traditional problem with parameter modes—and with the `READONLY` mode in particular—is that they tend to confuse the key pragmatic issue (does the implementation pass a value or a reference?) with two semantic issues: is the

3 Following the usual rules for parsing C declarations (footnote in Example 8.46), `r` is a pointer to a `huge_record` whose value is constant. If we wanted `r` to be a constant that points to a `huge_record`, we should need to say `huge_record* const r`.

callee allowed to change the formal parameter and, if so, will the changes be reflected in the actual parameter? C keeps the pragmatic issue separate, by forcing the programmer to pass references explicitly with pointers. Still, its `const` mode serves double duty: is the intent of `const foo* p` to protect the actual parameter from change, or to document the fact that the subroutine thinks of the formal parameter as a constant rather than a variable, or both?

Parameter Modes in Ada

Ada provides three parameter-passing modes, called `in`, `out`, and `in out`. `In` parameters pass information from the caller to the callee; they can be read by the callee but not written. `Out` parameters pass information from the callee to the caller. In Ada 83 they can be written by the callee but not read; in Ada 95 they can be both read and written, but they begin their life uninitialized. `In out` parameters pass information in both directions; they can be both read and written. Changes to `out` or `in out` parameters always change the actual parameter.

For parameters of scalar and access (pointer) types, Ada specifies that all three modes are to be implemented by copying values. For these parameters, then, `in` is call by value, `in out` is call by value/result, and `out` is simply *call by result* (the value of the formal parameter is copied into the actual parameter when the subroutine returns). For parameters of most constructed types, however, Ada specifically permits an implementation to pass either values or references. In most languages, these two different mechanisms would lead to different semantics: changes made to an `in out` parameter that is passed by reference will affect the actual parameter immediately; changes made to an `in out` parameter that is passed by value will not affect the actual parameter until the subroutine returns. As noted in Example 9.12, the difference can lead to different behavior in the presence of aliases.

One possible way to hide the distinction between reference and value/result would be to outlaw the creation of aliases, as Euclid does. Ada takes a simpler tack: a program that can tell the difference between value and reference-based implementations of (nonscalar, nonpointer) `in out` parameters is said to be *erroneous*—incorrect, but in a way that the language implementation is not required to catch.

Ada's semantics for parameter passing allow a single set of modes to be used not only for subroutine parameters but also for communication among concurrently executing tasks (to be discussed in Chapter 13). When tasks are executing on separate machines, with no memory in common, passing the address of an actual parameter is not a practical option. Most Ada compilers pass large arguments to subroutines by reference; they pass them to the entry points of tasks by copying.

References in C++

Programmers who switch to C after some experience with other languages are often frustrated by C's lack of reference parameters. As noted above, one can always arrange to modify an object by passing a pointer, but then the formal parameter is *declared as* a pointer, and must be explicitly dereferenced whenever it is used. C++ addresses this problem by introducing an explicit notion of a *reference*. Reference parameters are specified by preceding their name with an ampersand in the header of the function:

EXAMPLE 9.15
Reference parameters in C++

```
void swap(int &a, int &b) { int t = a; a = b; b = t; }
```

In the code of this swap routine, a and b are ints, not pointers to ints; no dereferencing is required. Moreover, the caller passes as arguments the variables whose values are to be swapped, rather than passing pointers to them. ■

As in C, a C++ parameter can be declared to be const to ensure that it is not modified. For large types, const reference parameters in C++ provide the same combination of speed and safety found in the READONLY parameters of Modula-3: they can be passed by address, and cannot be changed by the called routine.

References in C++ see their principal use as parameters, but they can appear in other contexts as well. Any variable can be declared to be a reference:

EXAMPLE 9.16
References as aliases in C++

```
int i;
int &j = i;
...
i = 2;
j = 3;
cout << i;          // prints 3
```

Here j is a reference to (an alias for) i. The initializer in the declaration is required; it identifies the object for which j is an alias. Moreover it is not possible later to change the object to which j refers; it will always refer to i.

Any change to i or j can be seen by reading the other. Most C++ compilers implement references with addresses. In this example, i will be assigned a location that contains an integer, while j will be assigned a location that contains the address of i. Despite their different implementation, however, there is no semantic difference between i and j; the exact same operations can be applied to either, with precisely the same results. ■

EXAMPLE 9.17
Simplifying code with an in-line alias

In C, programmers sometimes use a pointer to avoid repeated uses of the same complex expression:

```
{
    element* e = &ruby.chemical_composition.elements[1];
    e->name = "Al";
    e->atomic_number = 13;
    e->atomic_weight = 26.98154;
    e->metallic = true;
}
```

References avoid the need for pointer syntax:

```
{
    element& e = ruby.chemical_composition.elements[1];
    e.name = "Al";
    e.atomic_number = 13;
    e.atomic_weight = 26.98154;
    e.metallic = true;
}
```

EXAMPLE 9.18

Returning a reference from a function

Aside from function parameters, however, the most important use of references in C++ is for function returns. Section C-8.7 explains how references are used for I/O in C++. The overloaded << and >> operators return a reference to their first argument, which can in turn be passed to subsequent << or >> operations. The syntax

```
cout << a << b << c;
```

is short for

```
((cout.operator<<(a)).operator<<(b)).operator<<(c);
```

Without references, << and >> would have to return a pointer to their stream:

```
((cout.operator<<(a))->operator<<(b))->operator<<(c);
```

or

```
*(*(cout.operator<<(a)).operator<<(b)).operator<<(c);
```

This change would spoil the cascading syntax of the operator form:

```
*(*(cout << a) << b) << c;
```

Like pointers, references returned from functions introduce the opportunity to create dangling references in a language (like C++) with limited extent for local variables. In our I/O example, the return value is the same stream that was passed into `operator<<` as a parameter; since this outlives the function invocation, continued use of the reference is safe.

It should be noted that the ability to return references from functions is not new in C++: Algol 68 provides the same capability. The object-oriented features of C++, and its operator overloading, make reference returns particularly useful.

R-value References

One feature that *is* distinctive in C++ is the notion of an *r-value reference*, introduced in C++11. R-value references allow an argument that would normally be considered an r-value—typically, a built-up expression—to be passed to a function by reference. To see why this might be useful, consider the following declaration:

EXAMPLE 9.19
R-value references in C++11

```
obj o2 = o1;
```

Assuming that `o1` is also of class `obj`, the compiler will initialize `o2` by calling `obj`'s *copy constructor* method, passing `o1` as argument. As we shall see in Section 10.3, a constructor can be declared to take parameters like those of any other function. Historically, the parameter of `obj`'s copy constructor would have been a constant reference (`const obj&`), and the body of the constructor would have inspected this parameter to decide how to initialize `o2`. So far so good. Now consider the case in which objects of class `obj` contain pointers to dynamically allocated state. (The strings, vectors, lists, trees, and hash tables of the standard library all have such dynamic state.) If that state is mutable, the constructor will generally need to allocate and initialize a copy, so that neither object will be damaged by subsequent changes to the other. But now consider the declaration

```
obj o3 = foo("hi mom");
```

Assuming that `foo` has return type `obj`, the compiler will again create a call to the copy constructor, but this time it may pass a *temporary* object (call it *t*) used to hold the value returned from `foo`. As before, the constructor will allocate and initialize a copy of the state contained in *t*, but upon its return the copy in *t* will be destroyed (by calling its *destructor* method, which will presumably free the space it consumes in the heap). Wouldn't it be handy if we could *transfer* *t*'s state into `o3`, rather than creating a copy and then immediately destroying the original? This is precisely what r-value references allow.

In addition to the conventional copy constructor, with its `const obj&` parameter, C++11 allows the programmer to declare a *move constructor*, with an `obj&&` parameter (double ampersand, no `const`). The compiler will use the move constructor when—and only when—the parameter in a declaration is a "temporary"—a value that will no longer be accessible after evaluation of the expression in which it appears. In the declaration of `o3`, the return value of `foo` is such a temporary. If the dynamically allocated state of an `obj` object is accessed through a field named `payload`, the move constructor might be as simple as

```
obj::obj(obj&& other) {
    payload = other.payload;
    other.payload = nullptr;
}
```

The explicit `null`-ing of `other.payload` prevents `other`'s destructor from freeing the transferred state.

In some cases, the programmer may know that a value will never be used after passing it as a parameter, but the compiler may be unable to deduce this fact. To force the use of a move constructor, the programmer can wrap the value in a call to the standard library `move` routine:

```
obj o4 = std::move(o3);
```

The `move` routine generates no code: it is, in effect, a cast. Behavior is undefined if the program actually does contain a subsequent use of `o3`.

Like regular references, r-value references can be used in the declaration of arbitrary variables in C++. In practice, they seldom appear outside the parameters of move constructors and the analogous *move assignment* methods, which overload the = operator.

Closures as Parameters

A closure (a reference to a subroutine, together with its referencing environment) may be passed as a parameter for any of several reasons. The most obvious of these arises when the parameter is declared to be a subroutine (sometimes called a *formal subroutine*). In Ada one might write

EXAMPLE 9.20
Subroutines as parameters in Ada

```
1.  type int_func is access function (n : integer) return integer;
2.  type int_array is array (positive range <>) of integer;
3.  procedure apply_to_A (f : int_func; A : in out int_array) is
4.  begin
5.      for i in A'range loop
6.          A(i) := f(A(i));
6.      end loop;
8.  end apply_to_A;
        ...
9.      k : integer := 3;        -- in nested scope
        ...
10.     function add_k (m : integer) return integer is
11.     begin
12.         return m + k;
13.     end add_k;
        ...
14.     apply_to_A (add_k'access, B);
```

As discussed in Section 3.6.1, a closure needs to include both a code address and a referencing environment because, in a language with nested subroutines, we need to make sure that the environment available to `f` at line 6 is the same that would have been available to `add_k` if it had been called directly at line 14—in particular, that it includes the binding for `k`.

EXAMPLE 9.21
First-class subroutines in Scheme

Subroutines are routinely passed as parameters (and returned as results) in functional languages. A list-based version of `apply_to_A` would look something like this in Scheme (for the meanings of `car`, `cdr`, and `cons`, see Section 8.6):

```
(define apply-to-L
  (lambda (f l)
    (if (null? l) '()
        (cons (f (car l)) (apply-to-L f (cdr l))))))
```

Since Scheme is dynamically typed, there is no need to specify the type of `f`. At run time, a Scheme implementation will announce a dynamic semantic error in `(f (car l))` if `f` is not a function, and in `(null? l)`, `(car l)`, or `(cdr l)` if `l` is not a list. ■

EXAMPLE 9.22
First-class subroutines in OCaml

The code in OCaml and other ML dialects is similar, but the implementation uses inference (Section 7.2.4) to determine the types of `f` and `l` at compile time:

```
let rec apply_to_L f l =
  match l with
  | []        -> []
  | h :: t -> f h :: apply_to_L f t;;
```

■

EXAMPLE 9.23
Subroutine pointers in C and C++

As noted in Section 3.6, C and C++ have no need of subroutine closures, because their subroutines do not nest. Simple *pointers* to subroutines suffice. These are permitted both as parameters and as variables.

```
void apply_to_A(int (*f)(int), int A[], int A_size) {
    int i;
    for (i = 0; i < A_size; i++) A[i] = f(A[i]);
}
```

The syntax `f(n)` is used not only when `f` is the name of a function but also when `f` is a pointer to a subroutine; the pointer need not be dereferenced explicitly. ■

In object-oriented languages, one can approximate the behavior of a subroutine closure, even without nested subroutines, by packaging a method and its "environment" within an explicit object. We described these *object closures* in Section 3.6.3, noting in particular their integration with lambda expressions and the standard `function` class in C++11. Because they are ordinary objects, object closures require no special mechanisms to pass them as parameters or to store them in variables.

The *delegates* of C# extend the notion of object closures to provide type safety without the restrictions of inheritance. A delegate can be instantiated not only with a specified object method (subsuming the object closures of C++ and Java) but also with a static function (subsuming the subroutine pointers of C and C++) or with an anonymous nested delegate or lambda expression (subsuming true subroutine closures). If an anonymous delegate or lambda expression refers to objects declared in the surrounding method, then those objects have unlimited extent. Finally, as we shall see in Section 9.6.2, a C# delegate can actually contain a *list* of closures, in which case calling the delegate has the effect of calling *all* the entries on the list, in turn. (This behavior generally makes sense only when each entry has a `void` return type. It is used primarily when processing *events*.)

9.3.2 Call by Name

Explicit subroutine parameters are not the only language feature that requires a closure to be passed as a parameter. In general, a language implementation must pass a closure whenever the eventual use of the parameter requires the restoration of a previous referencing environment. Interesting examples occur in the *call-by-name* parameters of Algol 60 and Simula, the label parameters of Algol 60 and Algol 68, and the *call-by-need* parameters of Miranda, Haskell, and R.

IN MORE DEPTH

We consider call by name in more detail on the companion site. When Algol 60 was defined, most programmers programmed in assembly language (Fortran was only a few years old, and Lisp was even newer). The assembly languages of the day made heavy use of macros, and it was natural for the Algol designers to propose a parameter-passing mechanism that mimicked the behavior of macros, namely normal-order argument evaluation (Section 6.6.2). It was also natural, given common practice in assembly language, to allow a `goto` to jump to a label that was passed as a parameter.

Call-by-name parameters have some interesting and powerful applications, but they are more difficult to implement (and more expensive to use) than one might at first expect: they require the passing of closures, sometimes referred to as *thunks*. Label parameters are typically implemented by closures as well. Both call-by-name and label parameters tend to lead to inscrutable code; modern languages typically encourage programmers to use explicit formal subroutines and structured exceptions instead. Significantly, most of the arguments against call by name disappear in purely functional code, where side-effect freedom ensures that the value of a parameter will always be the same regardless of when it is evaluated. Leveraging this observation, Haskell (and its predecessor Miranda) employs normal-order evaluation for all parameters.

9.3.3 Special-Purpose Parameters

Figure 9.3 contains a summary of the common parameter-passing modes. In this subsection we examine other aspects of parameter passing.

Default (Optional) Parameters

In Section 3.3.6, we noted that *default* parameters provide an attractive alternative to dynamic scope for changing the behavior of a subroutine. A default parameter is one that need not necessarily be provided by the caller; if it is missing, then a preestablished default value will be used instead.

EXAMPLE 9.24
Default parameters in Ada

One common use of default parameters is in I/O library routines (described in Section C-8.7.3). In Ada, for example, the `put` routine for integers has the following declaration in the `text_IO` library package:

Parameter mode	Representative languages	Implementation mechanism	Permissible operations	Change to actual?	Alias?
value	C/C++, Pascal, Java/C# (value types)	value	read, write	no	no
`in, const`	Ada, C/C++, Modula-3	value or reference	read only	no	maybe
`out`	Ada	value or reference	write only	yes	maybe
value/result	Algol W	value	read, write	yes	no
`var, ref`	Fortran, Pascal, C++	reference	read, write	yes	yes
sharing	Lisp/Scheme, ML, Java/C# (reference types)	value or reference	read, write	yes	yes
r-value ref	C++11	reference	read, write	yes*	no*
`in out`	Ada, Swift	value or reference	read, write	yes	maybe
name	Algol 60, Simula	closure (thunk)	read, write	yes	yes
need	Haskell, R	closure (thunk) with memoization	read, write†	yes†	yes†

Figure 9.3 **Parameter-passing modes.** Column 1 indicates common names for modes. Column 2 indicates prominent languages that use the modes, or that introduced them. Column 3 indicates implementation via passing of values, references, or closures. Column 4 indicates whether the callee can read or write the formal parameter. Column 5 indicates whether changes to the formal parameter affect the actual parameter. Column 6 indicates whether changes to the formal or actual parameter, during the execution of the subroutine, may be visible through the other. *Behavior is undefined if the program attempts to use an r-value argument after the call. †Changes to arguments passed by need in R will happen only on the first use; changes in Haskell are not permitted.

```
type field is integer range 0..integer'last;
type number_base is integer range 2..16;
default_width : field       := integer'width;
default_base  : number_base := 10;
procedure put(item  : in integer;
              width : in field       := default_width;
              base  : in number_base := default_base);
```

Here the declaration of `default_width` uses the built-in type *attribute* `width` to determine the maximum number of columns required to print an integer in decimal on the current machine (e.g., a 32-bit integer requires no more than 11 columns, including the optional minus sign).

Any formal parameter that is "assigned" a value in its subroutine heading is optional in Ada. In our `text_IO` example, the programmer can call `put` with one, two, or three arguments. No matter how many are provided in a particular call, the code for `put` can always assume it has all three parameters. The implementation is straightforward: in any call in which actual parameters are missing, the compiler pretends as if the defaults had been provided; it generates a calling sequence that loads those defaults into registers or pushes them onto the stack, as appropriate. On a 32-bit machine, `put(37)` will print the string "37" in an 11-column field (with nine leading blanks) in base-10 notation. `Put(37, 4)` will print "37" in a four-column field (two leading blanks), and `put(37, 4, 8)` will print "45" ($37 = 45_8$) in a four-column field.

Because the `default_width` and `default_base` variables are part of the `text_IO` interface, the programmer can change them if desired. When using default values in calls with missing actuals, the compiler loads the defaults from the variables of the package. As noted in Section C-8.7.3, there are overloaded instances of `put` for all the built-in types. In fact, there are two overloaded instances of `put` for every type, one of which has an additional first parameter that specifies the output file to which to write a value.[4] It should be emphasized that there is nothing special about I/O as far as default parameters are concerned: defaults can be used in any subroutine declaration. In addition to Ada, default parameters appear in C++, C#, Common Lisp, Fortran 90, and Python.

Named Parameters

In all of our discussions so far we have been assuming that parameters are *positional*: the first actual parameter corresponds to the first formal parameter, the second actual to the second formal, and so on. In some languages, including Ada, C#, Common Lisp, Fortran 90, Python, and Swift, this need not be the case. These languages allow parameters to be *named*. Named parameters (also called *keyword* parameters) are particularly useful in conjunction with default parameters. Positional notation allows us to write `put(37, 4)` to print "37" in a four-column field, but it does not allow us to print in octal in a field of default width: any call (with positional notation) that specifies a base must also specify a width, explicitly, because the width parameter precedes the base in `put`'s parameter list. Named parameters provide the Ada programmer with a way around this problem:

EXAMPLE 9.25
Named parameters in Ada

```
put(item => 37, base => 8);
```

Because the parameters are named, their order does not matter; we can also write

```
put(base => 8, item => 37);
```

We can even mix the two approaches, using positional notation for the first few parameters, and names for all the rest:

```
put(37, base => 8);
```

In addition to allowing parameters to be specified in arbitrary order, omitting any intermediate default parameters for which special values are not required,

4 The real situation is actually a bit more complicated: The `put` routine for integers is nested inside `integer_IO`, a generic package that is in turn inside of `text_IO`. The programmer must *instantiate* a separate version of the `integer_IO` package for each variety (size) of integer type.

named parameter notation has the advantage of documenting the purpose of each parameter. For a subroutine with a very large number of parameters, it can be difficult to remember which is which. Named notation makes the meaning of arguments explicit in the call, as in the following hypothetical example:

EXAMPLE 9.26
Self-documentation with named parameters

```
format_page(columns => 2,
    window_height => 400, window_width => 200,
    header_font => Helvetica, body_font => Times,
    title_font => Times_Bold, header_point_size => 10,
    body_point_size => 11, title_point_size => 13,
    justification => true, hyphenation => false,
    page_num => 3, paragraph_indent => 18,
    background_color => white);
```

Variable Numbers of Arguments

Several languages, including Lisp, C and its descendants, and most of the scripting languages, allow the user to define subroutines that take a variable number of arguments. Examples of such subroutines can be found in Section C-8.7.3: the `printf` and `scanf` functions of C's `stdio` I/O library. In C, `printf` can be declared as follows:

```
int printf(char *format, ...) {
    ...
```

The ellipsis (`...`) in the function header is a part of the language syntax. It indicates that there are additional parameters following the format, but that their types and numbers are unspecified. Since C and C++ are statically typed, additional parameters are not type safe. They are type safe in Common Lisp and the scripting languages, however, thanks to dynamic typing.

Within the body of a function with a variable-length argument list, the C or C++ programmer must use a collection of standard routines to access the extra arguments. Originally defined as macros, these routines have implementations that vary from machine to machine, depending on how arguments are passed to functions; today the necessary support is usually built into the compiler. For `printf`, variable arguments would be used as follows in C:

EXAMPLE 9.27
Variable number of arguments in C

```
#include <stdarg.h>      /* macros and type definitions */
int printf(char *format, ...) {
    va_list args;
    va_start(args, format);
    ...
        char cp = va_arg(args, char);
        ...
        double dp = va_arg(args, double);
    ...
    va_end(args);
}
```

Here args is defined as an object of type va_list, a special (implementation-dependent) type used to enumerate the elided parameters. The va_start routine takes the last declared parameter (in this case, format) as its second argument. It initializes its first argument (in this case args) so that it can be used to enumerate the rest of the caller's actual parameters. At least one formal parameter must be declared; they can't all be elided.

Each call to va_arg returns the value of the next elided parameter. Two examples appear above. Each specifies the expected type of the parameter, and assigns the result into a variable of the appropriate type. If the expected type is different from the type of the actual parameter, chaos can result. In printf, the %X placeholders in the format string are used to determine the type: printf contains a large switch statement, with one arm for each possible X. The arm for %c contains a call to va_arg(args, char); the arm for %f contains a call to va_arg(args, double). All C floating-point types are extended to double-precision before being passed to a subroutine, so there is no need inside printf to worry about the distinction between floats and doubles. Scanf, on the other hand, must distinguish between pointers to floats and pointers to doubles. The call to va_end allows the implementation to perform any necessary cleanup operations (e.g., deallocation of any heap space used for the va_list, or repair of any changes to the stack frame that might confuse the epilogue code).

EXAMPLE 9.28
Variable number of arguments in Java

Like C and C++, C# and recent versions of Java support variable numbers of parameters, but unlike their parent languages they do so in a type-safe manner, by requiring all trailing parameters to share a common type. In Java, for example, one can write

```
static void print_lines(String foo, String... lines) {
    System.out.println("First argument is \"" + foo + "\".");
    System.out.println("There are " +
        lines.length + " additional arguments:");
    for (String str: lines) {
        System.out.println(str);
    }
}
...
print_lines("Hello, world", "This is a message", "from your sponsor.");
```

Here again the ellipsis in the method header is part of the language syntax. Method print_lines has two arguments. The first, foo, is of type String; the second, lines, is of type String.... Within print_lines, lines functions as if it had type String[] (array of String). The caller, however, need not package the second and subsequent parameters into an explicit array; the compiler does this automatically, and the program prints

```
First argument is "Hello, world".
There are 2 additional arguments:
This is a message
from your sponsor.
```

EXAMPLE 9.29
Variable number of arguments in C#

The parameter declaration syntax is slightly different in C#:

```
static void print_lines(String foo, params String[] lines) {
    Console.WriteLine("First argument is \"" + foo + "\".");
    Console.WriteLine("There are " +
        lines.Length + " additional arguments:");
    foreach (String line in lines) {
        Console.WriteLine(line);
    }
}
```

The calling syntax is the same. ■

9.3.4 Function Returns

The syntax by which a function indicates the value to be returned varies greatly. In languages like Lisp, ML, and Algol 68, which do not distinguish between expressions and statements, the value of a function is simply the value of its body, which is itself an expression.

In several early imperative languages, including Algol 60, Fortran, and Pascal, a function specified its return value by executing an assignment statement whose left-hand side was the name of the function. This approach has an unfortunate interaction with the usual static scope rules (Section 3.3.1): the compiler must forbid any immediately nested declaration that would hide the name of the function, since the function would then be unable to return. This special case is avoided in more recent imperative languages by introducing an explicit `return` statement:

EXAMPLE 9.30
`return` statement

```
return expression
```

In addition to specifying a value, `return` causes the immediate termination of the subroutine. A function that has figured out what to return but doesn't want to return yet can always assign the return value into a temporary variable, and then return it later:

```
rtn := expression
...
return rtn
```

■

Fortran separates termination of a subroutine from the specification of return values: it specifies the return value by assigning to the function name, and has a `return` statement that takes no arguments.

EXAMPLE 9.31
Incremental computation of a return value

Argument-bearing `return` statements and assignment to the function name both force the programmer to employ a temporary variable in incremental computations. Here is an example in Ada:

```
type int_array is array (integer range <>) of integer;
    -- array of integers with unspecified integer bounds
function A_max(A : int_array) return integer is
rtn : integer;
begin
    rtn := integer'first;
    for i in A'first .. A'last loop
        if A(i) > rtn then rtn := A(i); end if;
    end loop;
    return rtn;
end A_max;
```

Here rtn must be declared as a variable so that the function can read it as well as write it. Because rtn is a local variable, most compilers will allocate it within the stack frame of A_max. The return statement must then copy that variable's value into the return location allocated by the caller.

EXAMPLE 9.32

Explicitly named return values in Go

Some languages eliminate the need for a local variable by allowing the result of a function to have a name in its own right. In Go one can write

```
func A_max(A []int) (rtn int) {
    rtn = A[0]
    for i := 1; i < len(A); i++ {
        if A[i] > rtn { rtn = A[i] }
    }
    return
}
```

Here rtn can reside throughout its lifetime in the return location allocated by the caller. A similar facility can be found in Eiffel, in which every function contains an implicitly declared object named Result. This object can be both read and written, and is returned to the caller when the function returns.

EXAMPLE 9.33

Multivalue returns

Many early languages placed restrictions on the types of objects that could be returned from a function. In Algol 60 and Fortran 77, a function had to return a scalar value. In Pascal and early versions of Modula-2, it could return a scalar or a pointer. Most imperative languages are more flexible: Algol 68, Ada, C, Fortran 90, and many (nonstandard) implementations of Pascal allow functions to return values of composite type. ML, its descendants, and several scripting languages allow a function to return a *tuple* of values. In Python, for example, we might write

```
def foo():
    return 2, 3
...
i, j = foo()
```

In functional languages, it is commonplace to return a subroutine as a closure. Many imperative languages permit this as well. C has no closures, but allows a function to return a pointer to a subroutine.

✓ CHECK YOUR UNDERSTANDING

13. What is the difference between *formal* and *actual* parameters?
14. Describe four common parameter-passing modes. How does a programmer choose which one to use when?
15. Explain the rationale for `READONLY` parameters in Modula-3.
16. What parameter mode is typically used in languages with a reference model of variables?
17. Describe the parameter modes of Ada. How do they differ from the modes of other modern languages?
18. Give an example in which it is useful to return a reference from a function in C++.
19. What is an *r-value reference*? Why might it be useful?
20. List three reasons why a language implementation might implement a parameter as a closure.
21. What is a *conformant (open) array*?
22. What are *default* parameters? How are they implemented?
23. What are *named (keyword) parameters*? Why are they useful?
24. Explain the value of variable-length argument lists. What distinguishes such lists in Java and C# from their counterparts in C and C++?
25. Describe three common mechanisms for specifying the return value of a function. What are their relative strengths and drawbacks?

9.4 Exception Handling

Several times in the preceding chapters and sections we have referred to *exception-handling* mechanisms. We have delayed detailed discussion of these mechanisms until now because exception handling generally requires the language implementation to "unwind" the subroutine call stack.

An exception can be defined as an unexpected—or at least unusual—condition that arises during program execution, and that cannot easily be handled in the local context. It may be detected automatically by the language implementation, or the program may *raise* or *throw* it explicitly (the two terms are synonymous). The most common exceptions are various sorts of run-time errors. In an I/O library, for example, an input routine may encounter the end of its file before it can read a requested value, or it may find punctuation marks or letters on the input when it is expecting digits. To cope with such errors without an exception-handling mechanism, the programmer has basically three options, none of which is entirely satisfactory:

1. "Invent" a value that can be used by the caller when a real value could not be returned.
2. Return an explicit "status" value to the caller, who must inspect it after every call. Most often, the status is passed through an extra, explicit parameter. In some languages, the regular return value and the status may be returned together as a tuple.
3. Rely on the caller to pass a closure (in languages that support them) for an error-handling routine that the normal routine can call when it runs into trouble.

The first of these options is fine in certain cases, but does not work in the general case. Options 2 and 3 tend to clutter up the program, and impose overhead that we should like to avoid in the common case. The tests in option 2 are particularly offensive: they obscure the normal flow of events in the common case. Because they are so tedious and repetitive, they are also a common source of errors; one can easily forget a needed test. Exception-handling mechanisms address these issues by moving error-checking code "out of line," allowing the normal case to be specified simply, and arranging for control to branch to a *handler* when appropriate.

EXAMPLE 9.34
`ON` conditions in PL/I

Exception handling was pioneered by PL/I, which includes an executable statement of the form

```
ON condition
    statement
```

The nested statement (often a `GOTO` or a `BEGIN...END` block) is a handler. It is not executed when the `ON` statement is encountered, but is "remembered" for future reference. It will be executed later if exception *condition* (e.g., `OVERFLOW`) arises. Because the `ON` statement is executable, the binding of handlers to exceptions depends on the flow of control at run time.

If a PL/I exception handler is invoked and then "returns" (i.e., does not perform a `GOTO` to somewhere else in the program), then one of two things will happen. For exceptions that the language designers considered to be fatal, the program itself will terminate. For "recoverable" exceptions, execution will resume at the statement following the one in which the exception occurred. Unfortunately, experience with PL/I revealed that both the dynamic binding of handlers to exceptions and the automatic resumption of code in which an exception occurred were confusing and error-prone.

EXAMPLE 9.35
A simple `try` block in C++

Many more recent languages, including Ada, Python, PHP, Ruby, C++, Java, C#, and ML, provide exception-handling facilities in which handlers are lexically bound to blocks of code, and in which the execution of the handler *replaces* the yet-to-be-completed portion of the block. In C++ we might write

```
try {
    if (something_unexpected)
        throw my_error("oops!");
    ...
    cout << "everything's ok\n";

} catch (my_error e) {
    cout << e.explanation << "\n";
}
```

If something_unexpected occurs, this code will *throw* an exception of class my_error. This exception will be *caught* by the catch block, whose parameter, e, has a matching type (here assumed to have a string field named explanation). The catch block will then execute in place of the remainder of the try block. ■

EXAMPLE 9.36
Nested try blocks

Code blocks with handlers can nest:

```
try {
    ...
    try {
        ...
        if (something_unexpected)
            throw my_error("oops!");
        ...
        cout << "everything's ok\n";
        ...
    } catch (some_other_error e1) {
        cout << "not this one\n";
    }
    ...
} catch (my_error e) {
    cout << e.explanation << "\n";
}
```

When the exception is thrown, control transfers to the innermost *matching* handler within the current subroutine. ■

EXAMPLE 9.37
Propagation of an exception out of a called routine

If there is no matching handler in the current subroutine, then the subroutine returns abruptly and the exception is re raised at the point of call:

```
try {                                  void foo() {
    ...                                    ...
    foo();                                 if (something_unexpected)
    ...                                        throw my_error("oops!");
    cout << "everything's ok\n";           ...
                                       }
} catch (my_error e) {
    cout << e.explanation << "\n";
}
```

If the exception is not handled in the calling routine, it continues to propagate back up the dynamic chain. If it is not handled in the program's main routine, then a predefined outermost handler is invoked, and usually terminates the program. ▪

In a sense, the dependence of exception handling on the order of subroutine calls might be considered a form of dynamic binding, but it is a much more restricted form than is found in PL/I. Rather than say that a handler in a calling routine has been dynamically bound to an error in a called routine, we prefer to say that the handler is lexically bound to the expression or statement that *calls* the called routine. An exception that is not handled inside a called routine can then be modeled as an "exceptional return"; it causes the calling expression or statement to raise an exception, which is again handled lexically within its subroutine.

In practice, exception handlers tend to perform three kinds of operations. First, ideally, a handler will *compensate* for the exception in a way that allows the program to recover and continue execution. For example, in response to an "out of memory" exception in a storage management routine, a handler might ask the operating system to allocate additional space to the application, after which it could complete the requested operation. Second, when an exception occurs in a given block of code but cannot be handled locally, it is often important to declare a local handler that cleans up any resources allocated in the local block, and then "reraises" the exception, so that it will continue to propagate back to a handler that can (hopefully) recover. Third, if recovery is not possible, a handler can at least print a helpful error message before the program terminates.

As discussed in Section 6.2.1, exceptions are related to, but distinct from, the notion of multilevel returns. A routine that performs a multilevel return is functioning as expected; in Eiffel terminology, it is fulfilling its contract. A routine that raises an exception is *not* functioning as expected; it cannot fulfill its contract. Common Lisp and Ruby distinguish between these two related concepts, but most languages do not; in most, a multilevel return requires the outer caller to provide a trivial handler.

Common Lisp is also unusual in providing four different versions of its exception-handling mechanism. Two of these provide the usual "exceptional return" semantics; the others are designed to repair the problem and restart evaluation of some dynamically enclosing expression. Orthogonally, two perform their work in the referencing environment where the handler is declared; the others perform their work in the environment where the exception first arises. The latter option allows an abstraction to provide several alternative strategies for recovery from exceptions. The user of the abstraction can then specify, dynamically, which of these strategies should be used in a given context. We will consider Common Lisp further in Exercise 9.22 and Exploration 9.43. The "exceptional return" mechanism, with work performed in the environment of the handler, is known as `handler-case`; it provides semantics comparable to those of most other modern languages.

9.4.1 Defining Exceptions

In many languages, dynamic semantic errors automatically result in exceptions, which the program can then catch. The programmer can also define additional, application-specific exceptions. Examples of predefined exceptions include arithmetic overflow, division by zero, end-of-file on input, subscript and subrange errors, and null pointer dereference. The rationale for defining these as exceptions (rather than as fatal errors) is that they may arise in certain valid programs. Some other dynamic errors (e.g., return from a subroutine that has not yet designated a return value) are still fatal in most languages. In C++ and Common Lisp, exceptions are all programmer defined. In PHP, the `set_error_handler` function can be used to turn built-in semantic errors into ordinary exceptions. In Ada, some of the predefined exceptions can be *suppressed* by means of a pragma.

EXAMPLE 9.38 What *is* an exception?

An Ada exception is simply an object of the built-in `exception` type:

```
declare empty_queue : exception;
```

In Modula-3, exceptions are another "kind" of object, akin to constants, types, variables, or subroutines:

```
EXCEPTION empty_queue;
```

In most object-oriented languages, an exception is an instance of some predefined or user-defined class type:

```
class empty_queue {};
```

EXAMPLE 9.39 Parameterized exceptions

Most languages allow an exception to be "parameterized," so the code that raises the exception can pass information to the code that handles it. In object-oriented languages, the "parameters" are simply the fields of the class:

```
class duplicate_in_set {                    // C++
public:
    item dup;          // element that was inserted twice
    duplicate_in_set(item d) : dup(d) { }
};
...
throw duplicate_in_set(d);
```

In Modula-3, the parameters are included in the exception declaration, much as they are in a subroutine header (the Modula-3 `empty_queue` in Example 9.38 has no parameters). In Ada, the standard `Exceptions` library can be used to pass information from a `raise` statement to a handler. Without the library, an exception is simply a tag, with no value other than its name.

If a subroutine raises an exception but does not catch it internally, it may "return" in an unexpected way. This possibility is an important part of the routine's interface to the rest of the program. Consequently, several languages, including Modula-3, C++, and Java, include in each subroutine header a list of the exceptions that may propagate out of the routine. This list is mandatory in Modula-3: it is a run-time error if an exception arises that does not appear in the header and is not caught internally. The list is optional in C++: if it appears, the semantics are the same as in Modula-3; if it is omitted, all exceptions are permitted to propagate. Java adopts an intermediate approach: it segregates its exceptions into "checked" and "unchecked" categories. Checked exceptions must be declared in subroutine headers; unchecked exceptions need not. Unchecked exceptions are typically run-time errors that most programs will want to be fatal (e.g., subscript out of bounds)—and that would therefore be a nuisance to declare in every function—but that a highly robust program may want to catch if they occur in library routines.

9.4.2 Exception Propagation

EXAMPLE 9.40
Multiple handlers in C++

In most languages, a block of code can have a *list* of exception handlers. In C++:

```
try {                // try to read from file
    ...
    // potentially complicated sequence of operations
    // involving many calls to stream I/O routines
    ...
} catch(end_of_file e1) {
    ...
} catch(io_error e2) {
    // handler for any io_error other than end_of_file
    ...
} catch(...) {
    // handler for any exception not previously named
    // (in this case, the triple-dot ellipsis is a valid C++ token;
    // it does not indicate missing code)
}
```

When an exception arises, the handlers are examined in order; control is transferred to the first one that *matches* the exception. In C++, a handler matches if it names a class from which the exception is derived, or if it is a catch-all (`...`). In the example here, let us assume that `end_of_file` is a subclass of `io_error`. Then an `end_of_file` exception, if it arises, will be handled by the first of the three `catch` clauses. All other I/O errors will be caught by the second; all non-I/O errors will be caught by the third. If the last clause were missing, non-I/O errors would continue to propagate outward in the current subroutine, and then up the dynamic chain. ■

An exception that is declared in a recursive subroutine will be caught by the innermost handler for that exception at run time. If an exception propagates out of the scope in which it was declared, it can no longer be named by a handler, and thus can be caught only by a "catch-all" handler. In a language with concurrency, one must consider what will happen if an exception is not handled at the outermost level of a concurrent thread of control. In Modula-3 and C++, the entire program terminates abnormally; in Ada and Java, the affected thread terminates quietly; in C#, the behavior is implementation defined.

Handlers on Expressions

In an expression-oriented language such as ML or Common Lisp, an exception handler is attached to an expression, rather than to a statement. Since execution of the handler replaces the unfinished portion of the protected code when an exception occurs, a handler attached to an expression must provide a value for the expression. (In a statement-oriented language, the handler—like most statements—is executed for its side effects.) In the OCaml dialect of ML, a handler looks like this:

EXAMPLE 9.41
Exception handler in OCaml

```
let foo = try a / b with Division_by_zero -> max_int;;
```

Here `a / b` is the protected expression, `try` and `with` are keywords, `Division_by_zero` is an exception (a value built from the `exception` constructor), and `max_int` is an expression (in this case a constant) whose value replaces the value of the expression in which the `Division_by_zero` exception arose. Both the protected expression and the handler could in general be arbitrarily complicated, with many nested function calls. Exceptions that arise within a nested call (and are not handled locally) propagate back up the dynamic chain, just as they do in most statement-oriented languages. ■

Cleanup Operations

In the process of searching for a matching handler, the exception-handling mechanism must "unwind" the run-time stack by reclaiming the frames of any subroutines from which the exception escapes. Reclaiming a frame requires not only that its space be popped from the stack but also that any registers that were saved as part of the calling sequence be restored. (We discuss implementation issues in more detail in Section 9.4.3.)

In C++, an exception that leaves a scope, whether a subroutine or just a nested block, requires the language implementation to call *destructor* functions

DESIGN & IMPLEMENTATION

9.4 Structured exceptions

Exception-handling mechanisms are among the most complex aspects of modern language design, from both a semantic and a pragmatic point of view. Programmers have used subroutines since before there were computers (they appear, among other places, in the 19th-century notes of Countess Ada Augusta Byron). Structured exceptions, by contrast, were not invented until the 1970s, and did not become commonplace until the 1980s.

for any objects declared within that scope. Destructors (to be discussed in more detail in Section 10.3) are often used to deallocate heap space and other resources (e.g., open files). Similar functionality is provided in Common Lisp by an `unwind-protect` expression, and in Modula-3, Python, Java, and C# by means of `try... finally` constructs. Code in Python might look like this:

EXAMPLE 9.42
`finally` clause in Python

```
try:                                    # protected block
    my_stream = open("foo.txt", "r")    # "r" means "for reading"
    for line in my_stream:
        ...
finally:
    my_stream.close()
```

A `finally` clause will be executed whenever control escapes from the protected block, whether the escape is due to normal completion, an exit from a loop, a return from the current subroutine, or the propagation of an exception. We have assumed in our example that `my_stream` is not bound to anything at the beginning of the code, and that it is harmless to close a not-yet-opened stream.

9.4.3 Implementation of Exceptions

EXAMPLE 9.43
Stacked exception handlers

The most obvious implementation for exceptions maintains a linked-list stack of handlers. When control enters a protected block, the handler for that block is added to the head of the list. When an exception arises, either implicitly or as a result of a `raise` or `throw` statement, the language run-time system pops the innermost handler off the list and calls it. The handler begins by checking to see if it matches the exception that occurred; if not, it simply reraises it:

```
if exception matches duplicate_in_set
    ...
else
    reraise exception
```

To implement propagation back down the dynamic chain, each subroutine has an implicit handler that performs the work of the subroutine epilogue code and then reraises the exception.

EXAMPLE 9.44
Multiple exceptions per handler

If a protected block of code has handlers for several different exceptions, they are implemented as a single handler containing a multiarm `if` statement:

```
if exception matches end_of_file
    ...
elsif exception matches io_error
    ...
else
    ...         –– "catch-all" handler
```

The problem with this implementation is that it incurs run-time overhead in the common case. Every protected block and every subroutine begins with code to push a handler onto the handler list, and ends with code to pop it back off the list. We can usually do better.

The only real purpose of the handler list is to determine which handler is active. Since blocks of source code tend to translate into contiguous blocks of machine language instructions, we can capture the correspondence between handlers and protected blocks in the form of a table generated at compile time. Each entry in the table contains two fields: the starting address of a block of code and the address of the corresponding handler. The table is sorted on the first field. When an exception occurs, the language run-time system performs binary search in the table, using the program counter as key, to find the handler for the current block. If that handler reraises the exception, the process repeats: handlers themselves are blocks of code, and can be found in the table. The only subtlety arises in the case of the implicit handlers associated with propagation out of subroutines: such a handler must ensure that the reraise code uses the return address of the subroutine, rather than the current program counter, as the key for table lookup.

The cost of raising an exception is higher in this second implementation, by a factor logarithmic in the total number of handlers. But this cost is paid only when an exception actually occurs. Assuming that exceptions are unusual events, the net impact on performance is clearly beneficial: the cost in the common case is zero. In its pure form the table-based approach requires that the compiler have access to the entire program, or that the linker provide a mechanism to glue subtables together. If code fragments are compiled independently, we can employ a hybrid approach in which the compiler creates a separate table for each subroutine, and each stack frame contains a pointer to the appropriate table.

Exception Handling without Exceptions

It is worth noting that exceptions can sometimes be simulated in a language that does not provide them as a built-in. In Section 6.2 we noted that Pascal permitted `goto`s to labels outside the current subroutine, that Algol 60 allowed labels to be passed as parameters, and that PL/I allowed them to be stored in variables. These mechanisms permit the program to escape from a deeply nested context, but in a very unstructured way.

A more structured alternative can be found in the `call-with-current-continuation` (`call-cc`) routine of languages like Scheme and Ruby. As described in Section 6.2.2, `call-cc` takes a single argument *f*, which is itself a function. It calls *f*, passing as argument a continuation *c* (a closure) that captures the current program counter and referencing environment.. At any point in the future, *f* can call *c* to reestablish the saved environment. If nested calls have been made, control abandons them, as it does with exceptions. If we represent a protected block and its handlers as closures (lambda expressions), `call-cc` can be used to maintain a stack of continuations to which one should jump to emulate `raise`/`throw`. We explore this option further in Exercise 9.18.

EXAMPLE 9.45
setjmp and longjmp in C

Intermediate between the anarchy of nonlocal gotos and the generality of call/cc, C provides a pair of library routines entitled setjmp and longjmp. Setjmp takes as argument a buffer into which to capture a representation of the program's current state. This buffer can later be passed as the first argument to longjmp, to restore the captured state. Calls to setjmp return an integer: zero indicates "normal" return; nonzero values (provided as the second argument to longjmp) indicate exceptional "returns" from longjmp. Typical uses look like

```
if (!setjmp(buffer)) {
    /* protected code */
} else {
    /* handler */
}
```

or

```
switch (setjmp(buffer)) {
  case 0:
    /* protected code */
    break;
  case 1:
    /* handler 1 */
    break;
  ...
  case n:
    /* handler n */
    break:
}
```

When initially called, setjmp returns a 0, and control enters the protected code. If longjmp(buffer, v) is called anywhere within the protected code, or in anything called by that code, then setjmp will appear to return again, this time with a return value of v, causing control to enter a handler. Unlike the closure created by call/cc, the information captured by setjmp has limited extent: the behavior of longjmp(buffer, v) is undefined if the function containing the call to setjmp has returned. ■

The typical implementation of setjmp and longjmp saves the current machine registers in the setjmp buffer, and restores them in longjmp. There is no list of handlers; rather than "unwinding" the stack, the implementation simply tosses all the nested frames by restoring old values of the sp and fp. The problem with this approach is that the register contents at the beginning of the handler do not reflect the effects of the successfully completed portion of the protected code: they were saved before that code began to run. Any changes to variables that have

DESIGN & IMPLEMENTATION

9.5 setjmp

Because it saves multiple registers to memory, the usual implementation of setjmp is quite expensive—more so than entry to a protected block in the "obvious" implementation of exceptions described above. While implementors are free to use a more efficient, table-driven approach if desired, the usual implementation minimizes the complexity of the run-time system and eliminates the need for linker-supported integration of tables from separately compiled modules and libraries.

been written through to memory will be visible in the handler, but changes that were cached in registers will be lost. To address this limitation, C allows the programmer to specify that certain variables are `volatile`. A volatile variable is one whose value in memory can change "spontaneously," for example as the result of activity by an I/O device or a concurrent thread of control. C implementations are required to store volatile variables to memory whenever they are written, and to load them from memory whenever they are read. If a handler needs to see changes to a variable that may be modified by the protected code, then the programmer must include the `volatile` keyword in the variable's declaration.

✓ CHECK YOUR UNDERSTANDING

26. Describe three ways in which a language may allow programmers to declare exceptions.
27. Explain why it is useful to define exceptions as classes in C++, Java, and C#.
28. Explain the behavior and purpose of a `try... finally` construct.
29. Describe the algorithm used to identify an appropriate handler when an exception is raised in a language like Ada or C++.
30. Explain how to implement exceptions in a way that incurs no cost in the common case (when exceptions don't arise).
31. How do the exception handlers of a functional language like ML differ from those of an imperative language like C++?
32. Describe the operations that must be performed by the implicit handler for a subroutine.
33. Summarize the shortcomings of the `setjmp` and `longjmp` library routines of C.
34. What is a `volatile` variable in C? Under what circumstances is it useful?

9.5 Coroutines

Given an understanding of the layout of the run-time stack, we can now consider the implementation of more general control abstractions—*coroutines* in particular. Like a continuation, a coroutine is represented by a closure (a code address and a referencing environment), into which we can jump by means of a nonlocal `goto`, in this case a special operation known as transfer. The principal difference between the two abstractions is that a continuation is a constant—it does not change once created—while a coroutine changes every time it runs. When we `goto` a continuation, our old program counter is lost, unless we explicitly create a new continuation to hold it. When we transfer from one coroutine to another, our old program counter is saved: the coroutine we are leaving is updated to reflect it. Thus, if we perform a `goto` into the same continuation multiple times, each jump will start at precisely the same location, but if we perform a `transfer` into the same coroutine multiple times, each jump will take up where the previous one left off.

In effect, coroutines are execution contexts that exist concurrently, but that execute one at a time, and that transfer control to each other explicitly, by name. Coroutines can be used to implement iterators (Section 6.5.3) and threads (to be discussed in Chapter 13). They are also useful in their own right, particularly for certain kinds of servers, and for discrete event simulation. Threads have appeared, historically, as far back as Algol 68. Today they can be found in Ada, Java, C#, C++, Python, Ruby, Haskell, Go, and Scala, among many others. They are also commonly provided (though with somewhat less attractive syntax and semantics) outside the language proper by means of library packages. Coroutines are less common as a user-level programming abstraction. Historically, the two most important languages to provide them were Simula and Modula-2. We focus in the following subsections on the implementation of coroutines and (on the companion site) on their use in iterators (Section C-9.5.3) and discrete event simulation (Section C-9.5.4).

EXAMPLE 9.46
Explicit interleaving of concurrent computations

As a simple example of an application in which coroutines might be useful, imagine that we are writing a "screen saver" program, which paints a mostly black picture on the screen of an inactive laptop, and which keeps the picture moving, to avoid liquid-crystal "burn-in." Imagine also that our screen saver performs "sanity checks" on the file system in the background, looking for corrupted files. We could write our program as follows:

```
loop
    -- update picture on screen
    -- perform next sanity check
```

The problem with this approach is that successive sanity checks (and to a lesser extent successive screen updates) are likely to depend on each other. On most systems, the file-system checking code has a deeply nested control structure containing many loops. To break it into pieces that can be interleaved with the screen updates, the programmer must follow each check with code that saves the state of the nested computation, and must precede the following check with code that restores that state. ■

EXAMPLE 9.47
Interleaving coroutines

A much more attractive approach is to cast the operations as coroutines:[5]

5 Threads could also be used in this example, and might in fact serve our needs a bit better. Coroutines suffice because there is a small number of execution contexts (namely two), and because it is easy to identify points at which one should transfer to the other.

```
us, cfs : coroutine

coroutine check_file_system()
    -- initialize
    detach
    for all files
        ...
        transfer(us)
        ...
            transfer(us)
        ...
        transfer(us)
        ...

coroutine update_screen()
    -- initialize
    detach
    loop
        ...
        transfer(cfs)
        ...

begin           -- main
    us := new update_screen()
    cfs := new check_file_system()
    transfer(us)
```

The syntax here is based loosely on that of Simula. When first created, a coroutine performs any necessary initialization operations, and then detaches itself from the main program. The detach operation creates a coroutine object to which control can later be transfered, and returns a reference to this coroutine to the caller. The transfer operation saves the current program counter in the current coroutine object and resumes the coroutine specified as a parameter. The main body of the program plays the role of an initial, default coroutine.

Calls to transfer from within the body of check_file_system can occur at arbitrary places, including nested loops and conditionals. A coroutine can also call subroutines, just as the main program can, and calls to transfer may appear inside these routines. The context needed to perform the "next" sanity check is captured by the program counter, together with the local variables of check_file_system and any called routines, at the time of the transfer.

As in Example 9.46, the programmer must specify when to stop checking the file system and update the screen; coroutines make the job simpler by providing a transfer operation that eliminates the need to save and restore state explicitly. To decide where to place the calls to transfer, we must consider both performance and correctness. For performance, we must avoid doing too much work between calls, so that screen updates aren't too infrequent. For correctness, we must avoid doing a transfer in the middle of any check that might be compromised by file access in update_screen. Parallel threads (to be described in Chapter 13) would

DESIGN & IMPLEMENTATION

9.6 Threads and coroutines

As we shall see in Section 13.2.4, it is easy to build a simple thread package given coroutines. Most programmers would agree, however, that threads are substantially easier to use, because they eliminate the need for explicit transfer operations. This contrast—a lot of extra functionality for a little extra implementation complexity—probably explains why coroutines as an explicit programming abstraction are relatively rare.

eliminate the first of these problems by ensuring that the screen updater receives a share of the processor on a regular basis, but would complicate the second problem: we should need to synchronize the two routines explicitly if their references to files could interfere.

9.5.1 Stack Allocation

Because they are concurrent (i.e., simultaneously started but not completed), coroutines cannot share a single stack: their subroutine calls and returns, taken as a whole, do not occur in last-in-first-out order. If each coroutine is declared at the outermost level of lexical nesting (as was required in Modula-2), then their stacks are entirely disjoint: the only objects they share are global, and thus statically allocated. Most operating systems make it easy to allocate one stack, and to increase its portion of the virtual address space as necessary during execution. It is not as easy to allocate an arbitrary number of such stacks; space for coroutines was historically something of an implementation challenge, at least on machines with limited virtual address space (64-bit architectures ease the problem, by making virtual addresses relatively plentiful).

The simplest approach is to give each coroutine a fixed amount of statically allocated stack space. This approach was adopted in Modula-2, which required the programmer to specify the size and location of the stack when initializing a coroutine. It was a run-time error for the coroutine to need additional space. Some Modula-2 implementations would catch the overflow and halt with an error message; others would display abnormal behavior. If the coroutine used less (virtual) space than it was given, the excess was simply wasted.

If stack frames are allocated from the heap, as they are in most functional language implementations, then the problems of overflow and internal fragmentation are avoided. At the same time, the overhead of each subroutine call increases. An intermediate option is to allocate the stack in large, fixed-size "chunks." At each call, the subroutine calling sequence checks to see whether there is sufficient space in the current chunk to hold the frame of the called routine. If not, another chunk is allocated and the frame is put there instead. At each subroutine return, the epilogue code checks to see whether the current frame is the last one in its chunk. If so, the chunk is returned to a "free chunk" pool. To reduce the overhead of calls, the compiler can use the ordinary central stack if it is able to verify that a subroutine will not perform a transfer before returning [Sco91].

DESIGN & IMPLEMENTATION

9.7 Coroutine stacks

Many languages require coroutines or threads to be declared at the outermost level of lexical nesting, to avoid the complexity of noncontiguous stacks. Most thread libraries for sequential languages (the POSIX standard `pthread` library among them) likewise require or at least permit the use of contiguous stacks.

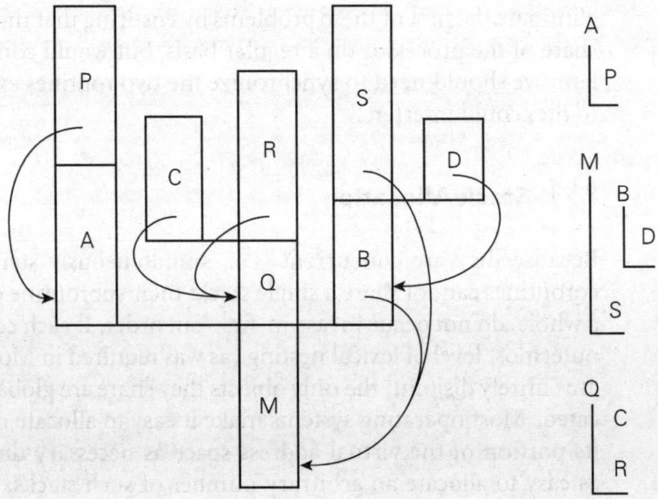

Figure 9.4 **A cactus stack.** Each branch to the side represents the creation of a coroutine (A, B, C, and D). The static nesting of blocks is shown at right. Static links are shown with arrows. Dynamic links are indicated simply by vertical arrangement: each routine has called the one above it. (Coroutine B, for example, was created by the main program, M. B in turn called subroutine S and created coroutine D.)

EXAMPLE 9.48
Cactus stacks

If coroutines can be created at arbitrary levels of lexical nesting (as they could in Simula), then two or more coroutines may be declared in the same nonglobal scope, and must thus share access to objects in that scope. To implement this sharing, the run-time system must employ a so-called *cactus stack* (named for its resemblance to the Saguaro cacti of the American Southwest; see Figure 9.4).

Each branch off the stack contains the frames of a separate coroutine. The dynamic chain of a given coroutine ends in the block in which the coroutine began execution. The *static* chain of the coroutine, however, extends down into the remainder of the cactus, through any lexically surrounding blocks. In addition to the coroutines of Simula, cactus stacks are needed for the threads of any language with lexically nested threads. "Returning" from the main block of a coroutine must generally terminate the program, as there is no indication of what routine to transfer to. Because a coroutine only runs when specified as the target of a transfer, there is never any need to terminate it explicitly. When a given coroutine is no longer needed, the programmer can simply reuse its stack space or, in a language with garbage collection, allow the collector to reclaim it automatically. ■

9.5.2 Transfer

To transfer from one coroutine to another, the run-time system must change the program counter (PC), the stack, and the contents of the processor's registers. These changes are encapsulated in the transfer operation: one coroutine calls transfer; a different one returns. Because the change happens inside transfer, changing the PC from one coroutine to another simply amounts to remembering the right return address: the old coroutine calls transfer from one location in the program; the new coroutine returns to a potentially different location. If transfer saves its return address in the stack, then the PC will change automatically as a side effect of changing stacks.

EXAMPLE 9.49
Switching coroutines

So how do we change stacks? The usual approach is simply to change the stack pointer register, and to avoid using the frame pointer inside of transfer itself. At the beginning of transfer we push all the callee-saves registers onto the current stack, along with the return address (if it wasn't already pushed by the subroutine call instruction). We then change the sp, pop the (new) return address (ra) and other registers off the new stack, and return:

```
transfer:
    push all registers other than sp (including ra)
    *current_coroutine := sp
    current_coroutine := r1      -- argument passed to transfer
    sp := *r1
    pop all registers other than sp (including ra)
    return
```

The data structure that represents a coroutine or thread is called a *context block*. In a simple coroutine package, the context block contains a single value: the coroutine's sp as of its most recent transfer. (A thread package generally places additional information in the context block, such as an indication of priority, or pointers to link the thread onto various scheduling queues. Some coroutine or thread packages choose to save registers in the context block, rather than at the top of the stack; either approach works fine.)

In Modula-2, the coroutine creation routine would initialize the coroutine's stack to look like the frame of transfer, with a return address and register contents initialized to permit a "return" into the beginning of the coroutine's code. The creation routine would set the sp value in the context block to point into this artificial frame, and return a pointer to the context block. To begin execution of the coroutine, some existing routine would need to transfer to it.

In Simula (and in the code in Example 9.47), the coroutine creation routine would begin to execute the new coroutine immediately, as if it were a subroutine. After the coroutine completed any application-specific initialization, it would perform a detach operation. Detach would set up the coroutine stack to look like the frame of transfer, with a return address that pointed to the following statement. It would then allow the creation routine to return to its own caller.

In all cases, transfer expects a pointer to a context block as argument; by dereferencing the pointer it can find the sp of the next coroutine to run. A global (static) variable, called current_coroutine in the code of Example 9.49, contains a pointer to the context block of the currently running coroutine. This pointer allows transfer to find the location in which it should save the old sp.

9.5.3 Implementation of Iterators

Given an implementation of coroutines, iterators are almost trivial: one coroutine is used to represent the main program; a second is used to represent the iterator. Additional coroutines may be needed if iterators nest.

IN MORE DEPTH

Additional details appear on the companion site. As it turns out, coroutines are overkill for iterator implementation. Most compilers use one of two simpler alternatives. The first of these keeps all state in a single stack, but sometimes executes in a frame other than the topmost. The second employs a compile-time code transformation to replace true iterators, transparently, with equivalent iterator objects.

9.5.4 Discrete Event Simulation

One of the most important applications of coroutines (and the one for which Simula was designed and named) is *discrete event simulation*. Simulation in general refers to any process in which we create an abstract model of some real-world system, and then experiment with the model in order to infer properties of the real-world system. Simulation is desirable when experimentation with the real world would be complicated, dangerous, expensive, or otherwise impractical. A *discrete event* simulation is one in which the model is naturally expressed in terms of events (typically interactions among various interesting objects) that happen at specific times. Discrete event simulation is usually not appropriate for continuous processes, such as the growth of crystals or the flow of water over a surface, unless these processes are captured at the level of individual particles.

IN MORE DEPTH

On the companion site we consider a traffic simulation, in which events model interactions among automobiles, intersections, and traffic lights. We use a separate coroutine for each trip to be taken by car. At any given time we run the coroutine with the earliest expected arrival time at an upcoming intersection. We keep inactive coroutines in a priority queue ordered by those arrival times.

9.6 Events

An *event* is something to which a running program (a process) needs to respond, but which occurs outside the program, at an unpredictable time. Events are commonly caused by inputs to a graphical user interface (GUI) system: keystrokes, mouse motions, button clicks. They may also be network operations or other asynchronous I/O activity: the arrival of a message, the completion of a previously requested disk operation.

In the I/O operations discussed in Section C-8.7, and in Section C-8.7.3 in particular, we assumed that a program looking for input will request it explicitly, and will wait if it isn't yet available. This sort of *synchronous* (at a specified time) and *blocking* (potentially wait-inducing) input is generally not acceptable for modern applications with graphical interfaces. Instead, the programmer usually wants a *handler*—a special subroutine—to be invoked when a given event occurs. Handlers are sometimes known as *callback* functions, because the run-time system calls back into the main program instead of being called *from* it. In an object-oriented language, the callback function may be a method of some *handler object*, rather than a static subroutine.

9.6.1 Sequential Handlers

Traditionally, event handlers were implemented in sequential programming languages as "spontaneous" subroutine calls, typically using a mechanism defined and implemented by the operating system, outside the language proper. To prepare to receive events through this mechanism, a program—call it *P*—invokes a setup_handler library routine, passing as argument the subroutine it wants to have invoked when the event occurs.

At the hardware level, asynchronous device activity during *P*'s execution will trigger an *interrupt* mechanism that saves *P*'s registers, switches to a different stack, and jumps to a predefined address in the OS kernel. Similarly, if some other process *Q* is running when the interrupt occurs (or if some action in *Q* itself needs to be reflected to *P* as an event), the kernel will have saved *P*'s state at the end of its last time slice. Either way, the kernel must arrange to invoke the appropriate event handler despite the fact that *P* may be at a place in its code where a subroutine call cannot normally occur (e.g., it may be halfway through the calling sequence for some other subroutine).

EXAMPLE 9.50
Signal trampoline

Figure 9.5 illustrates the typical implementation of spontaneous subroutine calls—as used, for example, by the Unix *signal* mechanism. The language run-time library contains a block of code known as the *signal trampoline.* It also includes a buffer writable by the kernel and readable by the runtime. Before delivering a signal, the kernel places the saved state of *P* into the shared buffer. It then switches back to *P*'s user-level stack and jumps into the signal trampoline. The trampoline creates a frame for itself in the stack and then calls the event handler using the normal subroutine calling sequence. (The correctness of this mechanism depends on there being nothing important in the stack beyond the location specified by the stack pointer register at the time of the interrupt.) When the event handler returns, the trampoline restores state (including all registers) from the buffer written by the kernel, and jumps back into the main program. To avoid recursive events, the kernel typically disables further signals when it jumps

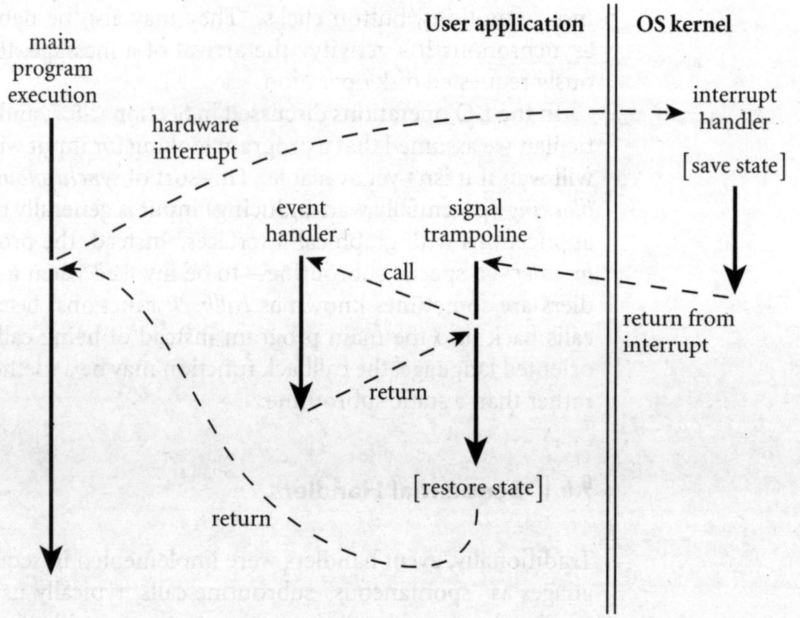

Figure 9.5 **Signal delivery through a trampoline.** When an interrupt occurs (or when another process performs an operation that should appear as an event), the main program may be at an arbitrary place in its code. The kernel saves state and invokes a *trampoline* routine that in turn calls the event handler through the normal calling sequence. After the event handler returns, the trampoline restores the saved state and returns to where the main program left off.

to the signal trampoline. Immediately before jumping back to the original program code, the trampoline performs a kernel call to reenable signals. Depending on the details of the operating system, the kernel may buffer some modest number of signals while they are disabled, and deliver them once the handler reenables them. ■

In practice, most event handlers need to share data structures with the main program (otherwise, how would they get the program to do anything interesting in response to the event?). We must take care to make sure neither the handler nor the main program ever sees these shared structures in an inconsistent state. Specifically, we must prevent a handler from looking at data when the main program is halfway through modifying it, or modifying data when the main program is halfway through reading it. The typical solution is to *synchronize* access to such shared structures by bracketing blocks of code in the main program with kernel calls that disable and reenable signals. We will use a similar mechanism to implement threads on top of coroutines in Section 13.2.4. More general forms of synchronization will appear in Section 13.3.

9.6.2 Thread-Based Handlers

In modern programming languages and run-time systems, events are often handled by a separate thread of control, rather than by spontaneous subroutine calls. With a separate handler thread, input can again be synchronous: the handler thread makes a system call to request the next event, and waits for it to occur. Meanwhile, the main program continues to execute. If the program wishes to be able to handle multiple events concurrently, it may create multiple handler threads, each of which calls into the kernel to wait for an event. To protect the integrity of shared data structures, the main program and the handler thread(s) will generally require a full-fledged synchronization mechanism, as discussed in Section 13.3: disabling signals will not suffice.

EXAMPLE 9.51
An event handler in C#

Many contemporary GUI systems are thread-based, though some have just one handler thread. Examples include the OpenGL Utility Toolkit (GLUT), the GNU Image Manipulation Program (GIMP) Tool Kit (Gtk), the JavaFX library, and the .NET Windows Presentation Foundation (WPF). In C#, an event handler is an instance of a *delegate* type—essentially, a list of subroutine closures (Section 3.6.3). Using Gtk#, the standard GUI for the Mono project, we might create and initialize a button as follows:

```
void Paused(object sender, EventArgs a) {
    // do whatever needs doing when the pause button is pushed
}
...
Button pauseButton = new Button("pause");
pauseButton.Clicked += new EventHandler(Paused);
```

`Button` and `EventHandler` are defined in the Gtk# library. `Button` is a class that represents the graphical widget. `EventHandler` is a delegate type, with which `Paused` is compatible. Its first argument indicates the object that caused the event; its second argument describes the event itself. `Button.Clicked` is the button's event handler: a field of `EventHandler` type. The `+=` operator adds a new closure to the delegate's list.[6] The graphics library arranges for a thread to call into the kernel to wait for user interface events. When our button is pushed, the call will return from the kernel, and the thread will invoke each of the entries on the delegate list. ■

EXAMPLE 9.52
An anonymous delegate handler

As described in Section 3.6.3, C# allows the handler to be specified more succinctly as an *anonymous delegate*:

```
pauseButton.Clicked += delegate(object sender, EventArgs a) {
    // do whatever needs doing
};
```
■

6 Technically, `Clicked` is of `event EventHandler` type. The `event` modifier makes the delegate private, so it can be invoked only from within the class in which it was declared. At the same time, it creates a public *property*, with `add` and `remove` *accessor* methods. These allow code outside the class to add handlers to the event (with `+=`) and remove them from it (with `-=`).

EXAMPLE 9.53
An event handler in Java

Other languages and systems are similar. In JavaFX, an event handler is typically an instance of a class that implements the EventHandler<ActionEvent> interface, with a method named handle:

```
class PauseListener implements EventHandler<ActionEvent> {
    public void handle(ActionEvent e) {
        // do whatever needs doing
    }
}
...
Button pauseButton = new Button();
pauseButton.setText("pause");
pauseButton.setOnAction(new PauseListener());
```

EXAMPLE 9.54
An anonymous inner class handler

Written in this form, the syntax is more cumbersome than it was in C#. We can simplify it some using an *anonymous inner class:*

```
pauseButton.setOnAction(new EventHandler<ActionEvent>() {
    public void handle(ActionEvent e) {
        // do whatever needs doing
    }
});
```

Here the definition of our PauseListener class is embedded, without the name, in a call to new, which is in turn embedded in the argument list of setOnAction. Like an anonymous delegate in C#, an anonymous class in Java can have only a single instance.

EXAMPLE 9.55
Handling an event with a lambda expression

We can simplify the syntax even further by using a Java 8 lambda expression:

```
pauseButton.setOnAction(e -> {
    // do whatever needs doing
});
```

This example leverages the *functional interface* convention of Java lambda expressions, described in Example 3.41. Using this convention, we have effectively matched the brevity of C#.

The action performed by a handler needs to be simple and brief, so the handler thread can call back into the kernel for another event. If the handler takes too long, the user is likely to find the application nonresponsive. If an event needs to initiate something that is computationally demanding, or that may need to perform additional I/O, the handler may create a new thread to do the work; alternatively, it may pass a request to some existing worker thread.

✓ CHECK YOUR UNDERSTANDING

35. What was the first high-level programming language to provide coroutines?
36. What is the difference between a *coroutine* and a *thread*?
37. Why doesn't the *transfer* library routine need to change the program counter when switching between coroutines?
38. Describe three alternative means of allocating coroutine stacks. What are their relative strengths and weaknesses?
39. What is a *cactus stack*? What is its purpose?
40. What is *discrete event simulation*? What is its connection with coroutines?
41. What is an *event* in the programming language sense of the word?
42. Summarize the two main implementation strategies for events.
43. Explain the appeal of *anonymous delegates* (C#) and *anonymous inner classes* (Java) for handling events.

9.7 Summary and Concluding Remarks

This chapter has focused on the subject of control abstraction, and on subroutines in particular. Subroutines allow the programmer to encapsulate code behind a narrow interface, which can then be used without regard to its implementation.

We began our study of subroutines in Section 9.1 by reviewing the management of the subroutine call stack. We then considered the *calling sequences* used to maintain the stack, with extra sections on the companion site devoted to *displays*; case studies of the LLVM and gcc compilers on ARM and x86, respectively; and the *register windows* of the SPARC. After a brief consideration of in-line expansion, we turned in Section 9.3 to the subject of parameters. We first considered parameter-passing *modes*, all of which are implemented by passing values, references, or closures. We noted that the goals of semantic clarity and implementation speed sometimes conflict: it is usually most efficient to pass a large parameter by reference, but the aliasing that results can lead to program bugs. In Section 9.3.3 we considered special parameter-passing mechanisms, including default (optional) parameters, named parameters, and variable-length parameter lists.

In the final three major sections we considered exception-handling mechanisms, which allow a program to "unwind" in a well-structured way from a nested sequence of subroutine calls; coroutines, which allow a program to maintain (and switch between) two or more execution contexts; and events, which allow a program to respond to asynchronous external activity. On the companion site we explained how coroutines are used for discrete event simulation. We also noted that they could be used to implement iterators, but here simpler alternatives exist. In Chapter 13, we will build on coroutines to implement *threads*, which run (or appear to run) in parallel with one another.

In several cases we can discern an evolving consensus about the sorts of control abstractions that a language should provide. The limited parameter-passing modes of languages like Fortran and Algol 60 have been replaced by more extensive or flexible options. Several languages augment the standard positional notation for arguments with default and named parameters. Less-structured error-handling mechanisms, such as label parameters, nonlocal `goto`s, and dynamically bound handlers, have been replaced by structured exception handlers that are lexically scoped within subroutines, and can be implemented at zero cost in the common (no-exception) case. The spontaneous subroutine call of traditional signal-handling mechanisms have been replaced by callbacks in a dedicated thread. In many cases, implementing these newer features has required that compilers and run-time systems become more complex. Occasionally, as in the case of call-by-name parameters, label parameters, or nonlocal `goto`s, features that were semantically confusing were also difficult to implement, and abandoning them has made compilers simpler. In yet other cases language features that are useful but difficult to implement continue to appear in some languages but not in others. Examples in this category include first-class subroutines, coroutines, iterators, continuations, and local objects with unlimited extent.

9.8 Exercises

9.1 Describe as many ways as you can in which functions in imperative programming languages differ from functions in mathematics.

9.2 Consider the following code in C++:

```
class string_map {
    string cached_key;
    string cached_val;
    const string complex_lookup(const string key);
        // body specified elsewhere
public:
    const string operator[](const string key) {
        if (key == cached_key) return cached_val;
        string rtn_val = complex_lookup(key);
        cached_key = key;
        cached_val = rtn_val;
        return rtn_val;
    }
};
```

Suppose that `string_map::operator[]` contains the only call to `complex_lookup` anywhere in the program. Explain why it would be unwise for the programmer to expand that call textually in-line and eliminate the separate function.

9.3 Using your favorite language and compiler, write a program that can tell the order in which certain subroutine parameters are evaluated.

9.4 Consider the following (erroneous) program in C:

```
void foo() {
    int i;
    printf("%d ", i++);
}

int main() {
    int j;
    for (j = 1; j <= 10; j++) foo();
}
```

Local variable `i` in subroutine `foo` is never initialized. On many systems, however, the program will display repeatable behavior, printing `0 1 2 3 4 5 6 7 8 9`. Suggest an explanation. Also explain why the behavior on other systems might be different, or nondeterministic.

9.5 The standard calling sequence for the c. 1980 Digital VAX instruction set employed not only a stack pointer (`sp`) and frame pointer (`fp`), but a separate *arguments pointer* (`ap`) as well. Under what circumstances might this separate pointer be useful? In other words, when might it be handy not to have to place arguments at statically known offsets from the `fp`?

9.6 Write (in the language of your choice) a procedure or function that will have four different effects, depending on whether arguments are passed by value, by reference, by value/result, or by name.

9.7 Consider an expression like `a + b` that is passed to a subroutine in Fortran. Is there any semantically meaningful difference between passing this expression as a reference to an unnamed temporary (as Fortran does) or passing it by value (as one might, for example, in Pascal)? That is, can the programmer tell the difference between a parameter that is a value and a parameter that is a reference to a temporary?

9.8 Consider the following subroutine in Fortran 77:

```
subroutine shift(a, b, c)
integer a, b, c
a = b
b = c
end
```

Suppose we want to call `shift(x, y, 0)` but we don't want to change the value of `y`. Knowing that built-up expressions are passed as temporaries, we decide to call `shift(x, y+0, 0)`. Our code works fine at first, but then (with some compilers) fails when we enable optimization. What is going on? What might we do instead?

9.9 In some implementations of Fortran IV, the following code would print a 3. Can you suggest an explanation? How do you suppose more recent Fortran implementations get around the problem?

```
c     main program
      call foo(2)
      print*, 2
      stop
      end
      subroutine foo(x)
          x = x + 1
          return
      end
```

9.10 Suppose you are writing a program in which all parameters must be passed by name. Can you write a subroutine that will swap the values of its actual parameters? Explain. (Hint: Consider mutually dependent parameters like `i` and `A[i]`.)

9.11 Can you write a `swap` routine in Java, or in any other language with only call-by-sharing parameters? What exactly should `swap` *do* in such a language? (Hint: Think about the distinction between the object to which a variable refers and the value [contents] of that object.)

9.12 As noted in Section 9.3.1, `out` parameters in Ada 83 can be written by the callee but not read. In Ada 95 they can be both read and written, but they begin their life uninitialized. Why do you think the designers of Ada 95 made this change? Does it have any drawbacks?

9.13 Taking a cue from Ada, Swift provides an `inout` parameter mode. The language manual does not specify whether `inout` parameters are to be passed by reference or value-result. Write a program that determines the implementation used by your local Swift compiler.

9.14 Fields of *packed* records (Example 8.8) cannot be passed by reference in Pascal. Likewise, when passing a subrange variable by reference, Pascal requires that all possible values of the corresponding formal parameter be valid for the subrange:

```
type small = 1..100;
     R = record x, y : small; end;
     S = packed record x, y : small; end;
var  a : 1..10;
     b : 1..1000;
     c : R;
     d : S;
procedure foo(var n : small);
begin
     n := 100;
     writeln(a);
end;
```

```
...
a := 2;
foo(b);       (* ok *)
foo(a);       (* static semantic error *)
foo(c.x);     (* ok *)
foo(d.x);     (* static semantic error *)
```

Using what you have learned about parameter-passing modes, explain these language restrictions.

9.15 Consider the following declaration in C:

```
double(*foo(double (*)(double, double[]), double)) (double, ...);
```

Describe in English the type of `foo`.

9.16 Does a program run faster when the programmer leaves optional parameters out of a subroutine call? Why or why not?

9.17 Why do you suppose that variable-length argument lists are so seldom supported by high-level programming languages?

9.18 Building on Exercise 6.35, show how to implement exceptions using `call-with-current-continuation` in Scheme. Model your syntax after the `handler-case` of Common Lisp. As in Exercise 6.35, you will probably need `define-syntax` and `dynamic-wind`.

9.19 Given what you have learned about the implementation of structured exceptions, describe how you might implement the nonlocal `goto`s of Pascal or the label parameters of Algol 60 (Section 6.2). Do you need to place any restrictions on how these features can be used?

9.20 Describe a plausible implementation of C++ destructors or Java `try... finally` blocks. What code must the compiler generate, at what points in the program, to ensure that cleanup always occurs when leaving a scope?

9.21 Use threads to build support for true iterators in Java. Try to hide as much of the implementation as possible behind a reasonable interface. In particular, hide any uses of `new thread`, `thread.start`, `thread.join`, `wait`, and `notify` inside implementations of routines named `yield` (to be called by an iterator) and in the standard Java `Iterator` interface routines (to be called in the body of a loop). Compare the performance of your iterators to that of the built-in iterator objects (it probably won't be good). Discuss any weaknesses you encounter in the abstraction facilities of the language.

9.22 In Common Lisp, multilevel returns use `catch` and `throw`; exception handling in the style of most other modern languages uses `handler-case` and `error`. Show that the distinction between these is mainly a matter of style, rather than expressive power. In other words, show that each facility can be used to emulate the other.

```
#include <signal.h>
#include <stdio.h>
#include <string.h>

char* days[7] = {"Sunday", "Monday", "Tuesday",
                 "Wednesday", "Thursday", "Friday", "Saturday"};
char today[10];

void handler(int n) {
    printf(" %s\n", today);
}

int main() {
    signal(SIGTSTP, handler);          // ^Z at keyboard
    for(int n = 0; ; n++) {
        strcpy(today, days[n%7]);
    }
}
```

Figure 9.6 **A problematic program in C to illustrate the use of signals.** In most Unix systems, the SIGTSTP signal is generated by typing control-Z at the keyboard.

9.23 Compile and run the program in Figure 9.6. Explain its behavior. Create a new version that behaves more predictably.

9.24 In C#, Java, or some other language with thread-based event handling, build a simple program around the "pause button" of Examples 9.51–9.54. Your program should open a small window containing a text field and two buttons, one labeled "pause", the other labeled "resume". It should then display an integer in the text field, starting with zero and counting up once per second. If the pause button is pressed, the count should suspend; if the resume button is pressed, it should continue.

Note that your program will need at least two threads—one to do the counting, one to handle events. In Java, the JavaFX package will create the handler thread automatically, and your main program can do the counting. In C#, some existing thread will need to call `Application.Run` in order to become a handler thread. In this case you'll need a second thread to do the counting.

9.25 Extend your answer to the previous problem by adding a "clone" button. Pushing this button should create an additional window containing another counter. This will, of course, require additional threads.

9.26–9.36 In More Depth.

9.9 Explorations

9.37 Explore the details of subroutine calls in the GNU Ada translator `gnat`. Pay particular attention to the more complex language features, including declarations in nested blocks (Section 3.3.2), dynamic-size arrays (Section 8.2.2), `in/out` parameters (Section 9.3.1), optional and named parameters (Section 9.3.3), generic subroutines (Section 7.3.1), exceptions (Section 9.4), and concurrency ("Launch-at-Elaboration," Section 13.2.3).

9.38 If you were designing a new imperative language, what set of parameter modes would you pick? Why?

9.39 Learn about references and the reference assignment operator in PHP. Discuss the similarities and differences between these and the references of C++. In particular, note that assignments in PHP can change the object to which a reference variable refers. Why does PHP allow this but C++ does not?

9.40 Learn about pointers to methods in C++. What are they useful for? How do they differ from a C# delegate that encapsulates a method?

9.41 Find manuals for several languages with exceptions and look up the set of predefined exceptions—those that may be raised automatically by the language implementation. Discuss the differences among the sets defined by different languages. If you were designing an exception-handling facility, what exceptions, if any, would you make predefined? Why?

9.42 Eiffel is an exception to the "replacement model" of exception handling. Its `rescue` clause is superficially similar to a `catch` block, but it must either `retry` the routine to which it is attached or allow the exception to propagate up the call chain. Put another way, the default behavior when control falls off the end of the `rescue` clause is to *reraise* the exception. Read up on "Design by Contract," the programming methodology supported by this exception-handling mechanism. Do you agree or disagree with the argument against replacement? Explain.

9.43 Learn the details of nonlocal control transfer in Common Lisp. Write a tutorial that explains `tagbody` and `go`; `block` and `return-from`; `catch` and `throw`; and `restart-case`, `restart-bind`, `handler-case`, `handler-bind`, `find-restart`, `invoke-restart`, `ignore-errors`, `signal`, and `error`. What do you think of all this machinery? Is it over-kill? Be sure to give an example that illustrates the use of `handler-bind`.

9.44 For Common Lisp, Modula-3, and Java, compare the semantics of `unwind-protect` and `try...finally`. Specifically, what happens if an exception arises within a cleanup clause?

9.45 As noted near the end of Section 9.6.2, an event-handler needs either to execute quickly or to pass its work off to another thread. A particularly elegant mechanism for the latter can be found in the `async` and `await` primitives of C# 5 and the similar `async` and `let!` of F#. Read up on the *asynchronous* programming model supported by these promitives. Explain their (implementation-level) connection to iterators (Section C-9.5.3). Write a GUI-based program or a network server that makes good use of them.

9.46 Compare and contrast the event-handling mechanisms of several GUI systems. How are handlers bound to events? Can you control the order in which they are invoked? How many event-handling threads does each system support? How and when are handler threads created? How do they synchronize with the rest of the program?

9.47–9.52 In More Depth.

9.10 Bibliographic Notes

Recursive subroutines became known primarily through McCarthy's work on Lisp [McC60].[7] Stack-based space management for recursive subroutines developed with compilers for Algol 60 (see, e.g., Randell and Russell [RR64]). (Because of issues of extent, subroutine space in Lisp requires more general, heap-based allocation.) Dijkstra [Dij60] presents an early discussion of the use of displays to access nonlocal data. Hanson [Han81] argues that nested subroutines are unnecessary.

Calling sequences and stack conventions for `gcc` are partially documented in the `texinfo` files distributed with the compiler (see *www.gnu.org/software/gcc*). Documentation for LLVM can be found at *llvm.org*. Several of the details described on the companion site were "reverse engineered" by examining the output of the two compilers.

The Ada language rationale [IBFW91, Chap. 8] contains an excellent discussion of parameter-passing modes. Harbison [Har92, Secs. 6.2–6.3] describes the Modula-3 modes and compares them to those of other languages. Liskov and Guttag [LG86, p. 25] liken call-by-sharing in Clu to parameter passing in Lisp. Call-by-name parameters have their roots in the lambda calculus of Alonzo Church [Chu41], which we consider in more detail in Section C-11.7.1. Thunks were first described by Ingerman [Ing61]. Fleck [Fle76] discusses the problems involved in trying to write a `swap` routine with call-by-name parameters (Exercise 9.10).

MacLaren [Mac77] describes exception handling in PL/I. The lexically scoped alternative of Ada, and of most more recent languages, draws heavily on the work of Goodenough [Goo75]. Ada's semantics are described formally by Luckam and

---

7 John McCarthy (1927–2011), long-time Professor at MIT and then Stanford Universities, was one of the founders of the field of Artificial Intelligence. He introduced Lisp in 1958, and also made key contributions to the early development of time-sharing and the use of mathematical logic to reason about computer programs. He received the ACM Turing Award in 1971.

Polak [LP80]. Clu's exceptions are an interesting historical precursor; details can be found in the work of Liskov and Snyder [LS79]. Meyer [Mey92a] discusses Design by Contract and exception handling in Eiffel. Friedman, Wand, and Haynes [FWH01, Chaps. 8–9] provide an excellent explanation of continuation-passing style in Scheme.

An early description of coroutines appears in the work of Conway [Con63], who used them to represent the phases of compilation. Birtwistle et al. [BDMN73] provide a tutorial introduction to the use of coroutines for simulation in Simula 67. Cactus stacks date from at least the mid-1960s; they were supported directly in hardware by the Burroughs B6500 and B7500 computers [HD68]. Murer et al. [MOSS96] discuss the implementation of iterators in the Sather programming language (a descendant of Eiffel). Von Behren et al. [vCZ+03] describe a system with chunk-based stack allocation.

Pratt [1989]. Other languages are an interesting [illegible] exception details in [illegible] found in the work of [illegible] and [illegible] [1979]. Meyer [illegible] discusses [illegible] exception handling in [illegible] [illegible] excellent description of continuation-passing style.

An early description of coroutines appears in the work of Conway [1963], who used them to represent the phases of compilation. [illegible] [illegible] coroutines [illegible] Simula [illegible] the [illegible] supported [illegible] hardware [illegible] [illegible] and [illegible] [illegible] program[illegible] language [illegible] [illegible] describes a system with cactus-stack allocation [illegible].

10 Data Abstraction and Object Orientation

In Chapter 3 we presented several stages in the development of data abstraction, with an emphasis on the scoping mechanisms that control the visibility of names. We began with global variables, whose lifetime spans program execution. We then added local variables, whose lifetime is limited to the execution of a single subroutine; nested scopes, which allow subroutines themselves to be local; and static variables, whose lifetime spans execution, but whose names are visible only within a single scope. These were followed by modules, which allow a collection of subroutines to share a set of static variables; module *types*, which allow the programmer to instantiate multiple instances of a given abstraction, and *classes*, which allow the programmer to define families of related abstractions.

Ordinary modules encourage a "manager" style of programming, in which a module exports an abstract type. Module types and classes allow the module itself to *be* the abstract type. The distinction becomes apparent in two ways. First, the explicit `create` and `destroy` routines typically exported from a manager module are replaced by creation and destruction of an instance of the module type. Second, invocation of a routine in a particular module instance replaces invocation of a general routine that expects a variable of the exported type as argument. Classes build on the module-as-type approach by adding mechanisms for *inheritance*, which allows new abstractions to be defined as refinements or extensions to existing ones, and *dynamic method binding*, which allows a new version of an abstraction to display newly refined behavior, even when used in a context that expects an earlier version. An instance of a class is known as an *object*; languages and programming techniques based on classes are said to be *object-oriented*.[1]

The stepwise evolution of data abstraction mechanisms presented in Chapter 3 is a useful way to organize ideas, but it does not completely reflect the historical development of language features. In particular, it would be inaccurate to suggest that object-oriented programming developed as an outgrowth of modules.

1 In previous chapters we used the term "object" informally to refer to almost anything that can have a name. In this chapter we will use it only to refer to an instance of a class.

Rather, all three of the fundamental concepts of object-oriented programming—encapsulation, inheritance, and dynamic method binding—have their roots in the Simula programming language, developed in the mid-1960s by Ole-Johan Dahl and Kristen Nygaard of the Norwegian Computing Center.[2] In comparison to modern object-oriented languages, Simula was weak in the data hiding part of encapsulation, and it was in this area that Clu, Modula, Euclid, and related languages made important contributions in the 1970s. At the same time, the ideas of inheritance and dynamic method binding were adopted and refined in Smalltalk over the course of the 1970s.

Smalltalk employed a distinctive "message-based" programming model, with dynamic typing and unusual terminology and syntax. The dynamic typing tended to make implementations relatively slow, and delayed the reporting of errors. The language was also tightly integrated into a graphical programming environment, making it difficult to port across systems. For these reasons, Smalltalk was less widely used than one might have expected, given the influence it had on subsequent developments. Languages like Eiffel, C++, Ada 95, Fortran 2003, Java, and C# represented to a large extent a reintegration of the inheritance and dynamic method binding of Smalltalk with "mainstream" imperative syntax and semantics. In an alternative vein, Objective-C combined Smalltalk-style messaging and dynamic typing, in a relatively pure and unadulterated form, with traditional C syntax for intra-object operations. Object orientation has also become important in functional languages, as exemplified by the Common Lisp Object System (CLOS [Kee89; Ste90, Chap. 28]) and the objects of OCaml.

More recently, dynamically typed objects have gained new popularity in languages like Python and Ruby, while statically typed objects continue to appear in languages like Scala and Go. Swift, the successor to Objective-C, follows the pattern of its predecessor (and of OCaml, in fact) in layering dynamically typed objects on top of an otherwise statically typed language.

In Section 10.1 we provide an overview of object-oriented programming and of its three fundamental concepts. We consider encapsulation and data hiding in more detail in Section 10.2. We then consider object initialization and finalization in Section 10.3, and dynamic method binding in Section 10.4. In Section 10.6 (mostly on the companion site) we consider the subject of *multiple inheritance*, in which a class is defined in terms of more than one existing class. As we shall see, multiple inheritance introduces some particularly thorny semantic and implementation challenges. Finally, in Section 10.7, we revisit the definition of object orientation, considering the extent to which a language can or should model ev-

---

2 Kristen Nygaard (1926–2002) was widely admired as a mathematician, computer language pioneer, and social activist. His career included positions with the Norwegian Defense Research Establishment, the Norwegian Operational Research Society, the Norwegian Computing Center, the Universities of Aarhus and Oslo, and a variety of labor, political, and social organizations. Ole-Johan Dahl (1931–2002) also held positions at the Norwegian Defense Research Establishment and the Norwegian Computing Center, and was the founding member of the Informatics department at Oslo. Together, Nygaard and Dahl shared the 2001 ACM Turing Award.

erything as an object. Most of our discussion will focus on Smalltalk, Eiffel, C++, and Java, though we shall have occasion to mention many other languages as well. We will return to the subject of dynamically typed objects in Section 14.4.4.

10.1 Object-Oriented Programming

EXAMPLE 10.1 list_node class in C++

Object-oriented programming can be seen as an attempt to enhance opportunities for code reuse by making it easy to define new abstractions as *extensions* or *refinements* of existing abstractions. As a starting point for examples, consider a collection of integers, implemented as a doubly linked list of records (we'll consider collections of other types of objects in Section 10.1.1). Figure 10.1 contains C++ code for the elements of our collection. The example employs a "module-as-type" style of abstraction: each element is a separate object of class `list_node`. The class contains both *data members* (`prev`, `next`, `head_node`, and `val`) and *subroutine members* (`predecessor`, `successor`, `insert_before` and `remove`). Subroutine members are called *methods* in many object-oriented languages; data members are also called *fields*. The keyword `this` in C++ refers to the object of which the currently executing method is a member. In Smalltalk and Objective-C, the equivalent keyword is `self`; in Eiffel it is `current`.

EXAMPLE 10.2 list class that uses list_node

Given the existence of the `list_node` class, we could define a list of integers as follows:

```
class list {
    list_node header;
public:
    // no explicit constructor required;
    // implicit construction of 'header' suffices
    int empty() {
        return header.singleton();
    }
    list_node* head() {
        return header.successor();
    }
    void append(list_node *new_node) {
        header.insert_before(new_node);
    }
    ~list() {                    // destructor
        if (!header.singleton())
            throw new list_err("attempt to delete nonempty list");
    }
};
```

To create an empty list, one could then write

```
list* my_list_ptr = new list;
```

```
class list_err {                              // exception
public:
    const char *description;
    list_err(const char *s) {description = s;}
};

class list_node {
    list_node* prev;
    list_node* next;
    list_node* head_node;
public:
    int val;                                  // the actual data in a node
    list_node() {                             // constructor
        prev = next = head_node = this;       // point to self
        val = 0;                              // default value
    }
    list_node* predecessor() {
        if (prev == this || prev == head_node) return nullptr;
        return prev;
    }
    list_node* successor() {
        if (next == this || next == head_node) return nullptr;
        return next;
    }
    bool singleton() {
        return (prev == this);
    }
    void insert_before(list_node* new_node) {
        if (!new_node->singleton())
            throw new list_err("attempt to insert node already on list");
        prev->next = new_node;
        new_node->prev = prev;
        new_node->next = this;
        prev = new_node;
        new_node->head_node = head_node;
    }
    void remove() {
        if (singleton())
            throw new list_err("attempt to remove node not currently on list");
        prev->next = next;
        next->prev = prev;
        prev = next = head_node = this;       // point to self
    }
    ~list_node() {                            // destructor
        if (!singleton())
            throw new list_err("attempt to delete node still on list");
    }
};
```

Figure 10.1 A simple class for list nodes in C++. In this example we envision a list of integers.

Records to be inserted into a list are created in much the same way:

```
list_node* elem_ptr = new list_node;
```

EXAMPLE 10.3
Declaration of in-line (expanded) objects

In C++, one can also simply declare an object of a given class:

```
list my_list;
list_node elem;
```

Our `list` class includes such an object (`header`) as a field. When created with `new`, an object is allocated in the heap; when created via elaboration of a declaration it is allocated statically or on the stack, depending on lifetime (Eiffel calls such objects "expanded"). Whether on the stack or in the heap, object creation causes the invocation of a programmer-specified initialization routine, known as a *constructor*. In C++ and its descendants, Java and C#, the name of the constructor is the same as that of the class itself. C++ also allows the programmer to specify a *destructor* method that will be invoked automatically when an object is destroyed, either by explicit programmer action or by return from the subroutine in which it was declared. The destructor's name is also the same as that of the class, but with a leading tilde (~). Destructors are commonly used for storage management and error checking.

EXAMPLE 10.4
Constructor arguments

If a constructor has parameters, corresponding arguments must be provided when declaring an in-line object or creating an object in the heap. Suppose, for example, that our `list_node` constructor had been written to take an explicit parameter:

```
class list_node {
    ...
    list_node(int v) {
        prev = next = head_node = this;
        val = v;
    }
```

Each in-line declaration or call to `new` would then need to provide a value:

```
list_node element1(0);                    // in-line
list_node *e_ptr = new list_node(13);     // heap
```

As we shall see in Section 10.3.1, C++ actually allows us to declare *both* constructors, and uses the usual rules of function overloading to differentiate between them: declarations without a value will call the no-parameter constructor; declarations with an integer argument will call the integer-parameter constructor.

Public and Private Members

The public label within the declaration of list_node separates members required by the implementation of the abstraction from members available to users of the abstraction. In the terminology of Section 3.3.4, members that appear after the public label are exported from the class; members that appear before the label are not. C++ also provides a private label, so the publicly visible portions of a class can be listed first if desired (or even intermixed). In many other languages, public data and subroutine members (fields and methods) must be individually so labeled (more on this in Section 10.2.2). Note that C++ classes are open scopes, as defined in Section 3.3.4; nothing needs to be explicitly imported.

In many languages—C++ among them—certain information can be left out of the initial declaration of a module or class, and provided in a separate file not visible to users of the abstraction. In our running example, we could declare the public methods of list_node without providing their bodies:

EXAMPLE 10.5
Method declaration without definition

```
class list_node {
    list_node* prev;
    list_node* next;
    list_node* head_node;
public:
    int val;
    list_node();
    list_node* predecessor();
    list_node* successor();
    bool singleton();
    void insert_before(list_node* new_node);
```

DESIGN & IMPLEMENTATION

10.1 What goes in a class declaration?

Two rules govern the choice of what to put in the declaration of a class, rather than in a separate definition. First, the declaration must contain all the information that a programmer needs in order to use the abstraction correctly. Second, the declaration must contain all the information that the compiler needs in order to generate code. The second rule is generally broader: it tends to force information that is not required by the first rule into (the private part of) the interface, particularly in languages that use a value model of variables, instead of a reference model. If the compiler must generate code to allocate space (e.g., in stack frames) to hold an instance of a class, then it must know the size of that instance; this is the rationale for including private fields in the class declaration. In addition, if the compiler is to expand any method calls in-line then it must have their code available. In-line expansion of the smallest, most common methods of an object-oriented program tends to be crucial for good performance.

```
        void remove();
        ~list_node();
};
```

This somewhat abbreviated class declaration might then be put in a .h "header" file, with method bodies relegated to a .cc "implementation" file. (C++ conventions for separate compilation are similar to those of C, which we saw in Section C-3.8. The file name suffixes used here are those expected by the GNU g++ compiler.) Within a .cc file, the header of a method definition must identify the class to which it belongs by using a :: *scope resolution* operator:

EXAMPLE 10.6
Separate method definition

```
void list_node::insert_before(list_node* new_node) {
    if (!new_node->singleton())
        throw new list_err("attempt to insert node already on list");
    prev->next = new_node;
    new_node->prev = prev;
    new_node->next = this;
    prev = new_node;
    new_node->head_node = head_node;
}
```

Tiny Subroutines

Object-oriented programs tend to make many more subroutine calls than do ordinary imperative programs, and the subroutines tend to be shorter. Lots of things that would be accomplished by direct access to record fields in a von Neumann language tend to be hidden inside object methods in an object-oriented language. Many programmers in fact consider it bad style to declare public fields, because doing so gives users of an abstraction direct access to the internal representation, and makes it impossible to change that representation without changing the user code as well. Arguably, we should make the `val` field of `list_node` private, with `get_val` and `set_val` methods to read and write it.

EXAMPLE 10.7
`property` and `indexer` methods in C#

C# provides a *property* mechanism specifically designed to facilitate the declaration of methods (called *accessors*) to "get" and "set" private fields. Using this mechanism, a C# version of our `val` field could be written as follows:

```
class list_node {
    ...
    int val;                  // val (lower case 'v') is private
    public int Val {
        get {                 // presence of get accessor and optional
            return val;       // set accessor means that Val is a property
        }
        set {
            val = value;      // value is a keyword: argument to set
        }
    }
    ...
}
```

Users of the `list_node` class can now access the (private) `val` field through the (public) `Val` property as if it were a field:

```
list_node n;
...
int a = n.Val;          // implicit call to get method
n.Val = 3;              // implicit call to set method
```

In effect, C# indexers provide the look of direct field access (from the perspective of a class's users) while preserving the ability to change the implementation. A similar *indexer* mechanism can make objects of arbitrary classes look like arrays, with conventional subscript syntax in both l-value and r-value contexts. An example appears in Sidebar 8.3.

In C++, operator overloading and references can be used to provide the equivalent of indexers, but not of properties. ■

Derived Classes

EXAMPLE 10.8
queue class derived from `list`

Suppose now that we already have a list abstraction, and would like a queue abstraction. We could define the queue from scratch, but much of the code would look the same as in Figure 10.1. In an object-oriented language we have the alternative of *deriving* the queue from the list, allowing it to *inherit* preexisting fields and methods:

```
class queue : public list {            // queue is derived from list
public:
    // no specialized constructor or destructor required
    void enqueue(int v) {
        append(new list_node(v));          // append is inherited from list
    }
    int dequeue() {
        if (empty())
            throw new list_err("attempt to dequeue from empty queue");
        list_node* p = head();             // head is also inherited
        p->remove();
        int v = p->val;
        delete p;
        return v;
    }
};
```

Here queue is said to be a *derived class* (also called a *child class* or *subclass*); `list` is said to be a *base class* (also called a *parent class* or *superclass*). The derived class inherits all the fields and methods of the base class, automatically. All the programmer needs to declare explicitly are members that a queue has but a `list` lacks—in this case, the `enqueue` and `dequeue` methods. We shall see examples shortly in which derived classes have extra fields as well. ■

In C++, public members of a base class are always visible inside the methods of a derived class. They are visible to *users* of the derived class only if the base class name is preceded with the keyword `public` in the first line of the derived class's declaration. Of course, we may not always *want* these members to be visible. In our queue example, we have chosen to pass integers to and from `enqueue` and `dequeue`, and to allocate and deallocate the `list_nodes` internally. If we want to keep these list nodes hidden, we must prevent the user from accessing the `head` and `append` methods of class `list`. We can do so by making `list` a *private* base class instead:

EXAMPLE 10.9

Hiding members of a base class

```
class queue : private list { ...
```

To make the `empty` method visible again, we can call it out explicitly:

```
public:
    using list::empty;
```

We will discuss the visibility of class members in more detail in Section 10.2.2. ■

When an object of a derived class is created in C++, the compiler arranges to call the constructor for the base class first, and then to call the constructor of the derived class. In our `queue` example, where the derived class lacks a constructor, the `list` constructor will still be called—which is, of course, what we want. We will discuss constructors further in Section 10.3.

By deriving new classes from old ones, the programmer can create arbitrarily deep *class hierarchies*, with additional functionality at every level of the tree. The standard libraries for Smalltalk and Java are as many as seven and eight levels deep, respectively. (Unlike C++, both Smalltalk and Java have a single root superclass, `Object`, from which all other classes are derived. C#, Objective-C, and Eiffel have a similar class; Eiffel calls it `ANY`.)

Modifying Base Class Methods

In addition to defining new fields and methods, and hiding those it no longer wants to be visible, a derived class can *redefine* a member of a base class simply by providing a new version. In our `queue` example, we might want to define a new `head` method that "peeks" at the first element of the queue, without removing it:

EXAMPLE 10.10

Redefining a method in a derived class

```
class queue : private list {
    ...
    int head() {
        if (empty())
            throw new list_err("attempt to peek at head of empty queue");
        return list::head()->val;
    }
```

Note that the `head` method of class `list` is still visible to methods of class `queue` (but not to its users!) when identified with the scope resolution operator (`list::`). ■

EXAMPLE 10.11
Accessing base class members

Other object-oriented languages provide other means of accessing the members of a base class. In Smalltalk, Objective-C, Java, and C#, one uses the keyword `base` or `super`:

```
list::head();           // C++
super.head();           // Java
base.head();            // C#
super head.             // Smalltalk
[super head]            // Objective-C
```

EXAMPLE 10.12
Renaming methods in Eiffel

In Eiffel, one must explicitly *rename* methods inherited from a base class, in order to make them accessible:

```
class queue
inherit
    list
        rename
            head as list_head
            ...     -- other renames
        end
```

Within methods of `queue`, the `head` method of `list` can be invoked as `list_head`. C++ and Eiffel cannot use the keyword `super`, because it would be ambiguous in the presence of multiple inheritance.

Objects as Fields of Other Objects

EXAMPLE 10.13
A queue that *contains* a list

As an alternative to deriving `queue` from `list`, we might choose to include a `list` as a *field* of a queue instead:

```
class queue {
    list contents;
public:
    bool empty() {
        return contents.empty();
    }
    void enqueue(const int v) {
        contents.append(new list_node(v));
    }
    int dequeue() {
        if (empty())
            throw new list_err("attempt to dequeue from empty queue");
        list_node* p = contents.head();
        p->remove();
        int v = p->val;
        delete p;
        return v;
    }
};
```

The practical difference is small in this example. The choice mainly boils down to whether we think of a queue as a special kind of list, or whether we think of a queue as an abstraction that *uses* a list as part of its implementation. The cases in which inheritance is most compelling are those in which we want to be able to use an object of a derived class (a "client," say) in a context that expects an object of a base class (a "person," say), and have that object behave in a special way by virtue of belonging to the derived class (e.g., include extra information when printed). We will consider these sorts of cases in Section 10.4.

10.1.1 Classes and Generics

The astute reader may have noticed that our various lists and queues have all embedded the assumption that the item in each list node is an integer. In practice, we should like to be able to have lists and queues of many kinds of items, all based on a single copy of the bulk of the code. In a dynamically typed language like Ruby or Python, this is natural: the val field would have no static type, and objects of any kind could be added to, and removed from, lists and queues.

In a statically typed language like C++, it is tempting to create a general-purpose list_node class that has no val field, and then derive subclasses (e.g., int_list_node) that add the values. While this approach can be made to work, it has some unfortunate limitations. Suppose we define a gp_list_node type, with the fields and methods needed to implement list operations, but without a val payload:

EXAMPLE 10.14 Base class for general-purpose lists

```
class gp_list_node {
    gp_list_node* prev;
    gp_list_node* next;
    gp_list_node* head_node;
public:
    gp_list_node();          // assume method bodies given separately
    gp_list_node* predecessor();
    gp_list_node* successor();
    bool singleton();
    void insert_before(gp_list_node* new_node);
    void remove();
    ~gp_list_node();
};
```

To create nodes that can be used in a list of integers, we will need a val field and some constructors:

```
class int_list_node : public gp_list_node {
public:
    int val;                 // the actual data in a node
    int_list_node() { val = 0; }
    int_list_node(int v) { val = v; }
    ...
```

Initialization of the `prev`, `next`, and `head_node` fields will remain in the hands of the `gp_list_node` constructor, which will be called automatically whenever we create a `int_list_node` object. The `singleton`, `insert_before`, and `remove` methods can likewise be inherited from `gp_list_node` intact, as can the destructor. ■

EXAMPLE 10.15 The problem with type-specific extensions

But what about `successor` and `predecessor`? If we leave these unchanged, they will continue to return values of type `gp_list_node`, not `int_list_node`:

```
int_list_node* p = ...              // whatever
int v = p->successor().val          // won't compile!
```

As far as the compiler is concerned, the successor of an `int_list_node` will have no `val` field. To fix the problem, we will need explicit casts:

```
    int_list_node* predecessor() {
        return static_cast<int_list_node*>(gp_list_node::predecessor());
    }
    int_list_node* successor() {
        return static_cast<int_list_node*>(gp_list_node::successor());
    }
```

In a similar vein, we can create a general-purpose list class:

```
class gp_list {
    gp_list_node head_node;
public:
    bool empty();               // method bodies again given separately
    gp_list_node* head();
    void append(gp_list_node *new_node);
    ~gp_list();
};
```

But if we extend it to create an `int_list` class, we will need a cast in the `head` method:

```
class int_list : public gp_list {
public:
    int_list_node* head() {     // redefinition; hides original
        return static_cast<int_list_node*>(gp_list::head());
    }
};
```

Assuming we write our code correctly, none of our casts will introduce bugs. They may, however, prevent the compiler from catching bugs if we write our code incorrectly:

```
class string_list_node : public gp_list_node {
    // analogous to int_list_node
    ...
};
...
string_list_node n("boo!");
int_list L;
L.append(&n);
cout << "0x" << hex << L.head()->val;
```

On the author's 64-bit Macbook, this code prints "0x6f6f6208." What happened? Method `int_list::append`, inherited from `gp_list`, expects a parameter of type `gp_list_node*`, and since `string_list_node` is derived from `gp_list_node`, a pointer to node `n` is acceptable. But when we peek at this node, the cast in `L.head()` tells the compiler not to complain when we treat the node (which can't be proven to be anything more specific than a `gp_list_node`) as if we were certain it held an `int`. Not coincidentally, the upper three bytes of `0x6f6f6208` contain, in reverse order, the ASCII codes of the characters "`boo`."

EXAMPLE 10.16
How do you name an unknown type?

Things get even worse if we try to define a general-purpose analogue of the queue from Examples 10.8–10.10:

```
class gp_queue : private gp_list {
public:
    using gp_list::empty;
    void enqueue(const ?? v);        // what is "??" ?
    ?? dequeue();
    ?? head();
};
```

How do we talk about the objects the queue is supposed to contain when we don't even know their type?

EXAMPLE 10.17
Generic lists in C++

The answer, of course, is generics (Section C-7.3.2)—templates, in C++. These allow us to define a `list_node<T>` class that can be instantiated for any data type `T`, without the need for either inheritance or type casts:

```
template<typename V>
class list_node {
    list_node<V>* prev;
    list_node<V>* next;
    list_node<V>* head_node;
public:
    V val;
    list_node<V>* predecessor() { ...
    list_node<V>* successor() { ...
    void insert_before(list_node<V>* new_node) { ...
    ...
};
```

```
template<typename V>
class list {
    list_node<V> header;
public:
    list_node<V>* head() { ...
    void append(list_node<V> *new_node) { ...
    ...
};

template<typename V>
class queue : private list<V> {
public:
    using list<V>::empty;
    void enqueue(const V v) { ...
    V dequeue() { ...
    V head() { ...
};

typedef list_node<int> int_list_node;
typedef list_node<string> string_list_node;
typedef list<int> int_list;
...
```

DESIGN & IMPLEMENTATION

10.2 Containers/collections

In object-oriented programming, an abstraction that holds a collection of objects of some given class is often called a *container*. Common containers include sorted and unsorted sets, stacks, queues, and dictionaries, implemented as lists, trees, hash tables, and various other concrete data structures. All of the major object-oriented languages include extensive container libraries. A few of the issues involved in their creation have been hinted at in this section: Which classes are derived from which others? When do we say that "X is a Y" instead of "X contains / uses a Y"? Which operations are supported, and what is their time complexity? How much "memory churn" (heap allocation and garbage collection) does each operation incur? Is everything type safe? How extensive is the use of generics? How easy is it to iterate over the contents of a container? Given these many questions, the design of safe, efficient, and flexible container libraries is a complex and difficult art. For an approach that builds on the `gp_list_node` base class of Example 10.14, but still leverages templates to avoid the need for type casts, see Exercise 10.8.

```
int_list_node n(3);
string_list_node s("boo!");
int_list L;
L.append(&n);          // ok
L.append(&s);          // will not compile!
```

In a nutshell, generics exist for the purpose of abstracting over unrelated types, something that inheritance does not support. In addition to C++, generics appear in most other statically typed object-oriented languages, including Eiffel, Java, C#, and OCaml.

✓ CHECK YOUR UNDERSTANDING

1. What are generally considered to be the three defining characteristics of object-oriented programming?
2. In what programming language of the 1960s does object orientation find its roots? Who invented that language? Summarize the evolution of the three defining characteristics since that time.
3. Name three important benefits of abstraction.
4. What are the more common names for *subroutine member* and *data member*?
5. What is a *property* in C#?
6. What is the purpose of the "private" part of an object interface? Why can't it be hidden completely?
7. What is the purpose of the `::` operator in C++?
8. Explain why in-line subroutines are particularly important in object-oriented languages.
9. What are *constructors* and *destructors*?
10. Give two other terms, each, for *base class* and *derived class*.
11. Explain why generics may be useful in an object-oriented language, despite the extensive polymorphism already provided by inheritance.

10.2 Encapsulation and Inheritance

Encapsulation mechanisms enable the programmer to group data and the subroutines that operate on them together in one place, and to hide irrelevant details from the users of an abstraction. In the preceding section (and likewise Section 3.3.5) we cast object-oriented programming as an extension of the "module-as-type" mechanisms of Simula and Euclid. It is also possible to cast object-oriented programming in a "module-as-manager" framework. In the first subsection below we consider the data-hiding mechanisms of modules in non-object-oriented languages. In the second subsection we consider the new data-hiding issues that arise when we add inheritance to modules. In the third subsection we briefly return to the module-as-manager approach, and show how several languages, including Ada 95 and Fortran 2003, add inheritance to records, allowing (static) modules to continue to provide data hiding.

10.2.1 Modules

Scope rules for data hiding were one of the principal innovations of Clu, Modula, Euclid, and other module-based languages of the 1970s. In Clu and Euclid, the declaration and definition (header and body) of a module always appeared together. In Modula-2, programmers had the option of placing the header and the body in separate files. Unfortunately, there was no way to divide the header into public and private parts; everything in it was public (i.e., exported). The only concession to data hiding was that pointer types could be declared in a header without revealing the structure of the objects to which they pointed. Compilers could generate code for the users of a module (Sidebar 10.1) without the hidden information, since pointers are all of equal size on most machines.

EXAMPLE 10.18
Data hiding in Ada

Ada increases flexibility by allowing the header of a package to be divided into public and private parts. Details of an exported type can be made *opaque* by putting them in the private part of the header and simply naming the type in the public part:

```
package foo is            -- header
    ...
    type T is private;
    ...
private         -- definitions below here are inaccessible to users
    ...
    type T is ...         -- full definition
    ...
end foo;
```

The private part provides the information the compiler needs to allocate objects "in line." A change to the body of a module never forces recompilation of any of the users of the module. A change to the private part of the module header may force recompilation, but it never requires changes to the source code of the users. A change to the public part of a header is a change to the module's interface: it will often require us to change the code of users. ■

Because they affect only the visibility of names, static, manager-style modules introduce no special code generation issues. Storage for variables and other data inside a module is managed in precisely the same way as storage for data immediately outside the module. If the module appears in a global scope, then its data can be allocated statically. If the module appears within a subroutine, then its data can be allocated on the stack, at known offsets, when the subroutine is called, and reclaimed when it returns.

Module types, as in Euclid and ML, are somewhat more complicated: they allow a module to have an arbitrary number of *instances*. The obvious implementation then resembles that of a record. If all of the data in the module have a statically known size, then each individual datum can be assigned a static offset within the module's storage. If the size of some of the data is not known until run time, then the module's storage can be divided into fixed-size and variable-size portions, with a dope vector (descriptor) at the beginning of the fixed-size portion. Instances of the module can be allocated statically, on the stack, or in the heap, as appropriate.

The "`this`" Parameter

One additional complication arises for subroutines inside a module. How do they know which variables to use? We could, of course, replicate the code for each subroutine in each instance of the module, just as we replicate the data. This replication would be highly wasteful, however, as the copies would vary only in the details of address computations. A better technique is to create a single instance of each module subroutine, and to pass that instance, at run time, the address of the storage of the appropriate module instance. This address takes the form of an extra, hidden first parameter for every module subroutine. A Euclid call of the form

EXAMPLE 10.19
The hidden `this` parameter

```
my_stack.push(x)
```

is translated as if it were really

```
push(my_stack, x)
```

where `my_stack` is passed by reference. The same translation occurs in object-oriented languages.

Making Do without Module Headers

As noted in Section C-3.8, Java packages and C/C++/C# namespaces can be spread across multiple compilation units (files). In C, C++, and C#, a single file can also contain pieces of more than one namespace. More significantly, many modern languages, including Java and C#, dispense with the notion of separate headers and bodies. While the programmer must still define the interface (and specify it via `public` declarations), there is no need to manually identify code that needs to be in the header for implementation reasons: instead the compiler is responsible for extracting this information automatically from the full text of the module. For software engineering purposes it may still be desirable to create preliminary "skeleton" versions of a module, against which other modules can be compiled, but this is optional. To assist in project management and documentation, many Java and C# implementations provide a tool that will extract from the complete text of a module the minimum information required by its users.

10.2.2 Classes

With the introduction of inheritance, object-oriented languages must supplement the scope rules of module-based languages to cover additional issues. For example, how much control should a base class exercise over the visibility of its members in derived classes? Should private members of a base class be visible to methods of a derived class? Should public members of a base class always be public members of a derived class (i.e., be visible to users of the derived class)?

We touched on these questions in Example 10.9, where we declared class `queue` as a `private list`, hiding public members of the base class from users of the derived class—except for method `empty`, which we made explicitly visible again with a `using` declaration. C++ allows the inverse strategy as well: methods of an otherwise `public` base class can be explicitly deleted from the derived class:

EXAMPLE 10.20
Hiding inherited methods

```
class queue : public list {
    ...
    void append(list_node *new_node) = delete;
```

Similar deletion mechanisms can be found in Eiffel, Python, and Ruby. ■

In addition to the `public` and `private` labels, C++ allows members of a class to be designated `protected`. A protected member is visible only to methods of its own class or of classes derived from that class. In our examples, a protected member *M* of `list` would be accessible not only to methods of `list` itself but also to methods of `queue`. Unlike public members, however, *M* would not be visible to arbitrary users of `list` or `queue` objects.

EXAMPLE 10.21
`protected` base class in C++

The `protected` keyword can also be used when specifying a base class:

```
class derived : protected base { ...
```

Here public members of the base class act like protected members of the derived class. ■

The basic philosophy behind the visibility rules of C++ can be summarized as follows:

- Any class can limit the visibility of its members. Public members are visible anywhere the class declaration is in scope. Private members are visible only inside the class's methods. Protected members are visible inside methods of the class or its descendants. (As an exception to the normal rules, a class can specify that certain other `friend` classes or subroutines should have access to its private members.)
- A derived class can restrict the visibility of members of a base class, but can never increase it.[3] Private members of a base class are never visible in a derived

3 A derived class can of course declare a new member with the same name as some existing member, but the two will then coexist, as discussed in Example 10.10.

class. Protected and public members of a public base class are protected or public, respectively, in a derived class. Protected and public members of a protected base class are protected members of a derived class. Protected and public members of a private base class are private members of a derived class.

- A derived class that limits the visibility of members of a base class by declaring that base class `protected` or `private` can restore the visibility of individual members of the base class by inserting a `using` declaration in the `protected` or `public` portion of the derived class declaration.
- A derived class can make methods (though not fields) of a base class inaccessible (to others and to itself) by explicitly `delete`-ing them.

Other object-oriented languages take different approaches to visibility. Eiffel is more flexible than C++ in the patterns of visibility it can support, but it does not adhere to the first of the C++ principles above. Derived classes in Eiffel can both restrict *and increase* the visibility of members of base classes. Every method (called a `feature` in Eiffel) can specify its own *export status*. If the status is `{NONE}` then the member is effectively private (called *secret* in Eiffel). If the status is `{ANY}` then the member is effectively public (called *generally available* in Eiffel). In the general case the status can be an arbitrary list of class names, in which case the feature is said to be *selectively available* to those classes and their descendants only. Any feature inherited from a base class can be given a new status in a derived class.

Java and C# follow C++ in the declaration of `public`, `protected`, and `private` members, but do not provide the `protected` and `private` designations for base classes; a derived class can neither increase *nor* restrict the visibility of members of a base class. It can, however, hide a field or *override* a method by defining a new one with the same name; the lack of a scope resolution operator makes the old member inaccessible to users of the new class. In Java, the overriding version of a method cannot have more restrictive visibility than the version in the base class.

The `protected` keyword has a slightly different meaning in Java than it does in C++: a `protected` member of a Java class is visible not only within derived classes but also within the entire package (namespace) in which the class is declared. A class member with no explicit access modifier in Java is visible throughout the package in which the class is declared, but *not* in any derived classes that reside in other packages. C# defines `protected` as C++ does, but provides an additional `internal` keyword that makes a member visible throughout the *assembly* in which the class appears. (An assembly is a collection of linked-together compilation units, comparable to a `.jar` file in Java.) Members of a C# class are `private` by default.

In Smalltalk and Objective-C, the issue of member visibility never arises: the language allows code at run time to attempt a call of any method name in any object. If the method exists (with the right number of parameters), then the invocation proceeds; otherwise a run-time error results. There is no way in these languages to make a method available to some parts of a program but not to others. In a related vein, Python class members are always public. In Ruby, fields are always private; more than that, they are accessible only to methods of the individual object to which they belong.

Static Fields and Methods

Orthogonal to the visibility implied by `public`, `private`, or `protected`, most object-oriented languages allow individual fields and methods to be declared `static`. Static class members are thought of as "belonging" to the class as a whole, not to any individual object. They are therefore sometimes referred to as *class* fields and methods, as opposed to *instance* fields and methods. (This terminology is most common in languages that create a special metaobject to represent each class—see Example 10.26. The class fields and methods are thought of as belonging to the metaobject.) A single copy of each static field is shared by all instances of its class: changes made to that field in methods of one object will be visible to methods of all other objects of the class. A static method, for its part, has no `this` parameter (explicit or implicit); it cannot access nonstatic (instance) fields. A nonstatic (instance) method, on the other hand, can access both static and nonstatic fields.

10.2.3 Nesting (Inner Classes)

Many languages allow class declarations to nest. This raises an immediate question: if `Inner` is a member of `Outer`, can `Inner`'s methods see `Outer`'s members, and if so, which instance do they see? The simplest answer, adopted in C++ and C#, is to allow access to only the static members of the outer class, since these have only a single instance. In effect, nesting serves simply as a means of information hiding. Java takes a more sophisticated approach. It allows a nested (*inner*) class to access arbitrary members of its surrounding class. Each instance of the inner class must therefore *belong to* an instance of the outer class.

EXAMPLE 10.22
Inner classes in Java

```
class Outer {
    int n;
    class Inner {
        public void bar() { n = 1; }
    }
    Inner i;
    Outer() { i = new Inner(); }          // constructor
    public void foo() {
        n = 0;
        System.out.println(n);            // prints 0
        i.bar();
        System.out.println(n);            // prints 1
    }
}
```

If there are multiple instances of `Outer`, each instance will have a different `n`, and calls to `Inner.bar` will access the appropriate `n`. To make this work, each instance of `Inner` (of which there may of course be an arbitrary number) must contain a hidden pointer to the instance of `Outer` to which it belongs. If a nested class in Java is declared to be `static`, it behaves as in C++ and C#, with access to only the static members of the surrounding class.

Java classes can also be nested inside methods. Such a *local* class has access not only to all members of the surrounding class but also to the parameters and variables of the method in which it is nested. The catch is that any parameters or variables that the nested class actually uses must be "effectively final"—either declared `final` explicitly or at least never modified (by the nested class, the surrounding method, or any other code) after the nested class is elaborated. This rule permits the implementation to make a copy of the referenced objects rather than maintaining a reference (i.e., a static link) to the frame of the surrounding method. ■

Inner and local classes in Java are widely used to create *object closures*, as described in Section 3.6.3. In Section 9.6.2 we used them as handlers for events. We also noted that a local class in Java can be *anonymous*: it can appear, in-line, inside a call to `new` (Example 9.54).

10.2.4 Type Extensions

Smalltalk, Objective-C, Eiffel, C++, Java, and C# were all designed from the outset as object-oriented languages, either starting from scratch or from an existing language without a strong encapsulation mechanism. They all support a module-as-type approach to abstraction, in which a single mechanism (the class) provides both encapsulation and inheritance. Several other languages, including Modula-3 and Oberon (both successors to Modula-2), CLOS, Ada 95/2005, and Fortran 2003, can be characterized as object-oriented extensions to languages in which modules already provide encapsulation. Rather than alter the existing module mechanism, these languages provide inheritance and dynamic method binding through a mechanism for *extending* records.

EXAMPLE 10.23
List and queue abstractions in Ada 2005

In Ada 2005, our list and queue abstractions could be defined as shown in Figure 10.2. To control access to the structure of types, we hide them inside Ada packages. The procedures `initialize`, `finalize`, `enqueue`, and `dequeue` of `g_list.queue` can convert their parameter `self` to a `list_ptr`, because `queue` is an extension of `list`. Package `g_list.queue` is said to be a *child* of package `g_list` because its name is prefixed with that of its parent. A child package in Ada is similar to a derived class in Eiffel or C++, except that it is still a manager, not a type. Like Eiffel, but unlike C++, Ada allows the body of a child package to see the private parts of the parent package.

All of the list and queue subroutines in Figure 10.2 take an explicit first parameter. Ada 95 and CLOS do not use "`object.method()`" notation. Python and Ada 2005 do use this notation, but only as syntactic sugar: a call to `A.B(C, D)`

```
generic
    type item is private;          -- Ada supports both type
    default_value : item;          -- and value generic parameters
package g_list is
    list_err : exception;
    type list_node is tagged private;
        -- 'tagged' means extendable; 'private' means opaque
    type list_node_ptr is access all list_node;
        -- 'all' means that this can point at 'aliased' nonheap data
    procedure initialize(self : access list_node; v : item := default_value);
        -- 'val' will get default value if second parameter is not provided
    procedure finalize(self : access list_node);
    function get_val(self : access list_node) return item;
    function predecessor(self : access list_node) return list_node_ptr;
    function successor(self : access list_node) return list_node_ptr;
    function singleton(self : access list_node) return boolean;
    procedure insert_before(self : access list_node; new_node : list_node_ptr);
    procedure remove(self : access list_node);

    type list is tagged private;
    type list_ptr is access all list;
    procedure initialize(self : access list);
    procedure finalize(self : access list);
    function empty(self : access list) return boolean;
    function head(self : access list) return list_node_ptr;
    procedure append(self : access list; new_node : list_node_ptr);
private
    type list_node is tagged record
        prev, next, head_node : list_node_ptr;
        val : item;
    end record;
    type list is tagged record
        head_node : aliased list_node;
        -- 'aliased' means that an 'all' pointer can refer to this
    end record;
end g_list;
...
package body g_list is
    -- definitions of subroutines
    ...
end g_list;
```

Figure 10.2 Generic list and queue abstractions in Ada 2005. The tagged types `list` and `queue` provide inheritance; the packages provide encapsulation. Declaring `self` to have type `access XX` (instead of `XX_ptr`) causes the compiler to recognize the subroutine as a method of the tagged type; `ptr.method(`*args*`)` is syntactic sugar for `method(ptr,`*args*`)` if `ptr` refers to an object of a tagged type. Function `delete_node` (next page) uses the `Unchecked_Deallocation` library package to create a type-specific routine for memory reclamation. The expression `list_ptr(self)` is a (type-safe) cast. *(continued)*

```
with g_list;                        -- import parent package
generic package g_list.queue is     -- dot means queue is child of g_list
    type queue is new list with private;
        -- 'new' means it's a subtype; 'with' means it's an extension
    type queue_ptr is access all queue;
    procedure initialize(self : access queue);
    procedure finalize(self : access queue);
    function empty(self : access queue) return boolean;
    procedure enqueue(self : access queue; v : item);
    function dequeue(self : access queue) return item;
    function head(self : access queue) return item;
private
    type queue is new list with null record;    -- no new fields
end g_list.queue;
...
with Ada.Unchecked_Deallocation;    -- for delete_node, below
package body g_list.queue is
    procedure initialize(self : access queue) is
    begin
        list_ptr(self).initialize;  -- call base class constructor
    end initialize;

    procedure finalize(self : access queue) is ...              -- similar
    function empty(self : access queue) return boolean is ...   -- to initialize

    procedure enqueue(self : access queue; v : item) is
    new_node : list_node_ptr;       -- local variable
    begin
        new_node := new list_node;
        new_node.initialize;        -- no automatic constructor calls
        list_ptr(self).append(new_node);
    end enqueue;

    procedure delete_node is new Ada.Unchecked_Deallocation
        (Object => list_node, Name => list_node_ptr);

    function dequeue(self : access queue) return item is
    head_node : list_node_ptr;
    rtn : item;
    begin
        if list_ptr(self).empty then raise list_err; end if;
        head_node := list_ptr(self).head;
        head_node.remove;
        rtn := head_node.val;
        delete_node(head_node);
        return rtn;
    end dequeue;

    function head(self : access queue) return item is ...   -- similar to delete
end g_list.queue;
```

Figure 10.2 *(continued)*

is interpreted as a call to `B(A, C, D)`, where `B` is declared as a three-parameter subroutine. Arbitrary Ada code can pass an object of type `queue` to any routine that expects a `list`; as in Java, there is no way for a derived type to hide the public members of a base type. ■

10.2.5 Extending without Inheritance

The desire to extend the functionality of an existing abstraction is one of the principal motivations for object-oriented programming. Inheritance is the standard mechanism that makes such extension possible. There are times, however, when inheritance is not an option, particularly when dealing with preexisting code. The class one wants to extend may not permit inheritance, for instance: in Java, it may be labeled `final`; in C#, it may be `sealed`. Even if inheritance is possible in principle, there may be a large body of existing code that uses the original class name, and it may not be feasible to go back and change all the variable and parameter declarations to use a new derived type.

EXAMPLE 10.24
Extension methods in C#

For situations like these, C# provides *extension methods*, which give the appearance of extending an existing class:

```
static class AddToString {
    public static int toInt(this string s) {
        return int.Parse(s);
    }
}
```

An extension method must be `static`, and must be declared in a `static` class. Its first parameter must be prefixed with the keyword `this`. The method can then be invoked as if it were a member of the class of which `this` is an instance:

```
int n = myString.toInt();
```

Together, the method declaration and use are syntactic sugar for

```
static class AddToString {
    public static int toInt (string s) {      // no 'this'
        return int.Parse(s);
    }
}
...
int n = AddToString.toInt(myString);
```

■

No special functionality is available to extension methods. In particular, they cannot access private members of the class that they extend, nor do they support dynamic method binding (Section 10.4). By contrast, several scripting languages, including JavaScript and Ruby, really do allow the programmer to add new methods to existing classes—or even to individual objects. We will explore these options further in Section 14.4.4.

CHECK YOUR UNDERSTANDING

12. What is meant by an *opaque* export from a module?
13. What are *private* types in Ada?
14. Explain the significance of the `this` parameter in object-oriented languages.
15. How do Java and C# make do without explicit class headers?
16. Explain the distinctions among `private`, `protected`, and `public` class members in C++.
17. Explain the distinctions among `private`, `protected`, and `public` base classes in C++.
18. Describe the notion of *selective availability* in Eiffel.
19. How do the rules for member name visibility in Smalltalk and Objective-C differ from the rules of most other object-oriented languages?
20. How do *inner* classes in Java differ from most other nested classes?
21. Describe the key design difference between the object-oriented features of Smalltalk, Eiffel, and C++ on the one hand, and Ada, CLOS, and Fortran on the other.
22. What are *extension methods* in C#? What purpose do they serve?

10.3 Initialization and Finalization

In Section 3.2 we defined the lifetime of an object to be the interval during which it occupies space and can thus hold data. Most object-oriented languages provide some sort of special mechanism to *initialize* an object automatically at the beginning of its lifetime. When written in the form of a subroutine, this mechanism is known as a *constructor*. Though the name might be thought to imply otherwise, a constructor does not allocate space; it initializes space that has already been allocated. A few languages provide a similar *destructor* mechanism to *finalize* an object automatically at the end of its lifetime. Several important issues arise:

Choosing a constructor: An object-oriented language may permit a class to have zero, one, or many distinct constructors. In the latter case, different constructors may have different names, or it may be necessary to distinguish among them by number and types of arguments.

References and values: If variables are references, then every object must be created explicitly, and it is easy to ensure that an appropriate constructor is called. If variables are values, then object creation can happen implicitly as a result of elaboration. In this latter case, the language must either permit objects to begin their lifetime uninitialized, or it must provide a way to choose an appropriate constructor for every elaborated object.

Execution order: When an object of a derived class is created in C++, the compiler guarantees that the constructors for any base classes will be executed, outermost first, before the constructor for the derived class. Moreover, if a class has members that are themselves objects of some class, then the constructors for the members will be called before the constructor for the object in which they are contained. These rules are a source of considerable syntactic and semantic complexity: when combined with multiple constructors, elaborated objects, and multiple inheritance, they can sometimes induce a complicated sequence of nested constructor invocations, with overload resolution, before control even enters a given scope. Other languages have simpler rules.

Garbage collection: Most object-oriented languages provide some sort of constructor mechanism. Destructors are comparatively rare. Their principal purpose is to facilitate manual storage reclamation in languages like C++. If the language implementation collects garbage automatically, then the need for destructors is greatly reduced.

In the remainder of this section we consider these issues in more detail.

10.3.1 Choosing a Constructor

Smalltalk, Eiffel, C++, Java, and C# all allow the programmer to specify more than one constructor for a given class. In C++, Java, and C#, the constructors behave like overloaded subroutines: they must be distinguished by their numbers and types of arguments. In Smalltalk and Eiffel, different constructors can have different names; code that creates an object must name a constructor explicitly. In Eiffel one might say

EXAMPLE 10.25
Naming constructors in Eiffel

```
class COMPLEX
creation
    new_cartesian, new_polar
feature {ANY}
    x, y : REAL

    new_cartesian(x_val, y_val : REAL) is
    do
        x := x_val; y := y_val
    end

    new_polar(rho, theta : REAL) is
    do
        x := rho * cos(theta)
        y := rho * sin(theta)
    end

    -- other public methods
```

```
feature {NONE}

    -- private methods

end -- class COMPLEX
...
a, b : COMPLEX
...
!!b.new_cartesian(0, 1)
!!a.new_polar(1, pi/2)
```

The `!!` operator is Eiffel's equivalent of `new`. Because class `COMPLEX` specified constructor ("creator") methods, the compiler will insist that every use of `!!` specify a constructor name and arguments. There is no straightforward analog of this code in C++; the fact that both constructors take two `real` arguments means that they could not be distinguished by overloading. ■

Smalltalk resembles Eiffel in the use of multiple named constructors, but it distinguishes more sharply between operations that pertain to an individual object and operations that pertain to a class of objects. Smalltalk also adopts an anthropomorphic programming model in which every operation is seen as being executed by some specific object in response to a request (a "message") from some other object. Since it makes little sense for an object *O* to create itself, *O* must be created by some other object (call it *C*) that represents *O*'s class. Of course, because *C* is an object, it must itself belong to some class. The result of this reasoning is a system in which each class definition really introduces a *pair* of classes and a pair of objects to represent them. Objective-C and CLOS have similar dual hierarchies, as do Python and Ruby.

EXAMPLE 10.26
Metaclasses in Smalltalk

Consider, for example, the standard class named `Date`. Corresponding to `Date` is a single object (call it *D*) that performs operations on behalf of the class. In particular, it is *D* that creates new objects of class `Date`. Because only objects execute operations (classes don't), we don't really need a name for *D*; we can simply use the name of the class it represents:

```
todaysDate <- Date today
```

This code causes *D* to execute the `today` constructor of class `Date`, and assigns a reference to the newly created object into a variable named `todaysDate`.

So what is the class of *D*? It clearly isn't `Date`, because *D represents* class `Date`. Smalltalk says that *D* is an object (in fact the only object) of the *metaclass* `Date class`. For technical reasons, it is also necessary for `Date class` to be represented by an object. To avoid an infinite regression, all objects that represent metaclasses are instances of a single class named `Metaclass`. ■

A few historic languages—notably Modula-3 and Oberon— provided no constructors at all: the programmer had to initialize everything explicitly. Ada 95 supports automatic calls to constructors and destructors (`Initialize` and `Finalize` routines) only for objects of types derived from the standard library type `Controlled`.

10.3.2 References and Values

Many object-oriented languages, including Simula, Smalltalk, Python, Ruby, and Java, use a programming model in which variables refer to objects. A few languages, including C++ and Ada, allow a variable to have a value that *is* an object. Eiffel uses a reference model by default, but allows the programmer to specify that certain classes should be `expanded`, in which case variables of those classes will use a value model. In a similar vein, C# and Swift use `struct` to define types whose variables are values, and `class` to define types whose variables are references.

With a reference model for variables, every object is created explicitly, and it is easy to ensure that an appropriate constructor is called. With a value model for variables, object creation can happen implicitly as a result of elaboration. In Ada, which doesn't provide automatic calls to constructors by default, elaborated objects begin life uninitialized, and it is possible to accidentally attempt to use a variable before it has a value. In C++, the compiler ensures that an appropriate constructor is called for every elaborated object, but the rules it uses to identify constructors and their arguments can sometimes be confusing.

EXAMPLE 10.27 Declarations and constructors in C++

If a C++ variable of class type `foo` is declared with no initial value, then the compiler will call `foo`'s zero-argument constructor (if no such constructor exists, but other constructors do, then the declaration is a static semantic error—a call to a nonexistent subroutine):

```
foo b;                  // calls foo::foo()
```

DESIGN & IMPLEMENTATION

10.3 The value/reference tradeoff

The reference model of variables is arguably more elegant than the value model, particularly for object-oriented languages, but generally requires that objects be allocated from the heap, and imposes (in the absence of compiler optimizations) an extra level of indirection on every access. The value model tends to be more efficient, but makes it difficult to control initialization. In languages with a reference model (including Java), an optimization known as *escape analysis* can sometimes allow the compiler to determine that references to a given object will always be contained within (will never escape) a given method. In this case the object can be allocated in the method's stack frame, avoiding the overhead of heap allocation and, more significantly, eventual garbage collection.

If the programmer wants to call a different constructor, the declaration must specify constructor arguments to drive overload resolution:

```
foo b(10, 'x');          // calls foo::foo(int, char)
foo c{10, 'x'};          // alternative syntax in C++11
```

EXAMPLE 10.28
Copy constructors

The most common argument list consists of a single object, of the same type as the object being declared:

```
foo a;
...
foo b(a);                // calls foo::foo(foo&)
foo c{a};                // alternative syntax
```

Usually the programmer's intent is to declare a new object whose initial value is "the same as" that of the existing object. In this case it may be more natural to write

```
foo a;                   // calls foo::foo()
...
foo b = a;               // calls foo::foo(foo&)
```

In recognition of this intent, a single-argument constructor (of matching type) is sometimes called a *copy constructor*. It is important to realize that the equals sign (=) in this most recent declaration of `b` indicates initialization, not assignment. The effect is exactly the same as in the declarations `foo b(a)` or `foo b{a}`. It is *not* the same as in the similar code fragment

```
foo a, b;                // calls foo::foo() twice
...
b = a;                   // calls foo::operator=(foo&)
```

Here `a` and `b` are initialized with the zero-argument constructor, and the later use of the equals sign indicates *assignment*, not initialization. The distinction is a common source of confusion in C++ programs. It arises from the combination of a value model of variables and an insistence that every elaborated object be initialized by a constructor. The rules are simpler in languages that use a uniform value model for class-type variables: if every object is created by an explicit call to `new` or its equivalent, each such call provides the "hook" at which to call a constructor.

EXAMPLE 10.29
Temporary objects

In C++, the requirement that every object be constructed (and likewise destructed) applies not only to objects with names but also to temporary objects. The following, for example, entails a call to both the `string(const char*)` constructor and the `~string()` destructor:

```
cout << string("Hi, Mom").length();      // prints 7
```

The destructor is called at the end of the output statement: the temporary object behaves as if its scope were just the line shown here.

In a similar vein, the following entails not only two calls to the default `string` constructor (to initialize `a` and `b`) and a call to `string::operator+()`, but also a constructor call to initialize the temporary object returned by `operator+()`—the object whose length is then queried by the caller:

```
string a, b;
...
(a + b).length();
```

As is customary for values returned from functions, the space for the temporary object is likely to be allocated (at a statically known offset) in the stack frame of the caller—that is, in the routine that calls both `operator+()` and `length()`. ■

EXAMPLE 10.30
Return value optimization

Now consider the code for some function `f`, returning a value of class type `foo`. If instances of `foo` are too big to fit in a register, the compiler will arrange for `f`'s caller to pass an extra, hidden parameter that specifies the location into which `f` should construct the return value. If the return statement itself creates a temporary object—

```
return foo( args )
```

—that object can easily be constructed at the caller-specified address. But suppose `f`'s source looks more like this:

```
foo rtn;
...        // complex code to initialize the fields of rtn
return rtn;
```

Because we have used a named, non-temporary variable, the compiler may need to invoke a copy constructor to copy `rtn` into the location in the caller's frame.[4] It is also permitted, however (if other `return` statements don't have conflicting needs), to construct `rtn` itself at the caller-specified location from the outset, and to elide the copy operation. This option is known as *return value optimization*. It turns out to significantly improve the performance of many C++ programs.

In Example 10.29, the value `a + b` was passed immediately to `length()`, allowing the compiler to use the same temporary object in the caller's frame as both the return value from `operator+()` and the `this` argument for `length()`. In other programs the compiler may need to invoke a copy constructor after a function returns:

```
foo c;
...
c = f( args );
```

4 The compiler may also use a move constructor ("R-value References," Section 9.3.1), if available. To avoid excess confusion, we limit the discussion here to copy constructors.

Here the location of `c` cannot be passed as the hidden parameter to `f` unless the compiler is able to prove that `c`'s value will not be used (via an alias, perhaps) during the call. The bottom line: returning an object from a function in C++ may entail zero, one, or two invocations of the return type's copy constructor, depending on whether the compiler is able to optimize either or both of the `return` statement and the subsequent use in the caller.

EXAMPLE 10.31
Eiffel constructors and expanded objects

While Eiffel has both dynamically allocated and `expanded` objects, its strategy with regard to constructors is somewhat simpler. Specifically, every variable is initialized to a default value. For built-in types (integer, floating-point, character, etc.), which are always `expanded`, the default values are all zero. For references to objects, the default value is `void` (null). For variables of `expanded` class types, the defaults are applied recursively to members. As noted above, new objects are created by invoking Eiffel's `!!` creation operator:

```
!!var.creator(args)
```

where `var` is a variable of some class type *T* and `creator` is a constructor for *T*. In the common case, `var` will be a reference, and the creation operator will allocate space for an object of class *T* and then call the object's constructor. This same syntax is permitted, however, when *T* is an `expanded` class type, in which case `var` will actually be an object, rather than a reference. In this case, the `!!`

DESIGN & IMPLEMENTATION

10.4 Initialization and assignment

Issues around initialization and assignment in C++ can sometimes have a surprising effect on performance—and potentially on program behavior as well. As noted in the body of the text, "`foo a = b`" is likely to be more efficient than "`foo a; a = b`"—and may lead to different behavior if `foo`'s copy constructor and assignment operator have not been designed to be semantically equivalent. Similar issues may arise with `operator+()` and `operator+=()`, `operator*()` and `operator*=()`, and the other analogous pairs of operations.

Similar issues may also arise when making function calls. A parameter that is passed by value typically induces an implicit call to a copy constructor. A parameter that is passed by reference does not, and may be equally acceptable, especially if declared to be `const`. (In C++11, the value parameter may also use a move constructor.) From a performance perspective, the cost of a copy or more constructor may or may not be outweighed by the cost of indirection and the possibility that code improvement may be inhibited by potential aliases. From a behavioral perspective, calls to different constructors and operators, induced by tiny source code changes, can be a source of very subtle bugs. C++ programmers must exercise great care to avoid side effects in constructors and to ensure that all intuitively equivalent methods have identical semantics in practice. Even then, performance tradeoffs may be very hard to predict.

operator simply passes to the constructor (a reference to) the already-allocated object. ■

10.3.3 Execution Order

As we have seen, C++ insists that every object be initialized before it can be used. Moreover, if the object's class (call it *B*) is derived from some other class (call it *A*), C++ insists on calling an *A* constructor before calling a *B* constructor, so that the derived class is guaranteed never to see its inherited fields in an inconsistent state. When the programmer creates an object of class *B* (either via declaration or with a call to `new`), the creation operation specifies arguments for a *B* constructor. These arguments allow the C++ compiler to resolve overloading when multiple constructors exist. But where does the compiler obtain arguments for the *A* constructor? Adding them to the creation syntax (as Simula did) would be a clear violation of abstraction. The answer adopted in C++ is to allow the header of the constructor of a derived class to specify base class constructor arguments:

EXAMPLE 10.32
Specification of base class constructor arguments

```
foo::foo( foo_params ) : bar( bar_args ) {
    ...
```

Here `foo` is derived from `bar`. The list *foo_params* consists of formal parameters for this particular `foo` constructor. Between the parameter list and the opening brace of the subroutine definition is a "call" to a constructor for the base class `bar`. The arguments to the `bar` constructor can be arbitrarily complicated expressions involving the `foo` parameters. The compiler will arrange to execute the `bar` constructor before beginning execution of the `foo` constructor. ■

EXAMPLE 10.33
Specification of member constructor arguments

Similar syntax allows the C++ programmer to specify constructor arguments or initial values for members of the class. In Figure 10.1, for example, we could have used this syntax to initialize `prev`, `next`, `head_node`, and `val` in the constructor for `list_node`:

DESIGN & IMPLEMENTATION

10.5 Initialization of "expanded" objects

C++ inherits from C a design philosophy that emphasizes execution speed, minimal run-time support, and suitability for "systems" programming, in which the programmer needs to be able to write code whose mapping to assembly language is straightforward and self-evident. The use of a value model for variables in C++ is thus more than an attempt to be backward compatible with C; it reflects the desire to allocate variables statically or on the stack whenever possible, to avoid the overhead of dynamic allocation, deallocation, and frequent indirection. In later sections we shall see several other manifestations of the C++ philosophy, including manual storage reclamation (Section 10.3.4) and static method binding (Section 10.4.1).

```
list_node() : prev(this), next(this), head_node(this), val(0) {
    // empty body -- nothing else to do
}
```

Given that all of these members have simple (pointer or integer) types, there will be no significant difference in the generated code. But suppose we have members that are themselves objects of some nontrivial class:

```
class foo : bar {
    mem1_t member1;        // mem1_t and
    mem2_t member2;        // mem2_t are classes
    ...
}

foo::foo( foo_params ) : bar( bar_args ), member1(mem1_init_val ),
        member2( mem2_init_val ) {
    ...
```

Here the use of embedded calls in the header of the `foo` constructor causes the compiler to call the copy constructors for the member objects, rather than calling the default (zero-argument) constructors, followed by `operator=` within the body of the constructor. Both semantics and performance may be different as a result.

EXAMPLE 10.34
Constructor forwarding

When the code of one constructor closely resembles that of another, C++ also allows the member-and-base-class-initializer syntax to be used to *forward* one constructor to another. In Example 10.4 we introduced a new integer-parameter constructor for the `list_node` class of Figure 10.1. Given the existence of this new constructor, we could re-write the default (no-parameter) constructor as

```
class list_node {
    ...
    list_node() : list_node(0) { }      // forward to (int) constructor
```

Any declaration of a `list_node` that does not provide an argument will now call the integer-parameter constructor with an argument of 0.

EXAMPLE 10.35
Invocation of base class constructor in Java

Like C++, Java insists that a constructor for a base class be called before the constructor for a derived class. The syntax is a bit simpler, however; the initial line of the code for the derived class constructor may consist of a "call" to the base class constructor:

```
super( args );
```

(C# has a similar mechanism.) As noted in Section 10.1, `super` is a Java keyword that refers to the base class of the class in whose code it appears. If the call to `super` is missing, the Java compiler automatically inserts a call to the base class's zero-argument constructor (in which case such a constructor must exist).

Because Java uses a reference model uniformly for all objects, any class members that are themselves objects will actually be *references*, rather than "expanded" objects (to use the Eiffel term). Java simply initializes such members to `null`. If the programmer wants something different, he or she must call `new` explicitly within the constructor of the surrounding class. Smalltalk and (in the common case) C# and Eiffel adopt a similar approach. In C#, members whose types are `structs` are initialized by setting all of their fields to zero or null. In Eiffel, if a class contains members of an `expanded` class type, that type is required to have a single constructor, with no arguments; the Eiffel compiler arranges to call this constructor when the surrounding object is created.

Smalltalk, Eiffel, CLOS, and Objective-C are all more lax than C++ regarding the initialization of base classes. The compiler or interpreter arranges to call the constructor (creator, initializer) for each newly created object automatically, but it does *not* arrange to call constructors for base classes automatically; all it does is initialize base class data members to default (zero or `null`) values. If the derived class wants different behavior, its constructor(s) must call a constructor for the base class explicitly.

10.3.4 Garbage Collection

EXAMPLE 10.36
Reclaiming space with destructors

When a C++ object is destroyed, the destructor for the derived class is called first, followed by those of the base class(es), in reverse order of derivation. By far the most common use of destructors in C++ is manual storage reclamation. Consider again the `queue` class of Figure10.8. Because our `queue` is derived from the `list` of Figure 10.2, its default destructor will call the explicit `~list` destructor, which will throw an exception if the list (i.e., the queue) is nonempty. Suppose instead that we wish to allow the destruction of a nonempty queue, and simply clean up its space. Since queue nodes are created by `enqueue`, and are used only within the code of the queue itself, we can safely arrange for the queue's destructor to delete any nodes that remain:

```
~queue() {
    while (!empty()) {
        list_node* p = contents.head();
        p->remove();
        delete p;
    }
}
```

Alternatively, since `dequeue` has already been designed to delete the node that contained the dequeued element:

```
~queue() {
    while (!empty()) {
        int v = dequeue();
    }
}
```

In modern C++ code, storage management is often facilitated through the use of *smart pointers* (Section 8.5.3). These arrange, in the destructor for a pointer, to determine whether any other pointers to the same object continue to exist—and if not, to reclaim that pointed-to object. ■

In languages with automatic garbage collection, there is much less need for destructors. In fact, the entire idea of destruction is suspect in a garbage-collected language, because the programmer has little or no control over when an object is going to be destroyed. Java and C# allow the programmer to declare a `finalize` method that will be called immediately before the garbage collector reclaims the space for an object, but the feature is not widely used.

✓ CHECK YOUR UNDERSTANDING

23. Does a constructor allocate space for an object? Explain.
24. What is a *metaclass* in Smalltalk?
25. Why is object initialization simpler in a language with a reference model of variables (as opposed to a value model)?
26. How does a C++ (or Java or C#) compiler tell which constructor to use for a given object? How does the answer differ for Eiffel and Smalltalk?
27. What is *escape analysis*? Describe why it might be useful in a language with a reference model of variables.
28. Summarize the rules in C++ that determine the order in which constructors are called for a class, its base class(es), and the classes of its fields. How are these rules simplified in other languages?
29. Explain the difference between initialization and assignment in C++.
30. Why does C++ need destructors more than Eiffel does?

10.4 Dynamic Method Binding

One of the principal consequences of inheritance/type extension is that a derived class *D* has all the members—data and subroutines—of its base class *C*. As long as *D* does not hide any of the publicly visible members of *C* (see Exercise 10.15), it makes sense to allow an object of class *D* to be used in any context that expects an object of class *C*: anything we might want to do to an object of class *C* we can also do to an object of class *D*. In other words, a derived class that does not hide any publicly visible members of its base class is a *subtype* of that base class.

EXAMPLE 10.37
Derived class objects in a base class context

The ability to use a derived class in a context that expects its base class is called *subtype polymorphism*. If we imagine an administrative computing system for a university, we might derive classes `student` and `professor` from class `person`:

```
class person { ...
class student : public person { ...
class professor : public person { ...
```

Because both student and professor objects have all the properties of a person object, we should be able to use them in a person context:

```
student s;
professor p;
...
person *x = &s;
person *y = &p;
```

Moreover a subroutine like

```
void person::print_mailing_label() { ...
```

would be polymorphic—capable of accepting arguments of multiple types:

```
s.print_mailing_label();     // i.e., print_mailing_label(s)
p.print_mailing_label();     // i.e., print_mailing_label(p)
```

As with other forms of polymorphism, we depend on the fact that print_mailing_label uses only those features of its formal parameter that all actual parameters will have in common. ■

EXAMPLE 10.38
Static and dynamic method binding

But now suppose that we have redefined print_mailing_label in each of the two derived classes. We might, for example, want to encode certain information (student's year in school, professor's home department) in the corner of the label. Now we have multiple versions of our subroutine—student::print_mailing_label and professor::print_mailing_label, rather than the single, polymorphic person::print_mailing_label. Which version we will get depends on the object:

```
s.print_mailing_label();     // student::print_mailing_label(s)
p.print_mailing_label();     // professor::print_mailing_label(p)
```

But what about

```
x->print_mailing_label();      // ??
y->print_mailing_label();      // ??
```

Does the choice of the method to be called depend on the types of the *variables* x and y, or on the classes of the *objects* s and p to which those variables refer? ■

The first option (use the type of the reference) is known as *static method binding*. The second option (use the class of the object) is known as *dynamic method binding*. Dynamic method binding is central to object-oriented programming. Imagine, for example, that our administrative computing program has created a list of persons who have overdue library books. The list may contain both students and professors. If we traverse the list and print a mailing label for each person, dynamic method binding will ensure that the correct printing routine is called for each individual. In this situation the definitions in the derived classes are said to *override* the definition in the base class.

Semantics and Performance

The principal argument against static method binding—and thus in favor of dynamic binding based on the type of the referenced object—is that the static approach denies the derived class control over the consistency of its own state. Suppose, for example, that we are building an I/O library that contains a `text_file` class:

EXAMPLE 10.39
The need for dynamic binding

```
class text_file {
    char *name;
    long position;             // file pointer
public:
    void seek(long whence);
    ...
};
```

Now suppose we have a derived class `read_ahead_text_file`:

```
class read_ahead_text_file : public text_file {
    char *upcoming_characters;
public:
    void seek(long whence);     // redefinition
    ...
};
```

The code for `read_ahead_text_file::seek` will undoubtedly need to change the value of the cached `upcoming_characters`. If the method is not dynamically dispatched, however, we cannot guarantee that this will happen: if we pass a `read_ahead_text_file` reference to a subroutine that expects a `text_file` reference as argument, and if that subroutine then calls `seek`, we'll get the version of `seek` in the base class. ■

Unfortunately, as we shall see in Section 10.4.3, dynamic method binding imposes run-time overhead. While this overhead is generally modest, it is nonetheless a concern for small subroutines in performance-critical applications. Smalltalk, Objective-C, Python, and Ruby use dynamic method binding for all methods. Java and Eiffel use dynamic method binding by default, but allow individual methods and (in Java) classes to be labeled `final` (Java) or `frozen` (Eiffel), in which case they cannot be overridden by derived classes, and can therefore employ an optimized implementation. Simula, C++, C#, and Ada 95 use static method binding by default, but allow the programmer to specify dynamic binding when desired. In these latter languages it is common terminology to distinguish between *overriding* a method that uses dynamic binding and (merely) *redefining* a method that uses static binding. For the sake of clarity, C# requires explicit use of the keywords `override` and `new` whenever a method in a derived class overrides or redefines (respectively) a method of the same name in a base class. Java and C++11 have similar annotations whose use is encouraged but not required.

10.4.1 Virtual and Nonvirtual Methods

In Simula, C++, and C#, which use static method binding by default, the programmer can specify that particular methods should use dynamic binding by labeling them as `virtual`. Calls to virtual methods are *dispatched* to the appropriate implementation at run time, based on the class of the object, rather than the type of the reference. In C++ and C#, the keyword `virtual` prefixes the subroutine declaration:[5]

EXAMPLE 10.40 Virtual methods in C++ and C#

```
class person {
public:
    virtual void print_mailing_label();
    ...
```

Ada 95 adopts a different approach. Rather than associate dynamic dispatch with particular methods, the Ada 95 programmer associates it with certain *references*. In our mailing label example, a formal parameter or an `access` variable (pointer) can be declared to be of the *class-wide* type `person'Class`, in which case all calls to all methods of that parameter or variable will be dispatched based on the class of the object to which it refers:

EXAMPLE 10.41 Class-wide types in Ada 95

```
type person is tagged record ...
type student is new person with ...
type professor is new person with ...

procedure print_mailing_label(r : person) is ...
procedure print_mailing_label(s : student) is ...
procedure print_mailing_label(p : professor) is ...

procedure print_appropriate_label(r : person'Class) is
begin
    print_mailing_label(r);
    -- calls appropriate overloaded version, depending
    -- on type of r at run time
end print_appropriate_label;
```

10.4.2 Abstract Classes

In most object-oriented languages it is possible to omit the body of a virtual method in a base class. In Java and C#, one does so by labeling both the class and the missing method as `abstract`:

EXAMPLE 10.42 Abstract methods in Java and C#

5 C++ also uses the `virtual` keyword in certain circumstances to prefix the name of a base class in the header of the declaration of a derived class. This usage supports the very different purpose of *shared multiple inheritance*, which we will consider in Section C-10.6.3.

```
abstract class person {
    ...
    public abstract void print_mailing_label();
    ...
```

EXAMPLE 10.43
Abstract methods in C++

The notation in C++ is somewhat less intuitive: one follows the subroutine declaration with an "assignment" to zero:

```
class person {
    ...
public:
    virtual void print_mailing_label() = 0;
    ...
```

C++ refers to abstract methods as *pure virtual* methods.

Regardless of declaration syntax, a *class* is said to be abstract if it has at least one abstract method. It is not possible to declare an object of an abstract class, because it would be missing at least one member. The only purpose of an abstract class is to serve as a base for other, *concrete* classes. A concrete class (or one of its intermediate ancestors) must provide a real definition for every abstract method it inherits. The existence of an abstract method in a base class provides a "hook" for dynamic method binding; it allows the programmer to write code that calls methods of (references to) objects of the base class, under the assumption that appropriate concrete methods will be invoked at run time. Classes that have no members other than abstract methods—no fields or method bodies—are called *interfaces* in Java, C#, and Ada 2005. They support a restricted, "mix-in" form of multiple inheritance, which we will consider in Section 10.5.[6]

10.4.3 Member Lookup

EXAMPLE 10.44
Vtables

With static method binding (as in Simula, C++, C#, or Ada 95), the compiler can always tell which version of a method to call, based on the type of the variable being used. With dynamic method binding, however, the object referred to by a reference or pointer variable must contain sufficient information to allow the code generated by the compiler to find the right version of the method at run time. The most common implementation represents each object with a record whose first field contains the address of a *virtual method table* (*vtable*) for the object's class (see Figure 10.3). The vtable is an array whose *i*th entry indicates the address of the code for the object's *i*th virtual method. All objects of a given concrete class share the same vtable.

EXAMPLE 10.45
Implementation of a virtual method call

Suppose that the `this` (`self`) pointer for methods is passed in register `r1`, that `m` is the third method of class `foo`, and that `f` is a pointer to an object of class `foo`. Then the code to call `f->m()` looks something like this:

---

6 Terminology differs in other languages. In Eiffel, an interface is called a *fully deferred* class. In Scala, it's called a *trait*.

```
class foo {
    int a;
    double b;
    char c;
public:
    virtual void k( ...
    virtual int l( ...
    virtual void m();
    virtual double n( ...
    ...
} F;
```

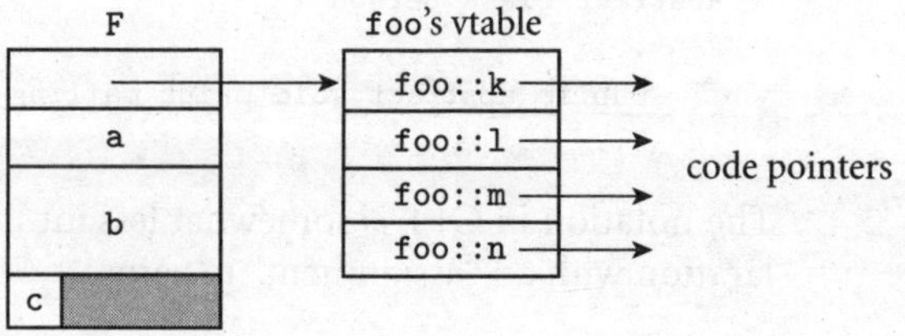

Figure 10.3 **Implementation of virtual methods.** The representation of object F begins with the address of the vtable for class foo. (All objects of this class will point to the same vtable.) The vtable itself consists of an array of addresses, one for the code of each virtual method of the class. The remainder of F consists of the representations of its fields.

```
class bar : public foo {
    int w;
public:
    void m() override;
    virtual double s( ...
    virtual char *t( ...
    ...
} B;
```

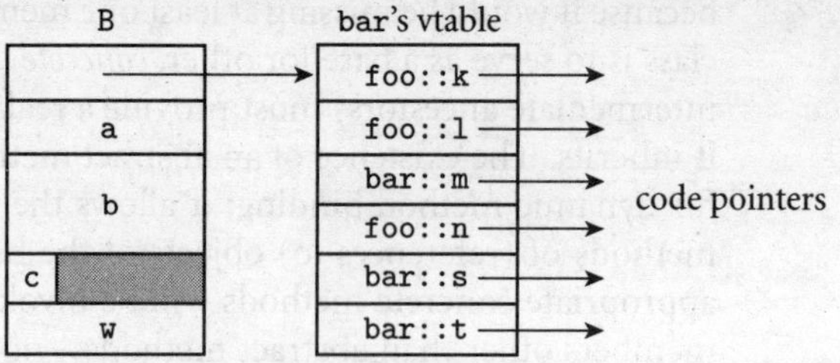

Figure 10.4 **Implementation of single inheritance.** As in Figure 10.3, the representation of object B begins with the address of its class's vtable. The first four entries in the table represent the same members as they do for foo, except that one—m—has been overridden and now contains the address of the code for a different subroutine. Additional fields of bar follow the ones inherited from foo in the representation of B; additional virtual methods follow the ones inherited from foo in the vtable of class bar.

```
r1 := f
r2 := *r1                  -- vtable address
r2 := *(r2 + (3−1) × 4)    -- assuming 4 = sizeof (address)
call *r2
```

On a typical modern machine this calling sequence is two instructions (both of which access memory) longer than a call to a statically identified method. The extra overhead can be avoided whenever the compiler can deduce the type of the relevant object at compile time. The deduction is trivial for calls to methods of object-valued variables (as opposed to references and pointers). ■

EXAMPLE 10.46
Implementation of single inheritance

If bar is derived from foo, we place its additional fields at the end of the "record" that represents it. We create a vtable for bar by copying the vtable for foo, replacing the entries of any virtual methods overridden by bar, and appending entries for any virtual methods introduced in bar (see Figure 10.4). If we have an object of class bar we can safely assign its address into a variable of type foo*:

```
class foo { ...
class bar : public foo { ...
...
foo F;
bar B;
foo* q;
bar* s;
...
q = &B;        // ok; references through q will use prefixes
               // of B's data space and vtable
s = &F;        // static semantic error; F lacks the additional
               // data and vtable entries of a bar
```

In C++ (as in all statically typed object-oriented languages), the compiler can verify the type correctness of this code statically. It may not know what the class of the object referred to by q will be at run time, but it knows that it will either be foo or something derived (directly or indirectly) from foo, and this ensures that it will have all the members that may be accessed by foo-specific code. ■

EXAMPLE 10.47
Casts in C++

C++ allows "backward" assignments by means of a dynamic_cast operator:

```
s = dynamic_cast<bar*>(q);      // performs a run-time check
```

If the run-time check fails, s is assigned a null pointer. For backward compatibility C++ also supports traditional C-style casts of object pointers and references:

```
s = (bar*) q;                   // permitted, but risky
```

With a C-style cast it is up to the programmer to ensure that the actual object involved is of an appropriate type: no dynamic semantic check is performed. ■

EXAMPLE 10.48
Reverse assignment in Eiffel and C#

Java and C# employ the traditional cast notation, but perform the dynamic check. Eiffel has a *reverse assignment* operator, ?=, which (like the C++ dynamic_cast) assigns an object reference into a variable if and only if the type at run time is acceptable:

DESIGN & IMPLEMENTATION

10.6 Reverse assignment

Implementations of Eiffel, Java, C#, and C++ support dynamic checks on reverse assignment by including in each vtable the address of a run-time *type descriptor*. In C++, dynamic_cast is permitted only on pointers and references of polymorphic types (classes with virtual methods), since objects of nonpolymorphic types do not have vtables. A separate static_cast operation can be used on nonpolymorphic types, but it performs no run-time check, and is thus inherently unsafe when applied to a pointer of a derived class type.

```
class foo ...
class bar inherit foo ...
...
f : foo
b : bar
...
f := b        -- always ok
b ?= f        -- reverse assignment: b gets f if f refers to a bar object
              -- at run time; otherwise b gets void
```

C# provides an as operator that performs a similar function. ■

As noted in Section 7.3, Smalltalk employs "duck typing": variables are *untyped* references, and a reference to any object may be assigned into any variable. Only when code actually attempts to invoke an operation (send a "message") at run time does the language implementation check to see whether the operation is supported by the object; if so, the object's type is assumed to be acceptable. The implementation is straightforward: fields of an object are never

DESIGN & IMPLEMENTATION

10.7 The fragile base class problem

Under certain circumstances, it can be desirable to perform method lookup at run time even when the language permits compile-time lookup. In Java, for example, dynamic lookup (or "just-in-time" compilation) can help to avoid important instances of the *fragile base class* problem, in which seemingly benign changes to a base class may break the behavior of a derived class.

Java implementations depend on the presence of a large standard library. This library is expected to evolve over time. Though the designers will presumably be careful to maximize backward compatibility—seldom if ever deleting any members of a class—it is likely that users of old versions of the library will on occasion attempt to run code that was written with a new version of the library in mind. In such a situation it would be disastrous to rely on static assumptions about the representation of library classes: code that tries to use a newly added library feature could end up accessing memory beyond the end of the available representation. Run-time method lookup, by contrast (or compilation performed against the currently available version of the library), will produce a helpful "member not found in your version of the class" dynamic error message.

A variety of other techniques can be used to guard against aspects of the fragile base class problem. In Objective-C, for example, modifications to a library class typically take the form of a separately compiled extension called a *category*, which is loaded into a program at run time. The loading mechanism updates the dictionary in which the runtime system performs dynamic method lookup. Without the category, attempts to use the new functionality will automatically elicit a "method not found" error.

public; methods provide the only means of object interaction. The representation of an object begins with the address of a type descriptor. The type descriptor contains a dictionary that maps method names to code fragments. At run time, the Smalltalk interpreter performs a lookup operation in the dictionary to see if the method is supported. If not, it generates a "message not understood" error—the equivalent of a type-clash error in Lisp. CLOS, Objective-C, Swift, and the object-oriented scripting languages provide similar semantics, and invite similar implementations. The dynamic approach is arguably more flexible than the static, but it imposes significant cost when methods are small, and delays the reporting of errors.

In addition to imposing the overhead of indirection, virtual methods often preclude the in-line expansion of subroutines at compile time. The lack of in-line subroutines can be a serious performance problem when subroutines are small and frequently called. Like C, C++ attempts to avoid run-time overhead whenever possible: hence its use of static method binding as the default, and its heavy reliance on object-valued variables, for which even virtual methods can be dispatched at compile time.

10.4.4 Object Closures

We have noted (in Section 3.6.4 and elsewhere) that object closures can be used in an object-oriented language to achieve roughly the same effect as subroutine closures in a language with nested subroutines—namely, to encapsulate a method with *context* for later execution. It should be noted that this mechanism relies, for its full generality, on dynamic method binding. Recall the `plus_x` object closure from Example 3.36, here adapted to the `apply_to_A` code of Example 9.23, and rewritten in generic form:

EXAMPLE 10.49
Virtual methods in an object closure

```
template<typename T>
class un_op {
public:
    virtual T operator()(T i) const = 0;
};

class plus_x : public un_op<int> {
    const int x;
public:
    plus_x(int n) : x(n) { }
    virtual int operator()(int i) const { return i + x; }
};

void apply_to_A(const un_op<int>& f, int A[], int A_size) {
    int i;
    for (i = 0; i < A_size; i++) A[i] = f(A[i]);
}
...
```

```
int A[10];
apply_to_A(plus_x(2), A, 10);
```

Any object derived from `un_op<int>` can be passed to `apply_to_A`. The "right" function will always be called because `operator()` is virtual. ■

EXAMPLE 10.50
Encapsulating arguments

A particularly useful idiom for many applications is to encapsulate a method *and its arguments* in an object closure for later execution. Suppose, for example, that we are writing a discrete event simulation, as described in Section C-9.5.4. We might like a general mechanism that allows us to schedule a call to an arbitrary subroutine, with an arbitrary set of parameters, to occur at some future point in time. If the subroutines we want to have called vary in their numbers and types of parameters, we won't be able to pass them to a general-purpose `schedule_at` routine. We can solve the problem with object closures, as shown in Figure 10.5. This technique is sufficiently common that C++11 supports it with standard library routines. The `fn_call` and `call_foo` classes of Figure 10.5 could be omitted in C++11. Function `schedule_at` would then be defined to take an object of class `std::function<void()>` (function object encapsulating a function to be called with zero arguments) as its first parameter. Object `cf`, which Figure 10.5 passes in that first parameter position, would be declared as

```
std::function<void()> cf = std::bind(foo, 3, 3.14, 'x');
```

The `bind` routine (an automatically instantiated generic function) encapsulates its first parameter (a function) together with the arguments that should eventually be passed to that function. The standard library even provides a "placeholder" mechanism (not shown here) that allows the programmer to bind only a subset of the function's parameters, so that parameters eventually passed to the function object can be used to fill in the remaining positions. ■

Object closures are commonly used in Java (and several other languages) to encapsulate start-up arguments for newly created threads of control (more on this in Section 13.2.3). They can also be used (as noted in Exploration 6.46) to implement iterators via the *visitor pattern*.

✓ CHECK YOUR UNDERSTANDING

31. Explain the difference between dynamic and static method binding (i.e., between *virtual* and *nonvirtual* methods).

32. Summarize the fundamental argument for dynamic method binding. Why do C++ and C# use static method binding by default?

33. Explain the distinction between *redefining* and *overriding* a method.

34. What is a *class-wide* type in Ada 95?

35. Explain the connection between dynamic method binding and polymorphism.

```
class fn_call {
public:
    virtual void operator()() = 0;
};
void schedule_at(fn_call& fc, time t) {
    ...
}
...
void foo(int a, double b, char c) {
    ...
}
class call_foo : public fn_call {
    int arg1;
    double arg2;
    char arg3;
public:
    call_foo(int a, double b, char c) :      // constructor
        arg1(a), arg2(b), arg3(c) {
        // member initialization is all that is required
    }
    void operator()() {
        foo(arg1, arg2, arg3);
    }
};
...
call_foo cf(3, 3.14, 'x');          // declaration/constructor call
schedule_at(cf, now() + delay);
    // at some point in the future, the discrete event system
    // will call cf.operator()(), which will cause a call to
    // foo(3, 3.14, 'x')
```

Figure 10.5 **Subroutine pointers and virtual methods.** Class `call_foo` encapsulates a subroutine pointer and values to be passed to the subroutine. It exports a parameter-less subroutine that can be used to trigger the encapsulated call.

36. What is an *abstract* method (also called a *pure* virtual method in C++ and a *deferred feature* in Eiffel)?
37. What is *reverse assignment*? Why does it require a run-time check?
38. What is a *vtable*? How is it used?
39. What is the *fragile base class* problem?
40. What is an *abstract* (*deferred*) *class*?
41. Explain the importance of virtual methods for object closures.

10.5 Mix-In Inheritance

When building an object-oriented system, it is often difficult to design a perfect inheritance tree, in which every class has exactly one parent. A `cat` may be an `animal`, a `pet`, a `family_member`, or an `object_of_affection`. A `widget` in the company database may be a `sortable_object` (from the reporting system's perspective), a `graphable_object` (from the window system's perspective), or a `storable_object` (from the file system's perspective); how do we choose just one?

In the general case, we could imagine allowing a class to have an arbitrary number of parents, each of which could provide it with both fields and methods (both abstract and concrete). This sort of "true" multiple inheritance is provided by several languages, including C++, Eiffel, CLOS, OCaml, and Python; we will consider it in Section 10.6. Unfortunately, it introduces considerable complexity in both language semantics and run-time implementation. In practice, a more limited mechanism, known as *mix-in inheritance*, is often all we really need.

EXAMPLE 10.51
The motivation for interfaces

Consider our `widgets`, for example. Odds are, the reporting system doesn't really define what a widget *is*; it simply needs to be able to *manipulate* widgets in certain well-defined ways—to sort them, for example. Likewise, the windowing system probably doesn't need to provide any state or functionality for widgets; it simply needs to be able to display them on a screen. To capture these sorts of requirements, a language with mix-in inheritance allows the programmer to define the *interface* that a class must provide in order for its objects to be used in certain contexts. For `widgets`, the reporting system might define a `sortable_object` interface; the window system might define a `graphable_object` interface; the file system might define a `storable_object` interface. No actual functionality would be provided by any of the interfaces: the designer of the `widget` class would need to provide appropriate implementations. ■

In effect—as we noted in Section 10.4.2—an interface is a class containing only abstract methods—no fields or method bodies. So long as it inherits from only one "real" parent, a class can "mix in" an arbitrary number of interfaces. If a formal parameter of a subroutine is declared to have an interface type, then any class that implements (inherits from) that interface can be passed as the corresponding actual parameter. The classes of objects that can legitimately be passed need not have a common class ancestor.

In recent years, mix-ins have become a common approach—arguably the dominant approach—to multiple inheritance. Though details vary from one language to another, interfaces appear in Java, C#, Scala, Objective-C, Swift, Go, Ada 2005, and Ruby, among others.

EXAMPLE 10.52
Mixing interfaces into a derived class

Elaborating on our `widget` example, suppose that we have been given general-purpose Java code that will sort objects according to some textual field, display a graphic representation of an object within a web browser window (hiding and refreshing as appropriate), and store references to objects by name in a dictionary data structure. Each of these capabilities would be represented by an interface.

If we have already developed some complicated class of `widget` objects, we can make use of the general-purpose code by mixing the appropriate interfaces into classes derived from `widget`, as shown in Figure 10.6.

10.5.1 Implementation

In a language like Ruby, Objective-C, or Swift, which uses dynamic method lookup, the methods of an interface can simply be added to the method dictionary of any class that implements the interface. In any context that requires the interface type, the usual lookup mechanism will find the proper methods. In a language with fully static typing, in which pointers to methods are expected to lie at known vtable offsets, new machinery is required. The challenge boils down to a need for multiple *views* of an object.

EXAMPLE 10.53
Compile-time implementation of mix-in inheritance

In Figure 10.6, method `dictionary.insert` expects a `storable_object` view of its parameter—a way to find the parameter's `get_stored_name` method. The `get_stored_name` method, however, is implemented by `augmented_widget`, and will expect an `augmented_widget` view of its `this` parameter—a way to find the object's fields and other methods. Given that `augmented_widget` implements three different interfaces, there is no way that a single vtable can suffice: its first entry can't be the first method of `sortable_object`, `graphable_object`, and `storable_object` simultaneously.

The most common solution, shown in Figure 10.7, is to include three extra vtable pointers in each `augmented_widget` object—one for each of the implemented interfaces. For each interface view we can then use a pointer to the place *within* the object where the corresponding vtable pointer appears. The offset of that pointer from the beginning of the object is known as the "`this` correction"; it is stored at the beginning of the vtable.

Suppose now that we wish to call `dictionary.insert` on an `augmented_widget` object `w`, whose address is currently in register r1. The compiler, which knows the offset c of `w`'s `storable_object` vtable pointer, will add c to r1 before passing it to `insert`. So far so good. What happens when `insert` calls `storable_object.get_stored_name`? Assuming that the `storable_object` view of `w` is available in, say, register r1, the compiler will generate code that looks something like this:

```
r2 := *r1              -- vtable address
r3 := *r2              -- this correction
r3 +:= r1              -- address of w
call *(r2+4)           -- method address
```

Here we have assumed that the `this` correction occupies the first four bytes of the vtable, and that the address of `get_stored_name` lies immediately after it, in the table's first regular slot. We have also assumed that `this` should be passed in register r3, and that there are no other arguments. On a typical modern machine this code is two instructions (a load and a subtraction)

```
public class widget { ...
}
interface sortable_object {
    String get_sort_name();
    bool less_than(sortable_object o);
    // All methods of an interface are automatically public.
}
interface graphable_object {
    void display_at(Graphics g, int x, int y);
    // Graphics is a standard library class that provides a context
    // in which to render graphical objects.
}
interface storable_object {
    String get_stored_name();
}
class named_widget extends widget implements sortable_object {
    public String name;
    public String get_sort_name() {return name;}
    public bool less_than(sortable_object o) {
        return (name.compareTo(o.get_sort_name()) < 0);
        // compareTo is a method of the standard library class String.
    }
}
class augmented_widget extends named_widget
        implements graphable_object, storable_object {
    ...         // more data members
    public void display_at(Graphics g, int x, int y) {
        ...     // series of calls to methods of g
    }
    public String get_stored_name() {return name;}
}
...
class sorted_list {
    public void insert(sortable_object o) { ...
    public sortable_object first() { ...
    ...
}
class browser_window extends Frame {
    // Frame is the standard library class for windows.
    public void add_to_window(graphable_object o) { ...
    ...
}
class dictionary {
    public void insert(storable_object o) { ...
    public storable_object lookup(String name) { ...
    ...
}
```

Figure 10.6 Interface classes in Java. By implementing the sortable_object interface in named_widget and the graphable_object and storable_object interfaces in augmented_widget, we obtain the ability to pass objects of those classes to and from such routines as sorted_list.insert, browser_window.add_to_window, and dictionary.insert.

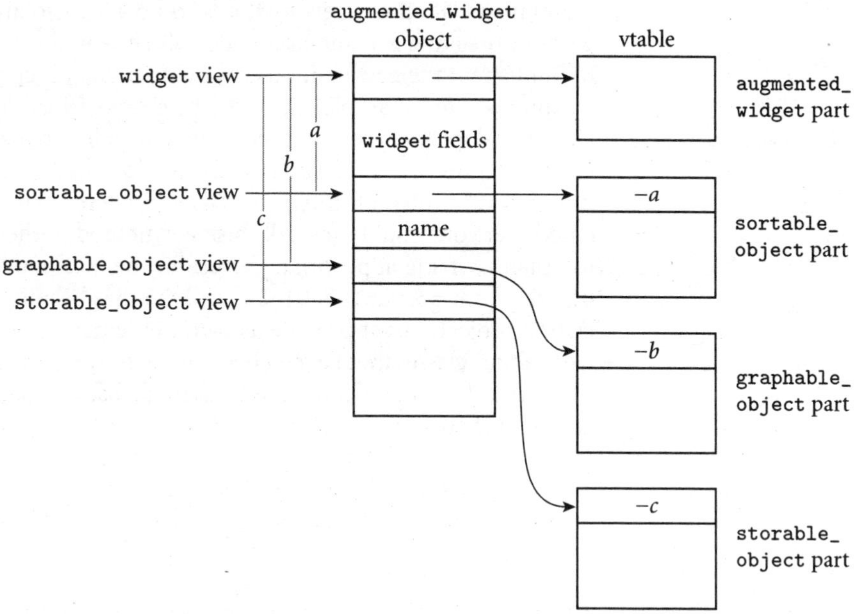

Figure 10.7 **Implementation of mix-in inheritance.** Objects of class augmented_widget contain four vtable addresses, one for the class itself (as in Figure 10.3), and three for the implemented interfaces. The view of the object that is passed to interface routines points directly at the relevant vtable pointer. The vtable then begins with a "this correction" offset, used to regenerate a pointer to the object itself.

longer than the code required with single inheritance. Once it executes, however, `augmented_widget.get_stored_name` will be running with exactly the parameter it expects: a reference to an `augmented_widget` object.

10.5.2 Extensions

The description of interfaces above reflects historical versions of Java, with one omission: in addition to abstract methods, an interface can define `static final` (constant) fields. Because such fields can never change, they introduce no run-time complexity or overhead—the compiler can, effectively, expand them in place wherever they are used.

Beginning with Java 8, interfaces have also been extended to allow `static` and `default` methods, both of which are given bodies—code—in the declaration of the interface. A `static` method, like a `static final` field, introduces no implementation complexity: it requires no access to object fields, so there is no ambiguity about what view to pass as `this`—there *is* no `this` parameter. Default methods are a bit more tricky. Their code is intended to be used by any class that does not override it. This convention is particularly valuable for library maintainers: it allows new methods to be added to an existing library interface without breaking existing user code, which would otherwise have to be updated to implement the new methods in any class that inherits from the interface.

EXAMPLE 10.54
Use of `default` methods

Suppose, for example, that we are engaged in a *localization* project, which aims to adapt some existing code to multiple languages and cultures. In the code of Figure 10.6, we might wish to add a new `get_local_name` method to the `storable_object` interface. Given a reference to a `storable_object`, updated user code could then call this new method, rather than `get_stored_name`, to obtain a string appropriate for use in the local context. A concrete class that inherits from `storable_object`, and that has been updated as part of the localization project, might provide its own implementation of `get_local_name`. But what about classes that haven't been updated yet (or that may never be updated)? These could leverage default methods to fall back on some general-purpose translation mechanism:

```
default String get_local_name() {
    return backup_translation(get_stored_name());
}
```

To use the default, each concrete class that inherits from `storable_object` would need to be recompiled, but its source code could remain unchanged. ■

Because a default method is defined within the interface declaration, it can see only the methods and (static) fields of the interface itself (along with any visible names from surrounding scopes). In particular, it has no access to other members of classes that inherit from the interface, and thus no need of an object view that would allow it to find those members. At the same time, the method *does* require access to the object's interface-specific vtable. In our `storable_object` example, the default `get_local_name` has to be able to find, and call, the version of `get_stored_name` defined by the concrete class. The usual way to implement this access depends on tiny *forwarding* routines: for each class *C* that inherits from `storable_object` and that needs the default code, the compiler generates a static, *C*-specific forwarding routine that accepts the concrete-class-specific `this` parameter, adds back in the `this` correction that the regular calling sequence just subtracted out, and passes the resulting pointer-to-vtable-pointer to the default method. ■

EXAMPLE 10.55
Implementation of `default` methods

As it turns out, the equivalent of default methods has long been provided by the Scala programming language, whose mix-ins are known as *traits*. In fact, traits support not only default methods but also mutable fields. Rather than try to create a view that would make these fields directly accessible, the Scala compiler generates, for each concrete class that inherits from the trait, a pair of hidden *accessor* methods analogous to the *properties* of C# (Example 10.7). References to the accessor methods are then included in the interface-specific vtable, where they can be called by default methods. In any class that does not provide its own definition of a trait field, the compiler creates a new private field to be used by the accessor methods.

10.6 True Multiple Inheritance

As described in Section 10.5, mix-in inheritance allows an interface to specify functionality that must be provided by an inheriting class in order for objects of that class to be used in a given context. Crucially, an interface does not, for the most part, *provide* that functionality itself. Even default methods serve mainly to orchestrate access to functionality provided by the inheriting class.

EXAMPLE 10.56
Deriving from two base classes

At times it can be useful to inherit real functionality from more than one base class. Suppose, for example, that our administrative computing system needs to keep track of information about every system user, and that the university provides every student with an account. It may then be desirable to derive class `student` from both `person` and `system_user`. In C++ we can say

```
class student : public person, public system_user { ...
```

Now an object of class `student` will have all the fields and methods of both a `person` and a `system_user`. The declaration in Eiffel is analogous:

```
class student
inherit
    person
    system_user
feature
    ...
```

True multiple inheritance appears in several other languages as well, including CLOS, OCaml, and Python. Many older languages, including Simula, Smalltalk, Modula-3, and Oberon, provided only single inheritance. Mix-in inheritance is a common compromise.

IN MORE DEPTH

Multiple inheritance introduces a wealth of semantic and pragmatic issues, which we consider on the companion site:

- Suppose two parent classes provide a method with the same name. Which one do we use in the child? Can we access both?
- Suppose two parent classes are both derived from some common "grandparent" class. Does the "grandchild" have one copy or two of the grandparent's fields?
- Our implementation of single inheritance relies on the fact that the representation of an object of the parent class is a prefix of the representation of an object of a derived class. With multiple inheritance, how can *each* parent be a prefix of the child?

Multiple inheritance with a common "grandparent" is known as *repeated* inheritance. Repeated inheritance with separate copies of the grandparent is known as *replicated* inheritance; repeated inheritance with a single copy of the grandparent is known as *shared* inheritance. Shared inheritance is the default in Eiffel. Replicated inheritance is the default in C++. Both languages allow the programmer to obtain the other option when desired.

10.7 Object-Oriented Programming Revisited

At the beginning of this chapter, we characterized object-oriented programming in terms of three fundamental concepts: encapsulation, inheritance, and dynamic method binding. Encapsulation allows the implementation details of an abstraction to be hidden behind a simple interface. Inheritance allows a new abstraction to be defined as an extension or refinement of some existing abstraction, obtaining some or all of its characteristics automatically. Dynamic method binding allows the new abstraction to display its new behavior even when used in a context that expects the old abstraction.

Different programming languages support these fundamental concepts to different degrees. In particular, languages differ in the extent to which they *require* the programmer to write in an object-oriented style. Some authors argue that a *truly* object-oriented language should make it difficult or impossible to write programs that are not object-oriented. From this purist point of view, an object-oriented language should present a *uniform object model* of computing, in which every data type is a class, every variable is a reference to an object, and every subroutine is an object method. Moreover, objects should be thought of in *anthropomorphic terms*: as active entities responsible for all computation.

Smalltalk and Ruby come close to this ideal. In fact, as described in the subsection below (mostly on the companion site), even such control-flow mechanisms as selection and iteration are modeled as method invocations in Smalltalk. On the other hand, Ada 95 and Fortran 2003 are probably best characterized as von Neumann languages that *permit* the programmer to write in an object-oriented style if desired.

So what about C++? It certainly has a wealth of features, including several (multiple inheritance, elaborate access control, strict initialization order, destructors, generics) that are useful in object-oriented programs and that are not found in Smalltalk. At the same time, it has a wealth of problematic wrinkles. Its simple types are not classes. It has subroutines outside of classes. It uses static method binding and replicated multiple inheritance by default, rather than the more costly `virtual` alternatives. Its unchecked C-style type casts provide a major loophole for type checking and access control. Its lack of garbage collection is a major obstacle to the creation of correct, self-contained abstractions. Probably most serious of all, C++ retains all of the low-level mechanisms of C, allowing the programmer to escape or subvert the object-oriented model of programming entirely. It has been suggested that the best C++ programmers are those who did *not* learn C first: they are not as tempted to write "C-style" programs in the newer language. On balance, it is probably safe to say that C++ is an object-oriented language in the same sense that Common Lisp is a functional language. With the possible exception of garbage collection, C++ provides all of the necessary tools, but it requires substantial discipline on the part of the programmer to use those tools "correctly."

10.7.1 The Object Model of Smalltalk

Historically, Smalltalk was considered the canonical object-oriented language. The original version of the language was designed by Alan Kay as part of his doctoral work at the University of Utah in the late 1960s. It was then adopted by the Software Concepts Group at the Xerox Palo Alto Research Center (PARC), and went through five major revisions in the 1970s, culminating in the Smalltalk-80 language.[7]

IN MORE DEPTH

We have mentioned several features of Smalltalk in previous sections. A somewhat longer treatment can be found on the companion site, where we focus in particular on Smalltalk's anthropomorphic programming model. A full introduction to the language is beyond the scope of this book.

CHECK YOUR UNDERSTANDING

42. What is *mix-in* inheritance? What problem does it solve?
43. Outline a possible implementation of mix-in inheritance for a language with statically typed objects. Explain in particular the need for interface-specific *views* of an object.
44. Describe how mix-ins (and their implementation) can be extended with default method implementations, static (constant) fields, and even mutable fields.
45. What does true multiple inheritance make possible that mix-in inheritance does not?

7 Alan Kay (1940–) joined PARC in 1972. In addition to developing Smalltalk and its graphical user interface, he conceived and promoted the idea of the laptop computer, well before it was feasible to build one. He became a Fellow at Apple Computer in 1984, and has subsequently held positions at Disney and Hewlett-Packard. He received the ACM Turing Award in 2003.

46. What is *repeated* inheritance? What is the distinction between *replicated* and *shared* repeated inheritance?

47. What does it mean for a language to provide a *uniform object model*? Name two languages that do so.

10.8 Summary and Concluding Remarks

This has been the last of our six core chapters on language design: names (Chapter 3), control flow (Chapter 6), type systems (Chapter 7), composite types (Chapter 8), subroutines (Chapter 9), and objects (Chapter 10).

We began in Section 10.1 by identifying three fundamental concepts of object-oriented programming: *encapsulation*, *inheritance*, and *dynamic method binding*. We also introduced the terminology of classes, objects, and methods. We had already seen encapsulation in the modules of Chapter 3. Encapsulation allows the details of a complicated data abstraction to be hidden behind a comparatively simple interface. Inheritance extends the utility of encapsulation by making it easy for programmers to define new abstractions as refinements or extensions of existing abstractions. Inheritance provides a natural basis for polymorphic subroutines: if a subroutine expects an instance of a given class as argument, then an object of any class derived from the expected one can be used instead (assuming that it retains the entire existing interface). Dynamic method binding extends this form of polymorphism by arranging for a call to one of the parameter's methods to use the implementation associated with the class of the actual object at run time, rather than the implementation associated with the declared class of the parameter. We noted that some languages, including Modula-3, Oberon, Ada 95, and Fortran 2003, support object orientation through a *type extension* mechanism, in which encapsulation is associated with modules, but inheritance and dynamic method binding are associated with a special form of record.

In later sections we covered object initialization and finalization, dynamic method binding, and (on the companion site) multiple inheritance in some detail. In many cases we discovered tradeoffs between functionality on the one hand and simplicity and execution speed on the other. Treating variables as references, rather than values, often leads to simpler semantics, but requires extra indirection. Garbage collection, as previously noted in Section 8.5.3, dramatically eases the creation and maintenance of software, but imposes run-time costs. Dynamic method binding requires (in the general case) that methods be dispatched using vtables or some other lookup mechanism. Fully general implementations of multiple inheritance tend to impose overheads even when unused.

In several cases we saw time/space tradeoffs as well. In-line subroutines, as previously noted in Section 9.2.4, can dramatically improve the performance of code with many small subroutines, not only by eliminating the overhead of the subroutine calls themselves, but by allowing register allocation, common subexpression analysis, and other "global" code improvements to be applied across calls. At the same time, in-line expansion generally increases the size of object code. Exercises C-10.28 and C-10.30 explore similar tradeoffs in the implementation of multiple inheritance.

Historically, Smalltalk was widely regarded as the purest and most flexible of the object-oriented languages. Its lack of compile-time type checking, however, together with its "message-based" model of computation and its need for dynamic method lookup, tended to make its implementations rather slow. C++, with its object-valued variables, default static binding, minimal dynamic checks, and high-quality compilers, was largely responsible for popularizing object-oriented programming in the 1990s. Today objects are ubiquitous—in statically typed, compiled languages like Java and C#; in dynamically typed languages like Python, Ruby, PHP, and JavaScript; and even in systems based on binary *components* or human-readable service invocations over the World Wide Web (more on these in the Bibliographic Notes).

10.9 Exercises

10.1 Some language designers argue that object orientation eliminates the need for nested subroutines. Do you agree? Why or why not?

10.2 Design a class hierarchy to represent syntax trees for the CFG of Figure 4.5. Provide a method in each class to return the value of a node. Provide constructors that play the role of the `make_leaf`, `make_un_op`, and `make_bin_op` subroutines.

10.3 Repeat the previous exercise, but using a variant record (union) type to represent syntax tree nodes. Repeat again using type extensions. Compare the three solutions in terms of clarity, abstraction, type safety, and extensibility.

10.4 Using the C# *indexer* mechanism, create a hash table class that can be indexed like an array. (In effect, create a simple version of the `System.Collections.Hashtable` container class.) Alternatively, use an overloaded version of `operator[]` to build a similar class in C++.

10.5 In the spirit of Example 10.8, write a *double-ended queue* (deque) abstraction (pronounced "deck"), derived from a doubly linked list base class.

10.6 Use templates (generics) to abstract your solutions to the previous two questions over the type of data in the container.

10.7 Repeat Exercise 10.5 in Python or Ruby. Write a simple program to demonstrate that generics are not needed to abstract over types. What happens if you mix objects of different types in the same deque?

10.8 When using the `list` class of Example 10.17, the typical C++ programmer will use a pointer type for generic parameter `V`, so that `list_nodes` point to the elements of the list. An alternative implementation would include `next` and `prev` pointers for the list within the elements themselves—typically by arranging for the element type to inherit from something like the `gp_list_node` class of Example 10.14. The result is sometimes called an *intrusive* list.

(a) Explain how you might build intrusive lists in C++ without requiring users to pepper their code with explicit type casts. Hint: given multiple inheritance, you will probably need to determine, for each concrete element type, the offset within the representation of the type at which the `next` and `prev` pointers appear. For further ideas, search for information on the `boost::intrusive::list` class of the popular Boost library.

(b) Discuss the relative advantages and disadvantages of intrusive and non-intrusive lists.

10.9 Can you emulate the inner class of Example 10.22 in C# or C++? (Hint: You'll need an explicit version of Java's hidden reference to the surrounding class.)

10.10 Write a package body for the list abstraction of Figure 10.2.

10.11 Rewrite the list and queue abstractions in Eiffel, Java, and/or C#.

10.12 Using C++, Java, or C#, implement a `Complex` class in the spirit of Example 10.25. Discuss the time and space tradeoffs between maintaining all four values (x, y, ρ, and θ) in the state of the object, or keeping only two and computing the others on demand.

10.13 Repeat the previous two exercises for Python and/or Ruby.

10.14 Compare Java `final` methods with C++ nonvirtual methods. How are they the same? How are they different?

10.15 In several object-oriented languages, including C++ and Eiffel, a derived class can hide members of the base class. In C++, for example, we can declare a base class to be `public`, `protected`, or `private`:

```
class B : public A { ...
    // public members of A are public members of B
    // protected members of A are protected members of B
...
class C : protected A { ...
    // public and protected members of A are protected members of C
...
class D : private A { ...
    // public and protected members of A are private members of D
```

In all cases, `private` members of `A` are inaccessible to methods of `B`, `C`, or `D`.

Consider the impact of `protected` and `private` base classes on dynamic method binding. Under what circumstances can a reference to an object of class `B`, `C`, or `D` be assigned into a variable of type `A*`?

10.16 What happens to the implementation of a class if we redefine a data member? For example, suppose we have

```
class foo {
public:
    int a;
    char *b;
};
...
class bar : public foo {
public:
    float c;
    int b;
};
```

Does the representation of a `bar` object contain one `b` field or two? If two, are both accessible, or only one? Under what circumstances?

10.17 Discuss the relative merits of classes and type extensions. Which do you prefer? Why?

10.18 Building on the outline of Example 10.28, write a program that illustrates the difference between copy constructors and `operator=` in C++. Your code should include examples of each situation in which one of these may be called (don't forget parameter passing and function returns). Instrument the copy constructors and assignment operators in each of your classes so that they will print their names when called. Run your program to verify that its behavior matches your expectations.

10.19 What do you think of the decision, in C++, C#, and Ada 95, to use static method binding, rather than dynamic, by default? Is the gain in implementation speed worth the loss in abstraction and reusability? Assuming that we sometimes want static binding, do you prefer the method-by-method approach of C++ and C#, or the variable-by-variable approach of Ada 95? Why?

10.20 If `foo` is an abstract class in a C++ program, why is it acceptable to declare variables of type `foo*`, but not of type `foo`?

10.21 Consider the Java program shown in Figure 10.8. Assume that this is to be compiled to native code on a machine with 4-byte addresses.

(a) Draw a picture of the layout in memory of the object created at line 15. Show all virtual function tables.

(b) Give assembly-level pseudocode for the call to `c.val` at line 19. You may assume that the address of `c` is in register `r1` immediately before the call, and that this same register should be used to pass the hidden `this` parameter. You may ignore the need to save and restore registers, and don't worry about where to put the return value.

```
1.  interface Pingable {
2.      public void ping();
3.  }

4.  class Counter implements Pingable {
5.      int count = 0;
6.      public void ping() {
7.          ++count;
8.      }
9.      public int val() {
10.         return count;
11.     }
12. }

13. public class Ping {
14.     public static void main(String args[]) {
15.         Counter c = new Counter();
16.         c.ping();
17.         c.ping();
18.         int v = c.val();
19.         System.out.println(v);
20.     }
21. }
```

Figure 10.8 A simple program in Java.

(c) Give assembly-level pseudocode for the call to `c.ping` at line 17. Again, assume that the address of `c` is in register `r1`, that this is the same register that should be used to pass `this`, and that you don't need to save or restore any registers.

(d) Give assembly-level pseudocode for the body of method `Counter.ping` (again ignoring register save/restore).

10.22 In Ruby, as in Java 8 or Scala, an interface (mix-in) can provide method code as well as signatures. (It can't provide data members; that would be multiple inheritance.) Explain why dynamic typing makes this feature more powerful than it is in the other languages.

10.23–10.31 In More Depth.

10.10 Explorations

10.32 Return for a moment to Exercise 3.7. Build a (more complete) C++ version of the singly linked list library of Figure 3.16. Discuss the issue of storage management. Under what circumstances should one delete the elements of a list when deleting the list itself? What should the destructor for `list_node` do? Should it delete its `data` member? Should it recursively delete node `next`?

10.33 The discussion in this chapter has focused on the classic "class-based" approach to object-oriented programming languages, pioneered by Simula and Smalltalk. There is an alternative, "object-based" approach that dispenses with the notion of class. In object-based programming, methods are directly associated with objects, and new objects are created using existing objects as *prototypes*. Learn about Self, the canonical object-based programming language, and JavaScript, the most widely used. What do you think of their approach? How does it compare to the class-based alternative? You may find it helpful to read the coverage of JavaScript in Section 14.4.4.

10.34 As described in Section C-5.5.1, performance on pipelined processors depends critically on the ability of the hardware to successfully predict the outcome of branches, so that processing of subsequent instructions can begin before processing of the branch has completed. In object-oriented programs, however, knowing the outcome of a branch is not enough: because branches are so often dispatched through vtables, one must also predict the *destination*. Learn how branch prediction works in one or more modern processors. How well do these processors handle object-oriented programs?

10.35 Explore the implementation of mix-in inheritance in a just-in-time (native code) Java compiler. Does it follow the strategy of Section 10.5? How efficient is it?

10.36 Explore the implementation of mix-in inheritance in Ruby. How does it differ from that of Java?

10.37 Learn about *type hierarchy analysis* and *type propagation*, which can sometimes be used to infer the concrete type of objects at compile time, allowing the compiler to generate direct calls to methods, rather than indirecting through vtables. How effective are these techniques? What fraction of method calls are they able to optimize in typical benchmarks? What are their limitations? (You might start with the papers of Bacon and Sweeney [BS96] and Diwan et al. [DMM96].)

10.38–10.39 In More Depth.

10.11 Bibliographic Notes

Appendix A contains bibliographic citations for the various languages discussed in this chapter, including Simula, Smalltalk, C++, Eiffel, Java, C#, Modula-3, Oberon, Ada 95, Fortran 2003, Python, Ruby, Objective-C, Swift, Go, OCaml, and CLOS. Other object-oriented versions of Lisp include Loops [BS83] and Flavors [Moo86].

Ellis and Stroustrup [ES90] provide extensive discussion of both semantic and pragmatic issues for historic versions of C++. Parts III and IV of Stroustrup's text [Str13] provide a comprehensive survey of the design and implementation of container classes in C++. Deutsch and Schiffman [DS84] describe techniques to implement Smalltalk efficiently. Borning and Ingalls [BI82] discuss multiple inheritance in an extension to Smalltalk-80. Strongtalk [Sun06] is a strongly typed successor to Smalltalk developed at Sun Microsystems in the 1990s, and since released as open source. Gil and Sweeney [GS99] describe optimizations that can be used to reduce the time and space complexity of multiple inheritance.

Dolby [Dol97] describes how an optimizing compiler can identify circumstances in which a nested object can be expanded (in the Eiffel sense) while retaining reference semantics. Bacon and Sweeney [BS96] and Diwan et al. [DMM96] discuss techniques to infer the concrete type of objects at compile time, thereby avoiding the overhead of vtable indirection. Driesen [Dri93] presents an alternative to vtables that requires whole-program analysis, but provides extremely efficient method dispatch, even in languages with dynamic typing and multiple inheritance.

Binary *component* systems allow code produced by arbitrary compilers for arbitrary languages to be joined together into a working program, often spanning a distributed collection of machines. CORBA [Sie00] is a component standard promulgated by the Object Management Group, a consortium of over 700 companies. .NET is a competing standard from Microsoft Corporation (*microsoft.com/net*), based in part on their earlier ActiveX, DCOM, and OLE [Bro96] products. JavaBeans [Sun97] is a CORBA-compliant binary standard for components written in Java.

With the explosion of web services, distributed systems have been designed to exchange and manipulate objects in human-readable form. SOAP [Wor12], originally an acronym for Simple Object Access Protocol, is a standard for web-based information transfer and method invocation. Its underlying data is typically encoded as XML (extensible markup language) [Wor06a]. In recent years, SOAP has largely been supplanted by REST (Representational State Transfer) [Fie00], a more informal set of conventions layered on top of ordinary HTTP. The underlying data in REST may take a variety of forms—most commonly JSON (JavaScript Object Notation) [ECM13].

Many of the seminal papers in object-oriented programming have appeared in the proceedings of the *ACM OOPSLA* conferences (Object-Oriented Programming Systems, Languages, and Applications), held annually since 1986, and published as special issues of *ACM SIGPLAN Notices*. Wegner [Weg90] enumerates the defining characteristics of object orientation. Meyer [Mey92b, Sec. 21.10] explains the rationale for dynamic method binding. Ungar and Smith [US91] describe Self, the canonical object-based (as opposed to class-based) language.

III

Alternative Programming Models

As we noted in Chapter 1, programming languages are traditionally though imperfectly classified into various imperative and declarative families. We have had occasion in Parts I and II to mention issues of particular importance to each of the major families. Moreover much of what we have covered—syntax, semantics, naming, types, abstraction—applies uniformly to all. Still, our attention has focused mostly on mainstream imperative languages. In Part III we shift this focus.

Functional and logic languages are the principal nonimperative options. We consider them in Chapters 11 and 12, respectively. In each case we structure our discussion around representative languages: Scheme and OCaml for functional programming, Prolog for logic programming. In Chapter 11 we also cover eager and lazy evaluation, and first-class and higher-order functions. In Chapter 12 we cover issues that make fully automatic, general purpose logic programming difficult, and describe restrictions used in practice to keep the model tractable. Optional sections in both chapters consider mathematical foundations: Lambda Calculus for functional programming, Predicate Calculus for logic programming.

The remaining two chapters consider concurrent and scripting models, both of which are increasingly popular, and cut across the imperative/declarative divide. Concurrency is driven by the hardware parallelism of internetworked computers and by the coming explosion in multithreaded processors and chip-level multiprocessors. Scripting is driven by the growth of the World Wide Web and by an increasing emphasis on programmer productivity, which places rapid development and reusability above sheer run-time performance.

Chapter 13 begins with the fundamentals of concurrency, including communication and synchronization, thread creation syntax, and the implementation of threads. The remainder of the chapter is divided between *shared-memory* models, in which threads use explicit or implicit synchronization mechanisms to manage a common set of variables, and (on the companion site) *message-passing* models, in which threads interact only through explicit communication.

The first half of Chapter 14 surveys problem domains in which scripting plays a major role: shell (command) languages, text processing and report generation, mathematics and statistics, the "gluing" together of program components, extension mechanisms for complex applications, and client and server-side Web scripting. The second half considers some of the more important language innovations championed by scripting languages: flexible scoping and naming conventions, string and pattern manipulation (extended regular expressions), and high level data types.

11 Functional Languages

Previous chapters of this text have focused largely on imperative programming languages. In the current chapter and the next we emphasize functional and logic languages instead. While imperative languages are far more widely used, "industrial-strength" implementations exist for both functional and logic languages, and both models have commercially important applications. Lisp has traditionally been popular for the manipulation of symbolic data, particularly in the field of artificial intelligence. OCaml is heavily used in the financial services industry. In recent years functional languages—statically typed ones in particular—have become increasingly popular for scientific applications as well. Logic languages are widely used for formal specifications and theorem proving and, less widely, for many other applications.

Of course, functional and logic languages have a great deal in common with their imperative cousins. Naming and scoping issues arise under every model. So do types, expressions, and the control-flow concepts of selection and recursion. All languages must be scanned, parsed, and analyzed semantically. In addition, functional languages make heavy use of subroutines—more so even than most von Neumann languages—and the notions of concurrency and nondeterminacy are as common in functional and logic languages as they are in the imperative case.

As noted in Chapter 1, the boundaries between language categories tend to be rather fuzzy. One can write in a largely functional style in many imperative languages, and many functional languages include imperative features (assignment and iteration). The most common logic language—Prolog—provides certain imperative features as well. Finally, it is easy to build a logic programming system in most functional programming languages.

Because of the overlap between imperative and functional concepts, we have had occasion several times in previous chapters to consider issues of particular importance to functional programming languages. Most such languages depend heavily on polymorphism (the implicit parametric kind—Sections 7.1.2, 7.3, and 7.2.4). Most make heavy use of lists (Section 8.6). Several, historically, were dynamically scoped (Sections 3.3.6 and C-3.4.2). All employ recursion (Section 6.6) for repetitive execution, with the result that program behavior and performance depend heavily on the evaluation rules for parameters (Section 6.6.2). All have a tendency to generate significant amounts of temporary data, which their implementations reclaim through garbage collection (Section 8.5.3).

Our chapter begins with a brief introduction to the historical origins of the imperative, functional, and logic programming models. We then enumerate fundamental concepts in functional programming and consider how these are realized in the Scheme dialect of Lisp and the OCaml dialect of ML. More briefly, we also consider Common Lisp, Erlang, Haskell, Miranda, pH, Single Assignment C, and Sisal. We pay particular attention to issues of evaluation order and higher-order functions. For those with an interest in the theoretical foundations of functional programming, we provide (on the companion site) an introduction to functions, sets, and the lambda calculus. The formalism helps to clarify the notion of a pure functional language, and illuminates the places where practical languages diverge from the mathematical abstraction.

11.1 Historical Origins

To understand the differences among programming models, it can be helpful to consider their theoretical roots, all of which predate the development of electronic computers. The imperative and functional models grew out of work undertaken by mathematicians Alan Turing, Alonzo Church, Stephen Kleene, Emil Post, and others in the 1930s. Working largely independently, these individuals developed several very different formalizations of the notion of an algorithm, or *effective procedure*, based on automata, symbolic manipulation, recursive function definitions, and combinatorics. Over time, these various formalizations were shown to be equally powerful: anything that could be computed in one could be computed in the others. This result led Church to conjecture that *any* intuitively appealing model of computing would be equally powerful as well; this conjecture is known as *Church's thesis*.

Turing's model of computing was the *Turing machine*, an automaton reminiscent of a finite or pushdown automaton, but with the ability to access arbitrary cells of an unbounded storage "tape."[1] The Turing machine computes in an imperative way, by changing the values in cells of its tape, just as a high-level imperative program computes by changing the values of variables. Church's model of computing is called the *lambda calculus*. It is based on the notion of parameterized expressions (with each parameter introduced by an occurrence of the

1 Alan Turing (1912–1954), after whom the Turing Award is named, was a British mathematician, philosopher, and computer visionary. As intellectual leader of Britain's cryptanalytic group during World War II, he was instrumental in cracking the German "Enigma" code and turning the tide of the war. He also helped lay the theoretical foundations of modern computer science, conceived the general-purpose electronic computer, and pioneered the field of Artificial Intelligence. Persecuted as a homosexual after the war, stripped of his security clearance, and sentenced to "treatment" with drugs, he committed suicide.

letter λ—hence the notation's name).[2] Lambda calculus was the inspiration for functional programming: one uses it to compute by substituting parameters into expressions, just as one computes in a high-level functional program by passing arguments to functions. The computing models of Kleene and Post are more abstract, and do not lend themselves directly to implementation as a programming language.

The goal of early work in computability was not to understand computers (aside from purely mechanical devices, computers did not exist) but rather to formalize the notion of an effective procedure. Over time, this work allowed mathematicians to formalize the distinction between a *constructive* proof (one that shows how to obtain a mathematical object with some desired property) and a *nonconstructive* proof (one that merely shows that such an object must exist, perhaps by contradiction, or counting arguments, or reduction to some other theorem whose proof is nonconstructive). In effect, a program can be seen as a constructive proof of the proposition that, given any appropriate inputs, there exist outputs that are related to the inputs in a particular, desired way. Euclid's algorithm, for example, can be thought of as a constructive proof of the proposition that every pair of non-negative integers has a greatest common divisor.

Logic programming is also intimately tied to the notion of constructive proofs, but at a more abstract level. Rather than write a general constructive proof that works for all appropriate inputs, the logic programmer writes a set of *axioms* that allow the *computer* to discover a constructive proof for each particular set of inputs. We will consider logic programming in more detail in Chapter 12.

11.2 Functional Programming Concepts

In a strict sense of the term, *functional programming* defines the outputs of a program as a mathematical function of the inputs, with no notion of internal state, and thus no side effects. Among the languages we consider here, Miranda, Haskell, pH, Sisal, and Single Assignment C are purely functional. Erlang is nearly so. Most others include imperative features. To make functional programming practical, functional languages provide a number of features that are often missing in imperative languages, including

- First-class function values and higher-order functions
- Extensive polymorphism
- List types and operators

2 Alonzo Church (1903–1995) was a member of the mathematics faculty at Princeton University from 1929 to 1967, and at UCLA from 1967 to 1990. While at Princeton he supervised the doctoral theses of, among many others, Alan Turing, Stephen Kleene, Michael Rabin, and Dana Scott. His codiscovery, with Turing, of undecidable problems was a major breakthrough in understanding the limits of mathematics.

- Structured function returns
- Constructors (aggregates) for structured objects
- Garbage collection

In Section 3.6.2 we defined a first-class value as one that can be passed as a parameter, returned from a subroutine, or (in a language with side effects) assigned into a variable. Under a strict interpretation of the term, first-class status also requires the ability to create (compute) new values at run time. In the case of subroutines, this notion of first-class status requires nested *lambda expressions* that can capture values defined in surrounding scopes, giving those values *unlimited extent* (i.e., keeping them alive even after their scopes are no longer active). Subroutines are second-class values in most imperative languages, but first-class values (in the strict sense of the term) in all functional programming languages. A *higher-order function* takes a function as an argument, or returns a function as a result.

Polymorphism is important in functional languages because it allows a function to be used on as general a class of arguments as possible. As we have seen in Sections 7.1 and 7.2.4, Lisp and its dialects are dynamically typed, and thus inherently polymorphic, while ML and its relatives obtain polymorphism through the mechanism of type inference. Lists are important in functional languages because they have a natural recursive definition, and are easily manipulated by operating on their first element and (recursively) the remainder of the list. Recursion is important because in the absence of side effects it provides the only means of doing anything repeatedly.

Several of the items in our list of functional language features (recursion, structured function returns, constructors, garbage collection) can be found in some but not all imperative languages. Fortran 77 has no recursion, nor does it allow structured types (i.e., arrays) to be returned from functions. Pascal and early versions of Modula-2 allow only simple and pointer types to be returned from functions. As we saw in Section 7.1.3, several imperative languages, including Ada, C, and Fortran 90, provide aggregate constructs that allow a structured value to be specified in-line. In most imperative languages, however, such constructs are lacking or incomplete. C# and several scripting languages—Python and Ruby among them—provide aggregates capable of representing an (unnamed) functional value (a lambda expression), but few imperative languages are so expressive. A pure functional language must provide completely general aggregates: because there is no way to update existing objects, newly created ones must be initialized "all at once." Finally, though garbage collection is increasingly common in imperative languages, it is by no means universal, nor does it usually apply to the local variables of subroutines, which are typically allocated in the stack. Because of the desire to provide unlimited extent for first-class functions and other objects, functional languages tend to employ a (garbage-collected) heap for *all* dynamically allocated data (or at least for all data for which the compiler is unable to prove that stack allocation is safe). C++11 and Java 8 provide lambda expressions, but without unlimited extent.

Because Lisp was the original functional language, and is still one of the most widely used, several characteristics of Lisp are commonly, though inaccurately, described as though they pertained to functional programming in general. We will examine these characteristics (in the context of Scheme) in Section 11.3. They include

- Homogeneity of programs and data: A program in Lisp is itself a list, and can be manipulated with the same mechanisms used to manipulate data.
- Self-definition: The operational semantics of Lisp can be defined elegantly in terms of an interpreter written in Lisp.
- Interaction with the user through a "read-eval-print" loop.

Many programmers—probably most—who have written significant amounts of software in both imperative and functional styles find the latter more aesthetically appealing. Moreover, experience with a variety of large commercial projects (see the Bibliographic Notes at the end of the chapter) suggests that the absence of side effects makes functional programs significantly easier to write, debug, and maintain than their imperative counterparts. When passed a given set of arguments, a pure function can always be counted on to return the same results. Issues of undocumented side effects, misordered updates, and dangling or (in most cases) uninitialized references simply don't occur. At the same time, many implementations of functional languages still fall short in terms of portability, richness of library packages, interfaces to other languages, and debugging and profiling tools. We will return to the tradeoffs between functional and imperative programming in Section 11.8.

11.3 A Bit of Scheme

Scheme was originally developed by Guy Steele and Gerald Sussman in the late 1970s, and has evolved through several revisions. The description here follows the 1998 R5RS (fifth revised standard), and should also be compliant with the 2013 R7RS.

Most Scheme implementations employ an interpreter that runs a "read-eval-print" loop. The interpreter repeatedly reads an expression from standard input (generally typed by the user), evaluates that expression, and prints the resulting value. If the user types

EXAMPLE 11.1
The read-eval-print loop

```
(+ 3 4)
```

the interpreter will print

```
7
```

If the user types

```
7
```

the interpreter will also print

```
7
```

(The number 7 is already fully evaluated.) To save the programmer the need to type an entire program verbatim at the keyboard, most Scheme implementations provide a `load` function that reads (and evaluates) input from a file:

```
(load "my_Scheme_program")
```

As we noted in Section 6.1, Scheme (like all Lisp dialects) uses *Cambridge Polish* notation for expressions. Parentheses indicate a function application (or in some cases the use of a macro). The first expression inside the left parenthesis indicates the function; the remaining expressions are its arguments. Suppose the user types

EXAMPLE 11.2 Significance of parentheses

```
((+ 3 4))
```

When it sees the inner set of parentheses, the interpreter will call the function +, passing 3 and 4 as arguments. Because of the outer set of parentheses, it will then attempt to call 7 as a zero-argument function—a run-time error:

```
eval: 7 is not a procedure
```

Unlike the situation in almost all other programming languages, extra parentheses change the semantics of Lisp/Scheme programs:

```
(+ 3 4)      ⟹ 7
((+ 3 4))    ⟹ error
```

Here the ⟹ means "evaluates to." This symbol is not a part of the syntax of Scheme itself.

EXAMPLE 11.3 Quoting

One can prevent the Scheme interpreter from evaluating a parenthesized expression by *quoting* it:

```
(quote (+ 3 4))  ⟹ (+ 3 4)
```

Here the result is a three-element list. More commonly, quoting is specified with a special shorthand notation consisting of a leading single quote mark:

```
'(+ 3 4)  ⟹ (+ 3 4)
```

EXAMPLE 11.4 Dynamic typing

Though every expression has a type in Scheme, that type is generally not determined until run time. Most predefined functions check dynamically to make sure that their arguments are of appropriate types. The expression

```
(if (> a 0) (+ 2 3) (+ 2 "foo"))
```

will evaluate to 5 if a is positive, but will produce a run-time type clash error if a is negative or zero. More significantly, as noted in Section 7.1.2, functions that make sense for arguments of multiple types are implicitly polymorphic:

```
(define min (lambda (a b) (if (< a b) a b)))
```

The expression (min 123 456) will evaluate to 123; (min 3.14159 2.71828) will evaluate to 2.71828.

EXAMPLE 11.5
Type predicates

User-defined functions can implement their own type checks using predefined *type predicate* functions:

```
(boolean? x)      ; is x a Boolean?
(char? x)         ; is x a character?
(string? x)       ; is x a string?
(symbol? x)       ; is x a symbol?
(number? x)       ; is x a number?
(pair? x)         ; is x a (not necessarily proper) pair?
(list? x)         ; is x a (proper) list?
```

(This is not an exhaustive list.)

EXAMPLE 11.6
Liberal syntax for symbols

A *symbol* in Scheme is comparable to what other languages call an identifier. The lexical rules for identifiers vary among Scheme implementations, but are in general much looser than they are in other languages. In particular, identifiers are permitted to contain a wide variety of punctuation marks:

```
(symbol? 'x$_%:&=*!)  ⟹ #t
```

The symbol #t represents the Boolean value true. False is represented by #f. Note the use here of quote ('); the symbol begins with x.

EXAMPLE 11.7
lambda expressions

To create a function in Scheme one evaluates a *lambda expression*:[3]

```
(lambda (x) (* x x))  ⟹ function
```

The first "argument" to lambda is a list of formal parameters for the function (in this case the single parameter x). The remaining "arguments" (again just one in this case) constitute the body of the function. As we shall see in Section 11.5, Scheme differentiates between functions and so-called *special forms*

3 A word of caution for readers familiar with Common Lisp: A lambda expression in Scheme *evaluates to* a function. A lambda expression in Common Lisp *is* a function (or, more accurately, is automatically coerced to be a function, without evaluation). The distinction becomes important whenever lambda expressions are passed as parameters or returned from functions: they must be quoted in Common Lisp (with function or #') to prevent evaluation. Common Lisp also distinguishes between a symbol's *value* and its meaning as a function; Scheme does not: if a symbol represents a function, then the function is the symbol's value.

(`lambda` among them), which resemble functions but have special evaluation rules. Strictly speaking, only functions have arguments, but we will also use the term informally to refer to the subexpressions that look like arguments in a special form. ■

A `lambda` expression does not give its function a name; this can be done using `let` or `define` (to be introduced in the next subsection). In this sense, a `lambda` expression is like the aggregates that we used in Section 7.1.3 to specify array or record values.

EXAMPLE 11.8
Function evaluation

When a function is called, the language implementation restores the referencing environment that was in effect when the `lambda` expression was evaluated (like all languages with static scope and first-class, nested subroutines, Scheme employs deep binding). It then augments this environment with bindings for the formal parameters and evaluates the expressions of the function body in order. The value of the last such expression (most often there *is* only one) becomes the value returned by the function:

```
((lambda (x) (* x x)) 3)  ⟹ 9
```
■

EXAMPLE 11.9
`if` expressions

Simple conditional expressions can be written using `if`:

```
(if (< 2 3) 4 5)   ⟹ 4
(if #f 2 3)        ⟹ 3
```

In general, Scheme expressions are evaluated in applicative order, as described in Section 6.6.2. Special forms such as `lambda` and `if` are exceptions to this rule. The implementation of `if` checks to see whether the first argument evaluates to `#t`. If so, it returns the value of the second argument, without evaluating the third argument. Otherwise it returns the value of the third argument, without evaluating the second. We will return to the issue of evaluation order in Section 11.5. ■

11.3.1 Bindings

EXAMPLE 11.10
Nested scopes with `let`

Names can be bound to values by introducing a nested scope:

```
(let ((a 3)
      (b 4)
      (square (lambda (x) (* x x)))
      (plus +))
  (sqrt (plus (square a) (square b))))   ⟹ 5.0
```

The special form `let` takes two or more arguments. The first of these is a list of pairs. In each pair, the first element is a name and the second is the value that the name is to represent within the remaining arguments to `let`. Remaining arguments are then evaluated in order; the value of the construct as a whole is the value of the final argument.

The scope of the bindings produced by `let` is `let`'s second argument only:

```
(let ((a 3))
  (let ((a 4)
        (b a))
    (+ a b)))     ⟹ 7
```

Here b takes the value of the *outer* a. The way in which names become visible "all at once" at the end of the declaration list precludes the definition of recursive functions. For these one employs letrec:

```
(letrec ((fact
          (lambda (n)
            (if (= n 1) 1
                (* n (fact (- n 1)))))))
  (fact 5))                          ⟹ 120
```

There is also a let* construct in which names become visible "one at a time" so that later ones can make use of earlier ones, but not vice versa. ■

EXAMPLE 11.11
Global bindings with define

As noted in Section 3.3, Scheme is statically scoped. (Common Lisp is also statically scoped. Most other Lisp dialects are dynamically scoped.) While let and letrec allow the user to create nested scopes, they do not affect the meaning of global names (names known at the outermost level of the Scheme interpreter). For these Scheme provides a special form called define that has the side effect of creating a global binding for a name:

```
(define hypot
  (lambda (a b)
    (sqrt (+ (* a a) (* b b)))))
(hypot 3 4)                         ⟹ 5
```

■

11.3.2 Lists and Numbers

EXAMPLE 11.12
Basic list operations

Like all Lisp dialects, Scheme provides a wealth of functions to manipulate lists. We saw many of these in Section 8.6; we do not repeat them all here. The three most important are car, which returns the head of a list, cdr ("coulder"), which returns the rest of the list (everything after the head), and cons, which joins a head to the rest of a list:

```
(car '(2 3 4))     ⟹ 2
(cdr '(2 3 4))     ⟹ (3 4)
(cons 2 '(3 4))    ⟹ (2 3 4)
```

Also useful is the null? predicate, which determines whether its argument is the empty list. Recall that the notation '(2 3 4) indicates a *proper* list, in which the final element is the empty list:

```
(cdr '(2))     ⟹ ()
(cons 2 3)     ⟹ (2 . 3)    ; an improper list
```

■

For fast access to arbitrary elements of a sequence, Scheme provides a `vector` type that is indexed by integers, like an array, and may have elements of heterogeneous types, like a record. Interested readers are referred to the Scheme manual [SDF+07] for further information.

Scheme also provides a wealth of numeric and logical (Boolean) functions and special forms. The language manual describes a hierarchy of five numeric types: `integer`, `rational`, `real`, `complex`, and `number`. The last two levels are optional: implementations may choose not to provide any numbers that are not real. Most but not all implementations employ arbitrary-precision representations of both integers and rationals, with the latter stored internally as (numerator, denominator) pairs.

11.3.3 Equality Testing and Searching

Scheme provides several different equality-testing functions. For numerical comparisons, `=` performs type conversions where necessary (e.g., to compare an integer and a floating-point number). For general-purpose use, `eqv?` performs a *shallow* comparison, while `equal?` performs a *deep* (recursive) comparison, using `eqv?` at the leaves. The `eq?` function also performs a shallow comparison, and may be cheaper than `eqv?` in certain circumstances (in particular, `eq?` is not required to detect the equality of discrete values stored in different locations, though it may in some implementations). Further details were presented in Section 7.4.

To search for elements in lists, Scheme provides two sets of functions, each of which has variants corresponding to the three general-purpose equality predicates. The functions `memq`, `memv`, and `member` take an element and a list as argument, and return the longest suffix of the list (if any) beginning with the element:

EXAMPLE 11.13
List search functions

```
(memq 'z '(x y z w))            ⟹ (z w)
(memv '(z) '(x y (z) w))        ⟹ #f        ; (eqv? '(z) '(z))    ⟹ #f
(member '(z) '(x y (z) w))      ⟹ ((z) w)   ; (equal? '(z) '(z))  ⟹ #t
```

The `memq`, `memv`, and `member` functions perform their comparisons using `eq?`, `eqv?`, and `equal?`, respectively. They return `#f` if the desired element is not found. It turns out that Scheme's conditional expressions (e.g., `if`) treat anything other than `#f` as true.[4] One therefore often sees expressions of the form

```
(if (memq desired-element list-that-might-contain-it) ...
```

■

4 One of the more confusing differences between Scheme and Common Lisp is that Common Lisp uses the empty list () for false, while most implementations of Scheme (including all that conform to the version 5 standard) treat it as true.

EXAMPLE 11.14
Searching association lists

The functions assq, assv, and assoc search for values in *association lists* (otherwise known as *A-lists*). A-lists were introduced in Section C-3.4.2 in the context of name lookup for languages with dynamic scoping. An A-list is a dictionary implemented as a list of pairs.[5] The first element of each pair is a key of some sort; the second element is information corresponding to that key. Assq, assv, and assoc take a key and an A-list as argument, and return the first pair in the list, if there is one, whose first element is eq?, eqv?, or equal?, respectively, to the key. If there is no matching pair, #f is returned.

11.3.4 Control Flow and Assignment

EXAMPLE 11.15
Multiway conditional expressions

We have already seen the special form if. It has a cousin named cond that resembles a more general if... elsif... else:

```
(cond
  ((< 3 2) 1)
  ((< 4 3) 2)
  (else 3))        ⟹ 3
```

The arguments to cond are pairs. They are considered in order from first to last. The value of the overall expression is the value of the second element of the first pair in which the first element evaluates to #t. If none of the first elements evaluates to #t, then the overall value is #f. The symbol else is permitted only as the first element of the last pair of the construct, where it serves as syntactic sugar for #t.

Recursion, of course, is the principal means of doing things repeatedly in Scheme. Many issues related to recursion were discussed in Section 6.6; we do not repeat that discussion here.

EXAMPLE 11.16
Assignment

For programmers who wish to make use of side effects, Scheme provides assignment, sequencing, and iteration constructs. Assignment employs the special form set! and the functions set-car! and set-cdr!:

```
(let ((x 2)                      ; initialize x to 2
      (l '(a b)))                ; initialize l to (a b)
  (set! x 3)                     ; assign x the value 3
  (set-car! l '(c d))            ; assign head of l the value (c d)
  (set-cdr! l '(e))              ; assign rest of l the value (e)
  ... x                ⟹ 3
  ... l                ⟹ ((c d) e)
```

The return values of the various varieties of set! are implementation-dependent.

EXAMPLE 11.17
Sequencing

Sequencing uses the special form begin:

5 For clarity, the figures in Section C-3.4.2 elided the internal structure of the pairs.

```
(begin
  (display "hi ")
  (display "mom"))
```

Here we have used begin to sequence display expressions, which cause the interpreter to print their arguments. ■

EXAMPLE 11.18
Iteration

Iteration uses the special form do and the function for-each:

```
(define iter-fib
  (lambda (n)
    ; print the first n+1 Fibonacci numbers
    (do ((i 0 (+ i 1))          ; initially 0, inc'ed in each iteration
         (a 0 b)                ; initially 0, set to b in each iteration
         (b 1 (+ a b)))         ; initially 1, set to sum of a and b
        ((= i n) b)             ; termination test and final value
      (display b)               ; body of loop
      (display " "))))          ; body of loop

(for-each
  (lambda (a b) (display (* a b)) (newline))
  '(2 4 6)
  '(3 5 7))
```

The first argument to do is a list of triples, each of which specifies a new variable, an initial value for that variable, and an expression to be evaluated and placed in a fresh instance of the variable at the end of each iteration. The second argument to do is a pair that specifies the termination condition and the expression to be returned. At the end of each iteration all new values of loop variables (e.g., a and b) are computed using the current values. Only after all new values are computed are the new variable instances created.

The function for-each takes as argument a function and a sequence of lists. There must be as many lists as the function takes arguments, and the lists must

DESIGN & IMPLEMENTATION

11.1 Iteration in functional programs

It is important to distinguish between iteration as a notation for repeated execution and iteration as a means of orchestrating side effects. One can in fact define iteration as syntactic sugar for tail recursion, and Val, Sisal, and pH do precisely that (with special syntax to facilitate the passing of values from one iteration to the next). Such a notation may still be entirely side-effect free, that is, entirely functional. In Scheme, assignment and I/O are the truly imperative features. We think of iteration as imperative because most Scheme programs that use it have assignments or I/O in their loops.

all be of the same length. For-each calls its function argument repeatedly, passing successive sets of arguments from the lists. In the example shown here, the unnamed function produced by the lambda expression will be called on the arguments 2 and 3, 4 and 5, and 6 and 7. The interpreter will print

```
6
20
42
()
```

The last line is the return value of for-each, assumed here to be the empty list. The language definition allows this value to be implementation-dependent; the construct is executed for its side effects.

Two other control-flow constructs have been mentioned in previous chapters. Delay and force (Section 6.6.2) permit the lazy evaluation of expressions. Call-with-current-continuation (call/cc; Section 6.2.2) allows the current program counter and referencing environment to be saved in the form of a closure, and passed to a specified subroutine. We will mention delay and force again in Section 11.5.

11.3.5 Programs as Lists

As should be clear by now, a program in Scheme takes the form of a list. In technical terms, we say that Lisp and Scheme are *homoiconic*—self-representing. A parenthesized string of symbols (in which parentheses are balanced) is called an *S-expression* regardless of whether we think of it as a program or as a list. In fact, an unevaluated program *is* a list, and can be constructed, deconstructed, and otherwise manipulated with all the usual list functions.

EXAMPLE 11.19
Evaluating data as code

Just as quote can be used to inhibit the evaluation of a list that appears as an argument in a function call, Scheme provides an eval function that can be used to evaluate a list that has been created as a data structure:

```
(define compose
  (lambda (f g)
    (lambda (x) (f (g x)))))
((compose car cdr) '(1 2 3))                              ⟹ 2

(define compose2
  (lambda (f g)
    (eval (list 'lambda '(x) (list f (list g 'x)))
          (scheme-report-environment 5))))
((compose2 car cdr) '(1 2 3))                             ⟹ 2
```

In the first of these declarations, compose takes as arguments a pair of functions f and g. It returns as result a function that takes as parameter a value x, applies g to it, then applies `f`, and finally returns the result. In the second declaration, `compose2` performs the same function, but in a different way. The function `list` returns a list consisting of its (evaluated) arguments. In the body of `compose2`, this list is the *unevaluated* expression `(lambda (x) (f (g x)))`. When passed to `eval`, this list evaluates to the desired function. The second argument of `eval` specifies the referencing environment in which the expression is to be evaluated. In our example we have specified the environment defined by the Scheme version 5 report [KCR+98]. ■

The original description of Lisp [MAE+65] included a *self-definition* of the language: code for a Lisp interpreter, written in Lisp. Though Scheme differs in many ways from this early Lisp (most notably in its use of lexical scoping), such a *metacircular* interpreter can still be written easily [AS96, Chap. 4]. The code is based on the functions `eval` and `apply`. The first of these we have just seen. The second, `apply`, takes two arguments: a function and a list. It achieves the effect of calling the function, with the elements of the list as arguments.

11.3.6 Extended Example: DFA Simulation in Scheme

EXAMPLE 11.20
Simulating a DFA in Scheme

To conclude our introduction to Scheme, we present a complete program to simulate the execution of a DFA (deterministic finite automaton). The code appears in Figure 11.1. Finite automata details can be found in Sections 2.2 and C-2.4.1. Here we represent a DFA as a list of three items: the start state, the transition function, and a list of final states. The transition function in turn is represented by a list of pairs. The first element of each pair is another pair, whose first element is a state and whose second element is an input symbol. If the current state and next input symbol match the first element of a pair, then the finite automaton enters the state given by the second element of the pair.

To make this concrete, consider the DFA of Figure 11.2. It accepts all strings of zeros and ones in which each digit appears an even number of times. To simulate this machine, we pass it to the function `simulate` along with an input string. As it runs, the automaton accumulates as a list a trace of the states through which it has traveled. Once the input is exhausted, it adds `accept` or `reject`. For example, if we type

```
(simulate
 zero-one-even-dfa   ; machine description
 '(0 1 1 0 1))       ; input string
```

then the Scheme interpreter will print

```
(q0 q2 q3 q2 q0 q1 reject)
```

If we change the input string to `010010`, the interpreter will print

```
(q0 q2 q3 q1 q3 q2 q0 accept)
```

■

```
(define simulate
  (lambda (dfa input)
    (letrec ((helper  ; note that helper is tail recursive,
               ; but builds the list of moves in reverse order
               (lambda (moves d2 i)
                 (let ((c (current-state d2)))
                   (if (null? i) (cons c moves)
                       (helper (cons c moves) (move d2 (car i)) (cdr i)))))))
      (let ((moves (helper '() dfa input)))
        (reverse (cons (if (is-final? (car moves) dfa)
                           'accept 'reject) moves))))))

;; access functions for machine description:
(define current-state car)
(define transition-function cadr)
(define final-states caddr)
(define is-final? (lambda (s dfa) (memq s (final-states dfa))))

(define move
  (lambda (dfa symbol)
    (let ((cs (current-state dfa)) (trans (transition-function dfa)))
      (list
       (if (eq? cs 'error)
           'error
           (let ((pair (assoc (list cs symbol) trans)))
             (if pair (cadr pair) 'error)))) ; new start state
       trans                                 ; same transition function
       (final-states dfa)))))                ; same final states
```

Figure 11.1 Scheme program to simulate the actions of a DFA. Given a machine description and an input symbol *i*, function `move` searches for a transition labeled *i* from the start state to some new state *s*. It then returns a new machine with the same transition function and final states, but with *s* as its "start" state. The main function, `simulate`, encapsulates a tail-recursive helper function that accumulates an inverted list of moves, returning when it has consumed all input symbols. The wrapper then checks to see if the helper ended in a final state; it returns the (properly ordered) series of moves, with `accept` or `reject` at the end. The functions `cadr` and `caddr` are defined as `(lambda (x) (car (cdr x)))` and `(lambda (x) (car (cdr (cdr x))))`, respectively. Scheme provides a large collection of such abbreviations.

✓ CHECK YOUR UNDERSTANDING

1. What mathematical formalism underlies functional programming?
2. List several distinguishing characteristics of functional programming languages.
3. Briefly describe the behavior of the Lisp/Scheme *read-eval-print* loop.
4. What is a *first-class* value?

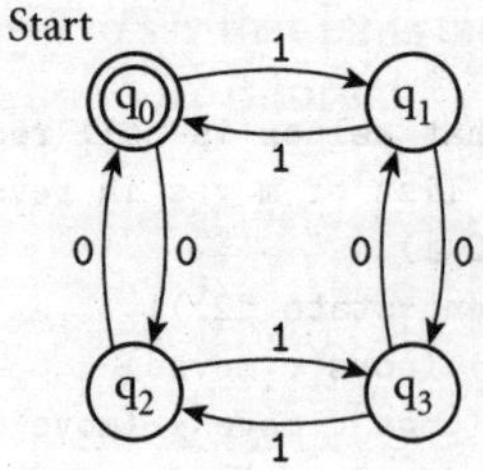


```
(define zero-one-even-dfa
  '(q0                                                        ; start state
    (((q0 0) q2) ((q0 1) q1) ((q1 0) q3) ((q1 1) q0)          ; transition fn
     ((q2 0) q0) ((q2 1) q3) ((q3 0) q1) ((q3 1) q2))
    (q0)))                                                    ; final states
```

Figure 11.2 DFA to accept all strings of zeros and ones containing an even number of each. At the bottom of the figure is a representation of the machine as a Scheme data structure, using the conventions of Figure 11.1.

5. Explain the difference between `let`, `let*`, and `letrec` in Scheme.
6. Explain the difference between `eq?`, `eqv?`, and `equal?`.
7. Describe three ways in which Scheme programs can depart from a purely functional programming model.
8. What is an *association list*?
9. What does it mean for a language to be *homoiconic*?
10. What is an *S-expression*?
11. Outline the behavior of `eval` and `apply`.

11.4 A Bit of OCaml

Like Lisp, ML has a complicated family tree. The original language was devised in the early 1970s by Robin Milner and others at Cambridge University. SML ("Standard" ML) and OCaml (Objective Caml) are the two most widely used dialects today. Haskell, the most widely used language for functional programming research, is a separate descendant of ML (by way of Miranda). F#, developed by Microsoft and others, is a descendant of OCaml.

Work on OCaml (and its predecessor, Caml) has been led since the early 1980s by researchers at INRIA, the French national computing research organization (the 'O' was added to the name with the introduction of object-oriented features in the early 1990s). Among the ML family languages, OCaml is known for the efficiency of the INRIA implementation and for its widespread commercial adoption: among other domains, OCaml is popular in the finance industry.

The INRIA OCaml distribution includes both a byte-code compiler (with accompanying virtual machine) and an optimizing native-code compiler for a variety of machine architectures. The interpreter can be used either interactively or to execute a previously written program. The easiest way to learn the language is to experiment with the interpreter interactively. The examples in the remainder of this section all work in that environment.

EXAMPLE 11.21
Interacting with the interpreter

The interpreter repeatedly reads an expression from standard input, evaluates that expression, and prints the resulting value. If the user types

```
3 + 4;;
```

the interpreter will print

```
- : int = 7
```

Double semicolons are used to indicate the end of a "top-level form"—an expression in the outermost scope. The output indicates that the user's expression (`-`) was an integer of value 7.

If the user types

```
7;;
```

the interpreter will also print

```
- : int = 7
```

(The number 7 is already fully evaluated.) Rather than type preexisting code into the interpreter directly, the programmer can instruct the interpreter to load it from a file:

```
#use "mycode.ml";;
```

The initial hash sign indicates that this is a directive to the interpreter, rather than an expression to be evaluated. ■

EXAMPLE 11.22
Function call syntax

To invoke a function, one types the function name followed by its argument(s):

```
cos 0.0;;          ⟹ 1.0
min 3 4;;          ⟹ 3
```

Here `cos` expects a single real-number argument; `min` expects two arguments of the same type, which must support comparison for ordering. As in our coverage of Scheme, we use ⟹ as shorthand to indicate the result of evaluation.

Note the absence of parentheses in function calls! Invocation is indicated simply by juxtaposition. An expression such as `foo (3, 4)` does *not* apply `foo` to the two arguments 3 and 4, but rather to the *tuple* `(3, 4)`. (A tuple is essentially a record whose elements are positional rather than named; more on this in Section 11.4.3.) ■

EXAMPLE 11.23
Function values

If we type in the name `cos` all by itself

```
cos;;
```

OCaml informs us that our expression is a function from `float`s to `float`s:

```
- : float -> float = <fun>
```

If we ask about `(+)` (which we must enclose in parentheses to avoid a syntax error), we learn that it is a function that maps *two* integers to a third:

```
- : int -> int -> int = <fun>
```

If we ask about `min`, we learn that it is polymorphic:

```
- : 'a -> 'a -> 'a = <fun>
```

As explained in Section 7.2.4, the `'a` is a *type parameter*; it indicates that the argument and result types of `min` can be arbitrary, so long as they are the same (of course, since `min` uses `<` internally, we will suffer a run-time exception if `'a` is a function type). ■

EXAMPLE 11.24
`unit` type

The lack of parentheses in function calls does raise the question: how do we distinguish a simple named value from a call to a zero-argument function? The answer is to insist that such functions take a dummy, placeholder argument, indicated by empty parentheses. A call to a function with no (useful) arguments then looks much like a call to a zero-argument function in C:

```
let c_three = 3;;
let f_three () = 3;;
```

Here `c_three` is a constant of type `int`; `f_three` is a function of type `unit -> int`. The former can be used in any context that expects an integer; the latter returns an integer when called with a `unit` argument:

```
c_three;;         ⟹ 3
f_three ();;      ⟹ 3
```

■

Lexical conventions in OCaml are straightforward: Identifiers are composed of upper- and lower-case letters, digits, underscores, and single quote marks; most are required to start with a lower-case letter or underscore (a few special kinds of names, including type constructors, variants, modules, and exceptions, must start with an upper-case letter). Comments are delimited with `(*... *)`, and are permitted to nest. Floating-point numbers are required to contain a decimal point: the expression `cos 0` will generate a type-clash error message.

Built-in types include Boolean values, integers, floating-point numbers, characters, and strings. Values of more complex types can be created using a variety of type constructors, including lists, arrays, tuples, records, variants, objects, and classes; several of these are described in Section 11.4.3. As discussed in Section 7.2.4, type checking is performed by *inferring* a type for every expression, and then checking that whenever two expressions need to be of the same type (e.g., because one is an argument and the other is the corresponding formal parameter), the inferences turn out to be the same. To support type inference, some operators that are overloaded in other languages are separate in OCaml. In particular, the usual arithmetic operations have both integer (`+`, `-`, `*`, `/`) and floating-point (`+.`, `-.`, `*.`, `/.`) versions.

11.4.1 Equality and Ordering

EXAMPLE 11.25
"Physical" and "structural" comparison

Like most functional languages, OCaml uses a reference model for names. When comparing two expressions, either or both of which may simply be a name, there are two different notions of equality. The so-called "physical" comparators, `==` and `!=`, perform what we called a "shallow" comparison in Section 7.4: they determine if the expressions refer to the same object, in the broad sense of the word. The so-called "structural" comparators, `=` and `<>`, perform what we called a "deep" comparison: they determine if the objects to which the expressions refer have the same internal structure or behavior. Thus the following expressions all evaluate to `true`:

physical (shallow)	structural (deep)
`2 == 2`	`2 = 2`
`"foo" != "foo"`	`"foo" = "foo"`
`[1; 2; 3] != [1; 2; 3]`	`[1; 2; 3] = [1; 1+1; 5-2]`

In the first line, there is (conceptually) only one 2 in the world, so references to it are both physically and structurally equivalent. In the second line, two character strings with the same constituent characters are structurally but not physically equivalent. In the third line, two lists are physically different even if they look syntactically the same; they are structurally equivalent if their corresponding elements are structurally equivalent. Significantly, expressions whose values are functions can be compared for physical (shallow) equality, but cause a run-time exception if compared for structural equality (equivalent behavior for functions is an undecidable problem). Structural comparison of cyclic structures can result in an infinite loop. ■

Comparison for ordering (<, >, <=, >=) is always based on deep comparison. It is defined in OCaml on all types other than functions. It does what one would normally expect on arithmetic types, characters, and strings (the latter works lexicographically); on other types the results are deterministic but not necessarily intuitive. In all cases, the results are consistent with the structural equality test (=): if `a = b`, then `a <= b` and `a >= b`; if `a <> b`, then `a < b` or `a > b`. As with the equality tests, comparison of functions will cause a run-time exception; comparison of cyclic structures may not terminate.

11.4.2 Bindings and Lambda Expressions

EXAMPLE 11.26
Outermost declarations

New names in OCaml are introduced with `let`. An outermost (top-level) `let` introduces a name that is visible throughout the remainder of its file or module:

```
let average = fun x y -> (x +. y) /. 2.;;
```

Here `fun` introduces a lambda expression. The names preceding the right arrow (`->`) are parameters; the expression following the arrow is the body of the function—the value it will return. To make programs a bit more readable, given the ubiquity of function declarations, OCaml provides the following somewhat simpler syntactic sugar:

DESIGN & IMPLEMENTATION

11.2 Equality and ordering in SML and Haskell

Unlike OCaml, SML provides a single equality operator: a built-in polymorphic function defined on some but not all types. Equality tests are deep for expressions of immutable types and shallow for those of mutable types. Tests on unsupported (e.g., function) types produce a compile-time error message rather than a run-time exception. The ordering comparisons, by contrast, are defined as overloaded names for a collection of built-in functions, each of which works on a different type.

As noted in Example 3.28 and Sidebar 7.7, Haskell unifies and extends the handling of equality and comparisons with a concept known as *type classes*.The equality operators (= and <>), for example, are declared (but not defined) in a predefined class `Eq`; any value that is passed to one of these operators will be inferred to be of some type in class `Eq`. Any value that is passed to one of the ordering operators (<, <=, >=, >) will similarly be inferred to be of some type in class `Ord`. This latter class is defined to be an extension of `Eq`; every type in class `Ord` must support the operators of class `Eq` as well. There is a strong analogy between type classes and the *interfaces* of languages with mix-in inheritance (Section 10.5).

```
let average x y = (x +. y) /. 2.;;
```

In either version of the function declaration, x and y will be inferred to be floats, because they are added with the floating-point +. operator. The programmer can document this explicitly if desired:

```
let average: float -> float -> float = fun x y -> (x +. y) /. 2.;;
```

or

```
let average (x:float) (y:float) :float = (x +. y) /. 2.;;
```

EXAMPLE 11.27
Nested declarations

Nested scopes are created with the `let...in...` construct. To compute the area of a triangle given the lengths of its sides, we might use the following function based on Heron's formula:

```
let triangle_area a b c =
  let s = (a +. b +. c) /. 2.0 in
  sqrt (s *. (s-.a) *. (s-.b) *. (s-.c));;
```

Here `s` is local to the expression following the `in`. It will be neither visible outside the `triangle_area` function nor in the body of its own definition (the expression between the inner = and the `in`).

EXAMPLE 11.28
A recursive nested function (reprise of Example 7.38)

In the case of recursion, of course, we do need a function to be visible within its declaration:

```
let fib n =
  let rec fib_helper f1 f2 i =
    if i = n then f2
    else fib_helper f2 (f1 + f2) (i + 1) in
  fib_helper 0 1 0;;
```

Here `fib_helper` is visible not only within the body of `fib`, but also within its own body.

11.4.3 Type Constructors

Lists

EXAMPLE 11.29
Polymorphic list operators

Programmers make heavy use of lists in most functional languages, and OCaml is no exception. Lists are naturally recursive, and lend themselves to manipulation with recursive functions. In scripting languages and dialects of Lisp, all of which are dynamically typed, lists can be heterogeneous—a single list may contain values of multiple, arbitrary types. In ML and its descendants, which perform all checking at compile time, lists must be homogeneous—all elements must have the same type. At the same time, functions that manipulate lists without performing operations on their members can take any kind of list as argument—they are naturally polymorphic:

```
let rec append l1 l2 =
  if l1 = [] then l2
  else hd l1 :: append (tl l1) l2;;

let rec member x l =
  if l = [] then false
  else if x = hd l then true
  else member x (tl l);;
```

Here append is of type `'a list -> 'a list -> 'a list`; member is of type `'a -> 'a list -> bool`. Empty brackets (`[]`) represent the empty list. The built-in `::` constructor is analogous to `cons` in Lisp: it takes an element and a list and tacks the former onto the beginning of the latter; its type is `'a -> 'a list -> 'a list`. The `hd` and `tl` functions are analogous to `car` and `cdr` in Lisp: they return the head and the remainder, respectively, of a list created by `::`. They are exported—together with many other useful routines (including append)—by the standard `List` library. (As it turns out, use of `hd` and `tl` is generally considered bad form in OCaml. Because they work only on nonempty lists, both functions must check their argument at run time and be prepared to throw an exception. OCaml's *pattern matching* mechanism, which we will examine in Section 11.4.4, allows the checking to be performed at compile time, and almost always provides a better way to write the code.) ■

EXAMPLE 11.30 List notation

Lists in OCaml are *immutable*: once created, their content never changes. List aggregates are most often written using "square bracket" notation, with semicolons separating the internal elements. The expression `[a; b; c]` is the same as `a :: b :: c :: []`. Note that if `a`, `b`, and `c` are all of the same type (call it `'t`), the expression `a :: b :: c` will still generate a type-clash error message: the right-hand operand of the second `::` needs to be of type `'t list`, not just `'t`.

The built-in at-sign constructor, `@`, behaves like an infix version of `append`. The expression `[a; b; c] @ [d; e; f; g]` is the same as `append [a; b; c] [d; e; f; g]`; it evaluates to `[a; b; c; d; e; f; g]`.

Since OCaml lists are homogeneous, one might wonder about the type of `[]`. To make it to be compatible with any list, it is given type `'a list`. ■

Arrays and Strings

While lists have a natural recursive definition and dynamically variable length, their immutability and linear-time access cost (for an arbitrary element) make them less than ideal for many applications. OCaml therefore provides a more conventional array type. The length of an array is fixed at elaboration time (i.e., when its declaration is encountered at run time), but its elements can be accessed in constant time, and their values can be changed by imperative code.

EXAMPLE 11.31 Array notation

Array aggregates look much like lists, but with vertical bars immediately inside the square brackets:

```
let five_primes = [| 2; 3; 5; 7; 11 |];;
```

Array indexing always starts at zero. Elements are accessed using the .() operator:

```
five_primes.(2);;        ⟹ 5
```

Unlike lists, arrays are mutable. Updates are made with the left-arrow assignment operator:

```
five_primes.(2) <- 4;;  ⟹ ()
five_primes.(2);;        ⟹ 4
```

Note that the assignment itself returns the unit value; it is evaluated for its side effect.

EXAMPLE 11.32
Strings as character arrays

Strings are essentially arrays of characters. They are delimited with double quotes, and indexed with the .[] operator:

```
let greeting = "hi, mom!";;
greeting.[7];;                ⟹ '!'
```

As of OCaml 4.02, strings are immutable by default, but there is a related bytes type that supports updates:

```
let enquiry = Bytes.of_string greeting;;
Bytes.set enquiry 7 '?';;  ⟹ ()
enquiry;;                    ⟹ "hi, mom?"
```

Tuples and Records

EXAMPLE 11.33
Tuple notation

Tuples, which we mentioned briefly in Example 11.22, are immutable, heterogeneous, but fixed-size collections of values of simpler types. Tuple aggregates are written by separating the component values with commas and surrounding them with parentheses. In a chemical database, the element Mercury might be represented by the tuple ("Hg", 80, 200.592), representing the element's chemical symbol, atomic number, and standard atomic weight. This tuple is said to be of type string * int * float; the stars, suggestive of multiplication, reflect the fact that tuple values are drawn from the Cartesian product of the string, int, and float domains.

Components of tuples are typically extracted via pattern matching (Section 11.4.4). In two-element tuples (often referred to as *pairs*), the components can also be obtained using the built-in polymorphic functions fst and snd:

```
fst ("Hg", 80);;     ⟹ "Hg"
snd ("Hg", 80);;     ⟹ 80
```

EXAMPLE 11.34
Record notation

Records are much like tuples, but the component values (fields) are named, rather than positional. The language implementation must choose an order for the internal representation of a record, but this order is not visible to the programmer. To introduce field names to the compiler, each record type must be declared:

```
type element =
  {name: string; atomic_number: int; atomic_weight: float};;
```

Record aggregates are enclosed in braces, with the fields (in any order) separated by semicolons:

```
let mercury =
  {atomic_number = 80; name = "Hg"; atomic_weight = 200.592};;
```

Individual fields of a record are easily accessed by name, using familiar "dot" notation:

```
mercury.atomic_weight;;      ⟹ 200.592
```

EXAMPLE 11.35
Mutable fields

At the programmer's discretion, fields can be declared to be mutable:

```
type sale_item = {name: string; mutable price: float};;
```

Like elements of an array, mutable fields can then be changed with the left-arrow operator:

```
let my_item = {name = "bike"; price = 699.95};;
my_item.price;;                  ⟹ 699.95
my_item.price <- 800.00;;        ⟹ ()
my_item;;                        ⟹ {name = "bike"; price = 800.}
```

EXAMPLE 11.36
References

As a convenience, the OCaml standard library defines a polymorphic `ref` type that is essentially a record with a single mutable field. The exclamation-point operator `!` is used to retrieve the object referred to by the reference; `:=` is used for assignment:

```
let x = ref 3;;
!x;;                             ⟹ 3
x := !x + 1;;                    ⟹ ()
!x;;                             ⟹ 4
```

Variant Types

Variant types, like records, must be declared, but instead of introducing a set of named fields, each of which is present in every value of the type, the declaration introduces a set of named *constructors* (variants), *one* of which will be present in each value of the type. In the simplest case, the constructors are all simply names, and the type is essentially an enumeration:

EXAMPLE 11.37
Variants as enumerations

```
type weekday = Sun | Mon | Tue | Wed | Thu | Fri | Sat;;
```

Note that constructor names must begin with a capital letter.

In more complicated examples, a constructor may specify a type for its variant. The overall type is then essentially a union:

EXAMPLE 11.38
Variants as unions

```
type yearday = YMD of int * int * int | YD of int * int;;
```

This code defines `YMD` as a constructor that takes a three-integer tuple as argument, and `YD` as a constructor that takes a two-integer tuple as argument. The intent is to allow days of the year to be specified either as (year, month, day) triples or as (year, day) pairs, where the second element of the pair may range from 1 to 366. In 2015 (a non–leap year), the Fourth of July could be represented either as `YMD (2015, 7, 4)` or as `YD (2015, 185)`, though the equality test `YMD (2015, 7, 4) = YD (2015, 185)` would fail. (We could, if desired, define a special equality operator for such constructed values—see Exercise 11.16.)

EXAMPLE 11.39
Recursive variants

Variant types are particularly useful for recursive structures, where different variants represent the base and inductive parts of a definition. The canonical example is a binary tree:

```
type 'a tree = Empty | Node of 'a * 'a tree * 'a tree;;
```

Given this definition, the tree

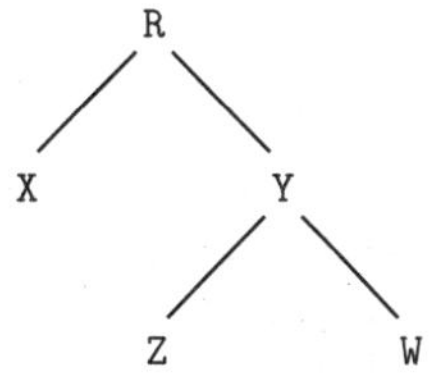

can be written `Node ('R', Node ('X', Empty, Empty), Node ('Y', Node ('Z', Empty, Empty), Node ('W', Empty, Empty)))`.

11.4.4 Pattern Matching

Pattern matching, particularly for strings, appears in many programming languages. Examples include Snobol, Icon, Perl, and the several other scripting languages that have adopted Perl's facilities (discussed in Section 14.4.2). ML is distinctive in extending pattern matching to the full range of constructed values—including tuples, lists, records, and variants—and integrating it with static typing and type inference.

EXAMPLE 11.40
Pattern matching of parameters

A simple example in OCaml occurs when passing parameters. Suppose, for example, that we need a function to extract the atomic number from an element represented as a tuple:

```
let atomic_number (s, n, w) = n;;
let mercury = ("Hg", 80, 200.592);;
atomic_number mercury;;                ⟹ 80
```

Here mercury, the argument to atomic_number, has been matched against the (single, tuple) parameter in the function definition, giving us names for its various fields, one of which we simply return. Since the other two fields are unused in the body of the function, we don't really have to give them names: the "wild card" (_) pattern can be used instead:

```
let atomic_number (_, n, _) = n;;
```

EXAMPLE 11.41
Pattern matching in local declarations

Pattern matching also works when declaring local names:

```
let atomic_number e =
  let (_, n, _) = e in n;;
```

In both versions of the atomic_number function, pattern matching allows us to associate names with the components of some larger constructed value. The real power of pattern matching, however, arises not in such simple cases, but in cases where the structure of the value to be matched may not be known until run time. Consider for example a function to return an in-order list of the nodes of a binary tree:

EXAMPLE 11.42
The match construct

```
type 'a tree = Empty | Node of 'a * 'a tree * 'a tree;;

let rec inorder t =
  match t with
  | Empty -> []
  | Node (v, left, right) -> inorder left @ [v] @ inorder right;;
```

DESIGN & IMPLEMENTATION

11.3 Type Equivalence in OCaml

Because of their use of type inference, ML-family languages generally provide the effect of structural type equivalence. Variants can be used to obtain the effect of name equivalence when desired:

```
type celsius_temp = CT of int;;
type fahrenheit_temp = FT of int;;
```

A value of type celsius_temp can then be obtained by using the CT constructor:

```
let freezing = CT(0);;
```

Unfortunately, celsius_temp does not automatically inherit the arithmetic operators and relations of int: the expression CT(0) + CT(20) will generate a type clash error message. Moreover, with the exception of the built-in comparison operators (<, >, <=, >=), there is no provision for overloading in OCaml: we can define cplus and fplus functions, but we cannot overload + itself.

The `match` construct compares a candidate expression (here `t`) with each of a series of patterns (here `Empty` and `Node (v, left, right)`). Each pattern is preceded by a vertical bar and separated by an arrow from an accompanying expression. The value of the overall construct is the value of the accompanying expression for the first pattern that matches the candidate expression. When applied to the tree of Example 11.39, our `inorder` function yields `['X'; 'R'; 'Z'; 'Y'; 'W']`.

EXAMPLE 11.43
Guards

In some cases, it can be helpful to *guard* a pattern with a Boolean expression. Suppose, for example, that we are looking for the value associated with a given key in a list of key-value pairs:

```
let rec find key l =
  match l with
  | [] -> raise Not_found
  | (k, v) :: rest when k = key -> v
  | head :: rest -> find key rest;;

let squares = [(1,1); (2,4); (3,9); (4,16); (5,25)];;
```

Given these definitions, `find 3 squares` will return the value 9; `find 6 squares` will raise a `Not_found` exception. Note that the patterns in a `match` are considered in program order: in our `find` function, we only use the third alternative when the guard in the second one fails.

EXAMPLE 11.44
The `as` keyword

When desired, a pattern can provide names at multiple levels of granularity. Consider, for example, the representation of a line segment as a pair of pairs indicating the coordinates of the endpoints. Given a segment `s`, we can name both the (two-component) points and the individual coordinates using the `as` keyword:

```
let (((x1, y1) as p1), ((x2, y2) as p2)) = s;;
```

If `s = ((1, 2), (3, 4))`, then after this declaration, we have `x1 = 1`, `y1 = 2`, `x2 = 3`, `y2 = 4`, `p1 = (1, 2)`, and `p2 = (3, 4)`.

EXAMPLE 11.45
The `function` keyword

One use case for `match` is sufficiently common to warrant its own syntactic sugar. An example can be seen in our `inorder` function, whose body consists of a `match` on the function's (single) parameter. The special `function` keyword eliminates the need to name the parameter explicitly:

```
let rec inorder = function
  | Empty -> []
  | Node (v, left, right) -> inorder left @ [v] @ inorder right;;
```

In many cases, an OCaml implementation can tell at compile time that a pattern match will succeed: it knows all necessary information about the structure of the value being matched against the pattern. In other cases, the implementation can tell that a match is doomed to fail, generally because the types of the pattern and the value cannot be unified. The more interesting cases are those in which the pattern and the value have the same type (i.e., could be unified), but the success of the match cannot be determined until run time. If `l` is of type `int list`, for example, then an attempt to "deconstruct" `l` into its head and tail may or may not succeed, depending on `l`'s value:

EXAMPLE 11.46
Run-time pattern matching

```
let head :: rest = l in ...
```

If `l` is `[]`, the attempted match will raise a `Match_failure` exception. ■

By default, the OCaml compiler will issue a compile-time warning for any pattern match whose options are not *exhaustive*—i.e., whose structure does not include all the possibilities inherent in the type of the candidate expression, and whose execution might therefore lead to a run-time exception. The compiler will also issue a warning if the pattern in a later arm of a multi-way `match` is completely covered by one in an earlier arm (implying that the latter will never be chosen).

A completely covered arm is probably an error, but harmless, in the sense that it will never result in a dynamic semantic error. Nonexhaustive cases may be intentional, if the programmer can predict that the pattern will always work at run time. The `append` function of Example 11.29 could have been written

EXAMPLE 11.47
Coverage of patterns

```
let rec append l1 l2 =
  if l1 = [] then l2
  else let h::t = l1 in h :: append t l2;;
```

This version of the code is likely to elicit a warning: the compiler will fail to realize that the `let` construct in the `else` clause will be elaborated only if `l1` is nonempty. (This example looks easy enough to figure out, but the general case is undecidable, and there is little point in providing special code to recognize easy cases.) Probably the best way to write the code is to use a two-way `match` instead of the `if... then... else`:

```
let rec append l1 l2 =
  match l1 with
  | []     -> l2
  | h::t -> h :: append t l2;;
```

Unlike either of the previous versions, this allows the compiler to verify that the matching is exhaustive. ■

In imperative languages, subroutines that need to produce more than one value often do so via modification of reference or result parameters. Functional languages, which need to avoid such side effects, must instead arrange to return multiple values from a function. In OCaml, these are easily composed into, and extracted from, a tuple. Consider, for example, a statistics routine that returns the mean and standard deviation of the values in a list:

EXAMPLE 11.48
Pattern matching against a tuple returned from a function

```
let stats l =
  let rec helper rest n sum sum_squares =
    match rest with
    | [] -> let nf = float_of_int n in
            (sum /. nf, sqrt (sum_squares /. nf))
    | h :: t ->
      helper t (n+1) (sum+.h) (sum_squares +. (h*.h)) in
  helper l 0 0.0 0.0;;
```

To obtain the statistics for a given list, we can pattern match against the value returned from function `stats`:

```
let (mean, sd) = stats [1.; 2.; 3.; 4.; 5.];;
```

To which the interpreter responds

```
val mean : float = 3.
val sd : float = 3.3166247903554
```

11.4.5 Control Flow and Side Effects

We have seen several examples of `if` expressions in previous sections. Because it must yield a value, almost every `if` expression has both a `then` part and an `else` part. The only exception is when the `then` part has `unit` type, and is executed for its side effect:

EXAMPLE 11.49
An `if` without an `else`

```
if a < 0 then print_string "negative"
```

Here the `print_string` call evaluates to `()`, as does, by convention, the implicit missing `else` clause; the overall expression thus has `unit` type.

I/O is a common form of side effect. OCaml provides standard library routines to read and print a variety of built-in types. It also supports formatted output in the style of C's `printf`.

EXAMPLE 11.50
Insertion sort in OCaml

While tail recursion and higher-order functions are strongly preferred when expressing repeated execution, iterative loops are also available. Perhaps their most common application is to update arrays in place:

```
let insertion_sort a =       (* sort array a without making a copy *)
  for i = 1 to Array.length a - 1 do
    let t = a.(i) in
    let j = ref i in
    while !j > 0 && t < a.(!j - 1) do
      a.(!j) <- a.(!j - 1);
      j := !j - 1
    done;
    a.(!j) <- t
  done;;
```

Note the use here of both `<-` assignment for array elements and `:=` assignment for references. (Keep in mind that the exclamation point indicates dereference, not logical negation.) Note also the use of semicolons to separate the assignments inside the `while` loop, and again to separate the `while` loop from the assignment to `a.(!j)`. The `for` and `while` loops both evaluate to `()`, as do both `<-` and `:=` assignments.

We have noted in previous sections that many routines in the OCaml standard library will raise exceptions in certain circumstances. We raised one ourselves in Example 11.43. A simple exception is declared as follows:

EXAMPLE 11.51
A simple exception

```
exception Not_found;;
```

EXAMPLE 11.52
An exception with arguments

In more complex cases, an exception can take arguments:

```
exception Bad_arg of float * string;;
```

This latter exception might be raised by a hypothetical trigonometry library:

```
let arc_cos x =
  if x < -1. || x > 1. then raise (Bad_arg (x, "in arc_cos"))
  else acos x;;
```

The predefined `acos` function simply returns a "not-a-number" value (`NaN`—Section C-5.2.2) when its argument has a magnitude larger than 1.

EXAMPLE 11.53
Catching an exception

Exceptions are caught in a `with` clause of a `try` expression:

```
let special_meals =
  [("Tim Smith", "vegan"); ("Fatima Hussain", "halal")];;

let meal_type p =
  try find p special_meals with Not_found -> "default";;

meal_type "Tim Smith";;         ⟹ "vegan"
meal_type "Peng Chen";;         ⟹ "default"
```

An exception with an argument is only slightly more complicated:

```
open Printf;;    (* formatted I/O library *)
let c = try arc_cos v with Bad_arg (arg, loc) ->
  (eprintf "Bad argument %f %s\n" arg loc; 0.0);;
```

Note that the expression after the arrow must have the same type as the expression between the `try` and `with`. Here we have printed an error message and then (after the semicolon) provided a value of 0.

11.4.6 Extended Example: DFA Simulation in OCaml

EXAMPLE 11.54
Simulating a DFA in OCaml

To conclude our introduction to OCaml, we reprise the DFA simulation program originally presented in Scheme in Example 11.20. The code appears in Figure 11.3. Finite automata details can be found in Sections 2.2 and C-2.4.1. Here we represent a DFA as a record with three fields: the start state, the transition function, and a list of final states. To represent the transition function we use a list of triples. The first two elements of each triple are a state and an input symbol. If these match the current state and next input symbol, then the finite automaton enters the state given by the third element of the triple.

To make all this concrete, consider the DFA of Figure 11.4. It accepts all strings of `a`s and `b`s in which each letter appears an even number of times. To simulate this machine, we pass it to the function `simulate` along with an input string. As it runs, the automaton accumulates as a list a trace of the states through which it has traveled. Once the input is exhausted, it packages the trace together in a tuple with either `Accept` or `Reject`. For example, if we type

```
simulate a_b_even_dfa ['a'; 'b'; 'b'; 'a'; 'b'];;
```

then the OCaml interpreter will print

```
- : state list * decision = ([0; 2; 3; 2; 0; 1], Reject)
```

If we change the input string to `abaaba`, the interpreter will print

```
- : state list * decision = ([0; 2; 3; 1; 3; 2; 0], Accept)
```

✓ CHECK YOUR UNDERSTANDING

12. Why does OCaml provide separate arithmetic operators for integer and floating-point values?
13. Explain the difference between *physical* and *structural* equality of values in OCaml.
14. How do lists in OCaml differ from those of Lisp and Scheme?
15. Identify the values that OCaml treats as *mutable*.
16. List three contexts in which OCaml performs *pattern matching*.
17. Explain the difference between *tuples* and *records* in OCaml. How does an OCaml record differ from a record (structure) in languages like C or Pascal?
18. What are OCaml *variants*? What features do they subsume from imperative languages such as C and Pascal?

```
open List;;      (* includes rev, find, and mem functions *)

type state = int;;
type 'a dfa = {
  current_state : state;
  transition_function : (state * 'a * state) list;
  final_states : state list;
};;
type decision = Accept | Reject;;

let move (d:'a dfa) (x:'a) : 'a dfa =
  { current_state = (
      let (_, _, q) =
        find (fun (s, c, _) -> s = d.current_state && c = x)
             d.transition_function in
      q);
    transition_function = d.transition_function;
    final_states = d.final_states;
  };;

let simulate (d:'a dfa) (input:'a list) : (state list * decision) =
  let rec helper moves d2 remaining_input : (state option * state list) =
    match remaining_input with
    | [] -> (Some d2.current_state, moves)
    | hd :: tl ->
        let new_moves = d2.current_state :: moves in
        try helper new_moves (move d2 hd) tl
        with Not_found -> (None, new_moves) in
  match helper [] d input with
  | (None, moves) -> (rev moves, Reject)
  | (Some last_state, moves) ->
      ( rev (last_state :: moves),
        if mem last_state d.final_states then Accept else Reject);;
```

Figure 11.3 OCaml program to simulate the actions of a DFA. Given a machine description and an input symbol *i*, function `move` searches for a transition labeled *i* from the start state to some new state *s*. If the search fails, `find` raises exception `Not_found`, which propagates out of `move`; otherwise `move` returns a new machine with the same transition function and final states, but with *s* as its "start" state. Note that the code is polymorphic in the type of the input symbols. The main function, `simulate`, encapsulates a tail-recursive `helper` function that accumulates an inverted list of moves, returning when it has consumed all input symbols. The encapsulating function then checks to see if the helper ended in a final state; it returns the (properly ordered) series of moves, together with an `Accept` or `Reject` indication. The built-in `option` constructor (Example 7.6) is used to distinguish between a real state (`Some s`) and an error state (`None`).

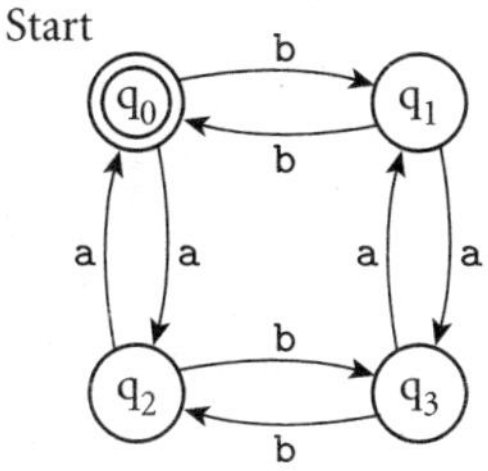


```
let a_b_even_dfa : char dfa =
  { current_state = 0;
    transition_function =
      [ (0, 'a', 2); (0, 'b', 1); (1, 'a', 3); (1, 'b', 0);
        (2, 'a', 0); (2, 'b', 3); (3, 'a', 1); (3, 'b', 2) ];
    final_states = [0];
  };;
```

Figure 11.4 DFA to accept all strings of `as` and `bs` containing an even number of each. At the bottom of the figure is a representation of the machine as an OCaml data structure, using the conventions of Figure 11.3.

11.5 Evaluation Order Revisited

In Section 6.6.2 we observed that the subcomponents of many expressions can be evaluated in more than one order. In particular, one can choose to evaluate function arguments before passing them to a function, or to pass them unevaluated. The former option is called *applicative-order* evaluation; the latter is called *normal-order* evaluation. Like most imperative languages, Scheme and OCaml use applicative order in most cases. Normal order, which arises in the macros and call-by-name parameters of imperative languages, is available in special cases.

EXAMPLE 11.55
Applicative and normal-order evaluation

Suppose, for example, that we have defined the following function in Scheme:

```
(define double (lambda (x) (+ x x)))
```

Evaluating the expression `(double (* 3 4))` in applicative order (as Scheme does), we have

```
    (double (* 3 4))
==> (double 12)
==> (+ 12 12)
==> 24
```

Under normal-order evaluation we would have

```
    (double (* 3 4))
⟹ (+ (* 3 4) (* 3 4))
⟹ (+ 12 (* 3 4))
⟹ (+ 12 12)
⟹ 24
```

Here we end up doing extra work: normal order causes us to evaluate (* 3 4) twice. ■

EXAMPLE 11.56
Normal-order avoidance of unnecessary work

In other cases, applicative-order evaluation can end up doing extra work. Suppose we have defined the following:

```
(define switch
  (lambda (x a b c)
    (cond ((< x 0) a)
          ((= x 0) b)
          ((> x 0) c))))
```

Evaluating the expression (switch -1 (+ 1 2) (+ 2 3) (+ 3 4)) in applicative order, we have

```
    (switch -1 (+ 1 2) (+ 2 3) (+ 3 4))
⟹ (switch -1 3 (+ 2 3) (+ 3 4))
⟹ (switch -1 3 5 (+ 3 4))
⟹ (switch -1 3 5 7)
⟹ (cond ((< -1 0) 3)
         ((= -1 0) 5)
         ((> -1 0) 7))
⟹ (cond (#t 3)
         ((= -1 0) 5)
         ((> -1 0) 7))
⟹ 3
```

(Here we have assumed that cond is built in, and evaluates its arguments lazily, even though switch is doing so eagerly.) Under normal-order evaluation we would have

```
    (switch -1 (+ 1 2) (+ 2 3) (+ 3 4))
⟹ (cond ((< -1 0) (+ 1 2))
         ((= -1 0) (+ 2 3))
         ((> -1 0) (+ 3 4)))
⟹ (cond (#t (+ 1 2))
         ((= -1 0) (+ 2 3))
         ((> -1 0) (+ 3 4)))
⟹ (+ 1 2)
⟹ 3
```

Here normal-order evaluation avoids evaluating (+ 2 3) or (+ 3 4). (In this case, we have assumed that arithmetic and logical functions such as + and < are built in, and force the evaluation of their arguments.) ■

In our overview of Scheme we differentiated on several occasions between special forms and functions. Arguments to functions are always passed by sharing (Section 9.3.1), and are evaluated before they are passed (i.e., in applicative order). Arguments to special forms are passed unevaluated—in other words, by name. Each special form is free to choose internally when (and if) to evaluate its parameters. `Cond`, for example, takes a sequence of unevaluated pairs as arguments. It evaluates their `car`s internally, one at a time, stopping when it finds one that evaluates to `#t`.

Together, special forms and functions are known as *expression types* in Scheme. Some expression types are *primitive*, in the sense that they must be built into the language implementation. Others are *derived*; they can be defined in terms of primitive expression types. In an `eval`/`apply`-based interpreter, primitive special forms are built into `eval`; primitive functions are recognized by `apply`. We have seen how the special form `lambda` can be used to create derived functions, which can be bound to names with `let`. Scheme provides an analogous special form, `syntax-rules`, that can be used to create derived special forms. These can then be bound to names with `define-syntax` and `let-syntax`. Derived special forms are known as *macros* in Scheme, but unlike most other macros, they are *hygienic*—lexically scoped, integrated into the language's semantics, and immune from the problems of mistaken grouping and variable capture described in Section 3.7. Like C++ templates (Section C-7.3.2), Scheme macros are Turing complete. They behave like functions whose arguments are passed by name (Section C-9.3.2) instead of by sharing. They are implemented, however, via logical expansion in the interpreter's parser and semantic analyzer, rather than by delayed evaluation with thunks.

11.5.1 Strictness and Lazy Evaluation

Evaluation order can have an effect not only on execution speed but also on program correctness. A program that encounters a dynamic semantic error or an infinite regression in an "unneeded" subexpression under applicative-order evaluation may terminate successfully under normal-order evaluation. A (side-effect-free) function is said to be *strict* if it is undefined (fails to terminate, or encounters an error) when any of its arguments is undefined. Such a function can safely evaluate all its arguments, so its result will not depend on evaluation order. A function is said to be *nonstrict* if it does not impose this requirement—that is, if it is sometimes defined even when one of its arguments is not. A *language* is said to be strict if it is defined in such a way that functions are always strict. A language is said to be nonstrict if it permits the definition of nonstrict functions. If a language always evaluates expressions in applicative order, then every function is guaranteed to be strict, because whenever an argument is undefined, its evaluation will fail and so will the function to which it is being passed. Contrapositively, a nonstrict language cannot use applicative order; it must use normal order to avoid evaluating unneeded arguments. Standard ML, OCaml, and (with the exception of macros) Scheme are strict. Miranda and Haskell are nonstrict.

Lazy evaluation, implemented automatically, gives us the advantage of normal-order evaluation (not evaluating unneeded subexpressions) while running within a constant factor of the speed of applicative-order evaluation for expressions in which everything is needed. The trick is to tag every argument internally with a "memo" that indicates its value, if known. Any attempt to evaluate the argument sets the value in the memo as a side effect, or returns the value (without recalculating it) if it is already set.

EXAMPLE 11.57
Avoiding work with lazy evaluation

Returning to the expression of Example 11.55, (double (* 3 4)) will be compiled in a lazy system as (double (f)), where f is a hidden closure with an internal side effect:

```
(define f
  (lambda ()
    (let ((done #f)                          ; memo initially unset
          (memo '())
          (code (lambda () (* 3 4))))
      (if done memo                          ; if memo is set, return it
          (begin
            (set! memo (code))               ; remember value
            (set! done #t)                   ; note that we set it
            memo)))))                        ; and return it
...
(double (f))
⟹ (+ (f) (f))
⟹ (+ 12 (f))        ; first call computes value
⟹ (+ 12 12)         ; second call returns remembered value
⟹ 24
```

Here (* 3 4) will be evaluated only once. While the cost of manipulating memos will clearly be higher than that of the extra multiplication in this case, if we were to replace (* 3 4) with a very expensive operation, the savings could be substantial. ■

Lazy evaluation is particularly useful for "infinite" data structures, as described in Section 6.6.2. It can also be useful in programs that need to examine only a prefix of a potentially long list (see Exercise 11.10). Lazy evaluation is used for all arguments in Miranda and Haskell. It is available in Scheme through explicit

DESIGN & IMPLEMENTATION

11.4 Lazy evaluation

One of the beauties of a purely functional language is that it makes lazy evaluation a completely transparent performance optimization: the programmer can think in terms of nonstrict functions and normal-order evaluation, counting on the implementation to avoid the cost of repeated evaluation. For languages with imperative features, however, this characterization does not hold: lazy evaluation is *not* transparent in the presence of side effects.

use of `delay` and `force`,[6] and in OCaml through the similar mechanisms of the standard `Lazy` library. It can also be achieved implicitly in Scheme (in certain contexts) through the use of macros. Where normal-order evaluation can be thought of as function evaluation using call-by-name parameters, lazy evaluation is sometimes said to employ "call by need." In addition to Miranda and Haskell, call by need can be found in the R scripting language, widely used by statisticians.

The principal problem with lazy evaluation is its behavior in the presence of side effects. If an argument contains a reference to a variable that may be modified by an assignment, then the value of the argument will depend on whether it is evaluated before or after the assignment. Likewise, if the argument contains an assignment, values elsewhere in the program may depend on when evaluation occurs. These problems do not arise in Miranda or Haskell because they are purely functional: there are no side effects. Scheme and OCaml leave the problem up to the programmer, but require that every use of a `delay`-ed expression be enclosed in `force`, making it relatively easy to identify the places where side effects are an issue.

11.5.2 I/O: Streams and Monads

A major source of side effects can be found in traditional I/O: an input routine will generally return a different value every time it is called, and multiple calls to an output routine, though they never return a value, must occur in the proper order if the program is to be considered correct.

One way to avoid these side effects is to model input and output as *streams*—unbounded-length lists whose elements are generated lazily. We saw an example of a stream in the infinite lists of Section 6.6.2 (an OCaml example appears in Exercise 11.18). If we model input and output as streams, then a program takes the form

EXAMPLE 11.58
Stream-based program execution

```
(define output (my_prog input))
```

When it needs an input value, function `my_prog` forces evaluation of the `car` (head) of `input`, and passes the `cdr` (tail) on to the rest of the program. To drive execution, the language implementation repeatedly forces evaluation of the `car` of `output`, prints it, and repeats:

```
(define driver
  (lambda (s)
    (if (null? s) '()      ; nothing left
        (begin
          (display (car s))
          (driver (cdr s))))))
(driver output)
```

6 Recall that `delay` is a special form that creates a [memo, closure] pair; `force` is a function that returns the value in the memo, using the closure to calculate it first if necessary.

EXAMPLE 11.59

Interactive I/O with streams

To make things concrete, suppose we want to write a purely functional program that prompts the user for a sequence of numbers (one at a time!) and prints their squares. If Scheme employed lazy evaluation of input and output streams (it doesn't), then we could write:

```
(define squares
  (lambda (s)
    (cons "please enter a number\n"
          (let ((n (car s)))
            (if (eof-object? n) '()
                (cons (* n n) (cons #\newline (squares (cdr s)))))))))
(define output (squares input)))
```

Prompts, inputs, and outputs (i.e., squares) would be interleaved naturally in time. In effect, lazy evaluation would *force* things to happen in the proper order: The `car` of `output` is the first prompt. The `cadr` of `output` (the head of the tail) is the first square, a value that requires evaluation of the `car` of `input`. The `caddr` of `output` (the head of the tail of the tail) is the second prompt. The `cadddr` of `output` (the head of the tail of the tail of the tail) is the second square, a value that requires evaluation of the `cadr` of `input`. ■

Streams formed the basis of the I/O system in early versions of Haskell. Unfortunately, while they successfully encapsulate the imperative nature of interaction at a terminal, streams don't work very well for graphics or random access to files. They also make it difficult to accommodate I/O of different kinds (since all elements of a list in Haskell must be of a single type). More recent versions of Haskell employ a more general concept known as *monads*. Monads are drawn from a branch of mathematics known as *category theory*, but one doesn't need to understand the theory to appreciate their usefulness in practice. In Haskell, monads are essentially a clever use of higher-order functions, coupled with a bit of syntactic sugar, that allow the programmer to chain together a sequence of *actions* (function calls) that have to happen in order. The power of the idea comes from the ability to carry a hidden, structured value of arbitrary complexity from one action to the next. In many applications of monads, this extra hidden value plays the role of mutable state: differences between the values carried to successive actions act as side effects.

EXAMPLE 11.60

Pseudorandom numbers in Haskell

As a motivating example somewhat simpler than I/O, consider the possibility of creating a pseudorandom number generator (RNG) along the lines of Example 6.45. In that example we assumed that `rand()` would modify hidden state as a side effect, allowing it to return a different value every time it is called. This idiom isn't possible in a pure functional language, but we can obtain a similar effect by passing the state to the function and having it return new state along with the random number. This is exactly how the built-in function `random` works in Haskell. The following code calls `random` twice to illustrate its interface.

```
twoRandomInts :: StdGen -> ([Integer], StdGen)
  -- type signature: twoRandomInts is a function that takes an
  -- StdGen (the state of the RNG) and returns a tuple containing
  -- a list of Integers and a new StdGen.
twoRandomInts gen = let
      (rand1, gen2) = random gen
      (rand2, gen3) = random gen2
  in ([rand1, rand2], gen3)

main = let
      gen = mkStdGen 123               -- new RNG, seeded with 123
      ints = fst (twoRandomInts gen)   -- extract first element
  in print ints                          -- of returned tuple
```

Note that gen2, one of the return values from the first call to `random`, has been passed as an argument to the second call. Then gen3, one of the return values from the second call, is returned to `main`, where it could, if we wished, be passed to another function. This mechanism works, but it's far from pretty: copies of the RNG state must be "threaded through" every function that needs a random number. This is particularly complicated for deeply nested functions. It is easy to make a mistake, and difficult to verify that one has not.

Monads provide a more general solution to the problem of threading mutable state through a functional program. Here is our example rewritten to use Haskell's standard `IO` monad, which includes a random number generator:

```
twoMoreRandomInts :: IO [Integer]
  -- twoMoreRandomInts returns a list of Integers.  It also
  -- implicitly accepts, and returns, all the state of the IO monad.
twoMoreRandomInts = do
  rand1 <- randomIO
  rand2 <- randomIO
  return [rand1, rand2]

main = do
  moreInts <- twoMoreRandomInts
  print moreInts
```

There are several differences here. First, the type of the `twoMoreRandomInts` function has become `IO [Integer]`. This identifies it as an *IO action*—a function that (in addition to returning an explicit list of integers) invisibly accepts and returns the state of the `IO` monad (including the standard RNG). Similarly, the type of `randomIO` is `IO Integer`. To thread the `IO` state from one action to the next, the bodies of `twoMoreRandomInts` and `main` use `do` notation rather than `let`. A `do` block packages a sequence of actions together into a single, compound action. At each step along the way, it passes the (potentially modified) state of the monad from one action to the next. It also supports the "assignment" operator, `<-`, which separates the explicit return value from the hidden state and opens a nested scope for its left-hand side, so all values "assigned" earlier in the sequence are visible to actions later in the sequence.

The `return` operator in `twoMoreRandomInts` packages an explicit return value (in our case, a two-element list) together with the hidden state, to be returned to the caller. A similar use of `return` presumably appears inside `randomIO`. Everything we have done is purely functional—`do` and `<-` are simply syntactic sugar—but the bookkeeping required to pass the state of the RNG from one invocation of `random` to the next has been hidden in a way that makes our code look imperative. ■

EXAMPLE 11.61
The state of the `IO` monad

So what does this have to do with I/O? Consider the `getChar` function, which reads a character from standard input. Like `rand`, we expect it to return a different value every time we call it. Haskell therefore arranges for `getChar` to be of type `IO Char`: it returns a character, but also accepts, and passes on, the hidden state of the monad.

In most Haskell monads, hidden state can be explicitly extracted and examined. The `IO` monad, however, is *abstract*: only part of its state is defined in library header files; the rest is implemented by the language run-time system. This is unavoidable because, in effect, *the hidden state of the* `IO` *monad encompasses the real world.* If this state were visible, a program could capture and reuse it, with the nonsensical expectation that we could "go back in time" and see what the user would have done in response to a different prompt last Tuesday. Unfortunately, `IO` state hiding means that a value of type `IO T` is permanently tainted: it can never be extracted from the monad to produce a "pure `T`." ■

EXAMPLE 11.62
Functional composition of actions

Because `IO` actions are just ordinary values, we can manipulate them in the same way as values of other data types. The most basic output action is `putChar`, of type `Char -> IO ()` (monadic function with an explicit character argument and no explicit return). Given `putChar`, we can define `putStr`:

```
putStr :: String -> IO ()
putStr s = sequence_ (map putChar s)
```

Strings in Haskell are simply lists of characters. The `map` function takes a function *f* and a list *l* as argument, and returns a list that contains the results of applying *f* to the elements of *l*:

```
map :: (a->b) -> [a] -> [b]
map f [] = []                          -- base case
map f (h:t) = f h : map f t            -- tail recursive case
                                       -- ':' is like cons in Scheme
```

The result of `map putChar s` is a list of actions, each of which prints a character: it has type `[IO ()]`. The built-in function `sequence_` converts this to a single action that prints a list. It could be defined as follows.

```
sequence_ :: [IO ()] -> IO ()
sequence_ [] = return ()                     -- base case
sequence_ (a:more) = do a; sequence_ more    -- tail recursive case
```

As before, do provides a convenient way to chain actions together. For brevity, we have written the actions on a single line, separated by a semicolon. ■

The entry point of a Haskell program is always the function `main`. It has type `IO ()`. Because Haskell is lazy (nonstrict), the action sequence returned by `main` remains hypothetical until the run-time system forces its evaluation. In practice, Haskell programs tend to have a small top-level structure of `IO` monad code that sequences I/O operations. The bulk of the program—both the computation of values *and the determination of the order in which I/O actions should occur*—is then purely functional. For a program whose I/O can be expressed in terms of streams, the top-level structure may consist of a single line:

EXAMPLE 11.63
Streams and the I/O monad

```
main = interact my_program
```

The library function `interact` is of type `(String -> String) -> IO ()`. It takes as argument a function from strings to strings (in this case `my_program`). It calls this function, passing the contents of standard input as argument, and writes the result to standard output. Internally, `interact` uses the function `getContents`, which returns the program's input as a lazily evaluated string: a stream. In a more sophisticated program, `main` may orchestrate much more complex I/O actions, including graphics and random access to files. ■

DESIGN & IMPLEMENTATION

11.5 Monads

Monads are very heavily used in Haskell. The `IO` monad serves as the central repository for imperative language features—not only I/O and random numbers but also mutable global variables and shared-memory synchronization. Additional monads (with accessible hidden state) support partial functions and various container classes (lists and sets). When coupled with lazy evaluation, monadic containers in turn provide a natural foundation for backtracking search, nondeterminism, and the functional equivalent of iterators. (In the list monad, for example, hidden state can carry the continuation needed to generate the tail of an infinite list.)

The inability to extract values from the `IO` monad reflects the fact that the physical world is imperative, and that a language that needs to interact with the physical world in nontrivial ways must include imperative features. Put another way, the `IO` monad (unlike monads in general) is more than syntactic sugar: by hiding the state of the physical world it makes it possible to express things that could not otherwise be expressed in a functional way, provided that we are willing to enforce a sequential evaluation order. The beauty of monads is that they confine sequentiality to a relatively small fraction of the typical program, so that side effects cannot interfere with the bulk of the computation.

11.6 Higher-Order Functions

A function is said to be a *higher-order function* (also called a *functional form*) if it takes a function as an argument, or returns a function as a result. We have seen several examples already of higher-order functions in Scheme: `call/cc` (Section 6.2.2), `for-each` (Example 11.18), `compose` (Example 11.19), and `apply` (Section 11.3.5). We also saw a Haskell version of the higher-order function `map` in Section 11.5.2. The Scheme version of `map` is slightly more general. Like `for-each`, it takes as argument a function and a *sequence* of lists. There must be as many lists as the function takes arguments, and the lists must all be of the same length. `Map` calls its function argument on corresponding sets of elements from the lists:

EXAMPLE 11.64
map function in Scheme

```
(map * '(2 4 6) '(3 5 7))  ⟹ (6 20 42)
```

Where `for-each` is executed for its side effects, and has an implementation-dependent return value, `map` is purely functional: it returns a list composed of the values returned by its function argument. ■

Programmers in Scheme (or in OCaml, Haskell, or other functional languages) can easily define other higher-order functions. Suppose, for example, that we want to be able to "fold" the elements of a list together, using an associative binary operator:

EXAMPLE 11.65
Folding (reduction) in Scheme

```
(define fold
  (lambda (f i l)
    (if (null? l) i     ; i is commonly the identity element for f
      (f (car l) (fold f i (cdr l))))))
```

Now `(fold + 0 '(1 2 3 4 5))` gives us the sum of the first five natural numbers, and `(fold * 1 '(1 2 3 4 5))` gives us their product. ■

EXAMPLE 11.66
Folding in OCaml

A similar `fold_left` function is defined by OCaml's `List` module:

```
fold_left (+) 0 [1; 2; 3; 4; 5];;          ⟹ 15
fold_left ( * ) 1 [1; 2; 3; 4; 5];;        ⟹ 120
```

(The spaces around `*` are required to distinguish it from a comment delimiter.) For non associative operators, an analogous `fold_right` function folds the list from right-to-left. It is not tail-recursive, however, and tends to be used less often. ■

EXAMPLE 11.67
Combining higher-order functions

One of the most common uses of higher-order functions is to build new functions from existing ones:

```
(define total (lambda (l) (fold + 0 l)))
(total '(1 2 3 4 5))                        ⟹ 15
```

```
(define total-all (lambda (l) (map total l)))
(total-all '((1 2 3 4 5)
             (2 4 6 8 10)
             (3 6 9 12 15)))                ⟹ (15 30 45)

(define make-double (lambda (f) (lambda (x) (f x x))))
(define twice (make-double +))
(define square (make-double *))
```

Currying

EXAMPLE 11.68
Partial application with currying

A common operation, named for logician Haskell Curry, is to replace a multiargument function with a function that takes a single argument and returns a function that expects the remaining arguments:

```
(define curried-plus (lambda (a) (lambda (b) (+ a b))))
((curried-plus 3) 4)                        ⟹ 7
(define plus-3 (curried-plus 3))
(plus-3 4)                                  ⟹ 7
```

Among other things, currying gives us the ability to pass a "partially applied" function to a higher-order function:

```
(map (curried-plus 3) '(1 2 3))             ⟹ (4 5 6)
```

EXAMPLE 11.69
General-purpose curry function

It turns out that we can write a general-purpose function in Scheme that "curries" its (binary) function argument:

```
(define curry (lambda (f) (lambda (a) (lambda (b) (f a b)))))
(((curry +) 3) 4)                           ⟹ 7
(define curried-plus (curry +))
```

DESIGN & IMPLEMENTATION

11.6 Higher-order functions

If higher-order functions are so powerful and useful, why aren't they more common in imperative programming languages? There would appear to be at least two important answers. First, much of the power of first-class functions depends on the ability to create new functions on the fly, and for that we need a function *constructor*—something like Scheme's `lambda` or OCaml's `fun`. Though they appear in several recent languages, function constructors are a significant departure from the syntax and semantics of traditional imperative languages. Second, the ability to specify functions as return values, or to store them in variables (if the language has side effects), requires either that we eliminate function nesting (something that would again erode the ability of programs to create functions with desired behaviors on the fly) or that we give local variables unlimited extent, thereby increasing the cost of storage management.

EXAMPLE 11.70

Tuples as OCaml function arguments

ML and its descendants make it especially easy to define curried functions—a fact that we glossed over in Section 11.4. Consider the following function in OCaml:

```
# let plus (a, b) = a + b;;
val plus : int * int -> int = <fun>
```

The first line here, which we have shown beginning with a # prompt, is entered by the user. The second line is printed by the OCaml interpreter, and indicates the inferred type of `plus`. Though one may think of `plus` as a function of two arguments, the OCaml definition says that all functions take a *single* argument. What we have declared is a function that takes a two-element *tuple* as argument. To call `plus`, we juxtapose its name and the tuple that is its argument:

```
# plus (3, 4);;
- : int = 7
```

The parentheses here are not part of the function call syntax; they delimit the tuple `(3, 4)`. ■

EXAMPLE 11.71

Optional parentheses on singleton arguments

We can declare a single-argument function without parenthesizing its formal argument:

```
# let twice n = n + n;;
val twice = fn : int -> int
# twice 2;;
- : int = 4
```

We can add parentheses in either the declaration or the call if we want, but because there is no comma inside, no tuple is implied:

```
# let double (n) = n + n;;
val double : int -> int = <fun>
# twice (2);;
- : int = 4
# twice 2;;
- : int = 4
# double (2);;
- : int = 4
# double 2;;
- : int = 4
```

Ordinary parentheses can be placed around any expression in OCaml. ■

EXAMPLE 11.72

Simple curried function in OCaml

Now consider the definition of a curried function:

```
# let curried_plus a = fun b -> a + b;;
val curried_plus : int -> int -> int = <fun>
```

Here the type of curried_plus is the same as that of the built-in + in Example 11.23—namely int -> int -> int. This groups implicitly as int -> (int -> int). Where plus is a function mapping a pair (tuple) of integers to an integer, curried_plus is a function mapping an integer to a function that maps an integer to an integer:

```
# curried_plus 3;;
- : int -> int = <fun>

# plus 3;;
Error: This expression has type int but an expression was expected of
       type int * int
```

EXAMPLE 11.73
Shorthand notation for currying

To make it easier to declare functions like curried_plus, ML-family languages, OCaml among them, allow a sequence of operands in the formal parameter position of a function declaration:

```
# let curried_plus a b = a + b;;
val curried_plus : int -> int -> int = <fun>
```

This form is simply shorthand for the declaration in the previous example; it does not declare a function of two arguments. Curried_plus has a single formal parameter, a. Its return value is a function with formal parameter b that in turn returns a + b.

EXAMPLE 11.74
Building fold_left in OCaml

Using tuple notation, a naive, non-curried fold function might be declared as follows in OCaml:

```
# let rec fold (f, i, l) =
    match l with
    | [] -> i
    | h :: t -> fold (f, f (i, h), t);;
val fold : ('a * 'b -> 'b) * 'b * 'a list -> 'b = <fun>
```

A curried version might be declared as follows:

```
# let rec curried_fold f i l =
    match l with
    | [] -> i
    | h :: t -> curried_fold f (f (i, h)) t;;
val curried_fold : ('a * 'b -> 'a) -> 'a -> 'b list -> 'a = <fun>
```

Note the difference in the inferred types of the functions. The advantage of the curried version is its ability to accept a partial list of arguments:

```
# curried_fold plus;;
- : int -> int list -> int = <fun>
# curried_fold plus 0;;
- : int list -> int = <fun>
# curried_fold plus 0 [1; 2; 3; 4; 5];;
- : int = 15
```

To obtain the behavior of the built-in `fold_left`, we need to assume that the function `f` is also curried:

```
# let rec fold_left f i l =
    match l with
    | [] -> i
    | h :: t -> fold_left f (f i h) t;;
val fold_left : ('a -> 'b -> 'a) -> 'a -> 'b list -> 'a = <fun>
# fold_left curried_plus 0 [1;2;3;4;5];;
- : int = 15
```

Note again the difference in the inferred type of the functions. ■

It is of course possible to define `fold_left` by nesting occurrences of the explicit `fun` notation within the function's body. The shorthand notation, with juxtaposed arguments, however, is substantially more intuitive and convenient.

EXAMPLE 11.75
Currying in OCaml vs Scheme

Note also that OCaml's syntax for function calls—juxtaposition of function and argument—makes the use of a curried function more intuitive and convenient than it is in Scheme:

```
fold_left (+) 0 [1; 2; 3; 4; 5];          (* OCaml *)
(((curried-fold +) 0) '(1 2 3 4 5))       ; Scheme
```

■

11.7 Theoretical Foundations

EXAMPLE 11.76
Declarative (nonconstructive) function definition

Mathematically, a function is a single-valued mapping: it associates every element in one set (the *domain*) with (at most) one element in another set (the *range*). In conventional notation, we indicate the domain and range of, say, the square root function by writing

$$\text{sqrt} : \mathcal{R} \longrightarrow \mathcal{R}$$

We can also define functions using conventional set notation:

$$\text{sqrt} \equiv \left\{(x, y) \in \mathcal{R} \times \mathcal{R} \mid y > 0 \wedge x = y^2\right\}$$

Unfortunately, this notation is *nonconstructive*: it doesn't tell us how to *compute* square roots. Church designed the lambda calculus to address this limitation. ■

IN MORE DEPTH

Lambda calculus is a *constructive* notation for function definitions. We consider it in more detail on the companion site. Any computable function can be written as a lambda expression. Computation amounts to macro substitution of arguments into the function definition, followed by reduction to simplest form via simple and mechanical rewrite rules. The order in which these rules are applied captures the distinction between applicative and normal-order evaluation, as described in Section 6.6.2. Conventions on the use of certain simple functions (e.g., the identity function) allow selection, structures, and even arithmetic to be captured as lambda expressions. Recursion is captured through the notion of *fixed points.*

11.8 Functional Programming in Perspective

Side-effect-free programming is a very appealing idea. As discussed in Sections 6.1.2 and 6.3, side effects can make programs both hard to read and hard to compile. By contrast, the lack of side effects makes expressions *referentially transparent*—independent of evaluation order. Programmers and compilers of a purely functional language can employ *equational reasoning*, in which the equivalence of two expressions at any point in time implies their equivalence at all times. Equational reasoning in turn is highly appealing for parallel execution: In a purely functional language, the arguments to a function can safely be evaluated in parallel with each other. In a lazy functional language, they can be evaluated in parallel with (the beginning of) the function to which they are passed. We will consider these possibilities further in Section 13.4.5.

Unfortunately, there are common programming idioms in which the canonical side effect—assignment—plays a central role. Critics of functional programming often point to these idioms as evidence of the need for imperative language features. I/O is one example. We have seen (in Section 11.5) that sequential access to files can be modeled in a functional manner using streams. For graphics and random file access we have also seen that the monads of Haskell can cleanly isolate the invocation of actions from the bulk of the language, and allow the full power of equational reasoning to be applied to both the computation of values and the determination of the order in which I/O actions should occur.

Other commonly cited examples of "naturally imperative" idioms include

Initialization of complex structures: The heavy reliance on lists in the Lisp and ML families reflects the ease with which functions can build new lists out of the components of old lists. Other data structures—multidimensional arrays in particular—are much less easy to put together incrementally, particularly if the natural order in which to initialize the elements is not strictly row-major or column-major.

Summarization: Many programs include code that scans a large data structure or a large amount of input data, counting the occurrences of various items or patterns. The natural way to keep track of the counts is with a dictionary data structure in which one repeatedly updates the count associated with the most recently noticed key.

In-place mutation: In programs with very large data sets, one must economize as much as possible on memory usage, to maximize the amount of data that will fit in memory or the cache. Sorting programs, for example, need to sort in place, rather than copying elements to a new array or list. Matrix-based scientific programs, likewise, need to update values in place.

These last three idioms are examples of what has been called the *trivial update problem*. If the use of a functional language forces the underlying implementation to create a new copy of the entire data structure every time one of its elements must change, then the result will be very inefficient. In imperative programs, the problem is avoided by allowing an existing structure to be modified in place.

One can argue that while the trivial update problem causes trouble in Lisp and its relatives, it does not reflect an inherent weakness of functional programming per se. What is required for a solution is a combination of convenient notation—to access arbitrary elements of a complex structure—and an implementation that is able to determine when the old version of the structure will never be used again, so it can be updated in place instead of being copied.

Sisal, pH, and Single Assignment C (SAC) combine array types and iterative syntax with purely functional semantics. The iterative constructs are defined as syntactic sugar for tail-recursive functions. When nested, these constructs can easily be used to initialize a multidimensional array. The semantics of the language say that each iteration of the loop returns a new copy of the entire array. The compiler can easily verify, however, that the old copy is never used after the return, and can therefore arrange to perform all updates in place. Similar optimizations could be performed in the absence of the imperative syntax, but require somewhat more complex analysis. Cann reports that the Livermore Sisal compiler

DESIGN & IMPLEMENTATION

11.7 Side effects and compilation

As noted in Section 11.2, side-effect freedom has a strong conceptual appeal: it frees the programmer from concern over undocumented access to nonlocal variables, misordered updates, aliases, and dangling pointers. Side-effect freedom also has the potential, at least in theory, to allow the compiler to generate faster code: like aliases, side effects often preclude the caching of values in registers (Section 3.5.1) or the use of constant and copy propagation (Sections C-17.3 and C-17.4).

So what are the technical obstacles to generating fast code for functional programs? The trivial update problem is certainly a challenge, as is the cost of heap management for values with unlimited extent. Type checking imposes significant run-time costs in languages descended from Lisp, but not in those descended from ML. Memoization is expensive in Miranda and Haskell, though so-called *strictness analysis* may allow the compiler to eliminate it in cases where applicative order evaluation is provably equivalent. These challenges are all the subject of continuing research.

was able to eliminate 99 to 100 percent of all copy operations in standard numeric benchmarks [Can92]. Scholz reports performance for SAC competitive with that of carefully optimized modern Fortran programs [Sch03].

Significant strides in both the theory and practice of functional programming have been made in recent years. Wadler [Wad98b] argued in the late 1990s that the principal remaining obstacles to the widespread adoption of functional languages were social and commercial, not technical: most programmers have been trained in an imperative style; software libraries and development environments for functional programming are not yet as mature as those of their imperative cousins. Experience over the past decade appears to have borne out this characterization: with the development of better tools and a growing body of practical experience, functional languages have begun to see much wider use. Functional features have also begun to appear in such mainstream imperative languages as C#, Python, and Ruby.

✓ CHECK YOUR UNDERSTANDING

19. What is the difference between *normal-order* and *applicative-order* evaluation? What is *lazy* evaluation?
20. What is the difference between a function and a *special form* in Scheme?
21. What does it mean for a function to be *strict*?
22. What is *memoization*?
23. How can one accommodate I/O in a purely functional programming model?
24. What is a *higher-order* function (also known as a *functional form*)? Give three examples.
25. What is *currying*? What purpose does it serve in practical programs?
26. What is the *trivial update problem* in functional programming?
27. Summarize the arguments for and against side-effect-free programming.
28. Why do functional languages make such heavy use of lists?

11.9 Summary and Concluding Remarks

In this chapter we have focused on the functional model of computing. Where an imperative program computes principally through iteration and side effects (i.e., the modification of variables), a functional program computes principally through substitution of parameters into functions. We began by enumerating a list of key issues in functional programming, including first-class and higher-order functions, polymorphism, control flow and evaluation order, and support for list-based data. We then turned to a pair of concrete examples—the Scheme dialect of Lisp and the OCaml dialect of ML—to see how these issues may be addressed in a programming language. We also considered, more briefly, the lazy evaluation and monads found in Haskell.

For imperative programming languages, the underlying formal model is often taken to be a Turing machine. For functional languages, the model is the lambda calculus. Both models evolved in the mathematical community as a means of formalizing the notion of an effective procedure, as used in constructive proofs. Aside from hardware-imposed limits on arithmetic precision, disk and memory space, and so on, the full power of lambda calculus is available in functional languages. While a full treatment of the lambda calculus could easily consume another book, we provided an overview on the companion site. We considered rewrite rules, evaluation order, and the Church-Rosser theorem. We noted that conventions on the use of very simple notation provide the computational power of integer arithmetic, selection, recursion, and structured data types.

For practical reasons, many functional languages extend the lambda calculus with additional features, including assignment, I/O, and iteration. Lisp dialects, moreover, are *homoiconic*: programs look like ordinary data structures, and can be created, modified, and executed on the fly.

Lists feature prominently in most functional programs, largely because they can easily be built incrementally, without the need to allocate and then modify state as separate operations. Many functional languages provide other structured data types as well. In Sisal and Single Assignment C, an emphasis on iterative syntax, tail-recursive semantics, and high-performance compilers allows multidimensional array-based functional programs to achieve performance comparable to that of imperative programs.

11.10 Exercises

11.1 Is the `define` primitive of Scheme an imperative language feature? Why or why not?

11.2 It is possible to write programs in a purely functional subset of an imperative language such as C, but certain limitations of the language quickly become apparent. What features would need to be added to your favorite imperative language to make it genuinely useful as a functional language? (Hint: What does Scheme have that C lacks?)

11.3 Explain the connection between short-circuit Boolean expressions and normal-order evaluation. Why is `cond` a special form in Scheme, rather than a function?

11.4 Write a program in your favorite imperative language that has the same input and output as the Scheme program of Figure 11.1. Can you make any general observations about the usefulness of Scheme for symbolic computation, based on your experience?

11.5 Suppose we wish to remove adjacent duplicate elements from a list (e.g., after sorting). The following Scheme function accomplishes this goal:

```
(define unique
  (lambda (L)
    (cond
      ((null? L) L)
      ((null? (cdr L)) L)
      ((eqv? (car L) (car (cdr L))) (unique (cdr L)))
      (else (cons (car L) (unique (cdr L)))))))
```

Write a similar function that uses the imperative features of Scheme to modify `L` "in place," rather than building a new list. Compare your function to the code above in terms of brevity, conceptual clarity, and speed.

11.6 Write tail-recursive versions of the following:

(a)
```
;; compute integer log, base 2
;; (number of bits in binary representation)
;; works only for positive integers
(define log2
  (lambda (n)
    (if (= n 1) 1 (+ 1 (log2 (quotient n 2))))))
```

(b)
```
;; find minimum element in a list
(define min
  (lambda (l)
    (cond
      ((null? l) '())
      ((null? (cdr l)) (car l))
      (#t (let ((a (car l))
                (b (min (cdr l))))
            (if (< b a) b a))))))
```

11.7 Write purely functional Scheme functions to

(a) return all *rotations* of a given list. For example, `(rotate '(a b c d e))` should return `((a b c d e) (b c d e a) (c d e a b) (d e a b c) (e a b c d))` (in some order).

(b) return a list containing all elements of a given list that satisfy a given predicate. For example, `(filter (lambda (x) (< x 5)) '(3 9 5 8 2 4 7))` should return `(3 2 4)`.

11.8 Write a purely functional Scheme function that returns a list of all permutations of a given list. For example, given `(a b c)`, it should return `((a b c) (b a c) (b c a) (a c b) (c a b) (c b a))` (in some order).

11.9 Modify the Scheme program of Figure 11.1 or the OCaml program of Figure 11.3 to simulate an NFA (nondeterministic finite automaton), rather than a DFA. (The distinction between these automata is described in Section 2.2.1.) Since you cannot "guess" correctly in the face of a multivalued transition function, you will need either to use explicitly coded backtracking to search for an accepting series of moves (if there is one), or keep track of *all* possible states that the machine could be in at a given point in time.

11.10 Consider the problem of determining whether two trees have the same *fringe*: the same set of leaves in the same order, regardless of internal structure. An obvious way to solve this problem is to write a function `flatten` that takes a tree as argument and returns an ordered list of its leaves. Then we can say

```
(define same-fringe
  (lambda (T1 T2)
    (equal (flatten T1) (flatten T2))))
```

Write a straightforward version of `flatten` in Scheme. How efficient is `same-fringe` when the trees differ in their first few leaves? How would your answer differ in a language like Haskell, which uses lazy evaluation for all arguments? How hard is it to get Haskell's behavior in Scheme, using `delay` and `force`?

11.11 In Example 11.59 we showed how to implement interactive I/O in terms of the lazy evaluation of streams. Unfortunately, our code would not work as written, because Scheme uses applicative-order evaluation. We can make it work, however, with calls to `delay` and `force`.

Suppose we define `input` to be a function that returns an "istream"—a promise that when forced will yield a pair, the `cdr` of which is an istream:

```
(define input (lambda () (delay (cons (read) (input)))))
```

Now we can define the driver to expect an "ostream"—an empty list or a pair, the `cdr` of which is an ostream:

```
(define driver
  (lambda (s)
    (if (null? s) '()
        (display (car s))
        (driver (force (cdr s))))))
```

Note the use of `force`.

Show how to write the function `squares` so that it takes an istream as argument and returns an ostream. You should then be able to type `(driver (squares (input)))` and see appropriate behavior.

11.12 Write new versions of `cons`, `car`, and `cdr` that operate on streams. Using them, rewrite the code of the previous exercise to eliminate the calls to `delay` and `force`. Note that the stream version of `cons` will need to avoid evaluating its second argument; you will need to learn how to define macros (derived special forms) in Scheme.

11.13 Write the standard quicksort algorithm in Scheme, without using any imperative language features. Be careful to avoid the trivial update problem; your code should run in expected time *n* log *n*.

Rewrite your code using arrays (you will probably need to consult a Scheme manual for further information). Compare the running time and space requirements of your two sorts.

11.14 Write `insert` and `find` routines that manipulate binary search trees in Scheme (consult an algorithms text if you need more information). Explain why the trivial update problem does *not* impact the asymptotic performance of `insert`.

11.15 Write an LL(1) parser generator in purely functional Scheme. If you consult Figure 2.24, remember that you will need to use tail recursion in place of iteration. Assume that the input CFG consists of a list of lists, one per nonterminal in the grammar. The first element of each sublist should be the nonterminal; the remaining elements should be the right-hand sides of the productions for which that nonterminal is the left-hand side. You may assume that the sublist for the start symbol will be the first one in the list. If we use quoted strings to represent grammar symbols, the calculator grammar of Figure 2.16 would look like this:

```
'(("program"  ("stmt_list" "$$"))
  ("stmt_list" ("stmt" "stmt_list") ())
  ("stmt"   ("id" ":=" "expr") ("read" "id") ("write" "expr"))
  ("expr"   ("term" "term_tail"))
  ("term"   ("factor" "factor_tail"))
  ("term_tail" ("add_op" "term" "term_tail") ())
  ("factor_tail" ("mult_op" "factor" "FT") ())
  ("add_op" ("+") ("-"))
  ("mult_op" ("*") ("/"))
  ("factor"  ("id") ("number") ("(" "expr" ")")))
```

Your output should be a parse table that has this same format, except that every right-hand side is replaced by a *pair* (a 2-element list) whose first element is the predict set for the corresponding production, and whose second element is the right-hand side. For the calculator grammar, the table looks like this:

```
(("program" (("$$" "id" "read" "write") ("stmt_list" "$$")))
 ("stmt_list"
  (("id" "read" "write") ("stmt" "stmt_list"))
  (("$$") ()))
 ("stmt"
  (("id") ("id" ":=" "expr"))
  (("read") ("read" "id"))
  (("write") ("write" "expr")))
 ("expr" (("(" "id" "number") ("term" "term_tail")))
```

```
("term" (("(" "id" "number") ("factor" "factor_tail")))
("term_tail"
 (("+" "-") ("add_op" "term" "term_tail"))
 (("$$" ")" "id" "read" "write") ()))
("factor_tail"
 (("*" "/") ("mult_op" "factor" "factor_tail"))
 (("$$" ")" "+" "-" "id" "read" "write") ()))
("add_op" (("+") ("+")) (("-") ("-")))
("mult_op" (("*") ("*")) (("/") ("/")))
("factor"
 (("id") ("id"))
 (("number") ("number"))
 (("(") ("(" "expr" ")"))))
```

(Hint: You may want to define a `right_context` function that takes a nonterminal B as argument and returns a list of all pairs (A, β), where A is a nonterminal and β is a list of symbols, such that for some potentially different list of symbols α, $A \longrightarrow \alpha\ B\ \beta$. This function is useful for computing FOLLOW sets. You may also want to build a tail-recursive function that recomputes FIRST and FOLLOW sets until they converge. You will find it easier if you do not include ϵ in either set, but rather keep a separate estimate, for each nonterminal, of whether it may generate ϵ.)

11.16 Write an equality operator (call it =/) that works correctly on the `yearday` type of Example 11.38. (You may need to look up the rules that govern the occurrence of leap years.)

11.17 Create addition and subtraction functions for the celsius and fahrenheit temperature types introduced in Sidebar 11.3. To allow the two scales to be mixed, you should also define conversion functions `ct_of_ft : fahrenheit_temp -> celsius_temp` and `ft_of_ct : celsius_temp -> fahrenheit_temp`. Your conversions should round to the nearest degree (half degrees round up).

11.18 We can use encapsulation within functions to delay evaluation in OCaml:

```
type 'a delayed_list =
  Pair of 'a * 'a delayed_list
| Promise of (unit -> 'a * 'a delayed_list);;

let head = function
| Pair (h, r) -> h
| Promise (f) -> let (a, b) = f() in a;;

let rest = function
| Pair (h, r) -> r
| Promise (f) -> let (a, b) = f() in b;;
```

Now given

```
let rec next_int n = (n, Promise (fun() -> next_int (n + 1)));;
let naturals = Promise (fun() -> next_int (1));;
```

we have

```
head naturals;;                      ⟹ 1
head (rest naturals);;               ⟹ 2
head (rest (rest naturals));;        ⟹ 3
...
```

The delayed list `naturals` is effectively of unlimited length. It will be computed out only as far as actually needed. If a value is needed more than once, however, it will be recomputed every time. Show how to use pointers and assignment (Example 8.42) to memoize the values of a `delayed_list`, so that elements are computed only once.

11.19 Write an OCaml version of Example 11.67. Alternatively (or in addition), solve Exercises 11.5, 11.7, 11.8, 11.10, 11.13, 11.14, or 11.15 in OCaml.

11.20–11.23 In More Depth.

11.11 Explorations

11.24 Read the original self-definition of Lisp [MAE+65]. Compare it to a similar definition of Scheme [AS96, Chap. 4]. What is different? What has stayed the same? What is built into `apply` and `eval` in each definition? What do you think of the whole idea? Does a metacircular interpreter really define anything, or is it "circular reasoning"?

11.25 Read the Turing Award lecture of John Backus [Bac78], in which he argues for functional programming. How does his FP notation compare to the Lisp and ML language families?

11.26 Learn more about monads in Haskell. Pay particular attention to the definition of lists. Explain the relationship of the list monad to list comprehensions (Example 8.58), iterators, continuations (Section 6.2.2), and backtracking search.

11.27 Read ahead and learn about *transactional memory* (Section 13.4.4). Then read up on STM Haskell [HMPH05]. Explain how monads facilitate the serialization of updates to locations shared between threads.

11.28 We have seen that Lisp and ML include such imperative features as assignment and iteration. How important are these? What do languages like Haskell give up (conversely, what do they gain) by insisting on a purely functional programming style? In a similar vein, what do you think of attempts in several recent imperative languages (notably Python and C#—see Sidebar 11.6) to facilitate functional programming with function constructors and unlimited extent?

11.29 Investigate the compilation of functional programs. What special issues arise? What techniques are used to address them? Starting places for your search might include the compiler texts of Appel [App97], Wilhelm and Maurer [WM95], and Grune et al. [GBJ$^+$12].

11.30–11.32 In More Depth.

11.12 Bibliographic Notes

Lisp, the original functional programming language, dates from the work of McCarthy and his associates in the late 1950s. Bibliographic references for Erlang, Haskell, Lisp, Miranda, ML, OCaml, Scheme, Single Assignment C, and Sisal can be found in Appendix A. Historically important dialects of Lisp include Lisp 1.5 [MAE$^+$65], MacLisp [Moo78] (no relation to the Apple Macintosh), and Interlisp [TM81].

The book by Abelson and Sussman [AS96], long used for introductory programming classes at MIT and elsewhere, is a classic guide to fundamental programming concepts, and to functional programming in particular. Additional historical references can be found in the paper by Hudak [Hud89], which surveys the field from the point of view of Haskell.

The lambda calculus was introduced by Church in 1941 [Chu41]. A classic reference is the text of Curry and Feys [CF58]. Barendregt's book [Bar84] is a standard modern reference. Michaelson [Mic89] provides an accessible introduction to the formalism, together with a clear explanation of its relationship to Lisp and ML. Stansifer [Sta95, Sec. 7.6] provides a good informal discussion and correctness proof for the fixed-point combinator **Y** (see Exercise C-11.21).

John Backus, one of the original developers of Fortran, argued forcefully for a move to functional programming in his 1977 Turing Award lecture [Bac78]. His functional programming notation is known as FP. Peyton Jones [Pey87, Pey92], Wilhelm and Maurer [WM95, Chap. 3], Appel [App97, Chap. 15], and Grune et al. [GBJ$^+$12, Chap. 7] discuss the implementation of functional languages. Peyton Jones's paper on the "awkward squad" [Pey01] is widely considered the definitive introduction to monads in Haskell.

While Lisp dates from the early 1960s, it is only in recent years that functional languages have seen widespread use in large commercial systems. Wadler [Wad98a, Wad98b] describes the situation as of the late 1990s, when the tide began to turn. Descriptions of many subsequent projects can be found in the proceedings of the Commercial Users of Functional Programming workshop (*cufp.galois.com*), held annually since 2004. The *Journal of Functional Programming* also publishes a special category of articles on commercial use. Armstrong reports [Arm07] that the Ericsson AXD301, a telephone switching system comprising more than two million lines of Erlang code, has achieved an astonishing "nine nines" level of reliability—the equivalent of less than 32 ms of downtime per year.

12 Logic Languages

Having considered functional languages in some detail, we now turn to logic languages. The overlap between imperative and functional concepts in programming language design has led us to discuss the latter at numerous points throughout the text. We have had less occasion to remark on features of logic programming languages. Logic of course is used heavily in the design of digital circuits, and most programming languages provide a logical (Boolean) type and operators. Logic is also heavily used in the formal study of language semantics, specifically in *axiomatic* semantics.[1] In the 1970s, with the work of Alain Colmeraurer and Philippe Roussel of the University of Aix–Marseille in France and Robert Kowalski and associates at the University of Edinburgh in Scotland, researchers also began to employ the process of logical deduction as a general-purpose model of computing.

We introduce the basic concepts of logic programming in Section 12.1. We then survey the most widely used logic language, Prolog, in Section 12.2. We consider, in turn, the concepts of resolution and unification, support for lists and arithmetic, and the search-based execution model. After presenting an extended example based on the game of tic-tac-toe, we turn to the more advanced topics of imperative control flow and database manipulation.

Much as functional programming is based on the formalism of lambda calculus, Prolog and other logic languages are based on *first-order predicate calculus.* A brief introduction to this formalism appears in Section C-12.3 on the companion site. Where functional languages capture the full capabilities of the lambda calculus, however (within the limits, at least, of memory and other resources), logic languages do not capture the full power of predicate calculus. We consider the relevant limitations as part of a general evaluation of logic programming in Section 12.4.

---

1 Axiomatic semantics models each statement or expression in the language as a *predicate transformer*—an inference rule that takes a set of conditions known to be true initially and derives a new set of conditions guaranteed to be true after the construct has been evaluated. The study of formal semantics is beyond the scope of this book.

12.1 Logic Programming Concepts

Logic programming systems allow the programmer to state a collection of *axioms* from which theorems can be proven. The user of a logic program states a theorem, or *goal*, and the language implementation attempts to find a collection of axioms and inference steps (including choices of values for variables) that together imply the goal. Of the several existing logic languages, Prolog is by far the most widely used.

EXAMPLE 12.1
Horn clauses

In almost all logic languages, axioms are written in a standard form known as a *Horn clause*. A Horn clause consists of a *head*,[2] or *consequent* term H, and a *body* consisting of terms B_i:

$$H \leftarrow B_1, B_2, \ldots, B_n$$

The semantics of this statement are that when the B_i are all true, we can deduce that H is true as well. When reading aloud, we say "H, if $B_1, B_2, \ldots,$ and B_n." Horn clauses can be used to capture most, but not all, logical statements. (We return to the issue of completeness in Section C-12.3.) ■

EXAMPLE 12.2
Resolution

In order to derive new statements, a logic programming system combines existing statements, canceling like terms, through a process known as *resolution*. If we know that A and B imply C, for example, and that C implies D, we can deduce that A and B imply D:

$$\begin{array}{l} C \leftarrow A, B \\ D \leftarrow C \\ \hline D \leftarrow A, B \end{array}$$

In general, terms like A, B, C, and D may consist not only of constants ("Rochester is rainy") but also of *predicates* applied to *atoms* or to *variables*: rainy(Rochester), rainy(Seattle), rainy(X). ■

EXAMPLE 12.3
Unification

During resolution, free variables may acquire values through *unification* with expressions in matching terms, much as variables acquire types in ML (Section 7.2.4):

$$\begin{array}{l} \text{flowery}(X) \leftarrow \text{rainy}(X) \\ \text{rainy}(\text{Rochester}) \\ \hline \text{flowery}(\text{Rochester}) \end{array}$$

In the following section we consider Prolog in more detail. We return to formal logic, and to its relationship to Prolog, in Section C-12.3. ■

---

2 Note that the word "head" is used for two different things in Prolog: the head of a Horn clause and the head of a list. The distinction between these is usually clear from context.

12.2 Prolog

Much as an imperative or functional language interpreter evaluates expressions in the context of a referencing environment in which various functions and constants have been defined, a Prolog interpreter runs in the context of a *database* of *clauses* (Horn clauses) that are assumed to be true.[3] Each clause is composed of *terms*, which may be constants, variables, or *structures*. A constant is either an atom or a number. A structure can be thought of as either a logical predicate or a data structure.

EXAMPLE 12.4
Atoms, variables, scope, and type

Atoms in Prolog are similar to symbols in Lisp. Lexically, an atom looks like an identifier beginning with a lowercase letter, a sequence of "punctuation" characters, or a quoted character string:

```
foo        my_Const     +      'Hi, Mom'
```

Numbers resemble the integers and floating-point constants of other programming languages. A variable looks like an identifier beginning with an uppercase letter:

```
Foo        My_var       X
```

Variables can be *instantiated* to (i.e., can take on) arbitrary values at run time as a result of unification. The scope of every variable is limited to the clause in which it appears. There are no declarations. Type checking is dynamic: it occurs only when a program attempts to use a value as an operand at run time.

EXAMPLE 12.5
Structures and predicates

Structures consist of an atom called the *functor* and a list of arguments:

```
rainy(rochester)
teaches(scott, cs254)
bin_tree(foo, bin_tree(bar, glarch))
```

Prolog requires the opening parenthesis to come immediately after the functor, with no intervening space. Arguments can be arbitrary terms: constants, variables, or (nested) structures. Internally, a typical Prolog implementation will represent each structure as a tree of Lisp-like `cons` cells. Conceptually, the programmer may prefer to think of certain structures (e.g., `rainy`) as logical predicates. We use the term "predicate" to refer to the combination of a functor and an "arity" (number of arguments). The predicate `rainy` has arity 1. The predicate `teaches` has arity 2.

EXAMPLE 12.6
Facts and rules

The clauses in a Prolog database can be classified as *facts* or *rules*, each of which ends with a period. A fact is a Horn clause without a right-hand side. It looks like a single term (the implication symbol is implicit):

---

3 In fact, for any given program, the database is assumed to characterize *everything* that is true. As we shall see in Section 12.4.3, this *closed world assumption* imposes certain limits on the expressiveness of the language.

```
rainy(rochester).
```

A rule has a right-hand side:

```
snowy(X) :- rainy(X), cold(X).
```

The token `:-` is the implication symbol; the comma indicates "and." Variables that appear in the head of a Horn clause are universally quantified: for all `X`, `X` is snowy if `X` is rainy and `X` is cold. ■

It is also possible to write a clause with an empty left-hand side. Such a clause is called a *query*, or a *goal*. Queries do not appear in Prolog programs. Rather, one builds a database of facts and rules and then initiates execution by giving the Prolog interpreter (or the compiled Prolog program) a query to be answered (i.e., a goal to be proven).

EXAMPLE 12.7
Queries

In most implementations of Prolog, queries are entered with a special `?-` version of the implication symbol. If we were to type the following:

```
rainy(seattle).
rainy(rochester).
?- rainy(C).
```

the Prolog interpreter would respond with

```
C = seattle
```

Of course, `C = rochester` would also be a valid answer, but Prolog will find `seattle` first, because it comes first in the database. (Dependence on ordering is one of the ways in which Prolog departs from pure logic; we discuss this issue further in Section 12.4.) If we want to find all possible solutions, we can ask the interpreter to continue by typing a semicolon:

```
C = seattle ;
C = rochester.
```

If there had been another possibility, the interpreter would have left off the final period and given us the opportunity to type another semicolon. Given

```
rainy(seattle).
rainy(rochester).
cold(rochester).
snowy(X) :- rainy(X), cold(X).
```

the query

```
?- snowy(C).
```

will yield only one solution. ■

12.2.1 Resolution and Unification

The *resolution principle*, due to Robinson [Rob65], says that if C_1 and C_2 are Horn clauses and the head of C_1 matches one of the terms in the body of C_2, then we can replace the term in C_2 with the body of C_1. Consider the following example.

EXAMPLE 12.8
Resolution in Prolog

```
takes(jane_doe, his201).
takes(jane_doe, cs254).
takes(ajit_chandra, art302).
takes(ajit_chandra, cs254).
classmates(X, Y) :- takes(X, Z), takes(Y, Z).
```

If we let `X` be `jane_doe` and `Z` be `cs254`, we can replace the first term on the right-hand side of the last clause with the (empty) body of the second clause, yielding the new rule

```
classmates(jane_doe, Y) :- takes(Y, cs254).
```

In other words, `Y` is a classmate of `jane_doe` if `Y` takes `cs254`.

Note that the last rule has a variable (`Z`) on the right-hand side that does not appear in the head. Such variables are existentially quantified: for all `X` and `Y`, `X` and `Y` are classmates if there exists a class `Z` that they both take.

The pattern-matching process used to associate `X` with `jane_doe` and `Z` with `cs254` is known as *unification*. Variables that are given values as a result of unification are said to be *instantiated*.

The unification rules for Prolog state that

- A constant unifies only with itself.
- Two structures unify if and only if they have the same functor and the same arity, and the corresponding arguments unify recursively.
- A variable unifies with anything. If the other thing has a value, then the variable is instantiated. If the other thing is an uninstantiated variable, then the two variables are associated in such a way that if either is given a value later, that value will be shared by both.

EXAMPLE 12.9
Unification in Prolog and ML

Unification of structures in Prolog is very much akin to ML's unification of the types of formal and actual parameters. A formal parameter of type `int * 'b list`, for example, will unify with an actual parameter of type `'a * real list` in ML by instantiating `'a` to `int` and `'b` to `real`.

EXAMPLE 12.10
Equality and unification

Equality in Prolog is defined in terms of "unifiability." The goal `=(A, B)` succeeds if and only if `A` and `B` can be unified. For the sake of convenience, the goal may be written as `A = B`; the infix notation is simply syntactic sugar. In keeping with the rules above, we have

```
?- a = a.
true.              % constant unifies with itself
?- a = b.
false.             % but not with another constant
?- foo(a, b) = foo(a, b).
true.              % structures are recursively identical
?- X = a.
X = a.             % variable unifies with constant
?- foo(a, b) = foo(X, b).
X = a.             % arguments must unify
```

EXAMPLE 12.11
Unification without instantiation

It is possible for two variables to be unified without instantiating them. If we type

```
?- A = B.
```

the interpreter will simply respond

```
A = B.
```

If, however, we type

```
?- A = B, A = a, B = Y.
```

(unifying A and B before binding a to A) the interpreter will linearize the string of unifications and make it clear that all three variables are equal to a:

```
A = B, B = Y, Y = a.
```

In a similar vein, suppose we are given the following rules:

```
takes_lab(S) :- takes(S, C), has_lab(C).
has_lab(D) :- meets_in(D, R), is_lab(R).
```

(S takes a lab class if S takes C and C is a lab class. Moreover D is a lab class if D meets in room R and R is a lab.) An attempt to resolve these rules will unify the head of the second with the second term in the body of the first, causing C and D to be unified, even though neither is instantiated. ■

12.2.2 Lists

EXAMPLE 12.12
List notation in Prolog

Like equality checking, list manipulation is a sufficiently common operation in Prolog to warrant its own notation. The construct [a, b, c] is syntactic sugar for the structure .(a, .(b, .(c, []))), where [] is the empty list and . is a built-in cons-like predicate. With minor syntactic differences (parentheses v. brackets; commas v. semicolons), this notation should be familiar to users of ML or Lisp. Prolog adds an extra convenience, however—an optional vertical bar that delimits the "tail" of the list. Using this notation, [a, b, c] could be expressed as [a | [b, c]], [a, b | [c]], or [a, b, c | []]. The vertical-bar notation is particularly handy when the tail of the list is a variable:

```
member(X, [X | _]).
member(X, [_ | T]) :- member(X, T).

sorted([]).           % empty list is sorted
sorted([_]).          % singleton is sorted
sorted([A, B | T]) :- A =< B, sorted([B | T]).
    % compound list is sorted if first two elements are in order and
    % remainder of list (after first element) is sorted
```

Here =< is a built-in predicate that operates on numbers. The underscore is a placeholder for a variable that is not needed anywhere else in the clause. Note that [a, b | c] is the *improper* list .(a, .(b, c)). The sequence of tokens [a | b, c] is syntactically invalid.

EXAMPLE 12.13
Functions, predicates, and two-way rules

One of the interesting things about Prolog resolution is that it does not in general distinguish between "input" and "output" arguments (there are certain exceptions, such as the is predicate described in the following subsection). Thus, given

```
append([], A, A).
append([H | T], A, [H | L]) :- append(T, A, L).
```

We can type

```
?- append([a, b, c], [d, e], L).
L = [a, b, c, d, e].
?- append(X, [d, e], [a, b, c, d, e]).
X = [a, b, c] ;
false.
?- append([a, b, c], Y, [a, b, c, d, e]).
Y = [d, e].
```

This example highlights the difference between functions and Prolog predicates. The former have a clear notion of inputs (arguments) and outputs (results); the latter do not. In an imperative or functional language we apply functions to arguments to generate results. In a logic language we search for values for which a predicate is true. (Not all logic languages are equally flexible. Mercury, for example, requires the programmer to specify in or out modes on arguments. These allow the compiler to generate substantially faster code.) Note that when the interpreter prints its response to our second query, it is not yet certain whether additional solutions might exist. Only after we enter a semicolon does it invest the effort to determine that there are none.

12.2.3 Arithmetic

EXAMPLE 12.14
Arithmetic and the is predicate

The usual arithmetic operators are available in Prolog, but they play the role of predicates, not of functions. Thus +(2, 3), which may also be written 2 + 3, is a two-argument structure, not a function call. In particular, it will not unify with 5:

```
?- (2 + 3) = 5.
false.
```

To handle arithmetic, Prolog provides a built-in predicate, `is`, that unifies its first argument with the arithmetic value of its second argument:

```
?- is(X, 1+2).
X = 3.
?- X is 1+2.
X = 3.                      % infix is also ok
?- 1+2 is 4-1.
false.                      % 1st argument (1+2) is already instantiated
?- X is Y.
ERROR                       % 2nd argument (Y) must already be instantiated
?- Y is 1+2, X is Y.
Y = X, X = 3.               % Y is instantiated before it is needed
```

12.2.4 Search/Execution Order

So how does Prolog go about answering a query (satisfying a goal)? What it needs is a sequence of resolution steps that will build the goal out of clauses in the database, or a proof that no such sequence exists. In the realm of formal logic, one can imagine two principal search strategies:

- Start with existing clauses and work forward, attempting to derive the goal. This strategy is known as *forward chaining.*
- Start with the goal and work backward, attempting to "unresolve" it into a set of preexisting clauses. This strategy is known as *backward chaining.*

If the number of existing rules is very large, but the number of facts is small, it is possible for forward chaining to discover a solution more quickly than backward chaining. In most circumstances, however, backward chaining turns out to be more efficient. Prolog is defined to use backward chaining.

EXAMPLE 12.15 Search tree exploration

Because resolution is associative and commutative (Exercise 12.5), a backward-chaining theorem prover can limit its search to sequences of resolutions in which terms on the right-hand side of a clause are unified with the heads of other clauses one by one in some particular order (e.g., left to right). The resulting search can be described in terms of a tree of subgoals, as shown in Figure 12.1. The Prolog interpreter (or program) explores this tree depth first, from left to right. It starts at the beginning of the database, searching for a rule *R* whose head can be unified with the top-level goal. It then considers the terms in the body of *R* as subgoals, and attempts to satisfy them, recursively, left to right. If at any point a subgoal fails (cannot be satisfied), the interpreter returns to the previous subgoal and attempts to satisfy it in a different way (i.e., to unify it with the head of a different clause).

```
rainy(seattle).
rainy(rochester).
cold(rochester).
snowy(X) :- rainy(X), cold(X).
```

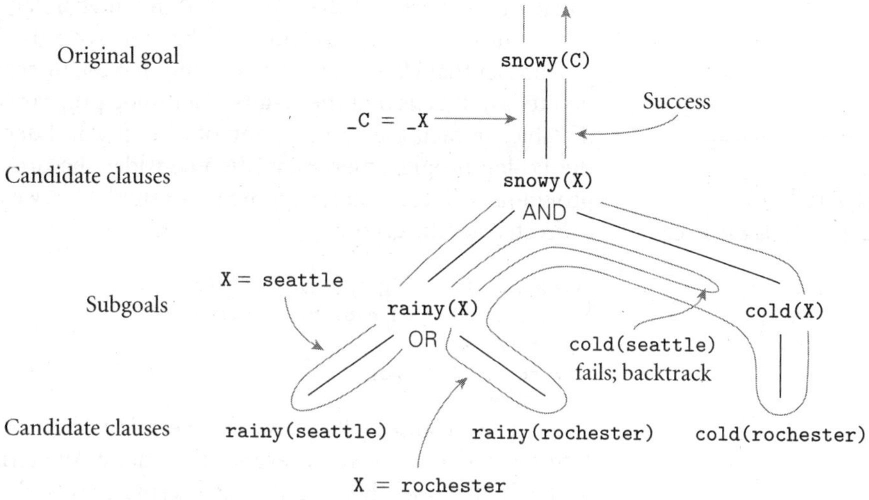

Figure 12.1 **Backtracking search in Prolog.** The tree of potential resolutions consists of alternating AND and OR levels. An AND level consists of subgoals from the right-hand side of a rule, all of which must be satisfied. An OR level consists of alternative database clauses whose head will unify with the subgoal above; one of these must be satisfied. The notation `_C = _X` is meant to indicate that while both `C` and `X` are uninstantiated, they have been associated with one another in such a way that if either receives a value in the future it will be shared by both.

EXAMPLE 12.16
Backtracking and instantiation

The process of returning to previous goals is known as *backtracking*. It strongly resembles the control flow of generators in Icon (Section C-6.5.4). Whenever a unification operation is "undone" in order to pursue a different path through the search tree, variables that were given values or associated with one another as a result of that unification are returned to their uninstantiated or unassociated state. In Figure 12.1, for example, the binding of `X` to `seattle` is broken when we backtrack to the `rainy(X)` subgoal. The effect is similar to the breaking of bindings between actual and formal parameters in an imperative programming language, except that Prolog couches the bindings in terms of unification rather than subroutine calls. ■

Space management for backtracking search in Prolog usually follows the single-stack implementation of iterators described in Section C-9.5.3. The interpreter pushes a frame onto its stack every time it begins to pursue a new subgoal *G*. If *G* fails, the frame is popped from the stack and the interpreter begins to backtrack. If *G* succeeds, control returns to the "caller" (the parent in the search tree), but *G*'s frame remains on the stack. Later subgoals will be given space *above* this dormant frame. If subsequent backtracking causes the interpreter to search for alternative ways of satisfying *G*, control will be able to resume where it last left off. Note that *G* will not fail unless all of its subgoals (and all of its siblings to the right in the search tree) have also failed, implying that there is nothing above *G*'s frame in the stack. At the top level of the interpreter, a semicolon typed by the user is treated the same as failure of the most recently satisfied subgoal.

The fact that clauses are ordered, and that the interpreter considers them from first to last, means that the results of a Prolog program are deterministic and predictable. In fact, the combination of ordering and depth-first search means that the Prolog programmer must often consider the order to ensure that recursive programs will terminate. Suppose for example that we have a database describing a directed acyclic graph:

EXAMPLE 12.17
Order of rule evaluation

```
edge(a, b).  edge(b, c).  edge(c, d).
edge(d, e).  edge(b, e).  edge(d, f).
path(X, X).
path(X, Y) :- edge(Z, Y), path(X, Z).
```

The last two clauses tell us how to determine whether there is a path from node `X` to node `Y`. If we were to reverse the order of the terms on the right-hand side of the final clause, then the Prolog interpreter would search for a node `Z` that is reachable from `X` before checking to see whether there is an edge from `Z` to `Y`. The program would still work, but it would not be as efficient. ■

EXAMPLE 12.18
Infinite regression

Now consider what would happen if in addition we were to reverse the order of the last two clauses:

```
path(X, Y) :- path(X, Z), edge(Z, Y).
path(X, X).
```

From a logical point of view, our database still defines the same relationships. A Prolog interpreter, however, will no longer be able to find answers. Even a simple query like `?- path(a, a)` will never terminate. To see why, consider Figure 12.2. The interpreter first unifies `path(a, a)` with the left-hand side of `path(X, Y) :- path(X, Z), edge(Z, Y)`. It then considers the goals on the right-hand side, the first of which (`path(X, Z)`), unifies with the left-hand side of the very same rule, leading to an infinite regression. In effect, the Prolog interpreter gets lost in an infinite branch of the search tree, and never discovers finite branches to the right. We could avoid this problem by exploring the tree in breadth-first order, but that strategy was rejected by Prolog's designers because of its expense: it can require substantially more space, and does not lend itself to a stack-based implementation. ■

12.2.5 Extended Example: Tic-Tac-Toe

EXAMPLE 12.19
Tic-tac-toe in Prolog

In the previous subsection we saw how the order of clauses in the Prolog database, and the order of terms within a right-hand side, can affect both the efficiency of

```
edge(a, b). edge(b, c). edge(c, d).
edge(d, e). edge(b, e). edge(d, f).
path(X, Y) :- path(X, Z), edge(Z, Y).
path(X, X).
```

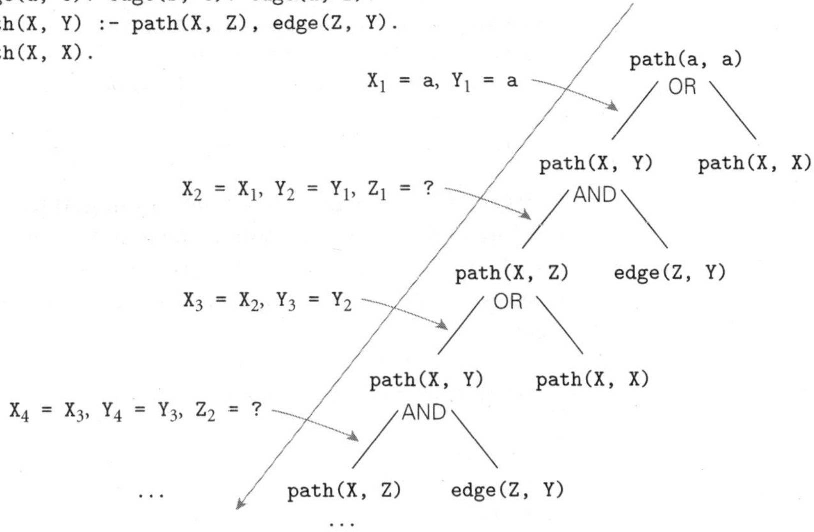

Figure 12.2 **Infinite regression in Prolog.** In this figure even a simple query like `?- path(a, a)` will never terminate: the interpreter will never find the trivial branch.

a Prolog program and its ability to terminate. Ordering also allows the Prolog programmer to indicate that certain resolutions are *preferred*, and should be considered before other, "fallback" options. Consider, for example, the problem of making a move in tic-tac-toe. (Tic-tac-toe is a game played on a 3×3 grid of squares. Two players, `X` and `O`, take turns placing markers in empty squares. A player wins if he or she places three markers in a row, horizontally, vertically, or diagonally.)

Let us number the squares from 1 to 9 in row-major order. Further, let us use the Prolog fact `x(n)` to indicate that player `X` has placed a marker in square n, and `o(m)` to indicate that player `O` has placed a marker in square m. For simplicity, let us assume that the computer is player `X`, and that it is `X`'s turn to move. We should like to be able to issue a query `?- move(A)` that will cause the Prolog interpreter to choose a good square `A` for the computer to occupy next.

Clearly we need to be able to tell whether three given squares lie in a row. One way to express this is:

```
ordered_line(1, 2, 3).    ordered_line(4, 5, 6).
ordered_line(7, 8, 9).    ordered_line(1, 4, 7).
ordered_line(2, 5, 8).    ordered_line(3, 6, 9).
ordered_line(1, 5, 9).    ordered_line(3, 5, 7).
```

```
line(A, B, C) :- ordered_line(A, B, C).
line(A, B, C) :- ordered_line(A, C, B).
line(A, B, C) :- ordered_line(B, A, C).
line(A, B, C) :- ordered_line(B, C, A).
line(A, B, C) :- ordered_line(C, A, B).
line(A, B, C) :- ordered_line(C, B, A).
```

It is easy to prove that there is no winning strategy for tic-tac-toe: either player can force a draw. Let us assume, however, that our program is playing against a less-than-perfect opponent. Our task then is never to lose, and to maximize our chances of winning if our opponent makes a mistake. The following rules work well:

```
move(A) :- good(A), empty(A).

full(A) :- x(A).
full(A) :- o(A).
empty(A) :- \+(full(A)).

% strategy:
good(A) :- win(A).            good(A) :- block_win(A).
good(A) :- split(A).          good(A) :- strong_build(A).
good(A) :- weak_build(A).
```

The initial rule indicates that we can satisfy the goal `move(A)` by choosing a good, empty square. The \+ is a built-in predicate that succeeds if its argument (a goal) cannot be proven; we discuss it further in Section 12.2.6. Square `n` is empty if we cannot prove it is full; that is, if neither `x(n)` nor `o(n)` is in the database.

The key to strategy lies in the ordering of the last five rules. Our first choice is to win:

```
win(A) :- x(B), x(C), line(A, B, C).
```

Our second choice is to prevent our opponent from winning:

```
block_win(A) :- o(B), o(C), line(A, B, C).
```

Our third choice is to create a "split"—a situation in which our opponent cannot prevent us from winning on the next move (see Figure 12.3):

```
split(A) :- x(B), x(C), different(B, C),
    line(A, B, D), line(A, C, E), empty(D), empty(E).
same(A, A).
different(A, B) :- \+(same(A, B)).
```

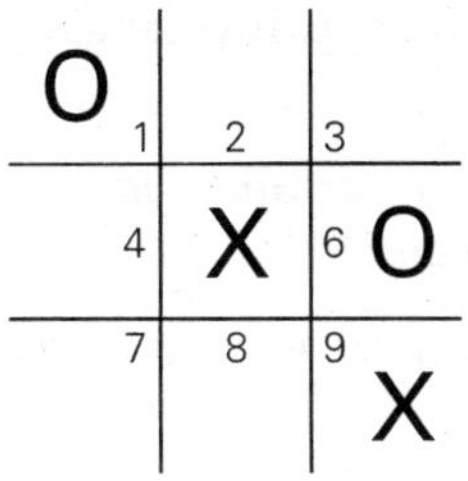

Figure 12.3 A "split" in tac-tac-toe. If X takes the bottom center square (square 8), no future move by O will be able to stop X from winning the game—O cannot block both the 2–5–8 line and the 7–8–9 line.

Here we have again relied on the built-in predicate \+.

Our fourth choice is to build toward three in a row (i.e., to get two in a row) in such a way that the obvious blocking move won't allow our opponent to build toward three in a row:

```
strong_build(A) :- x(B), line(A, B, C), empty(C), \+(risky(C)).
risky(C) :- o(D), line(C, D, E), empty(E).
```

Barring that, our fifth choice is to build toward three in a row in such a way that the obvious blocking move won't give our opponent a split:

```
weak_build(A) :- x(B), line(A, B, C), empty(C), \+(double_risky(C)).
double_risky(C) :- o(D), o(E), different(D, E), line(C, D, F),
    line(C, E, G), empty(F), empty(G).
```

If none of these goals can be satisfied, our final, default choice is to pick an unoccupied square, giving priority to the center, the corners, and the sides in that order:

```
good(5).
good(1).  good(3).  good(7).  good(9).
good(2).  good(4).  good(6).  good(8).
```

✓ CHECK YOUR UNDERSTANDING

1. What mathematical formalism underlies logic programming?
2. What is a *Horn clause*?
3. Briefly describe the process of *resolution* in logic programming.
4. What is a *unification*? Why is it important in logic programming?
5. What are *clauses*, *terms*, and *structures* in Prolog? What are *facts*, *rules*, and *queries*?

6. Explain how Prolog differs from imperative languages in its handling of arithmetic.

7. Describe the difference between *forward chaining* and *backward chaining*. Which is used in Prolog by default?

8. Describe the Prolog search strategy. Discuss *backtracking* and the *instantiation* of variables.

12.2.6 Imperative Control Flow

We have seen that the ordering of clauses and of terms in Prolog is significant, with ramifications for efficiency, termination, and choice among alternatives. In addition to simple ordering, Prolog provides the programmer with several explicit control-flow features. The most important of these features is known as the *cut*.

The cut is a zero-argument predicate written as an exclamation point: `!`. As a subgoal it always succeeds, but with a crucial side effect: it commits the interpreter to whatever choices have been made since unifying the parent goal with the left-hand side of the current rule, including the choice of that unification itself. For example, recall our definition of list membership:

EXAMPLE 12.20
The cut

```
member(X, [X | _]).
member(X, [_ | T]) :- member(X, T).
```

If a given atom `a` appears in list `L` *n* times, then the goal `?- member(a, L)` can succeed *n* times. These "extra" successes may not always be appropriate. They can lead to wasted computation, particularly for long lists, when `member` is followed by a goal that may fail:

```
prime_candidate(X) :- member(X, Candidates), prime(X).
```

Suppose that `prime(X)` is expensive to compute. To determine whether `a` is a prime candidate, we first check to see whether it is a member of the `Candidates` list, and then check to see whether it is prime. If `prime(a)` fails, Prolog will backtrack and attempt to satisfy `member(a, Candidates)` again. If `a` is in the `Candidates` list more than once, then the subgoal will succeed again, leading to reconsideration of the `prime(a)` subgoal, even though that subgoal is doomed to fail. We can save substantial time by cutting off all further searches for `a` after the first is found:

```
member(X, [X | _]) :- !.
member(X, [_ | T]) :- member(X, T).
```

The cut on the right-hand side of the first rule says that if X is the head of L, we should not attempt to unify member(X, L) with the left-hand side of the second rule; the cut commits us to the first rule.

EXAMPLE 12.21
\+ and its implementation

An alternative way to ensure that member(X, L) succeeds no more than once is to embed a use of \+ in the second clause:

```
member(X, [X | _]).
member(X, [H | T]) :- X \= H, member(X, T).
```

Here X \= H means X and H will not unify; that is, \+(X = H). (In some Prolog dialects, \+ is written not. This name suggests an interpretation that may be somewhat misleading; we discuss the issue in Section 12.4.3.) Our new version of member will display the same high-level behavior as before, but will be slightly less efficient: now the interpreter will actually consider the second rule, abandoning it only after (re)unifying X with H and reversing the sense of the test.

It turns out that \+ is actually implemented by a combination of the cut and two other built-in predicates, call and fail:

```
\+(P) :- call(P), !, fail.
\+(P).
```

The call predicate takes a term as argument and attempts to satisfy it as a goal (terms are first-class values in Prolog). The fail predicate always fails.

In principle, it is possible to replace all uses of the cut with uses of \+—to confine the cut to the implementation of \+. Doing so often makes a program easier to read. As we have seen, however, it often makes it less efficient. In some cases, explicit use of the cut may actually make a program *easier* to read. Consider our tic-tac-toe example. If we type semicolons at the program, it will continue to generate a series of increasingly poor moves from the same board position, even though we only want the first move. We can cut off consideration of the others by using the cut:

EXAMPLE 12.22
Pruning unwanted answers with the cut

```
move(A) :- good(A), empty(A), !.
```

To achieve the same effect with \+ we would have to do more major surgery (Exercise 12.8).

EXAMPLE 12.23
Using the cut for selection

In general, the cut can be used whenever we want the effect of if... then ... else:

```
statement :- condition, !, then_part.
statement :- else_part.
```

EXAMPLE 12.24
Looping with fail

The fail predicate can be used in conjunction with a "generator" to implement a loop. We have already seen (in Example 12.13) how to effect a generator by driving a set of rules "backward." Recall our definition of append:

```
append([], A, A).
append([H | T], A, [H | L]) :- append(T, A, L).
```

If we use write append(A, B, L), where L is instantiated but A and B are not, the interpreter will find an A and B for which the predicate is true. If backtracking forces it to return, the interpreter will look for *another* A and B; append will *generate* pairs on demand. (There is a strong analogy here to the generators of Icon, discussed in Section C-6.5.4.) Thus, to enumerate the ways in which a list can be partitioned into pairs, we can follow a use of append with fail:

```
print_partitions(L) :- append(A, B, L),
                       write(A), write(' '), write(B), nl,
                       fail.
```

The nl predicate prints a newline character. The query print_partitions([a, b, c]) produces the following output:

```
[] [a, b, c]
[a] [b, c]
[a, b] [c]
[a, b, c] []
false.
```

If we don't want the overall predicate to fail, we can add a final rule:

```
print_partitions(_).
```

Assuming this rule appears last, it will succeed after the output has appeared, and the interpreter will finish with "true." ■

EXAMPLE 12.25

Looping with an unbounded generator

In some cases, we may have a generator that produces an unbounded sequence of values. The following, for example, generates all of the natural numbers:

```
natural(1).
natural(N) :- natural(M), N is M+1.
```

We can use this generator in conjunction with a "test-cut" combination to iterate over the first *n* numbers:

```
my_loop(N) :- natural(I),
              write(I), nl,         % loop body (nl prints a newline)
              I = N, !.
```

So long as I is less than N, the equality (unification) predicate will fail and backtracking will pursue another alternative for natural. If I = N succeeds, however, then the cut will be executed, committing us to the current (final) choice of I, and successfully terminating the loop. ■

This programming idiom—an unbounded generator with a test-cut terminator—is known as *generate-and-test*. Like the iterative constructs of Scheme (Section 11.3.4), it is generally used in conjunction with side effects. One such side effect, clearly, is I/O. Another is modification of the program database.

Prolog provides a variety of I/O features. In addition to `write` and `nl`, which print to the current output file, the `read` predicate can be used to read terms from the current input file. Individual characters are read and written with `get` and `put`. Input and output can be redirected to different files using `see` and `tell`. Finally, the built-in predicates `consult` and `reconsult` can be used to read database clauses from a file, so they don't have to be typed into the interpreter by hand. (Some interpreters *require* this, allowing only queries to be entered interactively.)

EXAMPLE 12.26
Character input with `get`

The predicate `get` attempts to unify its argument with the next *printable* character of input, skipping over ASCII characters with codes below 32.[4] In effect, it behaves as if it were implemented in terms of the simpler predicates `get0` and `repeat`:

```
get(X) :- repeat, get0(X), X >= 32, !.
```

The `get0` predicate attempts to unify its argument with the single next character of input, regardless of value and, like `get`, cannot be resatisfied during backtracking. The `repeat` predicate, by contrast, can succeed an arbitrary number of times; it behaves as if it were implemented with the following pair of rules:

```
repeat.
repeat :- repeat.
```

Within the above definition of `get`, backtracking will return to `repeat` as often as needed to produce a printable character (one with ASCII code at least 32). In general, `repeat` allows us to turn any predicate with side effects into a generator.

12.2.7 Database Manipulation

EXAMPLE 12.27
Prolog programs as data

Clauses in Prolog are simply collections of terms, connected by the built-in predicates `:-` and `,`, both of which can be written in either infix or prefix form:

```
rainy(rochester).                 \
rainy(seattle).                    \   ≡ ','(rainy(rochester),
cold(rochester).                   /         ','(rainy(seattle),
snowy(X) :- rainy(X), cold(X).    /              ','(cold(rochester),
                                                     :-(snowy(X), ','(rainy(X),
                                                         cold(X))))))
```

4 Surprisingly, the ISO Prolog standard does not cover Unicode conformance.

Here the single quotes around the prefix commas serve to distinguish them from the commas that separate the arguments of a predicate.

EXAMPLE 12.28
Modifying the Prolog database

The structural nature of clauses and database contents implies that Prolog, like Scheme, is *homoiconic*: it can represent itself. It can also modify itself. A running Prolog program can add clauses to its database with the built-in predicate assert, or remove them with retract:

```
?- rainy(X).
X = seattle ;
X = rochester.
?- assert(rainy(syracuse)).
true.
?- rainy(X).
X = seattle ;
X = rochester ;
X = syracuse.
?- retract(rainy(rochester)).
true.
?- rainy(X).
X = seattle ;
X = syracuse.
```

There is also a retractall predicate that removes all matching clauses from the database.

EXAMPLE 12.29
Tic-tac-toe (full game)

Figure 12.4 contains a complete Prolog program for tic-tac-toe. It uses assert, retractall, the cut, fail, repeat, and write to play an entire game. Moves are added to the database with assert. They are cleared with retractall at the beginning of each game. This way the user can play multiple games without restarting the interpreter.

DESIGN & IMPLEMENTATION

12.1 Homoiconic languages

As we have noted, both Lisp/Scheme and Prolog are *homoiconic*. A few other languages, notably Snobol, Forth, and Tcl, share this property. What is its significance? For most programs the answer is: not much. So long as we write the sorts of programs that we'd write in other languages, the fact that programs and data look the same is really just a curiosity. It becomes something more if we are interested in *metacomputing*—the creation of programs that create or manipulate other programs, or that extend themselves. Metacomputing requires, at the least, that we have true first-class functions in the strict sense of the term—that is, that we be able to generate new functions whose behavior is determined dynamically. A homoiconic language can simplify metacomputing by eliminating the need to translate between internal (data structure) and external (syntactic) representations of programs or program extensions.

```
ordered_line(1, 2, 3).  ordered_line(4, 5, 6).  ordered_line(7, 8, 9).
ordered_line(1, 4, 7).  ordered_line(2, 5, 8).  ordered_line(3, 6, 9).
ordered_line(1, 5, 9).  ordered_line(3, 5, 7).
line(A, B, C) :- ordered_line(A, B, C).  line(A, B, C) :- ordered_line(A, C, B).
line(A, B, C) :- ordered_line(B, A, C).  line(A, B, C) :- ordered_line(B, C, A).
line(A, B, C) :- ordered_line(C, A, B).  line(A, B, C) :- ordered_line(C, B, A).

full(A) :- x(A).  full(A) :- o(A).  empty(A) :- \+(full(A)).
% NB: empty must be called with an already-instantiated A.
same(A, A).  different(A, B) :- \+(same(A, B)).

move(A) :- good(A), empty(A), !.

% strategy:
good(A) :- win(A).            good(A) :- block_win(A).     good(A) :- split(A).
good(A) :- strong_build(A).   good(A) :- weak_build(A).
good(5).  good(1).  good(3).  good(7).  good(9).  good(2).  good(4).  good(6).  good(8).

win(A) :- x(B), x(C), line(A, B, C).
block_win(A) :- o(B), o(C), line(A, B, C).
split(A) :- x(B), x(C), different(B, C), line(A, B, D), line(A, C, E), empty(D), empty(E).
strong_build(A) :- x(B), line(A, B, C), empty(C), \+(risky(C)).
weak_build(A) :- x(B), line(A, B, C), empty(C), \+(double_risky(C)).
risky(C) :- o(D), line(C, D, E), empty(E).
double_risky(C) :- o(D), o(E), different(D, E), line(C, D, F), line(C, E, G), empty(F), empty(G).

all_full :- full(1), full(2), full(3), full(4), full(5),
            full(6), full(7), full(8), full(9).
done :- ordered_line(A, B, C), x(A), x(B), x(C), write('I won.'), nl.
done :- all_full, write('Draw.'), nl.

getmove :- repeat, write('Please enter a move: '), read(X), empty(X), assert(o(X)).
makemove :- move(X), !, assert(x(X)).
makemove :- all_full.

printsquare(N) :- o(N), write(' o ').
printsquare(N) :- x(N), write(' x ').
printsquare(N) :- empty(N), write('   ').
printboard :- printsquare(1), printsquare(2), printsquare(3), nl,
              printsquare(4), printsquare(5), printsquare(6), nl,
              printsquare(7), printsquare(8), printsquare(9), nl.
clear :- retractall(x(_)), retractall(o(_)).

% main goal:
play :- clear, repeat, getmove, respond.
respond :- ordered_line(A, B, C), o(A), o(B), o(C),
           printboard, write('You won.'), nl.       % shouldn't ever happen!
respond :- makemove, printboard, done.
```

Figure 12.4 Tic-tac-toe program in Prolog.

EXAMPLE 12.30
The `functor` predicate

Individual terms in Prolog can be created, or their contents extracted, using the built-in predicates `functor`, `arg`, and `=..`. The goal `functor(T, F, N)` succeeds if and only if `T` is a term with functor `F` and arity `N`:

```
?- functor(foo(a, b, c), foo, 3).
true.
?- functor(foo(a, b, c), F, N).
F = foo,
N = 3.
?- functor(T, foo, 3).
T = foo(_G10, _G37, _G24).
```

In the last line of output, the atoms with leading underscores are placeholders for uninstantiated variables. ■

EXAMPLE 12.31
Creating terms at run time

The goal `arg(N, T, A)` succeeds if and only if its first two arguments (`N` and `T`) are instantiated, `N` is a natural number, `T` is a term, and `A` is the `N`th argument of `T`:

```
?- arg(3, foo(a, b, c), A).
A = c.
```

Using `functor` and `arg` together, we can create an arbitrary term:

```
?- functor(T, foo, 3), arg(1, T, a), arg(2, T, b), arg(3, T, c).
T = foo(a, b, c).
```

Alternatively, we can use the (infix) `=..` predicate, which "equates" a term with a list:

```
?- T =.. [foo, a, b, c].
T = foo(a, b, c).

?- foo(a, b, c) =.. [F, A1, A2, A3].
F = foo,
A1 = a,
A2 = b,
A3 = c.
```

Note that

```
?- foo(a, b, c) = F(A1, A2, A3).
```

and

```
?- F(A1, A2, A3) = foo(a, b, c).
```

do not work: the term preceding a left parenthesis must be an atom, not a variable.

EXAMPLE 12.32
Pursuing a dynamic goal

Using `=..` and `call`, the programmer can arrange to pursue (attempt to satisfy) a goal created at run time:

```
param_loop(L, H, F) :- natural(I), I >= L,
                       G =.. [F, I], call(G),
                       I = H, !.
```

The goal `param_loop(5, 10, write)` will produce the following output:

```
5678910
true.
```

If we want the numbers on separate lines we can write

```
?- param_loop(5, 10, writeln).
```

where

```
writeln(X) :- write(X), nl.
```

EXAMPLE 12.33
Custom database perusal

Taken together, the predicates described above allow a Prolog program to create and decompose clauses, and to add and subtract them from the database. So far, however, the only mechanism we have for *perusing* the database (i.e., to determine its contents) is the built-in search mechanism. To allow programs to

DESIGN & IMPLEMENTATION

12.2 Reflection

A *reflection* mechanism allows a program to reason about itself. While no widely used language is *fully reflective*, in the sense that it can inspect every aspect of its structure and current state, significant forms of reflection appear in several major languages, Prolog among them. Given the functor and arity of a starting goal, the `clause` predicate allows us to find everything related to that goal in the database. Using `clause`, we can in fact create a *metacircular interpreter* (Exercise 12.13)—an implementation of Prolog in itself—much as we could for Lisp using `eval` and `apply` (Section 11.3.5). We can also write evaluators that use nonstandard search orders (e.g., breadth-first or forward chaining; see Exercise 12.14). Other examples of rich reflection facilities appear in Java, C#, and the major scripting languages. As we shall see in Section 16.3.1, these allow a program to inspect and reason about its complete type structure. A few languages (e.g., Python) allow a program to inspect its source code as text, but this is not as powerful as the homoiconic inspection of Prolog or Scheme, which allows a program to *reason about* its own code structure directly.

"reason" in more general ways, Prolog provides a `clause` predicate that attempts to match its two arguments against the head and body of some existing clause in the database:

```
?- clause(snowy(X), B).
B = rainy(X), cold(X).
```

Here we have discovered that there is a single rule in the database whose head is a single-argument term with functor `snowy`. The body of that rule is the conjunction `B = rainy(X), cold(X)`. If there had been more such clauses, we would have had the opportunity to ask for them them by entering semicolons. Prolog requires that the first argument to `clause` be sufficiently instantiated that its functor and arity can be determined.

A clause with no body (a fact) matches the body `true`:

```
?- clause(rainy(rochester), true).
true.
```

Note that `clause` is quite different from `call`: it does not attempt to satisfy a goal, but simply to match it against an existing clause:

```
?- clause(snowy(rochester), true).
false.
```

Various other built-in predicates can also be used to "deconstruct" the contents of a clause. The `var` predicate takes a single argument; it succeeds as a goal if and only if its argument is an uninstantiated variable. The `atom` and `integer` predicates succeed as goals if and only if their arguments are atoms and integers, respectively. The `name` predicate takes two arguments. It succeeds as a goal if and only if its first argument is an atom and its second is a list composed of the ASCII codes for the characters of that atom.

12.3 Theoretical Foundations

EXAMPLE 12.34
Predicates as mathematical objects

In mathematical logic, a *predicate* is a function that maps constants (atoms) or variables to the values true and false. If rainy is a predicate, for example, we might have rainy(Seattle) = true and rainy(Tijuana) = false. *Predicate calculus* provides a notation and inference rules for constructing and reasoning about *propositions* (*statements*) composed of predicate applications, *operators* (and, or, not, etc.), and the *quantifiers* ∀ and ∃. Logic programming formalizes the search for variable values that will make a given proposition true.

IN MORE DEPTH

In conventional logical notation there are many ways to state a given proposition. Logic programming is built on *clausal form*, which provides a unique expression for every proposition. Many though not all clausal forms can be cast as a collection of Horn clauses, and thus translated into Prolog. On the companion site we trace the steps required to translate an arbitrary proposition into clausal form. We also characterize the cases in which this form can and cannot be translated into Prolog.

12.4 Logic Programming in Perspective

In the abstract, logic programming is a very compelling idea: it suggests a model of computing in which we simply list the logical properties of an unknown value, and then the computer figures out how to find it (or tells us it doesn't exist). Unfortunately, reality falls quite a bit short of the vision, for both theoretical and practical reasons.

12.4.1 Parts of Logic Not Covered

As noted in Section 12.3, Horn clauses do not capture all of first-order predicate calculus. In particular, they cannot be used to express statements whose clausal form includes a disjunction with more than one non-negated term. We can sometimes get around this problem in Prolog by using the \+ predicate, but the semantics are not the same (see Section 12.4.3).

12.4.2 Execution Order

EXAMPLE 12.35 Sorting incredibly slowly

In Section 12.2.4, we saw that one must often consider execution order to ensure that a Prolog search will terminate. Even for searches that terminate, naive code can be *very* inefficient. Consider the problem of sorting. A natural declarative

DESIGN & IMPLEMENTATION

12.3 Implementing logic

Predicate calculus is a significantly higher-level notation than lambda calculus. It is much more abstract—much less algorithmic. It is natural, therefore, that a language like Prolog not provide the full power of predicate calculus, and that it include extensions to make it more algorithmic. We may someday reach the point where programming systems are capable of discovering good algorithms from very high-level declarative specifications, but we are not there yet.

way to say that L2 is the sorted version of L1 is to say that L2 is a permutation of L1 and L2 is sorted:

```
declarative_sort(L1, L2) :- permutation(L1, L2), sorted(L2).
permutation([], []).
permutation(L, [H | T]) :- append(P, [H | S], L), append(P, S, W),
    permutation(W, T).
```

(The append and sorted predicates are defined in Section 12.2.2.) Unfortunately, Prolog's default search strategy may take exponential time to sort a list based on these rules: it will generate permutations until it finds one that is sorted. ■

While logic is inherently declarative, most logic languages explore the tree of possible resolutions in deterministic order. Prolog provides a variety of predicates, including the cut, fail, and repeat, to control that execution order (Section 12.2.6). It also provides predicates, including assert, retract, and call, to manipulate its database explicitly during execution.

EXAMPLE 12.36 Quicksort in Prolog

To obtain a more efficient sort, the Prolog programmer must adopt a less natural, "imperative" definition:

```
quicksort([], []).
quicksort([A | L1], L2) :- partition(A, L1, P1, S1),
    quicksort(P1, P2), quicksort(S1, S2), append(P2, [A | S2], L2).
partition(A, [], [], []).
partition(A, [H | T], [H | P], S) :- A >= H, partition(A, T, P, S).
partition(A, [H | T], P, [H | S]) :- A =< H, partition(A, T, P, S).
```

Even this sort is less efficient than one might hope in certain cases. When given an already-sorted list, for example, it takes quadratic time, instead of $O(n \log n)$. A good heuristic for quicksort is to partition the list using the median of the first, middle, and last elements. Unfortunately, Prolog provides no easy way to access the middle and final elements of a list (it has no arrays). ■

DESIGN & IMPLEMENTATION

12.4 Alternative search strategies

Some approaches to logic programming attempt to customize the run-time search strategy in a way that is likely to satisfy goals quickly. Darlington [Dar90], for example, describes a technique in which, when an intermediate goal *G* fails, we try to find alternative instantiations of the variables in *G* that will allow it to succeed, *before* backing up to previous goals and seeing whether the alternative instantiations will work in them as well. This "failure-directed search" seems to work well for certain classes of problems. Unfortunately, no general technique is known that will automatically discover the best algorithm (or even just a "good" one) for any given problem.

As we saw in Chapter 10, it can be useful to distinguish between the *specification* of a program and its *implementation*. The specification says what the program is to do; the implementation says how it is to do it. Horn clauses provide an excellent notation for specifications. When augmented with search rules (as in Prolog) they allow implementations to be expressed in the same notation.

12.4.3 Negation and the "Closed World" Assumption

A collection of Horn clauses, such as the facts and rules of a Prolog database, constitutes a list of things assumed to be true. It does not include any things assumed to be false. This reliance on purely "positive" logic implies that Prolog's `\+` predicate is different from logical negation. Unless the database is assumed to contain *everything* that is true (this is the *closed world assumption*), the goal `\+(T)` can succeed simply because our current knowledge is insufficient to prove `T`. Moreover, negation in Prolog occurs *outside* any implicit existential quantifiers on the right-hand side of a rule. Thus

EXAMPLE 12.37
Negation as failure

```
?- \+(takes(X, his201)).
```

where `X` is uninstantiated, means

$$? \ \neg\exists X[\mathsf{takes}(X, \mathsf{his201})]$$

rather than

$$? \ \exists X[\neg\mathsf{takes}(X, \mathsf{his201})]$$

If our database indicates that `jane_doe` takes `his201`, then the goal `takes(X, his201)` can succeed, and `\+(takes(X, his201))` will fail:

```
?- \+(takes(X, his201)).
false.
```

If we had a way to put the negation inside the quantifier, we might hope for an implementation that would respond

```
?- \+(takes(X, his201)).
X = ajit_chandra
```

or even

```
?- \+(takes(X, his201)).
X != jane_doe
```

A complete characterization of the values of X for which ¬takes(X, his201) is true would require a complete exploration of the resolution tree, something that Prolog does only when all goals fail, or when repeatedly prompted with semicolons. Mechanisms to incorporate some sort of "constructive negation" into logic programming are an active topic of research. ■

EXAMPLE 12.38
Negation and instantiation

It is worth noting that the definition of \+ in terms of failure means that variable bindings are lost whenever \+ succeeds. For example:

```
?- takes(X, his201).
X = jane_doe
?- \+(takes(X, his201)).
false.
?- \+(\+(takes(X, his201))).
true.                                   % no value for X provided
```

When takes first succeeds, X is bound to jane_doe. When the inner \+ fails, the binding is broken. Then when the outer \+ succeeds, a new binding is created to an uninstantiated value. Prolog provides no way to pull the binding of X out through the double negation. ■

✓ CHECK YOUR UNDERSTANDING

9. Explain the purpose of the cut (!) in Prolog. How does it relate to \+?
10. Describe three ways in which Prolog programs can depart from a pure logic programming model.
11. Describe the *generate-and-test* programming idiom.
12. Summarize Prolog's facilities for database manipulation. Be sure to mention assert, retract, and clause.
13. What sorts of logical statements cannot be captured in Horn clauses?
14. What is the *closed world assumption*? What problems does it cause for logic programming?

12.5 Summary and Concluding Remarks

In this chapter we have focused on the logic model of computing. Where an imperative program computes principally through iteration and side effects, and a functional program computes principally through substitution of parameters into functions, a logic program computes through the resolution of logical statements, driven by the ability to unify variables and terms.

Much of our discussion was driven by an examination of the principal logic language, Prolog, which we used to illustrate clauses and terms, resolution and unification, search/execution order, list manipulation, and high-order predicates for inspection and modification of the logic database.

Like imperative and functional programming, logic programming is related to constructive proofs. But where an imperative or functional program in some sense *is* a proof (of the ability to generate outputs from inputs), a logic program is a set of axioms from which the computer attempts to construct a proof. And where imperative and functional programming provide the full power of Turing machines and lambda calculus, respectively (ignoring hardware-imposed limits on arithmetic precision, disk and memory space, etc.), Prolog provides less than the full generality of resolution theorem proving, in the interests of time and space efficiency. At the same time, Prolog extends its formal counterpart with true arithmetic, I/O, imperative control flow, and higher-order predicates for self-inspection and modification.

Like Lisp/Scheme, Prolog makes heavy use of lists, largely because they can easily be built incrementally, without the need to allocate and then modify state as separate operations. And like Lisp/Scheme (but unlike ML and its descendants), Prolog is *homoiconic*: programs look like ordinary data structures, and can be created, modified, and executed on the fly.

As we stressed in Chapter 1, different models of computing are appealing in different ways. Imperative programs more closely mirror the underlying hardware, and can more easily be "tweaked" for high performance. Purely functional programs avoid the semantic complexity of side effects, and have proved particularly handy for the manipulation of symbolic (nonnumeric) data. Logic programs, with their highly declarative semantics and their emphasis on unification, are well suited to problems that emphasize relationships and search. At the same time, their de-emphasis of control flow can lead to inefficiency. At the current state of the art, computers have surpassed people in their ability to deal with low-level details (e.g., of instruction scheduling), but people are still better at inventing good algorithms.

As we also stressed in Chapter 1, the borders between language classes are often very fuzzy. The backtracking search of Prolog strongly resembles the execution of generators in Icon. Unification in Prolog resembles (but is more powerful than) the pattern-matching capabilities of ML and Haskell. (Unification is also used for type checking in ML and Haskell, and for template instantiation in C++, but those are *compile-time* activities.)

There is much to be said for programming in a purely functional or logic-based style. While most Scheme and Prolog programs make some use of imperative language features, those features tend to be responsible for a disproportionate share of program bugs. At the same time, there seem to be programming tasks—interactive I/O, for example—that are almost impossible to accomplish without side effects.

12.6 Exercises

12.1 Starting with the clauses at the beginning of Example 12.17, use resolution (as illustrated in Example 12.3) to show, in two different ways, that there is a path from `a` to `e`.

12.2 Solve Exercise 6.22 in Prolog.

12.3 Consider the Prolog `gcd` program in Figure 1.2. Does this program work "backward" as well as forward? (Given integers d and n, can you use it to generate a sequence of integers m such that $\texttt{gcd}(n, m) = d$?) Explain your answer.

12.4 In the spirit of Example 11.20, write a Prolog program that exploits backtracking to simulate the execution of a *non*deterministic finite automaton.

12.5 Show that resolution is commutative and associative. Specifically, if A, B, and C are Horn clauses, show that $(A \oplus B) = (B \oplus A)$ and that $((A \oplus B) \oplus C) = (A \oplus (B \oplus C))$, where $\oplus$ indicates resolution. Be sure to think about what happens to variables that are instantiated as a result of unification.

12.6 In Example 12.8, the query `?- classmates(jane_doe, X)` will succeed three times: twice with `X` = `jane_doe` and once with `X` = `ajit_chandra`. Show how to modify the `classmates(X, Y)` rule so that a student is not considered a classmate of himself or herself.

12.7 Modify Example 12.17 so that the goal `path(X, Y)`, for arbitrary already-instantiated `X` and `Y`, will succeed no more than once, even if there are multiple paths from `X` to `Y`.

12.8 Using only `\+` (no cuts), modify the tic-tac-toe example of Section 12.2.5 so it will generate only one candidate move from a given board position. How does your solution compare to the cut-based one (Example 12.22)?

12.9 Prove the claim, made in Example 12.19, that there is no winning strategy in tic-tac-toe—that either player can force a draw.

12.10 Prove that the tic-tac-toe strategy of Example 12.19 is optimal (wins against an imperfect opponent whenever possible, draws otherwise), or give a counterexample.

12.11 Starting with the tic-tac-toe program of Figure 12.4, draw a directed acyclic graph in which every clause is a node and an arc from A to B indicates that it is important, either for correctness or efficiency, that A come before B in the program. (Do not draw any other arcs.) Any topological sort of your graph should constitute an equally efficient version of the program. (Is the existing program one of them?)

12.12 Write Prolog rules to define a version of the `member` predicate that will generate all members of a list during backtracking, but without generating duplicates. Note that the cut and `\+` based versions of Example 12.20 will not suffice; when asked to look for an uninstantiated member, they find only the head of the list.

12.13 Use the `clause` predicate of Prolog to implement the `call` predicate (pretend that it isn't built in). You needn't implement all of the built-in predicates of Prolog; in particular, you may ignore the various imperative control-flow mechanisms and database manipulators. Extend your code by making the database an explicit argument to `call`, effectively producing a metacircular interpreter.

12.14 Use the `clause` predicate of Prolog to write a predicate `call_bfs` that attempts to satisfy goals breadth-first. (Hint: You will want to keep a queue of yet-to-be-pursued subgoals, each of which is represented by a stack that captures backtracking alternatives.)

12.15 Write a (list-based) *insertion sort* algorithm in Prolog. Here's what it looks like in C, using arrays:

```
void insertion_sort(int A[], int N)
{
    int i, j, t;
    for (i = 1; i < N; i++) {
        t = A[i];
        for (j = i; j > 0; j--) {
            if (t >= A[j-1]) break;
            A[j] = A[j-1];
        }
        A[j] = t;
    }
}
```

12.16 Quicksort works well for large lists, but has higher overhead than insertion sort for short lists. Write a sort algorithm in Prolog that uses quicksort initially, but switches to insertion sort (as defined in the previous exercise) for sublists of 15 or fewer elements. (Hint: You can count the number of elements during the `partition` operation.)

12.17 Write a Prolog sorting routine that is guaranteed to take $O(n \log n)$ time in the worst case. (Hint: Try *merge sort*; a description can be found in almost any algorithms or data structures text.)

12.18 Consider the following interaction with a Prolog interpreter:

```
?- Y = X, X = foo(X).
Y = foo(foo(foo(foo(foo(foo(foo(foo(foo(foo(foo(
foo(foo(foo(foo(foo(foo(foo(foo(foo(foo(foo(foo(
foo(foo(foo(foo(foo(foo(foo(foo(foo(foo(foo(foo(
foo(foo(foo(foo(foo(foo(foo(foo(foo(foo(foo(foo(
foo(foo(foo(foo(foo(foo(...
```

What is going on here? Why does the interpreter fall into an infinite loop? Can you think of any circumstances (presumably not requiring output) in which a structure like this one would be useful? If not, can you suggest how a Prolog interpreter might implement checks to forbid its creation? How expensive would those checks be? Would the cost in your opinion be justified?

12.19–12.21 In More Depth.

12.7 Explorations

12.22 Learn about alternative search strategies for Prolog and other logic languages. How do forward chaining solvers work? What are the prospects for intelligent hybrid strategies?

12.23 Between 1982 and 1992 the Japanese government invested large sums of money in logic programming. Research the *Fifth Generation* project, administered by the Japanese Ministry of International Trade and Industry (MITI). What were its goals? What was achieved? What was not? How tightly were the goals and outcomes tied to Prolog? What lessons can we learn from the project today?

12.24 Read ahead to Chapter 14 and learn about XSLT, a language used to manipulate data represented in XML, the extended markup language (of which XHTML, the latest standard for web pages, is an example). XSLT is generally described as declarative. Is it logic based? How does it compare to Prolog in expressive power, level of abstraction, and execution efficiency?

12.25 Repeat the previous question for SQL, the database query language (for an introduction, type "SQL tutorial" into your favorite Internet search engine).

12.26 Spreadsheets like Microsoft Excel are sometimes characterized as declarative programming. Is this fair? Ignoring extensions like Visual Basic macros, does the ability to define relationships among cells provide Turing complete expressive power? Compare the execution model to that of Prolog. How is the order of update for cells determined? Can data be pushed "both ways," as they can in Prolog?

12.27–12.30 In More Depth.

12.8 Bibliographic Notes

Logic programming has its roots in automated theorem proving. Much of the theoretical groundwork was laid by Horn in the early 1950s [Hor51], and by Robinson in the early 1960s [Rob65]. The breakthrough for computing came in the early 1970s, when Colmeraurer and Roussel at the University of Aix–Marseille in France and Kowalski and his colleagues at the University of Edinburgh in Scotland developed the initial version of Prolog. The early history of the language is recounted by Robinson [Rob83]. Theoretical foundations are covered by Lloyd [Llo87].

Prolog was originally intended for research in natural language processing, but it soon became apparent that it could serve as a general-purpose language. Several versions of Prolog have since evolved. The one described here is the widely used Edinburgh dialect. The ISO standard [Int95] is similar.

Several other logic languages have been developed, though none rivaled Prolog in popularity. OPS5 [BFKM86] used forward chaining. Gödel [HL94] includes modules, strong typing, a richer variety of logical operators, and enhanced control of execution order. Parlog is a parallel Prolog dialect; we will mention it briefly in Section 13.4.5. Mercury [SHC96] adopts a variety of features from ML-family functional languages, including static type inference, monad-like I/O, higher-order predicates, closures, currying, and lambda expressions. It is compiled, rather than interpreted, and requires the programmer to specify modes (`in`, `out`) for predicate arguments.

Database query languages stemming from Datalog [Ull85][UW08, Secs. 4.2–4.4] are implemented using forward chaining. CLP (Constraint Logic Programming) and its variants are largely based on Prolog, but employ a more general constraint-satisfaction mechanism in place of unification [JM94]. The Association for Logic Programming can be found on-line at *www.cs.nmsu.edu/ALP/*.

13 Concurrency

The bulk of this text has focused, implicitly, on *sequential* programs: programs with a single active execution context. As we saw in Chapter 6, sequentiality is fundamental to imperative programming. It also tends to be implicit in declarative programming, partly because practical functional and logic languages usually include some imperative features, and partly because people tend to develop imperative implementations and mental models of declarative programs (applicative order reduction, backward chaining with backtracking), even when language semantics do not require such a model.

By contrast, a program is said to be *concurrent* if it may have more than one active execution context—more than one "thread of control." Concurrency has at least three important motivations:

1. *To capture the logical structure of a problem.* Many programs, particularly servers and graphical applications, must keep track of more than one largely independent "task" at the same time. Often the simplest and most logical way to structure such a program is to represent each task with a separate thread of control. We touched on this "multithreaded" structure when discussing coroutines (Section 9.5) and events (Section 9.6); we will return to it in Section 13.1.1.
2. *To exploit parallel hardware, for speed.* Long a staple of high-end servers and supercomputers, multiple processors (or multiple cores within a processor) have become ubiquitous in desktop, laptop, and mobile devices. To use these cores effectively, programs must generally be written (or rewritten) with concurrency in mind.
3. *To cope with physical distribution.* Applications that run across the Internet or a more local group of machines are inherently concurrent. So are many embedded applications: the control systems of a modern automobile, for example, may span dozens of processors spread throughout the vehicle.

In general, we use the word *concurrent* to characterize any system in which two or more tasks may be underway (at an unpredictable point in their execution) at the same time. Under this definition, coroutines are not concurrent, because at any given time, all but one of them is stopped at a well-known place. A concurrent system is *parallel* if more than one task can be physically *active* at once; this requires more than one processor. The distinction is purely an implementation and performance issue: from a semantic point of view, there is no difference between true parallelism and the "quasiparallelism" of a system that switches between tasks at unpredictable times. A parallel system is *distributed* if its processors are associated with people or devices that are physically separated from one another in the real world. Under these definitions, "concurrent" applies to all three motivations above. "Parallel" applies to the second and third; "distributed" applies to only the third.

We will focus in this chapter on concurrency and parallelism. Parallelism has become a pressing concern since 2005 or so, with the proliferation of multicore processors. We will have less occasion to touch on distribution. While languages have been designed for distributed computing, most distributed systems run separate programs on every networked processor, and use message-passing library routines to communicate among them.

We begin our study with an overview of the ways in which parallelism may be used in modern programs. Our overview will touch on the motivation for concurrency (even on uniprocessors) and the concept of *races*, which are the principal source of complexity in concurrent programs. We will also briefly survey the architectural features of modern multicore and multiprocessor machines. In Section 13.2 we consider the contrast between shared-memory and message-passing models of concurrency, and between language and library-based implementations. Building on coroutines, we explain how a language or library can create and schedule threads. Section 13.3 focuses on low-level mechanisms for shared-memory synchronization. Section 13.4 extends the discussion to language-level constructs. Message-passing models of concurrency are considered in Section 13.5 (mostly on the companion site).

13.1 Background and Motivation

Concurrency is not a new idea. Much of the theoretical groundwork was laid in the 1960s, and Algol 68 includes concurrent programming features. Widespread interest in concurrency is a relatively recent phenomenon, however; it stems in part from the availability of low-cost multicore and multiprocessor machines, and in part from the proliferation of graphical, multimedia, and web-based applications, all of which are naturally represented by concurrent threads of control.

Levels of Parallelism

Parallelism arises at every level of a modern computer system. It is comparatively easy to exploit at the level of circuits and gates, where signals can propagate down thousands of connections at once. As we move up first to processors and cores, and then to the many layers of software that run on top of them, the *granularity* of parallelism—the size and complexity of tasks—increases at every level, and it becomes increasingly difficult to figure out what work should be done by each task and how tasks should coordinate.

For 40 years, microarchitectural research was largely devoted to finding more and better ways to exploit the *instruction-level* parallelism (ILP) available in machine language programs. As we saw in Chapter 5, the combination of deep, superscalar pipelines and aggressive speculation allows a modern processor to track dependences among hundreds of "in-flight" instructions, make progress on scores of them, and complete several in every cycle. Shortly after the turn of the century, it became apparent that a limit had been reached: there simply wasn't any more instruction-level parallelism available in conventional programs.

At the next higher level of granularity, so-called *vector parallelism* is available in programs that perform operations repeatedly on every element of a very large data set. Processors designed to exploit this parallelism were the dominant form of supercomputer from the late 1960s through the early 1990s. Their legacy lives on in the vector instructions of mainstream processors (e.g., the MMX, SSE, and AVX extensions to the x86 instruction set), and in modern graphical processing units (GPUs), whose peak performance can exceed that of the typical CPU (central processing unit—a conventional core) by a factor of more than 100.

Unfortunately, vector parallelism arises in only certain kinds of programs. Given the end of ILP, and the limits on clock frequency imposed by heat dissipation (Section C-5.4.4), general-purpose computing today must obtain its performance improvements from *multicore* processors, which require coarser-grain *thread-level* parallelism. The move to multicore has thus entailed a fundamental shift in the nature of programming: where parallelism was once a largely invisible implementation detail, it must now be written explicitly into high-level program structure.

Levels of Abstraction

On today's multicore machines, different kinds of programmers need to understand concurrency at different levels of detail, and use it in different ways.

The simplest, most abstract case arises when using "black box" parallel libraries. A sorting routine or a linear algebra package, for example, may execute in parallel without its caller needing to understand how. In the database world, queries expressed in SQL (Structured Query Language) often execute in parallel as well. Microsoft's .NET Framework includes a *Language-Integrated Query* mechanism (LINQ) that allows database-style queries to be made of program data structures, again with parallelism "under the hood."

At a slightly less abstract level, a programmer may know that certain tasks are mutually independent (because, for example, they access disjoint sets of

EXAMPLE 13.1
Independent tasks in C#

variables). Such tasks can safely execute in parallel.[1] In C#, for example, we can write the following using the Task Parallel Library:

```
Parallel.For(0, 100, i => { A[i] = foo(A[i]); });
```

The first two arguments to `Parallel.For` are "loop" bounds; the third is a delegate, here written as a lambda expression. Assuming `A` is a 100-element array, and that the invocations of `foo` are truly independent, this code will have the same effect as the obvious traditional `for` loop, except that it will run faster, making use of as many cores as possible (up to 100).

EXAMPLE 13.2
A simple race condition

If our tasks are *not* independent, it may still be possible to run them in parallel if we explicitly *synchronize* their interactions. Synchronization serves to eliminate *races* between threads by controlling the ways in which their actions can interleave in time. Suppose function `foo` in the previous example subtracts 1 from `A[i]` and also counts the number of times that the result is zero. Naively we might implement `foo` as

```
int zero_count;
public static int foo(int n) {
    int rtn = n - 1;
    if (rtn == 0) zero_count++;
    return rtn;
}
```

Consider now what may happen when two or more instances of this code run concurrently:

Thread 1	**Thread 2**
...	
r1 := zero_count	...
r1 := r1 + 1	r1 := zero_count
zero_count := r1	r1 := r1 + 1
...	zero_count := r1
	...

If the instructions interleave roughly as shown, both threads may load the same value of zero_count, both may increment it by one, and both may store the (only one greater) value back into zero_count. The result may be less than what we expect.

In general, a *race condition* occurs whenever two or more threads are "racing" toward points in the code at which they touch some common object, and the behavior of the system depends on which thread gets there first. In this particular example, the store of zero_count in Thread 1 is racing with the load in Thread 2.

1 Ideally, we might like the compiler to figure this out automatically, but the problem of independence is undecidable in the general case.

If Thread 1 gets there first, we will get the "right" result; if Thread 2 gets there first, we won't. ■

The most common purpose of synchronization is to make some sequence of instructions, known as a *critical section*, appear to be *atomic*—to happen "all at once" from the point of view of every other thread. In our example, the critical section is a load, an increment, and a store. The most common way to make the sequence atomic is with a *mutual exclusion lock*, which we *acquire* before the first instruction of the sequence and *release* after the last. We will study locks in Sections 13.3.1 and 13.3.5. In Sections 13.3.2 and 13.4.4 we will also consider mechanisms that achieve atomicity without locks.

At lower levels of abstraction, expert programmers may need to understand hardware and run-time systems in sufficient detail to *implement* synchronization mechanisms. This chapter should convey a sense of the issues, but a full treatment at this level is beyond the scope of the current text.

13.1.1 The Case for Multithreaded Programs

Our first motivation for concurrency—to capture the logical structure of certain applications—has arisen several times in earlier chapters. In Section C-8.7.1 we noted that interactive I/O must often interrupt the execution of the current program. In a video game, for example, we must handle keystrokes and mouse or joystick motions while continually updating the image on the screen. The standard way to structure such a program, as described in Section 9.6.2, is to execute the input handlers in a separate thread of control, which coexists with one or more threads responsible for updating the screen. In Section 9.5, we considered a screen saver program that used coroutines to interleave "sanity checks" on the file system with updates to a moving picture on the screen. We also considered discrete-event simulation, which uses coroutines to represent the active entities of some real-world system.

The semantics of discrete-event simulation require that events occur atomically at fixed points in time. Coroutines provide a natural implementation, because they execute one at a time: so long as we never switch coroutines in the middle of a to-be-atomic operation, all will be well. In our other examples, however—and indeed in most "naturally concurrent" programs—there is no need for coroutine semantics. By assigning concurrent tasks to threads instead of to coroutines, we acknowledge that those tasks can proceed in parallel if more than one core is available. We also move responsibility for figuring out which thread should run when from the programmer to the language implementation. In return, we give up any notion of trivial atomicity.

EXAMPLE 13.3
Multithreaded web browser

The need for multithreaded programs is easily seen in web-based applications. In a browser such as Chrome or Firefox (see Figure 13.1), there are typically many different threads simultaneously active, each of which is likely to communicate with a remote (and possibly very slow) server several times before completing its task. When the user clicks on a link, the browser creates a thread to request the specified document. For all but the tiniest pages, this thread will then receive a series of message "packets." As these packets begin to arrive the thread must format them for presentation on the screen. The formatting task is akin to typesetting: the thread must access fonts, assemble words, and break the words into lines. For many special tags within the page, the formatting thread will spawn additional threads: one for each image, one for the background if any, one to format each table, and possibly more to handle separate frames. Each spawned thread will communicate with the server to obtain the information it needs (e.g., the contents of an image) for its particular task. The user, meanwhile, can access items in menus to create new browser windows, edit bookmarks, change preferences, and so on, all in "parallel" with the rendering of page elements. ■

The use of many threads ensures that comparatively fast operations (e.g., display of text) do not wait for slow operations (e.g., display of large images). Whenever one thread *blocks* (waits for a message or I/O), the run-time or operating system will automatically switch execution on the core to run a different thread. In a *preemptive* thread package, these *context switches* will occur at other times as well, to prevent any one thread from hogging processor resources. Any reader who remembers early, more sequential browsers will appreciate the difference that multithreading makes in perceived performance and responsiveness, even on a single-core machine.

The Dispatch Loop Alternative

EXAMPLE 13.4
Dispatch loop web browser

Without language or library support for threads, a browser must either adopt a more sequential structure, or centralize the handling of all delay-inducing events in a single *dispatch loop* (see Figure 13.2). Data structures associated with the dispatch loop keep track of all the tasks the browser has yet to complete. The state of a task may be quite complicated. For the high-level task of rendering a page, the state must indicate which packets have been received and which are still outstanding. It must also identify the various subtasks of the page (images, tables, frames, etc.) so that we can find them all and reclaim their state if the user clicks on a "stop" button.

To guarantee good interactive response, we must make sure that no subaction of continue_task takes very long to execute. Clearly we must end the current action whenever we wait for a message. We must also end it whenever we read from a file, since disk operations are slow. Finally, if any task needs to compute for longer than about a tenth of a second (the typical human perceptual threshold), then we must divide the task into pieces, between which we save state and return to the top of the loop. These considerations imply that the condition at the top of the loop must cover the full range of asynchronous events, and that evaluations of the condition must be interleaved with continued execution of any tasks that were subdivided due to lengthy computation. (In practice we would probably need a more sophisticated mechanism than simple interleaving to ensure that neither input-driven nor compute-bound tasks hog more than their share of resources.) ■

```
procedure parse_page(address : url)
    contact server, request page contents
    parse_html_header()
    while current_token in {"<p>", "<h1>", "<ul>", ...,
            "<background", "<image", "<table", "<frameset", ...}
        case current_token of
            "<p>"     : break_paragraph()
            "<h1>"    : format_heading(); match("</h1>")
            "<ul>"    : format_list(); match("</ul>")
            ...
            "<background" :
                        a : attributes := parse_attributes()
                        fork render_background(a)
            "<image" :  a : attributes := parse_attributes()
                        fork render_image(a)
            "<table"  : a : attributes := parse_attributes()
                        scan forward for "</table>" token
                        token_stream s :=...     -- table contents
                        fork format_table(s, a)
            "<frameset" :
                        a : attributes := parse_attributes()
                        parse_frame_list(a)
                        match("</frameset>")
        ...
    ...
procedure parse_frame_list(a1 : attributes)
    while current_token in {"<frame", "<frameset", "<noframes>"}
        case current_token of
            "<frame" :  a2 : attributes := parse_attributes()
                        fork format_frame(a1, a2)
        ...
```

Figure 13.1 Thread-based code from a hypothetical Web browser. To first approximation, the parse_page subroutine is the root of a recursive descent parser for HTML. In several cases, however, the actions associated with recognition of a construct (background, image, table, frameset) proceed concurrently with continued parsing of the page itself. In this example, concurrent threads are created with the fork operation. An additional thread would likely execute in response to keyboard and mouse events.

The principal problem with a dispatch loop—beyond the complexity of subdividing tasks and saving state—is that it hides the algorithmic structure of the program. Every distinct task (retrieving a page, rendering an image, walking through nested menus) could be described elegantly with standard control-flow mechanisms, if not for the fact that we must return to the top of the dispatch loop at every delay-inducing operation. In effect, the dispatch loop turns the program "inside out," making the management of tasks explicit and the control flow within tasks implicit. The resulting complexity is similar to what we encountered when

```
type task_descriptor = record
    -- fields in lieu of thread-local variables, plus control-flow information
    ...
ready_tasks : queue of task_descriptor
...
procedure dispatch()
    loop
        -- try to do something input-driven
        if a new event E (message, keystroke, etc.) is available
            if an existing task T is waiting for E
                continue_task(T, E)
            else if E can be handled quickly, do so
            else
                allocate and initialize new task T
                continue_task(T, E)
        -- now do something compute bound
            if ready_tasks is nonempty
                continue_task(dequeue(ready_tasks), 'ok')

procedure continue_task(T : task, E : event)
    if T is rendering an image
        and E is a message containing the next block of data
            continue_image_render(T, E)
    else if T is formatting a page
        and E is a message containing the next block of data
            continue_page_parse(T, E)
    else if T is formatting a page
        and E is 'ok'        -- we're compute bound
            continue_page_parse(T, E)
    else if T is reading the bookmarks file
        and E is an I/O completion event
            continue_goto_page(T, E)
    else if T is formatting a frame
        and E is a push of the "stop" button
            deallocate T and all tasks dependent upon it
    else if E is the "edit preferences" menu item
        edit_preferences(T, E)
    else if T is already editing preferences
        and E is a newly typed keystroke
            edit_preferences(T, E)
    ...
```

Figure 13.2 Dispatch loop from a hypothetical non-thread-based Web browser. The clauses in continue_task must cover all possible combinations of task state and triggering event. The code in each clause performs the next coherent unit of work for its task, returning when (1) it must wait for an event, (2) it has consumed a significant amount of compute time, or (3) the task is complete. Prior to returning, respectively, code (1) places the task in a dictionary (used by dispatch) that maps awaited events to the tasks that are waiting for them, (2) enqueues the task in ready_tasks, or (3) deallocates the task.

trying to enumerate a recursive set with iterator objects in Section 6.5.3, only worse. Like true iterators, a thread package turns the program "right side out," making the management of tasks (threads) implicit and the control flow within threads explicit.

13.1.2 Multiprocessor Architecture

Parallel computer hardware is enormously diverse. A *distributed* system—one that we think of in terms of interactions among separate programs running on separate machines—may be as large as the Internet, or as small as the components of a cell phone. A parallel but *nondistributed* system—one that we think of in terms of a single program running on a single machine—may still be very large. China's Tianhe-2 supercomputer, for example, has more than 3 million cores, consumes over 17 MW of power, and occupies 720 square meters of floor space (about a fifth of an acre).

Historically, most parallel but nondistributed machines were *homogeneous*—their processors were all identical. In recent years, many machines have added programmable GPUs, first as separate processors, and more recently as separate portions of a single processor chip. While the cores of a GPU are internally homogeneous, they are very different from those of the typical CPU, leading to a globally *heterogeneous* system. Future systems may have cores of many other kinds as well, each specialized to particular kinds of programs or program components.

In an ideal world, programming languages and runtimes would map program fragments to suitable cores at suitable times, but this sort of automation is still very much a research goal. As of 2015, programmers who want to make use of the GPU write appropriate portions of their code in special-purpose languages like OpenCL or CUDA, which emphasize repetitive operations over vectors. A main program, running on the CPU, then ships the resulting "kernels" to the GPU explicitly.

In the remainder of this chapter, we will concentrate on thread-level parallelism for homogeneous machines. For these, many of the most important architectural questions involve the memory system. In some machines, all of physical memory is accessible to every core, and the hardware guarantees that every write is quickly visible everywhere. At the other extreme, some machines partition main memory among processors, forcing cores to interact through some separate message-passing mechanism. In intermediate designs, some machines share memory in a *noncoherent* fashion, making writes on one core visible to another only when both have explicitly flushed their caches.

From the point of view of language or library implementation, the principal distinction between shared-memory and message-passing hardware is that messages typically require the active participation of cores at both ends of the connection: one to send, the other to receive. On a shared-memory machine, a core can read and write remote memory without any other core's assistance.

On small machines (2–4 processors, say), main memory may be *uniform*—equally distant from all processors. On larger machines (and even on some very small machines), memory may be *nonuniform* instead—each bank may be physically adjacent to a particular processor or small group of processors. Cores in any processor can then access the memory of any other, but local memory is faster. Assuming all memory is cached, of course, the difference appears only on cache misses, where the penalty for local memory is lower.

Memory Coherence

As suggested by the notion of noncoherent memory, caches introduce a serious problem for shared-memory machines: unless we do something special, a core that has cached a particular memory location may run for an arbitrarily long time without seeing changes that have been made to that location by other cores. This problem—how to keep cached copies of a memory location consistent with

EXAMPLE 13.5

The cache coherence problem

DESIGN & IMPLEMENTATION

13.1 What, exactly, is a processor?

From roughly 1975 to 2005, a processor typically ran only one thread at a time, and occupied one full chip. Today, most vendors still use the term "processor" to refer to the physical device that "does the computing," and whose pins connect it to the rest of the computer, but the internal structure is much more complicated: there may be more than one chip inside the physical package, each chip may have multiple *cores* (each of which would have been called a "processor" in previous hardware generations), and each core may have multiple *hardware threads* (independent register sets, which allow the core's pipeline(s) to run a mix of instructions drawn from multiple software threads). A modern processor may also include many megabytes of on-chip cache, organized into multiple levels, and physically distributed and shared among the cores in complicated ways. Increasingly, processors may incorporate on-chip memory controllers, network interfaces, graphical processing units, or other formerly "peripheral" components, making continued use of the term "processor" problematic but no less common.

From a software perspective, the good news is that operating systems and programming languages generally model every concurrent activity as a thread, regardless of whether it shares a core, a chip, or a package with other threads. We will follow this convention for most of the rest of this chapter, ignoring the complexity of the underlying hardware. When we need to refer to the hardware on which a thread runs, we will usually call it a "core." The bad news is that a model of computing in which "everything is just a thread" hides details that are crucial to understanding and improving performance. Future chips are likely to include ever larger numbers of heterogeneous cores and complex on-chip networks. To use these chips effectively, language implementations will need to become much more sophisticated about scheduling threads onto the underlying hardware. How much of the task will need to be visible to the application programmer remains to be determined.

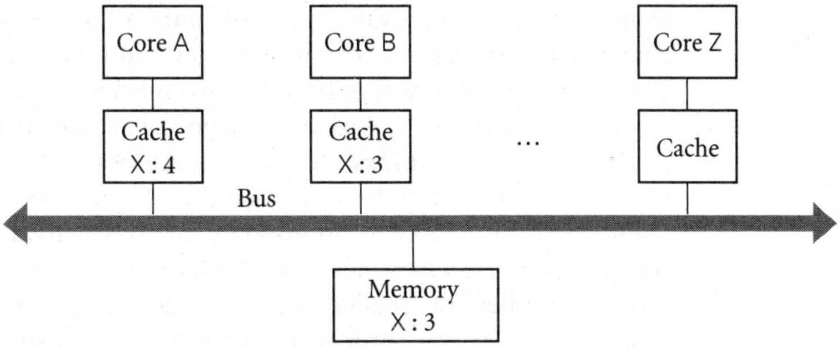

Figure 13.3 The cache coherence problem for shared-memory multicore and multiprocessor machines. Here cores A and B have both read variable X from memory. As a side effect, a copy of X has been created in the cache of each core. If A now changes X to 4 and B reads X again, how do we ensure that the result is a 4 and not the still-cached 3? Similarly, if Z reads X into its cache, how do we ensure that it obtains the 4 from A's cache instead of the stale 3 from memory?

one another—is known as the *coherence* problem (see Figure 13.3). On a simple bus-based machine, the problem is relatively easy to solve: the broadcast nature of the communication medium allows cache controllers to eavesdrop (*snoop*) on the memory traffic of other cores. When a core needs to write a cache line, it requests an *exclusive* copy, and waits for other cores to *invalidate* their copies. On a bus the waiting is trivial, and the natural ordering of messages determines who wins in the event of near-simultaneous requests. Cores that try to access a line in the wake of invalidation must go back to memory (or to another core's cache) to obtain an up-to-date copy. ■

Bus-based cache coherence algorithms are now a standard, built-in part of most commercial microprocessors. On large machines, the lack of a broadcast bus makes cache coherence a significantly more difficult problem; commercial implementations are available, but they are complex and expensive. On both small and large machines, the fact that coherence is not instantaneous (it takes time for notifications to propagate) means that we must consider the *order* in which updates to different locations appear to occur from the point of view of different processors. Ensuring a *consistent* view is a surprisingly difficult problem; we will return to it in Section 13.3.3.

As of 2015, there are multicore versions of every major instruction set architecture, including ARM, x86, Power, SPARC, x86-64, and IA-64 (Itanium). Small, cache-coherent multiprocessors built from these are available from dozens of manufacturers. Larger, cache-coherent shared-memory multiprocessors are available from several manufacturers, including Oracle, HP, IBM, and SGI.

Supercomputers

Though dwarfed financially by the rest of the computer industry, supercomputing has always played a disproportionate role in the development of computer technology and the advancement of human knowledge. Supercomputers have changed dramatically over time, and they continue to evolve at a very rapid pace. They have always, however, been parallel machines.

Because of the complexity of cache coherence, it is difficult to build large shared-memory machines. SGI sells machines with as many as 256 processors (2048 cores). Cray builds even larger shared-memory machines, but without the ability to cache remote locations. For the most part, however, the vector supercomputers of the 1960s–80s were displaced not by large multiprocessors, but by modest numbers of smaller multiprocessors or by very large numbers of commodity (mainstream) processors, connected by custom high-performance networks. As network technology "trickled down" into the broader market, these machines in turn gave way to *clusters* composed of both commodity multicore processors and commodity networks (Gigabit Ethernet or Infiniband). As of 2015, clusters have come to dominate everything from modest server farms up to all but the very fastest supercomputer sites. Large-scale on-line services like Google, Amazon, or Facebook are typically backed by clusters with tens or hundreds of thousands of cores (in Google's case, probably millions).

Today's fastest machines are constructed from special high-density multicore chips with low per-core operating power. The Tianhe-2 (the fastest machine in the world as of June 2015) uses a 2:3 mix of Intel 12-core Ivy Bridge and 61-core Phi processors, at 10 W and 5 W per core, respectively. Given current trends, it seems likely that future machines, both high-end and commodity, will be increasingly dense and increasingly heterogeneous.

From a programming language perspective, the special challenge of supercomputing is to accommodate nonuniform access times and (in most cases) the lack of hardware support for shared memory across the full machine. Today's supercomputers are programmed mostly with message-passing libraries (MPI in particular) and with languages and libraries in which there is a clear syntactic distinction between local and remote memory access.

✓ CHECK YOUR UNDERSTANDING

1. Explain the distinctions among *concurrent*, *parallel*, and *distributed*.
2. Explain the motivation for concurrency. Why do people write concurrent programs? What accounts for the increased interest in concurrency in recent years?
3. Describe the implementation levels at which parallelism appears in modern systems, and the levels of abstraction at which it may be considered by the programmer.
4. What is a *race condition*? What is *synchronization*?
5. What is a *context switch*? *Preemption*?
6. Explain the concept of a *dispatch loop*. What are its advantages and disadvantages with respect to multithreaded code?

7. Explain the distinction between a *multiprocessor* and a *cluster*; between a *processor* and a *core*.
8. What does it mean for memory in a multiprocessor to be *uniform*? What is the alternative?
9. Explain the *coherence problem* for multicore and multiprocessor caches.
10. What is a *vector machine*? Where does vector technology appear in modern systems?

13.2 Concurrent Programming Fundamentals

Within a concurrent program, we will use the term *thread* to refer to the active entity that the programmer thinks of as running concurrently with other threads. In most systems, the threads of a given program are implemented on top of one or more *processes* provided by the operating system. OS designers often distinguish between a *heavyweight* process, which has its own address space, and a collection of *lightweight* processes, which may share an address space. Lightweight processes were added to most variants of Unix in the late 1980s and early 1990s, to accommodate the proliferation of shared-memory multiprocessors.

We will sometimes use the word *task* to refer to a well-defined unit of work that must be performed by some thread. In one common programming idiom, a collection of threads shares a common "bag of tasks"—a list of work to be done. Each thread repeatedly removes a task from the bag, performs it, and goes back for another. Sometimes the work of a task entails adding new tasks to the bag.

Unfortunately, terminology is inconsistent across systems and authors. Several languages call their threads processes. Ada calls them tasks. Several operating systems call lightweight processes threads. The Mach OS, from which OSF Unix and Mac OS X are derived, calls the address space shared by lightweight processes a task. A few systems try to avoid ambiguity by coining new words, such as "actors," "fibers," or "filaments." We will attempt to use the definitions of the preceding two paragraphs consistently, and to identify cases in which the terminology of particular languages or systems differs from this usage.

13.2.1 Communication and Synchronization

In any concurrent programming model, two of the most crucial issues to be addressed are *communication* and *synchronization*. Communication refers to any mechanism that allows one thread to obtain information produced by another. Communication mechanisms for imperative programs are generally based on either *shared memory* or *message passing*. In a shared-memory programming model, some or all of a program's variables are accessible to multiple threads.

For a pair of threads to communicate, one of them writes a value to a variable and the other simply reads it. In a pure message-passing programming model, threads have no common state: for a pair of threads to communicate, one of them must perform an explicit send operation to transmit data to another. (Some languages—Ada, Go, and Rust, for example—provide both messages *and* shared memory.)

Synchronization refers to any mechanism that allows the programmer to control the relative order in which operations occur in different threads. Synchronization is generally implicit in message-passing models: a message must be sent before it can be received. If a thread attempts to receive a message that has not yet been sent, it will wait for the sender to catch up. Synchronization is generally not implicit in shared-memory models: unless we do something special, a "receiving" thread could read the "old" value of a variable, before it has been written by the "sender."

In both shared-memory and message-based programs, synchronization can be implemented either by *spinning* (also called *busy-waiting*) or by *blocking*. In busy-wait synchronization, a thread runs a loop in which it keeps reevaluating some condition until that condition becomes true (e.g., until a message queue becomes nonempty or a shared variable attains a particular value)—presumably as a result of action in some other thread, running on some other core. Note that busy-waiting makes no sense on a uniprocessor: we cannot expect a condition to become true while we are monopolizing a resource (the one and only core) required to make it true. (A thread on a uniprocessor may sometimes busy-wait for the completion of I/O, but that's a different situation: the I/O device runs in parallel with the processor.)

In blocking synchronization (also called *scheduler-based* synchronization), the waiting thread voluntarily relinquishes its core to some other thread. Before doing so, it leaves a note in some data structure associated with the synchronization condition. A thread that makes the condition true at some point in the future will find the note and take action to make the blocked thread run again. We will con-

DESIGN & IMPLEMENTATION

13.2 Hardware and software communication

As described in Section 13.1.2, the distinction between shared memory and message passing applies not only to languages and libraries but also to computer hardware. It is important to note that the model of communication and synchronization provided by the language or library need not necessarily agree with that of the underlying hardware. It is easy to implement message passing on top of shared-memory hardware. With a little more effort, one can also implement shared memory on top of message-passing hardware. Systems in this latter camp are sometimes referred to as *software distributed shared memory* (S-DSM).

	Shared memory	Message passing	Distributed computing
Language	Java, C# C/C++11	Go	Erlang
Extension	OpenMP		Remote procedure call
Library	`pthreads`, Windows threads	MPI	Internet libraries

Figure 13.4 Examples of parallel programming systems. There is also a very large number of experimental, pedagogical, or niche proposals for each of the regions in the table.

sider synchronization again briefly in Section 13.2.4, and then more thoroughly in Section 13.3.

13.2.2 Languages and Libraries

Thread-level concurrency can be provided to the programmer in the form of explicitly concurrent languages, compiler-supported extensions to traditional sequential languages, or library packages outside the language proper. All three options are widely used, though shared-memory languages are more common at the "low end" (for multicore and small multiprocessor machines), and message-passing libraries are more common at the "high end" (for massively parallel supercomputers). Examples of systems in widespread use are categorized in Figure 13.4.

For many years, almost all parallel programming employed traditional sequential languages (largely C and Fortran) augmented with libraries for synchronization or message passing, and this approach still dominates today. In the Unix world, shared memory parallelism has largely converged on the POSIX `pthreads` standard, which includes mechanisms to create, destroy, schedule, and synchronize threads. This standard became an official part of both C and C++ as of their 2011 versions. Similar functionality for Windows machines is provided by Microsoft's thread package and compilers. For high-end scientific computing, message-based parallelism has likewise converged on the MPI (Message Passing Interface) standard, with open-source and commercial implementations available for almost every platform.

While language support for concurrency goes back all the way to Algol 68 (and coroutines to Simula), and while such support was widely available in Ada by the late 1980s, widespread interest in these features didn't really arise until the mid-1990s, when the explosive growth of the World Wide Web began to drive the development of parallel servers and concurrent client programs. This development coincided nicely with the introduction of Java, and Microsoft followed with C# a few years later. Though not yet as influential, many other languages, including Erlang, Go, Haskell, Rust, and Scala, are explicitly parallel as well.

In the realm of scientific programming, there is a long history of extensions to Fortran designed to facilitate the parallel execution of loop iterations. By the turn of the century this work had largely converged on a set of extensions known as OpenMP, available not only in Fortran but also in C and C++. Syntactically, OpenMP comprises a set of *pragmas* (compiler directives) to create and synchronize threads, and to schedule work among them. On machines composed of a network of multiprocessors, it is increasingly common to see hybrid programs that use OpenMP within a multiprocessor and MPI across them.

In both the shared memory and message passing columns of Figure 13.4, the parallel constructs are intended for use within a single multithreaded program. For communication across program boundaries in distributed systems, programmers have traditionally employed library implementations of the standard Internet protocols, in a manner reminiscent of file-based I/O (Section C-8.7). For client-server interaction, however, it can be attractive to provide a higher-level interface based on *remote procedure calls* (RPC), an alternative we consider further in Section C-13.5.4.

In comparison to library packages, an explicitly concurrent programming language has the advantage of compiler support. It can make use of syntax other than subroutine calls, and can integrate communication and thread management more tightly with such concepts as type checking, scoping, and exceptions. At the same time, since most programs have historically been sequential, concurrent languages have been slow to gain widespread acceptance, particularly given that the presence of concurrent features can sometime make the sequential case more difficult to understand.

13.2.3 Thread Creation Syntax

Almost every concurrent system allows threads to be created (and destroyed) dynamically. Syntactic and semantic details vary considerably from one language or library to another, but most conform to one of six principal options: co-begin, parallel loops, launch-at-elaboration, fork (with optional join), implicit receipt, and early reply. The first two options delimit threads with special control-flow constructs. The others use syntax resembling (or identical to) subroutines.

At least one pedagogical language (SR) provided all six options. Most others pick and choose. Most libraries use fork/join, as do Java and C#. Ada uses both launch-at-elaboration and fork. OpenMP uses co-begin and parallel loops. RPC systems are typically based on implicit receipt.

Co-begin

EXAMPLE 13.6
General form of co-begin

The usual semantics of a compound statement (sometimes delimited with begin... end) call for sequential execution of the constituent statements. A co-begin construct calls instead for concurrent execution:

```
co-begin            -- all n statements run concurrently
```

```
    stmt_1
    stmt_2
    ...
    stmt_n
end
```

Each statement can itself be a sequential or parallel compound, or (commonly) a subroutine call.

EXAMPLE 13.7
Co-begin in OpenMP

Co-begin was the principal means of creating threads in Algol-68. It appears in a variety of other systems as well, including OpenMP:

```
#pragma omp sections
{
#   pragma omp section
    { printf("thread 1 here\n"); }

#   pragma omp section
    { printf("thread 2 here\n"); }
}
```

In C, OpenMP directives all begin with `#pragma omp`. (The `#` sign must appear in column one.) Most directives, like those shown here, must appear immediately before a loop construct or a compound statement delimited with curly braces.

Parallel Loops

Many concurrent systems, including OpenMP, several dialects of Fortran, and the Task Parallel Library for .NET, provide a loop whose iterations are to be executed concurrently. In OpenMP for C, we might say

EXAMPLE 13.8
A parallel loop in OpenMP

```
#pragma omp parallel for
for (int i = 0; i < 3; i++) {
    printf("thread %d here\n", i);
}
```

EXAMPLE 13.9
A parallel loop in C#

In C# with the Task Parallel Library, the equivalent code looks like this:

```
Parallel.For(0, 3, i => {
    Console.WriteLine("Thread " + i + "here");
});
```

The third argument to `Parallel.For` is a delegate, in this case a lambda expression. A similar `Foreach` method expects two arguments—an iterator and a delegate.

In many systems it is the programmer's responsibility to make sure that concurrent execution of the loop iterations is safe, in the sense that correctness will never depend on the outcome of race conditions. Access to global variables, for example, must generally be synchronized, to make sure that iterations do not conflict with one another. In a few languages (e.g., Occam), language rules prohibit conflicting accesses. The compiler checks to make sure that a variable written by one thread is neither read nor written by any concurrently active thread. In a similar but slightly more flexible vein, the `do concurrent` loop of Fortran 2008 constitutes an assertion on the programmer's part that iterations of the loop are mutually independent, and hence can safely be executed in any order, or in parallel. Several rules on the content of the loop—some but not all of them enforceable by the compiler—reduce the likelihood that programmers will make this assertion incorrectly.

Historically, several parallel dialects of Fortran provided other forms of parallel loop, with varying semantics. The `forall` loop of High Performance Fortran (HPF) was subsequently incorporated into Fortran 95. Like `do concurrent`, it indicates that iterations can proceed in parallel. To resolve race conditions, however, it imposes automatic, internal synchronization on the constituent statements of the loop, each of which must be an assignment or a nested `forall` loop. Specifically, all reads of variables in a given assignment statement, in all iterations, must occur before any write to the left-hand side, in any iteration. The writes of the left-hand side in turn must occur before any reads in the next assignment statement. In the following example, the first assignment in the loop will read $n-1$ elements of `B` and $n-1$ elements of `C`, and then update $n-1$ elements of `A`. Subsequently, the second assignment statement will read all n elements of `A` and then update $n-1$ of them:

EXAMPLE 13.10
`Forall` in Fortran 95

```
forall (i=1:n-1)
    A(i) = B(i) + C(i)
    A(i+1) = A(i) + A(i+1)
end forall
```

Note in particular that all of the updates to `A(i)` in the first assignment statement occur before any of the reads in the second assignment statement. Moreover in the second assignment statement the update to `A(i+1)` is *not* seen by the read of `A(i)` in the "subsequent" iteration: the iterations occur in parallel and each reads the variables on its right-hand side before updating its left-hand side. ■

For loops that iterate over the elements of an array, the `forall` semantics are ideally suited for execution on a vector machine. For more conventional multiprocessors, HPF provides an extensive set of *data distribution* and *alignment* directives that allow the programmer to scatter elements across the memory associated with a large number of processors. Within a `forall` loop, the computation in a given assignment statement is usually performed by the processor that "owns" the element on the assignment's left-hand side. In many cases an HPF or Fortran 95 compiler can prove that there are no dependences among certain (portions of) constituent statements of a `forall` loop, and can allow them to proceed without actually implementing synchronization.

OpenMP does not enforce the statement-by-statement synchronization of `forall`, but it does provide significant support for scheduling and data management. Optional "clauses" on `parallel` directives can specify how many threads to create, and which iterations of the loop to perform in which thread. They can also specify which program variables should be shared by all threads, and which should be split into a separate copy for each thread. It is even possible to specify that a private variable should be *reduced* across all threads at the end of the loop, using a commutative operator. To sum the elements of a very large vector, for example, one might write

EXAMPLE 13.11
Reduction in OpenMP

```
double A[N];
...
double sum = 0;
#pragma omp parallel for schedule(static) \
    default(shared) reduction(+:sum)
for (int i = 0; i < N; i++) {
    sum += A[i];
}
printf("parallel sum: %f\n", sum);
```

Here the `schedule(static)` clause indicates that the compiler should divide the iterations evenly among threads, in contiguous groups. So if there are t threads, the first thread should get the first N/t iterations, the second should get the next N/t iterations, and so on. The `default(shared)` clause indicates that all variables (other than `i`) should be shared by all threads, unless otherwise specified. The `reduction(+:sum)` clause makes `sum` an exception: every thread should have its own copy (initialized from the value in effect before the loop), and the copies should be combined (with `+`) at the end. If t is large, the compiler will probably sum the values using a tree of depth $\log(t)$.

Launch-at-Elaboration

In several languages, Ada among them, the code for a thread may be declared with syntax resembling that of a subroutine with no parameters. When the declaration is elaborated, a thread is created to execute the code. In Ada (which calls its threads `tasks`) we may write

EXAMPLE 13.12
Elaborated tasks in Ada

```
procedure P is
task T is
...
end T;
begin -- P
...
end P;
```

Task `T` has its own `begin... end` block, which it begins to execute as soon as control enters procedure `P`. If `P` is recursive, there may be many instances of `T` at the same time, all of which execute concurrently with each other and with whatever task is executing (the current instance of) `P`. The main program behaves like an initial default task.

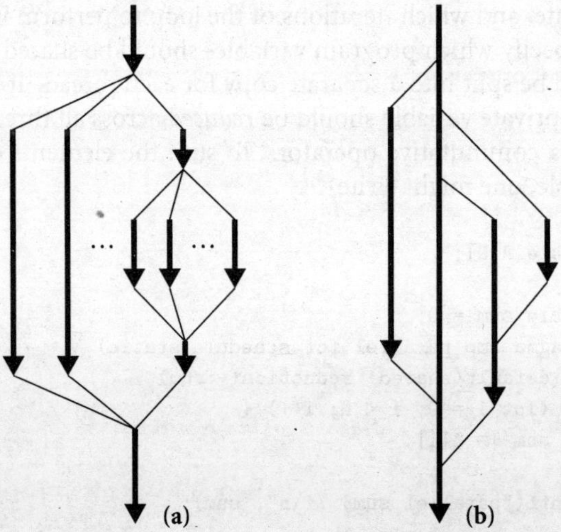

Figure 13.5 Lifetime of concurrent threads. With co-begin, parallel loops, or launch-at-elaboration (a), threads are always properly nested. With fork/join (b), more general patterns are possible.

When control reaches the end of procedure P, it will wait for the appropriate instance of T (the one that was created at the beginning of this instance of P) to complete before returning. This rule ensures that the local variables of P (which are visible to T under the usual static scope rules) are never deallocated before T is done with them. ■

Fork/Join

EXAMPLE 13.13 Co-begin vs fork/join

Co-begin, parallel loops, and launch-at-elaboration all lead to a concurrent control-flow pattern in which thread executions are properly nested (see Figure 13.5a). The fork operation is more general: it makes the creation of threads an explicit, executable operation. The companion join operation, when provided, allows a thread to wait for the completion of a previously forked thread. Because fork and join are not tied to nested constructs, they can lead to arbitrary patterns of concurrent control flow (Figure 13.5b). ■

EXAMPLE 13.14 Task types in Ada

In addition to providing launch-at-elaboration tasks, Ada allows the programmer to define task *types*:

```
task type T is
...
begin
...
end T;
```

The programmer may then declare variables of type access T (pointer to T), and may create new tasks via dynamic allocation:

```
pt : access T := new T;
```

The new operation is a fork: it creates a new thread and starts it executing. There is no explicit join operation in Ada, though parent and child tasks can always synchronize with one another explicitly if desired (e.g., immediately before the child completes its execution). As with launch-at-elaboration, control will wait automatically at the end of any scope in which task types are declared for all threads using the scope to terminate. ■

Any information an Ada task needs in order to do its job must be communicated through shared variables or through explicit messages sent after the task has started execution. Most systems, by contrast, allow parameters to be passed to a thread at start-up time. In Java one obtains a thread by constructing an object of some class derived from a predefined class called Thread:

EXAMPLE 13.15
Thread creation in Java 2

```
class ImageRenderer extends Thread {
    ...
    ImageRenderer( args ) {
        // constructor
    }
```

DESIGN & IMPLEMENTATION

13.3 Task-parallel and data-parallel computing

One of the most basic decisions a programmer has to make when writing a parallel program is how to divide work among threads. One common strategy, which works well on small machines, is to use a separate thread for each of the program's major tasks or functions, and to pipeline or otherwise overlap their execution. In a word processor, for example, one thread might be devoted to breaking paragraphs into lines, another to pagination and figure placement, another to spelling and grammar checking, and another to rendering the image on the screen. This strategy is often known as *task parallelism*. Its principal disadvantage is that it doesn't naturally scale to very large numbers of processors. For that, one generally needs *data parallelism*, in which more or less the same operations are applied concurrently to the elements of some very large data set. An image manipulation program, for example, may divide the screen into *n* small tiles, and use a separate thread to process each tile. A game may use a separate thread for every moving character or object.

A programming system whose features are designed for data parallelism is sometimes referred to as a data-parallel language or library. Task parallel programs are commonly based on co-begin, launch-at-elaboration, or fork/join: the code in different threads can be different. Data parallel programs are commonly based on parallel loops: each thread executes the same code, using different data. OpenCL and CUDA, unsurprisingly, are in the data-parallel camp: programmable GPUs are optimized for data parallel programs.

```
        public void run() {
            // code to be run by the thread
        }
    }
    ...
    ImageRenderer rend = new ImageRenderer( constructor_args );
```

Superficially, the use of new resembles the creation of dynamic tasks in Ada. In Java, however, the new thread does *not* begin execution when first created. To start it, the parent (or some other thread) must call the method named `start`, which is defined in `Thread`:

```
    rend.start();
```

`Start` makes the thread runnable, arranges for it to execute its `run` method, and returns to the caller. The programmer must define an appropriate `run` method in every class derived from `Thread`. The `run` method is meant to be called only by `start`; programmers should not call it directly, nor should they redefine `start`. There is also a `join` method:

```
    rend.join();        // wait for completion
```

The constructor for a Java thread typically saves its arguments in fields that are later accessed by `run`. In effect, the class derived from `Thread` functions as an *object closure*, as described in Section 3.6.3. Several languages, Modula-3 and C# among them, use closures more explicitly. Rather than require every thread to be derived from a common `Thread` class, C# allows one to be created from an arbitrary `ThreadStart` delegate:

EXAMPLE 13.16
Thread creation in C#

```
class ImageRenderer {
    ...
    public ImageRenderer( args ) {
        // constructor
    }
    public void Foo() {     // Foo is compatible with ThreadStart;
                            // its name is not significant
        // code to be run by the thread
    }
}
...
ImageRenderer rendObj = new ImageRenderer( constructor_args );
Thread rend = new Thread(new ThreadStart(rendObj.Foo));
```

If thread arguments can be gleaned from the local context, this can even be written as

```
Thread rend = new Thread(delegate() {
    // code to be run by the thread
});
```

(Remember, C# has unlimited extent for anonymous delegates.) Either way, the new thread is started and awaited just as it is in Java:

```
rend.Start();
...
rend.Join();
```

EXAMPLE 13.17 Thread pools in Java 5

As of Java 5 (with its `java.util.concurrent` library), programmers are discouraged from creating threads explicitly. Rather, tasks to be accomplished are represented by objects that support the `Runnable` interface, and these are passed to an `Executor` object. The `Executor` in turn farms them out to a managed pool of threads:

```
class ImageRenderer implements Runnable {
    ...
    // constructor and run() method same as before
}
...
Executor pool = Executors.newFixedThreadPool(4);
...
pool.execute(new ImageRenderer( constructor_args ));
```

Here the argument to `newFixedThreadPool` (one of a large number of standard `Executor` *factories*) indicates that `pool` should manage four threads. Each task specified in a call to `pool.execute` will be run by one of these threads. By separating the concepts of task and thread, Java allows the programmer (or run-time code) to choose an `Executor` class whose level of true concurrency and scheduling discipline are appropriate to the underlying OS and hardware. (In this example we have used a particularly simple pool, with exactly four threads.) C# has similar thread pool facilities. Like C# threads, they are based on delegates.

EXAMPLE 13.18 Spawn and sync in Cilk

A particularly elegant realization of `fork` and `join` appears in the Cilk programming language, developed by researchers at MIT, and subsequently developed into a commercial venture acquired by Intel. To fork a logically concurrent task in Cilk, one simply prepends the keyword `spawn` to an ordinary function call:

```
spawn foo( args );
```

At some later time, invocation of the built-in operation `sync` will join with all tasks previously spawned by the calling task. The principal innovation of Cilk is the mechanism for scheduling tasks. The language implementation includes a highly efficient thread pool mechanism that explores the task-creation graph depth first with a near-minimal number of context switches and automatic load balancing across threads. Java 7 added a similar but more restricted mechanism in the form of a `ForkJoinPool` for the `Executor` service. ■

Implicit Receipt

We have assumed in all our examples so far that newly created threads will run in the address space of the creator. In RPC systems it is often desirable to create a new thread automatically in response to an incoming request from some *other* address space. Rather than have an existing thread execute a receive operation, a server can *bind* a communication channel to a local thread body or subroutine. When a request comes in, a new thread springs into existence to handle it.

In effect, the `bind` operation grants remote clients the ability to perform a `fork` within the server's address space, though the process is often less than fully automatic. We will consider RPC in more detail in Section C-13.5.4.

Early Reply

EXAMPLE 13.19
Modeling subroutines with fork/join

We normally think of sequential subroutines in terms of a single thread, which saves its current context (its program counter and registers), executes the subroutine, and returns to what it was doing before. The effect is the same, however, if we have two threads—one that executes the caller and another that executes the callee. In this case, the call is essentially a fork/join pair. The caller waits for the callee to terminate before continuing execution. ■

Nothing dictates, however, that the callee has to terminate in order to release the caller; all it really has to do is complete the portion of its work on which re-

DESIGN & IMPLEMENTATION

13.4 Counterintuitive implementation

Over the course of 13 chapters we have seen numerous cases in which the implementation of a language feature may run counter to the programmer's intuition. Early reply—in which thread creation is usually delayed until the reply actually occurs—is but the most recent example. Others have included expression evaluation order (Section 6.1.4), subroutine in-lining (Section 9.2.4), tail recursion (Section 6.6.1), nonstack allocation of activation records (for unlimited extent—Section 3.6.2), out-of-order or even noncontiguous layout of record fields (Section 8.1.2), variable lookup in a central reference table (Section C-3.4.2), immutable objects under a reference model of variables (Section 6.1.2), and implementations of generics (Section 7.3.1) that share code among instances with different type parameters. A compiler may, particularly at higher levels of code improvement, produce code that differs dramatically from the form and organization of its input. Unless otherwise constrained by the language definition, an implementation is free to choose any translation that is provably equivalent to the input.

sult parameters depend. Drawing inspiration from the `detach` operation used to launch coroutines in Simula (Example 9.47), a few languages (SR and Hermes [SBG+91] among them) allow a callee to execute a reply operation that returns results to the caller *without* terminating. After an early reply, the two threads continue concurrently.

Semantically, the portion of the callee prior to the reply plays much the same role as the constructor of a Java or C# thread; the portion after the reply plays the role of the run method. The usual implementation is also similar, and may run counter to the programmer's intuition: since early reply is optional, and can appear in any subroutine, we can use the caller's thread to execute the initial portion of the callee, and create a new thread only when—and if—the callee replies instead of returning.

13.2.4 Implementation of Threads

As we noted near the beginning of Section 13.2, the threads of a concurrent program are usually implemented on top of one or more *processes* provided by the operating system. At one extreme, we could use a separate OS process for every thread; at the other extreme we could multiplex all of a program's threads on top of a single process. On a supercomputer with a separate core for every concurrent activity, or in a language in which threads are relatively heavyweight abstractions (long-lived, and created by the dozens rather than the thousands), the one-process-per-thread extreme is often acceptable. In a simple language on a uniprocessor, the all-threads-on-one-process extreme may be acceptable. Many language implementations adopt an intermediate approach, with a potentially very large number of threads running on top of some smaller but nontrivial number of processes (see Figure 13.6).

EXAMPLE 13.20 Multiplexing threads on processes

The problem with putting every thread on a separate process is that processes (even "lightweight" ones) are simply too expensive in many operating systems. Because they are implemented in the kernel, performing any operation on them requires a system call. Because they are general purpose, they provide features that most languages do not need, but have to pay for anyway. (Examples include separate address spaces, priorities, accounting information, and signal and I/O interfaces, all of which are beyond the scope of this book.) At the other extreme, there are two problems with putting all threads on top of a single process: first, it precludes parallel execution on a multicore or multiprocessor machine; second, if the currently running thread makes a system call that blocks (e.g., waiting for I/O), then none of the program's other threads can run, because the single process is suspended by the OS.

In the common two-level organization of concurrency (user-level threads on top of kernel-level processes), similar code appears at both levels of the system: the language run-time system implements threads on top of one or more processes in much the same way that the operating system implements processes on

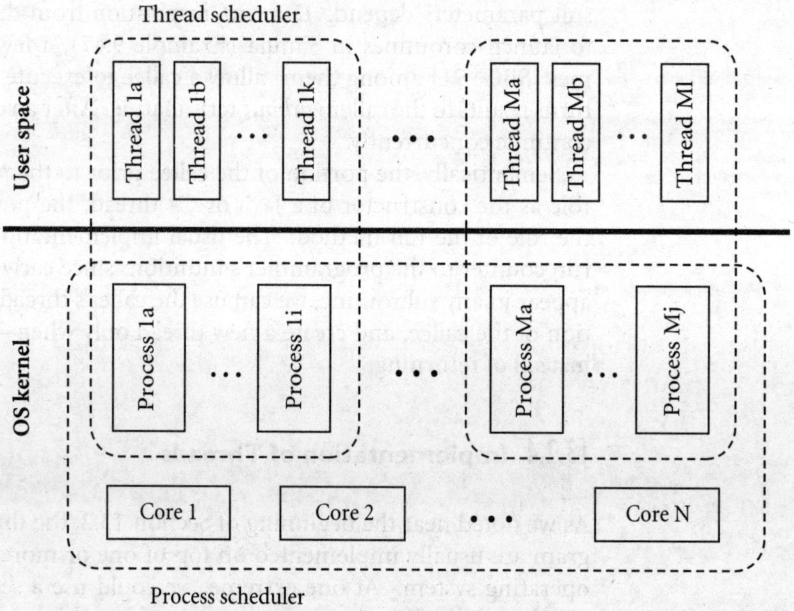

Figure 13.6 **Two-level implementation of threads.** A thread scheduler, implemented in a library or language run-time package, multiplexes threads on top of one or more kernel-level processes, just as the process scheduler, implemented in the operating system kernel, multiplexes processes on top of one or more physical cores.

top of one or more physical cores. We will use the terminology of threads on top of processes in the remainder of this section.

The typical implementation starts with coroutines (Section 9.5). Recall that coroutines are a sequential control-flow mechanism: the programmer can suspend the current coroutine and resume a specific alternative by calling the transfer operation. The argument to transfer is typically a pointer to the context block of the coroutine.

To turn coroutines into threads, we proceed in a series of three steps. First, we hide the argument to transfer by implementing a *scheduler* that chooses which thread to run next when the current thread yields the core. Second, we implement a *preemption* mechanism that suspends the current thread automatically on a regular basis, giving other threads a chance to run. Third, we allow the data structures that describe our collection of threads to be shared by more than one OS process, possibly on separate cores, so that threads can run on any of the processes.

Uniprocessor Scheduling

EXAMPLE 13.21 Cooperative multithreading on a uniprocessor

Figure 13.7 illustrates the data structures employed by a simple scheduler. At any particular time, a thread is either *blocked* (i.e., for synchronization) or *runnable*. A runnable thread may actually be running on some process or it may be awaiting

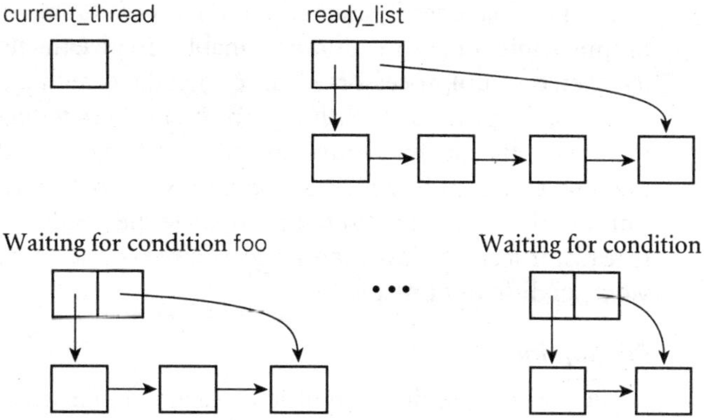

Figure 13.7 Data structures of a simple scheduler. A designated current_thread is running. Threads on the ready list are runnable. Other threads are blocked, waiting for various conditions to become true. If threads run on top of more than one OS-level process, each such process will have its own current_thread variable. If a thread makes a call into the operating system, its process may block in the kernel.

its chance to do so. Context blocks for threads that are runnable but not currently running reside on a queue called the *ready list*. Context blocks for threads that are blocked for scheduler-based synchronization reside in data structures (usually queues) associated with the conditions for which they are waiting. To yield the core to another thread, a running thread calls the scheduler:

```
procedure reschedule()
    t : thread := dequeue(ready_list)
    transfer(t)
```

Before calling into the scheduler, a thread that wants to run again at some point in the future must place its own context block in some appropriate data structure. If it is blocking for the sake of fairness—to give some other thread a chance to run—then it enqueues its context block on the ready list:

```
procedure yield()
    enqueue(ready_list, current_thread)
    reschedule()
```

To block for synchronization, a thread adds itself to a queue associated with the awaited condition:

```
procedure sleep_on(ref Q : queue of thread)
    enqueue(Q, current_thread)
    reschedule()
```

When a running thread performs an operation that makes a condition true, it removes one or more threads from the associated queue and enqueues them on the ready list.

Fairness becomes an issue whenever a thread may run for a significant amount of time while other threads are runnable. To give the illusion of concurrent activity, even on a uniprocessor, we need to make sure that each thread gets a frequent "slice" of the processor. With *cooperative multithreading*, any long-running thread must yield its core explicitly from time to time (e.g., at the tops of loops), to allow other threads to run. As noted in Section 13.1.1, this approach allows one improperly written thread to monopolize the system. Even with properly written threads, it leads to less than perfect fairness due to nonuniform times between yields in different threads.

Preemption

Ideally, we should like to multiplex each core fairly and at a relatively fine grain (i.e., many times per second) *without* requiring that threads call yield explicitly. On many systems we can do this in the language implementation by using timer signals for *preemptive multithreading*. When switching between threads we ask the operating system (which has access to the hardware clock) to deliver a signal to the currently running process at a specified time in the future. The OS delivers the signal by saving the context (registers and pc) of the process and transferring control to a previously specified *handler* routine in the language run-time system, as described in Section 9.6.1. When called, the handler modifies the state of the currently running thread to make it appear that the thread had just executed a call to the standard yield routine, and was about to execute its prologue. The handler then "returns" into yield, which transfers control to some other thread, as if the one that had been running had relinquished control of the process voluntarily.

Unfortunately, the fact that a signal may arrive at an arbitrary time introduces a race between voluntary calls to the scheduler and the automatic calls triggered by preemption. To illustrate the problem, suppose that a signal arrives when the currently running process has just enqueued the currently running thread onto the ready list in yield, and is about to call reschedule. When the signal handler "returns" into yield, the process will put the current thread into the ready list a second time. If at some point in the future the thread blocks for synchronization, its second entry in the ready list may cause it to run again immediately, when it should be waiting. Even worse problems can arise if a signal occurs in the middle of an enqueue, at a moment when the ready list is not even a properly structured queue. To resolve the race and avoid corruption of the ready list, thread packages commonly disable signal delivery during scheduler calls:

EXAMPLE 13.22
A race condition in preemptive multithreading

```
procedure yield()
    disable_signals()
    enqueue(ready_list, current_thread)
    reschedule()
    reenable_signals()
```

For this convention to work, *every* fragment of code that calls reschedule must disable signals prior to the call, and must reenable them afterward. (Recall that a similar mechanism served to protect data shared between the main program and event handlers in Section 9.6.1.) In this case, because reschedule contains a call to transfer, signals may be disabled in one thread and reenabled in another. ■

EXAMPLE 13.23
Disabling signals during context switch

It turns out that the sleep_on routine must also assume that signals are disabled and enabled by the caller. To see why, suppose that a thread checks a condition, finds that it is false, and then calls sleep_on to suspend itself on a queue associated with the condition. Suppose further that a timer signal occurs immediately after checking the condition, but before the call to sleep_on. Finally, suppose that the thread that is allowed to run after the signal makes the condition true. Since the first thread never got a chance to put itself on the condition queue, the second thread will not find it to make it runnable. When the first thread runs again, it will immediately suspend itself, and may never be awakened. To close this *timing window*—this interval in which a concurrent event may compromise program correctness—the caller must ensure that signals are disabled before checking the condition:

```
disable_signals()
if not desired_condition
    sleep_on(condition_queue)
reenable_signals
```

On a uniprocessor, disabling signals allows the check and the sleep to occur as a single, *atomic* operation. ■

Multiprocessor Scheduling

We can extend our preemptive thread package to run on top of more than one OS-provided process by arranging for the processes to share the ready list and related data structures (condition queues, etc.; note that each process must have a *separate* current_thread variable). If the processes run on different physical cores, then more than one thread will be able to run at once. If the processes share a single core, then the program will be able to make forward progress even when all but one of the processes are blocked in the operating system. Any thread that is runnable is placed in the ready list, where it becomes a candidate for execution by any of the application's processes. When a process calls reschedule, the queue-based ready list we have been using in our examples will give it the longest-waiting thread. The ready list of a more elaborate scheduler might give priority to interactive or time-critical threads, or to threads that last ran on the current core, and may therefore still have data in the cache.

Just as preemption introduced a race between voluntary and automatic calls to scheduler operations, true or quasiparallelism introduces races between calls in separate OS processes. To resolve the races, we must implement additional synchronization to make scheduler operations in separate processes atomic. We will return to this subject in Section 13.3.4.

CHECK YOUR UNDERSTANDING

11. Explain the differences among *coroutines*, *threads*, *lightweight processes*, and *heavyweight processes*.
12. What is *quasiparallelism*?
13. Describe the *bag of tasks* programming model.
14. What is *busy-waiting*? What is its principal alternative?
15. Name four explicitly concurrent programming languages.
16. Why don't message-passing programs require explicit synchronization mechanisms?
17. What are the tradeoffs between language-based and library-based implementations of concurrency?
18. Explain the difference between *data parallelism* and *task parallelism*.
19. Describe six different mechanisms commonly used to create new threads of control in a concurrent program.
20. In what sense is fork/join more powerful than *co-begin*?
21. What is a *thread pool* in Java? What purpose does it serve?
22. What is meant by a *two-level* thread implementation?
23. What is a *ready list*?
24. Describe the progressive implementation of scheduling, preemption, and (true) parallelism on top of coroutines.

13.3 Implementing Synchronization

As noted in Section 13.2.1, synchronization is the principal semantic challenge for shared-memory concurrent programs. Typically, synchronization serves either to make some operation *atomic* or to delay that operation until some necessary precondition holds. As noted in Section 13.1, atomicity is most commonly achieved with *mutual exclusion locks*. Mutual exclusion ensures that only one thread is executing some *critical section* of code at a given point in time. Critical sections typically transform a shared data structure from one consistent state to another.

Condition synchronization allows a thread to wait for a precondition, often expressed as a predicate on the value(s) in one or more shared variables. It is tempting to think of mutual exclusion as a form of condition synchronization (don't proceed until no other thread is in its critical section), but this sort of condition would require *consensus* among all extant threads, something that condition synchronization doesn't generally provide.

Our implementation of parallel threads, sketched at the end of Section 13.2.4, requires both atomicity and condition synchronization. Atomicity of operations on the ready list and related data structures ensures that they always satisfy a set of logical invariants: the lists are well formed, each thread is either running or resides in exactly one list, and so forth. Condition synchronization appears in the requirement that a process in need of a thread to run must wait until the ready list is nonempty.

It is worth emphasizing that we do not in general want to overly synchronize programs. To do so would eliminate opportunities for parallelism, which we generally want to maximize in the interest of performance. Moreover not all races are bad. If two processes are racing to `dequeue` the last thread from the ready list, we don't generally care which succeeds and which waits for another thread. We *do* care that the implementation of `dequeue` does not have *internal*, instruction-level races that might compromise the ready list's integrity. In general, our goal is to provide only as much synchronization as is necessary to eliminate "bad" races—those that might otherwise cause the program to produce incorrect results.

In the first subsection below we consider busy-wait synchronization. In the second we present an alternative, called *nonblocking synchronization*, in which atomicity is achieved without the need for mutual exclusion. In the third subsection we return to the subject of memory consistency (originally mentioned in Section 13.1.2), and discuss its implications for the semantics and implementation of language-level synchronization mechanisms. Finally, in Sections 13.3.4 and 13.3.5, we use busy-waiting among processes to implement a parallelism-safe thread scheduler, and then use this scheduler in turn to implement the most basic scheduler-based synchronization mechanism: namely, semaphores.

13.3.1 Busy-Wait Synchronization

Busy-wait condition synchronization is easy if we can cast a condition in the form of "location X contains value Y": a thread that needs to wait for the condition can simply read X in a loop, waiting for Y to appear. To wait for a condition involving more than one location, one needs atomicity to read the locations together, but given that, the implementation is again a simple loop.

Other forms of busy-wait synchronization are somewhat trickier. In the remainder of this section we consider *spin locks*, which provide mutual exclusion, and *barriers*, which ensure that no thread continues past a given point in a program until all threads have reached that point.

Spin Locks

Dekker is generally credited with finding the first two-thread mutual exclusion algorithm that requires no atomic instructions other than load and store. Dijkstra [Dij65] published a version that works for n threads in 1965. Peterson [Pet81] published a much simpler two-thread algorithm in 1981. Building on

```
type lock = Boolean := false;
procedure acquire_lock(ref L : lock)
    while not test_and_set(L)
        while L
            -- nothing -- spin
procedure release_lock(ref L : lock)
    L := false
```

Figure 13.8 **A simple test-and-`test_and_set` lock.** Waiting processes spin with ordinary read (`load`) instructions until the lock appears to be free, then use `test_and_set` to acquire it. The very first access is a `test_and_set`, for speed in the common (no competition) case.

Peterson's algorithm, one can construct a hierarchical n-thread lock, but it requires $O(n \log n)$ space and $O(\log n)$ time to get one thread into its critical section [YA93]. Lamport [Lam87][2] published an n-thread algorithm in 1987 that takes $O(n)$ space and $O(1)$ time in the absence of competition for the lock. Unfortunately, it requires $O(n)$ time when multiple threads attempt to enter their critical section at once.

While all of these algorithms are historically important, a practical spin lock needs to run in constant time and space, and for this one needs an atomic instruction that does more than load or store. Beginning in the 1960s, hardware designers began to equip their processors with instructions that read, modify, and write a memory location as a single atomic operation. The simplest such instruction is known as `test_and_set`. It sets a Boolean variable to `true` and returns an indication of whether the variable was previously `false`. Given `test_and_set`, acquiring a spin lock is almost trivial:

EXAMPLE 13.24 The basic test_and_set lock

```
while not test_and_set(L)
    -- nothing -- spin
```

In practice, embedding `test_and_set` in a loop tends to result in unacceptable amounts of communication on a multicore or multiprocessor machine, as the cache coherence mechanism attempts to reconcile writes by multiple cores attempting to acquire the lock. This overdemand for hardware resources is known as *contention*, and is a major obstacle to good performance on large machines.

EXAMPLE 13.25 Test-and-test_and_set

To reduce contention, the writers of synchronization libraries often employ a test-and-`test_and_set` lock, which spins with ordinary reads (satisfied by the cache) until it appears that the lock is free (see Figure 13.8). When a thread releases a lock there still tends to be a flurry of bus or interconnect activity as waiting

2 Leslie Lamport (1941–) has made a variety of seminal contributions to the theory of parallel and distributed computing, including synchronization algorithms, the notion of "happens-before" causality, Byzantine agreement, the Paxos consensus algorithm, and the temporal logic of actions. He also created the LaTeX macro package, with which this book was typeset. He received the ACM Turing Award in 2013.

threads perform their `test_and_sets`, but at least this activity happens only at the boundaries of critical sections. On a large machine, contention can be further reduced by implementing a *backoff* strategy, in which a thread that is unsuccessful in attempting to acquire a lock waits for a while before trying again. ▪

Many processors provide atomic instructions more powerful than `test_and_set`. Some can swap the contents of a register and a memory location atomically. Some can add a constant to a memory location atomically, returning the previous value. Several processors, including the x86, the IA-64, and the SPARC, provide a particularly useful instruction called `compare_and_swap` (`CAS`). This instruction takes three arguments: a location, an expected value, and a new value. It checks to see whether the expected value appears in the specified location, and if so replaces it with the new value, atomically. In either case, it returns an indication of whether the change was made. Using instructions like `atomic_add` or `compare_and_swap`, one can build spin locks that are *fair*, in the sense that threads are guaranteed to acquire the lock in the order in which they first attempt to do so. One can also build locks that work well—with no contention, even at release time—on arbitrarily large machines [MCS91, Sco13]. These topics are beyond the scope of the current text. (It is perhaps worth mentioning that fairness is a two-edged sword: while it may be desirable from a semantic point of view, it tends to undermine cache locality, and interacts very badly with preemption.)

An important variant on mutual exclusion is the *reader–writer lock* [CHP71]. Reader–writer locks recognize that if several threads wish to *read* the same data structure, they can do so simultaneously without mutual interference. It is only when a thread wants to *write* the data structure that we need to prevent other threads from reading or writing simultaneously. Most busy-wait mutual exclusion locks can be extended to allow concurrent access by readers (see Exercise 13.8).

Barriers

Data-parallel algorithms are often structured as a series of high-level steps, or *phases*, typically expressed as iterations of some outermost loop. Correctness often depends on making sure that every thread completes the previous step before any moves on to the next. A *barrier* serves to provide this synchronization.

EXAMPLE 13.26
Barriers in finite element analysis

As a concrete example, *finite element analysis* models a physical object—a bridge, let us say—as an enormous collection of tiny fragments. Each fragment of the bridge imparts forces to the fragments adjacent to it. Gravity exerts a downward force on all fragments. Abutments exert an upward force on the fragments that make up base plates. The wind exerts forces on surface fragments. To evaluate stress on the bridge as a whole (e.g., to assess its stability and resistance to failures), a finite element program might divide the fragments among a large collection of threads (probably one per core). Beginning with the external forces, the program would then proceed through a sequence of iterations. In each iteration, each thread would recompute the forces on its fragments based on the forces found in the previous iteration. Between iterations, the threads would

```
shared count : integer := n
shared sense : Boolean := true
per-thread private local_sense : Boolean := true

procedure central_barrier()
    local_sense := not local_sense
        -- each thread toggles its own sense
    if fetch_and_decrement(count) = 1
        -- last arriving thread
        count := n              -- reinitialize for next iteration
        sense := local_sense    -- allow other threads to proceed
    else
        repeat
            -- spin
        until sense = local_sense
```

Figure 13.9 A simple "sense-reversing" barrier. Each thread has its own copy of local_sense. Threads share a single copy of count and sense.

synchronize with a barrier. The program would halt when no thread found a significant change in any forces during the last iteration. ■

EXAMPLE 13.27 The "sense-reversing" barrier

The simplest way to implement a busy-wait barrier is to use a globally shared counter, modified by an atomic `fetch_and_decrement` instruction. The counter begins at *n*, the number of threads in the program. As each thread reaches the barrier it decrements the counter. If it is not the last to arrive, the thread then spins on a Boolean flag. The final thread (the one that changes the counter from 1 to 0) flips the Boolean flag, allowing the other threads to proceed. To make it easy to reuse the barrier data structures in successive iterations (known as barrier *episodes*), threads wait for alternating values of the flag each time through. Code for this simple barrier appears in Figure 13.9. ■

Like a simple spin lock, the "sense-reversing" barrier can lead to unacceptable levels of contention on large machines. Moreover the serialization of access to the counter implies that the time to achieve an *n*-thread barrier is $O(n)$. It is possible to do better, but even the fastest software barriers require $O(\log n)$ time to synchronize *n* threads [MCS91]. Large multiprocessors sometimes provide special hardware to reduce this bound to close to constant time.

EXAMPLE 13.28 Java 7 phasers

The Java 7 `Phaser` class provides unusually flexible barrier support. The set of participating threads can change from one phaser episode to another. When the number is large, the phaser can be *tiered* to run in logarithmic time. Moreover, arrival and departure can be specified as separate operations: in between, a thread can do work that (a) does not require that all other threads have arrived, and (b) does not have to be completed before any other threads depart. ■

13.3.2 Nonblocking Algorithms

When a lock is acquired at the beginning of a critical section, and released at the end, no other thread can execute a similarly protected piece of code at the same time. As long as every thread follows the same conventions, code within the critical section is atomic—it appears to happen all at once. But this is not the only possible way to achieve atomicity. Suppose we wish to make an arbitrary update to a shared location:

EXAMPLE 13.29
Atomic update with CAS

```
x := foo(x);
```

Note that this update involves at least two accesses to x: one to read the old value and one to write the new. We could protect the sequence with a lock:

```
acquire(L)
    r1 := x
    r2 := foo(r1)            -- probably a multi-instruction sequence
    x := r2
release(L)
```

But we can also do this without a lock, using `compare_and_swap`:

```
start:
    r1 := x
    r2 := foo(r1)            -- probably a multi-instruction sequence
    r2 := CAS(x, r1, r2)     -- replace x if it hasn't changed
    if !r2 goto start
```

If several cores execute this code simultaneously, one of them is guaranteed to succeed the first time around the loop. The others will fail and try again. This example illustrates that `CAS` is a *universal* primitive for single-location atomic update. A similar primitive, known as `load_linked/store_conditional`, is available on ARM, MIPS, and Power processors; we consider it in Exercise 13.7. ■

In our discussions thus far, we have used a definition of "blocking" that comes from operating systems: a thread that blocks gives up the core instead of actively spinning. An alternative definition comes from the theory of concurrent algorithms. Here the choice between spinning and giving up the core is immaterial: a thread is said to be "blocked" if it cannot make forward progress without action by other threads. Conversely, an operation is said to be *nonblocking* if in every reachable state of the system, any thread executing that operation is guaranteed to complete in a finite number of steps if it gets to run by itself (without further interference by other threads).

In this theoretical sense of the word, locks are inherently blocking, regardless of implementation: if one thread holds a lock, no other thread that needs that lock can proceed. By contrast, the `CAS`-based code of Example 13.29 is *nonblocking*: if the `CAS` operation fails, it is because some other thread has made progress.

Moreover if all threads but one stop running (e.g., because of preemption), the remaining thread is guaranteed to make progress.

We can generalize from Example 13.29 to design a variety of special-purpose concurrent data structures that operate without locks. Modifications to these structures often (though not always) follow the pattern

```
repeat
    prepare
    CAS                    -- (or some other atomic operation)
until success
clean up
```

If it reads more than one location, the "prepare" part of the algorithm may need to double-check to make sure that none of the values has changed (i.e., that all were read consistently) before moving on to the CAS. A read-only operation may simply return once this double-checking is successful.

In the CAS-based update of Example 13.29, the "prepare" part of the algorithm reads the old value of x and figures out what the new value ought to be; the "clean up" part is empty. In other algorithms there may be significant cleanup. In all cases, the keys to correctness are that (1) the "prepare" part is harmless if we need to repeat; (2) the CAS, if successful, logically completes the operation in a way that is visible to all other threads; and (3) the "clean up," if needed, can be performed by any thread if the original thread is delayed. Performing cleanup for another thread's operation is often referred to as *helping*.

EXAMPLE 13.30
The M&S queue

Figure 13.10 illustrates a widely used nonblocking concurrent queue. The dequeue operation does not require cleanup, but the enqueue operation does. To add an element to the end of the queue, a thread reads the current tail pointer to find the last node in the queue, and uses a CAS to change the next pointer of that node to point to the new node instead of being null. If the CAS succeeds (no other thread has already updated the relevant next pointer), then the new node has been inserted. As cleanup, the tail pointer must be updated to point to the new node, but any thread can do this—and will, if it discovers that tail->next is not null. ■

Nonblocking algorithms have several advantages over blocking algorithms. They are inherently tolerant of page faults and preemption: if a thread stops running partway through an operation, it never prevents other threads from making progress. Nonblocking algorithms can also safely be used in signal (event) and interrupt handlers, avoiding problems like the one described in Example 13.22. For several important data structures and algorithms, including stacks, queues, sorted lists, priority queues, hash tables, and memory management, nonblocking algorithms can also be faster than locks. Unfortunately, these algorithms tend to be exceptionally subtle and difficult to devise. They are used primarily in the implementation of language-level concurrency mechanisms and in standard library packages.

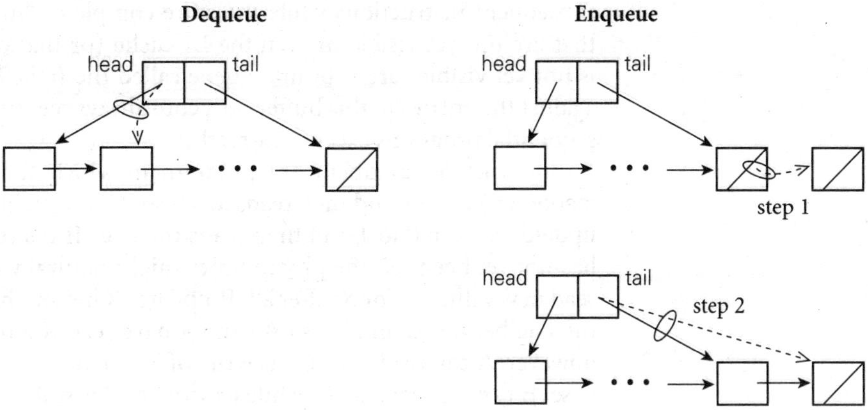

Figure 13.10 Operations on a nonblocking concurrent queue. In the dequeue operation (*left*), a single CAS swings the head pointer to the next node in the queue. In the enqueue operation (*right*), a first CAS changes the next pointer of the tail node to point at the new node, at which point the operation is said to have logically completed. A subsequent "cleanup" CAS, which can be performed by any thread, swings the tail pointer to point at the new node as well.

13.3.3 Memory Consistency

In all our discussions so far, we have depended, implicitly, on hardware memory coherence. Unfortunately, coherence alone is not enough to make a multiprocessor or even a single multicore processor behave as most programmers would expect. We must also worry, when more than one location is written at about the same time, about the *order* in which the writes become visible to different cores.

Intuitively, most programmers expect shared memory to be *sequentially consistent*—to make all writes visible to all cores in the same order, and to make any given core's writes visible in the order they were performed. Unfortunately, this behavior turns out to be very hard to implement efficiently—hard enough that most hardware designers simply don't provide it. Instead, they provide one of several *relaxed memory models*, in which certain loads and stores may appear to occur "out of order." Relaxed consistency has important ramifications for language designers, compiler writers, and the implementors of synchronization mechanisms and nonblocking algorithms.

The Cost of Ordering

The fundamental problem with sequential consistency is that straightforward implementations require both hardware and compilers to serialize operations that we would rather be able to perform in arbitrary order.

EXAMPLE 13.31
Write buffers and consistency

Consider, for example, the implementation of an ordinary store instruction. In the event of a cache miss, this instruction can take hundreds of cycles to complete. Rather than wait, most processors are designed to continue executing subsequent instructions while the store completes "in the background." Stores that are not yet visible in even the L1 cache (or that occurred after a store that is not yet visible) are kept in a queue called the *write buffer*. Loads are checked against the entries in this buffer, so a core always sees its own previous stores, and sequential programs execute correctly.

But consider a concurrent program in which thread A sets a flag (call it inspected) to true and then reads location X. At roughly the same time, thread B updates X from 0 to 1 and then reads the flag. If B's read reveals that inspected has not yet been set, the programmer might naturally assume that A is going to read new value (1) for X: after all, B updates X before checking the flag, and A sets the flag before reading X, so A cannot have read X already. On most machines, however, A can read X while its write of inspected is still in its write buffer. Likewise, B can read inspected while its write of X is still in its write buffer. The result can be very unintuitive behavior:

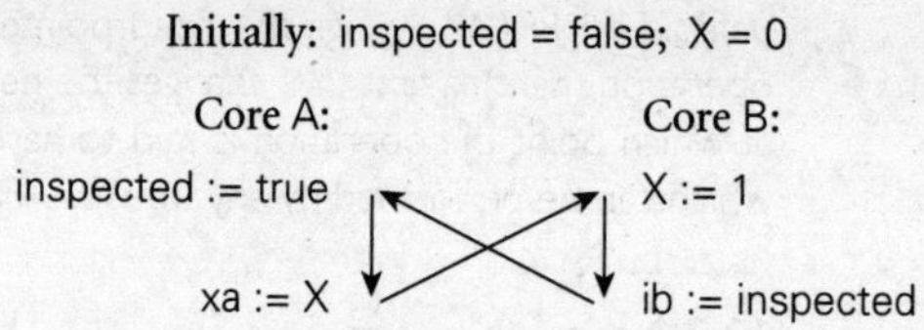

A's write of inspected precedes its read of X in program order. B's write of X precedes its read of inspected in program order. B's read of inspected appears to precede A's write of inspected, because it sees the unset value. And yet A's read of X appears to precede B's write of X as well, leaving us with xA = 0 and ib = false.

This sort of "temporal loop" may also be caused by standard compiler optimizations. Traditionally, a compiler is free to reorder instructions (in the absence of a data dependence) to improve the expected performance of the processor pipelines. In this example, a compiler that generates code for either A or B (without considering the other) may choose to reverse the order of operations on inspected and X, producing an apparent temporal loop even in the absence of hardware reordering. ■

Forcing Order with Fences and Synchronization Instructions

To avoid temporal loops, implementors of concurrent languages and libraries must generally use special *synchronization* or *memory fence* instructions. At some expense, these force orderings not normally guaranteed by the hardware.[3] Their presence also inhibits instruction reordering in the compiler.

In Example 13.31, both A and B must prevent their read from *bypassing* (completing before) the logically earlier write. Typically this can be accomplished by

3 Fences are also sometimes known as *memory barriers*. They are unrelated to the garbage collection barriers of Section 8.5.3 ("Tracing Collection"), the synchronization barriers of Section 13.3.1, or the RTL barriers of Section C-15.2.1.

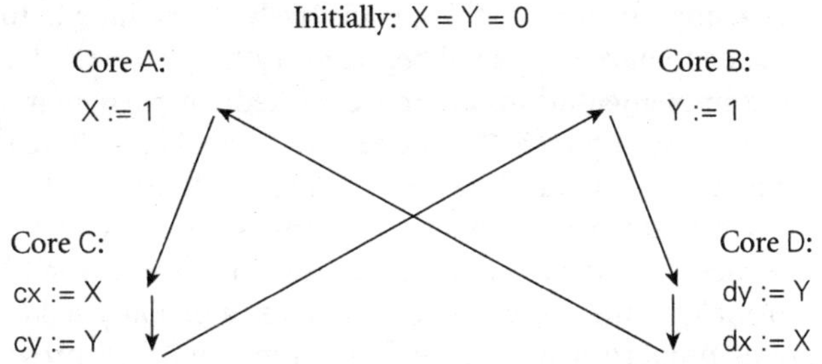

Figure 13.11 **Concurrent propagation of writes.** On some machines, it is possible for concurrent writes to reach cores in different orders. Arrows show apparent temporal ordering. Here C may read cy = 0 and cx = 1, while D reads dx = 0 and dy = 1.

identifying either the read or the write as a synchronization instruction (e.g., by implementing it with an `XCHG` instruction on the x86) or by inserting a fence between them (e.g., `membar StoreLoad` on the SPARC).

Sometimes, as in Example 13.31, the use of synchronization or fence instructions is enough to restore intuitive behavior. Other cases, however, require more significant changes to the program. An example appears in Figure 13.11. Cores A and B write locations X and Y, respectively. Both locations are read by cores C and D. If C is physically close to A in a distributed memory machine, and D is close to B, and if coherence messages propagate concurrently, we must consider the possibility that C and D will see the writes in opposite orders, leading to another temporal loop.

EXAMPLE 13.32
Distributed consistency

On machines where this problem arises, fences and synchronization instructions may not suffice to solve the problem. The language or library implementor (or even the application programmer) may need to bracket the writes of X and Y with (fenced) writes to some common location, to ensure that one of the original writes completes before the other starts. The most straightforward way to do this is to enclose the writes in a lock-based critical section. Even then, additional measures may be needed to ensure that the reads of X and Y are not executed out of order by either C or D.

Simplifying Language-Level Reasoning

For programs running on a single core, regardless of the complexity of the underlying pipeline and memory hierarchy, every manufacturer guarantees that instructions will appear to occur in *program order*: no instruction will fail to see the effects of some prior instruction, nor will it see the effects of any subsequent instruction. For programs running on a muilticore or multiprocessor machine, manufacturers also guarantee, under certain circumstances, that instructions executed on one core will be seen, in order, by instructions on other cores. Unfortunately, these circumstances vary from one machine to another. Some implementations of the MIPS and PA-RISC processors were sequentially consistent, as are IBM's z-Series mainframe machines: if a load on core B sees a value written by a store on core A, then, transitively, everything before the store on A is guaranteed to have happened before everything after the load on B. Other processors and implementations are more relaxed. In particular, most machines admit the loop of Example 13.31. The SPARC and x86 preclude the loop of Example 13.32 (Figure 13.11), but the Power, ARM, and Itanium all allow it.

Given this variation across machines, what is a language designer to do? The answer, first suggested by Sarita Adve and now embedded in Java, C++, and (less formally) other languages, is to define a *memory model* that captures the notion of a "properly synchronized" program, and then provide the illusion of sequential consistency for all such programs. In effect, the memory model constitutes a contract between the programmer and the language implementation: if the programmer follows the rules of the contract, the implementation will hide all the ordering eccentricities of the underlying hardware.

In the usual formulation, memory models distinguish between "ordinary" variable accesses and special *synchronization accesses*; the latter include not only lock acquire and release, but also reads and writes of any variable declared with a special synchronization keyword (`volatile` in Java or C#, `atomic` in C++). Ordering of operations across cores is based solely on synchronization accesses. We say that operation A *happens before* operation C ($A \prec_{HB} C$) if (1) A comes before C in program order in a single thread; (2) A and C are synchronization operations and the language definition says that A comes before C; or (3) there exists an operation B such that $A \prec_{HB} B$ and $B \prec_{HB} C$.

Two ordinary accesses are said to *conflict* if they occur in different threads, they refer to the same location, and at least one of them is a write. They are said to constitute a *data race* if they conflict and they are not ordered—the implementation might allow either one to happen first, and program behavior might change as a result. Given these definitions, the memory model contract is straightforward: *executions of data-race–free programs are always sequentially consistent.*

In most cases, an acquire of a mutual exclusion lock is ordered after the most recent prior release. A read of a `volatile` (`atomic`) variable is ordered after the write that stored the value that was read. Various other operations (e.g., the *transactions* we will study in Section 13.4.4) may also contribute to cross-thread ordering.

EXAMPLE 13.33
Using `volatile` to avoid a data race

A simple example of ordering appears in Figure 13.12, where thread A sets variable initialized to indicate that it is safe for thread B to use reference p. If initialized had not been declared as volatile, there would be no cross-thread ordering between A's write of true and B's loop-terminating read. Access to both initialized and p would then be data races. Under the hood, the compiler would have been free to move the write of true before the initialization of p (remember, threads are often separately compiled, and the compiler has no obvious way to tell that the writes to p and initialized have anything to do with one another). Similarly, on a machine with a relaxed hardware memory model, the processor and memory system would have been free to perform the writes in either order, regardless of the order specified by the compiler in machine code. On B's core, it would also have been possible for either the compiler or the hardware to read p

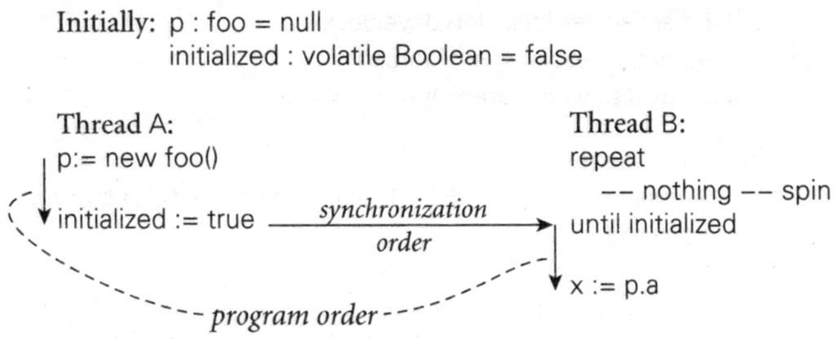

Figure 13.12 **Protecting initialization with a** volatile **flag.** Here labeling initialized as volatile avoids a data race, and ensures that B will not access p until it is safe to do so.

before confirming that initialized was true. The volatile declaration precludes all these undesirable possibilities.

Returning to Example 13.31, we might avoid a temporal loop by declaring both X and inspected as `volatile`, or by enclosing accesses to them in atomic operations, bracketed by lock acquire and release. In Example 13.32, `volatile` declarations on X and Y will again suffice to ensure sequential consistency, but the cost may be somewhat higher: on some machines, the compiler may need to use extra locks or special instructions to force a total order among writes to disjoint locations. ■

Synchronization races are common in multithreaded programs. Whether they are bugs or expected behavior depends on the application. Data races, on the other hand, are almost always program bugs. They are so hard to reason about—and so rarely useful—that the C++ memory model outlaws them altogether: given a program with a data race, a C++ implementation is permitted to display *any behavior whatsoever*. Ada has similar rules. For Java, by contrast, an emphasis on embedded applications motivated the language designers to constrain the behavior of racy programs in ways that would preserve the integrity of the underlying virtual machine. A Java program that contains a data race must continue to follow all the normal language rules, and any read that is not ordered with respect to a unique preceding write must return a value that might have been written by *some* previous write to the same location, or by a write that is unordered with respect to the read. We will return to the Java Memory Model in Section 13.4.3, after we have discussed the language's synchronization mechanisms.

13.3.4 Scheduler Implementation

EXAMPLE 13.34
Scheduling threads on processes

To implement user-level threads, OS-level processes must synchronize access to the ready list and condition queues, generally by means of spinning. Code for a simple *reentrant* thread scheduler (one that can be "reentered" safely by a second process before the first one has returned) appears in Figure 13.13. As in the code in Section 13.2.4, we disable timer signals before entering scheduler code, to

```
shared scheduler_lock : low_level_lock
shared ready_list : queue of thread
per-process private current_thread : thread

procedure reschedule()
    -- assume that scheduler_lock is already held and that timer signals are disabled
    t : thread
    loop
        t := dequeue(ready_list)
        if t ≠ null
            exit
        -- else wait for a thread to become runnable
        release_lock(scheduler_lock)
        -- window allows another thread to access ready_list (no point in reenabling
        -- signals; we're already trying to switch to a different thread)
        acquire_lock(scheduler_lock)
    transfer(t)
    -- caller must release scheduler_lock and reenable timer signals after we return

procedure yield()
    disable_signals()
    acquire_lock(scheduler_lock)
    enqueue(ready_list, current_thread)
    reschedule()
    release_lock(scheduler_lock)
    reenable_signals()

procedure sleep_on(ref Q : queue of thread)
    -- assume that caller has already disabled timer signals and acquired
    -- scheduler_lock, and will reverse these actions when we return
    enqueue(Q, current_thread)
    reschedule()
```

Figure 13.13 Pseudocode for part of a simple reentrant (parallelism-safe) scheduler. Every process has its own copy of current_thread. There is a single shared scheduler_lock and a single ready_list. If processes have dedicated cores, then the low_level_lock can be an ordinary spin lock; otherwise it can be a "spin-then-yield" lock (Figure 13.14). The loop inside reschedule busy-waits until the ready list is nonempty. The code for sleep_on cannot disable timer signals and acquire the scheduler lock itself, because the caller needs to test a condition and then block as a single atomic operation.

protect the ready list and condition queues from concurrent access by a process and its own signal handler. ■

EXAMPLE 13.35
A race condition in thread scheduling

Our code assumes a single "low-level" lock (scheduler_lock) that protects the entire scheduler. Before saving its context block on a queue (e.g., in yield or sleep_on), a thread must acquire the scheduler lock. It must then release the lock after returning from reschedule. Of course, because reschedule calls transfer, the lock will usually be acquired by one thread (the same one that disables timer signals) and released by another (the same one that reenables timer signals). The code for yield can implement synchronization itself, because its work is self-contained. The code for sleep_on, on the other hand, cannot, because a thread must generally check a condition and block if necessary as a single atomic operation:

```
disable_signals()
acquire_lock(scheduler_lock)
if not desired_condition
    sleep_on(condition_queue)
release_lock(scheduler_lock)
reenable_signals()
```

If the signal and lock operations were moved inside of sleep_on, the following race could arise: thread *A* checks the condition and finds it to be false; thread *B* makes the condition true, but finds the condition queue to be empty; thread *A* sleeps on the condition queue forever. ▪

A spin lock will suffice for the "low-level" lock that protects the ready list and condition queues, so long as every process runs on a different core. As we noted in Section 13.2.1, however, it makes little sense to spin for a condition that can only be made true by some other process using the core on which we are spinning. If we know that we're running on a uniprocessor, then we don't need a lock on the scheduler (just the disabled signals). If we *might* be running on a uniprocessor, however, or on a multiprocessor with fewer cores than processes, then we must be prepared to give up the core if unable to obtain a lock. The easiest way to do this is with a "spin-then-yield" lock, first suggested by Ousterhout [Ous82]. A simple example of such a lock appears in Figure 13.14. On a multiprogrammed machine, it might also be desirable to relinquish the core inside reschedule when the ready list is empty: though no other process of the current application will be able to do anything, overall system throughput may improve if we allow the operating system to give the core to a process from another application. ▪

EXAMPLE 13.36
A "spin-then-yield" lock

On a large multiprocessor we might increase concurrency by employing a separate lock for each condition queue, and another for the ready list. We would have to be careful, however, to make sure it wasn't possible for one process to put a thread into a condition queue (or the ready list) and for another process to attempt to transfer into that thread before the first process had finished transferring out of it (see Exercise 13.13).

Scheduler-Based Synchronization

The problem with busy-wait synchronization is that it consumes processor cycles—cycles that are therefore unavailable for other computation. Busy-wait synchronization makes sense only if (1) one has nothing better to do with the current core, or (2) the expected wait time is less than the time that would be required to switch contexts to some other thread and then switch back again. To ensure acceptable performance on a wide variety of systems, most concurrent

```
type lock = Boolean := false;

procedure acquire_lock(ref L : lock)
    while not test_and_set(L)
        count := TIMEOUT
        while L
            count −:= 1
            if count = 0
                OS_yield()          -- relinquish core and drop priority
                count := TIMEOUT

procedure release_lock(ref L : lock)
    L := false
```

Figure 13.14 A simple spin-then-yield lock, designed for execution on a multiprocessor that may be multiprogrammed (i.e., on which OS-level processes may be preempted). If unable to acquire the lock in a fixed, short amount of time, a process calls the OS scheduler to yield its core and to lower its priority enough that other processes (if any) will be allowed to run. Hopefully the lock will be available the next time the yielding process is scheduled for execution.

programming languages employ scheduler-based synchronization mechanisms, which switch to a different thread when the one that was running blocks.

In the following subsection we consider *semaphores*, the most common form of scheduler-based synchronization. In Section 13.4 we consider the higher-level notions of monitors, conditional critical regions, and transactional memory. In each case, scheduler-based synchronization mechanisms remove the waiting thread from the scheduler's ready list, returning it only when the awaited condition is true (or is likely to be true). By contrast, a spin-then-yield lock is still a busy-wait mechanism: the currently running process relinquishes the core, but remains on the ready list. It will perform a `test_and_set` operation every time the lock appears to be free, until it finally succeeds. It is worth noting that busy-wait synchronization is generally "level-independent"—it can be thought of as synchronizing threads, processes, or cores, as desired. Scheduler-based synchronization is "level-*dependent*"—it is specific to threads when implemented in the language run-time system, or to processes when implemented in the operating system.

EXAMPLE 13.37
The bounded buffer problem

We will use a *bounded buffer* abstraction to illustrate the semantics of various scheduler-based synchronization mechanisms. A bounded buffer is a concurrent queue of limited size into which *producer* threads insert data, and from which *consumer* threads remove data. The buffer serves to even out fluctuations in the relative rates of progress of the two classes of threads, increasing system throughput. A correct implementation of a bounded buffer requires both atomicity and condition synchronization: the former to ensure that no thread sees the buffer in an inconsistent state in the middle of some other thread's operation; the latter to force consumers to wait when the buffer is empty and producers to wait when the buffer is full. ■

```
type semaphore = record
    N : integer -- always non-negative
    Q : queue of threads

procedure P(ref S : semaphore)
    disable_signals()
    acquire_lock(scheduler_lock)
    if S.N > 0
        S.N -:= 1
    else
        sleep_on(S.Q)
    release_lock(scheduler_lock)
    reenable_signals()

procedure V(ref S : semaphore)
    disable_signals()
    acquire_lock(scheduler_lock)
    if S.Q is nonempty
        enqueue(ready_list, dequeue(S.Q))
    else
        S.N +:= 1
    release_lock(scheduler_lock)
    reenable_signals()
```

Figure 13.15 Semaphore operations, for use with the scheduler code of Figure 13.13.

13.3.5 Semaphores

Semaphores are the oldest of the scheduler-based synchronization mechanisms. They were described by Dijkstra in the mid-1960s [Dij68a], and appear in Algol 68. They are still heavily used today, particularly in library-based implementations of concurrency.

EXAMPLE 13.38 Semaphore implementation

A semaphore is basically a counter with two associated operations, P and V.[4] A thread that calls V atomically increments the counter. A thread that calls P waits until the counter is positive and then decrements it. We generally require that semaphores be fair, in the sense that threads complete P operations in the order that they started them. Implementations of P and V in terms of our scheduler operations appear in Figure 13.15. Note that we have elided the matching increment and decrement when a V allows a thread that is waiting in P to continue right away. ■

A semaphore whose counter is initialized to one and for which P and V operations always occur in matched pairs is known as a *binary semaphore.* It serves as

4 P stands for the Dutch word *passeren* (to pass) or *proberen* (to test); V stands for *vrijgeven* (to release) or *verhogen* (to increment). To keep them straight, speakers of English may wish to think of P as standing for "pause," since a thread will pause at a P operation if the semaphore count is negative. Algol 68 calls the P and V operations down and up, respectively.

```
shared buf : array [1..SIZE] of bdata
shared next_full, next_empty : integer := 1, 1
shared mutex : semaphore := 1
shared empty_slots, full_slots : semaphore := SIZE, 0

procedure insert(d : bdata)
    P(empty_slots)
    P(mutex)
    buf[next_empty] := d
    next_empty := next_empty mod SIZE + 1
    V(mutex)
    V(full_slots)

function remove() : bdata
    P(full_slots)
    P(mutex)
    d : bdata := buf[next_full]
    next_full := next_full mod SIZE + 1
    V(mutex)
    V(empty_slots)
    return d
```

Figure 13.16 Semaphore-based code for a bounded buffer. The mutex binary semaphore protects the data structure proper. The full_slots and empty_slots general semaphores ensure that no operation starts until it is safe to do so.

a scheduler-based mutual exclusion lock: the P operation acquires the lock; V releases it. More generally, a semaphore whose counter is initialized to k can be used to arbitrate access to k copies of some resource. The value of the counter at any particular time indicates the number of copies not currently in use. Exercise 13.19 notes that binary semaphores can be used to implement general semaphores, so the two are of equal expressive power, if not of equal convenience.

EXAMPLE 13.39
Bounded buffer with semaphores

Figure 13.16 shows a semaphore-based solution to the bounded buffer problem. It uses a binary semaphore for mutual exclusion, and two general (or *counting*) semaphores for condition synchronization. Exercise 13.17 considers the use of semaphores to construct an n-thread barrier. ■

✓ CHECK YOUR UNDERSTANDING

25. What is *mutual exclusion*? What is a *critical section*?

26. What does it mean for an operation to be *atomic*? Explain the difference between atomicity and *condition synchronization*.

27. Describe the behavior of a `test_and_set` instruction. Show how to use it to build a *spin lock*.

28. Describe the behavior of the `compare_and_swap` instruction. What advantages does it offer in comparison to `test_and_set`?

29. Explain how a *reader–writer lock* differs from an "ordinary" lock.
30. What is a *barrier*? In what types of programs are barriers common?
31. What does it mean for an algorithm to be *nonblocking*? What advantages do nonblocking algorithms have over algorithms based on locks?
32. What is *sequential consistency*? Why is it difficult to implement?
33. What information is provided by a *memory consistency model*? What is the relationship between hardware-level and language-level memory models?
34. Explain how to extend a preemptive uniprocessor scheduler to work correctly on a multiprocessor.
35. What is a *spin-then-yield* lock?
36. What is a *bounded buffer*?
37. What is a *semaphore*? What operations does it support? How do *binary* and *general* semaphores differ?

13.4 Language-Level Constructs

Though widely used, semaphores are also widely considered to be too "low level" for well-structured, maintainable code. They suffer from two principal problems. First, because their operations are simply subroutine calls, it is easy to leave one out (e.g., on a control path with several nested `if` statements). Second, unless they are hidden inside an abstraction, uses of a given semaphore tend to get scattered throughout a program, making it difficult to track them down for purposes of software maintenance.

13.4.1 Monitors

Monitors were suggested by Dijkstra [Dij72] as a solution to the problems of semaphores. They were developed more thoroughly by Brinch Hansen [Bri73], and formalized by Hoare [Hoa74] in the early 1970s. They have been incorporated into at least a score of languages, of which Concurrent Pascal [Bri75], Modula (1) [Wir77b], and Mesa [LR80] were probably the most influential.[5] They

5 Together with Smalltalk and Interlisp, Mesa was one of three influential languages to emerge from Xerox's Palo Alto Research Center in the 1970s. All three were developed on the Alto personal computer, which pioneered such concepts as the bitmapped display, the mouse, the graphical user interface, WYSIWYG editing, Ethernet networking, and the laser printer. The Mesa project was led by Butler Lampson (1943–), who played a key role in the later development of Euclid and Cedar as well. For his contributions to personal and distributed computing, Lampson received the ACM Turing Award in 1992.

```
monitor bounded_buf
imports bdata, SIZE
exports insert, remove

    buf : array [1..SIZE] of bdata
    next_full, next_empty : integer := 1, 1
    full_slots : integer := 0
    full_slot, empty_slot : condition

    entry insert(d : bdata)
        if full_slots = SIZE
            wait(empty_slot)
        buf[next_empty] := d
        next_empty := next_empty mod SIZE + 1
        full_slots +:= 1
        signal(full_slot)

    entry remove() : bdata
        if full_slots = 0
            wait(full_slot)
        d : bdata := buf[next_full]
        next_full := next_full mod SIZE + 1
        full_slots −:= 1
        signal(empty_slot)
        return d
```

Figure 13.17 Monitor-based code for a bounded buffer. Insert and remove are *entry* subroutines: they require exclusive access to the monitor's data. Because conditions are memory-less, both insert and remove can safely end their operation with a signal.

also strongly influenced the design of Java's synchronization mechanisms, which we will consider in Section 13.4.3.

A monitor is a module or object with operations, internal state, and a number of *condition variables*. Only one operation of a given monitor is allowed to be active at a given point in time. A thread that calls a busy monitor is automatically delayed until the monitor is free. On behalf of its calling thread, any operation may suspend itself by *wait*ing on a condition variable. An operation may also *signal* a condition variable, in which case one of the waiting threads is resumed, usually the one that waited first.

Because the operations (*entries*) of a monitor automatically exclude one another in time, the programmer is relieved of the responsibility of using P and V operations correctly. Moreover because the monitor is an abstraction, all operations on the encapsulated data, including synchronization, are collected together in one place. Figure 13.17 shows a monitor-based solution to the bounded buffer problem. It is worth emphasizing that monitor condition variables are not the same as semaphores. Specifically, they have no "memory": if no thread is waiting on a condition at the time that a signal occurs, then the signal has no effect.

EXAMPLE 13.40
Bounded buffer monitor

By contrast a V operation on a semaphore increments the semaphore's counter, allowing some future P operation to succeed, even if none is waiting now. ■

Semantic Details

Hoare's definition of monitors employs one thread queue for every condition variable, plus two bookkeeping queues: the *entry queue* and the *urgent queue*. A thread that attempts to enter a busy monitor waits in the entry queue. When a thread executes a signal operation from within a monitor, and some other thread is waiting on the specified condition, then the signaling thread waits on the monitor's urgent queue and the first thread on the appropriate condition queue obtains control of the monitor. If no thread is waiting on the signaled condition, then the signal operation is a no-op. When a thread leaves a monitor, either by completing its operation or by waiting on a condition, it unblocks the first thread on the urgent queue or, if the urgent queue is empty, the first thread on the entry queue, if any.

Many monitor implementations dispense with the urgent queue, or make other changes to Hoare's original definition. From the programmer's point of view, the two principal areas of variation are the semantics of the signal operation and the management of mutual exclusion when a thread waits inside a nested sequence of two or more monitor calls. We will return to these issues below.

Correctness for monitors depends on maintaining a *monitor invariant*. The invariant is a predicate that captures the notion that "the state of the monitor is consistent." The invariant needs to be true initially, and at monitor exit. It also needs to be true at every wait statement and, in a Hoare monitor, at signal operations as well. For our bounded buffer example, a suitable invariant would assert that full_slots correctly indicates the number of items in the buffer, and that those items lie in slots numbered next_full through next_empty − 1 (mod SIZE). Careful inspection of the code in Figure 13.17 reveals that the invariant does indeed hold initially, and that any time we modify one of the variables mentioned in the invariant, we always modify the others accordingly before waiting, signaling, or returning from an entry.

Hoare defined his monitors in terms of semaphores. Conversely, it is easy to define semaphores in terms of monitors (Exercise 13.18). Together, the two definitions prove that semaphores and monitors are equally powerful: each can express all forms of synchronization expressible with the other.

Signals as Hints and Absolutes

EXAMPLE 13.41

How to wait for a signal (hint or absolute)

In general, one signals a condition variable when some condition on which a thread may be waiting has become true. If we want to guarantee that the condition is still true when the thread wakes up, then we need to switch to the thread as soon as the signal occurs—hence the need for the urgent queue, and the need to ensure the monitor invariant at signal operations. In practice, switching contexts on a signal tends to induce unnecessary scheduling overhead: a signaling thread seldom changes the condition associated with the signal during the remainder of its operation. To reduce the overhead, and to eliminate the need to ensure the monitor invariant, Mesa specifies that signals are only *hints*: the language run-time system moves some waiting thread to the ready list, but the signaler retains control of the monitor, and the waiter must recheck the condition when it awakes. In effect, the standard idiom

```
if not desired_condition
    wait (condition_variable)
```

in a Hoare monitor becomes the following in Mesa:

```
while not desired_condition
    wait (condition_variable)
```

DESIGN & IMPLEMENTATION

13.5 Monitor signal semantics

By specifying that signals are hints, instead of absolutes, Mesa and Modula-3 (and similarly Java and C#, which we consider in Section 13.4.3) avoid the need to perform an immediate context switch from a signaler to a waiting thread. They also admit simpler, though less efficient implementations that lack a one-to-one correspondence between signals and thread queues, or that do not necessarily guarantee that a waiting thread will be the first to run in its monitor after the signal occurs. This approach can lead to complications, however, if we want to ensure that an appropriate thread always runs in the wake of a signal. Suppose an awakened thread rechecks its condition and discovers that it still can't run. If there may be some other thread that could run, the erroneously awakened thread may need to resignal the condition before it waits again:

```
if not desired_condition
    loop
        wait (condition_variable)
        if desired_condition
            break
        signal (condition_variable)
```

In effect the signal "cascades" from thread to thread until some thread is able to run. (If it is possible that *no* waiting thread will be able to run, then we will need additional logic to stop the cascading when every thread has been checked.) Alternatively, the thread that makes a condition (potentially) true can use a special broadcast version of the signal operation to awaken *all* waiting threads at once. Each thread will then recheck the condition and if appropriate wait again, without the need for explicit cascading. In either case (cascading signals or broadcast), signals as hints trade potentially high overhead in the worst case for potentially low overhead in the common case and a potentially simpler implementation.

Modula-3 takes a similar approach. An alternative appears in Concurrent Pascal, which specifies that a `signal` operation causes an immediate return from the monitor operation in which it appears. This rule keeps overhead low, and also preserves invariants, but precludes algorithms in which a thread does useful work in a monitor after `signal`ing a condition.

Nested Monitor Calls

In most monitor languages, a wait in a nested sequence of monitor operations will release mutual exclusion on the innermost monitor, but will leave the outer monitors locked. This situation can lead to *deadlock* if the only way for another thread to reach a corresponding signal operation is through the same outer monitor(s). In general, we use the term "deadlock" to describe any situation in which a collection of threads are all waiting for each other, and none of them can proceed. In this specific case, the thread that entered the outer monitor first is waiting for the second thread to execute a signal operation; the second thread, however, is waiting for the first to leave the monitor.

The alternative—to release exclusion on outer monitors when waiting in an inner one—was adopted by several early monitor implementations for uniprocessors, including the original implementation of Modula [Wir77a]. It has a significant semantic drawback, however: it requires that the monitor invariant hold not only at monitor exit and (perhaps) at signal operations, but also at any subroutine call that may result in a wait or (with Hoare semantics) a signal in a nested monitor. Such calls may not all be known to the programmer; they are certainly not syntactically distinguished in the source.

DESIGN & IMPLEMENTATION

13.6 The nested monitor problem

While maintaining exclusion on outer monitor(s) when waiting in an inner one may lead to deadlock with a signaling thread, releasing those outer monitors may lead to similar (if a bit more subtle) deadlocks. When a waiting thread awakens it must reacquire exclusion on both inner and outer monitors. The innermost monitor is of course available, because the matching signal happened there, but there is in general no way to ensure that unrelated threads will not be busy in the outer monitor(s). Moreover one of those threads may need access to the inner monitor in order to complete its work and release the outer monitor(s). If we insist that the awakened thread be the first to run in the inner monitor after the signal, then deadlock will result. One way to avoid this problem is to arrange for mutual exclusion across *all* the monitors of a program. This solution severely limits concurrency in multiprocessor implementations, but may be acceptable on a uniprocessor. A more general solution is addressed in Exercise 13.21.

13.4.2 Conditional Critical Regions

EXAMPLE 13.42
Original CCR syntax

Conditional critical regions (CCRs) are another alternative to semaphores, proposed by Brinch Hansen at about the same time as monitors [Bri73]. A critical region is a syntactically delimited critical section in which code is permitted to access a *protected* variable. A *conditional* critical region also specifies a Boolean condition, which must be true before control will enter the region:

```
region protected_variable, when Boolean_condition do
    ...
end region
```

No thread can access a protected variable except within a region statement for that variable, and any thread that reaches a region statement waits until the condition is true and no other thread is currently in a region for the same variable. Regions can nest, though as with nested monitor calls, the programmer needs to worry about deadlock. Figure 13.18 uses CCRs to implement a bounded buffer. ■

Conditional critical regions appeared in the concurrent language Edison [Bri81], and also seem to have influenced the synchronization mechanisms of Ada 95 and Java/C#. These later languages might be said to blend the features of monitors and CCRs, albeit in different ways.

Synchronization in Ada 95

The principal mechanism for synchronization in Ada, introduced in Ada 83, is based on message passing; we will describe it in Section 13.5. Ada 95 augments this mechanism with a notion of *protected object*. A protected object can have three types of methods: functions, procedures, and *entries*. Functions can only read the fields of the object; procedures and entries can read and write them. An

DESIGN & IMPLEMENTATION

13.7 Conditional critical regions

Conditional critical regions avoid the question of `signal` semantics, because they use explicit Boolean conditions instead of condition variables, and because conditions can be awaited only at the beginning of critical regions. At the same time, they introduce potentially significant inefficiency. In the general case, the code used to exit a conditional critical region must tentatively resume each waiting thread, allowing that thread to recheck its condition in its own referencing environment. Optimizations are possible in certain special cases (e.g., for conditions that depend only on global variables, or that consist of only a single Boolean variable), but in the worst case it may be necessary to perform context switches in and out of every waiting thread on every exit from a region.

```
buffer : record
    buf : array [1..SIZE] of bdata
    next_full, next_empty : integer := 1, 1
    full_slots : integer := 0

procedure insert(d : bdata)
    region buffer when full_slots < SIZE
        buf[next_empty] := d
        next_empty := next_empty mod SIZE + 1
        full_slots −:= 1

function remove() : bdata
    region buffer when full_slots > 0
        d : bdata := buf[next_full]
        next_full := next_full mod SIZE + 1
        full_slots +:= 1
    return d
```

Figure 13.18 **Conditional critical regions for a bounded buffer.** Boolean conditions on the region statements eliminate the need for explicit condition variables.

implicit reader–writer lock on the protected object ensures that potentially conflicting operations exclude one another in time: a procedure or entry obtains exclusive access to the object; a function can operate concurrently with other functions, but not with a procedure or entry.

Procedures and entries differ from one another in two important ways. First, an entry can have a Boolean expression *guard*, for which the calling task (thread) will wait before beginning execution (much as it would for the condition of a CCR). Second, an entry supports three special forms of call: *timed* calls, which abort after waiting for a specified amount of time, *conditional* calls, which execute alternative code if the call cannot proceed immediately, and *asynchronous* calls, which begin executing alternative code immediately, but abort it if the call is able to proceed before the alternative completes.

In comparison to the conditions of CCRs, the guards on entries of protected objects in Ada 95 admit a more efficient implementation, because they do not have to be evaluated in the context of the calling thread. Moreover, because all guards are gathered together in the definition of the protected object, the compiler can generate code to test them as a group as efficiently as possible, in a manner suggested by Kessels [Kes77]. Though an Ada task cannot wait on a condition in the middle of an entry (only at the beginning), it can *requeue* itself on another entry, achieving much the same effect. Ada 95 code for a bounded buffer would closely resemble the pseudocode of Figure 13.18; we leave the details to Exercise 13.23.

13.4.3 Synchronization in Java

EXAMPLE 13.43
`synchronized` statement in Java

In Java, every object accessible to more than one thread has an implicit mutual exclusion lock, acquired and released by means of `synchronized` statements:

```
synchronized (my_shared_obj) {
    ... // critical section
}
```

All executions of `synchronized` statements that refer to the same shared object exclude one another in time. `Synchronized` statements that refer to different objects may proceed concurrently. As a form of syntactic sugar, a method of a class may be prefixed with the `synchronized` keyword, in which case the body of the method is considered to have been surrounded by an implicit `synchronized (this)` statement. Invocations of nonsynchronized methods of a shared object—and direct accesses to public fields—can proceed concurrently with each other, or with a `synchronized` statement or method. ■

Within a `synchronized` statement or method, a thread can suspend itself by calling the predefined method `wait`. `Wait` has no arguments in Java: the core language does not distinguish among the different reasons why threads may be suspended on a given object (the `java.util.concurrent` library, which became standard with Java 5, does provide a mechanism for multiple conditions; more on this below). Like Mesa, Java allows a thread to be awoken for spurious reasons, or after a delay; programs must therefore embed the use of `wait` within a condition-testing loop:

EXAMPLE 13.44
`notify` as hint in Java

```
while (!condition) {
    wait();
}
```

A thread that calls the `wait` method of an object releases the object's lock. With nested `synchronized` statements, however, or with nested calls to `synchronized` methods, the thread does *not* release locks on any other objects. ■

To resume a thread that is suspended on a given object, some other thread must execute the predefined method `notify` from within a `synchronized` statement or method that refers to the same object. Like `wait`, `notify` has no arguments. In response to a `notify` call, the language run-time system picks an arbitrary thread suspended on the object and makes it runnable. If there are no such threads, then the `notify` is a no-op. As in Mesa, it may sometimes be appropriate to awaken *all* threads waiting in a given object; Java provides a built-in `notifyAll` method for this purpose.

If threads are waiting for more than one condition (i.e., if their `wait`s are embedded in dissimilar loops), there is no guarantee that the "right" thread will awaken. To ensure that an appropriate thread does wake up, the programmer may choose to use `notifyAll` instead of `notify`. To ensure that only *one* thread continues after wakeup, the first thread to discover that its condition has been satisfied must modify the state of the object in such a way that other awakened threads, when they get to run, will simply go back to sleep. Unfortunately, since all waiting threads will end up reevaluating their conditions every time one of them can run, this "solution" to the multiple-condition problem can be quite expensive.

The mechanisms for synchronization in C# are similar to the Java mechanisms just described. The C# `lock` statement is similar to Java's `synchronized`. It cannot be used to label a method, but a similar effect can be achieved (a bit more clumsily) by specifying a `Synchronized` *attribute* for the method. The methods `Pulse` and `PulseAll` are used instead of `notify` and `notifyAll`.

Lock Variables

In early versions of Java, programmers concerned with efficiency generally needed to devise algorithms in which threads were never waiting for more than one condition within a given object at a given time. The `java.util.concurrent` package, introduced in Java 5, provides a more general solution. (Similar solutions are possible in C#, but are not in the standard library.) As an alternative to `synchronized` statements and methods, modern Java programmers can create explicit `Lock` variables. Code that might once have been written

EXAMPLE 13.45
Lock variables in Java 5

```
synchronized (my_shared_obj) {
    ... // critical section
}
```

DESIGN & IMPLEMENTATION

13.8 Condition variables in Java

As illustrated by Mesa and Java, the distinction between monitors and CCRs is somewhat blurry. It turns out to be possible (see Exercise 13.22) to solve completely general synchronization problems in such a way that for every protected object there is only one Boolean condition on which threads ever spin. The solutions, however, may not be pretty: they amount to low-level use of semaphores, without the implicit mutual exclusion of *synchronized* statements and methods. For programs that are naturally expressed with multiple conditions, Java's basic synchronization mechanism (and the similar mechanism in C#) may force the programmer to choose between elegance and efficiency. The concurrency enhancements of Java 5 were a deliberate attempt to lessen this dilemma: `Lock` variables retain the distinction between mutual exclusion and condition synchronization characteristic of both monitors and CCRs, while allowing the programmer to partition waiting threads into equivalence classes that can be awoken independently. By varying the fineness of the partition the programmer can choose essentially any point on the spectrum between the simplicity of CCRs and the efficiency of Hoare-style monitors. Exercises 13.24 through 13.26 explore this issue further using bounded buffers as a running example.

may now be written

```
Lock l = new ReentrantLock();
l.lock();
try {
    ... // critical section
} finally {
    l.unlock();
}
```

A similar interface supports reader–writer locks. ■

Like semaphores, Java Lock variables lack the implicit release at end of scope associated with synchronized statements and methods. The need for an explicit release introduces a potential source of bugs, but allows programmers to create algorithms in which locks are acquired and released in non-LIFO order (see Example 13.14). In a manner reminiscent of the timed entry calls of Ada 95, Java Lock variables also support a tryLock method, which acquires the lock only if it is available immediately, or within an optionally specified timeout interval (a Boolean return value indicates whether the attempt was successful). Finally, a Lock variable may have an arbitrary number of associated Condition variables, making it easy to write algorithms in which threads wait for multiple conditions, without resorting to notifyAll:

EXAMPLE 13.46 Multiple Conditions in Java 5

```
Condition c1 = l.newCondition();
Condition c2 = l.newCondition();
...
c1.await();
...
c2.signal();
```

■

Java objects that use only synchronized methods (no locks or synchronized statements) closely resemble Mesa monitors in which there is a limit of one condition variable per monitor (and in fact objects with synchronized statements are sometimes referred to as monitors in Java). By the same token, a synchronized statement in Java that begins with a wait in a loop resembles a CCR in which the retesting of conditions has been made explicit. Because notify also is explicit, a Java implementation need not reevaluate conditions (or wake up threads that do so explicitly) on every exit from a critical section—only those in which a notify occurs.

The Java Memory Model

The Java Memory Model, which we introduced in Section 13.3.3, specifies exactly which operations are guaranteed to be ordered across threads. It also specifies, for every pair of reads and writes in a program execution, whether the read is permitted to return the value written by the write.

Informally, a Java thread is allowed to buffer or reorder its writes (in hardware or in software) until the point at which it writes a volatile variable or leaves a monitor (releases a lock, leaves a `synchronized` block, or `waits`). At that point all its previous writes must be visible to other threads. Similarly, a thread is allowed to keep cached copies of values written by other threads until it reads a `volatile` variable or enters a monitor (acquires a lock, enters a `synchronized` block, or wakes up from a `wait`). At that point any subsequent reads must obtain new copies of anything that has been written by other threads.

The compiler is free to reorder ordinary reads and writes in the absence of intrathread data dependences. It can also move ordinary reads and writes down past a subsequent `volatile` read, up past a previous `volatile` write, or into a `synchronized` block from above or below. It cannot reorder `volatile` accesses, monitor entry, or monitor exit with respect to one another.

If the compiler can prove that a `volatile` variable or monitor isn't used by more than one thread during a given interval of time, it can reorder its operations like ordinary accesses. For data-race-free programs, these rules ensure the appearance of sequential consistency. Moreover even in the presence of races, Java implementations ensure that reads and writes of object references and of 32-bit and smaller quantities are always atomic, and that every read returns the value written either by some unordered write or by some immediately preceding ordered write.

Formalization of the Java memory model proved to be a surprisingly difficult task. Most of the difficulty stemmed from the desire to specify meaningful semantics for programs with data races. The C++11 memory model, also introduced in Section 13.3.3, avoids this complexity by simply prohibiting such programs. To first approximation, C++ defines a *happens-before* ordering on memory accesses, similar to the ordering in Java, and then guarantees sequential consistency for programs in which all conflicting accesses are ordered. Modest additional complexity is introduced by allowing the programmer to specify weaker ordering on individual reads and writes of `atomic` variables; we consider this feature in Exploration 13.42.

13.4.4 Transactional Memory

All the general-purpose mechanisms we have considered for atomicity—semaphores, monitors, conditional critical regions—are essentially syntactic variants on locks. Critical sections that need to exclude one another must acquire and release the same lock. Critical sections that are mutually independent can run in parallel only if they acquire and release separate locks. This creates an unfortunate tradeoff for programmers: it is easy to write a data-race-free program with a single lock, but such a program will not *scale*: as cores and threads are added, the lock will become a bottleneck, and program performance will stagnate. To increase scalability, skillful programmers partition their program data into equivalence classes, each protected by a separate lock. A critical section must then acquire the locks for every accessed equivalence class. If different critical sections acquire locks in different orders, deadlock can result. Enforcing a common order can be difficult, however, because we may not be able to predict, when an operation starts, which data it will eventually need to access. Worse, the fact that correctness depends on locking order means that lock-based program fragments do not *compose*: we cannot take existing lock-based abstractions and safely call them from within a new critical section.

These issues suggest that locks may be too *low level* a mechanism. From a semantic point of view, the mapping between locks and critical sections is an implementation detail; all we really want is a composable atomic construct. Transactional memory (TM) is an attempt to provide exactly that.

Atomicity without Locks

Transactions have long been used, with great success, to achieve atomicity for database operations. The usual implementation is *speculative*: transactions in different threads proceed concurrently unless and until they *conflict* for access to some common record in the database. In the absence of conflicts, transactions run perfectly in parallel. When conflicts arise, the underlying system arbitrates between the conflicting threads. One gets to continue, and hopefully *commit* its updates to the database; the others *abort* and start over (after "rolling back" the work they had done so far). The overall effect is that transactions achieve significant parallelism at the implementation level, but appear to *serialize* in some global total order at the level of program semantics.

The idea of using more lightweight transactions to achieve atomicity for operations on in-memory data structures dates from 1993, when Herlihy and Moss proposed what was essentially a multiword generalization of the `load_linked`/`store_conditional`, instructions mentioned in Example 13.29. Their *transactional memory* (TM) began to receive renewed attention (and higher-level semantics) about a decade later, when it became clear to many researchers that multicore processors were going to be successful only with the development of simpler programming techniques.

EXAMPLE 13.47
A simple atomic block

The basic idea of TM is very simple: the programmer labels code blocks as atomic—

```
atomic {
    -- your code here
}
```

—and the underlying system takes responsibility for executing these blocks in parallel whenever possible. If the code inside the atomic block can safely be rolled back in the event of conflict, then the implementation can be based on speculation. ■

In some speculation-based systems, a transaction that needs to wait for some precondition can "deliberately" abort itself with an explicit retry primitive. The system will refrain from restarting the transaction until some previously read location has been changed by another thread. Transactional code for a bounded buffer would be very similar to that of Figure 13.18. We would simply replace

EXAMPLE 13.48
Bounded buffer with transactions

```
region buffer when full_slots < SIZE          region buffer when full_slots > 0
    ...                               and         ...
```

with

```
atomic                                          atomic
    if full_slots = SIZE then retry     and         if full_slots = 0 then retry
    ...                                             ...
```

TM avoids the need to specify object(s) on which to implement mutual exclusion. It also allows the condition test to be placed anywhere inside the atomic block.

Many different implementations of TM have been proposed, both in hardware and in software. As of 2015, hardware support is commercially available in IBM's z and p series machines, and in Intel's recent versions of the x86. Language-level support is available in Haskell and in several experimental languages and dialects. A formal proposal for transactional extensions to C++ is under consideration for the next revision of the language, expected in 2017 [Int15]. It will be several years before we know how much TM can simplify concurrency in practice, but current signs are promising.

An Example Implementation

There is a surprising amount of variety among software TM systems. We outline one possible implementation here, based, in large part, on the TL2 system of Dice et al. [DSS06] and the TinySTM system of Riegel et al. [FRF08].

Every active transaction keeps track of the locations it has read and the locations and values it has written. It also maintains a valid_time value that indicates the most recent *logical time* at which all of the values it has read so far were known to be correct. Times are obtained from a global clock variable that increases by one each time a transaction attempts to commit. Finally, threads share a global table of *ownership records* (orecs), indexed by hashing the address of a shared location. Each orec contains either (1) the most recent logical time at which any of the locations covered by (hashing to) that orec was updated, or (2) the ID t of a transaction that is currently trying to commit a change to one of those locations. In case (1), the orec is said to be *unowned*; in case (2) the orec—and, by extension, all locations that hash to it—is said to be *owned* by t.

EXAMPLE 13.49
Translation of an atomic block

The compiler translates each atomic block into code roughly equivalent to the following:

```
loop
    valid_time := clock
    read_set := write_map := ∅
    try
        -- your code here
        commit()
        break
    except when abort
        -- continue loop
```

In the body of the transaction (your code here), reads and writes of a location with address x are replaced with calls to read(x) and write(x, v), using the code

```
struct orec
    owned : Boolean
    val : union (time, transaction_id)

function read(x : address) : value
    if x ∈ write_map.domain then return write_map[x]
    loop
        repeat
            o : orec := orecs[hash(x)]
        until not o.owned
        t : time := o.val    -- when last modified
        if t > valid_time
            -- may be inconsistent with previous reads
            validate()    -- attempt to extend valid_time
        v : value := *x
        if o = orecs[hash(x)]
            read_set +:= {x}
            return v

procedure validate()
    t : time := clock
    for x : address ∈ read_set
        o : orec := orecs[hash(x)]
        if (not o.owned and o.val > valid_time)
                or (o.owned and o.val ≠ me)
            throw abort
    valid_time := t

procedure write(x : address, v : value)
    write_map[x] := v

procedure commit()
    try
        lock_map : map address → orec := ∅
        done : Boolean := false
        for x : address ∈ write_map.domain
            o : orec := orecs[hash(x)]
            if o ≠ ⟨true, me⟩
                if o.owned then throw abort
                if not CAS(&orecs[hash(x)], o, ⟨true, me⟩)
                    throw abort
                lock_map[x] := o
        n : time := 1 + fetch_and_increment(&clock)
        validate()
        done := true
        for ⟨x, v⟩ : ⟨address, value⟩ ∈ write_map
            *x = v                                  -- write back
    finally
        -- do this however control leaves the try block
        for ⟨x, o⟩ : ⟨address, orec⟩ ∈ lock_map
            orecs[hash(x)] := if done
                then ⟨false, n⟩                     -- update
                else o                              -- restore
```

Figure 13.19 Possible pseudocode for a software TM system. The read and write routines are used to replace ordinary loads and stores within the body of the transaction. The validate routine is called from both read and commit. It attempts to verify that no previously read value has since been overwritten and, if successful, updates valid_time. Various fence instructions (not shown) may be needed if the underlying hardware is not sequentially consistent.

shown in Figure 13.19. Also shown is the commit routine, called at the end of the try block above. ■

Briefly, a transaction buffers its (speculative) writes until it is ready to commit. It then locks all the locations it needs to write, verifies that all the locations it previously read have not been overwritten since, and then writes back and unlocks the locations. At all times, the transaction knows that all of its reads were mutually consistent at time valid_time. If it ever tries to read a new location that has been updated since valid_time, it attempts to *extend* this time to the current value of the global clock. If it is able to perform a similar extension at commit time, after having locked all locations it needs to change, then the aggregate effect of the transaction as a whole will be as if it had occurred instantaneously at commit time.

To implement retry (not shown in Figure 13.19), we can add an optional list of threads to every orec. A retrying thread will add itself to the list of every location in its `read_set` and then perform a P operation on a thread-specific semaphore. Meanwhile, any thread that commits a change to an orec with waiting threads performs a V on the semaphore of each of those threads. This mechanism will sometimes result in unnecessary wakeups, but these do not impact correctness. Upon wakeup, a thread removes itself from all thread lists before restarting its transaction.

Challenges

Many subtleties have been glossed over in our example implementation. The translation in Example 13.49 will not behave correctly if code inside the atomic block throws an exception (other than abort) or executes a return or an exit out of some surrounding loop. The pseudocode of Figure 13.19 also fails to consider that transactions may be nested.

Several additional issues are still the subject of debate among TM designers. What should we do about operations inside transactions (I/O, system calls, etc.) that cannot easily be rolled back, and how do we prevent such transactions from ever calling retry? How do we discourage programmers from creating transactions so large they almost always conflict with one another, and cannot run in parallel? Should a program ever be able to detect that transactions are aborting? How should transactions interact with locks and with nonblocking data structures? Should races between transactions and nontransactional code be considered program bugs? If so, should there be any constraints on the behavior that may result? These and similar questions will need to be answered by any production-quality TM-capable language.

13.4.5 Implicit Synchronization

In several shared-memory languages, the operations that threads can perform on shared data are restricted in such a way that synchronization can be implicit in the operations themselves, rather than appearing as separate, explicit operations. We have seen one example of implicit synchronization already: the `forall` loop of HPF and Fortran 95 (Example 13.10). Separate iterations of a `forall` loop proceed concurrently, semantically in lock-step with each other: each iteration reads all data used in its instance of the first assignment statement before any iteration updates its instance of the left-hand side. The left-hand side updates in turn occur before any iteration reads the data used in its instance of the second assignment statement, and so on. Compilation of `forall` loops for vector machines, while far from trivial, is more or less straightforward. On a more conventional multiprocessor, however, good performance usually depends on high-quality *dependence analysis*, which allows the compiler to identify situations in which statements within a loop do not in fact depend on one another, and can proceed without synchronization.

Dependence analysis plays a crucial role in other languages as well. In Sidebar 11.1 we mentioned the purely functional languages Sisal and pH (recall that iterative constructs in these languages are syntactic sugar for tail recursion). Because these languages are side-effect free, their constructs can be evaluated in any order, or concurrently, as long as no construct attempts to use a value that has yet to be computed. The Sisal implementation developed at Lawrence Livermore National Lab used extensive compiler analysis to identify promising constructs for parallel execution. It also employed tags on data objects that indicate whether the object's value had been computed yet. When the compiler was unable to guarantee that a value would have been computed by the time it was needed at run time, the generated code used tag bits for synchronization, spinning or blocking until they were properly set. Sisal's developers claimed (in 1992) that their language and compiler rivaled parallel Fortran in performance [Can92].

Automatic parallelization, first for vector machines and then for general-purpose machines, was a major topic of research in the 1980s and 1990s. It achieved considerable success with well-structured data-parallel programs, largely for scientific applications, and largely but not entirely in Fortran. Automatic identification of thread-level parallelism in more general, irregularly structured programs proved elusive, however, as did compilation for message-passing hardware. Research in this area continues, and has branched out to languages like Matlab and R.

Futures

EXAMPLE 13.50 future construct in Multilisp

Implicit synchronization can also be achieved without compiler analysis. The Multilisp [Hal85, MKH91] dialect of Scheme allowed the programmer to enclose any function evaluation in a special `future` construct:

```
(future (my-function my-args))
```

In a purely functional program, `future` is semantically neutral: assuming all evaluations terminate, program behavior will be exactly the same as if `(my-function my-args)` had appeared without the surrounding call. In the implementation, however, `future` arranges for the embedded function to be evaluated by a separate thread of control. The parent thread continues to execute until it actually tries to use the return value of `my-function`, at which point it waits for execution of the `future` to complete. If two or more arguments to a function are enclosed in `futures`, then evaluation of the arguments can proceed in parallel:

```
(parent (future (child1 args1 )) (future (child2 args2 )))
```

There were no additional synchronization mechanisms in Multilisp: `future` itself was the language's only addition to Scheme. Many subsequent languages and systems have provided `future` as part of a larger feature set. Using C#'s Task Parallel Library (TPL), we might write

EXAMPLE 13.51 Futures in C#

```
var description = Task.Factory.StartNew(() => GetDescription());
var numberInStock = Task.Factory.StartNew(() => GetInventory());
...
Console.WriteLine("We have " + numberInStock.Result
    + " copies of " + description.Result + " in stock");
```

Static library class `Task.Factory` is used to generate futures, known as "tasks" in C#. The `Create` method supports generic type inference, allowing us to pass a delegate compatible with `Func<T>` (function returning `T`), for any `T`. We've specified the delegates here as lambda expressions. If `GetDescription` returns a `String`, `description` will be of type `Task<String>`; if `GetInventory` returns an `int`, `numberInStock` will be of type `Task<int>`.

The Java standard library provides similar facilities, but the lack of delegates, properties (like `Result`), type inference (`var`), and automatic boxing (of the `int` returned by `GetInventory`) make the syntax quite a bit more cumbersome. Java also requires that the programmer pass newly created `Futures` to an explicitly created `Executor` object that will be responsible for running them. Scala provides syntax for futures as simple as that of C#, with even richer semantics.

EXAMPLE 13.52
Futures in C++11

Futures are also available in C++, where they are designed to interoperate with lambda expressions, object closures, and a variety of mechanisms for threading and asynchronous (delayed) computation. Perhaps the simplest use case employs the generic `async` function, which takes a function `f` and a list of arguments a_1, ..., a_n, and returns a future that will eventually yield `f(`a_1`, ..., `a_n`)`:

```
string ip_address_of(const char* hostname) {
    // do Internet name lookup (potentially slow)
}
...
```

DESIGN & IMPLEMENTATION

13.9 Side-effect freedom and implicit synchronization

In a partially imperative program (in Multilisp, C#, Scala, etc.), the programmer must take care to make sure that concurrent execution of `futures` will not compromise program correctness. The expression `(parent (future (child1` *args1* `)) (future (child2` *args2* `)))` may produce unpredictable behavior if the evaluations of `child1` and `child2` depend on one another, or if the evaluation of `parent` depends on any aspect of `child1` and `child2` other than their return values. Such behavior may be very difficult to debug. Languages like Sisal and Haskell avoid the problem by permitting only side-effect–free programs.

In a key sense, pure functional languages are ideally suited to parallel execution: they eliminate all artificial connections—all anti- and output dependences (Section C-17.6)—among expressions: all that remains is the actual *data flow*. Two principal barriers to performance remain: (1) the standard challenges of efficient code generation for functional programs (Section 11.8), and (2) the need to identify which potentially parallel code fragments are large enough and independent enough to merit the overhead of thread creation and implicit synchronization.

```
auto query = async(ip_address_of, "www.cs.rochester.edu");
...
cout << query.get() << "\n";      // prints "192.5.53.208"
```

Here variable `query`, which we declared with the `auto` keyword, will be inferred to have type `future<string>`. ■

In some ways the `future` construct of Multilisp resembles the built-in `delay` and `force` of Scheme (Section 6.6.2). Where `future` supports concurrency, however, `delay` supports lazy evaluation: it defers evaluation of its embedded function until the return value is known to be needed. Any use of a `delay`ed expression in Scheme must be surrounded by `force`. By contrast, synchronization on a Multilisp `future` is implicit—there is no analog of `force`.

A more complicated variant of the C++ `async`, not used in Example 13.52, allows the programmer to insist that the future be run in a separate thread—or, alternatively, that it remain unevaluated until `get` is called (at which point it will execute in the calling thread). When `async` is used as shown in our example, the choice of implementation is left to the run-time system—as it is in Multilisp.

Parallel Logic Programming

Several researchers have noted that the backtracking search of logic languages such as Prolog is also amenable to parallelization. Two strategies are possible. The first is to pursue in parallel the subgoals found in the right-hand side of a rule. This strategy is known as *AND parallelism*. The fact that variables in logic, once initialized, are never subsequently modified ensures that parallel branches of an AND cannot interfere with one another. The second strategy is known as *OR parallelism*; it pursues alternative resolutions in parallel. Because they will generally employ different unifications, branches of an OR must use separate copies of their variables. In a search tree such as that of Figure 12.1, AND parallelism and OR parallelism create new threads at alternating levels.

OR parallelism is *speculative*: since success is required on only one branch, work performed on other branches is in some sense wasted. OR parallelism works well, however, when a goal cannot be satisfied (in which case the entire tree must be searched), or when there is high variance in the amount of execution time required to satisfy a goal in different ways (in which case exploring several branches at once reduces the expected time to find the first solution). Both AND and OR parallelism are problematic in Prolog, because they fail to adhere to the deterministic search order required by language semantics. Parlog [Che92], which supports both AND and OR parallelism, is the best known of the parallel Prolog dialects.

CHECK YOUR UNDERSTANDING

38. What is a *monitor*? How do monitor *condition variables* differ from semaphores?
39. Explain the difference between treating monitor signals as *hints* and treating them as *absolutes*.
40. What is a *monitor invariant*? Under what circumstances must it be guaranteed to hold?
41. Describe the *nested monitor problem* and some potential solutions.
42. What is *deadlock*?
43. What is a *conditional critical region*? How does it differ from a monitor?
44. Summarize the synchronization mechanisms of Ada 95, Java, and C#. Contrast them with one another, and with monitors and conditional critical regions. Be sure to explain the features added to Java 5.
45. What is *transactional memory*? What advantages does it offer over algorithms based on locks? What challenges will need to be overcome before it enters widespread use?
46. Describe the semantics of the HPF/Fortran 95 `forall` loop. How does it differ from `do concurrent`?
47. Why might pure functional languages be said to provide a particularly attractive setting for concurrent programming?
48. What are *futures*? In what languages do they appear? What precautions must the programmer take when using them?
49. Explain the difference between AND *parallelism* and OR *parallelism* in Prolog.

13.5 Message Passing

Shared-memory concurrency has become ubiquitous on multicore processors and multiprocessor servers. Message passing, however, still dominates both distributed and high-end computing. Supercomputers and large-scale clusters are programmed primarily in Fortran or C/C++ with the MPI library package. Distributed computing increasingly relies on client–server abstractions layered on top of libraries that implement the TCP/IP Internet standard. As in shared-memory computing, scores of message-passing languages have also been developed for particular application domains, or for research or pedagogical purposes.

IN MORE DEPTH

Three central issues in message-based concurrency—naming, sending, and receiving—are explored on the companion site. A name may refer directly to a process, to some communication resource associated with a process (often called an *entry* or *port*), or to an independent *socket* or *channel* abstraction. A *send* operation may be entirely asynchronous, in which case the sender continues while the underlying system attempts to deliver the message, or the sender may wait, typically for acknowledgment of receipt or for the return of a reply. A *receive* operation, for its part, may be executed explicitly, or it may implicitly trigger execution of some previously specified handler routine. When implicit receipt is coupled with senders waiting for replies, the combination is typically known as *remote procedure call* (RPC). In addition to message-passing libraries, RPC systems typically rely on a language-aware tool known as a *stub compiler.*

13.6 Summary and Concluding Remarks

Concurrency and parallelism have become ubiquitous in modern computer systems. It is probably safe to say that most computer research and development today involves concurrency in one form or another. High-end computer systems have always been parallel, and multicore PCs and cellphones are now ubiquitous. Even on uniprocessors, graphical and networked applications are typically concurrent.

In this chapter we have provided an introduction to concurrent programming with an emphasis on programming language issues. We began with an overview of the motivations for concurrency and of the architecture of modern multiprocessors. We then surveyed the fundamentals of concurrent software, including communication, synchronization, and the creation and management of threads. We distinguished between shared-memory and message-passing models of communication and synchronization, and between language- and library-based implementations of concurrency.

Our survey of thread creation and management described some six different constructs for creating threads: co-begin, parallel loops, launch-at-elaboration, fork/join, implicit receipt, and early reply. Of these fork/join is the most common; it is found in a host of languages, and in library-based packages such as MPI and OpenMP. RPC systems typically use fork/join internally to implement implicit receipt. Regardless of the thread-creation mechanism, most concurrent programming systems implement their language- or library-level threads on top of a collection of OS-level processes, which the operating system implements in a similar manner on top of a collection of hardware cores. We built our sample implementation in stages, beginning with coroutines on a uniprocessor, then adding a ready list and scheduler, then timers for preemption, and finally parallel scheduling on multiple cores.

The bulk of the chapter focused on shared-memory programming models, and on synchronization in particular. We distinguished between atomicity and condition synchronization, and between busy-wait and scheduler-based implementations. Among busy-wait mechanisms we looked in particular at spin locks and barriers. Among scheduler-based mechanisms we looked at semaphores, monitors, and conditional critical regions. Of the three, semaphores are the simplest, and remain widely used, particularly in operating systems. Monitors and conditional critical regions provide better encapsulation and abstraction, but are not amenable to implementation in a library. Conditional critical regions might be argued to provide the most pleasant programming model, but cannot in general be implemented as efficiently as monitors.

We also considered the implicit synchronization provided by parallel functional languages and by parallelizing compilers for such data-parallel languages as High Performance Fortran. For programs written in a functional style, we considered the `future` mechanism introduced by Multilisp and subsequently incorporated into many other languages, including Java, C#, C++, and Scala.

As an alternative to lock-based atomicity, we considered nonblocking data structures, which avoid performance anomalies due to inopportune preemption and page faults. For certain common structures, nonblocking algorithms can outperform locks even in the common case. Unfortunately, they tend to be extraordinarily subtle and difficult to create.

Transactional memory (TM) was originally conceived as a general-purpose means of building nonblocking code for arbitrary data structures. Most recent implementations, however, have given up on nonblocking guarantees, focusing instead on the ability to specify atomicity without devising an explicit locking protocol. Like conditional critical regions, TM sacrifices performance for the sake of programmability. Prototype implementations are now available for a wide variety of languages, with hardware support in several commercial instruction sets.

Our section on message passing, mostly on the companion site, drew examples from several libraries and languages, and considered how processes name each other, how long they block when sending a message, and whether receipt is implicit or explicit. Distributed computing increasingly relies on remote procedure calls, which combine remote-invocation send (wait for a reply) with implicit message receipt.

As in previous chapters, we saw many cases in which language design and language implementation influence one another. Some mechanisms (cactus stacks, conditional critical regions, content-based message screening) are sufficiently complex that many language designers have chosen not to provide them. Other mechanisms (Ada-style parameter modes) have been developed specifically to facilitate an efficient implementation technique. And in still other cases (the semantics of no-wait send, blocking inside a monitor), implementation issues play a major role in some larger set of tradeoffs.

Despite the very long history of concurrent language design, until recently most multithreaded programs relied on library-based thread packages. Even C and C++ are now explicitly parallel, however, and it is hard to imagine any new languages being designed for purely sequential execution. As of 2015, explicitly parallel languages have yet to seriously undermine the dominance of MPI for high-end scientific computing, though this, too, may change in coming years.

13.7 Exercises

13.1 Give an example of a "benign" race condition—one whose outcome affects program behavior, but not correctness.

13.2 We have defined the *ready list* of a thread package to contain all threads that are runnable but not running, with a separate variable to identify the currently running thread. Could we just as easily have defined the ready list to contain *all* runnable threads, with the understanding that the one at the head of the list is running? (Hint: Think about multiprocessors.)

13.3 Imagine you are writing the code to manage a hash table that will be shared among several concurrent threads. Assume that operations on the table need to be atomic. You could use a single mutual exclusion lock to protect the entire table, or you could devise a scheme with one lock per hash-table bucket. Which approach is likely to work better, under what circumstances? Why?

13.4 The typical spin lock holds only one bit of data, but requires a full word of storage, because only full words can be read, modified, and written atomically in hardware. Consider, however, the hash table of the previous exercise. If we choose to employ a separate lock for each bucket of the table, explain how to implement a "two-level" locking scheme that couples a conventional spin lock for the table as a whole with a *single bit* of locking information for each bucket. Explain why such a scheme might be desirable, particularly in a table with external chaining.

13.5 Drawing inspiration from Examples 13.29 and 13.30, design a non-blocking linked-list implementation of a stack using `compare_and_swap`. (When `CAS` was first introduced, on the IBM 370 architecture, this algorithm was one of the driving applications [Tre86].)

13.6 Building on the previous exercise, suppose that stack nodes are dynamically allocated. If we read a pointer and then are delayed (e.g., due to preemption), the node to which the pointer refers may be reclaimed and then reallocated for a different purpose. A subsequent `compare-and-swap` may then succeed when logically it should not. This issue is known as the *ABA problem*.

Give a concrete example—an interleaving of operations in two or more threads—where the ABA problem may result in incorrect behavior for your stack. Explain why this behavior cannot occur in systems with automatic garbage collection. Suggest what might be done to avoid it in systems with manual storage management.

13.7 We noted in Section 13.3.2 that several processors, including the ARM, MIPS, and Power, provide an alternative to `compare_and_swap` (`CAS`) known as `load_linked/store_conditional` (`LL/SC`). A `load_linked` instruction loads a memory location into a register and stores certain bookkeeping information into hidden processor registers. A `store_conditional` instruction stores the register back into the memory location, but only if the location has not been modified by any other processor since the `load_linked` was executed. Like `compare_and_swap`, `store_conditional` returns an indication of whether it succeeded or not.

(a) Rewrite the code sequence of Example 13.29 using `LL/SC`.

(b) On most machines, an `SC` instruction can fail for any of several "spurious" reasons, including a page fault, a cache miss, or the occurrence of an interrupt in the time since the matching `LL`. What steps must a programmer take to make sure that algorithms work correctly in the face of such failures?

(c) Discuss the relative advantages of `LL/SC` and `CAS`. Consider how they might be implemented on a cache-coherent multiprocessor. Are there situations in which one would work but the other would not? (Hints: Consider algorithms in which a thread may need to touch more than one memory location. Also consider algorithms in which the contents of a memory location might be changed and then restored, as in the previous exercise.)

13.8 Starting with the test-and-`test_and_set` lock of Figure 13.8, implement busy-wait code that will allow readers to access a data structure concurrently. Writers will still need to lock out both readers and other writers. You may use any reasonable atomic instruction(s) (e.g., `LL/SC`). Consider the issue of fairness. In particular, if there are *always* readers interested in accessing the data structure, your algorithm should ensure that writers are not locked out forever.

13.9 Assuming the Java memory model,

(a) Explain why it is not sufficient in Figure 13.11 to label X and Y as `volatile`.

(b) Explain why it *is* sufficient, in that same figure, to enclose C's reads (and similarly those of D) in a `synchronized` block for some common shared object O.

(c) Explain why it is sufficient, in Example 13.31, to label both inspected and X as `volatile`, but not to label only one.

(Hint: You may find it useful to consult Doug Lea's Java Memory Model "Cookbook for Compiler Writers," at *gee.cs.oswego.edu/dl/jmm/cookbook.html*).

13.10 Implement the nonblocking queue of Example 13.30 on an x86. (Complete pseudocode can be found in the paper by Michael and Scott [MS98].)

Do you need fence instructions to ensure consistency? If you have access to appropriate hardware, port your code to a machine with a more relaxed memory model (e.g., ARM or Power). What new fences or atomic references do you need?

13.11 Consider the implementation of software transactional memory in Figure 13.19.

(a) How would you implement the read_set, write_map, and lock_map data structures? You will want to minimize the cost not only of insert and lookup operations but also of (1) "zeroing out" the table at the end of a transaction, so it can be used again; and (2) extending the table if it becomes too full.

(b) The validate routine is called in two different places. Expand these calls in-line and customize them to the calling context. What optimizations can you achieve?

(c) Optimize the commit routine to exploit the fact that a final validation is unnecessary if no other transaction has committed since valid_time.

(d) Further optimize commit by observing that the for loop in the finally clause really needs to iterate over orecs, not over addresses (there may be a difference, if more than one address hashes to the same orec). What data, ideally, should lock_map hold?

13.12 The code of Example 13.35 could fairly be accused of displaying poor abstraction. If we make *desired_condition* a delegate (a subroutine or object closure), can we pass it as an extra parameter, and move the signal and scheduler_lock management inside sleep_on? (Hint: Consider the code for the P operation in Figure 13.15.)

13.13 The mechanism used in Figure 13.13 to make scheduler code reentrant employs a single OS-provided lock for all the scheduling data structures of the application. Among other things, this mechanism prevents threads on separate processors from performing P or V operations on unrelated semaphores, even when none of the operations needs to block. Can you devise another synchronization mechanism for scheduler-related operations that admits a higher degree of concurrency but that is still correct?

13.14 Show how to implement a lock-based concurrent set as a singly linked sorted list. Your implementation should support insert, find, and remove operations, and should permit operations on separate portions of the list to occur concurrently (so a single lock for the entire list will not suffice). (Hint: You will want to use a "walking lock" idiom in which acquire and release operations are interleaved in non-LIFO order.)

13.15 (Difficult) Implement a nonblocking version of the set of the previous exercise. (Hint: You will probably discover that insertion is easy but deletion is hard. Consider a *lazy deletion* mechanism in which cleanup [physical removal of a node] may occur well after logical completion of the removal. For further details see the work of Harris [Har01].)

13.16 To make spin locks useful on a multiprogrammed multiprocessor, one might want to ensure that no process is ever preempted in the middle of a critical section. That way it would always be safe to spin in user space, because the process holding the lock would be guaranteed to be running on some other processor, rather than preempted and possibly in need of the current processor. Explain why an operating system designer might not want to give user processes the ability to disable preemption arbitrarily. (Hint: Think about fairness and multiple users.) Can you suggest a way to get around the problem? (References to several possible solutions can be found in the paper by Kontothanassis, Wisniewski, and Scott [KWS97].)

13.17 Show how to use semaphores to construct a scheduler-based n-thread barrier.

13.18 Prove that monitors and semaphores are equally powerful. That is, use each to implement the other. In the monitor-based implementation of semaphores, what is your monitor invariant?

13.19 Show how to use binary semaphores to implement general semaphores.

13.20 In Example 13.38 (Figure 13.15), suppose we replaced the middle four lines of procedure P with

```
if S.N = 0
    sleep_on(S.Q)
S.N −:= 1
```

and the middle four lines of procedure V with

```
S.N +:= 1
if S.Q is nonempty
    enqueue(ready_list, dequeue(S.Q))
```

What is the problem with this new version? Explain how it connects to the question of hints and absolutes in Section 13.4.1.

13.21 Suppose that every monitor has a separate mutual exclusion lock, so that different threads can run in different monitors concurrently, and that we want to release exclusion on both inner and outer monitors when a thread `waits` in a nested call. When the thread awakens it will need to reacquire the outer locks. How can we ensure its ability to do so? (Hint: Think about the order in which to acquire locks, and be prepared to abandon Hoare semantics. For further hints, see Wettstein [Wet78].)

13.22 Show how general semaphores can be implemented with conditional critical regions in which all threads wait for the same condition, thereby avoiding the overhead of unproductive wake-ups.

13.23 Write code for a bounded buffer using the protected object mechanism of Ada 95.

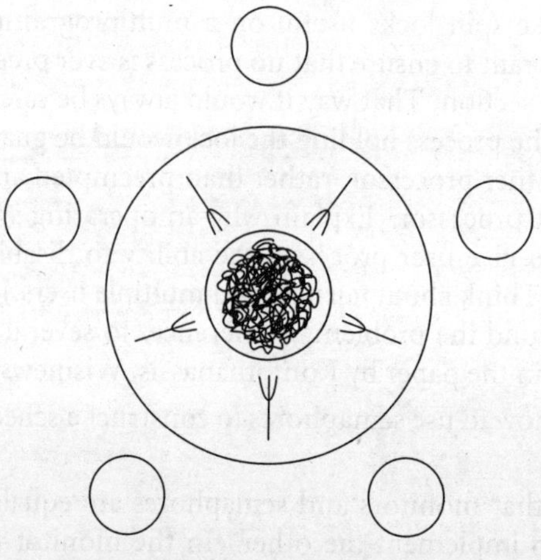

Figure 13.20 **The Dining Philosophers.** Hungry philosophers must contend for the forks to their left and right in order to eat.

13.24 Repeat the previous exercise in Java using `synchronized` statements or methods. Try to make your solution as simple and conceptually clear as possible. You will probably want to use `notifyAll`.

13.25 Give a more efficient solution to the previous exercise that avoids the use of `notifyAll`. (*Warning:* It is tempting to observe that the buffer can never be both full and empty at the same time, and to assume therefore that waiting threads are either all producers or all consumers. This need not be the case, however: if the buffer ever becomes even a temporary performance bottleneck, there may be an arbitrary number of waiting threads, including both producers and consumers.)

13.26 Repeat the previous exercise using Java `Lock` variables.

13.27 Explain how *escape analysis*, mentioned briefly in Sidebar 10.3, could be used to reduce the cost of certain `synchronized` statements and methods in Java.

13.28 The *dining philosophers problem* [Dij72] is a classic exercise in synchronization (Figure 13.20). Five philosophers sit around a circular table. In the center is a large communal plate of spaghetti. Each philosopher repeatedly thinks for a while and then eats for a while, at intervals of his or her own choosing. On the table between each pair of adjacent philosophers is a single fork. To eat, a philosopher requires both adjacent forks: the one on the left and the one on the right. Because they share a fork, adjacent philosophers cannot eat simultaneously.

Write a solution to the dining philosophers problem in which each philosopher is represented by a process and the forks are represented by shared data. Synchronize access to the forks using semaphores, monitors, or conditional critical regions. Try to maximize concurrency.

13.29 In the previous exercise you may have noticed that the dining philosophers are prone to deadlock. One has to worry about the possibility that all five of them will pick up their right-hand forks simultaneously, and then wait forever for their left-hand neighbors to finish eating.

Discuss as many strategies as you can think of to address the deadlock problem. Can you describe a solution in which it is provably impossible for any philosopher to go hungry forever? Can you describe a solution that is fair in a strong sense of the word (i.e., in which no one philosopher gets more chance to eat than some other over the long term)? For a particularly elegant solution, see the paper by Chandy and Misra [CM84].

13.30 In some concurrent programming systems, global variables are shared by all threads. In others, each newly created thread has a separate copy of the global variables, commonly initialized to the values of the globals of the creating thread. Under this private globals approach, shared data must be allocated from a special heap. In still other programming systems, the programmer can specify which global variables are to be private and which are to be shared.

Discuss the tradeoffs between private and shared global variables. Which would you prefer to have available, for which sorts of programs? How would you implement each? Are some options harder to implement than others? To what extent do your answers depend on the nature of processes provided by the operating system?

13.31 Rewrite Example 13.51 in Java.

13.32 AND parallelism in logic languages is analogous to the parallel evaluation of arguments in a functional language (e.g., Multilisp). Does OR parallelism have a similar analog? (Hint: Think about special forms [Section 11.5].) Can you suggest a way to obtain the effect of OR parallelism in Multilisp?

13.33 In Section 13.4.5 we claimed that both AND parallelism and OR parallelism were problematic in Prolog, because they failed to adhere to the deterministic search order required by language semantics. Elaborate on this claim. What specifically can go wrong?

13.34–13.38 In More Depth.

13.8 Explorations

13.39 The MMX, SSE, and AVX extensions to the x86 instruction set and the AltiVec extensions to the Power instruction set make vector operations available to general-purpose code. Learn about these instructions and research their history. What sorts of code are they used for? How are they related to vector supercomputers? To modern graphics processors?

13.40 The "Top 500" list (*top500.org*) maintains information, over time, on the 500 most powerful computers in the world, as measured on the Linpack performance benchmark. Explore the site. Pay particular attention to the historical trends in the kinds of machines deployed. Can you explain these trends? How many cases can you find of supercomputer technology moving into the mainstream, and vice versa?

13.41 In Section 13.3.3 we noted that different processors provide different levels of memory consistency and different mechanisms to force additional ordering when needed. Learn more about these hardware memory models. You might want to start with the tutorial by Adve and Gharachorloo [AG96].

13.42 In Sections 13.3.3 and 13.4.3 we presented a very high-level summary of the Java and C++ memory models. Learn their details. Also investigate the (more loosely specified) models of Ada and C#. How do these compare? How efficiently can each be implemented on various real machines? What are the challenges for implementors? For Java, explore the controversy that arose around the memory model in the original definition of the language (updated in Java 5—see the paper by Manson et al. [MPA05] for a discussion). For C++, pay particular attention to the ability to specify weakened consistency on loads and stores of `atomic` variables.

13.43 In Section 13.3.2 we presented a brief introduction to the design of *nonblocking* concurrent data structures, which work correctly without locks. Learn more about this topic. How hard is it to write correct nonblocking code? How does the performance compare to that of lock-based code? You might want to start with the work of Michael [MS98] and Sundell [Sun04]. For a more theoretical foundation, start with Herlihy's original article on *wait freedom* [Her91] and the more recent concept of *obstruction freedom* [HLM03], or check out the text by Herlihy and Shavit [HS12].

13.44 As possible improvements to reader-writer locks, learn about *sequence locks* [Lam05] and the *RCU* (read-copy update) synchronization idiom [MAK+01]. Both of these are heavily used in the operating systems community. Discuss the challenges involved in applying them to code written by "nonexperts."

13.45 The first software transactional memory systems grew out of work on nonblocking concurrent data structures, and were in fact nonblocking. Most recent systems, however, are lock based. Read the position paper by Ennals [Enn06] and the more recent papers of Marathe and Moir [MM08] and Tabba et al. [TWGM07]. What do you think? Should TM systems be nonblocking?

13.46 The most widely used language-level transactional memory is the *STM monad* of Haskell, supported by the Glasgow Haskell compiler and run-time system. Read up on its syntax and implementation [HMPH05]. Pay particular attention to the `retry` and `orElse` mechanisms. Discuss their similarities to—and advantages over—conditional critical regions.

13.47 Study the documentation for some of your favorite library packages (the C and C++ standard libraries, perhaps, or the .NET and Java libraries, or the many available packages for mathematical computing). Which routines can safely be called from a multithreaded program? Which cannot? What accounts for the difference? Why not make all routines thread safe?

13.48 Undertake a detailed study of several concurrent languages. Download implementations and use them to write parallel programs of several different sorts. (You might, for example, try Conway's Game of Life, Delaunay Triangulation, and Gaussian Elimination; descriptions of all of these can easily be found on the Web.) Write a paper about your experience. What worked well? What didn't? Languages you might consider include Ada, C#, Cilk, Erlang, Go, Haskell, Java, Modula-3, Occam, Rust, SR, and Swift. References for all of these can be found in Appendix A.

13.49 Learn about the supercomputing languages discussed in the Bibliographic Notes at the end of the chapter: Co-Array Fortran, Titanium, and UPC; and Chapel, Fortress, and X10. How do these compare to one another? To MPI and OpenMP? To languages with less of a focus on "high-end" computing?

13.50 In the spirit of the previous question, learn about the SHMEM library package, originally developed by Robert Numrich of Cray, Inc., and now standardized as OpenSHMEM (*openshmem.org*). SHMEM is widely used for parallel programming on both large-scale multiprocessors and clusters. It has been characterized as a cross between shared memory and message passing. Is this a fair characterization? Under what circumstances might a `shmem` program be expected to outperform solutions in MPI or OpenMP?

13.51 Much of this chapter has been devoted to the management of races in parallel programs. The complexity of the task suggests a tantalizing question: is it possible to design a concurrent programming language that is powerful enough to be widely useful, and in which programs are inherently race-free? For three very different takes on a (mostly) affirmative answer, see the work of Edward Lee [Lee06], the various concurrent dialects of Haskell [NA01, JGF96], and Deterministic Parallel Java (DPJ) [BAD$^+$09].

13.52–13.54 In More Depth.

13.9 Bibliographic Notes

Much of the early study of concurrency stems from a pair of articles by Dijkstra [Dij68a, Dij72]. Andrews and Schneider [AS83] provided an excellent snapshot of the field in the early 1980s. Holt et al. [HGLS78] is a useful reference for many of the classic problems in concurrency and synchronization.

Peterson's two-process synchronization algorithm appears in a remarkably elegant and readable two-page paper [Pet81]. Lamport's 1978 article on "Time, Clocks, and the Ordering of Events in a Distributed System" [Lam78] argued convincingly that the notion of global time cannot be well defined, and that distributed algorithms must therefore be based on causal *happens before* relationships among individual processes. Reader–writer locks are due to Courtois, Heymans, and Parnas [CHP71]. Java 7 phasers were inspired in part by the work of Shirako et al. [SPSS08]. Mellor-Crummey and Scott [MCS91] survey the principal busy-wait synchronization algorithms and introduce locks and barriers that scale without contention to very large machines.

The seminal paper on lock-free synchronization is that of Herlihy [Her91]. The nonblocking concurrent queue of Example 13.30 is due to Michael and Scott [MS96]. Herlihy and Shavit [HS12] and Scott [Sco13] provide modern, book-length coverage of synchronization and concurrent data structures. Adve and Gharachorloo introduce the notion of hardware memory models [AG96]. Pugh explains the problems with the original Java Memory Model [Pug00]; the revised model is described by Manson, Pugh, and Adve [MPA05]. The memory model for C++11 is described by Boehm and Adve [BA08]. Boehm has argued convincingly that threads cannot be implemented correctly without compiler support [Boe05]. The original paper on transactional memory is by Herlihy and Moss [HM93]. Harris, Larus, and Rajwar provide a book-length survey of the field as of late 2010 [HLR10]. Larus and Kozyrakis provide a briefer overview [LK08].

Two recent generations of parallel languages for high-end computing have been highly influential. The Partitioned Global Address Space (PGAS) languages include Co-Array Fortran (CAF), Unified Parallel C (UPC), and Titanium (a dialect of Java). They support a single global name space for variables, but employ an "extra dimension" of addressing to access data not on the local core. Much of the functionality of CAF has been adopted into Fortran 2008. The so-called HPCS languages—Chapel, Fortress, and X10—build on experience with the PGAS languages, but target a broader range of hardware, applications, and styles of parallelism. All three include transactional features. For all of these, a web search is probably the best source of current information.

MPI [Mes12] is documented in a variety of articles and books. The latest version draws several features from an earlier, competing system known as PVM (Parallel Virtual Machine) [Sun90, GBD+94]. Remote procedure call received increasing attention in the wake of Nelson's doctoral research [BN84]. The Open Network Computing RPC standard is documented in Internet RFC number 1831 [Sri95]. RPC also forms the basis of such higher-level standards as CORBA, COM, JavaBeans, and SOAP.

Software distributed shared memory (S-DSM) was originally proposed by Li as part of his doctoral research [LH89]. The TreadMarks system from Rice University was widely considered the most mature and robust of the various implementations [ACD+96].

14 Scripting Languages

Traditional programming languages are intended primarily for the construction of self-contained applications: programs that accept some sort of input, manipulate it in some well-understood way, and generate appropriate output. But most actual *uses* of computers require the coordination of multiple programs. A large institutional payroll system, for example, must process time-reporting data from card readers, scanned paper forms, and manual (keyboard) entry; execute thousands of database queries; enforce hundreds of legal and institutional rules; create an extensive "paper trail" for record-keeping, auditing, and tax preparation purposes; print paychecks; and communicate with servers around the world for on-line direct deposit, tax withholding, retirement accumulation, medical insurance, and so on. These tasks are likely to involve dozens or hundreds of separately executable programs. Coordination among these programs is certain to require tests and conditionals, loops, variables and types, subroutines and abstractions—the same sorts of logical tools that a conventional language provides *inside* an application.

On a much smaller scale, a graphic artist or photojournalist may routinely download pictures from a digital camera; convert them to a favorite format; rotate the pictures that were shot in vertical orientation; down-sample them to create browsable thumbnail versions; index them by date, subject, and color histogram; back them up to a remote archive; and then reinitialize the camera's memory. Performing these steps by hand is likely to be both tedious and error-prone. In a similar vein, the creation of a dynamic web page may require authentication and authorization, database lookup, image manipulation, remote communication, and the reading and writing of HTML text. All these scenarios suggest a need for programs that coordinate other programs.

It is of course possible to write coordination code in Java, C, or some other conventional language, but it isn't always easy. Conventional languages tend to stress efficiency, maintainability, portability, and the static detection of errors. Their type systems tend to be built around such hardware-level concepts as fixed-size integers, floating-point numbers, characters, and arrays. By contrast *scripting languages* tend to stress flexibility, rapid development, local customization, and dynamic (run-time) checking. Their type systems, likewise, tend to embrace such high-level concepts as tables, patterns, lists, and files.

General-purpose scripting languages like Perl, Python, and Ruby are sometimes called *glue languages*, because they were originally designed to "glue" existing programs together to build a larger system. With the growth of the World Wide Web, scripting languages have become the standard way to generate dynamic content, both on servers and with the client browser. They are also widely used to customize or extend the functionality of such "scriptable" systems as editors, spreadsheets, games, and presentation tools.

We consider the history and nature of scripting in more detail in Section 14.1. We then turn in Section 14.2 to some of the problem domains in which scripting is widely used. These include command interpretation (shells), text processing and report generation, mathematics and statistics, general-purpose program coordination, and configuration and extension. In Section 14.3 we consider several forms of scripting used on the World Wide Web, including CGI scripts, server- and client-side processing of scripts embedded in web pages, Java applets, and (on the companion site) XSLT. Finally, in Section 14.4, we consider some of the more interesting language features, common to many scripting languages, that distinguish them from their more traditional "mainstream" cousins. We look in particular at naming, scoping, and typing; string and pattern manipulation; and high-level structured data. We will not provide a detailed introduction to any one scripting language, though we will consider concrete examples in several. As in most of this book, the emphasis will be on underlying concepts.

14.1 What Is a Scripting Language?

Modern scripting languages have two principal sets of ancestors. In one set are the command interpreters or "shells" of traditional batch and "terminal" (command-line) computing. In the other set are various tools for text processing and report generation. Examples in the first set include IBM's JCL, the MS-DOS `command` interpreter, and the Unix `sh` and `csh` shell families. Examples in the second set include IBM's RPG and Unix's `sed` and `awk`. From these evolved Rexx, IBM's "Restructured Extended Executor," which dates from 1979, and Perl, originally devised by Larry Wall in the late 1980s, and still one of the most widely used general-purpose scripting languages. Other general-purpose scripting languages include Python, Ruby, PowerShell (for Windows), and AppleScript (for the Mac).

With the growth of the World Wide Web in the late 1990s, Perl was widely adopted for "server-side" web scripting, in which a web server executes a program (on the server's machine) to generate the content of a page. One early web-scripting enthusiast was Rasmus Lerdorf, who created a collection of scripts to track access to his personal home page. Originally written in Perl but soon redesigned as a full-fledged and independent language, these scripts evolved into PHP, now the most popular platform for server-side web scripting. PHP competitors include JSP (Java Server Pages), Ruby on Rails, and, on Microsoft platforms,

PowerShell. For scripting on the client computer, all major browsers implement JavaScript, a language developed by Netscape Corporation in the mid 1990s, and standardized by ECMA (the European standards body) in 1999 [ECM11].

In a classic paper on scripting [Ous98], John Ousterhout, the creator of Tcl, suggested that "Scripting languages assume that a collection of useful components already exist in other languages. They are intended not for writing applications from scratch but rather for combining components." Ousterhout envisioned a future in which programmers would increasingly rely on scripting languages for the top-level structure of their systems, where clarity, reusability, and ease of development are crucial. Traditional "systems languages" like C, C++, or Java, he argued, would be used for self-contained, reusable system components, which emphasize complex algorithms or execution speed. As a general rule of thumb that still seems reasonable today, he suggested that code could be developed 5 to 10 times faster in a scripting language, but would run 10 to 20 times faster in a traditional systems language.

Some authors reserve the term "scripting" for the glue languages used to coordinate multiple programs. In common usage, however, scripting is a broader and vaguer concept, encompassing not only web scripting but also *extension languages*. These are typically embedded within some larger host program, which they can then control. Many readers will be familiar with the Visual Basic "macros" of Microsoft Office and related applications. Others may be familiar with the Lisp-based extension language of the `emacs` text editor, or the widespread use of Lua in the computer gaming industry. Several other languages, including Tcl, Rexx, Python, and the Guile and Elk dialects of Scheme, have implementations designed to be embedded in other applications. In a similar vein, several widely used commercial applications provide their own proprietary extension languages. For graphical user interface (GUI) programming, the Tk toolkit, originally designed for use with Tcl, has been incorporated into several scripting languages, including Perl, Python, and Ruby.

One can also view XSLT (extensible stylesheet language transformations) as a scripting language, albeit somewhat different from the others considered in this chapter. XSLT is part of the growing family of XML (extensible markup language) tools. We consider it further in Section 14.3.5.

14.1.1 Common Characteristics

While it is difficult to define scripting languages precisely, there are several characteristics that they tend to have in common:

Both batch and interactive use. A few scripting languages (notably Perl) have a compiler that insists on reading the entire source program before it produces any output. Most other languages, however, are willing to compile or interpret their input line by line. Rexx, Python, Tcl, Guile, and (with short helper scripts) Ruby and Lua will all accept commands from the keyboard.

Economy of expression. To support both rapid development and interactive use, scripting languages tend to require a minimum of "boilerplate." Some make heavy use of punctuation and very short identifiers (Perl is notorious for this), while others (e.g., Rexx, Tcl, and AppleScript) tend to be more "English-like," with lots of words and not much punctuation. All attempt to avoid the extensive declarations and top-level structure common to conventional languages.

EXAMPLE 14.1

Trivial programs in conventional and scripting languages

Where a trivial program looks like this in Java:

```
class Hello {
    public static void main(String[] args) {
        System.out.println("Hello, world!");
    }
}
```

and like this in Ada:

```
with ada.text_IO; use ada.text_IO;
procedure hello is
begin
    put_line("Hello, world!");
end hello;
```

in Perl, Python, or Ruby it is simply

```
print "Hello, world!\n"
```

Lack of declarations; simple scoping rules. Most scripting languages dispense with declarations, and provide simple rules to govern the scope of names. In some languages (e.g., Perl) everything is global by default; optional declarations can be used to limit a variable to a nested scope. In other languages (e.g., PHP and Tcl), everything is local by default; globals must be explicitly imported. Python adopts the interesting rule that any variable that is assigned a value is local to the block in which the assignment appears. Special syntax is required to assign to a variable in a surrounding scope.

DESIGN & IMPLEMENTATION

14.1 Compiling interpreted languages

Several times in this chapter we will make reference to "the compiler" for a scripting language. As we saw in Examples 1.9 and 1.10, interpreters almost never work with source code; a front-end translator first replaces that source with some sort of intermediate form. For most implementations of most of the languages described in this chapter, the front end is sufficiently complex to deserve the name "compiler." Intermediate forms are typically internal data structures (e.g., a syntax tree) or "byte-code" representations reminiscent of those of Java.

Flexible dynamic typing. In keeping with the lack of declarations, most scripting languages are dynamically typed. In some (e.g., PHP, Python, Ruby, and Scheme), the type of a variable is checked immediately prior to use. In others (e.g., Rexx, Perl, and Tcl), a variable will be interpreted differently in different contexts. In Perl, for example, the program

EXAMPLE 14.2
Coercion in Perl

```
$a = "4";
print $a . 3 . "\n";      # '.' is concatenation
print $a + 3 . "\n";      # '+' is addition
```

will print

```
43
7
```

This contextual interpretation is similar to coercion, except that there isn't necessarily a notion of the "natural" type from which an object must be converted; the various possible interpretations may all be equally "natural." We shall have more to say about context in Perl in Section 14.4.3.

Easy access to system facilities. Most programming languages provide a way to ask the underlying operating system to run another program, or to perform some operation directly. In scripting languages, however, these requests are

DESIGN & IMPLEMENTATION

14.2 Canonical implementations

Because they are usually implemented with interpreters, scripting languages tend to be easy to port from one machine to another—substantially easier than compilers for which one must write a new code generator. Given a native compiler for the language in which the interpreter is written, the only difficult part (and it may indeed be difficult) is to implement any necessary modifications to the part of the interpreter that provides the interface to the operating system.

At the same time, the ease of porting an interpreter means that many scripting languages, including Perl, Python, and Ruby, have a single widely used implementation, which serves as the de facto language definition. Reading a book on Perl, it can be difficult to tell how a subtle program will behave. When in doubt, one may need to "try it out." Rexx and JavaScript are arguably the only widely used scripting languages that have both a formal definition codified by an international standards body and a nontrivial number of independent implementations. (Lua [and Scheme, if you count it as scripting] have detailed reference manuals and multiple implementations, though no formal blessing from a standards body. Dart has an ECMA standard, but as of 2015, only Google implementations. `Sed`, `awk`, and `sh` have all been standardized by POSIX [Int03b], but none of them can really be described as a full-fledged scripting language.)

much more fundamental, and have much more direct support. Perl, for one, provides well over 100 built-in commands that access operating system functions for input and output, file and directory manipulation, process management, database access, sockets, interprocess communication and synchronization, protection and authorization, time-of-day clock, and network communication. These built-in commands are generally a good bit easier to use than corresponding library calls in languages like C.

Sophisticated pattern matching and string manipulation. In keeping with their text processing and report generation ancestry, and to facilitate the manipulation of textual input and output for external programs, scripting languages tend to have extraordinarily rich facilities for pattern matching, search, and string manipulation. Typically these are based on *extended regular expressions*. We discuss them further in Section 14.4.2.

High-level data types. High-level data types like sets, bags, dictionaries, lists, and tuples are increasingly common in the standard library packages of conventional programming languages. A few languages (notably C++) allow users to redefine standard infix operators to make these types as easy to use as more primitive, hardware-centric types. Scripting languages go one step further by building high-level types into the syntax and semantics of the language itself. In most scripting languages, for example, it is commonplace to have an "array" that is indexed by character strings, with an underlying implementation based on hash tables. Storage is invariably garbage collected.

Much of the most rapid change in programming languages today is occurring in scripting languages. This can be attributed to several causes, including the continued growth of the Web, the dynamism of the open-source community, and the comparatively low investment required to create a new scripting language. Where a compiled, industrial-quality language like Java or C# requires a multiyear investment by a very large programming team, a single talented designer, working alone, can create a usable implementation of a new scripting language in only a year or two.

Due in part to this rapid change, newer scripting languages have been able to incorporate some of the most innovative concepts in language design. Ruby, for example, has a uniform object model (much like Smalltalk), true iterators (like Clu), lambda expressions, (like Lisp), array slices (like Fortran 90), structured exception handling, multiway assignment, and reflection. Python has many of these features as well, and a few that Ruby lacks, including Haskell-style list comprehensions.

14.2 Problem Domains

Some general-purpose languages—Scheme and Visual Basic, for example—are widely used for scripting. Conversely, some scripting languages, including Perl,

Python, and Ruby, are intended by their designers for general-purpose use, with features intended to support "programming in the large": modules, separate compilation, reflection, program development environments, and so on. For the most part, however, scripting languages tend to see their principal use in well-defined problem domains. We consider some of these in the following subsections.

14.2.1 Shell (Command) Languages

In the days of punch-card computing (through perhaps the mid 1970s), simple command languages allowed the user to "script" the processing of a card deck. A control card at the front of the deck, for example, might indicate that the upcoming cards represented a program to be compiled, or perhaps machine language for the compiler itself, or input for a program already compiled and stored on disk. A control card embedded later in the deck might test the exit status of the most recently executed program and choose what to do next based on whether that program completed successfully. Given the linear nature of a card deck, however (one can't in general back up), command languages for batch processing tended not to be very sophisticated. JCL, for example, had no iteration constructs.

With the development of interactive timesharing in the 1960s and early 1970s, command languages became much more sophisticated. Louis Pouzin wrote a simple command interpreter for CTSS, the Compatible Time Sharing System at MIT, in 1963 and 1964. When work began on the groundbreaking Multics system in 1964, Pouzin sketched the design of an extended command language, with quoting and argument-passing mechanisms, for which he coined the term "shell." The subsequent implementation served as inspiration for Ken Thompson in the design of the original Unix shell in 1973. In the mid-1970s, Stephen Bourne and John Mashey separately extended the Thompson shell with control flow and variables; Bourne's design was adopted as the Unix standard, taking the place (and the name) of the Thompson shell, `sh`.

In the late 1970s Bill Joy developed the so-called "C shell" (`csh`), inspired at least in part by Mashey's syntax, and introducing significant enhancements for interactive use, including history, aliases, and job control. The `tcsh` version of `csh` adds command-line editing and command completion. David Korn incorporated these mechanisms into a direct descendant of the Bourne shell, `ksh`, which is very similar to the standard POSIX shell [Int03b]. The popular "Bourne-again" shell, `bash`, is an open-source version of `ksh`. While `tcsh` is still popular in some quarters, `ksh`/`bash`/POSIX `sh` is substantially better for writing shell scripts, and comparable for interactive use.

In addition to features designed for interactive use, which we will not consider further here, shell languages provide a wealth of mechanisms to manipulate filenames, arguments, and commands, and to glue together other programs. Most of these features are retained by more general scripting languages. We consider a few of them here, using `bash` syntax. The discussion is of necessity heavily simplified; full details can be found in the `bash man` page, or in various on-line tutorials.

Filename and Variable Expansion

EXAMPLE 14.3
"Wildcards" and "globbing"

Most users of a Unix shell are familiar with "wildcard" expansion of file names. The following command will list all files in the current directory whose names end in `.pdf`:

```
ls *.pdf
```

The shell expands the pattern `*.pdf` into a list of all matching names. If there are three of them (say `fig1.pdf`, `fig2.pdf`, and `fig3.pdf`), the result is equivalent to

```
ls fig1.pdf fig2.pdf fig3.pdf
```

Filename expansion is sometimes called "globbing," after the original Unix `glob` command that implemented it. In addition to `*` wildcards, one can usually specify "don't care" or alternative characters or substrings. The pattern `fig?.pdf` will match (expand to) any file(s) with a single character between the `g` and the dot. The pattern `fig[0-9].pdf` will require that character to be a digit. The pattern `fig3.{eps,pdf}` will match both `fig3.eps` and `fig3.pdf`. ■

EXAMPLE 14.4
For loops in the shell

Filename expansion is particularly useful in loops. Such loops may be typed directly from the keyboard, or embedded in scripts intended for later execution. Suppose, for example, that we wish to create PDF versions of all our EPS figures:[1]

```
for fig in *.eps
do
    ps2pdf $fig
done
```

The `for` construct arranges for the shell variable `fig` to take on the names in the expansion of `*.eps`, one at a time, in consecutive iterations of the loop. The dollar sign in line 3 causes the value of `fig` to be expanded into the `ps2pdf` command before it is executed. (Interestingly, `ps2pdf` is itself a shell script that calls the `gs` Postscript interpreter.) Optional braces can be used to separate a variable name from following characters, as in `cp $foo ${foo}_backup`. ■

EXAMPLE 14.5
A whole loop on one line

Multiple commands can be entered on a single line if they are separated by semicolons. The following, for example, is equivalent to the loop in the previous example:

```
for fig in *.eps; do ps2pdf $fig; done
```

■

1 Postscript is a programming language developed at Adobe Systems, Inc. for the description of images and documents (we consider it again in Sidebar 15.1). Encapsulated Postscript (EPS) is a restricted form of Postscript intended for figures that are to be embedded in other documents. Portable Document Format (PDF, also by Adobe) is a self-contained file format that combines a subset of Postscript with font embedding and compression mechanisms. It is strictly less powerful than Postscript from a computational perspective, but much more portable, and faster and easier to render.

Tests, Queries, and Conditions

EXAMPLE 14.6

Conditional tests in the shell

The loop above will execute ps2pdf for every EPS file in the current directory. Suppose, however, that we already have some PDF files, and only want to create the ones that are missing:

```
for fig in *.eps
do
    target=${fig%.eps}.pdf
    if [ $fig -nt $target ]
    then
        ps2pdf $fig
    fi
done
```

The third line of this script is a variable assignment. The expression `${fig%.eps}` within the right-hand side expands to the value of `fig` with any trailing `.eps` removed. Similar special expansions can be used to test or modify the value of a variable in many different ways. The square brackets in line four delimit a conditional test. The `-nt` operator checks to see whether the file named by its left operand is newer than the file named by its right operand (or if the left operand exists but the right does not). Similar *file query* operators can be used to check many other properties of files. Additional operators can be used for arithmetic or string comparisons. ■

DESIGN & IMPLEMENTATION

14.3 Built-in commands in the shell

Commands in the shell generally take the form of a sequence of *words*, the first of which is the name of the command. Most commands are executable programs, found in directories on the shell's *search path*. A large number, however (about 50 in `bash`), are *builtins*—commands that the shell recognizes and executes itself, rather than starting an external program. Interestingly, several commands that are available as separate programs are duplicated as builtins, either for the sake of efficiency or to provide additional semantics. Conditional tests, for example, were originally supported by the external `test` command (for which square brackets are syntactic sugar), but these occur sufficiently often in scripts that execution speed improved significantly when a built-in version was added. By contrast, while the `kill` command is not used very often, the built-in version allows processes to be identified by small integer or symbolic names from the shell's *job control* mechanism. The external version supports only the longer and comparatively unintuitive process identifiers supplied by the operating system.

Pipes and Redirection

One of the principal innovations of Unix was the ability to chain commands together, "piping" the output of one to the input of the next. Like most shells, bash uses the vertical bar character (|) to indicate a pipe. To count the number of figures in our directory, without distinguishing between EPS and PDF versions, we might type

EXAMPLE 14.7
Pipes

```
for fig in *; do echo ${fig%.*}; done | sort -u | wc -l
```

Here the first command, a `for` loop, prints the names of all files with extensions (dot-suffixes) removed. The `echo` command inside the loop simply prints its arguments. The `sort -u` command after the loop removes duplicates, and the `wc -l` command counts lines. ■

Like most shells, bash also allows output to be redirected to a file, or input read from a file. To create a list of figures, we might type

EXAMPLE 14.8
Output redirection

```
for fig in *; do echo ${fig%.*}; done | sort -u > all_figs
```

The "greater than" sign indicates output redirection. If doubled (`sort -u >> all_figs`) it causes output to be appended to the specified file, rather than overwriting the previous contents.

In a similar vein, the "less than" sign indicates input redirection. Suppose we want to print our list of figures all on one line, separated by spaces, instead of on multiple lines. On a Unix system we can type

```
tr '\n' ' ' < all_figs
```

This invocation of the standard `tr` command converts all newline characters to spaces. Because `tr` was written as a simple filter, it does not accept a list of files on the command line; it only reads standard input. ■

For any executing Unix program, the operating system keeps track of a list of open files. By convention, *standard input* and *standard output* (`stdin` and `stdout`) are files numbers 0 and 1. File number 2 is by convention *standard error* (`stderr`), to which programs are supposed to print diagnostic error messages. One of the advantages of the `sh` family of shells over the `csh` family is the ability to redirect `stderr` and other open files independent of `stdin` and `stdout`. Consider, for example, the ps2pdf script. Under normal circumstances this script works silently. If it encounters an error, however, it prints a message to `stdout` and quits. This violation of convention (the message should go to `stderr`) is harmless when the command is invoked from the keyboard. If it is embedded in a script, however, and the output of the script is directed to a file, the error message may end up in the file instead of on the screen, and go unnoticed by the user. With bash we can type

EXAMPLE 14.9
Redirection of `stderr` and `stdout`

```
ps2pdf my_fig.eps 1>&2
```

Here 1>&2 means "make ps2pdf send file 1 (stdout) to the same place that the surrounding context would normally send file 2 (stderr)."

EXAMPLE 14.10
Heredocs (in-line input)

Finally, like most shells, bash allows the user to provide the input to a command in-line:

```
tr '\n' ' ' <<END
list
of
input
lines
END
```

The <<END indicates that subsequent input lines, up to a line containing only END, are to be supplied as input to tr. Such in-line input (traditionally called a "here document") is seldom used interactively, but is highly useful in shell scripts.

Quoting and Expansion

EXAMPLE 14.11
Problematic spaces in file names

Several examples in the preceding subsections have implicitly relied on the assumption that file names do not contain spaces. Returning to Example 14.4, we will encounter a "file not found" error if we try to run our loop in a directory that contains a file named two words.eps: ps2pdf will end up interpreting its arguments as two words instead of one, and will try to translate file two (which doesn't exist) into words.eps. To avoid problems like this, shells typically provide a *quoting* mechanism that will group words together into strings. We could fix Example 14.4 by typing

```
for fig in *.eps
do
    ps2pdf "$fig"
done
```

Here the double quotes around $fig cause it to be interpreted as a single word, even if it contains white space.

EXAMPLE 14.12
Single and double quotes

But this is not the only kind of quoting. Single (straight or forward) quotes also group text into words, but inhibit filename and variable expansion in the quoted text. Thus

```
foo=bar
single='$foo'
double="$foo"
echo $single $double
```

will print "$foo bar".

EXAMPLE 14.13
Subshells

Several other bracketing constructs in bash group the text inside, for various purposes. Command lists enclosed in parentheses are passed to a subshell for evaluation. If the opening parenthesis is preceded by a dollar sign, the output of the nested command list is expanded into the surrounding context:

```
for fig in $(cat my_figs); do ps2pdf ${fig}.eps; done
```

Here `cat` is the standard command to print the content of a file. Most shells use backward single quotes for the same purpose (`` `cat my_figs` ``); `bash` supports this syntax as well, for backward compatibility. ■

EXAMPLE 14.14
Brace-quoted blocks in the shell

Command lists enclosed in braces are treated by `bash` as a single unit. They can be used, for example, to redirect the output of a sequence of commands:

```
{ date; ls; } >> file_list
```

Unlike parenthesized lists, commands enclosed in braces are executed by the current shell. From a programming languages perspective, parentheses and braces behave "backward" from the way they do in C: parentheses introduce a nested dynamic scope in `bash`, while braces are purely for grouping. In particular, variables that are assigned new values within a parenthesized command list will revert to their previous values once the list has completed execution. ■

EXAMPLE 14.15
Pattern-based list generation

When not surrounded by white space, braces perform pattern-based list generation, in a manner similar to filename expansion, but without the connection to the file system. For example, `echo abc{12,34,56}xyz` prints `abc12xyz abc34xyz abc56xyz`. Also, as we have seen, braces serve to delimit variable names when the opening brace is preceded by a dollar sign. ■

In Example 14.6 we used square brackets to enclose a conditional expression. Double square brackets serve a similar purpose, but with more C-like expression syntax, and without filename expansion. Double parentheses are used to enclose arithmetic computations, again with C-like syntax.

The interpolation of commands in `$()` or backquotes, patterns in `{}`, and arithmetic expressions in `(())` are all considered forms of expansion, analogous to filename expansion and variable expansion. The splitting of strings into words is also considered a form of expansion, as is the replacement, in certain contexts, of tilde (`~`) characters with the name of the user's home directory. All told, these give us seven different kinds of expansion in `bash`.

All of the various bracketing constructs have rules governing which kinds of expansion are performed within. The rules are intended to be as intuitive as possible, but they are not uniform across constructs. Filename expansion, for example, does not occur within `[[]]`-bracketed conditions. Similarly, a double-quote character may appear inside a double-quoted string if escaped with a backslash, but a single-quote character may not appear inside a single-quoted string.

Functions

EXAMPLE 14.16
User-defined shell functions

Users can define functions in `bash` that then work like built-in commands. Many users, for example, define `ll` as a shortcut for `ls -l`, which lists files in the current directory in "long format":

```
function ll () {
    ls -l "$@"
}
```

Within the function, `$1` represents the first parameter, `$2` represents the second, and so on. In the definition of `ll`, `$@` represents the entire parameter list. Functions can be arbitrarily complex. In particular, `bash` supports both local variables and recursion. Shells in the `csh` family provide a more primitive `alias` mechanism that works via macro expansion.

The #! Convention

EXAMPLE 14.17

The `#!` convention in script files

As noted above, shell commands can be read from a *script* file. To execute them in the current shell, one uses the "dot" command:

```
. my_script
```

where `my_script` is the name of the file. Many operating systems, including most versions of Unix, allow one to turn a script file into an executable program, so that users can simply type

```
my_script
```

Two steps are required. First, the file must be marked *executable* in the eyes of the operating system. On Unix one types `chmod +x my_script`. Second, the file must be self-descriptive in a way that allows the operating system to tell which shell (or other interpreter) will understand the contents. Under Unix, the file must begin with the characters `#!`, followed by the name of the shell. The typical `bash` script thus begins with

```
#!/bin/bash
```

Specifying the full path name is a safety feature: it anticipates the possibility that the user may have a search path for commands on which some other program named `bash` appears before the shell. (Unfortunately, the requirement for full path names makes `#!` lines nonportable, since shells and other interpreters may be installed in different places on different machines.)

✓ CHECK YOUR UNDERSTANDING

1. Give a plausible one-sentence definition of "scripting language."
2. List the principal ways in which scripting languages differ from conventional "systems" languages.
3. From what two principal sets of ancestors are modern scripting languages descended?
4. What IBM creation is generally considered the first general-purpose scripting language?
5. What is the most popular language for server-side web scripting?

6. How does the notion of *context* in Perl differ from coercion?
7. What is *globbing*? What is a *wildcard*?
8. What is a *pipe* in Unix? What is *redirection*?
9. Describe the three standard I/O streams provided to every Unix process.
10. Explain the significance of the `#!` convention in Unix shell scripts.

DESIGN & IMPLEMENTATION

14.4 Magic numbers

When the Unix kernel is asked to execute a file (via the `execve` system call), it checks the first few bytes of the file for a "magic number" that indicates the file's type. Some values correspond to directly executable object file formats. Under Linux, for example, the first four bytes of an object file are `0x7f45_4c46` (⟨`del`⟩`ELF` in ASCII). Under Mac OS X they are `0xfeed_face`. If the first two bytes are `0x2321` (`#!` in ASCII), the kernel assumes that the file is a script, and reads subsequent characters to find the name of the interpreter.

The `#!` convention in Unix is the main reason that most scripting languages use `#` as the opening comment delimiter. Early versions of `sh` used the no-op command (`:`) as a way to introduce comments. Joy's C shell introduced `#`, whereupon some versions of `sh` were modified to launch `csh` when asked to execute a script that appeared to begin with a C shell comment. This mechanism evolved into the more general mechanism used in many (though not all) variants of Unix today.

14.2.2 Text Processing and Report Generation

Shell languages tend to be heavily string-oriented. Commands are strings, parsed into lists of words. Variables are string-valued. Variable expansion mechanisms allow the user to extract prefixes, suffixes, or arbitrary substrings. Concatenation is indicated by simple juxtaposition. There are elaborate quoting conventions. Few more conventional languages have similar support for strings.

At the same time, shell languages are clearly not intended for the sort of text manipulation commonly performed in editors like `emacs` or `vim`. Search and substitution, in particular, are missing, and many other tasks that editors accomplish with a single keystroke—insertion, deletion, replacement, bracket matching, forward and backward motion—would be awkward to implement, or simply make no sense, in the context of the shell. For repetitive text manipulation it is natural to want to automate the editing process. Tools to accomplish this task constitute the second principal class of ancestors for modern scripting languages.

```
# label (target for branch):
:top
/<[hH][123]>.*<\/[hH][123]>/ {         ;# match whole heading
    h                                  ;# save copy of pattern space
    s/\(<\/[hH][123]>\).*$/\1/         ;# delete text after closing tag
    s/^.*\(<[hH][123]>\)/\1/           ;# delete text before opening tag
    p                                  ;# print what remains
    g                                  ;# retrieve saved pattern space
    s/<[hH][123]>//                    ;# delete opening tag
    s/<\/[hH][123]>//                  ;# delete closing tag
    b top
}                                      ;# and branch to top of script
/<[hH][123]>/ {                        ;# match opening tag (only)
    N                                  ;# extend search to next line
    b top
}                                      ;# and branch to top of script
d                                      ;# if no match at all, delete
```

Figure 14.1 **Script in sed to extract headers from an HTML file.** The script assumes that opening and closing tags are properly matched, and that headers do not nest.

Sed

EXAMPLE 14.18
Extracting HTML headers with sed

As a simple text processing example, consider the problem of extracting all headers from a web page (an HTML file). These are strings delimited by `<h1>` ... `</h1>`, `<h2>` ... `</h2>`, and `<h3>` ... `</h3>` tags. Accomplishing this task in an editor like emacs, vim, or even Microsoft Word is straightforward but tedious: one must search for an opening tag, delete preceding text, search for a closing tag, mark the current position (as the starting point for the next deletion), and repeat. A program to perform these tasks in sed, the Unix "stream editor," appears in Figure 14.1. The code consists of a label and three commands, the first two of which are compound. The first compound command prints the first header, if any, found in the portion of the input currently being examined (what sed calls the *pattern space*). The second compound command appends a new line to the pattern space whenever it already contains a header-opening tag. Both compound commands, and several of the subcommands, use regular expression patterns, delimited by slashes. We will discuss these patterns further in Section 14.4.2. The third command (the lone d) simply deletes the pattern space. Because each compound command ends with a branch back to the top of the script, the second will execute only if the first does not, and the delete will execute only if neither compound does. ■

EXAMPLE 14.19
One-line scripts in sed

The editor heritage of sed is clear in this example. Commands are generally one character long, and there are no variables—no state of any kind beyond the program counter and text that is being edited. These limitations make sed best suited to "one-line programs," typically entered verbatim from the keyboard with the -e command-line switch. The following, for example, will read from standard input, delete blank lines, and (implicitly) print the nonblank lines to standard output:

```
/<[hH][123]>/ {
    # execute this block if line contains an opening tag
    do {
        open_tag = match($0, /<[hH][123]>/)
        $0 = substr($0, open_tag)       # delete text before opening tag
                                        # $0 is the current input line
        while (!/<\/[hH][123]>/) {      # print interior lines
            print                       #   in their entirety
            if (getline != 1) exit
        }
        close_tag = match($0, /<\/[hH][123]>/) + 4

        print substr($0, 0, close_tag)  # print through closing tag
        $0 = substr($0, close_tag + 1)  # delete through closing tag
    } while (/<[hH][123]>/)             # repeat if more opening tags
}
```

Figure 14.2 **Script in awk to extract headers from an HTML file.** Unlike the sed script, this version prints interior lines incrementally. It again assumes that the input is well formed.

```
sed -e'/^[[:space:]]*$/d'
```

Here ^ represents the beginning of the line and $ represents the end. The [[:space:]] expression matches any white-space character in the local character set, to be repeated an arbitrary number of times, as indicated by the Kleene star (*). The d indicates deletion. Nondeleted lines are printed by default. ■

Awk

In an attempt to address the limitations of sed, Alfred Aho, Peter Weinberger, and Brian Kernighan designed awk in 1977 (the name is based on the initial letters of their last names). Awk is in some sense an evolutionary link between stream editors like sed and full-fledged scripting languages. It retains sed's line-at-a-time filter model of computation, but allows the user to escape this model when desired, and replaces single-character editing commands with syntax reminiscent of C. Awk provides (typeless) variables and a variety of control-flow constructs, including subroutines.

An awk program consists of a sequence of *patterns*, each of which has an associated *action*. For every line of input, the interpreter executes, in order, the actions whose patterns evaluate to true. An example with a single pattern-action pair appears in Figure 14.2. It performs essentially the same task as the sed script of Figure 14.1. Lines that contain no opening tag are ignored. In a line with an opening tag, we delete any text that precedes the header. We then print lines until we find the closing tag, and repeat if there is another opening tag on the same line. We fall back into the interpreter's main loop when we're cleanly outside any header.

EXAMPLE 14.20
Extracting HTML headers with awk

Several conventions can be seen in this example. The current input line is available in the pseudovariable $0. The getline function reads into this variable

```
BEGIN {                             # "noise" words
    nw["a"] = 1;    nw["an"] = 1;   nw["and"] = 1;  nw["but"] = 1
    nw["by"] = 1;   nw["for"] = 1;  nw["from"] = 1; nw["in"] = 1
    nw["into"] = 1; nw["nor"] = 1;  nw["of"] = 1;   nw["on"] = 1
    nw["or"] = 1;   nw["over"] = 1; nw["the"] = 1;  nw["to"] = 1
    nw["via"] = 1;  nw["with"] = 1
}
{
    for (i=1; i <= NF; i++) {
        if ((!nw[$i] || i == 0 || $(i-1) ~ /[:-]$/) && ($i !~ /.+[A-Z]/)) {
            # capitalize
            $i = toupper(substr($i, 1, 1)) substr($i, 2)
        }
        printf $i " ";      # don't add trailing newline
    }
    printf "\n";
}
```

Figure 14.3 **Script in awk to capitalize a title.** The BEGIN block is executed before reading any input lines. The main block has no explicit pattern, so it is applied to every input line.

by default. The `substr(s, a, b)` function extracts the portion of string `s` starting at position `a` and with length `b`. If `b` is omitted, the extracted portion runs to the end of `s`. Conditions, like patterns, can use regular expressions; we can see an example in the `do ... while` loop. By default, regular expressions match against `$0`.

Perhaps the two most important innovations of `awk` are *fields* and *associative arrays*, neither of which appears in Figure 14.2. Like the shell, `awk` parses each input line into a series of words (fields). By default these are delimited by white space, though the user can change this behavior dynamically by assigning a regular expression to the built-in variable `FS` (field separator). The fields of the current input line are available in the pseudovariables `$1`, `$2`, ... The built-in variable `NR` gives the total number of fields. Awk is frequently used for field-based one-line programs. The following, for example, will print the second word of every line of standard input:

EXAMPLE 14.21
Fields in awk

```
awk '{print $2}'
```

EXAMPLE 14.22
Capitalizing a title in awk

Associative arrays will be considered in more detail in Section 14.4.3. Briefly, they combine the functionality of hash tables with the syntax of arrays. We can illustrate both fields and associative arrays with an example script (Figure 14.3) that capitalizes each line of its input as if it were a title. The script declines to modify "noise" words (articles, conjunctions, and short prepositions) unless they are the first word of the title or of a subtitle, where a subtitle follows a word ending with a colon or a dash. The script also declines to modify words in which any letter other than the first is already capitalized.

```
while (<>) {                                          # iterate over lines of input
    next if !/<[hH][123]>/;                           # jump to next iteration
    while (!/<\/[hH][123]>/) { $_ .= <>; }            # append next line to $_
    s/.*?(<[hH][123]>.*?<\/[hH][123]>)//s;
        # perform minimal matching; capture parenthesized expression in $1
    print $1, "\n";
    redo unless eof;     # continue without reading next line of input
}
```

Figure 14.4 Script in Perl to extract headers from an HTML file. For simplicity we have again adopted the strategy of buffering entire headers, rather than printing them incrementally.

Perl

Perl was originally developed by Larry Wall in 1987, while he was working at the National Security Agency. The original version was, to first approximation, an attempt to combine the best features of `sed`, `awk`, and `sh`. It was a Unix-only tool, meant primarily for text processing (the name stands for "practical extraction and report language"). Over the years Perl grew into a large and complex language, with an enormous user community. For many years it was clearly the most popular and widely used scripting language, though that lead has more recently been lost to Python, Ruby, and others. Perl is fast enough for much general-purpose use, and includes separate compilation, modularization, and dynamic library mechanisms appropriate for large-scale projects. It has been ported to almost every known operating system.

Perl consists of a relatively simple language core, augmented with an enormous number of built-in library functions and an equally enormous number of shortcuts and special cases. A hint at this richness of expression can be found in the standard language reference [CfWO12, p. 722], which lists (only) the 97 built-in functions "whose behavior varies the most across platforms." The cover of the third edition was emblazoned with the motto: "There's more than one way to do it."

EXAMPLE 14.23
Extracting HTML headers with Perl

We will return to Perl several times in this chapter, notably in Sections 14.2.4 and 14.4. For the moment we content ourselves with a simple text-processing example, again to extract headers from an HTML file (Figure 14.4). We can see several Perl shortcuts in this figure, most of which help to make the code shorter than the equivalent programs in `sed` (Figure 14.1) and `awk` (Figure 14.2). Angle brackets (<>) are the "readline" operator, used for text file input. Normally they surround a *file handle* variable name, but as a special case, empty angle brackets generate as input the concatenation of all files specified on the command line when the script was first invoked (or standard input, if there were no such files). When a readline operator appears by itself in the control expression of a `while` loop (but nowhere else in the language), it generates its input a line at a time into the pseudovariable `$_`. Several other operators work on `$_` by default. Regular expressions, for example, can be used to search within arbitrary strings, but when none is specified, `$_` is assumed.

The `next` statement is similar to `continue` in C or Fortran: it jumps to the bottom of the innermost loop and begins the next iteration. The `redo` statement also skips the remainder of the current iteration, but returns to the top of the loop, *without* reevaluating the control expression. In our example program, `redo` allows us to append additional input to the current line, rather than reading a new line. Because end-of-file is normally detected by an undefined return value from `<>`, and because that failure will happen only once per file, we must explicitly test for `eof` when using `redo` here. Note that `if` and its symmetric opposite, `unless`, can be used as either a prefix or a postfix test.

Readers familiar with Perl may have noticed two subtle but key innovations in the substitution command of line 4 of the script. First, where the expression `.*` (in `sed`, `awk`, and Perl) matches the longest possible string of characters that permits subsequent portions of the match to succeed, the expression `.*?` in Perl matches the *shortest* possible such string. This distinction allows us to easily isolate the first header in a given line. Second, much as `sed` allows later portions of a regular expression to refer back to earlier, parenthesized portions (line 4 of Figure 14.1), Perl allows such *captured* strings to be used *outside* the regular expression. We have leveraged this feature to print matched headers in line 6 of Figure 14.4. In general, the regular expressions of Perl are significantly more powerful than those of `sed` and `awk`; we will return to this subject in more detail in Section 14.4.2. ■

14.2.3 Mathematics and Statistics

As we noted in our discussions of `sed` and `awk`, one of the distinguishing characteristics of text processing and report generation is the frequent use of "one-line programs" and other simple scripts. Anyone who has ever entered formulas in the cells of a spreadsheet realizes that similar needs arise in mathematics and statistics. And just as shell and report generation tools have evolved into powerful languages for general-purpose computing, so too have notations and tools for mathematical and statistical computing.

In Section 8.2.1 ("Slices and Array Operations"), we mentioned APL, one of the more unusual languages of the 1960s. Originally conceived as a pen-and-paper notation for teaching applied mathematics, APL retained its emphasis on the concise, elegant expression of mathematical algorithms when it evolved into a programming language. Though it lacked both easy access to other programs and sophisticated string manipulation, APL displayed all the other characteristics of scripting described in Section 14.1.1, and one sometimes finds it listed as a scripting language.

The modern successors to APL include a trio of commercial packages for mathematical computing: Maple, Mathematica, and Matlab. Though their design philosophies differ, each provides extensive support for numerical methods, symbolic mathematics (formula manipulation), data visualization, and mathematical modeling. All three provide powerful scripting languages, with a heavy orientation toward scientific and engineering applications.

As the "3 Ms" are to mathematical computing, so the S and R languages are to statistical computing. Originally developed at Bell Labs by John Chambers and colleagues in the late 1970s, S is a commercial package widely used in the statistics community and in quantitative branches of the social and behavioral sciences. R is an open-source alternative to S that is largely though not entirely compatible with its commercial cousin. Among other things, R supports multidimensional array and list types, array slice operations, user-defined infix operators, call-by-need parameters, first-class functions, and unlimited extent.

14.2.4 "Glue" Languages and General-Purpose Scripting

From their text-processing ancestors, scripting languages inherit a rich set of pattern matching and string manipulation mechanisms. From command interpreter shells they inherit a wide variety of additional features including simple syntax; flexible typing; easy creation and management of subprograms, with I/O redirection and access to completion status; file queries; easy interactive and file-based I/O; easy access to command-line arguments, environment strings, process identifiers, time-of-day clock, and so on; and automatic interpreter start-up (the `#!` convention). As noted in Section 14.1.1, many scripting languages have interpreters that will accept commands interactively.

EXAMPLE 14.24
"Force quit" script in Perl

The combination of shell and text-processing mechanisms allows a scripting language to prepare input to, and parse output from, subsidiary processes. As a simple example, consider the (Unix-specific) "force quit" Perl script shown in Figure 14.5. Invoked with a regular expression as argument, the script identifies all of the user's currently running processes whose name, process id, or command-line arguments match that regular expression. It prints the information for each, and prompts the user for an indication of whether the process should be killed.

The second line of the code starts a subsidiary process to execute the Unix `ps` command. The command-line arguments cause `ps` to print the process id and name of all processes owned by the current user, together with their full command-line arguments. The pipe symbol (`|`) at the end of the command indicates that the output of `ps` is to be fed to the script through the `PS` file handle. The main `while` loop then iterates over the lines of this output. Within the loop, the `if` condition matches each line against `$ARGV[0]`, the regular expression provided on the script's command line. It also compares the first word of the line (the process id) against `$$`, the id of the Perl interpreter currently running the script.

Scalar variables (which in Perl include strings) begin with a dollar sign (`$`). Arrays begin with an at sign (`@`). In the first line of the `while` loop in Figure 14.5, the input line (`$_`, implicitly) is split into space-separated words, which are then assigned into the array `@words`. In the following line, `$words[0]` refers to the first element of this array, a scalar. A single variable name may have different values when interpreted as a scalar, an array, a hash table, a subroutine, or a file

```
$#ARGV == 0 || die "usage: $0 pattern\n";
open(PS, "ps -w -w -x -o'pid,command' |");  # 'process status' command
<PS>;                                       # discard header line
while (<PS>) {
    @words = split;             # parse line into space-separated words
    if (/$ARGV[0]/i && $words[0] ne $$) {
        chomp;                  # delete trailing newline
        print;
        do {
            print "? ";
            $answer = <STDIN>;
        } until $answer =~ /^[yn]/i;
        if ($answer =~ /^y/i) {
            kill 9, $words[0];  # signal 9 in Unix is always fatal
            sleep 1;            # wait for 'kill' to take effect
            die "unsuccessful; sorry\n" if kill 0, $words[0];
        }                       # kill 0 tests for process existence
    }
}
```

Figure 14.5 Script in Perl to "force quit" errant processes. Perl's text processing features allow us to parse the output of ps, rather than filtering it through an external tool like sed or awk.

handle. The choice of interpretation depends on the leading punctuation mark and on the *context* in which the name appears. We shall have more to say about context in Perl in Section 14.4.3.

Beyond the combination of shell and text-processing mechanisms, the typical glue language provides an extensive library of built-in operations to access features of the underlying operating system, including files, directories, and I/O; processes and process groups; protection and authorization; interprocess communication and synchronization; timing and signals; and sockets, name service, and network communication. Just as text-processing mechanisms minimize the need to employ external tools like sed, awk, and grep, operating system builtins minimize the need for other external tools.

At the same time, scripting languages have, over time, developed a rich set of features for internal computation. Most have significantly better support for mathematics than is typically found in a shell. Several, including Scheme, Python, and Ruby, support arbitrary precision arithmetic. Most provide extensive support for higher-level types, including arrays, strings, tuples, lists, and hashes (associative arrays). Several support classes and object orientation. Some support iterators, continuations, threads, reflection, and first-class and higher-order functions. Some, including Perl, Python, and Ruby, support modules and dynamic loading, for "programming in the large." These features serve to maximize the amount of code that can be written in the scripting language itself, and to minimize the need to escape to a more traditional, compiled language.

In summary, the philosophy of general-purpose scripting is to make it as easy as possible to construct the overall framework of a program, escaping to external tools only for special-purpose tasks, and to compiled languages only when performance is at a premium.

Python

As noted in Section 14.1, Rexx is generally considered the first of the general-purpose scripting languages, predating Perl and Tcl by almost a decade. Perl and Tcl are roughly contemporaneous: both were initially developed in the late 1980s. Perl was originally intended for glue and text-processing applications. Tcl was originally an extension language, but soon grew into glue applications as well. As the popularity of scripting grew in the 1990s, users were motivated to develop additional languages, to provide additional features, address the needs of specific application domains (more on this in subsequent sections), or support a style of programming more in keeping with the personal taste of their designers.

Python was originally developed by Guido van Rossum at CWI in Amsterdam, the Netherlands, in the early 1990s. He continued his work at CNRI in Reston, Virginia, beginning in 1995. After a series of subsequent moves, he joined Google in 2005. Recent versions of the language are owned by the Python Software Foundation. All releases are open source.

EXAMPLE 14.25
"Force quit" script in Python

Figure 14.6 presents a Python version of the "force quit" program from Example 14.24. Reflecting the maturation of programming language design, Python was from the beginning an object-oriented language.[2] It includes a standard library as rich as that of Perl, but partitioned into a collection of namespaces reminiscent of those of C++, Java, or C#. The first line of our script imports symbols from the `os`, `re`, `subprocess`, `sys`, and `time` library modules. The fifth line launches `ps` as an external program, and arranges for its output to be available to the script through a Unix pipe. We discard the initial (header) line of output from the subprocess by calling the output pipe's `readline` method. We then use a Python `for` loop to iterate over the remaining lines.

Perhaps the most distinctive feature of Python, though hardly the most important, is its reliance on indentation for syntactic grouping. Python not only uses line breaks to separate commands; it also specifies that the body of a structured statement consists of precisely those subsequent statements that are indented one more tab stop. Like the "more than one way to do it" philosophy of Perl, Python's use of indentation tends to arouse strong feelings among users: some strongly positive, some strongly negative.

The regular expression (`re`) library has all of the power available in Perl, but employs the somewhat more verbose syntax of method calls, rather than the built-in notation of Perl. The `search` routine returns a "match object" that captures,

---

2 Rexx and Tcl have object-oriented extensions, named Object Rexx and Incr Tcl, respectively. Perl 5 includes some (rather awkward) object-oriented features; Perl 6 will have more uniform object support.

```
import os, re, subprocess, sys, time
if len(sys.argv) != 2:
    sys.stderr.write('usage: ' + sys.argv[0] + ' pattern\n')
    sys.exit(1)
ps = subprocess.Popen(['/bin/ps', '-w', '-w', '-x',
                       '-o', 'pid,command'], stdout=subprocess.PIPE)
toss = ps.stdout.readline()          # discard header line
for line in ps.stdout:
    line = line.decode().rstrip()
    proc = int(re.search('\S+', line).group())
    if re.search(sys.argv[1], line) and proc != os.getpid():
        print(line + '? ', flush=True, end='')
        answer = sys.stdin.readline()
        while not re.search('^[yn]', answer, re.I):
            print('? ', flush=True, end='')
            answer = sys.stdin.readline()
        if re.search('^y', answer, re.I):
            os.kill(proc, 9)
            time.sleep(1)
            try:                     # expect exception if process
                os.kill(proc, 0)     # no longer exists
                sys.stderr.write('unsuccessful; sorry\n');
                sys.exit(1)
            except: pass             # do nothing on expected exception
```

Figure 14.6 Script in Python 3 to "force quit" errant processes. Compare with Figure 14.5.

lazily, the places in the string at which the pattern appears. If no match is found, `search` returns `None`, the empty object, instead. In a condition, `None` is interpreted as false, while a true match object is interpreted as true. The match object in turn supports a variety of methods, including group, which returns the substring corresponding to the first match. The `re.I` flag to `search` indicates case insensitivity. Note that group returns a string. Unlike Perl and Tcl, Python will not coerce this to an integer—hence the need for the explicit type conversion on the second line of the body of the `for` loop.

As in Perl, the `readline` method does not remove the newline character at the end of an input line; we use the `rstrip` method to do this. The `print` function adds a newline to the end of its argument list unless given a different end string. Unless explicitly instructed to `flush`, it also tends to buffer its output, waiting to call the OS until it has a large amount of data; this needs to be defeated for interactive IO.

The `sleep` and `kill` routines are available as library built-ins in Python, much as they are in Perl; there is no need to start a separate program. When given a signal number of 0, `kill` tests for process existence. Instead of returning a status code, however, as it does in Perl, Python's `kill` throws an exception if the process does not exist. We use a `try` block to catch this exception in the expected case. ■

While our "force quit" program may convey, at least in part, the "feel" of Perl and Python, it cannot capture the breadth of their capabilities. Python includes many of the more interesting features discussed in earlier chapters, including nested functions with static scoping, lambda expressions and higher-order functions, true iterators, list comprehensions, array slice operations, reflection, structured exception handling, multiple inheritance, and modules and dynamic loading. Many of these also appear in Ruby.

Ruby

Ruby was developed in Japan in the early 1990s by Yukihiro "Matz" Matsumoto. Matz writes that he "wanted a language more powerful than Perl, and more object-oriented than Python" [TFH13, Foreword]. The first public release was made available in 1995, and quickly gained widespread popularity in Japan. With the publication in 2001 of English-language documentation [TFH13, 1st ed.], Ruby spread rapidly elsewhere as well. Much of its success can be credited to the Ruby on Rails web-development framework. Originally released by David Heinemeier Hansson in 2004, Rails was subsequently adopted by several major players—notably Apple, which included it in the 10.5 "Leopard" release of the Mac OS, and Twitter, which used it for early versions of their infrastructure.

EXAMPLE 14.26
Method call syntax in Ruby

In keeping with Matz's original motivation, Ruby is a pure object-oriented language, in the sense of Smalltalk: everything—even instances of built-in types—is an object. Integers have more than 25 built-in methods. Strings have more than 75. Smalltalk-like syntax is even supported: `2 * 4 + 5` is syntactic sugar for `(2.*(4)).+(5)`, which is in turn equivalent to `(2.send('*', 4)).send('+', 5)`.[3] ■

EXAMPLE 14.27
"Force quit" script in Ruby

Figure 14.7 presents a Ruby version of our "force quit" program. Newline characters serve to end the current statement, but indentation is not significant. A dollar sign (`$`) at the beginning of an identifier indicates a global name. Though it doesn't appear in this example, an at sign (`@`) indicates an instance variable of the current object. Double at signs (`@@`) indicate an instance variable of the current *class*.

Probably the most distinctive feature of Figure 14.7 is its use of *blocks* and iterators. The `IO.popen` class method takes as argument a string that specifies the name and arguments of an external program. The method also accepts, in a manner reminiscent of Smalltalk, an *associated block*, specified as a multiline fragment of Ruby code delimited with curly braces. The associated block is essentially an extra parameter to popen, passed as a closure. The closure is invoked by popen, passing as parameter a file handle (an object of class `IO`) that represents the output of the external command. The `|ps|` at the beginning of the block specifies the name by which this handle is known within the block. In a similar vein, the `each`

3 Parentheses here are significant. Infix arithmetic follows conventional precedence rules, but method invocation proceeds from left to right. Likewise, parentheses can be omitted around argument lists, but the method-selecting dot (`.`) groups more tightly than the argument-separating comma (`,`), so `2.send '*', 4.send '+', 5` evaluates to 18, not 13.

```
ARGV.length() == 1 or begin
    $stderr.print("usage: #{$0} pattern\n"); exit(1)
end

pat = Regexp.new(ARGV[0])    # treat command-line arg as regular expression
IO.popen("ps -w -w -x -o'pid,command'") {|ps|
    ps.gets                  # discard header line
    ps.each {|line|
        pid = line.split[0].to_i
        if line =~ pat and pid != Process.pid then
            print line.chomp
            begin
                print "? "
                answer = $stdin.gets
            end until answer =~ /^[yn]/i
            if answer =~ /^y/i then
                Process.kill(9, pid)
                sleep(1)
                begin        # expect exception (process gone)
                    Process.kill(0, pid)
                    $stderr.print("unsuccessful; sorry\n"); exit(1)
                rescue       # handler -- do nothing
                end
            end
        end
    }
}
```

Figure 14.7 **Script in Ruby to "force quit" errant processes.** Compare with Figures 14.5 and 14.6.

method of object ps is an iterator that invokes the associated block (the code in braces beginning with `|line|`) once for every line of data. For those more comfortable with traditional `for` loop syntax, the iterator can also be written

```
for line in PS
    ...
end
```

In addition to (true) iterators, Ruby provides continuations, first-class and higher-order functions, and closures with unlimited extent. Its *module* mechanism supports an extended form of mix-in inheritance. Though a class cannot inherit data members from a module, it *can* inherit code. Run-time type checking makes such inheritance more or less straightforward. Methods of modules that have not been explicitly included into the current class can be accessed as qualified names; `Process.kill` is an example in Figure 14.7. Methods `sleep` and `exit` belong to module `Kernel`, which is included by class `Object`, and is thus available everywhere without qualification. Like popen, they are class methods, rather than instance methods; they have no notion of "current object." Variables `stdin` and `stderr` refer to global objects of class `IO`.

Regular expression operations in Ruby are methods of class `Regexp`, and can be invoked with standard object-oriented syntax. For convenience, Perl-like notation is also supported as syntactic sugar; we have used this notation in Figure 14.7.

The `rescue` clause of the innermost `begin` ... `end` block is an exception handler. As in the Python code of Figure 14.6, it allows us to determine whether the `kill` operation has succeeded by catching the (expected) exception that arises when we attempt to refer to a process after it has died. ■

14.2.5 Extension Languages

Most applications accept some sort of *commands*, which tell them what to do. Sometimes these commands are entered textually; more often they are triggered by user interface events such as mouse clicks, menu selections, and keystrokes. Commands in a graphical drawing program might save or load a drawing; select, insert, delete, or modify its parts; choose a line style, weight, or color; zoom or rotate the display; or modify user preferences.

An *extension language* serves to increase the usefulness of an application by allowing the user to create new commands, generally using the existing commands as building blocks. Extension languages are widely regarded as an essential feature of sophisticated tools. Adobe's graphics suite (Illustrator, Photoshop, InDesign, etc.) can be extended (scripted) using JavaScript, Visual Basic (on Windows), or AppleScript (on the Mac). Disney and Industrial Light & Magic use Python to extend their internal (proprietary) tools. The computer gaming industry makes heavy use of Lua for scripting of both commercial and open-source game engines. Many commercially available tools, including AutoCAD, Maya, Director, and Flash, have their own unique scripting languages. This list barely scratches the surface.

To admit extension, a tool must

- incorporate, or communicate with, an interpreter for a scripting language.
- provide hooks that allow scripts to call the tool's existing commands.
- allow the user to tie newly defined commands to user interface events.

With care, these mechanisms can be made independent of any particular scripting language. Microsoft's Windows Script interface allows almost any language to be used to script the operating system, web server, and browser. GIMP, the widely used GNU Image Manipulation Program, has a comparably general interface: it comes with a built-in interpreter for a dialect of Scheme, and supports plug-ins (externally provided interpreter modules) for Perl and Tcl, among others. There is a tendency, of course, for user communities to converge on a favorite language, to facilitate sharing of code. Microsoft tools are usually scripted with PowerShell; GIMP with Scheme; Adobe tools with Visual Basic on the PC, or AppleScript on the Mac.

```
(setq-default line-number-prefix "")
(setq-default line-number-suffix ") ")
(defun number-region (start end &optional initial)
  "Add line numbers to all lines in region.
With optional prefix argument, start numbering at num.
Line number is bracketed by strings line-number-prefix
and line-number-suffix (default \"\" and \") \")."
  (interactive "*r\np")       ; how to parse args when invoked from keyboard
  (let* ((i (or initial 1))
         (num-lines (+ -1 initial (count-lines start end)))
         (fmt (format "%%%dd" (length (number-to-string num-lines))))
                              ; yields "%1d", "%2d", etc. as appropriate
         (finish (set-marker (make-marker) end)))
    (save-excursion
      (goto-char start)
      (beginning-of-line)
      (while (< (point) finish)
        (insert line-number-prefix (format fmt i) line-number-suffix)
        (setq i (1+ i))
        (forward-line 1))
      (set-marker finish nil))))
```

Figure 14.8 Emacs Lisp function to number the lines in a selected region of text.

One of the oldest existing extension mechanisms is that of the emacs text editor, used to write this book. An enormous number of extension packages have been created for emacs; many of them are installed by default in the standard distribution. In fact much of what users consider the editor's core functionality is actually provided by extensions; the truly built-in parts are comparatively small.

EXAMPLE 14.28
Numbering lines with Emacs Lisp

The extension language for emacs is a dialect of Lisp called Emacs Lisp, or elisp, for short. An example script appears in Figure 14.8. It assumes that the user has used the standard *marking* mechanism to select a region of text. It then inserts a line number at the beginning of every line in the region. The first line is numbered 1 by default, but an alternative starting number can be specified with an optional parameter. Line numbers are bracketed with a prefix and suffix that are " " (empty) and ") " by default, but can be changed by the user if desired. To maintain existing alignment, small numbers are padded on the left with enough spaces to match the width of the number on the final line.

Many features of Emacs Lisp can be seen in this example. The `setq-default` command is an assignment that is visible in the current buffer (editing session) and in any concurrent buffers that haven't explicitly overridden the previous value. The `defun` command defines a new command. Its arguments are, in order, the command name, formal parameter list, documentation string, interactive specification, and body. The argument list for `number-region` includes the start and end locations of the currently marked region, and the optional initial line number. The documentation string is automatically incorporated into the on-line help system. The interactive specification controls how arguments are passed when the command is invoked through the user interface. (The command can also be called from other scripts, in which case arguments are passed in the conventional way.) The "`*`" raises an exception if the buffer is read-only. The "`r`" represents the beginning and end of the currently marked region. The "`\n`" separates the "`r`" from the following "`p`," which indicates an optional numeric *prefix argument*. When the command is bound to a keystroke, a prefix argument of, say, 10 can be specified by preceding the keystroke with "`C-u 10`" (control-U 10).

As usual in Lisp, the `let*` command introduces a set of local variables in which later entries in the list (`fmt`) can refer to earlier entries (`num-lines`). A *marker* is an index into the buffer that is automatically updated to maintain its position when text is inserted in front of it. We create the `finish` marker so that newly inserted line numbers do not alter our notion of where the to-be-numbered region ends. We set `finish` to `nil` at the end of the script to relieve `emacs` of the need to keep updating the marker between now and whenever the garbage collector gets around to reclaiming it.

The `format` command is similar to `sprintf` in C. We have used it, once in the declaration of `fmt` and again in the call to `insert`, to pad all line numbers out to an appropriate length. The `save-excursion` command is roughly equivalent to an exception handler (e.g., a Java `try` block) with a `finally` clause that restores the current focus of attention (`(point)`) and the borders of the marked region.

Our script can be supplied to `emacs` by including it in a personal start-up file (usually `~/.emacs`), by using the interactive `load-file` command to read some other file in which it resides, or by loading it into a buffer, placing the focus of attention immediately after it, and executing the interactive `eval-last-sexp` command. Once any of these has been done, we can invoke our command interactively by typing `M-x number-region` <RET> (meta-X, followed by the command name and the return key). Alternatively, we can *bind* our command to a keyboard shortcut:

```
(define-key global-map [?\C-#] 'number-region)
```

This one-line script, executed in any of the ways described above, binds our `number-region` command to key combination "control-number-sign". ■

✓ CHECK YOUR UNDERSTANDING

11. What is meant by the *pattern space* in `sed`?

12. Briefly describe the *fields* and *associative arrays* of `awk`.

13. In what ways did even early versions of Perl improve on `sed` and `awk`?

14. Explain the special relationship between `while` loops and file handles in Perl. What is the meaning of the empty file handle, `<>`?

15. Name three widely used commercial packages for mathematical computing.

16. List several distinctive features of the R statistical scripting language.
17. Explain the meaning of the `$` and `@` characters at the beginning of variable names in Perl. Explain the different meanings of `$`, `@`, and `@@` in Ruby.
18. Which of the languages described in Section 14.2.4 uses indentation to control syntactic grouping?
19. List several distinctive features of Python.
20. Describe, briefly, how Ruby uses *blocks* and *iterators*.
21. What capabilities must a scripting language provide in order to be used for extension?
22. Name several commercial tools that use extension languages.

14.3 Scripting the World Wide Web

Much of the content of the World Wide Web—particularly the content that is visible to search engines—is static: pages that seldom, if ever, change. But hypertext, the abstract notion on which the Web is based, was always conceived as a way to represent "the complex, the changing, and the indeterminate" [Nel65]. Much of the power of the Web today lies in its ability to deliver pages that move, play sounds, respond to user actions, or—perhaps most important—contain information created or formatted on demand, in response to the page-fetch request.

From a programming languages point of view, simple playback of recorded audio or video is not particularly interesting. We therefore focus our attention here on content that is generated on the fly by a program—a script—associated with an Internet URI (uniform resource identifier).[4] Suppose we type a URI into a browser on a client machine, and the browser sends a request to the appropriate web server. If the content is dynamically created, an obvious first question is: does the script that creates it run on the server or the client machine? These options are known as *server-side* and *client-side* web scripting, respectively.

Server-side scripts are typically used when the service provider wants to retain complete control over the content of the page, but can't (or doesn't want to) create the content in advance. Examples include the pages returned by search engines, Internet retailers, auction sites, and any organization that provides its clients with on-line access to personal accounts. Client-side scripts are typically used for tasks that don't need access to proprietary information, and are more

4 The term "URI" is often used interchangeably with "URL" (uniform resource locator), but the World Wide Web Consortium distinguishes between the two. All URIs are hierarchical (multipart) names. URLs are one kind of URIs; they use a naming scheme that indicates where to find the resource. Other URIs can use other naming schemes.

```
#!/usr/bin/perl

print "Content-type: text/html\n\n";
print "<!DOCTYPE html>\n";

print "<html lang=\"en\">\n";
$host = `hostname`; chop $host;
print "<head>\n";
print "<meta charset=\"utf-8\">\n";
print "<title>Status of ", $host, "</title>\n";
print "</head>\n<body>\n";
print "<h1>", $host, "</h1>\n";
print "<pre>\n", `uptime`, "\n", `who`;
print "</pre>\n</body>\n</html>\n";
```

Figure 14.9 **A simple CGI script in Perl.** If this script is named `status.perl`, and is installed in the server's `cgi-bin` directory, then a user anywhere on the Internet can obtain summary statistics and a list of users currently logged into the server by typing *hostname/cgi-bin/status.perl* into a browser window.

efficient if executed on the client's machine. Examples include interactive animation, error-checking of fill-in forms, and a wide variety of other self-contained calculations.

14.3.1 CGI Scripts

The original mechanism for server-side web scripting was the Common Gateway Interface (CGI). A CGI script is an executable program residing in a special directory known to the web server program. When a client requests the URI corresponding to such a program, the server executes the program and sends its output back to the client. Naturally, this output needs to be something that the browser will understand—typically HTML.

CGI scripts may be written in any language available on the server's machine, though Perl is particularly popular: its string-handling and "glue" mechanisms are ideally suited to generating HTML, and it was already widely available during the early years of the Web. As a simple if somewhat artificial example, suppose we would like to be able to monitor the status of a server machine shared by some community of users. The Perl script in Figure 14.9 creates a web page titled by the name of the server machine, and containing the output of the `uptime` and `who` commands (two simple sources of status information). The script's initial `print` command produces an HTTP message header, indicating that what follows is HTML. Sample output from executing the script appears in Figure 14.10. ■

EXAMPLE 14.29 Remote monitoring with a CGI script

EXAMPLE 14.30 Adder web form with a CGI script

CGI scripts are commonly used to process on-line forms. A simple example appears in Figure 14.11. The `form` element in the HTML file specifies the URI of the CGI script, which is invoked when the user hits the Submit button. Values previously entered into the `input` fields are passed to the script either as a trailing

```
<!DOCTYPE html>
<html lang="en">
<head>
<meta charset="utf-8">
<title>Status of sigma.cs.rochester.edu</title>
</head>
<body>
<h1>sigma.cs.rochester.edu</h1>
<pre>
22:10  up 5 days, 12:50, 5 users, load averages: 0.40 0.37 0.31

scott     console  Feb 13 09:21
scott     ttyp2    Feb 17 15:27
test      ttyp3    Feb 18 17:10
test      ttyp4    Feb 18 17:11
</pre>
</body>
</html>
```

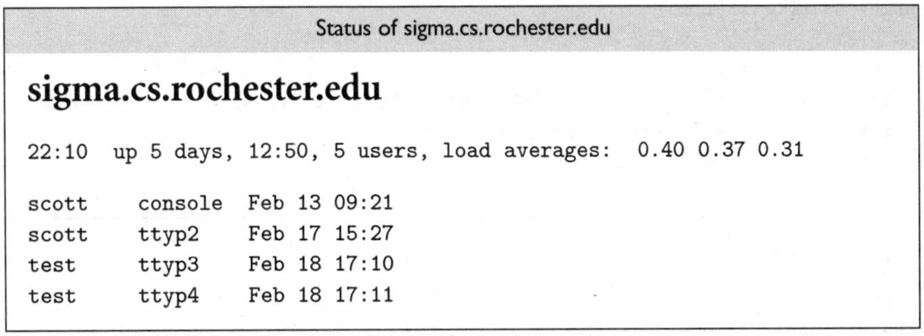

Figure 14.10 **Sample output from the script of Figure 14.9.** HTML source appears at top; the rendered page is below.

part of the URI (for a `get`-type form) or on the standard input stream (for a `post`-type form, shown here).[5] With either method, we can access the values using the `param` routine of the standard `CGI` Perl library, loaded at the beginning of our script.

14.3.2 Embedded Server-Side Scripts

Though widely used, CGI scripts have several disadvantages:

5 One typically uses `post` type forms for one-time requests. A `get` type form appears a little clumsier, because arguments are visibly embedded in the URI, but this gives it the advantage of repeatability: it can be "bookmarked" by client browsers.

```
<!DOCTYPE html>
<html lang="en">
<head><meta charset="utf-8"><title>Adder</title></head>
<body>
<form action="/cgi-bin/add.perl" method="post">
<p><input name="argA" size=3>First addend<br>
   <input name="argB" size=3>Second addend</p>
<p><input type="submit"></p>
</form>
</body>
</html>
```

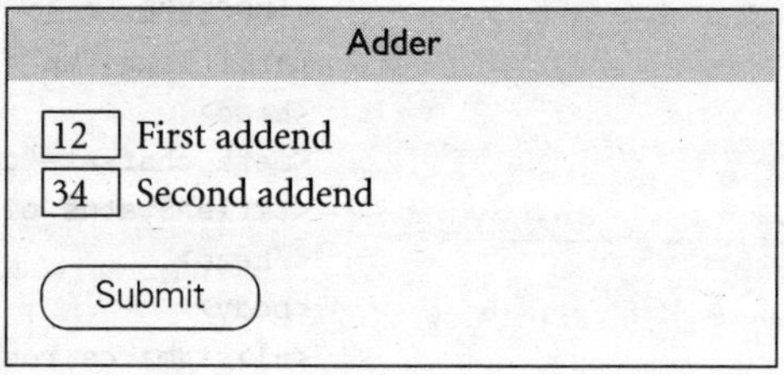


```
#!/usr/bin/perl

use CGI qw(:standard);      # provides access to CGI input fields
$argA = param("argA");  $argB = param("argB");  $sum = $argA + $argB;

print "Content-type: text/html\n\n";
print "<!DOCTYPE html>\n";

print "<html lang=\"en\">\n";
print "<head><meta charset=\"utf-8\"><title>Sum</title></head>\n<body>\n";
print "<p>$argA plus $argB is $sum</p>\n";
print "</body>\n</html>\n";
```

```
<!DOCTYPE html>
<html lang="en">
<head><meta charset="utf-8"><title>Sum</title></head>
<body>
<p>12 plus 34 is 46</p>
</body>
</html>
```

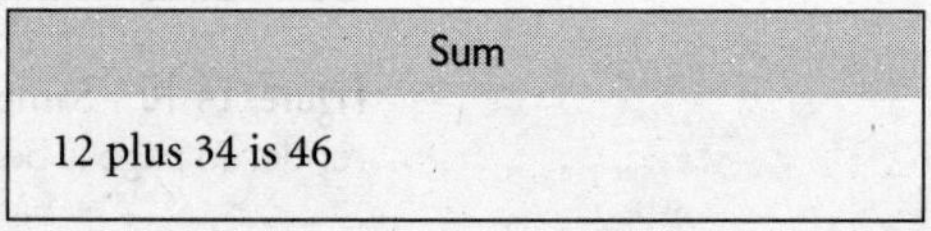

Figure 14.11 An interactive CGI form. Source for the original web page is shown at the upper left, with the rendered page to the right. The user has entered 12 and 34 in the text fields. When the Submit button is pressed, the client browser sends a request to the server for URI */cgi-bin/add.perl*. The values 12 and 13 are contained within the request. The Perl script, shown in the middle, uses these values to generate a new web page, shown in HTML at the bottom left, with the rendered page to the right.

- The web server must launch each script as a separate program, with potentially significant overhead (though a CGI script compiled to native code can be very fast once running).
- Because the server has little control over the behavior of a script, scripts must generally be installed in a trusted directory by trusted system administrators; they cannot reside in arbitrary locations as ordinary pages do.

```
<!DOCTYPE html>
<html lang="en">
<head>
<meta charset="utf-8">
<title>Status of <?php echo $host = chop(`hostname`) ?></title>
</head>
<body>
<h1><?php echo $host ?></h1>
<pre>
<?php echo `uptime`, "\n", `who` ?>
</pre>
</body>
</html>
```

Figure 14.12 **A simple PHP script embedded in a web page.** When served by a PHP-enabled host, this page performs the equivalent of the CGI script of Figure 14.9.

- The name of the script appears in the URI, typically prefixed with the name of the trusted directory, so static and dynamic pages look different to end users.
- Each script must generate not only dynamic content but also the HTML tags that are needed to format and display it. This extra "boilerplate" makes scripts more difficult to write.

To address these disadvantages, most web servers provide a "module-loading" mechanism that allows interpreters for one or more scripting languages to be incorporated into the server itself. Scripts in the supported language(s) can then be embedded in "ordinary" web pages. The web server interprets such scripts directly, without launching an external program. It then replaces the scripts with the output they produce, before sending the page to the client. Clients have no way to even know that the scripts exist.

Embeddable server-side scripting languages include PHP, PowerShell (in Microsoft Active Server Pages), Ruby, Cold Fusion (from Macromedia Corp.), and Java (via "Servlets" in Java Server Pages). The most common of these is PHP. Though descended from Perl, PHP has been extensively customized for its target domain, with built-in support for (among other things) e-mail and MIME encoding, all the standard Internet communication protocols, authentication and security, HTML and URI manipulation, and interaction with dozens of database systems.

EXAMPLE 14.31
Remote monitoring with a PHP script

The PHP equivalent of Figure 14.9 appears in Figure 14.12. Most of the text in this figure is standard HTML. PHP code is embedded between `<?php` and `?>` delimiters. These delimiters are not themselves HTML; rather, they indicate a *processing instruction* that needs to be executed by the PHP interpreter to generate replacement text. The "boilerplate" parts of the page can thus appear verbatim; they need not be generated by `print` (Perl) or `echo` (PHP) commands. Note that the separate script fragments are part of a single program. The `$host` variable, for example, is set in the first fragment and used again in the second.

```
<!DOCTYPE html>
<html lang="en">
<head><meta charset="utf-8"><title>20 numbers</title></head>
<body>
<p>
<?php
         for ($i = 0; $i < 20; $i++) {
             if ($i % 2) { ?>
<b><?php
                 echo " $i"; ?>
</b><?php
             } else echo " $i";
         }
 ?>
</p>
</body>
</html>
```

Figure 14.13 A fragmented PHP script. The if and for statements work as one might expect, despite the intervening raw HTML. When requested by a browser, this page displays the numbers from 0 to 19, with odd numbers written in bold.

EXAMPLE 14.32
A fragmented PHP script

PHP scripts can even be broken into fragments in the middle of structured statements. Figure 14.13 contains a script in which `if` and `for` statements span fragments. In effect, the HTML text between the end of one script fragment and the beginning of the next behaves as if it had been output by an `echo` command. Web designers are free to use whichever approach (`echo` or escape to raw HTML) seems most convenient for the task at hand. ■

Self-Posting Forms

EXAMPLE 14.33
Adder web form with a PHP script

By changing the `action` attribute of the `FORM` element, we can arrange for the Adder page of Figure 14.11 to invoke a PHP script instead of a CGI script:

```
<form action="add.php" method="post">
```

The PHP script itself is shown in the top half of Figure 14.14. Form values are made available to the script in an associative array (hash table) named `_REQUEST`. No special library is required. ■

EXAMPLE 14.34
Self-posting Adder web form

Because our PHP script is executed directly by the web server, it can safely reside in an arbitrary web directory, including the one in which the Adder page resides. In fact, by checking to see how a page was requested, we can merge the form and the script into a single page, and let it service its own requests! We illustrate this option in the bottom half of Figure 14.14. ■

```
<!DOCTYPE html>
<html lang="en">
<head><meta charset="utf-8"><title>Adder</title></head>
<body><p>
<?php
     $argA = $_REQUEST['argA']; $argB = $_REQUEST['argB'];
     $sum = $argA + $argB;
     echo "$argA plus $argB is $sum\n";
 ?>
</p></body></html>
```

```
<!DOCTYPE html>
<html lang="en">
<head><meta charset="utf-8">
<?php
    $argA = $_REQUEST['argA'];  $argB = $_REQUEST['argB'];
    if ($argA == "" || $argB == "") {
?>
        <title>Adder</title></head><body>
        <form action="adder.php" method="post">
        <p><input name="argA" size="3"> First addend<br>
           <input name="argB" size="3"> Second addend</p>
        <p><input type="submit"></p>
        </form></body></html>
<?php
    } else {
?>
        <title>Sum</title></head><body><p>
<?php
        $sum = $argA + $argB;
        echo "$argA plus $argB is $sum\n";
?>
        </p></body></html>
<?php
    }
?>
```

Figure 14.14 An interactive PHP web page. The script at top could be used in place of the script in the middle of Figure 14.11. The lower script in the current figure replaces both the web page at the top and the script in the middle of Figure 14.11. It checks to see if it has received a full set of arguments. If it hasn't, it displays the fill-in form; if it has, it displays results.

14.3.3 Client-Side Scripts

While embedded server-side scripts are generally faster than CGI scripts, at least when start-up cost predominates, communication across the Internet is still too slow for truly interactive pages. If we want the behavior or appearance of the page to change as the user moves the mouse, clicks, types, or hides or exposes windows, we really need to execute some sort of script on the client's machine.

Because they run on the web designer's site, CGI scripts and, to a lesser extent, embeddable server-side scripts can be written in many different languages. All the client ever sees is standard HTML. Client-side scripts, by contrast, require an interpreter on the client's machine. By virtue of having been "in the right place at the right time" historically, JavaScript is supported with at least some degree of consistency by almost all of the world's web browsers. Given the number of legacy browsers still running, and the difficulty of convincing users to upgrade or to install new plug-ins, pages intended for use outside a limited domain (e.g., the desktops of a single company) almost always use JavaScript for interactive features.

EXAMPLE 14.35
Adder web form in JavaScript

Figure 14.15 shows a page with embedded JavaScript that imitates (on the client) the behavior of the Adder scripts of Figures 14.11 and 14.14. Function `doAdd` is defined in the header of the page so it is available throughout. In particular, it will be invoked when the user clicks on the Calculate button. By default, the input values are character strings; we use the `parseInt` function to convert them to integers. The parentheses around `(argA + argB)` in the final assignment statement then force the use of integer addition. The other occurrences of `+` are string concatenation. To disable the usual mechanism whereby input data are submitted to the server when the user hits the enter or return key, we have specified a dummy behavior for the `onsubmit` attribute of the form.

Rather than replace the page with output text, as our CGI and PHP scripts did, we have chosen in our JavaScript version to append the output at the bottom. The HTML `SPAN` element provides a named place in the document where this output can be inserted, and the `getElementById` JavaScript method provides us with a reference to this element. The HTML *Document Object Model (DOM)*, standardized by the World Wide Web Consortium, specifies a very large number of other elements, attributes, and user actions, all of which are accessible in JavaScript. Through them, scripts can, at appropriate times, inspect or alter almost any aspect of the content, structure, or style of a page. ■

14.3.4 Java Applets and Other Embedded Elements

As an alternative to requiring client-side scripts to interact with the DOM of a web page, many browsers support an *embedding* mechanism that allows a browser plug-in to assume responsibility for some rectangular region of the page, in which it can then display whatever it wants. In other words, plug-ins are less a matter of scripting the browser than of bypassing it entirely. Historically, plug-ins were

```
<!DOCTYPE html>
<html lang="en">
<head><meta charset="utf-8"><title>Adder</title>
<script type="text/javascript">
function doAdd() {
    argA = parseInt(document.adder.argA.value)
    argB = parseInt(document.adder.argB.value)
    x = document.getElementById('sum')
    while (x.hasChildNodes())
        x.removeChild(x.lastChild)   // delete old content
    t = document.createTextNode(argA + " plus "
        + argB + " is " + (argA + argB))
    x.appendChild(t)
}
</script>
</head>
<body>
<form name="adder" onsubmit="return false">
<p><INPUT name="argA" size=3> First addend<br>
   <INPUT name="argB" size=3> Second addend</p>
<p><input type="button" onclick="doAdd()" value="Calculate"></p>
</form>
<p><span id="sum"></span></p>
</body>
</html>
```

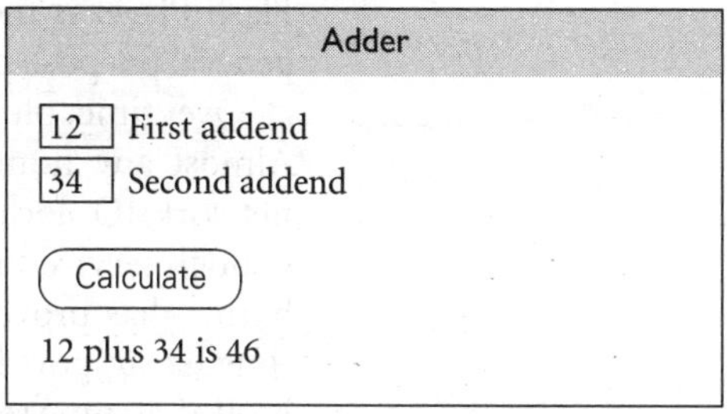

Figure 14.15 An interactive JavaScript web page. Source appears at left. The rendered version on the right shows the appearance of the page after the user has entered two values and hit the Calculate button, causing the output message to appear. By entering new values and clicking again, the user can calculate as many sums as desired. Each new calculation will replace the output message.

widely used for content—animations and video in particular—that were poorly supported by HTML.

EXAMPLE 14.36 Embedding an applet in a web page

Programs designed to be run by a Java plug-in are commonly known as *applets.* Consider, for example, an applet to display a clock with moving hands. Legacy browsers have supported several different applet tags, but as of HTML5 the standard syntax looks like this:

```
<embed type="application/x-java-applet" code="Clock.class">
```

The `type` attribute informs the browser that the embedded element is expected to be a Java applet; the `code` element provides the applet's URI. Additional attributes can be used to specify such properties as the required interpreter version number and the size of the needed display space. ■

As one might infer from the existence of the `type` attribute, `embed` tags can request execution by a wide variety of plug-ins—not just a Java Virtual Machine. As of 2015, the most widely used plug-in is Adobe's Flash Player. Though scriptable,

Flash Player is more accurately described as a multimedia display engine than a general purpose programming language interpreter.

Over time, plug-ins have proven to be a major source of browser security bugs. Almost any nontrivial plug-in requires access to operating system services—network IO, local file space, graphics acceleration, and so on. Providing just enough service to make the plug-in useful—but not enough to allow it to do any harm—has proven extremely difficult. To address this problem, extensive multimedia support has been built into the HTML5 standard, allowing the browser itself to assume responsibility for much of what was once accomplished with plug-ins. Security is still a problem, but the number of software modules that must be trusted—and the number of points at which an attacker might try to gain entrance—is significantly reduced. Many browsers now disable Java by default. Some disable Flash as well.

14.3.5 XSLT

Most readers will undoubtedly have had the opportunity to write, or at least to read, the HTML (hypertext markup language) used to compose web pages. HTML has, for the most part, a nested structure in which fragments of documents (*elements*) are delimited by *tags* that indicate their purpose or appearance. We saw in Section 14.2.2, for example, that top-level headings are delimited with `<h1>` and `</h1>`. Unfortunately, as a result of the chaotic and informal way in which the Web evolved, HTML ended up with many inconsistencies in its design, and incompatibilities among the versions implemented by different vendors.

DESIGN & IMPLEMENTATION

14.5 JavaScript and Java

Despite its name, JavaScript has no connection to Java beyond some superficial syntactic similarity. The language was originally developed by Brendan Eich at Netscape Corp. in 1995. Eich called his creation *LiveScript*, but the company chose to rename it as part of a joint marketing agreement with Sun Microsystems, prior to its public release. Trademark on the JavaScript name is actually owned by Oracle, which acquired Sun in 2010.

Netscape's browser was the market leader in 1995, and JavaScript usage grew extremely fast. To remain competitive, developers at Microsoft added JavaScript support to Internet Explorer, but they used the name *JScript* instead, and they introduced a number of incompatibilities with the Netscape version of the language. A common version was standardized as *ECMAScript* by the European standards body in 1997 (and subsequently by the ISO), but major incompatibilities remained in the Document Object Models provided by different browsers. These have been gradually resolved through a series of standards from the World Wide Web Consortium, but legacy pages and legacy browsers continue to plague web developers.

XML (extensible markup language) is a more recent and general language in which to capture structured data. Compared to HTML, its syntax and semantics are more regular and consistent, and more consistently implemented across platforms. It is *extensible*, meaning that users can define their own tags. It also makes a clear distinction between the *content* of a document (the data it captures) and the *presentation* of that data. Presentation, in fact, is deferred to a companion standard known as XSL (extensible stylesheet language). XSLT is a portion of XSL devoted to *transforming* XML: selecting, reorganizing, and modifying tags and the elements they delimit—in effect, scripting the processing of data represented in XML.

DESIGN & IMPLEMENTATION

14.6 How far can you trust a script?

Security becomes an issue whenever code is executed using someone else's resources. On a hosting machine, web servers are usually installed with very limited access rights, and with only a limited view of the host's file system. This strategy limits the set of pages accessible through the server to a well-defined subset of what would be visible to users logged into the hosting machine directly. By contrast, CGI scripts are separate executable programs, and can potentially run with the privileges of whoever installs them. To prevent users on the hosting machine from accidentally or intentionally passing their privileges to arbitrary users on the Internet, most system administrators configure their machines so that CGI scripts must reside in a special directory, and be installed by a trusted user. Embedded server-side scripts can reside in any file because they are guaranteed to run with the (limited) rights of the server itself.

A larger risk is posed by code downloaded over the Internet and executed on a client machine. Because such code is in general untrusted, it must be executed in a carefully controlled environment, sometimes called a *sandbox*, to prevent it from doing any damage. As a general rule, embedded JavaScript cannot access the local file system, memory management system, or network, nor can it manipulate documents from other sites. Java applets, likewise, have only limited ability to access external resources. Reality is a bit more complicated, of course: Sometimes, a script needs access to, say, a temporary file of limited size, or a network connection to a trusted server. Mechanisms exist to certify sites as *trusted*, or to allow a trusted site to certify the trustworthiness of pages from other sites. Scripts on pages obtained through a trusted mechanism may then be given extended rights. Such mechanisms must be used with care. Finding the right balance between security and functionality remains one of the central challenges of the Web, and of distributed computing in general. (More on this topic can be found in Section 16.2.4, and in Explorations 16.19 and 16.20.)

IN MORE DEPTH

XML can be used to create specialized markup languages for a very wide range of application domains. XHTML is an almost (but not quite) backward compatible variant of HTML that conforms to the XML standard. Web tools are increasingly being designed to generate XHTML.

On the companion site, we consider a variety of topics related to XML, with a particular emphasis on XSLT. We elaborate on the distinction between content and presentation, introduce the general notion of stylesheet languages, and describe the *document type definitions* (DTDs) and *schemas* used to define domain-specific applications of XML, using XHTML as an example.

Because tags are required to nest, an XML document has a natural tree-based structure. XSLT is designed to process these trees via recursive traversal. Though it can be used for almost any task that takes XML as input, perhaps its most common use is to transform XML into formatted output—often XHTML to be presented in a browser. As an extended example, we consider the formatting of an XML-based bibliographic database.

✓ CHECK YOUR UNDERSTANDING

23. Explain the distinction between *server-side* and *client-side* web scripting.
24. List the tradeoffs between CGI scripts and embedded PHP.
25. Why are CGI scripts usually installed only in a special directory?
26. Explain how a PHP page can service its own requests.
27. Why might we prefer to execute a web script on the server rather than the client? Why might we sometimes prefer the client instead?
28. What is the HTML *Document Object Model*? What is its significance for client-side scripting?
29. What is the relationship between JavaScript and Java?
30. What is an *applet*? Why applets are usually not considered an example of scripting?
31. What is HTML? XML? XSLT? How are they related to one another?

14.4 Innovative Features

In Section 14.1.1, we listed several common characteristics of scripting languages:

1. Both batch and interactive use

2. Economy of expression
3. Lack of declarations; simple scoping rules
4. Flexible dynamic typing
5. Easy access to other programs
6. Sophisticated pattern matching and string manipulation
7. High-level data types

Several of these are discussed in more detail in the subsections below. Specifically, Section 14.4.1 considers naming and scoping in scripting languages; Section 14.4.2 discusses string and pattern manipulation; and Section 14.4.3 considers data types. Items (1), (2), and (5) in our list, while important, are not particularly difficult or subtle, and will not be considered further here.

14.4.1 Names and Scopes

Most scripting languages (Scheme is the obvious exception) do not require variables to be declared. A few languages, notably Perl and JavaScript, permit optional declarations, primarily as a sort of compiler-checked documentation. Perl can be run in a mode (`use strict 'vars'`) that requires declarations. With or without declarations, most scripting languages use dynamic typing. Values are generally self-descriptive, so the interpreter can perform type checking at run time, or coerce values when appropriate.

Nesting and scoping conventions vary quite a bit. Scheme, Python, JavaScript, and R provide the classic combination of nested subroutines and static (lexical) scope. Tcl allows subroutines to nest, but uses dynamic scoping. Named subroutines (methods) do not nest in PHP or Ruby, and they are only sort of nest in Perl (more on this below as well), but Perl and Ruby join Scheme, Python, JavaScript, and R in providing first-class anonymous local subroutines. Nested blocks are statically scoped in Perl. In Ruby, they are part of the named scope in which they appear. Scheme, Perl, Python, Ruby, JavaScript, and R all provide unlimited extent for variables captured in closures. PHP, R, and the major glue languages (Perl, Tcl, Python, Ruby) all have sophisticated namespace mechanisms for information hiding and the selective import of names from separate modules.

What Is the Scope of an Undeclared Variable?

In languages with static scoping, the lack of declarations raises an interesting question: when we access a variable `x`, how do we know if it is local, global, or (if scopes can nest) something in-between? Existing languages take several different approaches. In Perl, all variables are global unless explicitly declared. In PHP, they are local unless explicitly imported (and all imports are global, since scopes do not nest). Ruby, too, has only two real levels of scoping, but as we saw in Section 14.2.4, it distinguishes between them using prefix characters on names: `foo` is a local variable; `$foo` is a global variable; `@foo` is an instance variable of the current object (the one whose method is currently executing); `@@foo` is an instance

```
i = 1;  j = 3
def outer():
    def middle(k):
        def inner():
            global i          # from main program, not outer
            i = 4
        inner()
        return i, j, k        # 3-element tuple
    i = 2                     # new local i
    return middle(j)          # old (global) j

print(outer())
print(i, j)
```

Figure 14.16 **A program to illustrate scope rules in Python.** There is one instance each of `j` and `k`, but two of `i`: one global and one local to `outer`. The scope of the latter is all of `outer`, not just the portion after the assignment. The `global` statement provides `inner` with access to the outermost `i`, so it can write it without defining a new instance.

variable of the current object's *class* (shared by all sibling instances). (Note: as we shall see in Section 14.4.3, Perl uses similar prefix characters to indicate *type*. These very different uses are a potential source of confusion for programmers who switch between the two languages.)

Perhaps the most interesting scope-resolution rule is that of Python and R. In these languages, a variable that is written is assumed to be local, unless it is explicitly imported. A variable that is only read in a given scope is found in the closest enclosing scope that contains a defining write. Consider, for example, the Python program of Figure 14.16. Here we have a set of nested subroutines, as indicated by indentation level. The main program calls `outer`, which calls `middle`, which in turn calls `inner`. Before its call, the main program writes both `i` and `j`. `Outer` reads `j` (to pass it to `middle`), but does not write it. It does, however, write `i`. Consequently, `outer` reads the global `j`, but has its own `i`, different from the global one. `Middle` reads both `i` and `j`, but it does not write either, so it must find them in surrounding scopes. It finds `i` in `outer`, and `j` at the global level. Inner, for its part, also writes the global `i`. When executed, the program prints

EXAMPLE 14.37
Scoping rules in Python

```
(2, 3, 3)
4 3
```

Note that while the tuple returned from `middle` (forwarded on by `outer`, and printed by the main program) has a 2 as its first element, the global `i` still contains the 4 that was written by `inner`. Note also that while the write to `i` in `outer` appears textually after the read of `i` in `middle`, its scope extends over all of `outer`, including the body of `middle`. ■

Interestingly, there is no way in Python for a nested routine to write a variable that belongs to a surrounding but nonglobal scope. In Figure 14.16, `inner` could not be modified to write `outer`'s `i`. R provides an alternative mechanism that

EXAMPLE 14.38
Superassignment in R

```
sub outer($) {                        # must be called with scalar arg
    $sub_A = sub {
        print "sub_A  $lex, $dyn\n";
    };
    my $lex = $_[0];                  # static local initialized to first arg
    local $dyn = $_[0];               # dynamic local initialized to first arg
    $sub_B = sub {
        print "sub_B  $lex, $dyn\n";
    };
    print "outer  $lex, $dyn\n";
    $sub_A->();
    $sub_B->();
}

$lex = 1; $dyn = 1;
print "main   $lex, $dyn\n";
outer(2);
print "main   $lex, $dyn\n";
```

Figure 14.17 **A program to illustrate scope rules in Perl.** The `my` operator creates a statically scoped local variable; the `local` operator creates a new dynamically scoped instance of a global variable. The static scope extends from the point of declaration to the lexical end of the block; the dynamic scope extends from elaboration to the end of the block's execution.

does provide this functionality. Rather than declare `i` to be `global`, R uses a "superassignment" operator. Where a normal assignment `i <- 4` assigns the value 4 into a local variable `i`, the superassignment `i <<- 4` assigns 4 into whatever `i` would be found under the normal rules of static (lexical) scoping.

Scoping in Perl

Perl has evolved over the years. At first, there were only global variables. Locals were soon added for the sake of modularity, so a subroutine with a variable named `i` wouldn't have to worry about modifying a global `i` that was needed elsewhere in the code. Unfortunately, locals were originally defined in terms of dynamic scoping, and the need for backward compatibility required that this behavior be retained when static scoping was added in Perl 5. Consequently, the language provides both mechanisms.

EXAMPLE 14.39
Static and dynamic scoping in Perl

Any variable that is not declared is global in Perl by default. Variables declared with the `local` operator are dynamically scoped. Variables declared with the `my` operator are statically scoped. The difference can be seen in Figure 14.17, in which subroutine `outer` declares two local variables, `lex` and `dyn`. The former is statically scoped; the latter is dynamically scoped. Both are initialized to be a copy of `foo`'s first parameter. (Parameters are passed in the pseudovariable `@_`. The first element of this array is `$_[0]`.)

Two lexically identical anonymous subroutines are nested inside `outer`, one before and one after the redeclarations of `$lex` and `$dyn`. References to these are stored in local variables sub_A and sub_B. Because static scopes in Perl extend from a declaration to the end of its block, sub_A sees the global $lex, while sub_B sees outer's $lex. In contrast, because the declaration of local $dyn occurs before either sub_A or sub_B is called, both see this local version. Our program prints

```
main   1, 1
outer  2, 2
sub_A  1, 2
sub_B  2, 2
main   1, 1
```

EXAMPLE 14.40
Accessing globals in Perl

In cases where static scoping would normally access a variable at an in-between level of nesting, Perl allows the programmer to force the use of a global variable with the our operator, whose name is intended to contrast with my:

```
($x, $y, $z) = (1, 1, 1);           # global scope
{                                   # middle scope
    my ($x, $y) = (2, 2);
    local $z = 3;
    {                               # inner scope
        our ($x, $z);               # use globals
        print "$x, $y, $z\n";
    }
}
```

Here there is one lexical instance of z and two of x and y—one global, one in the middle scope. There is also a dynamic z in the middle scope. When it executes

DESIGN & IMPLEMENTATION

14.7 Thinking about dynamic scoping

In Section 3.3.6, we described dynamic scope rules as introducing a new meaning for a name that remains visible, wherever we are in the program, until control leaves the scope in which the new meaning was created. This conceptual model mirrors the association list implementation described in Section C-3.4.2 and, as described in Sidebar 3.6, probably accounts for the use of dynamic scoping in early dialects of Lisp.

Documentation for Perl suggests a semantically equivalent but conceptually different model. Rather than saying that a local declaration introduces a new variable whose name hides previous declarations, Perl says that there is a *single* variable, at the global level, whose previous *value* is saved when the new declaration is encountered, and then automatically restored when control leaves the new declaration's scope. This model mirrors the underlying implementation in Perl, which uses a central reference table (also described in Section C-3.4.2). In keeping with this model and implementation, Perl does not allow a local operator to create a dynamic instance of a variable that is not global.

its `print` statement, the inner scope finds the `y` from the middle scope. It finds the global `x`, however, because of the `our` operator on line 6. Now what about `z`? The rules require us to start with static scoping, ignoring `local` operators. According, then, to the `our` operator in the inner scope, we are using the global `z`. Once we know this, we look to see whether a dynamic (`local`) redeclaration of `z` is in effect. In this case indeed it is, and our program prints `1, 2, 3`. As it turns out, the `our` declaration in the inner scope had no effect on this program. If only `x` had been declared `our`, we would still have used the global `z`, and then found the dynamic instance from the middle scope. ▪

14.4.2 String and Pattern Manipulation

When we first considered regular expressions, in Section 2.1.1, we noted that many scripting languages and related tools employ extended versions of the notation. Some extensions are simply a matter of convenience. Others increase the expressive power of the notation, allowing us to generate (match) nonregular sets of strings. Still other extensions serve to tie the notation to other language features.

We have already seen examples of extended regular expressions in `sed` (Figure 14.1), `awk` (Figures 14.2 and 14.3), Perl (Figures 14.4 and 14.5), Python (Figure 14.6), and Ruby (Figure 14.7). Many readers will also be familiar with `grep`, the stand-alone Unix pattern-matching tool (see Sidebar 14.8).

While there are many different implementations of extended regular expressions ("REs" for short), with slightly different syntax, most fall into two main groups. The first group includes `awk`, `egrep` (the most widely used of several different versions of `grep`), and the `regex` library for C. These implement REs as defined in the POSIX standard [Int03b]. Languages in the second group follow the lead of Perl, which provides a large set of extensions, sometimes referred to as "advanced REs." Perl-like advanced REs appear in PHP, Python, Ruby, JavaScript, Emacs Lisp, Java, and C#. They can also be found in third-party packages for C++ and other languages. A few tools, including `sed`, classic `grep`, and older Unix editors, provide so-called "basic" REs, less capable than those of `egrep`.

In certain languages and tools—notably `sed`, `awk`, Perl, PHP, Ruby, and JavaScript—regular expressions are tightly integrated into the rest of the language, with special syntax and built-in operators. In these languages an RE is typically delimited with slash characters, though other delimiters may be accepted in some cases (and Perl in fact provides slightly different semantics for a few alternative delimiters). In most other languages, REs are expressed as ordinary character strings, and are manipulated by passing them to library routines. Over the next few pages we will consider POSIX and advanced REs in more detail. Following Perl, we will use slashes as delimiters. Our coverage will of necessity be incomplete. The chapter on REs in the Perl book [CfWO12, Chap. 5] is over 100 pages long. The corresponding Unix `man` page totals some 40 pages.

POSIX Regular Expressions

EXAMPLE 14.41
Basic operations in POSIX REs

Like the "true" regular expressions of formal language theory, extended REs support concatenation, alternation, and Kleene closure. Parentheses are used for grouping:

```
/ab(cd|ef)g*/        matches abcd, abcdg, abefg, abefgg, abcdggg, etc.
```

EXAMPLE 14.42
Extra quantifiers in POSIX REs

Several other *quantifiers* (generalizations of Kleene closure) are also available: ? indicates zero or one repetitions, + indicates one or more repetitions, {*n*} indicates exactly *n* repetitions, {*n*,} indicates at least *n* repetitions, and {*n*, *m*} indicates *n*–*m* repetitions:

```
/a(bc)*/             matches a, abc, abcbc, abcbcbc, etc.
/a(bc)?/             matches a or abc
/a(bc)+/             matches abc, abcbc, abcbcbc, etc.
/a(bc){3}/           matches abcbcbc only
/a(bc){2,}/          matches abcbc, abcbcbc, etc.
/a(bc){1,3}/         matches abc, abcbc, and abcbcbc (only)
```

EXAMPLE 14.43
Zero-length assertions

Two *zero-length assertions*, ^ and $, match only at the beginning and end, respectively, of a target string. Thus while /abe/ will match abe, abet, babe, and label, /^abe/ will match only the first two of these, /abe$/ will match only the first and the third, and /^abe$/ will match only the first.

EXAMPLE 14.44
Character classes

As an abbreviation for the alternation of set of single characters (e.g., /a|e|i|o|u/), extended REs permit *character classes* to be specified with square brackets:

```
/b[aeiou]d/          matches bad, bed, bid, bod, and bud
```

DESIGN & IMPLEMENTATION

14.8 The grep command and the birth of Unix tools

Historically, regular expression tools have their roots in the pattern matching mechanism of the ed line editor, which dates from the earliest days of Unix. In 1973, Doug McIlroy, head of the department where Unix was born, was working on a project in computerized voice synthesis. As part of this project he was using the editor to search for potentially challenging words in an on-line dictionary. The process was both tedious and slow. At McIlroy's request, Ken Thompson extracted the pattern matcher from ed and made it a stand-alone tool. He named his creation grep, after the g/*re*/p command sequence in the editor: g for "global"; / / to search for a regular expression (*re*); p to print [HH97a, Chap. 9].

Thompson's creation was one of the first in a large suite of stream-based Unix tools. As described in Section 14.2.1, such tools are frequently combined with pipes to perform a variety of filtering, transforming, and formatting operations.

Ranges are also permitted:

```
/0x[0-9a-fA-F]+/        matches any hexadecimal integer
```

EXAMPLE 14.45
The dot (.) character

Outside a character class, a dot (`.`) matches any character other than a newline. The expression `/b.d/`, for example, matches not only `bad`, `bbd`, `bcd`, and so on, but also `b:d`, `b7d`, and many, many others, including sequences in which the middle character isn't printable. In a Unicode-enabled version of Perl, there are tens of thousands of options.

EXAMPLE 14.46
Negation and quoting in character classes

A caret (`^`) at the beginning of a character class indicates negation: the class expression matches anything *other* than the characters inside. Thus `/b[^aq]d/` matches anything matched by `/b.d/` except for `bad` and `bqd`. A caret, right bracket, or hyphen can be specified inside a character class by preceding it with a backslash. A backslash will similarly protect any of the special characters `| ( ) [ ] { } $ . * + ?` outside a character class.[6] To match a literal backslash, use two of them in a row:

```
/a\\b/                  matches a\b
```

EXAMPLE 14.47
Predefined POSIX character classes

Several character class expressions are predefined in the POSIX standard. As we saw in Example 14.19, the expression `[:space:]` can be used to capture white space. For punctuation there is `[:punct:]`. The exact definitions of these classes depend on the local character set and language. Note, too, that the expressions must be used *inside* a built-up character class; they aren't classes by themselves. A variable name in C, for example, might be matched by `/[[:alpha:]_][[:alpha:][:digit:]_]*/` or, a bit more simply, `/[[:alpha:]_][[:alnum:]_]*/`. Additional syntax, not described here, allows character classes to capture Unicode *collating elements* (multibyte sequences such as a character and associated accents) that collate (sort) as if they were single elements. Perl provides less cumbersome versions of most of these special classes.

Perl Extensions

EXAMPLE 14.48
RE matching in Perl

Extended REs are a central part of Perl. The built-in `=~` operator is used to test for matching:

```
$foo = "albatross";
if ($foo =~ /ba.*s+/) ...          # true
if ($foo =~ /^ba.*s+/) ...         # false (no match at start of string)
```

The string to be matched against can also be left unspecified, in which case Perl uses the pseudovariable `$_` by default:

6 Strictly speaking, `]` and `}` don't require a protective backslash unless there is a preceding unmatched (and unprotected) `[` or `{`, respectively.

```
$_ = "albatross";
if (/ba.*s+/) ...                    # true
if (/^ba.*s+/) ...                   # false
```

Recall that `$_` is set automatically when iterating over the lines of a file. It is also the default index variable in `for` loops. ■

EXAMPLE 14.49
Negating a match in Perl

The `!~` operator returns true when a pattern *does not* match:

```
if ("albatross" !~ /^ba.*s+/) ... # true
```

■

EXAMPLE 14.50
RE substitution in Perl

For substitution, the binary "mixfix" operator `s///` replaces whatever lies between the first and second slashes with whatever lies between the second and the third:

```
$foo = "albatross";
$foo =~ s/lbat/c/;                   # "across"
```

Again, if a left-hand side is not specified, `s///` matches and modifies `$_`. ■

Modifiers and Escape Sequences

Both matches and substitutions can be *modified* by adding one or more characters after the closing delimiter. A trailing `i`, for example, makes the match case-insensitive:

EXAMPLE 14.51
Trailing modifiers on RE matches

```
$foo = "Albatross";
if ($foo =~ /^al/i) ...              # true
```

A trailing g on a substitution replaces *all* occurrences of the regular expression:

```
$foo = "albatross";
$foo =~ s/[aeiou]/-/g;               # "-lb-tr-ss"
```

■

DESIGN & IMPLEMENTATION

14.9 Automata for regular expressions

POSIX regular expressions are typically implemented using the constructions described in Section 2.2.1, which transform the RE into an NFA and then a DFA. Advanced REs of the sort provided by Perl are typically implemented via backtracking search in the obvious NFA. The NFA-to-DFA construction is usually not employed because it fails to preserve some of the advanced RE extensions (notably the *capture* mechanism described in Examples 14.55–14.58) [CfWO12, pp. 241–246]. Some implementations use a DFA first to determine whether there *is* a match, and then an NFA or backtracking search to actually effect the match. This strategy pays the price of the slower automaton only when it's sure to be worthwhile.

Escape	Meaning
\0	NUL character
\a	alarm (BEL) character
\b	backspace (within character class)
\e	escape (ESC) character
\f	form-feed (FF) character
\n	newline
\r	return
\t	tab
NNN	character given by *NNN* in octal
\x{*abcd*}	character given by *abcd* in hexadecimal
\b	word boundary (outside character classes)
\B	not a word boundary
\A	beginning of string
\z	end of string
\Z	prior to final newline, or end of string if none
\d	digit (decimal)
\D	not a digit
\s	white space (space, tab, newline, return, form feed)
\S	not white space
\w	word character (letter, digit, underscore)
\W	not a word character

Figure 14.18 Regular expression escape sequences in Perl. Sequences in the top portion of the table represent individual characters. Sequences in the middle are zero-width assertions. Sequences at the bottom are built-in character classes. Note that these are only examples: Perl assigns a meaning to almost every backslash-character sequence.

For matching in multiline strings, a trailing `s` allows a dot (`.`) to match an embedded newline (which it normally cannot). A trailing `m` allows `$` and `^` to match immediately before and after such a newline, respectively. A trailing `x` causes Perl to ignore both comments and embedded white space in the pattern so that particularly complicated expressions can be broken across multiple lines, documented, and indented.

In the tradition of C and its relatives (Example 8.29), Perl allows nonprinting characters to be specified in REs using backslash *escape sequences.* Some of the most frequently used examples appear in the top portion of Figure 14.18. Perl also provides several zero-width assertions, in addition to the standard `^` and `$`. Examples are shown in the middle of the figure. The `\A` and `\Z` escapes differ from `^` and `$` in that they continue to match only at the beginning and end of the string, respectively, even in multiline searches that use the modifier `m`. Finally, Perl provides several built-in character classes, some of which are shown at the bottom of the figure. These can be used both inside and outside user-defined (i.e., bracket-delimited) classes. Note that `\b` has *different* meanings inside and outside such classes.

Greedy and Minimal Matches

The usual rule for matching in REs is sometimes called "left-most longest": when a pattern can match at more than one place within a string, the chosen match will be the one that starts at the earliest possible position within the string, and then extends as far as possible. In the string abcbcbcde, for example, the pattern /(bc)+/ can match in six different ways:

EXAMPLE 14.52
Greedy and minimal matching

```
abcbcbcde
abcbcbcde
abcbcbcde
abcbcbcde
abcbcbcde
abcbcbcde
```

The third of these is "left-most longest," also known as *greedy*. In some cases, however, it may be desirable to obtain a "left-most shortest" or *minimal* match. This corresponds to the first alternative above. ■

EXAMPLE 14.53
Minimal matching of HTML headers

We saw a more realistic example in Example 14.23 (Figure 14.4), which contains the following substitution:

```
s/.*?(<[hH][123]>.*?<\/[hH][123]>)//s;
```

Assuming that the HTML input is well formed, and that headers do not nest, this substitution deletes everything between the beginning of the string (implicitly $_) and the end of the first embedded header. It does so by using the *? quantifier instead of the usual *. Without the question marks, the pattern would match through (and the substitution would delete through) the end of the *last* header in the string. Recall that the trailing s modifier allows our headers to span lines.

In general, *? matches the smallest number of instances of the preceding subexpression that will allow the overall match to succeed. Similarly, +? matches at least one instance, but no more than necessary to allow the overall match to succeed, and ?? matches either zero or one instances, with a preference for zero. ■

Variable Interpolation and Capture

Like double-quoted strings, regular expressions in Perl support *variable interpolation.* Any dollar sign that does not immediately precede a vertical bar, closing parenthesis, or end of string is assumed to introduce the name of a Perl variable, whose value as a string is expanded prior to passing the pattern to the regular expression evaluator. This allows us to write code that generates patterns at run time:

EXAMPLE 14.54
Variable interpolation in extended REs

```
$prefix = ...
$suffix = ...
if ($foo =~ /^$prefix.*$suffix$/) ...
```

Note the two different roles played by $ in this example. ■

EXAMPLE 14.55
Variable capture in extended REs

The flow of information can go the other way as well: we can pull the values of variables out of regular expressions. We saw a simple example in the sed script of Figure 14.1:

```
s/^.*\(<[hH][123]>\)/\1/        ;# delete text before opening tag
```

The equivalent in Perl would look something like this:

```
$line =~ s/^.*(<[hH][123]>)/\1/;
```

Every parenthesized fragment of a Perl RE is said to *capture* the text that it matches. The captured strings may be referenced in the right-hand side of the substitution as \1, \2, and so on. Outside the expression they remain available (until the next substitution is executed) as $1, $2, and so on:

```
print "Opening tag: ", $1, "\n";
```

■

DESIGN & IMPLEMENTATION

14.10 Compiling regular expressions

Before it can be used as the basis of a search, a regular expression must be compiled into a deterministic or nondeterministic (backtracking) automaton. Patterns that are clearly constant can be compiled once, either when the program is loaded or when they are first encountered. Patterns that contain interpolated strings, however, must in the general case be recompiled whenever they are encountered, at potentially significant run-time cost. A programmer who knows that interpolated variables will never change can inhibit recompilation by attaching a trailing o modifier to the regular expression, in which case the expression will be compiled the first time it is encountered, and never thereafter. For expressions that must sometimes but not always be recompiled, the programmer can use the qr operator to force recompilation of a pattern, yielding a result that can be used repeatedly and efficiently:

```
for (@patterns) {               # iterate over patterns
    my $pat = qr($_);           # compile to automaton
    for (@strings) {            # iterate over strings
        if (/$pat/) {           # no recompilation required
            print;              # print all strings that match
            print "\n";
        }
    }
    print "\n";
}
```

EXAMPLE 14.56

Backreferences in extended REs

One can even use a captured string later in the RE itself. Such a string is called a *backreference*:

```
if (/.*?(<[hH]([123])>.*?<\/[hH]\2>)/) {
    print "header: $1\n";
}
```

Here we have used \2 to insist that the closing tag of an HTML header match the opening tag. ■

EXAMPLE 14.57

Dissecting a floating-point literal

One can, of course capture multiple strings:

```
if (/^([+-]?)((\d+)\.|(\d*)\.(\d+))(e([+-]?\d+))?$/) {
    # floating-point number
    print "sign:      ", $1, "\n";
    print "integer:   ", $3, $4, "\n";
    print "fraction: ", $5, "\n";
    print "mantissa: ", $2, "\n";
    print "exponent: ", $7, "\n";
}
```

As in the previous example, the numbering corresponds to the occurrence of left parentheses, read from left to right. With input `-123.45e-6` we see

```
sign:     -
integer:  123
fraction: 45
mantissa: 123.45
exponent: -6
```

Note that because of alternation, exactly one of $3 and $4 is guaranteed to be set. Note also that while we need the sixth set of parentheses for grouping (it has a `?` quantifier), we don't really need it for capture. ■

EXAMPLE 14.58

Implicit capture of prefix, match, and suffix

For simple matches, Perl also provides pseudovariables named `` $` ``, `$&`, and `$'`. These name the portions of the string before, in, and after the most recent match, respectively:

```
$line = <>;
chop $line;                     # delete trailing newline
$line =~ /is/;
print "prefix($`) match($&) suffix($')\n";
```

With input "`now is the time`", this code prints

```
prefix(now ) match(is) suffix( the time)
```

■

✓ **CHECK YOUR UNDERSTANDING**

32. Name a scripting language that uses dynamic scoping.
33. Summarize the strategies used in Perl, PHP, Ruby, and Python to determine the scope of variables that are not declared.
34. Describe the conceptual model for dynamically scoped variables in Perl.
35. List the principal features found in POSIX regular expressions, but not in the regular expressions of formal language theory (Section 2.1.1).
36. List the principal features found in Perl REs, but not in those of POSIX.
37. Explain the purpose of search *modifiers* (characters following the final delimiter) in Perl-type regular expressions.
38. Describe the three main categories of *escape sequences* in Perl-type regular expressions.
39. Explain the difference between *greedy* and *minimal* matches.
40. Describe the notion of *capture* in regular expressions.

14.4.3 Data Types

As we have seen, scripting languages don't generally require (or even permit) the declaration of types for variables. Most perform extensive run-time checks to make sure that values are never used in inappropriate ways. Some languages (e.g., Scheme, Python, and Ruby) are relatively strict about this checking; the programmer who wants to convert from one type to another must say so explicitly. If we type the following in Ruby,

EXAMPLE 14.59
Coercion in Ruby and Perl

```
a = "4"
print a + 3, "\n"
```

we get the following message at run time: "In '+': no implicit conversion of Fixnum into String (TypeError)." Perl is much more forgiving. As we saw in Example 14.2, the program

```
$a = "4";
print $a . 3 . "\n";            # '.' is concatenation
print $a + 3 . "\n";            # '+' is addition
```

prints 43 and 7.

In general, Perl (and likewise Rexx and Tcl) takes the position that programmers should check for the errors they care about, and in the absence of such checks the program should do something reasonable. Perl is willing, for example, to accept the following (though it prints a warning if run with the `-w` compile-time switch):

EXAMPLE 14.60
Coercion and context in Perl

```
$a[3] = "1";                    # (array @a was previously undefined)
print $a[3] + $a[4], "\n";
```

Here `$a[4]` is uninitialized and hence has value `undef`. In a numeric context (as an operand of `+`) the string `"1"` evaluates to 1, and `undef` evaluates to 0. Added together, these yield 1, which is converted to a string and printed. ■

EXAMPLE 14.61
Explicit conversion in Ruby

A comparable code fragment in Ruby requires a bit more care. Before we can subscript `a` we must make sure that it refers to an array:

```
a = []                          # empty array assignment
a[3] = "1"
```

If the first line were not present (and `a` had not been initialized in any other way), the second line would have generated an "undefined local variable" error. After these assignments, `a[3]` is a string, but other elements of `a` are `nil`. We cannot concatenate a string and `nil`, nor can we add them (both operators are specified in Ruby using the operator `+`). If we want concatenation, and `a[4]` may be `nil`, we must say

```
print a[3] + String(a[4]), "\n"
```

If we want addition, we must say

```
print Integer(a[3]) + Integer(a[4]), "\n"
```

■

As these examples suggest, Perl (and likewise Tcl) uses a value model of variables. Scheme, Python, and Ruby use a reference model. PHP and JavaScript, like Java, use a value model for variables of primitive type and a reference model for variables of object type. The distinction is less important in PHP and JavaScript than it is in Java, because the same variable can hold a primitive value at one point in time and an object reference at another.

Numeric Types

As we have seen in Section 14.4.2, scripting languages generally provide a very rich set of mechanisms for string and pattern manipulation. Syntax and interpolation conventions vary, but the underlying functionality is remarkably consistent, and heavily influenced by Perl. The underlying support for numeric types shows a bit more variation across languages, but the programming model is again remarkably consistent: users are, to first approximation, encouraged to think of numeric values as "simply numbers," and not to worry about the distinction between fixed and floating point, or about the limits of available precision.

Internally, numbers in JavaScript are always double-precision floating point; they are doubles by default in Lua as well. In Tcl they are strings, converted to integers or floating-point numbers (and back again) when arithmetic is needed. PHP uses integers (guaranteed to be at least 32 bits wide), plus double-precision floating point. To these Perl and Ruby add arbitrary precision (multiword) integers, sometimes known as *bignums*. Python has bignums too, plus support for complex numbers. Scheme has all of the above, plus precise rationals, maintained as ⟨numerator, denominator⟩ pairs. In all cases the interpreter "up-converts" as necessary when doing arithmetic on values with different representations, or when overflow would otherwise occur.

Perl is scrupulous about hiding the distinctions among different numeric representations. Most other languages allow the user to determine which is being used, though this is seldom necessary. Ruby is perhaps the most explicit about the existence of different representations: classes `Fixnum`, `Bignum`, and `Float` (double-precision floating point) have overlapping but not identical sets of built-in methods. In particular, integers have iterator methods, which floating-point numbers do not, and floating-point numbers have rounding and error checking methods, which integers do not. `Fixnum` and `Bignum` are both descendants of `Integer`.

Composite Types

The type constructors of compiled languages like C, Fortran, and Ada were chosen largely for the sake of efficient implementation. Arrays and records, in particular, have straightforward time- and space-efficient implementations, which we studied in Chapter 8. Efficiency, however, is less important in scripting languages. Designers have felt free to choose type constructors oriented more toward ease of understanding than pure run-time performance. In particular, most scripting languages place a heavy emphasis on *mappings*, sometimes called *dictionaries*, *hashes*, or *associative arrays*. As might be guessed from the third of these names, a mapping is typically implemented with a hash table. Access time for a hash remains $O(1)$, but with a significantly higher constant than is typical for a compiled array or record.

Perl, the oldest of the widely used scripting languages, inherits its principal composite types—the array and the hash—from `awk`. It also uses prefix characters on variable names as an indication of type: `$foo` is a scalar (a number, Boolean, string, or pointer [which Perl calls a "reference"]); `@foo` is an array; `%foo` is a hash; `&foo` is a subroutine; and plain `foo` is a filehandle or an I/O format, depending on context.

EXAMPLE 14.62
Perl arrays

Ordinary arrays in Perl are indexed using square brackets and integers starting with 0:

```
@colors = ("red", "green", "blue");      # initializer syntax
print $colors[1];                        # green
```

Note that we use the `@` prefix when referring to the array as a whole, and the `$` prefix when referring to one of its (scalar) elements. Arrays are self-expanding: assignment to an out-of-bounds element simply makes the array larger (at the cost of dynamic memory allocation and copying). Uninitialized elements have the value `undef` by default.

EXAMPLE 14.63
Perl hashes

Hashes are indexed using curly braces and character string names:

```
%complements = ("red" => "cyan",
                "green" => "magenta", "blue" => "yellow");
print $complements{"blue"};                # yellow
```

These, too, are self-expanding.

Records and objects are typically built from hashes. Where the C programmer would write `fred.age = 19`, the Perl programmer writes `$fred{"age"} = 19`. In object-oriented code, `$fred` is more likely to be a reference, in which case we have `$fred->{"age"} = 19`. ■

EXAMPLE 14.64

Arrays and hashes in Python and Ruby

Python and Ruby, like Perl, provide both conventional arrays and hashes. They use square brackets for indexing in both cases, and distinguish between array and hash initializers (aggregates) using bracket and brace delimiters, respectively:

```
colors = ["red", "green", "blue"]
complements = {"red" => "cyan",
               "green" => "magenta", "blue" => "yellow"}
print colors[2], complements["blue"]
```

DESIGN & IMPLEMENTATION

14.11 Typeglobs in Perl

It turns out that a global name in Perl can have multiple independent meanings. It is possible, for example, to use `$foo`, `@foo`, `%foo`, `&foo` and two different meanings of `foo`, all in the same program. To keep track of these multiple meanings, Perl interposes a level of indirection between the symbol table entry for `foo` and the various values `foo` may have. The intermediate structure is called a *typeglob*. It has one slot for each of `foo`'s meanings. It also has a name of its own: `*foo`. By manipulating typeglobs, the expert Perl programmer can actually modify the table used by the interpreter to look up names at run time. The simplest use is to create an alias:

```
*a = *b;
```

After executing this statement, `a` and `b` are indistinguishable; they both refer to the same typeglob, and changes made to (any meaning of) one of them will be visible through the other. Perl also supports *selective* aliasing, in which *one slot* of a typeglob is made to point to a value from a different typeglob:

```
*a = \&b;
```

The backslash operator (`\`) in Perl is used to create a pointer. After executing this statement, `&a` (the meaning of `a` as a function) will be the same as `&b`, but all other meanings of `a` will remain the same. Selective aliasing is used, among other things, to implement the mechanism that imports names from libraries in Perl.

(This is Ruby syntax; Python uses : in place of =>.)

EXAMPLE 14.65
Array access methods in Ruby

As a purely object-oriented language, Ruby defines subscripting as syntactic sugar for invocations of the [] (get) and []= (put) methods:

```
c = colors[2]                    # same as  c = colors.[](2)
colors[2] = c                    # same as  colors.[]=(2, c)
```

EXAMPLE 14.66
Tuples in Python

In addition to arrays (which it calls *lists*) and hashes (which it calls *dictionaries*), Python provides two other composite types: tuples and sets. A tuple is essentially an immutable list (array). The initializer syntax uses parentheses rather than brackets:

```
crimson = (0xdc, 0x14, 0x3c)     # R,G,B components
```

Tuples are more efficient to access than arrays: their immutability eliminates the need for most bounds and resizing checks. They also form the basis of multiway assignment:

```
a, b = b, a                      # swap
```

Parentheses can be omitted in this example: the comma groups more tightly than the assignment operator.

EXAMPLE 14.67
Sets in Python

Python sets are like dictionaries that don't map to anything of interest, but simply serve to indicate whether elements are present or absent. Unlike dictionaries, they also support union, intersection, and difference operations:

```
X = set(['a', 'b', 'c', 'd'])   # set constructor
Y = set(['c', 'd', 'e', 'f'])   #     takes array as parameter
U = X | Y                        # (['a', 'b', 'c', 'd', 'e', 'f'])
I = X & Y                        # (['c', 'd'])
D = X - Y                        # (['a', 'b'])
O = X ^ Y                        # (['a', 'b', 'e', 'f'])
'c' in I                         # True
```

EXAMPLE 14.68
Conflated types in PHP, Tcl, and JavaScript

PHP and Tcl have simpler composite types: they eliminate the distinction between arrays and hashes. An array is simply a hash for which the programmer chooses to use numeric keys. JavaScript employs a similar simplification, unifying arrays, hashes, and objects. The usual `obj.attr` notation to access a member of an object (what JavaScript calls a *property*) is simply syntactic sugar for `obj["attr"]`. So objects are hashes, and arrays are objects with integer property names.

EXAMPLE 14.69
Multidimensional arrays in Python and other languages

Higher-dimensional types are straightforward to create in most scripting languages: one can define arrays of (references to) hashes, hashes of (references to) arrays, and so on. Alternatively, one can create a "flattened" implementation by using composite objects as keys in a hash. Tuples in Python work particularly well:

```
matrix = {}                    # empty dictionary (hash)
matrix[2, 3] = 4               # key is (2, 3)
```

This idiom provides the appearance and functionality of multidimensional arrays, though not their efficiency. There exist extension libraries for Python that provide more efficient homogeneous arrays, with only slightly more awkward syntax. Numeric and statistical scripting languages, such as Maple, Mathematica, Matlab, and R, have much more extensive support for multidimensional arrays. ■

Context

In Section 7.2.2 we defined the notion of *type compatibility*, which determines, in a statically typed language, which types can be used in which *contexts*. In this definition the term "context" refers to information about how a value will be used. In C, for example, one might say that in the declaration

```
double d = 3;
```

the `3` on the right-hand side occurs in a context that expects a floating-point number. The C compiler *coerces* the `3` to make it a `double` instead of an `int`.

In Section 7.2.3 we went on to define the notion of *type inference*, which allows a compiler to determine the type of an expression based on the types of its constituent parts and, in some cases, the context in which it appears. We saw an extreme example in ML and its descendants, which use a sophisticated form of inference to determine types for most objects without the need for declarations.

In both of these cases—compatibility and inference—contextual information is used at compile time only. Perl extends the notion of context to drive decisions made at run time. More specifically, each operator in Perl determines, at compile time, and for each of its arguments, whether that argument should be interpreted as a *scalar* or a *list*. Conversely each argument (which may itself be a nested operator) is able to tell, at run time, which kind of context it occupies, and can consequently exhibit different behavior.

EXAMPLE 14.70
Scalar and list context in Perl

As a simple example, the assignment operator (`=`) provides a scalar or list context to its right-hand side based on the type of its left-hand side. This type is always known at compile time, and is usually obvious to the casual reader, because the left-hand side is a name and its prefix character is either a dollar sign (`$`), implying a scalar context, or an at (`@`) or percent (`%`) sign, implying a list context. If we write

```
$time = gmtime();
```

Perl's standard `gmtime()` library function will return the time as a character string, along the lines of `"Wed May 6 04:36:30 2015"`. On the other hand, if we write

```
@time_arry = gmtime();
```

the same function will return (30, 36, 4, 6, 4, 115, 3, 125, 0), a nine-element array indicating seconds, minutes, hours, day of month, month of year (with January = 0), year (counting from 1900), day of week (with Sunday = 0), day of year, and (as a 0/1 Boolean value) an indication of whether it's a leap year.

EXAMPLE 14.71
Using `wantarray` to determine calling context

So how does `gmtime` know what to do? By calling the built-in function `wantarray`. This returns true if the current function was called in a list context, and false if it was called in a scalar context. By convention, functions typically indicate an error by returning the empty array when called in a list context, and the undefined value (`undef`) when called in a scalar context:

```
if ( something went wrong ) {
    return wantarray ? () : undef;
}
```

14.4.4 Object Orientation

Though not an object-oriented language, Perl 5 has features that allow one to program in an object-oriented style.[7] PHP and JavaScript have cleaner, more conventional-looking object-oriented features, but both allow the programmer to use a more traditional imperative style as well. Python and Ruby are explicitly and uniformly object-oriented.

Perl uses a value model for variables; objects are always accessed via pointers. In PHP and JavaScript, a variable can hold either a value of a primitive type or a reference to an object of composite type. In contrast to Perl, however, these languages provide no way to speak of the reference itself, only the object to which it refers. Python and Ruby use a uniform reference model.

Classes are themselves objects in Python and Ruby, much as they are in Smalltalk. They are merely types in PHP, much as they are in C++, Java, or C#. Classes in Perl are simply an alternative way of looking at packages (namespaces). JavaScript, remarkably, has objects but no classes; its inheritance is based on a concept known as *prototypes*, initially introduced by the Self programming language.

Perl 5

Object support in Perl 5 boils down to two main things: (1) a "blessing" mechanism that associates a reference with a package, and (2) special syntax for method calls that automatically passes an object reference or package name as the initial argument to a function. While any reference can in principle be blessed, the usual convention is to use a hash, so that fields can be named as shown in Example 14.63.

---

7 More extensive features, currently under design for Perl 6, will not be covered here.

```
{   package Integer;

    sub new {
        my $class = shift;          # probably "Integer"
        my $self = {};              # reference to new hash
        bless($self, $class);
        $self->{val} = (shift || 0);
        return $self;
    }
    sub set {
        my $self = shift;
        $self->{val} = shift;
    }
    sub get {
        my $self = shift;
        return $self->{val};
    }
}
```

Figure 14.19 **Object-oriented programming in Perl.** Blessing a reference (object) into package `Integer` allows `Integer`'s functions to serve as the object's methods.

EXAMPLE 14.72
A simple class in Perl

As a very simple example, consider the Perl code of Figure 14.19. Here we have defined a package, `Integer`, that plays the role of a class. It has three functions, one of which (`new`) is intended to be used as a constructor, and two of which (`set` and `get`) are intended to be used as accessors. Given this definition we can write

```
$c1 = Integer->new(2);          # Integer::new("Integer", 2)
$c2 = new Integer(3);           # alternative syntax
$c3 = new Integer;              # no initial value specified
```

Both `Integer->new` and `new Integer` are syntactic sugar for calls to `Integer::new` with an additional first argument that contains the name of the package (class) as a character string. In the first line of function `new` we assign this string into the variable `$class`. (The `shift` operator returns the first element of pseudovariable `@_` [the function's arguments], and shifts the remaining arguments, if any, so they will be seen if `shift` is used again.) We then create a reference to a new hash, store it in local variable `$self`, and invoke the `bless` operator to associate it with the appropriate class. With a second call to `shift` we retrieve the initial value for our integer, if any. (The "or" expression [`||`] allows us to use 0 instead if no explicit argument was present.) We assign this initial value into the `val` field of `$self` using the usual Perl syntax to dereference a pointer and subscript a hash. Finally we return a reference to the newly created object. ■

EXAMPLE 14.73
Invoking methods in Perl

Once a reference has been blessed, Perl allows it to be used with method invocation syntax: `c1->get()` and `get c1()` are syntactic sugar for `Integer::get($c1)`. Note that this call passes a reference as the additional first parameter, rather than the name of a package. Given the declarations of `$c1`, `$c2`, and `$c3` from Example 14.72, the following code

```
print $c1->get, " ", $c2->get, " ", $c3->get, " ", "\n";
$c1->set(4);  $c2->set(5);  $c3->set(6);
print $c1->get, " ", $c2->get, " ", $c3->get, " ", "\n";
```

will print

```
2 3 0
4 5 6
```

As usual in Perl, if an argument list is empty, the parentheses can be omitted.

EXAMPLE 14.74
Inheritance in Perl

Inheritance in Perl is obtained by means of the `@ISA` array, initialized at the global level of a package. Extending the previous example, we might define a `Tally` class that inherits from `Integer`:

```
{   package Tally;
    @ISA = ("Integer");

    sub inc {
        my $self = shift;
        $self->{val}++;
    }
}
...
$t1 = new Tally(3);
$t1->inc;
$t1->inc;
print $t1->get, "\n";           # prints 5
```

The `inc` method of `t1` works as one might expect. However when Perl sees a call to `Tally::new` or `Tally::get` (neither of which is actually in the package), it uses the `@ISA` array to locate additional package(s) in which these methods may be found. We can list as many packages as we like in the `@ISA` array; Perl supports multiple inheritance. The possibility that `new` may be called through `Tally` rather than `Integer` explains the use of `shift` to obtain the class name in Figure 14.19. If we had used `"Integer"` explicitly we would not have obtained the desired behavior when creating a `Tally` object.

EXAMPLE 14.75
Inheritance via `use base`

Most often packages (and thus classes) in Perl are declared in separate modules (files). In this case, one must import the module corresponding to a superclass in addition to modifying `@ISA`. The standard `base` module provides convenient syntax for this combined operation, and is the preferred way to specify inheritance relationships:

```
{   package Tally;
    use base ("Integer");
    ...
```

PHP and JavaScript

While Perl's mechanisms suffice to create object-oriented programs, dynamic lookup makes them slower than equivalent imperative programs, and it seems fair to characterize the syntax as less than elegant. Objects are more fundamental to PHP and JavaScript.

PHP 4 provided a variety of object-oriented features, which were heavily revised in PHP 5. The newer version of the language provides a reference model of (class-typed) variables, interfaces and mix-in inheritance, abstract methods and classes, final methods and classes, static and constant members, and access control specifiers (`public`, `protected`, and `private`) reminiscent of those of Java, C#, and C++. In contrast to all other languages discussed in this subsection, class declarations in PHP must include declarations of all members (fields and methods), and the set of members in a given class cannot subsequently change (though one can of course declare derived classes with additional members).

JavaScript takes the unusual approach of providing objects—with inheritance and dynamic method dispatch—without providing classes. Such a language is said to be *object-based*, as opposed to object-oriented. Functions are first-class entities in JavaScript—objects, in fact. A method is simply a function that is referred to by a *property* (member) of an object. When we call `o.m`, the keyword `this` will refer to `o` during the execution of the function referred to by `m`. Likewise when we call `new f`, `this` will refer to a newly created (initially empty) object during the execution of `f`. A constructor in JavaScript is thus a function whose purpose is to assign values into properties (fields and methods) of a newly created object.

Associated with every constructor `f` is an object `f.prototype`. If object `o` was constructed by `f`, then JavaScript will look in `f.prototype` whenever we attempt to use a property of `o` that `o` itself does not provide. In effect, `o` inherits from `f.prototype` anything that it does not override. Prototype properties are commonly used to hold methods. They can also be used for constants or for what other languages would call "class variables."

EXAMPLE 14.76
Prototypes in JavaScript

Figure 14.20 illustrates the use of prototypes. It is roughly equivalent to the Perl code of Figure 14.19. Function `Integer` serves as a constructor. Assignments to properties of `Integer.prototype` serve to establish methods for objects constructed by `Integer`. Using the code in the figure, we can write

```
c2 = new Integer(3);
c3 = new Integer;

document.write(c2.get() + "  " + c3.get() + "<br>");
c2.set(4);  c3.set(5);
document.write(c2.get() + "  " + c3.get() + "<br>");
```

This code will print

```
3  0
4  5
```

■

```
function Integer(n) {
    this.val = n || 0;       // use 0 if n is missing (undefined)
}
function Integer_set(n) {
    this.val = n;
}
function Integer_get() {
    return this.val;
}
Integer.prototype.set = Integer_set;
Integer.prototype.get = Integer_get;
```

Figure 14.20 **Object-oriented programming in JavaScript.** The `Integer` function is used as a constructor. Assignments to members of its prototype object serve to establish methods. These will be available to any object created by `Integer` that doesn't have corresponding members of its own.

EXAMPLE 14.77
Overriding instance methods in JavaScript

Interestingly, the lack of a formal notion of class means that we can override methods and fields on an object-by-object basis:

```
c2.set = new Function("n", "this.val = n * n;");
    // anonymous function constructor
c2.set(3);  c3.set(4);      // these call different methods!
document.write(c2.get() + "  " + c3.get() + "<br>");
```

If nothing else has changed since the previous example, this code will print

```
9  4
```

EXAMPLE 14.78
Inheritance in JavaScript

To obtain the effect of inheritance, we can write

```
function Tally(n) {
    this.base(n);                       // call to base constructor
}
function Tally_inc() {
    this.val++;
}
Tally.prototype = new Integer;       // inherit methods
Tally.prototype.base = Integer;      // make base constructor available
Tally.prototype.inc = Tally_inc;     // new method
...
t1 = new Tally(3);
t1.inc();  t1.inc();
document.write(t1.get() + "<br>");
```

This code will print a 5.

ECMAScript 6, expected to become official in 2015, adds a formal notion of classes to the language, along with a host of other features. Classes are defined in a backward compatible way—essentially as syntactic sugar for constructors with prototypes.

Python and Ruby

As we have noted, both Python and Ruby are explicitly object-oriented. Both employ a uniform reference model for variables. Like Smalltalk, both incorporate an object hierarchy in which classes themselves are represented by objects. The root class in Python is called `object`; in Ruby it is `Object`.

EXAMPLE 14.79
Constructors in Python and Ruby

In both Python and Ruby, each class has a single distinguished constructor, which cannot be overloaded. In Python it is `__init__`; in Ruby it is `initialize`. To create a new object in Python one says `my_object = My_class(`*args*`)`; in Ruby one says `my_object = My_class.new(`*args*`)`. In each case the *args* are passed to the constructor. To achieve the effect of overloading, with different numbers or types of arguments, one must arrange for the single constructor to inspect its arguments explicitly. We employed a similar idiom in Perl (in the `new` routine of Figure 14.19) and JavaScript (in the `Integer` function of Figure 14.20). ■

Both Python and Ruby are more flexible than PHP or more traditional object-oriented languages regarding the contents (members) of a class. New fields can be added to a Python object simply by assigning to them: `my_object.new_field = value`. The set of methods, however, is fixed when the class is first defined. In Ruby only methods are visible outside a class ("put" and "get" methods must be used to access fields), and all methods must be explicitly declared. It is possible, however, to modify an existing class declaration, adding or overriding methods. One can even do this on an object-by-object basis. As a result, two objects of the same class may not display the same behavior.

EXAMPLE 14.80
Naming class members in Python and Ruby

Python and Ruby differ in many other ways. The initial parameter to methods is explicit in Python; by convention it is usually named `self`. In Ruby `self` is a keyword, and the parameter it represents is invisible. Any variable beginning with a single `@` sign in Ruby is a field of the current object. Within a Python method, uses of object members must name the object explicitly. One must, for example, write `self.print()`; just `print()` will not suffice. ■

Ruby methods may be `public`, `protected`, or `private`.[8] Access control in Python is purely a matter of convention; both methods and fields are universally accessible. Finally, Python has multiple inheritance. Ruby has mix-in inheritance: a class cannot obtain data from more than one ancestor. Unlike most other languages, however, Ruby allows an interface (mix-in) to define not only the signatures of methods but also their implementation (code).

✓ CHECK YOUR UNDERSTANDING

41. Contrast the philosophies of Perl and Ruby with regard to error checking and reporting.

---

8 The meanings of `private` and `protected` in Ruby are different from those in C++, Java, or C#: `private` methods in Ruby are available only to the current instance of an object; `protected` methods are available to any instance of the current class or its descendants.

42. Compare the numeric types of popular scripting languages to those of compiled languages like C or Fortran.
43. What are *bignums*? Which languages support them?
44. What are *associative arrays*? By what other names are they sometimes known?
45. Why don't most scripting languages provide direct support for records?
46. What is a *typeglob* in Perl? What purpose does it serve?
47. Describe the *tuple* and *set* types of Python.
48. Explain the unification of arrays and hashes in PHP and Tcl.
49. Explain the unification of arrays and objects in JavaScript.
50. Explain how tuples and hashes can be used to emulate multidimensional arrays in Python.
51. Explain the concept of *context* in Perl. How is it related to type compatibility and type inference? What are the two principal contexts defined by the language's operators?

DESIGN & IMPLEMENTATION

14.12 Executable class declarations

Both Python and Ruby take the interesting position that class declarations are executable code. Elaboration of a declaration executes the code inside. Among other things, we can use this mechanism to achieve the effect of conditional compilation:

```
class My_class                          # Ruby code
    def initialize(a, b)
        @a = a;   @b = b;
    end
    if expensive_function()
        def get()
            return @a
        end
    else
        def get()
            return @b
        end
    end
end
```

Instead of computing the expensive function inside get, on every invocation, we compute it once, ahead of time, and define an appropriate specialized version of get.

52. Compare the approaches to object orientation taken by Perl 5, PHP 5, JavaScript, Python, and Ruby.
53. What is meant by the *blessing* of a reference in Perl?
54. What are *prototypes* in JavaScript? What purpose do they serve?

14.5 Summary and Concluding Remarks

Scripting languages serve primarily to control and coordinate other software components. Though their roots go back to interpreted languages of the 1960s, for many years they were largely ignored by academic computer science. With an increasing emphasis on programmer productivity, however, and with the explosion of the World Wide Web, scripting languages have seen enormous growth in interest and popularity, both in industry and in academia. Many significant advances have been made by commercial developers and by the open-source community. Scripting languages may well come to dominate programming in the 21st century, with traditional compiled languages more and more seen as special-purpose tools.

In comparison to their traditional cousins, scripting languages emphasize flexibility and richness of expression over sheer run-time performance. Common characteristics include both batch and interactive use, economy of expression,

DESIGN & IMPLEMENTATION

14.13 Worse Is Better

Any discussion of the relative merits of scripting and "systems" languages invariably ends up addressing the tradeoffs between expressiveness and flexibility on the one hand and compile-time safety and performance on the other. It may also digress into questions of "quick-and-dirty" versus "polished" applications. An interesting take on this debate can be found in the widely circulated essays of Richard Gabriel (*www.dreamsongs.com/WorseIsBetter.html*). While working for Lucid Corp. in 1989, Gabriel found himself asking why Unix and C had been so successful at attracting users, while Common Lisp (Lucid's principal focus) had not. His explanation contrasts "The Right Thing," as exemplified by Common Lisp, with a "Worse Is Better" philosophy, as exemplified by C and Unix. "The Right Thing" emphasizes complete, correct, consistent, and elegant design. "Worse Is Better" emphasizes the rapid development of software that does most of what users need most of the time, and can be tuned and improved incrementally, based on field experience. Much of scripting, and Perl in particular, fits the "Worse Is Better" philosophy (Ruby and Scheme enthusiasts might beg to disagree). Gabriel, for his part, says he still hasn't made up his mind; his essays argue both points of view.

lack of declarations, simple scoping rules, flexible dynamic typing, easy access to other programs, sophisticated pattern matching and string manipulation, and high-level data types.

We began our chapter by tracing the historical development of scripting, starting with the command interpreter, or *shell* programs of the mid-1970s, and the text processing and report generation tools that followed soon thereafter. We looked in particular at the "Bourne-again" shell, `bash`, and the Unix tools `sed` and `awk`. We also mentioned such special-purpose domains as mathematics and statistics, where scripting languages are widely used for data analysis, visualization, modeling, and simulation. We then turned to the three domains that dominate scripting today: "glue" (coordination) applications, configuration and extension, and scripting of the World Wide Web.

For many years, Perl was the most popular of the general-purpose "glue" languages, but Python and Ruby have clearly overtaken it at this point. Several scripting languages, including Python, Scheme, and Lua, are widely used to extend the functionality of complex applications. In addition, many commercial packages have their own proprietary extension languages.

Web scripting comes in many forms. On the server side of an HTTP connection, the Common Gateway Interface (CGI) standard allows a URI to name a program that will be used to generate dynamic content. Alternatively, web-page-embedded scripts, often written in PHP, can be used to create dynamic content in a way that is invisible to users. To reduce the load on servers, and to improve interactive responsiveness, scripts can also be executed within the client browser. JavaScript is the dominant notation in this domain; it uses the HTML Document Object Model (DOM) to manipulate web-page elements. For more demanding tasks, many browsers can be directed to run a Java *applet*, which takes full responsibility for some portion of the "screen real estate," but this strategy comes with security concerns that are increasingly viewed as unacceptable. With the emergence of HTML5, most dynamic content—multimedia in particular—can be handled directly by the browser. At the same time, XML has emerged as the standard format for structured, presentation-independent information, with load-time transformation via XSL.

Because of their rapid evolution, scripting languages have been able to take advantage of many of the most powerful and elegant mechanisms described in previous chapters, including first-class and higher-order functions, unlimited extent, iterators, garbage collection, list comprehensions, and object orientation—not to mention extended regular expressions and such high-level data types as dictionaries, sets, and tuples. Given current trends, scripting languages are likely to become increasingly ubiquitous, and to remain a principal focus of language innovation.

14.6 Exercises

14.1 Does filename "globbing" provide the expressive power of standard regular expressions? Explain.

14.2 Write shell scripts to

(a) Replace blanks with underscores in the names of all files in the current directory.

(b) Rename every file in the current directory by prepending to its name a textual representation of its modification date.

(c) Find all `eps` files in the file hierarchy below the current directory, and create any corresponding `pdf` files that are missing or out of date.

(d) Print the names of all files in the file hierarchy below the current directory for which a given predicate evaluates to true. Your (quoted) predicate should be specified on the command line using the syntax of the Unix `test` command, with one or more at signs (`@`) standing in for the name of the candidate file.

14.3 In Example 14.16 we used `"$@"` to refer to the parameters passed to `ll`. What would happen if we removed the quote marks? (Hint: Try this for files whose names contain spaces!) Read the `man` page for `bash` and learn the difference between `$@` and `$*`. Create versions of `ll` that use `$*` or `"$*"` instead of `"$@"`. Explain what's going on.

14.4 (a) Extend the code in Figure 14.5, 14.6, or 14.7 to try to kill processes more gently. You'll want to read the `man` page for the standard `kill` command. Use a `TERM` signal first. If that doesn't work, ask the user if you should resort to `KILL`.

(b) Extend your solution to part (a) so that the script accepts an optional argument specifying the signal to be used. Alternatives to `TERM` and `KILL` include `HUP`, `INT`, `QUIT`, and `ABRT`.

14.5 Write a Perl, Python, or Ruby script that creates a simple *concordance*: a sorted list of significant words appearing in an input document, with a sublist for each that indicates the lines on which the word occurs, with up to six words of surrounding context. Exclude from your list all common articles, conjunctions, prepositions, and pronouns.

14.6 Write Emacs Lisp scripts to

(a) Insert today's date into the current buffer at the insertion point (current cursor location).

(b) Place quote marks (" ") around the word surrounding the insertion point.

(c) Fix end-of-sentence spaces in the current buffer. Use the following heuristic: if a period, question mark, or exclamation point is followed by a single space (possibly with closing quote marks, parentheses, brackets, or braces in-between), then add an extra space, unless the character preceding the period, question mark, or exclamation point is a capital letter (in which case we assume it is an abbreviation).

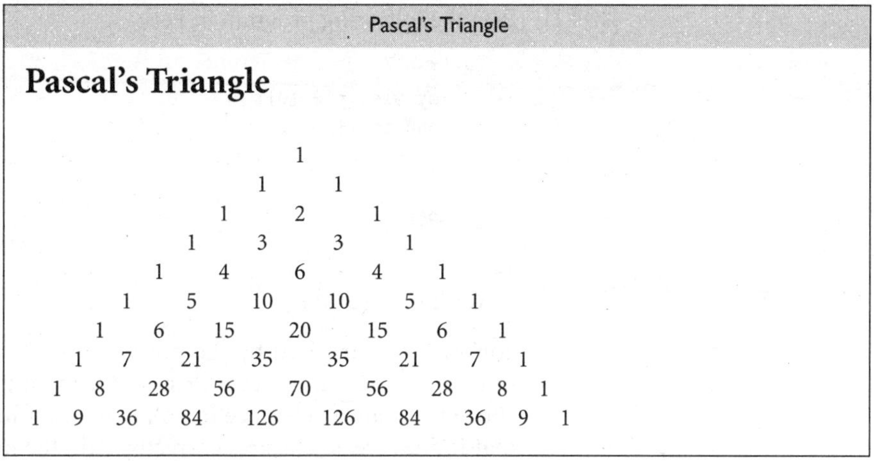

Figure 14.21 Pascal's triangle rendered in a web page (Exercise 14.8).

(d) Run the contents of the current buffer through your favorite spell checker, and create a new buffer containing a list of misspelled words.

(e) Delete one misspelled word from the buffer created in (d), and place the cursor (insertion point) on top of the first occurrence of that misspelled word in the current buffer.

14.7 Explain the circumstances under which it makes sense to realize an interactive task on the Web as a CGI script, an embedded server-side script, or a client-side script. For each of these implementation choices, give three examples of tasks for which it is clearly the preferred approach.

14.8 (a) Write a web page with embedded PHP to print the first 10 rows of Pascal's triangle (see Example C-17.10 if you don't know what this is). When rendered, your output should look like Figure 14.21.

(b) Modify your page to create a self-posting form that accepts the number of desired rows in an input field.

(c) Rewrite your page in JavaScript.

14.9 Create a fill-in web form that uses a JavaScript implementation of the Luhn formula (Exercise 4.10) to check for typos in credit card numbers. (But don't use real credit card numbers; homework exercises don't tend to be very secure!)

14.10 (a) Modify the code of Figure 14.15 (Example 14.35) so that it replaces the form with its output, as the CGI and PHP versions of Figures 14.11 and 14.14 do.

(b) Modify the CGI and PHP scripts of Figures 14.11 and 14.14 (Examples 14.30 and 14.34) so they appear to append their output to the bottom of the form, as the JavaScript version of Figure 14.15 does.

14.11 Run the following program in Perl:

```
sub foo {
    my $lex = $_[0];
    sub bar {
        print "$lex\n";
    }
    bar();
}

foo(2);  foo(3);
```

You may be surprised by the output. Perl 5 allows named subroutines to nest, but does not create closures for them properly. Rewrite the code above to create a reference to an anonymous local subroutine and verify that it does create closures correctly. Add the line `use diagnostics;` to the beginning of the original version and run it again. Based on the explanation this will give you, speculate as to how nested named subroutines are implemented in Perl 5.

14.12 Write a program that will map the web pages stored in the file hierarchy below the current directory. Your output should itself be a web page, containing the names of all directories and `.html` files, printed at levels of indentation corresponding to their level in the file hierarchy. Each `.html` file name should be a live link to its file. Use whatever language(s) seem most appropriate to the task.

14.13 In Section 14.4.1 we claimed that nested blocks in Ruby were part of the named scope in which they appear. Verify this claim by running the following Ruby script and explaining its output:

```
def foo(x)
    y = 2
    bar = proc {
        print x, "\n"
        y = 3
    }
    bar.call()
    print y, "\n"
end

foo(3)
```

Now comment out the second line (`y = 2`) and run the script again. Explain what happens. Restate our claim about scoping more carefully and precisely.

14.14 Write a Perl script to translate English measurements (in, ft, yd, mi) into metric equivalents (cm, m, km). You may want to learn about the `e` modifier on regular expressions, which allows the right-hand side of an `s///e` expression to contain executable code.

14.15 Write a Perl script to find, for each input line, the longest substring that appears at least twice within the line, without overlapping. (*Warning:* This is harder than it sounds. Remember that by default Perl searches for a *left-most longest* match.)

14.16 Perl provides an alternative `(?:...)` form of parentheses that supports grouping in regular expressions without performing capture. Using this syntax, Example 14.57 could have been written as follows:

```
if (/^([+-]?)((\d+)\.|(\d*)\.(\d+))(?:e([+-]?\d+))?$/) {
    # floating-point number
    print "sign:      ", $1, "\n";
    print "integer:   ", $3, $4, "\n";
    print "fraction:  ", $5, "\n";
    print "mantissa:  ", $2, "\n";
    print "exponent:  ", $6, "\n";              # not $7
}
```

What purpose does this extra notation serve? Why might the code here be preferable to that of Example 14.57?

14.17 Consider again the `sed` code of Figure 14.1. It is tempting to write the first of the compound statements as follows (note the differences in the three substitution commands):

```
/<[hH][123]>.*<\/[hH][123]>/ {     ;# match whole heading
    h                              ;# save copy of pattern space
    s/^.*\(<[hH][123]>\)/\1/       ;# delete text before opening tag
    s/\(<\/[hH][123]>\).*$/\1/     ;# delete text after closing tag
    p                              ;# print what remains
    g                              ;# retrieve saved pattern space
    s/^.*<\/[hH][123]>//           ;# delete through closing tag
    b top
```

Explain why this doesn't work. (Hint: Remember the difference between *greedy* and *minimal* matches [Example 14.53]. `Sed` lacks the latter.)

14.18 Consider the following regular expression in Perl: `/^(?:((?:ab)+)|a((?:ba)*))$/`. Describe, in English, the set of strings it will match. Show a natural NFA for this set, together with the minimal DFA. Describe the substrings that should be captured in each matching string. Based on this example, discuss the practicality of using DFAs to match strings in Perl.

14.19–14.21 In More Depth.

14.7 Explorations

14.22 Learn about TeX [Knu86] and LaTeX [Lam94], the typesetting system used to create this book. Explore the ways in which its specialized target domain—professional typesetting—influenced its design. Features you might wish to consider include dynamic scoping, the relatively impoverished arithmetic and control-flow facilities, and the use of macros as the fundamental control abstraction.

14.23 Research the security mechanisms of JavaScript and/or Java applets. What exactly are programs allowed to do and why? What potentially useful features have not been provided because they can't be made secure? What potential security holes remain in the features that *are* provided?

14.24 Learn about *web crawlers*—programs that explore the World Wide Web. Build a crawler that searches for something of interest. What language features or tools seem most useful for the task? *Warning:* Automated web crawling is a public activity, subject to strict rules of etiquette. Before creating a crawler, do a web search and learn the rules, and test your code *very* carefully before letting it outside your local subnet (or even your own machine). In particular, be aware that rapid-fire requests to the same server constitute a *denial of service attack*, a potentially criminal offense.

14.25 In Sidebar 14.9 we noted that the "extended" REs of `awk` and `egrep` are typically implemented by translating first to an NFA and then to a DFA, while those of Perl and its ilk are typically implemented via backtracking search. Some tools, including GNU `ggrep`, use a variant of the Boyer-Moore-Gosper algorithm [BM77, KMP77] for faster deterministic search. Find out how this algorithm works. What are its advantages? Could it be used in languages like Perl?

14.26 In Sidebar 14.10 we noted that nonconstant patterns must generally be recompiled whenever they are used. Perl programmers who wish to reduce the resulting overhead can inhibit recompilation using the `o` trailing modifier or the `qr` quoting operator. Investigate the impact of these mechanisms on performance. Also speculate as to the extent to which it might be possible for the language implementation to determine, automatically and efficiently, when recompilation should occur.

14.27 Our coverage of Perl REs in Section 14.4.2 was incomplete. Features not covered include look-ahead and look-behind (context) assertions, comments, incremental enabling and disabling of modifiers, embedded code, conditionals, Unicode support, nonslash delimiters, and the transliteration (`tr///`) operator. Learn how these work. Explain if (and how) they extend the expressive power of the notation. How could each be emulated (possibly with surrounding Perl code) if it were not available?

14.28 Investigate the details of RE support in PHP, Tcl, Python, Ruby, JavaScript, Emacs Lisp, Java, and C#. Write a paper that documents, as concisely as possible, the differences among these, using Perl as a reference for comparison.

14.29 Do a web search for Perl 6, a community-based effort that has been in the works for many years. Write a report that summarizes the changes with respect to Perl 5. What do you think of these changes? If you were in charge of the revision, what would you do differently?

14.30 Learn about AJAX, a collection of web technologies that allows a JavaScript program to interact with web servers "in the background," to dynamically update a page in a browser after its initial loading. What kinds of applications can you build in AJAX that you couldn't easily build otherwise? What features of JavaScript are most important for making the technology work?

14.31 Learn about Dart, a language developed at Google. Initially intended as a successor to JavaScript, Dart is now supported only as a language in which to develop code that will be *translated into* JavaScript. What explains the change in strategy? What are the odds that some other competitor to JavaScript will emerge in future years?

14.32–14.35 In More Depth.

14.8 Bibliographic Notes

Most of the major scripting languages and their predecessors are described in books by the language designers or their close associates: `awk` [AKW88], Perl [CfWO12], PHP [TML13], Python [vRD11], and Ruby [TFH13]. Several of these books have versions available on-line. Most of the languages are also described in a variety of other texts, and most have dedicated web sites: *perl.org*, *php.net*, *python.org*, *ruby-lang.org*. Extensive documentation for Perl is preinstalled on many machines; type `man perl` for an index.

Rexx [Ame96a] was standardized by ANSI, the American National Standards Institute. JavaScript [ECM11] is standardized by ECMA, the European standards body. Guile (*gnu.org/software/guile/*) is GNU's Scheme implementation for scripting. Standards for the World Wide Web, including HTML5, XML, XSL, XPath, and XSLT, are promulgated by the World Wide Web Consortium: *www.w3.org*. For those updating their pages to HTML5, the validation service at *validator.w3.org* is particularly useful. High-quality tutorials on many web-related topics can be found at *w3schools.com*.

Hauben and Hauben [HH97a] describe the historical roots of the Internet, including early work on Unix. Original articles on the various Unix shell languages include those of Mashey [Mas76], Bourne [Bou78], and Korn [Kor94]. The original reference on APL is by Iverson [Ive62]. Ousterhout [Ous98] makes the case for scripting languages in general, and Tcl in particular. Chonacky and Winch [CW05] compare and contrast Maple, Mathematica, and Matlab. Richard Gabriel's collection of "Worse Is Better" papers can be found at *www.dreamsongs.com/WorseIsBetter.html*. A similar comparison of Tcl and Scheme can be found in the introductory chapter of Abelson, Greenspun, and Sandon's on-line *Tcl for Web Nerds* guide (*philip.greenspun.com/tcl/index.adp*).

IV
A Closer Look at Implementation

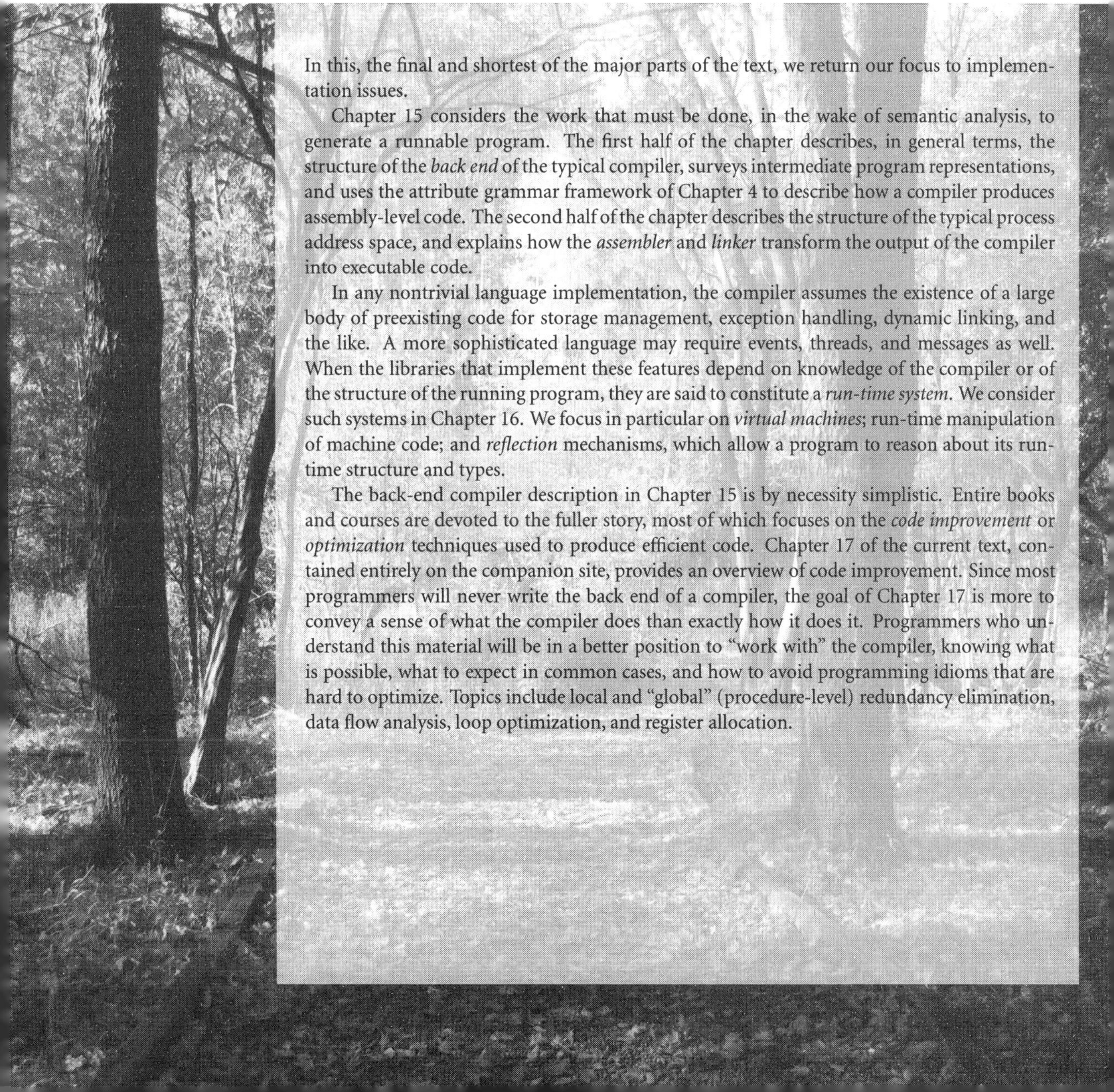

In this, the final and shortest of the major parts of the text, we return our focus to implementation issues.

Chapter 15 considers the work that must be done, in the wake of semantic analysis, to generate a runnable program. The first half of the chapter describes, in general terms, the structure of the *back end* of the typical compiler, surveys intermediate program representations, and uses the attribute grammar framework of Chapter 4 to describe how a compiler produces assembly-level code. The second half of the chapter describes the structure of the typical process address space, and explains how the *assembler* and *linker* transform the output of the compiler into executable code.

In any nontrivial language implementation, the compiler assumes the existence of a large body of preexisting code for storage management, exception handling, dynamic linking, and the like. A more sophisticated language may require events, threads, and messages as well. When the libraries that implement these features depend on knowledge of the compiler or of the structure of the running program, they are said to constitute a *run-time system*. We consider such systems in Chapter 16. We focus in particular on *virtual machines*; run-time manipulation of machine code; and *reflection* mechanisms, which allow a program to reason about its run-time structure and types.

The back-end compiler description in Chapter 15 is by necessity simplistic. Entire books and courses are devoted to the fuller story, most of which focuses on the *code improvement* or *optimization* techniques used to produce efficient code. Chapter 17 of the current text, contained entirely on the companion site, provides an overview of code improvement. Since most programmers will never write the back end of a compiler, the goal of Chapter 17 is more to convey a sense of what the compiler does than exactly how it does it. Programmers who understand this material will be in a better position to "work with" the compiler, knowing what is possible, what to expect in common cases, and how to avoid programming idioms that are hard to optimize. Topics include local and "global" (procedure-level) redundancy elimination, data flow analysis, loop optimization, and register allocation.

A Closer Look at Implementation

15 Building a Runnable Program

As noted in Section 1.6, the various phases of compilation are commonly grouped into a *front end* responsible for the analysis of source code, a *back end* responsible for the synthesis of target code, and often a "middle end" responsible for language- and machine-independent code improvement. Chapters 2 and 4 discussed the work of the front end, culminating in the construction of a syntax tree. The current chapter turns to the work of the back end, and specifically to code generation, assembly, and linking. We will continue with code improvement in Chapter 17.

In Chapters 6 through 10, we often discussed the code that a compiler would generate to implement various language features. Now we will look at how the compiler produces that code from a syntax tree, and how it combines the output of multiple compilations to produce a runnable program. We begin in Section 15.1 with a more detailed overview of the work of program synthesis than was possible in Chapter 1. We focus in particular on one of several plausible ways of dividing that work into phases. In Section 15.2 we then consider the many possible forms of intermediate code passed between these phases. On the companion site we provide a bit more detail on two concrete examples—the GIMPLE and RTL formats used by the GNU compilers. We will consider two additional intermediate forms in Chapter 16: Java bytecode and the Common Intermediate Language (CIL) used by Microsoft and other implementors of the Common Language Infrastructure.

In Section 15.3 we discuss the generation of assembly code from an abstract syntax tree, using attribute grammars as a formal framework. In Section 15.4 we discuss the internal organization of binary object files and the layout of programs in memory. Section 15.5 describes assembly. Section 15.6 considers linking.

15.1 Back-End Compiler Structure

As we noted in Chapter 4, there is less uniformity in back-end compiler structure than there is in front-end structure. Even such unconventional compilers as text processors, source-to-source translators, and VLSI layout tools must scan, parse, and analyze the semantics of their input. When it comes to the back end, however, even compilers for the same language on the same machine can have very different internal structure.

As we shall see in Section 15.2, different compilers may use different intermediate forms to represent a program internally. They may also differ dramatically in the forms of code improvement they perform. A simple compiler, or one designed for speed of compilation rather than speed of target code execution (e.g., a "just-in-time" compiler) may not do much improvement at all. A just-in-time or "load-and-go" compiler (one that compiles and then executes a program as a single high-level operation, without writing the target code to a file) may not use a separate linker. In some compilers, much or all of the code generator may be written automatically by a tool (a "code generator generator") that takes a formal description of the target machine as input.

15.1.1 A Plausible Set of Phases

EXAMPLE 15.1
Phases of compilation

Figure 15.1 illustrates a plausible seven-phase structure for a conventional compiler. The first three phases (scanning, parsing, and semantic analysis) are language dependent; the last two (target code generation and machine-specific code improvement) are machine dependent, and the middle two (intermediate code generation and machine-independent code improvement) are (to first approximation) dependent on neither the language nor the machine. The scanner and parser drive a set of action routines that build a syntax tree. The semantic analyzer traverses the tree, performing all static semantic checks and initializing various attributes (mainly symbol table pointers and indications of the need for dynamic checks) of use to the back end. ■

While certain code improvements can be performed on syntax trees, a less hierarchical representation of the program makes most code improvement easier. Our example compiler therefore includes an explicit phase for intermediate code generation. The code generator begins by grouping the nodes of the tree into *basic blocks*, each of which consists of a maximal-length set of operations that should execute sequentially at run time, with no branches in or out. It then creates a *control flow graph* in which the nodes are basic blocks and the arcs represent interblock control flow. Within each basic block, operations are represented as instructions for an idealized machine with an unlimited number of registers. We will call these *virtual registers*. By allocating a new one for every computed value, the compiler can avoid creating artificial connections between otherwise independent computations too early in the compilation process.

EXAMPLE 15.2
GCD program abstract syntax tree (reprise)

In Example 1.20 we used a simple greatest common divisor (GCD) program to illustrate the phases of compilation. The syntax tree for this program appeared in Figure 1.6; it is reproduced here (in slightly altered form) as Figure 15.2. A corresponding control flow graph appears in Figure 15.3. We will discuss techniques to generate this graph in Section 15.3 and Exercise 15.6. Additional examples of control flow graphs will appear in Chapter 17. ■

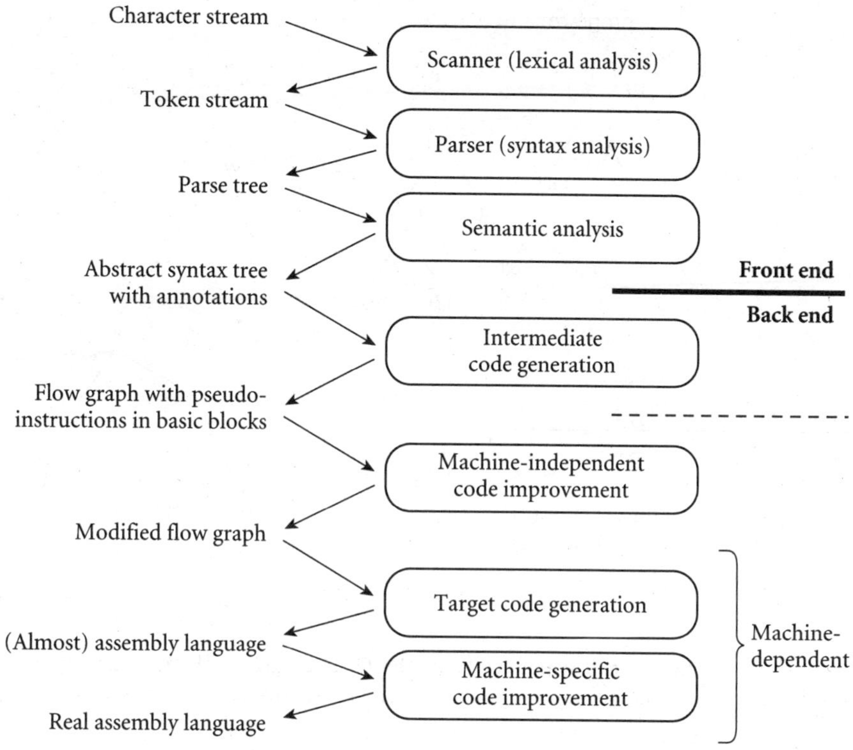

Figure 15.1 **A plausible set of compiler phases.** Here we have shown a sharper separation between semantic analysis and intermediate code generation than we considered in Chapter 1 (see Figure 1.3). Machine-independent code improvement employs an intermediate form that resembles the assembly language for an idealized machine with an unlimited number of registers. Machine-specific code improvement—register allocation and instruction scheduling in particular—employs the assembly language of the target machine. The dashed line shows a common "break point" between the front end and back end of a two-pass compiler. In some implementations, machine-independent code improvement may be located in a separate "middle end" pass.

The machine-independent code improvement phase of compilation performs a variety of transformations on the control flow graph. It modifies the instruction sequence within each basic block to eliminate redundant loads, stores, and arithmetic computations; this is *local code improvement*. It also identifies and removes a variety of redundancies across the boundaries between basic blocks within a subroutine; this is *global code improvement*. As an example of the latter, an expression whose value is computed immediately before an `if` statement need not be recomputed within the code that follows the `else`. Likewise an expression that appears within the body of a loop need only be evaluated once if its value will not change in subsequent iterations. Some global improvements change the number of basic blocks and/or the arcs among them.

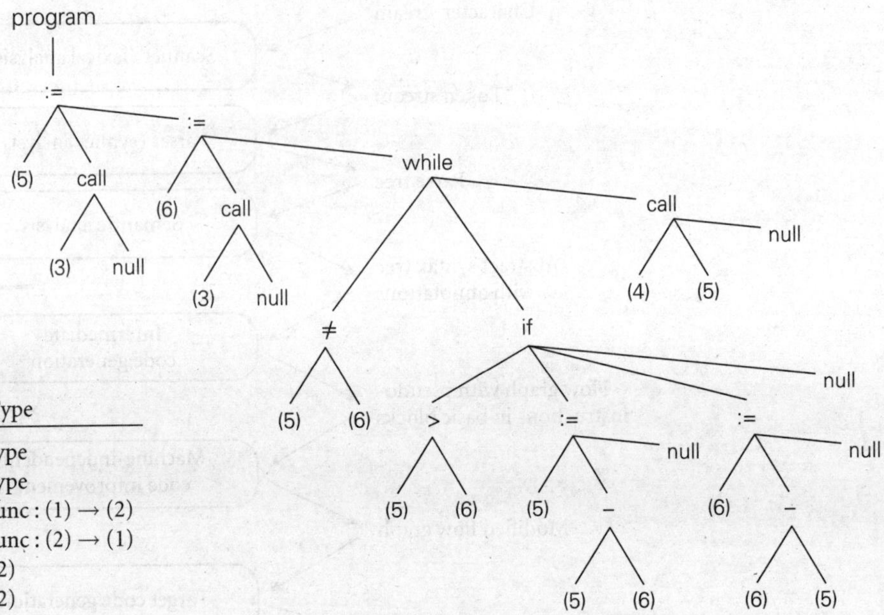

Index	Symbol	Type
1	`void`	type
2	`int`	type
3	`getint`	func : (1) → (2)
4	`putint`	func : (2) → (1)
5	`i`	(2)
6	`j`	(2)

Figure 15.2 **Syntax tree and symbol table for the GCD program.** The only difference from Figure 1.6 is the addition of explicit null nodes to indicate empty argument lists and to terminate statement lists.

It is worth noting that "global" code improvement typically considers only the current subroutine, not the program as a whole. Much recent research in compiler technology has been aimed at "truly global" techniques, known as *interprocedural code improvement.* Since programmers are generally unwilling to give up separate compilation (recompiling hundreds of thousands of lines of code is a very time-consuming operation), a practical interprocedural code improver must do much of its work at link time. One of the (many) challenges to be overcome is to develop a division of labor and an intermediate representation that allow the compiler to do as much work as possible during (separate) compilation, but leave enough of the details undecided that the link-time code improver is able to do its job.

Following machine-independent code improvement, the next phase of compilation is target code generation. This phase strings the basic blocks together into a linear program, translating each block into the instruction set of the target machine and generating branch instructions (or "fall-throughs") that correspond to the arcs of the control flow graph. The output of this phase differs from real assembly language primarily in its continued reliance on virtual registers. So long as the pseudoinstructions of the intermediate form are reasonably close to those of the target machine, this phase of compilation, though tedious, is more or less straightforward.

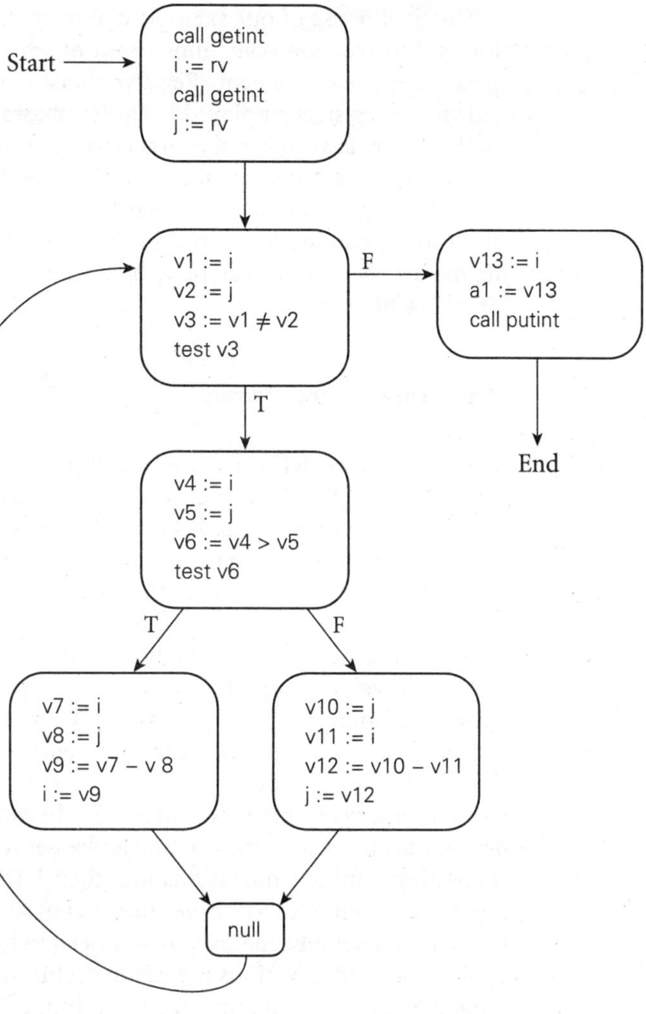

Figure 15.3 Control flow graph for the GCD program. Code within basic blocks is shown in the pseudo-assembly notation introduced in Sidebar 5.1, with a different virtual register (here named v1...v13) for every computed value. Registers a1 and rv are used to pass values to and from subroutines.

To reduce programmer effort and increase the ease with which a compiler can be ported to a new target machine, target code generators are sometimes generated automatically from a formal description of the machine. Automatically generated code generators all rely on some sort of pattern-matching algorithm to replace sequences of intermediate code instructions with equivalent sequences of target machine instructions. References to several such algorithms can be found in the Bibliographic Notes at the end of this chapter; details are beyond the scope of this book.

The final phase of our example compiler structure consists of register allocation and instruction scheduling, both of which can be thought of as machine-specific code improvement. Register allocation requires that we map the unlimited virtual registers employed in earlier phases onto the bounded set of architectural registers available in the target machine. If there aren't enough architectural registers to go around, we may need to generate additional loads and stores to multiplex a given architectural register among two or more virtual registers. Instruction scheduling (described in Sections C-5.5 and C-17.6) consists of reordering the instructions of each basic block in an attempt to fill the pipeline(s) of the target machine.

15.1.2 Phases and Passes

In Section 1.6 we defined a *pass* of compilation as a phase or sequence of phases that is serialized with respect to the rest of compilation: it does not start until previous phases have completed, and it finishes before any subsequent phases start. If desired, a pass may be written as a separate program, reading its input from a file and writing its output to a file. Two-pass compilers are particularly common. They may be divided between semantic analysis and intermediate code generation or between intermediate code generation and machine-independent code improvement. In either case, the first pass is commonly referred to as the "front end" and the second pass as the "back end."

Like most compilers, our example generates symbolic assembly language as its output (a few compilers, including those written by IBM for the Power family, generate binary machine code directly). The assembler (not shown in Figure 15.1) behaves as an extra pass, assigning addresses to fragments of data and code, and translating symbolic operations into their binary encodings. In most cases, the input to the compiler will have consisted of source code for a single compilation unit. After assembly, the output will need to be *linked* to other fragments of the application, and to various preexisting subroutine libraries. Some of the work of linking may be delayed until load time (immediately prior to program execution) or even until run time (during program execution). We will discuss assembly and linking in Sections 15.5 through 15.7.

15.2 Intermediate Forms

An *intermediate form* (IF) provides the connection between phases of machine-independent code improvement, and continues to represent the program during the various back-end phases.

IFs can be classified in terms of their *level*, or degree of machine dependence. High-level IFs are often based on trees or directed acyclic graphs (DAGs) that directly capture the hierarchical structure of modern programming languages.

A high-level IF facilitates certain kinds of machine-independent code improvement, incremental program updates (e.g., in a language-based editor), and direct interpretation (most interpreters employ a tree-based internal IF). Because the permissible structure of a tree can be described formally by a set of productions (as described in Section 4.6), manipulations of tree-based forms can be written as attribute grammars.

The most common medium-level IFs employ three-address instructions for a simple idealized machine, typically one with an unlimited number of registers. Often the instructions are embedded in a control flow graph. Since the typical instruction specifies two operands, an operator, and a destination, three-address instructions are sometimes called *quadruples.* Low-level IFs usually resemble the assembly language of some particular target machine, most often the physical machine on which the target code will execute.

EXAMPLE 15.3
Intermediate forms in Figure 15.1

Different compilers use different IFs. Many compilers use more than one IF internally, though in the common two-pass organization one of these is distinguished as "the" intermediate form by virtue of being the externally visible connection between the front end and the back end. In the example of Section 15.1.1, the syntax trees passed from semantic analysis to intermediate code generation constitute a high-level IF. Control flow graphs containing pseudo-assembly language (passed in and out of machine-independent code improvement) are a medium-level IF. The assembly language of the target machine (initially with virtual registers; later with architectural registers) serves as a low-level IF.

The distinction between "high-," "medium-," and "low-level" IFs is of course somewhat arbitrary: the plausible design space is very large, with a nearly continuous spectrum from abstract to machine-dependent. ■

Compilers that have back ends for several different target architectures tend to do as much work as possible on a high- or medium-level IF, so that the machine-independent parts of the code improver can be shared by different back ends. By contrast, some (but not all) compilers that generate code for a single architecture perform most code improvement on a comparatively low-level IF, closely modeled after the assembly language of the target machine.

In a multilanguage compiler family, an IF that is independent of both source language and target machine allows a software vendor who wishes to sell compilers for n languages on m machines to build just n front ends and m back ends, rather than $n \times m$ integrated compilers. Even in a single-language compiler family, a common, possibly language-dependent IF simplifies the task of porting to a new machine by isolating the code that needs to be changed. In a rich program development environment, there may be a variety of tools in addition to the passes of the compiler that understand and operate on the IF. Examples include editors, assemblers, linkers, debuggers, pretty-printers, and version-management software. In a language system capable of interprocedural (whole-program) code improvement, separately compiled modules and libraries may be compiled only to the IF, rather than the target language, leaving the final stages of compilation to the linker.

To be stored in a file, an IF requires a linear representation. Sequences of three-address instructions are naturally linear. Tree-based IFs can be linearized via ordered traversal. Structures like control flow graphs can be linearized by replacing pointers with indices relative to the beginning of the file.

15.2.1 GIMPLE and RTL

Many readers will be familiar with the gcc compilers. Distributed as open source by the Free Software Foundation, gcc is used very widely in both academia and industry. The standard distribution includes front ends for C, C++, Objective-C, Ada, Fortran, Go, and Java. Front ends for additional languages, including Cobol, Modula-2 and 3, Pascal and PL/I, are separately available. The C compiler is the original, and the one most widely used (gcc originally stood for "GNU C compiler"). There are back ends for dozens of processor architectures, including all commercially significant options. There are also GNU implementations, not based on gcc, for some two dozen additional languages.

IN MORE DEPTH

Gcc has three main IFs. Most of the (language-specific) front ends employ, internally, some variant of a high-level syntax tree form known as GENERIC. Early phases of machine-independent code improvement use a somewhat lower-level tree form known as GIMPLE (still a high-level IF). Later phases use a linear form known as RTL (register transfer language). RTL is a medium-level IF, but a bit higher level than most: it overlays a control flow graph on of a sequence of pseudoinstructions. RTL was, for many years, the principal IF for gcc. GIMPLE was introduced in 2005 as a more suitable form for machine-independent code improvement. We consider GIMPLE and RTL in more detail on the companion site.

15.2.2 Stack-Based Intermediate Forms

In situations where simplicity and brevity are paramount, designers often turn to stack-based languages. Operations in a such a language pop arguments from—and push results to—a common implicit stack. The lack of named operands means that a stack-based language can be very compact. In certain HP calculators (Exercise 4.7), stack-based expression evaluation serves to minimize the number of keystrokes required to enter equations. For embedded devices and printers, stack-based evaluation in Forth and Postscript serves to reduce memory and bandwidth requirements, respectively (see Sidebar 15.1).

Medium-level stack-based intermediate languages are similarly attractive when passing code from a compiler to an interpreter or virtual machine. Forty years ago, P-code (Example 1.15) made it easy to port Pascal to new machines, and helped to speed the language's adoption. Today, the compactness of Java bytecode helps minimize the download time for applets. Common Intermediate Language (CIL), the analogue of Java bytecode for .NET and other implementations of the Common Language Infrastructure (CLI), is similarly compact and machine independent. As of 2015, .NET runs only on the x86 and ARM, but the open-source Mono CLI is available for all the major instruction sets. We will consider Java bytecode and CIL in some detail in Chapter 16.

Unfortunately, stack-based IF is not well suited to many code improvement techniques: it limits the ability to eliminate redundancy or improve pipeline performance by reordering calculations. For this reason, languages like Java bytecode and CIL tend to be used mainly as an external format, not as a representation for code *within* a compiler.

EXAMPLE 15.4
Computing Heron's formula

In many cases, stack-based code for an expression will occupy fewer bytes, but specify more instructions, than corresponding three-address code. As a concrete example, consider Heron's formula to compute the area of a triangle given the lengths of its sides, a, b, and c:

$$A = \sqrt{s(s-a)(s-b)(s-c)}, \quad \text{where} \quad s = \frac{a+b+c}{2}$$

Figure 15.4 compares bytecode and three-address versions of this formula. Each line represents a single instruction. If we assume that a, b, c, and s are all among the first few local variables of the current subroutine, both the Java Virtual Machine (JVM) and the CLI will be able to move them to or from the stack with single-byte instructions. Consequently, the second-to-last instruction in the left column is the only one that needs more than a single byte (it takes three: one for

DESIGN & IMPLEMENTATION

15.1 Postscript

One of the most pervasive uses of stack-based languages today occurs in document preparation. Many document compilers (TEX, Microsoft Word, etc.) generate Postscript or the related Portable Document Format (PDF) as their target language. (Most document compilers employ some special-purpose intermediate language as well, and have multiple back ends, so they can generate multiple target languages.)

Postscript is stack-based. It is portable, compact, and easy to generate. It is also written in ASCII, so it can be read (albeit with some difficulty) by human beings. Postscript interpreters are embedded in most professional-quality printers. Issues of code improvement are relatively unimportant: most of the time required for printing is consumed by network delays, mechanical paper transport, and data manipulations embedded in (optimized) library routines; interpretation time is seldom a bottleneck. Compactness on the other hand is crucial, because it contributes to network delays.

```
push a        r2 := a
push b        r3 := b
push c        r4 := c
add           r1 := r2 + r3
add           r1 := r1 + r4
push 2        r1 := r1 / 2      -- s
divide
pop s
push s
push s        r2 := r1 – r2     -- s – a
push a
subtract
push s        r3 := r1 – r3     -- s – b
push b
subtract
push s        r4 := r1 – r4     -- s – c
push c
subtract
multiply      r3 := r3 × r4
multiply      r2 := r2 × r3
multiply      r1 := r1 × r2
push sqrt     call sqrt
call
```

Figure 15.4 Stack-based versus three-address IF. Shown are two versions of code to compute the area of a triangle using Heron's formula. At left is a stylized version of Java bytecode or CLI Common Intermediate Language. At right is corresponding pseudo-assembler for a machine with three-address instructions. The bytecode requires a larger number of instructions, but occupies less space.

the push operation and two to specify the sqrt routine). This gives us a total of 23 instructions in 25 bytes.

By contrast, three-address code for the same formula keeps a, b, c, and s in registers, and requires only 13 instructions. Unfortunately, in typical notation each instruction but the last will be four bytes in length (the last will be eight), and our 13 instructions will occupy 56 bytes. ■

15.3 Code Generation

EXAMPLE 15.5
Simpler compiler structure

The back-end structure of Figure 15.1 is too complex to present in any detail in a single chapter. To limit the scope of our discussion, we will content ourselves in this chapter with producing correct but naive code. This choice will allow us to consider a significantly simpler middle and back end. Starting with the structure of Figure 15.1, we drop the machine-independent code improver and then merge intermediate and target code generation into a single phase. This merged phase

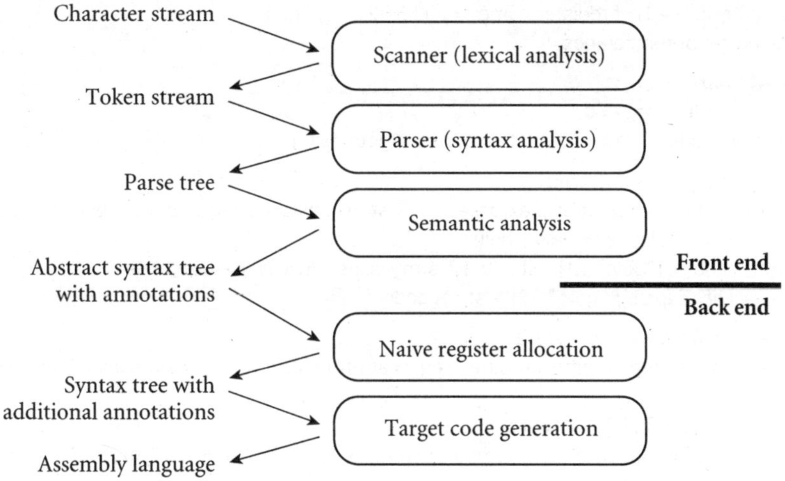

Figure 15.5 A simpler, nonoptimizing compiler structure, assumed in Section 15.3. The target code generation phase closely resembles the intermediate code generation phase of Figure 15.1.

generates pure, linear assembly language; because we are not performing code improvements that alter the program's control flow, there is no need to represent that flow explicitly in a control flow graph. We also adopt a much simpler register allocation algorithm, which can operate directly on the syntax tree prior to code generation, eliminating the need for virtual registers and the subsequent mapping onto architectural registers. Finally, we drop instruction scheduling. The resulting compiler structure appears in Figure 15.5. Its code generation phase closely resembles the intermediate code generation of Figure 15.1. ■

15.3.1 An Attribute Grammar Example

Like semantic analysis, intermediate code generation can be formalized in terms of an attribute grammar, though it is most commonly implemented via hand-written ad hoc traversal of a syntax tree. We present an attribute grammar here for the sake of clarity.

In Figure 1.7, we presented naive x86 assembly language for the GCD program. We will use our attribute grammar example to generate a similar version here, but for a RISC-like machine, and in pseudo-assembly notation. Because this notation is now meant to represent target code, rather than medium- or low-level intermediate code, we will assume a fixed, limited register set reminiscent of real machines. We will reserve several registers (`a1`, `a2`, `sp`, `rv`) for special purposes; others (`r1` .. `r`k) will be available for temporary values and expression evaluation.

EXAMPLE 15.6
An attribute grammar for code generation

Figure 15.6 contains a fragment of our attribute grammar. To save space, we have shown only those productions that actually appear in Figure 15.2. As in

```
reg_names : array [0..k−1] of register_name := ["r1", "r2", . . . , "rk"]
    -- ordered set of temporaries

program ⟶ stmt
    ▷ stmt.next_free_reg := 0
    ▷ program.code := ["main:"] + stmt.code + ["goto exit"]

while : stmt1 ⟶ expr stmt2 stmt3
    ▷ expr.next_free_reg := stmt2.next_free_reg := stmt3.next_free_reg := stmt1.next_free_reg
    ▷ L1 := new_label(); L2 := new_label()
      stmt1.code := ["goto" L1] + [L2 ":"] + stmt2.code + [L1 ":"] + expr.code
          + ["if" expr.reg "goto" L2] + stmt3.code

if : stmt1 ⟶ expr stmt2 stmt3 stmt4
    ▷ expr.next_free_reg := stmt2.next_free_reg := stmt3.next_free_reg := stmt4.next_free_reg :=
          stmt1.next_free_reg
    ▷ L1 := new_label(); L2 := new_label()
      stmt1.code := expr.code + ["if" expr.reg "goto" L1] + stmt3.code + ["goto" L2]
          + [L1 ":"] + stmt2.code + [L2 ":"] + stmt4.code

assign : stmt1 ⟶ id expr stmt2
    ▷ expr.next_free_reg := stmt2.next_free_reg := stmt1.next_free_reg
    ▷ stmt1.code := expr.code + [id.stp→name ":=" expr.reg] + stmt2.code

read : stmt1 ⟶ id1 id2 stmt2
    ▷ stmt1.code := ["a1 := &" id1.stp→name]      -- file
          + ["call" if id2.stp→type = int then "readint" else . . . ]
          + [id2.stp→name ":= rv"] + stmt2.code

write : stmt1 ⟶ id expr stmt2
    ▷ expr.next_free_reg := stmt2.next_free_reg := stmt1.next_free_reg
    ▷ stmt1.code := ["a1 := &" id.stp→name]       -- file
          + ["a2 :=" expr.reg]                      -- value
          + ["call" if id.stp→type = int then "writeint" else . . . ] + stmt2.code

writeln : stmt1 ⟶ id stmt2
    ▷ stmt1.code := ["a1 := &" id.stp→name] + ["call writeln"] + stmt2.code

null : stmt ⟶ ϵ
    ▷ stmt.code := null

'<>' : expr1 ⟶ expr2 expr3
    ▷ handle_op(expr1, expr2, expr3, "≠")

'>' : expr1 ⟶ expr2 expr3
    ▷ handle_op(expr1, expr2, expr3, ">")

'−' : expr1 ⟶ expr2 expr3
    ▷ handle_op(expr1, expr2, expr3, "−")

id : expr ⟶ ϵ
    ▷ expr.reg := reg_names[expr.next_free_reg mod k]
    ▷ expr.code := [expr.reg ":=" expr.stp→name]
```

Figure 15.6 **Attribute grammar to generate code from a syntax tree.** Square brackets delimit individual target instructions. Juxtaposition indicates concatenation within instructions; the '+' operator indicates concatenation of instruction lists. The handle_op macro is used in three of the attribute rules. *(continued)*

```
macro handle_op(ref result, L_operand, R_operand, op : syntax_tree_node)
    result.reg := L_operand.reg
    L_operand.next_free_reg := result.next_free_reg
    R_operand.next_free_reg := result.next_free_reg + 1
    if R_operand.next_free_reg < k
        spill_code := restore_code := null
    else
        spill_code := ["*sp :=" reg_names[R_operand.next_free_reg mod k]]
            + ["sp := sp − 4"]
        restore_code := ["sp := sp + 4"]
            + [reg_names[R_operand.next_free_reg mod k] ":= *sp"]
    result.code := L_operand.code + spill_code + R_operand.code
        + [result.reg ":=" L_operand.reg op R_operand.reg] + restore_code
```

Figure 15.6 *(continued)*

Chapter 4, notation like *while : stmt* on the left-hand side of a production indicates that a *while* node in the syntax tree is one of several kinds of *stmt* node; it may serve as the *stmt* in the right-hand side of its parent production. In our attribute grammar fragment, *program*, *expr*, and *stmt* all have a synthesized attribute code that contains a sequence of instructions. *Program* has an inherited attribute name of type string, obtained from the compiler command line. *Id* has a synthesized attribute stp that points to the symbol table entry for the identifier. *Expr* has a synthesized attribute reg that indicates the register that will hold the value of the computed expression at run time. *Expr* and *stmt* have an inherited attribute next_free_reg that indicates the next register (in an ordered set of temporaries) that is available for use (i.e., that will hold no useful value at run time) immediately before evaluation of a given expression or statement. (For simplicity, we will be managing registers as if they were a stack; more on this in Section 15.3.2.)

Because we use a symbol table in our example, and because symbol tables lie outside the formal attribute grammar framework, we must augment our attribute grammar with some extra code for storage management. Specifically, prior to evaluating the attribute rules of Figure 15.6, we must traverse the symbol table in order to calculate stack-frame offsets for local variables and parameters (two of which—`i` and `j`—occur in the GCD program) and in order to generate assembler directives to allocate space for global variables (of which our program has none). Storage allocation and other assembler directives will be discussed in more detail in Section 15.5.

15.3.2 Register Allocation

EXAMPLE 15.7
Stack-based register allocation

Evaluation of the rules of the attribute grammar itself consists of two main tasks. In each subtree we first determine the registers that will be used to hold various quantities at run time; then we generate code. Our naive register allocation strategy uses the next_free_reg inherited attribute to manage registers r1. . . r*k* as an expression evaluation stack. To calculate the value of (a + b) × (c − (d / e)), for example, we would generate the following:

```
r1 := a           -- push a
r2 := b           -- push b
r1 := r1 + r2     -- add
r2 := c           -- push c
r3 := d           -- push d
r4 := e           -- push e
r3 := r3 / r4     -- divide
r2 := r2 − r3     -- subtract
r1 := r1 × r2     -- multiply
```

Allocation of the next register on the "stack" occurs in the production *id : expr* $\longrightarrow \epsilon$, where we use expr.next_free_reg to index into reg_names, the array of temporary register names, and in macro handle_op, where we increment next_free_reg to make this register unavailable during evaluation of the right-hand operand. There is no need to "pop" the "register stack" explicitly; this happens automatically when the attribute evaluator returns to a parent node and uses the parent's (unmodified) next_free_reg attribute. In our example grammar, left-hand operands are the only constructs that tie up a register during the evaluation of anything else. In a more complete grammar, other long-term uses of registers would probably occur in constructs like `for` loops (for the step size, index, and bound).

In a particularly complicated fragment of code it is possible to run out of architectural registers. In this case we must *spill* one or more registers to memory. Our naive register allocator pushes a register onto the program's subroutine call stack, reuses the register for another purpose, and then pops the saved value back into the register before it is needed again. In effect, architectural registers hold the top *k* elements of an expression evaluation stack of effectively unlimited size. ■

It should be emphasized that our register allocation algorithm, while correct, makes very poor use of machine resources. We have made no attempt to reorganize expressions to minimize the number of registers used, or to keep commonly used variables in registers over extended periods of time (avoiding loads and stores). If we were generating medium-level intermediate code, instead of target code, we would employ virtual registers, rather than architectural ones, and would allocate a new one every time we needed it, never reusing one to hold a different value. Mapping of virtual registers to architectural registers would occur much later in the compilation process.

EXAMPLE 15.8
GCD program target code

Target code for the GCD program appears in Figure 15.7. The first few lines are generated during symbol table traversal, prior to attribute evaluation. Attribute program.name might be passed to the assembler, to tell it the name of the file into which to place the runnable program. A real compiler would probably also generate assembler directives to embed symbol-table information in the target program. As in Figure 1.7, the quality of our code is very poor. We will investigate

```
     -- first few lines generated during symbol table traversal
     .data          -- begin static data
i:   .word 0        -- reserve one word to hold i
j:   .word 0        -- reserve one word to hold j
     .text          -- begin text (code)
     -- remaining lines accumulated into program.code
main:
     a1 := &input   -- "input" and "output" are file control blocks
                    -- located in a library, to be found by the linker
     call readint   -- "readint", "writeint", and "writeln" are library subroutines
     i := rv
     a1 := &input
     call readint
     j := rv
     goto L1
L2:  r1 := i        -- body of while loop
     r2 := j
     r1 := r1 > r2
     if r1 goto L3
     r1 := j        -- "else" part
     r2 := i
     r1 := r1 − r2
     j := r1
     goto L4
L3:  r1 := i        -- "then" part
     r2 := j
     r1 := r1 − r2
     i := r1
L4:
L1:  r1 := i        -- test terminating condition
     r2 := j
     r1 := r1 ≠ r2
     if r1 goto L2
     a1 := &output
     r1 := i
     a2 := r1
     call writeint
     a1 := &output
     call writeln
     goto exit      -- return to operating system
```

Figure 15.7 Target code for the GCD program, generated from the syntax tree of Figure 15.2, using the attribute grammar of Figure 15.6.

techniques to improve it in Chapter 17. In the remaining sections of the current chapter we will consider assembly and linking. ■

✓ CHECK YOUR UNDERSTANDING

1. What is a *code generator generator*? Why might it be useful?
2. What is a *basic block*? A *control flow graph*?
3. What are *virtual registers*? What purpose do they serve?
4. What is the difference between *local* and *global* code improvement?
5. What is *register spilling*?
6. Explain what is meant by the "level" of an intermediate form (IF). What are the comparative advantages and disadvantages of high-, medium-, and low-level IFs?
7. What is the IF most commonly used in Ada compilers?
8. Name two advantages of a stack-based IF. Name one disadvantage.
9. Explain the rationale for basing a family of compilers (several languages, several target machines) on a single IF.
10. Why might a compiler employ more than one IF?
11. Outline some of the major design alternatives for back-end compiler organization and structure.
12. What is sometimes called the "middle end" of a compiler?
13. Why is management of a limited set of physical registers usually deferred until late in the compilation process?

15.4 Address Space Organization

Assemblers, linkers, and loaders typically operate on a pair of related file formats: *relocatable* object code and *executable* object code. Relocatable object code is acceptable as input to a linker; multiple files in this format can be combined to create an executable program. Executable object code is acceptable as input to a loader: it can be brought into memory and run. A relocatable object file includes the following descriptive information:

Import table: Identifies instructions that refer to named locations whose addresses are unknown, but are presumed to lie in other files yet to be linked to this one.

Relocation table: Identifies instructions that refer to locations within the current file, but that must be modified at link time to reflect the offset of the current file within the final, executable program.

Export table: Lists the names and addresses of locations in the current file that may be referred to in other files.

Imported and exported names are known as *external symbols.*

An executable object file is distinguished by the fact that it contains no references to external symbols (at least if statically linked—more on this below). It also defines a starting address for execution. An executable file may or may not be relocatable, depending on whether it contains the tables above.

Details of object file structure vary from one operating system to another. Typically, however, an object file is divided into several sections, each of which is handled differently by the linker, loader, or operating system. The first section includes the import, export, and relocation tables, together with an indication of how much space will be required by the program for noninitialized static data. Other sections commonly include code (instructions), read-only data (constants, jump tables for `case` statements, etc.), initialized but writable static data, and symbol table and layout information saved by the compiler. The initial descriptive section is used by the linker and loader. The symbol table section is used by debuggers and performance profilers (Sections 16.3.2 and 16.3.3). Neither of these tables is usually brought into memory at run time; neither is needed by most running programs (an exception occurs in the case of programs that employ *reflection* mechanisms [Section 16.3.1] to examine their own type structure).

In its runnable (loaded) form, a program is typically organized into several *segments.* On some machines (e.g., the 80286 or PA-RISC), segments were visible to the assembly language programmer, and could be named explicitly in instructions. More commonly on modern machines, segments are simply subsets of the address space that the operating system manages in different ways. Some of them—code, constants, and initialized data in particular—correspond to sections of the object file. Code and constants are usually read-only, and are often combined in a single segment; the operating system arranges to receive an interrupt if the program attempts to modify them. (In response to such an interrupt it will most likely print an error message and terminate the program.) Initialized data are writable. At load time, the operating system either reads code, constants, and initialized data from disk, or arranges to read them in at run time, in response to "invalid access" (page fault) interrupts or dynamic linking requests.

In addition to code, constants, and initialized data, the typical running program has several additional segments:

Uninitialized data: May be allocated at load time or on demand in response to page faults. Usually zero-filled, both to provide repeatable symptoms for programs that erroneously read data they have not yet written, and to enhance security on multiuser systems, by preventing a program from reading the contents of pages written by previous users.

Stack: May be allocated in some fixed amount at load time. More commonly, is given a small initial size, and is then extended automatically by the operating system in response to (faulting) accesses beyond the current segment end.

Heap: Like stack, may be allocated in some fixed amount at load time. More commonly, is given a small initial size, and is then extended in response to explicit requests (via system call) from heap-management library routines.

Files: In many systems, library routines allow a program to *map* a file into memory. The map routine interacts with the operating system to create a new segment for the file, and returns the address of the beginning of the segment. The contents of the segment are usually fetched from disk on demand, in response to page faults.

Dynamic libraries: Modern operating systems typically arrange for most programs to share a single copy of the code for popular libraries (Section C-15.7). From the point of view of an individual process, each such library tends to occupy a pair of segments: one for the shared code, one for *linkage information* and for a private copy of any writable data the library may need.

EXAMPLE 15.9
Linux address space layout

The layout of these segments for a contemporary 32-bit Linux system on the x86 appears in Figure 15.8. Relative placements and addresses may be different for other operating systems and machines. ■

15.5 Assembly

Some compilers translate source files directly into object files acceptable to the linker. More commonly, they generate assembly language that must subsequently be processed by an assembler to create an object file.

In our examples we have consistently employed a symbolic (textual) notation for code. Within a compiler, the representation would not be textual, but it would still be symbolic, most likely consisting of records and linked lists. To translate this symbolic representation into executable code, we must

1. Replace opcodes and operands with their machine language encodings.
2. Replace uses of symbolic names with actual addresses.

These are the principal tasks of an assembler.

In the early days of computing, most programmers wrote in assembly language. To simplify the more tedious and repetitive aspects of assembly programming, assemblers often provided extensive macro expansion facilities. With the ubiquity of modern high-level languages, such programmer-centric features have largely disappeared. Almost all assembly language programs today are written by compilers.

EXAMPLE 15.10
Assembly as a final compiler pass

When passing assembly language directly from the compiler to the assembler, it makes sense to use some internal (records and linked lists) representation. At the

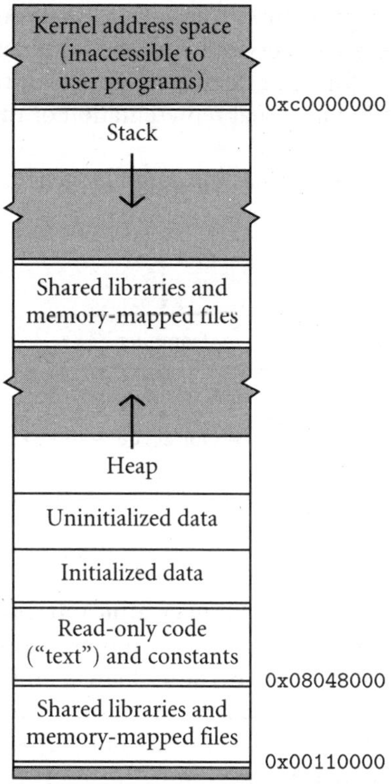

In early Unix systems with very limited memory, the stack grew downward from the bottom of the text segment; the number 0x08048000 is a legacy of these systems. The sections marked "Shared libraries and memory-mapped files" typically comprise multiple segments with varying permissions and addresses. (Modern Linux systems randomize the choice of addresses to discourage malware.) The top quarter of the address space belongs to the kernel. Just over 1 MB of space is left unmapped at the bottom of the address space to help catch program bugs in which small integer values are accidentally used as pointers.

Figure 15.8 Layout of 32-bit process address space in x86 Linux (not to scale). Double lines separate regions with potentially different access permissions.

same time, we must provide a textual front end to accommodate the occasional need for human input:

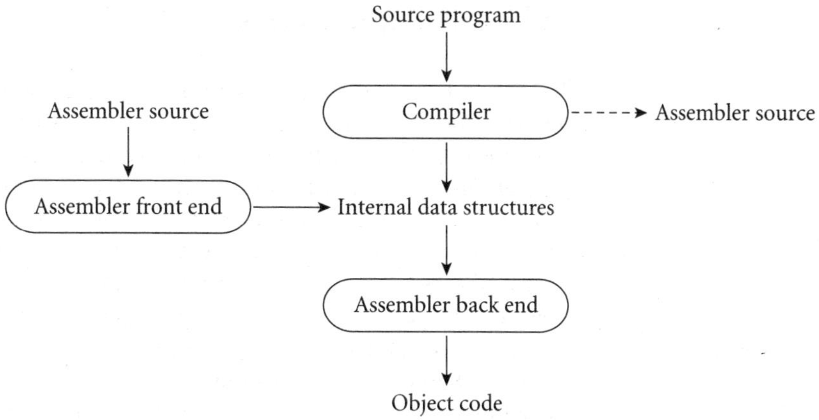

The assembler front end simply translates textual source into internal symbolic form. By sharing the assembler back end, the compiler and assembler front end avoid duplication of effort. For debugging purposes, the compiler will generally have an option to dump a textual representation of the code it passes to the assembler. ■

EXAMPLE 15.11
Direct generation of object code

An alternative organization has the compiler generate object code directly:

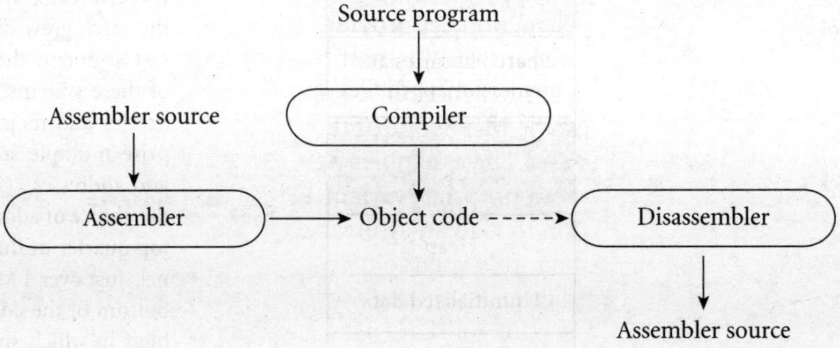

This organization gives the compiler a bit more flexibility: operations normally performed by an assembler (e.g., assignment of addresses to variables) can be performed earlier if desired. Because there is no separate assembly pass, the overall translation to object code may be slightly faster. The stand-alone assembler can be relatively simple. If it is used only for small, special-purpose code fragments, it probably doesn't need to perform instruction scheduling or other machine-specific code improvement. Using a disassembler instead of an assembly language dump from the compiler ensures that what the programmer sees corresponds precisely to what is in the object file. If the compiler uses a fancier assembler as a back end, then any program modifications effected by the assembler will not be visible in the assembly language dumped by the compiler. ■

15.5.1 Emitting Instructions

The most basic task of the assembler is to translate symbolic representations of instructions into binary form. In some assemblers this is an entirely straightforward task, because there is a one-to-one correspondence between mnemonic operations and instruction op-codes. Many assemblers, however, make minor changes to their input in order to improve performance or to extend the instruction set in ways that make the assembly language easier for human beings to read. The GNU assembler, `gas`, is among the more conservative, but even it takes a few liberties.

EXAMPLE 15.12
Compressing `nop`s

For example, some compilers generate `nop` instructions to cache-align certain basic blocks (e.g., function prologues). To reduce the number of cycles these consume, `gas` will combine multiple consecutive `nop`s into multibyte instructions that have no effect. (On the x86, there are 2-, 4-, and 7-byte variants of the `lea` instruction that can be used to move a register into itself.) ■

EXAMPLE 15.13
Relative and absolute branches

For jumps to nearby addresses, `gas` uses an instruction variant that specifies an offset from the `pc`. For jumps to distant addresses (or to addresses not known until link time), it uses a longer variant that specifies an absolute address. A few x86 instructions (not typically generated by modern compilers) don't have the longer variant. For these, some assemblers will reverse the sense of the conditional test to hop over an unconditional jump. `Gas` simply fails to handle them. ■

EXAMPLE 15.14
Pseudoinstructions

At the more aggressive end of the spectrum, SGI's assembler for the MIPS instruction set provides a large number of *pseudoinstructions* that translate into different real instructions depending on their arguments, or that correspond to multi-instruction sequences. For example, there are two integer `add` instructions on the MIPS: one of them adds two registers; the other adds a register and a constant. The assembler provides a single pseudoinstruction, which it translates into the appropriate variant. In a similar vein, the assembler provides a pseudoinstruction to load an arbitrary constant into a register. Since all instructions are 32 bits long, this pseudoinstruction must be translated into a pair of real instructions when the constant won't fit in 16 bits. Some pseudoinstructions may generate even longer sequences. Integer division can take as many as 11 real instructions, to check for errors and to move the quotient from a temporary location into the desired register. ■

In effect, the SGI assembler implements a "cleaned-up" variant of the real machine. In addition to providing pseudoinstructions, it reorganizes instructions to hide the existence of delayed branches (Section C-5.5.1) and to improve the expected performance of the processor pipeline. This reorganization constitutes a final pass of *instruction scheduling* (Sections C-5.5.1 and C-17.6). Though the job could be handled by the compiler, the existence of pseudoinstructions like the integer division example argues strongly for doing it in the assembler. In addition to having two branch delays that might be filled by neighboring instructions, the expanded division sequence can be used as a source of instructions to fill nearby branch, load, or functional unit delays.

EXAMPLE 15.15
Assembler directives

In addition to translating from symbolic to binary instruction representations, most assemblers respond to a variety of *directives*. `Gas` provides more than 100 of these. A few examples follow.

Segment switching: The `.text` directive indicates that subsequent instructions and data should be placed in the code (text) segment. The `.data` directive indicates that subsequent instructions and data should be placed in the initialized data segment. (It is possible, though uncommon, to put instructions in the data segment, or data in the code segment.) The `.space` *n* directive indicates that *n* bytes of space should be reserved in the uninitialized data segment. (This latter directive is usually preceded by a label.)

Data generation: The `.byte`, `.hword`, `.word`, `.float`, and `.double` directives each take a sequence of arguments, which they place in successive locations in the current segment of the output program. They differ in the types of operands. The related `.ascii` directive takes a single character string as argument, which it places in consecutive bytes.

Symbol identification: The `.globl` *name* directive indicates that *name* should be entered into the table of exported symbols.

Alignment: The `.align` *n* directive causes the subsequent output to be aligned at an address evenly divisible by 2^n.

15.5.2 Assigning Addresses to Names

Like compilers, assemblers commonly work in several phases. If the input is textual, an initial phase scans and parses the input, and builds an internal representation. In the most common organization there are two additional phases. The first identifies all internal and external (imported) symbols, assigning locations to the internal ones. This phase is complicated by the fact that the length of some instructions (on a CISC machine) or the number of real instructions produced by a pseudoinstruction (on a RISC machine) may depend on the number of significant bits in an address. Given values for symbols, the final phase produces object code.

Within the object file, any symbol mentioned in a `.globl` directive must appear in the table of exported symbols, with an entry that indicates the symbol's address. Any symbol referred to in a directive or an instruction, but not defined in the input program, must appear in the table of imported symbols, with an entry that identifies all places in the code at which such references occur. Finally, any instruction or datum whose value depends on the placement of the current file within the address space of a running program must be listed in the relocation table.

EXAMPLE 15.16
Encoding of addresses in object files

Historically, assemblers distinguished between *absolute* and *relocatable* words in an object file. Absolute words were known at assembly time; they did not need to be changed by the linker. Examples include constants and register–register instructions. A relocatable word, in contrast, needed to be modified by adding to it the address within the final program of the code or data segment of the object file in which it appeared. A CISC jump instruction, for example, might consist of a 1-byte `jmp` opcode followed by a 4-byte target address. For a local target, the address bytes in the object file would contain the symbol's offset within the file. The linker would finalize the address by adding the address of the file's code segment in the final version of the program.

On modern machines, this single form of relocation no longer suffices. Addresses are encoded into instructions in many different ways, and these encodings must be reflected in the relocation table and the import table. On a 32-bit ARM processor, for example, an unconditional branch (`b`) instruction has a 24-bit offset field. The processor left-shifts this field by two bits, sign-extends it, and then adds it to the address of the branch instruction itself to obtain the target address.[1]

1 The size of the offset implies that branches on ARM are limited to jumps of $\leq$ 32 MB in either direction. If the linker discovers that a target is farther away than that, it must generate "veneer" code that loads the target address into `r12` (which is reserved for this purpose) and then performs and indirect branch.

To relocate such an instruction, the linker must add the address of the target code segment and the offset within it of the target instruction, subtract the address of the current code segment and the offset within it of the branch instruction, perform a two-bit right arithmetic shift, and truncate the result to 24 bits. In a similar vein, a 32-bit load on ARM requires a two-instruction sequence analogous to that of Example 15.14; if the loaded quantity is relocatable, the linker must recalculate the 16-bit operands of both instructions. Modern assemblers and object file formats reflect this diversity of relocation modes. ■

15.6 Linking

Most language implementations—certainly all that are intended for the construction of large programs—support separate compilation: fragments of the program can be compiled and assembled more or less independently. After compilation, these fragments (known as *compilation units*) are "glued together" by a *linker*. In many languages and environments, the programmer explicitly divides the program into modules or files, each of which is separately compiled. More integrated environments may abandon the notion of a file in favor of a database of subroutines, each of which is separately compiled.

The task of a linker is to join together compilation units. A *static linker* does its work prior to program execution, producing an executable object file. A *dynamic linker* (described in Section C-15.7) does its work after the (first part of the) program has been brought into memory for execution.

Each to-be-linked compilation unit must be a relocatable object file. Typically, some files will have been produced by compiling fragments of the application being constructed, while others will be preexisting library packages needed by the application. Since most programs make use of libraries, even a "one-file" application typically needs to be linked.

Linking involves two subtasks: relocation and the resolution of external references. Some authors refer to relocation as *loading*, and call the entire "joining together" process "link-loading." Other authors (including the current one) use "loading" to refer to the process of bringing an executable object file into memory for execution. On very simple machines, or on machines with very simple operating systems, loading entails relocation. More commonly, the operating system uses virtual memory to give every program the impression that it starts at some standard address. In many systems loading also entails a certain amount of linking (Section C-15.7).

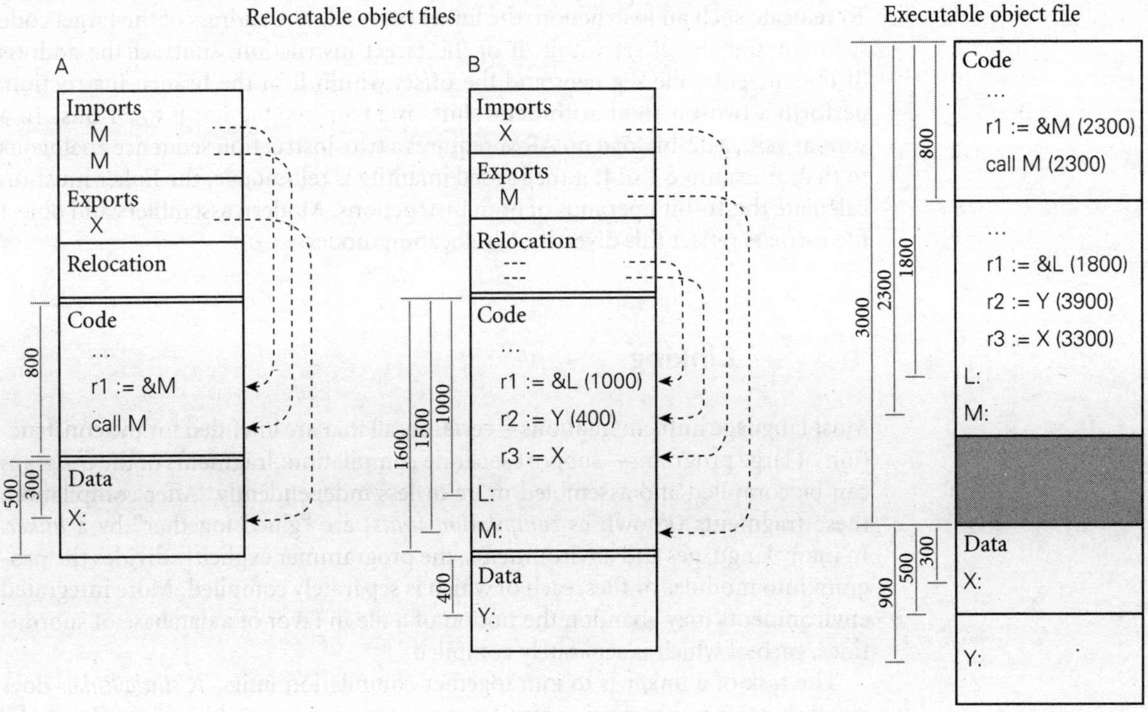

Figure 15.9 **Linking relocatable object files** A **and** B **to make an executable object file.** For simplicity of presentation, A's code section has been placed at offset 0, with B's code section immediately after, at offset 800 (addresses increase down the page). To allow the operating system to establish different protections for the code and data segments, A's data section has been placed at the next page boundary (offset 3000), with B's data section immediately after (offset 3500). External references to M and X have been set to use the appropriate addresses. Internal references to L and Y have been updated by adding in the starting addresses of B's code and data sections, respectively.

15.6.1 Relocation and Name Resolution

Each relocatable object file contains the information required for linking: the import, export, and relocation tables. A static linker uses this information in a two-phase process analogous to that described for assemblers in Section 15.5. In the first phase, the linker gathers all of the compilation units together, chooses an order for them in memory, and notes the address at which each will consequently lie. In the second phase, the linker processes each unit, replacing unresolved external references with appropriate addresses, and modifying instructions that need to be relocated to reflect the addresses of their units. These phases are illustrated pictorially in Figure 15.9. Addresses and offsets are assumed to be written in hexadecimal notation, with a page size of 4K (1000_{16}) bytes.

EXAMPLE 15.17
Static linking

Libraries present a bit of a challenge. Many consist of hundreds of separately compiled program fragments, most of which will not be needed by any particular application. Rather than link the entire library into every application, the linker needs to search the library to identify the fragments that are referenced from the main program. If these refer to additional fragments, then those must be included also, recursively. Many systems support a special library format for relocatable object files. A library in this format may contain an arbitrary number of code and data sections, together with an index that maps symbol names to the sections in which they appear.

15.6.2 Type Checking

Within a compilation unit, the compiler enforces static semantic rules. Across the boundaries between units, it uses module headers to enforce the rules pertaining to external references. In effect, the header for module *M* makes a set of promises regarding *M*'s interface to its users. When compiling the body of *M*, the compiler ensures that those promises are kept. Imagine what could happen, however, if we compiled the body of *M*, and then changed the numbers and types of parameters for some of the subroutines in its header file before compiling some user module *U*. If both compilations succeed, then *M* and *U* will have very different notions of how to interpret the parameters passed between them; while they may still link together, chaos is likely to ensue at run time. To prevent this sort of problem, we must ensure whenever *M* and *U* are linked together that both were compiled using the same version of *M*'s header.

In most module-based languages, the following technique suffices. When compiling the body of module *M* we create a dummy symbol whose name uniquely characterizes the contents of *M*'s header. When compiling the body of *U* we create a reference to the dummy symbol. An attempt to link *M* and *U* together will succeed only if they agree on the name of the symbol.

EXAMPLE 15.18
Checksumming headers for consistency

One way to create the symbol name that characterizes *M* is to use a textual representation of the time of the most recent modification of *M*'s header. Because files may be moved across machines, however (e.g., to deliver source files to geographically distributed customers), modification times are problematic: clocks on different machines may be poorly synchronized, and file copy operations often

DESIGN & IMPLEMENTATION

15.2 Type checking for separate compilation

The encoding of type information in symbol names works well in C++, but is too strict for use in C: it would outlaw programming tricks that, while questionable, are permitted by the language definition. Symbol-name encoding is facilitated in C++ by the use of structural equivalence for types. In principle, one could use it in a language with name equivalence, but given that such languages generally have well-structured modules, it is simpler just to use a checksum of the header.

change the modification time. A better candidate is a *checksum* of the header file: essentially the output of a hash function that uses the entire text of the file as key. It is possible in theory for two different but valid files to have the same checksum, but with a good choice of hash function the odds of this error are exceedingly small. ■

The checksum strategy does require that we know when we're using a module header. Unfortunately, as described in Section C-3.8, we don't know this in C and C++: headers in these languages are simply a programming convention, supported by the textual inclusion mechanism of the language's preprocessor. Most implementations of C do not enforce consistency of interfaces at link time; instead, programmers rely on configuration management tools (e.g., Unix's `make`) to recompile files when necessary. Such tools are typically driven by file modification times.

Most implementations of C++ adopt a different approach, sometimes called *name mangling*. The name of each imported or exported symbol in an object file is created by concatenating the corresponding name from the program source with a representation of its type. For an object, the type consists of the class name and a terse encoding of its structure. For a function, it consists of an encoding of the types of the arguments and the return value. For complicated objects or functions of many arguments, the resulting names can be very long. If the linker limits symbols to some too-small maximum length, the type information can be compressed by hashing, at some small loss in security [SF88].

One problem with any technique based on file modification times or checksums is that a trivial change to a header file (e.g., modification of a comment, or definition of a new constant not needed by existing users of the interface) can prevent files from linking correctly. A similar problem occurs with configuration management tools: a trivial change may cause the tool to recompile files unnecessarily. A few programming environments address this issue by tracking changes at a granularity smaller than the compilation unit [Tic86]. Most just live with the need to recompile.

15.7 Dynamic Linking

On a multiuser system, it is common for several instances of a program (e.g., an editor or web browser) to be executing simultaneously. It would be highly wasteful to allocate space in memory for a separate, identical copy of the code of such a program for every running instance. Many operating systems therefore keep track of the programs that are running, and set up memory mapping tables so that all instances of the same program share the same read-only copy of the program's code segment. Each instance receives its own writable copy of the data segment. Code segment sharing can save enormous amounts of space. It does not work, however, for instances of programs that are similar but not identical.

Many sets of programs, while not identical, have large amounts of library code in common—for example to manage a graphical user interface. If every application has its own copy of the library, then large amounts of memory may be wasted. Moreover, if programs are statically linked, then much larger amounts of disk space may be wasted on nearly identical copies of the library in separate executable object files.

IN MORE DEPTH

In the early 1990s, most operating system vendors adopted *dynamic linking* in order to save space in memory and on disk. We consider this option in more detail on the companion site. Each dynamically linked library resides in its own code and data segments. Every program instance that uses a given library has a private copy of the library's data segment, but shares a single system-wide read-only copy of the library's code segment. These segments may be linked to the remainder of the code when the program is loaded into memory, or they may be linked incrementally on demand, during execution. In addition to saving space, dynamic linking allows a programmer or system administrator to install backward-compatible updates to a library without rebuilding all existing executable object files: the next time it runs, each program will obtain the new version of the library automatically.

CHECK YOUR UNDERSTANDING

14. What are the distinguishing characteristics of a *relocatable* object file? An *executable* object file?
15. Why do operating systems typically *zero-fill* pages used for uninitialized data?
16. List four tasks commonly performed by an *assembler*.
17. Summarize the comparative advantages of assembly language and object code as the output of a compiler.
18. Give three examples of *pseudoinstructions* and three examples of *directives* that an assembler might be likely to provide.
19. Why might an assembler perform its own final pass of instruction scheduling?
20. Explain the distinction between *absolute* and *relocatable* words in an object file. Why is the notion of "relocatability" more complicated than it used to be?
21. What is the difference between *linking* and *loading*?
22. What are the principal tasks of a *linker*?
23. How can a linker enforce type checking across compilation units?
24. What is the motivation for *dynamic* linking?

15.8 Summary and Concluding Remarks

In this chapter we focused our attention on the back end of the compiler, and on *code generation*, *assembly*, and *linking* in particular.

Compiler middle and back ends vary greatly in internal structure. We discussed one plausible structure, in which semantic analysis is followed by, in order, intermediate code generation, machine-independent code improvement, target code generation, and machine-specific code improvement (including register allocation and instruction scheduling). The semantic analyzer passes a syntax tree to the intermediate code generator, which in turn passes a *control flow graph* to the machine-independent code improver. Within the nodes of the control flow graph, we suggested that code be represented by instructions in a pseudo-assembly language with an unlimited number of *virtual registers*. In order to delay discussion of code improvement to Chapter 17, we also presented a simpler back-end structure in which code improvement is dropped, naive register allocation happens early, and intermediate and target code generation are merged into a single phase. This simpler structure provided the context for our discussion of code generation.

We also discussed intermediate forms (IFs). These can be categorized in terms of their *level*, or degree of machine independence. On the companion site we considered GIMPLE and RTL, the IFs of the Free Software Foundation GNU compilers. A well-defined IF facilitates the construction of *compiler families*, in which front ends for one or more languages can be paired with back ends for many machines. In many systems that compile for a virtual machine (to be discussed at greater length in Chapter 16), the compiler produces a stack-based medium-level IF. While not generally suitable for use inside the compiler, such an IF can be simple and very compact.

Intermediate code generation is typically performed via ad hoc traversal of a syntax tree. Like semantic analysis, the process can be formalized in terms of attribute grammars. We presented part of a small example grammar and used it to generate code for the GCD program introduced in Chapter 1. We noted in passing that target code generation is often automated, in whole or in part, using a *code generator generator* that takes as input a formal description of the target machine and produces code that performs pattern matching on instruction sequences or trees.

In our discussion of assembly and linking we described the format of *relocatable* and *executable* object files, and discussed the notions of *name resolution* and *relocation*. We noted that while not all compilers include an explicit assembly phase, all compilation systems must make it possible to generate assembly code for debugging purposes, and must allow the programmer to write special-purpose routines in assembler. In compilers that use an assembler, the assembly phase is sometimes responsible for instruction scheduling and other low-level code improvement. The linker, for its part, supports separate compilation, by "gluing" together object files produced by multiple compilations. In many modern systems, significant portions of the linking task are delayed until load time or even run time, to allow programs to share the code segments of large, popular libraries. For many languages the linker must perform a certain amount of semantic checking, to guarantee type consistency. In more aggressive optimizing compilation systems (not discussed in this text), the linker may also perform interprocedural code improvement.

As noted in Section 1.5, the typical programming environment includes a host of additional tools, including debuggers, performance profilers, configuration and version managers, style checkers, preprocessors, pretty-printers, testing systems, and perusal and cross-referencing utilities. Many of these tools, particularly in well-integrated environments, are directly supported by the compiler. Many make use, for example, of symbol-table information embedded in object files. Performance profilers and testing systems often rely on special instrumentation code inserted by the compiler at subroutine calls, loop boundaries, and other key points in the code. Perusal, style-checking, and pretty-printing programs may share the compiler's scanner and parser. Configuration tools often rely on lists of interfile dependences, again generated by the compiler, to tell when a change to one part of a large system may require that other parts be recompiled.

15.9 Exercises

15.1 If you were writing a two-pass compiler, why might you choose a high-level IF as the link between the front end and the back end? Why might you choose a medium-level IF?

15.2 Consider a language like Ada or Modula-2, in which a module *M* can be divided into a specification (header) file and an implementation (body) file for the purpose of separate compilation (Section 10.2.1). Should *M*'s specification itself be separately compiled, or should the compiler simply read it in the process of compiling *M*'s body and the bodies of other modules that use abstractions defined in *M*? If the specification is compiled, what should the output consist of?

15.3 Many research compilers (e.g., for SR [AO93], Cedar [SZBH86], Lynx [Sco91], and Modula-3 [Har92]) have used C as their IF. C is well documented and mostly machine independent, and C compilers are much more widely available than alternative back ends. What are the disadvantages of generating C, and how might they be overcome?

15.4 List as many ways as you can think of in which the back end of a just-in-time compiler might differ from that of a more conventional compiler. What design goals dictate the differences?

15.5 Suppose that k (the number of temporary registers) in Figure 15.6 is 4 (this is an artificially small number for modern machines). Give an example of an expression that will lead to register spilling under our naive register allocation algorithm.

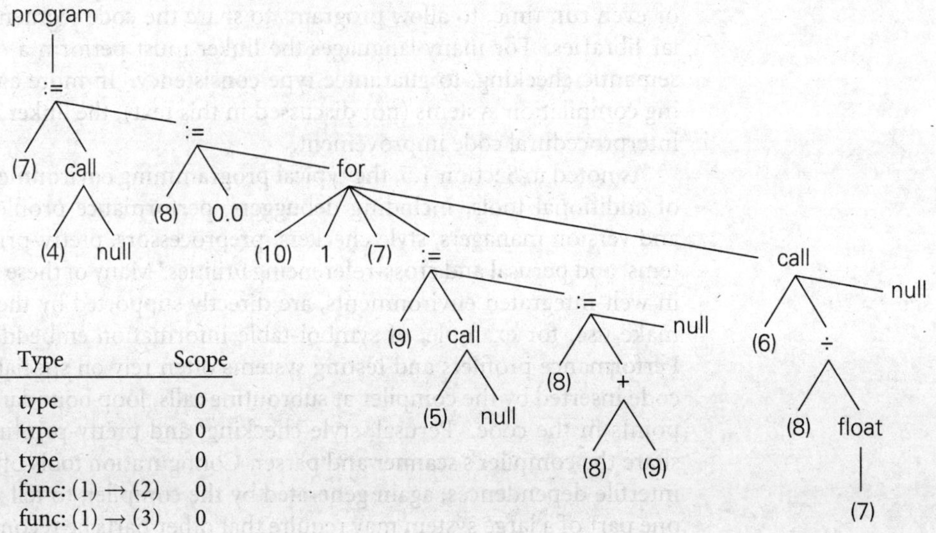

Index	Symbol	Type	Scope
1	`void`	type	0
2	`int`	type	0
3	`real`	type	0
4	`getint`	func: (1) → (2)	0
5	`getreal`	func: (1) → (3)	0
6	`putreal`	func: (3) → (1)	0
7	`n`	2	1
8	`sum`	3	1
9	`x`	3	1
10	`i`	2	2

Figure 15.10 Syntax tree and symbol table for a program that computes the average of `N` real numbers. The children of the for node are the index variable, the lower bound, the upper bound, and the body.

15.6 Modify the attribute grammar of Figure 15.6 in such a way that it will generate the control flow graph of Figure 15.3 instead of the linear assembly code of Figure 15.7.

15.7 Add productions and attribute rules to the grammar of Figure 15.6 to handle Ada-style `for` loops (described in Section 6.5.1). Using your modified grammar, hand-translate the syntax tree of Figure 15.10 into pseudo-assembly notation. Keep the index variable and the upper loop bound in registers.

15.8 One problem (of many) with the code we generated in Section 15.3 is that it computes at run time the value of expressions that could have been computed at compile time. Modify the grammar of Figure 15.6 to perform a simple form of *constant folding*: whenever both operands of an operator are compile-time constants, we should compute the value at compile time and then generate code that uses the value directly. Be sure to consider how to handle overflow.

15.9 Modify the grammar of Figure 15.6 to generate jump code for Boolean expressions, as described in Section 6.4.1. You should assume short-circuit evaluation (Section 6.1.5).

15.10 Our GCD program did not employ subroutines. Extend the grammar of Figure 15.6 to handle procedures without parameters (feel free to adopt any reasonable conventions on the structure of the syntax tree). Be sure to generate appropriate prologue and epilogue code for each subroutine, and to save and restore any needed temporary registers.

15.11 The grammar of Figure 15.6 assumes that all variables are global. In the presence of subroutines, we should need to generate different code (with fp-relative displacement mode addressing) to access local variables and parameters. In a language with nested scopes we should need to dereference the static chain (or index into the display) to access objects that are neither local nor global. Suppose that we are compiling a language with nested subroutines, and are using a static chain. Modify the grammar of Figure 15.6 to generate code to access objects correctly, regardless of scope. You may find it useful to define a to_register subroutine that generates the code to load a given object. Be sure to consider both l-values and r-values, and parameters passed by both value and result.

15.12–15.15 In More Depth.

15.10 Explorations

15.16 Investigate and describe the IF of the compiler you use most often. Can you instruct the compiler to dump it to a file which you can then inspect? Are there tools other than the compiler phases that operate on the IF (e.g., debuggers, code improvers, configuration managers, etc.)? Is the same IF used by compilers for other languages or machines?

15.17 Implement Figure 15.6 in your favorite programming language. Define appropriate data structures to represent a syntax tree; then generate code for some sample trees via ad hoc tree traversal.

15.18 Augment your solution to the previous exercise to handle various other language features. Several interesting options have been mentioned in earlier exercises. Others include functions, first-class subroutines, `case` statements, records, arrays (particularly those of dynamic size), and iterators.

15.19 Find out what tools are available on your favorite system to inspect the content of object files (on a Unix system, use `nm` or `objdump`). Consider some program consisting of a modest number (three to six, say) of compilation units. Using the appropriate tool, list the imported and exported symbols in each compilation unit. Then link the files together. Draw an address map showing the locations at which the various code and data segments have been placed. Which instructions within the code segments have been changed by relocation?

15.20 In your favorite C++ compiler, investigate the encoding of type information in the names of external symbols. Are there strange strings of characters at the end of every name? If so, can you "reverse engineer" the algorithm used to generate them? For hints, type "C++ name mangling" into your favorite search engine.

15.21–15.25 In More Depth.

15.11 Bibliographic Notes

Standard compiler textbooks (e.g., those by Aho et al. [ALSU07], Cooper and Torczon [CT04], Grune et al. [GBJ+12], Appel [App97], or Fischer et al. [FCL10]) are an accessible source of information on back-end compiler technology. More detailed information can be found in the text of Muchnick [Muc97]. Fraser and Hanson provide a wealth of detail on code generation and (simple) code improvement in their `lcc` compiler [FH95].

RTL and GIMPLE are documented in the `gcc` Internals Manual, available from *www.gnu.org/onlinedocs*. Java bytecode is documented by Lindholm and Yellin [LYBB14]. The Common Intermediate Language is described by Miller and Ragsdale [MR04].

Ganapathi, Fischer, and Hennessy [GFH82] and Henry and Damron [HD89] provide early surveys of automatic code generator generators. The most widely used technique from that era was based on LR parsing, and was due to Glanville and Graham [GG78]. Fraser et al. [FHP92] describe a simpler approach based on dynamic programming. Documentation for the LLVM Target-Independent Code Generator can be found at *llvm.org/docs/CodeGenerator.html*.

Beck [Bec97] provides a good turn-of-the-century introduction to assemblers, linkers, and software development tools. Gingell et al. describe the implementation of shared libraries for the SPARC architecture and the SunOS variant of Unix [GLDW87]. Ho and Olsson describe a particularly ambitious dynamic linker for Unix [HO91]. Tichy presents a compilation system that avoids unnecessary recompilations by tracking dependences at a granularity finer than the source file [Tic86].

16 Run-Time Program Management

Every nontrivial implementation of a high-level programming language makes extensive use of libraries. Some library routines are very simple: they may copy memory from one place to another, or perform arithmetic functions not directly supported by the hardware. Others are more sophisticated. Heap management routines, for example, maintain significant amounts of internal state, as do libraries for buffered or graphical I/O.

In general, we use the term *run-time system* (or sometimes just *runtime*, without the hyphen) to refer to the set of libraries on which the language implementation depends for correct operation. Some parts of the runtime, like heap management, obtain all the information they need from subroutine arguments, and can easily be replaced with alternative implementations. Others, however, require more extensive knowledge of the compiler or the generated program. In simpler cases, this knowledge is really just a set of conventions (e.g., for the subroutine calling sequence) that the compiler and runtime both respect. In more complex cases, the compiler generates program-specific *metadata* that the runtime must inspect to do its job. A tracing garbage collector (Section 8.5.3), for example, depends on metadata identifying all the "root pointers" in the program (all global, static, and stack-based pointer or reference variables), together with the type of every reference and of every allocated block.

Many examples of compiler/runtime integration have been discussed in previous chapters; we review these in Sidebar 16.1. The length and complexity of the list generally means that the compiler and the run-time system must be developed together.

Some languages (notably C) have very small run-time systems: most of the user-level code required to execute a given source program is either generated directly by the compiler or contained in language-independent libraries. Other languages have extensive run-time systems. C#, for example, is heavily dependent on a run-time system defined by the Common Language Infrastructure (CLI) standard [Int12a].

EXAMPLE 16.1
The CLI as a run-time system and virtual machine

Like any run-time system, the CLI depends on data generated by the compiler (e.g., type descriptors, lists of exception handlers, and certain content from the symbol table). It also makes extensive assumptions about the structure of

DESIGN & IMPLEMENTATION

16.1 Run-time systems

Many of the most interesting topics in language implementation revolve around the run-time system, and have been covered in previous chapters. To set the stage for virtual machines, we review those topics here.

Garbage Collection (Section 8.5.3). As noted in the chapter introduction, a tracing garbage collector must be able to find all the "root pointers" in the program, and to identify the type of every reference and every allocated block. A compacting collector must be able to *modify* every pointer in the program. A generational collector must have access to a list of old-to-new pointer references, maintained by write barriers in the main program. A collector for a language like Java must call appropriate `finalize` methods. And in implementations that support concurrent or incremental collection, the main program and the collector must agree on some sort of locking protocol to preserve the consistency of the heap.

Variable Numbers of Arguments (Section 9.3.3). Several languages allow the programmer to declare functions that take an arbitrary number of arguments, of arbitrary type. In C, a call to `va_arg(my_args, arg_type)` must return the next argument in the previously identified list `my_args`. To find the argument, `va_arg` must understand which arguments are passed in which registers, and which arguments are passed on the stack (with what alignment, padding, and offset). If the code for `va_arg` is generated entirely in-line, this knowledge may be embedded entirely in the compiler. If any of the code is in library routines, however, those routines are compiler-specific, and thus a (simple) part of the run-time system.

Exception Handling (Section 9.4). Exception propagation requires that we "unwind" the stack whenever control escapes the current subroutine. Code to deallocate the current frame may be generated by the compiler on a subroutine-by-subroutine basis. Alternatively, a general-purpose routine to deallocate any given frame may be part of the run-time system. In a similar vein, the closest exception handler around a given point in the program may be found by compiler-generated code that maintains a stack of active handlers, or by a general-purpose run-time routine that inspects a table of program-counter-to-handler mappings generated at compile time. The latter approach avoids any run-time cost when entering and leaving a protected region (`try` block).

Event Handling (Section 9.6). Events are commonly implemented as "spontaneous" subroutine calls in a single-threaded program, or as "callbacks" in a separate, dedicated thread of a concurrent program. Depending on implementation strategy, they may be able to exploit knowledge of the compiler's subroutine calling conventions. They also require synchronization between the main program and the event handler, to protect the consistency of shared data structures. A truly asynchronous call—one that may interrupt execution of the main program at any point—may need to save the entire register set of the machine. Calls that occur only at well-defined "safe points" in the program (implemented via polling) may be able to save a smaller amount of state. In either case, calls to any handler not at the outermost level of lexical nesting may need to interpret a closure to establish the proper referencing environment.

Coroutine and Thread Implementation (Sections 9.5 and 13.2.4). Code to create a coroutine or thread must allocate and initialize a stack, establish a referencing environment, perform any set-up needed to handle future exceptions, and invoke a specified start-up routine. Routines like transfer, yield, reschedule, and sleep_on (as well as any scheduler-based synchronization mechanisms) must likewise understand a wealth of details about the implementation of concurrency.

Remote Procedure Call (Section C-13.5.4). Remote procedure call (RPC) merges aspects of events and threads: from the server's point of view, an RPC is an event executed by a separate thread in response to a request from a client. Whether built into the language or implemented via a stub compiler, it requires a run-time system (dispatcher) with detailed knowledge of calling conventions, concurrency, and storage management.

Transactional Memory (Section 13.4.4). A software implementation of transactional memory must buffer speculative updates, track speculative reads, detect conflicts with other transactions, and validate its view of memory before performing any operation that might be compromised by inconsistency. It must also be prepared to roll back its updates if aborted, or to make them permanent if committed. These operations typically require library calls at the beginning and end of every transaction, and at most read and write instructions in between. Among other things, these calls must understand the layout of objects in memory, the meaning of metadata associated with objects and transactions, and the policy for arbitrating between conflicting transactions.

Dynamic Linking (Section C-15.7). In any system with separate compilation, the compiler generates symbol table information that the linker uses to resolve external references. In a system with fully dynamic (lazy) linking, external references are (temporarily) filled with pointers to the linker, which must then be part of the run-time system. When the program tries to call a routine that has not yet been linked, it actually calls the linker, which resolves the reference dynamically. Specifically, the linker looks up symbol table information describing the routine to be called. It then patches, in a manner consistent with the language's subroutine calling conventions, the linkage tables that will govern future calls.

compiler-generated code (e.g., parameter-passing conventions, synchronization mechanisms, and the layout of run-time stacks). The coupling between compiler and runtime runs deeper than this, however: the CLI programming interface is so complete as to fully hide the underlying hardware.[1] Such a runtime is known as a *virtual machine.* Some virtual machines—notably the Java Virtual Machine (JVM)—are language-specific. Others, including the CLI, are explicitly intended for use with multiple languages. In conjunction with development of their version of the CLI,[2] Microsoft introduced the term *managed code* to refer to programs that run on top of a virtual machine. ■

Virtual machines are part of a growing trend toward run-time management and manipulation of programs using compiler technology. This trend is the subject of this chapter. We consider virtual machines in more detail in Section 16.1. To avoid the overhead of emulating a non-native instruction set, many virtual machines use a *just-in-time* (JIT) compiler to translate their instruction set to that of the underlying hardware. Some may even invoke the compiler after the program is running, to compile newly discovered components or to optimize code based on dynamically discovered properties of the program, its input, or the underlying system. Using related technology, some language implementations perform *binary translation* to retarget programs compiled for one machine to run on another machine, or *binary rewriting* to instrument or optimize programs that have already been compiled for the current machine. We consider these various forms of late binding of machine code in Section 16.2. Finally, in Section 16.3, we consider run-time mechanisms to inspect or modify the state of a running program. Such mechanisms are needed by symbolic debuggers and by profiling and performance analysis tools. They may also support *reflection*, which allows a program to inspect and reason about its *own* state at run time.

16.1 Virtual Machines

A *virtual machine* (VM) provides a complete programming environment: its application programming interface (API) includes everything required for correct execution of the programs that run above it. We typically reserve use of the term "VM" to environments whose level of abstraction is comparable to that of a computer implemented in hardware. (A Smalltalk or Python interpreter, for example, is usually not described as a virtual machine, because its level of abstraction is too high, but this is a subjective call.)

Every virtual machine API includes an instruction set architecture (ISA) in which to express programs. This may be the same as the instruction set of some

---

1 In particular, the CLI defines the instruction set of compiler's target language: the Common Intermediate Language (CIL) described in Section C-16.1.2.

2 CLI is an ECMA and ISO standard. CLR—the Common Language Runtime—is Microsoft's implementation of the CLI. It is part of the .NET framework.

existing physical machine, or it may be an artificial instruction set designed to be easier to implement in software and to generate with a compiler. Other portions of the VM API may support I/O, scheduling, or other services provided by a library or by the operating system (OS) of a physical machine.

In practice, virtual machines tend to be characterized as either *system* VMs or *process* VMs. A system VM faithfully emulates all the hardware facilities needed to run a standard OS, including both privileged and unprivileged instructions, memory-mapped I/O, virtual memory, and interrupt facilities. By contrast, a process VM provides the environment needed by a single user-level process: the unprivileged subset of the instruction set and a library-level interface to I/O and other services.

System VMs are often managed by a *virtual machine monitor* (VMM) or *hypervisor*, which multiplexes a single physical machine among a collection of "guest" operating systems, each of which runs in its own virtual machine. The first widely available VMM was IBM's CP/CMS, which debuted in 1967. Rather than build an operating system capable of supporting multiple users, IBM used the CP ("control program") VMM to create a collection of virtual machines, each of which ran a lightweight, single-user operating system (CMS). In recent years, VMMs have played a central role in the rise of cloud computing, by allowing a hosting center to share physical machines among a large number of (mutually isolated) guest OSes. The center can monitor and manage its workload more easily if customer workloads were running on bare hardware—it can even migrate running OSes from one machine to another, to balance load among customers or to clear machines for hardware maintenance. System VMs are also increasingly popular on personal computers, where products like VMware Fusion and Parallels Desktop allow users to run programs on top of more than one OS at once.

It is process VMs, however, that have had the greatest impact on programming language design and implementation. As with system VMs, the technology is decades old: the P-code VM described in Example 1.15, for example, dates from the early 1970s. Process VMs were originally conceived as a way to increase program portability and to quickly "bootstrap" languages on new hardware. The traditional downside was poor performance due to interpretation of the abstract instruction set. The tradeoff between portability and performance remained valid through the late 1990s, when early versions of Java were typically an order of magnitude slower than traditionally compiled languages like Fortran or C. With the introduction of just-in-time compilation, however, modern implementations of the Java Virtual Machine (JVM) and the Common Language Infrastructure (CLI) have come to rival the performance of traditional languages on native hardware. We will consider these systems in Sections 16.1.1 and 16.1.2.

Both the JVM and the CLI use a stack-based intermediate form (IF): Java bytecode and CLI Common Intermediate Language (CIL), respectively. As described in Section 15.2.2, the lack of named operands means that stack-based IF can be very compact—a feature of particular importance for code (e.g., applets) distributed over the Internet. At the same time, the need to compute everything in stack order means that intermediate results cannot generally be saved in registers and reused. In many cases, stack-based code for an expression will occupy fewer bytes, but specify more instructions, than corresponding code for a register-based machine.

16.1.1 The Java Virtual Machine

Development of the language that eventually became Java began in 1990–1991, when Patrick Naughton, James Gosling, and Mike Sheridan of Sun Microsystems began work on a programming system for embedded devices. An early version of this system was up and running in 1992, at which time the language was known as Oak. In 1994, after unsuccessful attempts to break into the market for cable TV set-top boxes, the project was retargeted to web browsers, and the name was changed to Java.

The first public release of Java occurred in 1995. At that time code in the JVM was entirely interpreted. A JIT compiler was added in 1998, with the release of Java 2. Though not standardized by any of the usual agencies (ANSI, ISO, ECMA), Java is sufficiently well defined to admit a wide variety of compilers and JVMs. Oracle's `javac` compiler and HotSpot JVM, released as open source in 2006, are by far the most widely used. The Jikes RVM (Research Virtual Machine) is a self-hosting JVM, written in Java itself, and widely used for VM research. Several companies have their own proprietary JVMs and class libraries, designed to provide a competitive edge on particular machines or in particular markets.

Architecture Summary

The interface provided by the JVM was designed to be an attractive target for a Java compiler. It provides direct support for all (and only) the built-in and

DESIGN & IMPLEMENTATION

16.2 Optimizing stack-based IF

As we shall see in Section C-16.1.2, code for the CLI was not intended for interpretation; it is almost always JIT compiled. As a result, the extra instructions sometimes needed to capture an expression in stack-based form are not a serious problem: reasonably straightforward code improvement algorithms (to be discussed in Chapter 17) allow the JIT compiler to transform the left side of Figure 15.4 into good machine code at load time. In the judgment of the CLI designers, the simplicity and compactness of the stack-based code outweigh the cost of the code improvement. For Java, the need for compact mobile code (e.g., browser applets) was a compelling advantage, even in early implementations that were interpreted rather than JIT compiled.

The higher level of abstraction of stack-based code also enhances portability. Three-address instructions might be a good fit for execution on SPARC machines, but not on the x86 (a two-address machine).

reference types defined by the Java language. It also enforces both definite assignment (Section 6.1.3) and type safety. Finally, it includes built-in support for many of Java's language features and standard library packages, including exceptions, threads, garbage collection, reflection, dynamic loading, and security.

Of course, nothing requires that Java bytecode be produced from Java source. Compilers targeting the JVM exist for many other languages, including Ruby, JavaScript, Python, and Scheme (all of which are traditionally interpreted), as well as C, Ada, Cobol, and others, which are traditionally compiled.[3] There are even assemblers that allow programmers to write Java bytecode directly. The principal requirement, for both compilers and assemblers, is that they generate correct *class files*. These have a special format understood by the JVM, and must satisfy a variety of structural and semantic constraints.

At start-up time, a JVM is typically given the name of a class file containing the static method `main`. It loads this class into memory, verifies that it satisfies a variety of required constraints, allocates any static fields, links it to any preloaded library routines, and invokes any initialization code provided by the programmer for classes or static fields. Finally, it calls `main` in a single thread. Additional classes (needed by the initial class) may be loaded either immediately or lazily on demand. Additional threads may be created via calls to the (built-in) methods of class `Thread`. The three following subsections provide additional details on JVM storage management, the format of class files, and the Java bytecode instruction set.

Storage Management

Storage allocation mechanisms in the JVM mirror those of the Java language. There is a global *constant pool*, a set of registers and a stack for each thread, a *method area* to hold executable bytecode, and a heap for dynamically allocated objects.

Global data The method area is analogous to the code ("text") segment of a traditional executable file, as described in Section 15.4. The constant pool contains both program constants and a variety of symbol table information needed by the JVM and other tools. Like the code of methods, the constant pool is read-only to user programs. Each entry begins with a one-byte tag that indicates the kind of information contained in the rest of the entry. Possibilities include the various built-in types; character-string names; and class, method, and field references.

EXAMPLE 16.2
Constants for "Hello, world"

Consider, for example, the trivial "Hello, world" program:

3 Compilation of type-unsafe code, as in C, is problematic; we will return to this issue in Section C-16.1.2.

```
class Hello {
    public static void main(String args[]) {
        System.out.println("Hello, world!");
    }
};
```

When compiled with OpenJDK's javac compiler, the constant pool for this program has 28 separate entries, shown in Figure 16.1. Entry 18 contains the text of the output string; entry 3 indicates that this text is indeed a Java string. Many of the additional entries (7, 11, 14, 21–24, 26, 27) give the textual names of files, classes, methods, and fields. Others (9, 10, 13) are the names of structures elsewhere in the class file; by pointing to these entries, the structures can be self-descriptive. Four of the entries (8, 12, 25, 28) are *type signatures* for methods and fields. In the format shown here, "V" indicates void; "L*name*;" is a fully qualified class. For methods, parentheses surround the list of argument types; the return type follows. Most of the remaining entries are references to classes (5, 6, 16, 19), fields (2), and methods (1, 4). The final three entries (15, 17, 20) give name and type for fields and methods. The surprising amount of information for such a tiny program stems from Java's rich naming structure, the use of library classes, and the deliberate retention of symbol table information to support lazy linking, reflection, and debugging. ■

Per-thread data A program running on the JVM begins with a single thread. Additional threads are created by allocating and initializing a new object of the build-in class Thread, and then calling its start method. Each thread has a small set of base registers, a stack of method call frames, and an optional traditional stack on which to call native (non-Java) methods.

Each frame on the method call stack contains an array of local variables, an *operand stack* for evaluation of the method's expressions, and a reference into the constant pool that identifies information needed for dynamic linking of called methods. Space for formal parameters is included among the local variables. Variables that are not live at the same time can share a slot in the array; this means that the same slot may be used at different times for data of different types.

Because Java bytecode is stack oriented, operands and results of arithmetic and logic instructions are kept in the operand stack of the current method frame, rather than in registers. Implicitly, the JVM instruction set requires four registers per thread, to hold the program counter and references to the current frame, the top of the operand stack, and the base of the local variable array.

Slots in the local variable array and the operand stack are always 32 bits wide. Data of smaller types are padded; long and double data take two slots each. The maximum depth required for the operand stack can be determined statically by the compiler, making it easy to preallocate space in the frame.

Heap In keeping with the type system of the Java language, a datum in the local variable array or the operand stack is always either a reference or a value of a built-in scalar type. Structured data (objects and arrays) must always lie in the

```
const #1 = Method  #6.#15;          //  java/lang/Object."<init>":()V
const #2 = Field   #16.#17;         //  java/lang/System.out:Ljava/io/PrintStream;
const #3 = String  #18;             //  Hello, world!
const #4 = Method  #19.#20;         //  java/io/PrintStream.println:(Ljava/lang/String;)V
const #5 = class   #21;             //  Hello
const #6 = class   #22;             //  java/lang/Object
const #7 = Asciz   <init>;
const #8 = Asciz   ()V;
const #9 = Asciz   Code;
const #10 = Asciz  LineNumberTable;
const #11 = Asciz  main;
const #12 = Asciz  ([Ljava/lang/String;)V;
const #13 = Asciz  SourceFile;
const #14 = Asciz  Hello.java;
const #15 = NameAndType #7:#8;       //  "<init>":()V
const #16 = class  #23;              //  java/lang/System
const #17 = NameAndType #24:#25;     //  out:Ljava/io/PrintStream;
const #18 = Asciz  Hello, world!;
const #19 = class  #26;              //  java/io/PrintStream
const #20 = NameAndType #27:#28;     //  println:(Ljava/lang/String;)V
const #21 = Asciz  Hello;
const #22 = Asciz  java/lang/Object;
const #23 = Asciz  java/lang/System;
const #24 = Asciz  out;
const #25 = Asciz  Ljava/io/PrintStream;;
const #26 = Asciz  java/io/PrintStream;
const #27 = Asciz  println;
const #28 = Asciz  (Ljava/lang/String;)V;
```

Figure 16.1 **Content of the JVM constant pool for the program in Example 16.2.** The "Asciz" entries (zero-terminated ASCII) contain null-terminated character-string names. Most other entries pair an indication of the kind of constant with a reference to one or more additional entries. This output was produced by Sun's `javap` tool.

heap. They are allocated, dynamically, using the `new` and `newarray` instructions. They are reclaimed automatically via garbage collection. The choice of collection algorithm is left to the implementor of the JVM.

To facilitate sharing among threads, the Java language provides the equivalent of monitors with a lock and a single, implicit condition variable per object, as described in Section 13.4.3. The JVM provides direct support for this style of synchronization. Each object in the heap has an associated mutual exclusion lock; in a typical implementation, the lock maintains a set of threads waiting for entry to the monitor. In addition, each object has an associated set of threads that are waiting for the monitor's condition variable.[4] Locks are acquired with the `monitorenter` instruction and released with the `monitorexit` instruction. Most

4 To save space, a JIT compiler will typically omit the monitor information for any object it can prove is never used for synchronization.

JVMs insist that these calls appear in matching nested pairs, and that every lock acquired within a given method be released within the same method (any correct compiler for the Java language will follow these rules).

Consistency of access to shared objects is governed by the Java memory model, which we considered briefly in Section 13.3.3. Informally, each thread behaves as if it kept a private cache of the heap. When a thread releases a monitor or writes a `volatile` variable, the JVM must ensure that all previous updates to the thread's cache have been written back to memory. When a thread enters a monitor or reads a `volatile` variable, the JVM must (in effect) clear the thread's cache so that subsequent reads cause locations to be reloaded from memory. Of course, actual implementations don't perform explicit write-backs or invalidations; they start with the memory model provided by the hardware's cache coherence protocol and use memory barrier (fence) instructions where needed to avoid unacceptable orderings.

Class Files

Physically, a JVM class file is stored as a stream of bytes. Typically these occupy some real file provided by the operating system, but they could just as easily be a record in a database. On many systems, multiple class files may be combined into a Java archive (`.jar`) file.

Logically, a class file has a well-defined hierarchical structure. It begins with a "magic number" (`0x_cafe_babe`), as described in Sidebar 14.4. This is followed by

- Major and minor version numbers of the JVM for which the file was created
- The constant pool
- Indices into the constant pool for the current class and its superclass
- Tables describing the class's superinterfaces, fields, and methods

Because the JVM is both cleaner and more abstract than a real machine, the Java class file structure is both cleaner and more abstract than a typical object file (Section 15.4). Conspicuously missing is the extensive *relocation* information required to cope with the many ways that addresses are embedded into instructions on a typical real machine. In place of this, bytecode instructions in a class file contain references to symbolic names in the constant pool. These become references into the method area when code is dynamically linked. (Alternatively, they may become real machine addresses, appropriately encoded, when the code is JIT compiled.) At the same time, class files contain extensive information not typically found in an executable object file. Examples include access flags for classes, fields, and methods (`public`, `private`, `protected`, `static`, `final`, `synchronized`, `native`, `abstract`, `strictfp`); symbol table information that is built into the structure of the file (rather than an optional add-on); and special instructions for such high-level notions as throwing an exception or entering or leaving a monitor.

Bytecode

The bytecode for a method (or for a constructor or a class initializer) appears in an entry in the class file's method table. It is accompanied by the following:

- An indication of the number of local variables, including parameters
- The maximum depth required in the operand stack
- A table of exception handler information, each entry of which indicates
  - The bytecode range covered by this handler
  - The address (index in the code) of the handler itself
  - The type of exception caught (an index into the constant pool)
- Optional information for debuggers: specifically, a table mapping bytecode addresses to line numbers in the original source code and/or a table indicating which source code variable(s) occupy which JVM local variables at which points in the bytecode.

Instruction Set Java bytecode was designed to be both simple and compact. Orthogonality was a strictly secondary concern. Every instruction begins with a single-byte *opcode*. Arguments, if any, occupy subsequent bytes, with values given in big-endian order. With two exceptions, used for `switch` statements, arguments are unaligned, for compactness. Most instructions, however, actually don't need an argument. Where typical hardware performs arithmetic on values in named registers, bytecode pops arguments from, and pushes result to, the operand stack of the current method frame. Moreover, even loads and stores can often use a single byte. There are, for example, special one-byte integer store instructions for each of the first four entries in the local variable array. Similarly, there are special instructions to push the values −1, 0, 1, 2, 3, 4, and 5 onto the operand stack.

As of Java 8, the JVM defines 205 of the 256 possible opcode values. Five of these serve special purposes (unused, `nop`, debugger breakpoints, implementation dependent). The remainder can be organized into the following categories:

Load/store: move values back and forth between the operand stack and the local variable array.

Arithmetic: perform integer or floating point operations on values in the operand stack.

Type conversion: "widen" or "narrow" values among the built-in types (`byte`, `char`, `short`, `int`, `long`, `float`, and `double`). Narrowing may result in a loss of precision but never an exception.

Object management: create or query the properties of objects and arrays; access fields and array elements.

Operand stack management: push and pop; duplicate; swap.

Control transfer: perform conditional, unconditional, or multiway branches (`switch`).

Method calls: call and return from ordinary and `static` methods (including constructors and initializers) of classes and interfaces. An `invokedynamic` instruction, introduced in the Java 7 JVM, allows run-time customization of linkage conventions for individual call sites. It is used both for Java 8 `lambda` expressions and for the implementation of dynamically typed languages on top of the JVM.

Exceptions: `throw` (no instructions required for `catch`).

Monitors: enter and exit (`wait`, `notify`, and `notifyAll` are invoked via method calls).

EXAMPLE 16.3

Bytecode for a list insert operation

As a concrete example, consider the following definitions for an integer set, represented as a sorted linked list:

```
public class LLset {
    node head;
    class node {
        public int val;
        public node next;
    }
    public LLset() {            // constructor
        head = new node();  // head node contains no real data
        head.next = null;
    }
    ...
}
```

An `insert` method for this class appears in Figure 16.2. Java source is on the left; a symbolic representation of the corresponding bytecode is on the right. The line at the top of the bytecode indicates a maximum depth of 3 for the operand stack and four entries in the local variable array, the first two of which are arguments: the `this` pointer and the integer `v`. Perusal of the code reveals numerous examples of the special one-byte load and store instructions, and of instructions that operate implicitly on the operand stack.

Verification Safety was one of the principal concerns in the definition of the Java language and virtual machine. Many of the things that can "go wrong" while executing machine code compiled from a more traditional language cannot go wrong when executing bytecode compiled from Java. Some aspects of safety are obtained by limiting the expressiveness of the byte-code instruction set or by checking properties at load time. One cannot jump to a nonexistent address, for example, because method calls specify their targets symbolically by name, and branch targets are specified as indices within the code attribute of the current method. Similarly, where hardware allows displacement addressing from the frame pointer to access memory outside the current stack frame, the JVM checks at load time to make sure that references to local variables (specified by constant indices into the local variable array) are within the bounds declared.

```
                                      Code:
public void insert(int v) {            Stack=3, Locals=4, Args_size=2
    node n = head;                     0:   aload_0             // this
                                       1:   getfield       #4; //Field head:LLLset$node;
                                       4:   astore_2
    while (n.next != null              5:   aload_2             // n
           && n.next.val < v) {        6:   getfield       #5; //Field LLset$node.next:LLLset$node;
                                       9:   ifnull         31  // conditional branch
                                       12:  aload_2
                                       13:  getfield       #5; //Field LLset$node.next:LLLset$node;
                                       16:  getfield       #6; //Field LLset$node.val:I
                                       19:  iload_1             // v
                                       20:  if_icmpge      31
        n = n.next;                    23:  aload_2
                                       24:  getfield       #5; //Field LLset$node.next:LLLset$node;
                                       27:  astore_2
    }                                  28:  goto           5
    if (n.next == null                 31:  aload_2
        || n.next.val > v) {           32:  getfield       #5; //Field LLset$node.next:LLLset$node;
                                       35:  ifnull         49
                                       38:  aload_2
                                       39:  getfield       #5; //Field LLset$node.next:LLLset$node;
                                       42:  getfield       #6; //Field LLset$node.val:I
                                       45:  iload_1
                                       46:  if_icmple      76
        node t = new node();           49:  new            #2; //class LLset$node
                                       52:  dup
                                       53:  aload_0
                                       54:  invokespecial  #3; //Method LLset$node."<init>":(LLLset;)V
                                       57:  astore_3
        t.val = v;                     58:  aload_3             // t
                                       59:  iload_1
                                       60:  putfield       #6; //Field LLset$node.val:I
        t.next = n.next;               63:  aload_3
                                       64:  aload_2
                                       65:  getfield       #5; //Field LLset$node.next:LLLset$node;
                                       68:  putfield       #5; //Field LLset$node.next:LLLset$node;
        n.next = t;                    71:  aload_2
                                       72:  aload_3
                                       73:  putfield       #5; //Field LLset$node.next:LLLset$node;
    } // else v already in set         76:  return
}
```

Figure 16.2 **Java source and bytecode for a list insertion method.** Output on the right was produced by Oracle's `javac` (compiler) and `javap` (disassembler) tools, with additional comments inserted by hand.

Other aspects of safety are guaranteed by the JVM during execution. Field access and method call instructions throw an exception if given a null reference. Similarly, array load and store instructions throw an exception if the index is not within the bounds of the array.

When it first loads a class file, the JVM checks the top-level structure of the file. Among other things, it verifies that the file begins with the appropriate "magic number," that the specified sizes of the various sections of the file are all within bounds, and that these sizes add up to the size of the overall file. When it links the class file into the rest of the program, the JVM checks additional constraints. It verifies that all items in the constant pool are well formed, and that nothing inherits from a `final` class. More significantly, it performs a host of checks on the bytecode of the class's methods. Among other things, the bytecode verifier ensures that every variable is initialized before it is read, that every operation is type-safe, and that the operand stacks of methods never overflow or underflow. All three of these checks require *data flow analysis* to determine that desired properties (initialization status, types of slots in the local stack frame, depth of the operand stack) are the same on every possible path to a given point in the program. We will consider data flow in more detail in Section C-17.4.

DESIGN & IMPLEMENTATION

16.3 Verification of class files and bytecode

Java compilers are required to generate code that satisfies all the constraints defined by the Java class file specification. These include well-formedness of the internal data structures, type safety, definite assignment, and lack of underflow or overflow in the operand stack. A JVM, however, has no way to tell whether a given class file was generated by a correct compiler. To protect itself from potentially incorrect (or even malicious) class files, a JVM must *verify* that any code it runs follows all the rules. Under normal operation, this means that certain checks (e.g., data flow for definite assignment) are performed twice: once by the Java compiler, to provide compile-time error messages to the programmer, and again by the JVM, to protect against buggy compilers or alternative sources of bytecode.

To improve program start-up times and avoid unnecessary work, most JVMs delay the loading (and verification) of class files until some method in that file is actually called (this is the Java equivalent of the *lazy linking* described in Section C-15.7.2). In order to effect this delay, the JVM must wait until a call occurs to verify the last few properties of the code at the call site (i.e., that it refers to a method that really exists, and that the caller is allowed to call).

16.1.2 The Common Language Infrastructure

As early as the mid-1980s, Microsoft recognized the need for interoperability among programming languages running on Windows platforms. In a series of product offerings spanning a decade and a half, the company developed increasingly sophisticated versions of its Component Object Model (COM), first to communicate with, then to call, and finally to share data with program components written in multiple languages.

With the success of Java, it became clear by the mid to late 1990s that a system combining a JVM-style run-time system with the language interoperability of COM could have enormous technical and commercial potential. Microsoft's .NET project set out to realize this potential. It includes a JVM-like virtual machine whose specification—the Common Language Infrastructure (CLI)—is standardized by ECMA and the ISO. While development of the CLI has clearly been driven by Microsoft, other implementations—notably from the open-source Mono project, led by Xamarin, Inc.—are available for non-Windows platforms.

IN MORE DEPTH

We consider the CLI in more detail on the companion site. Among other things, we describe the Common Type System, which governs cross-language interoperability; the architecture of the virtual machine, including its support for generics; the Common Intermediate Language (CIL—the CLI analogue of Java bytecode); and Portable Executable (PE) *assemblies*, the CLI analogue of `.jar` files.

CHECK YOUR UNDERSTANDING

1. What is a *run-time system*? How does it differ from a "mere" library?
2. List some of the major tasks that may be performed by a run-time system.
3. What is a *virtual machine*? What distinguishes it from interpreters of other sorts?
4. Explain the distinction between *system* and *process* VMs. What other terms are sometimes used for system VMs?
5. What is *managed code*?
6. Why do many virtual machines use a stack-based intermediate form?
7. Give several examples of special-purpose instructions provided by Java bytecode.
8. Summarize the architecture of the Java Virtual Machine.
9. Summarize the content of a Java class file.
10. Explain the validity checks performed on a class file at load time.

16.2 Late Binding of Machine Code

In the traditional conception (Example 1.7), compilation is a one-time activity, sharply distinguished from program execution. The compiler produces a target program, typically in machine language, which can subsequently be executed many times for many different inputs.

In some environments, however, it makes sense to bring compilation and execution closer together in time. A *just-in-time* (JIT) compiler translates a program from source or intermediate form into machine language immediately before each separate run of the program. We consider JIT compilation further in the first subsection below. We also consider language systems that may compile new pieces of a program—or recompile old pieces—after the program begins its execution. In Sections 16.2.2 and 16.2.3, we consider *binary translation* and *binary rewriting* systems, which perform compiler-like operations on programs *without* access to source code. Finally, in Section 16.2.4, we consider systems that may download program components from remote locations. All these systems serve to delay the binding of a program to its machine code.

16.2.1 Just-in-Time and Dynamic Compilation

To promote the Java language and virtual machine, Sun Microsystems coined the slogan "write once, run anywhere"—the idea being that programs distributed as Java bytecode could run on a very wide range of platforms. Source code, of course, is also portable, but byte code is much more compact, and can be interpreted without additional preprocessing. Unfortunately, interpretation tends to be expensive. Programs running on early Java implementations could be as much as an order of magnitude slower than compiled code in other languages. Just-in-time compilation is, to first approximation, a technique to retain the portability of bytecode while improving execution speed. Like both interpretation and dynamic linking (Section 15.7), JIT compilation also benefits from the delayed discovery of program components: program code is not bloated by copies of widely shared libraries, and new versions of libraries are obtained automatically when a program that needs them is run.

Because a JIT system compiles programs immediately prior to execution, it can add significant delay to program start-up time. Implementors face a difficult tradeoff: to maximize benefits with respect to interpretation, the compiler should produce good code; to minimize start-up time, it should produce that code very quickly. In general, JIT compilers tend to focus on the simpler forms of target code improvement. Specifically, they often limit themselves to the so-called *local* improvements, which operate within individual control-flow constructs. Improvements at the *global* (whole method) and *interprocedural* (whole program) level may be expensive to consider.

Fortunately, the cost of JIT compilation is typically lessened by the existence of an earlier source-to-byte-code compiler that does much of the "heavy lifting."[5] Scanning is unnecessary in a JIT compiler, since bytecode is not textual. Parsing is trivial, since class files have a simple, self-descriptive structure. Many of the properties that a source-to-byte-code compiler must infer at significant expense (type safety, agreement of actual and formal parameter lists) are embedded directly in the structure of the bytecode (objects are labeled with their type, calls are made through method descriptors); others can be verified with simple data flow analysis. Certain forms of machine-independent code improvement may also be performed by the source-to-byte-code compiler (these are limited to some degree by stack-based expression evaluation).

All these factors allow a JIT compiler to be faster—and to produce better code—than one might initially expect. In addition, since we are already committed to invoking the JIT compiler at run time, we can minimize its impact on program start-up latency by running it a bit at a time, rather than all at once:

- Like a lazy linker (Section C-15.7.2), a JIT compiler may perform its work incrementally. It begins by compiling only the class file that contains the program entry point (i.e., `main`), leaving *hooks* in the code that call into the run-time system wherever the program is supposed to call a method in another class file. After this small amount of preparation, the program begins execution. When execution falls into the runtime through an unresolved hook, the runtime invokes the compiler to load the new class file and to link it into the program.
- To eliminate the latency of compiling even the original class file, the language implementation may incorporate both an interpreter and a JIT compiler. Execution begins in the interpreter. In parallel, the compiler translates portions of the program into machine code. When the interpreter needs to call a method, it checks to see whether a compiled version is available yet, and if so calls that version instead of interpreting the bytecode. We will return to this technique below, in the context of the HotSpot Java compiler and JVM.
- When a class file is JIT compiled, the language implementation can cache the resulting machine code for later use. This amounts to guessing, speculatively, that the versions of library routines employed in the current run of the program will still be current when the program is run again. Because languages like Java and C# require the appearance of late binding of library routines, this guess must be checked in each subsequent run. If the check succeeds, using a cached copy saves almost the entire cost of JIT compilation.

Finally, JIT compilation affords the opportunity to perform certain kinds of code improvement that are usually not feasible in traditional compilers. It is customary, for example, for software vendors to ship a single compiled version of an

---

5 While a JIT compiler could, in principle, operate on source code, we assume throughout this discussion that it works on a medium-level IF like Java bytecode or CIL.

application for a given instruction set architecture, even though implementations of that architecture may differ in important ways, including pipeline width and depth; the number of physical (renaming) registers; and the number, size, and speed of the various levels of cache. A JIT compiler may be able to identify the processor implementation on which it is running, and generate code that is tuned for that specific implementation. More important, a JIT compiler may be able to *in-line* calls to dynamically linked library routines. This optimization is particularly important in object-oriented programs, which tend to call many small methods. For such programs, dynamic in-lining can have a dramatic impact on performance.

Dynamic Compilation

We have noted that a language implementation may choose to delay JIT compilation to reduce the impact on program start-up latency. In some cases, compilation *must* be delayed, either because the source or bytecode was not created or discovered until run time, or because we wish to perform optimizations that depend on information gathered during execution. In these cases, we say the language implementation employs *dynamic compilation*. Common Lisp systems have used dynamic compilation for many years: the language is typically compiled, but a program can extend itself at run time. Optimization based on run-time statistics is a more recent innovation.

Most programs spend most of their time in a relatively small fraction of the code. Aggressive code improvement on this fraction can yield disproportionately large improvements in program performance. A dynamic compiler can use statistics gathered by run-time *profiling* to identify *hot paths* through the code, which it then optimizes in the background. By rearranging the code to make hot paths contiguous in memory, it may also improve the performance of the instruction cache. Additional run-time statistics may suggest opportunities to unroll loops (Exercise C-5.21), assign frequently used expressions to registers (Sections C-5.5.2 and C-17.8), and schedule instructions to minimize pipeline stalls (Sections C-5.5.1 and C-17.6).

EXAMPLE 16.4
When is in-lining safe?

In some situations, a dynamic compiler may even be able to perform optimizations that would be unsafe if implemented statically. Consider, for example, the in-lining of methods from dynamically linked libraries. If `foo` is a `static` method of class `C`, then calls to `C.foo` can safely be in-lined. Similarly, if `bar` is a `final` method of class `C` (one that cannot be overridden), and `o` is an object of class `C`, then calls to `o.bar` can safely be in-lined. But what if `bar` is not `final`? The compiler can still in-line calls to `o.bar` if it can prove that `o` will never refer to an instance of a class derived from `C` (which might have a different implementation of `bar`). Sometimes this is easy:

```
C o = new C( args );
o.bar();                // no question what type this is
```

Other times it is not:

```
static void f(C o) {
    o.bar();
}
```

Here the compiler can in-line the call only if it knows that `f` will never be passed an instance of a class derived from `C`. A dynamic compiler can perform the optimization if it verifies that there exists no class derived from `C` anywhere in the (current version of the) program. It must keep notes of what it has done, however: if dynamic linking subsequently extends the program with code that defines a new class `D` derived from `C`, the in-line optimization may need to be undone. ■

In some cases, a dynamic compiler may choose to perform optimizations that may be unsafe even in the current program, provided that profiling suggests they will be profitable and run-time checks can determine whether they are safe.

EXAMPLE 16.5
Speculative optimization

Suppose, in the previous example, there already exists a class `D` derived from `C`, but profiling indicates that every call to `f` so far has passed an instance of class `C`. Suppose further that `f` makes many calls to methods of parameter `o`, not just the one shown in the example. The compiler might choose to generate code along the following lines:

```
static void f(C o) {
    if (o.getClass() == C.class) {
        ... // code with in-lined calls -- much faster
    } else {
        ... // code without in-lined calls
    }
}
```

■

An Example System: the HotSpot Java Compiler

HotSpot is Oracle's principal JVM and JIT compiler for desktop and server systems. It was first released in 1999, and is available as open source.

HotSpot takes its name from its use of dynamic compilation to improve the performance of hot code paths. Newly loaded class files are initially interpreted. Methods that are executed frequently are selected by the JVM for compilation and are subsequently patched into the program on the fly. The compiler is aggressive about in-lining small routines, and will do so in a deep, iterative fashion, repeatedly in-lining routines that are called from the code it just finished in-lining. As described in the preceding discussion of dynamic compilation, the compiler will also in-line routines that are safe only for the current set of class files, and will dynamically "deoptimize" in-lined calls that have been rendered unsafe by the loading of new derived classes.

The HotSpot compiler can be configured to operate in either "client" or "server" mode. Client mode is optimized for lower start-up latency. It is appropriate for systems in which a human user frequently starts new programs. It translates Java bytecode to static single assignment (SSA) form (a medium-level IF described in Section C-17.4.1) and performs a few straightforward machine-independent optimizations. It then translates to a low-level IF, on which it performs instruction scheduling and register allocation. Finally, it translates this IF to machine code.

Server mode is optimized to generate faster code. It is appropriate for systems that need maximum throughput and can tolerate slower start-up. It applies most classic global and interprocedural code improvement techniques to the SSA version of the program (many of these are described in Chapter 17), as well as other improvements specific to Java. Many of these improvements make use of profiling statistics.

Particularly when running in server mode, HotSpot can rival the performance of traditional compilers for C and C++. In effect, aggressive in-lining and profile-driven optimization serve to "buy back" both the start-up latency of JIT compilation and the overhead of Java's run-time semantic checks.

Other Example Systems

EXAMPLE 16.6
Dynamic compilation in the CLR

Like HotSpot, Microsoft's CIL-to-machine-code compiler performs dynamic optimization of hot code paths. The .NET source-to-CIL compilers are also explicitly available to programs through the `System.CodeDom.Compiler` API. A program running on the CLR can directly invoke the compiler to translate C# (or Visual Basic, or other .NET languages) into CIL PE assemblies. These can then be loaded into the running program. As they are loaded, the CLR JIT compiler translates them to machine code. As noted in Sections 3.6.4 and 11.2, C# includes lambda expressions reminiscent of those in functional languages:

```
Func<int, int> square_func = x => x * x;
```

Here `square_func` is a function from integers to integers that multiplies its parameter (`x`) by itself, and returns the product. It is analogous to the following in Scheme:

```
(let ((square-func (lambda (x) (* x x)))) ...
```

Given the C# declaration, we can write

```
y = square_func(3);          // 9
```

But just as Lisp allows a function to be represented as a list, so too does C# allow a lambda expression to be represented as a syntax tree:

```
Expression<Func<int, int>> square_tree = x => x * x;
```

Various methods of library class `Expression` can now be used to explore and manipulate the tree. When desired, the tree can be converted to CIL code:

```
square_func = square_tree.Compile();
```

These operations are roughly analogous to the following in Scheme:

```
(let* ((square-tree '(lambda (x) (* x x)))   ; note the quote mark
       (square-func (eval square-tree (scheme-report-environment 5))))
  ...
```

The difference in practice is that while Scheme's `eval` checks the syntactic validity of the `lambda` expression and creates the metadata needed for dynamic type checking, the typical implementation leaves the function in list (tree) form, and interprets it when called. C#'s `Compile` is expected to produce CIL code; when called it will be JIT compiled and directly executed. ■

EXAMPLE 16.7
Dynamic compilation in CMU Common Lisp

Many Lisp dialects and implementations have employed an explicit mix of interpretation and compilation. Common Lisp includes a `compile` function that takes the name of an existing (interpretable) function as argument. As a side effect, it invokes the compiler on that function, after which the function will (presumably) run much faster:

```
(defun square (x) (* x x))       ; outermost level function declaration
(square 3)                       ; 9
(compile 'square)
(square 3)                       ; also 9 (but faster :-)
```

CMU Common Lisp, a widely used open-source implementation of the language, incorporates two interpreters and a compiler with two back ends. The so-called "baby" interpreter understands a subset of the language, but works stand-alone. It handles simple expressions at the read-eval-print loop, and is used to bootstrap the system. The "grown-up" interpreter understands the whole language, but needs access to the front end of the compiler. The bytecode compiler translates source code to an intermediate form reminiscent of Java bytecode or CIL. The native code compiler translates to machine code. In general, programs are run by the "grown-up" interpreter unless the programmer invokes the compiler explicitly from the command line or from within a Common Lisp program (with `compile`). The compiler, when invoked, produces native code unless otherwise instructed. Documentation indicates that the bytecode version of the compiler runs twice as fast as the native code version. Bytecode is portable and 6× denser than native code. It runs 50× slower than native code, but 10× faster than the interpreter. ■

EXAMPLE 16.8
Compilation of Perl

Like most scripting languages, Perl 5 compiles its input to an internal syntax tree format, which it then interprets. In several cases, the interpreter may need to call back into the compiler during execution. Features that force such dynamic compilation include `eval`, which compiles and then interprets a string; `require`, which loads a library package; and the `ee` version of the substitution command, which performs expression evaluation on the replacement string:

```
$foo = "abc";
$foo =~ s/b/2 + 3/ee;          # replace b with the value of 2 + 3
print "$foo\n";                # prints a5c
```

Perl can also be directed, via library calls or the `perlcc` command-line script (itself written in Perl), to translate source code to either bytecode or machine code. In the former case, the output is an "executable" file beginning with `#! /usr/bin/perl` (see the Sidebar 14.4 for a discussion of the `#!` convention). If invoked from the shell, this file will feed itself back into Perl 5, which will notice that the rest of the file contains bytecode instead of source, and will perform a quick reconstruction of the syntax tree, ready for interpretation.

If directed to produce machine code, `perlcc` generates a C program, which it then runs through the C compiler. The C program builds an appropriate syntax tree and passes it directly to the Perl interpreter, bypassing both the compiler and the byte-code-to-syntax-tree reconstruction. Both the bytecode and machine code back ends are considered experimental; they do not work for all programs.

Perl 6, still under development as of 2015, is intended to be JIT compiled. Its virtual machine, called Parrot, is unusual in providing a large register set, rather than a stack, for expression evaluation. Like Perl itself—but unlike the JVM and CLR—Parrot allows variables to be treated as different types in different contexts. Work is underway to target other scripting languages to Parrot, with the eventual goal or providing interoperability similar to that of the .NET languages. ■

✓ CHECK YOUR UNDERSTANDING

11. What is a *just-in-time* (JIT) compiler? What are its potential advantages over interpretation or conventional compilation?
12. Why might one prefer bytecode over source code as the input to a JIT compiler?
13. What distinguishes *dynamic compilation* from just-in-time compilation?
14. What is a *hot path*? Why is it significant?
15. Under what circumstances can a JIT compiler expand virtual methods in-line?
16. What is *deoptimization*? When and why is it needed?
17. Explain the distinction between the function and expression tree representations of a lambda expression in C#.
18. Summarize the relationship between compilation and interpretation in Perl.

16.2.2 Binary Translation

Just-in-time and dynamic compilers assume the availability of source code or of bytecode that retains all of the semantic information of the source. There are times, however, when it can be useful to recompile object code. This process is known as *binary translation*. It allows already-compiled programs to be run on a machine with a different instruction set architecture. Some readers may recall

Apple's Rosetta system, which allowed programs compiled for older PowerPC-based Macintosh computers to run on newer x86-based Macs. Rosetta built on experience with a long line of similar translators.

The principal challenge for binary translation is the loss of information in the original source-to-object-code translation. Object code typically lacks both type information and the clearly delineated subroutines and control-flow constructs of source code and bytecode. While most of this information appears in the compiler's symbol table, and may sometimes be included in the object file for debugging purposes, vendors usually delete it before shipping commercial products, and a binary translator cannot assume it will be present.

The typical binary translator reads an object file and reconstructs a control flow graph of the sort described in Section 15.1.1. This task is complicated by the lack of explicit information about basic blocks. While branches (the ends of basic blocks) are easy to identify, beginnings are more difficult: since branch targets are sometimes computed at run time or looked up in dispatch tables or virtual function tables, the binary translator must consider the possibility that control may sometimes jump into the middle of a "probably basic" block. Since translated code will generally not lie at the same address as the original code, computed branches must be translated into code that performs some sort of table lookup, or falls back on interpretation.

Static binary translation is not always possible for arbitrary object code. In addition to computed branches, problems include self-modifying code (programs that write to their own instruction space), dynamically generated code (e.g., for single-pointer closures, as described in Example C-9.61), and various forms of introspection, in which a program examines and reasons about its own state (we will consider this more fully in Section 16.3). Fortunately, many common idioms can be identified and treated as special cases, and for the (comparatively rare) cases that can't be handled statically, a binary translator can always delay some translation until run time, fall back on interpretation, or simply inform the user that translation is not possible. In practice, binary translation has proved remarkably successful.

Where and When to Translate

Most binary translators operate in user space, and limit themselves to the non-privileged subset of the machine's instruction set. A few are built at a lower level.

EXAMPLE 16.9
The Mac 68K emulator

When Apple converted from the Motorola 680x0 processor to the PowerPC in 1994, they built a 68K interpreter into the operating system. A subsequent release the following year augmented the interpreter with a rudimentary binary translator that would cache frequently executed instruction sequences in a small (256KB) buffer. By placing the interpreter (emulator) in the lowest levels of the operating system, Apple was able to significantly reduce its time to market: only the most performance-critical portions of the OS were rewritten for the PowerPC, leaving the rest as 68K code. Additional portions were rewritten over time. ■

EXAMPLE 16.10
The Transmeta Crusoe processor

In the late 1990s, Transmeta Corp. developed an unusual system capable of running unmodified x86 operating systems and applications by means of binary translation. Their Crusoe and Efficeon processors, sold from 2000 to 2005, ran proprietary "Code Morphing" software directly on top of a wide-instruction-word ISA (distantly related to the Itanium). This software, designed in conjunction with the hardware, translated x86 code to native code on the fly, and was entirely invisible to systems running above it. ■

Binary translators display even more diversity in their choice of what and when to translate. In the simplest case, translation is a one-time, off-line activity akin to conventional compilation. In the late 1980s, for example, Hewlett Packard Corp. developed a binary translator to retarget programs from their "Classic" HP 3000 line to the PA-RISC processor. The translator depended on the lack of dynamic linking in the operating system: all pieces of the to-be-translated program could be found in a single executable. ■

EXAMPLE 16.11 Static binary translation

EXAMPLE 16.12 Dynamic binary translation

In a somewhat more ambitious vein, Digital Equipment Corp. (DEC) in the early 1990s constructed a pair of translators for their newly developed Alpha processor: one (`mx`) to translate Unix programs originally compiled for MIPS-based workstations, the other (VEST) to translate VMS programs originally compiled for the VAX. Because VMS supported an early form of shared libraries, it was not generally possible to statically identify all the pieces of a program. VEST and `mx` were therefore designed as "open-ended" systems that could intervene, at run time, to translate newly loaded libraries. Like the HP system, DEC's translators saved new, translated versions of their applications to disk, for use in future runs. ■

EXAMPLE 16.13 Mixed interpretation and translation

In a subsequent project in the mid-1990s, DEC developed a system to execute shrink-wrapped Windows software on Alpha processors. (Early versions of Microsoft's Windows NT operating system were available for both the x86 and the

DESIGN & IMPLEMENTATION

16.4 Emulation and interpretation

While the terms *interpretation* and *emulation* are often used together, the concepts are distinct. *Interpretation*, as we have seen, is a language implementation technique: an interpreter is a program capable of executing programs written in the to-be-implemented language. *Emulation* is an end goal: faithfully imitating the behavior of some existing system (typically a processor or processor/OS pair) on some other sort of system. An emulator may use an interpreter to execute the emulated processor's instruction set. Alternatively, it may use binary translation, special hardware (e.g., a field-programmable gate array—FPGA), or some combination of these.

Emulation and interpretation are also distinct from *simulation*. A simulator models some complex system by capturing "important" behavior and ignoring "unimportant" detail. Meteorologists, for example, simulate the Earth's weather systems, but they do not emulate them. An emulator is generally considered correct if it does exactly what the original system does. For a simulator, one needs some notion of accuracy: how close is close enough?

Alpha, but most commercial software came in x86-only versions.) DEC's FX!32 included both a binary translator and a highly optimized interpreter. When the user tried to run an x86 executable, FX!32 would first interpret it, collecting usage statistics. Later, in the background, it would translate hot code paths to native code, and store them in a database. Once translated code was available (later in the same execution or during future runs), the interpreter would run it in lieu of the original.

EXAMPLE 16.14
Transparent dynamic translation

Modern emulation systems typically take an intermediate approach. A fast, simple translator creates native versions of basic blocks or subroutines on demand, and caches them for repeated use within a given execution. For the sake of transparency (to avoid modification of programs on disk), and to accommodate dynamic linking, translated code is usually not retained from one execution to the next. Systems in this style include Apple's Rosetta; HP's Aries, which retargets PA-RISC code to the Itanium; and Intel's IA-32 EL, which retargets x86 code to the Itanium.

EXAMPLE 16.15
Translation and virtualization

Among the most widely used emulators today is the open-source QEMU (quick emulation) system. In the language of Section 16.1, QEMU is a *system* virtual machine. Like other system VMs, it runs as a user-level process that emulates bare hardware on which to run a guest operating system (and that system's workload). Unlike most system VMs, QEMU can emulate hardware very different from that of the underlying physical machine. For the sake of good performance, it makes heavy use of binary translation, converting large blocks of guest system instructions into equivalent blocks of native instructions.

Dynamic Optimization

In a long-running program, a dynamic translator may revisit hot paths and optimize them more aggressively. A similar strategy can also be applied to programs that don't need translation—that is, to programs that already exist as machine code for the underlying architecture. This sort of *dynamic optimization* has been reported to improve performance by as much as 20% over already-optimized code, by exploiting run-time profiling information.

EXAMPLE 16.16
The Dynamo dynamic optimizer

Much of the technology of dynamic optimization was pioneered by the Dynamo project at HP Labs in the late 1990s. Dynamo was designed to transparently enhance the performance of applications for the PA-RISC instruction set. A subsequent version, DynamoRIO, was written for the x86. Dynamo's key innovation was the concept of a *partial execution trace*: a hot path whose basic blocks can be reorganized, optimized, and cached as a linear sequence.

An example of such a trace appears in Figure 16.3. Procedure print_matching takes a set and a predicate as argument, and prints all elements of the set that match the predicate. At run time, Dynamo may discover that the procedure is frequently called with a particular predicate p that is almost never true. The hot path through the flow graph (left side of the figure) can then be turned into the trace at the right. If print_matching is sometimes called with a different predicate p, it will use a separate copy of the code. Branches out of the trace (in the

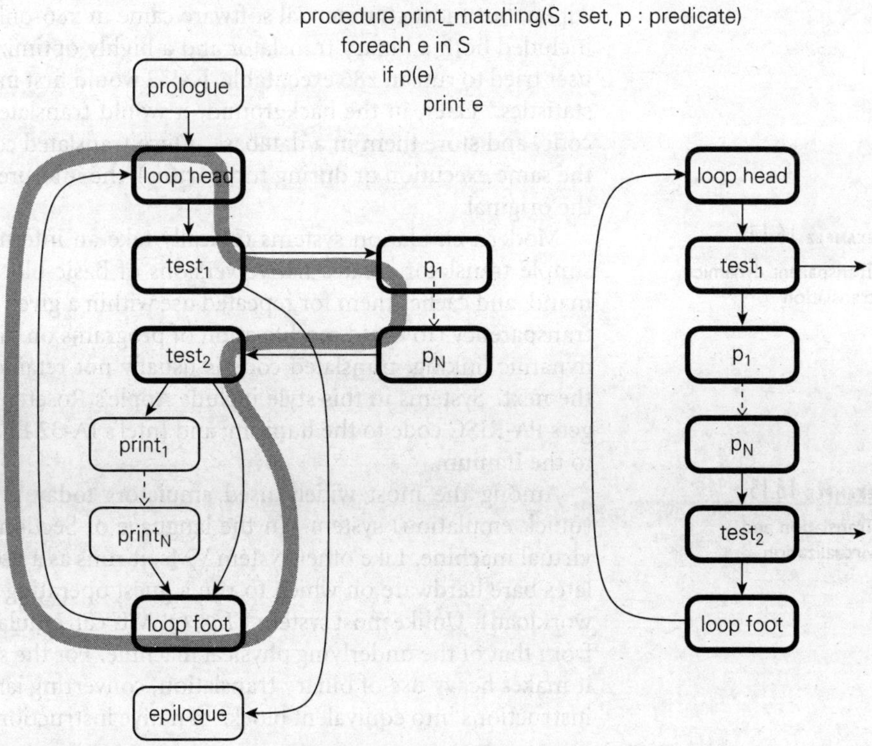

Figure 16.3 **Creation of a partial execution trace.** Procedure print_matching (shown at top) is often called with a particular predicate, p, which is usually false. The control flow graph (*left*, with hot blocks in bold and the hot path in grey) can be reorganized at run time to improve instruction-cache locality and to optimize across abstraction boundaries (*right*).

loop-termination and predicate-checking tests) jump either to other traces or, if appropriate ones have not yet been created, back into Dynamo.

By identifying and optimizing traces, Dynamo is able to significantly improve locality in the instruction cache, and to apply standard code improvement techniques across the boundaries between separately compiled modules and dynamically loaded libraries. In Figure 16.3, for example, it will perform register allocation jointly across print_matchings and the predicate p. It can even perform instruction scheduling across basic blocks if it inserts appropriate *compensating code* on branches out of the trace. An instruction in block test_2, for example, can be moved into the loop footer if a copy is placed on the branch to the right. Traces have proved to be a very powerful technique. They are used not only by dynamic optimizers, but by dynamic translators like Rosetta as well, and by binary instrumentation tools like Pin (to be discussed in Section 16.2.3). ■

16.2.3 Binary Rewriting

While the goal of a binary optimizer is to improve the performance of a program without altering its behavior, one can also imagine tools designed to *change* that behavior. *Binary rewriting* is a general technique to modify existing executable programs, typically to insert instrumentation of some kind. The most common form of instrumentation collects profiling information. One might count the number of times that each subroutine is called, for example, or the number of times that each loop iterates (Exercise 16.5). Such counts can be stored in a buffer in memory, and dumped at the end of execution. Alternatively, one might log all memory references. Such a log will generally need to be sent to a file as the program runs—it will be too long to fit in memory.

In addition to profiling, binary rewriting can be used to

- Simulate new architectures: operations of interest to the simulator are replaced with code that jumps into a special run-time library (other code runs at native speed).
- Evaluate the coverage of test suites, by identifying paths through the code that are not explored by a series of tests.
- Implement *model checking* for parallel programs, a process that exposes race conditions (Example 13.2) by forcing a program through different interleavings of operations in different threads.
- "Audit" the quality of a compiler's optimizations. For example, one might check whether the value loaded into a register is always the same as the value that was already there (such loads suggest that the compiler may have failed to realize that the load was redundant).
- Insert dynamic semantic checks into a program that lacks them. Binary rewriting can be used not only for simple checks like null-pointer dereference and arithmetic overflow, but for a wide variety of memory access errors as well, including uninitialized variables, dangling references, memory leaks, "double deletes" (attempts to deallocate an already deallocated block of memory), and access off the ends of dynamically allocated arrays.

More ambitiously, as described in Sidebar 16.5, binary rewriting can be used to "sandbox" untrusted code so that it can safely be executed in the same address space as the rest of the application.

EXAMPLE 16.17
The ATOM binary rewriter

Many of the techniques used by rewriting tools were pioneered by the ATOM binary rewriter for the Alpha processor. Developed by researchers at DEC's Western Research Lab in the early 1990s, ATOM was a static tool that modified a program for subsequent execution.

To use ATOM, a programmer would write *instrumentation* and *analysis* subroutines in C. Instrumentation routines would be called by ATOM during the rewriting process. By calling back into ATOM, these routines could arrange for the rewritten application to call analysis routines at instructions, basic blocks, subroutines, or control flow edges of the programmer's choosing. To make room for inserted calls, ATOM would move original instructions of the instrumented program; to facilitate such movement, the program had to be provided as a set of relocatable modules. No other changes were made to the instrumented program; in particular, data addresses were always left unchanged. ■

An Example System: the Pin Binary Rewriter

For modern processors, ATOM has been supplanted by Pin, a binary rewriter developed by researchers at Intel in the early 2000s, and distributed as open source. Designed to be largely machine independent, Pin is available not only for the x86, x86-64, and Itanium, but also for ARM.

Pin was directly inspired by ATOM, and has a similar programming interface. In particular, it retains the notions of instrumentation and analysis routines. It also borrows ideas from Dynamo and other dynamic translation tools. Most significantly, it uses an extended version of Dynamo's trace mechanism to instrument previously unmodified programs at run time; the on-disk representation of the program never changes. Pin can even be *attached* to an already-running application, much like the symbolic debuggers we will study in Section 16.3.2.

Like Dynamo, Pin begins by writing an initial trace of basic blocks into a run-time trace cache. It ends the trace when it reaches an unconditional branch, a predefined maximum number of conditional branches, or a predefined maximum number of instructions. As it writes, it inserts calls to analysis routines (or in-line versions of short routines) at appropriate places in the code. It also maintains a mapping between original program addresses and addresses in the trace, so it can modify address-specific instructions accordingly. Once it has finished creating a trace, Pin simply jumps to its first instruction. Conditional branches that exit the trace are set to link to other traces, or to jump back into Pin.

Indirect branches are handled with particular care. Based on run-time profiling, Pin maintains a set of predictions for the targets of such branches, sorted most likely first. Each prediction consists of an address in the original program (which serves as a key) and an address to jump to in the trace cache. If none of the predictions match, Pin falls back to table lookup in its mapping between original and trace cache addresses. If match is still not found, Pin falls back on an instruction set interpreter, allowing it to handle even dynamically generated code.

To reduce the need to save registers when calling analysis routines, and to facilitate in-line expansion of those routines, Pin performs its own register allocation for the instructions of each trace, using similar allocations whenever possible for traces that link to one another. In multithreaded programs, one register is statically reserved to point to a thread-specific buffer, where registers can be spilled when necessary. Condition codes are not saved across calls to analysis routines unless their values are needed afterward. For routines that can be called anywhere within a basic block, Pin hunts for a location where the cost of saving and restoring is minimized.

16.2.4 Mobile Code and Sandboxing

Portability is one of the principal motivations for late binding of machine code. Code that has been compiled for one machine architecture or operating system cannot generally be run on another. Code in a byte code (Java bytecode, CIL) or scripting language (JavaScript, Visual Basic), however, is compact and machine independent: it can easily be moved over the Internet and run on almost any platform. Such *mobile code* is increasingly common. Every major browser supports JavaScript; most enable the execution of Java applets as well. Visual Basic macros are commonly embedded not only in pages meant for viewing with Internet Explorer, but also in Excel, Word, and Outlook documents distributed via email. Cell phone apps may use mobile code to distribute games, productivity tools, and interactive media that run within an existing process.

In some sense, mobile code is nothing new: almost all our software comes from other sources; we download it over the Internet or perhaps install it from a DVD. Historically, this usage model has relied on trust (we assume that software from a well-known company will be safe) and on the very explicit and occasional nature of installation. What has changed in recent years is the desire to download code frequently, from potentially untrusted sources, and often without the conscious awareness of the user.

Mobile code carries a variety of risks. It may access and reveal confidential information (spyware). It may interfere with normal use of the computer in annoying ways (adware). It may damage existing programs or data, or save copies of itself that run without the user's intent (malware of various kinds). In particular

DESIGN & IMPLEMENTATION

16.5 Creating a sandbox via binary rewriting

Binary rewriting provides an attractive means to implement a sandbox. While there is in general no way to ensure that code does what it is supposed to do (one is seldom sure of that even with one's own code), a binary rewriter can

- Verify the address of every load and store, to make sure untrusted code accesses only its own data, and to avoid alignment faults
- Similarly verify every branch and call, to prevent control from leaving the sandbox by any means other than returning
- Verify all opcodes, to prevent illegal instruction faults
- Double-check the parameters to any arithmetic instruction that may generate a fault
- Audit (or forbid) all system calls
- Instrument backward jumps to limit the amount of time that untrusted code can run (and in particular to preclude any infinite loops)

egregious cases, it may use the host machine as a "zombie" from which to launch attacks on other users.

To protect against unwanted behavior, both accidental and malicious, mobile code must be executed in some sort of *sandbox*, as described in Sidebar 14.6. Sandbox creation is difficult because of the variety of resources that must be protected. At a minimum, one needs to monitor or limit access to processor cycles, memory outside the code's own instructions and data, the file system, network interfaces, other devices (passwords, for example, may be stolen by snooping the keyboard), the window system (e.g., to disable pop-up ads), and any other potentially dangerous services provided by the operating system.

Sandboxing mechanisms lie at the boundary between language implementation and operating systems. Traditionally, OS-provided virtual memory techniques might be used to limit access to memory, but this is generally too expensive for many forms of mobile code. The two most common techniques today—both of which rely on technology discussed in this chapter—are binary rewriting and execution in an untrusting interpreter. Both cases are complicated by an inherent tension between safety and utility: the less we allow untrusted code to do, the less useful it can be. No single policy is likely to work in all cases. Applets may be entirely safe if all they can do is manipulate the image in a window, but macros embedded in a spreadsheet may not be able to do their job without changing the user's data. A major challenge for future work is to find a way to help users—who cannot be expected to understand the technical details—to make informed decisions about what and what not to allow in mobile code.

✓ CHECK YOUR UNDERSTANDING

19. What is *binary translation*? When and why is it needed?
20. Explain the tradeoffs between static and dynamic binary translation.
21. What is *emulation*? How is it related to interpretation and simulation?
22. What is *dynamic optimization*? How can it improve on static optimization?
23. What is *binary rewriting*? How does it differ from binary translation and dynamic optimization?
24. Describe the notion of a *partial execution trace*. Why is it important to dynamic optimization and rewriting?
25. What is *mobile code*?
26. What is *sandboxing*? When and why is it needed? How can it be implemented?

16.3 Inspection/Introspection

Symbol table metadata makes it easy for utility programs—just-in-time and dynamic compilers, optimizers, debuggers, profilers, and binary rewriters—to *inspect* a program and reason about its structure and types. We consider debuggers and profilers in particular in Sections 16.3.2 and 16.3.3. There is no reason, however, why the use of metadata should be limited to outside tools, and indeed it is not: Lisp has long allowed a program to reason about its own internal structure and types (this sort of reasoning is sometimes called *introspection*). Java and C# provide similar functionality through a *reflection* API that allows a program to peruse its own metadata. Reflection appears in several other languages as well, including Prolog (Sidebar 12.2) and all the major scripting languages. In a dynamically typed language such as Lisp, reflection is essential: it allows a library or application function to type check its own arguments. In a statically typed language, reflection supports a variety of programming idioms that were not traditionally feasible.

16.3.1 Reflection

EXAMPLE 16.18
Finding the concrete type of a reference variable

Trivially, reflection can be useful when printing diagnostics. Suppose we are trying to debug an old-style (nongeneric) queue in Java, and we want to trace the objects that move through it. In the `dequeue` method, just before returning an object `rtn` of type `Object`, we might write

```
System.out.println("Dequeued a " + rtn.getClass().getName());
```

If the dequeued object is a boxed `int`, we will see

```
Dequeued a java.lang.Integer
```

More significantly, reflection is useful in programs that manipulate other programs. Most program development environments, for example, have mechanisms to organize and "pretty-print" the classes, methods, and variables of a program. In a language with reflection, these tools have no need to examine source code: if they load the already-compiled program into their own address space, they can use the reflection API to query the symbol table information created by the compiler. Interpreters, debuggers, and profilers can work in a similar fashion. In a distributed system, a program can use reflection to create a general-purpose *serialization* mechanism, capable of transforming an almost arbitrary structure into a linear stream of bytes that can be sent over a network and reassembled at the other end. (Both Java and C# include such mechanisms in their standard library, implemented on top of the basic language.) In the increasingly dynamic world of Internet applications, one can even create conventions by which a program can "query" a newly discovered object to see what methods it implements, and then choose which of these to call.

There are dangers, of course, associated with the undisciplined use of reflection. Because it allows an application to peek inside the implementation of a class (e.g., to list its private members), reflection violates the normal rules of abstraction and information hiding. It may be disabled by some security policies (e.g., in sandboxed environments). By limiting the extent to which target code can differ from the source, it may preclude certain forms of code improvement.

EXAMPLE 16.19

What *not* to do with reflection

Perhaps the most common pitfall of reflection, at least for object-oriented languages, is the temptation to write `case` (`switch`) statements driven by type information:

```
procedure rotate(s : shape)
    case shape.type of                    -- don't do this in Java!
        square: rotate_square(s)
        triangle: rotate_triangle(s)
        circle:                           -- no-op
        ...
```

While this kind of code is common (and appropriate) in Lisp, in an object-oriented language it is much better written with subtype polymorphism:

```
    s.rotate()                            -- virtual method call
```

Java Reflection

Java's root class, `Object`, supports a `getClass` method that returns an instance of `java.lang.Class`. Objects of this class in turn support a large number of reflection operations, among them the `getName` method we used in Example 16.18. A call to `getName` returns the *fully qualified* name of the class, as it is embedded in the package hierarchy. For array types, naming conventions are taken from the JVM:

EXAMPLE 16.20

Java class-naming conventions

```
int[] A = new int[10];
System.out.println(A.getClass().getName());       // prints "[I"
String[] C = new String[10];
System.out.println(C.getClass().getName());       // "[Ljava.lang.String;"
Foo[][] D = new Foo[10][10];
System.out.println(D.getClass().getName());       // "[[LFoo;"
```

Here Foo is assumed to be a user-defined class in the default (outermost) package. A left square bracket indicates an array type; it is followed by the array's element type. The built-in types (e.g., `int`) are represented in this context by single-letter names (e.g., `I`). User-defined types are indicated by an `L`, followed by the fully qualified class name and terminated by a semicolon. Notice the similarity of the second example (`C`) to entry #12 in the constant pool of Figure 16.1: that entry gives the parameter types (in parentheses) and return type (`V` means `void`) of `main`. As every Java programmer knows, `main` expects an array of strings.

EXAMPLE 16.21

Getting information on a particular class

A call to `o.getClass()` returns information on the concrete type of the object referred to by `o`, not on the abstract type of the reference `o`. If we want a `Class` object for a particular type, we can create a dummy object of that type:

```
Object o = new Object();
System.out.println(o.getClass().getName());      // "java.lang.Object"
```

Alternatively, we can append the pseudo field name `.class` to the name of the type itself:

```
System.out.println(Object.class.getName());      // "java.lang.Object"
```

In the reverse direction, we can use static method `forName` of class `Class` to obtain a `Class` object for a type with a given (fully qualified) character string name:

```
Class stringClass = Class.forName("java.lang.String");
Class intArrayClass = Class.forName("[I");
```

Method `forName` works only for reference types. For built-ins, one can either use the `.class` syntax or the `.TYPE` field of one of the standard wrapper classes:

```
Class intClass = Integer.TYPE;
```

Given a `Class` object `c`, one can call `c.getSuperclass()` to obtain a `Class` object for `c`'s parent. In a similar vein, `c.getClasses()` will return an array of `Class` objects, one for each public class declared within `c`'s class. Perhaps more interesting, `c.getMethods()`, `c.getFields()`, and `c.getConstructors()` will return arrays of objects representing all `c`'s public methods, fields, and constructors (including those inherited from ancestor classes). The elements of these arrays are instances of classes `Method`, `Field`, and `Constructor`, respectively. These are declared in package `java.lang.reflect`, and serve roles analogous to that of `Class`. The many methods of these classes allow one to query almost any aspect of the Java type system, including modifiers (`static`, `private`, `final`, `abstract`, etc.), type parameters of generics (but not of generic instances—those are erased), interfaces implemented by classes, exceptions thrown by methods, and much more. Perhaps the most conspicuous thing that is *not* available through the Java reflection API is the bytecode that implements methods. Even this, however, can be examined using third-party tools such as the Apache Byte Code Engineering Library (BCEL) or ObjectWeb's ASM, both of which are open source.

EXAMPLE 16.22

Listing the methods of a Java class

Figure 16.4 shows Java code to list the methods declared in (but not inherited by) a given class. Also shown is output for `AccessibleObject`, the parent class of `Method`, `Field`, and `Constructor`. (The primary purpose of this class is to

```
import static java.lang.System.out;

public static void listMethods(String s)
        throws java.lang.ClassNotFoundException {
    Class c = Class.forName(s);     // throws if class not found
    for (Method m : c.getDeclaredMethods()) {
        out.print(Modifier.toString(m.getModifiers()) + " ");
        out.print(m.getReturnType().getName() + " ");
        out.print(m.getName() + "(");
        boolean first = true;
        for (Class p : m.getParameterTypes()) {
            if (!first) out.print(", ");
            first = false;
            out.print(p.getName());
        }
        out.println(") ");
    }
}
```

Sample output for `listMethods("java.lang.reflect.AccessibleObject")`:

```
public java.lang.annotation.Annotation getAnnotation(java.lang.Class)
public boolean isAnnotationPresent(java.lang.Class)
public [Ljava.lang.annotation.Annotation; getAnnotations()
public [Ljava.lang.annotation.Annotation; getDeclaredAnnotations()
public static void setAccessible([Ljava.lang.reflect.AccessibleObject;, boolean)
public void setAccessible(boolean)
private static void setAccessible0(java.lang.reflect.AccessibleObject, boolean)
public boolean isAccessible()
```

Figure 16.4 **Java reflection code to list the methods of a given class.** Sample output is shown below below the code.

control whether the reflection interface can be used to override access control [`private`, `protected`] for the given object.) ■

EXAMPLE 16.23
Calling a method with reflection

One can even use reflection to call a method of an object whose class is not known at compile time. Suppose that someone has created a stack containing a single integer:

```
Stack s = new Stack();
s.push(new Integer(3));
```

Now suppose we are passed this stack as a parameter `u` of `Object` type. We can use reflection to explore the concrete type of `u`. In the process we will discover that its second method, named `pop`, takes no arguments and returns an `Object` result. We can call this method using `Method.invoke`:

```
Method uMethods[] = u.getClass().getMethods();
Method method1 = uMethods[1];
Object rtn = method1.invoke(u);      // u.pop()
```

A call to `rtn.getClass().getName()` will return `java.lang.Integer`. A call to `((Integer) rtn).intValue()` will return the value 3 that was originally pushed into `s`.

Other Languages

C#'s reflection API is similar to that of Java: `System.Type` is analogous to `java.lang.Class`; `System.Reflection` is analogous to `java.lang.reflect`. The pseudo function `typeof` plays the role of Java's pseudo field `.class`. More substantive differences stem from the fact that PE assemblies contain a bit more information than is found in Java class files. We can ask for names of formal parameters in C#, for example, not just their types. More significantly, the use of reification instead of erasure for generics means that we can retrieve precise information on the type parameters used to instantiate a given object. Perhaps the biggest difference is that .NET provides a standard library, `System.Reflection.Emit`, to create PE assemblies and to populate them with CIL. The functionality of `Reflection.Emit` is roughly comparable to that of the BCEL and ASM tools mentioned in the previous subsection. Because it is part of the standard library, however, it is available to any program running on the CLI.

All of the major scripting languages (Perl, PHP, Tcl, Python, Ruby, JavaScript) provide extensive reflection mechanisms. The precise set of capabilities varies some from language to language, and the syntax varies quite a bit, but all allow a program to explore its own structure and types. From the programmer's point of view, the principal difference between reflection in Java and C# on the one hand, and in scripting languages on the other, is that the scripting languages—like Lisp—are dynamically typed. In Ruby, for example, we can discover the class of an object, the methods of a class or object, and the number of parameters expected by each method, but the parameters themselves are untyped until the method is called. In the following code, method p prints its argument to standard output, followed by a newline:

EXAMPLE 16.24
Reflection facilities in Ruby

```
squares = {2=>4, 3=>9}
p squares.class                         # Hash
p Hash.public_instance_methods.length   # 146 -- Hashes have many methods
p squares.public_methods.length         # 146 -- those same methods
m = Hash.public_instance_methods[12]
p m                                     # ":store"
p squares.method(m).arity               # 2 -- key and value to be stored
```

As in Java and C#, we can also invoke a method whose name was not known at compile time:

```
squares.store(1, 1)                 # static invocation
p squares                           # {2=>4, 3=>9, 1=>1}
squares.send(m, 0, 0)               # dynamic invocation
p squares                           # {2=>4, 3=>9, 1=>1, 0=>0}
```

As suggested at the beginning of this section, reflection is in some sense more "natural" in scripting languages (and in Lisp and Prolog) than it is in Java or C#: detailed symbol table information is needed at run time to perform dynamic type checks; in an interpreted implementation, it is also readily available. Lisp programmers have known for decades that reflection was useful for many additional purposes. The designers of Java and C# clearly felt these purposes were valuable enough to justify adding reflection (with considerably higher implementation complexity) to a compiled language with static typing.

Annotations and Attributes

Both Java and C# allow the programmer to extend the metadata saved by the compiler. In Java, these extensions take the form of *annotations* attached to declarations. Several annotations are built into the programming language. These play the role of pragmas. In Example C-7.65, for example, we noted that the Java compiler will generate warnings when a generic class is assigned into a variable of the equivalent nongeneric class. The warning indicates that the code is not statically type-safe, and that an error message is possible at run time. If the programmer is certain that the error cannot arise, the compile-time warning can be disabled by prefixing the method in which the assignment appears with the annotation `@SuppressWarnings("unchecked")`.

In general, a Java annotation resembles an interface whose methods take no parameters, throw no exceptions, and return values of one of a limited number of predefined types. An example of a user-defined annotation appears in Figure 16.5. If we run the program it will print

EXAMPLE 16.25 User-defined annotations in Java

```
author:    Michael Scott
date:      July, 2015
revision:  0.1
docString: Illustrates the use of annotations
```

EXAMPLE 16.26 User-defined annotations in C#

The C# equivalent of Figure 16.5 appears in Figure 16.6. Here user-defined annotations (known as *attributes* in C#) are classes, not interfaces, and the syntax for attaching an attribute to a declaration uses square brackets instead of an @ sign.

In effect, annotations (attributes) serve as compiler-supported comments, with well-defined structure and an API that makes them accessible to automated perusal. As we have seen, they may be read by the compiler (as pragmas) or by reflective programs. They may also be read by independent tools. Such tools can be surprisingly versatile.

EXAMPLE 16.27 javadoc

An obvious use is the automated creation of documentation. Java annotations (first introduced in Java 5) were inspired at least in part by experience with the

```
import static java.lang.System.out;
import java.lang.annotation.*;

@Retention(RetentionPolicy.RUNTIME)
@interface Documentation{
    String author();
    String date();
    double revision();
    String docString();
}

@Documentation(
    author = "Michael Scott",
    date = "July, 2015",
    revision = 0.1,
    docString = "Illustrates the use of annotations"
)
public class Annotate {
    public static void main(String[] args) {
        Class<Annotate> c = Annotate.class;
        Documentation a = c.getAnnotation(Documentation.class);
        out.println("author:    " + a.author());
        out.println("date:      " + a.date());
        out.println("revision:  " + a.revision());
        out.println("docString: " + a.docString());
    }
}
```

Figure 16.5 **User-defined annotations in Java.** `Retention` is a built-in annotation *for annotations*. It indicates here that `Documentation` annotations should be saved in the class file produced by the Java compiler, where they will be available to run-time reflection.

earlier `javadoc` tool, which produces HTML-formatted documentation based on structured comments in Java source code. The `@Documented` annotation, when attached to the declaration of a user-defined annotation, indicates that `javadoc` should include the annotation when creating its reports. One can easily imagine more sophisticated documentation systems that tracked the version history and bug reports for a program over time. ■

EXAMPLE 16.28 Intercomponent communication

The various communication technologies in .NET make extensive use of attributes to indicate which methods should be available for remote execution, how their parameters should be marshalled into messages, which classes need serialization code, and so forth. Automatic tools use these attributes to create appropriate stubs for remote communication, as described (in language-neutral terms) in Section C-13.5.4. ■

EXAMPLE 16.29 Attributes for LINQ

In a similar vein, the .NET LINQ mechanism uses attributes to define the mapping between classes in a user program and tables in a relational database, allow-

```
using System;
using System.Reflection;

[AttributeUsage(AttributeTargets.Class)]
    // Documentation attribute can applied only to classes
public class DocumentationAttribute : System.Attribute {
    public string author;
    public string date;     // these should perhaps be properties
    public double revision;
    public string docString;
    public DocumentationAttribute(string a, string d, double r, string s) {
        author = a;  date = d;  revision = r;  docString = s;
    }
}

[Documentation("Michael Scott",
    "July, 2015", 0.1, "Illustrates the use of attributes")]
public class Attr {
    public static void Main(string[] args) {
        System.Reflection.MemberInfo tp = typeof(Attr);
        object[] attrs =
            tp.GetCustomAttributes(typeof(DocumentationAttribute), false);
            // false means don't search ancestor classes and interfaces
        DocumentationAttribute a = (DocumentationAttribute) attrs[0];
        Console.WriteLine("author:     " + a.author);
        Console.WriteLine("date:       " + a.date);
        Console.WriteLine("revision:   " + a.revision);
        Console.WriteLine("docString:  " + a.docString);
    }
}
```

Figure 16.6 **User-defined attributes in C#.** This code is roughly equivalent to the Java version in Figure 16.5. `AttributeUsage` is a predefined attribute indicating properties of the attribute to whose declaration it is attached.

ing an automatic tool to generate SQL queries that implement iterators and other language-level operations. ■

In an even more ambitious vein, independent tools can be used to modify or analyze programs based on annotations. One could imagine inserting logging code into certain annotated methods, or building a testing harness that called annotated methods with specified arguments and checked for expected results (Exercise 16.11). JML, the Java Modeling Language, allows the programmer to specify preconditions, post-conditions, and invariants for classes, methods, and statements, much like those we considered under "Assertions" in Section 4.1. JML builds on experience with an earlier multilanguage, multi-institution project known as Larch. Like `javadoc`, JML uses structured comments rather than the newer compiler-supported annotations to express its specifications, so they are not automatically included in class files. A variety of tools can be used, however,

EXAMPLE 16.30
The Java Modeling Language

to verify that a program conforms to its specifications, either statically (where possible) or at run time (via insertion of semantic checks).

EXAMPLE 16.31
Java annotation processors

Java 5 introduced a program called `apt` designed to facilitate the construction of annotation processing tools. The functionality of this tool was subsequently integrated into Sun's Java 6 compiler. Its key enabling feature is a set of APIs (in `javax.annotation.processing`) that allow an *annotation processor* class to be added to a program in such a way that the compiler will run it at compile time. Using reflection, the class can peruse the static structure of the program (including annotations and full information on generics) in much the same way that traditional reflection mechanisms allow a running program to peruse its own types and structure.

16.3.2 Symbolic Debugging

Most programmers are familiar with symbolic debuggers: they are built into most programming language interpreters, virtual machines, and integrated program development environments. They are also available as stand-alone tools, of which the best known is probably GNU's `gdb`. The adjective *symbolic* refers to a debugger's understanding of high-level language syntax—the symbols in the original program. Early debuggers understood assembly language only.

In a typical debugging session, the user starts a program under the control of the debugger, or *attaches* the debugger to an already running program. The debugger then allows the user to perform two main kinds of operations. One kind inspects or modifies program data; the other controls execution: starting, stopping, stepping, and establishing *breakpoints* and *watchpoints*. A breakpoint specifies that execution should stop if it reaches a particular location in the source code. A watchpoint specifies that execution should stop if a particular variable is read or written. Both breakpoints and watchpoints can typically be made *conditional*, so that execution stops only if a particular Boolean predicate evaluates to true.

Both data and control operations depend critically on symbolic information. A symbolic debugger needs to be able both to parse source language expressions and to relate them to symbols in the original program. In `gdb`, for example, the command `print a.b[i]` needs to parse the to-be-printed expression; it also needs to recognize that `a` and `i` are in scope at the point where the program is currently stopped, and that `b` is an array-typed field whose index range includes the current value of `i`. Similarly, the command `break 123 if i+j == 3` needs to parse the expression `i+j`; it also needs to recognize that there is an executable statement at line 123 in the current source file, and that `i` and `j` are in scope at that line.

Both data and control operations also depend on the ability to manipulate a program from outside: to stop and start it, and to read and write its data. This control can be implemented in at least three ways. The easiest occurs in interpreters. Since an interpreter has direct access to the program's symbol table and is "in the loop" for the execution of every statement, it is a straightforward matter to move back and forth between the program and the debugger, and to give the latter access to the former's data.

The technology of dynamic binary rewriting (as in Dynamo and Pin) can also be used to implement debugger control [ZRA+08]. This technology is relatively new, however, and is not widely employed in production debugging tools.

For compiled programs, the third implementation of debugger control is by far the most common. It depends on support from the operating system. In Unix, it employs a kernel service known as `ptrace`. The `ptrace` kernel call allows a debugger to "grab" (attach to) an existing process or to start a process under its control. The tracing process (the debugger) can intercept any signals sent to the traced process by the operating system and can read and write its registers and memory. If the traced process is currently running, the debugger can stop it by sending it a signal. If it is currently stopped, the debugger can specify the address at which it should resume execution, and can ask the kernel to run it for a single instruction (a process known as *single stepping*) or until it receives another signal.

Perhaps the most mysterious parts of debugging from the user's perspective are the mechanisms used to implement breakpoints, watchpoints, and single stepping. The default implementation, which works on any modern processor, relies

DESIGN & IMPLEMENTATION

16.6 DWARF

To enable symbolic debugging, the compiler must include symbol table information in each object file, in a format the debugger can understand. The DWARF format, used by many systems (Linux among them) is among the most versatile available [DWA10, Eag12]. Originally developed by Brian Russell of Bell Labs in the late 1980s, DWARF is now maintained by the independent DWARF Committee, led by Michael Eager. Version 5 is expected to appear in late 2015.

Unlike many proprietary formats, DWARF is designed to accommodate a very wide range of (statically typed) programming languages and an equally wide variety of machine architectures. Among other things, it encodes the representation of all program types, the names, types, and scopes of all program objects (in the broad sense of the term), the layout of all stack frames, and the mapping from source files and line numbers to instruction addresses.

Much emphasis has been placed on terse encoding. Program objects are described hierarchically, in a manner reminiscent of an AST. Character string names and other repeated elements are captured exactly once, and then referenced indirectly. Integer constants and references employ a variable-length encoding, so small values take fewer bits. Perhaps most important, stack layouts and source-to-address mappings are encoded not as explicit tables, but as finite automata that *generate* the tables, line by line. For the tiny `gcd` program of Example 1.20, a human-readable representation of the DWARF debugging information (as produced by Linux's `readelf` tool) would fill more than four full pages of this book. The binary encoding in the object file takes only 571 bytes.

on the ability to modify the memory space of the traced process—in particular, the portion containing the program's code. As an example, suppose the traced process is currently stopped, and that before resuming it the debugger wishes to set a breakpoint at the beginning of function `foo`. It does so by replacing the first instruction of the function's prologue with a special kind of `trap`.

EXAMPLE 16.32
Setting a breakpoint

Trap instructions are the normal way a process requests a service from the operating system. In this particular case, the kernel interprets the trap as a request to stop the currently running process and return control to the debugger. To resume the traced process in the wake of the breakpoint, the debugger puts back the original instruction, asks the kernel to single-step the traced process, replaces the instruction yet again with a `trap` (to reenable the breakpoint), and finally resumes the process. For a conditional breakpoint, the debugger evaluates the condition's predicate when the breakpoint occurs. If the breakpoint is unconditional, or if the condition is true, the debugger jumps to its command loop and waits for user input. If the predicate is false, it resumes the traced process automatically and transparently. If the breakpoint is set in an inner loop, where control will reach it frequently, but the condition is seldom true, the overhead of switching back and forth between the traced process and the debugger can be very high. ■

EXAMPLE 16.33
Hardware breakpoints

Some processors provide hardware support to make breakpoints a bit faster. The x86, for example, has four *debugging registers* that can be set (in kernel mode) to contain an instruction address. If execution reaches that address, the processor simulates a trap instruction, saving the debugger the need to modify the address space of the traced process and eliminating the extra kernel calls (and the extra round trip between the traced process and the debugger) needed to restore the original instruction, single-step the process, and put the trap back in place. In a similar vein, many processors, including the x86, can be placed in *single-stepping mode*, which simulates a trap after every user-mode instruction. Without such support, the debugger (or the kernel) must implement single-stepping by repeatedly placing a (temporary) breakpoint at the next instruction. ■

EXAMPLE 16.34
Setting a watchpoint

Watchpoints are a bit trickier. By far the easiest implementation depends on hardware support. Suppose we want to drop into the debugger whenever the program modifies some variable `x`. The debugging registers of the x86 and other modern processors can be set to simulate a trap whenever the program writes to `x`'s address. When the processor lacks such hardware support, or when the user asks the debugger to set more breakpoints or watchpoints than the hardware can support, there are several alternatives, none of them attractive. Perhaps the most obvious is to single step the process repeatedly, checking after each instruction to see whether `x` has been modified. If the processor also lacks a single-step mode, the debugger will want to place its temporary breakpoints at successive store instructions rather than at every instruction (it may be able to skip some of the store instructions if it can prove they cannot possibly reach the address of `x`). Alternatively, the debugger can modify the address space of the traced process to make `x`'s page unwritable. The process will then take a segmentation fault on every write to that page, allowing the debugger to intervene. If the write is actually to x, the debugger jumps to its command loop. Otherwise it performs the write on the process's behalf and asks the kernel to resume it. ■

Unfortunately, the overhead of repeated context switches between the traced process and the debugger dramatically impacts the performance of software watchpoints: slowdowns of 1000× are not uncommon. Debuggers based on dynamic binary rewriting have the potential to support arbitrary numbers of watchpoints at speeds close to those admitted by hardware watchpoint registers. The idea is straightforward: the traced program runs as partial execution traces in a trace cache managed by the debugger. As it generates each trace, the debugger adds instructions at every store, in-line, to check whether it writes to x's address and, if so, to jump back to the command loop.

16.3.3 Performance Analysis

Before placing a debugged program into production use, one often wants to understand—and if possible improve—its performance. Tools to profile and analyze programs are both numerous and varied—far too much so to even survey them here. We focus therefore on the run-time technologies, described in this chapter, that feature prominently in many analysis tools.

EXAMPLE 16.35
Statistical sampling

Perhaps the simplest way to measure, at least approximately, the amount of time spent in each part of the code is to *sample* the program counter (PC) periodically. This approach was exemplified by the classic `prof` tool in Unix. By linking with a special `prof` library, a program could arrange to receive a periodic timer signal—once a millisecond, say—in response to which it would increment a counter associated with the current PC. After execution, the `prof` post-processor would correlate the counters with an address map of the program's code and produce a statistical summary of the percentage of time spent in each subroutine and loop. ■

EXAMPLE 16.36
Call graph profiling

While simple, `prof` had some serious limitations. Its results were only approximate, and could not capture fine-grain costs. It also failed to distinguish among calls to a given routine from multiple locations. If we want to know which of A, B, and C is the biggest contributor to program run time, it is not particularly helpful to learn that all three of them call D, where most of the time is actually spent. If we want to know whether it is A's Ds, B's Ds, or C's Ds that are so expensive, we can use the (slightly) more recent `gprof` tool, which relies on compiler support to instrument procedure prologues. As the instrumented program runs, it logs the number of times that D is called from each location. The `gprof` post-processor then assumes that the total time spent in D can accurately be apportioned among the call sites according to the relative number of calls. More sophisticated tools log not only the caller and callee but also the stack *backtrace* (the contents of the dynamic chain), allowing them to cope with the case in which D consumes twice as much time when called from A as it does when called from B or C (see Exercise 16.13). ■

If our program is underperforming for algorithmic reasons, it may be enough to know where it is spending the bulk of its time. We can focus our attention on improving the source code in the places it will matter most. If the program is underperforming for other reasons, however, we generally need to know *why*. Is it cache misses due to poor locality, perhaps? Branch mispredictions? Poor use of the processor pipeline? Tools to address these and similar questions generally rely on more extensive instrumentation of the code or on some sort of hardware support.

EXAMPLE 16.37
Finding basic blocks with low IPC

As an example of instrumentation, consider the task of identifying basic blocks that execute an unusually small number of instructions per cycle. To find such blocks we can combine (1) the aggregate time spent in each block (obtained by statistical sampling), (2) a count of the number of times each block executes (obtained via instrumentation), and (3) static knowledge of the number of instructions in each block. If basic block i contains k_i instructions and executes n_i times during a run of a program, it contributes $k_i n_i$ dynamic instructions to that run. Let $N = \sum_i k_i n_i$ be the total number of instructions in the run. If statistical sampling indicates that block i accounts for x_i% of the time in the run and x_i is significantly larger than $(k_i n_i)/N$, then something strange is going on—probably an unusually large number of cache misses.

EXAMPLE 16.38
Haswell performance counters

Most modern processors provide a set of *performance counters* that can be used to good effect by performance analysis tools. The Intel Haswell processor, for example, has built-in counters for clock ticks (both total and when running) and instructions executed. It also has four general-purpose counters, which can be configured by the kernel to count any of more than 250 different kinds of *events*, including branch mispredictions; TLB (address translation) misses; and various kinds of cache misses, interrupts, executed instructions, and pipeline stalls. Finally, it has counters for the number of Joules of energy consumed by the processor cores, caches, and memory. Unfortunately, performance counters are generally a scarce resource (one might often wish for many more of them). Their number, type, and mode of operation varies greatly from processor to processor; direct access to them is usually available only in kernel mode; and operating systems do not always export that access to user-level programs with a convenient or uniform interface. Tools to access the counters and interpret their values are available from most manufacturers—Intel among them. Portable tools are an active topic of research.

✓ CHECK YOUR UNDERSTANDING

27. What is *reflection*? What purposes does it serve?
28. Describe an inappropriate use of reflection.
29. Name an aspect of reflection supported by the CLI but not by the JVM.
30. Why is reflection more difficult to implement in Java or C# than it is in Perl or Ruby?
31. What are *annotations* (Java) or *attributes* (C#)? What are they used for?

32. What are `javadoc`, `apt`, `JML`, and `LINQ`, and what do they have to do with annotation?
33. Briefly describe three different implementation strategies for a symbolic debugger.
34. Explain the difference between *breakpoints* and *watchpoints*. Why are watchpoints potentially much more expensive?
35. Summarize the capabilities provided by the Unix `ptrace` mechanism.
36. What is the principal difference between the Unix `prof` and `gprof` tools?
37. For the purposes of performance analysis, summarize the relative strengths and limitations of statistical sampling, instrumentation, and hardware performance counters. Explain why statistical sampling and instrumentation might profitably be used together.

16.4 Summary and Concluding Remarks

We began this chapter by defining a run-time system as the set of libraries, essential to many language implementations, that depend on knowledge of the compiler or the programs it produces. We distinguished these from "ordinary" libraries, which require only the arguments they are passed.

We noted that several topics covered elsewhere in the book, including garbage collection, variable-length argument lists, exception and event handling, coroutines and threads, remote procedure calls, transactional memory, and dynamic linking are often considered the purview of the run-time system. We then turned to virtual machines, focusing in particular on the Java Virtual Machine (JVM) and the Common Language Infrastructure (CLI). Under the general heading of late binding of machine code, we considered just-in-time and dynamic compilation, binary translation and rewriting, and mobile code and sandboxing. Finally, under the general heading of inspection and introspection, we considered reflection mechanisms, symbolic debugging, and performance analysis.

Through all these topics we have seen a steady increase in complexity over time. Early Basic interpreters parsed and executed one source statement at a time. Modern interpreters first translate their source into a syntax tree. Early Java implementations, while still interpreter-based, relied on a separate source-to-byte-code compiler. Modern Java implementations, as well as implementations of the CLI, enhance performance with a just-in-time compiler. For programs that extend themselves at run time, the CLI allows the source-to-byte-code compiler to be invoked dynamically as well, as it is in Common Lisp. Recent systems may profile and reoptimize already-running programs. Similar technology may allow separate tools to translate from one machine language to another, or to instrument code for testing, debugging, security, performance analysis, model checking, or architectural simulation. The CLI provides extensive support for cross-language interoperability.

Many of these developments have served to blur the line between the compiler and the run-time system, and between compile-time and run-time operations. It seems safe to predict that these trends will continue. More and more, programs will come to be seen not as static artifacts, but as dynamic collections of malleable components, with rich semantic structure amenable to formal analysis and reconfiguration.

16.5 Exercises

16.1 Write the formula of Example 15.4 as an expression tree (a syntax tree in which each operator is represented by an internal node whose children are its operands). Convert your tree to an *expression DAG* by merging identical nodes. Comment on the redundancy in the tree and how it relates to Figure 15.4.

16.2 We assumed in Example 15.4 and Figure 15.4 that a, b, c, and s were all among the first few local variables of the current method, and could be pushed onto or popped from the operand stack with a single one-byte instruction. Suppose that this is not the case: that is, that the push and pop instructions require three bytes each. How many bytes will now be required for the code on the left side of Figure 15.4?

Most stack-based languages, Java bytecode and CIL among them, provide a swap instruction that reverses the order of the top two values on the stack, and a duplicate instruction that pushes a second copy of the value currently at top of stack. Show how to use swap and duplicate to eliminate the pop and the pushes of s in the left side of Figure 15.4. Feel free to exploit the associativity of multiplication. How many instructions is your new sequence? How many bytes?

16.3 The speculative optimization of Example 16.5 could in principle be statically performed. Explain why a dynamic compiler might be able to do it more effectively.

16.4 Perhaps the most common form of run-time instrumentation counts the the number of times that each basic block is executed. Since basic blocks are short, adding a load-increment-store instruction sequence to each block can have a significant impact on run time.

We can improve performance by noting that certain blocks imply the execution of other blocks. In an if... then ... else construct, for example, execution of either the then part or the else part implies execution of the conditional test. If we're smart, we won't actually have to instrument the test.

Describe a general technique to minimize the number of blocks that must be instrumented to allow a post-processor to obtain an accurate count for each block. (This is a difficult problem. For hints, see the paper by Larus and Ball [BL92].)

16.5 Visit *software.intel.com/en-us/articles/pintool-downloads* and download a copy of Pin. Use it to create a tool to profile loops. When given a (machine code) program and its input, the output of the tool should list the number of times that each loop was encountered when running the program. It should also give a histogram, for each loop, of the number of iterations executed.

16.6 Outline mechanisms that might be used by a binary rewriter, without access to source code, to catch uses of uninitialized variables, "double deletes," and uses of deallocated memory (e.g., dangling pointers). Under what circumstances might you be able to catch memory leaks and out-of-bounds array accesses?

16.7 Extend the code of Figure 16.4 to print information about

(a) fields
(b) constructors
(c) nested classes
(d) implemented interfaces
(e) ancestor classes, and their methods, fields, and constructors
(f) exceptions thrown by methods
(g) generic type parameters

16.8 Repeat the previous exercise in C#. Add information about parameter names and generic instances.

16.9 Write an interactive tool that accepts keyboard commands to load specified class files, create instances of their classes, invoke their methods, and read and write their fields. Feel free to limit keyboard input to values of built-in types, and to work only in the global scope. Based on your experience, comment on the feasibility of writing a command-line interpreter for Java, similar to those commonly used for Lisp, Prolog, or the various scripting languages.

16.10 In Java, if the concrete type of `p` is `Foo`, `p.getClass()` and `Foo.class` will return the same thing. Explain why a similar equivalence could not be guaranteed to hold in Ruby, Python, or JavaScript. For hints, see Section 14.4.4.

16.11 Design a "test harness" system based on Java annotations. The user should be able to attach to a method an annotation that specifies parameters to be passed to a test run of the method, and values expected to be returned. For simplicity, you may assume that parameters and return values will all be strings or instances of built-in types. Using the annotation processing facility of Java 6, you should automatically generate a new method, `test()` in any class that has methods with `@Test` annotations.

This method should call the annotated methods with the specified parameters, test the return values, and report any discrepancies. It should also call the `test` methods of any nested classes. Be sure to include a mechanism to invoke the `test` method of every top-level class. For an extra challenge, devise a way to specify multiple tests of a single method, and a way to test exceptions thrown, in addition to values returned.

16.12 C++ provides a `typeid` operator that can be used to query the concrete type of a pointer or reference variable:

```
if (typeid(*p) == typeid(my_derived_type)) ...
```

Values returned by `typeid` can be compared for equality but not assigned. They also support a `name()` method that returns an (implementation-dependent) character string name for the type. Give an example of a program fragment in which these mechanisms might reasonably be used.

Unlike more extensive reflection mechanisms, `typeid` can be applied only to (instances of) classes with at least one virtual method. Give a plausible explanation for this restriction.

16.13 Suppose we wish, as described at the end of Example 16.36, to accurately attribute sampled time to the various contexts in which a subroutine is called. Perhaps the most straightforward approach would be to log not only the current PC but also the stack *backtrace*—the contents of the dynamic chain—on every timer interrupt. Unfortunately, this can dramatically increase profiling overhead. Suggest an equivalent but cheaper implementation.

16.14–16.17 In More Depth.

16.6 Explorations

16.18 Learn about the Java *security policy* mechanism. What aspects of program behavior can the programmer enable/proscribe? How are such policies enforced? What is the relationship (if any) between security policies and the verification process described in Sidebar 16.3?

16.19 Learn about `taint` mode in Perl and Ruby. How does it compare to sandbox creation via binary rewriting, as described in Sidebar 16.5? What sorts of security problems does it catch? What sorts of problems does it *not* catch?

16.20 Learn about *proof-carrying code*, a technique in which the supplier of mobile code includes a proof of its safety, and the user simply verifies the proof, rather than regenerating it (start with the work of Necula [Nec97]). How does this technique compare to other forms of sandboxing? What properties can it guarantee?

16.21 Investigate the *MetaObject Protocol* (MOP), which underlies the Common Lisp Object System. How does it compare to the reflection mechanisms of Java and C#? What does it allow you to do that these other languages do not?

16.22 When using a symbolic debugger and moving through a program with breakpoints, one often discovers that one has gone "too far," and must start the program over from the beginning. This may mean losing all the effort that had been put into reaching a particular point. Consider what it would take to be able to run the program not only forward but *backward* as well. Such a *reverse execution* facility might allow the user to narrow in on the source of bugs much as one narrows the range in binary search. Consider both the loss of information that happens when data is overridden and the nondeterminism that arises in parallel and event-driven programs.

16.23 Download and experiment with one of the several available packages for performance counter sampling in Linux (try *sourceforge.net/projects/perfctr/*, *perfmon2.sourceforge.net/*, or *www.intel.com/software/pcm*). What do these packages allow you to measure? How might you use the information? (Note: you may need to install a kernel patch to make the program counters available to user-level code.)

16.24–16.25 In More Depth.

16.7 Bibliographic Notes

Aycock [Ayc03] surveys the history of just-in-time compilation. Documentation on the HotSpot compiler and JVM can be found at Oracle's web site: *www.oracle.com/technetwork/articles/javase/index-jsp-136373.html*. The JVM specification is by Lindholm et al. [LYBB14]. Sources of information on the CLI include the ECMA standard [Int12a, MR04] and the .NET pages at *msdn.microsoft.com*.

Arnold et al. [AFG+05] provide an extensive survey of adaptive optimization techniques for programs on virtual machines. Deutsch and Schiffman [DS84] describe the ParcPlace Smalltalk virtual machine, which pioneered such mechanisms as just-in-time compilation and the caching of JIT-compiled machine code. Various articles discuss the binary translation technology of Apple's 68K emulator [Tho95], DEC's FX!32 [HH97b], and its earlier VEST and `mx` [SCK+93].

Probably the best source of information on binary rewriting is the text by Hazelwood [Haz11]. The original papers on Dynamo, Atom, Pin, and QEMU are by Bala et al. [BDB00], Srivastava and Eustace [SE94], Luk et al. [LCM+05], and Bellard [Bel05], respectively. Duesterwald [Due05] surveys issues in the design of a dynamic binary optimizer, drawing on her experience with the Dynamo project. Early work on sandboxing via binary rewriting is reported by Wahbe et al. [WLAG93].

The DWARF standard is available from *dwarfstd.org* [DWA10]; Eager provides a gentler introduction [Eag12]. Ball and Larus [BL92] describe the minimal instrumentation required to profile the execution of basic blocks. Zhao et al. [ZRA+08] describe the use of dynamic instrumentation (based on DynamoRIO) to implement watchpoints efficiently. Martonosi et al. [MGA92] describe a performance analysis tool that builds on the idea outlined in Example 16.37.

17 Code Improvement

In Chapter 15 we discussed the generation, assembly, and linking of target code in the back end of a compiler. The techniques we presented led to correct but highly suboptimal code: there were many redundant computations, and inefficient use of the registers, multiple functional units, and cache of a modern microprocessor. This chapter takes a look at *code improvement*: the phases of compilation devoted to generating *good* (fast) code. As noted in Section 1.6.4, code improvement is often referred to as *optimization*, though it seldom makes anything optimal in any absolute sense.

Our study will consider simple *peephole* optimization, which "cleans up" generated target code within a very small instruction window; *local* optimization, which generates near-optimal code for individual basic blocks; and *global* optimization, which performs more aggressive code improvement at the level of entire subroutines. We will not cover interprocedural improvement; interested readers are referred to other texts (see the Bibliographic Notes at the end of the chapter). Moreover, even for the subjects we cover, our intent will be more to "demystify" code improvement than to describe the process in detail. Much of the discussion will revolve around the successive refinement of code for a single subroutine. This extended example will allow us to illustrate the effect of several key forms of code improvement without dwelling on the details of how they are achieved.

IN MORE DEPTH

Chapter 17 can be found in its entirety on the companion site.

Programming Languages Mentioned

This appendix provides brief descriptions, bibliographic references, and (in many cases) URLs for on-line information concerning each of the principal programming languages mentioned in this book. The URLs are accurate as of June 2015, though they are subject to change as people move files around. Some additional URLs can be found in the bibliographic references.

Bill Kinnersley maintains an index of on-line materials for approximately 2500 programming languages at *people.ku.edu/~nkinners/LangList/Extras/langlist.htm*.

Figure A.1 shows the genealogy of some of the more influential or widely used programming languages. The date for each language indicates the approximate time at which its features became widely known. Arrows indicate principal influences on design. Many influences, of course, cannot be shown in a single figure.

Ada: Originally intended to be the standard language for all software commissioned by the U.S. Department of Defense [Ame83], now standardized by the ISO [Int12b]. Prototypes designed by teams at several sites; final '83 language developed by a team at Honeywell's Systems and Research Center in Minneapolis and Alsys Corp. in France, led by Jean Ichbiah. A very large language, descended largely from Pascal. Design rationale articulated in a remarkably clear companion document [IBFW91]. Ada 95 was a revision developed under government contract by a team at Intermetrics, Inc. It fixed several subtle problems in the earlier language, and added objects, shared-memory synchronization, and many other features. Ada 2005 and Ada 2012 add a host of additional features; for a summary see *ada2012.org/comparison.html*. Freely available implementation (`gnat`) distributed as part of the GNU compiler collection (`gcc`). Additional resources at *adaic.org/* and *ada-europe.org/*.

Algol 60: The original block-structured language. The definition by Naur et al. [NBB+63] is considered a landmark of clarity and conciseness. It includes the original use of Backus-Naur Form (BNF).

Algol 68: A large and relatively complex successor to Algol 60, designed by a committee led by A. van Wijngaarden. Includes (among other things) structures and unions, expression-based syntax, reference parameters, a reference model of variables, and concurrency. The official definition [vMP+75] uses

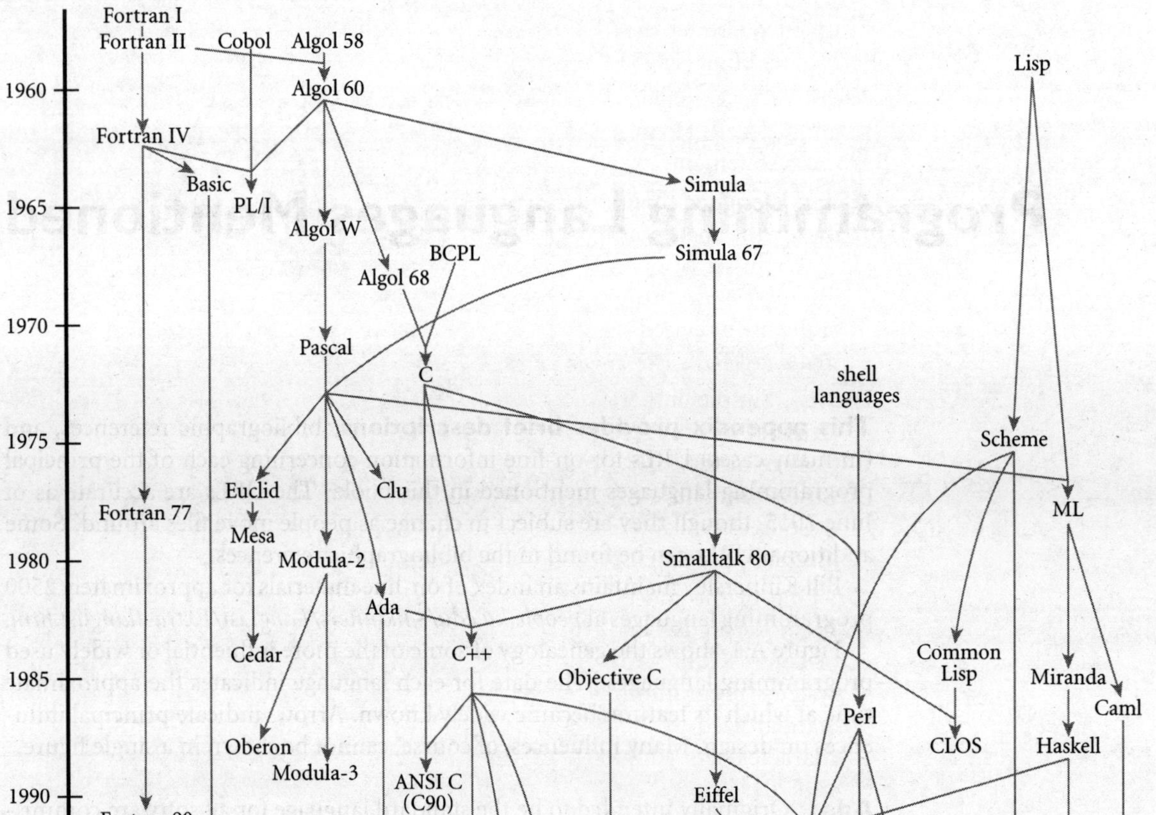

Figure A.1 **Genealogy of selected programming languages.** Dates are approximate. Arrows that continue at the botton of the page indicate ongoing evolution.

unconventional terminology and is very difficult to read; other sources (e.g., Pagan's book [Pag76]) are more accessible.

Algol W: A smaller, simpler alternative to Algol 68, proposed by Niklaus Wirth and C. A. R. Hoare [WH66, Sit72]. The precursor to Pascal. Introduced the `case` statement.

APL: Designed by Kenneth Iverson in the late 1950s and early 1960s, primarily for the manipulation of numeric arrays. Functional. Extremely concise. Powerful set of operators. Employs an extended character set. Intended for interactive use. Original syntax [Ive62] was nonlinear; implementations generally use a revised syntax due to a team at IBM [IBM87]. On-line resources at *sigapl.org/*.

Basic: Simple imperative language, originally intended for interactive use. Original version developed by John Kemeny and Thomas Kurtz of Dartmouth College in the early 1960s. Dozens of dialects exist. Microsoft's Visual Basic, which bears little resemblance to the original, is the most widely used today (resources available at *msdn.microsoft.com/en-us/library/sh9ywfdk.aspx*). Minimal subset defined by ANSI standard [Ame78].

C: One of the most successful imperative languages. Originally defined by Brian Kernighan and Dennis Ritchie of Bell Labs as part of the development of Unix [KR88]. Concise syntax. Unusual declaration syntax. Intended for systems programming. Weak type checking. No dynamic semantic checks. Standardized by ANSI/ISO in 1990 [Ame90]. Extensions for international character sets adopted in 1994. More extensive changes adopted in 1999 and 2011 [Int99, Int11]. Popular open-source implementations include `gcc` (*gnu.org/software/gcc/*) and `clang/llvm` (*clang.llvm.org/*).

C#: Object-oriented language originally designed by Anders Hejlsberg, Scott Wiltamuth, and associates at Microsoft Corporation in the late 1990s and early 2000s [HTWG11, Mic12, ECM06a]. Versions 1 and 2 standardized by ECMA and the ISO [ECM06a]; subsequent versions defined directly by Microsoft. Serves as the principal language for the .NET platform, a runtime and middleware system for multilanguage distributed computing. Includes most of Java's features, plus many from C++ and Visual Basic, including both reference and value types, both contiguous and row-pointer arrays, both virtual and nonvirtual methods, operator overloading, delegates, generics, local type inference, an "unsafe" superset with pointers, and the ability to invoke methods of dynamically typed objects across language boundaries. Commercial resources at *msdn.microsoft.com/en-us/vstudio/hh388566.aspx*. Freely available implementation at *mono-project.com/docs/about-mono/languages/csharp/*.

C++: The first object-oriented successor to C to gain widespread adoption. Still widely considered the one most suited to "industrial strength" computing. Originally designed by Bjarne Stroustrup of Bell Labs (now at Texas A&M University). A large language. Standardized by the ISO in 1998; major revision in 2011; updated in 2014. Includes (among other things) generalized reference types, both static and dynamic method binding, extensive facilities for overloading and coercion, multiple inheritance, and Turing-complete generics. No automatic garbage collection. Many texts exist; aside from the ISO standard [Int14b], Stroustrup's is the most comprehensive [Str13]. Freely available implementations included in the `gcc` and `clang/llvm` distributions (see C). Stroustrup's own resource page is at *stroustrup.com/C++.html.*

Caml and OCaml: Caml is a dialect of ML developed by Guy Cousineau and colleagues at INRIA (the French National research institute) beginning in the late 1980s. Evolved into Objective Caml (OCaml) around 1996, under the leadership of Xavier Leroy; the revised language adds modules and object orientation. Regarded by many as "more practical" than SML (the other principal ML dialect), OCaml is widely used in industry. See also F#. On-line resources at *caml.inria.fr/*.

Cedar: See Mesa and Cedar.

Cilk: Concurrent extension of C and C++ developed by Charles Leiserson and associates at MIT beginning in the mid 1990s, and commercialized by Cilk Arts, Inc. in 2006; acquired by Intel in 2009. Extensions to C are deliberately minimal: a function can be `spawned` as a separate task; completion of subtasks can be awaited *en masse* with `sync`; tasks can synchronize with each other to a limited degree with `inlets`. Implementation employs a novel, provably efficient *work-stealing* scheduler. On-line resources at *supertech.csail.mit.edu/cilk/* and */software.intel.com/en-us/intel-cilk-plus.*

CLOS: The Common Lisp Object System [Kee89; Sei05, Chaps. 16–17]. A set of object-oriented extensions to Common Lisp, incorporated into the ANSI standard language (see Common Lisp).

Clu: Developed by Barbara Liskov and associates at MIT in the late 1970s [LG86]. Designed to provide an unusually powerful set of features for data abstraction [LSAS77]. Also includes iterators and exception handling. Documentation and freely available implementations at *pmg.csail.mit.edu/CLU.html*.

Cobol: Originally developed by the U.S. Department of Defense in the late 1950s and early 1960s by a team led by Grace Murray Hopper. Long the most widely used programming language in the world. Standardized by ANSI in 1968; revised in 1974 and 1985. Intended principally for business data processing. Introduced the concept of structures. Elaborate I/O facilities. Cobol 2002 and 2014 [Int14a] add a variety of modern language features, including object orientation.

Common Lisp: Large, widely used dialect of Lisp (see also Lisp). Includes (among other things) static scoping, an extensive type system, exception handling, and object-oriented features (see CLOS). For years the standard reference was the book by Guy Steele, Jr. [Ste90]. Subsequently standardized by ANSI [Ame96b]; recent text by Seibel [Sei05] Abridged hypertext version of the standard available at *lispworks.com/documentation/HyperSpec/Front/index.htm*.

CSP: See Occam.

Eiffel: An object-oriented language developed by Bertrand Meyer and associates at the Société des Outils du Logiciel à Paris [Mey92b, ECM06b]. Includes (among other things) multiple inheritance, automatic garbage collection, and powerful mechanisms for renaming of data members and methods in derived classes. On-line resources at *eiffel.com/*.

Erlang: A functional language with extensive support for distribution, fault tolerance, and message passing. Developed by Joe Armstrong and colleagues at Ericsson Computer Science Laboratory starting in the late 1980s [Arm13]. Distributed as open source since 1998. Used to implement a variety of products from Ericsson and other companies, particularly in the European telecom industry. On-line resources at *erlang.org/*.

Euclid: Imperative language developed by Butler Lampson and associates at the Xerox Palo Alto Research Center in the mid-1970s [LHL$^+$77]. Designed to eliminate many of the sources of common programming errors in Pascal, and to facilitate formal verification of programs. Has closed scopes and module types.

F#: A descendant of OCaml developed by Don Syme and colleagues at Microsoft Research. First public release was in 2005 [SGC13]. Differences from OCaml are primarily to accommodate integration with the .NET framework. On-line resources at *research.microsoft.com/fsharp/* and *msdn.microsoft.com/en-us/library/dd233154.aspx*.

Forth: A small and rather ingenious stack-based language designed for interpretation on machines with limited resources [Bro87, Int97]. Originally developed by Charles H. Moore in the late 1960s. Has a loyal following in the instrumentation and process-control communities.

Fortran: The original high-level imperative language. Developed in the mid-1950s by John Backus and associates at IBM. Important historical versions include Fortran I, Fortran II, Fortran IV, Fortran 77, and Fortran 90. The latter two were documented in a pair of ANSI standards. Fortran 90 [MR96] (updated in 1995) was a major revision to the language, adding (among other things) recursion, pointers, new control constructs, and a wealth of array operations. Fortran 2003 adds object orientation. Fortran 2008 [Int10] (approved in 2010) adds several generics, co-arrays (arrays with an explicit extra "location" dimension for distributed-memory machines), and a `DO CONCURRENT` construct for loops whose iterations are independent. Fortran 77 continues to be widely used. Freely available `gfortran` implementation conforms to all modern standards, and is distributed as part of the gcc compiler suite (*gnu.org/software/gcc/fortran/*). Support for the older g77 front end was discontinued as of gcc version 3.4.

Go: A statically typed language developed by Robert Griesemer, Rob Pike, Ken Thompson, and colleagues at Google, beginning in 2007. Intended to combine the simplicity of scripting languages with the efficiency of compilation, and motivated in part by the perception that C++ had grown too large and complicated. Includes garbage collection, strong typing, local type inference, type extension and interfaces as an alternative to classes, variable-length and associative arrays, and message-based concurrency. In active use both within and outside Google. Online resources at *golang.org/*.

Haskell: The leading purely functional language. Descended from Miranda. Designed by a committee of researchers beginning in 1987. Includes curried functions, higher order functions, nonstrict semantics, static polymorphic typing, pattern matching, list comprehensions, modules, monadic I/O, type classes, and layout (indentation)-based syntactic grouping. Haskell 98 was for many years the standard; superceded by Haskell 2010 [PJ10]. On-line resources at *haskell.org/*. Several concurrent variants have also been devised, including Concurrent Haskell [JGF96] and pH [NA01].

Icon: The successor to Snobol. Developed by Ralph Griswold (Snobol's principal designer) at the University of Arizona [GG96]. Adopts more conventional control-flow constructs, but with powerful iteration and search facilities based on pattern matching and backtracking. On-line resources at *cs.arizona.edu/icon/*.

Java: Object-oriented language based largely on a subset of C++. Developed by James Gosling and associates at Sun Microsystems in the early 1990s [AG06, GJS+14]. Intended for the construction of highly portable, architecture-neutral programs. Defined in conjunction with an intermediate *bytecode* format intended for execution on a Java *virtual machine* [LYBB14]. Includes (among other things) a reference model of (class-typed) variables, mix-in inheritance, threads, and extensive predefined libraries for graphics, communication, and other activities. On-line resources at *docs.oracle.com/javase/*.

JavaScript: Simple scripting language developed by Brendan Eich at Netscape Corp. in the mid 1990s for the purpose of client-side web scripting. Has no connection to Java beyond superficial syntactic similarity. Embedded in most commercial web browsers. Microsoft's JScript is very similar. The two were merged into a single ECMA standard in 1997; subsequently revised and cross-standardized by the ISO [ECM11].

Lisp: The original functional language [McC60]. Developed by John McCarthy in the late 1950s as a realization of Church's lambda calculus. Many dialects exist. The two most common today are Common Lisp and Scheme (see separate entries). Historically important dialects include Lisp 1.5 [MAE+65], MacLisp [Moo78], and Interlisp [TM81].

Lua: Lightweight scripting language intended primarily for extension/embedded settings. Originally developed by Roberto Ierusalimschy, Waldemar Celes, and Luiz Henrique de Figueiredo at the Pontifical Catholic University of Rio de Janeiro. Intended to be simple, fast, and easy to extend and to port to new environments. The standard implementation is also quite small—well under 1 MB for the interpreter and all the standard libraries. Heavily used in the gaming industry and in a wide variety of other fields. Online resources at *lua.org/*.

Mesa and Cedar: Mesa [LR80] was a successor to Euclid developed in the 1970s at Xerox's Palo Alto Research Center by a team led by Butler Lampson. Includes monitor-based concurrency. Along with Interlisp and Smalltalk, one of three companion projects that pioneered the use of personal workstations, with bitmapped displays, mice, and a graphical user interface. Cedar [SZBH86] was a successor to Mesa with (among other things) complete type safety, exceptions, and automatic garbage collection.

Miranda: Purely functional language designed by David Turner in the mid-1980s [Tur86]. Descended from ML; has type inference and automatic currying. Adds list comprehensions (Section 8.6), and uses lazy evaluation for all arguments. Uses indentation and line breaks for syntactic grouping. On-line resources at *miranda.org.uk/*.

ML: Functional language with "Pascal-like" syntax. Originally designed in the mid- to late 1970s by Robin Milner and associates at the University of Edinburgh as the meta-language (hence the name) for a program verification system. Pioneered aggressive compile-time type inference and polymorphism. Has a few imperative features. Several dialects exist; the most widely used are Standard ML [MTHM97] and OCaml (see separate entry). Standard ML of New Jersey, a project of Princeton University and Bell Labs, has produced freely available implementations for many platforms (*smlnj.org/*).

Modula and Modula-2: The immediate successors to Pascal, developed by Niklaus Wirth. The original Modula [Wir77b] was an explicitly concurrent monitor-based language. It is sometimes called Modula (1) to distinguish it from its successors. The more influential Modula-2 [Wir85b] was originally designed with coroutines (Section 9.5), but no real concurrency. Both languages provide mechanisms for module-as-manager style data abstractions. Modula-2 was standardized by the ISO in 1996 [Int96]. Freely available implementation for several platforms available from *nongnu.org/gm2/*.

Modula-3: A major extension to Modula-2 developed by Luca Cardelli, Jim Donahue, Mick Jordan, Bill Kalsow, and Greg Nelson at the Digital Systems Research Center and the Olivetti Research Center in the late 1980s [Har92]. Intended to provide a level of support for large, reliable, and maintainable systems comparable to that of Ada, but in a simpler and more elegant form. On-line resources at *modula3.org/*.

Oberon: A deliberately minimal language designed by Niklaus Wirth [Wir88b, RW92]. Essentially a subset of Modula-2 [Wir88a], augmented with a mechanism for type extension (Section 10.2.4) [Wir88c]. On-line resources at *oberon.ethz.ch/*.

Objective-C: An object-oriented extension to C based on Smalltalk-style "messaging." Designed by Brad Cox and StepStone corporation in the early 1980s. Adopted by NeXT Software, Inc., in the late 1980s for their

NeXTStep operating system and programming environment. Adopted by Apple as the principal development language for Mac OS X after Apple acquired NeXT in 1997. Substantially simpler than other object-oriented descendants of C. Distinguished by fully dynamic method dispatch and unusual messaging syntax. Freely available implementation included in the gcc distribution (see C). On-line documentation can be found with a search at *developer.apple.com/library/mac/navigation*. Future development at Apple is moving to Swift (see separate entry).

OCaml: See Caml.

Occam: A concurrent language [JG89] based on CSP [Hoa78], Hoare's notation for message-based communication using guarded commands and synchronization send. The language of choice for systems built from INMOS Corporation's *transputer* processors, once widely used in Europe. Uses indentation and line breaks for syntactic grouping. On-line resources at *wotug.org/occam/*.

Pascal: Designed by Niklaus Wirth in the late 1960s [Wir71], largely in reaction to Algol 68, which was widely perceived as bloated. Heavily used in the 1970s and 1980s, particularly for teaching. Introduced subrange and enumeration types. Unified structures and unions. For many years, the standard reference was Wirth's book with Kathleen Jensen [JW91]; subsequently standardized by ISO and ANSI [Int90]. Freely available implementation available at *gnu-pascal.de/gpc/h-index.html*.

Perl: A general-purpose scripting language designed by Larry Wall in the late 1980s [CfWO12]. Includes unusually extensive mechanisms for character string manipulation and pattern matching based on (extended) regular expressions. Borrows features from C, sed, awk [AKW88], and various Unix *shell* (command interpreter) languages. Is famous/infamous for having multiple ways of doing almost anything. Enjoyed an upsurge in popularity in the late 1990s as a server-side web scripting language. Version 5 released in 1995; version 6 still under development as of 2015. On-line resources at *perl.org/*.

PHP: A descendant of Perl designed for server-side web scripting. Scripts are typically embedded in web pages. Originally created by Rasmus Lerdorf in 1995 to help manage his personal home page. The name is now officially a recursive acronym (PHP: Hypertext Preprocessor). More recent versions due to Andi Gutmans and Zeev Suraski, in cooperation with Lerdorf. Includes built-in support for a wide range of Internet protocols and for access to dozens of different commercial database systems. Version 5 (2004) added extensive object-oriented features, mix-in inheritance, iterator objects, autoloading, structured exception handling, reflection, overloading, and optional type declarations for parameters. On-line resources at *php.net/*.

PL/I: A large, general-purpose language designed in the mid-1960s as a successor to Fortran, Cobol, and Algol [Bee70]. Never managed to displace its predecessors; kept alive largely through IBM corporate influence.

Postscript: A stack-based language for the description of graphics and print operations [Ado90]. Developed and marketed by Adobe Systems, Inc. Based in part on Forth [Bro87]. Generated by many word processors and drawing programs. Most professional-quality printers contain a Postscript interpreter.

Prolog: The most widely used logic programming language. Developed in the early 1970s by Alain Colmeraurer and Philippe Roussel of the University of Aix–Marseille in France and Robert Kowalski and associates at the University of Edinburgh in Scotland. Many dialects exist. Partially standardized in 1995 [Int95]. Numerous implementations, both free and commercial, are available; popular freely available versions include GNU Prolog (*gprolog.org/*) and SWI-Prolog (*swi-prolog.org/*).

Python: A general-purpose, object-oriented scripting language designed by Guido van Rossum in the early 1990s. Uses indentation for syntactic grouping. Includes dynamic typing, nested functions with lexical scoping, lambda expressions and higher order functions, true iterators, list comprehensions, array slices, reflection, structured exception handling, multiple inheritance, and modules and dynamic loading. On-line resources at *python.org/*.

R: Open-source scripting language intended primarily for statistical analysis. Based on the proprietary S statistical programming language, originally developed by John Chambers and others at Bell Labs. Supports first-class and higher order functions, unlimited extent, call-by-need, multidimensional arrays and slices, and an extensive library of statistical functions. On-line resources at *r-project.org/*.

Ruby: An elegant, general-purpose, object-oriented scripting language designed by Yukihiro "Matz" Matsumoto, beginning in 1993. First released in 1995. Inspired by Ada, Eiffel, and Perl, with traces of Python, Lisp, Clu, and Smalltalk. Includes dynamic typing, arbitrary precision arithmetic, true iterators, user-level threads, first-class and higher order functions, continuations, reflection, Smalltalk-style messaging, mix-in inheritance, autoloading, structured exception handling, and support for the Tk windowing toolkit. The text by Thomas and Hunt is a standard reference [TFH13]. On-line resources at *ruby-lang.org/*.

Rust: A statically typed language for systems programming, initially developed by Graydon Hoare and colleagues at Mozilla Research. Syntactically reminiscent of C, but with a strong emphasis on type safety, memory safety (without automatic garbage collection), and concurrency. Includes local type inference, Haskell-like type traits, generics, mix-in inheritance, pattern matching, and inter-thread communication based on ownership transfer. Statically prohibits both null and dangling pointers. On-line resources at *rust-lang.org/*.

Scala: Object-oriented functional language developed by Martin Odersky and associates at the École Polytechnique Fédérale de Lausanne in Switzerland, beginning in 2001. Intended for implementation on top of the Java Virtual Machine, and motivated in part by perceived shorcomings in Java. Provides arguably the most aggressive integration of functional features into an imperative language. Has first-class and higher order functions, local type inference, lazy evaluation, pattern matching, currying, tail recursion, rich generics (with covariance and contravariance), message-based concurrency, trait-based inheritance (sort of a cross between classes and interfaces). Heavily used in both industry and academia. Development funded by the European Research Council. On-line resources at *scala-lang.org/*.

Scheme: A small, elegant dialect of Lisp (see also Lisp) developed in the mid-1970s by Guy Steele and Gerald Sussman. Has static scoping and true first-class functions. Widely used for teaching. The sixth revised standard (R6RS) [SDF+07], released in 2007, substantially increased the size of the language; in the wake of subsequent objections, the R7RS standard [SCG+13] codifies a small core language similar to the R5RS version and a larger set of extensions. Earlier version standardized by the IEEE and ANSI [Ins91]. The book by Abelson and Sussman [AS96], long used for introductory programming classes at MIT and elsewhere, is a classic guide to fundamental programming concepts, and to functional programming in particular. On-line resources at *community.schemewiki.org/*.

Simula: Designed at the Norwegian Computing Center, Oslo, in the mid-1960s by Ole-Johan Dahl, Bjørn Myhrhaug, and Kristen Nygaard [BDMN73, ND78]. Extends Algol 60 with *classes* and *coroutines*. The name of the language reflects its suitability for discrete-event simulation (Section C-9.5.4). Free Simula-to-C translator available at *directory.fsf.org/project/cim/*.

Single Assignment C (SAC): A purely functional language designed for high performance computing on array-based data [Sch03]. Developed by Sven-Bodo Scholz and associates at University of Hertfordshire and several other institutions beginning in 1994. Similar in spirit to Sisal, but with syntax based as heavily as possible on C. On-line resources at *www.sac-home.org/*.

Sisal: A functional language with "imperative-style" syntax. Developed by James McGraw and associates at Lawrence Livermore National Laboratory in the early to mid-1980s [FCO90, Can92]. Intended primarily for high-performance scientific computing, with automatic parallelization. A descendant of the dataflow language Val [McG82]. No longer under development at LLNL; available open-source from *sisal.sourceforge.net/*.

Smalltalk: Considered by many to be the quintessential object-oriented language. Developed by Alan Kay, Adele Goldberg, Dan Ingalls, and associates at the Xerox Palo Alto Research Center throughout the 1970s, culminating in the Smalltalk-80 language [GR89]. Anthropomorphic programming model based on "messages" between active objects. On-line resources at *smalltalk.org/*.

SML: See ML.

Snobol: Developed by Ralph Griswold and associates at Bell Labs in the 1960s [GPP71], culminating in SNOBOL4. Intended primarily for processing character strings. Included an extremely rich set of string-manipulating primitives and a novel control-flow mechanism based on the notions of *success* and *failure*. On-line archive at *snobol4.org/*.

SR: Concurrent programming language developed by Greg Andrews and colleagues at the University of Arizona in the 1980s [AO93]. Integrated not only sequential and concurrent programming but also shared memory, semaphores, message passing, remote procedures, and rendezvous into a single conceptual framework and simple syntax. On-line archive at *cs.arizona.edu/sr/*.

Swift: Dynamic object-oriented language developed by Apple as a successor to Objective-C. Includes garbage collection, local type inference, array bounds checking, associative arrays, tuples, first class lambda expressions with unlimited extent, generics, and both value and reference variables of object type. On-line resources at *developer.apple.com/swift/*.

Tcl/Tk: Tool command language (pronounced "tickle"). Scripting language designed by John Ousterhout in the late 1980s [Ous94, WJH03]. Keyword-based syntax resembles Unix command-line invocations and switches; punctuation is relatively spare. Uses dynamic scoping. Supports reflection, recursive invocation of interpreter. Tk (pronounced "tee-kay") is a set of Tcl commands for graphical user interface (GUI) programming. Designed by Ousterhout as an extension to Tcl, Tk has also been embedded in Ruby, Perl, and several other languages. On-line resources at *tcl.tk/*.

Turing: Derived from Euclid by Richard Holt and associates at the University of Toronto in the early 1980s [HMRC88]. Originally intended as a pedagogical language, but could be used for a wide range of applications. Descendants, also developed by Holt's group, include Turing Plus and Object-Oriented Turing.

XSL: Extensible Stylesheet Language, standardized by the World Wide Web Consortium. Serves as the standard stylesheet language for XML (Extensible Markup Language), the standard for self-descriptive tree-structured data, of which XHTML is a dialect. Includes three substandards: XSLT (XSL Transformations) [Wor14], which specifies how to translate from one dialect of XML to another; XPath [Wor07], used to name elements of an XML document; and XSL-FO (XSL Formatting Objects) [Wor06b], which specifies how to format documents. XSLT, though highly specialized to the transformation of XML, is a Turing complete programming language [Kep04]. Standards and additional resources at *w3.org/Style/XSL/*.

B Language Design and Language Implementation

Throughout this text, we have had occasion to remark on the many connections between language design and language implementation. Some of the more direct connections have been highlighted in separate sidebars. We list those sidebars here.

Chapter 1: Introduction

Chapter 2: Programming Language Syntax

Chapter 3: Names, Scopes, and Bindings

Chapter 12: Logic Languages

Chapter 13: Concurrency

Chapter 14: Scripting Languages

Chapter 15: Building a Runnable Program

Chapter 16: Run-Time Program Management

Chapter 17: Code Improvement

Numbered Examples

Chapter 1: Introduction

Chapter 2: Programming Language Syntax

The Binding of Referencing Environments

Macro Expansion

Separate Compilation

Chapter 4: Semantic Analysis

The Role of the Semantic Analyzer

Attribute Grammars

Evaluating Attributes

Action Routines

Space Management for Attributes

Tree Grammars and Syntax Tree Decoration

Chapter 5: Target Machine Architecture

The Memory Hierarchy

Data Representation

Instruction Set Architecture (ISA)

Functional Programming in Perspective

Chapter 12: Logic Languages

Logic Programming Concepts

Prolog

Logic Programming in Perspective

Chapter 13: Concurrency

Background and Motivation

Concurrent Programming Fundamentals

Chapter 14: Scripting Languages

What Is a Scripting Language?

Innovative Features

Chapter 15: Building a Runnable Program

Back-End Compiler Structure

Intermediate Forms

Code Generation

Address Space Organization

Assembly

Linking

Chapter 16: Run-Time Program Management

Virtual Machines

Late Binding of Machine Code

Inspection/Introspection

Chapter 17: Code Improvement

Bibliography

[ACD$^+$96] Cristiana Amza, Alan L. Cox, Sandhya Dwarkadas, Pete Keleher, Honghui Lu, Ramakrishnan Rajamony, Weimin Yu, and Willy Zwaenepoel. TreadMarks: Shared memory computing on networks of workstations. *IEEE Computer*, 29(2):18–28, February 1996.

[Ado90] Adobe Systems, Inc. *PostScript Language Reference Manual*. Addison-Wesley, Reading, MA, second edition, 1990.

[AF84] Krzysztof R. Apt and Nissim Francez. Modeling the distributed termination convention of CSP. *ACM Transactions on Programming Languages and Systems*, 6(3):370–379, July 1984.

[AFG$^+$05] Matthew Arnold, Stephen J. Fink, David Grove, Michael Hind, and Peter F. Sweeney. A survey of adaptive optimization in virtual machines. *Proceedings of the IEEE*, 93(2):449–466, February 2005.

[AG96] Sarita V. Adve and Kourosh Gharachorloo. Shared memory consistency models: A tutorial. *IEEE Computer*, 29(12):66–76, December 1996.

[AG05] David Abrahams and Aleksey Gurtovoy. *C++ Template Metaprogramming: Concepts, Tools, and Techniques from Boost and Beyond*. Addison-Wesley, Boston, MA, 2005.

[AG06] Ken Arnold and James Gosling. *The Java Programming Language*. Addison-Wesley Professional, fourth edition, 2006.

[AH95] Ole Agesen and Urs Hölzle. Type feedback v. concrete type inference: A comparison of optimization techniques for object-oriented languages. In *Proceedings of the Tenth ACM SIGPLAN Conference on Object-Oriented Programming Systems, Languages, and Applications*, pages 91–107, Austin, TX, October 1995.

[AK02] Randy Allen and Ken Kennedy. *Optimizing Compilers for Modern Architectures: A Dependence-Based Approach*. Morgan Kaufmann, San Francisco, CA, 2002.

[AKW88] Alfred V. Aho, Brian W. Kernighan, and Peter J. Weinberger. *The AWK Programming Language*. Addison-Wesley, Reading, MA, 1988.

[All69] Frances E. Allen. Program optimization. *Annual Review in Automatic Programming*, 5:239–307, 1969.

[ALSU07] Alfred V. Aho, Monica S. Lam, Ravi Sethi, and Jeffrey D. Ullman. *Compilers: Principles, Techniques, and Tools*. Addison-Wesley, Boston, MA, second edition, 2007.

[Ame78] American National Standards Institute, New York, NY. *Programming Language Minimal BASIC*, 1978. ANSI X3.60–1978.

[Ame83] American National Standards Institute, New York, NY. *Reference Manual for the Ada Programming Language*, January 1983. ANSI/MIL 1815 A–1983.

[Ame90] American National Standards Institute, New York, NY. *Programming Language C*, 1990. ANSI/ISO 9899–1990 (revision and redesignation of ANSI X3.159–1989).

[Ame96a] American National Standards Institute, New York, NY. *Information Technology—Programming Language REXX*, 1996. ANSI INCITS 274-1996/AMD1-2000 (R2001).

[Ame96b] American National Standards Institute, New York, NY. *Programming Language—Common Lisp*, 1996. ANSI X3.226:1994. Available at *lispworks.com/documentation/common-lisp.html*.

[AO93] Gregory R. Andrews and Ronald A. Olsson. *The SR Programming Language: Concurrency in Practice*. Benjamin/Cummings, Redwood City, CA, 1993.

[App91] Andrew W. Appel. *Compiling with Continuations*. Cambridge University Press, Cambridge, England, 1991.

[App97] Andrew W. Appel. *Modern Compiler Implementation.* Cambridge University Press, Cambridge, England, 1997. Text available in ML, Java, and C versions. C version specialized by Maia Ginsburg; Java version (second edition, 2002) specialized by Jens Palsberg.

[Arm07] Joe Armstrong. What's all this fuss about Erlang? The Pragmatic Programmers, 2007. Available at *pragprog.com/articles/erlang.html.*

[Arm13] Joe Armstrong. *Programming Erlang: Software for a Concuirrent World.* Pragmatic Bookshelf, second edition, 2013.

[AS83] Gregory R. Andrews and Fred B. Schneider. Concepts and notations for concurrent programming. *ACM Computing Surveys*, 15(1):3–43, March 1983.

[AS96] Harold Abelson and Gerald Jay Sussman. *Structure and Interpretation of Computer Programs.* MIT Press, Cambridge, MA, second edition, 1996. With Julie Sussman. Full text and supplementary resources available at *mitpress.mit.edu/sicp/.*

[Ass93] Association for Computing Machinery, New York, NY. *Proceedings of the Second ACM SIGPLAN History of Programming Languages (HOPL) Conference*, Cambridge, MA, April 1993. In *ACM SIGPLAN Notices*, 28(3), March 1993.

[Ass07] Association for Computing Machinery, New York, NY. *Proceedings of the Third ACM SIGPLAN History of Programming Languages (HOPL) Conference*, San Diego, CA, June 2007.

[Atk73] M. Stella Atkins. Mutual recursion in Algol 60 using restricted compilers. *Communications of the ACM*, 16(1):47–48, 1973.

[AU72] Alfred V. Aho and Jeffrey D. Ullman. *The Theory of Parsing, Translation and Compiling.* Prentice-Hall, Englewood Cliffs, NJ, 1972. Two-volume set.

[AWZ88] Bowen Alpern, Mark N. Wegman, and F. Kenneth Zadeck. Detecting equality of variables in programs. In *Conference Record of the Fifteenth ACM Symposium on Principles of Programming Languages*, pages 1–11, San Diego, CA, January 1988.

[Ayc03] John Aycock. A brief history of just-in-time. *ACM Computing Surveys*, 35(2):97–113, June 2003.

[BA08] Hans-J. Boehm and Sarita V. Adve. Foundations of the C++ concurrency memory model. In *Proceedings of the SIGPLAN 2008 Conference on Programming Language Design and Implementation*, pages 68–78, Tucson, ZA, June 2008.

[Bac78] John W. Backus. Can programming be liberated from the von Neumann style? A functional style and its algebra of programs. *Communications of the ACM*, 21(8):613–641, August 1978. The 1977 Turing Award lecture.

[BAD+09] Robert L. Bocchino, Jr., Vikram S. Adve, Danny Dig, Sarita Adve, Stephen Heumann, Rakesh Komuravelli, Jeffrey Overbey, Patrick Simmons, Hyojin Sung, and Mohsen Vakilian. A type and effect system for deterministic parallel Java. In *Proceedings of the Twenty-Fourth ACM SIGPLAN Conference on Object-Oriented Programming, Systems, Languages, and Applications*, Orlando, FL, October 2009.

[Bag89] Rajive Bagrodia. Synchronizatiom of asynchronous processes in CSP. *ACM Transactions on Programming Languages and Systems*, 11(4):585–597, October 1989.

[BALL90] Brian N. Bershad, Thomas E. Anderson, Edward D. Lazowska, and Henry M. Levy. Lightweight remote procedure call. *ACM Transactions on Computer Systems*, 8(1):37–55, February 1990.

[Ban97] Utpal Banerjee. *Dependence Analysis*, volume 3 of *Loop Transformations for Restructuring Compilers.* Kluwer Academic Publishers, Boston, MA, 1997.

[Bar84] Hendrik Pieter Barendregt. *The Lambda Calculus: Its Syntax and Semantics*, volume 103 of *Studies in Logic and the Foundations of Mathematics.* North-Holland, Amsterdam, The Netherlands, revised edition, 1984.

[BCR04] David F. Bacon, Perry Cheng, and V. T. Rajan. A unified theory of garbage collection. In *Proceedings of the Nineteenth ACM SIGPLAN Conference on Object-Oriented Programming, Systems, Languages, and Applications*, pages 50–68, Vancouver, BC, Canada, October 2004.

[BDB00] Vasanth Bala, Evelyn Duesterwald, and Sanjeev Banerjia. Dynamo: A transparent dynamic optimization system. In *Proceedings of the SIGPLAN 2000 Conference on Programming Language Design and Implementation*, pages 1–12, Vancouver, BC, Canada, June 2000.

[BDMN73] Graham M. Birtwistle, Ole-Johan Dahl, Bjørn Myhrhaug, and Kristen Nygaard. *SIMULA Begin.* Auerback Publishers, Inc., Philadelphia, PA, 1973.

[Bec97] Leland L. Beck. *System Software: An Introduction to Systems Programming.* Addison-Wesley, Reading, MA, third edition, 1997.

[Bee70] David Beech. A structural view of PL/I. *ACM Computing Surveys*, 2(1):33–64, March 1970.

[Bel05] Fabrice Bellard. QEMU, a fast and portable dynamic translator. In *Proceedings of the USENIX 2005 Annual Technical Conference*, pages 41–46, Anaheim, CA, April 2005.

[Ben00] John L. Bentley. *Programming Pearls*. Addison-Wesley Professional, 2000. First edition, 1986.

[Ber85] Robert L. Bernstein. Producing good code for the case statement. *Software—Practice and Experience*, 15(10):1021–1024, October 1985. A correction, by Sampath Kannan and Todd A. Proebsting, appears in Volume 24, Number 2.

[BFKM86] Lee Brownston, Robert Farrell, Elaine Kant, and Nancy Martin. *Programming Expert Systems in OPS5: An Introduction to Rule-Based Programming*. Addison-Wesley, Reading, MA, 1986.

[BGS94] David F. Bacon, Susan L. Graham, and Oliver J. Sharp. Compiler transformations for high-performance computing. *ACM Computing Surveys*, 26(4):345–420, December 1994.

[BHJL07] Andrew Black, Norman Hutchinson, Eric Jul, and Henry Levy. The development of the Emerald programming language. In *HOPL III Proceedings* [Ass07], pages 11-1–11-51.

[BHPS61] Yehoshua Bar-Hillel, Micha A. Perles, and Eliahu Shamir. On formal properties of simple phrase structure grammars. *Zeitschrift feur Phonetik, Sprachwissenschaft und Kommunikationsforschung*, 14:143–172, 1961.

[BI82] Alan H. Borning and Daniel H. H. Ingalls. Multiple inheritance in Smalltalk-80. In *AAAI-82: The National Conference on Artificial Intelligence*, pages 234–237, Pittsburgh, PA, August 1982.

[BL92] Thomas Ball and James R. Larus. Optimally profiling and tracing programs. In *Conference Record of the Nineteenth ACM Symposium on Principles of Programming Languages*, pages 59–70, Albuquerque, NM, January 1992.

[BM77] Robert S. Boyer and J. Strother Moore. A fast string searching algorithm. *Communications of the ACM*, 20(10):762–772, October 1977.

[BN84] Andrew D. Birrell and Bruce J. Nelson. Implementing remote procedure calls. *ACM Transactions on Computer Systems*, 2(1):39–59, February 1984.

[BO11] Randal E Bryant and David O'Hallaron. *Computer Systems: A Programmer's Perspective*. Prentice-Hall, Boston, MA, second edition, 2011.

[Boe05] Hans-J. Boehm. Threads cannot be implemented as a library. In *Proceedings of the SIGPLAN 2005 Conference on Programming Language Design and Implementation*, pages 261–268, Chicago, IL, June 2005.

[BOSW98] Gilad Bracha, Martin Odersky, David Stoutamire, and Philip Wadler. Making the future safe for the past: Adding genericity to the Java programming language. In *Proceedings of the Thirteenth ACM SIGPLAN Conference on Object-Oriented Programming, Systems, Languages, and Applications*, pages 183–200, Vancouver, BC, Canada, October 1998.

[Bou78] Stephen R. Bourne. An introduction to the UNIX shell. *Bell System Technical Journal*, 57(6, Part 2):2797–2822, July–August 1978.

[Bri73] Per Brinch Hansen. *Operating System Principles*. Prentice-Hall, Englewood Cliffs, NJ, 1973.

[Bri75] Per Brinch Hansen. The programming language Concurrent Pascal. *IEEE Transactions on Software Engineering*, SE–1(2):199–207, June 1975.

[Bri81] Per Brinch Hansen. The design of Edison. *Software—Practice and Experience*, 11(4):363–396, April 1981.

[Bro87] Leo Brodie. *Starting FORTH: An Introduction to the FORTH Language and Operating System for Beginners and Professionals*. Prentice-Hall Software Series. Prentice-Hall, Englewood Cliffs, NJ, second edition, 1987.

[Bro96] Kraig Brockschmidt. How OLE and COM solve the problems of component software design. *Microsoft Systems Journal*, 11(5):63–82, May 1996.

[BS83] Daniel G. Bobrow and Mark J. Stefik. The LOOPS manual. Technical report, Xerox Palo Alto Research Center, Palo Alto, CA, 1983.

[BS96] David F. Bacon and Peter F. Sweeney. Fast static analysis of C++ virtual function calls. In *Proceedings of the Eleventh ACM SIGPLAN Conference on Object-Oriented Programming, Systems, Languages, and Applications*, pages 324–341, San Jose, CA, October 1996.

[BW88] Hans-Juergen Boehm and Mark Weiser. Garbage collection in an uncooperative environment. *Software—Practice and Experience*, 18(9):807–820, September 1988.

[CAC+81] Gregory Chaitin, Marc Auslander, Ashok Chandra, John Cocke, Martin Hopkins, and Peter Markstein. Register allocation via coloring. *Computer Languages*, 6(1):47–57, 1981.

[Cai82] R. Cailliau. How to avoid getting SCHLONKED by Pascal. *ACM SIGPLAN Notices*, 17(12):31–40, December 1982.

[Can92] David Cann. Retire Fortran? A debate rekindled. *Communications of the ACM*, 35(8):81–89, August 1992.

[CDW04] Hao Chen, Drew Dean, and David Wagner. Model checking one million lines of C code. In *Proceedings of the Network and Distributed System Security Symposium*, pages 171–185, San Diego, CA, February 2004.

[Cer89] Paul Ceruzzi. *Beyond the Limits—Flight Enters the Computer Age*. MIT Press, Cambridge, MA, 1989.

[CF58] Haskell B. Curry and Robert Feys. *Combinatory Logic*, volume 1 of *Studies in Logic and the Foundations of Mathematics*. North-Holland, Amsterdam, The Netherlands, 1958. With two sections by William Craig.

[CFR+91] Ronald Cytron, Jeanne Ferrante, Barry K. Rosen, Mark N. Wegman, and F. Kenneth Zadeck. Efficiently computing static single assignment form and the control dependence graph. *ACM Transactions on Programming Languages and Systems*, 13(4):451–490, October 1991.

[CfWO12] Tom Christiansen, brian d foy, Larry Wall, and Jon Orwant. *Programming Perl*. O'Reilly Media, Sebastopol, CA, fourth edition, 2012.

[Che92] Andrew Cheese. *Parallel Execution of Parlog*. Springer-Verlag, Berlin, Germany, 1992.

[Cho56] Noam Chomsky. Three models for the description of language. *IRE Transactions on Information Theory*, IT-2(3):113–124, September 1956.

[Cho62] Noam Chomsky. Context-free grammars and pushdown storage. In *Quarterly Progress Report No. 65*, pages 187–194. MIT Research Laboratory for Electronics, Cambridge, MA, 1962.

[CHP71] Pierre-Jacques Courtois, F. Heymans, and David L. Parnas. Concurrent control with 'readers' and 'writers'. *Communications of the ACM*, 14(10):667–668, October 1971.

[Chu41] Alonzo Church. *The Calculi of Lambda-Conversion*. Annals of Mathematical Studies #6. Princeton University Press, Princeton, NJ, 1941.

[CL83] Robert P. Cook and Thomas J. LeBlanc. A symbol table abstraction to implement languages with explicit scope control. *IEEE Transactions on Software Engineering*, SE–9(1):8–12, January 1983.

[Cle86] J. Craig Cleaveland. *An Introduction to Data Types*. Addison-Wesley, Reading, MA, 1986.

[CLFL94] Jeffrey S. Chase, Henry M. Levy, Michael J. Feeley, and Edward D. Lazowska. Sharing and protection in a single-address-space operating system. *ACM Transactions on Computer Systems*, 12(4):271–307, November 1994.

[CM84] K. Mani Chandy and Jayadev Misra. The drinking philosophers problem. *ACM Transactions on Programming Languages and Systems*, 6(4):632–646, October 1984.

[CM03] William F. Clocksin and Christopher S. Mellish. *Programming in Prolog*. Springer-Verlag, Berlin, Germany, fifth edition, 2003.

[Coh81] Jacques Cohen. Garbage collection of linked data structures. *ACM Computing Surveys*, 13(3):341–367, September 1981.

[Con63] Melvin E. Conway. Design of a separable transition-diagram compiler. *Communications of the ACM*, 6(7):396–408, July 1963.

[Cou84] Bruno Courcelle. Attribute grammars: Definitions, analysis of dependencies, proof methods. In Bernard Lorho, editor, *Methods and Tools for Compiler Construction: An Advanced Course*, pages 81–102. Cambridge University Press, Cambridge, England, 1984.

[CS69] John Cocke and Jacob T. Schwartz. Programming languages and their compilers: Preliminary notes. Technical report, Courant Institute of Mathematical Sciences, New York University, New York, NY, 1969.

[CS01] Bradford L. Chamberlain and Lawrence Snyder. Array language support for parallel sparse computation. In *Proceedings of the Fifteenth International Conference on Supercomputing*, pages 133–145, Sorrento, Italy, June 2001.

[CT04] Keith D. Cooper and Linda Torczon. *Engineering a Compiler*. Morgan Kaufmann, San Francisco, CA, 2004.

[CW85] Luca Cardelli and Peter Wegner. On understanding types, data abstraction, and polymorphism. *ACM Computing Surveys*, 17(4):471–522, December 1985.

[CW05] Norman Chonacky and David Winch. Maple, Mathematica, and Matlab: The 3M's without the tape. *Computing in Science and Engineering*, 7(1):8–16, 2005.

[Dar90] Jared L. Darlington. Search direction by goal failure in goal-oriented programming. *ACM Transactions on Programming Languages and Systems*, 12(2):224–252, April 1990.

[Dav63] Martin Davis. Eliminating the irrelevant from mechanical proofs. In *Proceedings of a Symposium in Applied Mathematics*, volume 15, pages 15–30. American Mathematical Society, Providence, RI, 1963.

[DB76] L. Peter Deutsch and Daniel G. Bobrow. An efficient incremental automatic garbage collector. *Communications of the ACM*, 19(9):522–526, September 1976.

[DDH72] Ole-Johan Dahl, Edsger W. Dijkstra, and Charles Antony Richard Hoare. *Structured Programming*. A.P.I.C.

Studies in Data Processing #8. Academic Press, New York, NY, 1972.

[DeR71] Franklin L. DeRemer. Simple LR(k) grammars. *Communications of the ACM*, 14(7):453–460, July 1971.

[DGAFS+80] Robert B. K. Dewar, Jr. Gerald A. Fisher, Edmond Schonberg, Robert Froehlich, Stephen Bryant, Clinton F. Goss, and Michael Burke. The NYU Ada translator and interpreter. In *Proceedings of the ACM SIGPLAN Symposium on the Ada Programming Language*, pages 194–201, Boston, MA, December 1980.

[Dij60] Edsger W. Dijkstra. Recursive programming. *Numerische Mathematik*, 2:312–318, 1960. Reprinted as pages 221–228 of *Programming Systems and Languages*, Saul Rosen, editor. McGraw-Hill, New York, NY, 1967.

[Dij65] Edsger W. Dijkstra. Solution of a problem in concurrent programming control. *Communications of the ACM*, 8(9):569, September 1965.

[Dij68a] Edsger W. Dijkstra. Co-operating sequential processes. In F. Genuys, editor, *Programming Languages*, pages 43–112. Academic Press, London, England, 1968.

[Dij68b] Edsger W. Dijkstra. Go To statement considered harmful. *Communications of the ACM*, 11(3):147–148, March 1968.

[Dij72] Edsger W. Dijkstra. Hierarchical ordering of sequential processes. In Charles Antony Richard Hoare and Ronald H. Perrott, editors, *Operating Systems Techniques*, A.P.I.C. Studies in Data Processing #9, pages 72–93. Academic Press, London, England, 1972. Also *Acta Informatica*, 1(8):115–138, 1971.

[Dij75] Edsger W. Dijkstra. Guarded commands, nondeterminacy, and formal derivation of programs. *Communications of the ACM*, 18(8):453–457, August 1975.

[Dij76] Edsger W. Dijkstra. *A Discipline of Programming*. Prentice-Hall, Englewood Cliffs, NJ, 1976.

[Dij82] Edsger W. Dijkstra. How do we tell truths that might hurt? *ACM SIGPLAN Notices*, 17(5):13–15, May 1982.

[Dio78] Bernard A. Dion. *Locally Least-Cost Error Correctors for Context-Free and Context-Sensitive Parsers*. Ph. D. dissertation, University of Wisconsin–Madison, 1978. Computer Sciences Technical Report #344.

[DMM96] Amer Diwan, J. Eliot B. Moss, and Kathryn S. McKinley. Simple and effective analysis of statically typed object-oriented programs. In *Proceedings of the Eleventh ACM SIGPLAN Conference on Object-Oriented Programming, Systems, Languages, and Applications*, pages 292–305, San Jose, CA, October 1996.

[Dol97] Julian Dolby. Automatic inline allocation of objects. In *Proceedings of the SIGPLAN '97 Conference on Programming Language Design and Implementation*, pages 7–17, Las Vegas, NV, June 1997.

[Dri93] Karel Driesen. Selector table indexing and sparse arrays. In *Proceedings of the Eighth ACM SIGPLAN Conference on Object-Oriented Programming Systems, Languages, and Applications*, pages 259–270, Washington, DC, September 1993.

[DRSS96] Steven Dawson, C. R. Ramakrishnan, Steven Skiena, and Terrence Swift. Principles and practice of unification factoring. *ACM Transactions on Programming Languages and Systems*, 18(5):528–563, September 1996.

[DS84] L. Peter Deutsch and Allan M. Schiffman. Efficient implementation of the Smalltalk-80 system. In *Conference Record of the Eleventh ACM Symposium on Principles of Programming Languages*, pages 297–302, Salt Lake City, UT, January 1984.

[DSS06] Dave Dice, Ori Shalev, and Nir Shavit. Transactional locking II. In *Proceedings of the Twentieth International Symposium on Distributed Computing*, pages 194–208, Stockholm, Sweden, September 2006.

[Due05] Evelyn Duesterwald. Design and engineering of a dynamic binary optimizer. *Proceedings of the IEEE*, 93(2):436–448, February 2005.

[DWA10] DWARF Debugging Information Format Committee. *DWARF Debugging Information Format, Version 4*, June 2010. Available as *dwarfstd.org/doc/DWARF4.pdf*.

[Dya95] Lev J. Dyadkin. Multibox parsers: No more handwritten lexical analyzers. *IEEE Software*, 12(5):61–67, September 1995.

[Eag12] Michael J. Eager. Introduction to the DWARF debugging format. The Pragmatic Programmers, April 2012. Available as *dwarfstd.org/doc/Debugging%20using%20DWARF-2012.pdf*.

[Ear70] Jay Earley. An efficient context-free parsing algorithm. *Communications of the ACM*, 13(2):94–102, February 1970.

[ECM06a] ECMA International, Geneva, Switzerland. *C# Language Specification*, fourth edition, June 2006. ECMA-334, ISO/IEC 23270. Available as *ecma-international.org/publications/files/ECMA-ST/Ecma-334.pdf*.

[ECM06b] ECMA International, Geneva, Switzerland. *Eiffel: Analysis, Design and Programming Language*, second edition, June 2006. ECMA-367. Available at *ecma-international.org/publications/standards/Ecma-367.htm*.

[ECM11] ECMA International, Geneva, Switzerland. *ECMAScript Language Specification*, 5.1 edition, June 2011. ECMA-262, ISO/IEC 16262:2011. Available as *ecma-international.org/publications/files/ECMA-ST/Ecma-262.pdf*.

[ECM13] ECMA International, Geneva, Switzerland. *The JSON Data Interchange Format*, October 2013. ECMA-404. Available as *ecma-international.org/publications/files/ECMA-ST/ECMA-404.pdf*.

[Eng84] Joost Engelfriet. Attribute grammars: Attribute evaluation methods. In Bernard Lorho, editor, *Methods and Tools for Compiler Construction: An Advanced Course*, pages 103–138. Cambridge University Press, Cambridge, England, 1984.

[Enn06] Robert Ennals. Software transactional memory should not be lock free. Technical Report IRC-TR-06-052, Intel Research Cambridge, 2006.

[ES90] Margaret A. Ellis and Bjarne Stroustrup. *The Annotated C++ Reference Manual*. Addison-Wesley, Reading, MA, 1990.

[Eve63] R. James Evey. Application of pushdown store machines. In *Proceedings of the 1963 Fall Joint Computer Conference*, pages 215–227, Las Vegas, NV, November 1963. AFIPS Press, Montvale, NJ.

[FCL10] Charles N. Fischer, , Ron K. Cytron, and Richard J. LeBlanc, Jr. *Crafting a Compiler*. Addison-Wesley, Boston, MA, second edition, 2010.

[FCO90] John T. Feo, David Cann, and Rod R. Oldehoeft. A report on the Sisal language project. *Journal of Parallel and Distributed Computing*, 10(4):349–365, December 1990.

[FG84] Alan R. Feuer and Narain Gehani, editors. *Comparing and Assessing Programming Languages: Ada, C, Pascal*. Prentice-Hall Software Series. Prentice-Hall, Englewood Cliffs, NJ, 1984.

[FH95] Christopher W. Fraser and David R. Hanson. *A Retargetable C Compiler: Design and Implementation*. Benjamin/Cummings, Redwood City, CA, 1995.

[FHP92] Christopher W. Fraser, David R. Hanson, and Todd A. Proebsting. Engineering a simple, efficient code generator generator. *ACM Letters on Programming Languages and Systems*, 1(3):213–226, September 1992.

[Fie00] Roy Thomas Fielding. *Architectural Styles and the Design of Network-based Software Architectures*. Ph. D. dissertation, University of California, Irvine, 2000.

[Fin96] Raphael A. Finkel. *Advanced Programming Language Design*. Addison-Wesley, Menlo Park, CA, 1996.

[FL80] Charles N. Fischer and Richard J. LeBlanc, Jr. Implementation of runtime diagnostics in Pascal. *IEEE Transactions on Software Engineering*, SE–6(4):313–319, July 1980.

[Fle76] Arthur C. Fleck. On the impossibility of content exchange through the by-name parameter transmission technique. *ACM SIGPLAN Notices*, 11(11):38–41, November 1976.

[FMQ80] Charles N. Fischer, Donn R. Milton, and Sam B. Quiring. Efficient LL(1) error correction and recovery using only insertions. *Acta Informatica*, 13(2):141–54, February 1980.

[Fra80] Nissim Francez. Distributed termination. *ACM Transactions on Programming Languages and Systems*, 2(1):42–55, January 1980.

[FRF08] Pascal Felber, Torvald Riegel, and Christof Fetzer. Dynamic performance tuning of word-based software transactional memory. In *Proceedings of the Thirteenth ACM SIGPLAN Symposium on Principles and Practice of Parallel Programming*, pages 237–246, Salt Lake City, UT, February 2008.

[FSS83] Stefan M. Freudenberger, Jacob T. Schwartz, and Micha Sharir. Experience with the SETL optimizer. *ACM Transactions on Programming Languages and Systems*, 5(1):26–45, January 1983.

[FWH01] Daniel P. Friedman, Mitchell Wand, and Christopher T. Haynes. *Essentials of Programming Languages*. MIT Press, Cambridge, MA, second edition, 2001.

[FY69] Robert R. Fenichel and Jerome C. Yochelson. A Lisp garbage collector for virtual memory computer systems. *Communications of the ACM*, 12(11):611–612, November 1969.

[GBD+94] Al Geist, Adam Beguelin, Jack Dongarra, Weicheng Jiang, Robert Manchek, and Vaidyalingam S. Sunderam. *PVM: Parallel Virtual Machine: A Users' Guide and Tutorial for Networked Parallel Computing*. MIT Press, Cambridge, MA, 1994. Available at *netlib.org/pvm3/book/pvm-book.html*.

[GBJ+12] Dick Grune, Henri E. Bal, Ceriel J. H. Jacobs, Koen G. Langendoen, and Kees van Reeuwijk. *Modern*

Compiler Design. Springer-Verlag, New York, NY, second edition, 2012.

[GDDC97] David Grove, Greg DeFouw, Jeffrey Dean, and Craig Chambers. Call graph construction in object-oriented languages. In *Proceedings of the Twelfth ACM SIGPLAN Conference on Object-Oriented Programming, Systems, Languages, and Applications*, pages 108–124, Atlanta, GA, October 1997.

[GFH82] Mahadevan Ganapathi, Charles N. Fischer, and John L. Hennessy. Retargetable compiler code generation. *ACM Computing Surveys*, 14(4):573–592, December 1982.

[GG78] R. Steven Glanville and Susan L. Graham. A new method for compiler code generation. In *Conference Record of the Fifth Annual ACM Symposium on Principles of Programming Languages*, pages 231–240, Tucson, AZ, January 1978.

[GG96] Ralph E. Griswold and Madge T. Griswold. *The Icon Programming Language*. Peer-to-Peer Communications, San Jose, CA, third edition, 1996. Out of print; available on-line at *cs.arizona.edu/icon/lb3.htm*. Previous editions published by Prentice-Hall.

[GJL+03] Ronald Garcia, Jaakko Järvi, Andrew Lumsdaine, Jeremy Siek, and Jeremiah Willcock. A comparative study of language support for generic programming. In *Proceedings of the Eighteenth ACM SIGPLAN Conference on Object-Oriented Programming, Systems, Languages, and Applications*, pages 115–134, Anaheim, CA, October 2003.

[GJS+14] James Gosling, Bill Joy, Guy Steele, Gilad Bracha, and Alex Buckley. *The Java Language Specification*. Addison-Wesley, Reading, MA, Java SE 8 edition, 2014. Available at *docs.oracle.com/javase/specs/*.

[GL05] Samuel Z. Guyer and Calvin Lin. Client-driven pointer analysis. *Science of Computer Programming*, 58(1–2):83–114, October 2005.

[GLDW87] Robert A. Gingell, Meng Lee, Xuong T. Dang, and Mary S. Weeks. Shared libraries in SunOS. In *Proceedings of the 1987 Summer USENIX Conference*, pages 131–145, Phoenix, AZ, June 1987.

[GM86] Phillip B. Gibbons and Steven S. Muchnick. Efficient instruction scheduling for a pipelined architecture. In *Proceedings of the SIGPLAN '86 Symposium on Compiler Construction*, pages 11–16, Palo Alto, CA, July 1986.

[Gol84] Adele Goldberg. *Smalltalk-80: The Interactive Programming Environment*. Addison-Wesley Series in Computer Science. Addison-Wesley, Reading, MA, 1984.

[Gol91] David Goldberg. What every computer scientist should know about floating-point arithmetic. *ACM Computing Surveys*, 23(1):5–48, March 1991.

[Gol12] David Goldberg. Computer arithmetic. In Hennessy and Patterson [HP12], Appendix J. Available as *booksite.mkp.com/9780123838728/references/appendix_j.pdf*.

[Goo75] John B. Goodenough. Exception handling: Issues and a proposed notation. *Communications of the ACM*, 18(12):683–696, December 1975.

[Gor79] Michael J. C. Gordon. *The Denotational Description of Programming Languages: An Introduction*. Springer-Verlag, New York, NY, 1979.

[GPP71] Ralph E. Griswold, J. F. Poage, and I. P. Polonsky. *The Snobol4 Programming Language*. Prentice-Hall, Englewood Cliffs, NJ, second edition, 1971.

[GR62] Seymour Ginsburg and H. Gordon Rice. Two families of languages related to ALGOL. *Journal of the ACM*, 9(3):350–371, 1962.

[GR89] Adele Goldberg and David Robson. *Smalltalk-80: The Language*. Addison-Wesley Series in Computer Science. Addison-Wesley, Reading, MA, 1989.

[Gri81] David Gries. *The Science of Programming*. Texts and Monographs in Computer Science. Springer-Verlag, New York, NY, 1981.

[GS99] Joseph (Yossi) Gil and Peter F. Sweeney. Space- and time-efficient memory layout for multiple inheritance. In *Proceedings of the Fourteenth ACM SIGPLAN Conference on Object-Oriented Programming, Systems, Languages, and Applications*, pages 256–275, Denver, CO, November 1999.

[GSB+93] William E. Garrett, Michael L. Scott, Ricardo Bianchini, Leonidas I. Kontothanassis, R. Andrew McCallum, Jeffrey A. Thomas, Robert Wisniewski, and Steve Luk. Linking shared segments. In *Proceedings of the USENIX Winter '93 Technical Conference*, pages 13–27, San Diego, CA, January 1993.

[GTW78] Joseph A. Goguen, James W. Thatcher, and Eric G. Wagner. An initial algebra approach to the specification, correctness, and implementation of abstract data types. In Raymond T. Yeh, editor, *Current Trends in Programming Methodology*, volume 4, pages 80–149. Prentice-Hall, Englewood Cliffs, NJ, 1978.

[Gut77] John Guttag. Abstract data types and the development of data structures. *Communications of the ACM*, 20(6):396–404, June 1977.

[Hal85] Robert H. Halstead, Jr. Multilisp: A language for concurrent symbolic computation. *ACM Transactions on Programming Languages and Systems*, 7(4):501–538, October 1985.

[Han81] David R. Hanson. Is block structure necessary? *Software—Practice and Experience*, 11(8):853–866, August 1981.

[Han93] David R. Hanson. A brief introduction to Icon. In *HOPL II Proceedings* [Ass93], pages 359–360.

[Har92] Samuel P. Harbison. *Modula-3*. Prentice-Hall, Englewood Cliffs, NJ, 1992.

[Har01] Timothy L. Harris. A pragmatic implementation of non-blocking linked-lists. In *Proceedings of the Fifteenth International Symposium on Distributed Computing (DISC)*, pages 300–314, Lisbon, Portugal, October 2001.

[Haz11] Kim Hazelwood. *Dynamic Binary Modification: Tools, Techniques, and Applications*. Synthesis Lectures on Computer Architecture. Morgan & Claypool Publishers, March 2011.

[HD68] E. A. Hauck and B. A. Dent. Burroughs' B6500/B7500 stack mechanism. In *Proceedings of the AFIPS Spring Joint Computer Conference*, volume 32, pages 245–251, 1968. Reprinted as pages 244–250 of Siewiorek, Bell, and Newell [SBN82].

[HD89] Robert R. Henry and Peter C. Damron. Algorithms for table-driven code generators using tree-pattern matching. Technical Report 89-02-03, Computer Science Department, University of Washington, Seattle, WA, February 1989.

[Hen14] Laurie Hendren, editor. *ACM SIGPLAN International Workshop on Libraries, Languages, and Compilers for Array Programming*, Edinburgh, Scotland, June 2014. Held in conjunction with the *Thirty-Fifth ACM SIGPLAN Conference on Programming Language Design and Implementation*.

[Her91] Maurice P. Herlihy. Wait-free synchronization. *ACM Transactions on Programming Languages and Systems*, 13(1):124–149, January 1991.

[HGLS78] Richard C. Holt, G. Scott Graham, Edward D. Lazowska, and Mark A. Scott. *Structured Concurrent Programming with Operating Systems Applications*. Addison-Wesley Series in Computer Science. Addison-Wesley, Reading, MA, 1978.

[HH97a] Michael Hauben and Ronda Hauben. *Netizens: On the History and Impact of Usenet and the Internet*. Wiley/IEEE Computer Society Press, New York, NY, 1997. Available at *columbia.edu/~hauben/netbook/*.

[HH97b] Raymond J. Hookway and Mark A. Herdeg. DIGITAL FX!32: Combining emulation and binary translation. *DIGITAL Technical Journal*, 9(1):3–12, 1997.

[Hin01] Michael Hind. Pointer analysis: Haven't we solved this problem yet? In *Proceedings of the ACM SIGPLAN–SIGSOFT Workshop on Program Analysis for Software Tools and Engineering*, pages 54–61, Snowbird, UT, June 2001.

[HJBG81] John L. Hennessy, Norman Jouppi, Forest Baskett, and John Gill. MIPS: A VLSI processor architecture. In *Proceedings of the CMU Conference on VLSI Systems and Computations*, pages 337–346. Computer Science Press, Rockville, MD, October 1981.

[HL94] Patricia M. Hill and John W. Lloyd. *The Gödel Programming Language*. Logic Programming Series. MIT Press, Cambridge, MA, 1994.

[HLM03] Maurice Herlihy, Victor Luchangco, and Mark Moir. Obstruction-free synchronization: Double-ended queues as an example. In *Proceedings of the Twenty-Third International Conference on Distributed Computing Systems*, pages 522–529, Providence, RI, May 2003.

[HLR10] Tim Harris, James R. Larus, and Ravi Rajwar. *Transactional Memory*. Synthesis Lectures on Computer Architecture. Morgan & Claypool Publishers, second edition, December 2010.

[HM93] Maurice P. Herlihy and J. Eliot B. Moss. Transactional memory: Architectural support for lock-free data structures. In *Proceedings of the Twentieth International Symposium on Computer Architecture*, pages 289–300, San Diego, CA, May 1993.

[HMPH05] Tim Harris, Simon Marlow, Simon Peyton Jones, and Maurice Herlihy. Composable memory transactions. In *Proceedings of the Tenth ACM SIGPLAN Symposium on Principles and Practice of Parallel Programming*, pages 48–60, Chicago, IL, June 2005.

[HMRC88] Richard C. Holt, Philip A. Matthews, J. Alan Rosselet, and James R. Cordy. *The Turing Programming Language: Design and Definition*. Prentice-Hall, Englewood Cliffs, NJ, 1988.

[HMU07] John E. Hopcroft, Rajeev Motwani, and Jeffrey D. Ullman. *Introduction to Automata Theory, Languages, and Computation*. Pearson/Addison-Wesley, Boston, MA, third edition, 2007.

[HO91] W. Wilson Ho and Ronald A. Olsson. An approach to genuine dynamic linking. *Software—Practice and Experience*, 21(4):375–390, April 1991.

[Hoa69] Charles Antony Richard Hoare. An axiomatic basis of computer programming. *Communications of the ACM*, 12(10):576–580+, October 1969.

[Hoa74] Charles Antony Richard Hoare. Monitors: An operating system structuring concept. *Communications of the ACM*, 17(10):549–557, October 1974.

[Hoa75] Charles Antony Richard Hoare. Recursive data structures. *International Journal of Computer and Information Sciences*, 4(2):105–132, June 1975.

[Hoa78] Charles Antony Richard Hoare. Communicating Sequential Processes. *Communications of the ACM*, 21(8):666–677, August 1978.

[Hoa81] Charles Antony Richard Hoare. The emperor's old clothes. *Communications of the ACM*, 24(2):75–83, February 1981. The 1980 Turing Award lecture.

[Hoa89] Charles Antony Richard Hoare. Hints on programming language design. In Cliff B. Jones, editor, *Essays in Computing Science*, pages 193–216. Prentice-Hall, New York, NY, 1989. Based on a keynote address presented at the *First ACM Symposium on Principles of Programming Languages*, Boston, MA, October 1973.

[Hor51] Alfred Horn. On sentences which are true of direct unions of algebras. *Journal of Symbolic Logic*, 16(1):14–21, March 1951.

[Hor87] Ellis Horowitz. *Programming Languages: A Grand Tour*. Computer Software Engineering Series. Computer Science Press, Rockville, MD, third edition, 1987.

[HP12] John L. Hennessy and David A. Patterson. *Computer Architecture: A Quantitative Approach*. Morgan Kaufmann, San Francisco, CA, fifth edition, 2012. Third edition, 2003.

[HS12] Maurice Herlihy and Nir Shavit. *The Art of Multiprocessor Programming*. Morgan Kaufmann, San Francisco, CA, revised edition, 2012.

[HTWG11] Anders Hejlsberg, Mads Torgersen, Scott Wiltamuth, and Peter Golde. *The C# Programming Language*. Addison-Wesley, Boston, MA, fourth edition, 2011.

[Hud89] Paul Hudak. Conception, evolution, and application of functional programming languages. *ACM Computing Surveys*, 21(3):359–411, September 1989.

[IBFW91] Jean Ichbiah, John G. P. Barnes, Robert J. Firth, and Mike Woodger. *Rationale for the Design of the Ada Programming Language*. Cambridge University Press, Cambridge, England, 1991.

[IBM87] IBM Corporation. *APL2 Programming: Language Reference*, 1987. SH20-9227.

[IEE87] IEEE Standards Committee. IEEE standard for binary floating-point arithmetic. *ACM SIGPLAN Notices*, 22(2):9–25, February 1987.

[Ing61] Peter Z. Ingerman. Thunks: A way of compiling procedure statements with some comments on procedure declarations. *Communications of the ACM*, 4(1):55–58, January 1961.

[Ins91] Institute of Electrical and Electronics Engineers, New York, NY. *IEEE/ANSI Standard for the Scheme Programming Language*, 1991. IEEE 1178-1990. Available at *http://standards.ieee.org/findstds/standard/1178-1990.html*.

[Int90] International Organization for Standardization, Geneva, Switzerland. *Information Technology—Programming Languages—Pascal*, 1990. ISO/IEC 7185:1990 (revision and redesignation of ANSI/IEEE 770X). Available as *pascal-central.com/docs/iso7185.pdf*.

[Int95] International Organization for Standardization, Geneva, Switzerland. *Information Technology—Programming Languages—Prolog—Part 1: General Core*, 1995. ISO/IEC 13211-1:1995.

[Int96] International Organization for Standardization, Geneva, Switzerland. *Information Technology—Programming Languages—Part 1: Modula-2, Base Language*, 1996. ISO/IEC 10514-1:1996.

[Int97] International Organization for Standardization, Geneva, Switzerland. *Programming Language Forth*, 1997. ISO/IEC 15145:1997 (revision and redesignation of ANSI X3.215–1994).

[Int99] International Organization for Standardization, Geneva, Switzerland. *Programming Language—C*, December 1999. ISO/IEC 9899:1999(E).

[Int03a] International Organization for Standardization, Geneva, Switzerland. *The C Rationale*, April 2003. ISO/IEC JTC 1/SC 22/WG 14, revision 5.10.

[Int03b] International Organization for Standardization, Geneva, Switzerland. *Information Technology—Portable Operating System Interface (POSIX)*, fourth edition, August 2003. ISO/IEC 9945-1:2003. Also IEEE standard 1003.1, 2004 Edition, and The Open Group Technical Standard Base Specifications, Issue 6. Available at *pubs.opengroup.org/onlinepubs/009695399/*.

[Int10] International Organization for Standardization, Geneva, Switzerland. *Information Technology—Programming Languages—Fortran—Part 1: Base Language*, 2010. ISO/IEC 1539-1:2010.

[Int11] International Organization for Standardization, Geneva, Switzerland. *Programming Languages—C*, December 2011. ISO/IEC 9899:2011.

[Int12a] International Organization for Standardization, Geneva, Switzerland. *Information Technology—Common Language Infrastructure (CLI)*, February 2012. ISO/IEC 23271:2012. Also ECMA-335, 6th Edition, June 2012. Available at *ecma-international.org/publications/standards/Ecma-335.htm*.

[Int12b] International Organization for Standardization, Geneva, Switzerland. *Information Technology—Programming Languages—Ada*, December 2012. ISO/IEC 8652:2012. Available at *ada-auth.org/standards/ada12.html*.

[Int14a] International Organization for Standardization, Geneva, Switzerland. *Information Technology—Programming Languages, Their Environments and System Software Interfaces—Programming Language COBOL*, 2014. ISO/IEC 1989:2014.

[Int14b] International Organization for Standardization, Geneva, Switzerland. *Information Technology—Programming Languages—C++*, 2014. ISO/IEC 14882:2014.

[Int15] International Organization for Standardization, Geneva, Switzerland. *Technical Specification for C++ Extensions for Transactional Memory*, May 2015. ISO/IEC JTC 1/SC 22/WG 21 N4514.

[Ive62] Kenneth E. Iverson. *A Programming Language*. John Wiley and Sons, New York, NY, 1962.

[JBW$^+$87] David Jefferson, Brian Beckman, Fred Wieland, Leo Blume, Mike DiLoreto, Phil Hontalas, Pierre Laroche, Kathy Sturdevant, Jack Tupman, Van Warren, John Wedel, Herb Younger, and Steve Bellenot. Distributed simulation and the Time Warp operating system. In *Proceedings of the Eleventh ACM Symposium on Operating Systems Principles*, pages 77–93, Austin, TX, November 1987.

[JF10] Jaakko Järvi and John Freeman. C++ lambda expressions and closures. *Science of Computer Programming*, 75(9):762–772, September 2010.

[JG89] Geraint Jones and Michael Goldsmith. *Programming in occam2*. Prentice-Hall International Series in Computer Science. Prentice-Hall, Englewood Cliffs, NJ, second edition, 1989.

[JGF96] Simon Peyton Jones, Andrew Gordon, and Sigbjorn Finne. Concurrent Haskell. In *Proceedings of the Twenty-Third ACM Symposium on Principles of Programming Languages*, pages 295–308, St. Petersburg Beach, FL, January 1996.

[JL96] Richard Jones and Rafael Lins. *Garbage Collection: Algorithms for Automatic Dynamic Memory Management*. John Wiley and Sons, New York, NY, 1996.

[JM94] Joxan Jaffar and Michael J. Maher. Constraint logic programming: A survey. *Journal of Logic Programming*, 20:503–581, May–July 1994.

[Joh75] Stephen C. Johnson. Yacc—Yet another compiler compiler. Technical Report 32, Computing Science, AT&T Bell Laboratories, Murray Hill, NJ, 1975.

[JOR75] Mehdi Jazayeri, William F. Ogden, and William C. Rounds. The intrinsically exponential complexity of the circularity problem for attribute grammars. *Communications of the ACM*, 18(12):697–706, December 1975.

[JPAR68] Walter L. Johnson, James H. Porter, Stephanie I. Ackley, and Douglas T. Ross. Automatic generation of efficient lexical processors using finite state techniques. *Communications of the ACM*, 11(12):805–813, December 1968.

[JW91] Kathleen Jensen and Niklaus Wirth. *Pascal User Manual and Report: ISO Pascal Standard*. Springer-Verlag, New York, NY, fourth edition, 1991. Revised by Andrew B. Mickel and James F. Miner. ISBN 0-387-97649-3.

[Kas65] T. Kasami. An efficient recognition and syntax analysis algorithm for context-free languages. Technical Report AFCRL-65-758, Air Force Cambridge Research Laboratory, Bedford, MA, 1965.

[KCR$^+$98] Richard Kelsey, William Clinger, Jonathan Rees, H. Abelson, R. K. Dybvig, C. T. Haynes, G. J. Rozas, N. I. Adams IV, D. P. Friedman, E. Kohlbecker, G. L. Steele, Jr., D. H. Bartley, R. Halstead, D. Oxley, G. J. Sussman, G. Brooks, C. Hanson, K. M. Pitman, and M. Wand. Revised^5 report on the algorithmic language Scheme. *Higher-Order and Symbolic Computation*, 11(1):7–105, 1998. Edited by Kelsey, Clinger, and Rees. Available at *schemers.org/Documents/Standards/R5RS/*.

[Kee89] Sonya E. Keene. *Object-Oriented Programming in Common Lisp: A Programmer's Guide to CLOS*. Addison-Wesley, Reading, MA, 1989. Contributions by Dan Gerson.

[Kep04] Stephan Kepser. A simple proof for the Turing-completeness of XSLT and XQuery. In *Proceedings, Extreme Markup Languages 2004*, Montréal, Canada, August

2004. Available as *conferences.idealliance.org/extreme/html/2004/Kepser01/EML2004Kepser01.html*.

[Ker81] Brian W. Kernighan. Why Pascal is not my favorite programming language. Technical Report 100, Computing Science, AT&T Bell Laboratories, Murray Hill, NJ, 1981. Reprinted as pages 170–186 of Feuer and Gehani [FG84].

[Kes77] Joep L. W. Kessels. An alternative to event queues for synchronization in monitors. *Communications of the ACM*, 20(7):500–503, July 1977.

[Kle56] Stephen C. Kleene. Representation of events in nerve nets and finite automata. In Claude E. Shannon and John McCarthy, editors, *Automata Studies*, number 34 in Annals of Mathematical Studies, pages 3–41. Princeton University Press, Princeton, NJ, 1956.

[KMP77] Donald E. Knuth, James H. Morris, and Vaughan R. Pratt. Fast pattern matching in strings. *SIAM Journal of Computing*, 6(2):323–350, June 1977.

[Knu65] Donald E. Knuth. On the translation of languages from left to right. *Information and Control*, 8(6):607–639, December 1965.

[Knu68] Donald E. Knuth. Semantics of context-free languages. *Mathematical Systems Theory*, 2(2):127–145, June 1968. Correction appears in Volume 5, pages 95–96.

[Knu84] Donald E. Knuth. Literate programming. *The Computer Journal*, 27(2):97–111, May 1984.

[Knu86] Donald E. Knuth. *The TeXbook*. Addison-Wesley, Reading, MA, 1986.

[Kor94] David G. Korn. `ksh`: An extensible high level language. In *Proceedings of the USENIX Very High Level Languages Symposium*, pages 129–146, Santa Fe, NM, October 1994.

[KP78] Brian W. Kernighan and Phillip J. Plauger. *The Elements of Programming Style*. McGraw-Hill, New York, NY, second edition, 1978.

[KR88] Brian W. Kernighan and Dennis M. Ritchie. *The C Programming Language*. Prentice-Hall, Englewood Cliffs, NJ, second edition, 1988.

[Krá73] Jaroslav Král. The equivalence of modes and the equivalence of finite automata. *ALGOL Bulletin*, 35:34–35, March 1973.

[KS01] Andrew Kennedy and Don Syme. Design and implementation of generics for the .NET Common Language Runtime. In *Proceedings of the SIGPLAN 2001 Conference on Programming Language Design and Implementation*, pages 1–12, Snowbird, UT, June 2001.

[KWS97] Leonidas I. Kontothanassis, Robert Wisniewski, and Michael L. Scott. Scheduler-conscious synchronization. *ACM Transactions on Computer Systems*, 15(1):3–40, February 1997.

[Lam78] Leslie Lamport. Time, clocks, and the ordering of events in a distributed system. *Communications of the ACM*, 21(7):558–565, July 1978.

[Lam87] Leslie Lamport. A fast mutual exclusion algorithm. *ACM Transactions on Computer Systems*, 5(1):1–11, February 1987.

[Lam94] Leslie Lamport. *LaTeX: A Document Preparation System*. Addison-Wesley Professional, Reading, MA, second edition, 1994.

[Lam05] Christoph Lameter. Effective synchronization on Linux/NUMA systems. In *Proceedings of the Gelato Federation Meeting*, San Jose, CA, May 2005.

[LCM+05] Chi-Keung Luk, Robert Cohn, Robert Muth, Harish Patil, Artur Klauser, Geoff Lowney, Steven Wallace, Vijay Janapa Reddi, and Kim Hazelwood. Pin: Building customized program analysis tools with dynamic instrumentation. In *Proceedings of the SIGPLAN 2005 Conference on Programming Language Design and Implementation*, pages 190–200, Chicago, IL, June 2005.

[Lee06] Edward A. Lee. The problem with threads. *Computer*, 39(5):33–42, May 2006.

[Les75] Michael E. Lesk. Lex—A lexical analyzer generator. Technical Report 39, Computing Science, AT&T Bell Laboratories, Murray Hill, NJ, 1975.

[LG86] Barbara Liskov and John Guttag. *Abstraction and Specification in Program Development*. MIT Press, Cambridge, MA, 1986.

[LH89] Kai Li and Paul Hudak. Memory coherence in shared virtual memory systems. *ACM Transactions on Computer Systems*, 7(4):321–359, November 1989.

[LHL+77] Butler W. Lampson, J. J. Horning, R. L. London, J. G. Mitchell, and G. J. Popek. Report on the programming language Euclid. *ACM SIGPLAN Notices*, 12(2):1–79, February 1977.

[LK08] James Larus and Christos Kozyrakis. Transactional memory. *Communications of the ACM*, 51(7):80–88, July 2008.

[LL12] Kenneth C. Louden and Kenneth A. Lambert. *Programming Languages: Principles and Practice*. Cengage Learning, Boston, MA, third edition, 2012.

[Llo87] John W. Lloyd. *Foundations of Logic Programming.* Springer-Verlag, Berlin, West Germany, second edition, 1987.

[Lom75] David B. Lomet. Scheme for invalidating references to freed storage. *IBM Journal of Research and Development,* 19(1):26–35, January 1975.

[Lom85] David B. Lomet. Making pointers safe in system programming languages. *IEEE Transactions on Software Engineering,* SE–11(1):87–96, January 1985.

[LP80] David C. Luckam and W. Polak. Ada exception handling: An axiomatic approach. *ACM Transactions on Programming Languages and Systems,* 2(2):225–233, April 1980.

[LR80] Butler W. Lampson and David D. Redell. Experience with processes and monitors in Mesa. *Communications of the ACM,* 23(2):105–117, February 1980.

[LRS74] Philip M. Lewis II, Daniel J. Rosenkrantz, and Richard E. Stearns. Attributed translations. *Journal of Computer and System Sciences,* 9(3):279–307, December 1974.

[LS68] Philip M. Lewis II and Richard E. Stearns. Syntax-directed transduction. *Journal of the ACM,* 15(3):465–488, July 1968.

[LS79] Barbara Liskov and Alan Snyder. Exception handling in CLU. *IEEE Transactions on Software Engineering,* SE–5(6):546–558, November 1979.

[LS83] Barbara Liskov and Robert Scheifler. Guardians and actions: Linguistic support for robust, distributed programs. *ACM Transactions on Programming Languages and Systems,* 5(3):381–404, July 1983.

[LSAS77] Barbara Liskov, Alan Snyder, Russel Atkinson, and J. Craig Schaffert. Abstraction mechanisms in CLU. *Communications of the ACM,* 20(8):564–576, August 1977.

[LYBB14] Tim Lindholm, Frank Yellin, Gilad Bracha, and Alex Buckley. *The Java Virtual Machine Specification.* Addison-Wesley Professional, Java SE 8 edition, 2014. Available at *docs.oracle.com/javase/specs/*.

[Mac77] M. Donald MacLaren. Exception handling in PL/I. In David B. Wortman, editor, *Proceedings of an ACM Conference on Language Design for Reliable Software,* pages 101–104, Raleigh, NC, 1977.

[MAE+65] John McCarthy, Paul W. Abrahams, Daniel J. Edwards, Timothy P. Hart, and Michael I. Levin. *LISP 1.5 Programmer's Manual.* MIT Press, Cambridge, MA, second edition, 1965. Available as *softwarepreservation.org/projects/LISP/book/LISP%201.5%20Programmers%20Manual.pdf*.

[Mai90] Harry G. Mairson. Deciding ML typability is complete for deterministic exponential time. In *Conference Record of the Seventeenth Annual ACM Symposium on Principles of Programming Languages,* pages 382–401, San Francisco, CA, January 1990.

[MAK+01] Paul E. McKenney, Jonathan Appavoo, Andi Kleen, Orran Krieger, Rusty Russel, Dipankar Sarma, and Maneesh Soni. Read-copy update. In *Proceedings of the Ottawa Linux Symposium,* pages 338–367, Ottawa, ON, Canada, July 2001.

[Mas76] John R. Mashey. Using a command language as a high-level programming language. In *Proceedings of the Second International IEEE Conference on Software Engineering,* pages 169–176, San Francisco, CA, October 1976.

[Mas87] Henry Massalin. Superoptimizer: A look at the smallest program. In *Proceedings of the Second International Conference on Architectural Support for Programming Languages and Operating Systems,* pages 122–126, Palo Alto, CA, October 1987.

[McC60] John McCarthy. Recursive functions of symbolic expressions and their computation by machine, Part I. *Communications of the ACM,* 3(4):184–195, April 1960.

[McG82] James R. McGraw. The VAL language: Description and analysis. *ACM Transactions on Programming Languages and Systems,* 4(1):44–82, January 1982.

[McK04] Kathryn S. McKinley, editor. *20 Years of the ACM SIGPLAN Conference on Programming Language Design and Implementation, 1979–1999.* ACM Press, New York, NY, 2004. Also *ACM SIGPLAN Notices,* 39(4), April 2004.

[MCS91] John M. Mellor-Crummey and Michael L. Scott. Algorithms for scalable synchronization on shared-memory multiprocessors. *ACM Transactions on Computer Systems,* 9(1):21–65, February 1991.

[Mes12] Message Passing Interface Forum. *MPI: A Message-Passing Interface Standard,* September 2012. Version 3.0. Available as *mpi-forum.org/docs/mpi-3.0/mpi30-report.pdf*.

[Mey92a] Bertrand Meyer. Applying "design by contract". *IEEE Computer,* 25(10):40–51, October 1992.

[Mey92b] Bertrand Meyer. *Eiffel: The Language.* Prentice-Hall, Englewood Cliffs, NJ, 1992.

[MF08] Jacob Matthews and Robert Bruce Findler. An operational semantics for Scheme. *Journal of Functional Programming,* 18(1):47–86, 2008.

[MGA92] Margaret Martonosi, Anoop Gupta, and Thomas Anderson. MemSpy: Analyzing memory system bottlenecks in programs. In *Proceedings of the 1992 ACM SIGMETRICS Joint International Conference on Measurement and Modeling of Computer Systems*, pages 1–12, Newport, RI, June 1992.

[Mic68] Donald Michie. 'Memo' functions and machine learning. *Nature*, 218(5136):19–22, April 1968.

[Mic89] Greg Michaelson. *An Introduction to Functional Programming through Lambda Calculus.* International Computer Science Series. Addison-Wesley, Wokingham, England, 1989.

[Mic12] Microsoft Corporation. *C# Language Specification, Version 5.0*, 2012. Available at *msdn.microsoft.com/en-us/library/ms228593.aspx.*

[Mil78] Robin Milner. A theory of type polymorphism in programming. *Journal of Computer and System Sciences*, 17(3):348–375, December 1978.

[MKH91] Eric Mohr, David A. Kranz, and Robert H. Halstead, Jr. Lazy task creation: A technique for increasing the granularity of parallel programs. *IEEE Transactions on Parallel and Distributed Systems*, 2(3):264–280, July 1991.

[MLB76] Michael Marcotty, Henry F. Ledgard, and Gregor V. Bochmann. A sampler of formal definitions. *ACM Computing Surveys*, 8(2):191–276, June 1976.

[MM08] Virendra J. Marathe and Mark Moir. Toward high performance nonblocking software transactional memory. In *Proceedings of the Thirteenth ACM SIGPLAN Symposium on Principles and Practice of Parallel Programming*, pages 227–236, Salt Lake City, UT, February 2008.

[Moo78] David A. Moon. *MacLisp Reference Manual.* MIT Artificial Intelligence Laboratory, 1978.

[Moo86] David A. Moon. Object-oriented programming with Flavors. In *OOPSLA '86 Conference Proceedings: Object-Oriented Programming Systems, Languages, and Applications*, pages 1–8, Portland, OR, September 1986.

[Mor70] Howard L. Morgan. Spelling correction in systems programs. *Communications of the ACM*, 13(2):90–94, 1970.

[MOSS96] Stephan Murer, Stephen Omohundro, David Stoutamire, and Clemens Szyperski. Iteration abstraction in Sather. *ACM Transactions on Programming Languages and Systems*, 18(1):1–15, January 1996.

[MPA05] Jeremy Manson, William Pugh, and Sarita V. Adve. The Java memory model. In *Proceedings of the Thirty Second ACM Symposium on Principles of Programming Languages*, pages 378–391, Long Beach, CA, January 2005.

[MR96] Michael Metcalf and John Reid. *Fortran 90/95 Explained.* Oxford University Press, London, England, 1996.

[MR04] James S. Miller and Susann Ragsdale. *The Common Language Infrastructure Annotated Standard.* Addison-Wesley, Boston, MA, 2004. Based on ECMA-335, 2nd Edition, 2002.

[MS96] Maged M. Michael and Michael L. Scott. Simple, fast, and practical non-blocking and blocking concurrent queue algorithms. In *Proceedings of the Fifteenth Annual ACM Symposium on Principles of Distributed Computing*, pages 267–275, Philadelphia, PA, May 1996.

[MS98] Maged M. Michael and Michael L. Scott. Nonblocking algorithms and preemption-safe locking on multiprogrammed shared memory multiprocessors. *Journal of Parallel and Distributed Computing*, 51:1–26, 1998.

[MTAB13] Leo A. Meyerovich, Matthew E. Torok, Eric Atkinson, and Rastislav Bodík. Parallel schedule synthesis for attribute grammars. In *Proceedings of the Eighteenth ACM SIGPLAN Symposium on Principles and Practice of Parallel Programming*, pages 187–196, Shenzhen, China, February 2013.

[MTHM97] Robin Milner, Mads Tofte, Robert Harper, and David MacQueen. *The Definition of Standard ML—Revised.* MIT Press, Cambridge, MA, 1997.

[Muc97] Steven S. Muchnick. *Advanced Compiler Design and Implementation.* Morgan Kaufmann, San Francisco, CA, 1997.

[MYD95] Bruce J. McKenzie, Corey Yeatman, and Lorraine De Vere. Error repair in shift-reduce parsers. *ACM Transactions on Programming Languages and Systems*, 17(4):672–689, July 1995.

[NA01] Rishiyur S. Nikhil and Arvind. *Implicit Parallel Programming in pH.* Morgan Kaufmann, San Francisco, CA, 2001.

[NBB+63] Peter Naur (ed.), J. W. Backus, F. L. Bauer, J. Green, C. Katz, J. McCarthy, A. J. Perlis, H. Rutishauser, K. Samelson, B. Vauquois, J. H. Wegstein, A. van Wijngaarden, and M. Woodger. Revised report on the algorithmic language ALGOL 60. *Communications of the ACM*, 6(1):1–23, January 1963. Original version appeared in the May 1960 issue.

[ND78] Kristen Nygaard and Ole-Johan Dahl. The development of the Simula languages. In *HOPL I Proceedings* [Wex78], pages 439–493.

[Nec97] George C. Necula. Proof-carrying code. In *Conference Record of the Twenty-Fourth ACM Symposium on Principles of Programming Languages*, pages 106–119, Paris, France, January 1997.

[Nel65] Theodor Holm Nelson. Complex information processing: A file structure for the complex, the changing, and the indeterminate. In *Proceedings of the Twentieth ACM National Conference*, pages 84–100, Cleveland, OH, August 1965.

[NK15] Tobias Nipkow and Gerwin Klein. *Concrete Semantics with Isabelle/HOL*. Springer Science+Business Media, Berlin, Germany, 2015.

[Ous82] John K. Ousterhout. Scheduling techniques for concurrent systems. In *Proceedings of the Third International Conference on Distributed Computing Systems*, pages 22–30, Miami/Ft. Lauderdale, FL, October 1982.

[Ous94] John K. Ousterhout. *Tcl and the Tk Toolkit*. Addison-Wesley Professional, Reading, MA, 1994.

[Ous98] John K. Ousterhout. Scripting: Higher-level programming for the 21st century. *IEEE Computer*, 31(3):23–30, March 1998.

[Pag76] Frank G. Pagan. *A Practical Guide to Algol 68*. John Wiley and Sons, London, England, 1976.

[Par72] David L. Parnas. On the criteria to be used in decomposing systems into modules. *Communications of the ACM*, 15(12):1053–1058, December 1972.

[Pat85] David A. Patterson. Reduced instruction set computers. *Communications of the ACM*, 28(1):8–21, January 1985.

[PD80] David A. Patterson and David R. Ditzel. The case for the reduced instruction set computer. *ACM SIGARCH Computer Architecture News*, 8(6):25–33, October 1980.

[PD12] Larry L. Peterson and Bruce S. Davie. *Computer Networks: A Systems Approach*. Morgan Kaufmann, San Francisco, CA, fifth edition, 2012.

[Pet81] Gary L. Peterson. Myths about the mutual exclusion problem. *Information Processing Letters*, 12(3):115–116, June 1981.

[Pey87] Simon L. Peyton Jones. *The Implementation of Functional Programming Languages*. Prentice-Hall, Englewood Cliffs, NJ, 1987.

[Pey92] Simon L. Peyton Jones. Implementing lazy functional languages on stock hardware: The Spineless Tagless G-machine. *Journal of Functional Programming*, 2(2):127–202, 1992.

[Pey01] Simon Peyton Jones. Tackling the Awkward Squad: Monadic input/output, concurrency, exceptions, and foreign-language calls in Haskell. In Tony Hoare, Manfred Broy, and Ralf Steinbruggen, editors, *Engineering Theories of Software Construction*, pages 47–96. IOS Press, 2001. Originally presented at the *Marktoberdorf Summer School*, 2000. Revised and corrected version available as *research.microsoft.com/~simonpj/papers/marktoberdorf/mark.pdf*.

[PH12] David A. Patterson and John L. Hennessy. *Computer Organization and Design: The Hardware-Software Interface*. Morgan Kaufmann, San Francisco, CA, fourth, revised edition, 2012.

[Pie02] Benjamin C. Pierce. *Types and Programming Languages*. MIT Press, Cambridge, MA, 2002.

[PJ10] *Haskell 2010 Language Report*, April 2010. Available at *haskell.org/onlinereport/haskell2010/*.

[PQ95] Terrence J. Parr and R. W. Quong. ANTLR: A predicated-*LL*(*k*) parser generator. *Software—Practice and Experience*, 25(7):789–810, July 1995.

[Pug00] William Pugh. The Java memory model is fatally flawed. *Concurrency—Practice and Experience*, 12(6):445–455, May 2000.

[Rad82] George Radin. The 801 minicomputer. In *Proceedings of the First International Symposium on Architectural Support for Programming Languages and Operating Systems*, pages 39–47, Palo Alto, CA, March 1982.

[Rep84] Thomas Reps. *Generating Language-Based Environments*. MIT Press, Cambridge, MA, 1984. Winner of the 1983 ACM Doctoral Dissertation Award.

[RF93] B. Ramakrishna Rau and Joseph A. Fisher. Instruction-level parallel processing: History, overview, and perspective. *Journal of Supercomputing*, 7(1/2):9–50, May 1993.

[Rob65] John Alan Robinson. A machine-oriented logic based on the resolution principle. *Journal of the ACM*, 12(1):23–41, January 1965.

[Rob83] John Alan Robinson. Logic programming—Past, present, and future. *New Generation Computing*, 1(2):107–124, 1983.

[RR64] Brian Randell and Lawford J. Russell, editors. *ALGOL 60 Implementation: The Translation and Use of ALGOL 60 Programs on a Computer*. A.P.I.C. Studies in Data Processing #5. Academic Press, New York, NY, 1964.

[RS59] Michael O. Rabin and Dana S. Scott. Finite automata and their decision problems. *IBM Journal of Research and Development*, 3(2):114–125, 1959.

[RS70] Daniel J. Rosenkrantz and Richard E. Stearns. Properties of deterministic top-down grammars. *Information and Control*, 17(3):226–256, October 1970.

[RT88] Thomas Reps and Timothy Teitelbaum. *The Synthesizer Generator: A System for Constructing Language-Based Editors*. Springer-Verlag, New York, NY, 1988.

[Rub87] Frank Rubin. 'GOTO considered harmful' considered harmful. *Communications of the ACM*, 30(3):195–196, March 1987. Further correspondence appears in Volume 30, Numbers 6, 7, 8, 11, and 12.

[Rut67] Heinz Rutishauser. *Description of ALGOL 60*. Springer-Verlag, New York, NY, 1967.

[RW92] Martin Reiser and Niklaus Wirth. *Programming in Oberon—Steps Beyond Pascal and Modula*. Addison-Wesley, Reading, MA, 1992.

[SBG+91] Robert E. Strom, David F. Bacon, Arthur P. Goldberg, Andy Lowry, Daniel M. Yellin, and Shaula Alexander Yemini. *Hermes: A Language for Distributed Computing*. Prentice-Hall, Englewood Cliffs, NJ, 1991.

[SBN82] Daniel P. Siewiorek, C. Gordon Bell, and Allen Newell. *Computer Structures: Principles and Examples*. McGraw-Hill, New York, NY, 1982.

[SCG+13] Alex Shinn, John Cowan, Arthur A. Gleckler, Steven Ganz, Aaron W. Hsu, Bradley Lucier, Emmanuel Medernach, Alexey Radul, Jeffrey T. Read, David Rush, Benjamin L. Russel, Olin Shivers, Alaric Snell-Pym, Gerald J. Sussman, Richart Kelsey, William Clinger, Jonathan Rees, Michael Sperber, R. Kent Dybvig, Matthew Flatt, and Anton van Stratten. *Revised^7 Report on the Algorithmic Language Scheme*, July 2013. Edited by Shinn, Cowan, and Gleckler. Available at *trac.sacrideo.us/wg/wiki/R7RSHomePage/*.

[Sch03] Sven-Bodo Scholz. Single assignment C—Efficient support for high-level array operations in a functional setting. *Journal of Functional Programming*, 13(6):1005–1059, 2003.

[SCK+93] Richard L. Sites, Anton Chernoff, Matthew B. Kirk, Maurice P. Marks, and Scott G. Robinson. Binary translation. *Communications of the ACM*, 36(2):69–81, February 1993.

[Sco91] Michael L. Scott. The Lynx distributed programming language: Motivation, design, and experience. *Computer Languages*, 16(3/4):209–233, 1991.

[Sco13] Michael L. Scott. *Shared-Memory Synchronization*. Synthesis Lectures on Computer Architecture. Morgan & Claypool Publishers, June 2013.

[SDB84] Mayer D. Schwartz, Norman M. Delisle, and Vimal S. Begwani. Incremental compilation in Magpie. In *Proceedings of the SIGPLAN '84 Symposium on Compiler Construction*, pages 122–131, Montreal, Quebec, Canada, June 1984.

[SDDS86] Jacob T. Schwartz, Robert B. K. Dewar, Ed Dubinsky, and Edmond Schonberg. *Programming with Sets: An Introduction to SETL*. Texts and Monographs in Computer Science. Springer-Verlag, New York, NY, 1986.

[SDF+07] Michael Sperber, R. Kent Dybvig, Matthew Flatt, Anton van Straaten, Richard Kelsey, William Clinger, Jonathan Rees, Robert Bruce Findler, and Jacob Matthews. *Revised^6 Report on the Algorithmic Language Scheme*, September 2007. Edited by Sperber, Dybvig, Flatt, and van Stratten. Available at *r6rs.org/*.

[SE94] Amitabh Srivastava and Alan Eustace. ATOM: A system for building customized program analysis tools. In *Proceedings of the SIGPLAN 1994 Conference on Programming Language Design and Implementation*, pages 196–205, Orlando, FL, June 1994.

[Seb15] Robert W. Sebesta. *Concepts of Programming Languages*. Pearson/Addison-Wesley, Boston, MA, eleventh edition, 2015.

[Sei05] Peter Seibel. *Practical Common Lisp*. Apress L. P., 2005.

[Set96] Ravi Sethi. *Programming Languages: Concepts and Constructs*. Addison-Wesley, Reading, MA, second edition, 1996.

[SF80] Marvin H. Solomon and Raphael A. Finkel. A note on enumerating binary trees. *Journal of the ACM*, 27(1):3–5, January 1980.

[SF88] Michael L. Scott and Raphael A. Finkel. A simple mechanism for type security across compilation units. *IEEE Transactions on Software Engineering*, SE–14(8):1238–1239, August 1988.

[SFL+94] Ioannis Schoinas, Babak Falsafi, Alvin R. Lebeck, Steven K. Reinhardt, James R. Larus, and David A. Wood. Fine-grain access control for distributed shared memory. In *Proceedings of the Sixth International Conference on Architectural Support for Programming Languages and Operating Systems*, pages 297–306, San Jose, CA, October 1994.

[SG96] Daniel J. Scales and Kourosh Gharachorloo. Shasta: A low overhead, software-only approach for supporting fine-grain shared memory. In *Proceedings of the Seventh International Conference on Architectural Support for Programming Languages and Operating Systems*, pages 174–185, Cambridge, MA, October 1996.

[SGC13] Don Syme, Adam Granicz, and Antonio Cisternino. *Expert F# 3.0.* Apress, Berkeley, CA, 2013.

[SH92] A. S. M. Sajeev and A. John Hurst. Programming persistence in χ. *IEEE Computer*, 25(9):57–66, September 1992.

[SHC96] Zoltan Somogyi, Fergus Henderson, and Thomas Conway. The execution algorithm of Mercury: An efficient purely declarative logic programming language. *Journal of Logic Programming*, 29(1–3):17–64, October–December 1996.

[Sie00] Jon Siegel. *CORBA 3 Fundamentals and Programming.* John Wiley and Sons, New York, NY, 2000.

[Sip13] Michael Sipser. *Introduction to the Theory of Computation.* Cengage Learning, Boston, MA, third edition, 2013.

[Sit72] Richard L. Sites. Algol W reference manual. Technical Report STAN-CS-71-230, Computer Science Department, Stanford University, Stanford, CA, February 1972.

[SK95] Kenneth Slonneger and Barry L. Kurtz. *Formal Syntax and Semantics of Programming Languages: A Laboratory Based Approach.* Addison-Wesley, Reading, MA, 1995.

[SMC91] Joel H. Saltz, Avi Mirchandaney, and Kay Crowley. Run-time parallelization and scheduling of loops. *IEEE Transactions on Computers*, 40(5):603–612, May 1991.

[SPSS08] Jun Shirako, David Peixotto, Vivek Sarkar, and William N. Scherer III. Phasers: A unified deadlock-free construct for collective and point-to-point synchronization. In *Proceedings of the Twenty-Second International Conference on Supercomputing*, pages 277–288, Island of Kos, Greece, June 2008.

[SR13] Mehran Sahami and Steve Roach, editors. *Computer Science Curricula 2013: Curriculum Guidelines for Undergraduate Degree Programs in Computer Science.* Joint Task Force on Computing Curricula, Association for Computing Machinery (ACM) and the IEEE Computer Society, December 2013. Available as *acm.org/education/CS2013-final-report.pdf*.

[Sri95] Raj Srinivasan. RPC: Remote procedure call protocol specification version 2. Internet Request for Comments #1831, August 1995. Available at *rfc-archive.org/getrfc.php?rfc=1831.*

[SS71] Dana S. Scott and Christopher Strachey. Toward a mathematical semantics for computer language. In Jerome Fox, editor, *Proceedings, Symposium on Computers and Automata*, pages 19–46. Polytechnic Institute of Brooklyn Press, New York, NY, 1971.

[SSA13] Eric Schkufza, Rahul Sharma, and Alex Aiken. Stochastic superoptimization. In *Proceedings of the Eighteenth International Conference on Architectural Support for Programming Languages and Operating Systems*, pages 305–316, Houston, TX, March 2013.

[SSD13] Andrew Sutton, Bjarne Stroustrup, and Gabriel Dos Reis. *Concepts Lite: Constraining Templates with Predicates*, March 2013. Document number N3580, Concepts working group, International Organization for Standardization. Available as *open-std.org/jtc1/sc22/wg21/docs/papers/2013/n3580.pdf*.

[Sta95] Ryan D. Stansifer. *The Study of Programming Languages.* Prentice-Hall, Englewood Cliffs, NJ, 1995.

[Ste90] Guy L. Steele Jr. *Common Lisp—The Language.* Digital Press, Bedford, MA, second edition, 1990. Available at *cs.cmu.edu/Groups/AI/html/cltl/cltl2.html.*

[Sto77] Joseph E. Stoy. *Denotational Semantics: The Scott-Strachey Approach to Programming Language Semantics*, volume 1. MIT Press, Cambridge, MA, 1977.

[Str13] Bjarne Stroustrup. *The C++ Programming Language.* Addison-Wesley Professional, fourth edition, 2013. Second edition, 1991.

[Sun90] Vaidyalingam S. Sunderam. PVM: A framework for parallel distributed computing. *Concurrency—Practice and Experience*, 2(4):315–339, December 1990.

[Sun97] Sun Microsystems, Mountain View, CA. *JavaBeans*, August 1997. Version 1.01-A. Available at *oracle.com/technetwork/articles/javaee/spec-136004.html.*

[Sun04] Håkan Sundell. *Efficient and Practical Non-Blocking Data Structures.* Ph. D. dissertation, Department of Computing Science, Chalmers University of Technology and Göteborg University, Göteborg, Sweden, 2004. Available as *cs.chalmers.se/~tsigas/papers/Haakan-Thesis.pdf*.

[Sun06] Sun Microsystems. Strongtalk: Smalltalk with a need for speed. *strongtalk.org*, 2006.

[SW67] Herbert Schorr and William M. Waite. An efficient machine-independent procedure for garbage collection in various list structures. *Communications of the ACM*, 10(8):501–506, August 1967.

[SW94] James E. Smith and Shlomo Weiss. PowerPC 601 and Alpha 21064: A tale of two RISCs. *IEEE Computer*, 27(6):46–58, June 1994.

[SZBH86] Daniel C. Swinehart, Polle T. Zellweger, Richard J. Beach, and Robert B. Hagmann. A structural view of the

Cedar programming environment. *ACM Transactions on Programming Languages and Systems*, 8(4):419–490, October 1986.

[Tan78] Andrew S. Tanenbaum. A comparison of Pascal and ALGOL 68. *The Computer Journal*, 21(4):316–323, November 1978.

[TFH13] Dave Thomas, Chad Fowler, and Andy Hunt. *Programming Ruby 1.9 & 2.0—The Pragmatic Programmers' Guide*. The Pragmatic Programmers, LLC, Dallas, TX, 2013.

[Tho95] Tom Thompson. Building the better virtual CPU. *Byte*, 20(8):149–150, August 1995.

[Tic86] Walter F. Tichy. Smart recompilation. *ACM Transactions on Programming Languages and Systems*, 8(3):273–291, July 1986.

[TM81] Warren Teitelman and Larry Masinter. The Interlisp programming environment. *IEEE Computer*, 14(4):25–33, April 1981.

[TML13] Kevin Tatroe, Peter MacIntyre, and Rasmus Lerdorf. *Programming PHP*. O'Reilly Media, Sebastopol, CA, third edition, 2013.

[TR81] Timothy Teitelbaum and Thomas Reps. The Cornell Program Synthesizer: A syntax-directed programming environment. *Communications of the ACM*, 24(9):563–573, September 1981.

[Tre86] R. Kent Treiber. Systems programming: Coping with parallelism. Technical Report RJ 5118, IBM Almaden Research Center, April 1986.

[Tur86] David A. Turner. An overview of Miranda. *ACM SIGPLAN Notices*, 21(12):158–166, December 1986.

[TW12] Andrew S. Tanenbaum and David J. Wetherall. *Computer Networks*. Pearson Higher Education, fifth edition, 2012.

[TWGM07] Fuad Tabba, Cong Wang, James R. Goodman, and Mark Moir. NZTM: Nonblocking zero-indirection transactional memory. In *Second ACM SIGPLAN Workshop on Transactional Computing*, Portland, OR, August 2007. Available as *cs.rochester.edu/meetings/TRANSACT07/papers/tabba.pdf*.

[Ull85] Jeffrey D. Ullman. Implementation of logical query languages for databases. *ACM Transactions on Database Systems*, 10(3):289–321, September 1985.

[US91] David Ungar and Randall B. Smith. SELF: The power of simplicity. *Lisp and Symbolic Computation*, 4(3):187–205, July 1991.

[UW08] Jeffrey D. Ullman and Jennifer Widom. *A First Course in Database Systems*. Pearson/Prentice-Hall, Upper Saddle River, NJ, third edition, 2008.

[vCZ+03] Rob von Behren, Jeremy Condit, Feng Zhou, George C. Necula, and Eric Brewer. Capriccio: Scalable threads for internet services. In *Proceedings of the Nineteenth ACM Symposium on Operating Systems Principles*, pages 268–281, Bolton Landing (Lake George), NY, October 2003.

[VF82] Thomas R. Virgilio and Raphael A. Finkel. Binding strategies and scope rules are independent. *Computer Languages*, 7(2):61–67, 1982.

[VF94] Jack E. Veenstra and Robert J. Fowler. Mint: A front end for efficient simulation of shared-memory multiprocessors. In *Proceedings of the Second International Workshop on Modeling, Analysis and Simulation of Computer and Telecommunication Systems*, pages 201–207, Durham, NC, January 1994.

[vMP+75] A. van Wijngaarden, B. J. Mailloux, J. E. L. Peck, C. H. A. Koster, M. Sintzoff, C. H. Lindsey, L. G. L T. Meertens, and R. G. Fisker. Revised report on the algorithmic language ALGOL 68. *Acta Informatica*, 5(1–3):1–236, 1975. Also *ACM SIGPLAN Notices*, 12(5):1–70, May 1977.

[vRD11] Guido van Rossum and Fred L. Drake, Jr. (Editor). *The Python Language Reference Manual (version 3.2)*. Network Theory, Ltd., Bristol, UK, 2011.

[Wad98a] Philip Wadler. An angry half-dozen. *ACM SIGPLAN Notices*, 33(2):25–30, February 1998. NB: table of contents on cover of issue is incorrect.

[Wad98b] Philip Wadler. Why no one uses functional languages. *ACM SIGPLAN Notices*, 33(8):23–27, August 1998.

[Wat77] David Anthony Watt. The parsing problem for affix grammars. *Acta Informatica*, 8(1):1–20, 1977.

[Web89] Fred Webb. Fortran story—The real scoop. Submitted to `alt.folklore.computers`, 1989. Quoted by Mark Brader in the ACM *RISKS* on-line forum, volume 9, issue 54, December 12, 1989.

[Weg90] Peter Wegner. Concepts and paradigms of object-oriented programming. *OOPS Messenger*, 1(1):7–87, August 1990. Expanded version of the keynote address from *OOPSLA '89*.

[Wet78] Horst Wettstein. The problem of nested monitor calls revisited. *ACM Operating Systems Review*, 12(1):19–23, January 1978.

[Wex78] Richard L. Wexelblat, editor. *Proceedings of the ACM SIGPLAN History of Programming Languages (HOPL) Conference*, ACM Monograph Series, 1981, Los Angeles, CA, June 1978. Academic Press, New York, NY.

[WH66] Niklaus Wirth and Charles Antony Richard Hoare. A contribution to the development of ALGOL. *Communications of the ACM*, 9(6):413–431, June 1966.

[Wil92a] Paul R. Wilson. Pointer swizzling at page fault time: Efficiently and compatibly supporting huge address spaces on standard hardware. In *Proceedings of the International Workshop on Object Orientation in Operating Systems*, pages 364–377, Paris, France, September 1992.

[Wil92b] Paul R. Wilson. Uniprocessor garbage collection techniques. In *Proceedings of the International Workshop on Memory Management*, volume 637 of *Lecture Notes in Computer Science*, pages 1–42. Springer-Verlag, Berlin, Germany, 1992. Workshop held at St. Malo, France, September 1992. Expanded version available as *ftp://ftp.cs.utexas.edu/pub/garbage/bigsurv.ps*.

[Win93] Glynn Winskel. *The Formal Semantics of Programming Languages*. MIT Press, Cambridge, MA, 1993.

[Wir71] Niklaus Wirth. The programming language Pascal. *Acta Informatica*, 1(1):35–63, 1971.

[Wir76] Niklaus Wirth. *Algorithms + Data Structures = Programs*. Prentice-Hall, Englewood Cliffs, NJ, 1976.

[Wir77a] Niklaus Wirth. Design and implementation of Modula. *Software—Practice and Experience*, 7(1):67–84, January–February 1977.

[Wir77b] Niklaus Wirth. Modula: A language for modular multiprogramming. *Software—Practice and Experience*, 7(1):3–35, January–February 1977.

[Wir80] Niklaus Wirth. The module: A system structuring facility in high-level programming languages. In Jeffrey M. Tobias, editor, *Language Design and Programming Methodology*, volume 79 of *Lecture Notes in Computer Science*, pages 1–24. Springer-Verlag, Berlin, West Germany, 1980. Proceedings of a symposium held at Sydney, Australia, September 1979.

[Wir85a] Niklaus Wirth. From programming language design to computer construction. *Communications of the ACM*, 28(2):159–164, February 1985. The 1984 Turing Award lecture.

[Wir85b] Niklaus Wirth. *Programming in Modula-2*. Texts and Monographs in Computer Science. Springer-Verlag, New York, NY, third, corrected edition, 1985.

[Wir88a] Niklaus Wirth. From Modula to Oberon. *Software—Practice and Experience*, 18(7):661–670, July 1988.

[Wir88b] Niklaus Wirth. The programming language Oberon. *Software—Practice and Experience*, 18(7):671–690, July 1988.

[Wir88c] Niklaus Wirth. Type extensions. *ACM Transactions on Programming Languages and Systems*, 10(2):204–214, April 1988. Relevant correspondence appears in Volume 13, Number 4.

[Wir07] Niklaus Wirth. Modula-2 and Oberon. In *HOPL III Proceedings* [Ass07], pages 3-1–3-10.

[WJ93] Paul R. Wilson and Mark S. Johnstone. Real-time non-copying garbage collection. In *OOPSLA '93 Workshop on Memory Management and Gargage Collection*, Washington, DC, September 1993.

[WJH03] Brent B. Welch, Ken Jones, and Jeffrey Hobbs. *Practical Programming in Tcl and Tk*. Prentice-Hall, Upper Saddle River, NJ, fourth edition, 2003. Sample chapters from previous editions available on-line at *beedub.com/book/*.

[WLAG93] Robert Wahbe, Steven Lucco, Thomas E. Anderson, and Susan L. Graham. Efficient software-based fault isolation. In *Proceedings of the Fourteenth ACM Symposium on Operating Systems Principles*, pages 203–216, Asheville, NC, December 1993.

[WM95] Reinhard Wilhelm and Dieter Maurer. *Compiler Design*. Addison-Wesley, Wokingham, England, 1995. Translated from the German by Stephen S. Wilson.

[WMWM87] Janet H. Walker, David A. Moon, Daniel L. Weinreb, and Mike McMahon. The Symbolics Genera programming environment. *IEEE Software*, 4(6):36–45, November 1987.

[Wol96] Michael Wolfe. *High Performance Compilers for Parallel Computing*. Addison-Wesley, Redwood City, CA, 1996.

[Wor05] World Wide Web Consortium. *Character Model for the World Wide Web 1.0: Fundamentals*, February 2005. Available at *w3.org/TR/charmod/*.

[Wor06a] World Wide Web Consortium. *Extensible Markup Language (XML) 1.1 (Second Edition)*, September 2006. Available at *w3.org/TR/xml11/*.

[Wor06b] World Wide Web Consortium. *Extensible Stylesheet Language (XSL) Version 1.1*, December 2006. Available at *w3.org/TR/xsl/*.

[Wor07] World Wide Web Consortium. *XML Path Language (XPath) 2.0*, January 2007. Available at *w3.org/TR/xpath20/*.

[Wor12] World Wide Web Consortium. SOAP current status. *w3.org/standards/techs/soap*, 2012.

[Wor14] World Wide Web Consortium. *XSL Transformations (XSLT) Version 3.0*, October 2014. Available at *w3.org/TR/xslt-30/*.

[WSH77] Jim Welsh, W. J. Sneeringer, and Charles Antony Richard Hoare. Ambiguities and insecurities in Pascal. *Software—Practice and Experience*, 7(6):685–696, November–December 1977.

[YA93] Jae-Heon Yang and James H. Anderson. Fast, scalable synchronization with minimal hardware support (extended abstract). In *Proceedings of the Twelfth Annual ACM Symposium on Principles of Distributed Computing*, pages 171–182, Ithaca, NY, August 1993.

[You67] Daniel H. Younger. Recognition and parsing of context-free languages in time n^3. *Information and Control*, 10(2):189–208, February 1967.

[YTEM04] Junfeng Yang, Paul Twohey, Dawson Engler, and Madanlal Musuvathi. Using model checking to find serious file system errors. In *Proceedings of the Sixth USENIX Symposium on Operating Systems Design and Implementation*, pages 273–288, San Francisco, CA, December 2004.

[Zho96] Neng-Fa Zhou. Parameter passing and control stack management in Prolog implementation revisited. *ACM Transactions on Programming Languages and Systems*, 18(6):752–779, November 1996.

[ZRA$^+$08] Qin Zhao, Rodric Rabbah, Saman Amarasinghe, Larry Rudolph, and Weng-Fai Wong. How to do a million watchpoints: Efficient debugging using dynamic instrumentation. In *Proceedings of the Seventeenth International Conference on Compiler Construction*, pages 147–162, Budapest, Hungary, March 2008.

[Younger] Daniel H. Younger. Recognition and parsing of context-free languages in time n^3. *Information and Control*, 10(2):189–208, February 1967.

[YTEM04] [illegible] Yang, [illegible] Twohey, Dawson Engler, and Madanlal Musuvathi. Using model checking to find serious file system errors. In *Proceedings of the Sixth USENIX Symposium on Operating Systems Design and Implementation*, pages [illegible], San Francisco, CA, December 2004.

[Zhang96] Xiao [illegible] Zhang. [illegible] parsing and control [illegible] management in [illegible] implementation [illegible] *Transactions on Programming Languages and Systems*, 18(6):732–[illegible], November 1996.

[ZRA+08] Qin Zhao, Rodric Rabbah, Saman Amarasinghe, Larry Rudolph, and Weng-Fai Wong. How to do a million watchpoints: Efficient debugging using dynamic instrumentation. In *Proceedings of the 17th International Conference on Compiler Construction*, pages 147–162, Budapest, Hungary, March 2008.

[Wor14] World Wide Web Consortium. [illegible] *Language* [illegible] 2.0, January [illegible]. Available as [illegible]

[Wor14] World Wide Web Consortium. SOAP current status. [illegible] /standards/techs/soap [illegible]

[illegible] [illegible] Consortium. [illegible] 7.0 [illegible] October 2014. Available at [illegible] /Unicode7.0.0/

[illegible] [illegible] Wirth [illegible] Anthony [illegible] Richard [illegible] *Software—Practice and Experience*, 7(6):685–[illegible], November–December 1977.

[YA93] Jae-Heon Yang and James H. Anderson. Fast, scalable synchronization with minimal hardware support. In *Proceedings of the Twelfth Annual ACM Symposium on Principles of Distributed Computing*, pages 171–182, Ithaca, NY, August 1993.

Index

In each entry, pages in the main text are listed first, followed by pages on the companion site. The "ff" designation indicates that coverage continues on following pages.

B

C

E

H

I

M

S

T

U